Encyclopedia of the
AMERICAN CIVIL WAR
A Political, Social, and Military History
Volume I

Encyclopedia of the
AMERICAN CIVIL WAR
A Political, Social, and Military History
Volume I

David S. Heidler and Jeanne T. Heidler
Editors

Foreword by
James M. McPherson

David J. Coles
Associate Editor

Gary W. Gallagher
James M. McPherson
Mark E. Neely, Jr.
Editorial Board

Cartography by
Donald Frazier
Richard J. Thompson, Jr.

ABC-CLIO

Santa Barbara, California
Denver, Colorado
Oxford, England

Library of Congress Cataloging-in-Publication Data

Heidler, David Stephen, 1955-
    Encyclopedia of the American Civil War : a political, social, and
military history / David S. Heidler and Jeanne T. Heidler, editors ;
David J. Coles, associate editor ; Gary W. Gallagher, James M.
McPherson, Mark E. Neely, Jr., editorial board.
            p. cm.
Includes bibliographical references and index.
        ISBN 1-57607-066-2 (set : alk. paper)
    1. United States--History--Civil War, 1861-1865--Encyclopedias. I.
Heidler, Jeanne T. II. Coles, David J. III. Title.
        E468 .H47 2000
        973.7'03--dc21
                                                                00-011195

ISBN 1-57607-066-2 (alk. paper)

04 03 02 01 00 10 9 8 7 6 5 4 3 2 1

ABC-CLIO, Inc.
130 Cremona Drive, P.O. Box 1911
Santa Barbara, California 93116-1911

This book is printed on acid-free paper.
Manufactured in the United States of America.

This book is also available on the World Wide Web as an e-book. Visit www.abc-clio.com for details.

To

Thomas A. Belser, Jr.
Joseph H. Harrison, Jr.
Robert R. Rea

Our Great Triumvirate

CONTRIBUTORS

Gretchen A. Adams
University of New Hampshire

Frank Alduino
Anne Arundel Community College

Donald Altschiller
Mugar Memorial Library, Boston
University

William L. Anderson
Western Carolina University

Byron Andreasen
University of Illinois at Urbana—
Champaign

Brad Arnold
Virginia Military Institute

Steven M. Avella
Marquette University

Rolando Avila
The University of Texas—Pan American

Catherine O. Badura
Valdosta State University

Anne J. Bailey
Georgia College & State University

Jean Harvey Baker
Goucher College

Daniel P. Barr
Kent State University

Christopher Bates
University of California—Los Angeles

James S. Baugess
Columbus State Community College

Harry M. Bayne
Brewton Parker College

Jonathan M. Beagle
University of New Hampshire

Terry L. Beckenbaugh
University of Arkansas

W. Robert Beckman
Illinois State University

James R. Belpedio
Becker College

Robert Patrick Bender
University of Arkansas

Kurt O. Berends
Calvin College

Jennifer L. Bertolet
George Washington University

Eugene H. Berwanger
Colorado State University

Paul M. Bessell
George Washington Masonic National
Memorial

Alexander M. Bielakowski
Kansas State University

Andrew Paul Bielakowski
University of Toronto

Louis Bielakowski
Independent scholar

Judith Bielecki
Washburn-Norlans Foundation

John David Bladek
University of Washington

Frederick J. Blue
Youngstown State University

Arnold D. Blumberg
Johns Hopkins University

Kenneth J. Blume
Albany College of Pharmacy

Eric L. Bobo
University of Southern Mississippi

Lori Bogle
United States Naval Academy

Ray E. Boomhower
Indiana Historical Society

Lincoln Bramwell
University of Utah

Russell K. Brown
Groveton, Georgia

William H. Brown
North Carolina State Archives

Gary L. Browne
University of Maryland—Baltimore
County

Judkin Jay Browning
Independent scholar

Susannah U. Bruce
Kansas State University

Stephen P. Budney
University of Mississippi

Robert W. Burg
Purdue University

Frank J. Byrne
The Ohio State University

Lauren Cooke Burgess
Independent scholar

Mike Butler
University of Mississippi

Chris M. Calkins
Petersburg National Battlefield

Bill Cameron
United States Army (Retired)

Heidi Campbell-Shoaf
Independent scholar

Jack J. Cardoso
State University College at Buffalo

Rosemarie S. Cardoso
Art Education, Clarence, New York

David Carlson
Georgia Military College

Stephen A. Carney
Kent State University

Ruth C. Carter
University of Pittsburgh Library System
(Retired)

Joan E. Cashin
The Ohio State University

JoAnn E. Castagna
University of Iowa

Albert Castel, Emeritus
Western Michigan University

Adrienne Caughfield
Texas Christian University

Mark R. Cheathem
Mississippi State University

H. Lee Cheek, Jr.
Lee University

CONTRIBUTORS

Robert H. Churchill
Rutgers University

Paul A. Cimbala
Fordham University

Mary Lynn Cluff
University of Phoenix

Thomas Burnell Colbert
Marshalltown Community College

David J. Coles
Longwood College

Michael J. Connolly
St. Anselm College

Rory Cornish
Northeast Louisiana University

Janet L. Coryell
Western Michigan University

Karen L. Cox
Independent scholar

Lynda Lasswell Crist
Rice University

Edward R. Crowther
Adams State College

Thomas F. Curran
Saint Louis University

Enrico Dal Lago
National University of Ireland, Galway

C. David Dalton
College of the Ozarks

Michael S. Davis
Kansas State University

William C. Davis
Independent scholar

Thomas A. DeBlack
Arkansas Tech University

Christine Dee
Harvard University

Kenneth A. Deitreich
West Virginia University

Frank E. Deserino
University College, London

Charles Ellis Dickson
Independent scholar

Richard Digby-Junger
Western Michigan University

Laurent Ditmann
Spelman College

James G. Downhour
Southern Illinois University

Alan C. Downs
Georgia Southern University

Dorothy L. Drinkard
East Tennessee State University

Hubert F. Dubrulle
University of Puget Sound

Russell Duncan
University of Copenhagen

John P. Dunn
Valdosta State University

R. Blake Dunnavent
Lubbock Christian University

Robert N. Dykstra
SUNY—Albany

Gary T. Edwards
University of Memphis

David P. Eldridge
Mississippi State University

Stephen D. Engle
Florida Atlantic University

Paul D. Escott
Wake Forest University

Nicole Etcheson
University of Texas at El Paso

Damon R. Eubank
Campbellsville University

Warner D. Farr
U.S. Army Special Operations Command

Carol Faulkner
Pamona College

William B. Feis
Buena Vista University

Eric Fettmann
Independent scholar

Phyllis F. Field
Ohio University

Roy E. Finkenbine
University of Detroit Mercy

Steven Fisher
University of Denver

Jane Flaherty
Texas A & M University

Chris E. Fonvielle, Jr.
University of North Carolina—
    Wilmington

Franklin Forts
University of Georgia

Buck T. Foster
Mississippi State University

Daniel L. Fountain
University of Mississippi

Lisa Tendrich Frank
University of Florida

Donald S. Frazier
McMurry University

John C. Fredriksen
Independent scholar

Derek W. Frisby
University of Alabama

Gary W. Gallagher
University of Virginia

J. Matthew Gallman
Gettysburg College

Douglas G. Gardner
Miami University

Samantha Jane Gaul
Virginia Tech

Peter S. Genovese
Bowling Green State University

David J. Gerleman
Southern Illinois University

Charles Dana Gibson
Independent scholar

William Gillette
Rutgers University

James M. Gillispie
University of Mississippi

Lesley J. Gordon
University of Akron

Mark R. Grandstaff
Brigham Young University

Jennifer L. Gross
University of Georgia

Carl J. Guarneri
St. Mary's College of California

K. R. Constantine Gutzman
John Jay College—CUNY

Richard C. Halseth
Independent scholar

Ron Hamilton
Indiana University—Indianapolis

Edward John Harcourt
Vanderbilt University

William C. Harris
North Carolina State University

Jennifer Harrison
North Carolina Wesleyan College

Lowell H. Harrison
Western Kentucky University

Dale F. Harter
The Library of Virginia

William T. Hartley
University of Tennessee

Charles L. Heath, Jr.
Institute for Historical and Cultural
  Research, East Carolina University

David S. Heidler
Independent scholar

Jeanne T. Heidler
United States Air Force Academy

David C. R. Heisser
Daniel Library, The Citadel

Earl J. Hess
Lincoln Memorial University

Wallace C. Hettle
University of Northern Iowa

Bernard Hirschhorn
Independent scholar

Wolfgang C. Hochbruck
University of Stuttgart, Germany

Randolph Hollingsworth
University of Kentucky

Peter C. Holloran
New England Historical Association

James V. Holton
Polk County Historical Museum, Bartow,
  Florida

Ari Hoogenboom
Brooklyn College and Graduate Center
  City University of New York

Charles F. Howlett
Amityville (NY) Public Schools /
  University College, Adelphi University

Leonne M. Hudson
Kent State University

James L. Isemann
Southeast Community College, Lincoln,
  NE

Kathryn Allamong Jacob
Schlesinger Library, Harvard University

James Robbins Jewell
West Virginia University

Robert W. Johannsen
University of Illinois at Urbana-
  Champagne

Charles Thomas Johnson
Valdosta State University

Timothy D. Johnson
Lipscomb University

Trevor M. Jones
Early American Museum, Mahomet, IL

Mauriel P. Joslyn
Independent scholar

Jerry Keenan
Independent scholar

Christian B. Keller
Pennsylvania State University

Jeff Kinard
Independent scholar

Charles E. Kinzer
Longwood College

James C. Klotter
Georgetown College

Willard Carl Klunder
Wichita State University

Joe Knetsch
Florida Department of Environmental
  Protection

Paul E. Kuhl
Winston Salem University

Alan K. Lamm
Mount Olive College

Scott M. Langston
Southwest Baptist University

Lisa Lauterbach Laskin
Harvard University

Mark A. Lause
University of Cincinnati

Dennis S. Lavery
Department of the Army

Elizabeth D. Leonard
Colby College

Kevin M. Levin
St. Anne's—Belfield School

Frank R.Levstik
Kentucky Department of Libraries and
  Archives

Daniel Liestman
Kansas State University Libraries

Brad D. Lookingbill
Columbia College

Richard D. Loosbrock
Chadron State College

M. Philip Lucas
Cornell College

Kenneth L. Lyftogt
University of Northern Iowa

Sharon S. MacDonald
Illinois State University

Ronald G. Machoian
Independent scholar

Bruce D. Mactavish
Washburn University

Brock Magoon
Independent scholar

Dane Magoon
Southern Illinois University

Jonathan L. Mahaffey
Appalachian State University

Sr. Mary Denis Maher, CSA
Ursuline College

Wayne Mahood, Emeritus
SUNY—Genesee

Jo Ann Manfra
Worcester Polytechnic Institute

John F. Marszalek
Mississippi State University

James Marten
Marquette University

Bruce E. Matthews
Auburn University

John Mayfield
Samford University

Joseph M. McCarthy
Suffolk University

James L. McDonough
Auburn University

David McGee
University of Georgia

Stanley S. McGowen
Sam Houston State University

John E. McKay
Independent scholar

Brian D. McKnight
Mississippi State University

James H. Meredith
United States Air Force Academy

Nathan R. Meyer
Eureka, Illinois

Christopher C. Meyers
Georgia Military College

Carl H. Moneyhon
University of Arkansas at Little Rock

James M. Morris
Christopher Newport University

Malcolm Muir, Jr.
Austin Peay State University

Earl F. Mulderink III
Southern Utah University

William H. Mulligan, Jr.
Murray State University

R. Boyd Murphree
Florida State Archives

Diane Neal
University of Central Oklahoma

Frank Nickell
Southeast Missouri State University

Alan T. Nolan
Indiana Historical Society

David A. Norris
Independent scholar

Greg O'Brien
University of Southern Mississippi

Broeck N. Oder
Santa Catalina School, Monterey, CA

Matthew Pacer
Kansas State University

Dave Page
Independent scholar

Christopher M. Paine
Indiana University Southeast

William A. Pannapacker
Harvard University

Sue C. Patrick
University of Wisconsin—Barron
County

Donald K. Pickens
University of North Texas

Michael D. Pierce
Tarleton State University

Walter E. Pittman
University of West Alabama

Brian C. Pohanka
Independent scholar

W. Scott Poole
University of South Carolina—Aiken

David A. Powell
Independent scholar

J. Tracy Power
South Carolina Department of Archives
and History

Thomas Lynwood Powers
University of South Carolina Sumter

Dorothy O. Pratt
University of Notre Dame

James M. Prichard
Kentucky Department of Libraries &
Archives

David A. Proctor
North Florida Community College

Jeffery S. Prushankin
University of Arkansas

Ethan S. Rafuse
University of Missouri—Kansas City

Edward Ragan
Syracuse University

Steven J. Ramold
University of Nebraska—Lincoln

Chad A. Reisig
Claremont Graduate University

Kent D. Richards, Emeritus
Central Washington University

Curtis Richardson
Northern Illinois University

William H. Roberts
The Ohio State University

James I. Robertson, Jr.
Virginia Polytechnic Institute & State
University

Glenn Robins
University of Southern Mississippi

Junius P. Rodriguez
Eureka College

Alicia E. Rodriquez
California State University, Bakersfield

Charles P. Roland
University of Kentucky

Todd Anthony Rosa
George Washington University

Michael A. Ross
Loyola University New Orleans

Anne Sarah Rubin
American University

Susan Sessions Rugh
Brigham Young University

Robert D. Sampson
University of Illinois at Urbana-
Champaign

Charles W. Sanders, Jr.
Kansas State University

Stanley Sandler
Virginia Military Institute

Richard A. Sauers
Superior (WI) Public Museums

Robert Saunders, Jr.
Troy State University Dothan

Elizabeth D. Schafer
Independent scholar

Jane E. Schultz
Indiana University-Purdue University

Angela Schwarz
University of Duisberg, Germany

Mark E. Scott
Independent scholar

Paul Searls
University of Vermont

Philip Lee Secrist
Kennesaw State University

Peter J. Sehlinger
Indiana University, Indianapolis

Edward Sharp
University of North Carolina at
Greensboro

William L. Shea
University of Arkansas at Monticello

Dana B. Shoaf
Independent scholar

Rae Sikula
Cudahy Library, Loyola University of
Chicago

Larry C. Skogen
Independent scholar

James L. Sledge III
Truett-McConnell College

Adam I. P. Smith
Queen Mary and Westfield College,
University of London

Duane A. Smith
Fort Lewis College

Elbert B. Smith, Emeritus
University of Maryland

G. Judson Smith, Jr.
Alexander H. Stephens State Historic
Park

Gene A. Smith
Texas Christian University

Gerald J. Smith
Paine College

Michael Thomas Smith
Louisburg College

Timothy B. Smith
Mississippi State University

Mark Snell
Shepherd College

Irvin D. Solomon
Florida Gulf Coast University

Richard J. Sommers
Independent scholar

Ian M.Spurgeon
Kansas State University

Kenneth R. Stevens
Texas Christian University

Christopher S. Stowe
The University of Toledo

Reginald C. Stuart
St. Bonaventure University

David M. Sullivan
Independent scholar

Stephen C. Svonavec
Francis Marion University

Katherine L. Swimm
University of Mississippi

Wiley Sword
Independent scholar

Craig L. Symonds
United States Naval Academy

John Syrett
Trent University

Bruce Tap
Independent scholar

Robert A. Taylor
Florida Institute of Technology

Teresa A. Thomas
Fitchburg State College

J. Mark Thompson
University of North Carolina at
Pembroke

William A. Tidwell
Independent scholar

Eric Tscheschlok
Auburn University

Adam-Max Tuchinsky
University of North Carolina at Chapel
Hill

Spencer C. Tucker
Virginia Military Institute

Minoa Uffelman
Austin Peay State University

David J. Ulbrich
Kansas State University

Gregory J. W. Urwin
Temple University

Antoinette G. Van Zelm
Independent scholar

Wendy Hamand Venet
Georgia State University

Eric H. Walther
University of Houston

Matthew S. Warshauer
Central Connecticut State University

Zack C. Waters
Independent scholar

Tim J. Watts
Kansas State University

Clive Webb
University of Sussex at Brighton

Jim Weeks
Pennsylvania State University

William Weisberger
Independent scholar

Stephen G. Weisner
Springfield Technical Community
College

Mark A. Weitz
Auburn University—Montgomery

David P. Werlich
Southern Illinois University—
Carbondale

Kristy Armstrong White
Northeast Mississippi Museum
Association

Clay Williams
Old Capitol Museum, Jackson, MS

David Williams
Valdosta State University

Teresa C. Williams
Valdosta State University

Brian S. Wills
University of Virginia's College at Wise

Mary Ellen Wilson
Middle Georgia College

Thomas A. Wing
Fort Smith National Historic Site

Robert S. Wolff
Central Connecticut State University

Thomas E. Woods, Jr.
Suffolk Community College

Eddie Woodward
The Library of Virginia

CONTRIBUTORS

Robert Wooster
Texas A&M University—Corpus Christi

Susan Wyly-Jones
Harvard University

Ben Wynne
University of Mississippi

Mitchell Yockelson
National Archives

Duane C. Young
De Montford University

David T. Zabecki
American Military University

Kathleen R. Zebley
University of North Carolina at Pembroke

Qingsong Zhang
Independent scholar

Gregory R. Zieren
Austin Peay State University

CONTENTS

ENCYCLOPEDIA OF THE AMERICAN CIVIL WAR
A Political, Social, and Military History

VOLUME I

List of Entries, xv

Foreword by James W. McPherson, xxv

Preface, xxvii

Introduction: An Overview of the American Civil War, xxix

Encyclopedia of the American Civil War

A–C, 1

VOLUME II

D–I, 545

VOLUME III

J–Q, 1055

VOLUME IV

R–Z, 1589

VOLUME V

List of Documents, 2177

Source Documents, 2187

Appendices

I: Confederate States of America—General Officers, 2461

II: Confederate States of America—Government (1861–1865), 2467

III: United States of America—General Officers, 2475

IV: United States of America—Government (1857–1865), 2481

V: Battlefield Location Maps, 2497

Chronology of the American Civil War, 2513

Glossary, 2547

Bibliography, 2549

Index, 2613

LIST OF ENTRIES

Abbot, Henry Larcom
Abbott, Henry Livermore
Abercrombie, John Joseph
Abolitionist Movement
Abolitionists
Acoustic Shadows
Adams, Charles Francis
Adams, Charles Francis, Jr.
Adams, Daniel Weisiger
Adams, Henry Brooks
Adams, John
Adams, William Wirt
African-American Sailors
African-American Soliders, C.S.A.
African-American Suffrage
Alabama
Alabama Claims
Alabama, CSS
Albemarle Sound
Albert, Prince
Alcott, Louisa May
Aldie, Virginia, Battle of
Alexander, Edward Porter
Alexandria, Louisiana, Destruction of
Alger, Russell Alexander
Allatoona, Battle of
Alleghany Mountain, [West] Virginia, Battle of
Allen, Henry Watkins
Allen, William Wirt
Alton Federal Military Prison
Amelia Court House/Jetersville
American Party
American Red Cross
Ames, Adelbert
Ammen, Jacob
Anaconda Plan
Anderson, George Thomas
Anderson, James Patton
Anderson, Joseph Reid
Anderson, Richard Heron
Anderson, Robert
Anderson, William "Bloody Bill"
Andersonville
Andrew, John Albion
Andrews, George Leonard
Andrews's Raid
"Annals of the War"
Anthony, Susan Brownell
Antietam, Battle of
Appomattox Court House
Archer, James Jay
Arkansas
Arkansas, CSS
Arkansas Post, Battle of
Arlington
Armistead, Lewis Addison
Armories, Arsenals, and Foundries
Armstrong, Frank Crawford
Army of Kansas
Army of Kentucky
Army of Middle Tennessee

Army of Mississippi
Army of Missouri
Army of Mobile
Army of New Mexico
Army of Northern Virginia
Army of Tennessee
Army of the Cumberland
Army of the Gulf
Army of the James
Army of the Kanawha
Army of the Northwest, Confederate
Army of the Ohio
Army of the Peninsula
Army of the Potomac
Army of the Shenandoah, C.S.A.
Army of the Shenandoah, U.S.A.
Army of the Tennessee
Army of the West
Army of Virginia
Army of West Tennessee
Army Organization, C.S.A.
Army Organization, U.S.A.
Army, United States
Art of the Civil War
Artillery
Asboth, Alexander S.
Ashby, Turner
Ashley, James Mitchell
Atchison, David Rice
Atlanta Campaign
Atlanta, Georgia
Augur, Christopher Columbus
Averasboro (Averasborough), Battle of
Averell, William Woods
Averell's Raids
Ayres, Romeyn Beck

Babcock, Orville Elias
Bagby, George William
Bailey, Joseph
Bailey, Theodorus
Baird, Absalom
Baker, Edward Dickinson
Baker, La Fayette Curry
Baldwin, John Brown
Balloons
Ball's Bluff, Battle of
Baltimore & Ohio Railroad
Baltimore, Maryland
Baltimore Riot
Banks, Nathaniel Prentiss
Barksdale, Ethelbert
Barksdale, William E.
Barlow, Francis Channing
Barnard, George Norman
Barnard, John Gross
Barnes, Joseph K.
Barringer, Rufus
Barry, William Farquhar
Bartlett, Joseph Jackson
Bartlett, William Francis
Barton, Clara

Barton, Seth Maxwell
Bartow, Francis Stebbins
Bate, William Brimage
Bates, Edward
Baton Rouge, Battle of
"Battle Hymn of the Republic"
Battles and Leaders of the Civil War
Baxter Springs, Battle of
Baylor, John Robert
Bayonet
Beale, Richard Lee Turbeville
Bean's Station, Tennessee, Engagement at
Beatty, Samuel
Beauregard, Pierre Gustave Toutant
Bedini, Gaetano
Bee, Barnard Elliott
Beecher, Henry Ward
Belknap, William Worth
Bell, John
Belle Isle
Belmont, Battle of
Bennett House
Benjamin, Judah Philip
Bennett, James Gordon
Benning, Henry Lewis
Bentonville, Battle of
Berdan, Hiram
Bermuda Hundred Campaign
Berry, Hiram Gregory
Berryville, Virginia
Bickerdyke, Mary Ann Ball
Bickley, George Washington Leigh
Bierce, Ambrose Gwinett
Big Bethel, Battle of
Big Black River, First Battle of
Bigelow, John
Birney, David Bell
Birney, William
Blackford's (Boteler's) Ford
Blackwell, Elizabeth
Blaine, James Gillespie
Blair, Austin
Blair, Francis Preston
Blair, Francis Preston, Jr.
Blair, Montgomery
Blakely, Alabama, Battle of
Blockade of the C.S.A
Blockade Runners
Blunt, James Gilpatrick
Bonds
Bonham, Milledge Luke
Booneville, Mississippi, Battle of
Boonville, Missouri, Battle of
Booth, John Wilkes
Border States
Botts, John Minor
Boudinot, Elias Cornelius
Bounty System
Boutwell, George Sewall
Bowen, John Stevens
Boyce, William Waters

Boyd, Maria Isabella "Belle"
Bradford, Augustus Williamson
Bradley, Amy Morris
Brady, Mathew B.
Bragg, Braxton
Bragg, Edward Stuyvesant
Bragg, Thomas
Bramlette, Thomas Elliott
Branch, Lawrence O'Bryan
Brandy Station, Battle of
Brannan, John Milton
Bratton, John
Breckinridge, John Cabell
Breckinridge, Robert Jefferson
Brentwood, Tennessee
Brevet Rank
Brice's Cross Roads/Guntown, Battle of
Bright, Jesse David
Bright, John
Bristoe Station, Battle of
Brooke, John Mercer
Brooke, John Rutter
Brooks, Preston Smith
Brooks, William Thomas Harbaugh
Brough, John
Brown, Albert Gallatin
Brown, Isaac Newton
Brown, John
Brown, John Calvin
Brown, Joseph Emerson
Brown, William Wells
Browning, Orville Hickman
Brownlow, William Gannaway
Brownsville, Texas
Bryant, William Cullen
Buchanan, Franklin
Buchanan, James
Buchanan, Robert Christie
Buck and Ball
Buckingham, William Alfred
Buckner, Simon Bolivar
Buell, Don Carlos
Buford, Abraham
Buford, John
Buford, Napoleon Bonaparte
Bull Run, First Battle of
Bull Run, Second Battle of
Bulloch, James Dunwody
Bummers
Burbridge, Stephen Gano
Burnett, Henry Lawrence
Burns, Anthony
Burns, John Lawrence
Burnside, Ambrose Everett
Butler, Andrew Pickens
Butler, Benjamin Franklin
Butler, Matthew Calbraith
Butler's Proclamation
Butterfield, Daniel

Cadwalader, George
Cairo
Caldwell, John Curtis
Calhoun, John Caldwell
California
Cameron, James

Cameron, Simon
Camp Chase
Camp Douglas, Illinois
Camp Jackson Massacre
Camp Morton
Camp Nelson, Kentucky
Campbell, John Archibald
Campbell's Station, Tennessee, Battle of
Canby, Edward Richard Sprigg
Cane Hill, Battle of
Cannon, William
Carey, Henry Charles
Carlin, William Passmore
Carlisle, Pennsylvania
Carnegie, Andrew
Carnifex Ferry, Battle of
Carolinas Campaign
Carondelet, USS
Carr, Eugene Asa
Carrick's Ford
Carrington, Henry Beebe
Carroll, Anna Ella
Carroll, Samuel Sprigg
Carson, Christopher Houston "Kit"
Carthage, Battle of
Caruthers, Robert Looney
Casey, Silas
Cass, Lewis
Castle Thunder
Casualties
Catholics
Catlett's Station, Battle of
Catron, John
Cavalry, C.S.A.
Cavalry, U.S.A.
Cedar Creek, Battle of
Cedar Mountain, Battle of
Centralia Massacre
Chalmers, James Ronald
Chamberlain, Joshua Lawrence
Chambersburg, Burning of
Chambersburg Raid
Champion's Hill, Battle of
Chancellorsville, Battle of
Chandler, Zachariah
Chantilly, Battle of
Chaplains
Chaplains, African-American
Charleston (Illinois) Riot
Charleston Mercury
Chase, Salmon Portland
Chattahoochee River, Georgia,
  Operations around
Chattanooga Campaign
Chattanooga, Tennessee
Cheat Mountain, Virginia
Cheatham, Benjamin Franklin
Cherokee Indians
Chesapeake Affair
Chesnut, James
Chesnut, Mary Boykin
Cheyenne Indians
Chicago Tribune
Chickamauga, Battle of
Chickasaw Bluffs, Battle of
Chickasaw Indians

Chinese-American Soldiers
Chivington, John Milton
Choctaw Indians
Churches
Cincinnati, Siege of
City Point, Virginia
Civil Liberties, C.S.A.
Civil Liberties, U.S.A.
Clark, Charles
Clark, Henry Toole
Class Conflict, C.S.A.
Class Conflict, U.S.A.
Clay, Cassius Marcellus
Clay, Clement Claiborne, Jr.
Clay, Henry
Clay-Clopton, Virginia Caroline Tunstall
Clayton, Henry Delamar
Clayton, Powell
Cleburne, Patrick Ronayne
Clingman, Thomas Lanier
Cloyd's Mountain, Battle of
Cobb, Howell
Cobb, Thomas Reade Rootes
Coburn, Abner
Cold Harbor, Battle of
Colfax, Schuyler
Colquitt, Alfred Holt
Colt, Samuel
Columbia, South Carolina, Burning of
Columbus, Kentucky
Commissary
Comstock, Cyrus Ballou
Confederate Diaspora
Confiscation Acts
Congress, C.S.A.
Congress, U.S.A.
Conkling, Roscoe
Connor, Patrick Edward
Conscription, C.S.A.
Conscription, U.S.A.
Constitution, C.S.A.
Constitutional Union Party
Contrabands
Cook, Philip
Cooke, Jay
Cooke, John Esten
Cooke, Philip St. George
Cooper, Samuel
Cooperationists
Copperheads
Corinth, Battle of
Corinth, Mississippi
Corinth, Siege of
Corse, John Murray
Cotton
Couch, Darius Nash
Courts, C.S.A.
Courts, U.S.A.
Covert Action, Confederate
Covert Operations, U.S.A.
Cox, Jacob Dolson
Cox, Samuel Sullivan
Crampton's Gap, Battle of
Crater, Battle of the
Crawford, Samuel J.
Creek Indians

Crimping
Crittenden Compromise
Crittenden, George Bibb
Crittenden, John Jordan
Crittenden, Thomas Leonidas
Crocker, Marcellus Monroe
Crook, George
Cross Keys, Battle of
Cullum, George Washington
Cumming, Kate
Currency, C.S.A.
Curtin, Andrew Gregg
Curtis, Benjamin Robbins
Curtis, Newton Martin
Curtis, Samuel Ryan
Cushing, Alonzo Hersford
Cushing, William Barker
Cushman, Pauline
Custer, George Armstrong
Cyclorama

Dabney, Robert Lewis
Dabney's Mills/Hatcher's Run (Virginia),
    Battle of
Dahlgren Guns
Dahlgren, John Adolph Bernard
Dallas, Georgia, Battle of
Dalton, Georgia, First Battle of
Dana, Charles Anderson
Dana, Napoleon Jackson Tecumseh
Dana, Richard Henry, Jr
Daniel, Peter Vivian
Daughters of the Regiment
Davids
Davis Bend, Mississippi
Davis, Charles Henry
Davis, David
Davis, George
Davis, Henry Winter
Davis, Jefferson
Davis, Jefferson Columbus
Davis, Varina Howell
De Bow, James Dunwoody Brownson
De Bow's Review
De Bray, Xavier Blanchard
De Forest, John William
De Leon, Edwin
De Trobriand, Regis
Decorations
Deep Bottom Run/Strawberry Plains,
    Virginia, Second Battle of
Democratic Party
Dennison, William
Departments, Military, C.S.A.
Departments, Military, U.S.A.
Desertion
Devens, Charles, Jr.
Devils
Devin, Thomas Casimer
Dickinson, Anna Elizabeth
Dilger, Hubert
Diplomacy, C.S.A.
Diplomacy, U.S.A.
Disease
Divers, Bridget
Dix, Dorothea Lynde

Dix, John Adams
"Dixie"
Dodge, Grenville Mellen
Donelson, Andrew Jackson
Doolittle, James Rood
Doubleday, Abner
Douglas, Stephen Arnold
Douglass, Frederick
Dow, Neal
Dranesville, Battle of
Dred Scott Case
Drewry's Bluff, Virginia, Battle of
Dudley, Thomas Haines
Duffié, Alfred Napoléon Alexandre
Duke, Basil Wilson
Du Pont, Samuel Francis
Durant, Thomas Jefferson

Eads, James Buchanan
Early, Jubal Anderson
Early's Washington Raid
Edmonds, Sarah Emma
Edmondson, Isabella "Belle"
Egypt
Election of 1856
Election of 1858
Election of 1860
Election of 1862
Election of 1864
Elections of 1863, C.S.A.
Ellet, Charles, Jr.
Elliott, Washington Lafayette
Ellis, John Willis
Ellsworth, Elmer Ephraim
Elmira Prison
Elzey, Arnold
Emancipation Proclamation
Emerson, Ralph Waldo
Emory, William Hemsley
Enchantress Affair
Enrolled Missouri Militia
Ericsson, John
Espionage
Etheridge, Annie
Evans, Augusta Jane
Evans, Clement Anselm
Evans, George Henry
Evans, Nathan George
Everett, Edward
Ewell, Richard Stoddert
Ewing, Hugh Boyle
Ewing, Thomas, Jr.
Ex parte Merryman
Ex parte Milligan
Ezra Church, Battle of

Fair Oaks/Seven Pines
Fair Oaks, Battle of Second
Fairbanks, Erastus
Fairfax Court House
Falling Waters, Battle of
Farmville/High Bridge, Battle of
Farnsworth, Elon John
Farragut, David Glasgow
Fayetteville Arsenal
Fenton, Reuben Eaton

Ferrero, Edward
Fessenden, Francis
Fessenden, James Deering
Fessenden, William Pitt
Field, Charles William
Fillmore, Millard
Financing, C.S.A.
Financing, U.S.A.
Finegan, Joseph
Finley, Clement Alexander
Finley, Jesse Johnson
Fire-eaters
Fisher's Hill, Battle of
Fisk, Clinton Bowen
Fitzhugh, George
Five Forks, Battle of
Flags
Flanagin, Harris
Florida
Florida, CSS
Floyd, John Buchanan
Fogg, George Gilman
Fogg, Isabella Morrison
Foote, Andrew Hull
Foote, Henry Stuart
Force, Manning Ferguson
Ford, Antonia
Foreign Visitors
Forrest's Raids
Forrest, Nathan Bedford
Forster, William Edward
Fort Anderson
Fort Craig
Fort Delaware Prison
Fort Donelson, Battle of
Fort Fisher
Fort Henry, Battle of
Fort Huger/Hill's Point
Fort Jefferson and Fort Taylor
Fort Macon
Fort McAllister, Reduction of
Fort Monroe
Fort Myers, Battle of
Fort Pickens
Fort Pillow
Fort Pillow Massacre
Fort Pulaski, Reduction of
Fort Sanders, Battle of
Fort Smith, Arkansas
Fort Stedman, Battle of
Fort Stevens, District of Columbia
Fort Sumter, Bombardment of
Fort Wagner, Battle of
Fort Warren, Massachusetts
Fortifications
Foster, Robert Sanford
Foster, Stephen Collins
Fox, Gustavus Vasa
Frank Leslie's Illustrated Newspaper
Franklin, Battle of
Franklin, William Buel
Fredericksburg, First Battle of
Fredericksburg, Second Battle of
Free Soil Party
Freedmen's Bureau
Freeport Doctrine

Frietschie, Barbara
Frémont, Jessie Benton
Frémont, John Charles
French, Samuel Gibbs
French, William Henry
Front Royal, Battle of
Fry, James Barnett
Fry, Speed Smith
Fugitive Slave Act of 1850
Furman, James Clement

Gaines' Mill, Battle of
Galvanized Yankees
Galveston, Texas
Gamble, Hamilton Rowan
Gardner, Alexander
Gardner, Franklin
Gardner, James
Garnett, Richard Brooke
Garnett, Robert Selden
Garrard, Kenner
Garrett, Robert & Sons
Garrison, William Lloyd
Gatling Gun
Geary, John White
General Orders, No. 100
Georgia
German-Americans
Getty, George Washington
Gettysburg Address
Gettysburg, Battle of
Gibbon, John
Giddings, Joshua Reed
Gillmore, Quincy Adams
Gilmer, Jeremy Francis
Gilmer, John Adams
Gilmore, James Roberts
Gist, States Rights
Gladstone, William
Glasgow, Missouri, Battle of
Globe Tavern, Virginia
Glorieta Pass, Battle of
Goldsboro, North Carolina
Gordon, George Henry
Gordon, John Brown
Gorgas, Josiah
Gosport Navy Yard
Govan, Daniel Chevilette
Gracie, Archibald, Jr.
Grady, Henry Woodfin
Graham, Charles Kinnaird
Grand Review
Granger, Gordon
Grant, Lewis Addison
Grant, Ulysses Simpson
Gratiot Street and Myrtle Street Federal
    Military Prisons (St. Louis)
Gray, Henry
Great Britain
Greeley, Horace
Green, Tom
Greenbacks
Greenbrier River, Virginia, Battle of
Greene, George Sears
Greenhow, Rose O'Neal
Gregg, David McMurtrie

Gregg, Maxcy
Gregg, William
Gresham, Walter Quintin
Grier, Robert Cooper
Grierson, Benjamin Henry
Grierson's Raid
Griffin, Charles
Griffing, Josephine Sophia White
Grimes, Bryan
Grimké, Angelina
Grimké, Sarah Moore
Grinnell, Josiah Bushnell
Griswoldville, Georgia, Battle of
Grose, William
Grover, Cuvier
Groveton, Virginia, Battle of
Grow, Galusha Aaron
Guerrilla Warfare
Gurowski, Count Adam
Guthrie, James

Habeas Corpus, Writ of (C.S.A.)
Habeas Corpus, Writ of (U.S.A.)
Hahn, Georg Michael Decker
Hall, Maria M. C.
Halleck, Henry Wager
Halpine, Charles Graham
Halstead, Murat
Hamblin, Joseph Eldridge
Hamilton, Andrew Jackson
Hamilton, Schuyler
Hamlin, Hannibal
Hammond, James Henry
Hammond, William Alexander
Hampton Roads Peace Conference
Hampton, Wade
Hancock, Winfield Scott
Hanover Court House, Battle Of
Hanover, Pennsylvania, Battle of
Hardee, William Joseph
Hardin, Martin Davis
Hardtack
Harper's Ferry, [West] Virginia
Harper's Weekly
Harris, Ellen Osborne
Harris, Isham Green
Harris, Nathaniel Harrison
Harrison, Benjamin
Harrison's Landing, Virginia
Hartford, USS
Hartranft, John Frederick
Hartsuff, George Lucas
Harvey, Cordelia Perrine
Harvey, Louis Powell
Hatch, Edward
Hatch, John Porter
Hatcher's Run/Burgess Mill, Virginia,
    Battle of
Hatteras Inlet, Capture Of
Haupt, Herman
Hawes, Richard
Hawkins, John Parker
Hawley, Harriet Foote
Hawley, Joseph Roswell
Haw's Shop, Battle of
Hawthorne, Nathaniel

Hay, John Milton
Hayes, Rutherford Birchard
Hayne, Paul Hamilton
Hays, Alexander
Hazen, William Babcock
Hébert, Paul Octave
Heintzelman, Samuel Peter
Helena, Battle of
Helm, Benjamin Hardin
Helper, Hinton Rowan
Hendricks, Thomas Andrews
Herndon, William Henry
Herron, Francis Jay
Heth, Henry
Hicks, Thomas Holliday
Higginson, Thomas Wentworth
Hill, Adams Sherman
Hill, Ambrose Powell
Hill, Benjamin Harvey
Hill, Daniel Harvey
Hincks, Edward Winslow
Hindman, Thomas Carmichael
Hines, Thomas H.
Hitchcock, Ethan Allen
Hodgers, Jennie
Hoffman, William
Hoge, Jane Blaikie
Hoke, Robert Frederick
Holcombe, James Philemon
Holden, William Woods
Hollins, George Nichols
Holly Springs Raid
Holmes, Oliver Wendell, Jr.
Holmes, Theophilus Hunter
Holt, Joseph
Homer, Winslow
Homestead Act
Honey Hill, South Carolina, Battle of
Honey Springs, Battle of
Hood, John Bell
Hood's Second Sortie (Battle of
    Atlanta)
Hooker, Joseph
Hopkins, Juliet Opie
Hotchkiss, Jedediah
Hotze, Henry
Housatonic
Houston, Sam
Hovey, Alvin Peterson
Howard, Joseph, Jr.
Howard, Oliver Otis
Howe, Julia Ward
Howe, Samuel Gridley
Hudson, Frederic
Huger, Benjamin
Humphreys, Andrew Atkinson
Hunley
Hunt, Henry Jackson
Hunter, David
Hunter, Robert Mercer Taliaferro
Hunton, Eppa
Huntsville, Alabama
Hurlbut, Stephen Augustus
Huse, Caleb

Imboden and Jones's Raid

Imboden, John Daniel
Immigrants
Immigration
Impressment
Indian Brigade
Indian Territory
Ingalls, Rufus
Invalid Corps
Irish-Americans
Irish Bend/Bayou Teche
Irish Brigade
Iron Brigade
Ironclads
Irwinville, Georgia
Island No. 10, Battle of
Italian-Americans
Iuka, Battle of
Iverson, Alfred, Jr.
Iverson, Alfred

Jackson, Claiborne Fox
Jackson, Mississippi, Capture of
Jackson, Battle of
Jackson, Thomas Jonathan
Jacksonville, Florida
Jenkins, Albert Gallatin
Jenkins' Ferry, Battle of
Jenkins, Micah
Jews
Johnson, Andrew
Johnson, Bushrod Rust
Johnson, Edward
Johnson Farm (Darbytown and New
   Market Roads)
Johnson, George W.
Johnson, Herschel Vespasian
Johnson, Reverdy
Johnson, Richard W.
Johnson's Island
Johnsonville, Tennessee
Johnston, Joseph Eggleston
Joint Committee on the Conduct of the
   War
Jones, Catesby ap Roger
Jones, Charles Colcock, Jr.
Jones, John Beauchamp
Jones, John Robert
Jones, John William
Jones, Samuel
Jones, William Edmonson
Jonesboro, Battle of
J. R. Williams
Julian, George Washington

Kane, Thomas Leiper
Kansas
Kansas-Nebraska Act
Kautz, August Valentine
Kean, Robert Garlick Hill
Kearny, Philip
Kearsarge, USS
Keene, Laura
Keitt, Lawrence Massillon
Kell, John Mcintosh
Kelley, Benjamin Franklin
Kelly's Ford, Virginia, Battle of

Kemper, James Lawson
Kenner, Duncan Farrar
Kennesaw Mountain, Battle of
Kentucky
Kernstown, First Battle of
Kernstown, Virginia, Second Battle of
Kershaw, Joseph Brevard
Keyes, Erasmus Darwin
Kilpatrick-Dahlgren Raid
Kilpatrick, Hugh Judson
Kimball, Nathan
King, John Haskell
King, Rufus
Kirkwood, Samuel Jordan
Knights of the Golden Circle
Knipe, Joseph Farmer
Knoxville Campaign
Kryzanowski, Wladimir

Labor
Ladies Memorial Associations
Lamar, Charles Augustus Lafayette
Lamar, Lucius Quintus Cincinnatus
Lamon, Ward Hill
Lane, Harriet Rebecca
Lane, James Henry
Lane, James Henry
Lane, Joseph
Langston, John Mercer
Law, Evander McIvor
Lawler, Michael Kelly
Lawrence, Kansas
Lawton, Alexander Robert
Lecompton Constitution
Ledlie, James Hewett
Lee, Fitzhugh
Lee, George Washington Custis
Lee, Robert Edward
Lee, Samuel Philips
Lee, Stephen Dill
Lee, William Henry Fitzhugh
Legal Tender Acts
Leggett, Mortimer Dormer
Leisure
Lemmon v. People
Letcher, John
Lexington, Missouri, Battle of
Lexington, Tennessee, Battle of
Libby Prison
Lieber, Francis
Lincoln, Abraham
Lincoln Assassination
Lincoln, Mary Todd
Lincoln, Robert Todd
Lincoln's Reconstruction Policy
Lindsay, William Schaw
Livermore, Mary Ashton Rice
Locke, David Ross
Logan, John Alexander
Logan's Cross Roads/Mill Springs/Beech
   Grove, Kentucky, Battle of
Logistics
Lomax, Lunsford Lindsay
Long, Armistead Lindsay
Longfellow, Henry Wadsworth
Longstreet, James

Lookout Mountain, Battle of
Lopez, Narciso
Loring, William Wing
Lost Cause
Louisiana
Lovejoy, Georgia, Battle of
Lovejoy, Owen
Lovell, Mansfield
Lowe, Thaddeus Sobieski Constantine
Lowell, Charles Russell
Lowell, James Russell
Loyalty Oaths
Lubbock, Francis Richard
Lynch, Patrick Neison
Lynchburg Campaign
Lyon, Nathaniel
Lyons, Richard Bickerton Pemell,
   Second Baron and First Earl Lyons
Lytle, William Haines

MacArthur, Arthur, Jr.
Mackenzie, Ranald Slidell
Maffitt, John Newland
Magoffin, Beriah
MaGrath, Andrew Gordon
Magruder, John Bankhead
Mahan, Dennis Hart
Mahone, William
Mallet, John William
Mallory, Stephen Russell
Malvern Hill, Battle of
Manigault, Arthur Middleton
Mann, Ambrose Dudley
Mansfield, Joseph King Fenno
Mansfield, Louisiana, Battle of
Marine Corps, C.S.A.
Marine Corps, U.S.A.
Marks' Mills, Battle of
Marmaduke, John Sappington
Marshall, Humphrey
Martin, William Thompson
Martindale, John Henry
Martinsburg, Virginia
Maryland
Mason, James Murray
Masons
Matamoros, Mexico
Maum Guinea
Maury, Dabney Herndon
Maury, Matthew Fontaine
Maxey, Samuel Bell
Maximilian, Ferdinand
McArthur, John
McCallum, Daniel Craig
McCausland, John A.
McClellan, George Brinton
McClernand, John Alexander
McCooks of Ohio
McCulloch, Ben
McCulloch, Hugh
McDowell, Irvin
McDowell, Virginia, Battle of
McGowan, Samuel
McGuire, Hunter Holmes
McIntosh, John Baillie
McKay, Charlotte Johnson

McKinley, William
McLaws, Lafayette
McLean, John
McLean, Wilmer
McNeill, John Hanson and Jesse
McPherson, James Birdseye
Meade, George Gordon
Meagher, Thomas Francis
Mechanicsville, Battle of
Medal of Honor
Medicine
Medill, Joseph
Meigs, Montgomery C.
Melville, Herman
Memminger, Christopher Gustavus
Memorials, C.S.A.
Memorials, U.S.A.
Memphis, Naval Battle of
Mercier, Henri
Meredith, Solomon
Meridian Campaign
Merritt, Wesley
Merryman, John
Mexico
Miles, Nelson Appleton
Miles, William Porcher
Milligan, Lambdin P.
Milliken's Bend, Battle of
Milroy, Robert Huston
Milton, John
Mine Run Campaign
Minie Ball
Minié, Claude Étienne
Missionary Ridge, Battle of
Mississippi
Missouri
Mitchel, Ormsby Macknight
Mobile Bay
Mobile Campaign
Monitor, USS
Monitor versus *Virginia*
Monocacy, Maryland, Battle of
Montague, Robert Latane
Montgomery, James
Moore, Andrew Barry
Moore, Samuel Preston
Moore, Thomas Overton
Moorefield, West Virginia, Battle of
Morgan, Edwin Denison
Morgan, George Washington
Morgan, J. Pierpont
Morgan, James Dada
Morgan, John Hunt
Morgan's Raids
Mormons
Morrill, Justin Smith
Morrill Land Grant Act
Morton, Oliver Perry
Mosby, John Singleton
Mott, Gershom
Mott, Lucretia
Mower, Joseph Anthony
Mud March
Mudd, Samuel Alexander
Munford, Thomas Taylor
Munfordville, Battle of

Murrah, Pendleton
Music
Myer, Albert James
Myers, Abraham Charles

Napoleon III
Nashville, Battle of
Nashville, Tennessee
Nast, Thomas A.
National Tribune
Nativism
Natural Bridge, Florida, Battle of
Navy, C.S.A.
Navy, U.S.A.
Negley, James Scott
Nelson, Samuel
New Bern, Battle of
New Ironsides
New Jersey
New Market, Battle of
New Market Heights/Chaffin's
    Farm/Fort Harrison, Battle of
New Mexico Territory
New Orleans, Capture of
New York, Attempt to Burn
New York City Draft Riots
New York Times
New York Tribune
Newsom, Ella King
Newspapers
Newton, John
Nicolay, John George
North Anna, Battle of
North Carolina
Northrop, Lucius Bellinger
Nurses

Oak Grove (Henrico), Virginia
Oglesby, Richard James
Old Capitol Prison
Olmsted, Frederick Law
Olustee, Battle of
Opdycke, Emerson
Ord, Edward Otho Cresap
Order of American Knights
Ordnance, Naval
Orphan Brigade
Ostend Manifesto
Osterhaus, Peter J.
O'Sullivan, Timothy H.
Ould, Robert

Page, Charles Anderson
Paine, Halbert Eleazer
Palmer, John McCauley
Palmer, William Jackson
Palmerston, John Temple, Third
    Viscount
Palmito Ranch, Battle of
Parke, John Grubb
Parker, Ely Samuel
Parker, Joel
Parker, Theodore
Parker's Cross Roads
Parsons, Emily Elizabeth
Parsons, Lewis Baldwin

Patrick, Marsena Rudolph
Patterson, Robert
Paul, Gabriel René
Pay, C.S.A.
Pay, U.S.A.
Pea Ridge, Battle of
Peabody, George
Peace Democrats
Peace Movements
Peachtree Creek, Battle of
Pearson, Richmond Mumford
Pegg, Thomas
Pegram, John
Pelham, John
Pember, Phoebe Yates Levy
Pemberton, John Clifford
Pender, William Dorsey
Pendleton, George Hunt
Pendleton, William Nelson
Peninsula Campaign
Pennington, William
Pennsylvania
Pennypacker, Galusha
Pensacola, Florida
Perry, Edward Aylesworth
Perry, Madison Starke
Perryville/Chaplin Hills, Battle of
Personal Liberty Laws
Petersburg, Siege of
Petigru, James Louis
Pettigrew, James Johnston
Pettus, Edmund Winston
Pettus, John Jones
Pensions, Civil War
Phelan, James
Phelps, John Wolcott
Phelps's Raid
Philippi, Battle of
Phillips, Eugenia Levy
Phillips, Wendell
Phillips, William Addison
Photography
Pickens, Francis Wilkinson
Picket
Pickett, George Edward
Piedmont, Virginia, Battle of
Pierce, Franklin
Pierpont, Francis Harrison
Pike, Albert
Pillow, Gideon Johnson
Pilot Knob, Battle of
Pinkerton, Allan
Planter
Pleasant Hill, Louisiana, Battle of
Pleasants, Henry
Pleasonton, Alfred
Plum Point Bend, Naval Battle of
Plymouth, Battle of
Point Lookout Prison
Poison Spring, Battle of
Polignac, Camille Armand Jules Marie,
    Prince de
Polk, Leonidas
Pollard, Edward Alfred
Pomeroy, Samuel Clarke
Pook's "Turtles"

Pope, John
Poplar Springs Church (Peeble's Farm
    or Pegram's Farm)
Popular Sovereignty
Port Gibson, Battle of
Port Hudson, Louisiana Campaign
Port Republic, Battle of
Port Royal Sound/Hilton Head, Battle of
Porter, David Dixon
Porter, Fitz John
Porter, William David
Potter, Robert Brown
Powell, Lewis Thornton ("Payne")
Prairie Grove, Battle of
Prentiss, Benjamin Mayberry
Preston, John Smith
Preston, William
Price, Sterling
Price's Missouri Raid
Prigg v. Pennsylvania
Princeton, Virginia
Prisoner Exchanges
Prisoner Paroles
Prisoners of War
Prisons, C.S.A.
Prisons, U.S.A.
Privateers
Prize Cases
Pryor, Roger Atkinson

Quaker Guns
Quakers
Quantrill, William Clarke
Quartermaster
Quitman, John Anton

Radical Republicans
Railroads, C.S.A.
Railroads, U.S.A.
Rains, Gabriel James
Rains, George Washington
Ramseur, Stephen Dodson
Randolph, George Wythe
Ransom, Matt Whitaker
Ransom, Robert, Jr.
Ransom, Thomas Edward Greenfield
Rappahannock Station, Battle of
Rations, C.S.A.
Rations, U.S.A.
Rawlins, John Aaron
Raymond, Battle of
Raymond, Henry Jarvis
Reagan, John Henninger
Reams' Station, Virginia
Rebel Yell
Rector, Henry Massey
Red River Campaign
Reeder, Andrew Horatio
Refugee Home Society
Reid, Whitelaw
Religion
Reno, Jesse Lee
Republican Party
Resaca, Battle of
Reynolds, Arabella "Belle"
Reynolds, John Fulton

Reynolds, Joseph Jones
Rhett, Robert Barnwell, Sr.
Rich Mountain, Battle of
Richardson, Albert Deane
Richardson, Israel Bush
Richmond Campaign (Overland
    Campaign)
Richmond Examiner
Richmond, Kentucky, Battle of
Richmond, Virginia
Richmond, Virginia, Surrender of
Richmond Whig
Ricketts, James Brewerton
Rifles
Rio Grande Campaign
Riots, C.S.A.
Riots, U.S.A.
Ripley, James Wolfe
Ripley, Roswell Sabine
Riverine Warfare, U.S.N.
Rives, Alfred Landon
Rives, William Cabell
Roanoke Island, North Carolina
Robertson, Jerome Bonaparte
Robinson, Charles
Robinson, John Cleveland
Rock Island Prison
Rocky Face Ridge, Battle of
Rodes, Robert Emmett
Rodgers, John, Jr.
Rodman Gun
Rodman, Thomas Jefferson
Roebuck, John Arthur
Root, George Frederick
Rosecrans, William Starke
Ross, John
Rosser, Thomas Lafayette
Rost, Pierre Adolphe
Rousseau, Lovell Harrison
Ruffin, Edmund
Ruger, Thomas Howard
Russell, David Allen
Russell, Lord John
Russell, William Howard
Russian-American Relations

Sabine Pass, Texas, First Battle of
Sabine Pass, Texas, Second Battle of
Sacramento, Kentucky, Battle of
Salem Church/Salem Heights, Battle of
Salisbury Prison
Salm-Salm, Prince Felix Constantin
    Alexander Johann Nepomuk
Salomon, Friedrich
Saltville, Battle of
Sand Creek Massacre
Sandersville, Battle of
Santa Rosa Island
Savage's Station, Battle of
Savannah, Georgia
Savannah, Siege of
Saxton, Rufus
Sayler's Creek/Harper's Farm, Battle of
Schenck, Robert Cumming
Schofield, John McAllister
Schurz, Carl

Scott, Dred
Scott, William Campbell
Scott, Winfield
Secession
Secessionville, Battle of
Secret Service, C.S.A.
Secret Service, U.S.A.
Seddon, James Alexander
Sedgwick, John
Seligman, Joseph
Selma, Alabama
Seminole Indians
Semmes, Raphael
Seven Days' Battles
Seward, Frederick William
Seward, William Henry
Seymour, Horatio
Seymour, Thomas Hart
Seymour, Truman B.
Sharpshooters
Shaw, Robert Gould
Shelby, Joseph Orville
Shenandoah, CSS
Shenandoah Valley Campaign (1862)
Shenandoah Valley Campaign
    (1864–1865)
Shepley, George Foster
Sheridan, Philip Henry
Sherman, John
Sherman, Thomas West
Sherman, William Tecumseh
Sherman's March to the Sea
Sherwood, Isaac Ruth
Shields, James
Shiloh, Battle of
Shorter, John Gill
Shoup, Francis Asbury
Sibley, Henry Hastings
Sibley, Henry Hopkins
Sickles, Daniel Edgar
Sigel, Franz
Signal Corps
Simms, William Gilmore
Sims, Thomas
Sioux Indians
Sister Nurses
Slaves
Slemmer, Adam Jacoby
Slidell, John
Slocum, Henry Warner
Slang
Small Arms
Smalley, George Washburn
Smalls, Robert
Smith, Andrew Jackson
Smith, Caleb Blood
Smith, Charles Ferguson
Smith, Charles Henry (C.S.A.)
Smith, Charles Henry (U.S.A.)
Smith, Edmund Kirby
Smith, Gerrit
Smith, Giles Alexander
Smith, Gustavus Woodson
Smith, James Youngs
Smith, John Eugene
Smith, Martin Luther

Smith, Morgan Lewis
Smith, Thomas Kilby
Smith, Truman
Smith, William
Smith, William Farrar
Smith, William Sooy
Smoothbores
Soldiers' Votes
Sons of Confederate Veterans
Sons of Liberty, Order of
Sorrel, Gilbert Moxley
Soulé, Pierre
South Carolina
South Mountain, Maryland, Battle of
Southern Illustrated News
Southern Literary Messenger
Southern Unionism
Spanish Fort, Battle of
Sparrow, Edward
Spaulding, Elbridge Gerry
Speed, Joshua
Spinner, Francis Elias
Spotsylvania Court House, Battle of
Sprague, Kate Chase
Sprague, William
Springfield Armory
Springfield Rifle
St. Albans, Vermont, Raid
St. John, Isaac Munroe
Stahel-Szamvald, Julius
Stanley, David Sloane
Stanly, Edward
Stannard, George Jerrison
Stanton, Edwin
Stanton, Elizabeth Cady
Star of the West
Stearns, George Luther
Steedman, James Blair
Steele, Frederick
Stephens, Alexander Hamilton
Steuart, George Hume
Stevens, Isaac Ingalls
Stevens, Thaddeus
Stevenson, Carter Littlepage
Stewart, Alexander Peter
Stoeckl, Edouard de
Stone, Charles Pomeroy
Stone, Sarah Katherine, "Kate"
Stone, William Milo
Stoneman, George H., Jr.
Stoneman's Raid (April–May 1863)
Stoneman's Raid (July 1864)
Stoneman's Raid (December 1864–January 1865)
Stoneman's Raid (March–April 1865)
Stones River, Battle of
Stonewall Brigade
Stonewall, CSS
Stowe, Harriett Beecher
Strader v. Graham, 10 How. 82 (1851)
Strategy, C.S.A.
Strategy, U.S.A.
Streight's Raid
Stringham, Silas H.
Strong, George Templeton
Stuart, James Ewell Brown

Stuart's Dumfries (Virginia) Raid
Stuart's Ride around McClellan
Studebaker, Clement
Sturgis, Samuel Davis
Suffolk, Virginia, Siege of
Sultana
Sumner, Charles
Sumner, Edwin Vose
Sumter, CSS
Supreme Court, U.S.
Surratt, John Harrison, Jr.
Surratt, Mary Eugenia
Sutlers
Sweeny, Thomas William
Swinton, William
Sykes, George

Tactics
Taliaferro, William Booth
Taney, Roger Brooke
Tappan, Lewis
Tattnall, Josiah
Tax-in-Kind
Taylor, Richard
Taylor, Susie King
Tecumseh, USS
Telegraph
Tennessee
Tennessee, CSS
Terry, Alfred Howe
Texas
Texas Rangers
Thayer, John Milton
Thayer, Sylvanus
Thirteenth Amendment
Thomas, George Henry
Thomas, Lorenzo
Thomas, William Holland
Thompson, Jacob
Thompson, Meriwether Jeff
Thompson's Station/Spring Hill
Thoreau, Henry David
Thornwell, James H.
Tidball, John Caldwell
Tilden, Samuel Jones
Tilghman, Lloyd
Timrod, Henry
Tod, David
Todd, George
Todd's Tavern, Battle of
Tompkins, Sally Louisa
Tom's Brook, Battle of
Toombs, Robert Augustus
Torbert, Alfred Thomas Archimedes
Torpedoes
Totopotomy Creek, Battle of
Totten, Joseph Gilbert
Townsend, George Alfred
Tredegar Irons Works
Trenholm, George
Trent Affair
Trevilian Station, Battle of
Trimble, Isaac Ridgeway
Trumbull, Lyman
Truth, Sojourner
Tubman, Harriet

Tucker, John Randolph
Tullahoma Campaign
Tupelo, Battle of
Turchin, John Basil
Turchin, Nadine
Turner, John Wesley
Twiggs, David Emanuel
Tyler, John
Tyler, Robert Ogden

Ullmann, Daniel
Uncle Tom's Cabin
Underground Railroad
Underwood, Adin Ballou
Uniforms, Insignia, and Equipment
Union Leagues
Unionists, Southern
United Daughters of the Confederacy
United States Christian Commission
United States Colored Troops
United States Sanitary Commission
Upton, Emory
Utoy Creek, Battle of

Val Verde, New Mexico, Battle of
Vallandigham, Clement Laird
Van Cleve, Horatio Phillips
Van Dorn, Earl
Van Lew, Elizabeth
Vance, Zebulon Baird
Vanderbilt, Cornelius
Velazquez, Loreta Janeta
Vermont Brigade
Verot, Jean Pierre Augustin
Veterans' Organizations
Vicksburg Campaign
Victor, Orville James
Villard, Henry
Virginia
Virginia, CSS
Virginia Military Institute
von Steinwehr, Baron Adolf Wilhelm August Friedrich

Waddell, James Iredell
Wade, Benjamin Franklin
Wade-Davis Bill
Wakeman, Sarah Rosetta
Walker, James Alexander
Walker, John George
Walker, Leroy Pope
Walker, Mary Edwards
Walker, Robert John
Walker, William
Walker, William Henry Talbot
Wallace, Lewis (Lew)
Wallace, William Henry
Walthall, Edward Cary
War Correspondents
War Democrats
War of the Rebellion: Official Records
Ware Bottom Church, Virginia
Warren, Gouverneur Kemble
Washburn, Francis
Washburn, Israel, Jr.
Washburn, Cadwallader Colder

Washburne, Elihu Benjamin
Washington, D.C.
Washington Peace Conference
Watie, Stand
Watterson, Henry
Watts, Thomas Hill
Waud, Alfred Rudolph
Wauhatchie, Battle at (Brown's Ferry)
Wayne, James Moore
Waynesboro, Georgia
Waynesboro, Virginia, Battle of
Weaver, James Baird
Webb, Alexander Stewart
Webb, James Watson
Webster, Daniel
Weed, Thurlow
Weitzel, Godfrey
Weld, Theodore Dwight
Weldon & Petersburg Railroad
Welles, Gideon
West Point, Mississippi, Battle of
West Virginia
Western Sanitary Commission
Westport, Battle of
Wheat, Chatham Roberdeau
Wheaton, Frank
Wheeler, Joseph
Wheeler's Middle Tennessee Raid
Wheeler's Raid
Whiting, William Henry Chase

Whitman, Walt[er]
Whittier, John Greenleaf
Wickham, Williams Carter
Wigfall, Louis Trezevant
Wilcox, Cadmus Marcellus
Wild, Edward Augustus
Wilder, John Thomas
Wilderness, Battle of the
Wilkes, Charles
Willcox, Orlando Bolivar
Williams, Alphesus Starkey
Williamsburg, Battle of
Willich, August (von)
Wilmington, North Carolina
Wilmot, David
Wilmot Proviso
Wilson, Henry
Wilson, James Harrison
Wilson's Creek, Missouri
Wilson's Selma Raid
Winchester, First Battle of
Winchester, Second Battle of
Winchester, Third Battle of (Opequon)
Winder, Charles Sidney
Winder, John Henry
Winslow, John Ancrum
Wirz, Henry
Wise, Henry Alexander
Withers, Jones Mitchell
Wittenmyer, Annie Turner

Wofford, William Tatum
Women
Women Soldiers
Wood, Fernando
Wood, John Taylor
Wood, Thomas John
Woods, Charles Robert
Woodson's Cavalry
Woodward, George Washington
Wool, John Ellis
Worden, John Lorimer
Wright, Ambrose Ransom
Wright, Horatio Gouverneur

Yancey, William Lowndes
Yates, Richard
Yazoo Expedition
Yazoo Pass Expedition
Yellow Bayou (Bayou de Glaize),
    Louisiana
Yellow Tavern, Battle of
Yorktown
Young, Brigham
Young, John Russell
Young, Pierce Manning Butler
Yulee, David Levy

Zollicoffer, Felix
Zook, Samuel Kosciuszko
Zouaves

FOREWORD

By James M. McPherson

An advertising slogan popular during the years of my youth was: "When better cars are built, Buick will build them." The clear message was that, while there were many makes of automobiles on the market, Buick was the best.

That slogan comes to mind when reading the *Encyclopedia of the American Civil War*. Readers can choose from several reference works on the Civil War, but this one is the best. Comprehensive, authoritative, well written, cross-referenced, its 1600+ articles range from a column to several pages in length, covering every conceivable subject and significant person connected with the causes, course, and consequences of the war—from the Free Soil Party and the Wilmot Proviso to the Freedmen's Bureau and the Thirteenth Amendment; from John C. Calhoun and George Fitzhugh to Duncan Kenner and the Confederacy's last-ditch effort to enlist African-American soldiers; from the firing on *Star of the West* in January 1861 to the CSS *Shenandoah*'s rampage among American whalers in the Pacific during the summer of 1865.

Even the most learned and dedicated Civil War aficionados will find something here that they did not know before. Test yourself: What do you know about the battles of Alleghany Mountain, Glasgow, Greenbrier River, Ware Bottom Church, or Yellow Bayou? You can read about them in these pages. Can you identify Gaetano Bedini, Virginia Caroline Tunstall Clay-Clopton, Xavier Blanchard De Bray, Antonia Ford, Cordelia Perrine Harvey, or William Holland Thomas? Look them up in this encyclopedia and you will be prepared to win the Civil War *Jeopardy* sweepstakes. Most readers of this foreword know something of Braxton Bragg, but how many are familiar with Edward Stuyvesant Bragg and Thomas Bragg? How many can describe the Charleston (Illinois) Riot or Phelps's Raid? Can you explain the issues at stake in the case of *Lemmon v. People* and relate them to the causes of the war? With this encyclopedia in hand, you can answer all of these questions and many, many more. Arranged alphabetically, the entries cover a broad range of categories: persons; states; military campaigns and battles; the names of ships; the various armies (of Northern Virginia, of the Potomac, etc.); famous units like the Stonewall Brigade and the Iron Brigade; important legislation and proclamations; names of newspapers and magazines; names of important organizations; prisoner-of-war camps; key events such as the Centralia Massacre, the burning of Columbia, the assassination of Lincoln; and categories such as casualties; class conflict (C.S.A. and U.S.A.); United States Colored Troops; African-American Soldiers (C.S.A.); photography; the Underground Railroad; armories, arsenals, and foundries; and scores of others. In short, nothing of importance or interest is left out. Cross-references and a brief bibliography at the end of each article refer the reader to other relevant articles in this encyclopedia and to outside sources for further research. Another valuable feature are the documents that provide a primary-source accompaniment to many of the articles. These documents give a sense of immediacy to the subjects of the articles; they also suggest sources and ideas for further reading and research.

For good reason, the Civil War is the most written-about subject in American history. Northern victory assured the survival of the United States as one nation, indivisible, and ended the anomaly of slavery in a country founded on a charter of freedom. A blend of triumph and tragedy, courage and cowardice, heroes and knaves, selfless sacrifice and selfish profiteering, the war shaped and defined the America that has emerged in the 135 years since the guns fell silent. This reference work will broaden and deepen the knowledge of this titanic conflict for novice and expert alike.

PREFACE

We have sought with this encyclopedia to fashion a comprehensive source for a boundless subject. At most for both serious scholars and interested amateurs, we hope to provide a reference of first resort for those seeking information either on broad areas or specific topics. More than 1,600 essays describe and explain a myriad of aspects that cover the coming of the war, its conduct, and its consequences in a political, military, and social context. In addition to full biographies of major and minor military, political, diplomatic, and cultural figures, these essays include descriptions of more than sixty major engagements as well as important skirmishes and their role in the larger military setting. We have also tried to cover broad areas such as strategy and tactics, social trends, and technological innovations. Primary documents are provided in a separate section, maps depict military aspects, and illustrations furnish both portraiture and vivid scenes from the period. Appendices supply the executive officers of both the United States and Confederate States, general officers of each army, a glossary of terms unique to military usage or peculiar to the period, and an extensive bibliography.

We are grateful to our editorial board for guidance and advice. Our associate editor, David J. Coles, provided insightful assistance in identifying potential contributors and reviewing work once it came to hand. While indebted to all our contributors, we are especially appreciative of those whose special exertions materially advanced this project to its completion. Albert Castel, Warner Farr, Dave Sullivan, Spencer Tucker, and Dave Zabecki were among those who took time from busy schedules to read material and offer suggestions for its improvement. Elizabeth Leonard not only made a significant contribution herself, she introduced us to several scholars whose expertise proved invaluable in deepening the texture of this work. Jane Schultz and Wendy Venet number among those contributors whose special command of areas in the field helped us round out our list and bring it to a conclusion. Jack Davis was an early friend to the project, as were Paul Cimbala, John Marszalek, Greg Urwin, and David Williams, all of whom made valuable suggestions for additions to the list and provided introductions to scholars who could write on specialized subjects. Many contributors gave us leads to illustrations, and Judith Bielecki, JoAnn Castagna, Paul Cimbala, Paul Kuhl, David Williams, and Dave Zabecki even went so far as to send camera-ready prints or negatives with permissions. Don Frazier's cartography again proved peerless and his timing flawless. We could not have completed the enterprise without John Fredriksen's valuable and timely contributions, and we owe special thanks to Jean Harvey Baker and Richard J. Sommers for their extraordinary efforts as much as for their impeccable work. Finally, we are humbled by the professionalism and high consideration of several authors who made their valuable contributions to the project in spite of dire health crises. Wishing to preserve their privacy, we have thanked them privately, painfully aware that our acknowledgments both public and private are inadequate notice of their splendid sacrifices and pale expressions of our deep appreciation.

The support of friends and family was so ample that it eludes the proper expression of thanks. Cyrus K. Heidler was always standing by to help ease the weariness of long labors. Friends like Kathryn E. Holland Braund, Steve Engle, and Reg Stuart had kind words ready when such were sorely needed. And Joseph and Sarah Twiggs have been in this, as in all things, wise and witty, and though at some remove, always near when needed and always cheerful wherever.

—*David S. Heidler and Jeanne T. Heidler*

INTRODUCTION

More than any other event, the American Civil War went far in defining a United States that had been imperfectly and incompletely shaped by its first seventy years. For seven decades, the presence of slavery in a republic founded upon principles of human freedom increasingly befuddled the political system and unraveled the social fabric. Although slavery in the South had given rise to antislavery movements in the North as early as the American Revolution, notably among religious groups such as the Quakers, a fresh vigor characterized abolitionist activities in the 1830s. Although the abolitionists divided along radical and moderate lines and argued among themselves about the viability of political solutions to the moral blight of slavery, the abolitionists became a moral force of growing influence and gradually made a deep impression on Northern sentiments. The movement also provoked a proslavery reaction from Southern whites that enlarged the breach between North and South. Southerners came to feel beleaguered and isolated as moderate Northerners increasingly exhibited the attitude that slavery was wrong and at least should not be extended to the nation's western territories.

Arguments over these western territories goaded the country into a series of disruptive crises. Each was settled with an unsatisfying compromise that left most Southerners feeling materially cheated and many Northerners morally embarrassed. In 1854, efforts to organize the vast Midwest region called the Nebraska Territory led to the ill-conceived Kansas-Nebraska Act. It was a project designed to secure Southern support for the organization of what by prior agreement would have been a free territory. Two territories, Kansas and Nebraska, would be created from the region under the principal of popular sovereignty, which was to say that each territory would decide for itself whether to admit or prohibit slavery. This cynical calculation for Southern endorsement was apparent from the start. Kansas, the southernmost section of the region, was obviously supposed to become a slave state, while Nebraska to the north would apparently become a free state. The plan instantly went awry, however, when the fate of Kansas became a point of occasionally violent contention between armed antislavery and proslavery factions that went far in turning the territory into a battleground.

Antislavery Northerners were enraged while Southerners took Northern reaction as another instance of bad faith. Consequently, all previous compromises on the slavery issue were imperiled, and any future compromises were preemptively questionable. The party system was immediately altered. Democrats began to drift into Northern and Southern wings, sometimes hostile and always suspicious of each other. The Whig Party simply disintegrated with much of its Northern element forming into the new Republican Party. This new party's initial reason for existence was to mount a robust objection to slavery, but within two years its program would expand to attract Northern yeomen farmers and businessmen as well as antislavery advocates. Although it was an exclusively sectional party, it contended successfully against Northern Democrats in state and local contests, became a powerful force in Congress, and mounted a serious bid for the presidency in 1856.

Democrat James Buchanan won the 1856 election, but he had been in office only two days when the Supreme Court made a ruling in the *Dred Scott* Case on 6 March 1857. Scott was a slave who sued for his freedom on the basis that his owner had taken him to live for five years in the free state of Illinois and the free Wisconsin Territory. In addition to denying Scott his freedom, Chief Justice Roger Taney's comprehensive decision went further to declare that Congress had no authority to prohibit slavery in the territories, even if territorial inhabitants desired such a prohibition. The ruling seriously eroded the power of popular sovereignty to exclude slavery from any territories in the Union, thus depriving Northern Democrats of a convenient way to sidestep confrontations with their Southern wing over slavery. Republicans decried the decision and condemned the Court, thus giving Southerners additional evidence that the North would not respect any measures—even Supreme Court decisions—that did not assail slavery.

The most disruptive issue distracting the Buchanan administration, however, was the ongoing controversy over Kansas. When Buchanan attempted to obtain statehood for the troubled territory, proslavery forces at Lecompton, Kansas, drafted a constitution that not only reflected their views on slavery but also removed the possibility of a territorial referendum excluding it from the new state. Illinois senator Stephen A. Douglas, leading Democrat in Congress and a proponent of popular sovereignty, objected to the Lecompton Constitution so strenuously that he earned the lasting enmity of President Buchanan. Douglas was forced to defend his Senate seat in 1858 against the Republican challenger Abraham Lincoln, doing so in a series of joint appearances across Illinois that would be immortalized as the Lincoln-Douglas Debates. Douglas kept his Senate seat, but Lincoln's declarations on slavery struck such a sympathetic chord among Northerners that he would emerge from the contest a national figure. Stating a

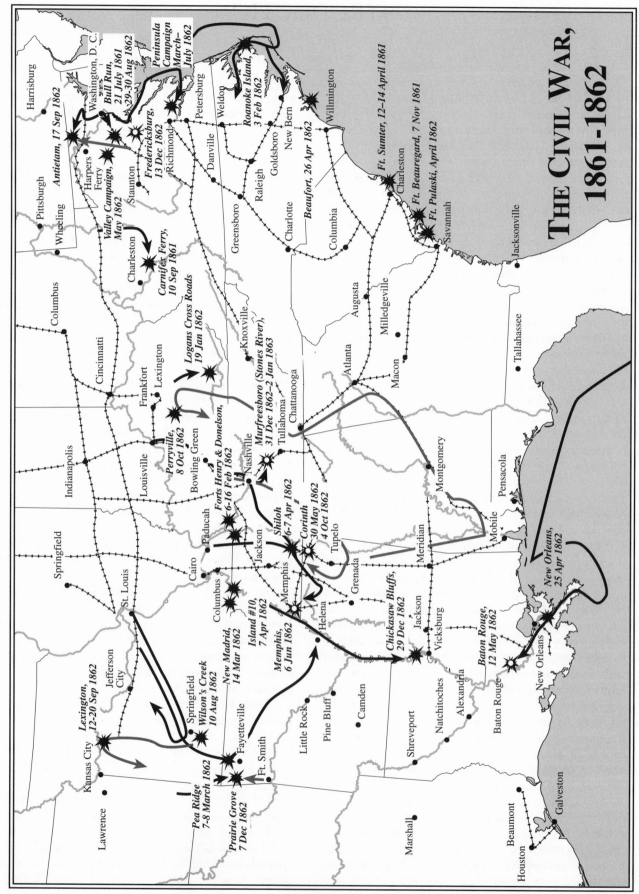

THE CIVIL WAR, 1861-1862

Harrisburg

Pittsburgh

Wheeling

Washington, D.C.

Bull Run, 21 July 1861 & 29-30 Aug 1862

Peninsula Campaign March–July 1862

Antietam, 17 Sep 1862

Harpers Ferry

Valley Campaign, May 1862

Staunton

Fredericksburg, 13 Dec 1862

Richmond

Petersburg

Weldon

Danville

Roanoke Island, 3 Feb 1862

New Bern

Goldsboro

Beaufort, 26 Apr 1862

Willmington

Ft. Sumter, 12–14 April 1861

Ft. Beauregard, 7 Nov 1861

Charleston

Ft. Pulaski, April 1862

Savannah

Jacksonville

Columbus

Cincinnatti

Frankfort

Lexington

Charleston

Carnifex Ferry, 10 Sep 1861

Logans Cross Roads 19 Jan 1862

Knoxville

Greensboro

Raleigh

Charlotte

Columbia

Augusta

Milledgeville

Macon

Tallahassee

Indianapolis

Louisville

Perryville, 8 Oct 1862

Bowling Green

Forts Henry & Donelson, 6-16 Feb 1862

Nashville

Murfreesboro (Stones River), 31 Dec 1862–2 Jan 1863

Tullahoma

Chattanooga

Atlanta

Montgomery

Pensacola

Springfield

Paducah

Cairo

Jackson

Shiloh, 6-7 Apr 1862

Corinth 30 May 1862 4 Oct 1862

Tupelo

Meridian

Mobile

New Orleans, 25 Apr 1862

St. Louis

Columbus

New Madrid, 14 Mar 1862

Memphis

Island #10, 7 Apr 1862

Memphis, 6 Jun 1862

Helena

Grenada

Chickasaw Bluffs, 29 Dec 1862

Jackson

Vicksburg

Baton Rouge, 12 May 1862

New Orleans

Jefferson City

Springfield

Wilson's Creek 10 Aug 1862

Fayetteville

Ft. Smith

Little Rock

Pine Bluff

Camden

Natchitoches

Shreveport

Alexandria

Baton Rouge

Lexington, 12-20 Sep 1862

Kansas City

Lawrence

Pea Ridge 7-8 March 1862

Prairie Grove 7 Dec 1862

Marshall

Beaumont

Houston

Galveston

moderate antislavery position, Lincoln insisted that slavery could not be molested where it existed, but it must not be allowed to spread to areas where it did not; even as he condemned slavery, he refused to denounce slaveholders. Prominent members of the Republican Party began taking Lincoln's measure as a possible presidential candidate for 1860.

Moderation of Lincoln's type reflected the majority opinion in the North, but the increasing tensions of the sectional dispute saw dramatic and extreme occurrences overwhelm the demeanor of such moderation. Ultimately, Southerners were unable to distinguish between temperate opposition to slavery and radical abolitionism. The most notorious episode of the latter was John Brown's October 1859 raid on the federal armory at Harper's Ferry in western Virginia. Brown intended to mount an invasion of the South, arming liberated slaves to commit insurrection and bring about the violent destruction of slavery. The raid failed, but Brown's subsequent trial revealed that some prominent Northern abolitionists had backed the scheme. For Southerners, such a revelation was bad enough, yet worse was the mantle of martyrdom that many Northerners settled on Brown's shoulders even as the hangman was placing the noose around his neck. Pealing bells and cannon salutes provided the backdrop for large gatherings that heard Brown compared to Christ, his gallows likened to the cross.

The election of 1860 was held in the shadow of these ominous events. The Democrats soon found themselves divided over both a candidate and a platform, and an abortive convention in Charleston, South Carolina, and then a discordant one in Baltimore, Maryland, failed to mend the rift. Instead, two Democratic Party candidates would emerge from the brawl, Stephen A. Douglas and John C. Breckinridge, the latter bearing the onus of being the "Southern" candidate. Whigs and other disaffected political strays, untethered by the roiling sectional dispute, cobbled together a Constitutional Union Party to nominate John Bell, touted as a candidate who would avoid the distracting slavery controversy to restore the Union to amity. And the Republicans on the third ballot of their convention in Chicago nominated Abraham Lincoln, who in November 1860 became the sixteenth president-elect of the United States.

The outcome of the 1860 election triggered a grave crisis. Four days after Abraham Lincoln's election, South Carolina's legislature unanimously called a special convention that met in Charleston. On 20 December 1860, the convention unanimously chose to secede from the Union, and six additional Deep South states had followed by early February 1861. That month representatives from these states met at Montgomery, Alabama, to form the Confederate States of America and choose their president, former U.S. Senator Jefferson Davis of

Mississippi, and vice president, Alexander H. Stephens of Georgia. Basic American ideals of self-determination as manifested in the Declaration of Independence guided the Southerners toward secession and in their mind justified them in the act. Southern secessionists drew parallels from the American Revolution's defiance of the British Empire in 1776. Furthermore, to the secessionists the Union that was formed in the aftermath of the Revolution was a voluntary formation that could be voluntarily disbanded. Separated from Northern assaults on its "peculiar institution" of slavery, the South would seek to forge its own fate, confident that it would do so more agreeably as a separate nation.

Meanwhile, Lincoln would not take office until 4 March 1861, and elderly President James Buchanan confronted the emergency. Unswerving in his loyalty to the Union, Buchanan rejected the idea that secession was legal. Yet, he also insisted that the Constitution did not empower the president to employ force to preserve the Union. In any event, the United States's small peacetime army was widely scattered and mainly occupied with policing the western frontier. Buchanan was not alone in hoping that compromise and reconciliation would avert the storm. Indeed, the specter of war was a powerful incentive for compromise, and serious efforts for reconciliation were played out in Washington in tandem with the secession crisis. One was the set of initiatives sponsored by Kentucky senator John J. Crittenden as proposed constitutional amendments protecting slavery and thus designed to accommodate Southern apprehensions. This compromise effort failed in part because Lincoln declared his opposition to it on the grounds that its provisions would violate Republican promises to halt the spread of slavery into the territories. The other major effort was the Washington Peace Conference, a meeting attended mainly by fading luminaries of another time—former president John Tyler was its presiding officer—and whose informal appellation of "The Old Gentlemen's Convention" indicated the futility of its labors.

Even after his inauguration, Lincoln remained hopeful that reconciliation was still possible, and he fundamentally continued Buchanan's policy of watchful waiting. Yet political compromises fashioned to postpone a final reckoning became at the end only another source of confusion and dissatisfaction themselves, and the final reckoning loomed as the republic remained divided. And Lincoln could not wait forever. Federal authority over forts in the South brought the secession crisis to its conclusion. Seceding states had taken over almost all U. S. property within their borders so that when Lincoln became president, there were only two important garrisons in the South still in federal possession. One was lightly manned Fort Sumter in Charleston Harbor, whose supplies would be exhausted by mid-

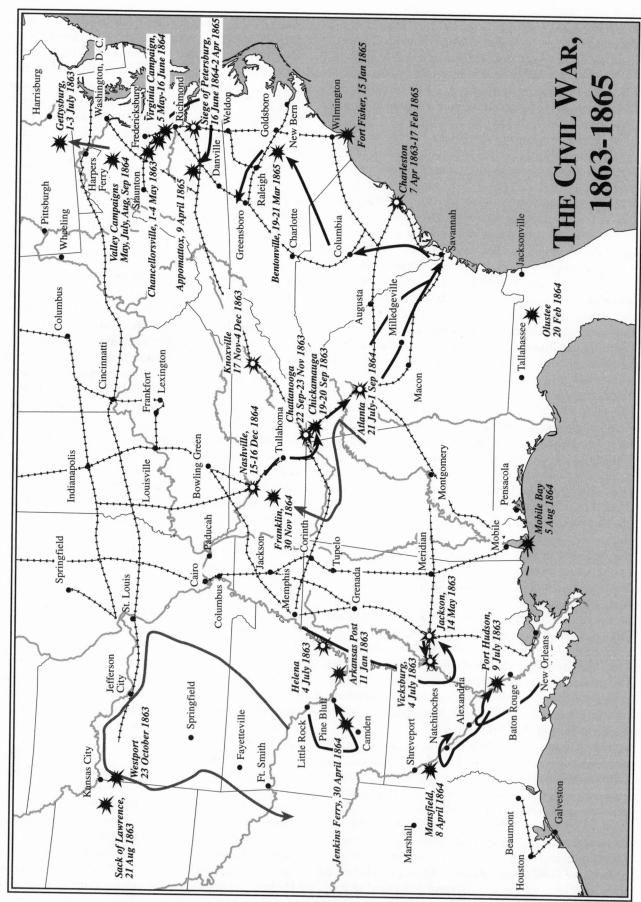

THE CIVIL WAR, 1863-1865

Harrisburg

Washington, D. C.

Gettysburg,
1-3 July 1863

Fredericksburg

Virginia Campaign,
5 May-16 June 1864

Richmond

Siege of Petersburg,
16 June 1864-2 Apr 1865

Weldon

Danville

Goldsboro

New Bern

Wilmington

Fort Fisher, 15 Jan 1865

Harpers
Ferry

Staunton

Valley Campaigns
May, July, Aug, Sep 1864

Greensboro

Raleigh

Bentonville, 19-21 Mar 1865

Charlotte

Charleston
7 Apr 1863-17 Feb 1865

Pittsburgh

Wheeling

Chancellorsville, 1-4 May 1863

Appomattox, 9 April 1865

Columbia

Savannah

Jacksonville

Columbus

Cincinnatti

Lexington

Augusta

Milledgeville

Olustee
20 Feb 1864

Frankfort

Knoxville
17 Nov-4 Dec 1863

Chattanooga
22 Sep-23 Nov 1863

Chickamauga
19-20 Sep 1863

Macon

Tallahassee

Nashville,
15-16 Dec 1864

Tullahoma

Atlanta
21 July-1 Sep 1864

Indianapolis

Louisville

Bowling Green

Montgomery

Pensacola

Franklin,
30 Nov 1864

Corinth

Mobile

Mobile Bay
5 Aug 1864

Paducah

Springfield

St. Louis

Cairo

Jackson

Memphis

Tupelo

Meridian

Columbus

Grenada

Jackson,
14 May 1863

Jefferson
City

Westport
23 October 1863

Springfield

Fayetteville

Little Rock

Pine Bluff

Helena
4 July 1863

Arkansas Post
11 Jan 1863

Camden

Vicksburg,
4 July 1863

Natchitoches

Alexandria

Port Hudson,
9 July 1863

Baton Rouge

New Orleans

Kansas City

Sack of Lawrence,
21 Aug 1863

Ft. Smith

Jenkins Ferry, 30 April 1864

Shreveport

Mansfield,
8 April 1864

Marshall

Beaumont

Houston

Galveston

April. Buchanan's attempt to reinforce Sumter in January had failed when batteries drove off the *Star of the West*. Now, after giving up the dim hope that force would not be necessary, Lincoln ultimately elected to hold the fort and informed South Carolina authorities that an expedition would supply though not reinforce it. The Confederate government deemed the gesture as aggression, and on 12 April 1861 batteries opened fire on Fort Sumter, an act that many Northerners found so provocative that it gave Lincoln a significant psychological advantage in both the domestic and foreign arenas. By making the South appear to be the aggressor against the Union, Lincoln was able to summon patriots to protect the flag. On 15 April he called on the states for 75,000 men to suppress the rebellion. On 19 April, Lincoln proclaimed a blockade of Southern seaports, extending its range on 27 April. Young men gathered into armies, and brothers braced to strike down brothers. The Civil War had begun.

For the next four years, the country would test the limits of its endurance and the durability of its central ideas. The remarkable will and resolution of both sides prolonged a contest that became a horrifying nightmare from the first shots. Every day of those four years marked the delivery to countless firesides of doleful messages announcing that the boy who had gone away to fight would never be coming home.

From the Southern perspective, Lincoln's call for volunteers amounted to unprovoked aggression against the Confederacy. Soon Virginia, Arkansas, Tennessee, and North Carolina joined the Confederacy, although they did so with considerable anxiety and debate. The western counties of Virginia, in fact, refused to join the state in secession and themselves seceded from Virginia in mid-1861, eventually to become the state of West Virginia. Furthermore, the border states of Missouri, Kentucky, Maryland, and Delaware did not secede. The Confederacy was thus deprived of border state factories, horses, and mules as well as control of strategic waterways such as the Ohio River. From the Ohio, the Cumberland and Tennessee Rivers would provide avenues of invasion for Union gunboats. Lincoln adopted a deft balance of inducement and force in dealing with the border states. To protect the capital, he imposed martial law in parts of Maryland. He was careful about Kentucky, but he sent troops to western Virginia and Missouri to aid Unionists in protecting their regions for the Union. These areas of vague and tenuous loyalty would experience an especially ugly aspect of the Civil War when guerrilla warfare erupted and preyed on civilian as well as military targets. Missouri would be especially plagued with tragic atrocities and grisly retribution.

In the coming conflict, the Confederacy had the advantage of interior lines, and the Union faced the hard task of conquering and occupying an immense amount of territory. If it could endure long enough to discourage the North, the Confederacy could win by surviving. In the face of Northern invasion, Southerners also would be spurred by the need to protect hearth and home. Also during the war, Confederate commerce raiders such as the notorious *Alabama* plied global waters to capture or destroy more than 250 Northern ships, an accomplishment that so damaged the American merchant marine that it would not recover for the remainder of the century.

Northern advantages, however, especially derived from a war of attrition. With only a marginal manufacturing capability, the South would experience serious shortages of the most basic items that would diminish the Confederate ability to wage war. The South's substandard railroad system caused chronic supply problems, and logistical difficulties would only compound when invading Union armies destroyed what railroad lines existed. The North contained not only ample farms but also a diversified and large manufacturing potential. The United States would build a large navy that effectively blockaded Southern ports even as it protected grain exports abroad and facilitated imports from European factories. The Union's larger population of about 22 million to the Confederacy's 9 million people (including about 3.5 million slaves) would be bolstered by European immigrants, many of whom immediately enlisted in Union armies.

Eventually, these Northern advantages would prove irresistible, but at the outset of the conflict Southern victory was a definite possibility. Many thought it would be a short war, and many young men rushed to the colors in both the North and South, fearful that the glorious conflict would conclude before they could see action. Lincoln's initial call for volunteers had anticipated that they would be needed for only ninety days. At the end of May, the Confederate government relocated its capital from Montgomery, Alabama, to Richmond, Virginia—a move that would have profound strategic implications for the coming war—and Northerners, eagerly expecting a swift settlement with one big battle, entreated their raw soldiers to march "On to Richmond!"

The hastily raised Union army of about 30,000 men was hardly ready to go on the offensive, but under pressure from newspapers and the public, Lincoln decided the army should move against a smaller Confederate army near Bull Run and Manassas Junction, about thirty miles southwest of Washington. The resulting battle of First Bull Run (there would another battle at the same place thirteen months later) on 21 July 1861 was a Confederate victory that ended with many Union soldiers in panicked flight. Yet Confederate forces were too fatigued to pursue and exploit their triumph. Worse, the victory at Bull Run amplified Southerners' conceit

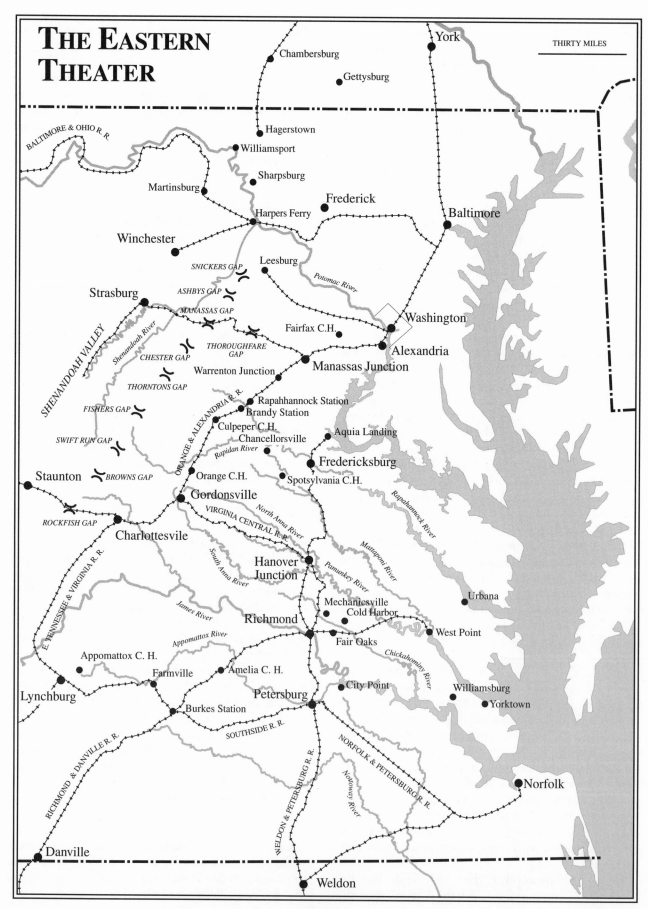

THE EASTERN THEATER

THIRTY MILES

York

Chambersburg

Gettysburg

BALTIMORE & OHIO R. R.

Hagerstown

Williamsport

Sharpsburg

Frederick

Martinsburg

Baltimore

Harpers Ferry

Winchester

Leesburg

SNICKERS GAP

Potomac River

ASHBYS GAP

Strasburg

MANASSAS GAP

Washington

THOROUGHFARE GAP

Fairfax C.H.

Alexandria

CHESTER GAP

SHENANDOAH VALLEY

Warrenton Junction

Manassas Junction

THORNTONS GAP

Shenandoah River

Rapahhannock Station

FISHERS GAP

Brandy Station

ORANGE & ALEXANDRIA R. R.

Culpeper C.H.

Aquia Landing

Chancellorsville

SWIFT RUN GAP

Rapidan River

Fredericksburg

Staunton

BROWNS GAP

Orange C.H.

Spotsylvania C.H.

Gordonsville

Rapahhannock River

ROCKFISH GAP

VIRGINIA CENTRAL R. R.

North Anna River

Charlottesville

Mattaponi River

South Anna River

Hanover Junction

E. TENNESSEE & VIRGINIA R. R.

Pamunkey River

Urbana

James River

Mechanicsville

Cold Harbor

Richmond

West Point

Appomattox River

Fair Oaks

Appomattox C. H.

Chickahominy River

Farmville

Amelia C. H.

Williamsburg

Lynchburg

City Point

Yorktown

Petersburg

Burkes Station

SOUTHSIDE R. R.

NORFOLK & PETERSBURG R. R.

RICHMOND & DANVILLE R. R.

WELDON & PETERSBURG R. R.

Nottoway River

Norfolk

Danville

Weldon

about their superiority over the "mongrel" hordes of the North. With many believing that the war was won, enlistments decreased and preparations for a lengthy contest no longer seemed necessary. In the North the fantasy of a quick end to this crisis died at Bull Run, and the Lincoln administration dedicated the country's resources to the towering job of winning the war.

Eventually Union strategy would be honed to embrace something resembling a modern, coordinated war effort. Aging General Winfield Scott had been ridiculed in the press for his proposal of the so-called Anaconda Plan, and Lincoln himself had thought the idea envisioned a needlessly protracted war. Yet a modification of Scott's idea was in due time implemented. The Union was already planning to choke the South with the blockade, and its fixation on capturing the Confederate capital at Richmond remained a constant. Yet the strategy would also move to cut the Confederacy in half by controlling the Mississippi River and at the end would further fragment the rebellion by invading Georgia and the Carolinas. Finally, under the strategic vision of Ulysses S. Grant, the North would apply its inexhaustible resources in men and materiel to engage the South simultaneously on as many fronts as possible to pulverize it into capitulation.

Immediately after First Bull Run, though, Lincoln had to restore confidence and rehabilitate the main Union army that had returned to Washington a shattered mob. In the hopes that competent and charismatic leadership would rebuild this force and bring order to the entire military organization, Lincoln turned to West Point graduate Major General George B. McClellan. Eventually made general-in-chief of all Union armies, McClellan was young, energetic, and confident. The newspapers dubbed him "The Young Napoleon," and his flair for organization and meticulous attention to detail soon whipped the force he renamed the Army of the Potomac into impressive fighting trim. The men loved him, but he became so cautious about their welfare that he became too attentive to risks. When Lincoln pressed him to action, McClellan adopted a contemptuous manner toward the president that was beyond inappropriate. Lincoln nonetheless was resolved to be charitable if McClellan could win the war.

Mistaken in his belief that Confederate forces in northern Virginia outnumbered his own, McClellan resolved to avoid a direct confrontation and instead planned a waterborne approach to Richmond. The Peninsula campaign was the ambitious result in the spring of 1862. McClellan's large army of almost 100,000 men was ferried to the end of Virginia's York Peninsula from whence it moved slowly up toward Richmond. McClellan would claim that Lincoln's insistence on keeping back forces to protect the capital hopelessly subverted the Peninsula campaign. Yet Lincoln was

adamant, especially when Thomas "Stonewall" Jackson's epic maneuvers in the Shenandoah Valley seemed to imperil Washington. When Confederate general Joseph E. Johnston attacked McClellan in the battle of Seven Pines, it was an indecisive engagement that nonetheless rattled the Young Napoleon even as it left Johnston seriously wounded. General Robert E. Lee, given command of the forces he named the Army of Northern Virginia, soon launched a series of furious attacks known as the Seven Days' battles (25 June–1 July 1862). Lee drove McClellan away from Richmond, and Lincoln gave up on the Peninsula campaign and at least temporarily cast aside McClellan.

The Western theater offered more encouraging events for the Union, especially as they led to the emergence of an able general in Ulysses S. Grant. Although Grant was not a prepossessing figure and his prewar career both in military and civilian pursuits had branded him a failure, his audacity, ingenuity, and determination soon revealed him to be a unique commodity among Union general officers. In February 1862, his capture of Fort Henry on the Tennessee River and Fort Donelson on the Cumberland River pierced the Confederate defense of the entire region, especially Tennessee. Emboldened by such success, Grant brashly moved on the important railroad junction at Corinth, Mississippi, and was handed a stunning setback when Confederate forces under Albert Sidney Johnston nearly destroyed his army at the battle of Shiloh on 6 April 1862. Yet Johnston was mortally wounded at Shiloh, a loss that many regarded as a crippling blow to the Confederacy. For his part, Grant was able to hold on until reinforcements allowed him to turn the tide the next day. Nonetheless, the near disaster at Shiloh was a mistake that had some calling for Grant's hide. Lincoln would have none of it, and he refused to act on stories that labeled Grant a drunkard. The country was too much in need of generals who fought and, even better, won. Lincoln would not discard any who did so.

Other Union successes in the West were heartening as well. In the spring of 1862, David G. Farragut's naval forces conducted a joint operation with the army to capture New Orleans. Soon much of the Mississippi River was crawling with Union gunboats, and the Confederacy anxiously sought to protect a cramped region between Vicksburg and Port Hudson to keep available the imperative supplies of livestock and stores in Louisiana and Texas. In the fall of 1862, a Confederate invasion of Kentucky ended at the muddled battle of Perryville, which at least had the effect of requiring Southern forces to retreat into east Tennessee.

In the East, Lincoln supplanted George McClellan with a general who had won in the West. General John Pope had waged a successful assault against Island No. 10 on the Mississippi River, and in the wake of the

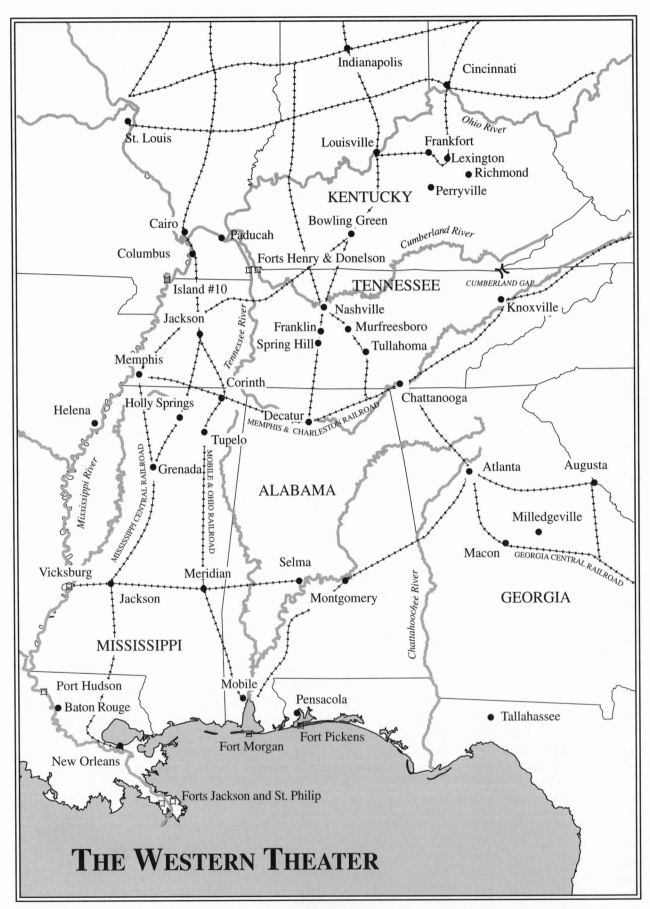

Indianapolis

Cincinnati

Ohio River

St. Louis

Louisville

Frankfort

Lexington

Richmond

KENTUCKY

Perryville

Cairo

Bowling Green

Paducah

Cumberland River

Columbus

Forts Henry & Donelson

Island #10

TENNESSEE

CUMBERLAND GAP

Jackson

Nashville

Knoxville

Tennessee River

Franklin

Murfreesboro

Spring Hill

Tullahoma

Memphis

Corinth

Chattanooga

Helena

Holly Springs

Decatur

MEMPHIS & CHARLESTON RAILROAD

Tupelo

Atlanta

Augusta

MISSISSIPPI CENTRAL RAILROAD

Grenada

ALABAMA

Milledgeville

MOBILE & OHIO RAILROAD

Macon

GEORGIA CENTRAL RAILROAD

Mississippi River

Selma

Vicksburg

Meridian

GEORGIA

Jackson

Montgomery

Chattahoochee River

MISSISSIPPI

Port Hudson

Mobile

Pensacola

Baton Rouge

Fort Morgan

Fort Pickens

Tallahassee

New Orleans

Forts Jackson and St. Philip

THE WESTERN THEATER

Peninsula disappointment, Lincoln tapped him to command a new Federal army to march on Richmond. Yet Pope proved more boastful than resourceful, and Robert E. Lee handed him and his army a sundering defeat at the battle of Second Bull Run on 29–30 August 1862. In the wake of this disaster, Lincoln reluctantly reinstated McClellan as the army's principal commander.

In the autumn of 1862, Lee hoped that by moving north of the Potomac River he would advance not only Confederate military fortunes, but also Confederate diplomatic efforts to secure foreign recognition. The possibility of foreign intervention on the Confederacy's behalf promised the surest path to ultimate victory. Many in Europe's ruling classes were repelled by American democracy and consequently intrigued by Southern chivalry with its aristocratic pretensions.

At the outset of Lee's invasion of western Maryland, McClellan, with characteristic caution, made only tentative moves to counter it until a copy of Lee's battle plans was found by Union soldiers and delivered to head-quarters. Moving with unusual dispatch, McClellan descended on the hastily congregated Southern army at Antietam Creek on 17 September 1862 and fought there for twelve hours to produce the bloodiest single day of the war. Although Antietam ended in a stalemate, it did produce conclusive consequences. Immediately, Lee was forced to move back across the Potomac, his invasion a failure and its objectives unrealized. McClellan's failure to exploit fully the remarkable advantage handed him in the discovery of Lee's lost order, and the subsequent return of his habitual caution, led Lincoln again to remove him from command, this for the last time.

And in a larger sense, the battle of Antietam was truly decisive. The Confederacy would never again be so near the chance of obtaining British and French recognition, a diplomatic achievement that might have led to indis-pensable military alliances. After Antietam, Britain rightly had second thoughts about the potential for Confederate military success. British reservations were also reinforced when Lincoln used the modest Union success at Antietam as a reason to announce the prelim-inary Emancipation Proclamation on 23 September 1862. In this preliminary document, Lincoln promised that should the rebellion continue, on 1 January 1863 emancipation would become final. Thus the Civil War became not only a moral crusade, it also became a revo-lution growing out of the exercise to suppress a rebellion.

The effect of the proclamation on the diplomatic situation was instantly telling. The South had counted on British dependence on cotton to sway the working class of England to support the Confederacy. Yet, the great abundance of southern cotton yields in the years before the war had glutted British warehouses. Eighteen months into the war, British cotton reserves would begin

to dwindle, but then the strong antislavery sentiments among British common folk made them violently oppose official intervention on behalf of the South, and the British government accordingly took heed. The moral imperative of the Emancipation Proclamation both bolstered and sealed this British attitude toward the Union. Although Anglo-American relations were occa-sionally vexed by incidents such as the *Trent* Affair and the construction in British shipyards of Confederate commerce raiders and possible warships, the adroit U.S. minister Charles Francis Adams was able to maintain civil, if not always congenial, relations with his British hosts.

Napoleon III of France followed the British lead in ultimately refusing to recognize the Confederacy. Instead Napoleon took advantage of American preoccupations to establish a puppet regime in Mexico under Austrian Archduke Maximilian. The venture certainly excited American displeasure, but until the war ended, there was little the United States could do. In 1865, however, the armies that had recently defeated the Confederacy were prepared to march into Mexico, and Napoleon equivo-cated as long as he could before abruptly abandoning Maximilian in 1867 to his fate before a Mexican firing squad.

Domestically, the Emancipation Proclamation changed almost everything, even as its limited scope of freeing slaves only in those areas in rebellion changed almost nothing, at least right away. For one thing, it paved the way for the enlistment of significant numbers of African-Americans into the U.S. military. At first, however, public reactions to the proclamation were mixed. Many abolitionists protested that Lincoln had issued a meaningless manifesto, while many ordinary Northerners, reflecting the racism of the time, grumbled that the war was to preserve the Union, not to end slavery. A significant number of Union soldiers deserted, and the 1862 congressional elections seemed to repu-diate the administration's call for emancipation. Yet in spite of all that, Lincoln's gesture moved the war from a limited political goal of preserving the Union to its larger meaning as a fight for representative democracy and human freedom. Its participants consequently found themselves engulfed in and overwhelmed by a drama as profoundly affecting as any that has ever impinged on the American experience. Some understood and accepted this great change better than others, but the country as well as the world would eventually see the moral imperative of emancipation as a shining moment in the history of human affairs. The Civil War, in the doing of it, would mark the country's most tragic time, but the war, in the meaning of it, became its finest hour.

Emancipation and all its ramifications were played out in the context of striving for Union victory. Lincoln's search for a general to win the war continued,

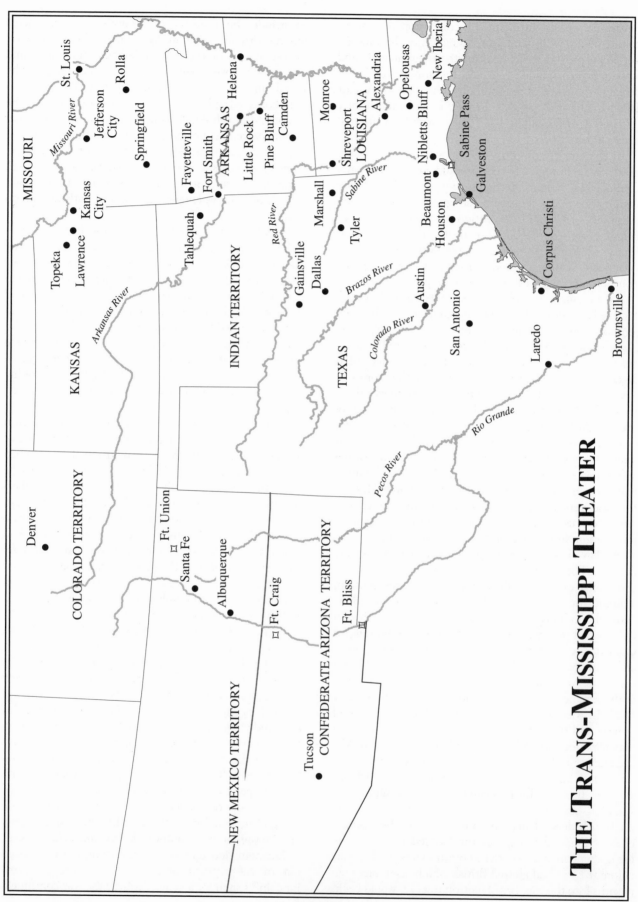

THE TRANS-MISSISSIPPI THEATER

with gruesome results on the battlefield. After McClellan's disappointing indecision following Antietam, General Ambrose E. Burnside replaced him as commander of the Army of the Potomac. At Fredericksburg, Virginia, on 13 December 1862, Burnside used up more than 10,000 Union soldiers with repeated assaults against Lee's unassailable position. Lincoln was never more forlorn than during the bleak Christmas that followed this ghastly engagement. After Burnside staged another, though less costly, misadventure, Joseph Hooker replaced him. Hooker resembled McClellan in his flair for organization as well as insubordination, yet Hooker was aggressive, at least to a point. When he tried to force Lee out of his stronghold at Fredericksburg, Hooker brought on the battle of Chancellorsville on 2–4 May 1863. Lee seized the initiative by dividing his numerically inferior force, sending "Stonewall" Jackson to attack the Union right flank, a move that caught "Fighting Joe" Hooker completely by surprise. Often described as Lee's most dazzling victory, Chancellorsville nonetheless was a tragic business for the Confederacy because during the battle Jackson's own men mistook him for the enemy and mortally wounded him.

The loss of Stonewall Jackson was a dire blow. More than ever, Lee believed another invasion of the North was necessary to win a conclusive victory on Union soil that would secure Southern independence and end the war. During this perilous period, Lincoln again was faced with the necessity of replacing the commander of the Army of the Potomac. Hooker had become quarrelsome, difficult, and apparently ineffective after his humiliation at Chancellorsville. Consequently, the president selected General George Gordon Meade, even as Lee was moving briskly into Pennsylvania. Chance and opportunity rather than deliberate design threw the two armies together at the small seminary village of Gettysburg, Pennsylvania. During the first three days of July 1863, Lee repeatedly tried to dislodge Meade from strong positions south of Gettysburg along Cemetery Ridge. On the last day, 3 July 1863, the most famous assault of the war occurred. What would become known as Pickett's Charge sent about 15,000 Confederates directly against the Union line, a majestically brave gesture the failure of which broke the back of the Army of Northern Virginia. Lee was forced to retreat south of the Potomac River.

At the same time as the titanic clash at Gettysburg, a more prolonged but equally significant military drama was ending in the West. Vicksburg, Mississippi, had rightly gained the label "The Gibraltar of the Confederacy" because of its impregnable situation on the Mississippi River. The city protected the Confederacy's only remaining route to its western regions with their indispensable supplies. Ulysses S. Grant had the chore of capturing Vicksburg, a task that presented such strategic and tactical problems that his management of the campaign produced a military masterpiece. Still, the operations were lengthy, ultimately necessitating a siege of Vicksburg that featured a nerve-shattering bombardment of the city's starving population. On 4 July 1863, the day after Lee's defeat in Pennsylvania, Vicksburg and its entire garrison of irreplaceable Confederate troops surrendered. When Port Hudson fell on 9 July, the Mississippi River was completely in federal hands.

Beyond their military significance, the twin victories at Gettysburg and Vicksburg produced political consequences of the first order. Peace movements in the North that were bolstered by the lack of Union military success were quieted, at least for a time. The Union reaped benefits abroad as well. The British government seized warships apparently slated for delivery to the Confederate navy, and Napoleon III halted the Confederacy's plans to purchase naval vessels from France.

That fall at Gettysburg, Lincoln delivered a brief address at dedication ceremonies for a national cemetery. In the most eloquent pronouncement of the war, the president praised the soldiers whose deaths had marked "the last full measure of devotion" to liberty and pledged the country to finish the work and secure "a new birth of freedom." Thus, as 1863 drew to a close, the Confederacy was to be stalked continually by the specter of impending defeat. Southern armies would fight on for another sixteen months, however, compelling the Union to adopt a fully coordinated and relentless policy of military engagement and destruction.

In one of 1863's few bright spots for the South, that fall Confederate forces under Braxton Bragg defeated Union forces at Chickamauga, Georgia. The whipped Union army was very nearly annihilated, but elements of it under George H. Thomas held a key position long enough to allow the remainder to flee into Chattanooga. Bragg was besieging the city, and the Union army was trapped there when Lincoln ordered Grant to take charge in east Tennessee. Aided by reinforcements rapidly transported toward Chattanooga by railroad, Grant was able to score signal victories in November at Missionary Ridge and Lookout Mountain. Not only was the siege of Chattanooga thus raised, but also Bragg was forced to retreat into north Georgia, his veteran army badly shaken by the inability to exploit its hard-won victory at Chickamauga. As the Union laid plans to invade Georgia, Bragg's troubled tenure as commander of the Confederate Army of Tennessee ended when Jefferson Davis replaced him with Joseph E. Johnston.

Lincoln also made some command changes. Convinced that he had found the man who could win the war in the hard-driving Grant, the president appointed him general-in-chief and summoned him to Washington. Although Meade remained in command of the Army of the Potomac, many, including Lincoln, were dissatisfied with his caution after Gettysburg. Grant proved himself willing to use all the weapons in the North's arsenal, including its vast economic, material, and manpower resources. It this last, Grant would demonstrate an unswerving determination to endure enormous casualties in applying remorseless pressure against all points of the Confederate military. Set upon all at once, the South's armies would fall prey to the numerical superiority of Union forces and be destroyed in detail. Grant, like Lincoln, realized that the destruction of the Confederate military presence would end the war, not the mere occupation of selected regions or particular cities.

As part of this coordinated strategy, William Tecumseh Sherman would invade Georgia, first to seize the important rail center at Atlanta. During the spring and summer of 1864, Sherman's forces commenced a deft game of maneuver and deadly confrontation with Johnston's forces in the mountains and passes of northern Georgia. Yet as Johnston continued to retreat toward Atlanta in a search for ground that would allow him to halt Sherman's advance, Jefferson Davis impatiently replaced him with John Bell Hood. The aggressive and impetuous Hood tried to stop Sherman with direct confrontation, a design that badly mauled the Confederate army and allowed Sherman to capture Atlanta in September 1864.

It was a crucial victory, for it occurred in time to affect positively Lincoln's chances in the presidential election of 1864. As the fall elections loomed, Lincoln had despaired that the bleak military picture would cause his defeat and bring to office the Democratic Party nominee, George B. McClellan. Lincoln's fears were not without foundation, for Grant's overland move against Lee's army, begun in the spring of 1864, had produced shocking losses. With more than 100,000 men, Grant had repeatedly struck Lee at a cost to the Union army of almost 50,000 casualties. This devil's arithmetic was calculated on the certainty that Lee's losses, proportionately similar, would remain gaping holes in the Army of Northern Virginia, while Grant could replace his with a steady stream of new recruits and draftees. On 3 June 1864, a Union assault at Cold Harbor left almost 7,000 Union soldiers killed or wounded in a matter of minutes. Though his attack at Cold Harbor was a mistake rather than a deliberate expenditure—Grant, who would always regret his decision to attack at Cold Harbor, thought that Lee's army was more brittle than it obviously was—Northerners were dismayed by the butchery. As Grant besieged Lee at Petersburg just southeast of Richmond, a considerable sentiment arose during that summer's intense presidential campaign that Lincoln and

his general had managed only a bloody stalemate. Sherman's victory in Atlanta helped to diminish that attitude, and Lincoln won a second term in November. It was the final blow to any hope in the Confederacy of ending the war on Southern terms.

And in its final, anguished months, parts of the Confederacy would suffer a terrible fate. By living off the countryside, Sherman was able to move far away from his line of supply and cut a wide swath through Georgia all the way to Savannah on the coast. On this March to the Sea, Sherman's "bummers" not only stripped the land of foodstuffs, they destroyed anything that could be of military value to the Confederacy. Gutted buildings and ruined railroads lay in the wake of an army that, as Sherman put it, was committed to making the South feel the hard fist of war. Hearing of such destruction, Southern soldiers far from their homes began to leave their posts and head for their families. After his capture of Savannah, Sherman marched northward into South Carolina to commence a campaign of destruction that visited upon the seat of secession an almost biblical retribution. Meanwhile, in Virginia's Shenandoah Valley, Union practitioners of the hard war policy smashed one of Lee's most important sources of supply. A force under Philip Sheridan was so destructive that he claimed a crow flying over the Shenandoah Valley would have to carry its own supplies.

In the spring of 1865, Grant's overwhelming preponderance broke Lee's lines at Petersburg and finally gave the Army of the Potomac the prize of Richmond. As Jefferson Davis and the remnants of the Confederate government fled, Lee tried to run westward, but he was trapped near Appomattox Court House in Virginia. On 9 April, Lee formally surrendered the Army of Northern Virginia to Grant, who followed Lincoln's instructions for leniency, the first step as Lincoln saw it to an amicable restoration of the nation. In the weeks that followed, other Confederate forces in the field also surrendered. The Civil War, or at least the fighting of it, was over.

In a sense, though, the most important work lay before the country. At this pivotal moment, an assassin's bullet struck down Lincoln even before the last Southern armies had surrendered. To bind up wounds, to forget scars, and to allay antagonisms would now be all the harder. The fate of emancipated slaves would depend on political uncertainties and suffer under the weight of ancient prejudices in both the North and the South. The legions of dead soldiers would remain as ghosts in memory, compelling some to preserve old allegiances and promote outmoded ideas. The country would stumble through the years of Reconstruction only partially realizing the vision of those who saw an opportunity to remake both the North and the South into places of racial and social equality. Indeed, that work yet continues.

Yet, by ultimately reaffirming and reanimating their

commitment to liberty and Union, those who survived the incredible ordeal emerged transformed by the experience, as was their country. Both Northerners and Southerners, both white and black, would, in a new birth of freedom, continue to redefine that country. They would people its vast reaches, contract its continent by lacing it with steel rails, and look beyond its borders to weigh the burdens of global power. Having survived what Lincoln called the "fiery trial" and a "mighty scourge," in the end, they were all Americans, and there was nothing they could not do.

Encyclopedia of the
AMERICAN CIVIL WAR
A Political, Social, and Military History

Volume I
A–C

After the war he returned to the Corps of Engineers and his regular rank of major. Commanding an engineer battalion at Willett's Point, New York, gave him the chance to establish the Engineer School of Application. He became a ubiquitous presence on commissions and boards, traveled extensively, and retired from the army in August 1895 as a colonel, respected by his colleagues and honored by Congress with promotion to brigadier general, retired.

Abbot continued his engineering career as a consultant and took rank with the successful minority on the board that recommended the construction of locks for the Panama Canal. When he died on 1 October 1927, he left a legacy of engineering innovations marked, in part, by exemplary service in the Civil War.

—*David S. Heidler and Jeanne T. Heidler*

See also Petersburg Campaign.
For further reading:
Abbot, C. G. *Biographical Memoir of Henry Larcom Abbot, 1831–1927* (1930).

ABBOT, HENRY LARCOM
(1831–1927)
Union officer

Born 31 August 1831 in Beverly, Massachusetts, to Joseph H. and Fanny Larcom Abbot, Henry L. Abbot was descended from notable Revolutionary War veterans. The recipient of an excellent preparatory education in Boston, he graduated from West Point in 1854, second in his class of forty-six. He was a promising addition to the Army Corps of Engineers, surveying railroad routes in California and Oregon and contributing to innovative methods of flood control and dredging on the Mississippi River.

At the start of the Civil War, Abbot was attached to General Irvin McDowell's headquarters as a first lieutenant of topographical engineers. He was wounded at First Bull Run, earning a brevet, and he participated in McClellan's Peninsula campaign, winning another brevet at Yorktown. As a captain in June 1862, Abbot briefly served as General John G. Barnard's aide during the construction of Washington's defenses, and afterward accompanied General Nathaniel Banks's expedition to New Orleans as its chief topographical engineer.

In January 1863 Abbot was breveted to colonel and placed in command of the 1st Connecticut Heavy Artillery in defense of Washington. He and the 1st Connecticut remained at this post until the Virginia campaign. Beginning in March 1864, Abbot commanded Ulysses S. Grant's siege artillery, including the celebrated "Dictator," a massive mortar that could hurl a shot more than two miles.

By the time he mustered out of the Volunteer forces in September 1865, Abbot had won seven brevets for merit and bravery and stood at the rank of major general.

ABBOTT, HENRY LIVERMORE
(1842–1864)
Union officer

Born in Lowell, Massachusetts, on 21 January 1842, Henry Abbott grew up in a large, prosperous, and well-educated family. His father, Josiah Gardner Abbott, was a successful attorney and politically active member of the Democratic Party, and his mother, Caroline, was a member of the socially prominent Livermore family. Henry, the third of eleven children, proved to be something of a prodigy and enrolled in Harvard at age fourteen with his older brother Edward in 1856. He graduated in 1860 and was reading law in his father's office when the Civil War broke out.

Abbott did not immediately follow his older and younger brothers to war when they joined the 2d Massachusetts Infantry as officers. Instead he waited, and, after serving a brief stint in the militia, he followed his friend Oliver Wendell Holmes, Jr., in signing up with the 20th Massachusetts on 10 July 1861. Abbott became a second lieutenant in the regiment at the end of August and accompanied it, when he was healthy, for the remainder of his service in the war. He thus participated in the Union catastrophe that October at Ball's Bluff, where he distinguished himself by demonstrating remarkable composure under fire as the regiment suffered staggering losses (almost 30 percent killed or wounded and 37 percent captured). Promoted to first lieutenant on 8 November 1861, he was with the regiment in the Peninsula campaign, fighting at Fair Oaks and later protecting General George McClellan's retreat to the James River during the Seven Days. At Glendale,

Abbott suffered a serious wound in his right arm that compelled his recuperation at home.

Although he had rejoined the 20th Massachusetts before the battle of Antietam, he nevertheless missed the Maryland campaign when he was hospitalized at Frederick, Maryland, because of a combination of typhoid fever and grief over his brother, who had been killed at Cedar Mountain. By the end of the year, he was back in action, courageously leading his regiment during the vicious fighting to occupy Fredericksburg, Virginia, and on 13 December he participated in the Union assault on Marye's Heights. Apparently charmed after his injury at Glendale, Abbott survived unscathed and was promoted to captain on 28 December.

The following spring he fought at the second battle of Fredericksburg, which coincided with the Chancellorsville campaign, and in July on the third day at Gettysburg, his regiment helped to repulse the Confederate attack. This last action so eviscerated the 20th Massachusetts that command of it devolved on Abbott, the senior of the three officers who had emerged uninjured from the fight. He would remain in this command until his death. On 10 October 1863, he was promoted to major, and four days later fought in the sharp action at Bristoe Station. With the onset of Ulysses S. Grant's overland march on Richmond in the spring of 1864, Abbott's luck was exhausted. He was mortally wounded in the Wilderness on 6 May.

Abbott's service and exploits had been distinguished enough to earn him some notoriety, so news of his death caused consternation at the highest levels of command. He was soon memorialized with a brevet promotion to brigadier general of volunteers, antedated to the day he was killed. His burial in his hometown of Lowell, Massachusetts, was especially somber, for, as Oliver Wendell Holmes, Jr., would later remark, Abbott was a friend whose death "seemed to end a portion of our life also."

—*David S. Heidler and Jeanne T. Heidler*

See also Holmes, Oliver Wendell, Jr.
For further reading:
Scott, Robert Garth, ed. *Fallen Leaves: The Civil War Letters of Major Henry Livermore Abbott* (1991).

ABERCROMBIE, JOHN JOSEPH
(1798–1877)
Union general

John J. Abercrombie's origins, beginning with both the place and date of his birth, have been the source of considerable confusion. He may have been a native of Maryland, born on 4 March 1798 in Baltimore, or he may have been born in Tennessee on 24 March 1798. Though he was later related by marriage to celebrated people, such as father-in-law General Robert

Patterson (for whom he served as aide-de-camp in the Mexican-American War) and his brother-in-law Brigadier General Francis E. Patterson, much of Abercrombie's early life remains unknown.

Abercrombie attended West Point, graduating thirty-seventh of forty in the class of 1822, and served at posts in various regions of the country during the 1820s. In the ensuing years, he fought in the Black Hawk War, the Second Seminole War, and the Mexican-American War, in which he was wounded. Having earned a brevet in both the Seminole and Mexican-American conflicts, he had reached the rank of colonel in the 7th U.S. Infantry as of 25 February 1861. He saw action in the Civil War's earliest engagements. On 20 June 1861, he was placed in command of the 6th Brigade, 2d Division of the Department of Pennsylvania, and led his brigade at Falling Waters on 2 July 1861. He then commanded the 2d Brigade in Nathaniel Banks's division in the Shenandoah Valley from mid-July to mid-August 1861.

Promoted to brigadier general of volunteers on 31 August 1861, Abercrombie was part of General Charles Stone's disastrous reconnaissance at Ball's Bluff in October 1861. In that operation, his 1st Brigade of Volunteers crossed from the Maryland side of the Potomac River opposite Edward's Ferry and fought a brief engagement there on 21 October before recrossing the river the following day. During an otherwise tragic series of events, Abercrombie demonstrated initiative and competence in placing his people and repulsing a Confederate attack. He praised his men, but noted that "there were instances when the officers exhibited less zeal than the men," especially when it was discovered that some officers had "absented themselves and were found on the Maryland side when their regiments were recalled."

In the spring of 1862, Abercrombie commanded the 2d Brigade, 1st Division of V Corps, headquartered at Warrenton Junction. Demonstrating a sense of the enemy more astute than that of George McClellan's intelligence operatives, Abercrombie conducted a reconnaissance on the Rappahannock River to ascertain Confederate strength there. He estimated that reports of 7,000 rebels in the area were likely an exaggeration that doubled their actual numbers.

In the Peninsula campaign, he led the 2d Brigade at Fair Oaks on 31 May–1 June 1862 and ably protected the Union right flank. Although wounded at Fair Oaks, Abercrombie was present on the crest of Malvern Hill in support of the Union left. At the height of the battle, he rode to his batteries to direct them personally to increase their elevation for the protection of the men in his front.

After the Peninsula campaign, Abercrombie's field service was limited to directing operations from various headquarters situated in the environs of Washington or northern Virginia. Doubtless his age (he was 65 in 1863)

John Abercrombie (*Library of Congress*)

and his wounds, the latest from Fair Oaks, dictated his reduced activity in the field. At the close of his service in 1864, he commanded the depot at White House supporting Ulysses S. Grant's march on Richmond. On 20 June 1864, the day that he relinquished this command to Brigadier General George W. Getty, Abercrombie fended off an attack mounted by Wade Hampton's legion. It was Abercrombie's last combat of the war; he was mustered out of the U.S. volunteers four days later.

In March 1865, Abercrombie was awarded a final brevet to brigadier general in the regular army, an honor that marked the nation's gratitude as he neared retirement. Leaving the army on 12 June 1865, Abercrombie took up residence in Roslyn, Long Island, where he died on 3 January 1877.

—*David S. Heidler and Jeanne T. Heidler*

See also Patterson, Robert.
For further reading:
The War of the Rebellion: A Compilation of the Official Records of the Union and Confederate Armies (1880–1901).

ABOLITIONIST MOVEMENT

The abolitionist movement, or abolitionism, flourished in the United States between 1830 and 1865. Its aim was the immediate emancipation of the slaves in the American South. For most of its history, abolitionism was a movement at the margins of American politics, and abolitionists were a dissenting minority. Abolitionism is distinguished from a more general antislavery attitude, which characterized a much larger group of people, and which focused on preventing the expansion of slavery into the western territories of the United States.

Abolitionism had its historical roots in the Enlightenment's doctrine of human rights and in the evangelical attack on the morality of slavery that characterized the Great Awakening of the 1730s and 1740s. Early abolitionists included the Quakers, who, throughout the eighteenth century, engaged in an uncompromising battle against slavery, which they saw as a moral abomination in opposition to God's plans for human progress. Eighteenth-century abolitionism gained momentum during the revolutionary period and reached its peak between 1784 and 1804, when slavery was abolished in the Northern states and many slaves were manumitted in the South. After 1804, the new economic opportunities brought by the cotton boom and increasing fears of slave rebellion made Southern slaveholders tighten their control over their slaves.

By 1810 this early wave of militant abolitionism had died out and opposition to slavery had embraced the idea of gradual, compensated emancipation. In 1816 a group of antislavery advocates, who sought the end of slavery, but at the same time feared the consequences of emancipation for the white population, formed the American Colonization Society with the aim of transporting free blacks to Africa. Although racist in principle, the movement received widespread support from Christian antislavery advocates throughout the late 1810s and 1820s, and served as an important forum for meeting and discussion on the subject of slavery for future abolitionists, such as William Lloyd Garrison.

In the 1820s America was undergoing tremendous transformation. In the North, early industrialization, improvement in the communication system, and the spread of mass culture and popular publications influenced almost every aspect of social life. As people strove to make sense of these momentous transformations, several morally committed individuals dedicated themselves to showing Americans the contradictions of the society in which they lived and called for a variety of social reforms. Especially in New England, where change brought by early industrialization was more pronounced, organized movements for reform, such as temperance, affected a large part of the population.

Related to the reformist ferment, a new evangelical revival swept across America in the 1820s; preachers like Charles G. Finney and Lyman Beecher urged individuals to abandon their sinful lives and look for God's salvation through contribution to the moral improvement of society. Evangelical ministers and evangelical converts touched by the new revivalist wave effectively constituted the most important influence on the abolitionist movement; several abolitionist leaders were educated in New England by evangelical preachers, who gave them a strong sense of moral and religious commitment and a will to fight moral degradation and the evil represented by sin, such as the one of owning slaves.

While white abolitionism was not yet an active force in the 1820s, black abolitionism was gaining ground. African-American abolitionists rejected the plans for colonization as racist and considered the idea of gradual emancipation as a way of postponing the solution of the problem posed by the existence of slavery in the South. In 1829, David Walker, a former slave from North Carolina living in Boston, published his "Appeal to the Colored Citizens of the World," in which he denounced colonization and urged slaves to take up arms and rebel against their masters. Two years later, Nat Turner's rebellion in Virginia caused Southern slaveholders to suspect that Walker's pamphlet had managed to circulate among the slaves.

The conventional date for the beginning of the renewed abolitionist movement in antebellum America is January 1831, when William Lloyd Garrison started the publication of the antislavery journal, *The Liberator*, which soon became as influential as David Walker's "Appeal." Garrison published his paper from his native Boston, where he had been influenced by evangelical preachers and had been involved in numerous antislavery activities. In time, he had become convinced that the only possible solution to the problem of the existence of slavery in the South was its immediate abolition. From the pages of the *Liberator*, Garrison repeatedly denounced slavery as a scandal and a sin, condemned colonization, and urged Americans to embrace the cause of "immediate, unconditional, uncompensated emancipation." In 1832 in Boston, Garrison and twelve friends, who were equally committed to abolitionism, founded the New England Anti-Slavery Society; the organization was devoted to immediatism and, unlike earlier antislavery societies founded in the post-Revolutionary era, included both whites and blacks.

Between 1831 and 1833, abolitionist groups sprang up in two other areas of the North, apart from New England. One group was based in New York, where their main representatives were Arthur and Lewis Tappan, both wealthy merchants and committed evangelicals, and Joshua Leavitt. The other group was based in upstate New York and northeastern Ohio and included James G. Birney, Elizur Wright, and Theodore D. Weld, who was a disciple of evangelical preacher Charles G. Finney. In 1833 sixty-two representatives of the three abolitionist groups gathered in Philadelphia and founded the American Anti-Slavery Society, the first national organization whose aim was the immediate emancipation of slaves in the South. Its "Declaration of Sentiments," written by Garrison, endorsed the Christian attitude of nonviolent resistance and condemned slavery as a violation of the principles stated in the Declaration of Independence and as a sin in the eyes of God. At the same time, the "Declaration of Sentiments" urged abolitionists to persuade citizens in the Northern states to endorse the abolition of slavery through the tactic of "moral suasion" and the spread of antislavery literature. A year after its foundation, the American Anti-Slavery Society, controlled by the wealthy New York–based Tappan brothers, started publishing its own periodical, *The Emancipator*, which was circulated nationally; several other periodicals, such as the *Anti-Slavery Reporter* and the *Anti-Slavery Standard*, joined the *Emancipator* in an impressive flow of publications, which also included pamphlets and books aimed at showing Americans the evils of slavery.

As early as 1833, abolitionists confronted mobs of hostile Northerners, who assaulted them and attempted to silence them. Typically, the mobs included professionals, such as lawyers, physicians, and businessmen, whom abolitionists called "gentlemen of property and standing," and who considered the call for immediate emancipation of the Southern slaves as socially disruptive and revolutionary. In 1835, after the American Anti-Slavery Society launched a postal campaign for the spreading of abolitionist literature, anti-abolitionist violence increased dramatically throughout the North; riots were reported in Utica, Cincinnati, Philadelphia, and Boston, where William Lloyd Garrison was dragged through the city streets. Anti-abolitionist violence reached its peak in 1837, when a mob killed antislavery newspaper editor Elijah P. Lovejoy at Alton, Illinois, and subsided after 1838. Meanwhile, angry Southerners pressed the president and Congress to censor abolitionist literature, which flooded the postal offices of both North and South. In 1837, in response to Southern requests, Congress adopted the "gag rule," according to which antislavery petitions would not be taken into consideration. Even though the rule remained valid until 1844, it did not prevent abolitionists from continuing their campaign, which by 1838 registered a total of 415,000 petitions sent to the capital.

After 1835, in spite of a successful record in the influence of public opinion, abolitionists manifested signs of deep ideological divisions within the American Anti-Slavery Society, as they realized that immediatism and moral suasion had not achieved the aim of changing the national attitude against slavery. In the debates about the implementation of new tactics, Garrison and his followers emerged as radical supporters of doctrines of nonresistance and moral revolution. "Garrisonians" thought that American values were the expression of the nation's profound corruption and that reform was needed in several spheres to bring about a new society. Consequently, they did not restrict themselves to the battle against slavery, but became involved in other movements for social reform—and they kept a general attitude of questioning accepted authority, whether it came from husbands, religious ministers, or government officials.

Garrisonians welcomed women within the abolitionist movement and encouraged them to join the American Anti-Slavery Society. Some of the best-known female abolitionists were Lydia Maria Child and Angelina and Sarah Grimké. Hundreds of others were actively involved in the society's activities, especially in the 1837 petitions campaign. In the late 1830s and 1840s, they started to merge the fight against slavery with the battle for women's rights and equality. While Garrisonians supported their battle as part of the necessary moral revolution of society, anti-Garrisonians, mainly including abolitionists from New York, considered the movement for women's rights extraneous to abolitionism and unnecessary, given that American society was fundamentally sound, apart from the flaws related to the existence of slavery.

Between 1838 and 1840, Garrisonians and anti-Garrisonians confronted each other not just over women's rights, but also on the equally important issue of political action. While Garrisonians continued to show an antigovernment attitude and rely on moral suasion, anti-Garrisonians went as far as conceiving the possibility of a third party based on abolitionist principles. At the 1840 meeting of the American Anti-Slavery Society, anti-Garrisonians were defeated in the elections of the executive committee by the Garrisonian faction and abandoned the organization; most of them ended up in the American and Foreign Anti-Slavery Society, founded by Arthur and Lewis Tappan. Garrisonians remained in control of the original American Anti-Slavery Society, which, even though greatly diminished in numbers, remained a far more radical organization in its principles.

With the split of 1840, the abolitionist movement lost both its unity and its momentum. Within the Garrisonian faction, women became increasingly convinced that they needed their own organization to be able to fight effectively for their rights; in 1848, a group of female abolitionists, headed by Garrisonians Elizabeth Cady Stanton and Susan B. Anthony, gathered at Seneca Falls, New York, and started the first women's rights movement in American history. They demanded equal participation with men in professional activities and the right to vote. Although they continued to be supported by Garrisonian abolitionists, women had started to follow a distinct trajectory from their initial participation in the American Anti-Slavery Society.

By 1848, African-American abolitionists had become disillusioned and convinced that their goals did not fully coincide with the goals of the American Anti-Slavery Society, which they had enthusiastically supported throughout the 1830s. Even though Garrisonians had made a genuine effort at fighting racial prejudice, several African-Americans felt that white abolitionists tended to patronize them. After 1843, black activists organized in a Negro National Convention Movement to fight discrimination and promote the advancement of the free people of color. African-Americans could count among themselves some of the most famous abolitionists, such as Frederick Douglass, Harriet Tubman, and Sojourner Truth, who toured the Northern cities and gave public lectures on their experience in slavery.

In 1840 at Albany, New York, a small group of abolitionists founded the Liberty Party, a political organization dedicated to the cause of immediate emancipation, and elected as candidate for the forthcoming elections James G. Birney. As a political force, the Liberty Party was never able to challenge the hegemony of Democrats and Whigs in Congress, and, after garnering a record of 60,000 votes in the 1844 elections, gradually disappeared from the scene. Several anti-Garrisonian abolitionists ended up reluctantly voting for the Free-Soil Party and then for the Republican Party. Garrisonians, instead, continued to be skeptical about political involvement throughout the crisis of the 1850s. However, the effects of the 1850 Fugitive Slave Act and the internecine fighting in Kansas convinced most of them to abandon the doctrine of moral suasion and support active resistance of the slaves toward slaveowners.

Most abolitionists applauded John Brown's revolutionary attack on Harper's Ferry, and, after the election of Lincoln and the secession of the Southern states, sided with the Union. However, as soon as it became clear that the Republican government had not started a war for the destruction of slavery, they denounced the Lincoln administration and increased their demands for immediate emancipation. After the Emancipation Proclamation of 1863, abolitionists began a campaign for securing the achievement of emancipation through a constitutional amendment. In July 1865, after the passage of the Thirteenth Amendment, which prohibited the existence of slavery, Garrison abandoned the American Anti-Slavery Society, declaring that it had fulfilled its aim. The organization continued to exist under the direction of Wendell Phillips until 1870, after the passage of the Fourteenth and Fifteenth Amendment, which guaranteed the protection of the rights of black citizens in the United States.

—*Enrico Dal Lago*

See also Abolitionists; Emancipation Proclamation; Free Soil Party; Fugitive Slave Act; Republican Party; Thirteenth Amendment; Underground Railroad.

For further reading:

Aptheker, Herbert. *Abolitionism: A Revolutionary Movement* (1989).

Goodman, Paul. *Of One Blood: Abolitionists and the Origins of Racial Equality* (1998).

Stewart, James B. *Holy Warriors: The Abolitionists and American Slavery* (1996).

Walters, Ronald. *The Antislavery Appeal: American Abolitionism after 1830* (1978).

ABOLITIONISTS

Although they were never large in number, abolitionists exerted extraordinary influence in catalyzing debates and issues that brought on the American Civil War. These individuals differed from others who opposed slavery because they favored immediately ending slavery without compensating slave owners for the loss of their "property" and without relocating freed slaves outside the United States. Free blacks, manumitted slaves, slaves who had escaped bondage, and whites of both sexes joined the cause of immediate abolitionism, and they constantly argued over means and ends. Black abolitionists, for example, did not find compelling the white abolitionist strategy of moral suasion. In 1843 at a convention in Buffalo, New York, and again in 1850, they encouraged Southern slave revolts that they pledged to join once they were under way. Slowly, their arguments made inroads on the consciousness of white abolitionists, who increasingly favored direct action or political activism by the end of the 1850s. Indeed, an association of abolitionists styling itself the "Secret Six" supported John Brown's seizure of the U.S. arsenal at Harper's Ferry in 1859.

The posture of moral suasion embraced by white abolitionists rooted itself in the soil of reform, especially in New England and New York after the War of 1812. Animated by evangelicalism and its emphasis on individual moral responsibility, abolitionists tried to show that slaveholding was a sin in the eyes of God, and immediate repentance offered the only remedy. Since such moral appeals had resulted in countless religious conversions and seemed to be effective in related reform movements such as temperance, white abolitionists clung to persuasion until the 1850s.

Abolitionists tended to eschew partisan politics, too, because political parties inclined toward corruption and moved toward solutions by compromise. To the abolitionists, since slaveholding was a sin, it could not be the subject of mediation. Beginning around 1840, some abolitionists did move toward formal politics and associated themselves with the Liberty Party in 1840, with the Free Soil Party in 1848, and, after 1854, with the Republican Party, but abolitionists did not play a determining role in shaping policy or platforms.

Abolitionists did fashion organizations to spread their ideas. In December 1833, leading abolitionists such as William Lloyd Garrison, Arthur Tappan, and Lewis Tappan established the American Anti-Slavery Society, which labored to organize local antislavery societies, to produce antislavery publications, and to convert ministers to abolitionism. Although the society focused most of its labors in the free states, it did disseminate abolitionist literature through the mails to the Southern states.

By 1840, the American Anti-Slavery Society had fractured. Those who followed Garrison and Abby Kelly believed that the abolition of slavery was just one of a myriad of reforms that needed to be undertaken. This group tended to favor women's rights and included those abolitionists who favored social and legal equality for emancipated slaves. The other faction, led by the Tappans, believed that society was basically healthy and that the emancipation of slaves was the last remaining hurdle needed to redeem the promise of the United States. They did not link abolitionism to other reforms or to further attempts to ameliorate the conditions of African-Americans.

This division among whites reflected some differences between whites and blacks over the goals of abolitionism. For many of the Tappan faction, once slavery was ended, the work was done. Black abolitionists understood that freedom from slavery did not mean the ending of white racism, and they tended to endorse other reforms, including guarantees of voting rights. Black abolitionists also found frustrating the condescension of white abolitionists and the difficulty white abolitionists had in appraising slavery and racism as systems rather than as the moral failings of individuals.

An African-American organization offered one solution to the racial divide in abolitionism. Founded in 1830, the National Negro Convention not only worked for abolitionism, it also crusaded against Northern racism. Like African-American churches in the North, this organization, run by blacks, helped to harbor runaway slaves and offered blacks a community largely free from white interference.

Yet black and white abolitionists could and did work together, such as when they pursued the release and repatriation of African slaves taken into custody by the U.S. Navy after they had seized control of the slave ship *Amistad.* Although white abolitionists did not embrace

Seven noted abolitionsists depicted in *Pioneers of Freedom*, an 1866 carte-de-viste photograph. (*Library of Congress*)

violence, they believed that the Africans in this instance had acted appropriately to effect their freedom. And the *Amistad* mutiny and aftermath allowed abolitionists who employed moral suasion, legal arguments, or direct action to play important and interrelated parts in a saga that actually resulted in real freedom for persons held in bondage.

In the 1850s, abolitionists continued to occupy the fringes of Northern society and Northern opinion, although antislavery, as opposed to abolitionism, became an increasingly mainstream point of view. The Republican Party embraced an antislavery theme, but abolitionists did not believe attempts to confine slavery to the Southern states would lead to its quick end. Abolitionists proved willing to endorse slave violence and other forms of direct action to end slavery. Garrison even hoped that Northern states, weary of the power Southern states wielded in national counsels, would themselves secede from the Union, leaving the South to

contend with slaves who, according to Garrison, would rebel and earn their freedom. Others, like Lysander Spooner, a Boston attorney, encouraged non-slave-holding whites and Southern slaves to make common cause and overthrow the slave regime.

Spooner's discourses, along with the links between abolitionists and John Brown, illustrate how abolitionists contributed to the coming of the Civil War. No one acted on Spooner's call, and Brown's raid failed. Yet repeated efforts at agitation might have one day provoked the slave rebellion that Southern whites feared. Mainstream Northerners' disavowals of abolitionists could not diminish the growing Southern belief that abolitionists were more than a fringe element. Worse for Southerners was the possibility that the new abolitionist message of direct action might attract enough converts to effect emancipation, even as their message of moral suasion had not done so in the previous thirty years. As the South perceived that possibility becoming more likely, the destruction of the Union and the war that followed it did so as well.

—*Edward R. Crowther*

See also Abolitionist Movement; Brown, John; Garrison, William Lloyd; Tappan, Lewis.
For further reading:
Dillon, Merton L. *The Abolitionists: The Growth of a Dissenting Minority* (1974).
———. *Elijah P. Lovejoy, Abolitionist Editor* (1961).
———. *Slavery Attacked: Southern Slaves and their Allies, 1619–1865* (1990).
Friedman, Lawrence J. *Gregarious Saints: Self and Community in American Abolitionism, 1830–1870* (1982).
Kraditor, Aileen S. *Means and Ends in American Abolitionism: Garrison and His Critics on Strategy and Tactics, 1834–1850* (1969).
Renehan, Edward J., Jr. *The Secret Six: The True Tale of the Men Who Conspired with John Brown* (1995).
Stewart, James Brewer. *Holy Warriors: The Abolitionists and American Slavery* (1997).

ACOUSTIC SHADOWS

An acoustic shadow is an area where sound from nearby locations is prevented from reaching because of atmospheric phenomena or terrain features. On several occasions in the Civil War, acoustic shadows had important effects on major battles. Some nineteenth-century writers referred to these cases as "silent battles." Commanders depended on the sounds of battle to know where to send troops or respond to threats to their lines, and acoustic shadows contributed to several disastrous command decisions.

There are four major causes of acoustic shadows: wind direction; absorption of sound by woods or other obstacles; variation in the temperature of the air at different altitudes; and differences in wind speed at different altitudes. Most acoustic shadows are due to wind direction or the absorption of sound. Sound carries better downwind than it does upwind. Sound absorption by thick woods, hills, or mountains can significantly affect the audibility of sound.

Sound travels faster in warm air than in cool air. Usually, the air gets cooler at higher altitudes. Sound waves near the ground, therefore, travel faster than they would at a higher altitude. If anything makes part of a sound wave travel faster than another part, it causes the entire sound wave to change direction. This phenomenon is called refraction. Refraction often causes a sound wave to move upward, away from the hearing of people on the ground. However, if there is a temperature inversion, the air is warmer at a higher altitude than a lower one. This causes the opposite of normal refraction, and sends sound waves toward the ground, making them carry farther than normal.

Changes in wind speed also cause acoustic shadows. Winds tend to blow faster as they get higher from the ground, away from friction caused by trees and other obstacles. Higher wind speeds increase the velocity of the upper part of a sound wave and push it back toward the ground. It is possible for a sound wave to bounce upward after hitting the ground, and sometimes repeatedly bounce up and down, causing alternating areas of sound or silence to people listening on the ground.

Acoustic shadows were reported as having affected the battles at Fort Donelson, Seven Pines, Gaines's Mill, Perryville, Iuka, Chancellorsville, Gettysburg, and Five Forks, among others.

At Iuka on 18 September 1862, a force under Confederate major general Sterling Price attacked Brigadier General William Rosecrans. Rosecrans's men barely managed to hold their own until the fighting broke off at dark. More Union forces under Major General Edward Ord were only four miles away in Price's rear, upwind from the battle. Rosecrans was furious about Ord's failure to reinforce him, which he felt would have enabled him to crush Price's army. Ord saw smoke rising from the battle, which he thought was only Rosecrans burning captured materiel, because no noise of the battle reached his position.

At Chancellorsville on 2 May 1863, "Stonewall" Jackson's surprise attack shattered Union general Joseph Hooker's right flank, only three miles from his headquarters. Hooker heard little or none of the battle and knew nothing of the collapse of his right until the first panic-stricken soldiers streamed into view near his headquarters.

Acoustic shadows were also noted during naval battles. Witnesses of the battle between the *Monitor* and the *Virginia* on 9 March 1862 had a plain view of the action from the shore but heard nothing. An extreme example of acoustic shadowing was reported after the battle of Port Royal on 7 November 1861. Union soldiers aboard a transport ship upwind of the fighting saw the flashes and smoke of the naval bombardment but heard nothing except during brief times when the steady wind slowed down. On the other hand, residents of St. Augustine, Florida, heard the same bombardment 150 miles away in the other direction.

Acoustic shadows played a major role in the battle of Five Forks on 1 April 1865. Confederate major generals George Pickett and Fitzhugh Lee left their commands to attend a shad bake held by Brigadier General Thomas Rosser. While Pickett was away, his men were hit by a strong Union assault led by Major General Philip Sheridan. The weakened Confederate lines reeled under the impact, and they needed the authority of a division commander to meet the crisis. Pickett and Lee, separated from the front lines by only a mile and a half of thick pine forest, heard nothing of the fighting until it was too late. The loss of the rebel right flank that day forced the abandonment of Petersburg and Richmond and led to the surrender at Appomattox on 9 April.

—*David A. Norris*

See also Chancellorsville, Battle of; Five Forks, Battle of; Iuka, Battle of.

For further reading:

De Motte, John B. "The Cause of a Silent Battle." In *Battles and Leaders of the Civil War* (1887).
Koerner, Brendan I. "The Battle Was Lost in a Zone of Silence: Acoustics Helps Explain Civil War Blunders." *U.S. News and World Report* (1998).
Ross, Charles. "Ssh! Battle in Progress." *Civil War Times Illustrated* (1996).
Suhr, Robert Collins. "Small But Savage Battle of Iuka." *America's Civil War* (1999).

ADAMS, CHARLES FRANCIS
(1807–1886)
U.S. minister to Great Britain

On 25 November 1863 Charles Francis Adams, America's minister to the Court of St. James, wrote to his son: "The war has done us much good. It has cured us of much of the spirit of vaunting and braggadocio which peace and prosperity had pampered, and has left us moderate but firm." Then, in analyzing his contribution, he continued: "The prejudices and distrust that prevailed here at the outset against every act of the Administration are slowly yielding to the conviction that it deserves confidence. All the little that I have contributed to this result has been to nourish by a steady and uniform bearing, as well under adverse as under favorable circumstances, the growth of this opinion in the British Cabinet. I believe that now it is firmly planted there. If our arms favor us in any moderate degree for the future, I think we may hope to steer clear of farther trouble in this kingdom." In his best self-deprecating style, Charles Francis Adams modestly summed up a great achievement. His steady and firm course had helped keep the two nations from war and the British government from assisting the Southern cause of independence in any decisive fashion.

Charles Francis Adams, the son of President John Quincy Adams and Louisa Catherine (Johnson) Adams, was born on 18 August 1807. His early life took him to St. Petersburg, Russia, where his father was serving, and there young Adams learned French, German, and Russian, preferring to speak French to his native English. His father's duties in Belgium and France also afforded young Charles exposure to European politics during the exciting "Hundred Days," when Napoleon briefly reclaimed his throne in 1815. John Quincy Adams's appointment to the Court of St. James meant that Charles would attend English public schools, a not altogether pleasant experience. Although his academic performance did not always please his parents, the young scholar had a chance to mature and learn much about English public life. Upon returning to the United States during his father's tenure as secretary of state, Charles was placed in the Boston Latin School and later Harvard University, graduating from the latter in 1825, at the young age of eighteen.

After spending three years in Washington while his father was president, Charles decided to settle down and study law under the brief tutelage of Daniel Webster. He was admitted to the practice of law in January 1829. He married his beloved Abigail, the daughter of the influential Peter C. Brooks of Boston (whose other sons-in-law were Reverend Nathaniel Frothingham and Edward Everett), on 5 September 1829. Aside from his law practice, Charles assumed the care of most of his father's property, alleviating the elder statesman from the woes of financial management while he served eighteen years in the United States Congress. Charles also found time to write some articles for the *North American Review*, the leading literary magazine of the day.

During this time Charles wrote pamphlets on national topics and became interested in the abolitionist cause. His interest in politics got him elected to the Massachusetts legislature in 1840 as a Whig. He served three years in the state house of representatives and two in the senate. Along with Stephen Phillips, Charles Sumner, and others, he helped to establish the Boston *Whig*, which became the voice of the "Conscience Whigs," those who strongly opposed slavery and the so-called Southern policy of the "Cotton Whigs." With such divisions besetting the Whig Party, Adams was soon attracted to the new Free Soil Party and was actually named its vice presidential candidate in 1848. The failure of this party to materialize into a more permanent organization led Adams and others to join the newly formed Republican Party. In 1858 Adams was nominated for his father's seat in the United States Congress and was easily elected over two rival candidates. In

Congress he became aligned with his friend William Seward and took to the campaign trail with him in the 1860 presidential election. Although he preferred Seward for the Republican nomination, Adams joined the majority in backing Abraham Lincoln for the post and worked hard throughout the Northeast for his election. Adams's own reelection to Congress put him into a leadership position and made his role pivotal in the negotiations to prevent the South from leaving the Union. Adams's controversial policy of moderation in these negotiations led some, such as Charles Sumner, to think of him as weak and break off social and political relations with him.

Seward's appointment as secretary of state, a post some thought Adams deserved, soon placed Adams in the forefront of events. His old friend nominated him for the post of minister to the Court of St. James. Adams had few illusions about the difficulty of representing the United States in Great Britain. It was already known that Prime Minister Lord Palmerston had no love for the young republic and that many in the British ministry, including William Gladstone, were pro-Southern in sympathy. These men and Foreign Minister Lord John Russell would have to be met on their own terms and under trying conditions. Even prior to presenting his credentials, Adams learned that Great Britain had already granted belligerent status to the Confederacy. Although this gesture by the British was designed primarily to preserve their neutral status in shipping, Seward and many in America took it as a direct insult to the United States. Belligerent status, however, did not confer official recognition and thereby sovereignty. It only instituted the right to realize certain defined goals within the international community. At the same time, the British declared their neutrality in the American conflict, and this in effect recognized the Union's blockade of Southern ports. Adams handled this situation with directness and firmness and soon earned not only the respect of Lord Russell but also established an informal understanding with him. In his first extended meeting with Russell, Adams complained that the British recognition of Confederate belligerency encouraged a government that actually lacked an organized military or naval establishment. Adams's steady handling of the affair won Russell's admiration and achieved something of a diplomatic triumph. Russell from then on kept representatives of the Confederacy at arm's length.

Much of Adams's anxiety during his tenure as minister resulted from Union reverses on the battlefield. He wrote to his son on 7 September 1861: "The feeling here which at one time was leaning our way has been very much changed by the disaster at Bull's run, and by the steady operation of the press against us. Great Britain always looks to her own interest as a paramount law of her action in foreign affairs. She might deal quite summarily with us, were it not for the European complications which are growing more and more embarrassing." Major Union victories inspired the opposite feelings, and although each victory elated him, Adams was careful to maintain a level posture. After the fall of Vicksburg, he noted, "I tried to bear up under the intelligence with a suitable degree of moderation. I ventured to indulge a slight sense of satisfaction."

Aside from the vicissitudes caused by uncertain battles, Adams had to handle several delicate situations. The most notable was the *Trent* Affair. In this case, the Union vessel *San Jacinto* intercepted the British mail-packet *Trent* and seized its two Confederate passengers, John Slidell and James M. Mason, special commissioners on their way to Europe to procure supplies, arms, and if possible, allies. The capture of the two envoys by Captain Charles Wilkes caused an international uproar. Adams, who believed that British neutrality had been violated, nevertheless obeyed Seward's commands and presented the Union case to the British government. The British demanded that the prisoners be released and that the United States formally apologize for its violation of the rights of neutrals. After postponing a response to let matters cool, Adams finally notified the British that Wilkes had acted without orders and that the prisoners would be released. Yet he also noted that the United States government held that neutrals who knowingly carried enemy envoys with their contraband dispatches were subject to seizure under the laws of nations and that such captures should be adjudicated before an international tribunal. This response, while capitulating to British demands for the surrender of the prisoners and an admission of a wrongful act, saved face for Seward and Lincoln by asserting a justification for the seizure that was recognized by international law. At the same time Adams's reply assuaged British ire by recognizing long-held British principles concerning the rights of blockading nations. Indeed, as one historian has observed, "The *Trent* Affair served to underline the importance of a naval blockade as England's most formidable offensive weapon."

Adams also had to deal with problems arising from the construction and release of Confederate raiders, such as the *Alabama*, and the Laird rams. In the former case, Adams failed to stop the release, and the *Alabama*'s career of destruction became a persistent source of Anglo-American irritation that lingered for years after the war. In the latter case, steady pressure from Adams and Lord Russell's willingness to lessen tensions led to a unique solution. The British government purchased the rams instead of releasing them to their putative buyers in Egypt. Such an indication of British sympathy toward the Northern cause greatly lessened the strain between the two countries.

In addition to ships being built for the Confederacy in

Britain, there was the problem of vessels under British registry trading with the South. The Bahamas and Bermuda were regular stops for ships engaged in this trade. These ports also carried on a regular trade with Southern blockade runners. The running of contraband arms and goods through Mexico, especially at Matamoros, disturbed Adams and the State Department. Here an old legal doctrine known as "continuous voyage" came into play when the United States seized the *Peterhoff*, which had been plying this trade. The principle of continuous voyage did not deem shipment by land as part of a "voyage." In this case, the announcement by Lloyds of London that they would no longer underwrite such voyages brought this potentially dangerous situation under control.

Adams displayed poise and reserve that played well with his British hosts. He also benefitted from European turmoil in the early 1860s. Concern about the aims of Napoleon III, the rise of German nationalism, uprisings in Poland, reform in Russia, and its own colonial ventures, did not give the British government the freedom to act as the British public sometimes demanded. It was also not lost on the British government that Canada was essentially a hostage to the United States. An expected cotton shortage in Britain was not the factor the South believed it would be to bring the British to their aid. As it turned out, a surplus of cotton from the 1860 harvest had augmented British reserves, and by the time those were expended the harvests from India began to fill the void. Meanwhile, Adams's contacts with Richard Cobden, John Bright, and others kept him well informed about the mood in Manchester, Lancaster, and Liverpool.

Although tending to modesty, Charles Francis Adams's evaluation of his tenure was accurate. It was his calm, steady, and firm demeanor that impressed the British Cabinet, especially Lord Russell, and members of Parliament on both sides of the aisle.

Adams's contributions to American diplomacy continued after the war with the signing of the Treaty of Washington in 1871. In this episode Adams led the campaign to reject the concept of "indirect damages" resulting from the *Alabama* claims. Again he ran afoul of his former colleague, Charles Sumner, who had insisted on their inclusion in any settlement. That the final treaty reflected Adams's ideas gives silent witness to his solid judgment. Moreover, without the acceptance of Adams's counsel, the final arbitration of the *Alabama* claims may never have taken place or may have been inordinately delayed.

Weary of public life, Adams avoided a movement to have him run against Ulysses S. Grant for the presidency and spent the remainder of his days editing his father's diary and other family papers. He died on 21 November 1886.

—*Joe Knetsch*

See also Adams, Charles Francis, Jr.; Adams, Henry Brooks; *Alabama* Claims; *Alabama,* CSS; Diplomacy, U.S.A.; Great Britain.

For further reading:

Crook, D. P. *Diplomacy during the American Civil War* (1975).

Duberman, Martin. *Charles Francis Adams, 1807–1886* (1968).

Ford, W. C., ed. *A Cycle of Adams Letters, 1861–1865* (1920).

ADAMS, CHARLES FRANCIS, JR.
(1835–1915)
Union officer

Born in Boston, the son of Charles Francis and Abigail Brooks Adams, Charles Francis Adams, Jr., graduated from Harvard in 1856. After a brief career as a lawyer, during which time he established a hearty reputation as a partygoing patrician with regular attendance at Boston's Tiger Ball, Adams abandoned his legal career for the grand tour of Europe. In 1860 he traveled across America, making several valuable political contacts, including a brief meeting with Lincoln. Adams took up journalism and wrote an economic critique of Southern cotton producers entitled "King Cotton" for the *Atlantic* magazine in 1861.

Although a member of the Massachusetts Militia, Adams did not leap into military service. Instead, he busied himself drafting a diplomatic strategy on the cotton issue for his father to use in negotiating with the British after Lincoln appointed the elder Adams minister to London. Yet Adams joined the 1st Massachusetts Cavalry by December 1861. He was stationed on the Sea Islands, later the site of the Port Royal experiment, and found the area populated by thousands of former slaves. There was little armed resistance from the Confederates, though, and little of Adams's early service involved combat. As the war intensified and tactics changed, Union cavalry correspondingly saw more activity. In the June 1862 battle at Johns Island, South Carolina, Adams was forced to retreat, but in a letter home he assured his father that the retreat was orderly and that "we should have whipped them dreadfully had they followed us."

The 1st Massachusetts suffered severe losses at Antietam and the following summer, in July 1863, Adams escorted infantry on a forty-mile forced march to Gettysburg, Pennsylvania, reaching that place in less than twenty-four hours. Determined to "bear up the reeling fortunes" of the Union, he upon the next morning witnessed the scene of "twenty thousand fellow creatures wounded or dead around us … yet the elements seemed electrified with a certain magnetic influence of victory, as the great army sank down overwearied in its tracks." Later that month, however, Adams soberly wrote, "I no longer believe in a collapse of the rebellion."

In 1864 Adams became an officer in the 5th Massachusetts Cavalry, the first black cavalry regiment from that state. Although the descendent of generations of antislavery advocates, including Presidents John Adams and John Quincy Adams, the latter of whom had acted as defense counsel in the *Amistad* case, Charles Francis Adams, Jr., never evinced the same confidence in his regiment's black soldiers as did some others. He had no doubt that the "one good to result from this war must be the freedom and regeneration of the African race," but he firmly believed that black troops required different treatment than did white soldiers. He observed, "Patience, kindness, and self-control have not been my characteristics as an officer." However, after months in command he wrote that he hoped "to see the Army become for the black race a school of skilled labor and of self reliance, as well as an engine of war."

Adams's health began a precipitous decline in spring 1865 as he suffered from malarial fevers. He saw little active duty until his regiment occupied Richmond. Despite a brief incident involving horse theft by some of his regiment—an episode that nearly got Adams arrested and court-martialed—he finished out the war and returned home in June 1865, weighing barely 130 pounds, distressed by the carnage he had witnessed, and disheartened by Lincoln's assassination. Adams gradually recovered his health and eventually married Mary Hone Ogden and fathered five children.

Charles Francis Adams's career was filled with contradictions. He was a crusading journalist against the powerful railroad combinations and then an investor in, and later president of, the Union Pacific Railroad, in which position he made a substantial fortune. He attempted a second career as a reformer in the 1890s by employing his writing talent to support the Anti-Imperialist League. He wrote and lectured on the Civil War, served as an overseer of Harvard College, and became president of the Massachusetts Historical Society. Adams resided in Quincy and Lincoln, Massachusetts, until his death in 1915. Leaving his autobiography to be published posthumously, he managed to ignite yet another controversy from the grave. When the book appeared in 1916 it included blunt criticism of General Joseph Hooker and other Union officers.

—Teresa Thomas

See also Adams, Charles Francis; Adams, Henry Brooks.

For further reading:

Adams, Charles F., Jr. *The Double Anniversary: '76 and '63. A Fourth of July Address Delivered at Quincy, Massachusetts, by Charles F. Adams, Jr.* (1869).

Adams, Charles F., Jr. *Charles Francis Adams, 1835–1915: An Autobiography* (1916).

Crowninshield, Benjamin W. *A History of the First Regiment of Massachusetts Cavalry Volunteers* (1891).

Ford, Worthington Chauncey, ed. *A Cycle of Adams Letters 1861–1865* (1920).

Kirkland, Edward Chase. *Charles Francis Adams Junior 1835–1915: The Patrician at Bay* (1965).

ADAMS, DANIEL WEISIGER
(1821–1872)
Confederate general

Born to George Adams and Anna Weisiger Adams in Frankfort, Kentucky, Daniel Adams moved with his family to Natchez, Mississippi, as a child. Before being admitted to the Mississippi bar, Adams attended the University of Virginia. After a brief stint in Mississippi politics, he moved to Louisiana. As the secession crisis loomed, Adams was active in efforts to prevent Louisiana from seceding. When these efforts failed and Louisiana joined the Confederacy, however, Adams actively helped prepare his adopted state for war.

Governor Thomas E. Moore appointed Adams to a three-member commission to make defensive and offensive preparations. Following his service on this body, Adams began his military service as a lieutenant colonel of the 1st Louisiana Regulars. On 30 October 1861 he became the colonel of the regiment. His promotion occurred while Adams was stationed at Pensacola, Florida. He divided his time between this city and Mobile, Alabama, during the first months of the war.

Adams moved north in early 1862 and commanded the 1st Brigade, 2d Division, II Corps, at Shiloh after its commander, Brigadier General Adley H. Gladden, was mortally wounded early in the battle. Adams lost his right eye in the attack on the Federal center and was temporarily left for dead. For his service in this battle Adams was promoted to brigadier general on 23 May 1862.

After recovering from his wounds, Adams served under William J. Hardee as the commander of the 2d Louisiana Brigade at Perryville. A few months later at Stones River, Adams commanded the 1st Brigade, 1st Division of Hardee's Corps. Once again Adams suffered serious wounds (this time in the left arm) that knocked him out of action for several months.

In September 1863 Adams commanded a brigade of Breckinridge's Division of D. H. Hill's Corps. During the battle, he was seriously wounded in the arm, and after most of his possessions were stolen by Northern soldiers, he was captured by a Union officer. By summer 1864 he had been exchanged. He then commanded a cavalry brigade guarding railroads out of Alabama, before being given command of the District of Central Alabama on 24 September. With Confederate commands disintegrating in early 1865, Adams's authority gradually widened, until on 11 March 1865 he received command of all forces in Alabama above the Department of the Gulf. His limited resources kept him from preventing the raids by Union cavalry Brigadier General James Wilson against Selma, Alabama, on 2 April 1865, and Montgomery, Alabama, on 16 April 1865.

After surrendering in May 1865, Adams received his parole at Meridian, Mississippi, on 9 May 1865.

Following a brief trip to England after the war, Adams returned to New Orleans, where he practiced law until his death in 1872. Adams was the younger brother of fellow Confederate general William Wirt Adams.

—*David S. Heidler and Jeanne T. Heidler*

See also Adams, William Wirt; Chickamauga, Battle of; Hardee, William J.; Wilson, James Harrison; Wilson's Selma Raid.

For further reading:
Cozzens, Peter. *No Better Place to Die: The Battle of Stones River* (1991).
———. *This Terrible Sound; The Battle of Chickamauga* (1992).
Tourgee, Albion. *The Story of a Thousand, Being a History of the Services of the One Hundred Fifth Ohio Volunteer Infantry, in the War for the Union* (1896).
Watts, T. H. "To the People of Alabama." *Montgomery Weekly Mail* (1865).

ADAMS, HENRY BROOKS
(1838–1918)
Intellectual and historian

Henry Adams was the great grandson of John Adams, the second president of the United States, and the grandson of John Quincy Adams, the sixth president. His father was Charles Francis Adams, Sr., who married the youngest daughter of Peter Chardon Brooks, thought to be the wealthiest man in Boston at the time. A member of the Boston Brahmin aristocracy, Adams was born into one of the most dominant political families in the first hundred years of the American republic.

After graduating from Harvard University in 1858, Adams took the Brahmin obligatory Grand Tour of Europe, where he studied for two years, mainly in Berlin. Returning to America after finishing his studies, Adams found the United States, in the months before the 1860 elections, teetering toward civil war. Charles Francis Adams, a Republican in the House of Representatives, joined William Seward of New York in campaigning for their fellow Republican Abraham Lincoln. Henry Adams voted for Lincoln on 6 November, and his father won reelection by a sizable margin. He joined his father in Washington, D.C., by early December, and for a time he served both as his father's private secretary and covertly as the Washington correspondent of the Boston newspaper *Daily Advertiser,* which had strong Republican affiliations.

Adams served his father in Washington until the congressman was appointed envoy extraordinary and minister plenipotentiary to England on 20 March 1861. Adams eventually accompanied his father to England, serving as the elder Adams's private secretary. Unbeknownst to his father, Adams also served as a foreign correspondent for the *New York Times* in violation of State Department regulations.

When the minister delayed his departure to London

for six weeks until his eldest son, John Quincy, was married, the Confederate diplomats to England took the opportunity to influence England's Proclamation of Neutrality in the American civil conflict. The England that Adams was visiting in the early 1860s was at its apogee of economic and military power and thus was more concerned about protecting its position and wealth than it was concerned with moral imperatives. Because of England's prominence in the world, the American diplomatic ministry in London was the most critical one, especially since Confederate cotton was a vital component of the British textile industry.

At the heart of the Union's foreign relationship with England was the contention that the Confederate cause was nothing more than a rebellion and any foreign emissary from those rebelling states was illegitimate and should not be recognized by the British foreign ministry. Charles F. Adams, Sr., found, however, that the British government and people were at best indifferent not only to this Union argument but to their overall cause as well. Compounding the complexity of the situation was Secretary of State Seward's impetuous involvement in diplomatic affairs with England, manifested especially in his aggressive memorandum that practically declared war on any European power that recognized Confederate legations. As he would prove to do throughout his service in London, Adams's father always managed to avoid completely rupturing relations with the British, which proved a difficult proposition as the Union army bungled through one military defeat after another until Antietam. The claim of a victory there gave Lincoln the opportunity to issue the Emancipation Proclamation in 1862, which was to prove a major turning point in Anglo-American relations.

Later victories at Vicksburg and Gettysburg discouraged the British from ever providing aid to the Confederate cause and further cemented the relations between the U.S. government and England. When the most intense pressure was off the Union ministry, Adams found life in London pleasurable, as he enjoyed the association with prominent Englishman and Americans alike. Adams's experiences as his father's secretary during the United States' most turbulent period and his life in London, which was the English-speaking world's intellectual capital, proved to be influential to his later writings, especially in his masterpiece *The Education of Henry Adams*, which was privately published in September 1918 and won the Pulitzer Prize posthumously.

In *The Education*, Adams wrote about the complexity of his feelings during this time in his life, "Of the year 1862 Henry Adams could never think without a shudder. The war alone did not greatly distress him; already in his short life he was used to seeing people wade in blood, and he could plainly discern in history,

that man from the beginning had found his chief amusement in bloodshed; but the ferocious joy of destruction at its best requires that one should kill what one hates, and young Adams neither hated nor wanted to kill his friends the rebels, while he wanted nothing so much as to wipe England off the earth."

Adams's memoirs remain a classic in American literature.

—*James H. Meredith*

See also Adams, Charles Francis; Adams, Charles Francis, Jr.; Diplomacy, U.S.A.; Great Britain.

For further reading:
Adams, Henry. *The Education of Henry Adams, Henry Adams: Novels, Mont Saint Michel, and The Education* (1983).
———. *Henry Adams: Selected Letters* (1992).
Samuels, Ernest. *Henry Adams* (1989).

ADAMS, JOHN
(1825–1864)
Confederate general

Born to Irish immigrant parents in Nashville, Tennessee, Adams moved with his family to Pulaski, Tennessee, while still a child. He lived there until entering the United States Military Academy in 1841. He graduated five years later, twenty-fifth of fifty-nine in the Class of 1846. He received a commission in the 1st Dragoons and was sent immediately to Mexico to serve in the war that erupted there. During the Mexican War, Adams received a brevet promotion to first lieutenant for bravery at the battle of Santa Cruz de Rosales. Following the war, he served in several frontier posts in California, New Mexico, and Minnesota. In the midst of these moves around the frontier, Adams married Georgia McDougal and started what would become a family of six children.

When the Civil War began, Adams was in command of Fort Crook, California, as a captain. Hearing of Tennessee's secession, Adams immediately resigned his commission and boarded a steamer for New York City, arriving there in late summer 1861. General Winfield Scott recommended to Secretary of State William Henry Seward that Adams be arrested as a political prisoner before he could join the Confederate army. Adams made his way south, however, and received an appointment as a captain in the Confederate cavalry.

Adams commanded briefly at Memphis where his main duty was housing and feeding prisoners of war. He then served in western Kentucky and subsequently in Mississippi. Adams was promoted to colonel in May 1862 and commanded a brigade of William Wing Loring's division during the Vicksburg campaign the following year. After Vicksburg, he commanded a brigade under Joseph Johnston at Jackson, Mississippi. Upon the organization of Johnston's Army of Tennessee in December 1863, Adams commanded a brigade in Leonidas Polk's division and fought in northern Mississippi and Alabama before rejoining the main Army of Tennessee in the attempt to stop William T. Sherman's Atlanta campaign.

In the Atlanta campaign, Adams was commended for bravery for his actions at Rocky Face Ridge and Resaca, but he failed to prevent the federal crossing of the Chattahoochee River in July 1864. After Atlanta fell Adams commanded a brigade in John Bell Hood's march into Tennessee. At the battle of Franklin on 30 November 1864, a wounded right arm did not deter Adams from leading a cavalry charge on the Union breastworks. Union soldiers, awed by his bravery, did not shoot at him until he grabbed a set of Union colors. Struck nine times, he died atop the Union works. He was buried near his home in Pulaski, Tennessee.

—*David S. Heidler and Jeanne T. Heidler*

See also Army of Tennessee; Franklin, Battle of.

For further reading:

McDonough, James L., and Thomas L. Connelly. *Five Tragic Hours: The Battle of Franklin* (1983).

Sword, Wiley. *Embrace an Angry Wind: The Confederacy's Last Hurrah; Spring Hill, Franklin and Nashville* (1992).

ADAMS, WILLIAM WIRT
(1819–1888)
Confederate general

Born in Frankfort, Kentucky, to George Adams and Anna Weisiger Adams, William Wirt Adams (generally called Wirt Adams throughout his life) moved briefly to Texas as a young man, where he served in the army of the Republic of Texas in 1839. From Texas he moved to Mississippi, where he became a prominent banker, planter, and state legislator. Adams became active in the secession movement in Mississippi, and after that state's secession, the governor sent Adams as part of a commission to urge Louisiana to secede.

Following the formation of the Confederate States of America, Confederate president Jefferson Davis offered Adams the position of postmaster general, but he refused. Instead, Adams raised and became the colonel of the 1st Mississippi Cavalry. Adams and his men guarded part of the Confederate retreat from Kentucky in spring 1862 and fought at Shiloh. Shortly afterward Adams became Major General Earl Van Dorn's chief of artillery and in that capacity fought at Iuka in September, where he was commended for a trap he set for Union soldiers. October 1862 found him again in command of his cavalry regiment, and he fought at Corinth in Frank Armstrong's cavalry brigade. In 1863 Adams fought in the Vicksburg campaign, particularly in the failed effort to repulse Colonel Benjamin H. Grierson's raid in April and May. He was involved in several skirmishes outside

Vicksburg in June, and on 25 September received a promotion to brigadier general for his actions in the campaign. Throughout the late summer and fall of 1863, Adams operated throughout Mississippi.

Serving under Nathan Bedford Forrest for the remainder of the war, Adams saw action in the weak Confederate attempt to prevent William T. Sherman from taking Meridian, Mississippi, in February 1864. During Sherman's Atlanta campaign, Adams commanded a cavalry division guarding rail lines out of Mississippi and Alabama. In fall 1864 he commanded the Northern District of Mississippi.

Adams surrendered in May 1865 and was paroled. He lived the remainder of his life in Vicksburg and Jackson, Mississippi. He served in state government and as the postmaster of Jackson. In 1888 a Jackson newspaper editor with whom Adams had been feuding killed him in a fight in Jackson.

—*David S. Heidler and Jeanne T. Heidler*

See also Forrest, Nathan Bedford; Grierson's Raid; Meridian Campaign; Van Dorn, Earl.

For further reading:

Bearss, Margie Riddle. *Sherman's Forgotten Campaign: The Meridian Expedition* (1987).

Brown, D. Alexander. *Grierson's Raid: A Cavalry Adventure of the Civil War* (1954).

AFRICAN-AMERICAN SAILORS

In 1861, faced with the daunting task of blockading hundreds of miles of Confederate coast with a minuscule force, the United States Navy turned to African-Americans to fill their ranks. As the navy rapidly acquired ships to carry out the blockade, a shortage of sailors became a critical problem. African-American seamen proved the solution. Not only did large numbers of African-Americans possess maritime skills, but also black sailors had a tradition of service with the navy going back to the Revolutionary War. African-American sailors had served with distinction in all of America's previous wars and represented a small percentage of the navy's manpower in 1861. Blacks were also numerous in the antebellum merchant marine's manpower, filling jobs in a disreputable occupation considered beneath the dignity of most Americans.

The number of African-Americans who enlisted in the Union navy is subject to debate. The total number of navy enlistments (regardless of race) is estimated at roughly 118,000. The first research into African-American Civil War sailors in the late 1940s fixed the percentage of black sailors at 25 percent (about 32,000) of the navy's total enlisted force. Later research in the 1970s guessed the number of enlistees at 9 percent (roughly 10,000). Contemporary research conducted by the National Park Service estimates the number of African-Americans in the Union navy at about 24,000

(16 percent). The number of black Union sailors will probably never be known for certain as navy documents generally did not classify sailors by race, a remarkable fact in a highly race-conscious era.

The recruitment of African-American sailors was markedly different from the enlisting of black soldiers into the Union armies. First, African-American sailors had served the United States from the start. Northern racists initially opposed the enlistment of black soldiers because the war was a conflict over the Union, not slavery. But African-American sailors had a long tradition of service to the nation and their entrance into the navy in large numbers caused little stir. While pubic pressure and federal policy kept black soldiers out of the war, African-American sailors fought for the Union. Second, naval service was not considered socially elevating. While soldiers were usually held in low esteem by the general public, at least some generals (such as George Washington or Andrew Jackson) had risen to the presidency and the army enjoyed a modicum of social standing. Sailors, however, were considered the dregs of society. Thus, the public objected to black soldiers as the elevation of an inferior people to a minimal status with whites. Slaves and seaman, however, shared a common low social standing. Also, whereas the states recruited the army's volunteer regiments, the navy retained its recruiting responsibilities unto itself. Thus, the states had no say in the recruiting of African-American sailors at federal installations, and the enlistment of black sailors occurred out of sight of the general public.

Lastly, the African-American sailors who enlisted in the navy represented an almost opposite demographic background than did black soldiers. Black soldiers were overwhelmingly rural southern slaves who fled from slavery to enlist in the Union army. African-American sailors, however, were mostly urban northern free blacks. While the largest demographic group of African-Americans in the Union army comprised slaves from the Mississippi River valley, a common African-American sailor was a skilled laborer from New York or Boston. Also, unique to African-American sailors, large numbers of foreign-born blacks came to the United States to enlist in the navy. Nearly one in eight African-American sailors came from a foreign land.

Once enlisted in the service, African-American sailors had a much different experience than their counterparts in the army. First, African-American sailors fought from the very first days of the war. While the army resisted black recruits in large numbers until 1863, black sailors served the nation from the opening shots to the bitter end. Second, while the army segregated its black troops into separate "colored" units, the navy fully integrated African-American sailors into its ship crews. This was not an attempt at social equalization; rather it

was simply impracticable to segregate African-American sailors into specific portions of a vessel or onto vessels manned only by black seamen. The integration of crews generated less overt racism than in the army. Living side by side on crowded vessels and sharing common dangers led black and white sailors to at best learn respect for each other or at least keep their prejudices to themselves. The army did little to quell racism in its ranks, but the navy enjoyed relatively harmonious race relations.

The navy also paid its black sailors equal wages to its white crewmen in sharp contrast to the army. For most of the war white army privates received $13 per month in pay along with free uniforms. Until 1864, however, black soldiers received only $10 per month plus a $3 deduction to pay for uniforms and food. The navy, however, always paid the same wages. Along with fair wages, African-American sailors also shared equally in prize moneys when Confederate merchant ships and blockade-runners were captured. Prize money was so lucrative a sailor lucky to participate in a rich capture could receive several years' wages in a matter of hours. The navy provided other benefits in equal portions. For instance, many black army regiments received substandard weapons, uniforms, and food, leading to unnecessary deaths from combat, disease, and exposure. The fully integrated navy crews, however, enjoyed not only a common standard of equipment, clothing, and sustenance, but also a superior supply system that provided replenishment on a fairly regular schedule.

Navy medical care also surpassed its army equivalent. The army chronically lacked physicians, especially to support its black regiments. The navy enjoyed a much larger medical service, however, and smaller percentage of African-American sailors died by disease than black soldiers. The army in general lost roughly one in every fifteen recruits to disease and one in every seven black soldiers to various ailments. Navy doctors, operating with better facilities, drugs, and equipment, limited deaths to disease to one in every forty recruits with relatively minor differences between white and African-American sailors.

African-American sailors shared in the dangers of combat alongside their white shipmates. In many instances the army relegated black troops to relatively unimportant supporting roles such as felling trees, digging trenches, and building roads because the army derided their skills as soldiers. African-American sailors, integrated among navy crews, received every opportunity to demonstrate their bravery under fire. Eight African-American sailors received the Medal of Honor during the Civil War.

Lastly, the navy equally applied its criminal justice system to its African-American recruits. Often the army unjustly prosecuted black soldiers or ignored injustices inflicted upon them by white officers and men. The navy, however, equally applied its criminal justice procedures to both punish and protect African-American sailors. Whites who assaulted or abused black sailors faced navy justice equal to crimes against white personnel. While blacks in the North enjoyed few legal privileges, the navy permitted African-American sailors to testify in court against white defendants or, if charged with an offense, to cross-examine white witnesses. The navy, eager to preserve its source of manpower, even granted beneficial treatment to black sailors accused of violations. When charged with a crime, African-American sailors generally received less severe punishment than white sailors in the form of shorter prison sentences, lower fines, and a higher acquittal rate. Fewer African-American sailors received the death penalty or life sentences in prison relative to their percentage of the navy population.

The Union navy achieved its Civil War goals only with the assistance of African-American sailors. Filling the manpower gap at a time when the navy desperately needed skilled personnel, African-Americans proved their worth to the Union. Whether fighting on river or sea, African-American sailors demonstrated that courage, loyalty, and ability knew no race.

—Steven J. Ramold

See also African-American Soldiers, C.S.A.; Navy, U.S.A..
For further reading:
Canney, Donald L. *Lincoln's Navy: The Ships, Men, and Organization, 1861–1865* (1998).
Quarles, Benjamin. *The Negro in the Civil War* (1989).
Ramold, Steven J. "Valuable Men for Certain Kinds of Duty: African-Americans in the Civil War Navy" (Ph.D. dissertation, 1999).
Valuska, David L. "The Negro in the Union Navy, 1861–1865" (Ph.D. dissertation, 1973).

AFRICAN-AMERICAN SOLDIERS, C.S.A.

Throughout the Civil War, the Confederate government and military were increasingly preoccupied with obtaining new white recruits to fill depleted ranks. At the national level, legislation such as the Conscription Acts of 1862 and 1864 tried to deal with this problem. Within the army measures were implemented to remove whites from regimental support roles such as teamsters, cooks, and musicians, and to detail them to front line duty. Body servants or free blacks often filled the resulting vacancies. Slave labor and conscripted free blacks were also utilized extensively in the Confederate military to perform duties such as building fortifications, expanding river defenses, repairing rail networks, and assisting in the manufacture of armaments. All such measures were designed to free up whites for service in the Confederate army.

The burdens of the Civil War greatly strained the relations between the southern states and their central government. The logistics of fielding and equipping an army became the paramount concern, not just for the national government, but for the state governments as well. Throughout the war the state governments, particularly those most vulnerable to Union invasion, acted according to their individual needs, insisting that their primary obligation was the protection and defense of their citizens, even when that conflicted with Confederate policy. For instance, when Tennessee and Louisiana seceded, their governors saw no other option than to enlist or draft all able bodied men of fighting age, whether white or black, into home guards, militias, and state defense forces. These groups were separate from other state forces incorporated into the Confederate army, and their training and supply were somewhat inferior to that of the Regular Army. Yet it remains that over time Southern states realized that tapping slave and free black populations was the only way to replenish depleted manpower. No specific Confederate law prohibited the practice, but ironically these state actions threatened the very foundation of the Confederacy's reason for existence.

For this reason, the Confederacy found it difficult to assign a meaningful role to slaves and free blacks in the war. Racism and the stigma of slavery were traditions built over centuries, and they continued to dictate white Southerners' perceptions of African-Americans. An extensive legal framework defined African-Americans as property. Although the Confederate government refused to enlist blacks as soldiers, they were often put to other tasks. Measures such as the Negro Musicians Bill in 1863, and the Regimental Cooks Bills of 1862 and 1863, allowed the government to move whites from support functions to the front lines. Going any further in the use of African-Americans was unthinkable to the majority of white Southerners. The Confederate Congress would not even discuss the matter because to contemplate black southern combat soldiers made meaningless for the planter class the very foundation for secession. On the facade, the Confederate Congress—constantly aware of its labor problems—claimed that the issue of black soldiers was not for debate, as they saw this as an affront to the very reason for secession from the Union. Howell Cobb of Georgia, a former member of the Confederate Congress, was so vehemently against the arming of black Southerners that even as the war drew to a close he wrote, "the day you make them soldiers would be the beginning of the end of the revolution."

Nonetheless, there are numerous examples of slaves and free blacks being utilized in the war effort as military support staff. In the early months of the war, some free blacks joined military companies such as Harvey's Scouts (who rode with Nathan Bedford Forrest) and the 3d Georgia Infantry Regiment. In addition, some free blacks from New Orleans also offered their services to the Confederacy. Besides free blacks, slaves also served and

African-American laborers on the James River, Virginia (*National Archives*)

occasionally bore arms as body servants. These were slaves whose prewar career did not generally involve working in the fields, but in the plantation house. Often they grew up with the children of their masters and had close, though often ambivalent, relationships with them, and so when the war began it was a natural consequence for them to accompany their masters into the military whether they wanted to or not.

Several of the Confederate state governments specifically targeted their black population for use in state defense. With its pivotal position as an inland gateway to the Deep South, Tennessee would be a prime target for the Union. The people of Tennessee were divided in their loyalties, as the eastern half of the state generally supported the Union, while elites in the western half supported the Confederacy. Shortly after its secession from the Union, Tennessee's state legislature tried to meet the problems of defense by authorizing Governor Isham G. Harris, "to accept into the armed forces of the state all male persons of color." The number of recruits that were obtained is not known, but some of these men did apply for and receive black Confederate pensions in the postwar period.

The state of Louisiana, with its own unique geographic, social, and governmental systems, held the largest Creole and free black communities in the South. Here, Governor Thomas O. Moore in 1861, and his successor, Henry W. Allen in 1864, specifically authorized the use of black Southerners as soldiers. Although Moore was thinking of their use as more of a supportive role, he did allow the organization of the Native Guards in 1861, but Allen went so far as to make a request to the Confederate secretary of war James A. Seddon, for the immediate organization of black regiments. Best known of these were the Native Guards, a regiment that was both officered and manned by the free black population of New Orleans. This occurred prior to the official enlistment of blacks in the Union army. Ironically, following the fall of New Orleans in 1862, many of the members of the Native Guards would join the Union army as part of the early Northern efforts to recruit blacks.

Another example of the utilization of black Southerners in the early part of the war can be seen in South Carolina. South Carolina's planter class were uncompromising on the crucial issues of slavery and states rights, but this did not deter groups of slaves and free blacks from participating in that state's regiments. Members from the state's free black communities in Columbia and Charleston petitioned Governor Francis

Pickens to allow them to "render service where we can be most useful." Pickens ordered one such group to assist with the artillery barrage of Fort Sumter after they said "they would be ready whenever called upon to assist in preparing the State a defense against any action that may be brought against her." However, as in Tennessee, South Carolina also encompassed geographical and cultural distinctions where the influence of low and upcountry elites impinged on governmental policy towards the state's black population.

A more serious attempt to directly enlist black Southerners into the army as soldiers occurred in January 1864. Major General Patrick Cleburne, an Irish-born division commander in the Army of Tennessee, circulated a document calling for the enlistment of slaves. Cleburne proposed "that we immediately commence training a large reserve of the most courageous of our slaves, and further that we guarantee freedom within a reasonable time to every slave in the South who shall remain true to the Confederacy in this war." Cleburne stressed the Confederacy's need for additional troops, and added: "[w]e can only get a sufficiency [of numbers] by making the negro share the danger and hardships of the war."

While Jefferson Davis would not consider the plan at that time, military necessity eventually ended his reluctance. In late 1864, Secretary of State Judah Benjamin also called for the enlistment of slaves, and in January 1865, Robert E. Lee added his support for the immediate employment of black soldiers. "We must decide," the general wrote, "whether slavery shall be extinguished by our enemies and the slave be used against us, or use them ourselves at the risk of the effects which may be produced upon our social institutions."

On 13 March 1865, the Confederate Congress finally authorized the recruitment of "Negro Soldiers." In exchange for their "loyal service," a loosely defined emancipation would be their reward with the defeat of the Union. In Richmond, Majors James W. Pegram and Thomas P. Turner were the first to recruit the city's slaves into military companies. A Richmond newspaper noted in late March that the black recruits "move with evident pride and satisfaction to themselves" and that "the knowledge of the military art they already exhibit was something remarkable." During the retreat from Richmond, some of the black soldiers were involved in a rear guard action on 5 April, near Paineville, while others were seen constructing earthworks the following day. The remnants of these companies were evidently disbanded or captured before the final capitulation, as the only known blacks listed on the Appomattox surrender rolls are a handful of cooks, teamsters, and musicians.

When considering the issue of African-American soldiers in Confederate service, the question of numbers remains inconclusive, a natural consequence when considering that many Southern records were lost or destroyed at the war's conclusion. Aside from the service of the Louisiana Native Guards at the outbreak of the war, and the several companies of African-Americans organized in Richmond in March 1865, there is little documentation indicating that blacks served as combat soldiers in southern armies in anything but the most negligible numbers. Their main role in the Confederate military was that of support staff, servants, cooks, teamsters, and musicians. The most contentious question of why black Southerners might support the Confederacy remains a riddle. The majority of these participants were either conscripted, coerced, or in a few cases saw the war as a means of economic advancement. Yet, perhaps the answer in part also lies in the same motives of many Southern whites who went to war. They wanted to protect their families and their communities. In the case of some body servants, there was the paternalistic relationship between master and slave. But obviously absent from such motives was any loyalty to the Confederacy or to its peculiar institution.

—*Frank E. Deserino*

See also African-American Sailors; African-American Suffrage; Cleburne, Patrick Ronayne; Slaves; United States Colored Troops.

For further reading:

Berlin, Ira, ed. *Freedom: A Documentary History of Emancipation, 1861-1867. Series II: The Black Military Experience* (1982).

Brewer, James H. *The Confederate Negro: Virginia's Craftsmen and Military Laborers, 1861-1865* (1969).

Durden, Robert F. *The Gray and the Black* (1972).

Helsley, Alexia J. *South Carolina's African-American Confederate Pensioners 1923-1925* (1998).

Jordan, Ervin L., Jr. *Black Confederates and Afro-Yankees in Civil War Virginia* (1995).

McPherson, James M. *The Negro's Civil War: How American Negroes Felt and Acted During the War for the Union* (1965).

Trudeau, Noah Andre. *Like Men of War: Black Troops in the Civil War, 1862-1865* (1998).

AFRICAN-AMERICAN SOLDIERS, U.S.A.
See United States Colored Troops

AFRICAN-AMERICAN SUFFRAGE

The issue of extending to African-Americans the right to vote tested the egalitarian meaning of the Civil War. In 1861 less than one-tenth of African-Americans in the North lived in states where they could legally vote. These states were Maine, Massachusetts, New Hampshire, New York (where a discriminatory $250 property qualification applied), Rhode Island, and Vermont. Exclusion from the ballot box generally reflected a belief, reiterated by the Supreme Court in its decision in the *Dred Scott* Case (1857), that African-Americans could not be citizens because of inherent racial differences. Abolitionists had persistently challenged this idea, arguing not only that all men should be free but that they should enjoy freedom equally—that is, without civil or political disabilities based on race. Even with the emergence of a sectional northern Republican Party in the 1850s, egalitarians made little headway. While Republican legislators in several states pushed to equalize suffrage, popular referenda in the decade before the war in New York, Michigan, Iowa, and Wisconsin defeated their proposals by large margins. Only in areas settled by New Englanders did the suffrage issue fail to divide Republican voters seriously.

When African-Americans served the Union cause during the war as guides, scouts, cooks, teamsters, laborers, nurses, and, above all, as soldiers, they challenged existing stereotypes about their race. Wartime hostility toward the South and its institutions also diminished open defenses of racism by moderate Republicans, especially as captured African-American soldiers faced execution or enslavement at Confederate hands. Abolitionists meanwhile argued that the North's wartime suffering would be meaningless unless the nation repented the sin of slavery and pledged itself to freedom and equality for all. Thus, wartime conditions facilitated moves toward not only emancipation of Southern slaves but also equal rights.

In 1862 Attorney General Edward Bates delivered an opinion that contradicted the *Dred Scott* decision by declaring that African-Americans were citizens. The right to establish qualifications to vote, however, rested with the individual states. Although some abolitionists doubted that newly freed slaves were prepared to vote, Wendell Phillips and Frederick Douglass argued that the freedmen were no less capable than the impoverished immigrants currently entering the electorate in the North; possession of the ballot would be essential for blacks to achieve equal access to education and economic opportunity. Because white Southerners were unlikely to embrace African-American suffrage, abolitionists and their radical Republican allies favored the idea that the Southern states, by seceding, had lost their rights as states, which would permit Congress to regulate their suffrage until these rights were regained.

In 1864 radicals, led principally by Senator Charles Sumner, tested sentiment in Congress on African-American suffrage. Attempts to remove the term *white* from the suffrage provisions for Montana Territory and the District of Columbia went down to defeat. Democrats, recognizing the ability of the race issue to divide Republicans, stressed it incessantly. They accused Republicans of pursuing equality to perpetuate their own political power and predicted a race war endangering the Republic if equal rights prevailed. Acknowledging the existence of prejudice, President Abraham Lincoln's Ten Per Cent Plan for reconstruction permitted white Southerners who pledged future loyalty to the United States to reorganize state governments. Petitioned by representatives of New Orleans's large free black community, however, Lincoln privately inquired of Louisiana governor Michael Hahn whether African-Americans who had served in the Union army or owned property might not vote. Even a qualified suffrage for African-Americans, however, was anathema to most Southern whites.

Radical Republicans, deploring Lincoln's deference to former Rebels, articulated a different approach to Reconstruction in the Wade-Davis Bill. Fearful of the race issue, its sponsors proposed granting political power to whites who had never supported the Confederacy, but not African-Americans. Lincoln's pocket veto of the Wade-Davis Bill angered radicals, some of whom joined a movement to secure a more radical Republican candidate for president in 1864. Wendell Phillips tirelessly toured the country, proclaiming that there could be no peace without justice for African-Americans and that they deserved to participate in a government they defended with their lives. Phillips and other radicals, including Frederick Douglass and Elizabeth Cady Stanton, promoted John C. Frémont as the nominee of a radical Democratic Party. Many abolitionists (including powerful antislavery editors William Lloyd Garrison and Theodore Tilton) refused to abandon Lincoln, however, despite his perceived ideological shortcomings.

At the end of the war, the suffrage issue remained unresolved. Despite Garrison's recommendation that the American Antislavery Society disband upon the passage of the Thirteenth Amendment abolishing slavery, Phillips's supporters within the society voted to continue the quest for equal rights. Radical Republicans in Wisconsin, Minnesota, and Connecticut prepared for referenda to revise their state suffrage provisions to permit African-Americans to vote. Although all would fail, as had the prewar referenda, the war had heightened a partisanship that soon would be harnessed on behalf of African-American suffrage. The nation's ultimate commitment to African-American suffrage in the Fifteenth Amendment (1870), however, would owe as much to political calculations as an acceptance of ideals of equality.

—*Phyllis F. Field*

See also Bates, Edward; Douglass, Frederick; *Dred Scott* Case; Emancipation Proclamation; Freedmen's Bureau; Frémont, John C.; Garrison, William Lloyd; Hahn, Michael; Lincoln's Reconstruction Policy; Phillips, Wendell; Thirteenth Amendment; Wade-Davis Bill.

For further reading:
Dykstra, Robert R. *Bright Radical Star: Black Freedom and White Supremacy on the Hawkeye Frontier* (1993).
McPherson, James M. *The Struggle for Equality: Abolitionists and the Negro in the Civil War and Reconstruction* (1964).
Voegeli, V. Jacque. *Free But Not Equal: The Midwest and the Negro During the Civil War* (1967).

ALABAMA

Alabama was established as a separate territory in 1817 and was admitted into the Union as the twenty-second state in 1819. By 1820 Alabama's population was more than 125,000, including about 500 free African-Americans. By 1830 there were 300,000 residents, 38 percent of them slaves, and cotton was the principal money crop. Agriculture dominated Alabama, and Mobile was second to only New Orleans as a cotton port. Until the Civil War, domestic politics centered on removal of the Indians, land policy, the banking system, and the question of slavery.

The state suffered severely for almost a decade in the economic depression that followed the panic of 1837. During the late 1840s and 1850s efforts were made to create a more modern, industrialized economy. Coal and iron were boated out of the mountains because Alabama, lagging far behind other states, had only 165 miles of railroad track as late as 1852. By 1860 that had increased to 743 miles; however, the mountain regions remained unpenetrated, and the northern and southern portions of the state were not linked for lack of a standard gauge. In the mineral district before the Civil War, only seventeen forges, nine primitive furnaces, and one crude rolling mill were engaged in ironmaking. Until the Civil War, the vast majority of investment remained in cotton and slaves. The population was almost 1 million, with nearly half that number African-American. All but 5 percent of the population lived in rural areas.

By the late 1850s, slavery and other sectional issues had long been important in Alabama politics; however, the state was still secure in the Union. Andrew Barry Moore, a moderate Democrat, was elected governor without any opposition and was reelected two years later. A series of events, beginning with John Brown's raid in Virginia in October 1859, drove Alabamians toward the radical Southern rights stance of William Lowndes Yancey.

On 24 February 1860, the legislature called for a state convention in the event of a Republican presidential victory. Within a year, events on the national level made secession inevitable in Alabama. Alabama delegates walked out of the Democratic National Convention at Charleston when supporters of Illinois senator Stephen A. Douglas would not accept a platform protecting slavery in the territories. The presidential campaign of 1860 brought Alabama to the point of secession. In the general election, Kentuckian John C. Breckinridge won the state with 48,000 votes. Union-minded Democrats supported Douglas, who received 13,000 votes, and Whigs cast 27,000 votes for Constitutional Union candidate, John Bell of Tennessee.

With Lincoln's election, Governor Moore—now a secessionist—called for the election of delegates to a 7 January 1861 state convention. Moore sent commissioners to other slave states to counter Union supporters or "cooperationists" who advocated pan-Southern action. Voters elected a clear majority of "immediate secessionists" (fifty-four) over cooperationists (forty-six). The cooperationists, largely from northern Alabama, were vulnerable to invasion in the event of war, and their livelihood did not center on slavery.

At the state convention—under the leadership of Yancey and Thomas Hill Watts—secessionists claimed that Alabama, as a sovereign state, had the right to secede. On 11 January, Alabama was voted out of the Union, followed by a petition inviting other Southern states to send delegates to a 4 February convention in Montgomery. The vote on the secession ordinance was sixty-nine to thirty-one. Many cooperationists refused to sign the official copy of the secession ordinance, though most of them recognized secession as legal and binding. Among farmers from the north part of the state, there was talk of seceding from Alabama and inviting neighboring citizens in Georgia and Tennessee to join them in forming a free state under the Indian name of Nickajack.

By the end of January, six lower states had cut their ties with the Union. Montgomery hosted the convention that created the Confederate States of America. It was chosen due largely to its central location and convenient railroad and river facilities. Thirty-seven delegates began secret deliberation on 4 February. Within days a provisional constitution was drafted and a vice president, Alexander Hamilton Stephens of Georgia, and a president, Jefferson Davis of Mississippi, were elected.

The Provisional Constitution provided that until otherwise decided Montgomery would serve as the capital of the Confederacy. Yet Montgomery's inadequate accommodations and hot climate were a source of constant complaint, and Virginia's entry into the Confederacy soon prompted a move to Richmond. Some argued for the move on the grounds that Virginia's security and consequently that of the entire Confederacy was dependent on situating the capital in Richmond. Others concluded that Virginia would be the scene of crisis, and the government needed to be there to offer logistical, as well as political support for Virginians who would bear the brunt of campaigning.

Montgomery nevertheless remained important. The city was a stop on a major railroad line, and thousands of troops passed through each month. The city included seven military hospitals and served as a major supply depot.

Confederate volunteers in Alabama, like those in other Southern states, anticipated a short war. Loyalists in the hill country who took a position of neutrality were threatened in those counties that lagged in filling their ranks of volunteers for the Confederacy. To deal with this, the state legislature passed a conscription act in

1862 and appropriated several million dollars for military operations and for the support of the families of soldiers. As a result, neutralists hardened into Unionists and many joined the Union army. Historians disagree on the extent of Unionism in Alabama, but statistics show that 2,578 white Alabamians joined the Union army. Otherwise, 75,000 whites served in the Confederate army. In addition, 10,000 African-American Alabamians fought for the Union.

Alabama saw its share of fighting toward the end of the Civil War, including the largest naval engagement of the war in Mobile Bay in August 1864. Mobile was the leading port on the Gulf Coast after the fall of New Orleans in 1862. Blockade runners shipped cotton to Havana in exchange for military supplies and other items. Union admiral David Glasgow Farragut began his attack in Mobile Bay running past Forts Morgan and Gaines on 5 August. All but one of eighteen Union gunboats passed safely into the bay, leading to Fort Morgan's capitulation on 23 August. Though Mobile Bay was under Union control, Mobile's citizens held out until the end of the war and made it the last coastal city in the Confederacy to fall. Two of the last land battles of the Civil War took place at Fort Blakeley and Spanish Fort on the eastern side of Mobile Bay, between 27 March and 9 April 1865.

In early 1865, Union general James Harrison Wilson attacked the Confederacy's second largest arsenal in Selma, Alabama. Selma produced cannon, cartridges, shovels, uniforms, and other war materiel in machine shops, iron mills, and cotton mills. By the time of Wilson's attack, Confederate opposition consisted mainly of old men and boys, and Federal troops easily took control of the town, setting fire to its public buildings, storehouses, business district, and more than a hundred private homes. Selma was left with more damage than all other Alabama towns combined. On 4 May 1865, General Richard Taylor surrendered remaining Confederate forces at Citronell.

Following the collapse of the Confederacy and the refusal of the state legislature to ratify the Fourteenth Amendment to the U.S. Constitution, Alabama in 1867 was placed under military rule. In 1868 the state ratified a new constitution that protected the civil rights of African-Americans, and Alabama was readmitted to the Union. Moreover, the Civil War dealt a mortal blow to Alabama's feudal society. Planters were forced to substitute tenant farming or peonage for slavery; however, they never recovered completely from the emancipation of their labor force. Soybeans and cattle supplanted the production of cotton.

From 1868 to 1874 Alabama was in political turmoil. To many whites, the Reconstruction period was tragic; to many blacks, it was a period of opportunity and hope. Among white Alabamians, a struggle ensued between those who defied the notion of African-Americans having political rights and power and those willing to cooperate with African-Americans and their Northern allies. African-Americans demanded access to education and were given it, but most whites insisted that schools be racially separate. Although African-Americans participated in the constitutional conventions and in the state legislatures, their political power was not as strong as that of African-Americans in South Carolina, Mississippi, or Louisiana. In 1874 the white Democrats of Alabama, most of whom had been supporters of the Confederacy, regained control of the state political machinery. African-Americans were left with little political power until the Civil Rights movement of the 1960s.

—*Kevin M. Levin*

See also Army of Mobile; Blakely, Alabama, Battle of; Mobile Bay; Mobile Campaign; Selma, Alabama; Wilson's Selma Raid.

For further reading:
Fleming, Walter L. *Civil War and Reconstruction in Alabama* (1905).
McMillan, Malcolm C. *Constitutional Development in Alabama, 1798–1901* (1955).
Rogers, William W., Robert D. Ward, and Leah R. Atkins. *Alabama: The History of a Deep South State* (1994).

ALABAMA CLAIMS

During the Civil War, in addition to procuring certain supplies for the war effort, the Confederate States of America also purchased ships in Great Britain and then took those ships to other ports for outfitting as warships. Confederate purchasing agent James D. Bulloch was the most successful at this practice, and two of the ships he purchased, the CSS *Alabama* and the CSS *Florida*, did serious damage to the U.S. merchant fleet during the war. Other vessels purchased later, like the CSS *Shenandoah*, also caused serious losses to U.S. shippers.

While these purchases were taking place, the U.S. minister to Great Britain, Charles Francis Adams, protested vigorously to the British government that allowing such practices to take place violated British neutrality in the conflict. At times the British government seemed to agree and even made an unsuccessful attempt to prevent the *Alabama* from leaving Great Britain. Off and on throughout the war, however, the Confederacy was able to procure such ships, and the damage to U.S. shipping continued.

During the war, Adams made a formal claim to the British government that the United States should be paid for damage to American shipping as a result of the activities of the *Alabama*. As a result of that claim, which was rejected, all subsequent claims made by the United States for damages inflicted by all of the other British-built ships have generally been lumped together as the "*Alabama* claims."

After the war, the British government of Lord Palmerston refused to negotiate the continued claims of the United States and refused to submit the matter to arbitration by neutral parties. Many other men in the British government, however, saw such a stand as short-sighted. They argued that Palmerston's position established the precedent that neutral powers like the United States could allow Britain's enemies to purchase warships in those neutral ports. To give weight to that argument, the U.S. Congress made it plain after the war that such purchases would be allowed.

The British government changed in 1866, and President Andrew Johnson's secretary of state, William Henry Seward, immediately opened negotiations with Great Britain regarding the *Alabama* claims. When the two governments reached an agreement in 1868, Seward's efforts were thwarted in the Senate by the chairman of the Senate Committee on Foreign Relations, Charles Sumner. Sumner argued that the monetary settlement was not large enough (he demanded that since so much long-term damage had been done to American merchant shipping that the British government should pay for half the cost of the Civil War) and that the British should include an apology in the agreement. Sumner's ultimate goal apparently was to secure Canada in payment of the *Alabama* claims.

The incoming Ulysses S. Grant administration took up the negotiations. Grant's secretary of state, Hamilton Fish, opened negotiations with British emissary John Rose in 1870. The British government still believed that it was to its advantage to settle with the United States and, as part of a settlement, to have a statement agreed upon by both countries that neutrality would prevent either nation from allowing the enemies of either from outfitting warships in the neutral country.

Fish and Rose reached an agreement in early 1871 to submit the *Alabama* claims as well as other matters of dispute between the two countries to a commission of five representatives from each country. Thrown into the negotiations were New England fishing rights along the Canadian coast and U.S. navigation rights on the St. Lawrence River. The joint commission negotiated the Treaty of Washington in the spring of 1871, and the treaty was ratified by the U.S. Senate on 24 May 1871.

The Treaty of Washington contained a statement of regret from the British government regarding the damage done by the Confederate ships, and a statement by both nations that neither side would allow such an occurrence in the future. The treaty also allowed for temporary fishing rights for New Englanders and navigation of the St. Lawrence. As for the monetary claims regarding the damage done by the *Alabama* and the other ships, the claims were submitted to a commission of one representative from the United States, one from Great Britain,

and one each from Switzerland, Brazil, and Italy. Charles Francis Adams was the American representative. Caleb Cushing, former U.S. attorney general, served as counsel for the United States regarding legal matters of the settlement. The commission reached an agreement that the United States should be paid $15,500,000 in gold for damages caused by the Confederate ships. The British made the payment in 1873, thus ensuring that the United States as a neutral power would never give material aid to enemies of Great Britain.

—*David S. Heidler and Jeanne T. Heidler*

See also Adams, Charles Francis; *Alabama*, CSS; Bulloch, James Dunwody; Diplomacy, U.S.A.; *Florida*, CSS; *Shenandoah*, CSS.

For further reading:
Cook, Adrian. *The Alabama Claims: American Politics and Anglo-American Relations, 1865–1872* (1975).

ALABAMA, CSS
Confederate commerce raider

On 1 August 1861, Confederate purchasing agent James D. Bulloch contracted for a ship with John Laird & Sons at Liverpool, England. First identified as Hull No. 290, she was launched on 15 May 1862 as the *Enrica*. United States diplomats in Britain learned she was intended for the Confederacy and brought pressure on the British government to impound her, but Bulloch managed to get her to sea on 30 July, before she could be seized. Rendezvousing with two other ships, she received her ordnance and other supplies at the Portuguese island of Terceira in the Azores. There her captain, Raphael Semmes, joined her and on 24 August placed her into commission as the *Alabama*.

A sleek, three-masted, bark-rigged sloop of oak with a copper hull, the *Alabama* was probably the finest cruiser of her class in the world. She weighed 1,050 tons and was 220 feet in length overall, 31 feet 9 inches in beam, and 14 feet in depth of hold. She had a screw propeller that could be detached so that she might make faster speed under sail alone. She could make 13 knots under steam and sail and 10 knots under sail. Captain Semmes characterized her as "a very perfect ship of her class." A well-built vessel, she survived several bad storms, including a hurricane.

The *Alabama* had a fully equipped machine shop to enable her crew to make all ordinary repairs themselves and could carry coal sufficient for eighteen days of continuous steaming. Semmes preferred to rely on sail where possible. In fact, all but about a half dozen of her subsequent captures were taken under sail alone. If able to provision from captured prizes, the *Alabama* could remain at sea a long time.

The *Alabama* mounted eight guns: six 32-pounders in broadside and two pivot-guns (a 7-inch, 110-

The CSS *Alabama*, from an undated print (*Library of Congress*)

pounder rifled Blakeley, and a smoothbore 8-inch, 68-pounder) amidships. She had a 120-man crew and twenty-four officers.

The *Alabama* first cruised in the Azores and took a number of prizes. She then sailed to the Newfoundland Banks where she was also quite successful. Semmes then took her into the Caribbean, where she intercepted and took the *Ariel*, her most important prize. The *Alabama* then sailed to Galveston, Texas, where on 11 January 1863 she lured out, engaged, and then sank the Union warship *Hatteras*.

Captain Semmes then returned the *Alabama* to the West Indies. She next spent several months off the coast of Latin America, where she took additional prizes before sailing for South Africa. Learning that the more powerful U.S. Navy steamer *Vanderbilt* was searching for him, Semmes then took the *Alabama* into the Pacific, hopeful of inflicting serious damage on U.S.-Asian trade. She sailed all the way to India but took few prizes because U.S. merchant captains, having been warned of her presence, stayed in port. Semmes was also experiencing increasing disciplinary problems with his crew, and the ship herself badly needed an overhaul in a modern shipyard.

The *Alabama* sailed to France by way of Cape Town, dropping anchor at Cherbourg on 11 June 1864. Since her commissioning, she had sailed 75,000 miles, taken sixty-six prizes, and sunk a Union warship. Twenty-five Union warships had searched for her, costing the Federal government over $7 million. Her exploits had also been a considerable boost to Confederate morale.

On 19 June 1864 after the French denied him access to a dry dock, Semmes took the *Alabama* out to engage the Union warship *Kearsarge*, which had taken up position off the harbor. The ensuing battle was one of the most spectacular Civil War naval engagements. Superior Union gunnery, chain armor aboard the *Kearsarge*, and poor cannon powder on the *Alabama* all spelled disaster for the Confederate commerce raider. Having been repeatedly holed, the *Alabama* went down. She suffered forty-one casualties: Nine were killed and twenty wounded in the engagement, and twelve others subsequently drowned.

In 1984 the French navy located the *Alabama*'s resting place. Although she is within French territorial waters, British preservationist groups want the wreck, if raised, to be displayed at Birkenhead where she was built. The United States government had asserted ownership, however, and in 1989 Congress passed the CSS *Alabama* Preservation Act. The fight over the *Alabama* continues.

—*Spencer C. Tucker*

See also Bulloch, James Dunwody; *Kearsarge*, USS; Navy, C.S.A.; Semmes, Raphael.
For further reading:
Robinson, Charles M., III. *Shark of the Confederacy. The Story of the CSS Alabama* (1995).
Semmes, Raphael. *Memoirs of Service Afloat During the War Between the States* (1987).

Silverstone, Paul H. *Warships of the Civil War Navies* (1989).
Sinclair, Arthur. *Two Years on the Alabama* (1895).
Summersell, Charles G. *CSS Alabama: Builder, Captain, and Plans* (1985).
Tucker, Spencer C. *Raphael Semmes and the Alabama* (1996).

ALBEMARLE, CSS

One of the Confederate navy's most successful ironclads, the *Albemarle* played a key role in the capture of Plymouth, North Carolina, on 17–20 April 1864. The *Albemarle's* contractor was Gilbert Elliott, a nineteen-year-old shipbuilder and engineer. The designer and supervisor of construction was John L. Porter, who had worked on the conversion of the *Merrimack* into the CSS *Virginia*. The *Albemarle* was built in a former cornfield on the Roanoke River at Edwards Ferry, North Carolina. Construction, begun in spring 1863, was painfully slow. The remote yard had to compete with other ironclads for workers, transportation of supplies, and other resources. Elliott scrounged railroad rails and even scrap nuts and bolts to be rolled into armor plate.

The *Albemarle* was 152 feet long, with a beam of 45 feet and a draft of 8 feet. Built of solid 8-by-10 pine timbers, and covered with 4-inch planks and two layers of 2-inch thick iron plating, the vessel was powered by two 200-horsepower engines. Her armament consisted of two 6.4-inch Brooke rifles, mounted at the bow and stern. An 18-foot oak prow, also covered with iron plates, could be used as a ram.

The Confederate navy assigned Commander James W. Cooke to the *Albemarle*. Early in 1864, Brigadier General Robert F. Hoke planned an attack on the nearby Union-held town of Plymouth, and persuaded Cooke to bring the still unfinished *Albemarle* down the river to help him. Hoke surrounded Plymouth on 17 April 1864, and began his attack, which continued the next day. When Cooke ordered the *Albemarle* to cast off late on 17 April, workmen still labored aboard the vessel. The rudder broke during the trip, and the engines broke down, resulting in hours of delay. It was 2:30 A.M. on 19 April when the *Albemarle* reached Plymouth and steered for the Union gunboats, *Miami* and *Southfield*. Commander C. W. Flusser had stretched chains and spars between the two gunboats to snag the *Albemarle* between them. Cooke avoided this trap and rammed the *Southfield*, which sank quickly. The *Albemarle* and the *Miami* dueled at close range until a Federal shell bounced off the *Albemarle's* armor and exploded on the deck of the *Miami*, killing Flusser. The

Battle between the *Sassacus* and the *Albermarle*, May 1864, from an undated painting (*National Archives*)

Miami and two smaller Union vessels retreated down the river.

Plymouth held out until 10 A.M. on 20 April, when Brigadier General W. H. Wessells surrendered. Perhaps the *Albemarle* was the deciding factor in Hoke's victory, for she had deprived the Federals of the protection of the Union navy's heavy guns while adding her own 100-pounders to Hoke's field artillery. The fall of Plymouth threatened Union control of all of eastern North Carolina. In nearby Washington, the Union garrison looted and set fire to the town before fleeing to New Bern. Hoke followed and began an attack on New Bern in early May.

Cooke and Hole planned to have the *Albemarle* steam to New Bern to help in the attack. On 5 May 1864 Cooke found his way blocked by seven Union gunboats in Albemarle Sound. After a two-and-a-half-hour battle, the *Albemarle* and the Federal flotilla fought to a draw. The combined Union flotilla failed to destroy the ram, but the *Albemarle* was damaged and unable to push past the Union vessels. Hoke was soon ordered to break off his operations and rejoin Lee in Virginia.

The *Albemarle* remained a threat to the Union navy. Lieutenant William B. Cushing was chosen to lead a raid against the ram. Cushing designed a special boom tipped with a torpedo and fitted onto a steam launch. On the night of 27 October 1864 Cushing and his twenty-five men steamed into the Roanoke River and neared the *Albemarle*. At the last minute, a sleeping sentinel was awakened by his barking dog. Cushing came under musket fire from shore, and a bonfire lit to reveal the raiders also showed a protective log boom surrounding the *Albemarle*. Cushing steamed full speed to jump the boat over the boom and detonated the torpedo against the ironclad's hull, sinking her in eight feet of water. Cushing and one other man escaped; two drowned, and the rest were captured.

Thus, the *Albemarle* became the only Confederate ironclad to be destroyed by enemy action—the others were either captured or scuttled to avoid capture. Without the *Albemarle*, Plymouth fell to the Union again on 31 October. The Confederates never again had a chance to regain control of the sounds of North Carolina.

The *Albemarle* was raised in 1865, towed to the Norfolk Navy Yard, and sold at auction in 1867.

—David A. Norris

See also Albemarle Sound; Cushing, William Barker; Plymouth, Battle of.

For further reading:
Barrett, John G. *The Civil War in North Carolina* (1963).
Cushing, W. B. "The Destruction of the *Albemarle*." In *Battles and Leaders of the Civil War*, vol. 4.
Elliott, Gilbert. "The First Battle of the Confederate Ram *Albemarle*." In *Battles and Leaders of the Civil War*, vol. 4.
Elliott, Robert G. *Ironclad of the Roanoke* (1994).
Holden, Edgar. "The *Albemarle* and the *Sassacus*." In *Battles and Leaders of the Civil War*, vol. 4.
Official Record. Naval Records. Series I, vols. 9–10.
Still, William N., Jr. *Iron Afloat: The Story of the Confederate Armorclads* (1985).

ALBEMARLE SOUND
(5 May 1864)

Plymouth, North Carolina, was captured on 20 April 1864 by three Confederate brigades under Brigadier General Robert F. Hoke, aided by the CSS *Albemarle*. Hoke intended to follow up his victory by mounting an attack on New Bern, where most of the remaining Union forces in North Carolina were. Commander James W. Cooke, captain of the *Albemarle*, planned to bring his vessel again to help Hoke in the attempt to take New Bern.

Bringing the *Albemarle* to New Bern would be difficult for Cooke. The Rebel ram faced a long trip steaming across the rough waters of the Albemarle, Croatan, and Pamlico sounds. The final leg of the journey was a trip up the Neuse River, dodging Federal obstructions, before joining the fighting at New Bern. Cooke also knew that whatever gunboats could be sent by the Union navy would be waiting for him.

Hoke was already embroiled in the attack on New Bern when the *Albemarle* left Plymouth on 5 May 1864. The ram was accompanied by two smaller steamers, the *Bombshell* and the *Cotton Plant*. The *Bombshell* had been an Erie Canal boat before being added to the Union navy. The vessel had been sunk during the battle of Plymouth, but had been raised and repaired by the Confederates. The *Bombshell* carried coal and supplies, and the *Cotton Plant* towed several launches loaded with soldiers.

Cooke soon learned that his way to New Bern was blocked off Sandy Point, North Carolina, by a force of seven Union vessels under Captain Melancton Smith. Smith had four double-enders, the *Mattabesett*, *Sassacus*, *Wyalusing*, and *Miami*, and three smaller steamers, the *Whitehead*, *Ceres*, and *Commodore Hull*. Although none of Smith's vessels was an ironclad—Union ironclads drew too much water to pass through the inlets along North Carolina's coast—he massed sixty guns against the *Albemarle*'s two.

The *Albemarle* opened fire at about 5 P.M. Cooke's first two shots smashed the *Mattabesett*'s launch, tore through her rigging, and wounded six men. The *Albemarle* then tried to ram the *Sassacus*, but the Confederate ship was difficult to steer and missed. The *Sassacus* unloaded a full broadside at the *Albemarle*, but the shots bounced harmlessly off the ram's armor. Cooke had ordered his tenders to steam upriver to safety; the *Cotton Plant* did, but the *Bombshell* for some reason did not and was captured by the *Sassacus*.

After taking the *Bombshell*, the *Sassacus* was about a mile from the ram. Lieutenant Commander F. A. Roe ordered the *Sassacus* to run full steam to ram the *Albemarle*. The *Sassacus* struck the *Albemarle* with a great crash that threatened to capsize the ram. The *Sassacus's* bow remained entangled with the *Albemarle*. The Rebel gunners fired a 100-pounder shot that tore through the *Sassacus*, exploding her starboard boiler and filling the ship's interior with scalding steam. The *Sassacus* finally parted from the *Albemarle* and drifted downstream without steam power, continuing to fire at the *Albemarle* until out of range.

The fighting continued until about 7:30 P.M., although none of the Federal fleet engaged the *Albemarle* as aggressively as the *Sassacus*. Cooke then steered for Plymouth. The *Albemarle* had taken many hits from the Union vessels, had run out of fuel, and had suffered damage to her steering. Her stern Brooke rifle was broken off at the muzzle. The smokestack was torn with so many shot holes that it could not provide enough draft for the engines to work efficiently. Bacon, lard, and butter had to be used as fuel to get up enough steam for the *Albemarle* to return to Plymouth.

Although Smith failed to capture the *Albemarle*, his flotilla prevented her from reaching New Bern to join Hoke. At any rate, news soon reached Plymouth that Hoke had been ordered to break off his attack on New Bern and return with his men to Virginia to join Robert E. Lee's army, which was facing a spring offensive.

The *Albemarle* remained a threat to the Union navy until she was sunk at her moorings in Plymouth in a raid led by Lieutenant William B. Cushing on 27 October 1864. With the *Albemarle* gone, the Federals once again took control of the sound and the region around it. The smokestack of the *Albemarle*, bearing holes from the battle of 5 May, is on display at the North Carolina Museum of History in Raleigh.

—David A. Norris

See also Albemarle, CSS.
For further reading:
Elliott, Robert G. *Ironclad of the Roanoke* (1994).
Holden, Edgar. "The 'Albemarle' and the 'Sassacus.'" In *Battles and Leaders of the Civil War*, vol. 4.
Nichols, Roy F., ed. "Fighting in North Carolina Waters." *North Carolina Historical Review* (1963).
Official Records. Naval Records Series I:9.
Still, William N., Jr. *Iron Afloat: The Story of the Confederate Armorclads* (1985).

ALBERT, PRINCE
(1819–1861)
Royal consort to Queen Victoria

As Queen Victoria's husband and advisor, Prince Albert played a significant role in bringing the *Trent* Affair to a peaceful resolution. Asked by his wife to read and emend a draft of the British Cabinet's demand for redress from the American government, Albert softened its wording. His emendations probably did not prove decisive in preventing the outbreak of war; nonetheless, they made British demands easier for the Americans to swallow.

Born on 26 August 1819 at Rosenau, his father's residence near Coburg in present-day Germany, Albert was the second son of Duke Ernest of Saxe-Coburg-Gotha, and Louise, daughter of Duke Augustus of Saxe-Gotha-Altenburg. Starting in 1836, King Leopold I of Belgium arranged several meetings between his nephew Albert and his niece, Princess Victoria of England. After several elaborately staged encounters, Victoria grew enamored of Albert. In 1840 Albert and Victoria, now Queen Victoria, were married in London.

Albert's official and unofficial position in Britain proved difficult to settle, particularly as Britain had never before had a prince consort. The government could not decide whether Albert was merely a private person who had married the queen or whether it should recognize him as a public figure with public duties of his own. Many British politicians sought to limit what they saw as a foreign influence on the queen, while others advocated that the talents of the well-educated prince could contribute to the public good. Albert's personality—intelligent, disciplined, ambitious, and serious—rubbed many British acquaintances the wrong way. His interest in administrative efficiency and desire to expand the role of the monarchy antagonized British statesmen who saw him as an interloper. As a foreign prince from a minor German state, Albert never enjoyed much popularity in the country at large. Not until 1857 would an act of Parliament officially make Albert the prince consort, thereby recognizing his position as a public figure and the queen's advisor.

Very close in private life, Victoria and Albert formed an intimate political partnership. Although Albert was better educated, Victoria often possessed a better understanding of the British mood. While Victoria acted as the queen, Albert served as her private secretary and main advisor. Albert had many interests and exerted his influence in a number of areas (for instance, he took the lead in organizing the Great Exhibition of 1851). In particular, he constantly advised Victoria on foreign policy. It was in this capacity that he played an important role in the American Civil War.

On 27 November 1861 the British mail steamer *Trent* reached Southampton, England, bearing news of its famous encounter with the USS *San Jacinto*. Anticipating that this type of crisis would arise, Prime Minister Lord Palmerston had already consulted the law officers of the Crown about whether the Federals could seize the Confederate commissioners from a British vessel. The law officers had described such an act as a violation of international law. Nevertheless, Palmerston invited them to deliver their opinion again at a Cabinet meeting on 29 November. Presented with this legal opinion, the Cabinet decided to demand an apology and the restoration of the Confederate commissioners. If the U.S. government refused, the British would recall Lord Lyons, their minister in Washington, D.C.

The Cabinet reconvened on 30 November to write the official dispatch that Lyons would give to Henry Seward, the American secretary of state. The fourteen members of the Cabinet who attended the meeting offered a number of revisions to the draft submitted by Lord John Russell, the foreign secretary. That night, Russell forwarded a new draft of the dispatch to Queen Victoria for her comments. Victoria entrusted the draft to Albert, who had just fallen ill with typhoid fever. Initially, the *Trent* Affair had outraged the prince consort. Given time to consider the matter, however, he concluded that Britain probably would not attain its ends by threatening the United States. Writing in the Queen's name, Albert jotted down a note to the Cabinet, in which he described the Cabinet draft as "somewhat meagre." Borrowing the idea from a *London Times* editorial, Albert advised that the dispatch to the United States express the hope that "the American captain [of the USS *San Jacinto*] did not act under instructions, or, if he did, that he misapprehended them." Albert hoped that by framing the communication in this way, the British government would allow the United States to back down without losing face. Both Palmerston and Russell agreed that softening the dispatch in this manner would prove useful and make British demands more palatable. Having amended the dispatch accordingly, the Cabinet sent it to Lyons.

It is unlikely that Albert's revisions to the British note prevented war between the United States and Great Britain. Other members of the Cabinet also had a hand in softening the dispatch. Russell, for instance, advised Lyons to avoid menacing Seward. Nevertheless, Albert's dramatic intervention had a palpable impact. After reading the British dispatch, Seward told Lyons that its "courteous and friendly" wording would make it easier for him to convince the American Cabinet and public to accept British demands.

After writing his note, Albert confessed he felt so weak that he could barely hold his pen. He never wrote another political memorandum. His illness took a turn for the worse, and he declined precipitously. On 14 December 1861, he died at Windsor.

—*Hubert F. Dubrulle*

See also Adams, Charles Francis; Diplomacy, U.S.A.; Great Britain; Lyons, Richard Bickerton Pemell; *Trent* Affair.
For further reading:
Bennett, Daphne. *King without a Crown* (1983).
Bolitho, Hector. *Albert, Prince Consort* (1964).
Hobhouse, Hermione. *Prince Albert, His Life and Work* (1983).
James, Robert Rhodes. *Albert, Prince Consort: A Biography* (1983).
Martin, Theodore. *The Life of His Royal Highness the Prince Consort* (1880).
Pound, Reginald. *Albert: A Biography of the Prince Consort* (1973).
Weintraub, Stanley. *Uncrowned King: The Life of Prince Albert* (1997).

ALCOTT, LOUISA MAY
(1832–1888)
Author

Best known as the author of the classic *Little Women* (1868), Louisa May Alcott incorporated the Civil War into her writing in numerous ways. The daughter of Bronson Alcott, Louisa was reared in Concord, Massachusetts, where the Hawthornes were good friends and Henry David Thoreau was one of her teachers.

Alcott began publishing in literary and women's magazines before she turned twenty. Eventually she graduated to such respected journals as *The Atlantic Monthly* and *The Commonwealth*. In addition to her stories and articles about domesticity, she created mystery thrillers under pseudonyms such as A. M. Barnard, and contributed regularly to magazines for children such as *The Little Pilgrim*, *Youth's Companion*, *Our Young Folks*, and *Merry's Museum*, which she edited for a time in the late 1860s.

Not surprisingly given her background, Alcott was sympathetic to the abolitionist cause. After John Brown was hanged for his attack on Harper's Ferry, she published a poem in the abolitionist newspaper *The Liberator* entitled "With a Rose, That Bloomed on the Day of John Brown's Martyrdom." As befitting a member of the reform-minded, activist New England elite, she contributed to the Union war effort by sewing uniforms and acting in amateur theatricals to raise money for the United States Sanitary Commission. She became a nurse late in 1862 at the Union Hotel Hospital in Georgetown, just in time to help receive the casualties from the battle of Fredericksburg. After a few weeks, she developed typhoid and was rushed back to Concord. Her active participation in the Civil War was over (although she joined the League of Loyal Women) and she would be a semi-invalid for the rest of her life.

Alcott spent the next several years writing books, articles, and stories about the Civil War. She placed some of her domestic thrillers in Civil War settings, but much better known were the books she published under her own name. She reworked letters she had written while serving at the hospital into a series of stories featuring a character called Nurse Tribulation Periwinkle. These were collected in the book *Hospital Sketches* in 1863. More war stories followed in *On Picket Duty, and Other Tales*, and in incidental pieces she wrote for adult, as well as juvenile, magazines. One of her wartime stories, "Nelly's Hospital," appeared just as the war ended in a new children's periodical called *Our Young Folks*. It told the story of a little girl who, animated by sympathy for her wounded brother, decides to create her own hospital in which she will treat all the "wounded" animals she finds in the neighborhood. Aided by the gardener's son, she gathers mice, spiders, birds, and insects into her "U.S. Sanitary Commission" wagon and nurses them back to health. "Nelly's Hospital" captured perfectly the ways in which Civil War–era children incorporated the war into their own lives through play and support for family members in the army.

The same determination to show the domestic side of the Civil War appeared in Alcott's most famous work, *Little Women*. Although its account of Meg, Jo, Beth, and Amy ranged far beyond the Civil War home front—linking, as one modern critic argues, "the cause of domestic reform to patriotism and abolition"—it also offered a moving portrayal of a Northern family whose comfortable lives have been disrupted by the patriarch's absence. The girls make do with sparse Christmases and restricted opportunities, and Mrs. March busies herself with long hours of work for the local branch of the Sanitary Commission. In an early scene that reflected one of the realities of the Civil War home front, the family huddles near a fire for the ceremonial reading of a letter from Mr. March. Such letters were full of news about camp life, the next campaign, hopeful assurances that the war would soon be over, and earnest advice from absent fathers. "Very few letters written in those hard times were not touching, especially those which fathers sent home," wrote Alcott.

Alcott's chief contribution to the Civil War effort did not come from her brief stint as an army nurse. Rather, it came in the form of her deep understanding of the ways that the war affected every element of life on the Northern home front. Never out of print since its publication, *Little Women* remains one of the most telling portrayals of the Civil War experience of Northern families.

—*James Marten*

For further reading:
Alcott, Louisa May. *Little Women* (1868–1869).
Elbert, Sarah. *A Hunger for Home: Louisa May Alcott and "Little Women"* (1984).
Saxton, Martha. *Louisa May: A Modern Biography of Louisa May Alcott* (1977).
Stein, Madeleine B. *Louisa May Alcott: A Biography* (1996).

ALDIE, VIRGINIA, BATTLE OF
(17 June 1863)

In June 1863, Robert E. Lee moved the Army of Northern Virginia out of its works near Fredericksburg to begin a second invasion of the North in as many years. Joseph Hooker, chastened by the defeat at Chancellorsville, kept the Army of the Potomac massed across the Rappahannock River at Falmouth until he could discern Lee's plans.

Hooker gave his cavalry commander General Alfred Pleasonton the job of finding out Lee's purpose. Lee needed to postpone such a discovery as long as possible, so he directed General Jeb Stuart's cavalry to screen the army as it headed north. Pleasonton, emboldened by his surprise of Stuart at Brandy Station on 9 June, undertook his probing with enthusiasm. Stuart, still stinging from Brandy Station, saw his assignment of shielding Lee's army as a way to redeem himself. The result was a series of violent cavalry clashes in the third week of June, beginning at Aldie, Virginia.

Lee wanted to get the bulk of his army west of the Blue Ridge as quickly as possible. On his right, James Longstreet's I Corps trudged north from Culpeper toward Snicker's Gap. Stuart also rambled north, east of Longstreet, between the Northern and Southern armies. He deployed Beverly Robertson, Fitz Lee, and W. F. H. "Rooney" Lee's brigades (this last commanded by John Chambliss in the stead of the wounded Lee) across a broad front. On 17 June, part of Fitz Lee's brigade commanded by Colonel Thomas Munford was scouting near Aldie. Munford posted pickets outside the town and then led the bulk of the troopers to forage on the Snicker's Gap road to the west. In the early afternoon, General H. Judson Kilpatrick's brigade, riding ahead of David M. Gregg's division, stumbled into Munford's pickets and began what Alfred Pleasonton described as "a pretty sharp fight."

Thomas Rosser first heard the musket fire back at Aldie. He wheeled the 5th Virginia toward the guns and soon came upon the field where Kilpatrick was driving back the gray pickets. Rosser now did some driving of his own, pushing Kilpatrick back through Aldie and hastily setting up a defensive line. Munford soon returned and managed a skillful mix of charges and retrogrades that badly mauled the persistent Kilpatrick. At the end of four hours, the Rebel line had stalled the Federal advance, but Kilpatrick was being reinforced. Moreover, Stuart, several miles to the west at Middleburg, called Munford back because he was surrounding Alfred Duffié's Rhode Island cavalry regiment there. So Munford pulled away from Aldie in the late afternoon along the Snicker's Gap Road. The Confederates had suffered about 100 casualties; Kilpatrick's brigade, approximately 300, a jolt that gave David Gregg pause and consequently doomed Duffié's Rhode Islanders.

Pleasonton had ordered Alfred Duffié's 1st Rhode Island Cavalry to ride through Thoroughfare Gap toward Middleburg, there to join with Gregg's division, which was supposed to be moving west from Aldie. With Gregg engaged at Aldie, however, Duffié soon found himself alone in a neighborhood teeming with Confederates. He had brushed against Chambliss's pickets as he came through Thoroughfare, so he knew that a Confederate brigade was trailing his rear. Chambliss kept his distance, however, and because Duffié expected to meet Gregg any minute, Duffié was unalarmed. Following his instructions, he swung north and reached Middleburg at 4:00 P.M. Stuart and his staff were in Middleburg, and Stuart was initially surprised by the sudden appearance of Union cavalry. Duffié drove into the town and pushed Stuart out of it, an embarrassment that the Confederate cavalry would avenge with a will. Duffié found himself virtually surrounded in Middleburg with Chambliss and Robertson joined in overwhelming numbers that grew with the arrival of Munford from Aldie. Duffié sent calls for help toward Aldie, but his couriers fell to capture. After suffering three bludgeoning assaults, he extricated himself from the town he had three hours earlier resolved to hold at all costs. Of the 275 men of the 1st Rhode Island, he was able to fight his way out with only 31, fleeing across Little River to the northeast. About 100 of those that Duffié had left behind would eventually make their way back to Union lines, but it remained obvious that Duffié had essentially lost his entire regiment at Middleburg. "I cannot understand Duffié's conduct," said Pleasonton.

On 18 June, Pleasanton belatedly sent Colonel J. Irwin Gregg of the 16th Pennsylvania with a brigade to Duffié's relief at Middleburg. After a heated contest, Gregg gained possession of the town for all of three hours before he responded at 6:00 P.M. to an order to return to Aldie. He had half-executed that order when it was countermanded, so he camped halfway between the two towns. The next day, Gregg again took Middleburg after a violent action that consumed much of the day and cost him about 100 casualties.

Stuart had to pull back toward the Shenandoah, however, as he faced an increasingly determined press by Pleasonton's cavalry. On the morning of 20 June, Pleasonton learned from a captured Confederate that Longstreet had finally moved through Ashby's Gap into the Shenandoah Valley, apparently leaving Stuart alone east of the Blue Ridge. Pleasonton wanted to take his entire corps "and throw it on Stuart's whole force, and cripple it up." Accordingly, on the next day, David Gregg's division pressured Wade Hampton and Beverly Robertson out of their lines at Goose Creek. They retired toward Upperville. Farther north, John Buford threatened to turn Stuart's entire left flank and thus forced Chambliss and "Grumble" Jones to fall back toward Upperville as well, with Buford in pursuit. Thus on 21 June, the last collision of a four-day cavalry contest played out as scattered Union and Confederate forces concentrated at Upperville, the Union intention now being to "cripple up" Stuart as much as it had been to discover Lee's intentions. After putting up a stout resistance, Stuart remained mindful of the need to keep his screen intact, so he pulled back again to stronger positions at Ashby's Gap.

The clashes at Aldie, Middleburg, and Upperville allowed Lee to move north screened as much by the gray cavalry as by the Blue Ridge. Pleasonton, however, was able to tell Hooker that Lee was in the Shenandoah Valley obviously headed for the Potomac and beyond. In the longer view, Stuart was able to persuade Lee to consent to detaching his cavalry from the main Confederate column as it moved into southern Pennsylvania. Aware of Lee's instruction that his cavalry rejoin the army once Hooker also crossed the Potomac, Stuart struck out toward the east in another of his famous raids. This raid, however, would prove more costly to his own army than to the Federals. When Union and Confederate forces collided at Gettysburg, Lee's indispensable cavalry would not be there.

—*David S. Heidler and Jeanne T. Heidler*

See also Cavalry, C.S.A.; Cavalry, U.S.A.; Duffié, Alfred; Gregg, David McMurtrie; Kilpatrick, Hugh Judson; Munford, Thomas Taylor; Pleasonton, Alfred; Rosser, Thomas Lafayette; Stuart, James Ewell Brown.

For further reading:
O'Neill, Robert F. *The Cavalry Battles of Aldie, Middleburg and Upperville: Small but Important Riots, June 10–27, 1863* (1993). Starr, Stephen Z. *The Union Cavalry in the Civil War* (1979–1985).

ALEXANDER, EDWARD PORTER
(1835–1910)
Confederate general

Edward Porter Alexander was born to Leopold Alexander and Sarah Gilbert Alexander in Washington, Georgia. Porter entered the U.S. Military Academy and graduated third of thirty-eight in the class of 1857. During Porter's time as a cadet, Robert E. Lee served as superintendent. Commissioned an engineering officer, Porter taught briefly at the academy before going west to participate in the Mormon expedition. Before reaching Albert Sidney Johnston's army, Porter learned of the termination of the expedition and returned to West Point to teach. During his time at the academy, Alexander participated in a number of weapons' experiments and was charged with developing a flag signal system for the U.S. Army. The system he arrived at would be used by both the Union and Confederacy during the Civil War.

In 1860 Alexander was sent to the Pacific Northwest, where he served briefly in Washington before being sent to San Francisco. While there in early 1861, Alexander heard of the secession of Georgia and resigned his commission. Upon his return east, he accepted a captain's commission in the Confederate engineers.

Alexander's first important assignment in the

E. Porter Alexander (*Library of Congress*)

Confederate Army was to organize and train a Confederate signal service. While still in the process of training his new recruits, he was ordered in July 1861 to report to Major General P. G. T. Beauregard at Manassas Junction, Virginia. Arriving a short time before the beginning of the battle of First Bull Run, Alexander supervised the erection of his signal towers, placed his men, and prepared for battle. During the engagement on 21 July 1861, Porter's signals had a direct impact on the movement of Confederate troops to meet the Northern attack.

During the fall of 1861, Alexander served under Joseph Johnston in northern Virginia as acting chief of artillery. He was also active in intelligence gathering, dealing extensively with spies operating around Washington.

Promoted to major, Alexander was chief of ordnance under Johnston during the early phases of the Peninsula campaign in the spring of 1862. Though charged with distributing weapons and ammunition, he fought at the battle of Williamsburg on 5 May 1862 and was commended by James Longstreet for his actions there.

Continuing as chief of ordnance under Robert E. Lee in the Army of Northern Virginia, Alexander distributed ammunition to the widely dispersed units in preparation for the Seven Days' battles. Most of his work done and his interest in intelligence gathering unabated, Alexander volunteered to go up in a hot air balloon at Gaines' Mill on 27 June. He ascended several times over the next several days, bringing down valuable information regarding the positions of George McClellan's army.

Still chief of ordnance through the fall of 1862, Alexander was at Second Bull Run and in the invasion of Maryland. Promoted to major in November, Alexander was given an artillery battalion to command. A colonel by the time of the battle of Fredericksburg in December 1862, Alexander had command of the batteries on Marye's Heights and was largely responsible for the resounding Confederate victory.

Not accompanying his corps commander Longstreet to North Carolina in the spring of 1863, Alexander traveled around Joseph Hooker's flank with Stonewall Jackson at Chancellorsville. After the initial attack that pushed back Hooker's lines upon one another and after Jackson had been wounded reconnoitering his lines, Alexander spent the entire night into the following morning finding the right location for the guns to commence the attack at dawn.

After Hooker's retreat, Alexander was fairly inactive, but at the beginning of what would become the Gettysburg campaign, Longstreet gave him command of the I Corps' reserve artillery. Alexander was quite busy during 2 and 3 July at this pivotal battle. On 2 July his artillery supported that part of the I Corps' attack through the Peach Orchard. The following day Alexander would see his greatest test of the war.

Called upon to command the artillery barrage that would attempt to knock out Federal guns in preparation for the charge that would bear George Pickett's name, Alexander gathered as much ammunition as possible, spent the predawn hours of 3 July finding the best locations for his guns, and began the firing at 1:00 P.M. For about half an hour, the two sides exchanged almost continuous fire. Shortly before 1:30, Alexander sent word to Pickett to begin the advance while the artillery still had sufficient ammunition to support the charge. A few minutes later the Union guns slackened, and hoping that perhaps some had been knocked out, Alexander again urged Pickett to hurry. The ill-fated charge failed, largely because the Federal guns were still firmly in place waiting only for the charge to commence.

In the late summer of 1863, Alexander followed Longstreet to Georgia, where he arrived too late to participate at Chickamauga, but served as Longstreet's chief of artillery in the Knoxville campaign and in the Department of East Tennessee in early 1864. Promoted brigadier general in February 1864, Alexander returned with Longstreet to Virginia in the spring of 1864 and served as chief of artillery, I Corps, Army of Northern Virginia, for the remainder of the war. He fought in all the major battles opening Ulysses S. Grant's Virginia campaign. When Grant attempted to move across the James River to assault Petersburg, Alexander was able to move his artillery quickly through the lines and had his guns in place when the main attack commenced.

During the siege of Petersburg, Alexander worked constantly to devise ways to use his artillery effectively from the trenches. He experimented with various types of mortars to some effect. As June wore on, Alexander also became convinced that Union forces were tunneling in an attempt to break the Confederate lines. Before acting on this belief, however, he was hit in the arm by a sharpshooter. As he departed to convalesce, he informed Lee of his suspicion, and unsuccessful efforts were made to thwart the Union plan. Upon recovery, Alexander returned to the army, primarily supervising the defense of Richmond along the James River. He joined the retreat of the Army of Northern Virginia in April 1865 and surrendered at Appomattox Court House.

After the war, Alexander engaged in various pursuits. He served briefly as a college professor before devoting most of the rest of his life to different business ventures, including one in the railroad industry. He became a wealthy planter on islands off the coast of South Carolina but spent much of his time in Savannah, Georgia. He also wrote, most notably, a memoir of the war that became a classic military analysis of Confederate successes and failures.

—*David S. Heidler and Jeanne T. Heidler*

See also Artillery; Balloons; Chancellorsville, Battle of; Fredericksburg, Battle of; Gettysburg, Battle of; Petersburg Campaign.

For further reading:
Alexander, Edward Porter. *Fighting for the Confederacy: The Personal Recollections of General Edward Porter Alexander* (1989).
———. *Military Memoirs of a Confederate: A Critical Narrative* (1907).
Golay, Michael. *To Gettysburg and Beyond: The Parallel Lives of Joshua Lawrence Chamberlain and Edward Porter Alexander* (1994).
Klein, Maury. *Edward Porter Alexander* (1971).

ALEXANDRIA, LOUISIANA, DESTRUCTION OF
(May 1864)

Situated in central Louisiana on the Red River opposite Pineville, Alexandria suffered almost total devastation during Nathaniel Banks's Red River campaign of 1864. When initially occupied by Federal forces under Brigadier General A. J. Smith along with a flotilla of gunboats under Admiral David D. Porter, the town was looted by Smith's rough westerners and Porter's sailors. Banks arrived four days later, stopped the plundering, and tried to secure the region by adminis-

tering loyalty oaths and recruiting from the local population with substantial bounties as enticements.

After his defeat by Richard Taylor at Mansfield on 8 April 1864, Banks fought a defensive engagement at Pleasant Hill and then retreated to Alexandria, reaching there on 26 April. Banks would have preferred to continue his retreat toward the Mississippi, but he had to await the arrival of Porter's fleet that had ranged up the river as far as Blair's Landing. The gunboats did not arrive until 28 April, and both Banks and Porter could have been in serious trouble had Taylor's force remained at full strength. Instead, General Edmund Kirby Smith had detached parts of it for operations in Arkansas, and by the time he sent it back to Louisiana, the Federals were beyond reach and Alexandria was in ruins. For the time being, the best Taylor could do was harass Banks with skirmishes around the town.

When Porter finally did arrive, his gunboats had been badly beaten up by raking fire from the banks as he moved down the river. The main problem once he reached Alexandria was the Red River. Its level had fallen so quickly and considerably that an impassable rapids prevented the gunboats from moving any farther down the river. As news came that Taylor was working to seal off Banks's avenues of retreat, Porter became concerned that the army would abandon him.

Lieutenant Colonel Joseph Bailey, 4th Wisconsin Cavalry and acting engineer of the 19th Army Corps, had anticipated this problem during the retreat. Even before the engagement at Pleasant Hill, he had submitted a plan to build a dam at Alexandria to raise the level of the water so Porter's vessels could pass. When it was learned that Porter had scuttled the ironclad *Eastport* after it had grounded on a snag, Bailey was dispatched to help the admiral raise the vessel and relate to him the plan for the dam at Alexandria. When the flotilla reached Alexandria, Bailey examined the falls and, after some effort, persuaded Banks to authorize the construction. Banks remained dubious, however, and with good reason. At the point Bailey proposed to place his dam, the river was 758 feet wide, 4 to 6 feet deep, and with a strong current running about 10 miles per hour. Nonetheless, Bailey put details from a dozen different regiments (prominently including the 97th and 99th Colored Infantry) to work with materials stripped from Alexandria and the nearby woods. Confederate brigadier general St. John Liddell, who occupied the bank opposite this construction site, would later be criticized by Taylor for allowing the work to proceed fairly unimpeded, but Liddell claimed that there was little he could do without artillery. Bailey built not only the dam at the base of the falls, but completed two wing dams on each side of the river at their head. Moreover, he was able to complete the dam in an astonishing ten days to raise the Red River at the base of the falls more than five feet and more than a foot at their head. It was enough to float Porter's eight remaining gunboats free and allow the army to proceed south to safety. In June, Congress voted a resolution of thanks to Colonel Bailey for his work on the Red River that had rescued Porter's vessels "from imminent peril."

As the army evacuated Alexandria on 13 May, Andrew J. Smith's men set fire to it. In this action, which was taken with considerable planning and care about where to place combustibles, they continued a practice of looting and destruction that had marked their retreat during the campaign. They had laid waste to Grand Ecore while passing through it, and now they did such a thorough job of razing Alexandria that, after the fires had burned out, there were reportedly only two houses left standing. Banks did nothing to stop the destruction, although some of his soldiers before departing tried to save some homes. Smith's command had served under Sherman, and their behavior in this campaign, especially at Alexandria, has been attributed to the hard war policy they learned under him and that he would make even more infamous during his campaign in Georgia later that year.

—*David S. Heidler and Jeanne T. Heidler*

See also Bailey, Joseph; Banks, Nathaniel Prentice; Mansfield, Louisiana, Battle of; Pleasant Hill, Louisiana, Battle of; Porter, David Dixon; Red River Campaign; Smith, Andrew Jackson; Taylor, Richard.

For further reading:
Johnson, Ludwell H. *Red River Campaign: Politics and Cotton in the Civil War* (1958).
Parrish, T. Michael. *Richard Taylor: Soldier Prince of Dixie* (1992).
Taylor, Richard. *Destruction and Reconstruction: Personal Experiences of the Late War* (1879; reprint, 1983).

ALGER, RUSSELL ALEXANDER
(1836–1907)
Union officer

Born on 27 February 1836 in the Western Reserve of Ohio, Russell A. Alger exemplified a certain type of American during the Civil War era. He began life in a log cabin, fended largely for himself in his youth, was drawn to the law, but made a fortune in timber. He was also of the prime age to be swept into the Civil War. He willingly thrust himself into the conflict, but almost three decades after it, he would have to endure a public controversy about the way he had left it.

Alger's main service was as colonel of the 5th Michigan Cavalry, part of George Armstrong Custer's celebrated 2d Cavalry Brigade of the Army of the Potomac. Custer's unit sustained more losses than any other mounted force during the war, and the 5th Michigan was second only to the 1st Michigan Cavalry in casualties. Alger participated in the advance from the

Rappahannock River to the Rapidan River in September 1863, seeing action near Culpeper and Raccoon Ford.

During the early part of 1864 he was in Washington, where as a special commissioner he became involved in plans for the distribution of Abraham Lincoln's December 1863 Amnesty Proclamation. Alger suggested that cavalry units carry the proclamation directly to the enemy to encourage desertion by speeding its proliferation among war-weary Confederates.

In May 1864, Alger and the 5th Michigan crossed the Rapidan River at Ely's Ford as part of Ulysses S. Grant's Richmond campaign. He saw action at Todd's Tavern, where his regiment assisted in driving rebel forces from the field. The 5th Michigan helped destroy Confederate supplies and transportation facilities by tearing up sections of the Richmond & Fredericksburg Railroad. At Yellow Tavern on 11 May, Alger's regiment took heavy losses, and he reportedly was nearby when a sharpshooter mortally wounded Jeb Stuart. At the end of June, Alger fought at Trevilian Station, where his pursuit of fleeing Confederates left him and about forty of his men separated from their brigade with a large Confederate force in between. He fought his way back into Union lines near Louisa Court House.

The 5th Michigan joined Philip Sheridan's raid of the Shenandoah Valley in the summer of 1864, and it was this service under Sheridan that tarnished Alger's reputation. He already had been ill earlier in the year when sickness had required his handing over the command of the regiment during late May. In August 1864, the illness became so serious that it put Alger into an infirmary and required his reassignment to light administrative duties in Washington. He resigned from the army on 20 September 1864, receiving an honorable discharge and eventually the award for bravery of two brevet ranks to major general of volunteers. Alger moved to Detroit and began a political carrier that made him Michigan's governor in 1884 and saw him mentioned for president in the 1888 Republican convention. He became commander in chief of the Grand Army of the Republic in 1889.

Nevertheless, during the presidential race of 1892, newspaper allegations implied that he had been dismissed from the army for dereliction. The accounts cited charges lodged in 1864 by George A. Custer and apparently supported by Sheridan. After the war Alger had given $10,000 to a financially embarrassed Sheridan, and the generosity did not help appearances.

Although Alger enjoyed the support of many influential defenders, the matter remained unresolved to linger as an unsubstantiated blemish. In spite of the charges, William McKinley appointed Alger secretary of war in 1897. During his tenure, the War Department published the monumental *The War of the Rebellion: A Compilation of the Official Records of the Union and Confederate Armies.*

When the foibles of the war with Spain in 1898 were laid at Alger's door, he resigned under pressure from the president in 1899. Elected by the Michigan legislature to the Senate in 1902, he died in office on 24 January 1907.

—*David S. Heidler and Jeanne T. Heidler*

See also *The War of the Rebellion: A Compilation of the Official Records of the Union and Confederate Armies.*

For further reading:
Bell, Rodney Ellis. "A Life of Russell Alexander Alger, 1836–1907" (Ph.D. dissertation, 1957).

ALLATOONA, BATTLE OF
(5 October 1864)

After Major General William T. Sherman's successful capture of Atlanta in September 1864, the Confederate Army of Tennessee was forced to change its very fighting nature. Jefferson Davis, having finally lost confidence in General Joseph E. Johnston during the battle for the city, replaced him with the more aggressive John Bell Hood on 17 July. This change to a more aggressive officer did little to alter either the inevitable loss of Atlanta or the overall campaign. Having ingeniously maneuvered and fought his way through rugged northwest Georgia, Sherman seemed unassailable in Atlanta; nothing could dislodge him, except for defeat in open battle or the severing of his supply lines.

The Confederates could no longer engage the massive Union force in open battle, especially since they no longer had the defensive advantages of north Georgia's mountainous terrain at their disposal. And except for foolhardiness, they had no reason to fight a major engagement because they had already lost Atlanta, the one thing worth defending in that area. Hood, therefore, moved his troops back northward through Georgia, attempting to disrupt Sherman's vital supply line and in the hopes of drawing small Union forces out of Atlanta to defend their rear where he could defeat them piecemeal.

The initial strategy called for Hood's men almost to retrace the route Sherman had taken during his advance from Chattanooga to Atlanta, keeping the main body of his meager forces west of the Western and Atlantic rail line. Hood intended to destroy critical bridges, passes, and supply centers north toward Tennessee. On 29 September, Hood's army forded the Chattahoochee River and began to tear up railroad track from Big

Allatoona Pass, Georgia, *ca.* 1864 (Photograph by Mathew Brady Studio / *Library of Congress*)

Shanty to Acworth. Because of its initial surprise, Hood's plan worked well, destroying more than eight miles of track and taking more than 600 prisoners. Flush with success, Hood ordered Confederate Lieutenant General Alexander P. Stewart's troops to capture the large Union supply center at Allatoona Pass, a 180-foot deep gash through the Allatoona Mountain range northwest of Atlanta. Stewart gave Major General Samuel G. French's division, a force of 3,276 men, the assignment first to take the pass and then to destroy the railroad bridge over the Etowah River.

Aware that Hood was on the move, Sherman hurriedly moved his troops. In his memoirs Sherman wrote: "[L]earning that heavy masses of infantry, artillery, and cavalry, had been seen from Kenesaw (marching north), I inferred that Allatoona was their objective." He also observed that the objective contained more than a million rations of bread. Sherman sent Brigadier General John M. Corse to reinforce this vulnerable supply center, which action provided a total of 2,025 soldiers to defend what was already a highly defensible position. That many of Corse's troops were using Henry repeating rifles did not hurt his situation as well.

With the element of surprise gone and an almost equivalence in firepower between the two opposing forces, French's soldiers were walking into a far more difficult situation than they could ever have imagined. After exchanging messages concerning French's request for Corse's surrender, the Confederates attacked from the west and north, mounting a furious assault against the determined Union defenders. By midday, they had managed to push the Federals back into the mountaintop fort and were seemingly making significant progress in forcing a capitulation until Federal troops rallied. French, finally recognizing the futility of his position, withdrew to regroup with Hood's main force. The battle for Allatoona Pass was over.

In the end, Corse's casualties were 706, while French lost 897. Unfit for a major battle, Hood's army moved westward toward the Coosa and Oostenaula rivers and later toward Gadsden, Alabama.

Although Sherman later denied it, he was supposed to have sent a message to Corse stating: "Hold the Fort; I am coming." Whether it is true or not, this phrase became part of the refrain for the revival hymn "Hold the Fort" by Phillip B. Bliss. By this stage in the war, whatever Sherman did seemed to carry with it legendary implications.

—James Meredith

For further reading:
O'Connor, Richard. *Hood: Cavalier General* (1949).
Scaife, William R. "Hood's March to Tennessee: October–December 1864." In *The Civil War Battlefield Guide* (1998).
Sherman, William T. *Memoirs of William T. Sherman* (1990).

ALLEGHANY MOUNTAIN, [WEST] VIRGINIA, BATTLE OF
(13 December 1861)

In late November 1861, the Confederate Army of the Northwest withdrew eastward from Camp Bartow on the Greenbrier River to the mountaintop garrison known as Camp Alleghany (sometimes spelled Allegheny). From there, a large portion of the army under Major General William W. Loring continued on, uniting with Jackson's Army of the Valley at Winchester. Colonel Edward Johnson, with six regiments of infantry, two batteries of artillery, and a detachment of cavalry, some 1,200 in all, remained on the mountain to hold the Confederate line.

Brigadier General Robert H. Milroy had recently replaced Joseph J. Reynolds as commander of the Union garrison at Cheat Mountain. Possibly inspired by Loring's departure, Milroy determined to move against his Southern counterparts at Camp Alleghany, fifteen miles to the east, and at dawn on 13 December 1861 he did so. Milroy's plan divided his army in two. One column consisting of about 930 men under Colonel Gideon C. Moody, would march twelve miles, turning the Confederate left flank. The other column, numbering around 830 men and under Milroy's supervision, traveled only five miles, turning the Confederate right and rear. Moody was to attack at the sound of Milroy's guns.

Difficult terrain, however, put Moody's brigade hours behind. Consequently, when Milroy ran into Confederate pickets, Moody was not in place and the planned simultaneous assault had to be aborted. The firing on their right alerted the Southerners, and Johnson ordered elements of his various regiments to occupy the crest of the mountain on the right or eastern edge of the camp.

The morning was clear and cold, the frost thick and white on the ground. The Southerners almost froze in the piercing wind awaiting the attack. The Union troops advanced, gaining a foothold in the timbers that skirted the mountain summit. The Confederates counterattacked and pushed the Federals back into the woods, thus inaugurated an indeterminable amount of charges and countercharges. The fighting was largely hand to hand and "the roar of the musketry was incessant and deafening." The opposing forces could scarcely see one another for the smoke. Command control was lost and units became intermingled. "The men fought on their own hook, each loading and firing as fast as possible…."

And in the middle of it all was Edward Johnson. Although Johnson sustained no wounds or injuries, by the end of the battle his clothes were riddled with holes. When his men were nearly out of ammunition, Johnson and his forces made a determined rush, and amid deafening shouts the Southerners drove the Federals, inflicting severe losses. Years later, John S. Robson of the

52d Virginia, recalled that, in the final charge in this sector, Johnson with a musket in one hand and "swinging a big club in the other…led his line right up among the enemy, driving them headlong down the mountain, killing and wounding many with the bayonet and capturing a large number of prisoners."

The lack of anticipated cooperation by Moody's column on the Confederate left had a demoralizing effect on the Federals. By the time Moody's unit came up, the Southerners were waiting for them. After repulsing Milroy on his right, Johnson, with the advantage of interior lines, quickly moved the bulk of his force to the left. Moody's men formed their lines and quickly advanced. When the Federals got to within 200 yards of the Confederate entrenchments, the fire became so hot that the Northerners were compelled to make for the shelter of logs, trees, and whatever protection could be found. As opposed to the earlier charge and counter-charge on the Confederate right, this portion of the battle was a firefight, lasting approximately five hours, the Southerners firing from the cover of their entrenchments, and the Federals firing from under the cover of the fallen timbers.

In the end, Southern leadership, determination, and firepower, combined with the plunging morale of the Northern soldiers, brought the same result on the Confederate left. "They were met on both points with the most determined heroism," wrote Johnson, "and, after a contest lasting from 7:00 A.M. until near 2:00 P.M., repulsed with great loss." The Federals returned to Cheat Mountain, according to Sergeant Major Ambrose Bierce, "a beaten, dispirited and exhausted force, feeble from fatigue and savage from defeat." The Southerners did not pursue and remained at Camp Alleghany through the winter.

Confederate losses amounted to 20 killed, 98 wounded, and 28 missing. The Federals lost 20 killed, 107 wounded, and 10 missing.

Johnson was lauded for his personal bravery. According to the 17 December 1861 *Daily Dispatch*, Edward Johnson "covered himself with glory, and is entitled to the appellation of the Hero of the Alleghany." One month later, Edward "Alleghany" Johnson was elevated to brigadier general, effective 13 December 1861.

—*Eddie Woodward*

See also Army of the Northwest; Johnson, Edward.
For further reading:
Bierce, Ambrose. "On a Mountain." In *Collected Works* (1909–1912).
Driver, Robert J. *52d Virginia Infantry* (1986).
Hamilton, W.D. "Camp Baldwin Expedition." In *History of the Thirty-Second Regiment, Ohio Veteran Volunteer Infantry* (1896).
———. *Recollections of a Cavalryman of the Civil War after Fifty Years, 1861–1865* (1915).
Hotchkiss, J., ed. *Virginia. Confederate Military History* (1899; reprint, 1987).
Lessor, W. Hunter, Kim A. McBride, and Janet G. Brasher. "Cheat Summit Fort and Camp Allegheny: Early Civil War Encampments in West Virginia." In *Look to the Earth: Historical Archaeology and the American Civil War* (1994).
Robson, John S. *How a One-Legged Rebel Lives* (1898).
Woodward, Edward V. "Holding the Alleghany Line: Edward Johnson, the Army of the Northwest, and the Battle of Alleghany Summit." (Thesis, 1998).

ALLEN, HENRY WATKINS
(1820–1866)
Confederate general; governor of Louisiana

Born in Virginia to Thomas Allen, a physician, and Ann Watkins Allen, Henry Watkins Allen moved to Missouri as a child with his parents. He eventually moved to Mississippi, was admitted to the bar, traveled briefly to the Republic of Texas, and finally returned to Mississippi to become a planter. A restless spirit, however, took him to Louisiana, where he wrote extensively and became involved in state politics. He traveled extensively, spending a brief time in Massachusetts during which he attended classes at Harvard Law School. In 1859 Allen went to Italy, hoping to enlist in Garibaldi's revolutionary force, only to find the insurrection over when he arrived.

Returning to the United States just as the Civil War began, Allen immediately enlisted in the Confederate army, rising quickly from private to colonel of the 4th Louisiana Regiment. Initially, the regiment garrisoned coastal fortifications in Louisiana, but in February 1862 it was summoned north to reinforce Albert Sidney Johnston's army as it retreated into northern Mississippi. Allen commanded the 4th Louisiana Regiment at the battle of Shiloh, in which he was wounded in the face in an attack on the Hornet's Nest, and at Baton Rouge on 5 August 1862, where he was wounded again, this time more severely.

In the failed Confederate attempt to retake Baton Rouge, Allen commanded the Louisiana Brigade. He was wounded in both legs, the damage to the right leg being so severe that Allen would never again walk without crutches. He remained in active service, though, first as the military governor of Jackson, Mississippi, and then as a brigadier general beginning on 19 August 1863 under Edmund Kirby Smith. In 1864, however, Allen was elected governor of Louisiana and left military service.

As governor, Allen proved tremendously effective in rebuilding Louisiana's shattered economy. Working to keep both the military forces and civilians supplied with necessities, Allen opened trade with Mexico, particularly utilizing the state's large supply of cotton. He also established state-run supply points for civilians and encouraged industry with state funds and incentives. Concerned about the defense of the state, he sent out a call on 16 March 1864 to all able-bodied Louisiana males to be ready at a moment's notice to defend the state. He also reorganized the militia to make it more responsive to emergencies and suggested to the Confederate War Department the enlistment of black men. The United States Army was using black soldiers against the Confederacy, he argued, so the Confederate army should also use the resource.

As the war drew to a close, Allen used his influence to bring about the surrender of the trans-Mississippi Confederate forces to save his state from any further destruction. He attended a conference in May 1865 in Marshall, Texas, with the governors of Texas, Arkansas, and Missouri to urge the surrender of remaining Confederate military forces in the region. Following capitulation, Allen moved to Mexico and started an American newspaper in Mexico City. He died there in 1866, and his body was returned to Baton Rouge for burial.

—*David S. Heidler and Jeanne T. Heidler*

See also Baton Rouge, Battle of; Louisiana.
For further reading:
Cassidy, Vincent H. *Henry Watkins Allen of Louisiana* (1964).
Chandler, Luther Edward. "The Career of Henry Watkins Allen." (Ph.D. dissertation, 1940).
Dorsey, Sarah A. *Recollections of Henry Watkins Allen* (1866).

ALLEN, WILLIAM WIRT
(1835–1894)
Confederate general

William Wirt Allen was born in New York City to Wade Hampton Allen and Eliza Sayre Allen. Wade Allen was a successful businessman and had agricultural interests in the South. William Allen was educated in Alabama before being sent to Princeton, from which he graduated in 1854. On graduation he became an Alabama planter. Opposing secession, Allen nevertheless became a first lieutenant in the 1st Montgomery Mounted Rifles.

In 1862 Allen achieved the rank of major in the same unit and, after fighting bravely at Shiloh, was promoted to colonel of the 1st Alabama Cavalry. He commanded this regiment in Braxton Bragg's invasion of Kentucky in fall 1862 and was wounded at Perryville. Back in command in December at Stones River, Allen led a brigade and again suffered serious wounds.

In February 1864 Allen was promoted to brigadier general and commanded one of Joseph Wheeler's cavalry brigades. As a part of the Army of Tennessee, he fought to defend Atlanta in the summer of 1864. During the early months of 1865, he commanded a division of Joseph Johnston's army in the Carolinas and was promoted to major general on 4 March 1865. He surrendered his force in May 1865 at Concord, North Carolina, and was paroled from Charlotte, North Carolina.

Following the war, Allen returned to planting and served in Alabama state government as a U.S. marshal. He died at Sheffield, Alabama.

—*David S. Heidler and Jeanne T. Heidler*

See also Wheeler, Joseph.
For further reading:
Barrett, John G. *Sherman's March through the Carolinas* (1996).
Glatthaar, Joseph T. *The March to the Sea and Beyond: Sherman's Troops in the Savannah and Carolinas Campaigns* (1985).

ALTON FEDERAL MILITARY PRISON

With Union prison facilities in St. Louis overtaxed by the end of the war's first year, Adjutant General Lorenzo Thomas authorized Major General Henry Halleck to seek the permission of Illinois governor Richard Yates to utilize the condemned and abandoned Alton State Penitentiary, northeast of St. Louis near the Mississippi River. Yates agreed, and the Alton Prison received its first military prisoners on 9 February 1862.

Within three days the facility experienced overcrowding. When opened in 1831, the state penitentiary had a maximum capacity of 800 inmates. In its second career as a military prison, it usually housed between 1,000 and 1,500 persons at any given time, and at one point held almost 1,900 prisoners.

As was true of all Civil War prisons, Alton remained overcrowded, unsanitary, and disease-ridden throughout the conflict. Although Alton primarily housed captured soldiers, its inmates consisted of some political prisoners, including about two dozen women.

—*Thomas F. Curran*

See also Andersonville Prison; Belle Isle Prison; Camp Chase Prison; Camp Douglas Prison; Camp Morton Prison; Elmira Prison; Fort Delaware Prison; Fort Warren Prison; Gratiot Street and Myrtle Street Prisons; Johnson's Island Prison; Libby Prison; Old Capitol Prison; Prisoner Exchanges; Prisoner Paroles; Prisoners of War; Prisons, C.S.A.; Prisons, U.S.A.; Rock Island Prison; Salisbury Prison; Yates, Richard.
For further reading:
Frost, Griffin. *Camp and Prison Journal.* (1867; reprint 1994).
Hesseltine, William B. *Civil War Prisons: A Study in War Psychology* (1930).
Speers, Lonnie R. *Portals to Hell: Military Prisons of the Civil War* (1997).

AMELIA COURT HOUSE/JETERSVILLE
(3–5 April 1865)

The near-confrontation at Jetersville, Virginia, on 5 April 1865 capped the initial segment of the retreat of the Army of Northern Virginia from Richmond and Petersburg to Appomattox. Having concentrated his army at Amelia Court House, a rail station thirty-nine miles southwest of Richmond,

General Robert E. Lee began a march toward Danville along the Richmond & Danville Railroad. As the Confederates approached the next station, at Jetersville, they discovered a strong Federal force under General Philip Sheridan entrenched across the railroad. Deciding not to risk an open engagement, Lee ordered a night march farther west to Farmville, where supplies awaited and from whence he still hoped to proceed south and ultimately rendezvous with Confederate forces under General Joseph Johnston.

After the disaster at Five Forks and the loss of the Southside Railroad at Sutherland Station on 1–2 April, Lee ordered a withdrawal of some 55,000 Confederate troops from the 28-mile front held during the siege of Petersburg and Richmond. His first objective was to concentrate his army, and he chose to do so at Amelia Court House, a station on the Danville Railroad roughly equidistant from all points on the defense line. Aware that Lee intended to march to Danville, and concerned that he might unite with Johnston's Army of Tennessee, General Ulysses S. Grant immediately sent a Federal contingent of about 63,000 troops under Generals Sheridan, George G. Meade, and Ord in pursuit from Petersburg westward along the Southside Railroad. Grant hoped to secure Burkeville, the junction between the Southside Railroad and the Richmond & Danville Railroad, before the Confederates arrived there and thus cut Lee's intended route of retreat.

Making an all-night march on 2–3 April along three main routes, the Confederates reached Amelia generally unmolested, although rearguard actions did include a cavalry engagement at Namozine Church between the Confederate forces under Major General W. H. F. "Rooney" Lee and the Federals under Major General George Custer. Before the evacuation, Robert E. Lee had requisitioned 350,000 food rations to be sent from Richmond to Amelia, but upon arrival at the station the commander was dismayed to find that confusion in the transmission of the orders had resulted instead in a delivery of ordnance stores. The mistake proved costly because Lee was compelled to spend all of 4 April in bivouac at Amelia to let his troops forage for food. The fleeting opportunity to turn south ahead of the Union pursuit was lost.

While Lee's men foraged, the Federal Army of the Shenandoah, a cavalry force under Major General Philip Sheridan, moved rapidly to the west along a route just south of the Confederate position. By 5:00 P.M. on 4 April, Sheridan had gained footing on the Richmond & Danville Railroad north of Burkeville at Jetersville, a station about seven miles below Amelia. Sheridan was soon reinforced by the II and V Infantry Corps from Meade's Army of the Potomac. These troops spent the morning and early afternoon of 5 April digging entrenchments in a front facing northeast and extending ultimately about two miles on either side of the railroad.

The Confederate forage wagons returned to Amelia early on 5 April with little for the troops to eat. Lee's army was hungry and had lost its day's lead on the Federals. Lee would later term this delay "fatal." At 1:00 P.M. he directed the Army of Northern Virginia to take up the march for Danville along the railroad with Lieutenant General James Longstreet's I Corps in the van.

Hearing skirmish fire as they neared Jetersville, Lee and Longstreet halted the Confederate column and conferred with the commander's son, Rooney Lee, whose cavalry had discovered Sheridan's forces. Longstreet readied three divisions for battle, but Lee, advised that more Federal infantry were soon to arrive, judged the enemy position too strong to warrant an attack. Here Lee changed his original plans, deciding to make another night march around the Union left flank and west about 20 miles to Farmville. There he could obtain supplies and rations, then turn south and reach the Danville Railroad at Keysville. The orders were given and the Confederate column withdrew.

Sheridan and Meade remained entrenched through the night of 5 April. The Federals had been unable to mount an offensive during the day, as Meade's VI Corps did not reach the field until about 6:00 P.M. Leaving his reserve force, Ord's Army of the James, at Burkeville, General Grant arrived in Jetersville by 10:30 P.M. The next morning the Federals advanced up the railroad only to find the enemy gone. When the trailing elements of Lee's column were observed heading west across nearby Flat Creek, however, the Union infantry quickly changed front behind it and the chase was resumed.

—*Charles E. Kinzer*

See also Appomattox Court House; Farmville/High Bridge, Battle of; Five Forks, Battle of; Namozine Church; Sayler's Creek/Harper's Farm, Battle of.
For further reading:
Calkins, Chris M. *The Appomattox Campaign: March 29–April 9, 1865* (1997).

AMERICAN PARTY

The American Party (or the Know-Nothings, as members were commonly known), played a key role in the transformation of the second American political party system during the mid-1850s. Originally founded as a secret nativist society, by 1854 the Know-Nothings had supplanted the Whigs as the major opposition party to the Democrats. In their meteoric rise they threatened to overwhelm the newly formed Republican Party and even to capture the presidency. By the end of 1856, however, the American Party had all but vanished as a political power, sacrificed on the alter of sectionalism and destroyed by the chaos of political realignment.

The Know-Nothings grew out of a nativist organization in New York City called the Order of the Star Spangled Banner. It was a secret society devoted to denying political participation to Catholics and the foreign born, and to defeating the old, corrupt Whig and Democratic Parties, which the society accused of catering to the immigrant vote. Energized by unrest over the waves of primarily Irish and German immigrants pouring into the United States (2.9 million immigrants entered the country between 1845 and 1854), the Know-Nothings spread throughout much of the eastern and border states in 1853 and 1854, gradually moving into politics in support of their anti-Catholic, antiforeign, and antiparty agenda. Still unknown by much of the population, the Know-Nothing Party was catapulted into prominence through the silent campaign of its initiates in the autumn elections of 1854. Its most amazing victories came in Massachusetts, where members waged a "dark lantern" crusade, voting for fellow Know-Nothings not even listed on the ballot. Seemingly out of nowhere the party managed to capture all but three seats in the state legislature and the entire congressional delegation, and to elect the governor and a United States senator. Know-Nothings earned less spectacular, but still significant, victories in New York, Pennsylvania, Maryland, and Ohio. Thus, the Know-Nothings stood on the verge of national power.

In 1854 the Know-Nothings officially became the American Party, and Northern and Southern members convened at the party's first convention in Philadelphia in June 1855. In a meeting marked by the chaos that was to become so familiar to Americans during the political breakdown of the 1850s, Northern and Southern Know-Nothings battled over the party's platform. While in agreement over their nativist and antiparty beliefs, the issue of slavery proved divisive. The main controversy concerned the recently adopted Kansas-Nebraska Act, which opened up the old Louisiana Purchase territory to so-called popular sovereignty. This was an old idea that now threatened to allow slavery into the territories where it was previously restricted by the Missouri Compromise of 1820. The American Party had three major divisions over slavery. Many of the Northern men were free-soil adherents. Led by Henry Wilson of Massachusetts, they attempted to force the party to take a stand against the Kansas-Nebraska Act. A group of Southerners, convinced by the previous month's loss in Virginia's gubernatorial race in which they had been savaged by Democrat Henry Alexander Wise for being secret abolitionists, believed that the party had to take a strong stand defending slavery in the territories. A third group of both Northern and Southern moderates, centered on Kenneth Rayner of North Carolina and

Henry Fuller of Pennsylvania, tried to steer a middle road in the vain hope of removing slavery from the political arena. This struggle over the platform effectively split the party, as Wilson and his backers bolted the convention after passage of a plank that failed to meet their demands for a restoration of the Missouri Compromise. This left the proslavery Southerners and moderates to control the party. The nativist tenets upon which the American Party had been founded had not been strong enough to hold the Know-Nothings together.

Following this breakup, the Know-Nothings tried on several occasions to reunite, but a disastrous two-month battle in the U.S. House of Representatives over the election of the Speaker in 1855–1856, and the nomination of the old Whig Millard Fillmore for president in February 1856 fractured the party forever. Southerners largely stayed with Fillmore, a New Yorker, but the majority of Northerners deserted and joined the Republicans over the summer of 1856. In the 1856 election Fillmore finished third behind Democrat James Buchanan and Republican John C. Frémont, capturing only Maryland. By this time the nativist party of 1854 had become a shell of its former self, controlled by old Whigs and little resembling the party that had so amazed Americans two years earlier. Following the 1856 election the American Party survived for a year in a few Southern states, and then died. Its remnants were awakened from the dead in 1860 in the form of the Constitutional Union Party, but it too had little in common with the old Know-Nothings and the nativism responsible for the American Party's initial popularity.

—*John David Bladek*

See also Democratic Party; Popular Sovereignty; Republican Party.

For further reading:
Anbinder, Tyler. *Nativism and Slavery: The Northern Know Nothings and the Politics of Slavery* (1992).
Baker, Jean H. *Ambivalent Americans: The Know-Nothing Party in Maryland* (1977).
Bladek, John David. "Virginia is Middle Ground: The Know Nothing-Party and the Virginia Gubernatorial Election of 1855." *Virginia Magazine of History and Biography* (1998).
Cantrell, Greg. "Southern and Nativist: Kenneth Rayner and the Ideology of 'Americanism.'" *North Carolina Historical Review* (1992).
Holt, Michael F. *The Rise and Fall of the American Whig Party: Jacksonian Politics and the Onset of the Civil War* (1999).

AMERICAN RED CROSS

The American Red Cross did not officially exist during the Civil War, but the origins of the American chapter stem from the incidents of war, especially those involving Clara Barton, numerous women's organizations (mainly relief oriented), and the U.S. Sanitary Commission. The idea behind the American Red Cross began with local aid organizations such as the Women's Central Association of Relief, various local organizations that sought to meet the needs of Union armies, the Catholic Sisters of Mercy, the Sisters of the Holy Cross, and others. In addition, the horrors of the Austro-Prussian War and the activities of Florence Nightingale during the Crimean War impressed many people in the United States, who thus became aware of the need to create better conditions for wounded and encamped soldiers.

The Women's Central Association of Relief pressured the federal government early in the war to create a sanitary commission to care for the soldiers' needs. President Lincoln and army officials initially thought that such an organization would prove to be either useless or a hindrance. Public pressure, though, forced the hand of government, and in June 1861 the federal government sanctioned the U.S. Sanitary Commission. Under the supervision of the Army Medical Service, the commission inspected hospitals and camps, suggesting improvements to the Army Medical Service.

The Sanitary Commission, however, was only one step toward the formation of the American Red Cross. Clara Barton also played a vital role that led to the creation of the American Red Cross. Appalled by the ravages of war, Barton strove to help wounded soldiers and locate those who were missing, especially after seeing the casualty figures from the first battle of Bull Run. She found, however, that the authorities did not want her help. When she contacted the governor of Massachusetts, he resisted her idea of working on the front lines.

Undeterred, Barton went directly to Washington. She already possessed supplies and had assistants to help her distribute them on the front lines. All she needed was official approval to do so. She approached Colonel Daniel Rucker, a member of the Quartermaster Corps, who was intrigued by her knowledge and impressed with the supplies already at her disposal. Her preparation convinced him to allow her and her assistants access to the front. Her first direct experience with the war occurred at Fredericksburg, Virginia, during the Peninsula campaign in 1862, when officers and soldiers welcomed her help, and her supplies were quickly distributed. She also began administering medicine, cleaning wounds, applying fresh dressings, or simply speaking a few words of comfort to a dying soldier. Convinced that some organization such as the International Red Cross was needed to care for soldiers, Clara committed herself to the establishment of an American version after the war.

All local relief organizations, the Sanitary Commission, Clara Barton, and other individuals contributed to the creation of the American Red Cross after the Civil War. Their combined experiences, as well as the destruction of the war, helped establish the

American organization, but it was Barton who took the final steps. On 21 May 1881, she founded the American Association of the Red Cross, and in March 1882 the U.S. government approved the organization. It then officially became the American Red Cross.

Barton also lectured and lobbied for the U.S. government's support of the 1864 Geneva Convention, a treaty that stipulated fair treatment of wounded soldiers and prisoners.

The American chapter of the Red Cross operated under the articles of the 1864 convention that had established the International Red Cross. Accordingly, it was affiliated with the International Red Cross and the League of Red Cross Societies. Today, the Red Cross plays a large role in relief activities, caring for victims of war and natural disasters.

—*Matthew Pacer*

See also Barton, Clara; Blackwell, Elizabeth; Disease; Medicine; United States Christian Commission; United States Sanitary Commission.
For further reading:
Barton, Clara. *The Red Cross* (1898).
Burton, David H. *Clara Barton: In the Service of Humanity* (1995).
Dulles, Foster R. *The American Red Cross: A History* (1950).

AMES, ADELBERT
(1835–1933)
Union general

Adelbert Ames served in the Union army during the American Civil War and established an outstanding record while rising from second lieutenant to brevet brigadier general. As governor of Mississippi during Reconstruction, he battled unsuccessfully to establish a democratic society. At his death in 1933, he was the last surviving Civil War officer.

The son of a prosperous clipper ship captain, Ames was born in Rockland, Maine, on 31 October 1835. He entered West Point in July 1856 and graduated in May 1861 near the top of his class. During the course of the Civil War, Ames fought in seven major military campaigns and sixteen battles, including First Bull Run, the Peninsula campaign, Gaines's Mill, Malvern Hill, Antietam, Fredericksburg, Chancellorsville, Gettysburg, Petersburg, Cold Harbor, and Fort Fisher. He earned a reputation as a stern disciplinarian who led by example and often joined his troops in the heat of battle. He began the war as a second lieutenant in the U.S. Artillery Corps and ended as commander of the Tenth Army Corps with the rank of brevet major general.

After the Confederate surrender, Ames was stationed in South Carolina, where he experienced the hatred of Southern whites while working to halt widespread violence against former slaves. In 1868, Ames took

Adelbert Ames (*Library of Congress*)

1876 moved to impeach him. Exhausted from struggling against political violence and fed up with the absence of a federal commitment to racial equality and the protection of political rights, Ames resigned the governorship on 28 March 1876.

During the second half of his long life, Ames amassed a sizable fortune from business interests in flour milling, textile manufacturing, and real estate. He frequently attended military reunions and died in 1933, immensely proud of his military, political, and business careers.

—*Bruce D. Mactavish*

See also Fort Fisher.
For further reading:
Ames, Blanch. *Adelbert Ames, 1835–1933: General, Senator, Governor* (1964).
Current, Richard N. *Three Carpetbag Governors* (1967).
Harris, William C. *The Day of the Carpetbagger: Republican Reconstruction in Mississippi* (1979).

AMMEN, JACOB
(1807–1894)
Union general

Born to David Ammen and Sally Houtz Ammen in Fincastle, Virginia, Jacob Ammen moved with his family to Ohio when he was ten years old. He was educated locally before receiving an appointment to the U.S. Military Academy in 1827. He graduated twelfth of thirty-three from the class of 1831. Commissioned an artillery officer, Ammen resigned from the army after six years, serving most of that time as an instructor at West Point but also a short time from 1832 to 1833 as an artillery officer in Charleston Harbor. For the next 18 years, Ammen spent most of his time teaching at various universities including what would become Transylvania University and Indiana University.

Immediately before the Civil War, Ammen made his living as a civil engineer. With Abraham Lincoln's call for volunteers on 15 April 1861, Ammen organized a company of the 12th Ohio and became its captain. Two months later Ammen was made the colonel of the 24th Ohio.

For the first months of the war, the 24th served in the campaign in western Virginia. In November 1861 the 24th was transferred to the Army of the Ohio. On the second day of the battle of Shiloh, 7 April, Ammen commanded the 10th Brigade of the 4th Division, protecting the extreme left flank of Don Carlos Buell's army. He was commended by both his division commander, Brigadier General William Nelson, and Major General Buell for his actions there.

Ammen continued to command the 10th Brigade during the siege of Corinth. He was promoted to brigadier general in July 1862, but was forced to take a leave of absence that fall as a result of ill health. For the remainder

charge of Union occupational forces at Vicksburg, Mississippi, and in 1869 President Grant appointed him provisional governor of Mississippi and commander of the Fourth Military District. Governor Ames used his political and military authority to establish and protect the political, economic, and social rights of freedmen and freedwomen. He favored racial equality, universal manhood suffrage, and a system of state-supported schools for all children. Ames responded to frequent racial violence in Mississippi by using troops to protect black citizens, directing military commissions to convict perpetrators, and removing from office state and local officials who violated the rights of black Mississippians. The Republican-controlled state legislature appointed Ames senator in 1870, a position he held until 1873. In 1874, Ames once again became governor of Mississippi after a hard-fought victory over James Lusk Alcorn. His inaugural address emphasized his continued commitment to full economic rights for all Mississippians. Such ideals brought Ames into direct conflict with the rising tide of Democratic political terrorism sweeping the state. Lacking the assistance of Federal troops, he was unable to stop the organized campaign of violence, intimidation, and assassination that brought Redeemer Democrats into office. The Democratic-controlled legislature fabricated a series of charges against Ames and in of the war, Ammen held a variety of jobs, primarily staff or desk jobs, because of the feebleness of his health.

In the spring of 1863, he assumed command of Camp Douglas, a prisoner-of-war camp in Chicago. By the summer, Ammen was transferred to East Tennessee, where he participated in Ambrose Burnside's campaign there. At the end of the year, Ammen was given command of the District of Central Kentucky. In the spring of 1864, Ammen was given command of the 4th Division, XXIII Corps, commanded by Major General John Schofield and headquartered in Knoxville, Tennessee. The primary job of the division in the spring was to combat against raids perpetrated by Confederate cavalryman Joseph Wheeler. The following fall, while still in East Tennessee, Ammen guarded Federal positions against the campaign of John C. Breckinridge.

In January 1865, citing failing business interests but probably as much a result of his bad health, Ammen resigned from the army. After the war he worked as a civil engineer and a Maryland farmer. He traveled to Central America in 1874 as part of a government-appointed commission to look at possible canal locations. He retired to Lockland, Ohio, in 1891 and died there on 6 February 1894.

—*David S. Heidler and Jeanne T. Heidler*

See also Corinth, Battle of; Shiloh, Battle of.
For further reading:
Wessen, Ernest James, ed. *Papers of Brigadier General Jacob Ammen* (1957).

ANACONDA PLAN

When South Carolinians fired on Fort Sumter on 12 April 1861, the U.S. Army, numbering some 16,000 men, was suddenly expected to subdue the rebellious South, a region measuring 750,000 square miles and inhabited by 9 million people. Initially, many Northerners, including President Abraham Lincoln, expected that the conflict would be over in a few months. However, U.S. Army General-in-Chief Winfield Scott saw the magnitude of the future conflict more clearly. In 1861, he predicted that the Civil War would last more than two years, require 300,000 Union soldiers, and cost 100,000 casualties as a result of both combat and disease. Aside from insufficient manpower and material, the Union's military and political leaders did not possess a coherent plan for victory. As part of his responsibilities as general-in-chief, Scott made a significant contribution to the Union's cause by formulating the so-called Anaconda Plan, a grand strategic or political plan for the subjugation of the Confederacy. Something of a misnomer, the term "Anaconda" came into use after 1861 among Union leaders and skeptical Union press to describe Scott's strategy.

Born in 1786, Winfield Scott started his military career in 1808 as a captain of artillery and served with

distinction in the War of 1812. He rose to the rank of brigadier general by the age of thirty and fought in several battles and wars against Indians. In 1835, his three-volume *Infantry Tactics* appeared. Scott took part in diplomatic missions to England and Canada in 1838, and he was promoted to general-in-chief of the army in 1841. During the Mexican-American War, he brilliantly commanded the U.S. landing at Vera Cruz and the subsequent campaign in 1847. In Mexico, he clearly demonstrated intelligent leadership, a knack for organization, an appreciation for logistics, and a comprehension of strategic and political issues. Scott accepted the Whig Party's presidential nomination in 1852. Consequently, Winfield Scott brought more than fifty years of experience in domestic, foreign, and military affairs to the situation facing the Union army in the Civil War's early months.

For Scott, war was a game of chess. Opposing armies would maneuver to bring each other into checkmate and obtain victories without necessarily destroying all the enemy forces or losing all their own forces. The overall political or grand strategic goal of victory could be achieved by limited means. Scott's strategic thinking was consistent with his strategy employed in the Mexican-American War. Using the continent as a chessboard, Scott designed his Anaconda Plan to accomplish a political goal: forcing the Confederacy into peace negotiations rather than the purely military goal of defeating its armed forces on the battlefield. Scott favored conciliation with the Confederacy rather than its destruction in a total war.

Scott's plan was influenced by the moderate strategic theories of Baron Antoine Henri Jomini, a Swiss military thinker who had served with both Napoleon's French forces and the opposing Russian forces. Jomini's interpretation of Napoleonic warfare influenced U.S. military leaders during the mid-nineteenth century. Jomini did not want needlessly bloody battles. Instead, he advocated the use of interior lines and control of geography to allow a preponderance of force to be exerted against an enemy's weak points.

Scott's Anaconda Plan called for the Union army and navy to exert constant pressure on the South and gradually strangle it to death. It consisted of two main parts. First, exploiting its great advantage in number of ships and experienced leaders, the Union fleet would impose a naval blockade, causing economic hardship in the South. As the South's commercial activities decreased, its valuable cash crops such as tobacco and cotton could not be used to trade with the Europeans. Second, the Union naval and land forces would open the Mississippi and other Southern rivers and split the South into two parts. Controlling these rivers would deprive the Confederate army of its interior lines of communication and transportation as well as allow the Union army to employ these same lines of communication and trans-

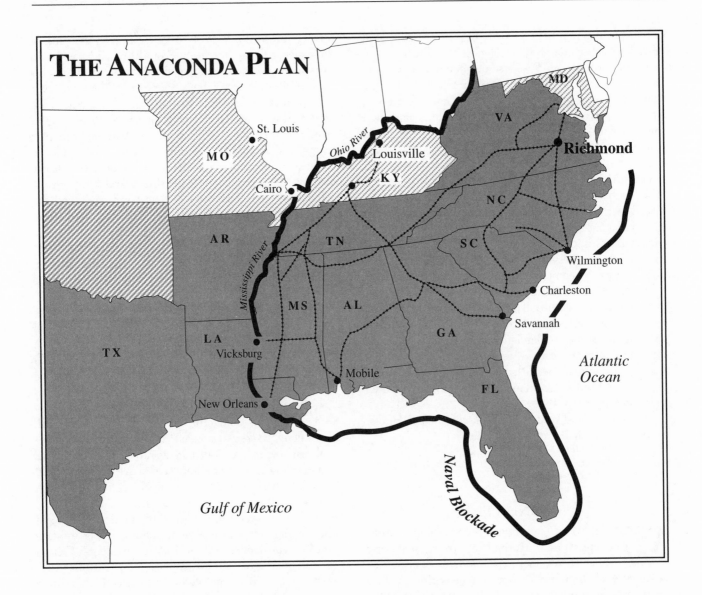

THE ANACONDA PLAN

portation. Consequently, a war of attrition would take its toll as the isolated and enveloped Confederacy lost its logistical capabilities.

Contemporaries scoffed at Scott and his Anaconda Plan. The North's public and their representatives impatiently clamored for a dramatic military confrontation culminating in a Confederate defeat. Naysayers believed that Scott's grand strategy was too passive and too elaborate. The plan did have some weaknesses and shortcomings. For example, its implementation would not have directly damaged the South's will to fight. Moreover, the Anaconda Plan did not strike any blows against the Confederacy's agricultural base in the Deep South. Lastly, the plan did not anticipate occupation and control of conquered Confederate territory. Ultimately, four years of bloody battles and bitter occupations were also needed to achieve the political goal of victory by means of a strategy of annihilation. The Confederacy's military forces had to be bludgeoned into

submission in a methodical, destructive, total war.

These weaknesses and shortcomings notwithstanding, Winfield Scott's Anaconda Plan did indeed influence the strategy that the Union military eventually used to win the Civil War. The Union's naval blockade handicapped the Confederacy's commercial activities. With the capture of New Orleans in April 1862 and Vicksburg in July 1863, Union control of the Mississippi split the South into two parts.

—*David Ulbrich*

See also Scott, Winfield.
For further reading:
Eisenhower, John S. D. *Agent of Destiny: The Life and Times of General Winfield Scott* (1997).
Johnson, Timothy D. *Winfield Scott: The Quest for Military Glory* (1998).
Marszalek, John F. "Where Did Winfield Scott Find His Anaconda?" *Lincoln Herald* (1987).
Ropp, Theodore. "Anacondas Anyone?" *Military Affairs* (1963).
Scott, Winfield. *Memoirs of Lieutenant-General Scott, LL. D.* (1864; reprint, 1970).

ANDERSON, GEORGE THOMAS
(1824–1901)
Confederate general

Born in Covington, Georgia, to Joseph Stewart Anderson and Lucy Cunningham Anderson, George Thomas Anderson was educated at Emory College. At the outbreak of the Mexican War in 1848 he received a commission as a second lieutenant in the Georgia Mounted Volunteers and served in Winfield Scott's Mexico City campaign. Anderson returned to his family's home after the war. In 1855 he decided to return to the military and accepted a captain's commission in the 1st United States Cavalry. He served for three years, resigning his commission in 1858 and again returning home to the family plantation.

At the outbreak of the Civil War, Anderson helped to raise the 11th Georgia Regiment and was made the regiment's colonel. During the summer of 1861 Anderson took his regiment to Virginia, where it served without seeing combat for the remainder of the year. In February 1862 Anderson was given command of a brigade that included the 11th and was composed entirely of Georgia troops. Initially, the brigade was part of the division commanded by Major General Gustavus W. Smith, but during the early phases of the Peninsula campaign it was placed under Major General David R. Jones. As part of a force under the overall command of John B. Magruder, Anderson and his men occupied the Confederate works at Yorktown in an effort to delay Union general George B. McClellan's movement up the Peninsula. Anderson and his brigade also fought during the Seven Days' battles, being especially conspicuous at Malvern Hill.

Upon the organization of the Army of Northern Virginia into two corps, Anderson and his brigade came under the command of James Longstreet. In late August 1862 Anderson led his brigade at Second Bull Run where he was slightly injured. He was back in command by mid-September, however, in time to fight in the defense of Turner's Gap at South Mountain and then at Antietam. Anderson was commended for his actions in the latter battle.

In November 1862 Anderson was formally promoted to brigadier general. He had commanded a brigade for almost a year. At Fredericksburg a month later, he continued to command the same brigade in the division under John Bell Hood. In spring 1863, along with much of Longstreet's corps, Anderson went to Suffolk, Virginia, but was back with the Army of Northern Virginia in time to begin the invasion of the North that would culminate in the battle of Gettysburg.

As was the case with the remainder of Longstreet's corps, Anderson arrived too late to fight on the first day of the battle of Gettysburg. Anderson and his brigade were part of Hood's division that attacked the Union left

on the afternoon of 2 July. In the fierce fighting in the Devil's Den at the base of Little Roundtop Anderson was seriously wounded.

After a convalescence of several months, in October 1863 Anderson was sent to Tennessee to join much of the remainder of Longstreet's corps. He distinguished himself in the Knoxville campaign. In the spring he returned with the corps to command his brigade in the Wilderness campaign and all the subsequent battles of Ulysses S. Grant's campaign against Robert E. Lee. At the end of June he settled into the trenches of Petersburg with his brigade where he would spend much of the remainder of the war.

In the meantime Anderson had entered into a dispute with the governor of Georgia, Joseph Brown. In spring 1864 Anderson and the officers of his brigade took offense at the efforts of Brown to withhold troops and supplies from the Confederate government. When Brown called the state legislature into session to acquiesce in his efforts, Anderson and his officers circulated a petition among the soldiers of the brigade, who were all from Georgia units, protesting Brown's actions. Anderson then forwarded the petition to Brown with the assurance that virtually every soldier in the brigade had signed it. Brown fired back, angrily accusing Anderson of trying to gain the favor of the Richmond government to secure a promotion to major general. In the intensity of preparations for the coming campaign the dispute ended there, although the episode provided a clear example of the damage done to morale when soldiers learn of the failure of home governments to support their efforts in the field. Anderson ended the war by surrendering with what was left of the Army of Northern Virginia at Appomattox Court House.

After the war Anderson returned to Georgia, where he tried to rebuild his fortunes. Landless, he accepted a number of positions, including working for the Georgia Railroad in Atlanta. He became somewhat prominent in civic affairs in the city and served briefly as the boom town's chief of police. In his later years he moved to Anniston, Alabama, where he also occupied several civic offices. He died in Anniston on 4 April 1901.

—*David S. Heidler and Jeanne T. Heidler*

See also Georgia; Gettysburg, Battle of.
For further reading:
Boney, F. N. *Rebel Georgia* (1997).
Pfanz, Harry W. *Gettysburg, The Second Day* (1987).

ANDERSON, JAMES PATTON
(1822–1872)
Confederate general; congressman

James Patton Anderson was the son of William Preston Anderson and Margaret Adair Anderson. He was born in Winchester, Tennessee, in 1822. His father having died when James was still a boy, Anderson was brought up by his grandfather, who had him educated at Jefferson College in Pennsylvania. As a young man, Anderson moved to Mississippi where he became a physician and county sheriff. While engaged in these occupations, Anderson studied law and was admitted to the Mississippi bar. In 1847 he raised the 1st Battalion Mississippi Rifles to fight in the Mexican War and became the unit's lieutenant colonel and then colonel.

Upon his return to the United States, Anderson became involved in Mississippi politics, served in the state legislature, and became a protege of Jefferson Davis. After losing his bid for reelection to the state legislature, Anderson was appointed by President Franklin Pierce—probably at the urging of the president's secretary of war, Jefferson Davis—to serve as U.S. marshal in the Washington Territory and to take the territorial census. Anderson became so popular in Washington that he was selected as the territory's congressional delegate. He served in that position from 1855 to 1857. When offered the position of territorial governor by President James Buchanan, however, Anderson refused because of his desire in the midst of the sectional crisis to return to the South.

Anderson moved to Florida to manage the plantation of an elderly aunt and there became involved in Florida politics. Jefferson County, Florida, sent him as one of its delegates to the secession convention and then as a congressman to the Provisional Confederate Congress.

Within a few months, however, Anderson resigned his seat to join the 1st Florida Regiment stationed under Braxton Bragg at Pensacola. In February 1862 he received a promotion to brigadier general. He led a brigade at Shiloh and in defense of Corinth. In Bragg's invasion of Kentucky, he temporarily commanded a division that constituted the left of Bragg's morning attack on 8 October 1862 at Perryville. At Stones River he was again in command of his brigade when he captured a portion of the Union artillery. Leading a division the following year at Chickamauga, Georgia, Anderson was commended for his bravery there, and a few months later he led the same division at Chattanooga, Tennessee.

In February 1864 Anderson received a promotion to major general and was placed in charge of the District of Florida. In summer 1864 John Bell Hood summoned him from Florida after replacing Joseph Johnston in the defense of Atlanta. Anderson fought at Ezra Church and Utoy Creek before suffering a severe wound at Jonesboro. Physicians judged that his injuries would preclude further service, but as Sherman made his way through the Carolinas in the early months of 1865, Anderson ignored this advice and returned to the army. He surrendered at Greensboro, North Carolina, but stubbornly refused a parole.

Following the war Anderson worked as the editor of an agricultural newspaper and as a tax collector in Tennessee.

—*David S. Heidler and Jeanne T. Heidler*

See also Perryville, Battle of; Stones River, Battle of.
For further reading:
Anderson, James Patton. "Autobiography." (Transcript, Southern Historical Collection, University of North Carolina).
Hoffman, John. *The Confederate Collapse at the Battle of Missionary Ridge: The Reports of James Patton Anderson and His Brigade Commanders* (1985).

ANDERSON, JOSEPH REID
(1813–1892)
Confederate general; industrialist

Joseph Reid Anderson was born in Virginia to William Anderson and Anne Thomas Anderson. He graduated fourth of forty-nine in the United States Military Academy Class of 1836. Upon graduation, he entered the 3d Artillery but within months transferred to the Army Corps of Engineers. In less than a year, however, he resigned this commission to work as an engineer for the state of Virginia. In 1841 he opened his own engineering firm and became the superintendent of the Tredegar Iron Works. Over the next decade and a half, Anderson gradually gained financial control of the iron works until he owned it outright by 1858.

In addition to his business pursuits, Anderson became involved in Virginia politics. Originally a Whig, he became a Democrat in 1857 and served in the Virginia House of Delegates. Although he was not a radical, he did strongly support efforts to organize Southern commercial ventures before the war. Once Virginia seceded, he used these commercial connections to supply the Confederacy with war materiel.

To further support the war effort, Anderson accepted a commission as a major of artillery in the Confederate army in August 1861. A month later he received a promotion to brigadier general and a transfer to Wilmington, North Carolina. Concern that his absence would hurt the Tredegar Iron Works prompted the Confederate War Department to make his field command contingent on the iron works' smooth operation. Even while in North Carolina, Anderson remained apprehensive about the safety of Virginia and sent suggestions to the Confederate War Department about the best ways to block the James River to Union gunboats.

In early 1862 Anderson briefly commanded the District of Cape Fear and the District of North Carolina before bringing the Third North Carolina Brigade to the York Peninsula to join in the defense of Richmond. As Union general Irvin McDowell's army moved south from Washington in May 1862, Anderson commanded the

Joseph Reid Anderson (*Library of Congress*)

Army of the Rappahannock guarding the crossings around Fredericksburg, Virginia. During the Seven Days' battles, he commanded the 3d Brigade of A. P. Hill's division until he was wounded at Frayser's Farm on 30 June 1862. Because of his injury and the need to maximize the output from the Tredegar Works, Anderson resigned his commission in July 1862.

For the remainder of the war, Anderson dedicated all of his time to the operation of the iron works, keeping it at full production almost to the moment the Union army entered Richmond. The ammunition and artillery pieces produced there became an essential part of the Confederate war effort. Upon Richmond's surrender, the federal government confiscated the facility and did not relinquish it until 1867.

After the iron works returned to his ownership, Anderson spent much of the rest of his life managing it. He also remained active in Richmond affairs and efforts to industrialize the South. He died in New Hampshire in 1892, and his body was returned to Richmond for burial.

—*David S. Heidler and Jeanne T. Heidler*

See also Tredegar Iron Works; Wilmington, North Carolina.
For further reading:
Dew, Charles B. *Ironmaker to the Confederacy: Joseph R. Anderson and the Tredegar Iron Works* (1966).

ANDERSON, RICHARD HERON
(1821–1879)
Confederate general

Born to William Wallace Anderson and Mary Jane MacKenzie Anderson in South Carolina, Richard Anderson graduated fortieth of fifty-six in the 1842 class of the United States Military Academy. During the Mexican-American War, he fought in Winfield Scott's campaign to take Mexico City. He received a brevet to first lieutenant for his actions in this campaign. During the 1850s, Anderson served in a number of frontier posts and was promoted to captain in 1855. From 1858 to 1859, he served as a member of Colonel Albert Sidney Johnston's Utah expedition, following which he was stationed in Nebraska Territory. When he heard of the secession of his home state of South Carolina, Anderson resigned his commission and accepted a major's commission in the Confederate army.

Initially assigned to the Department of South Carolina and Florida, Anderson served under P. G. T. Beauregard in Charleston, South Carolina, during the Fort Sumter crisis and was present when that fort surrendered. When Beauregard moved from Charleston to assume command of the Confederate forces at Manassas Junction during the summer of 1861, Anderson assumed command at Charleston. He received a promotion to brigadier general in July 1861.

In early 1862 Anderson transferred to Richmond, where he commanded a brigade under James Longstreet in the Peninsula campaign and earned a promotion to the rank of major general. He remained a part of the Army of Northern Virginia for the remainder of the war, fighting in every major engagement of that army.

During the Peninsula campaign, Anderson commanded the guard for the Confederate retreat from Yorktown and held the Union army briefly at Williamsburg. Anderson moved north after this action to guard the Rappahannock River crossings from Irvin McDowell's move south from Washington. He left that position just in time to participate on 31 May 1862 in Joseph Johnston's attack on McClellan at Fair Oaks. James Longstreet commended Anderson for his actions there and during the Seven Days' battles.

Anderson received a promotion to major general in July 1862. After McClellan's retreat to the James River, Lee sent Jackson and Longstreet north to engage the Union army under John Pope. Anderson was temporarily left behind to guard Richmond against any renewal of hostilities by McClellan. When it became apparent that McClellan had no intention of attacking, Anderson joined General Longstreet's corps in time for the descent on Pope at Second Bull Run.

Lee followed this victory with his first invasion of the North, and Anderson's division was temporarily detached to join with Stonewall Jackson's capture of Harper's Ferry in western Virginia. That goal accomplished, Anderson's division departed for the rendezvous with Lee's army at Sharpsburg. Anderson arrived at 7 A.M. on 17 September 1862, in time to participate in the early phases of the battle. He was wounded early in the day, however, and did not lead his men in their support of D. H. Hill at the sunken road. At the battle of Fredericksburg, Anderson commanded the Confederate far left and as a result had little part in the fighting. When Longstreet was sent to the Carolinas following Fredericksburg, Anderson's division remained with Lee. He moved out of Fredericksburg on 29 April 1863 to protect the approaches from Chancellorsville. He remained in that position, digging in for several days, and prevented Hooker from moving forward while Jackson moved around the Union army. Lee commended Anderson for his actions during the battle of Chancellorsville in May 1863.

With Stonewall Jackson's death at the battle of Chancellorsville, Anderson's division was moved to A. P. Hill's Corps. On the second day of the fighting at Gettysburg, Anderson and his division, temporarily attached to Longstreet, attacked the Union right of Daniel Sickles's corps that had moved off of Cemetery Ridge. The following day, part of Anderson's division participated in Pickett's Charge.

In May 1864 Anderson temporarily rose to the rank of lieutenant general and corps commander when James Longstreet was severely wounded at the battle of the Wilderness. In command of Longstreet's corps, Anderson was ordered by Lee to move out of Confederate lines to Spotsylvania Court House before General Grant could reach that point. Anderson managed to move his men to the position earlier and with greater speed than Lee had anticipated, but Anderson was nonetheless barely ahead of the lead elements of the Union army.

When Longstreet returned to command of his corps in October 1864, Anderson was moved to help supervise Richmond's defenses. When Confederate forces evacuated their entrenchments at Petersburg, Anderson commanded the right of the retreat. Most of his command was either devastated or scattered at Sayler's Creek, and the remainder was put under Longstreet and John B. Gordon. Absent a command, Anderson received permission to return home. He departed for South Carolina on 7 April 1865, two days before Lee's surrender on 9 April at Appomattox.

The period after the war was difficult for Anderson. His failure at several endeavors left him dying in virtual poverty in Beaufort, South Carolina.

—*David S. Heidler and Jeanne T. Heidler*

See also Sayler's Creek, Battle of.
For further reading:
Elliott, Joseph Cantey. *Lieutenant General Richard Heron*

Anderson: Lee's Noble Soldier (1985).
Walker, Cornelius Irvine. *The Life of Lieutenant General Richard Heron Anderson, of the Confederate States Army* (1917).

ANDERSON, ROBERT
(1805–1871)
Union officer

Robert Anderson was born near Louisville, Kentucky, the son of a Revolutionary War officer. He graduated from West Point, fifteenth in a class of thirty-seven, in 1825, and was commissioned a lieutenant with the 3d U.S. Artillery. Anderson went on to distinguish himself by fighting in the Black Hawk War of 1832, winning a brevet promotion to captain; he also earned praise for his performance against the Seminole Indians from 1836 to 1838.

Anderson subsequently served as assistant adjutant general in the Eastern Division, 1838–1841, where he rose to captain. During the Mexican-American War, he campaigned under Winfield Scott throughout the advance upon Mexico City in 1847. Valorous behavior at Molino del Rey brought him a second brevet promotion to major and a severe wound. After the war, Anderson fulfilled a number of routine assignments without fanfare, and sought to supplement his meager income by translating several French artillery texts for the army. By 1857 he had risen to the rank of major and gained a reputation as a deeply religious, highly conscientious soldier. In 1845 he married Elizabeth Bayard Clinch of Georgia and came into possession of several slaves. Moreover, like many officers of Southern birth (his family was originally Virginian), he espoused pro-slavery and pro-Southern sympathies. As events would prove, the slight, nondescript Anderson was also possessed of an unimpeachable sense of loyalty and devotion to the United States.

By November 1860, the escalating tide of secession emboldened Southern resentment toward the North, and isolated army garrisons became objects of derision. Such was the state of affairs around Charleston, South Carolina, when the War Department ordered Anderson to take charge of the three small forts in the harbor. His appointment was a calculated move, for they anticipated that a pro-Southern officer would use tact and discretion in dealing with Charleston authorities. Although he accepted the assignment, Anderson keenly felt the weight of his predicament and was determined not to initiate any moves that might precipitate a war.

In his dealings with local authorities, Anderson proved polite, even sympathetic, but to no avail. He also believed that it was only a matter of time before the government ordered him to hand his post over to the Southerners. However, attitudes hardened toward the presence of a Union garrison after 20 December 1860, when an ordinance of secession was passed. Anderson at this point deemed his position untenable, and on the night of 26 December he abandoned Fort Moultrie and Castle Pinckney, spiking the guns. He then relocated the 137 men of his command to Fort Sumter, an unfinished work on an island in the middle of Charleston harbor. The beleaguered garrison set about fortifying their position while awaiting further instructions from Washington.

As events unfolded, the administration of James Buchanan proved unable to handle the growing secession crisis. They ignored or overlooked Anderson's pleas for both reinforcements and supplies throughout the winter and early spring of 1861. Bereft of orders, Anderson took it upon himself to maintain the status quo as long as his possession of Fort Sumter was not compromised. He politely rebuffed Confederate demands for his surrender, but in a most conciliatory fashion. His determination to avoid provoking hostilities was underscored on 9 January 1861, when Confederate shore batteries fired upon and drove off the much-needed supply ship *Star of the West*. This greatly exacerbated his logistical problems, and he went so far as to advise Southern emissaries that he would be forced to capitulate on 15 April 1861 if supplies were not forthcoming.

It fell upon the newly installed administration of Abraham Lincoln to break the impasse. The president probably realized that Anderson's garrison was doomed in the event of war, so he orchestrated a scheme to maximize political benefit from their demise. He thereupon declared that an expedition was being mounted for the express purpose of resupplying Fort Sumter and not reinforcing it. If the Confederates had the audacity to violate this humane mission, he expected Southern aggression to mobilize and unify his Northern political base.

Lincoln's reasoning proved correct. Unwilling to tolerate a Union garrison further, and determined to prevent its being supplied, on 12 April 1861 General Pierre G. T. Beauregard sent an ultimatum to Anderson demanding his immediate surrender. Anderson, unmoved as always, politely declined. One hour later, at 4:30 A.M., Confederate gunners fired the first shots of the Civil War. Discarding his past deference, Anderson replied in kind and allowed his subordinate, Captain Abner Doubleday, the honor of returning the first Union shot. The ensuing 36-hour bombardment severely damaged Fort Sumter before Anderson struck his colors on 14 April 1861. The garrison then surrendered with honors of war and was paroled and allowed to leave. Miraculously, Union forces sustained only two fatalities—a gunner who died when his cannon exploded as it fired a salute to the lowering American flag and another soldier mortally wounded by the explosion. But, as Lincoln anticipated, the Confederates were tarred as aggressors and bolstered Northern sentiment for war.

Anderson's stand at Fort Sumter made him a national hero overnight, and he was promoted to brigadier general on 15 May 1861. He subsequently commanded the Department of Kentucky (later the Department of the Cumberland) for several months as the neutrality of that essential border state hung in the balance. Anderson worked carefully on behalf of the federal government until his health gave out and he was replaced by General William T. Sherman on 8 October 1861. He saw no further action until April 1865, when he donned the uniform of a brevet major general of volunteers and hoisted the American flag over Fort Sumter after the Confederate surrender. Anderson then relocated to Europe in an attempt to improve his health; he died in Nice, France, and was interred at West Point.

—*John C. Fredriksen*

See also Doubleday, Abner; Fort Sumter.
For further reading:
Garrison, Webb S. *Lincoln's Little War* (1997).
Klein, Maury. *Days of Defiance: Sumter, Secession, and the Coming of the Civil War* (1997).

ANDERSON, WILLIAM "BLOODY BILL"
(1839–1864)
Confederate guerrilla leader

Born in Kentucky in 1839, the oldest of six children born to William Anderson, Sr., and Martha Anderson, William, Jr., migrated with his family from Missouri to his father's land claim east of Council Grove, Kansas, in 1857. By the time he reached 21 he had acquired a land claim of his own and was accompanying wagon trains west on the Santa Fe Trail and apparently engaging in selling stolen ponies and horses. With the outbreak of the Civil War he began a career in banditry, first with pro-Union, antislavery Jayhawkers, then with pro-Confederate, proslavery Bushwhackers. In both cases his object was financial. Like other such irregular forces operating in Kansas, they were enriched themselves under the guise of fighting for liberty.

After his father died the victim of a shotgun blast to the chest over a matter of "family honor"—his mother had died in 1860 when struck by lightning—Bill and his brother Jim took the remainder of the family back to Missouri but not before mortally wounding the object of the family's "dishonor" in July 1862. Here in western Missouri they resumed their guerrilla warfare, now against pro-Unionists in the area, especially along the Santa Fe Trail. Bill eventually headed up his own 30-to-40-man guerrilla band as its "captain."

Anderson's notoriety as a guerrilla began in 1863 when he joined the band led by William Clarke Quantrill. This move was triggered by the death of his 14-year-old sister Josephine and injuries to his 16-year-old sister Mary Ellen and 10-year-old sister Janie in the collapse of a temporary Union jail in Kansas City on 13 August 1863. The jail was a three-story brick building being used to house women suspected of aiding the pro-Confederate guerrillas. It collapsed when a weakened adjoining building fell in on it. Believing that the Union soldiers had deliberately weakened the structure and acting out of revenge with some 450 other partisans, Anderson (along with Frank James, Cole Younger, and others) played a leading role in Quantrill's retaliatory raid on Lawrence, Kansas, on 21 August of that year. Quantrill's last order to his men was to "Kill every man big enough to carry a gun." Close to 200 unarmed men and boys were killed—Anderson personally killing fourteen—and the business district of the town was put to the torch.

In Texas that winter Anderson got married and broke with Quantrill. In the spring of 1864 led about 50 guerrillas back to Missouri, there to burn, loot, and slaughter Union soldiers and pro-Union civilians in the central part of the state. This orgy of violence climaxed on 27 September 1864, at the little town of Centralia when Anderson's gang, joining with those of Thomas Todd, Si Gordon, and others, first looted the town and held up a stagecoach. They then stopped a North Missouri train a mile out of town, stripped 24 unarmed Union soldiers of their uniforms and shot them down in cold blood (except for Sergeant Tom Goodman, whom they spared to exchange for one of their men captured four days before). When a Union force chasing them fell into their trap three miles southeast of Centralia, Anderson's men killed over 100 soldiers, mutilating some. The guerrillas thereafter returned to Centralia to kill more soldiers before riding off.

Anderson and his guerrillas then went on to serve with Confederate generals Sterling Price and Joseph Shelby in their unsuccessful raid into Missouri that ended decisively at Westport on 23 October. Caught in a Union ambush outside of Albany, Missouri, on 7 October 1864, Anderson, now referred to as "the blood-drenched savage," was cut down by two shots to the head as he led his guerrilla column into the fray. The next day his body was placed on public exhibition in nearby Richmond and photographed with his head propped up, wearing a "guerrilla shirt," and with pistols in both hands. It was also reported that he was decapitated by Unionist militiamen, his head stuck atop of a pole, his body dragged through town behind a horse.

Thus ended the short and violent career of the Confederacy's most noted and brutal guerrilla partisan other than William Quantrill. Anderson claimed to have tied a knot in a silken cord for every man he killed (the knots totaling 54 by his death) and to have decorated the bridle of his horse with the scalps of Federal soldiers. He was buried that day in an unmarked grave in the

Richmond cemetery. Today an incorrectly dated headstone marks his grave.

—*James M. Morris*

See also Centralia Massacre; Guerrilla Warfare; Lawrence, Kansas; Missouri; Quantrill, William Clarke.

For further reading:

Brownlee, Richard S. *Gray Ghosts of the Confederacy: Guerrilla Warfare in the West, 1861–1865* (1958).

Castel, Albert, and Thomas Goodrich. *Bloody Bill Anderson: The Short, Savage Life of a Civil War Guerrilla* (1998).

Goodrich, Thomas. *Black Flag: Guerrilla Warfare on the Western Border, 1861–1865* (1995).

Harris, Charles F. "Catalyst for Terror: The Collapse of the Women's Prison in Kansas City." *Missouri Historical Review* (1995).

Leslie, Edward. *The Devil Knows How to Ride: The True Story of William Clarke Quantrill and His Confederate Raiders* (1996).

Monaghan, Jay. *Civil War on the Western Border, 1854–1865* (1955).

Schultz, Duane. *Quantrill's War: The Life and Times of William Clarke Quantrill, 1837–1865* (1996).

ANDERSONVILLE
(1864–1865)
Confederate military prison

Construction of Andersonville prison, officially known as Camp Sumter, began in southern Georgia in January 1864. Between February 1864 and May 1865, 45,613 United States prisoners were held at Andersonville, and nearly 13,000 men died there.

Filth, vermin, disease, malnutrition, exposure to the elements, and a stench that was said to cause prisoners to vomit upon entering the grounds characterized Andersonville prison. Conditions such as these were endemic to many hastily constructed Civil War military penitentiaries, but Andersonville's reputation for its exceptionally brutal conditions has made it the best known of all Civil War prisons.

Until 1863 prisoners of war were exchanged under a cartel between the Confederate and United States governments. After the agreement collapsed, the need to construct large military prison camps developed. The site for Andersonville, selected by Confederate captain W. Sidney Winder, was chosen because of its distance from battle lines, access to railroad lines, and its ample supply of pure water and lumber in the Georgia pine forest.

Although plans dictated that barracks be built at the prison, the inflated price of lumber meant that Confederate officials could not afford to purchase the board feet needed for such construction. Instead, a stockade that surrounded 16.5 acres of land enclosed the prisoners beneath the open sky. Built with slave labor, the stockade was constructed of pine logs cut to a length of 25 feet. Logs hewn to a thickness of 12 inches were placed into the ground at a depth of 5 feet, leaving a wall

View from the main gate of prisoners drawing rations at Andersonville, 17 August 1864
(Photograph by A. J. Riddle / *National Archives*)

of 15 feet surrounding the grounds. A stream about five feet wide flowed through the prison and supplied the inmates with water.

The first prisoners arrived at Andersonville on 25 February 1864, before construction of the facility was completed. In June 1864, while the prison held over 23,000 men, the stockade was enlarged to enclose a total of 26 acres of land. With no buildings in which inmates could take shelter, captives were exposed to the elements. Using scraps of lumber, logs, blankets, and whatever materials they could scavenge, prisoners built crude structures, which they called "shebangs," that served as inadequate housing.

A lack of sanitary practices and overcrowding plagued the prison. Workers in the prison bakery, which was located upstream of the stockade, discarded refuse into the stream, thus contaminating the water supply before it reached the inmates. Men bathing and defecating in

and near the stream were another source of contamination. The prison was built to accommodate 10,000 men; however, by the end of July 1864, Confederate officials crowded over 31,000 prisoners into the stockade. In August 1864 Andersonville's inmate population reached its high of nearly 33,000. Such a high population taxed limited facilities and resources. Prisoners standing and walking near the stream eroded its banks and created a three-and-a-half-acre swamp in the center of the prison. The swamp, which served as a toilet area, resulted not only in a portion of land rendered uninhabitable, but also created an unbearable stench and a source of disease where maggots were said to breed 15 to 18 inches deep.

Many prisoners who arrived at Andersonville sickly and weak found conditions at the prison camp compounded their misery. Meager, nutritionally inadequate, and uncooked rations resulted in a variety of illnesses and contributed to the deaths of many inmates.

A burial party at Andersonville prison, 17 August 1864. (Photograph by A. J. Riddle / *National Archives*)

Scurvy, which was widespread in the camp, as well as malnutrition, intensified the suffering of thousands of men who were plagued with and died from respiratory ailments and from various intestinal tract disorders and diseases, including diarrhea and dysentery.

Along with disease, violence perpetrated by prison guards, as well as by inmates resulted in many deaths. Guards were known to kill prisoners who made the unfortunate mistake of venturing too close to the stockade's deadline.

The degree to which Confederates deliberately brutalized Union prisoners, however, has been debated. Because of a shortage of Confederate soldiers available to serve as guards, Andersonville's prison guards were posted only to ensure that inmates would not escape, and not necessarily to maintain order. As a result, inmates terrorized, stole from, and killed fellow prisoners. The largest and most notorious of these raiders was a band of men that arrived in April 1864 under the leadership of William "Mosby" Collins of Pennsylvania.

After suffering the attacks of Mosby's raiders for some months, inmates appealed to the commander of the prison for relief. He eventually decided to allow prisoners to organize themselves, and to arrest and try the suspected criminals.

In July the so-called Regulators arrested twenty-four members of the raider gang. A jury made up of twelve inmates heard evidence against the raiders and brought a sentence of death against six of the ringleaders. On 11 July, the guilty men were executed by hanging. The eighteen who were not convicted were forced to run a gauntlet of their fellow prisoners armed with clubs. Three men died from the beatings they received.

In early September 1864, as Unions troops advanced deeper into the South and closer to Andersonville, Confederate officials transferred most of the camps' inmates to other Southern penitentiaries. By December 1864 only 1,359 prisoners who were too sick to travel remained in Andersonville. Additional men, however, were transferred to the prison in late December. On 4

May 1865 Colonel George C. Gibbs, who had taken command of the prison in October 1864, paroled the remaining inmates.

Noteworthy among Andersonville's prison officials was Captain Henry Wirz, who commanded the interior of the prison. In the aftermath of the war, Wirz, a native of Switzerland, was arrested and tried by a military court for crimes connected to his service at Andersonville. It appears that much of testimony of former prisoners against Wirz, who was hated by inmates, lacked credibility. Wirz did not receive a fair trial. Nevertheless, he was found guilty and sentenced to death. On 10 November 1865, he was hanged in Washington, D.C.

Today, the prison grounds and the adjoining cemetery are part of the 395-acre Andersonville National Historic Site.

—*Alicia Rodriquez*

See also Prisoner Exchanges; Prisoner Paroles; Prisoners of War; Prisons, C.S.A.; Wirz, Henry.

For further reading:
Hesseltine, William Best. *Civil War Prisons: A Study in War Psychology* (1998).
Marvel, William. *Andersonville: The Last Depot* (1994).
Speer, Lonnie R. *Portals to Hell: Military Prisons of the Civil War* (1997).

ANDREW, JOHN ALBION
(1818–1867)
Governor of Massachusetts

John A. Andrew was born in Windham, Maine, on 31 May 1818, the son of a farmer and merchant. After graduating from Bowdoin College in 1837, he studied law in Boston and was admitted to the Massachusetts bar in 1840. As a young lawyer, Andrew was an active abolitionist opponent of the war with Mexico and the Fugitive Slave Act. As a Conscience Whig allied with Charles Francis Adams, Charles Sumner, and Theodore Parker, Andrew moved easily to the Free Soil Party in 1848 and was an organizer of the Republican Party in 1856. Elected as a Republican state legislator from Boston in 1857, Andrew became prominent as a defender of John Brown. His legal defense efforts led a U.S. Senate committee investigating the Harper's Ferry raid to summon Andrew to Washington. In 1860 he was chairman of the Massachusetts delegation at the Republican Convention in Chicago and was instrumental in switching many votes from Seward to Lincoln. Later that year, Andrew was elected governor by the largest popular majority of the era.

Upon taking office, Governor Andrew obtained an emergency appropriation from the legislature to expand the state militia before the attack on Fort Sumter. Despite Andrew's distrust of the new administration and Secretary of War Simon Cameron, Massachusetts was the first state to respond to Lincoln's call for volunteers in April 1861. The 6th Massachusetts Regiment battled a Baltimore mob on 19 April while boarding trains to defend Washington, D.C. The zealous Andrew became one of the strongest and most effective wartime governors and was reelected to five terms spanning 1861 to 1866.

Perhaps his chief achievement was in persuading Secretary of War Edwin M. Stanton to authorize African-American troops. When enlistments of black troops in Massachusetts proved inadequate, Andrew's agents recruited in other states despite the objections of Stanton, General Ulysses S. Grant, and some governors. By May 1863, the 54th Massachusetts Regiment became the first regular army regiment of black soldiers (led by Colonel Robert Gould Shaw and other white officers) in the Union army. Andrew championed the 178,000 African-American soldiers who served in the Union army when Stanton ruled that they were not entitled to a Federal enlistment bounty and were paid less than white troops. In this imbroglio, the clearsighted Andrew also opposed the War Department's action authorizing Massachusetts general Benjamin F. Butler to recruit six regiments in the New England states (called the Department of New England) while the region's governors recruited troops at the same time with subsequent confusion and expense. When Stanton replaced Cameron in January 1862, Andrew persuaded the War Department to abolish the Department of New England and ended his quarrel with General Butler.

Andrew also defended another despised minority when he adopted a pro-Catholic stance in 1862. By showing his support for Irish Catholic soldiers, he won a following among Catholic and anti-nativist voters. Andrew patiently resolved disputes in the 9th Massachusetts Volunteer Infantry and other Irish units and persuaded the legislature to repeal discriminatory laws aimed at Irish immigrants and passed with Know-Nothing and Republican Party support in 1857–1859. Consequently, Colonel Patrick R. Guiney, commanding the 9th Massachusetts, broke with most Irish Catholics in the state to support Andrew and other Republican candidates.

Governor Andrew encountered other problems from an unexpected quarter, the 20th Massachusetts Volunteer Infantry, dubbed the "Harvard Regiment" because so many officers were Harvard graduates, including Oliver Wendell Holmes, Jr., and the grandson of Paul Revere. The 20th was also labeled the "Copperhead Regiment" because of the antiabolitionist views of many of its Harvard-educated officers even though two of its companies were made up of abolitionist Germans.

In 1865 Andrew honored the 54th Regiment's heroic service at Fort Wagner, South Carolina, on 18 July 1863 by appointing the committee that authorized the Shaw

Memorial unveiled on Boston Common on Decoration Day 1897. This monumental bronze relief of Shaw and his black troops, sculpted by Augustus Saint-Gaudens, was the first significant public celebration of African-American service in the Civil War.

Governor Andrew presided over the first national convention of the Unitarian Church and retired from public office. His farewell address in January 1866 included his support for a lenient reconstruction policy. Returning to his law practice, he continued his interests in temperance, divorce, and usury reforms. But exhausted by the war years, Andrew died suddenly in Boston on 30 October 1867 and was buried at Mount Auburn Cemetery in Cambridge and later interred in Hingham, Massachusetts.

John Andrew's skill in coping with the conflicting demands of Garrisonian abolitionists, pro-war and Copperhead Democrats, African-American leaders, a vigilant local press, the patronage pressures in commissioning officers, the public welfare needs on the home front, and an often inefficient and inconstant War Department is, perhaps, his great legacy.

—*Peter C. Holloran*

See also Butler, Benjamin Franklin; Parker, Theodore; Shaw, Robert Gould; Sumner, Charles.
For further reading:
Chandler, Peleg W. *Memoir of the Hon. John Albion Andrew* (1880).
Hamrogue, John M. "John A. Andrew, Abolitionist Governor, 1861–1865" (Ph.D. dissertation, 1974).
O'Connor, Thomas H. *Civil War Boston: Homefront and Battlefield* (1997).
Pearson, Henry Greenleaf. *The Life of John A. Andrew, Governor of Massachusetts, 1861–1865* (1904).
Samito, Christian G. *Commanding Boston's Irish Ninth: The Civil War Letters of Colonel Patrick R. Guiney, Ninth Massachusetts Volunteer Infantry* (1998).

ANDREWS, GEORGE LEONARD
(1828–1899)
Union general

George Leonard Andrews was born to Manasseh Andrews and Harriet Leonard Andrews in Bridgewater, Massachusetts. He attended the State Normal School at Bridgewater before accepting an appointment to the U.S. Military Academy, from which he graduated first of forty-two in the class of 1851. After commissioning in the Corps of Engineers, Andrews served on the Fort Warren project in Boston and as an instructor at West Point before resigning his commission in 1855. Before the Civil War, he worked as a civil engineer.

At the outbreak of hostilities, Andrews accepted a commission as the lieutenant colonel of the 2d Massachusetts. During the Shenandoah Valley campaign of the spring of 1862, Andrews commanded the 2d under Nathaniel Prentiss Banks. Andrews was promoted to colonel of the regiment on 13 June 1862 and led it at the battles of Cedar Mountain and Antietam. At the latter engagement, the 2d Massachusetts supported Major General Joseph Hooker on the Union right.

On 10 November 1862, Andrews was promoted to brigadier general and assigned to Banks's Louisiana expedition. He was sent by Banks to New York City in December 1862 to prepare the transports for shipment of the army. Upon his arrival in New Orleans in early 1863, Andrews was made Banks's chief of staff.

During the summer of 1863, Andrews participated in the siege and capture of Port Hudson, and upon its surrender on 9 July 1863, Andrews was placed in command. The following day, he was given command of the Corps d'Afrique, a unit of African-American soldiers. At the same time that Andrews was charged with raising this new unit from surrounding plantations, he commanded the District of Baton Rouge and Port Hudson, headquartered at Port Hudson. Until February 1865 he held this command, during which he sent out parties to outlying plantations on and near the Mississippi River to recruit young male slaves for African-American units.

In February 1865 Andrews was relieved from his command at Port Hudson and ordered to report to New Orleans. He was made provost-marshal general of the Army of the Gulf, a position he held until the end of the war. He fought in the Mobile campaign of the spring of 1865, for which he was commended by Major General Edward R. S. Canby.

Andrews was one of the commissioners appointed by Canby in May 1865 to receive the surrender of Lieutenant General Richard Taylor. Andrews became Canby's chief of staff in June and spent the next weeks supervising the paroling of prisoners at Shreveport, Louisiana.

Andrews left the army in August 1865 and spent the next two years as a Mississippi planter. He returned to Massachusetts in 1867 where he worked for several years as a U.S. marshal. He became a professor of French at the U.S. Military Academy in 1871, a position he occupied for over twenty years. He retired to Brookline, Massachusetts, where he died on 4 April 1899. His remains were taken to Arlington National Cemetery for burial.

—*David S. Heidler and Jeanne T. Heidler*

See also African-American Soldiers, C.S.A.; Banks, Nathaniel Prentiss; Mobile Campaign; Port Hudson.
For further reading:
Hollingsworth, Harold M. "George Andrews—Carpetbagger." *Tennessee Historical Quarterly* (1969).

ANDREWS, JAMES
See Andrews's Raid

ANDREWS'S RAID
(12 April 1862)

Both Union and Confederate troops sabotaged railroads to impede enemy supply and troop transport. The Andrews's Raid, popularly known as the "Great Locomotive Chase," was one of the best-known attempts at railroad destruction during the Civil War. The Civil War was the first U.S. war in which railroads were used. Because tracks linked major cities, control of the railroad provided a strategic advantage.

In the spring of 1862, the Confederate defense line stretched from Richmond, Virginia, to Corinth, Mississippi. General Joseph E. Johnston was at Richmond, relying on railroads to connect with forces in the Deep South that were commanded by General P. G. T. Beauregard. The rail line between Richmond and Memphis, passing through east Tennessee, was the quickest route. From Memphis, supplies could be diverted to or received from such major centers as New Orleans, Mobile, Montgomery, Charleston, and Savannah. Union strategists realized that controlling the Tennessee railroad would hinder Confederate troops in Virginia. Brigadier General Ormsby M. Mitchel planned to move Union troops from western Tennessee to the eastern part of the state, expelling Confederates from Chattanooga. From there, he planned to launch an assault against Virginia and defeat the Confederacy. To achieve this, he wanted to damage the rail lines from Atlanta to Chattanooga.

Previously, an effort to destroy the Western & Atlantic Railroad's bridges in Georgia had failed because the operatives did not show up as planned in Atlanta. On 7 April 1862, Mitchel asked James J. Andrews, a furtive character with a mysterious past, to recruit volunteers for a second attempt. Andrews had admirably performed spying missions for General Don Carlos Buell and had also smuggled quinine to Union troops. Mitchel ordered Andrews to steal a train to burn railroad bridges, destroy tracks, and cut telegraph lines along the Georgia State Railroad south of Chattanooga. At the same time, Mitchel planned to secure Huntsville, Alabama, and move east to meet up with Andrews and his men behind Federal lines in Chattanooga. (The Andrews's Raiders are sometimes also referred to as the Mitchel's Raiders.) Twenty-two Ohio soldiers from General Joshua W. Sill's brigade accepted Andrews's invitation. Traveling from Shelbyville, Tennessee, wearing civilian clothes, they walked through rain and mud in small groups to Chattanooga where they boarded a southbound train. By midnight on 11 April, the raiders reached Marietta, Georgia, where they rendezvoused with Andrews. Several of the volunteers were delayed by the weather, and two had been impressed into the Confederate army. The next morning, they bought tickets to Big Shanty (Kennesaw), Georgia, twenty-five miles north of Atlanta. When they arrived, they discovered that a Confederate camp was located by the tracks, a fact that Andrews had been unaware of, and he told his men to proceed cautiously.

While the train's crew and passengers ate breakfast at a restaurant, the Union raiders separated the steam locomotive named the General, the tender, and three boxcars from the train and opened the throttle to leave the station. A Confederate sentry observed the train thieves, but was unsure if they were railroad employees or saboteurs. When he realized that they were stealing the engine, he was unable to notify other stations because Big Shanty did not have a telegraph. Inside the restaurant, the General's conductor, Captain William A. Fuller, and crew heard the train and rushed outside to see the engine departing while Confederate soldiers fired rifles at it. Fuller, engineer Jeff Cain, and shop foreman Anthony Murphy began running after the General, and two miles up the track, they found a handcar. The handcar derailed at a spot where the raiders had broken the rails. Placing the handcar back on the tracks, the train crew reached Etowah, Georgia, where they found the engine Yonah sitting on a siding. The raiders had not stopped to disable the Yonah because they feared it would raise suspicions. While the train crew steamed up the Yonah, the raiders stopped to cut telegraph wires at several places so that any pursuers could not warn stations up the tracks. Andrews had obtained a timetable for the railroad and put the General on a siding at Kingston, Georgia, so that a scheduled southbound express train could pass. However, two more trains arrived that were not listed on the timetable, and an anxious Andrews insisted that he be allowed to pass, stating that he had orders to deliver a trainload of gunpowder to Confederate General P. G. T. Beauregard. When Andrews demanded to know the cause of the delay, the station agent told him that General Mitchel had captured Huntsville and Confederate train traffic had been diverted to the Georgia route.

After sixty-five minutes of waiting, the raiders were permitted to continue. Five minutes later, Fuller and his men were stopped by the three southbound trains. They abandoned the Yonah on a siding and traveled to a junction two miles north of Kingston where they took the engine named William L. Smith, but were halted by broken rails that the raiders had thrown on the tracks. Fuller and Murphy raced on foot, stopping the engine Texas at Adairsville and then pursuing the General in reverse. The raiders released two boxcars to block the Texas. When they tried to burn bridges, the rain-soaked wood refused to catch fire, and they left a boxcar aflame on one bridge. After pushing the boxcars onto a siding, the Texas began a pursuit that reached speeds of sixty miles per hour, with the pursuers catching glimpses of the General. Depleted of wood and water, the General lost steam two miles north of Ringgold, just south of the Tennessee border. The approximately ninety-mile chase ended with the raiders abandoning the General and running into the woods.

Search parties located and captured most of the raiders within days and placed them in jails at Chattanooga and Atlanta. Two raiders floated down the Chattahoochee and Apalachicola rivers to the coast, and others who eluded capture headed north to rejoin their regiments. Andrews and seven men were tried as spies and hanged in Atlanta in June. If they had worn uniforms, they would have been considered prisoners of war. Six raiders were exchanged for Confederate prisoners and were awarded the U.S. Army's first Medal of Honor in March 1863. The remaining raiders, except Andrews, later received Medals of Honor, including posthumous presentations.

The surviving Andrews's Raiders wrote articles and books about their adventures, attended anniversary celebrations of the raid, and were honored guests at Grand Army of the Republic conventions. The General was displayed at the 1888 national grand encampment in Columbus, Ohio. The Confederate pursuers joined the raiders to speak to audiences about the chase. In May 1891, several raiders also attended dedication services for the Ohio Monument at the National Cemetery in Chattanooga. Topped by a bronze replica of the General, the monument was placed next to the graves of the executed raiders. Historical markers were placed at significant Andrews's Raid sites in Tennessee and Georgia. In April 1962, a steam engine reenacted the chase for the Civil War Centennial, and President John F. Kennedy hosted ceremonies at the White House for the raiders' descendants. The General toured the United States before being housed at the Big Shanty Museum in Kennesaw. The Texas was displayed in the lobby of the Atlanta Cyclorama. Embellished as a folk legend, the Andrews's Raid was the subject of books and movies, including Walt Disney's *The Great Locomotive Chase* (1956).

—*Elizabeth D. Schafer*

See also Covert Activities, C.S.A.; Espionage; Railroads, C.S.A.; Railroads, U.S.A..

For further reading:
Epstein, Samuel, and Beryl Epstein. *The Andrews Raid or the Great Locomotive Chase April 12, 1862* (1956).
Gregg, Frank M. *Andrews Raiders* (1891).
O'Neill, Charles. *Wild Train: The Story of the Andrews Raiders* (1956).
Pittenger, William. *Daring and Suffering: A History of the Great Railroad Adventure* (1863).
Wilson, John A. *Adventures of Alf. Wilson: A Thrilling Episode of the Dark Days of the Rebellion* (1897).

"ANNALS OF THE WAR"

Considered by many historians to be one of the finest postwar series of recollections by veterans of the Civil War, the "Annals of the War" was the brainchild of Philadelphia journalist Alexander K. McClure. An active Republican politician, McClure owned the Philadelphia *Times*, a daily paper in the city. To increase circulation, McClure contacted Civil War generals and civilian leaders and asked them to contribute to a series about the war that he wished to publish in a new paper.

The new paper, the Philadelphia *Weekly Times*, began publication on 3 March 1877. Each weekly issue featured the series "Annals of the War" on the front page. The first issue included an article written by Gideon Welles entitled "The First Ironclad." Contributors from the Union side included James H. Wilson, William B. Franklin, Andrew A. Humphreys, Samuel W. Crawford, Noble D. Preston, and David H. Strother. To balance the perspectives, McClure made sure that former Confederates wrote articles for the Annals. These men included John E. Cooke, Henry B. McClellan, Armistead L. Long, James Longstreet, Walter H. Taylor, Henry Heth, and John H. Reagan.

Subjects included the controversies surrounding the battle of Gettysburg, the fighting at Bristoe Station, the Knoxville campaign, Chancellorsville, Second Manassas, Petersburg, and a wide array of other battles and campaigns. Some writers delved into the subject of blacks in Confederate armies; others wrote of amazing adventures of scouts behind the lines. Boston Corbett wrote of the death of John Wilkes Booth, and Matoaca Gay penned a short piece about social life in Richmond during the war.

In 1879, McClure published a hardbound book that contained fifty-five of the articles included thus far in the series. The series continued to attract a wide reading audience but a planned second volume was never published. "Annals of the War" finally ground to a halt in 1888. The entire series included more than 800 contributions, ranging in size from an entire page to a single column. The series proved to be a valuable contribution to the history of the Civil War as seen by men and women who took part in this great epic of U.S. history.

—*Richard A. Sauers*

See also National Tribune.
For further reading:
McClure, Alexander K., ed. *The Annals of the War Written by Leading Participants North and South* (1879; reprint 1994).

ANTHONY, SUSAN BROWNELL
(1820–1906)

Abolitionist; suffragist

Susan Brownell Anthony was born in Adams, Massachusetts, the daughter of Daniel and Lucy Anthony. Anthony's early career was as a schoolteacher, but when she left home in 1852 to run her family's farm in Center Falls, New York, she became interested in the temperance, antislavery, and women's rights movements. Anthony met Elizabeth Cady Stanton in 1851, a meeting that began a close working and personal relationship that would last for both their lives. Anthony attended her first women's rights convention in 1852 in Syracuse, New York, and threw herself into her work as a reformer for the rest of the 1850s.

Beginning in 1856, she lectured for the American Anti-Slavery Society throughout New York state and in January 1861, with tensions over slavery and the sectional conflict mounting, she was mobbed when speaking in Albany and Buffalo. Anthony's continued commitment was clear when she wrote Martha Coffin Wright, reformer and sister of Lucretia Mott, "There was a more determined union to put down a speech, not to the mind of the masses—but we must face it through."

Anthony and other women's rights supporters halted their conventions for the duration of the Civil War, but remained interested in the abolition of slavery. Disappointed with the limited nature of President Lincoln's Emancipation Proclamation, Anthony founded the Women's National Loyal League with Stanton on 14 May 1863 in New York City. Anthony served as the secretary, while Stanton held the office of president. The goals of the League were to collect a million signatures on a petition calling for the abolition of slavery throughout the United States, a petition that they later revised to call for a constitutional amendment: "believing slavery the great cause of the present rebellion, and an institution fatal to the life of Republican government, earnestly pray your honorable bodies to immediately abolish it throughout the United states; and to adopt measures for so amending the Constitution, as forever to prohibit its existence in any portion of our common country." The League collected 400,000 signatures by the summer of 1864. Anthony also opposed Lincoln's reelection in 1864, supporting the more avowedly antislavery candidate, John C. Frémont.

After the war, Anthony continued her agitation on behalf of rights for women and African-Americans, joining the American Equal Rights Association. In 1867 she and Stanton headed to Kansas, where both women's and African-American suffrage were to be put to a referendum. Anthony and Stanton could not gain the support of the Republican Party or their fellow abolitionists in agitating for the passage of the women's suffrage referendum. The relationship between Stanton and Anthony and the Equal Rights Association grew worse in 1869, when the Association endorsed the Fifteenth Amendment, even though it did not include a provision for women's suffrage. Stanton and Anthony broke with the Association to form the National Woman Suffrage Association later that year.

In 1870 financial woes forced Anthony to give up the *Revolution*, the paper she, Stanton, and George Francis Train began after the Kansas campaign. Anthony embarked on a lecture tour until 1876 to pay off debts

from this paper. She also continued her work for the National Woman Suffrage Association, campaigning for a federal amendment for women's suffrage and aiding state campaigns. With Stanton and Matilda Joslyn Gage, she compiled the multivolume *History of Woman Suffrage*, published between 1881 and 1885.

When the divided women's rights movement reunited in 1890 to form the National American Woman Suffrage Association, Anthony served first as vice president and then in 1892 she began a term as president that lasted until 1900. Anthony also worked throughout her career on behalf of working women's rights and coeducation. When she moved permanently to Rochester, New York, in 1890, she became a trustee of the State Industrial School and encouraged the University of Rochester to admit women. Anthony became the most famous nineteenth-century suffragist. Though criticized and mocked early in her career for lacking the charm or oratorical ability of Elizabeth Cady Stanton, she was much admired at the time of her death for her devotion to the cause of women's rights.

—*Carol Faulkner*

See also African-American Suffrage; Election of 1864; Frémont, John C.; Mott, Lucretia; Stanton, Elizabeth Cady.
For further reading:

Anthony, Susan B., Matilda Joslyn Gage, and Elizabeth Cady Stanton, eds. *A History of Woman Suffrage* (1970).
DuBois, Ellen Carol. *Feminism and Suffrage: The Emergence of an Independent Women's Movement in America 1848–1861* (1978).
Gordon, Ann D. *The Selected Papers of Elizabeth Cady Stanton and Susan B. Anthony: In the School of Anti-Slavery 1840–1866* (1997).
Sherr, Lynn. *Failure Is Impossible: Susan B. Anthony in Her Own Words* (1996).
Venet, Wendy Hamand. *Neither Ballots nor Bullets: Women Abolitionists and the Civil War* (1991).

ANTIETAM, BATTLE OF
(17 September 1862)

The battle of Antietam, outside Sharpsburg, Maryland, on 17 September 1862, was America's bloodiest day. Combined, Union and Confederate soldiers inflicted upon one another 22,719 casualties: 12,401 for Major General George McClellan's Army of the Potomac and 10,318 for General Robert E. Lee's Army of Northern Virginia. Although his forces were vastly superior in numbers, General McClellan spent the days both before and after the battle convinced that Lee possessed unseen divisions that awaited any false step. The result at Antietam, as at the battle of South Mountain, was that McClellan never committed his forces thoroughly to the fight. Rather than attack Lee's positions simultaneously, he fought them piecemeal. Reserve troops, numbering some 20,000, were kept out of the fight to meet these phantom divisions of

Confederate soldiers. While McClellan lacked resolve during the battle, Lee had resolve to spare, so much so that historians question the wisdom of giving battle in the first place. With but one means of escape, Lee stood ground against an army he knew to be vastly superior in size to his own.

Even contemporaries, however, understood that the meaning of the battle was somehow more than could be gleaned from the wisdom or folly of the commanders on that day. For the troops who fought, Antietam was the place that invested everyday names like "the cornfield" or "the west woods" with images of battlefield chaos and horror. In October, Mathew Brady opened his exhibition of photographs entitled "The Dead of Antietam" in New York City. A writer for the *New York Times* noted, "Mr. Brady has done something to bring home to us the terrible reality and earnestness of war. If he has not brought bodies and laid them in our door-yards and along the streets, he has done something very like it…."

Lee's army had crossed into Maryland just ten days earlier, beset by straggling and relegated to a diet of green apples and raw corn. Confederate leaders believed that a major victory, in the wake of the battle of Second Bull Run and occurring on Northern soil, might convince Britain and France to recognize Confederate independence. Continued victories might also encourage Northern voters to reject Republican candidates in favor of peace Democrats during the fall congressional elections. There were important tactical reasons as well. By taking the fight to the North, Lee was able to provision his troops from a region untouched by the war and guarantee that any battles would scar Northern farms rather than Southern ones. If he were successful at severing rail lines at Harper's Ferry and Harrisburg, the eastern states would be cut off from their western counterparts, at least temporarily. Finally, Confederate leaders—both political and military—wanted to boost Southern morale by going on the offensive. It is sometimes also argued that Lee also hoped to raise the rebellion in western Maryland. Confederate troops sang "Maryland, My Maryland" as they crossed the Potomac River, and Lee pointedly encouraged Marylanders to throw off their

Middle Bridge, photographed shortly after the battle (Photograph by Alexander Gardner / *Library of Congress*)

Hagerstown

LONGSTREET

SOUTH MOUNTAIN

CATOCTIN MOUNTAIN

Antietam Creek

Monocacy River

M A R Y L A N D

Turner's Gap

Martinsburg

Sharpsburg

McLAWS

Frederick

14 September

Cooksville

11–12 September

Crampton's Gap

JACKSON

Damascus

Harper's Ferry

13–15 September

Brookeville

WALKER

McCLELLAN

Leesburg

White's Ferry

Rockville

4–5 September

LEE

V I R G I N I A

Shenandoah River

Washington

STUART

Potomac River

1 September

Chantilly

**THE ANTIETAM
CAMPAIGN
SEPTEMBER 1862**

29–30 August

Manassas Junction

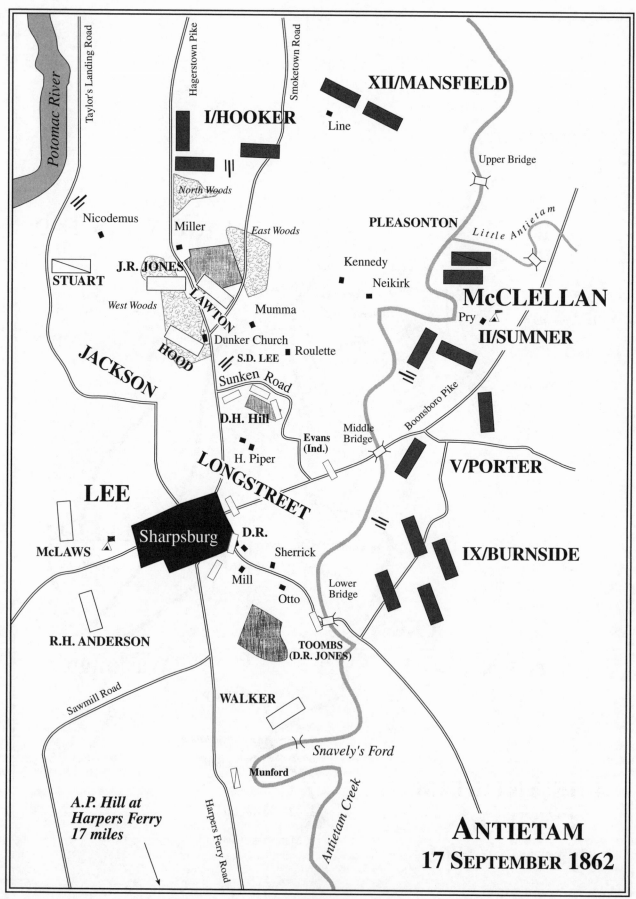

Potomac River

Taylor's Landing Road

Hagerstown Pike

Smoketown Road

XII/MANSFIELD

I/HOOKER

Line

North Woods

Upper Bridge

Nicodemus

Miller

East Woods

PLEASONTON

Little Antietam

J.R. JONES

Kennedy

Neikirk

STUART

LAWTON

West Woods

Mumma

McCLELLAN

JACKSON

HOOD

Dunker Church

Roulette

Pry

II/SUMNER

S.D. LEE

Sunken Road

Boonsboro Pike

D.H. HILL

Evans (Ind.)

Middle Bridge

H. Piper

LONGSTREET

V/PORTER

LEE

Sharpsburg

D.R.

Sherrick

McLAWS

Mill

Otto

Lower Bridge

IX/BURNSIDE

R.H. ANDERSON

TOOMBS (D.R. JONES)

Sawmill Road

WALKER

Snavely's Ford

A.P. Hill at Harpers Ferry 17 miles

Munford

Harpers Ferry Road

Antietam Creek

ANTIETAM 17 SEPTEMBER 1862

Confederate dead along the Hagerstown road (Photograph by Alexander Gardner / *Library of Congress*)

"foreign yoke." Privately, however, Lee reported to Confederate president Jefferson Davis that western Maryland farmers would not fight to support slave-holding states because they had no slaves themselves. Unbeknown to Lee and Davis, President Abraham Lincoln awaited a Union victory to issue his proclamation freeing all slaves in the Confederacy if Southern states did not return to the Union by the end of the year.

The battle of Antietam was the result of a chain of circumstance that began shortly after Lee's 43,000 troops entered Maryland. Having detached troops under Major General T. J. "Stonewall" Jackson, Major General Lafayette McLaws, and Brigadier General John G. Walker to subdue the Federal garrison at Harper's Ferry, Lee accompanied the remainder under Major General James Longstreet and Major General D. H. Hill to capture Boonsboro. These plans were detailed in Special Order 191, dated on 9 September, calling for all forces to converge on Harper's Ferry and Boonsboro several days later. On 13 September in a field outside Frederick, two Indiana soldiers discovered a copy of those orders, reportedly wrapped around three cigars. The discovery of Lee's plans allowed McClellan to pursue the Confederate force, which was already a day behind its plans. At the battle of South Mountain on 14 September, Lee's forces fought a delaying action that allowed him to entrench his forces outside Sharpsburg.

Meanwhile, the Harper's Ferry garrison—more than 12,000 Federal troops—surrendered the following day under the punishing fire from the surrounding hills.

The stage was set for the battle of Antietam as Lee entrenched his troops in a bend of the Potomac River between the town of Sharpsburg and Antietam Creek. The creek and the ridges surrounding it provided a strong natural fortification. Three bridges—the Upper, Middle, and Rohrbach's (later known as Burnside's)—spanned the creek. On the 15th, 70,000 Federal troops arrived, taking positions opposite the ridge fortified by Lee. Although D. H. Hill, Longstreet, and Jackson (who had marched directly from Harper's Ferry) could field only 26,000 troops, McClellan estimated Lee's Army of Northern Virginia at 120,000 troops total. On the 16th, the forces exchanged artillery fire while McClellan, in his customarily cautious fashion, surveyed the terrain and planned the battle for the following day. McClellan himself later recounted more than one version of his battle plans, so it is impossible to know how far the events of the 17th deviated from his plan. One thing is certain: McClellan intended the first blow to fall on the Confederate left.

Late in the afternoon on the 16th, McClellan sent Major General Joseph Hooker's I Corps of 8,600 men across the Antietam via the Upper Bridge. From there they swung north, bivouacking near the Hagerstown turnpike in preparation for a dawn assault on the Confederate left. Around midnight, Major General Joseph K. F. Mansfield's XII Corps followed Hooker, establishing a position from which he could support the I Corps on the following day. These moves did not go unnoticed; overnight Lee reinforced his left, bringing its strength to 7,700 men. Thus McClellan's forces allowed Lee precious time to amass his forces to receive the blow.

The battle of Antietam occurred in three stages on 17 September as McClellan sent his troops in successive attacks against the Confederate left, center, and right. Beginning at dawn, Hooker's troops advanced toward their objectives, crossing the Hagerstown turnpike and seizing the plateau upon which sat a whitewashed church belonging to a German Baptist sect known locally as the Dunkers. In Hooker's plan of attack, Brigadier General Abner Doubleday's 1st Division would march south on the turnpike while Brigadier General James B. Ricketts's 2d Division would advance through the East Woods and the Miller farm's thirty-acre cornfield. Brigadier General George G. Meade's 3d Division would form the center, providing support for Doubleday and Ricketts while advancing through the East Woods. To meet the Federal force, Stonewall Jackson had spread two divisions under Brigadier General Alexander R. Lawton and Brigadier General John R. Jones from the West Woods across the turnpike, running just south of the Miller cornfield to the Mumma farm. Four reserve brigades waited inside the West Woods to stage a counterattack. Confederate artillery near the Dunker Church and on Nicodemus Hill, flanking the approach along the turnpike, completed Jackson's preparations.

At dawn, Meade's 1st Brigade of Pennsylvanians under Brigadier General Truman Seymour began to advance through the East Woods, exchanging fire with Colonel James A. Walker's brigade of Alabama, Georgia, and North Carolina troops. No sooner had Walker's men forced back their opponents than the first of Ricketts's infantry advanced into Miller's field. Confederate artillery directed by Colonel Stephen Lee near the Dunker Church inflicted heavy casualties on the advancing troops. Around 6:00 A.M., Brigadier General Abram Duryea's brigade (the 97th, 104th, and 105th New York and the 107th Pennsylvania) marched through the standing corn directly into volleys from Colonel Marcellus Douglass's brigade of the 13th, 26th, 31st, 38th, 60th, and 61st Georgia Regiments. Firing upon one another at a range of 250 yards, both sides were so badly mauled that the firing simply stopped with neither side achieving an advantage. Some of Walker's troops, the 12th and 21st Georgia as well as the 21st North Carolina, managed to find a position from which to put Duryea's forces under flanking fire, but only at the cost of receiving fire from Meade's men in the East Woods. Duryea had endured enough, however. When

reinforcements failed to materialize, he ordered his troops to withdraw back through the cornfield.

Those reinforcements, brigades under Brigadier General George L. Hartstuff and Colonel William A. Christian, advanced haphazardly. A shell wounded Hartstuff while Christian fled the line in terror. Colonel Richard Coulter rallied Hartstuff's men, but they emerged from the East Woods and the cornfield into the same fire as previous troops had encountered with the added hazard that Colonel Lee's artillery had ranged the field in the previous engagement. Despite their losses, Federal forces outnumbered their opponents, whose line began to buckle. Lawton then threw in Brigadier General Harry T. Hays's Louisiana "Tiger" brigade, forcing the Federals back to the East Woods and inflicting on the 12th Massachusetts 67 percent casualties, the highest casualty rate of any unit that day.

Brigadier General John Gibbon's 4th Brigade in Doubleday's division advanced down the turnpike, pushing Jackson's men east of the turnpike back behind the edge of the cornfield. Troops from the 7th Wisconsin and the 19th Indiana crossed the turnpike and advanced toward the West Woods. Yet as his remaining regiments, the 6th and 7th Wisconsin, cleared the edge of the cornfield, they came under a withering fire from Rebels that had been concealed in a pasture. The Federal advance was completely halted, however, by a charge of 1,150 troops under Brigadier General William E. Starke from the West Woods. By taking up positions just west of the turnpike, Starke's troops could fire upon Doubleday's men easily but were themselves exposed. After Starke was mortally wounded, his forces withdrew.

Fortunately for Confederate forces, two divisions under Major General Lafayette McLaws and Major General Robert H. Anderson arrived just after 7:00 A.M., having completed a night march from Harper's Ferry. Around 7:15, Lee then ordered Colonel George T. Anderson to move his Georgia brigade from the army's right to reinforce Jackson's left. For Hooker's men, the battle on the Confederate left was proceeding at great cost, but still forcing Jackson's corps backward slowly. At 7:00 A.M., Brigadier General John Bell Hood's division of 2,300 men advanced through the West Woods, gathered other Confederate troops, and pushed Federal forces back through the cornfield again. The assault cost Hood's units dearly: 60 percent were casualties, but the dramatic charge prevented Confederate lines from rupturing. Two hours and 2,500 casualties later, Hooker's troops were back where they had begun. Of the cornfield, later Hooker wrote that "every stalk in the northern and greater part of the field was cut as closely as could have been done with a knife."

Hooker called for support from Mansfield's XII Corps of 7,200 men to support his retreating line. Hood had

Bodies of Confederate dead gathered for burial (Photograph by Alexander Gardner / *Library of Congress*)

also called for reinforcement during his advance, but none arrived in time to secure his position. When later asked where his troops were, Hood replied, "Dead on the field." Brigadier General Roswell S. Ripley's brigade did shift from the Confederate center in time to prevent a complete rout. Hood's forces, uniting with Ripley's, formed a new line, one that was quickly reinforced when D. H. Hill sent two additional divisions under Brigadier General Alfred H. Colquitt and Colonel D. K. McRae to their assistance. Together, these troops were more than a match for Mansfield's 1st Division, half of whom were new recruits. Mansfield himself was mortally wounded in one exchange, leaving command of the corps to Brigadier General Alpheus S. Williams. McRae's men, however, broke under the advance of Brigadier General George Sears Greene's 2d Division on their flank. Hill worked frantically to pull his men back through the cornfield before they were overrun. Hood did the same. Outnumbered, they regrouped in the West Woods, where they had begun the day.

The assault on the Confederate left began to lurch into the center after Hill committed McRae and Colquitt's troops to the battle. Major General Edwin V.

Sumner received the order to send two of his divisions into battle at 7:20 A.M., when word of Hood's counterattack reached McClellan. Major General John Sedgwick's 2d Division led the way, fording Antietam Creek between the Upper and Middle bridges. On the battlefield, Williams's XII Corps was stretched by then from the West Woods across the road to the East Woods. Sumner led Sedgwick's men through the East Wood with all intention of crossing the turnpike, turning left, and forcing Confederate troops into the Union right wing of Major General Ambrose Burnside's IX Corps. But Sumner's lead division advanced without Brigadier General William H. French's 3d Division, which had become separated at the East Woods. Having lost contact with Sumner, French ordered his men to reinforce the XII Corps troops around the East Woods, while Sedgwick's men advanced alone.

Sumner's incautious plan—he apparently failed to gather sufficient intelligence on the field from I and XII Corps commanders—led his troops to disaster. Marching in three parallel lines across what Sumner assumed was clear ground, Sedgwick's 5,400 men were exposed to a flanking attack from their left shortly after

Mass burial of Confederate dead in a rifle pit (Photograph by Alexander Gardner / *Library of Congress*)

9:00 A.M. First, Major John Pelham's Virginia horse artillery commenced fire on the advancing soldiers from behind the West Woods. Jackson then seized the opportunity that Sumner presented to him. With 3,000 troops of McLaws's division joining the 1,400 remaining troops of Brigadier General Jubal A. Early's Virginia brigade and Brigadier General Maxcy Gregg's South Carolina brigade, rebel soldiers slammed into the left and rear of Sedgwick's division, scattering some of his men back across the turnpike while cornering the rest in the West Woods. Finding themselves under fire from three directions, those troops trapped in the woods beat a retreat to the north. Even so, another flanking attack by Brigadier General Paul J. Semmes's Georgia and Virginia troops from the west, as well as continued artillery fire, introduced a sense of sheer panic into the retreating Federal forces. At the North Woods, however, I Corps troops and artillery stopped the Confederate advance, but all ground gained west of the turnpike that day had been lost.

Both sides took this chance to reinforce their troops and renew the offensive. Brigadier General Alpheus S. Williams, now in command of the XII Corps, sent the 2d Massachusetts and the 13th New Jersey into the fray. Lee had earlier ordered Brigadier General John G. Walker's division, composed primarily of North Carolina soldiers, from the Confederate right to reinforce Jackson and McLaws. These new forces clashed around 10:00 A.M. in the area between the cornfield and the West Woods, but shortly thereafter Walker's men were forced backward by two brigades of Brigadier General George S. Greene's 2d Division. Again, Federal troops surged forward, seizing ground in the West Woods.

Meanwhile, as Sumner directed Sedgwick's division on the Federal right, French's division, unable to locate Sumner and Sedgwick, had taken up positions facing the Rebel center. With Greene's men on his right, and Major General Israel B. Richardson's 1st Division of Sumner's corps on his left, French confronted Major General D. H. Hill's men entrenched in a sunken road that branched

Unburied dead near the Dunker church (Photograph by Alexander Gardner / *Library of Congress*)

off the Hagerstown turnpike. Hill commanded roughly 2,500 men, less than half the number of French's forces, but Hill's men were concealed in the sunken road, ready to fire down a gradual ridge at any advancing Federal troops. The first Federal brigade to approach—the 1st Delaware, 5th Maryland, and 4th New York—were cut down. The second, composed of the 14th Connecticut, 108th New York, and 130th Pennsylvania, came under heavy fire as well, but beat off a counterattack by the Alabama brigade of Brigadier General Robert E. Rodes. The third brigade—the 8th Ohio, 14th Indiana, and 7th West Virginia—advanced only to meet the same hail of fire directed from the sunken road. Of French's 5,700 men, 1,750 became casualties in less than an hour.

Richardson's division, numbering 4,000 men, was ordered forward to continue the assault on the Confederate center. For his part, Lee sent his final

reserve of Major General Richard H. Anderson's division, some 3,400 men, to reinforce Hill. Richardson's first assault, that of Brigadier General Thomas F. Meagher's "Irish Brigade" and the 29th Massachusetts, met the same fate as the previous three attempts. A fatal error by Confederate troops on the right of the sunken road then transformed their defensive haven into a shooting gallery. Richardson's second brigade, under Brigadier General John C. Caldwell, began a gradual flanking move on the sunken road position that, at that point, was swollen with reinforcements. As Colonel Carnot Posey ordered his Mississippi troops to fall back to ease the overcrowding on the right of the line, others sensed in this movement the beginnings of a general retreat. A similar disaster occurred on the left-hand side of the sunken road. Lieutenant Colonel J. N. Lightfoot of the 6th Alabama misinterpreted an order for his own troops to shift position and relayed an order of withdrawal throughout Rodes's command. The remaining Confederate troops were then exposed to fire from three directions, transforming the sunken road into "Bloody Lane." Those who could escape the trench fled headlong toward Sharpsburg, but many were cut down before they had the chance.

Elsewhere on the battlefield, Federal troops under George Sears Greene that had seized ground near the Dunker Church advanced, unaware that Sedgwick's division, which Greene assumed was protecting his right, had been routed earlier. Suddenly, the 49th North Carolina appeared on Greene's right, while a counterattack planned by Longstreet to relieve the pressure on Hill caught him unawares on the left. Longstreet's relief force, a composite command of 675 men under Colonel John R. Cooke, helped to scatter Greene's men back across the turnpike and then staged a counterattack against Federal troops in the center. This effort failed, but Cooke's men easily repelled an ill-conceived charge toward the Dunker Church by Colonel William H. Irwin's brigade of New York and Maine troops from VI Corps. Still outnumbered, the collapse of the center was stemmed by Hill himself, who led one brief counterattack of perhaps 200 men. These battles in and around Bloody Lane cost the Confederate command 2,600 casualties. Although the assaults by Cooke and Hill provided time for artillery units to seal the breech in the line, the remaining troops were scattered and disorganized. Had further pressure from the Federals been forthcoming, the line would have broken.

The only portent of battle on the Confederate right was the exchange of artillery and skirmishing fire between Burnside's IX Corps and Longstreet's troops. Confederate infantry was positioned on the opposite side of Rohrbach's Bridge, a triple-arched, stone bridge over Antietam Creek. From their position, they could shoot down the ridge at any forces trying to cross the river. Burnside's orders were to cross the creek, capture Sharpsburg, and seize the only serviceable ford (Boteler's) across the Potomac available to Lee's troops if they were forced to retreat. The defenses had been staffed at dawn by the divisions of Brigadier General David R. Jones and Brigadier General John G. Walker. Yet by 10:00 A.M., when Burnside finally received the order to advance, Lee had already pulled out all of Walker's men and Colonel George T. Anderson's Georgia brigade to reinforce other positions. When the attack finally came, Jones had but 3,000 men of whom the 400 men of the 2d and 20th Georgia in the command of Brigadier General Robert Toombs defended Rohrbach's Bridge itself. The opposing force, Burnside's corps of 12,500 infantry, outnumbered their adversaries, but suffered disadvantages due to the terrain. The road approaching the bridge ran parallel to Antietam Creek;

thus forces approaching by the clearest path were exposed to the greatest fire.

Around 10:00 A.M., Burnside and Brigadier Jacob D. Cox received the order to advance. Colonel Henry W. Kingsbury's 11th Connecticut Regiment led the way to provide covering fire for the advance of Colonel George Crook's Ohio brigade of the Kanawha division. This attack failed as advancing troops were picked off from the opposite shore. Meanwhile, Brigadier General Isaac P. Rodman's 3d Division, plus the remaining Kanawha brigade of Ohioans, struggled downstream through thick brush in search of Snavely's Ford, by which they hoped to outflank Jones's position. The ford, however, was difficult to locate; it proved to be two miles downstream. A second assault directed at the bridge by one of Brigadier General Samuel D. Sturgis's brigades, led by the 2d Maryland and 6th New Hampshire, was cut down by Confederate rifle and artillery fire. Finally Cox ordered Sturgis's other brigade under Brigadier General Edward Ferrero to charge directly downhill to take the bridge. At 12:30 P.M., the 51st New York and 51st Pennsylvania plunged downhill toward the bridge, taking up positions on the east side. The Georgia troops opposite, now running low on ammunition, yielded just enough ground for the two Federal regiments to charge across the bridge. Shortly after 1:00 P.M., Burnside's forces, including Rodman's division, converged on the west side of what after the battle was known as Burnside's Bridge.

At this point, a dispute between Sumner and Major General William B. Franklin occurred about whether to press the attack against Hill's troops in the Confederate center. Franklin had arrived on the scene with five brigades of his VI Corps, eager to join Sumner's troops in a final assault. Sumner refused, arguing that his troops were already too close to the breaking point. When McClellan sent a courier with a message suggesting he pursue the attack, an exasperated Sumner replied, "Go back, young man, and tell General McClellan I have no command! Tell him my command, Banks' command, and Hooker's command are all cut up and demoralized. Tell him General Franklin has the only organized command on this part of the field." After reviewing the situation, McClellan sided with Sumner, and the attack was postponed.

Lee, on the other hand, had asked Stonewall Jackson around noon to fashion a counterattack that would relieve the pressure on the center. Jackson planned a two-prong attack in which 5,000 infantry and cavalry under Major General J. E. B. Stuart would try to outflank the right wing of McClellan's forces while the 48th North Carolina from John G. Walker's division would push forward from the West Woods. This effort failed to achieve Jackson's objective of unraveling the Federal right wing because Federal I Corps batteries heavily

Soldiers at Antietam, September 1862 (*Library of Congress*)

outgunned Stuart's artillery. After a two-hour delay in bringing ammunition and supporting troops across the bridge, 8,000 troops from Burnside's IX Corps at 3:00 P.M. advanced on the remnants of Jones's men, now numbering perhaps 2,800. The Federal plan was to outflank the weakened Confederate right and cut Lee off from Boteler's Ford. Outnumbered, Jones's forces were slowly pushed backward despite the assistance of artillery that poured rounds into the advancing Union troops. Colonel Harrison S. Fairchild's brigade of New York soldiers pushed all the way to the outskirts of Sharpsburg, whereupon the Army of Northern Virginia received a reprieve from certain defeat.

Having left Harper's Ferry at 6:30 A.M., A. P. Hill arrived with 3,000 troops after a punishing seventeen-mile march. Hill's troops, some wearing captured Federal uniforms from the Harper's Ferry garrison, slammed into the 16th Connecticut on Burnside's left shortly after 3:30 P.M. These troops were part of Colonel Edward Harland's brigade, like Fairchild's, a part of Rodman's division. Having demolished that force, Hill's men then dispatched the 4th Rhode Island and Colonel Hugh Ewing's brigade of Ohio soldiers from the Kanawha division in fierce fighting near the Otto family cornfield. The sudden pressure on their flank forced Burnside's men (including those that had begun to enter

Lincoln visits the Antietam battlefield, 3 October 1862 (Photograph by Alexander Gardner / *Library of Congress*)

Sharpsburg) to retreat from the pursuit of Confederates under the command of A. P. Hill, Toombs, and Longstreet. Federal troops finally regrouped on a ridge with their backs to Antietam Creek. The third stage of the battle was complete.

On the morning of 18 September, Lee's battered forces were drawn up, prepared to meet a Federal offensive that never came. Throughout the night of the 17th, both sides had tended to their wounded, but nothing could be done for those trapped between the lines. Many survivors remembered the cries of agony that punctuated the night. On the 18th, an improvised truce held while the two sides exchanged their wounded and began the ghastly task of burying the dead. Outside the makeshift field hospitals, rows of bodies grew steadily throughout the day, but a more macabre sight were the burial pits given over solely to the amputated limbs of the wounded. By afternoon, Lee had given orders to fall back across the Potomac under cover of night. To the occasional and improvised refrain of "Damn My Maryland," the Army of Northern Virginia departed.

McClellan's men suffered 12,401 casualties, including 2,108 dead, 9,540 wounded, and 753 missing. Lee's men lost 10,318, including 1,546 dead, 7,752 wounded, and 1,108 missing. According to historian Stephen Sears, these figures amount to 25 percent of the overall Federal force and 31 percent of the Confederate. On no day before or since have U.S. military forces fallen in such numbers.

At the battle of Antietam, Union and Confederate forces fought to a tactical draw because Lee's line outside Sharpsburg held. McClellan never delivered the final blow that would have scattered Confederate troops into the Potomac. Later, Generals Burnside and Cox both testified before a congressional committee that Burnside had offered to take the remaining troops of IX Corps (numbering roughly 9,000–9,500) and attack the Confederate right at dawn on the 18th if McClellan could supply an additional 5,000 men. These numbers could have been drawn from I, II, and XII Corps troops that had fought the previous day or from V and VI Corps that had seen little action. Sears estimates that the I, II, IX, and XII Corps combined had approximately 30,000 infantrymen available on the morning of the 18th. Another 20,300 were available from V and VI Corps because only one brigade of twelve had seen significant action the day before. In addition, the 1st Division of IV Corps, under Major General Darius N. Couch, arrived midday on the 18th from Crampton's Gap, bringing an additional 6,000 experienced troops. Earlier that morning, Brigadier Andrew A. Humphreys had also arrived with 6,000 newly recruited Pennsylvania troops for V Corps. All told, McClellan commanded 50,000 combat-ready soldiers at dawn with an additional 12,000 arriving by the middle of the day, yet no attempt was made to assault Lee's battered line.

McClellan's failure to pursue his numerical advantage is often ascribed to his continued belief in Lee's phantom reserve. McClellan had significant battlefield advantages that make his hesitation incomprehensible. The natural barrier of Antietam Creek no longer protected the Confederate right. Moreover, Lee's line had been pushed back so far that he risked catastrophe; if Lee's position was overrun, McClellan's forces could threaten his only escape at Boteler's Ford long before his troops could retreat across the Potomac. Lee's decision to remain in Maryland, courting absolute disaster not just for the Army of Northern Virginia but for the Confederacy itself, is similarly inexplicable.

For more than a month, from 17 September to 26 October, McClellan declined to pursue Lee across the Potomac. Urged on by prodding from both Major General Henry W. Halleck, general-in-chief of the U.S. Army, and President Abraham Lincoln, McClellan dithered, citing shortages of equipment and the fear of overextending his forces. In his official report on the Maryland campaign, Halleck wrote, "The long inactivity of so large an army in the face of a defeated foe, and during the most favorable season for rapid movements and a vigorous campaign, was a matter of great disappointment and regret." For McClellan, however, Antietam was his greatest victory. That the Army of Northern Virginia escaped his grasp McClellan attributed to the cowardly surrender of the Harper's Ferry garrison. Had Federal forces there held out one day longer, McClellan wrote in his official report of 15 October, he could have captured the Confederates that had seized Maryland Heights above the town, preventing the garrison's surrender. Thereby he would have been able to tie up the Confederate troops besieging the town from Loudoun and Bolivar Heights. "I would have had," he wrote, "35,000 or 40,000 less men to encounter at Antietam, and must have captured or destroyed all opposed to me. As it was, I had to engage an army fresh from a recent and to them a great victory, and to reap the disadvantages of their being freshly and plentifully supplied with ammunition and supplies." Having

inflated his opponent's numbers, McClellan similarly inflated the casualties inflicted by his men, reporting to Halleck that he had inflicted some 30,000 casualties, nearly three times those suffered by Lee's forces at Antietam. In November, McClellan was relieved of command by Halleck and Secretary of War Edwin Stanton in favor of Ambrose Burnside.

The battle of Antietam was, however, a tremendous strategic success for the Union army. The battle had cost the Union army dearly, and Confederate forces more so. McClellan had inadvertently demonstrated that the path to strategic victory would not lie solely in brilliant tactics or battlefield heroism, but in the slow attrition of men that the more populous North could afford but the South could not. On 23 September, Lincoln published his Emancipation Proclamation, threatening to abolish slavery in all areas loyal to the Confederacy. Antietam, then, became the moment when the "war between the states" became "a battle for freedom."

—*Robert S. Wolff*

See also Emancipation Proclamation; Gaines's Mill, Battle of; Lee, Robert E.; Maryland; McClellan, George B.; South Mountain, Battle of.

For further reading:
Foote, Shelby. *The Civil War: A Narrative. Fort Sumter to Perryville* (1958).
Frassanito, William A. *Antietam: The Photographic Legacy of America's Bloodiest Day* (1978).
Gallagher, Gary W., ed. *Antietam: Essays on the 1862 Maryland Campaign* (1989).
Sears, Stephen W. *Landscape Turned Red: The Battle of Antietam* (1983).

APPOMATTOX COURT HOUSE

The small Virginia town of Appomattox Court House, ninety miles east of Richmond, was the site of the surrender of the Army of Northern Virginia to Federal forces on 9 April 1865. A twelve-day campaign drew both armies away from the metropolitan area of the Confederate capital, before the Confederate army finally gave in to increasing Federal pressure and superior numbers. The Confederate surrender was the end of the Civil War in Virginia and marked the beginning of the end of the war across the South.

The Federal forces that gathered for the spring campaign in 1865 numbered just over 76,000 and were under the overall command of Lieutenant General Ulysses S. Grant. Grant's army consisted of the Army of the Potomac, under Major General George G. Meade, the Army of the Shenandoah, under Major General Philip H. Sheridan, and the Army of the James, under Major General E. O. C. Ord. The Confederate forces of approximately 57,800 were led by General Robert E. Lee and his Army of Northern Virginia. The Confederate ranks also included soldiers from the Department of Richmond, under Lieutenant General Richard S. Ewell,

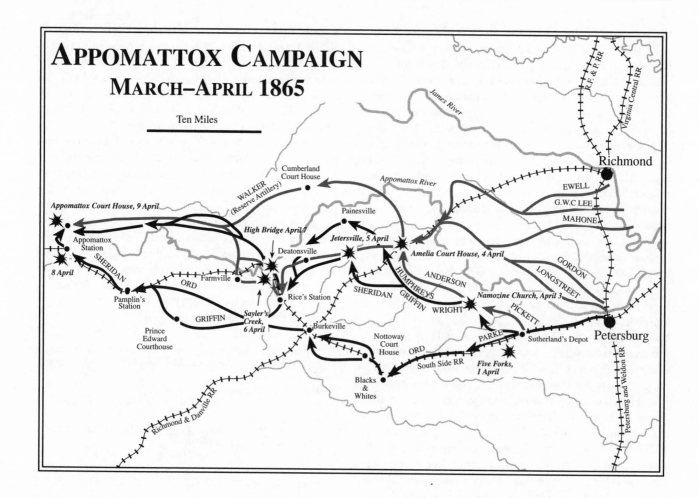

APPOMATTOX CAMPAIGN
MARCH–APRIL 1865

Ten Miles

and the Department of North Carolina and Southern Virginia, under Brigadier General Henry Wise.

The Campaign —The Appomattox campaign began on 29 March 1865. Federal and Confederate forces had been entrenched around Petersburg since late spring 1864, but both sides expected decisive action in 1865.

The immediate goal of the Federal army at this time was to capture the Southside Railroad to cut off Petersburg from its major supply route. The larger objective of the campaign was to force Lee to stretch his thin forces to the point where the Confederates would have to abandon Petersburg and Richmond. Accordingly, Grant sent infantry and cavalry forces to the southwest of Petersburg, planning to flank and draw the Confederate forces out of their entrenchments. In the final days of March, several actions took place at Quaker Road, White Oak Road, and Dinwiddie Court House, all of which were preliminary to the decisive battle at Five Forks on 1 April.

The Confederate defeat at Five Forks left Petersburg and Richmond vulnerable to the strong Federal forces that now circled the two cities from the south. Lee advised President Jefferson Davis that the Confederate government should abandon the capital immediately,

and on 2 April, a stream of political and civilian refugees began to pour out of the city. Petersburg was also evacuated that day, and Federal forces occupied both cities on 3 April. As for the Confederate army, its best hope was to move southwest out of Virginia and attempt to join Joseph Johnston's forces in North Carolina. With this goal, Lee's forces began a westward retreat, trying to stay ahead of the rapidly advancing Federal army.

In addition to meeting up with Johnston, Lee had the more immediate problem of feeding and supplying his troops. Over the next three days, the army moved west, toward Amelia Court House, engaging with Federal forces at Sutherland Station, Namozine Church, and Jetersville. Supplies were to be sent from Richmond to meet the army at Amelia. When the army arrived on 4 April however, there was no food waiting—ordnance and other supplies had been sent instead. The delay caused by this error cost Lee his small lead on the Federal forces. He was forced to redirect his army toward the next potential supply depot, Farmville.

On 6 April, as Lee's army neared Farmville another fierce battle took place at Sayler's Creek, culminating in another Confederate defeat. Some soldiers did receive rations at Farmville on 7 April, but the appearance of

Federal troops at Appomattox Court House, April 1865 (Photograph by Timothy O'Sullivan / *Library of Congress*)

Federal troops forced the Confederates to move on, abandoning their supplies. Lee hoped that by crossing the Appomattox River and destroying the bridges he could cut off the Federal pursuit. One bridge was not destroyed in time however, and the Federals were able to maintain their chase across the river. The Confederates had to keep going, fighting a holding action at Cumberland Church and making a hard night march toward their next supply stop, Appomattox Station. Meanwhile, fast-moving Federal cavalry remained south of the river and kept moving west to head off the Confederate forces.

By 7 April, Grant had begun to think that the Confederates might consider surrendering. He was told that the captured General Ewell claimed that the Confederates should have surrendered earlier, when they could have negotiated better terms. By the 7th, Grant had also been informed of Sheridan's intention to capture several Confederate supply trains waiting at

Appomattox Station. As a result of this information, Grant opened communications with Lee by sending a note requesting the surrender of his army, since further Confederate resistance appeared futile.

Lee was also considering his options, which were few and difficult. Ten days into this campaign, Lee's army was rapidly losing its effectiveness. Lack of proper nourishment and hard marching were taking their toll physically, and men began literally to drop from exhaustion. Morale was plummeting; the precarious position of the Confederacy had to have been evident to soldiers with the loss of Richmond, the flight of the government, and the Army's own difficult campaign all combining to present a bleak prospect for their future. Soldiers began to desert in large numbers.

Surrender was a painful choice, but Lee's other options were hardly more palatable. Should they not get through to North Carolina, the Army of Northern Virginia could engage in one final bloody battle that would probably destroy it completely; alternatively, soldiers could be ordered to return to their states to carry on the war by other means. That night, Lee responded to Grant's note, saying only that in the interest of avoiding more bloodshed, he would like to know what terms Grant would offer.

Grant's next communication, received by Lee on 8 April, stated that the only condition upon which he would insist was that soldiers be disqualified from taking up arms against the U.S. government until properly exchanged. In this message, Grant offered to meet with Lee or a representative to arrange the surrender.

Despite the formidable realities of his situation, Lee replied to Grant that perhaps the Federal commander had misunderstood; he still did not think that "the emergency has risen to call for the surrender of this Army" and had not proposed to arrange a surrender with his last note. However, he was willing to discuss peace terms generally and offered to meet with Grant the following morning at 10:00 A.M. Grant's response, received on the morning of 9 April, was brief—he was not authorized to treat generally for peace, only for the surrender of the army, so there would be no point in meeting unless it was to discuss surrender.

On the night of 8 April, Lee and his corps commanders decided to make one final attempt to break through the next morning. In their front, General John Gordon's Confederate infantry division, supported by Fitzhugh Lee's cavalry, faced only Federal cavalry and would make the initial assault. A breakthrough here was considered the only feasible option. James Longstreet's corps held the Confederate rear.

Unknown to the Confederates, however, Federal infantry was marching hard through that night to join Sheridan's cavalry and reinforce their precarious position. More Federal infantry rapidly approached the Confederate rear guard. Once the forces were engaged very early on 9 April, Gordon sent word back to Lee that he did not think he could hold his position without support.

While waiting for the expected 10:00 A.M. meeting with Grant, Lee informally polled some of his commanders for their opinions on the situation. Longstreet and William Mahone counseled surrender. E. Porter Alexander opposed that view and encouraged Lee to disperse his forces and to carry on the fight however possible. Lee responded that to allow that would be to let loose on the countryside an undisciplined mob of soldiers who would rob and plunder to support themselves. Such actions would certainly bring retaliation from the enemy, and he could not allow such a state of affairs to develop. Later that morning, Lee received Grant's note turning down the proposed meeting, yet the grim news from Gordon had left him little room to negotiate. Now with his forces pressed in on one another, there appeared to be no other option but to request explicitly a surrender conference, which Lee did in a final note.

The response at Grant's headquarters was subdued. Only a feeble cheer and some tears greeted the news that Lee would meet to discuss surrender, although Grant did declare that his migraine headache had miraculously disappeared. Further communications proposed that Lee and his staff should find a location; Grant would meet them where they indicated. White truce flags went out from both sides. As the news of the truce took time to disseminate, there was some disagreement whether particular units should surrender directly to one another or wait for orders. By the early afternoon of 9 April, much of the fighting had stopped in Virginia. It is estimated that at this time the Confederates had approximately 10,000 effective soldiers in the field; Union forces numbered more than 60,000.

The Surrender —At midday, Lee and his aide Colonel Charles Marshall rode out on the road to Appomattox Court House. The first white civilian they encountered was local resident Wilmer McLean, who, when asked, initially offered a nearby outbuilding for the conference. When the shabby, unfurnished structure was declared unsuitable, McLean proffered his own, more comfortable home. What Marshall and Lee probably did not know is that McLean's reluctance may have been a result of his earlier war experiences. By a remarkable coincidence, the McLean family had left a previous home after the house had served as a Confederate hospital and General P. G. T. Beauregard's headquarters during First Bull Run, the first battle of the war in Virginia. Hoping to avoid the rest of the war, McLean had moved his family to Appomattox Court House in 1863.

A half-hour after Lee and Marshall arrived, Grant and his staff arrived at the McLean house at approximately 2:00 P.M. By all accounts, the contrast between the two commanders was extraordinary. Lee presented a dignified figure, tall and dressed in his best uniform, with a fine sword. In comparison, Grant was muddy from his long ride, wearing a simple soldier's coat with only three-star shoulder straps to indicate his rank, and was swordless. While only Marshall accompanied Lee, Grant had a small entourage of staff and officers. These included Sheridan and Ord, as well as J. A. Rawlins, Rufus Ingalls, M. R. Morgan, Robert T. Lincoln (the president's son), Adam Badeau, Orville Babcock, Horace Porter, Seth Williams, Theodore Bowers, and Ely Parker. There is some debate about other Federal officers and journalists who may or may not have been in the parlor during the conference.

After brief conversation about their mutual service in Mexico, Lee called Grant's attention to the matter at hand by requesting his terms for surrender. Grant replied that they were as he had stated earlier: men and officers who surrendered were to be paroled and could not take up arms again until properly exchanged. Their arms and

The McLean House, Appomattox, April 1865 (Photograph by Timothy O'Sullivan / *Library of Congress*)

supplies were to be turned over as captured property. Lee asked Grant to write out the terms. In the written proposal, Grant added that officers would not have to surrender side arms and may also keep their horses. Grant also stated that soldiers could go home and would not be disturbed by U.S. authority as long as they maintained their parole.

With this last condition, Grant exceeded his charter of negotiating only the surrender of the army. He effectively said that Confederate soldiers would not be treated as traitors by the U.S. government. Although Lincoln would probably have endorsed this decision, it was not Grant's to make.

Lee commented that the terms would have a most happy effect on his army, but noted that in the Confederate army all cavalry and artillery horses were privately owned (as opposed to the army-owned Federal horses); did the terms mean that only officers could keep their horses? Grant considered, and he agreed that, as

horses would be necessary in the coming months to the many small farmers in the ranks, they could be retained by all who claimed ownership. Marshall drafted a note of agreement, which Lee signed. Copies of the surrender terms and agreement were made, signed, and distributed. Marshall commented afterward: "There was no theatrical display about it. It was in itself perhaps the greatest tragedy that ever occurred in the history of the world, but it was the simplest, plainest, and most thoroughly devoid of any attempt at effect, that you can imagine."

After the signing, the meeting began to dissolve into individual conversations between the officers present. Lee and Grant discussed the return of Federal prisoners, and the provision of rations by the well-supplied Federal army to the starving Confederate forces. There was no discussion of Lee's surrendering his sword, despite popular myth to the contrary. Lee met the other officers in the room, shaking hands with each before leaving the

McLean house at approximately 3:00 P.M. Lee's ride back to his camp through Confederate lines brought throngs of soldiers to the roadside, a few cheers, some tears, and much disbelief that the four years of intense combat had ended so abruptly.

After Grant left the McLean house, Federal officers descended upon it, buying and taking the furniture as souvenirs. McLean tried to prevent the chaos, but his parlor was left a shambles. Grant cabled the news to Washington at 4:30 P.M. As word of the surrender spread through Federal lines, great rejoicing commenced, culminating in the firing of artillery salutes. Grant, sensitive to the proximity of his vanquished foe, quickly ordered the excessive exultation stopped.

The formal surrender ceremony took place on 12 April. General Joshua Chamberlain was given the honor of receiving the surrender, in this final encounter between the two armies. As the Confederate soldiers marched between the two lines of Federal soldiers, Chamberlain ordered his troops to display a carry arms salute. Confederate general John Gordon responded with an order in kind—"honor answering honor." Confederate arms were stacked, banners laid on the ground, and the Southern soldiers began to go home. Approximately 28,000 Confederate soldiers surrendered at Appomattox. This number is higher than the effective number in the field at the truce because of the return of stragglers and deserters in the days between the cessation of hostilities and the surrender ceremony.

The surrender that took place at Appomattox Court House is remarkable for its lack of rancor between the two previously bitter enemies and for the dignity of the proceedings. Upon the appearance of flags of truce on the morning of the 9th, Confederate and Federal officers met between the lines to exchange greetings, information, and flasks. After the surrender, Federal soldiers freely shared the contents of their haversacks with their hungry Confederate counterparts. The surrender ceremony was marked by a profound respect on both sides. The choices made by the commanders of the two armies reflected an awareness of the long-term effects of the war on the nation. Grant could have treated the defeated Confederates far more harshly and deprived them of the basic necessities for starting their civilian lives again. Lee could have allowed his army to become a guerrilla fighting force, a decision that would have further embittered the two sides. Both commanders strove to set examples for their armies and their country to follow.

Other forces remained in the field, and it would be another year before Andrew Johnson could proclaim the insurrection at an end. Nonetheless, the end of the war in Virginia signaled the beginning of the end of the Confederate States of America.

—*Lisa Lauterbach Laskin*

See also Amelia Court House/Jetersville; Farmville/High Bridge; Grant, Ulysses S.; Lee, Robert E.; McLean, Wilmer; Namozine Church; Richmond, Surrender of; Sayler's Creek/Harper's Farm, Battle of.

For further reading:
Adams, Charles Francis. "Lee at Appomattox." In *Lee at Appomattox and Other Papers* (1902).
Calkins, Chris M. *The Appomattox Campaign: March 29–April 9, 1865* (1997).
Cauble, Frank P. *The Surrender Proceedings: April 9, 1865, Appomattox Court House* (1987).
Chamberlain, Joshua Lawrence. *The Passing of the Armies: An Account of the Final Campaign of the Army of the Potomac, Based upon Personal Reminiscences of the Fifth Army Corps* (1915; reprint, 1994).
Grant, U.S. *Personal Memoirs of U.S. Grant* (1885).
Marshall, Charles. *An Aide-de-Camp of Lee: Being the Papers of Colonel Charles Marshall, Sometime Aide-de-Camp, Military Secretary, and Assistant Adjutant General on the Staff of Robert E. Lee, 1862–1865* (1927).

ARCHER, JAMES JAY
(1817–1864)
Confederate general

Born to John Archer and Ann Stump Archer in Harford County, Maryland, James Archer was educated at Princeton, and at Bacon College in Kentucky, before studying law and opening a practice in Maryland. At the outbreak of the Mexican-American War, Archer accepted a captain's commission, commanding a company of Maryland volunteers. He fought with distinction during the Mexico City campaign, earning a brevet promotion to major for his actions during the taking of Chapultepec.

After seven years in civilian life as a lawyer, Archer decided to return to the army and became a captain in the 9th Infantry in 1855. He saw service primarily in the Pacific Northwest. At the outbreak of the Civil War, Archer's sympathies lay with the South, and in May 1861 he resigned his commission. In the fall of 1861, he was commissioned colonel of the 5th Texas Infantry as part of the Texas Brigade of John Bell Hood.

He commanded the 5th in the early days of the Peninsula campaign in the spring of 1862 and was recognized for gallantry during the battle of Seven Pines on 31 May 1862. On 3 June 1862 he was promoted brigadier general and commander of the Texas Brigade that became known as Archer's brigade.

As part of A. P. Hill's division, Archer commanded his brigade at the Seven Days' battles, during which he was especially conspicuous at Mechanicsville and Gaines' Mill. In August 1862, Archer fought at Cedar Mountain and Second Bull Run and led his brigade in Robert E. Lee's invasion of Maryland in September 1862, going as part of A. P. Hill's division to take Harper's Ferry and then marching quickly to Antietam. Archer became ill on the march, and temporarily relinquished command of his brigade. He fought at Fredericksburg and Chancellorsville before leading his brigade north again as part of A. P. Hill's corps into Pennsylvania.

At Gettysburg, Archer's brigade was a part of the division commanded by Major General Henry Heth. On the first day of the battle, 1 July, Archer led his brigade against the center of the Federal line on Seminary Ridge, pushing forward so quickly that his brigade was virtually enveloped before they could be supported by other parts of the division. Archer was captured.

Transported to Johnson's Island in Ohio, Archer was held there until June 1864 when he was transferred to Fort Delaware and then finally exchanged in August 1864. During his imprisonment, Archer's health had suffered, but he was determined to return to active command. Given command of his former brigade, Archer received orders on 9 August to report to the Army of the Tennessee under John Bell Hood in Atlanta. Ten days later this order was revoked, possibly as a result of Archer's bad health, and he was ordered to report to the Army of Northern Virginia in Petersburg, Virginia. Archer's health continued to deteriorate, however, and he died in Richmond on 24 October 1864.

—*David S. Heidler and Jeanne T. Heidler*

See also Gettysburg, Battle of; Harper's Ferry; Hood, John Bell.
For further reading:
Craig, David R. "James J. Archer: The Little Gamecock" (M.A. thesis, 1983).
Schoeberlein, Robert W. "A Marylander at the Northwest Frontier." *Maryland Historical Magazine* (1995).

ARKANSAS

Arkansas seceded from the Union on 6 May 1861, following months of bitter debate among its people. Like other border states, many citizens held strong Union sympathies. They successfully blocked the efforts of delegates to the first secession convention (3–18 March 1861) to secede, but Lincoln's call for troops following the capture of Fort Sumter broadened support for secession and led to the state's leaving the Union. In the next four years, Arkansas contributed as many as 60,000 men to the Confederate cause. Its forty-six infantry regiments, seventeen cavalry regiments, and thirteen batteries of artillery fought in every theater of action.

For both the Confederacy and the Union, Arkansas possessed considerable strategic value. Its location made it important for carrying out Confederate ambitions in Missouri and the Indian Territory. For the United States government, its occupation was essential for protecting Missouri and St. Louis. As a result, northern Arkansas became an immediate focus of military activity.

In summer 1861 Governor Henry Rector ordered troops there. These troops fought under General Ben McCulloch on 10 August 1861 at Oak Hills, Missouri. That bloody battle temporarily halted the Federal effort to push Confederate forces out of Missouri.

Following Oak Hills, Confederate forces fell back into Arkansas. The Federals reorganized, and before the end of 1861 their Army of the Southwest under General Samuel R. Curtis had pushed into northwestern Arkansas. On 7 March 1862, General Earl Van Dorn's Confederate forces attacked Curtis at Pea Ridge. The two-day battle failed to dislodge Curtis, and Van Dorn, responding to requests by General Albert S. Johnston for reinforcements, removed his army east of the Mississippi River.

After regrouping, Curtis's army reentered Arkansas on the White River on 29 April 1862. His goal was Little Rock. Van Dorn's move had left Arkansas unprotected, but the state's new military commander, Major General Thomas C. Hindman, scraped up a force to resist Curtis. A combination of low water on the White River and a lucky shot by Confederate artillery that sank the USS *Mound City* at St. Charles on 17 June and turned back a Federal flotilla moving up-river to join Curtis thwarted Federal plans. Curtis's column moved overland to the Mississippi and occupied the town of Helena on 12 July.

With Curtis out of the way, Hindman hoped to regain control of northwestern Arkansas. His plan was approved by General Theophilus Holmes, who had replaced him because of civilian complaints about harsh measures, such as declaring martial law, and Hindman marched back into northwest Arkansas in the autumn of 1862. Determined not to allow the Confederates to return, General Curtis ordered the Federal Army of the Frontier to deal with Hindman. The two forces collided at Prairie Grove on 7 and 8 December. Neither side defeated the other on the field, but Hindman's badly supplied army retreated south. After Prairie Grove, the Confederates never reoccupied the northwest, although small-unit operations continued there until the war's end, and Confederate raids into Missouri passed through in 1863 and 1864.

After Prairie Grove, the Confederate effort in Arkansas became unfocused, and their authorities lacked clear strategic goals. They made decisions that accomplished little and squandered men. Brigadier General Thomas J. Churchill decided to build up a small fort on the Arkansas River to threaten Federal operations on the Mississippi River, but the Federals responded with a massive force that captured Fort Hindman and most of its inadequate garrison on 11 June 1863. On 4 July 1863, General Holmes attacked the Federals at Helena, hoping to divert men from the siege of Vicksburg. The battle was ill timed—Vicksburg surrendered that day—and badly planned. The Confederates were driven back with severe losses.

Federal strategy appeared to have clearer goals, especially following the victory at Vicksburg. The Federals sought control over the Arkansas River as an avenue into the Indian Territory and to serve as a barrier to Confederate operations north of the river. They also had the resources to achieve these goals. On 1 September 1863, General James G. Blunt captured the river town of Fort Smith as a part of his operations in the Indian Territory. On 10 September, Major General Frederick Steele occupied Little Rock in a virtually unopposed march from Helena. Four days later the Federals occupied the city of Pine Bluff.

The Union occupation of Little Rock, Helena, and Fort Smith encouraged local Unionists to reorganize a loyal state government in Arkansas. Following a January 1864 state convention endorsed by President Abraham Lincoln, the Unionists held an election and chose as governor Isaac Murphy, one of the delegates to the 1861 convention who had refused to support secession. The Federal occupation also encouraged many civilians to switch sides. By the end of the war, 8,289 whites had enlisted in the Union army. The Federal presence also effectively ended slavery behind Union lines, and some 6,000 freedmen from Arkansas also joined the Union army.

After the capture of Little Rock, General Steele's primary mission was to hold the Arkansas River and he did little to disturb the Confederates who had fled into southwestern Arkansas. Only orders to cooperate with General Nathaniel Banks's Red River expedition in the spring of 1864 led him in that direction. Steele got as far as Camden, but after the defeat of Banks's army in Louisiana at Mansfield and Pleasant Hill on 8 and 9 April 1864, his advance halted. Following attacks upon his supply lines at Poison Springs on 17 April and Marks' Mills on 25 April, he retreated toward Little Rock. A major battle at Jenkins' Ferry on 28 April stopped Confederate pursuit and allowed him to escape back to the capital city.

Confederate authorities never despaired completely and from the fall of Little Rock to the end of the war they probed Federal lines, even mounting an unsuccessful attack on Pine Bluff shortly after its occupation in September 1863. After the Red River campaign they used southwestern Arkansas as a base from which General Sterling Price carried out his raid into Missouri in the summer of 1864. Nonetheless, they found they could do little to change the military situation. They did not have enough men to challenge the Federal occupation and, increasingly, they had to deal with internal problems produced by defeat and the collapse of the domestic economy. Confederate conscription in spring 1862 had hastened the disillusionment, and opposition to Confederate authority developed to the point of requiring military force to suppress it.

When the Confederacy's eastern armies surrendered in April 1865, most Arkansas soldiers and civilians had no desire to continue the war. Despite official efforts to stop it, desertion quickly depleted Confederate units in the state. Civilians plundered military warehouses. When E. Kirby Smith formally surrendered forces in the Trans-Mississippi District on 2 June 1865, little of the Confederacy remained intact within Arkansas.

—*Carl H. Moneyhon*

See also Arkansas Post, Battle of; Curtis, Samuel R.; Fort Smith, Arkansas; Helena, Arkansas, Battle of; Hindman, Thomas C.; Holmes, Theophilus; McCulloch, Ben; Pea Ridge, Battle of; Poison Spring, Battle of; Prairie Grove, Battle of; Rector, Henry M.; Steele, Frederick; Van Dorn, Earl.

For further reading:

Christ, Mark, ed. *Rugged and Sublime: The Civil War in Arkansas* (1994).

Dougan, Michael. *Confederate Arkansas: The People and Policies of a Frontier State in Wartime* (1976).

Moneyhon, Carl H. *The Impact of the Civil War and Reconstruction:Persistence in the Midst of Ruin* (1994).

Shea, William L., and Earl J. Hess. *Pea Ridge: Civil War Campaign in the West* (1992).

Thomas, David Y. *Arkansas in War and Reconstruction, 1861–1874* (1926).

ARKANSAS, CSS

The *Arkansas* was the most successful Confederate ironclad on the Mississippi. She contributed greatly to the revival of Southern fortunes in the west in the summer of 1862. In her twenty-three-day career, the *Arkansas* was undefeated by Union forces but ultimately was wrecked by her own unsophisticated technology.

On 16 August 1861 the Confederate Congress appropriated $160,000 to construct two ironclads at Memphis to defend the Mississippi. Similar in appearance to the CSS *Virginia*, the rams were smaller, but still measured 165 feet in length and 35 feet in width. When loaded the *Arkansas* drew at least 14 feet of water. Contractor John T. Shirley intended to have both rams finished in four months, but a shortage of trained laborers and materials prevented him from meeting this deadline. By April 1862, when Memphis was captured by Union forces, neither ironclad was finished. One was burned, while the other, the *Arkansas*, was towed down the Mississippi and up the Yazoo River to be completed. On 26 May 1862 Lieutenant Isaac Newton Brown took command. When he arrived, work on the *Arkansas* was at a standstill. The Yazoo River had overflowed its banks, and the *Arkansas* was moored to a submerged levy four miles from dry land.

Brown demonstrated enormous energy and creativity. He had the *Arkansas* towed to Yazoo City. Local planters provided laborers and forges. A sunken barge loaded with railroad rails for the *Arkansas*'s armor was raised. The rails were bolted to the superstructure, with alternating rails reversed, so that bulbs and flanges interlocked for maximum strength. Brown's workers were unable to curve the rails to conform to the shape of the *Arkansas*'s stern and quarter, so they bolted thinner boiler plates there. Armament consisted of ten guns of mixed calibers. Henry K. Stevens, the first lieutenant, drew plans for the gun carriages from memory and had them constructed from unseasoned cypress wood. Gunpowder had to be produced locally from sulphur, saltpeter, and charcoal.

An iron ram extended ten feet forward of the *Arkansas*'s bow. She was powered by 450-horsepower short-stroke screw engines salvaged from a sunken steamer. They drove two screws, but Brown quickly discovered that if one engine stopped, the remaining screw could only propel the Arkansas in a circle. Work with the ill-tempered engines was made more difficult by the lack of insulating material; temperatures in the fire-room reached 130 degrees.

Short of her intended complement of 200 men, the *Arkansas* boasted only 100 sailors, although they were experienced, having served on Confederate gunboats. Sixty soldiers were recruited from the army to work the guns, but the *Arkansas* was still undermanned when she sailed into battle. Nonetheless, on 12 July 1862 Brown took the *Arkansas* downstream toward the Mississippi. The Yazoo had fallen to fifteen feet and would soon trap the *Arkansas*, but by 15 July Brown was ready to enter the Mississippi and move downstream to the Confederate fortress of Vicksburg.

Between the *Arkansas* and Vicksburg were the combined fleets of Admiral David Farragut, who had captured New Orleans and run past the fortifications at Vicksburg, and Captain Charles H. Davis, whose river gunboats had conquered the upper Mississippi. Warned by deserters that the "Arkansas Traveler" was coming out, three Union ships had been sent up the Yazoo to reconnoiter. At first mistaking the *Arkansas* for an ordinary steamer, the Union vessels ran back for the fleet under fire from the Confederate ironclad. The ironclad *Carondelet* was badly damaged and forced ashore. The gunboat *Tyler* was cut up badly, and the ram *Queen of the West* ran away without attempting a collision. The firing was heard by the rest of the Union flotilla, but they believed that they were hearing only the *Tyler* firing on Confederate shore positions. When they realized that the monster ironclad was coming, most Union ships were unprepared to move.

Brown hove in close to the line of anchored ships and fired broadsides as fast as his guns could be loaded. As the *Arkansas* ran through the fleet, she received hits as fast as she dealt them out. The sixteen Union warships suffered smashed boilers and cut steam lines, but one-eighth of the *Arkansas*'s crew was also struck down. Her smokestack was riddled and the draft failed. Losing power, she slid past the last ships and rounded for Vicksburg.

Farragut was beside himself with fury and embarrass-

ment. Not only had his command been surprised, but the *Arkansas* was now between him and New Orleans. Worried about falling water levels in the Mississippi, Farragut determined to run back past Vicksburg while he could. The *Arkansas*'s position was marked, and Farragut's fleet began to sail past Vicksburg as dusk fell. As each ship passed the *Arkansas*'s anchorage, it fired broadsides at the ironclad; Brown, however, had shifted his anchor and thus escaped what would have been certain destruction.

On 22 July Davis tried again to sink the *Arkansas* with the ironclad *Essex* and ram *Queen of the West*. The *Essex* exchanged fire with the *Arkansas*, but got the worst of the exchange and drifted without power down the Mississippi. The *Queen of the West* slammed into the *Arkansas*, dislocating her temperamental engines but doing no other damage. Farragut towed the disabled *Essex* to Baton Rouge for repairs and left for deeper waters.

Brown commenced repairs on the badly damaged *Arkansas* before departing for a much-needed leave. Soon after his departure, Stevens was ordered to take the ironclad downriver to support the land attack on Baton Rouge. Leaving Vicksburg on 3 August, the *Arkansas* reached Baton Rogue two days later, just as her starboard engine broke down. After she had run aground, the ironclad's crew worked desperately to repair the engine. Early on 6 August, they spotted the *Essex* coming up to fight. As the *Arkansas* moved out into the river, one of her propeller shafts broke, and the ironclad again circled helplessly until it ran aground. Fearing that the *Essex* would pour fire into the lightly armored stern, Stevens ordered the *Arkansas* abandoned and then blew her up.

—*Tim J. Watts*

See also Ironclads; Riverine Warfare.
For further reading:
Coleman, S. B., and Paul Stevens. "A July Morning with the Rebel Ram *Arkansas*." *U.S. Naval Institute Proceedings* (1962).
Flynt, David. "Run the Fleet: The Career of the C.S. Ram *Arkansas*." *Journal of Mississippi History* (1989).
Huffstot, Robert S. "The Brief, Glorious Career of the CSS *Arkansas*." *Civil War Times Illustrated* (1968).
Parrish, Tom Z. *The Saga of the Confederate Ram Arkansas: The Mississippi Valley Campaign, 1862* (1987).
Still, William N., Jr. "Confederate Shipbuilding in Mississippi." *Journal of Mississippi History* (1968).

ARKANSAS POST, BATTLE OF
(11 January 1863)

In late 1862 Confederate forces at Vicksburg controlled navigation on the Mississippi River. One-hundred miles to the north, Confederate supremacy was not as certain. In September 1862 Major General Theophilus H. Holmes, commander of the Trans-Mississippi Department, ordered Colonel John W.

Dunnington to ensure Confederate control of the Arkansas and White rivers. Rebel engineers chose a site twenty-five miles above the mouth of the Arkansas River and 117 miles below Little Rock to construct an earthen fort. By the middle of November 1862 the Post of Arkansas (as the Confederates called it) or Fort Hindman (as it was known to the Federals) was nearly complete.

When completed, Arkansas Post formed a hollow square, 190 feet on each side with a bastion at each corner, surrounded by a ditch 20 feet wide and 8 feet deep. Artillery firepower consisted of four 10-pounder Parrott rifles, four 6-pounder smoothbores, and three 9-inch Columbiads. The fort was on a bluff 25 feet above the Arkansas River, 50 miles from its mouth. Inside the fort were some 5,000 Confederates under the command of General Thomas J. Churchill. Arkansas Post not only defended the Arkansas and White rivers, but also disrupted Federal commerce on those rivers. In late December 1862, just a month after construction was completed, the Union steamer *Blue Wing* was forced to surrender to Confederate artillery fire from the Arkansas shore and was taken to Arkansas Post. The Federal army had to capture Arkansas Post to protect its commerce.

The man to do this was Major General John A. McClernand, a political general (one who gained his commssion through political position or connections) from Illinois. McClernand had spent the first year of the war as General Ulysses S. Grant's second in command, and badly wanted an independent command. September 1862 saw him in Washington, D.C., meeting with cabinet officials and President Lincoln in an attempt to get a separate command. His friendship with the president helped him acquire his independent status. In October 1862 McClernand was authorized to recruit an army in the Midwest and use it against Vicksburg. The general wished to capture Arkansas Post, however, before turning his attention to Vicksburg.

After several delays, General McClernand assumed command of his force, which he called the Army of the Mississippi, on 2 January 1863. This Federal army numbered approximately 32,000 men and was divided into two army corps. General George W. Morgan commanded the First Corps and General William T. Sherman the Second. Accompanying the army was a naval flotilla under the command of Admiral David D. Porter. On 4 January, McClernand, Sherman, and Porter met at Milliken's Bend to determine the army's movements. At this council of war, the three men agreed to reduce Arkansas Post.

Their plan called for an expedition to sail up the Mississippi until it met the White River, then continue up that river. From there the flotilla was to move up the Arkansas River, which ran into the White. At a suitable place below the fort the troops would disembark.

Morgan's 1st Corps would form the left wing and Sherman's 2d Corps the right. Sherman's men were to march behind the fort, linking up with the Arkansas River above the bastion. Morgan's troops would establish a line below the fort connecting with Sherman's men and the Arkansas River. This would encircle the fortress, forcing its surrender.

By 8 January, the Federal expedition had reached the White River undetected. At about 5 P.M. on 9 January, the flotilla landed about three miles from Arkansas Post and the soldiers disembarked. Late that afternoon, Confederate general Churchill received word that a large Federal fleet was approaching. Churchill ordered his men to draw ammunition and prepare three days' rations—his troops were to be prepared for action at a minute's notice. Meanwhile, the Federal army spent 10 January getting into position. As the moon rose on the tenth, Admiral Porter commenced a naval bombardment of the fort in preparation for the next day's assault.

On 11 January, the navy began the assault by again bombarding the fortress at about 1 P.M. A half hour later the infantry moved in. As the Federal lines advanced, the heavily outnumbered Confederates poured a destructive fire into the blue columns. Admiral Porter's gunboats passed by the fort and opened a reverse fire upon the enemy. By 3:30 P.M. the Union attackers were within 100 yards of the fort, and artillery fire from within it had ceased. As the Yankee assault bore down upon the fortress, it was obvious that further resistance was futile, and white flags of surrender appeared.

The Federal expedition netted almost 5,000 prisoners, seven enemy flags, seventeen pieces of artillery, thousands of small arms, and a great deal of ammunition. The Union casualties numbered 134 killed, 898 wounded, and 29 missing. Along with preserving Federal commerce on the Arkansas River, this victory also provided a much-needed victory that rejuvenated the Federal army and boosted Union morale.

—*Christopher C. Meyers*

See also Army of Mississippi; Holmes, Theophilus; McClernand, John A.; Morgan, George W.; Porter, David Dixon; Sherman, William Tecumseh.
For further reading:
Bearss, Edwin. "The Battle of the Post of Arkansas." *The Arkansas Historical Quarterly* (1959).
Coleman, Roger. *The Arkansas Post Story* (1987).
Walker, John W. *Excavation of the Arkansas Post Branch of the Bank of the State of Arkansas* (1971).

ARLINGTON

The Civil War was Arlington National Cemetery's *raison d'etre*. Hundreds of Confederate dead and thousands of Union dead lie in Arlington, the largest of the nation's burial grounds. In April 1861 these acres on the Virginia heights overlooking the Potomac

Brigadier General Gustavus A. DeRussey (*third from left*) and staff on the portico of Arlington House, May 1864
(*Library of Congress*)

River and Washington, D.C., were not planted with the dead, but with crops. Robert E. Lee was doing his best to make his wife's estate a model farm.

Mary Anne Custis Lee inherited Arlington in 1857 upon the death of her father, George Washington Parke Custis, the adopted grandson of George Washington. She grew up in Arlington House. After her wedding there in 1831 to Robert E. Lee, scion of an equally august Virginia family, she continued to live at Arlington while Lee was stationed throughout the west. Six of their seven children were born in the house. Mrs. Lee's pride was her beautiful rose garden to the east of the mansion.

When he resigned his commission in the United States Army in April 1861 and left for Richmond, Lee urged his wife to prepare to follow him. He was certain that Arlington, so strategically located, would soon be occupied by Union soldiers. Within weeks, Mrs. Lee received

word that Federal troops would soon arrive. Taking away whatever family relics she could and storing the rest in the attic and cellar, she and her daughters headed south. Neither she nor her husband would ever again set foot in Arlington House, their home of thirty years.

In 1862, Congress levied taxes on real estate in the "insurrectionary" districts. Because the real goal was confiscation of Southerners' property rather than raising revenue, tax collectors refused to accept payment from anyone but the owner himself or herself. When Mrs. Lee, who was an invalid confined to a wheelchair, sent a cousin with her payment, it was refused. With uncommon speed, the 1,100-acre Arlington estate went on the auction block for default of taxes and was sold to the United States government for $26,800.

By the time the government became the owner of Arlington, the war had already created an urgent need for national cemeteries, especially in Washington. After each major battle in the surrounding countryside, the dead and dying were brought into the capital. Scores of Union soldiers and captured Confederates died every week in the makeshift hospitals that filled the city. Authority for military cemeteries rested with Quartermaster General Montgomery C. Meigs. Although he was raised in Georgia and owed his promotions to Southern friends in Congress, once the war began, Meigs turned virulently anti-Southern. He saved his deepest hatred for his old commander, Robert E. Lee. When in 1864 Secretary of War Edwin Stanton ordered Meigs to create a national cemetery near Washington, Meigs ordered no surveys of other sites, but immediately recommended that the 200 acres of the Arlington estate closest to the house be transformed into a burying ground for the Union dead.

Meigs ordered the first soldiers' graves dug in Mrs. Lee's rose garden in May 1864. By the end of 1864, over 7,000 graves spread across the area known as the Field of the Dead. Among them was the grave of Meigs's son, John Rodgers Meigs, killed by Confederate guerrillas. By the war's end, more than 16,000 Union graves surrounded Arlington House on three sides. The markers above the majority of them are inscribed simply "Unknown U.S. Soldier."

Immediately after the war, Meigs ordered a huge vault dug in what was left of Mrs. Lee's rose garden. Into the enormous pit went the skeletal remains of all the unidentified war dead gathered up from Bull Run and other battlefields near Washington. Though Meigs was loath to admit it, among the skeletons of the 2,111 or more bodies in the common grave under the huge granite marker intended to honor the Union's "army of martyrs" some Confederate bones were almost certainly commingled.

By the end of the war, several hundred Confederate dead, mostly prisoners of war who died in local hospitals, lay in graves scattered about Arlington. Meigs refused their relatives entry to the cemetery. On the first Decoration Day (now Memorial Day) in 1868, Meigs ordered that the Southern women who came to decorate the Confederate graves be turned away. Not until a new generation of leaders took up the reins of power and another war intervened would the Confederate dead at Arlington be recognized.

In 1898 President William McKinley, speaking in Atlanta, extolled the many Confederate veterans who had rallied to the flag and fought side by side with former Union men in the Spanish-American War. Old differences should be buried, McKinley told the crowd, and the bravery and sacrifice of all the dead should be recognized. In 1900 Congress authorized a Confederate section within Arlington National Cemetery. More than 400 Confederate dead were gathered from all over the cemetery and from graves in Alexandria and at the Soldiers' Home and were reinterred in the new Confederate section. In 1906 the United Daughters of the Confederacy won permission to erect a memorial in the midst of the Southern dead. Sculpted by Moses Ezekiel, himself a Confederate veteran, and dedicated in 1914, the Confederate Monument, the largest memorial in the cemetery, takes its theme from the verse from Isaiah carved around the pedestal: "They shall beat their swords into plowshares, and their spears into pruning hooks."

Among the 200,000 veterans of America's wars and their dependents buried at Arlington National Cemetery, 20,000 are the Civil War dead. The more than four million tourists who visit the cemetery each year traverse sixteen miles of roads, most named for heroes of the Civil War—Grant, Sherman, Sheridan, McClellan, McPherson, Farragut. This cemetery that was created as an act of revenge upon Robert E. Lee by Montgomery Meigs, who is also buried there and for whom a drive is named, has become the most hallowed ground in America.

—*Kathryn Allamong Jacob*

For further reading:
Ashabranner, Brent. *A Grateful Nation: The Story of Arlington National Cemetery* (1990).
Hinkle, John Vincent. *Arlington: Monument to Heroes* (1970).

ARMISTEAD, LEWIS ADDISON
(1817–1863)

Confederate general

Lewis A. Armistead was born in New Bern, North Carolina, on 18 February 1817 to General Walker Keith and Elizabeth Armistead. Armistead's ancestors, originally named Armstädt, came from Hessen-Darmstädt, now a part of Germany. The Armistead name early became prominent in U.S. military circles. Lewis's father and five brothers served during the War of 1812. One of them, Major George Armistead, was the commander of Fort McHenry during the British attack on the installation. The Armisteads were also related to four U.S. presidents: James Monroe, William Henry Harrison, John Tyler, and Benjamin Harrison.

Lewis Armistead entered West Point in 1834, but left in 1836. Two versions of the story regarding his departure exist. In one, he was dismissed after an altercation with Jubal Early during which he broke a plate over Early's head. A second version cites poor grades as reason for dismissal. Three years later Armistead joined the army as a second lieutenant, beginning a military career that would take him from the swamps of Florida, to the hills of Mexico City, and finally to the farmlands of Pennsylvania. During the Seminole Wars of 1835–1842,

Armistead fought under the command of his father Walker Keith Armistead and shortly thereafter was promoted to first lieutenant, a rank he held when the war with Mexico broke out in 1846. Armistead was decorated for heroism three times during the war, most notably for his actions at Chapultepec were he was "the first to leap into the Great Ditch." For his service that day he was brevetted to the rank of major. After the war, Armistead served on the western frontier, earning a reputation as a casual, friendly, but highly disciplined officer who believed that "obedience to duty was the first qualification of a soldier." During this time he cultivated many lasting friendships, most significant of which was his close association with Winfield Scott Hancock of Pennsylvania.

The outbreak of Civil War in the spring of 1861 left Armistead with a difficult choice. He had developed strong friendships with men like Hancock and others who chose to remain loyal to the Union. In the end, however, his devotion to his home state took precedence, and on 26 May 1861 he resigned his commission in the U.S. Army. Armistead, who by now was a widower and older than most of his comrades, accepted a colonelcy in the Confederate army and command of the 57th Virginia Infantry. Less than a year later, on 1 April 1862 he was promoted to brigadier general in the Army of Northern Virginia. In Armistead's first action, the battle of Seven Pines, he served with distinction and his brigade quickly won a reputation as one of the toughest units in the Army of Northern Virginia. Later, at the battle of Malvern Hill, Armistead would "charge with a yell" and help to turn the tide in favor of the Confederacy. His toughness extended beyond the battlefield. Soldiers either straggling or caught in dereliction of duty were disciplined by their superior officer who himself was directly responsible for their actions. Armistead believed that the private must answer to the officer, but the officer to him. This devotion to discipline was tempered by his soft-spoken manner, creating a blend that made him one of the most popular officers in the Army of Northern Virginia.

During the Antietam campaign, Armistead served as provost marshal for Lee's army. Later, he participated in the battles of Fredericksburg and Chancellorsville. Armistead's roles in these engagements, however, were minor compared with the immortality he would gain at Gettysburg. On the third day of the battle, 3 July 1863, Armistead led one of General George Pickett's brigades in the charge against the Union center commanded by Armistead's close friend Winfield Scott Hancock. With his hat on the point of his sword and uttering "Men! Remember what you are fighting for—your homes, your friends, and your sweethearts!" Armistead moved forward. Eventually he and a handful of men succeeded in reaching and scaling the stone wall that protected a

battery of Union guns. It was while taking these guns, that Armistead fell mortally wounded. After the battle he was removed to a Federal field hospital where he died on 5 July 1863. On his deathbed he requested that his watch and other valuables be given to his friend Hancock who had also been wounded that day, though he would survive the war. Shortly after his death, Lewis Armistead's body was claimed by friends and taken to Baltimore, where he was buried in the family cemetery plot at St. Paul's Church.

—*Charles Thomas Johnson*

See also Gettysburg, Battle of.
For further reading:
Poindexter, James E. "General Armistead's Portrait Presented." *Southern Historical Society Papers* (1909).
Schuricht, Herrmann. *History of the German Element in Virginia* (1898–1900).

ARMORIES, ARSENALS, AND FOUNDRIES

An elaborate complex of armories, arsenals, foundries, laboratories, and depots provided the North and South with the weapons, ammunition, and equipment necessary to wage the Civil War. The functions of armories and arsenals were not strictly distinctive during the war, for both armories and arsenals not only stored arms, but both in some instances were capable of producing them as well. Laboratories were both research and production facilities, and depots were repositories for distributing ordnance.

The United States military listed the following extant armories and arsenals in 1859: Allegheny Arsenal, Pittsburgh, Pennsylvania; Augusta Arsenal, Georgia; Baton Rouge Arsenal, Louisiana; Benicia Arsenal, California; Charleston Arsenal, South Carolina; Detroit Arsenal, Dearbornville, Michigan; Fayetteville Arsenal, North Carolina; Fort Monroe Arsenal, Old Point Comfort, Virginia; Frankford Arsenal, Philadelphia, Pennsylvania; Harper's Ferry Armory, Virginia; Kennebec Arsenal, Augusta, Maine; Little Rock Arsenal, Arkansas; Mount Vernon Arsenal, Alabama; New York Arsenal, Governor's Island, New York; Pikesvilee Arsenal, Maryland; Saint Louis Arsenal, Missouri; San Antonio Arsenal, Texas; Springfield Armory, Massachusetts; Vancouver Arsenal, Washington Territory; Washington Arsenal, Washington, D.C.; Watertown Arsenal, Massachusetts; and Watervliet Arsenal, New York.

The combined inventory of these armories and arsenals included a total of 561,400 muskets and 48,862 rifles. James Buchanan's secretary of war during the secession crisis, the Virginian John B. Floyd, was later accused of ordering a controversial series of transfers that moved weapons from Northern armories and arsenals to Southern ones. Yet such a stratagem would have had little effect in the long term. In arms production and maintenance, as in everything else, the

Ruins of the federal armory at Harper's Ferry, Virginia, October 1862 (Photograph by S. A. Holmes / *Library of Congress*)

Confederate States could not match the potential of the North. From 1 January 1861 to 30 June 1866, Union arsenals and foundries supplied a prodigious amount of weaponry and equipment, including 7,892 cannon, 11,787 artillery carriages, 4,022,130 small arms, 1,022,176,474 cartridges for small arms, 1,220,555,435 percussion caps, 2,862,177 rounds of fixed artillery ammunition, 14,507,682 cannon primers and fuses, 12,875,294 pounds of artillery projectiles, 26,440,054 pounds of gunpowder, 6,395,152 pounds of potassium nitrate, and 90,416,295 pounds of lead. The U.S. Ordnance Department also produced an enormous amount of parts for repairing damaged items or replacing those lost or destroyed.

As for the South, records of production are not as complete, but the circumstantial evidence of Confederate armies relatively well supplied with arms indicates a titanic achievement by the Confederacy's

Ordnance Department. Federal arsenals in the South were among the Federal property seceding states immediately seized. The Confederacy would superintend the operation of these facilities during the war with astounding results, considering the Ordnance Department had to cope with dire shortages. In addition to arsenals at Charleston, Fayetteville, Augusta, Mount Vernon, Baton Rouge, Little Rock, and San Antonio, there were also the large Tredegar Irons Works in Richmond and arsenals in Apalachicola, Florida, and Selma, Alabama, the last of which came on line later in the war (1863). The Tredegar plant was the principal foundry for the Confederacy and the only one capable of casting the largest guns, although it did not have the Rodman technique. In Alabama, in addition to Selma's arsenal, the facilities there included a naval ordnance works, ten iron foundries, eight machine-shops, a shovel factory, a card factory for carding cotton, two wagon factories, a horseshoe factory, and a large rolling-mill. With abundant iron and coal mines only forty-five miles away at Montevallo and linked by the Alabama & Tennessee Railroad, Selma could produce almost anything, including 7- and 6-inch rifled cannon. At the Augusta Arsenal, Gabriel W. Rains produced heavy artillery and field pieces, and in February 1862, the War Department reported that government armories at Richmond (augmented by equipment taken down from Harper's Ferry) and Fayetteville were supplying 1,500 muskets and rifles per month. As a testament to the chronic dearth of manpower, authorities calculated that the rate of supply could have been doubled had they possessed enough skilled labor. The government competed with private workshops for workmen in their arsenals and foundries, but the high priority given to arms production prompted the Confederacy to grant wholesale draft exemptions to persons working in foundries.

Foundries, establishments that could cast metals, were an integral part of arms production. Foundries were part of an arsenal's manufacturing plant, but in the North and South, scores of private firms received government contracts. The Union and Confederacy contracted with private foundries to cast heavy artillery as well as cooking utensils, railroad spikes, tools, and nails. At the outbreak of the war, the biggest three foundries in the North were the Fort Pitt Foundry directed by Charles Knap, the West Point Foundry Association directed by Robert Parrott, and the South Boston Foundry directed by Cyrus Anger.

In the South, the arsenal and foundry eventually became vulnerable military targets, so they continued to operate until Federal military conquests either put them out of operation by occupation or deprived them of areas that provided imperative raw materials. Facilities in western Virginia were the objectives of frequent raids, while the Harper's Ferry Armory's workshops were burned and the site was mainly used as an ordnance depot. The Little Rock Arsenal would be occupied by Federals troops, and foundries in Atlanta and in Rome, Georgia, would invite destruction by Sherman's forces as he advanced to the sea. When Sherman moved into the Carolinas, his forces destroyed the Fayetteville Arsenal. In Alabama, Selma not only was an important weapons manufacturer, it was also the repository for all the iron and coal distributed through Georgia, Alabama, and Mississippi, so it became a prime target for James H. Wilson's sweeping cavalry raid in March–April 1865.

—David S. Heidler and Jeanne T. Heidler

See also Artillery; Fayetteville Arsenal; Rifles; Small Arms; Springfield Armory; Springfield Rifle.
For further reading:
Albaugh, William A., and Edward N. Simmons. *Confederate Arms* (1957; reprint, 1987).
Davis, Carl L. *Arming the Union: Small Arms in the Civil War* (1973).
Downey, Fairfax. *The Sound of the Guns: The Story of the American Artillery* (1955).
Edwards, William B. *Civil War Guns: The Complete Story of Federal and Confederate Small Arms: Design, Manufacture, Identification, Procurement, Issue, Employment, Effectiveness, and Postwar Disposal* (1997).
McKee, W. Reid, and M.E. Mason, Jr. *Civil War Projectiles II: Small Arms & Artillery* (1980).
Murphy, John M., and Howard M. Madaus. *Confederate Rifles & Muskets: Infantry Small Arms Manufactured in the Southern Confederacy, 1861–1865* (1996).
Naisawald, L. Van Loan, *Grape and Canister: The Story of the Field Artillery of the Army of the Potomac* (1983).
Olmstead, Edwin, Wayne Stark, and Spencer Tucker. *The Big Guns. Civil War Siege, Seacoast and Naval Cannon* (1997).
Peterson, Harold L. *Round Shot and Rammers: An Introduction to Muzzle-loading Land Artillery in the United States* (1969).
Tucker, Spencer C. *Arming the Fleet: U.S. Navy Ordnance in the Muzzle-loading Era.* (1989).
Wilson, Eugene K. "James H. Burton and the Development of the Confederate Small Arms Industry" (Thesis, 1976).

ARMSTRONG, FRANK CRAWFORD
(1835–1909)
Confederate general

Frank Crawford Armstrong was born to Frank W. Armstrong, an army officer, and Anne Millard Armstrong in Indian Territory (present-day Oklahoma) in 1835. While still a boy, he suffered the loss of his father, and his mother remarried General Persifor F. Smith. Armstrong went to Massachusetts to school, and upon the completion of his education, chose a military career. He received a commission as a second lieutenant of cavalry. Before the Civil War, he served at a number of frontier military posts and was a part of Albert Sidney Johnston's expedition to Utah to subdue the Mormons.

At the beginning of the Civil War, Armstrong did not immediately resign his commission. Promoted to captain in June 1861, he fought as a Union officer at the battle of First Bull Run. He resigned his commission on 13 August 1861 and accepted a commission in the Confederate army. The Confederate War Department sent him to the western theater, where he served as aide to Brigadier General Ben McCulloch at the battle of Wilson's Creek in August 1861. In December 1861 Armstrong fought at the battle of Chustenahlah in the Cherokee Nation. His connection with the Cherokees from his upbringing in Indian Territory made him useful in bringing many of those people to the Confederate side.

By early 1862 Armstrong was serving as Brigadier General McCulloch's adjutant general headquartered at Fort Smith. He was standing nearby when McCulloch was killed by Union sharpshooters at the battle of Pea

Ridge on 7 March 1862. After this battle, Armstrong briefly served as the colonel of the 3d Louisiana Infantry. In June 1862 he received a promotion to acting brigadier general with command of Major General Sterling Price's cavalry.

On 25 July 1862 Armstrong attacked the Union position at Courtland, Alabama, taking over 150 prisoners and Union supplies with the loss of only eight casualties. General Price commended Armstrong for his actions at Courtland. On 1 September 1862, while commanding 1,600 cavalry, he defeated another Union force at Bolivar, Tennessee, capturing seventy-one prisoners. He also cut part of Union communications in the area by destroying railroad track and bridges. Price again commended him in the strongest terms. Armstrong commanded Price's cavalry later in September 1862 at Iuka and in October at Corinth.

In January 1863, after fighting in the battle of Stones River, Armstrong received a permanent promotion to brigadier general. In March 1863 he fought at the battle of Spring Hill and as the commander of the 1st Brigade of Nathan Bedford Forrest's cavalry at the battle of Brentwood, Tennessee.

Armstrong temporarily commanded a division at Chickamauga, Georgia, but was back in command of a cavalry brigade attached to Leonidas Polk during the Atlanta campaign. He moved with John Bell Hood into Tennessee in the fall of 1864, fought at Franklin, and guarded the Confederate army's retreat from Nashville in December 1864. Armstrong was captured during Wilson's Raid on Selma, Alabama, on 2 April 1865.

After the war Armstrong lived in Texas and the Indian Territory, working for the government in various Indian posts. He died in Bar Harbor, Maine, in 1909.

—*David S. Heidler and Jeanne T. Heidler*

See also Brentwood, Tennessee; Cherokee Indians.

ARMY OF KANSAS

The Army of Kansas was composed of forces within a geographical area that included Kansas, the Indian Territory west of Arkansas, and the Nebraska, Dakota, and Colorado territories.

Created on 9 November 1861, the Department of Kansas was commanded by Major General David Hunter and consisted of five newly formed regiments of Kansas and Wisconsin infantry and five new cavalry regiments from Kansas and Ohio. Three regiments each of infantry and cavalry from the regular establishment rounded out the forces. The department was merged into the Department of the Mississippi on 11 March 1862, but was recreated on 2 May 1862 with Brigadier General James G. Blunt commanding.

In August 1862 forces were organized into three brigades commanded by Brigadier General Frederick Salomon (1st Brigade), Colonel William Weer (2d Brigade), and Colonel W. F. Cloud (3d Brigade). When the department again was subsumed on 19 September 1862, this time into the Department of Missouri, these brigades were reformed with forces of the Department of Missouri into the Army of the Frontier under Brigadier General John M. Schofield.

The Department of Kansas was yet again revived on 1 January 1864 under Major General Samuel R. Curtis. That summer five districts (North Kansas, South Kansas, Upper Arkansas, Nebraska, and Colorado) were established and remained in place until war's end in April 1865. Meanwhile, the Department of Kansas was merged into the Department of Missouri on 30 January 1865.

In spite of all these organizational changes, the soldiers in the region were frequently described as the Army of Kansas, even in those times when no such entity officially existed.

—*David S. Heidler and Jeanne T. Heidler*

See also Departments, Military; Kansas.
For further reading:
Miller, Edward A. *Lincoln's Abolitionist General: The Biography of David Hunter* (1997).

ARMY OF KENTUCKY

There were three embodiments of a Union military force known either officially or informally as the Army of Kentucky. The first was created from recruits collected by Lovell H. Rousseau near Danville, Kentucky, during the state's early neutrality. That neutrality guided Federal behavior, constraining it to the creation of a Department of Kentucky under Kentucky native Brigadier General Robert Anderson. The breaching of Kentucky's neutrality in the summer of 1861, however, saw the forces of Rousseau and those similarly recruited by William Nelson organized into the Army of Kentucky on 25 August 1861. The army was placed under Major General Gordon Granger and consisted of two brigades commanded by Brigadier Generals Mahlon D. Manson and Charles Cruft. This Army of Kentucky was routed and much of it captured at the battle of Richmond, Kentucky, on 30 August 1861, thus ending the first army's existence.

The second Army of Kentucky had only a brief existence. It consisted of three divisions under Stephen G. Burbridge (later under Andrew Jackson Smith), Green Clay Smith (later under Quincy A. Gillmore), and Absalom Baird. When this second Army of Kentucky was dismantled by reassignments to other forces and departments, a third Army of Kentucky, as it was informally called, came into being in February 1863. It was essentially a reorganization of Baird's division with his two brigades from the second Army of Kentucky being joined by William P. Reed's brigade from the District of Western Kentucky and George Crook's from West

Virginia. Baird's division formed the nucleus for Gordon Granger's reserve corps that became until October 1863 part of the Army of the Cumberland.

The third "Army of Kentucky" that fought with such distinction at Chickamauga was composed of elements of Baird's division by then under the command of James Steedman. During the critical stage of the battle's second day, Granger had three brigades of his reserve corps protecting the Union flank near McAffee's Church. He boldly moved two of them into the fray and managed to save the Union position from complete collapse. Some accounts refer to these brigades as the reserve corps and others as the Army of the Kentucky, the latter likely because Gordon Granger's original command remained so closely identified with him.

A Confederate Army of Kentucky existed, beginning in late August 1862. It was the force Edmund Kirby Smith led into Kentucky simultaneous to Braxton Bragg's invasion of the state. The army was composed of divisions under C. L. Stevenson, Henry Heth, Patrick Cleburne, and Thomas J. Churchill. John Hunt Morgan led its cavalry. It was this Confederate Army of Kentucky that ironically met and routed the first Union Army of Kentucky at the battle of Richmond. It would later join with Bragg's forces for the indecisive but critical battle of Perryville.

—*David S. Heidler and Jeanne T. Heidler*

See also Baird, Absalom; Chickamauga, Battle of; Granger, Gordon S.; Kentucky; Richmond, Kentucky, Battle of.

For further reading:

Baird, John A. *Profile of a Hero: The Story of Absalom Baird, His Family, and the American Military Tradition* (1977).

Coulter, E. Merton. *The Civil War and Readjustment in Kentucky* (1926).

Falaise, Louis De. "General Stephen Gano Burbridge's Command in Kentucky." *Register of the Kentucky Historical Society* (1971).

Hafendorfer, Kenneth A. *Perryville: Battle for Kentucky* (1981).

Harrison, Lowell H. *The Civil War in Kentucky* (1975).

Lambert, D. Warren. *When the Ripe Pears Fell: The Battle of Richmond, Kentucky* (1995).

McDonough, James Lee. *War in Kentucky: From Shiloh to Perryville* (1994).

ARMY OF MIDDLE TENNESSEE

The Confederate Army of Middle Tennessee was organized on 28 October 1862 by combining the approximately 4,000 men of Major General John C. Breckinridge's corps with Nathan Bedford Forrest's cavalry operating in the region for which the force was named. Breckinridge's corps had already seen considerable service. Organized in March 1861, it was originally under the command of George B. Crittenden, already under a cloud for his role in the Confederate disaster at Logan's Cross Roads the previous January. At the end of March, Breckinridge replaced Crittenden as corps commander because of charges of the latter's chronic

drunkenness. Under Breckinridge, the outfit fought at Shiloh, Corinth, and Baton Rouge before returning to middle Tennessee in the fall of 1862.

Headquartered at Murfreesboro, Breckinridge's task was to guard against additional Federal encroachment while Braxton Bragg and Edmund Kirby Smith carried out their invasions of Kentucky. Therefore Forrest's cavalry, with two batteries assigned, was given the job of watching the approaches to Murfreesboro from Nashville. He was to place his cavalry close to Nashville to exploit any chances to harass the Union troops in the area. Mainly, though, Breckinridge wanted the Confederate cavalry to watch for any Federal moves toward the army's position from anywhere east or west of Nashville or from the Tennessee River. In November, Joseph Wheeler assumed command of the Army of Middle Tennessee's cavalry.

The Army of Middle Tennessee's infantry was formed into three brigades. The 1st Brigade was commanded by Colonel R. W. Hanson and consisted of the 2d, 4th, 6th, and 9th Kentucky Regiments as well as two batteries. Acting as a reserve, it was placed on the Shelbyville road near that town. The 2d Brigade was commanded by Colonel John B. Palmer and consisted of the 18th and 32d Tennessee, 32d Alabama, 4th Florida, and two batteries. It formed the right wing of the army and was encamped to protect the Lebanon and Nashville turnpike. The 3d Brigade, commanded by Colonel F. M. Walker, consisted of the 20th, 28th, and 45th Tennessee, the 60th North Carolina, and two batteries. It formed the left wing of the army and guarded the ground between the road leading to Nashville and the one leading to Franklin.

After failing to win a decisive victory at Perryville and thus failing in his invasion of Kentucky, Bragg returned to Murfreesboro, where the Army of Middle Tennessee was absorbed into the Army of Tennessee as the 1st Division of William Hardee's II Corps. It thus ceased to exist as an organizational entity. As part of II Corps, it consisted of four brigades commanded by Gideon Pillow, William Preston, Daniel W. Adams, and R. W. Hanson. During the Stones River campaign, it numbered about 7,000 men.

—*David S. Heidler and Jeanne T. Heidler*

See also Army of Tennessee; Breckinridge, John C.; Tennessee.

ARMY OF MISSISSIPPI

The Army of Mississippi was not a continuous classification throughout the Civil War. Many armies such as the Union Army of the Tennessee, Confederate Army of Northern Virginia, and Confederate Army of Tennessee had definite dates of origin and lasted throughout the war. The Army of Mississippi was not so resilient, however. Actually, three

Confederate Armies of (the) Mississippi existed in the Civil War. The first, the progenitor of the Confederacy's great western army, the Army of Tennessee, was created by General P. G. T. Beauregard on 5 March 1862 from troops in the Western Department (or Department No. 2). The force initially consisted of the two corps led by Major Generals Leonidas Polk and Braxton Bragg. On 29 March, the Central Army of Kentucky directly under General Albert Sydney Johnston, the department commander, reinforced the Army of the Mississippi. Johnston on this date took charge of the Army of the Mississippi, with Beauregard relegated to second-in-command.

The troops that would constitute the Army of Mississippi were widely scattered over the western Confederacy. Soldiers of Leonidas Polk's Corps were spread from Columbus, Kentucky, to Memphis along the great river as well as into the interior of the Confederate heartland. Braxton Bragg's men defended the Gulf Coast, principally at Pensacola, Mobile, and New Orleans. During the closing days of March 1862, the army concentrated in northeastern Mississippi, a major effort made possible by the steamboat, railroad, and telegraph. However, the army was green; probably 80 percent of the men had never heard a gun fired in anger. Bragg referred to the army as a mob.

The first action of this army, so designated by official representation, came at Shiloh on 6–7 April 1862. As the army assembled at Corinth, Mississippi, it was reorganized and its principal units renamed. Polk's troops, initially dubbed the First Grand Division, became after 29 March the I Corps, Bragg commanded II Corps and Major General William Hardee III Corps. The Reserve Corps was initially placed under George Crittenden, but he relinquished command on 31 March to Brigadier General John C. Breckinridge.

In personnel, the Army of Mississippi at Shiloh officially numbered 44,699. Its main strength was situated in its line infantry of the volunteer state regiments raised almost entirely in areas west of the Appalachians. On 6 April, the army listed in its order of battle 76 infantry regiments or battalions from the following states: Alabama, 10; Arkansas, 10; Florida, 1; Kentucky, 5; Louisiana, 12; Mississippi, 9; Missouri, 1; Tennessee, 26; and Texas, 2. Also present were two regiments and one battalion of the small regular Confederate army. The infantry was equipped with a wide array of weaponry, from shotguns to state-of-the-art British .577 Enfield rifles that had been run through the blockade.

In artillery, Johnston's army could muster 22 batteries and companies from the following states: Alabama, 3; Arkansas, 5; Georgia, 1; Kentucky, 2; Louisiana, 2; Mississippi, 4; and Tennessee, 5. Many of the artillery pieces in the Army of the Mississippi were guns of Southern origin, made at Nashville, Memphis, or New Orleans.

In cavalry, Johnston counted 9 regiments, squadrons, and other units of varying size from the following states: Alabama, 1; Georgia, 1; Kentucky, 2; Mississippi, 3; Tennessee, 1; and Texas, 1. The Army of Mississippi was the source of some of the finest cavalrymen that the war produced, including Nathan Bedford Forrest, John Hunt Morgan, and Joseph Wheeler.

Lacking time for training, the army embarked almost immediately on an offensive to destroy the Army of the Tennessee under Major General Ulysses S. Grant at Pittsburg Landing. The resulting battle of Shiloh, one of the greatest bloodlettings of the war, showed that the Confederate army would fight bravely, if not especially skillfully. Lacking more than a veneer of experienced officers, the army paid a terrible price for its callowness. Its losses at Shiloh totaled 10,694. Among the casualties was the army's commander, Albert Sidney Johnston, the only four-star American ever killed in action.

Under Johnston's replacement, P. G. T. Beauregard, the Army of Mississippi fell back to Corinth, and pressed heavily by Union forces in May, retreated to Tupelo, Mississippi. Disappointed in the apparent passivity of its commander, President Jefferson Davis replaced Beauregard temporarily on 27 June with Bragg and then on 5 July with William Hardee who moved the army to Chattanooga. On 15 August, command passed back to Bragg, who reorganized the force. Bragg left the forces in Mississippi under Major Generals Earl Van Dorn and Sterling Price. The second Confederate force called the Army of Mississippi was formed on 7 December 1862 out of Major General Earl Van Dorn's Army of West Tennessee and the corps (sometimes called the Army of the West) commanded by Major General Sterling Price. Prior to its designation as the Army of Mississippi (the label would lie idle for several months), the force was troubled by the lack of cooperation between Van Dorn and Price. Price fought the interesting yet unimportant battle of Iuka on 19 September 1862. Eventually, Jefferson Davis himself rectified the command situation in Mississippi. He gave Van Dorn command of the 22,000-man army, and the Confederates subsequently attacked and lost at Corinth on 3–4 October 1862. Van Dorn was relieved and replaced by Lieutenant General John C. Pemberton who commanded the army through the Vicksburg campaign, although in January 1863 he reorganized his forces and dropped the designation Army of Mississippi. The forces fought its largest and most important battle at Champion's Hill on 16 May, where Grant defeated Pemberton and sealed Vicksburg's fate. Most of the army, 28,000 strong, withdrew and subsequently surrendered with the city on 4 July 1863. Most of the army was paroled and exchanged, which put the units back into the ranks by 1864. Lieutenant General Leonidas Polk took command of the forces in Mississippi and endeavored to thwart Major General William T. Sherman's Meridian campaign in February 1864.

Thus a third Army of Mississippi came into existence under Polk. It joined the Army of Tennessee on 12 May 1864 during the Atlanta campaign. Following Polk's death in action on 14 June at Pine Mountain, Georgia, the organization was renamed on 26 July as Stewart's Corps to reflect more accurately its size (about 20,000) and its new commander Lieutenant General Alexander P. Stewart.

While little continuity emerges regarding the various names, a definite pattern exists regarding geography and units that made up the army. A history of the Army of Mississippi can be used loosely to describe the western-most portion of the Western theater. For instance, when General Braxton Bragg split the Confederate army at Tupelo, Mississippi, in July 1862 and moved to Tennessee for his subsequent march into Kentucky, he split the Western theater into two parts. The Army of Tennessee fought the remainder of the war in the easternmost portion of the Western theater, while the Army of Mississippi fought the western battles. This split in the Western theater remained until May 1864, when the two armies again united into the Army of Tennessee, the Army of Mississippi becoming the third corps. Thus, from July 1862 to May 1864, the Army of Mississippi fought on its own in its own theater. Many historians argue convincingly that it was in this westernmost area of the Western theater that the war was won and lost, making the operations of the Army of Mississippi highly significant.

Historians have pointed out that the Army of Mississippi is frequently mentioned in the *Official Records* as the Army of the Mississippi. Several Union organizations (under John McClernand, John Pope, William S. Rosecrans, Ulysses S. Grant, and William T. Sherman) also bore the name Army (or Division) of the Mississippi.

—*Malcolm Muir and Timothy B. Smith*

See also Champions Hill, Battle of; Corinth, Battle of; Departments, Military, C.S.A.; Departments, Military, U.S.A.; Iuka, Battle of; Shiloh, Battle of; Vicksburg Campaign.

For further reading:
Bearss, Edwin C. *The Vicksburg Campaign* (1985).
Bearss, Margie Riddle. *Sherman's Forgotten Campaign: The Meridian Expedition* (1987).
Cozzens, Peter. *The Darkest Days of the War: The Iuka Corinth Campaign* (1997).
Sword, Wiley. *Shiloh: Bloody April* (1974).

ARMY OF MISSOURI

The Confederate Army of Missouri began with at least 12,000 men, but the short-lived, largely blue-coated army relied so heavily on foraging men, as well as uniforms and supplies, that its commanders likely had only a vague idea how large it was at any given point. Passing through Federally occupied territory during Price's Missouri Raid, the army surely added thousands to its ranks, but the army's itinerary surely caused it to lose thousands who simply went home as the certainty of defeat loomed so largely. Although 20,000 men probably passed through its ranks, the army rarely had more than 12,000 at any one time and regularly functioned with far fewer effectives.

In August 1864, Confederate Trans-Mississippi commander General Edmund Kirby Smith authorized General Sterling Price, heading the Department of Arkansas, to organize its cavalry division with supplemental forces into this new army. From 16 to 18 September, Price reorganized the mounted Confederate forces in Arkansas into three divisions.

General Joseph O. Shelby commanded the smallest division of nearly 3,400 men. Within it, Colonel David Shanks commanded Shelby's old "Iron Brigade" with Colonel Sidney D. Jackman taking another, and Colonel Charles H. Tyler slated to organize a new brigade to be raised in Missouri.

The largest division of almost 5,100 men was commanded by Brigadier General James F. Fagan, an infantry commander who was promoted to a mounted command over experienced cavalrymen. Fagan's division had four brigades, including the largest in Price's army, that of Brigadier General William Lewis Cabell, who had served the Richmond government well before going west. Colonels William Slemmons, Archibald S. Dobbins, and Thomas H. McCray commanded the other three brigades.

The final 3,800-man division was commanded by Brigadier General John S. Marmaduke, who had earned a reputation as "the cavalier general" for his two 1863 mounted raids into Missouri. His most reliable brigade belonged to Brigadier General John Bullock Clark, Jr., the son of a Missouri politician expelled from the U.S. Congress in 1861. Marmaduke's other brigade belonged to Colonel Thomas R. Freeman.

Among the ranks of Price's army were such distinguished figures as Thomas C. Reynolds, exiled governor of Missouri's Confederate state government; Trusten Polk, who had been expelled from the U.S. Senate; and Brigadier General Merriwether Jeff Thompson, the former mayor of St. Joseph, who had recently been paroled after a year's captivity. Many of these officers and men had served alongside each other, and their official hope was to liberate what they saw as a Confederate state.

While Price's officers were accomplished leaders, the bitter legacy of guerrilla war and reprisals that had raged in the state predisposed the Army of Missouri to be avengers rather than liberators. Of the five Missouri brigadiers, Jackman and Freeman had both led guerrillas themselves. As regimental commanders, Colonels John Truesdale Coffee and William O. Coleman had fought primarily as irregulars, and DeWitt Clinton Hunter had actually participated in the Baxter Springs Massacre. Others with ties to partisan warfare included Colonels John Q. A. Burbridge, Colton Green, David Shanks, Moses W. Smith, Alonzo Slayback, Benjamin Elliott, Sol Kitchen, William L. Jeffries, Robert R. Lawther, J. A. Schnable, and Timothy Reeves (also spelled Reves).

This army, then, was not merely a Trans-Mississippi version of the eastern Confederate forces. Viewing Missouri as a seceded state, the Army of Missouri readily "conscripted" thousands of unwilling civilians as recruits and rarely recognized lines between civilians and combatants or between prisoners of war and active enemies. No Confederate army of comparable size and importance so persistently left in its wake a trail of murdered civilians and prisoners, particularly African-Americans and Germans.

Problems of logistics and poor management crippled the Army of Missouri. In a region where adult white men carried arms in peacetime, the complaints of Confederate officers that the army had not armed their men likely meant not that they remained unarmed but that the lack of standardized arms meant an unmanageably wild variety of ammunition. Later recruits, of course, would have only what arms they could bring to the army. More seriously, Price had been unable to mount the entire command, and those few on foot—fewer than 200 in Shelby's division—slowed the entire column to the pace of infantry. Still worse, confiscations continued to swell the size of Price's supply train to 500 wagons. Price usually ran the army from the back of an ambulance owing to malaria or—if his critics were to be believed—the bottle. All bode very poorly for an army dependent on speed for its success.

Arguably, the achievements of the Army of Missouri were politically self-defeating, and its military successes depended most directly on the ineptness of Federal generalship.

—*Mark A. Lause*

See also Price, Sterling; Price's Missouri Raid.
For further reading:
Hinton, Richard J. *Rebel Invasion of Missouri and Kansas, and the Campaign of the Army of the Border against General Sterling Price, in October and November 1864* (1865).
Monaghan, Jay. *Civil War on the Western Border* (1955).
Sallee, Scott E. "Missouri! One Last Time: Sterling Price's 1864 Missouri Expedition, 'A Just and Holy Cause.'" *Blue and Gray Magazine* (1991).

ARMY OF MOBILE

Prior to the creation of the Army of Mobile, troops in the vicinity of that city were commanded by Brigade General Jones M. Withers and were designated as the District of Alabama (October 1861) in Braxton Bragg's Department of Alabama and West Florida. On 20 December 1861, Withers's area of responsibility was extended westward to include Pascagoula Bay and the part of Mississippi east of the Pascagoula River. On 27 January 1862, Withers's command officially became the Army of Mobile and was charged with the defense of the Gulf Coast between the Pascagoula and Perdido rivers. The army consisted of 10,056 men with 9,278 present for duty. It contained the 2d, 18th, 19th, 20th, 21st, 22d, 23d, 24th, and 25th Alabama Infantry Regiments, the 2d Alabama Battalion, a company of Alabama infantry, a battalion of Mississippi volunteers, a company of Mississippi infantry, six companies of the Alabama Mounted Volunteers, the 1st Battalion of Alabama Artillery, and the 2d Battalion of Alabama Light Artillery.

Authorities consistently calculated the army as under-manned and its capabilities limited, not only by a paucity of resources but also because of a rapid turnover in its command. Withers was relieved in February 1861, when he and elements of the Army of Mobile were shifted to the 2d Division of Bragg's II Corps, Army of Mississippi, in which they would fight at Shiloh. Meanwhile Brigadier General Samuel Jones, commanding from Pensacola, absorbed Mobile's department, and temporary commanders of lesser rank supervised the Army of Mobile. Colonel John B. Villepeague took command on 28 February 1862, but was soon relieved for duty with the Army of Mississippi. His replacement was Colonel W. L. Powell, commander of the 2d Brigade, who was himself replaced at the end of April 1862 by Brigadier General James E. Slaughter. At roughly the same time, Major General John H. Forney succeeded Samuel Jones as commander of what now was designated as the District of the Gulf. Forney established his headquarters in Mobile.

By the fall of 1862 the Army of Mobile was still being reported in Confederate returns, but it had been reduced to nearly half its original size by detachments to other armies and postings to nearby garrisons. Ultimately, in June 1863 the District of the Gulf came under its final commander, Major General Dabney H. Maury. By this time, the organizational entity labeled the Army of Mobile had been subsumed by the patchwork collection of troops that remained in defense of the city. They were generally referred to as the Mobile garrison.

—*David S. Heidler and Jeanne T. Heidler*

ARMY OF NEW MEXICO

The Confederate Army of New Mexico was actually a glorified brigade of less than 4,000 men under the command of Brigadier General Henry Hopkins Sibley that was given the task of conquering the New Mexico Territory (now Arizona and New Mexico). Confederate interest in New Mexico, spurred by dreams of access to California gold and Pacific ports, originated in July 1861, when John R. Baylor led the 2d Texas Mounted Rifles into New Mexico and captured the 700-man Union garrison of Fort Fillmore. At this time, Henry Hopkins Sibley, just resigned from Federal army service in New Mexico, persuaded Confederate president Jefferson Davis of the feasibility of conquering the area. Commissioned brigadier general, Sibley organized and proclaimed the Army of New Mexico (also known as Sibley's Arizona Brigade, Sibley's New Mexico Brigade, or simply Sibley's Brigade) at Fort Bliss, Texas, on 14 December 1861. The army consisted of the 4th, 5th, and 7th Regiments of Texas Volunteer Cavalry, Baylor's command, and assorted support units—an aggregate of approximately 3,700 men.

Relatively well trained for that stage of the war, but plagued by logistical shortages, Sibley's force was largely ill clothed, chronically low on food for both man and mount, and short of appropriate weapons (two companies carried only revolvers and nine-foot lances). Hoping to live off the land and captured Federal stores, the Army of New Mexico pushed northward into New Mexico in January 1862. By mid-February 1862, Sibley's force confronted approximately 3,800 Federals under Colonel Edward R. S. Canby at Fort Craig. Canby commanded about 1,200 regulars, most of the remainder being New Mexico and Colorado volunteers and militia in disparate states of discipline. Having left garrisons at several locations, Sibley took only 2,600 men into battle at Valverde near Fort Craig on 21 February 1862. The day-long battle was furious, and Sibley, who was ill or intoxicated, turned over command to Colonel Thomas Green, who drove the Unionists back to Fort Craig with a final furious assault near sunset.

Having suffered approximately 200 casualties, Sibley then bypassed Fort Craig, moving up the Rio Grande Valley toward the bountiful supply depots at Albuquerque and Santa Fe. With little enthusiasm for fighting, significant numbers had deserted the Union forces, and Sibley's campaign seemed poised for complete success, as Confederate forces spread as far west as Tucson, Arizona. However, quick-thinking Federal quartermasters in Albuquerque and Santa Fe destroyed or evacuated virtually all supplies, so the capture of these locations on 4 and 23 March, respectively, hardly alleviated the Army of New Mexico's dire logistics. Additionally, the Confederates had become progressively dispersed by garrisoning captured areas, so that only 600 men actually occupied Santa Fe. Conversely, Canby received modest but steady reinforcements that allowed him to move northward with his own forces at Fort Craig, while also directing 1,300 men from Fort Union (northeast of Santa Fe) to move on the Confederate-held territorial capital.

On 26 through 28 March 1862, 600 Confederates

under W. R. Scurry clashed with 1,300 Federals under John Slough and John Chivington at the battle of Glorieta Pass, twenty miles southeast of Santa Fe. Although driven from the main field, the Unionists captured the Confederate supply train and killed hundreds of horses and mules, leaving the Army of New Mexico virtually bereft of supplies and mounts.

In Santa Fe, the just-arrived Sibley surveyed the remains of his army and learned that Canby and 1,200 Federals were now approaching Albuquerque. Sibley concentrated his depleted force at Albuquerque and contemplated three options: starvation in Albuquerque, an attack on Canby's now-united forces that outnumbered him two to one, or retreat down the Rio Grande River.

On 12 April 1862, the Army of New Mexico left Albuquerque, moving down the west bank of the Rio Grande, shadowed on the east bank by Canby. Although in constant visual contact, only desultory skirmishing resulted, for Canby's supply situation precluded taking prisoners. Thus "escorted," Sibley's men suffered terribly, water shortages causing some to slaughter their few animals and drink the blood. By early May, Sibley and 1,700 survivors staggered back to Fort Bliss in Texas and eventually on to San Antonio. Hopes of renewing the campaign ended when the Union's "California Column" reached New Mexico.

Its ambitions dashed, the Army of New Mexico later fought as Sibley's Brigade and Green's Brigade, but its greatest days lay behind, in the Union-held Rio Grande Valley. If successful, the Army of New Mexico's exploits might have ranked with Scott's 1847 Mexico campaign, but, in failure, it remains a quixotic sidelight of the war.

—*Broeck N. Oder*

See also Baylor, John Robert; Canby, Edward R. S.; Fort Craig, Battle of; Glorieta Pass, Battle of; New Mexico; Sibley, Henry Hopkins; Val Verde, Battle of.

For further reading:
Frazier, Donald S. *Blood and Treasure: Confederate Empire in the Southwest* (1995).
Hall, Martin H. *The Confederate Army of New Mexico* (1978).
———. *Sibley's New Mexico Campaign* (1960).
Johnson, Robert U., and Clarence C. Buel. *Battles and Leaders of the Civil War*, vol. 2 (1956).
Josephy, Alvin M. *The Civil War in the American West* (1991).
Thompson, Jerry. *Henry Hopkins Sibley: Confederate General of the West* (1987).

ARMY OF NORTHERN VIRGINIA

The most famous and most successful of all the Confederate armies had its origins in the Department of Alexandria, a command created in April 1861 encompassing most of northern Virginia and also known as the Department of the Potomac. After P. G. T. Beauregard took command of the department in June, its field army became known as the Army of the

Potomac. This army, merged with Joseph E. Johnston's Army of the Shenandoah, won the first major battle of the war at First Bull Run in July, and the combined force, under Johnston's command, kept its new name in the Department of the Potomac.

When a new Department of Northern Virginia was created in October 1861, Johnston was assigned to command it, with department headquarters at Manassas and the Army of the Potomac as its principal army. After Johnston was seriously wounded at Fair Oaks/Seven Pines in May 1862, Robert E. Lee left his position as military advisor to President Jefferson Davis to take command of the army and the department, a post he would hold for the rest of the war.

Within a month the renamed Army of Northern Virginia would drive the Federal Army of the Potomac, under George B. McClellan, from the outskirts of Richmond in the Seven Days' battles (25 June–1 July 1862). Though Confederate casualties were heavy, and Lee's complicated and ambitious plans often went astray on the battlefield, the campaign helped save the capital and gave a much-needed boost to Southern morale.

It also marked the beginning of a remarkable ten-month period in which Lee took the initiative from the Federals in the East and his army fought a series of battles that transformed it into one of the greatest armies in American military history. Lee soon reorganized the Army of Northern Virginia to reflect his strategic and tactical vision, transferring or shifting generals and units, and settled on two infantry wings under James Longstreet and Thomas J. "Stonewall" Jackson, a large cavalry division under James E. B. "Jeb" Stuart, and artillery batteries assigned to specific brigades or divisions.

Lee soon took his army north to oppose the Army of Virginia, a new Federal force under John Pope that had been organized to operate between Richmond and Washington. He took a bold gamble by dividing his force in the face of Pope's large army. After Jackson captured or destroyed a huge cache of Union supplies at Manassas Junction, his wing was attacked by Pope on the old Manassas battlefield. The Confederates held their position until Longstreet arrived to help deliver a crushing blow to the Federals, whose retreat turned into a rout toward Washington late on the second day of the battle of Second Bull Run/Second Manassas (29–30 August 1862).

This victory helped convince Lee, Davis, and other authorities in Richmond that the time was right for an invasion of Maryland, to carry the war into Northern territory and perhaps to encourage foreign intervention on behalf of the Confederacy. The Army of Northern Virginia crossed the Potomac River in early September with its ranks reduced by widespread straggling and weakened by its losses during the summer. Lee, still willing to take enormous risks, separated his forces again, sending Jackson to capture the arsenal and garrison at Harper's Ferry while the rest of the army faced the Army of the Potomac, once again under McClellan. He concentrated his forces at the town of Sharpsburg, on the banks of Antietam Creek, and endured the bloodiest single day of the entire war at Antietam/Sharpsburg (17 September 1862). The Confederates held off a succession of piecemeal Federal assaults until timely reinforcements arrived on the field at a critical moment, saving the Army of Northern Virginia from almost certain destruction. The battle ended in a draw, though Lee's withdrawal back across the Potomac and the army's appalling losses gave some Southerners cause for concern if not alarm.

There was a significant lull in the Eastern theater after Antietam as both major armies there spent the fall of 1862 recuperating from several months of hard campaigning and looking toward their next battle, which many believed would not come until spring. Lee took advantage of the opportunity to organize his army into two permanent infantry corps, the first under Longstreet and the second under Jackson, and a cavalry corps, under Stuart.

By December 1862 the Army of the Potomac, this time under Ambrose E. Burnside, attempted another advance toward Richmond, this time by way of Fredericksburg, a town on the Rappahannock River between the two capitals. The Army of Northern Virginia established a strong defensive position along the river and easily repulsed wave after wave of Federal attacks launched against its lines in the remarkably one-sided battle of Fredericksburg (11–13 December 1862).

By the spring of 1863, Lee and the Army of Northern Virginia confronted a revitalized Army of the Potomac under new commander Joseph Hooker, who confidently predicted victory. The two armies met west of Fredericksburg in the Wilderness, a nearly impenetrable forest dense with thickets and underbrush. Lee boldly divided his army in two and pinned the Federals in place with a third of his force while Jackson, with the rest of the army, marched around Hooker's flank and launched a slashing attack that threatened to rout almost half of the Army of the Potomac. After heavy fighting, in which Hooker never committed all his troops, the Federals withdrew across the Rappahannock River. The four-day battle of Chancellorsville (1–4 May 1863) was the army's most impressive victory, marred only by the death of Jackson, who was accidentally wounded by his own men. Soon afterward, a confident Lee wrote to one of his generals, "there never were such men in an army before. They will go anywhere and do anything if properly led." One of his soldiers claimed at about the same time, "This is the best army in the world I expect. We are all satisfied with General Lee and he is always ready for a fight." That confidence would cost Lee and his men dearly in their next campaign.

Lee now proposed another invasion of the North—this time advancing as far as Pennsylvania—which would take the war out of Virginia and into Northern territory once again, and perhaps winning a smashing victory that would end the war. He also realized that it was not feasible to continue operating with an army split into two large and unwieldy corps and decided to reorganize it. Longstreet retained the I Corps, Richard S. Ewell was promoted to command Jackson's old II Corps, and A. P. Hill was promoted to command a new III Corps, created from units in the I and II Corps. The army's artillery had already been reorganized in the months before Chancellorsville, with the creation of battalions assigned to each corps.

The Army of Northern Virginia, about 75,000 strong, crossed over the Potomac River in mid-June and by the end of the month was scattered among several towns in southern Pennsylvania. By then the Confederates faced an Army of the Potomac numbering about 95,000 and commanded by yet another new general, George G. Meade. Lee concentrated his force near Gettysburg, a town at the center of an extensive road network in southern Pennsylvania.

The three days of battle at Gettysburg (1–3 July 1863) have often been called "the High Water Mark of the Confederacy," an assessment more justified after 1865 than it was in the summer of 1863. The Confederates launched a fierce attack on the first day, pushing the Federals through the streets of Gettysburg and eventually to Cemetery Ridge due south of the town, where Meade rallied his troops and established a strong defensive position that evening. Heavy fighting on the second day, in the area between Cemetery Ridge and the Confederate position on Seminary Ridge, also lasted until nightfall but accomplished little, as the Federals managed to hold their ground under intense pressure from repeated assaults. Lee, who still believed that the Army of the Potomac would break if he sent enough troops against it at the right place, planned a massive frontal assault against Meade's center, on Cemetery Ridge, for the afternoon of 3 July. The attack, known to history as "Pickett's Charge," had little if any chance of success and was a bloody failure that ended the battle. After suffering enormous casualties—more than a third of its officers and men killed, wounded, or captured in three days—the army soon withdrew from Pennsylvania and recrossed the Potomac into Virginia. Though Lee, his soldiers, the Confederate authorities, and the Southern people were naturally disappointed by the outcome, they were still confident that the Army of Northern Virginia would still help win the Confederacy's independence.

The army fought no pitched battles for the rest of 1863 and, except for minor clashes at Bristoe Station, Rappahannock Station, and Mine Run, spent its time waiting for an opportunity to resume the offensive the next spring. Lee did send Longstreet and I Corps to reinforce Braxton Bragg's Army of Tennessee, and, although this detached force participated in the Confederate victory at Chickamauga (19–20 September 1863) and the Knoxville campaign (November–December 1863), it accomplished little before returning to Virginia the following April.

By that time, the Army of the Potomac would be directed by Ulysses S. Grant, who had just been promoted to command all the armies of the United States. Although the army was still officially under Meade, Grant established his headquarters in the field with it and became Lee's principal opponent for the remainder of the war. When Grant made a move toward Richmond and entered the same Wilderness where Lee had been so successful against Hooker the year before, the Confederates attacked. Two days of battle in the Wilderness (5–6 May 1864), characterized by fierce but inconclusive combat in which neither side held an advantage for long, ended in a draw. This first phase of the Overland campaign marked a change in Lee's generalship, as he would thereafter take a more defensive stance than he preferred in the hope of preventing unnecessary losses that could not be replaced.

Grant now made an attempt to get the Army of the Potomac between Lee and Richmond, but the Army of Northern Virginia blocked his path at Spotsylvania Court House. Several days of bloody battle there at Spotsylvania (8–19 May 1864), most notably in an incredible hand-to-hand battle for the center of the Confederate lines that lasted for almost twenty-four hours on 12 May, resulted in staggering losses for both armies but did little to slow the momentum of the Army of the Potomac.

Within two weeks the Army of Northern Virginia would find itself in essentially the same position as it held when Lee took command in June 1862: facing the Army of the Potomac within sight of Richmond. At Cold Harbor both armies dug makeshift entrenchments, and two days of preliminary fighting there convinced Grant that the Confederates were demoralized by being maneuvered so close to their capital. He ordered a frontal assault against a strong Confederate position on the morning of 3 June, hoping to break Lee's lines and open the way to Richmond. The Army of Northern Virginia held its lines, easily repulsing the Federals and inflicting heavy casualties on the attackers. Three days of fighting at Cold Harbor (1–3 June 1864) ended with the Army of the Potomac no closer to its goal.

In just under a month of almost daily combat from the Wilderness to Cold Harbor, major and minor actions had now killed, wounded, or made prisoners of about 30,000 Confederates in the Army of Northern Virginia.

Thirty-seven of Lee's general officers—most notably Longstreet, seriously wounded by his own men at the Wilderness, and Stuart, mortally wounded at Yellow Tavern—were among these losses. These casualties, in officers and among the rank and file, would soon prove to be catastrophic.

Grant, realizing that he could not break Lee's lines by sheer force, now used his superior numbers in conjunction with other Federal forces to try and force the Confederates to choose between saving Richmond or saving Petersburg, a vital railroad center south of the capital. When the Army of the Potomac and the Army of Northern Virginia constructed an elaborate system of earthworks and trenches facing each other around Petersburg in mid-June, they initiated a siege that would last for the next ten months (June 1864–April 1865).

The remarkable battle of the Crater (30 July 1864), in which the Federals exploded four tons of gunpowder under Lee's army, was an excellent opportunity to break through his lines and capture Petersburg. Grant's assault, however, was decisively defeated by a fierce Confederate counterattack and actually had little real impact on the siege. The stalemate continued throughout the summer, fall, and winter, and would do so with few major breaks until the spring of 1865. The two armies, within yards of each other, occupied an extensive line of trenches, rifle pits, and batteries, and spent most of their days waiting for the decisive battle that never came.

Lee, hoping to take some pressure off the Army of Northern Virginia and to save the vital Shenandoah Valley for the Confederacy, sent his II Corps, under Jubal A. Early, to the valley in June. Early, facing a Federal army under Philip H. Sheridan, was soundly defeated in three battles that fall—at Winchester (19 September 1864), Fisher's Hill (22 September 1864), and Cedar Creek (19 October 1864)—and the remnants of his corps returned to Lee in December.

The sharp decline in Confederate morale that followed the fall of Atlanta, Early's crushing defeats in the Shenandoah Valley, Lincoln's reelection, the March to the Sea, and the twin disasters at Franklin and Nashville only confirmed to many that the Army of Northern Virginia was indeed, in the words of one of its officers, "the last hope of the South." Many of Lee's soldiers, however, whether veterans or conscripts, began to desert in greater numbers throughout the fall and into the winter of 1864–1865 as it became more and more evident that the Confederacy was dying. Lee's appointment to the position of general in chief of the Confederate armies, made in February 1865, might have had some impact if it had made earlier in the war but was by that point an empty gesture.

The spring campaign was mercifully short. Lee made one last desperate attempt to break through Grant's lines near Petersburg at Fort Stedman (25 March 1865). That assault, the last serious offensive move undertaken by the Army of Northern Virginia, was repulsed with heavy casualties. A week later, at Five Forks (1 April 1865), Grant defeated a third of Lee's army, capturing or driving it from the crossroads. A Federal assault all along the lines at Petersburg on the morning of 2 April broke Lee's defenses in several places and forced the evacuation of Richmond by the next morning. "If we, the Army of Northern Virginia, are defeated, all is lost," one of Lee's gloomy soldiers wrote in his diary that night. Lee retreated southwest, hoping to somehow reach Joseph E. Johnston and the remnants of the Army of Tennessee in North Carolina, but was so closely pursued by Grant that escape was impossible. Within days, Federals captured or scattered about a quarter of his entire army at Sayler's Creek/Harper's Farm (6 April 1865). When the Army of Northern Virginia reached the small town of Appomattox Court House, Lee found Federal cavalry blocking his retreat to the west with Grant's infantry close behind him. He met Grant at Wilmer McLean's house on Palm Sunday, 9 April, and finally surrendered the Army of Northern Virginia—about 28,000 officers and men, according to best estimates—to the Army of the Potomac.

Though Lee's surrender to Grant did not technically end the Civil War, it deprived the Confederacy of its last viable fighting force and its best general. In the years to come, the name "Appomattox" would eventually come to signify the end of the war.

—*J. Tracy Power*

See also Anderson, Richard Heron; Antietam, Battle of; Appomattox Court House; Brandy Station; Bull Run, First Battle of; Bull Run, Second Battle of; Cedar Creek; Cedar Mountain; Chambersburg Raid; Chancellorsville, Battle of; Cold Harbor; Crater, Battle of the; Early, Jubal Anderson; Ewell, Richard Stoddert; Fisher's Hill; Five Forks; Fort Stedman; Fredericksburg, First Battle of; Fredericksburg, Second Battle of; Gaines's Mill; Gettysburg, Battle of; Glendale, Battle of; Gordon, John Brown; Groveton, Virginia, Battle of; Hampton, Wade; Hill, Ambrose Powell; Jackson, Thomas Jonathan; Knoxville Campaign; Lee, Fitzhugh; Lee, Robert Edward; Longstreet, James; Malvern Hill; Mechanicsville; Mine Run Campaign; Petersburg Campaign; Rappahannock Station; Savage's Station; Sayler's Creek; Seven Days'; Shenandoah Valley Campaign (1862); Shenandoah Valley Campaign (1864-1865); South Mountain, Battle of; Spotsylvania; Stonewall Brigade; Stuart, James Ewell Brown; Stuart's Dumfries Raid; Stuart's Ride Around McClellan; Wilderness, Battle of the; Winchester, Second Battle of; Winchester, Third Battle of; Yellow Tavern.

For further reading:

Alexander, Edward Porter. *Fighting for the Confederacy: The Personal Recollections of General Edward Porter Alexander* (1989).

———. *Military Memoirs of a Confederate: A Critical Narrative* (1907).

Allen, William. *The Army of Northern Virginia in 1862* (1892).

Casler, John O. *Four Years in the Stonewall Brigade* (1971).

Freeman, Douglas Southall. *Lee's Lieutenants: A Study in Command* (1942–1944).

Gallagher, Gary W. *Lee and His Generals in War and*

Memory (1998).

———, ed. *Lee the Soldier* (1996).

Hattaway, Herman, and Archer Jones. *How the North Won: A Military History of the Civil War* (1983).

Hewitt, Janet B., et al., eds. *Supplement to the Official Records of the Union and Confederate Armies* (1994–2000).

Lee, R. E. *Lee's Dispatches: Unpublished Letters of General Robert E. Lee, C.S.A. to Jefferson Davis and the War Department of The Confederate States of America 1862–1865* (1957).

———. *The Wartime Papers of R. E. Lee* (1961).

McCarthy, Carlton. *Detailed Minutiae of Soldier Life in the Army of Northern Virginia 1861–1865* (1882).

McMurry, Richard M. *Two Great Rebel Armies: An Essay in Confederate Military History* (1989).

Power, J. Tracy. *Lee's Miserables: Life in the Army of Northern Virginia from the Wilderness to Appomattox* (1998).

Taylor, Walter H. *Four Years With General Lee* (1877).

———. *General Lee: His Campaigns in Virginia 1861–1865 with Personal Reminiscences* (1906).

U.S. War Department. *The War of the Rebellion: A Compilation of the Official Records of the Union and Confederate Armies* (1880–1901).

Woodworth, Steven E. *Davis and Lee at War* (1995).

ARMY OF TENNESSEE

This hard-bitten army was the Confederacy's military mainstay in the Southern heartland. That it ultimately failed to withstand an ever-increasing and resilient Union opponent reflected more the flaws in the army's leadership than it revealed any absence of resolution or valor on the part of its soldiers. Created in late November 1862 by combining the Army of Kentucky and the Army of Mississippi, it would fight major engagements at Stones River and Chickamauga, unsuccessfully lay siege to occupied Chattanooga, and then execute a skillful retrograde through the mountains of North Georgia to fight a series of battles in the defense of Atlanta. After the fall of Atlanta, the army moved north into Tennessee to fight at Franklin and Nashville. By then it was a badly mauled shadow of its former self, stumbling as much as marching toward its surrender near Durham, North Carolina, an event that occurred fifteen days after Lee's Army of Northern Virginia had surrendered at Appomattox Court House.

The Army of Tennessee's creation grew from the failure of Braxton Bragg and Edmund Kirby Smith's invasion of Kentucky in the fall of 1862. The two distinct southern armies that had fought together at Perryville in September were designated as the Army of Tennessee upon their return to that state. Bragg was placed in command. The army was organized into two corps under Lieutenant General Leonidas Polk and Lieutenant General William J. Hardee and four brigades of cavalry, commanded by Brigadier Generals Joseph Wheeler (the overall cavalry commander), Alexander Buford, John Pegram, and John Wharton. Almost immediately after its formation, the army was reduced by the need to send Carter Stevenson's division of 10,000 men

to Vicksburg, so Polk's corps consisted of two divisions under Major Generals B. F. Cheatham and Jones M. Withers, while Hardee's contained three divisions under Major Generals John C. Breckinridge, Patrick R. Cleburne, and John P. McCown, this last part of the original Army of Kentucky or Kirby Smith's Corps as it was also known. It was in this configuration and at a strength of less than 40,000 that the army fought the furious and stalemated battle of Stones River at the end of the year.

Retreating to Tullahoma after Stones River, the Army of Tennessee was reinforced and by the summer of 1863 numbered 43,700 men, a figure that included Nathan Bedford Forrest's cavalry division. After William S. Rosecrans's campaign of maneuver had displaced Bragg from his positions in middle Tennessee, James Longstreet's Corps was detached from the Army of Northern Virginia to reinforce the Army of Tennessee. It was also bolstered by the arrival from Mississippi of brigades under John Gregg and Evander McNair, and a brigade under Major General W. H. T. Walker, who was placed in command of the Reserve Corps. These arrivals accounted for a considerable addition to the army and required its significant reorganization. It was formed into a Right Wing under Polk (D. H. Hill's corps and Walker's Reserve Corps) and a Left Wing under Longstreet (Simon Bolivar Buckner's corps and Longstreet's corps under John Bell Hood). The infantry numbered almost 48,000 men, and Wheeler's corps with Forrest's division accounted for nearly 15,000 cavalry.

It was thus with confidence that Bragg tried to exploit the scattered nature of Rosecrans's Army of the Cumberland as it moved through the mountainous terrain of the Tennessee-Alabama-Georgia border. The attempt to cut up Rosecrans in detail, however, brought on the concentration of the armies at Chickamauga on 19–20 September where the Army of Tennessee won its greatest victory. Bragg's failure to exploit this victory with a decisive blow squandered his greatest opportunity and enraged his subordinates. His unhappy facility for blaming his staff for his failures shook the army to its roots when it brought about another major reorganization. The personal intervention of President Jefferson Davis, who visited the army's gloomy headquarters after Chickamauga, hastened the rearrangement. Leonidas Polk was relieved of command and in late October was transferred to the command of the Department of Alabama, Mississippi, and East Louisiana. Buckner's request for reassignment was swiftly granted, and on 14 December he was detached to command the District of the Gulf in Mobile. D. H. Hill's outspoken criticism of Bragg and his insistence that Bragg be removed so irritated the president that he relieved Hill instead. As it was then reconstituted after Chickamauga, the Army of Tennessee consisted of three corps under Longstreet,

Hardee, and Breckinridge, but even this arrangement proved temporary. In November, Longstreet was detached to lay siege to Ambrose Burnside's occupation of Knoxville.

Bragg's failure at Chattanooga indicated how low the army's morale had sunk following such carping, command dislocation, impermanence. On 25 November, the army's center was routed at Missionary Ridge and the whole of it streamed south toward Dalton, Georgia, where on 2 December Bragg finally was relieved of command to be replaced by Joseph E. Johnston. The army's new commander left much of its organization in place and tried to repair the damage of the post-Chickamauga contretemps. Hardee remained in command of Polk's former I Corps, Hood commanded II Corps, and Polk fatefully rejoined the army with his Army of Mississippi that became III Corps, Army of Tennessee. He would be killed at Pine Mountain on 14 June.

Under Johnston's skillful management, the army executed a series of complicated retrogrades through the mountains of north Georgia as William T. Sherman began his inexorable advance on Atlanta, but criticism of Johnston's defensive withdrawal led Davis to replace his with the impetuous Hood on 18 July 1864. There had never been any doubt that the Army of Tennessee would fight—just if Johnston would—so Hood rushed it to combat in a rash but unsuccessful effort to drive Sherman from the environs of Atlanta. In this way, Hood went far in breaking his army as an effective combat force and then completed the job by taking it into Tennessee where it would fight George H. Thomas's army at Franklin and Nashville. After the latter battle, Hood asked to be relieved of command and was briefly replaced by Richard Taylor. Finally on 25 February 1865, Joseph E. Johnston resumed command of the shattered remnants of the Army of Tennessee.

Depleted now by abominable morale as well as casualties and at less than half its fighting size, the army was joined by all available troops in the Department of South Carolina, Georgia, and Florida, more to trail Sherman's march through the Carolinas than effectively oppose it. Johnston's command comprised a geographical expanse of considerable dimension, but his manpower was a pitiful testimony to the final limitations and fatal weariness of the Confederacy. With less than 20,000 effectives, he forlornly reorganized the Army of Tennessee again on 9 April, the day that Lee was surrendering at Appomattox. Hardee, Alexander P. Stewart, and Stephen D. Lee commanded ragged corps and Wade Hampton led the cavalry, but the war was over. A ceasefire on 18 April was the prelude to Johnston's surrender of the Army of Tennessee to Sherman at Bennett's House on 26 April 1865.

—*David S. Heidler and Jeanne T. Heidler*

See also Atlanta Campaign; Bragg, Braxton; Carolinas Campaign; Chattanooga Campaign; Chickamauga, Battle of; Hood, John Bell; Johnston, Joseph E.; Stones River, Battle of; Tullahoma Campaign

For further reading:
Connelly, Thomas. *Autumn of Glory: The Army of Tennessee, 1862–1865* (1971).
Cumming, Kate. *A Journal of Hospital Life in the Confederate Army of Tennessee* (1866).
Horn, Stanley. *The Army of Tennessee* (1952).
Madaus, Howard M. *The Battle Flags of the Confederate Army of Tennessee* (1976).
McWhiney, Grady. *Braxton Bragg and Confederate Defeat* (1969).
Sykes, E. T. "Walthall's Brigade—A Cursory Sketch with Personal Experiences of Walthall's Brigade, Army of Tennessee, C.S.A., 1862–1865." *Publications of the Mississippi Historical Society* (1917).

ARMY OF THE CUMBERLAND

Union general Don Carlos Buell's Army of the Ohio became the Army of the Cumberland on 24 October 1862, when General Order No. 168, Adjutant General's Office, reorganized the Department of the Cumberland. The new department included east Tennessee from the Tennessee River and the parts of Alabama and Georgia that would come under Federal control by military occupation. The Army of the Ohio had already seen hard action at Shiloh in April and Perryville in October. In October 1861 its official classification became XIV Corps. Yet from the start the army was also called the Army of the Cumberland, possibly because it contained in part elements of the force that had operated in the old Department of the Cumberland (15 August–9 November 1861) under Robert Anderson and William T. Sherman.

William S. Rosecrans took command of the Army of the Cumberland on 30 October 1862. On 19 December under General Order No. 41, the army was arranged into three wings, with the right wing commanded by Alexander McCook, the left wing by Thomas L. Crittenden, and the center wing by George H. Thomas. The cavalry was commanded by Brigadier General David Stanley. It was in this arrangement that the army would fight the fierce engagement at Stone's River at the end of 1862.

The Army of the Cumberland was reorganized into three corps on 9 January 1863 with Thomas commanding XIV Corps; McCook, XX Corps; and Crittenden, XXI Corps. Rosecrans in June created the Reserve Corps from the Army of Kentucky commanded by Major General Gordon Granger. During June 1863, the army conducted the Tullahoma campaign, a skillful series of maneuvers and skirmishes against Braxton Bragg in middle Tennessee that kept Bragg from reinforcing besieged Vicksburg. Yet on 20 September, the Army of the Cumberland suffered a stunning defeat at

Headquarters of the Army of the Cumberland, Missionary Ridge (Photograph by Mathew Brady Studio / *National Archives*)

Chickamauga and retreated into Chattanooga where XI and XII Corps from the Army of the Potomac would reinforce it. The army was again reorganized on 9 October when XX and XXI Corps were merged with the Reserve Corps to create a new IV Corps under Gordon Granger. The most important change came at the army's head. Rosecrans's calamitous performance in the fall of 1863 prompted Ulysses S. Grant to replace him with George H. Thomas on 20 October. Thomas, with William T. Sherman's Army of the Tennessee and under the personal direction of Grant, would lift the siege of Chattanooga at the end of November, setting the stage for the 1864 Atlanta campaign.

In April 1864, the Army of the Cumberland revived XX Corps by merging the Army of the Potomac's XI and XII Corps and placing the new unit under Joseph Hooker. Also in that month, Granger was replaced at the head of IV Corps by Oliver O. Howard, and the army's cavalry was organized into four divisions of three brigades each. At the outset of the Atlanta campaign, the army was composed of IV, XIV, and XX Corps, totaling close to 61,000 men and boasting artillery that numbered 130 guns. Howard would command IV Corps until he assumed command of the Army of the Tennessee on 27 July, when the corps devolved upon David Stanley. John M. Palmer commanded XIV Corps until 7 August, when General Richard W. Johnson succeeded him. Johnson was in turn succeeded by brevet Major General Jefferson C. Davis on 22 August. Hooker was followed in command of XX Corps by Brigadier General Alpheus S. Williams on 28 July, and Williams was replaced on 27 August by General Henry W. Slocum.

From the spring of 1864 to the fall of Atlanta in September, the Army of the Cumberland would see some of its hardest fighting, suffering almost 23,000 casualties, of whom more than 3,000 were killed. After the Atlanta campaign, the army was essentially dismantled. Thomas took what was still designated as the Army of the Cumberland but actually was only its IV Corps and the 4th Division of XX Corps to harry John Bell Hood's advance into Tennessee. In November and December 1864, the Army of the Cumberland with XXIII Corps (John Schofield's Army of the Ohio) defeated Hood at Franklin and Nashville. Meanwhile, XIV and XX Corps (again under Williams) were placed under Slocum and formed Sherman's right wing in the epic March to the Sea. These two corps would be officially constituted as Slocum's Army of Georgia on 28 March 1865.

—*David S. Heidler and Jeanne T. Heidler*

See also Rosecrans, William Starke; Thomas, George Henry.
For further reading:
Cist, Henry M. *The Army of the Cumberland* (1882).
Van Horne, Thomas B. *History of the Army of the Cumberland: Its Organization, Campaigns, and Battles, Written at the Request of Major-General George H. Thomas Chiefly from His Private Military Journal and Official and Other Documents Furnished by Him* (1875).

ARMY OF THE GULF

The Union Department of the Gulf was organized on 23 February 1862 to span the Gulf Coast west of Pensacola, Florida, and into the interior as it was occupied by Federal troops. Forces in the department were frequently and somewhat loosely described as the Army of the Gulf. Originally, it comprised Benjamin F. Butler's New Orleans Expeditionary Corps. Butler commanded the department and stirred controversy during the initial occupation of New Orleans where the department's headquarters were situated. On 17 December 1862, Nathaniel P. Banks succeeded him and remained in command until 23 September 1864, when Stephen G. Hurlbut took charge. At war's end, Banks resumed command briefly from 22 April until 3 June 1865, when Edward R. S. Canby was placed in command. The department had been embraced by the Military Division of West Mississippi on 7 May 1864 and remained there until 17 May 1865, but even during that time it had continued to function as a discrete organizational entity.

Upon the establishment of the Defenses of New Orleans on 16 December 1862, a major reorganization of the Army of the Gulf followed early the following year. Most of its regiments became part of XIX Corps (organized on 5 January 1863 to date from 14 December 1862) under Banks. From then to its discontinuance as a part of the department on 7 November 1864, XIX Corps formed the heart of the body troops called the Army of the Gulf. After Banks the corps was commanded by Major General William B. Franklin (21 August 1863–2 May 1864), Brigadier General William H. Emory (2 May–2 July 1864), Brigadier General Benjamin S. Roberts (2 July–6 July 1864), Brigadier General Michael K. Lawler (6 July–7 July 1864), and finally Major General John J. Reynolds to 7 November 1864.

Shortly after its organization the corps consisted of four divisions and seven unattached regiments at Brashear City, Key West, Tortugas, and West Florida. Among its unique features were six newly organized regiments of Louisiana African-American troops. It boasted nineteen batteries of light artillery, a regiment of heavy artillery, and five regiments of cavalry. Returns for the corps totaled 55,229, with 44,832 present, and 35,670 present for duty.

This force participated in the campaigns against Port Hudson, the Texas Coast, and—joined by XIII, XVI, and XVII Corps—in Banks's abortive Red River campaign of 1864 during his tenure as commander of the department. After the Red River campaign, the 1st and 2d Divisions of XIX Corps departed for Virginia to participate in the Shenandoah Valley campaign. The balance of the corps remained in Louisiana, and with XIII and XVI Corps fought in Canby's assault on Fort Blakely, Spanish Fort, and Mobile in the spring of 1865.

—*David S. Heidler and Jeanne T. Heidler*

See also Departments, Military, U.S.A.; Mobile Campaign; New Orleans, Capture of; Port Hudson Campaign; Red River Campaign.

For further reading:

Gregg, Jo Chandler. *Life in the Army in the Departments of Virginia, and the Gulf, including Observations in New Orleans: With an Account of the Author's Life and Experience in the Ministry* (1866).

ARMY OF THE JAMES

This Union force was created in April 1864 to assist in General Ulysses S. Grant's overland campaign against Richmond. The Army of the James was in the Department of Virginia and North Carolina, which had been created on 15 July 1863 by combining the separate departments of the two states. At the time of the establishment of the Army of the James, the department was under the command of Major General Benjamin F. Butler, who also commanded the army.

The Army of the James was composed of the X and XVIII Corps and a cavalry division under August V. Kautz. The X Corps was a celebrated outfit, originally organized on 3 September 1862 as the Department of the South. Under General Quincy A. Gillmore, it had participated in the failed attack on Fort Wagner outside Charleston, South Carolina, on 18 July 1863 with the 54th Massachusetts leading the assault. The XVIII Corps had been organized in the Department of North Carolina on 24 December 1862. By the time it was transferred to Virginia in spring 1864, it had absorbed the VII Corps when that unit was discontinued on 1 August 1863. When the X and XVIII Corps assembled at Yorktown in April 1864, they totaled 33,898 officers and men and boasted eighty-two artillery pieces.

Brigadier General Alfred H. Terry briefly commanded the X Corps until Gillmore resumed command on 4 May 1864. Terry commanded the corps four additional times, stepping in each time to fill voids created by the departure of other officers. He would be the corps's last commander when its white troops were merged into the new XXIV Corps and its African-American troops into the new XXV Corps. The other commanders of X Corps were W. T. H. Brooks (21 June–18 July 1864), David B. Birney (28 July–10 October 1864), and Adelbert Ames (4 November–18 November 1864).

Major General William F. Smith commanded the XVIII Corps as part of the Army of the James from 2 May to 10 July 1864. He was succeeded by Brigadier General J. H. Martindale (10 July–21 July 1864), Major General E. O. C. Ord (21 July–4 September 1864), and Major General John Gibbon (4 September–22 September 1864). Ord returned to command on 22 September and remained until the end of the month when Brigadier General Charles A. Heckman briefly commanded (29 September–1 October 1864). Finally Brevet Major General Godfrey Weitzel took command on 1 October and continued in charge until the corps's discontinuance on 3 December 1864. Like the X Corps, the XVIII Corps's white troops were moved to XXIV Corps, Ord commanding, and its African-Americans to XV Corps, Weitzel commanding.

The army's cavalry division was modest in number—Philip Sheridan described it as "Kautz's small cavalry division"—and never numbered more than about 2,300. In participating in raids and skirmishes during the Bermuda Hundred campaign, it performed some marginal service.

The Army of the James fought well, but it was badly led from the top. Butler was occasionally impetuous and frequently inept, so the army's career was mainly checkered and its people generally unhappy. In October 1864 Assistant Adjutant General Edward W. Smith chastised officers for their "laziness and inattention" in failing to file timely reports. Butler often meted out equally harsh discipline for both small and serious matters. Consequently, the army did not fulfill many of Grant's expectations. It offered little assistance on his southern flank as the Army of the Potomac began the march on Richmond from the north. Instead, the Army of the James suffered such severe defeats in the Bermuda Hundred campaign that Grant detached considerable parts of it to aid the Army of the Potomac in the main advance on the Army of Northern Virginia. Parts of the X and the entire XVIII Corps fought at Cold Harbor with dreadful losses. Returning to Bermuda Hundred, these detached elements again functioned as the Army of the James in the Petersburg campaign.

The reorganization of the Army of the James on 3 December 1864 formed the army into the XXIV and XXV Corps. Butler led detachments from the XXIV Corps on a failed expedition to take Fort Fisher, North Carolina, but a second foray on 15 January 1865 under Terry was successful. The units detached to form Terry's expedition—the 2d Division and Abbot's Brigade of XXIV Corps and Paine's (African-American) Brigade of XXV corps—stayed in North Carolina and became part of a restored X Corps.

Ord replaced the discredited Butler as commander of the Army of the James in January 1865. The Army of the James assisted in the final assault on Richmond in April, and African-American troops of the XXV Corps were the first to enter the captured city. As part of the Union pursuit of the Army of Northern Virginia, XXIV Corps was engaged on the morning of Lee's surrender and reportedly fired the last infantry volley in the campaign. After the war, the XXV Corps formed part of the Army of Occupation in Texas, remaining at that duty until January 1866, when the corps was discontinued.

—*David S. Heidler and Jeanne T. Heidler*

See also Bermuda Hundred Campaign; Butler, Benjamin Franklin; Departments, Military, U.S.A.; Petersburg Campaign.

For further reading:
Longacre, Edward G. *Army of Amateurs: General Benjamin F. Butler and the Army of the James, 1863–1865* (1997).
Smith, William Farrar. *From Chattanooga to Petersburg under Generals Grant and Butler; A Contribution to the History of the War and a Personal Vindication* (1893).

ARMY OF THE KANAWHA

Confederate forces in the Kanawha Valley region of western Virginia were organized into the Army of the Kanawha in the first months of the war. Former Virginia governor Henry A. Wise had been given command on 6 June 1861 of troops he had raised and others from the Confederate Provisional Army. Styling itself Wise's Legion, the unit was only marginally structured with militia and provisional army soldiers mingled in fluidly shifting companies. The Legion was badly supplied, ravaged by disease, especially measles, and depleted by desertion when local men ran away after being ordered out of the Kanawha to protect, for instance, the Virginia Central Railroad. At most the outfit numbered only about 1,800 men.

To bolster this meager military presence, former governor John B. Floyd was authorized to raise troops and was given overall command of the Army of the Kanawha on 11 August. Floyd's army consisted of the 45th and 50th Virginia Infantry and the 8th Cavalry Regiment. Efforts to meld Wise's Legion into the Army of the Kanawha, however, foundered because of Wise's ego and Floyd's tactlessness. The two had never like one another, and now these political rivals found themselves military ones as well. Only the Federals would profit.

By the time Floyd came into the region, Wise had already been forced to retreat from the Kanawha as Jacob D. Cox's Federals moved into the valley and occupied Charleston. Situated in Lewisburg at the time of Floyd's appointment, Wise gave only a formal nod to his new superior's status. Moreover, he commenced a series of complaints about his belief that Floyd intended "to destroy my command, and not only transfer to himself the State volunteers and militia, but by constant detachments of my Legion, to merge it also in his brigade, to be commanded by his field officers, and be torn to pieces by maladministration, and to sink me, the second in command, even below his majors and captains."

The Army of the Kanawha was under the overall command of the Northwest Army under Robert E. Lee with headquarters at Valley Mountain. It was to this authority that Wise directed his pleas that his command remain an independent one, and it was from that remove that Lee tried to cope with the Wise-Floyd antagonism that threatened to endanger the entire region. Lee wanted Wise and Floyd to cooperate against William S. Rosecrans's positions at Gauley Bridge, but even his legendary tact could not resolve the discord. "Feeling assured of the patriotism and zeal of the officers and men composing the Army of the Kanawha," he wrote to Wise, "I have never apprehended any embarrassment or interference in the execution of their respective duties believing they would make everything yield to the welfare of the republic.

Nonetheless, Lee was compelled to delineate the lines

of command, which he did on 21 August by directing that Colonel C. Q. Tompkins's 22d Virginia and Colonel John McCausland's 36th Virginia would be assigned to Floyd. The Wise Legion was by the same order placed under the "immediate command" of Henry Wise, but everybody would be subject to the orders of the commanding general of the Army of the Kanawha, which meant John B. Floyd. It was to no avail, and Floyd remained undermanned, bereft of any meaningful cooperation from the Wise Legion. On 10 September, the Army of the Kanawha barely managed to hold its positions when Rosecrans attacked it at Carnifex Ferry. That night Floyd had to withdraw.

President Jefferson Davis, the War Department, and Lee finally threw up their hands in the face of Wise's recalcitrance. On 12 September, Adjutant and Inspector General Samuel Cooper conveyed Davis's order that Lee had the authority to transfer Wise's Legion to any command other than General Floyd's. It was an admission that the two men would never work together. Accordingly to make up for the absence of Wise's Legion, Colonel William Phillips's Georgia Legion and Colonel D. R. Russell's 20th Mississippi Infantry reinforced Floyd. The resolution of the Army of the Kanawha's command problems came too late to salvage the military situation in the region.

Wise's Legion was subsequently sent to Norfolk and from there to North Carolina to help defend Roanoke. The Army of the Kanawha itself soon ceased to be when Floyd took the 20th Mississippi, 36th Virginia, and 50th Virginia to Bowling Green, Kentucky. There these units and the 51st and 56th Virginia were incorporated into William J. Hardee's Central Army of Kentucky as its 3d Division. By year's end, only two regiments of the old Army of the Kanawha remained at Lewisburg: Colonel Henry Heth's 45th Virginia and Tompkins's 22d Virginia.

—David S. Heidler and Jeanne T. Heidler

See also Carnifex Ferry, Battle of; Floyd, John Buchanan; Wise, Henry Alexander.

For further reading:
Simpson, Craig M. *A Good Southerner: The Life of Henry A. Wise of Virginia* (1985).

ARMY OF THE NORTHWEST, CONFEDERATE
(June 1861–May 1862)

On 8 June 1861, the Southern troops operating in northwestern Virginia, near what would become the border of present-day Virginia and West Virginia, were designated the Confederate Army of the Northwest and placed under the command of Brigadier General Robert S. Garnett. The army's ominous 11 July 1861 debut against Union Generals George B. McClellan and William S. Rosecrans resulted in a Confederate defeat at Rich Mountain and included the surrender of a large portion of the Southern army under Colonel John Pegram. While evacuating his position at Laurel Hill on 13 July, Garnett's retreating army was again attacked at Carrick's Ford on the Cheat River. Garnett was killed in that engagement, the first general on either side to die in battle. Brigadier General Henry Rootes Jackson temporarily took charge of the shattered army. On 21 July Major General William W. Loring officially took command.

Although the size and regiments were continually fluctuating, in general the Army of the Northwest was separated into two components: the Monterey Division on the western front and the Huntersville Division in the rear defending transportation, communications, and the interior.

In late July, General Robert E. Lee, commander of all Virginia forces, traveled personally to this sector to oversee operations. Late summer and fall 1861 were an unusually cold and damp season in this mountainous region. Snow fell in late August. Frozen or thawing roads made transportation nearly impossible. Soldiers struggled to survive as military operations and campaigning became all but impossible. For this and other reasons, Loring remained inactive. After considerable prompting by Lee and a favorable change in the weather, Loring advanced, and on 12–13 September the army again suffering a severe setback with the ill-fated Cheat Mountain campaign. A few days later, Lee traveled to the nearby Army of the Kanawha to mediate between his two feuding generals, John B. Floyd and Henry Wise. Soon after, Loring and five regiments of the Army of the Northwest followed Lee for a combined movement against the Federal forces in the Sewell Mountain campaign. (Unfortunately for the Confederacy, Lee chose to deal with these two commands piecemeal instead of uniting them in one coordinated effort.) Henry R. Jackson and the rest of the Army of the Northwest remained at Camp Bartow on the Greenbrier River.

On 3 October 1861, Federal forces under the command of Brigadier General Joseph J. Reynolds attacked the Confederates at Camp Bartow. The advance was repulsed and the Federal army retreated to their garrison at Cheat Mountain. Both sides seemed to settle down into winter quarters.

In late November, Loring's forces returned and again the Army of the Northwest was divided. Loring, under orders from the Army of the Northwest's departmental commander Major General Thomas J. Jackson, took the majority of the army to Winchester and then on to Romney. This would result in the infamous Loring-Jackson confrontation, concluding in Loring's transfer out of the department on 9 February 1862. This division never returned to the Army of the Northwest, being absorbed into the Army of the Valley.

The remainder of the Army of the Northwest (the

Monterey Division) withdrew to the mountain pass, where the Staunton and Parkersburg Turnpike crossed the summit of Alleghany Mountain. Command of the small mountain garrison fell to Colonel Edward Johnson. There, at Camp Alleghany, Johnson and his 1,800 men were again attacked by the Union garrison at Cheat Mountain, this time under Brigadier General Robert H. Milroy. And again, the Federal forces were repulsed.

This action concluded campaigning in the region for the winter of 1861–1862. Except for a raid on Huntersville in early January and scouting or occasional skirmishing, both sides remained inactive. In early spring, newly appointed Brigadier General Edward Johnson and his six regiments, still designated as the Army of the Northwest, gradually moved eastward toward a union with Jackson's Army of the Valley.

On 8 May 1862, with Johnson directing the Confederate operations, the combined two armies won a victory at McDowell, again over Milroy. Near the end of the engagement, Edward Johnson received a serious ankle wound. The wound was so serious that he was unable to remain with his small army. Subsequently, Johnson's army, the last of the northwestern command, was incorporated into Jackson's Army of the Valley and the Confederate Army of the Northwest ceased to exist.

—*Eddie Woodward*

See also Johnson, Edward.

For further reading:

Freeman, Douglas Southall. *Lee's Lieutenants: A Study in Command* (1942–1944).

Hall, James E. *Diary of a Confederate Soldier* (1961).

Hotchkiss, Jed. *Virginia. Confederate Military History*. vol. IV (1899; reprint, 1987).

Pryor, Shepherd Green. *A Post of Honor: The Pryor Letters, 1861–63* (1989).

Woodward, Edward V. "Holding the Alleghany Line: Edward Johnson, the Army of the Northwest, and the Battle of Alleghany Summit" (Thesis, 1998).

ARMY OF THE OHIO

Some confusion surrounds what constituted the body of soldiers known as the Union Army of the Ohio at any given time during the Civil War. The force was nominally a creation of the large Department of the Ohio, which went through several reorganizations during the war's first year. It is therefore useful to review those reorganizations to describe the initial creation of the Army of the Ohio as well as its subsequent reincarnation.

The Department of the Ohio was created on 3 May 1861 to embrace Illinois, Indiana, and Ohio. Six days later, portions of what is now West Virginia and Pennsylvania were added to it, as was Missouri on 6 June 1861. Illinois was transferred to the Western Department on 3 July. The Department of the Ohio's boundaries were again readjusted on 19 September 1861 to embrace Ohio, Indiana, and the area of Kentucky

within fifteen miles of Cincinnati. Finally on 9 November, it took on the final shape of its first existence to include Ohio, Michigan, Indiana, and Kentucky east of the Cumberland River.

The department's new commander was Brigadier General Don Carlos Buell, who took over from Brigadier General Ormsby Mitchell on 15 November 1861. Buell's force would be designated as the Army of the Ohio. General in Chief George B. McClellan resisted the idea of organizing the Union armies into corps, so army structure consisted of divisions numbered according to when they were formed. Although eastern armies abandoned this structure in favor of corps organization in the spring of 1862, it remained in the western armies until the following December. Consequently, the Army of the Ohio had several numbered divisions, each with three numbered brigades. It was under this rudimentary and unsatisfactory organization that the Army of the Ohio fought at Shiloh in April 1862. This structure would remain in place until corps organization was introduced in 1863 for the western armies.

In March 1862, the Department of the Ohio ceased to exist when it was divided between the Department of the Mississippi and the Mountain Department. The department was revived on 19 August 1862, but in the interim the troops in Buell's Army of the Ohio had operated under William S. Rosecrans as part of Rosecrans's new Department of the Cumberland. This new incarnation of the Cumberland department came into being on 24 October 1862 and should not be confused with the original Department of the Cumberland under Robert Anderson and then William T. Sherman. With this change, the Army of the Ohio officially became XIV Corps. Yet because it now contained some elements from the earlier Department of the Cumberland and because of its association with the new department of the same name, XIV Corps (or the original Army of the Ohio) was frequently referred to as the Army of the Cumberland. The army fought at Stones River under this appellation.

The Department of the Ohio was recreated on 19 August 1862 under Major General Horatio Wright. It embraced Illinois, Indiana, Ohio, Michigan, briefly Wisconsin, and Kentucky east of the Tennessee River, including Cumberland Gap. By then, troops of the original Army of the Ohio were scattered geographically and organizationally. Some elements, for instance, made up the whole of the Army of the Kentucky that performed with high distinction at Chickamauga. When Ambrose Burnside assumed command of the department on 25 March 1863, IX Army Corps was dispatched from the east to participate in operations in east Tennessee. Eventually IX Corps was merged with regiments from Kentucky under George L. Hartsuff to form XXIII Corps, which would capture Knoxville and then withstand James Longstreet's siege of that city.

Placed under John Schofield on 4 April 1864, XXIII Corps, numbering about 12,800 men, was the Army of the Ohio that participated in the Atlanta campaign. It was sharply engaged at Resaca, Kennesaw Mountain, and Utoy Creek. As Sherman began his March to the Sea, the Army of the Ohio, numbering about 10,000 men, joined with George H. Thomas's army to fight in the battle of Franklin. It mainly formed the reserve at the battle of Nashville. In these operations, the Army of the Ohio in its last embodiment had scored its most memorable accomplishments.

After campaigning in Tennessee with Thomas, the bulk of Schofield's Army of the Ohio (officially still XXIII Corps) was transferred to the east. Original plans called for it to join the Army of the Potomac's siege at Petersburg, Virginia, but it finally wound up in North Carolina to assist in William T. Sherman's advance northward from Savannah. There it would remain, forming the core of the Department of North Carolina. Considerably diminished by regiments mustering out, it was discontinued on 1 August 1865.

—*David S. Heidler and Jeanne T. Heidler*

See also Atlanta Campaign; Buell, Don Carlos; Franklin, Battle of; Kennesaw Mountain, Battle of; Resaca, Battle of; Schofield, John M.; Utoy Creek, Battle of.

For further reading:
Castel, Albert E.. *Decision in the West: The Atlanta Campaign of 1864* (1992).
Fry, James B. *Operations of the Army Under Buell from June 10th to October 30th, 1862 and the "Buell Commission"* (1884).
McDonough, James L. *Schofield: Union General in the Civil War and Reconstruction* (1972).
Schofield, John McAllister. *Forty Six Years in the Army* (1897).
Weigley, Russell F. "The Military Thought of John M. Schofield." *Military Affairs* (1959).

ARMY OF THE PENINSULA

The Confederate government placed Virginia's York Peninsula in the Department of the Peninsula on 26 May 1861. John Bankhead Magruder was put in command of the department, and from his headquarters at Yorktown he commanded a scattered group of garrisons and camps that was labeled the Army of the Peninsula. This force has the distinction of having fought at Big Bethel on 10 June 1861, reportedly the first land engagement of the war in the east.

By January 1862, the Army of the Peninsula consisted of two divisions. The 1st Division, under Brigadier General Gabriel J. Rains, posted at Yorktown and Ship Point. The 13th Alabama, 2d Florida, 6th Georgia, 23d Georgia, 14th Louisiana, a Louisiana Zouave battalion, 2d Mississippi, 15th North Carolina, 32d Virginia (2 companies), 53d Virginia (8 companies), 115th Virginia Militia, Maurin's Louisiana battery, Nelson's battery, and the 1st Virginia Artillery (3 companies) embodied the division, as well as six independent companies of heavy artillery.

The 2d Division, under Brigadier General Lafayette McLaws, included the 8th Alabama, Cobb's Legion, 10th Georgia, 16th Georgia, Greenville Guards, 2d Louisiana, 5th Louisiana, 10th Louisiana, 14th Virginia, 32d Virginia, one company of the 53d Virginia, four companies of Virginia Cavalry, and five companies of 1st Virginia Artillery at Mulberry Point. The 6th Virginia, 9th Virginia Militia, 21st Virginia Militia, 87th Virginia Militia, one company of the 3d Virginia Cavalry, and one company of the 1st Virginia Artillery were at Gloucester Point with four batteries of heavy artillery. Encamped at Williamsburg were the 1st Louisiana Battalion, two companies of the 32d Virginia, and one company of the 53d Virginia, while the 61st Virginia Militia and a company of Virginia Cavalry were stationed in Matthews County. Six companies of the 3d Virginia Cavalry were at Lebanon Church and around Yorktown, and the 52d Virginia Militia, one company of the 1st Virginia Artillery, and two independent companies of Virginia Artillery were at Jamestown Island. The returns for the army listed its effective strength at about 11,000 men.

These were the forces that were fated to face the first phase of George B. McClellan's Peninsula campaign in the spring of 1862. On 27 March, Richmond dispatched the 14th and 26th Alabama (the latter without arms) to Yorktown, and on 11 April, 4,000 additional men under D. H. Hill joined the Army of the Peninsula to bring its aggregate strength up to about 31,000. Magruder warned that number would not be nearly enough to oppose the vast blue host assembling in his front. He calculated that he had about 23,000 effective men on a 14-mile front to resist what he estimated to be between 100,000 and 200,000 enemy troops.

Even though Magruder's estimation of enemy strength was somewhat exaggerated, his appraisal of the situation was not. Confederate forces swiftly consolidated to face McClellan's offensive, and one result was the incorporation of the Army of the Peninsula into Joseph E. Johnston's main force. Thus, on 26 April 1862, the Army of the Peninsula ceased to exist as an organizational entity. Thereafter it would be referred to as Johnston's Right Wing.

—*David S. Heidler and Jeanne T. Heidler*

See also Big Bethel, Battle of; Magruder, John B.; Peninsula Campaign.

For further reading:
Casdorph, Paul D. *Prince John Magruder: His Life and Campaigns* (1996).

ARMY OF THE POTOMAC

After the defeat of Union arms at the battle of Bull Run (First Manassas) in July 1861, George B. McClellan was placed in command of Union forces in and around Washington, D.C., and immediately threw himself into the task of building an army. As

Officers of the 1st Massachusetts Cavalry at Army of the Potomac headquarters, August 1864 (*Left to right*) unknown;
Captain Edward A. Flint; Captain Charles Francis Adams, Jr.; Lieutenant George H. Teague (*Library of Congress*)

regiments poured into Washington, McClellan established a system by which they would be organized into provisional brigades and receive instruction. By 4 August 1861, twelve brigades had been organized and were rigorously training under McClellan's direction. Two weeks later, McClellan formally conferred upon his command the name it would carry through the hardest fighting of the Civil War, the Army of the Potomac.

In November 1861 McClellan replaced Winfield Scott as general in chief of all the Union armies, but did not relinquish command of the Army of the Potomac. On 15 October he had organized the army into twelve divisions and remained deeply involved in its training as he worked to organize the rest of the Union war machine. On 20 November McClellan displayed his work in a spectacular grand review of the Army of the Potomac at Munson's Hill, Virginia, but shortly thereafter decided to postpone the commencement of operations until spring 1862.

Frustration with military inactivity led Congress in December to establish the Joint Committee on the Conduct of the War (JCCW). The JCCW was dominated by radical Republicans who were ignorant of, and had nothing but contempt for, military science, and who demanded a hard war against the South. It did not take long for the members of the JCCW to develop a powerful distaste for McClellan and his "pets" in the Army of the Potomac high command, a sentiment that was fully reciprocated. To the radicals, these officers were too conservative in their politics and generalship. Throughout the war, the JCCW would be a thorn in the side of the Army of the Potomac, as the radicals used its investigative powers to promote generals who shared their views on strategy, tactics, and politics, and to make life difficult for any officer who did not.

As the JCCW pursued its investigations in early 1862, the issue of organizing the Army of the Potomac into corps emerged as a major source of tension between McClellan and the politicians. Skeptical of the senior division commanders, the leading candidates for corps command who proved all too willing to cooperate with the JCCW, McClellan resisted calls for the organization of corps. His uneasiness about organizing corps was exacerbated when he submitted his plan for operating against Richmond from the lower Chesapeake Bay to a council of war in March. Of the four senior division commanders, Irvin McDowell, Edwin Sumner, and Samuel Heintzelman opposed the plan, while Erasmus

Keyes only conditionally approved it. The other division commanders endorsed the plan. Lincoln, who was beginning to have reservations about McClellan, accepted the vote of the majority, but then issued orders mandating the organization of corps with McDowell, Sumner, Heintzelman, and Keyes as their commanders. Three days later the president removed McClellan as general in chief so that he could focus exclusively on the Army of the Potomac.

During the Peninsula campaign, McClellan managed to secure permission to organize two new corps, which he gave to his friends Fitz John Porter and William Franklin. The army reached the outskirts of Richmond in late May 1862. Then, at the battle of Fair Oaks (Seven Pines), the Confederate commander, Joseph E. Johnston, was wounded and replaced by Robert E. Lee. Lee's strategic and tactical brilliance would make the road to Union victory a long, bloody, and frustrating ordeal.

When Lee drove McClellan from the gates of Richmond in the Seven Days' battles, Lincoln organized the Army of Virginia under John Pope for operations along the direct overland route from Washington to Richmond. In August Lincoln and his new general in chief, Henry W. Halleck, ordered McClellan's army back to northern Virginia to cooperate with Pope. Friction between Pope, a favorite of the Radical Republicans, and McClellan plagued the operation from the outset and helped Lee defeat Pope's army at the second battle of Bull Run (Manassas). Pope blamed an Army of the Potomac "cabal" for his failure and, backed by the Radical Republicans and the Lincoln administration, engineered an unfair court-martial to cashier Fitz John Porter from the service for disobedience of orders.

After Second Bull Run, Lincoln placed McClellan in command of Pope's army and the Army of the Potomac and directed him to deal with Lee's invasion of Maryland. McClellan immediately abolished the Army of Virginia as an independent force and integrated its units into the Army of the Potomac. Then, for the push westward into Maryland, he organized the army into three wings commanded by Franklin, Sumner, and Ambrose Burnside. Although he successfully turned back Lee's invasion, McClellan infuriated Lincoln by failing to destroy Lee's army or recross the Potomac until over a month after the battle of Antietam. Lincoln removed him from command in November 1862.

McClellan's replacement, Burnside, organized the army into three "grand" divisions under Sumner, Franklin, and Joseph Hooker. Burnside, however, proved inept as an army commander, and under his leadership the Army of the Potomac suffered its worst defeat of the war at Fredericksburg on 13 December 1862. This disaster was followed in January by an attempt to flank Lee that bad weather transformed into a miserable "Mud March." Morale plunged, desertion became rampant,

and several generals implored Lincoln to replace Burnside before the army melted away. Impressed by his acceptance of full responsibility for the Fredericksburg debacle, Lincoln chose to sustain Burnside until, in an effort to stamp out dissension, the general drafted orders removing several officers from their posts or cashiering them from the service altogether. Endorse the orders, Burnside told the president, or accept his resignation. Lincoln did neither, although he did relieve Burnside from command of the Army of the Potomac.

As Burnside's replacement, Lincoln chose Hooker, a hard fighter of high ambition but low character. During Burnside's tenure in command, Hooker had actively intrigued against him, as he had against almost anyone else who stood between Hooker and command of the Army of the Potomac. He earlier had also cultivated a positive relationship with the Radical Republicans by criticizing and firmly establishing his independence from McClellan and the rest of the army high command.

By the time Hooker assumed command, Lincoln and Halleck had fundamentally reoriented Union strategy. They accepted McClellan's argument that the prospects for success operating along the overland route from Washington to Richmond were not great and the most effective way to attack the Confederate capital was via the Peninsula. But to do the latter meant either dividing Union forces in Virginia or uncovering Washington. Lincoln and Halleck were unwilling to do either. Consequently, they decided to keep the Army of the Potomac concentrated on the overland route from Washington to Richmond, where they were to make Lee's army the target of their operations. Lincoln and Halleck recognized that Lee's ability, geography, logistics, and the strength of the tactical defensive made it highly unlikely that a decisive victory could be achieved by following the new "headquarters doctrine." Yet Lee's aggressive generalship and demonstrated preference for operating as far north as possible might well, they surmised, produce an opportunity to catch the Confederate army far from its base and deliver a crippling blow. Along with the change in strategy, there had been tremendous turnover in the Army of the Potomac high command by the time Hooker took over. Not only had McClellan and Burnside come and gone, but all six of the original corps commanders were no longer with the army. John Reynolds now commanded the 1st Corps, Darius Couch commanded the 2d, Dan Sickles commanded the 3d, George Meade commanded the 5th, and John Sedgwick commanded the 6th. (The 4th Corps had been left in garrison on the Peninsula the previous summer.) Also now with the army were Oliver Otis Howard's 11th Corps and Henry Slocum's 12th Corps. Despite this turnover, with the exception of Hooker, his chief of staff Daniel Butterfield, and Sickles, the army high command was still dominated by

Army of the Potomac near Falmouth, Virginia, as sketched by Alfred R. Waud (*Library of Congress*)

conservative McClellanites like Reynolds, Couch, Meade, Sedgwick, Gouverneur K. Warren, and Winfield Scott Hancock.

Whatever skepticism greeted Hooker's ascension to command quickly dissipated as a result of his spectacular success restoring the army's fighting spirit. He improved the soldiers' diets by adding fresh vegetables and soft bread to their rations, instituted liberal furlough policies, improved sanitation, built hospitals, and made sure the men received their pay. Hooker also abandoned Burnside's grand division scheme and returned to corps organization. To promote unit pride and facilitate control on the battlefield, he instituted a system of corps and division badges: a circle for the 1st Corps, trefoil for the 2d, lozenge for the 3d, Maltese cross for the 5th, cross for the 6th, crescent for the 11th, and star for the 12th. Within each corps, the 1st Division's patch was red, the 2d's white, and the 3d's blue.

By April 1863 the army was again ready for action. Unfortunately, at the battle of Chancellorsville in May Hooker lost his nerve and the army suffered yet another humiliating defeat. Hooker's subsequent actions in response to Lee's decision to undertake another invasion

of the North did little to restore confidence in his generalship. Consequently, to the delight of the majority of the corps commanders and the dismay of the radicals, Lincoln replaced Hooker with Meade on 28 June.

In the three days of fighting at Gettysburg in the week that followed, Meade's leadership, mistakes by the enemy, and the inspiration that came from fighting on Northern soil enabled the army to win its first clear and unambiguous battlefield victory over Lee. Meade, however, frustrated Lincoln by failing to pursue Lee's army with the vigor the president hoped for. Then in November Meade further antagonized the politicians, but won the hearts of his army, when he refused to assault an impregnable Rebel position at Mine Run.

Political discontent with Meade contributed to an ugly imbroglio that illustrated and exacerbated tensions between the JCCW and the Army of the Potomac and within the Army's high command. Radical favorite Sickles instigated the controversy by accusing Meade of wanting to surrender the field at Gettysburg to the Confederates (which was patently false) and claiming that his own actions (which in fact nearly lost the battle) had saved the army by preventing Meade from

A group of scouts and guides for the Army of the Potomac at Berlin (now Brunswick), Maryland, October 1862
(Photograph by Alexander Gardner / *National Archives*)

doing this. Relishing the opportunity to diminish Meade, a conservative West Pointer, the JCCW zealously pursued the matter in spring 1864, seeking out testimony from officers hostile to Meade and sympathetic to Sickles. The JCCW also undertook an investigation of Chancellorsville that was designed to rehabilitate Hooker by pinning the blame for the defeat on Sedgwick, a McClellan loyalist.

As the Army spent the winter of 1863–1864 encamped in the vicinity of Culpeper, Virginia, the beleaguered Meade decided to reorganize his command. He abolished the 1st and 3d Corps (the 11th and 12th had been sent to Tennessee the previous September) and assigned their units to one of the three remaining corps: Hancock's 2d; Warren's 5th; and Sedgwick's 6th. Aided by his chief of staff, Andrew A. Humphreys, Meade also implemented reforms that dramatically improved the army's administration. Better living conditions, an array of inducements offered by the government, and a determination to see the war through to the end helped convince over half of the thousands of veterans whose enlistments were scheduled to expire in 1864 to reenlist.

When Ulysses S. Grant became general in chief of the Federal armies in the spring of 1864, many speculated

that he would replace Meade as the commander of the Army of the Potomac. Grant did choose to accompany the Army on its final campaign, but he technically left Meade in place as the army's commander. These 1864 spring and summer campaigns introduced the Army of the Potomac to a brutal, unrelenting form of war unprecedented in the American experience. Over 60,000 men fell in continuous fighting and bad weather that made the army's drive from the Wilderness to Petersburg an unceasing horror. Combat effectiveness plummeted as experienced veterans fell and were replaced by garrison soldiers, conscripts, and substitutes. Then, after a useless assault at Cold Harbor, even experienced officers and men began to exhibit what became known as Cold Harbor syndrome, a reluctance to assault entrenchments. Nonetheless, they remained determined to fight on until victory was won. Although they still retained a powerful affection for McClellan, in the November 1864 election the Army of the Potomac expressed this determination by voting overwhelmingly for Lincoln.

By the time the siege of Petersburg began, Grant was exercising almost complete control over the army. Under Grant, the Army maintained a bulldog grip on

Petersburg until April 1865, when Lee abandoned the town and Richmond. The army vigorously pursued Lee and managed to cut off his retreat near Appomattox Court House. There Lee surrendered on 9 April 1865, bringing an end to four years of war. Its mission accomplished, on 23 May the North's greatest army marched down Pennsylvania Avenue in the Grand Review. Shortly thereafter, the Army of the Potomac was officially disbanded and the men whose courage, skill, and determination on the battlefields of Virginia, Maryland, and Pennsylvania had preserved the Union returned to their homes to build modern America.

—*Ethan S. Rafuse*

See also Antietam, Battle of; Appomattox Court House; Army of Virginia; Burnside, Ambrose E.; Chancellorsville, Battle of; Fredericksburg, Battle of; Gettysburg, Battle of; Grand Review; Grant, Ulysses S.; Heintzelman, Samuel Peter; Hooker, Joseph; Joint Committee on the Conduct of the War; Keyes, Erasmus Darwin; McClellan, George B.; McDowell, Irvin; Meade, George Gordon; Petersburg Campaign; Sickles, Daniel; Sumner, Edwin V.

For further reading:
———. *The Army of the Potomac: Glory Road* (1952).
Catton, Bruce. *Mr. Lincoln's Army* (1951).
———. *A Stillness at Appomattox* (1953).
Grant, Ulysses S. *Personal Memoirs of U. S. Grant* (1885).
Hattaway, Herman, and Archer Jones. *How the North Won: A Military History of the Civil War* (1983).
McClellan, George B. *McClellan's Own Story: The War for the Union, the Soldiers Who Fought It, the Civilians Who Directed It, and His Relations to It and to Them* (1887).
Meade, George Gordon. *Life and Letters of George Gordon Meade, Major-General United States Army* (1913; reprint, 1994).
Tap, Bruce. *Over Lincoln's Shoulder: The Committee on the Conduct of the War* (1998).
U.S. War Department. *The War of the Rebellion: A Compilation of the Official Records of the Union and Confederate Armies* (1880–1901).

ARMY OF THE SHENANDOAH, C.S.A.

Virginia State troops had already been gathering for a month in the Shenandoah Valley when Colonel Thomas J. Jackson was placed in command of them on 28 April 1861. Jackson continued recruiting activities, and on 24 May 1861, Major General Joseph E. Johnston took command of the force designated as the Army of the Shenandoah. By the end of June 1861 it consisted of four infantry brigades and the 1st Virginia Cavalry, 334 strong, under Colonel J. E. B. Stuart.

Colonel T. J. Jackson's 1st Brigade included the 2d, 4th, 5th, 27th Virginia Infantry, and Pendleton's battery for a strength of 2,256 officers and men. Colonel F. S. Bartow's 2d Brigade included the 7th, 8th, 9th Georgia Infantry, Duncan's and Pope's Kentucky Battalions, and Alburtis's battery for a strength of 2,608. Brigadier General Bernard E. Bee's 3d Brigade included the 4th

Alabama Infantry, 2d Mississippi Infantry, 11th Mississippi Infantry, 1st Tennessee Infantry, and Imboden's battery for a strength of 2,882. And Colonel Arnold Elzey's 4th Brigade included the 1st Maryland Battalion of Infantry, 3d Tennessee Infantry, 10th Virginia Infantry, 13th Virginia Infantry, and Grove's battery for a strength of 2,311. The 33d Virginia Infantry was not brigaded but would fight with Jackson's division at First Bull Run. The aggregate strength of the Army of the Shenandoah was 10,057.

This force fought at Falling Waters on 2 July and subsequently was engaged at Bunker Hill and Charles Town before slipping from the valley to join P. G. T. Beauregard's Confederate Army of the Potomac to fight at First Bull Run on 21 July 1861. By then, Colonel Elzey's brigade had been placed under the command of Edmund Kirby Smith. The arrival of the Army of the Shenandoah on the Confederate left helped to turn the course of the battle for the South, and it was Jackson's Virginians who were described by Bee as standing like a stone wall, thus giving Jackson the most famous nickname of the war.

After the battle of First Bull Run, the Army of the Shenandoah was incorporated into the Confederate Army of the Potomac, which the following spring Robert E. Lee would name the Army of Northern Virginia.

—*David S. Heidler and Jeanne T. Heidler*

See also Bull Run, First Battle of; Falling Waters; Jackson, Thomas J.; Johnston, Joseph E.; Smith, Edmund Kirby.

For further reading:
Downs, Alan Craig. "Gone Past All Redemption? The Early War Years of General Joseph Eggleston Johnston" (Ph.D. dissertation, 1991).
Henderson, G. F. R. *Stonewall Jackson and the American Civil War* (1898).
Johnston, Joseph E. *Narrative of Military Operations Directed during the Late War between the States* (1874; reprint, 1959).
Robertson, James I., Jr. *Stonewall Jackson: The Man, The Soldier, The Legend* (1997).
Symonds, Craig L. *Joseph E. Johnston: A Civil War Biography* (1992).
Woodward, Harold R., Jr. *Defender of the Valley. Brigadier General John Daniel Imboden, C.S.A.* (1996).

ARMY OF THE SHENANDOAH, U.S.A.

In the summer of 1864, Union general in chief Ulysses S. Grant reorganized forces in the East to make command structures more efficient. He merged the Department of the Susquehanna, the Middle Department, the Department of Washington, and the Department of West Virginia into the Middle Military Division and named Brigadier General Philip Sheridan as temporary commander on 5 August. Given the task of clearing Confederate forces under Jubal Early from the Shenandoah Valley, Sheridan took command of the Army of the Shenandoah, which consisted of the Army of the Potomac's VI Corps under Major General Horatio G. Wright and the 1st and 2d Divisions (commanded by Brigadier Generals William Dwight and Cuvier Grover) of XIX Corps under Brigadier General William H. Emory. The VI Corps included divisions under Brigadier Generals David A. Russell, George W. Getty, and James B. Ricketts. Major General George Crook's Army of West Virginia, designated as VIII Corps, was also part of the army. Colonel Joseph Thoburn and Isaac Duval commanded its divisions. The army boasted twelve batteries of artillery.

Sheridan brought with him from the Army of the Potomac Wesley Merritt's 1st and James H. Wilson's 3d Cavalry Divisions. Brigadier General Alfred Torbert took command of the cavalry forces in the Army of the Shenandoah, which were soon bolstered by two additional divisions under Alfred N. Duffié and William Woods Averell from the Army of West Virginia. The total strength of the army was about 40,000 men when it began the Shenandoah Valley campaign of 1864.

The army's activities in the Shenandoah Valley gave the Union a series of brilliant victories marked by hard-won fights at Opequon, Fisher's Hill, and Cedar Creek. Sharp skirmishes were a constant feature of the campaign, and total casualties were heavy in both the infantry and cavalry. General David Russell was killed at Opequon, and James Ricketts was seriously wounded at Cedar Creek.

After successfully concluding the Shenandoah Valley campaign, the Army of the Shenandoah was dismantled by the return of detached elements to the Army of the Potomac. It remained to be mentioned, however, as the name occasionally applied to Merritt's cavalry corps, which was sometimes referred to as the cavalry of the Army of the Shenandoah. Upon its return to service in the siege of Petersburg, this corps consisted of Thomas C. Devin's and George A. Custer's divisions with the addition of Crooks's division. In the final campaign of 1865 it had thirty-seven regiments of cavalry for a strength of about 13,800, and distinguished itself in actions from Five Forks to Appomattox.

—*David S. Heidler and Jeanne T. Heidler*

See also Cedar Creek, Battle of; Early, Jubal; Fisher's Hill, Battle of; Merritt, Wesley; Shenandoah Valley Campaign (August 1864–March 1865); Sheridan, Philip H.; Torbert, Alfred T. A.; Winchester (Opequon), Third Battle of.

For further reading:

Bushong, Millard K. *Old Jube: A Biography of General Jubal A. Early* (1988).
Heatwole, John L. *The Burning: Sheridan in the Shenandoah Valley* (1998).
Morris, Roy, Jr. *Sheridan: The Life and Wars of General Phil Sheridan* (1992).
Osborne, Charles C. *Jubal: The Life and Times of General Jubal A. Early, C.S.A., Defender of the Lost Cause* (1992).
Sheridan, Philip Henry. *Personal Memoirs of P. H. Sheridan, General, U. S. Army. New and Enl. Ed. With an Account of his Life from 1871 to His Death, in 1888,* by Brigadier-General Michael V. Seridan (1904).
Stackpole, Edward J. *Sheridan in the Shenandoah: Jubal Early's Nemesis* (1992).

ARMY OF THE TENNESSEE

Union brigadier general Ulysses S. Grant commanded the forerunner of the Department and Army of the Tennessee from 1 August 1861 to 14 February 1862, when he was succeeded by Brigadier General William T. Sherman. During this time it was designated as the Military District of Cairo (Kentucky) and included Cairo, Bird's Point, and Cape Girardeau, Missouri, as well as assorted other posts.

On 16 October 1862, the Department of the Tennessee was created and embraced Cairo, Forts Henry and Donelson, northern Mississippi, and the regions of Kentucky and Tennessee that lay west of the Tennessee River. Grant was placed in command, and all troops in the department were organized into XIII Army Corps on 24 October 1862. This massive organization constituted the entire Army of the Tennessee and was thus too unwieldy. On 18 December 1862, XIII Corps was consequently arranged into four new corps, designated as XIII, XV, XVI, and XVII Corps. General John A. McClernand was placed in command of XIII Corps; General William T. Sherman, of XV Corps; Major General Stephen A. Hurlbut, of XVI Corps; and Major General James B. McPherson, of XVII Corps. On 24 October 1863, Grant was succeeded in command by Sherman, who in turn was succeeded on 26 March 1864 by McPherson, who was killed during the Atlanta campaign on 22 July 1864. Major General John A. Logan commanded the army for five days until Major General O. O. Howard took command and remained in that position until 19 May 1865. Logan resumed command until 1 August 1865, when the organization was discontinued.

The Army of the Tennessee was a large force whose separate components were often detached for service in various operations. As a result, it is easy to confuse both the organizational structure of the army and its nomenclature. For instance, Sherman early took the right wing of McClernand's XIII Corps with parts of his XV Corps on the Yazoo expedition that included the failed attack at Chickasaw Bluffs. And in January 1863, McClernand assailed Arkansas Post with part of his XIII Corps and Sherman's XV Corps, although he referred to these detached forces of the Army of the Tennessee as I and II Corps of the Army of the Mississippi.

The Army of the Tennessee was actively engaged in the lengthy Vicksburg campaign of 1863. During that campaign, McClernand's bravado so irritated Grant that he relieved him from command of XIII Corps, replacing him with General E. O. Ord. After the fall of Vicksburg, the corps was briefly stationed at Jackson, Mississippi, and then was moved to New Orleans. Detachments scattered it along the Gulf from Texas to Louisiana, and parts of the corps would participate in the Red River Expedition of April 1864.

As for XV Corps, after Vicksburg the bulk of it would move to Memphis and from there to Chattanooga to participate in the raising of the Confederate siege in November 1863. By then Sherman's promotion on 27 October to command the Army of the Tennessee had placed General Frank P. Blair in charge of XV Corps. After Chattanooga, it advanced on Knoxville to assist Ambrose Burnside's resistance to James Longstreet's siege there. The corps arrived after Longstreet had already retreated. Under General John A. Logan, XV Corps with two divisions of XVI Corps and XVII Corps (minus two divisions left in the Mississippi Valley) took part in the Atlanta campaign as the Army of the Tennessee.

With Howard in command, the Army of the Tennessee formed the right wing of Sherman's March to the Sea. During this operation it consisted of XV and XVII Corps with the two divisions of XVI Corps that had participated in the Atlanta campaign integrated into them. After occupying Savannah, Sherman's force began its march through the Carolinas on 1 February. The Army of the Tennessee thus was part of the force present when Joseph E. Johnston surrendered on 26 April 1865 at Bennett House near Durham, North Carolina. The army participated in the Grand Review in Washington and was discontinued in August 1865.

—*David S. Heidler and Jeanne T. Heidler*

See also Atlanta Campaign; Carolinas Campaign; Chattanooga Campaign; Sherman's March to the Sea; Vicksburg Campaign.

For further reading:

Cannan, John. *The Atlanta Campaign, May–November, 1864* (1991).

Castel, Albert E. *Decision in the West: The Atlanta Campaign of 1864* (1992).

Cozzens, Peter. *The Civil War in the West: From Stones River to Chattanooga* (1996).

———. *The Shipwreck of Their Hopes: The Battles for Chattanooga* (1994).

Glatthaar, Joseph T. *The March to the Sea and Beyond: Sherman's Troops in the Savannah and Carolinas Campaigns* (1985).

Meyers, Christopher C. " 'Two Generals Cannot Command This Army': John A. McClernand and the Politics of Command in Grant's Army of the Tennessee." *Columbiad* (1998).

Miers, Earl Schenck. *The Web of Victory: Grant at Vicksburg* (1955; reprint, 1983).

ARMY OF THE WEST

A creation of Brigadier General Nathaniel Lyon, the Army of the West survived little longer than did the general himself. In June 1861 Federal forces took the field in Missouri, pursuing the pro-Southern forces of Governor Claiborne Jackson into southwest Missouri. Arriving in Springfield, Missouri, on 13 July, Brigadier General Lyon took command of the Union forces there, designating them the Army of the West. Within a month, Lyon led this army at Wilson's Creek.

In June 1861 Lyon had sent two columns from St. Louis to capture Southern supporters within Missouri. The newly enlisted Missouri volunteer regiments, which overwhelmingly consisted of German and German-American volunteers, made up the majority of Lyon's forces. Lyon led one column to Jefferson City, defeated Jackson's forces at Boonville, and pursued the Confederates south. The second column headed south to secure southwest Missouri for the Union. Lyon took command of both columns when they assembled in Springfield, Missouri. On 24 July he reorganized these columns into four brigades and designated them the Army of the West.

As July wore on, grave problems plagued the army as it camped near Springfield. It faced critical supply shortages, and Lyon's appeals for supplies and reinforcements seemed to fall on deaf ears. Additionally, most of the troops, consisting of three-month volunteers, were reaching the end of their enlistments. Meanwhile, rumors circulated that Southern forces were moving north toward Springfield. Lyon chose to march out and face them.

Lyon led the army south out of Springfield on 1 August. The next day they encountered the Southern forces at Dug Springs, Missouri, and drove the Confederates back. Having won the initial engagement, Lyon pushed on to Curran Post Office. The army's lack of food and the danger of being cut off by the enemy, however, forced Lyon to return to Springfield, arriving on 6 August. The Confederates under Generals Sterling Price and Benjamin McCulloch also moved north and encamped at Wilson's Creek, ten miles south of Lyon's position.

The army's situation had become serious. Lyon still had not received support from St. Louis. He felt the enemy to his front made any retreat dangerous, but he feared that he could not defend Springfield with his forces, as discharges continued to eat away at his ranks. By 9 August Lyon had decided to risk a withdrawal, but after consulting with Colonel Franz Sigel, he chose to attack instead.

Lyon divided the army of 5,400 effectives into two columns for the attack. Lyon commanded the northern column and was to strike the Confederate camp from the northwest with three brigades. The first, Major Samuel Sturgis's brigade, consisted of Plummer's battalion of regulars, a battalion of the 2d Missouri Infantry, Kansas Rangers, Company B, 1st U.S. Cavalry, and Battery F, 2d U.S. Artillery. Lieutenant Colonel George Andrews commanded the 2d Brigade that included Steele's battalion of regulars, the 1st Missouri Volunteers, and DuBois's battery. Colonel George W. Deitzler led the 3d Brigade containing the 1st and 2d Kansas Volunteers. In addition, Lyon's force included the 1st Iowa and two units of home guard cavalry.

While Lyon attacked the Confederates from the northeast, Sigel was to strike the Confederates from the southwest with his brigade. It included the 3d and 5th Missouri Volunteers, Backoff's battalion of Missouri Artillery, Carr's Cavalry, Company I, 1st U.S. Artillery, and Company C, 2d U.S. Dragoons. The two columns were to catch the Confederates between them.

The Army of the West marched out of Springfield on 9 August. The next morning, both columns struck the Confederates. Lyon's troops fought well for most of the morning, however, the Confederates routed Sigel's brigade, driving it from the field. The northern column fought on, unaware of Sigel's fate. Late in the morning, Lyon was killed leading a charge. Command passed to Sturgis, who called a retreat, leading the column back to Springfield.

As senior officer, Sigel took command of the army in Springfield and withdrew toward Rolla on 11 August. Along the march, however, Sturgis regained command when a number of officers, criticizing Sigel's performance at Wilson's Creek, called for his removal. Reaching Rolla on 19 August, the Army of the West returned by rail to St. Louis where General John C. Frémont chose to disband it and shifted its forces to northern Missouri. Although the army existed less than a month, its actions at Wilson's Creek aided the Union forces in retaining control of Missouri.

—*James G. Downhour*

See also Lyon, Nathaniel; Wilson's Creek.

For further reading:
Bearss, Edwin C. *The Battle of Wilson's Creek* (1992).
Welcher, Frank J. *The Union Army, 1861–1865: Organization and Operations* (1989).

ARMY OF VIRGINIA

The Federal Army of Virginia was formed on 26 June 1862 by the consolidation of three independent departments–the Mountain Department, the Department of the Shenandoah, and the Department of the Rappahannock. Major General John Pope was given command of this new army. Pope had connections with Mary Todd Lincoln's family, and had received an early appointment to brigadier general. He was in charge of the forces that captured Island No. 10 and then commanded the left wing of the Union army that captured Corinth, Mississippi, in May 1862.

Pope's new command consisted of three corps. The I Corps was led by Major General John C. Frémont, and was composed of troops that had been in the Mountain Department of western Virginia. Frémont, Pope's senior

in rank, refused to serve and was soon replaced by Major General Franz Sigel, a German-born soldier, who, though inept in the field, was a symbol of support for the war effort. His division commanders were Robert C. Schenck, Adolph von Steinwehr, and Carl Schurz. Brigadier General Robert H. Milroy led an independent brigade, and a cavalry brigade under the command of Colonel John Beardsley completed the corps organization.

Major General Nathaniel P. Banks led II Corps, formerly the Department of the Shenandoah. Banks was a political general from Massachusetts who had served as both governor and Speaker of the House of Representatives. Although ill suited for military success, Banks was an ardent supporter of the Lincoln administration. His troops had been defeated by Stonewall Jackson in May and had been driven across the Potomac River into Maryland. Brigadier Generals Alpheus S. Williams and James Cooper (soon replaced by Christopher C. Augur), led the two divisions of infantry. Brigadier General John P. Hatch (later replaced by John Buford) commanded the cavalry attached to II Corps.

Major General Irvin McDowell was in charge of the army's III Corps. McDowell was the general defeated at First Bull Run and thereafter was a corps commander and placed in command of the Department of the Rappahannock. His two four-brigade divisions were led by Brigadier Generals Rufus King and James B. Ricketts. Brigadier General George D. Bayard commanded the cavalry brigade.

Pope's army numbered some 51,000 troops. Lincoln hoped that this army would move south to threaten Southern communications and draw off troops from Richmond, allowing McClellan's Army of the Potomac a chance to attack the Confederate capital. However, McClellan's withdrawal during the Seven Days' battles forced Pope to scrap any offensive plans and remain in northern Virginia, waiting for the Army of the Potomac to reinforce him. With the strength of these combined forces, Pope could attack Richmond from the north.

Pope took active command and issued orders that included permission for his troops to provision themselves off the country through which they passed, and one designed to hold citizens responsible for acts of Confederate irregulars behind the lines. Another order allowed Pope's officers to arrest all male citizens suspected of disloyalty.

After McClellan retreated to Harrison's Landing, Lee sent Jackson's corps north to watch Pope. Seeing an opportunity to attack, Jackson crossed the Rapidan River and headed for Culpeper to strike Banks's corps. Banks attacked first at Cedar Mountain on 9 August. After a hard battle Banks was repulsed, but Federal reinforcements prohibited a Confederate advance, and Jackson retreated south.

When McClellan's corps began to move north by water to Aquia Creek to join Pope, Lee and Longstreet's Corps joined Jackson to attack Pope. Lee planned a rapid forward march and crossing of the Rapidan on 18 August to force Pope to withdraw westward, but Pope learned of the advance and quickly withdrew behind the Rappahannock River. Reinforcements from the Army of the Potomac here joined the Army of Virginia. To breach this line, Jackson's corps made a circuitous march behind Pope's right flank and destroyed his supply base at Manassas Junction.

Jackson then withdrew to the old battlefield of Manassas and managed to hide his divisions while waiting for Longstreet to join him. Pope, blinded by his misuse of cavalry, retreated to catch Jackson. On 28 August Jackson struck at Rufus King's division at Brawner's Farm. The next day, Pope's troops began assaulting Jackson's line even as Longstreet's troops arrived on the battlefield. On 30 August Longstreet struck Pope's exposed left flank and drove the Union army from the field. A sharp engagement at Chantilly on 1 September essentially ended the Second Bull Run campaign as the defeated Union armies withdrew to Washington.

Here, Pope was replaced and McClellan placed in command of the defenses of the city. Pope's three corps were merged into the Army of the Potomac. Sigel's command became the XI Army Corps. Banks was replaced and his corps became the XII Army Corps. Joseph Hooker replaced McDowell, and his corps was renumbered the I Army Corps.

—*Richard A. Sauers*

See also Bull Run, Second Battle of; Pope, John.
For further reading:
Gordon, George H. *History of the Campaign of the Army of Virginia, Under John Pope: From Cedar Mountain to Alexandria, 1862* (1879).
Hennessy, John J. *Return to Bull Run: The Campaign and Battle of Second Manassas* (1993).
Ropes, John C. *The Army Under Pope* (1881).

ARMY OF WEST TENNESSEE

The Army of West Tennessee was the official designation of a Confederate force that existed for about two months at the end of 1862. It was also the name applied to the Union army under the command of Major General Ulysses S. Grant, starting in February 1862, that fought at Shiloh in April. Actually, the Union army derived its name from the fact that it was under the District of West Tennessee, a geographical setting that by September 1862 embraced several other forces as well. For instance, the Districts of Jackson and Corinth became the 3d Division of the district, Memphis the 1st Division, and Mississippi the 4th Division. (On 26 October 1863, these would be incorporated into the District of Tennessee, XIII Army Corps.)

In any case, the Union Army of West Tennessee was much more substantial in comparison to the Confederate force. Reflecting the absence of corps organizations in the western Union armies before December 1862, it consisted of six divisions of three brigades each. The 1st Division was commanded by John McClernand except for a brief period in May and early June. Major General C. F. Smith originally commanded the 2d Division, but at Shiloh the division was under Brigadier General W. H. L. Wallace, who was mortally wounded. Ultimately it was placed under Major General Edward O. C. Ord. Major General Lewis Wallace commanded the 3d Division, Brigadier General Stephen A. Hurlbut commanded the 4th, Brigadier General William T. Sherman commanded the 5th, and Brigadier General Benjamin Prentiss commanded the 6th.

The Confederate Army of West Tennessee was created by merging Sterling Price's Army of the West with Earl Van Dorn's troops from Mississippi and eastern Louisiana. As constituted on 28 September 1862, the army operated somewhat like two corps, although the force was cobbled together so quickly that its parts retained separate identities. Price's Army of the West was designated as Price's corps and included the 1st Division, four brigades strong, under Brigadier General Louis Hébert, and Brigadier General Dabney Maury's division. Brigadier General Mansfield Lovell commanded the troops officially called the District of Mississippi. Colonel William H. Jackson led the cavalry, and Van Dorn was in overall command. This Confederate Army of West Tennessee made the furious but failed assault at Corinth on 3–4 October, ironically attacking William S. Rosecrans's 2d Division of the Union Army of West Tennessee.

Corinth was this Confederate army's largest engagement. Not until 16 October was it officially named the Army of West Tennessee, and then the attempt was made to place it into the structure of two actual corps. Yet discipline in the force was bad and relations between its general officers was worse. On 22 November, the War Department in Richmond asked in some exasperation what the army intended to call itself. Neither Price's persistent Army of the West nor Van Dorn's Army of West Tennessee seemed appropriate, given the outfit's situation following the retreat from Corinth. The War Department suggested "Army of Northern Mississippi." Two days later, Adjutant General Samuel Cooper curtly observed that all other names aside from I and II Corps of the Department of Mississippi were "improper."

On 7 December 1862, two days after elements of the Army of West Tennessee had fought a skirmish at Coffeeville, its brief existence came to an end. The secretary of war directed that the army would consist of two corps, designated I and II Corps, to be commanded respectively by Van Dorn and Price. Mansfield Lovell was relieved and was instructed to await further orders.

—*David S. Heidler and Jeanne T. Heidler*

See also Corinth, Battle of; Lovell, Mansfield; Price, Sterling; Shiloh, Battle of; Van Dorn, Earl.

ARMY ORGANIZATION, C.S.A.

At first glance, a Confederate field army looked indistinguishable from its Northern opponent. Like the Federal army, a Southern army was built on infantry regiments, grouped into brigades, with those brigades grouped into divisions. Artillery was also initially not organized or grouped above the battery level, and was usually attached to infantry brigades on a one-battery-per-brigade basis.

Subtle differences distinguished the armies, however. Some of those differences proved to be advantages and contributed significantly to early Southern victories over more numerous enemies, while others were liabilities that remained uncorrected. The Confederacy overall raised fewer regiments than did the Union and made an effort to keep those regimental ranks filled up with draftees and recruits. The result was that Confederate units at the tactical level were often as strong or stronger then their foes, despite a significant, overall Union advantage in numbers. With fewer subordinates to command, the job of a Confederate brigade or divisional commander was less complicated. More Southern manpower could be brought to bear in a fight than might be the case for a Northern army. Regimental strengths remained relatively strong until the last year of the war, when the depletion of Southern manpower simply meant that there were no more troops to send forward. Confederate regiments had eroded to mere fragments by the end of the war.

The Confederacy was also much quicker to mass artillery into battalions of four batteries each and attach them to the divisional and corps level. Robert E. Lee's Army of Northern Virginia had reorganized most of its artillery by mid-1862, and the value of this organization proved its worth at both Second Bull Run and Antietam, where the timely intervention of Confederate artillery battalions helped stem powerful Union attacks. The Federals always had more—and usually better—cannon, but the superior Confederate organization meant that Southern artillery would not be dominated by those enemy advantages. The Confederates also formed an artillery reserve, but, unlike their Northern foes, rarely used it to its greatest advantage. By 1863 the Confederacy had done away with the idea of a central army artillery reserve entirely, preferring instead to mass more guns at the corps level.

The South did not formally adopt the army corps model as quickly as the Federals did, but in practice used it all the time. The western Confederate armies under Braxton Bragg created a logical and sensible corps structure soon after the battle of Shiloh in 1862. In Virginia, the Confederates relied on "wings," informal groupings of divisions that were de facto corps. Here the South relied on the superiority of its senior leadership, for both these wings were much larger than the normal Federal corps, with four or five divisions to command instead of the Union's two or three. As long as superior leaders such as James Longstreet and Thomas J. Jackson were present, this system worked well, but with Jackson's death in 1863, General Lee realized that the structure was too large for most commanders, and revised the army into three corps of three divisions each. In the west, with a much smaller infantry force to work with, the Confederate Army of Tennessee usually contained two corps of two or three divisions each. Only for the Atlanta campaign, when all available force was gathered to defend the Deep South, did the Army of Tennessee's strength increase to three corps.

At the divisional and brigade level, other distinguishing Southern characteristics may be noted. Confederate brigades were more likely to contain regiments all from the same state, an idea that Confederate president Davis felt fostered more esprit de corps and had some political advantages back home. Further, Confederate divisions tended to be larger then their Union counterparts, with four or five brigades instead of two or three. This difference meant that a Confederate division was likely to have twice as many men as a Union one, and sometimes a single Confederate division might be as strong as a Union corps. Hence, while weaker in numbers overall, the available Confederate strength was better concentrated at the vanguard.

Confederate cavalry was brigaded much earlier than Federal cavalry, another massing of force that helped contribute significantly to the early Southern dominance by that arm. Also, Confederates more liberally recruited the mounted arm than did their Northern opponents. For example, throughout much of 1863, the Army of Tennessee boasted more cavalry than did the Federal Army of the Cumberland. By the latter part of the war, however, the imbalance was reversed. In the last year of the war, the Confederacy could not find sufficient horses to mount a large portion of its troops, could not arm them with repeaters and breechloading carbines to match Federal firepower, and suffered from serious desertion problems. All added up to a Union dominance in cavalry operations not previously seen.

In the East, Confederate cavalry was also hampered by the fact that no formal corps structure was created to command the expanded force, meaning that J. E. B. Stuart had to manage the affairs of 10,000 men in up to seven brigades without any intermediate commanders. This decided liability was not remedied until the spring of 1864.

In the west, the exact opposite problem arose. By 1863 the Army of Tennessee had no less than two cavalry corps, commanded by Generals Joseph Wheeler and Nathan B. Forrest, with no sole commander of all mounted troops. A more logical situation would have been to merge the two corps into a single entity, but Forrest, for one, was politically difficult and refused to serve under Wheeler's command. This unfortunate situation allowed the most significant advantage the Army of Tennessee possessed— its superiority in the mounted arm—to be rendered largely useless in practical terms. General Bragg, for instance, was badly surprised at both Tullahoma and at the crossing of the Tennessee River in 1863.

—*David A. Powell*

See also Army Organization, U.S.A.
For further reading:
Beringer, Richard E., Herman Hattaway, Archer Jones, and William N. Still, Jr. *Why the South Lost the Civil War* (1986).
Hattaway, Herman, and Archer Jones. *How the North Won: A Military History of the Civil War* (1983).

ARMY ORGANIZATION, U.S.A.

The basic building block of the Civil War army was the infantry regiment. Recruited initially by the states, each regiment numbered about 1,000 men organized into ten companies. Most regiments received at least some recruits during the war, and so ended up with between 1,500 to 2,000 men on their rolls by war's end. In reality, however, disease and combat kept up a continual attrition, so that regiments rarely numbered more than 500 men, and often less than 200. Cavalry regiments were similarly recruited, with an initial strength of about 1,200 men. Artillery, while nominally organized in regiments, was most often recruited and deployed by battery, a unit ranging between four to six guns and approximately eighty to 120 men.

At the start of the war, Union army organization was primitive at best. Four regiments were grouped together into brigades, and two to three brigades were assigned to divisions. Initially, the division was the largest subunit organized, meaning that an army commander could expect to command five or six such divisions directly. When only the initial rush of recruits was available, this structure proved adequate to manage the approximately 35,000 to 40,000 men who filled a typical Federal army in 1861.

Cavalry and artillery initially were adjuncts to the infantry. Cavalry was rarely even brigaded, but instead was usually superintended directly by the army commander. Artillery was most often assigned to an infantry brigade one battery at a time. Consequently, it was difficult to mass either branch on a battlefield, as these units were scattered all throughout the army.

By 1862, however, the Union armies were simply too large to abide such informality. In March of that year, the Union Army of the Potomac numbered over 100,000 men in twelve infantry divisions and thus defied management by one man. The situation required the creation of army corps. Corps were the relatively permanent grouping of two to four divisions into a single tactical and administrative unit, putting into place a middle management between the army commander and his divisions and brigades. Some artillery was assigned to a central reserve, but most of it was still parceled out at the brigade or division level. Cavalry remained informally assigned directly to the corps or remained under the army commander's direct supervision, but formal brigade or divisional groupings for the mounted arm remained a distant development.

Organizational development in the west tended to lag behind that in the east. Smaller-sized forces were committed there in the first two years of the war, and the much greater distances in the west necessitated dispersion rather than concentration. Hence, western armies tended to number 40,000 to 60,000 men, remaining easier to manage with less formal organizational structure.

The year 1863 saw little change to the main structure of the army, but significant changes did occur in the way the supporting arms—cavalry and artillery—were arranged. Union general John Pope, much maligned for his mishandling of the Second Bull Run campaign, took a significant step when he forged several Union cavalry regiments into three formal mounted brigades in the fall of 1862. Yet it was General Joseph E. Hooker who finally placed the mounted arm into a discrete cavalry corps in 1863. With the creation of an independent cavalry corps, massing approximately 12,000 mounted men together for the first time, Hooker created an instrument that later commanders would use to great effect. No longer would Federal cavalry always be outnumbered and outfought.

Similarly, artillery batteries were removed from direct divisional or brigade control and assigned directly to corps commanders in their own brigades. This step allowed the corps commander to mass the five or six batteries in his corps into a single force, and use it where most needed at rapid notice. In the east, Union practice continued to include a significant artillery reserve directly under the army commander, a useful practice for reinforcing any particularly threatened corps or massing for an attack. Together, these three steps: the infantry corps, the cavalry corps, and the artillery brigades and reserve all constituted the final form of Union army organization. It was an effective, flexible structure that allowed the army commander to focus on fighting his opponent rather than overwhelming him with administrative detail.

The western armies eventually adopted all the innovations of the Federals in Virginia, though not as quickly. For instance, at Chickamauga in September

1863, artillery batteries were most often still assigned at the brigade level, though nominally they were grouped into battalions under division command. No independent artillery reserve existed. By 1864, however, there was virtually no difference in organization between theaters.

One significant drawback to the Union organization was the failure to maintain the strength of infantry regiments in the field. Given the political nature of how these units were first raised, state politicians often found it more advantageous to raise new units (which meant more political appointments of high rank) rather than send recruits to existing units in the field. As the war dragged on, veteran units dwindled in size to mere shadows of their initial strength. To maintain brigades at anything like a reasonable strength, these skeleton units were often merged into one brigade, meaning that a single brigade might number eight or ten regiments by late 1864. This duplicated the administrative difficulties that the corps structure was supposed to alleviate, although at an admittedly smaller scale. Newly arrived units, still large due to their lack of time in service, often outnumbered the rest of their new brigade put together. Far better from a tactical standpoint would have been to fill up existing veteran units with a steady stream of recruits.

By contrast, the basic Union staff organization remained superior to that of its opponents throughout the war. In the Army of the Potomac, for example, the army staff evolved into a quite modern organization of several hundred men, including a military intelligence section that, from 1863 on, did a splendid job of keeping the Union army commander informed of his opponent's organization and strength. Confederate staffs remained much more informal, to the detriment of their commanders.

—*David A. Powell*

See also Army Organization, C.S.A.
For further reading:
Beringer, Richard E., Herman Hattaway, Archer Jones, and William N. Still, Jr. *Why The South Lost the Civil War* (1986).
Hattaway, Herman, and Archer Jones. *How the North Won: A Military History of the Civil War* (1983).

ARMY, UNITED STATES
(1861–1865)

When the Civil War began, the army of the United States was scattered around the country in numerous small posts. A mere 12,698 men, not including officers, were authorized by Congress to hold down three million square miles of territory. The army consisted then of ten regiments of infantry, five of cavalry (including "Dragoons" and "Mounted Rifles"), and three of artillery. The artillery found in the west, however, was often acting either as ad hoc cavalry or infantry. One hundred eighty-three companies (or batteries) of the total of 198 available garrisoned seventy-nine outposts on the frontier. The remaining fifteen were allotted to Atlantic coastal fortresses, twenty-three Federal arsenals, and the line of the Canadian border. The largest formation at any post, and then rarely seen, was a battalion of a few companies.

However, the North possessed a huge advantage over the South in human and material resources in early 1861, an advantage that would eventually prove decisive. In manufactures the North enjoyed marked advantages in the ability to produce the goods needed for war, possessing as it did "close to 90 percent of the nation's industrial capacity." Additionally, the Union outnumbered the South by nearly four to one in potential military manpower.

Data from the 1860 Census shows that the populations of the two sections of the country contrasted sharply. The South contained 5,447,220 whites, 132,760 free blacks, and 3,521,110 black slaves, for a total of 9,103,332 persons. Of these, only 1,064,193 white men between the ages of eighteen and forty-five constituted the military population of the South. In contrast, the population of the loyal states and territories was 21,475,373 whites, 355,310 free blacks, and 432,650 black slaves, for a total of 22,339,989 persons. Of these, 4,559,872 white men aged eighteen to forty-five constituted the military population of the North. The North's population advantage of nearly 2.5:1 would be telling for agriculture and manufacturing, but its advantage of 4.28:1 in military population was overwhelming, with 2,494,592 whites serving in the army and 101,207 more serving as sailors and marines. The total of 2,595,799 made up 57 percent of the total Northern population of military age.

In April 1861 President Lincoln resorted to the only measure available to him under the Law of 1795 and called out 75,000 militia for three months. However, following the fiasco at Bull Run, this was rarely done again. Continuing a trend begun after the War of 1812, the North's new regiments were largely made up by calling out "Volunteers" for longer periods of service, and not by either calling out large numbers of militia or increasing appreciably the size of the regular forces. In May 1861 Lincoln did increase the regular army to 22,714 men by adding nine regiments of infantry, one of artillery, and one of cavalry, but after that little was done for them. He also called for 42,000 three-year Volunteers, the first of many such calls.

In July 1861 the North began to convert its manpower advantage into a huge army of Volunteer regiments, which compared favorably with any fielded by European industrial powers at the time. Congress legalized President Lincoln's increase in the regular establishment and his call for the first three-year Volunteers, and then called for 500,000 additional Volunteers. Following the pattern set as early as the American Revolution, this manpower was organized into regiments of infantry, cavalry, and artillery, nominally of 1,000 men each—but always far fewer in reality, especially after active campaigning. Each regiment in turn usually consisted of ten companies, or artillery batteries, and a small headquarters termed a "Field and Staff." The regiments of artillery were administrative only, and batteries served independently attached to larger formations.

There were exceptions to the general organization in the regular army that played havoc with attempts at homogeneity in drill and tactics. The regular cavalry was increased to twelve companies, as was the artillery. While the ten original infantry regiments were organized, as were the Volunteers, with ten companies, the nine new infantry regiments raised in 1861 were organized with twenty-four companies divided into three battalions, or nominally 2,400 men. However, the disruption this multiplicity of organization caused was often alleviated in practice. Lone regular regiments or battalions were often employed as General Officer's Escorts, such as the battalion of the 4th U.S. Cavalry in Major General James H. Wilson's Cavalry Corps in 1865. Groups of regiments were organized into discrete brigades of Regulars, such as the 1st and 2d Brigades of the 2d Division, V Corps, at Gettysburg in 1863.

The army was not a static force. The exertions of campaigning and attrition through casualties, desertions, and disease reduced the initial force quickly, so that as the war dragged on, more calls for Volunteers were needed. In July 1862 Congress called for an additional 300,000 Volunteers. The results were disappointing, and to redress the shortfall, in August a "draft" for 300,000 men was levied on state militias for a term of nine months' service. States responded even less enthusiastically. However, the use of federal, state, and local bounties, or cash incentives to induce enlistment, filled most of the original call out. Given this history, the Enrollment Act was passed on 3 March 1863, the first compulsory citizen conscription in U.S. history. Inequities in the system, such as allowing the hiring of substitutes and the payment of $300 directly to the government for exemptions, led to the notion that the struggle was becoming a rich man's war and a poor man's fight. Draft riots also erupted, notably in New York City during the summer. Still, the scheme raised only 10 percent of the total manpower enlisted for the war: 86,724 men paid the $300 commutation and were exempted, while only 118,010 substitutes were enlisted, and only 52,068 men were actually drafted.

One of President Lincoln's more successful war measures was the Emancipation Proclamation. This document cut the bonds of Southern blacks to the South and spurred the recruiting of black troops. Of the 178,975 "Colored Troops" that served in the Union army, 99,337 were recruited in the South, thus diminishing Southern resources because most blacks were engaged in agricultural pursuits. Black troops made up nearly 12 percent of the Union army in service in 1864 and 1865, and could be justly proud of their record. One in three were casualties. They served in 449 engagements, including thirty-nine major battles. They were organized into 120 regiments of infantry, seven of cavalry, twelve of heavy artillery, and ten batteries of light artillery. One entire corps—the XXV Corps organized on 3 December 1864 under Major General Godfrey Weitzel—was composed of black troops previously belonging to X and XVIII Corps. The black troops of Kautz's division of XXV Corps were the first to enter Richmond after its fall.

The total Union force organized by war's end amounted to 272 regiments, forty-five separate battalions, and seventy-eight independent companies of cavalry; sixty-one regiments, eight battalions, and thirty-six companies of heavy artillery; nine battalions and 432 batteries of light artillery; thirteen regiments, one battalion, and seven companies of engineers; four regiments, three battalions, and thirty-five companies of "Sharp Shooters"; and a staggering 2,144 regiments, sixty battalions, and 351 companies of infantry. This amounted to a grand total of 3,559 independent units. By the war's end, when the Confederacy could muster barely 180,000 men under arms, the Union still had over one million of these men in uniform. From the over 2.5 million men who served the Union under all enlistment terms, 110,070 died in battle, while 249,458 more died from disease or other causes.

—Duane C. Young

See also Army of Mississippi; Army of the Gulf; Army of the James; Army of the Kanawha; Army of the Northwest Confederate; Army of the Ohio; Army of the Peninsula; Army of the Potomac; Army of the Shenandoah (U.S.A); Army of the Tennessee; Army of the West; Army of Virginia; Army Organization, U.S.A.; Artillery.

For further reading:
Cornish, Dudley Taylor. *The Sable Arm: Negro Troops in the Union Army, 1861–1865* (1966).
Dyer, Frederick H. *A Compendium of the War of the Rebellion* (1908).
Fox, William F. *Regimental Losses in the American Civil War, 1861–1865* (1889).
Ganoe, William A. *The History of the United States Army* (1942; reprint, 1964).
McPherson, James M. *Ordeal by Fire: The Civil War and Reconstruction* (1992).
Randall, James G., and David Herbert Donald. *The Civil War and Reconstruction* (1969).
Segal, David R. *Recruiting For Uncle Sam: Citizenship and Military Manpower Policy* (1989).
Shannon, Fred A. *The Organization and Administration of the Union Army, 1861–1865* (1928).
United States Department of the Census. *Population of the United States in 1860* (1864).

ART OF THE CIVIL WAR

To consider the art of the Civil War is to accept that the North had an embarrassment of riches. With a larger population, some art organizations, and burgeoning art schools, the North had a greater number of men and women practicing art. More European artists immigrated to the major cities of the North, where wealthy patrons lived, and more young artists traveled to European capitals for academic training. More publishing houses flourished, and printing firms employed and trained many engravers and lithographers.

The South had a smaller, more agrarian population and relatively fewer trained artists. Before the war, graphic images were obtained from the North and Europe or from small publishing houses in Baltimore or New Orleans.

Once the North tightened the noose of the blockade, paper, printing ink, canvas, and art materials became scarce. With all able Southern men joining the Confederate army, the Southern government had difficulty finding engravers to print Confederate money, postage stamps, and notes, to say nothing of newspaper illustrations and prints.

Southerners did not lack an appreciation for prints and artwork. However, during the war and after, their energies had to focus on survival. During the postwar period, Civil War prints, paintings, and sculpture would help heal the divisive wounds and glorify the leaders and combatants of both the North and South.

The immediacy of the sketches, engravings, and photographs from the front lines served the purpose of bringing the war to the public as soon as possible. It would be later in comfortable studios, often with the service of paid models, that the large oil paintings of notables and battle scenes would be completed.

At the start of the Civil War, the art and illustrations that Americans saw were derivative and often poorly executed. In the North, publications such as *Harper's Weekly, Frank Leslie's Illustrated Newspaper,* and the *New York Illustrated News* hired talented combat artists who followed the armies, witnessed the bloody battles, camped with the soldiers and lived in the heart of the war. However, their talent was poorly served by the primitive printing process of the day.

In the field, artists would sketch and draw what they objectively saw in pencil, crayon, watercolor, and pen and ink. These drawings would be rushed to the editorial offices in New York using whatever mode was available—horse, train, boat, messenger, or bribery. In New York, wood engravers, often less skilled, would quickly copy the drawing on a thick block of wood and carve away the negative areas, leaving the raised surfaces to carry the ink to the newsprint. The sensitive line of pencil and pen, as well as significant detail and informa-

tion, would often be lost in the transfer to the cruder medium of wood engraving.

At that time, the technique for reproducing photographs did not exist. It was long after the war that photographs were studied by artists and were used to produce paintings, drawings, lithographs, and wood engravings of a higher artistic level.

The most complete visual history of the war was published by the editors of *Century Magazine* in 1887–1888. Called *Battles and Leaders of the Civil War,* this four-volume set is considered to be the definitive account of the war and has the richest collection of illustrations. *Century* editors used seventy artists who created over 1,000 pictures from their field sketches; former soldiers who became artists after the war; and professional illustrators who used artists' sketch books. Also used were photographs by Mathew Brady and Alexander Gardner and the oral descriptions by veterans to produce accurate and skillful representations of the war era.

The artists joined the journalists to risk dysentery, gunfire, deprivation, and the ire of commanders to make a graphic portrayal of war for the rest of the country. Most of the more accomplished artists were from Eastern Seaboard cities, and many had received classical training in the artistic capitals of Europe. After the battles, the artists and journalists enjoyed being considered part of the rakish Bohemian Brigade. They shared information, and often the artists drew maps and diagrams for the writers.

Since salaries were meager (from $15 to $35 a week), only Winslow Homer, the best known of the artists, would receive $60 dollars for a double-page spread. The war provided tremendous impetus to Homer's career. He had completed an apprenticeship in lithography in 1857 when he was twenty-one. At the start of the war he was attending night school at the National Academy of Design in New York. He had published some drawings in *Ballou's Pictorial* and in *Harper's Weekly.* In 1861 the latter commissioned him to make drawings of Lincoln's inauguration. He was then sent to cover the Peninsula campaign when the war began. He sketched countless scenes of battle and the soldier's life in the field. He returned to New York and began work on paintings such as *Sharpshooter on Picket Duty, Rations,* and *Home Sweet Home.* Some of these works were exhibited at the National Academy in 1863. He continued with his Civil War themes, with his *Prisoners from the Front* being perhaps his best work. It was exhibited at the Paris International Exposition of 1867 and is now in the collections of the Metropolitan Museum of Art in New York. After travel in Europe, Homer shifted his art to sea and marine scenes, returning only briefly in 1878 to painting of "negro life" in Virginia in a work called *Visit from the Old Mistress,* which was exhibited in the Paris

A *Harper's Weekly* depiction of their artist, Alfred R. Waud, at work (*Library of Congress*)

Exhibition of 1878 and is now in the National Gallery of Art in Washington, D.C.

Many artists, however, were not paid when their work was not published. Artists were also responsible for travel and accommodations. Many artists carried letters of introduction to commanders. The artists moved about all fronts of the war. For example, Theodore R. Davis of *Harper's Weekly* accompanied General Sherman's march through Georgia and was considered the artist who saw more of the war than any other.

By 1861, Henri Lovi of Cincinnati estimated that he had ridden horseback 1,000 miles in three months. He complained to the editors at *Frank Leslie's Illustrated Newspaper,* "Riding from ten to fifteen miles daily through mud and underbrush and then working until midnight by the dim light of a tallow dip…I am nearly 'played out' and as soon as the Pittsburg landing is worked up and Corinth settled, I must beg a furlough for

rest and repairs. I am deranged about the stomach, ragged, unkempt and unshorn, and need the co-joined skill and services of the apothecary, the tailor and the barber and above all the attentions of home.…"

Some artists, such as Alfred R. Waud, were gifted writers as well. Waud accompanied General Custer on a raid, and his article "A Day in Camp" was as skillful as his line and wash drawings portraying the scene. Some of the hundreds of Civil War artists became famous after the war. Winslow Homer, George Caleb Bingham, Eastman Johnson, William Morris Hunt, Albert Bierstadt, Thomas Moran, and Thomas Nast are familiar names of artists who covered the Union at war.

Naval artists also had their part. The navies of the North and South launched ingenious warships in the form of gunboats and odd submarines. Xanthus Smith and other maritime artists painted dramatic pictures of fierce battles on the seas and rivers. Unlike life with the armies and access to all the battles, on the seas the artists found a less than hospitable terrain. With close quarters and firm discipline, naval ships did not often carry journalists, photographers, or artists.

On 8 March 1862, at Hampton Roads off Newport News, Virginia, the ironclad Confederate vessel CSS *Virginia* (formerly the USS *Merrimack*), a massive mound of deadly power, shelled and rammed the wooden ships of the Union navy. Xanthus Russell Smith, who had served on a wooden frigate, later painted the 9 March battle between the *Virginia* and the USS *Monitor*. In the painting, the stately wooden ships were a background for the squat and deadly steam-driven ironclads. Julian O. Davidson, who had been to sea, showed marine paintings with close attention to the technical details of the new line of ironclad vessels. Davidson produced a variety of naval illustrations that the Boston-based Louis Prang Company printed in a chromolithography series of Civil War prints. These artists, regardless of their training—classical European or naive primitive—painted large military battles in oil or quick pencil sketches, often drawn in the noisy fury of battle, and brought a dimension of emotion, humanity, and heroic drama of the tragic epic.

More dominant and immediate was the work of photographers. Mathew B. Brady's name is synonymous with photographs of President Lincoln and the Civil War, but he was a single player. While Brady had received permission from the president to privately document the impending war, many anonymous photographers were in the field with the Confederate armies as well.

Brady's colleague was Alexander Gardner. Scottish by birth, he probably met Brady during the 1851 World's Fair, as Gardner was one of the early experts in wet-plate photography. In 1856 Gardner sailed for New York City, his fare paid by Brady. He was Brady's closest associate during the war.

Gardner entered Brady's world of photography when Brady was nationally known as photographer to politicians, millionaires, and visiting royalty. His ornate studios in New York and Washington were hung with a who's who of reigning celebrities. In 1858, Alexander Gardner was manager of Brady's Washington studio. With the start of war in 1861, Brady, "the Lincoln photographer," convinced Lincoln and the war department that it was imperative to record the history of the war as it happened by means of photography. Disappointed at having to finance the venture himself, he believed that it would be a profitable investment.

Photographic technology was only twenty-two years old when the Civil War began. On 21 July 1861, at the battle of First Bull Run there appeared strange-looking hooded black wagons drawn by horses. Called "what's-its" by the soldiers, these black-hooded laboratories were ingenious, efficient photo processing laboratories manned by Brady's photographic artists. Photography in the middle of a battlefield was a daunting task. A photographer would set up the heavy studio camera on the tripod and view the objects to be filmed. In the wagon, the assistant would coat a sheet of clean glass with the liquid collodian, let it dry, then dip it in silver nitrate. These tasks had to be done in near darkness so as not to expose the plate. The glass plate was placed into a lightproof holder, rushed to the photographer, and slotted into the back of the camera. Then the black cloth was pulled over the camera and the photographer's head, and the plate was exposed for approximately ten seconds, then rushed back to the wagon for developing. Dust, humidity, and timing were all obstacles to be overcome by those Civil War photographers. The entire procedure had to be accomplished within ten to twenty minutes or the image would be lost. Alexander Gardner worked in one of those Brady wagons and reportedly took three-quarters of the photographs of the Army of the Potomac. However, Brady's name appears as the photographer.

Brady had no taste for the war and after a short time at the Bull Run debacle he returned to his New York portrait studio. The cost of supplying and photographing the war, coupled with his poor business practices, caused his financial ruin, resulting in his bankruptcy by 1873. His hope of reaping riches from his Civil War photographs was dashed by a glut of pictures. More than a million exposures were made, and the public could not get enough of the war pictures, but by the end of the horrific conflict the Americans had no desire to see the painful images.

Alexander Gardner left Brady in 1863 and set up a studio similar to Brady's in Washington where, for the remainder of the war, he sporadically photographed battles and the tragic aftermaths. Gardner photographed Lincoln's funeral and the famous pictures of the hanging of the assassination conspirators.

Gardner closed his studio and became a field photographer for the Union Pacific Railroad. His black laboratory wagon followed the covered wagons on the Chisolm Trail into the western frontier. He became famous for some of the best photographs of the western frontier.

Southern photographers were also on hand at the start of the war. F. K. Houston of Charleston, South Carolina, photographed the vanquished Fort Sumter; he was followed by James Osburn and F. E. Durbec. Perhaps because of limited supplies, they did not continue to photograph Civil War subjects.

Brady's failing eyesight led him to relegate the camera work to his talented staff. The bulk of the photos were taken by Gardner, his son James, Timothy O'Sullivan, William Pywell, George N. Barnard, David Woodbury, E. Guy Fox, and others. Gardner's and O'Sullivan's work developed into true art, and they left Brady when he denied them credit for their work. The only official government photographer working for the U.S. Military Railroad was a Captain A. J. Russell, who is credited with work of high quality. These were artists who captured the static scenes of scarred and blasted fields littered with broken equipment, although they would frequently move bodies to improve the composition of a photograph and add drama to the scene. They took thousands of *carte de viste* photos of young, smartly dressed recruits and grizzled veterans in rag-tag uniforms. They captured homey scenes of encampments, barbers working outdoors, cooks stirring pots, soldiers playing cards at their leisure in front of their tents, the dead and dying in field hospitals, and generals whose names are now a part of the American pageant. The results of their work often had an ignominious end. When the demand for Civil War photographs waned, thousands of the glass-plate negatives were sold for use as windows in greenhouses. As the seasons changed, the captured faces in the glass—the corpse-strewn battlefields of Antietam, Fredericksburg, Vicksburg, Gettysburg; the sunken gunboats; the ruined cities; and the heroic and battle-weary soldiers—were burned away by the rays of the sun. These negatives became the ghostly pentimento of this tragic civil war.

To produce lithographs, the artist would draw on smooth stone slabs with a grease pencil. It offered a more sensitive surface for detail and shading than woodcut engraving, but it was time-consuming, as the stone required inking with a brayer for each print. After several hundred prints the original image would fade.

Engravings on copper or steel plates were the most demanding of skill and time. The artist was required to scratch and carve incised lines into hard sheets of treated copper with engraving tools. Ink would be rubbed into these lines, excess ink would be wiped away, and the plate would be placed into a press with a sheet of dampened paper. The plate and paper, sandwiched between felt blankets, would be drawn through the press, forcing the damp paper into the incised lines and creating a richly detailed engraving.

Among the most popular and accessible American art forms—priced for as little as twenty-five cents and sold in general stores and on street corners—were prints by Currier and Ives. This company, started in 1835, achieved great success through mass-producing familiar American scenes as well as Civil War battle prints. Rare was the household that did not have a Currier and Ives print on the wall.

Established artists would sell paintings to the firm, which then had them copied on lithographic stones and printed as black-and-white prints. In the New York City factory, the prints would move down an assembly line, where workers would dab bright colors on the print through a stencil. Although Currier and Ives prints were

not always historically accurate, they filled a demand by the masses for Civil War art. By the mid-1880s, the Louis Prang Company of Boston and the firm of Kurz and Allison of Chicago had also printed a series of battle scenes that are still used today as graphic illustrations for book covers.

None of the art produced during the Civil War was officially sponsored by the governments of either side. It did not occur to these mid–nineteenth-century administrations to utilize art as propaganda, nor could they afford it. Initially it was the artists and the few patrons who documented the war. After the war, the growing number of veterans' organizations continued to stimulate and encourage the creation of Civil War art. Other factors also contributed to these efforts, such as a curiosity about the war by those who had not experienced it directly, and a desire to honor those who had fought.

One defining image from all the art produced for and about the Confederacy is an engraving called *The Burial of Latane*. William DeHartburn Washington, an artist from Richmond, Virginia, completed an oil painting in 1864 portraying the burial of a young doctor who was killed as his unit repulsed the Union forces just north of Richmond. Captain Latane, sword drawn and charging the retreating forces, was killed by a fusillade of gunfire. His brother, a comrade in arms, transported his body to a nearby plantation, where the mistress of the plantation, with the help of the slaves and other women, tenderly put the young officer to rest as if he were one of their beloved sons. Reported by the press and memorialized in a widely read poem, the incident moved the artist to paint the burial scene with the women and girls performing the service and mourning the unknown soldier. This image would strike the heart of all those Southerners who lost a loved one far from home and among strangers. Ironically, it was a Northern engraver, A. G. Campbell, working from a photograph, and a New York City publishing house that produced the print that evoked such an unparalleled response, particularly among the women of the South. Universal sorrow, the skill of the engraver, and active promotion and marketing of the print created a symbol of the Lost Cause. *The Burial of Latane* portrayed a woman's view of the war, sustained the Southern identity, and became an enduring image for decades after the war.

From 1785 to 1903, military cyclorama paintings were a popular art form in the great capitals of Europe. Brought to the United States in 1790, this kind of touring painting was displayed on the interior walls of specially constructed round buildings. Stretching up to fifty feet in height and encircling the viewer for nearly four hundred feet in length, the canvas would envelop the viewer in an immense painting in the round. At first, experienced European artists did the research, visited battle sites, and interviewed the soldiers and officers. Teams of painters would work for months to create the battle scene vistas that would draw millions of viewers in American cities. They paid between twenty-five and fifty cents for admission. Many major battles—Antietam, Second Bull Run, Shiloh, the clash of the *Monitor* and the *Virginia,* and others—were the subject matter of these colossal canvasses. Few have survived, and those that have are rarely exhibited.

Around 1882, Paul Philippoteaux, a Frenchman who had worked on European cycloramas, came to Gettysburg to do research on the battle. With a team of five artists he completed the first of four cycloramas of the battle of Gettysburg. He exhibited the first work to great acclaim in Chicago in 1883. One of Philippoteaux's Gettysburg cycloramas is on display at the Gettysburg National Military Park. Another cyclorama, *The Battle of Atlanta,* by William Wehner and his team of European artists, was restored in 1982 and is on view in modern facilities near the Atlanta battleground.

As an art form the cyclorama never attained the level of museum quality. As a spectacle it was hyped and promoted in the florid language of the time. The sheer size and weight of the canvas, the need for a special building, and the growing distaste among Americans for the illustrated carnage doomed this once-popular kind of painting. The arrival of new technology heralded by D. W. Griffith's movie *The Birth of a Nation* in 1915 closed the door on the cyclorama, a unique form of artistic storytelling.

For decades after the war, to heal the wounds, confront the terrible losses, and glorify the survivors of this national cataclysm, thousands of statues, obelisks, plaques, busts, tombs, canons, and pillars were carved and constructed in twenty-five states and the District of Columbia. In almost every hamlet, town, and city that sent soldiers to the war there are examples of sculpture in parks, town squares, cemeteries, and battle sites. The National Park Service and numerous other organizations maintain and administrate various buildings and battle-grounds throughout these states.

The largest and most imposing of all Civil War sculpture is carved into the granite of a mountain near Atlanta called Stone Mountain. The equestrian figures of Robert E. Lee, "Stonewall" Jackson, and Jefferson Davis were conceived and begun by Gutzon Borglum, who later designed and created Mount Rushmore. This impressive sculpture, later completed by Walker Hancock, measures 90 feet high by 190 feet long. It is a spectacular feat of engineering and carving.

Augustus Saint-Gaudens was commissioned to create a sculptural monument for Boston honoring Colonel Robert Gould Shaw, the leader of the 54th Massachusetts, the black regiment that stormed Fort Wagner. A masterpiece, this bas relief took fourteen

years to complete. It depicts Shaw on horseback accompanied by a column of his men and is sculpted with attention to detail and honest realism. Saint-Gaudens's equestrian statue of General William T. Sherman being led by the winged female figure of American victory was placed on New York's Fifth Avenue near the entrance to Central Park. The figure of the horse and rider and the striding Victory create an unmistakable feeling of forward movement and progress. This gilded statue rides high above pedestrians, taxis, and hansom cabs on one of the busiest, most affluent, and modern city corners in the world.

The nation's capital, with a wealth of sculpture, is home to one of America's most familiar monuments, the Lincoln Memorial. The white marble sculpture of the seated Abraham Lincoln by America's acknowledged leading sculptor, Daniel Chester French, is a powerful symbol for all Americans. From within the stone emerges the sad but rugged character of the man who held the country together through its bloody struggle.

The Hudson River school of painting, rooted in European themes, was the predominant style of painting in the period before the war. English-born Thomas Cole was painting in this manner in 1825. The majestic American landscape was painted as a vision from a palette arranged by God.

By the 1850s a more natural and realistic style emerged as artists like George Caleb Bingham portrayed the reality of American life and work in everyday scenes. Unlike the Europeans, who had a long art history of military themes, the antimilitary American artists were more likely to paint idyllic landscapes and upon these arcadian backgrounds superimpose the war scene. An example would be a painting by Albert Bierstadt entitled *Guerilla Warfare (Picket Duty in Virginia)* (1862), in which five Union soldiers fire upon Confederate troops in the distance. The rolling hills bathed in summer haze, the carefully painted lush grasses, and beautifully rendered trees provide a theatrical set upon which the soldiers casually play at war.

Conrad Wise Chapman, an ardent son of Virginia, returned from Italy at age nineteen to fight as well as record scenes of camp life. After recovery from a head wound, he was transferred in October 1863 to Charleston, South Carolina. Later, he was to paint a series of thirty-one oils of the harbor during the siege. These landscapes and seascapes are peaceful depictions of the harbor watched over by the lone sentry at his post atop the ramparts. His work, in the Museum of the Confederacy, is considered the most important of the Confederacy.

John Ross Key, who also painted a work called *The Bombardment of Fort Sumter* in 1864, fell victim to the same philosophy that so many Civil War painters employed. They sought to reduce the carnage and destruction to a lovely landscape that just happened to be a background for columns of marching soldiers and prancing horses. Critics were no better in the assessment of these works of Civil War art, much of which was sentimental, idealized, and sanitized views of a horrific national explosion. The artists Gilbert Gaul, Peter F. Rothermel, William B. T. Trego, Walton Taber, and Thure deThulstrup seemed to portray the battle scenes with more visual realism, honesty, and artistic skill than others.

Winslow Homer, considered the greatest of the Civil War painters, after his brief sojourn to the front for *Harper's Weekly*, almost exclusively concentrated his paintings' subject matter on genre scenes of the soldiers' life in camp. He had no interest in being a painter of military battles; his forte was being a painter of the people. Perhaps if we strip away the pretensions of glory formed in the idealized portraits of military leaders, the carefully painted rows of nameless soldiers marching to their deaths, the stiff and static generals astride their foaming steeds, safely behind the lines, we would accept Lincoln's observation that it was "the people's war."

—*Rosemarie S. Cardoso*

See also Battles and Leaders of the Civil War; Brady, Mathew B.; Cyclorama; *Frank Leslie's Illustrated Newspaper*; Gardner, Alexander; *Harper's Weekly*; Homer, Winslow; Nast, Thomas; Photography; Waud, Alfred Rudolph.

For further reading:

Blay, John S. *The Civil War A Pictorial Profile* (1958).

Gardner, Alexander. *Gardner's Photographic Sketchbook of the Civil War* (1959).

Holzer, Harold, and Mark E. Neely, Jr. *Mine Eyes Have Seen the Glory* (1993).

Jacobson, Doranne. *The Civil War in Art: A Visual Odyssey* (1996).

Ketchum, Richard M., ed. *The American Heritage Picture History of the Civil War* (1960).

McSpadden, J. Walker. *Famous Sculptors of America* (1968).

Neely, Mark E. Jr., Harold Holzer, and Gabor S. Boritt. *The Confederate Image: Prints of the Lost Cause* (1987).

Sears, Stephen W. *The American Heritage Century Collection of Civil War Art* (1974).

Starr, Louis M. *Bohemian Brigade: Civil War Newsmen in Action* (1987).

Ward, Geoffrey C., et al. *The Civil War: An Illustrated History* (1990).

Williams, Herman Warner, Jr. *The Civil War: The Artists' Record* (1961).

ARTILLERY

Land-based artillery was typed variously by its design, projectile, trajectory, deployment, and bore. The two most general classifications were *heavy*, massive large caliber cannons used in garrison, siege, and seacoast roles, and *light*, mobile horse-drawn weapons used most often with infantry in the field. A cannon's trajectory—the arc of its projectile's flight—and basic design provided more specific classifications.

Guns were long-barreled weapons capable of firing heavy projectiles in relatively flat trajectories. Howitzers had shorter barrels, a powder chamber smaller in diameter than the bore of the piece, and achieved a higher trajectory than guns. Mortars had very short, thick-walled barrels and lobbed large caliber projectiles at an extremely high trajectory. Columbiads were the heaviest weapons, usually deployed in garrison, siege, and seacoast roles, and were capable of firing tremendous projectiles great distances.

Both rockets and hand grenades also saw limited use. Some evidence supports the view that the Confederates used British-designed Congreve rockets early in the war. However, they found the Congreves, which resembled very large bottle rockets, so highly inaccurate that they soon abandoned them. The Union army fielded the spin-stabilized Hale rocket in both 6- and 16-pound weights. Although the Hale could achieve a maximum range of about 2,200 yards, it, like the Congreve, was far from accurate, and carried an insufficient warhead to inflict significant damage.

Numerous hand grenade patents also emerged during the war, but the Ketcham was the most commonly used hand-thrown ordnance. Significant numbers of Ketchams were manufactured by the Federal arsenals in 1-, 2-, 3-, and 5-pound weights. The Ketcham was stabilized by cardboard fins and detonated by a percussion fuse in its nose. Other types of grenades included the Adams and Excelsior patents, as well as common 6-pound spherical cannon balls that were lit and either rolled or thrown at nearby enemy positions.

Both smoothbore and rifled weapons saw extensive use during the war. The majority were muzzle loading, although a limited number of breech-loading pieces were also fielded. Smoothbore cannons fired spherical projectiles attached by tinned iron straps to wooden bases called *sabots*. This arrangement, when attached to a powder bag, was what was known as fixed ammunition. Fixed ammunition afforded smoothbore gunners a speed advantage over their rifled-gun counterparts, who usually had to load their powder charge and projectile separately.

Smoothbore ammunition classifications included solid shot, common shell, case shot, canister, and grapeshot. Solid shot consisted of solid-cast iron balls used for battering down brick or masonry fortifications. The tendency of solid shot to carom across hard ground also proved particularly deadly for long-range antipersonnel purposes. Common shells were hollow iron projectiles filled with a bursting charge, detonated by either time or impact fuses and designed to explode into numerous fragments. Case shot, also known as shrapnel for its English inventor, Henry Shrapnel, was also a hollow iron sphere but with thinner walls and filled with iron or lead balls designed to scatter upon detonation. It too was fuse detonated.

An eight-inch Parrot gun (*foreground*), with a Rodman gun beyond; Battery Rogers at Hunting Creek and the Potomac, Alexandria, Virginia. (*Library of Congress*)

A canister round was a tinned iron can filled with iron or lead balls sealed with a heavy iron plate at either end and nailed to a wooden sabot. In effect a huge shotgun cartridge, canister was particularly effective against attacking infantry and cavalry at close ranges. In many instances gunners loaded "double canister" when threatened with being overrun. Grapeshot was typically fired from the larger garrison, siege, and seacoast artillery. A stand of grapeshot, as the projectile was called, consisted of nine large iron balls arranged in three tiers and held in place by two heavy iron plates at either end with two iron rings around the middle. A long bolt passing through the middle of the stand through each end plate secured the projectile until it was fired. When fired, the

bolt would bend or fracture, thus releasing the stand's deadly components with an effect similar to canister but on a larger scale. Grapeshot was particularly effective in wrecking ships' rigging as well as against personnel.

Rifled cannon projectiles were most commonly cylindrical, and resembled modern artillery ordnance in appearance. Rather than a wooden sabot, rifled projectiles were usually cast with integral lead, copper, or brass expansion rings designed to grip the bore's rifling upon firing. The advent of rifled artillery sparked a rush to the U.S. Patent Office as inventors submitted scores of designs for "improved" projectiles and their various components, including fuses and sabots. Capable of greater range and accuracy than smoothbore weapons,

A modified 12-pounder breech-loading Whitworth gun, location unknown (*Library of Congress*)

rifled artillery was most effective firing case shot and shell, as well as—to a limited extent—solid shot, also known as bolts. Bolts were most useful against armored and masonry targets but relatively ineffective against infantry, owing to their tendency to bury themselves in the earth rather than bounce along the ground in the manner of spherical solid shot. The spin afforded by rifled barrels also tended to make grapeshot and canister impractical, because of their tendency to sling their components in unpredictable patterns.

Explosive shell and case projectiles relied on either time or percussion fuses to ignite their bursting charges. The simplest time fuse consisted of a 2-inch paper tube of compressed gunpowder inserted into either a wooden or metal fuse adapter that in turn was fitted into a hole in the projectile. Time fuses of various patents were fitted to both spherical and rifled shell and case shot. The paper fuses were color coded to indicate their various burning times and were ignited by the cannon's firing. The Borman time fuse was a threaded soft metal disc filled with an internal powder train graduated from one to five seconds burning time. Preparatory to loading, the gunner punched a hole into the fuse at the appropriate second

mark indicated on its face. This exposed the powder trail to the flames generated by the cannon's ignition.

As their detonation relied on direct impact with a target, percussion fuses were impractical for use with spherical ammunition, as round balls tended to spin unpredictably after firing. Screwed into the nose of the projectile and designed to explode on impact, percussion fuses were best suited to rifled artillery. Their basic principle relied on a sliding powder-filled plunger that, through inertia, would fly forward on impact against the front of the fuse. The impact would then explode a percussion cap very similar to those used on percussion muskets. There were several varieties of percussion fuses and some combined both time and percussion characteristics. Parrott, Hotchkiss, and Schenkl were three of the most widely used percussion patents.

As a general rule the Union, with its superior manufacturing capabilities, produced ammunition more reliable than the ordnance in the Confederates' limber chests. But owing to the many variables inherent in its manufacture, components, and use, explosive ammunition used by both sides was always subject to malfunction. Despite the often ingenious efforts of their inventors, explosive shells were prone either to explode before leaving the muzzle of the cannon or not explode at all.

Field artillery usually consisted of 12-pounder smoothbores and 10- and sometimes 20-pounder rifled guns. Their two-wheeled "stock trail" field carriages were most typically constructed of wood with iron fittings. The Model 1841 bronze 6-pounder guns and 12-pounder howitzers were already obsolete in 1861, and as the war progressed were eventually removed from Federal service. The ordnance-starved Confederacy, however, continued to field both until the war's end. Although seeing rather limited use, the 12-pounder mountain howitzer was designed for easy disassembly for transport on muleback in difficult terrain. At only 37 inches in length and weighing a diminutive 220 pounds, the mountain howitzer shared the same bore size and thus the same ammunition as its larger 12-pounder cousins. The mountain howitzer's short barrel precluded long-range accuracy, but by virtue of its design it could be deployed in areas inaccessible to conventional artillery.

By far the most popular field cannon among gunners of both sides was the bronze 12-pounder smooth-bore Model 1857 Napoleon. Namesake of Napoleon III, under whose auspices it was originally designed for the French army, the Model 1857 was a hybrid gun-howitzer, being somewhat smaller and lighter than the earlier model 12-pounder, yet taking the same powder charge. In Federal service it replaced both the 6-pounder and the 12-pounder howitzer. The South relied heavily on captured Napoleons and also manufactured simplified Napoleons cast without the muzzle swell found on Federal models. The Napoleon fired shot, shell, case, and canister with equal ease.

Some debate arose among gunners concerning the relative merits and liabilities between smoothbore and rifled artillery. The Napoleon was unsurpassed as a relatively short-range antipersonnel weapon. Firing fixed ammunition, it was somewhat faster to load than rifled field guns. Also, its projectile was some two pounds heavier, allowing for a significantly stronger blasting charge. The Napoleon's 4.62-inch smooth bore was particularly well suited to the use of canister, and it was more effective than rifled guns in heavily wooded terrain. In addition, many contemporary observers noted that rifled projectiles tended to bury themselves and explode harmlessly in the earth upon impact, thus negating their effectiveness. The smoothbores' spherical projectiles, however, tended to bounce across the ground, causing considerable destruction before detonating. For their part, the rifles' proponents viewed such drawbacks a small price to pay for their pieces' far superior accuracy and range.

The two most commonly used rifled field artillery pieces were the 3-inch, 10-pounder Parrotts and Ordnance Rifles. Patented in 1861 by Robert P. Parrott, superintendent of the West Point Foundry of Cold Spring, New York, the Parrott was originally produced in 2.9-inch caliber, but later models were standardized as 3-

The "Dictator," a flatcar-mounted mortar, was used during the siege of Petersburg.
(Photograph by David Knox / *Library of Congress*)

inch weapons. Parrotts are easily distinguished by the wrought-iron reinforcing band around the breech of their inherently brittle cast-iron tubes. The reinforcing band did much to improve the Parrott's reliability, but throughout the war Parrotts managed to explode with annoying and often dangerous regularity. Still, the Parrott was accurate and relatively inexpensive to produce. Two models of Parrott rifles were produced during the war—the Model 1861, easily identified by its muzzle swell, and the simpler Model 1863, cast without a muzzle swell. The Parrott design sufficiently impressed Confederate ordnance officers to prompt them to produce their own copies at Richmond's Tredegar Works. Twenty-pounder (3.67-inch) Parrotts also saw field service.

Adopted by the Federal Ordnance Department in 1861, the wrought-iron 3-inch Ordnance Rifle, often mistakenly referred to as the Rodman, was originally patented by John Griffen in 1855. The majority of the Ordnance Rifles were manufactured at the Phoenix Iron Company of Phoenixville, Pennsylvania. The foundry's president, Samuel J. Reeves, received his own patent in 1862 for additional improvements in the weapon's production. The Ordnance Rifle, with its strikingly modern, streamlined appearance, accuracy, and reliability, was considered the best muzzle-loading rifled field gun of the day. Ordnance Rifles made up 41 percent of the Federal guns at Gettysburg. The Ordnance Rifle most often fired projectiles of the Hotchkiss and Schenkl patents, but would also accept 3-inch Parrott ammunition. Confederate inventors also produced a number of unique designs, such as the Archer, Mullane, Reed, and Reed-Braun patents, for use in captured Ordnance Rifles.

The James Rifles saw rather less use during the war. Designed by General Charles T. James of the Rhode Island militia to accept his own unique patented projec-

Army engineers remove an 8-inch Columbiad gun from Fort McAllister, Savannah, Georgia, in December 1864.
(*Library of Congress*)

A 12-pounder howitzer captured from the Confederates by Butterfield's Brigade near Hanover Court House, 27 May 1862
(*Library of Congress*)

tile, the 14-pounder (3.8-inch) James Rifles were cast by the Ames Manufacturing Company of Chicopee, Massachusetts. The James, however, exhibited a number of drawbacks, and after 1862 became an increasing rarity in the field. The James patent projectile with its soft lead sabot proved the first culprit in the gun's demise. Early in the war gunners delivering covering fire over the heads of their own infantry found that their ammunition tended to fling off its lead sabot upon leaving the muzzles of their guns. The resulting casualties among their own troops caused by this rain of deadly shrapnel from the rear understandably cost the James much in the way of reputation. Although the ammunition problem was remedied by the substitution of Hotchkiss pattern projectiles, the material of its manufacture eventually doomed the James. Despite sharing a similar appearance to the Ordnance Rifle, the James was of the softer cast bronze, rather than wrought iron. Its rifling, therefore, tended to erode quickly after heavy use with a consequent loss in accuracy.

Two breech-loading rifles were introduced during the war. Both the Armstrong and Whitworth rifles were designed and manufactured in England and were imported in limited numbers. The majority saw use in Confederate service. Despite their advanced designs, neither the Armstrong nor Whitworth's breech-loading mechanisms afforded any significant advantage in their speed of loading. Crews often found them overly complicated, difficult to operate, and prone to fouling and breakage. In addition, neither weapon employed fixed ammunition. Both weapons, however, won reputations for unsurpassed range and accuracy.

The Armstrong employed a projectile either fitted with three rows of small brass studs intended to mate with its bore's rifling or lead driving bands. Armstrongs were manufactured in a number of calibers, the most common being 3-inch 10-pounder weapons. The weapons developed by the prolific English weapons designer Sir Joseph Whitworth were also produced in a number of calibers, the most common probably the 12-pounder (2.75-inch) models with a few large caliber Whitworths also seeing some action. Although some Whitworths were manufactured as muzzle-loading weapons, all shared their inventor's unique twisting hexagonal bore and corresponding ammunition. The efficiency of the Whitworth system allowed gunners to

Parrot gun at an unknown location, early 1860s (*Library of Congress*)

achieve ranges of almost six miles—an advantage often lost in practical use owing to the era's primitive aiming. The Whitworth's streamlined, hexagonal projectiles also shared the disadvantage of most rifled field gun projectiles in that they were not large enough to accommodate a significant blasting charge. They were most effective firing bolts that could be delivered accurately at high velocity in much flatter trajectories than conventional artillery. Troops noted that the Whitworth projectiles' hexagonal shape, coupled with its high rate of speed, lent it an unnerving high-pitched whine that added much to its fearsome reputation.

Classified as heavy artillery, siege and garrison cannons were of heavier caliber and less mobile than field artillery. Siege artillery, however, was usually mounted on

relatively mobile wooden carriages similar in design to the field artillery's. The great weight of the more permanently fixed garrison and seacoast weapons necessitated that their carriages be constructed of heavy timber or iron. The two most common types of mounts were the casement and the barbette carriages. The tracked casement carriage was similar to naval carriages, as it was used primarily in older, permanent masonry forts with gun ports. Its design facilitated the limited movement necessary to retract the cannon into the fort for loading. The more common barbette carriages were most often employed in open earthen or masonry fortifications. Their design employed small wheels on tracks and either a front or center pivot or *pintle*. This arrangement allowed gunners to traverse their weapons for a wide angle of fire.

Some of the most common seacoast smoothbores were the iron Model 1829 32-pounder and the Model 1831 42-pounder guns. Both weapons were typically mounted on wooden, front pintle, barbette carriages for garrison use. Experiences early in the war quickly led artillerists to the conclusion that rifled weapons, with their higher velocities, were far superior to the older smoothbore cannons against masonry targets. As a result, some smoothbore guns were rifled to accept James projectiles.

The West Point Foundry also produced its famous Parrott rifles in massive 6.4-inch (100-pound), 8-inch (200-pound), and 10-inch (250–300-pound) versions. Mounted on wrought iron, front pintle, barbette carriages, these huge weapons shared not only the accuracy of the smaller Parrotts, but, unfortunately, their propensity to burst during firing. The bursting of such larger guns was an ongoing concern for weapons designers of the era, owing to the comparatively primitive metallurgy of the day and the volatility of black powder propellant charges. One solution was the "built-up" gun—a cannon manufactured of separate components fused together to provide added strength. The Parrott was an example of the built-up gun, but other designs proved more successful, including the British-designed Blakely and Armstrong rifles and the Confederate-designed Brooke rifles.

A few 5-inch (80-pound) Whitworth rifles also saw service in Confederate coastal defenses.

First developed by American Colonel George Bomford and introduced in 1811, the cast-iron smoothbore Columbiads were some of the largest cannons to see service in the war. Primarily a seacoast weapon, the Columbiad combined various aspects of the gun and howitzer. Early Columbiads shared a similar powder chamber to the howitzer and all were capable of firing in both high howitzer and low gun trajectories. The Columbiad's design underwent a number of modifications both before and during the war, resulting in a wide variety of types and calibers. The Models of 1844 and 1858 were cast in 8-inch (65-pound) and 10-inch (128-pound) calibers, as was the Model 1861 Rodman, which was also cast in a 15-inch (428-pound) version. At least one 20-inch Rodman was produced in 1864. Named for their inventor, Thomas Jefferson Rodman, these innovative weapons introduced a number of improvements in casting and overall design and both Union and Confederate foundries produced them in significant numbers. Most Columbiads were mounted on massive wrought-iron, center pintle, barbette carriages.

Mortars were classified as siege, garrison, and seacoast artillery and were cast in a number of sizes. They fired heavy spherical time-fused shell and case ammunition. The Coehorn, named for its inventor, the seventeenth-century Dutch artillerist Baron van Menno Coehoorn,

was the smallest weapon of this class and saw wide use. The standard 24-pound Coehorn consisted of a short 16.32-inch bronze tube mounted on a simple wooden bed with four handles. Weighing a mere 296 pounds, the Coehorn could be carried by as few as two men. It was particularly well suited for trench warfare, owing to its mobility and ability to throw projectiles in a high arc into opposing earthworks. The Confederates produced somewhat simplified iron Coehorns in both 24- and 12-pound models. The iron Model 1841 8- and 10-inch siege models were much heavier mortars than the Coehorns, and in 1861 were augmented by still more massive weapons, the 10- and 13-inch seacoast mortars. The tube of the largest of these, the 13-inch seacoast mortar, weighed 17,120 pounds and could hurl a 220-pound projectile 4,325 yards at a 45 degree elevation. Owing partially to transportation difficulties, few of these mortars were actually installed in seacoast fortifications by war's end. They did, however, see use on special mortar boats operating along the Mississippi River, and the most famous mortar of all, the "Dictator," was mounted on a special railroad flatcar for use during the siege of Petersburg.

—*Jeff Kinard*

See also Armories, Arsenals, and Foundries; Dahlgren Guns; Ordnance, Naval; Rodman Gun; Springfield Armory; Tredegar Iron Works.

For further reading:

Coggins, Jack. *Arms and Equipment of the Civil War* (1989).
Peterson, Harold L. *Round Shot and Rammers: An Introduction to Muzzle-loading Land Artillery in the United States* (1969).
Thomas, Dean S. *Cannons* (1985).

ASBOTH, ALEXANDER SANDOR
(1811–1868)
Union general

A veteran of the Hungarian Revolution of 1848, Alexander Sandor Asboth fled to the United States, befriended powerful politicians, and rose rapidly in rank at the outbreak of the Civil War. He led divisions at the battle of Pea Ridge and during the advance on Corinth in early 1862, before questions about his competence relegated him to minor commands for the remainder of the war.

Born in Keszthely, Hungary, on 18 December 1811, Asboth studied engineering and worked as a civil servant, before participating in the unsuccessful 1848 revolt against Austria as an aide to Louis Kossuth. He fled his homeland after the uprising's failure, traveling first to Turkey, before receiving asylum in the United States. Upon his arrival Asboth continued to work for Hungarian independence, establishing several factories in New York to produce supplies for the continued struggle.

During the 1850s Asboth remained in New York,

where he fortuitously befriended John C. Frémont. Upon the outbreak of the Civil War, the famed Pathfinder appointed the dashing, militarily experienced Hungarian as his chief of staff with the rank of brigadier general. This appointment, however, would not be confirmed until early 1862.

Asboth's first serious engagement was at the battle of Pea Ridge in March 1862, where he commanded the 2d Division of Samuel Curtis's Army of the Southwest. Suffering a serious arm wound in the battle, the Hungarian performed erratically, urging Curtis to withdraw from the field after the first day's fighting. Asboth next led troops in the Union advance on Corinth, Mississippi, which was followed successively by garrison duty in Mississippi, as commander of fortifications at Memphis, and, in early 1863, as commander of the District of Columbus in western Kentucky. In the latter position he strove to defend the supply lines of Ulysses Grant's army against attacks from Confederate guerrillas. Asboth's actions again led to questions about his competence. He often bombarded his superiors with exaggerated or pessimistic reports, and asked for reinforcements after noting that he had driven Confederate forces from his district.

Ultimately, in August 1863 the Hungarian was relieved of his command. He briefly commanded a division in William Sherman's XVI Corps, before being transferred to Edward Ord's XIII Corps, and eventually to Nathaniel Banks's Department of the Gulf. In November 1863, Banks finally placed Asboth in command of the District of West Florida, with his headquarters at Fort Barrancas, near Pensacola. Asboth would spend the remainder of the war in this remote location. Despite his eagerness to return to a more active theater, Asboth generally performed well in his new position. He worked to organize a regiment of cavalry from Unionist refugees, encouraged black enlistments, and mounted a number of raids into the Confederate-held interior.

The only significant military engagement in which Asboth participated while in Florida was the 27 September 1864 raid on Marianna. With 700 men from the 2d Maine Cavalry, 1st Florida Infantry, and the 82d and 86th United States Colored Infantry, Asboth left Barrancas on 18 September, with the objectives of capturing isolated Confederate outposts, recruiting men for his black and Unionist regiments, and collecting supplies and mounts for his command. Upon reaching Marianna, the Federals fought a heated engagement with a small Rebel force composed primarily of a home guard company referred to as the Cradle and the Grave. Asboth's troops captured the town, killing or capturing most of the defenders, but while leading a charge their commander suffered two serious wounds, one breaking his cheekbone and the other his left arm.

After several months' recuperation, Asboth returned to his command in early 1865. He received a major general's brevet in March, and was mustered out of volunteer service five months later. His postwar career proved tragically brief. Though still suffering from his Marianna wound, Asboth was appointed minister to Argentina in early 1866. While in Buenos Aires he attempted to mediate an end to a war that pitted Paraguay against Argentina, Brazil, and Uruguay. Despite failing health, Asboth was appointed minister to Uruguay in October 1867. Over the next several months his condition deteriorated, and he died on 21 January 1868 in Buenos Aires.

—*David J. Coles*

See also Immigrants; Pea Ridge, Battle of.
For further reading:

Hess, Earl J. "Alexander Asboth: One of Lincoln's Hungarian Heroes?" *Lincoln Herald* (1982).
Shea, William L., and Earl J. Hess. *Pea Ridge: Civil War Campaign in the West* (1992).
Vasvary, Edmund. *Lincoln's Hungarian Heroes: The Participation of Hungarians in the Civil War, 1861–1865* (1939).

ASHBY, TURNER
(1828–1862)
Confederate officer

Born on 23 October 1828, in Fauquier County, Virginia, Turner Ashby was from a wealthy Virginia planter family. His grandfather, Captain "Jack" Ashby, had earned fame in the American Revolutionary War. Taught by his mother and hired tutors, Ashby had little formal education. After the early death of his father, he and his brothers managed the family farm, Rose Hill.

As sectional tensions heightened, Ashby formed a volunteer cavalry company, his reputation as a horseman attracting many recruits. Following John Brown's 1859 raid at Harper's Ferry, Ashby took his company there, and subsequently it patrolled the Potomac River crossings to prevent other such raids.

Following the secession of Virginia, Ashby's company became part of Colonel Angus W. McDonald's 7th Virginia Cavalry Regiment. McDonald knew a fighter when he saw one and on 25 June 1861, he recommended Ashby for promotion to lieutenant colonel. The next day, Ashby's brother Richard, out searching for a Northern sympathizer, was mortally wounded by a Union patrol. Turner came upon the scene before his brother died and was convinced that Richard had been stabbed after he had fallen. He vowed vengeance.

Ashby soon developed a reputation for reckless bravery in battle equalled by few other commanders, North or South, yet he was reportedly so soft-spoken, mild mannered, and gentlemanly when not in a fight,

Turner Ashby (*Library of Congress*)

that those who met him could not remember anything he had said. When rheumatism forced McDonald to retire, Ashy became colonel of the regiment and exercised virtually independent command in the region west of Harper's Ferry. Ashby was a poor disciplinarian, however, and his units had a reputation for going their own way and looting.

On 16 October 1861 Ashby planned to attack Federal troops active in the vicinity of his camp on Bolivar Heights near Harper's Ferry. With no more than 550 men, of whom 300 were militia, and two artillery pieces, he drove Union troops from the vicinity. Ashby performed a variety of other missions until the spring of 1862 when Major General Thomas J. "Stonewall" Jackson gave him command of his cavalry. Ashby speedily built up this force to twenty-one companies. Ashby played a key role in Jackson's Shenandoah Valley campaign, securing vital intelligence on Union forces and masking Jackson's weakness.

After participating in the withdrawal from Winchester, Virginia, on 11 March, Ashby reported to Jackson ten days later the mistaken impression that Federal troops were retiring northward and only a meager Union presence remained in that city. This faulty information contributed to Jackson's decision to attack and to his subsequent repulse in the battle of Kernstown

on 23 March 1862. Afterward, some of Ashby's cavalry became demoralized. Discipline was lax and the companies operated as semi-independent commands with control exercised by individual captains, some of whom were incompetent. Federal troops captured one company of sixty men and mounts, and they came on another company hors de combat ("out of the fight") on applejack and quickly scattered it.

Under pressure from Richmond and believing Ashby a poor disciplinarian who attached little importance to drill, Jackson dispersed Ashby's cavalry within his command. An angry Ashby then threatened to resign. Despite Ashby's shortcomings, Jackson could ill afford to lose him. He was invaluable in scouting in front or commanding the rear guard, only he could hold the diverse cavalry units together, and his bravery in battle was an important example for the army. Ashby's men boasted that within a single month he had engaged the Federals on twenty-eight separate occasions. So, following a private meeting between the two men on 24 April 1862, Jackson relented and restored the whole of the cavalry to Ashby's command. Having promised Jackson that he would discipline his men, Ashby now fought harder than ever, and Jackson was instrumental in securing his promotion to brigadier general on 23 May.

Late in the afternoon on 6 June, two miles south of Harrisonburg, Virginia, Ashby was leading several companies of infantry on foot in a rear-guard action against Union troops. He had just shouted, "Forward, my brave men!" when he was struck and killed by a Union bullet. Jackson, who received the news at Port Republic, was visibly shaken by it. He later observed of Ashby, "As a partisan officer I never knew his superior; his daring was proverbial; his powers of endurance almost incredible; his tone of character heroic; and his sagacity almost intuitive in divining the purpose and movements of the enemy." Ashby's death was indeed a heavy blow to Jackson's army.

—*Spencer C. Tucker*

See also Cavalry, C.S.A.; Jackson, Thomas J.; Kernstown, Battle of; Shenandoah Valley Campaign.
For further reading:
Freeman, Douglas Southall. "Manassas to Malvern Hill." In *Lee's Lieutenants: A Study in Command,* vol. 1 (1942–1944).

ASHLEY, JAMES MITCHELL
(1824–1896)
U.S. congressman

Born to John C. Ashley and Mary Kilpatrick Ashley in Allegheny County, Pennsylvania, James Mitchell Ashley received no formal schooling. His father was a circuit minister, and by traveling with his father into the upper South, the younger Ashley saw slavery firsthand. As a teenager, he left home for life aboard a steamboat on the Ohio River, first as a crew member and then as a clerk for the company. After leaving that job, he traveled throughout the South, where he developed a strong abhorrence of the institution of slavery. He frequently spoke out against the institution during his travels, a habit that caused him to be forced out of the state of Virginia.

Returning north, Ashley took up residence in Ohio, where he became a printer and then a journalist. At the same time, Ashley began the study of law and entered into several business pursuits. His antislavery views also led him into Ohio politics, starting as a Democrat, then as a member of the Free Soil Party, and soon after its founding, as a member of the Republican Party. He served as an Ohio delegate in 1856 to the first Republican National Convention, where he supported the candidacy of John C. Frémont. In 1858, Ashley was elected from Toledo to the U.S. House of Representatives.

Ashley served five consecutive terms in Congress during which time he introduced a number of controversial measures and gained a reputation as one of that body's more eccentric members. Early in his congressional career he took up the unpopular issue of civil rights for African-Americans, believing that the best place for the federal government to address this issue was in the territories. Eventually rising to the position of chairman of the Committee on Territories, he used that forum to urge legislation on that issue.

From the very beginning of the Civil War, Ashley championed treating the seceded states harshly as punishment for rebelling against the legal government. Many of the measures he advocated for the reconstruction of the Union were embodied in the Wade-Davis Bill in 1864 and later enacted in the Reconstruction Acts of 1867.

During the war, Ashley quickly became a vocal part of that group of congressional representatives known as the Radical Republicans. He saw the war as an opportunity to end the evil of slavery and worked tirelessly during the conflict to bring about that goal. In the spring of 1862, he helped sponsor the bill that ultimately abolished slavery in Washington, D.C., and was a guiding force behind what would become the Thirteenth Amendment to the Constitution, which abolished slavery in the United States. Ashley was also an early advocate of African-American suffrage and worked to make such a measure a part of the reconstruction legislation introduced in Congress in 1864.

During the war, Ashley frequently corresponded with those officers he considered right-minded on the political issues of the day. He supported the resolution of Congress that recommended that officers not be required to return runaway slaves. He also sought to determine through his contacts in the army how many officers supported the issues espoused by the Radical Republicans and what preponderance of George McClellan supporters the army still contained, particularly in later phases of the war.

After the war, Ashley quickly became a vocal opponent of the new president, Andrew Johnson. Ashley developed a theory that indicated that Johnson had been directly involved in the assassination of Abraham Lincoln. He based this supposition on his belief that every previous vice president who had become president because of the death of a president had been involved in that death. To him John Tyler had conspired to kill William Henry Harrison, Millard Fillmore had been involved in the death of Zachary Taylor, and therefore it followed that Andrew Johnson was implicated in the death of Abraham Lincoln. Besides the fact that Ashley opposed Johnson's lenient reconstruction plan for the South, he believed that Johnson was a conspirator in murder as well.

In December 1866, before the new, more radical Congress that had been elected the month before took its seat, Ashley introduced a resolution in Congress that a committee be appointed to determine charges for impeachment of Andrew Johnson. Though the measure failed at that time, Ashley was among that group of Radical Republicans who were determined to return articles of impeachment against Johnson as soon as the new Congress was seated. Perhaps the most dogged of the group, Ashley introduced the early measures that resulted in the articles that brought Johnson to trial in the Senate.

Ashley's singlemindedness on this issue discredited him somewhat in the eyes of his constituents when Johnson was acquitted, and Ashley was defeated for reelection in 1868. His loyalty to that cause, however, was rewarded in 1869 when the new president, Ulysses S. Grant, appointed Ashley territorial governor of Montana. Early in Grant's administration, however, Ashley openly criticized some of the president's decisions and was removed from his governorship in 1870. His opposition to Grant led him to join the Liberal Republicans in 1872 and attend as a delegate that group's convention the same year. This participation was his last major political activity. He returned to business pursuits in Toledo, where he became one of the founders and ultimately president of the Toledo, Ann Arbor & Northern Michigan Railroad. Ashley retired in 1893 and died in Toledo on 16 September 1896.

—*David S. Heidler and Jeanne T. Heidler*

See also Congress, U.S.A.; Radical Republicans; Wade-Davis Bill.

For further reading:

Horowitz, Robert F. *The Great Impeacher: A Political Biography of James M. Ashley* (1979).
Trefousse, Hans Louis. *Impeachment of a President; Andrew Johnson, the Blacks, Reconstruction* (1975).

ATCHISON, DAVID RICE
(1807–1886)
United States senator

David Rice Atchison left his native state of Kentucky shortly after graduating from Transylvania University in 1825 to practice law in Liberty, Missouri. During the 1830s and early 1840s, Atchison gained prominence as a Democratic state legislator, circuit court judge, and militia officer. In 1843 he was appointed to fill a vacancy in the U.S. Senate and continued to represent Missouri there for the next thirteen years.

In Congress, Atchison rose to a position of power and influence. He was highly regarded by his colleagues, who elected him president pro tempore of the Senate sixteen times between 1846 and 1854. An advocate of territorial expansion, Atchison pushed for American annexation of Texas in 1845 and occupation of the Oregon Country in 1846, and he supported President James K. Polk's expansionist aims during the Mexican-American War. He likewise advocated the extension of slavery, insisting that Southern slaveholders had a constitutional right to carry their peculiar institution into the nation's territorial possessions. Thus, he strenuously opposed the Wilmot Proviso, which was intended to outlaw slavery in the Mexican Cession. He also objected to the Compromise of 1850, seeing in it no sufficient guarantees for Southern slave property in the territories. Amid these controversies, Atchison gravitated to the militant Southern rights movement led by John C. Calhoun, with its doctrine of unobstructed slavery expansion. Following Calhoun's death, Atchison emerged as the most outspoken champion of Southern rights in the Senate.

The territorial issue divided the Democratic Party in Missouri and provided the backdrop for the state's 1850 Senate race, which pitted Atchison against his hated rival, Thomas Hart Benton. Though Benton had long reigned as chief potentate of Missouri's Democracy, he had lost popular support after the Mexican-American War by favoring congressional restrictions against slavery in the territories. Running on the strength of his Southern rights credentials, Atchison was able to win the election and deny his nemesis a sixth term in the Senate.

In Washington Atchison was part of an influential bloc of Southern senators that included Andrew P. Butler of South Carolina and Virginians James M. Mason and Robert M. T. Hunter. Dubbed the "F Street Mess" because they lodged in the same boardinghouse on F Street, the foursome composed the Capitol's most formidable proslavery phalanx. In 1853–1854 Atchison and his messmates led Southern opposition to the organization of Nebraska Territory as free soil. As a precondition for organization they demanded unimpeded access for slaveowners through the repeal of the Missouri Compromise (which would have banned slavery from the territory). Thus, Atchison had a key role in framing the provisions of the Kansas-Nebraska Act that rescinded the 36 degree 30 minute parallel of latitude restriction on slavery, while opening the new territories to slaveholders on the basis of popular sovereignty.

Thereafter Atchison labored intensively to bring Kansas into the Union as a slave state. In 1855–1856 (while still a member of the Senate), he had a direct hand in fomenting violent confrontation in "Bleeding Kansas" as the head the Missouri border ruffians, proslavery posses who rode across the Kansas border to bully and harass free-soil settlers there. These guerrilla bands also used fraud and intimidation to rig elections, hoping to create a proslavery territorial government, despite the free-soil sentiments of most Kansas residents. When free-soil elements ultimately prevailed, Atchison left politics and retired to his Missouri home and farm.

With the advent of the Civil War, Atchison warmly embraced the Confederate cause and was active in the failed secession movement led by Missouri's governor, Claiborne F. Jackson. When Jackson established a rump secessionist government loyal to the Confederacy, Atchison acted as an intermediary with Confederate authorities, appealing to President Jefferson Davis—a former colleague in the Senate—for official recognition of the state's pro-Southern government. After the battle of Pea Ridge, Arkansas, in March 1862, which left Missouri under firm Union control, Atchison moved to Grayson County, Texas. There he spent the balance of the war in relative obscurity. He returned to Missouri in 1867, settling in Clinton County. Aside from taking part in occasional speaking engagements, Atchison made no effort to revive his public career in postbellum years. He neither sought political office nor resumed his law practice, preferring instead to devote his energies solely to agricultural pursuits.

—*Eric Tscheschlok*

See also Kansas; Kansas-Nebraska Act; Missouri; Popular Sovereignty.

For further reading:
Parrish, William E. *David Rice Atchison of Missouri, Border Politician* (1961).
Potter, David M. *The Impending Crisis, 1848–1861* (1976).
Rawley, James A. *Race and Politics: "Bleeding Kansas" and the Coming of the Civil War* (1969).

ATLANTA CAMPAIGN
(May–September 1864)

In the early spring of 1864, Union major general William Tecumseh Sherman saw that Georgia, and Atlanta specifically, held the key to bringing the war to an end. Confederate General Robert E. Lee's forces in Virginia, the main focus of the war to that point, were able to hold the Union forces away from Richmond

Fortifications at Atlanta, 1864 (*Library of Congress*)

largely because of the supplies that flowed steadily up from the transportation and logistical center of Atlanta.

With Lieutenant General Ulysses S. Grant's blessing, Sherman set about building an overwhelming force from his headquarters in Chattanooga, Tennessee, a little more than 100 miles northwest of Atlanta. Other Union commands were asked to supply what men they could spare, and by late April 1864, three grand armies with more than 98,000 men stood ready to invade Georgia. A steady stream of reinforcements brought this force to more than 112,000 by June. To oppose him stood Confederate general Joseph Eggleston Johnston with but a single grand army of just two corps' strength, numbering just under 50,000 men. Reinforcements from Alabama, including Major General Leonidas Polk's entire corps and other commands not then under direct siege, bolstered Johnston's total strength to three corps with just under 65,000 men by late June.

Besides being understaffed and underequipped, Johnston faced an equally serious situation. His own combatant forces would be forced to protect the railroads leading to and from Atlanta and keep their own supply lines intact. One key factor lay in their favor, however: Johnston was a master of defensive strategy, rarely successful in the advance, but almost supernatural in his ability to know the exact moment to withdraw, just at the point where fierce resistance would damage his enemy the most while keeping his own forces intact. Unusual for a combat commander, he was also a humanist who deeply cared about his men and sought to minimize casualties even at the advantage of the enemy. Johnston had another serious disadvantage, the enmity of Confederate president Jefferson Davis, who blamed him for the loss of Vicksburg the previous summer and all too readily listened to whomever had a complaint about his tactics.

On 7 May 1864, the Union forces marched out of Chattanooga and the Ringgold area toward the southeast, through Tunnel Hill and just to the west of Dalton. The Atlanta campaign would consist of nine individual battles or local campaigns, as well as nearly five months of unbroken skirmishes and small actions.

About thirty miles southeast of Chattanooga, Dalton was shielded from a direct advance by a long, shear cliff face locally known as Rocky Face Ridge and called the "Georgian Gibraltar" by Union troops. Three gaps in the otherwise foreboding mountain ridge were large enough to allow an army to pass through in a reasonable amount of time, but they could be easily blockaded with a relatively small force of infantry and artillery.

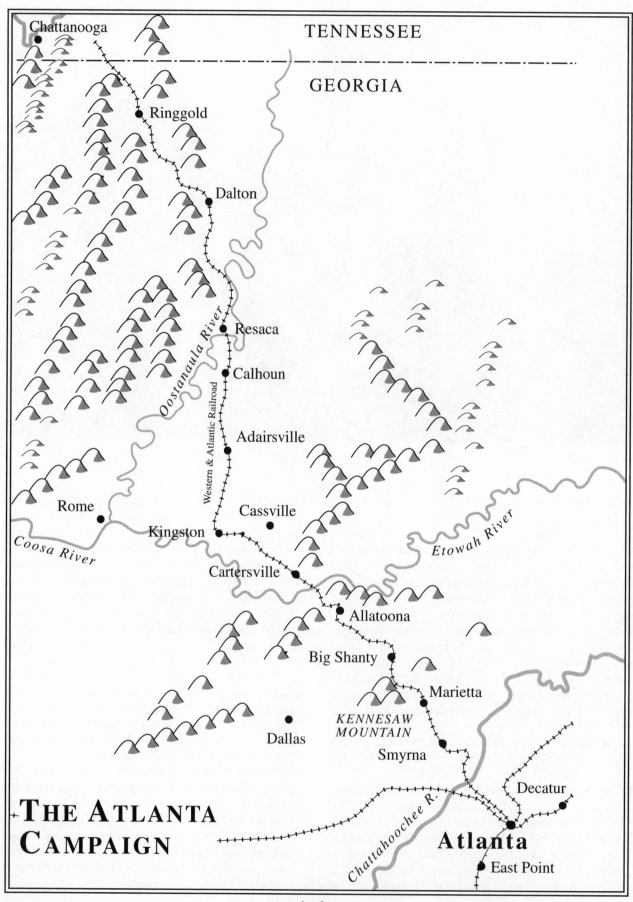

Chattanooga

TENNESSEE

GEORGIA

Ringgold

Dalton

Resaca

Oostanaula River

Calhoun

Western & Atlantic Railroad

Adairsville

Rome

Cassville

Kingston

Coosa River

Cartersville

Etowah River

Allatoona

Big Shanty

Marietta

KENNESAW MOUNTAIN

Dallas

Smyrna

Decatur

THE ATLANTA CAMPAIGN

Chattahoochee R.

Atlanta

East Point

Sherman had explored most of this area while on detached duty in Marietta in 1844 and recalled the lay of the land in great detail. Johnston's army could be trapped by the rocky ridge that was then their refuge if Union forces could get to the level open ground between it and Atlanta. Sherman sent two of his armies to distract Johnston by a strong direct assault at the northernmost gap, Mill Creek, while his third army slipped through the southernmost gap, Snake Creek, to cut off Johnston's retreat to Resaca.

Johnston expected that Sherman would merely feint toward Dalton and then race south to try and cut Confederate forces off from the rail line to Atlanta. Consequently, Johnston ordered preparation of defensive works on "good ground" seventeen miles south, just north and west of Resaca. In addition, he ordered a series of "military roads" prepared between the two positions, so that he could rapidly shuttle his troops into the new positions when Sherman made his move.

On 8 May 1864, having received notice from his cavalry scouts that Sherman's forces were on the march toward him, Johnston positioned Lieutenant General John Bell Hood's army corps on top of the ridgeline and across Crow Valley to Pickett Top and refused southward over Hamilton Mountain directly north of Dalton. William J. Hardee's corps took up positions just to the west of Dalton, directly on top of the impressive ridgeline. The Confederate line here snaked along roughly five miles of hill and valley, forming an almost fishhook shape with Rocky Face Ridge as the shank and Dalton just below the point. A detached division guarded the railway just to the northeast of Dalton, and a smaller detachment took up post above Dug Gap, two miles below the city.

Union major general George H. Thomas's Army of the Cumberland moved down the railway from Ringgold on 8 May and took up a position just to the west of Mill Creek Gap, while Major General John M. Schofield's Army of the Ohio moved in from the north and took up a position across Crow Valley. The distraction caused by these highly visible movements and the ridgeline screening him from the Confederate positions allowed Union major general James Birdseye McPherson to march the Army of the Tennessee quickly south through Snake Creek Gap.

Later that day, two small demonstrations were mounted by the Union troops against the strong Confederate position just south of Mill Creek Gap and against the weaker position at Dug Gap. The attack at Mill Creek nearly turned into a full battle, with part of Oliver O. Howard's IV Army Corps actually making it to the top of the northern end of the ridgeline before being violently repulsed. Both attacks were ultimately unsuccessful, though the attack at Dug Gap degenerated at one point into hand-to-hand combat, actually a compar-

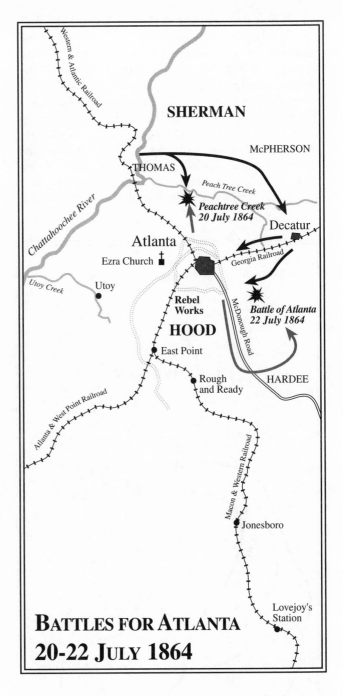

BATTLES FOR ATLANTA 20-22 JULY 1864

atively rare event during the war, and featured the Confederates at one point rolling large boulders down the steep mountainside at the onrushing Union force.

Early in the morning of 9 May, McPherson's men emerged from Snake Creek Gap and marched quickly toward Resaca, but the sight of Confederate cavalry and infantry troops in the area along with the well-prepared roads gave McPherson pause. Afraid that he would be caught in the open ground and unsure just how strong a force he was facing at that moment (less than one division of infantry and a few cavalry), McPherson became unusually cautious and elected to withdraw and entrench at the mouth of Snake Creek Gap. Sherman considered this act to be one of the major mistakes of the campaign; if McPherson had moved into Resaca, Johnston would have been surrounded, and the campaign might well have ended with his capitulation.

At the same time that McPherson made his move, Thomas and Schofield both launched strong attacks on the Confederate line, reinforcing the previous day's assault directly against Mill Creek Gap and down the eastern slope of Rocky Face Ridge in Crow Valley. Multiple Federal assaults over the next three days were successfully repulsed, leading Sherman to order a gradual

withdrawal of forces from the fight to follow McPherson's route down to Resaca. Johnston fully expected this, and by the afternoon of 11 May, while the battle was still fully under way, he began ordering his units also to break off gradually and march to their prepared positions outside Resaca. By midnight on the 12th, nearly all his army had moved south, staying intact as fighting units and taking all their supplies with them.

Resaca was the only site of the campaign, where all the armies of both sides clashed at the same battleground. The small hamlet of Resaca straddled a single rail line running almost due north-south. Johnston was tied to the railroad both by the need to protect his avenue of supply and to prevent Sherman from acquiring a speedy approach to Atlanta.

The area around Resaca was primarily farm fields and other open areas surrounded by thick woods with an abundance of entangling underbrush. Johnston's defensive position had two major weaknesses. First, to the rear of his lines was the Oostanaula River, making a hasty withdrawal nearly impossible. Second, the railroad he had to defend lay nearly underfoot and all along the Confederate line, also limiting his chances for tactical maneuver. His advantage was chiefly that his forces were in close proximity and well protected on his flanks by the river.

Sherman placed his forces in a semicircle that was anchored by the river on the right and curved around to face the northernmost Confederates directly. His position had little immediate advantage over the Confederate line, but units traveling through Snake Creek Gap quickly reinforced it.

Johnston's plan—to defend the river and rail line from heavily fortified positions—was clear. Sherman's purpose was less so. Starting early on the afternoon of 13 May, Union forces mounted uncoordinated and seemingly random attacks against the Confederate left, right, center, and the right again on the morning of the 15th. The incredibly rough terrain before the Confederate lines blunted most of these assaults as much as armed resistance did. On the afternoon of 14 May, an attack on the bend of the Confederate line was Brigadier General Henry M. Judah's 2d Division, XIII Corps, and Brigadier General Absalom Baird's 3d Division, XIV Corps, nearly annihilated by coordinated artillery and long-range rifle fire. It had only taken a few minutes for the Federals to lose more than 600 men even before they could move through the muck. Judah was dismissed from the army four days later for his alleged incompetence during the battle.

The unsuccessful Union assaults failed to push back the Confederate line at all. Several divisions of Hood's army corps stepped out on the late afternoon of 15 May in a counterattack on the Union left, but were withdrawn after Johnston learned of the only Union success of the

**BATTLES FOR ATLANTA
28 JULY –1 SEPT. 1864**

Camp of the 2d Massachusetts Infantry on the grounds of the Atlanta City Hall, 1864
(Photograph by George N. Barnard / *Library of Congress*)

battle: Brigadier General Thomas W. Sweeney's 2d Division (Major General Grenville M. Dodge's XVI Army Corps) had crossed the Oostanaula River a few miles south at Lay's Ferry and was threatening to cut the railroad and block the Confederate line of retreat. Within hours Johnston had evacuated his forces intact across the river and was marching south toward Cassville, destroying all bridges behind him. The last, the railroad bridge just below Resaca, was set afire at 3:30 A.M.

Johnston, ever the wily strategist, came up with a unique plan while pulling back from Resaca on the night of 15 May. He would send Hardee's corps with most of the army's supply wagons and ambulances straight through Adairsville to Kingston, fifteen miles down the main road. Meanwhile, Hood's and Polk's corps moved down a little-used route to the small town of Cassville, just ten miles away. To ensure the safety of the supply train, Major General Benjamin F. Cheatham's division was placed across the road about three miles north of Adairsville. Hood and Polk were ordered to march rapidly and "tightly"—to give the appearance that only a small force had passed down their path—and to be ready to launch a sudden counterattack when the unsuspecting Union forces appeared.

Sherman followed Johnston southward, delayed by the long river crossings necessary for his large force and by an almost comical spat between Schofield and Major General Joseph Hooker over which one had the right of way on the narrow roads. The Union forces had not paused to regroup after raking the Resaca battleground. They headed south with McPherson's Army of the Tennessee wide to the Union right, Thomas's Army of the Cumberland marching straight down the railway, and Schofield's Army of the Ohio (also known as and consisting only of the XXIII Army Corps) wide to the left. Expecting Johnston to make a stand at Adairsville, Sherman ordered his widely separated columns to close together just north of the small crossroads town. The lead elements of the Union force arrived in Adairsville after a brief but spirited skirmish with Cheatham's division on the morning of 18 May.

Sherman was apparently deceived by the Confederate diversionary tactic. Eager to engage Johnston before the Confederate force reached good defensive ground south of the Etowah River, Sherman hastily pushed all his units except Hooker's XX and Schofield's XXIII Army Corps down the single road to Kingston. These two corps were ordered down the road to Cassville, to protect the flank of the main Union column.

Just to the west of the main Union line of advance, a single infantry division commanded by Union brigadier general Jefferson C. Davis (2d Division, XIV Army Corps) and supported by Brigadier General Kenner Garrard's 2d Cavalry Division marched in and captured the important industrial center of Rome on 18 May after a one-day battle with Confederate major general Samuel G. French's division.

At Cassville, Johnston ordered Polk to place his corps across the road about one-half mile northeast of the town square, with Hood's corps positioned about one mile east and parallel to the road, so as to hit the Union flank as it approached. On the morning of 19 May, just as Schofield's corps was walking into the trap, a small unit of Union cavalry led from the east by Brigadier General Edward M. McCook stumbled into Hood's troops and a brief skirmish erupted. Fearful that McCook was supported by infantry, Hood suddenly pulled back from his ambush position to one facing east, supporting Polk's right. Johnston believed that the chance for surprise was lost and ordered both corps to a low range of hills southeast of the town.

Hood defended his overreaction to the end of his life, insisting that he had infantry to his rear and that he would have been unable to launch his attack on the main column of Union troops on the Cassville road. Surprisingly enough, he was partly correct; close behind McCook were two brigades of Union infantry supported by a single battery of horse artillery wandering around lost. They were looking for a road leading into the east side of Cassville when they ran into the rear column of Hood's corps.

On the Confederate left, Hardee put up a stiff resistance against the massed Union forces near Kingston, but shortly after the Cassville disaster, and at the urging of Hood and Polk, Johnston ordered all forces to disengage and withdraw south of the Etowah River and into the Allatoona Mountains. Johnston's forces finally halted about eleven miles southeast of Cassville and set up a strong defensive position around the railroad gap at Allatoona Pass, just northwest of the small town of Acworth. As usual, Johnston ordered the railroad bridge across the Etowah burned as they retreated. Sherman moved in and occupied Cassville and Kingston, giving his men a few days to rest while he studied the ground ahead.

Sherman had ridden the area around Allatoona extensively as a young officer assigned to Marietta; he knew the potential for making the gap into a natural fortress. Changing tactics, he abandoned his line of march straight down the railroad and moved westward, toward the small town of Dallas. It is not clear whether he was trying to pull Johnston behind him into more open terrain (which is doubtful) or whether he was trying to take a more western approach into Atlanta. The real danger for Sherman was that, by abandoning the railroad, he was lengthening his own supply column, making it more vulnerable to a rear attack by Johnston's troops and cavalry.

Ordered up and out by buglers on the morning of 22 May, the three grand armies moved out of camp at Cassville and Kingston in their usual three columns. Thomas and Schofield moved nearly due south while McPherson swung far to the right in order to approach Dallas from due west. The huge columns of massed Union infantry in a front nearly twenty miles wide were hard to conceal, and the move west was soon discovered by Confederate major general Joseph Wheeler's cavalry corps. By the afternoon of 23 May, Johnston ordered Hardee to good defensive ground just east of Dallas and Polk at a tiny crossroads nearby called New Hope. Hood remained entrenched at Allatoona Pass overnight and then was ordered to New Hope when Johnston realized that all the Union forces were headed toward Dallas. On his arrival, Polk shifted his men slightly to the west, tying in with Hardee and forming a strong defensive line nearly four miles long from directly south of Dallas to one mile east of New Hope.

Hood scurried into line just before the forward Union skirmishers and scouts came into view. Confederate major general Carter L. Stevenson's division set up on the right, Major General Thomas C. Hindman's division set up on the higher ground on the left, and Major General Alexander P. Stewart's division deployed directly in front of the small, log New Hope Church in the center. Just before 10:00 A.M. on 25 May, Confederate skirmishers encountered the forward elements of Hooker's XX Army Corps rapidly marching toward New Hope. They attempted to burn a bridge over Pumpkinvine Creek to set up a delaying action, but were quickly overrun by Union brigadier general John W. Geary's 2d Division.

Warned that action was imminent, Stewart deployed his men in line astride the crossroads, ordering them to dig in as rapidly as possible. Brigadier General Marcellus Stovall's Georgia Brigade was positioned on an open hilltop in the church's graveyard and was unable or unwilling to dig in at all, but Brigadier General Henry D. Clayton's and Brigadier General Alpheus Baker's Alabama Brigades in the center and right of the line

threw up hasty works of felled trees and earthen embankments. Sixteen guns from Captain McDonald Oliver's Eufaula Alabama and Captain Charles E. Fenner's Louisiana Batteries were massed within Stewart's roughly one-half mile front.

Sherman ordered Hooker to push through what he believed was a small force and march directly on to Dallas, remarking that "There haven't been twenty rebels there today" to the front of him. Just before 4:00 P.M., a severe thunderstorm started to blow in over the New Hope area. Marching steadily on through the mounting wind and pounding thunder came Geary's 2d Division, with Major General Daniel Butterfield's 3d

Federal soliders relax in a captured Confederate fort near Atlanta, 1864
(Photograph by George N. Barnard / *Library of Congress*)

Battery M, 5th U.S. Artillery, manning a captured Confederate fort near Atlanta, 1864 (*Library of Congress*)

Division to his left and Brigadier General Alpheus S. Williams's 1st Division on his right, all spread across a one-half mile front in column formation and unknowingly beating down directly on the massed Confederate front of Stewart's division.

Just after 5:00 P.M., as Geary's skirmishers drove back Hood's, Union buglers sounded out the call to go forward double-quick. Stumbling and falling through the thick brush and unable to see what lay ahead, the men from Ohio, Pennsylvania, and New York hoped to brush straight through what they believed was a weak line of Confederate militia and detached infantry brigades. Just as the monsoon-force rains began, Williams's men broke out of the thickest part of the woods and rushed straight for the Confederate line.

Stewart had wisely ordered the artillery to load with double-canister and had positioned his 4,000 men nearly shoulder to shoulder on a very tight front, anticipating quite accurately that Hooker would be compacted in heavy infantry formations on his approach. As lightning crackled all around and sheets of rain poured down, the shouting mass of more than 16,000 blue-coated infantry burst into sight less than 100 feet in front of Stewart's lines. Immediately the Confederate line opened up and disappeared again in a thick cloud of bluish gray rifle and cannon smoke. Williams's men took the brunt of the concentrated fire, losing most of their more than 800 casualties in the first ten minutes of battle.

For more than three hours, this one-sided slaughter went on, into the dark and stormy evening. Geary, Butterfield, and Williams all ordered repeated assaults, trying to break through what was obviously the main Confederate army line, only to be thrown back each time by murderous artillery and rifle fire. Stewart's Confederate forces started running out of ammunition, the sixty round per man standard issue being depleted in as little as thirty minutes in some cases. Stewart brought his reserve forces in line primarily for their ammunition supply, and runners searched the wounded and dead for any extra cartridges. Hooker finally admitted defeat about 7:30 P.M., pulling his men back a short distance to dig in for the night.

Throughout the long night, as Union men dug in with shovels, bayonets, tin cups, or bare hands, sporadic rifle and artillery fire broke out, but no further assaults by either side were mounted. Hooker's command lost more than 1,600 men in the short fight. (Most references support this figure, but one source claims less than 700.) Confederate losses amounted to "between 300 and 400" as reported by Stewart. One bitter Union infantryman remarked that Hooker had sent them into a "hell hole;" the name sticks as a common reference to the brutal fight there and at Pickett's Mill.

After the blow he received at New Hope Church, Sherman returned to his standard tactic of rapid flanking maneuver and ordered three divisions under the direct command of Howard to the far left in an attempt to turn the Confederate right. Johnston soon learned of the flanking attempt and ordered two divisions to shift to the right of Hood's line, covering the probable Union line of attack. To the far right of the newly extended Confederate line was one of Johnston's best, Major General Patrick R. Cleburne's division, taking up positions on a hilltop overlooking the small settlement of Pickett's Mill.

Although his scouts reported fresh earthworks and Howard himself rode forward and observed gray-uniformed troops moving in on the hill before them, the Union commander was somewhat convinced that he had reached the flank or rear of the Confederate line of battle and possibly believed that only a small picket outpost was entrenching. His uncertainty is obvious in a message sent about 3:30 P.M., "I am now turning the enemy's right flank, I think." Just after noon on 27 May, Howard brought his three divisions in line of attack on a hilltop just north of the small mill community, again forming the men into the same narrow, deep, heavy infantry formations that had failed so miserably two days earlier at New Hope Church.

At this point, the Confederate line curved to the east following the ridgeline atop a low rounded hill overlooking a steep, densely overgrown ravine. As the battle unfolded, two brigades of Cleburne's force were shifted to the far right of the line, refusing at right angles to the line to prevent any possibility of being flanked.

At 4:30 P.M. the Union line, or at least most of it, stepped off into the thick, entangling underbrush. There were serious communication and land navigation problems, and one brigade ended up marching completely away from the growing sounds of battle, "to get rations." That particular brigade's commander, Brigadier General Nathaniel McLean of Kentucky, was a political enemy of Howard and on this day chose a particularly poor way of demonstrating his contempt.

Howard's leading brigade, Brigadier General William B. Hazen's 2d Brigade (Brigadier General Thomas J. Wood's 3d Division, Howard's IV Army Corps), easily drove away the Confederate pickets and moved into the ravine. The growth was so thick that the colors had to be encased to prevent them from being torn to pieces, and Hazen was forced to resort to his compass to stay moving in the right direction. Emerging suddenly in an open field, his troops first encountered a weak skirmish line of about 1,000 dismounted cavalrymen from Confederate brigadier general John Kelly's and Brigadier General William Hume's cavalry divisions, who they mistook as unentrenched infantry. Steadily overpowering the cavalrymen, Hazen's men rushed cheering across the open ground upward to what they thought was an undefended rocky ridgeline. Just before the Union infantry gained the heights, Confederate brigadier

general Hiram M. Granbury's Texas Brigade suddenly stood up and began pouring a galling fire into the face of the onrushing line.

Hazen's men kept up the pressure, although suffering appalling casualties from a two-gun battery (Confederate captain Thomas J. Key's Arkansas battery) to their right at the point of the ravine and from two more regiments rushing in to support Granbury, Colonel George Baucum's 8th Brigade, 19th Arkansas Consolidated Regiment, to his left and Brigadier General Mark P. Lowrey's Alabama-Mississippi Brigade to his right. Hazen managed to stay in the fight for about fifty minutes before being forced to withdraw, leaving his more than 500 wounded and dead in place in the open ravine.

As Hazen withdrew, Union colonel William H. Gibson's 1st Brigade advanced over nearly the same ground and met the same fate. Far from hitting a weakened Confederate line, as 3d Division commander Brigadier General Thomas J. Wood had hoped, Gibson's men advanced as far as the Confederate line itself before being thrown violently back. Roughly an hour of combat resulted in nothing more than an additional 687 Union casualties. Another brigade, Union colonel Frederick Knefler's 3d, was sent in about 6:30 P.M. to cover Gibson's retreat and to recover as many wounded as possible. They too were subjected to intense, nearly point-blank fire from the Confederate positions as soon as they entered the entangled ravine.

The major assaults ended by 7:00 P.M., but occasional firefights erupted until 10:00 P.M., when Granbury was ordered to "clear his front." The Texans fixed bayonets and with wild rebel yells charged forward into the darkened ravine, killing or capturing many of the remaining Union troops. The remaining Union troops either "skedaddled" or "retreated in good order, with no pursuit [by the Texans] even being attempted," depending on whose account you read. Both sides encamped for the night after the firing died down about 11:00 P.M., their attention still fixed on the body-strewn battleground eerily lit up by dead pine trees set afire during the hot exchange.

Total Union losses for the day's action totaled 1,689 killed, wounded, captured, or missing; Cleburne reported 398 killed or wounded. This failed action so upset Sherman that he apparently "forgot" to mention it in both his official report and his postwar memoirs.

The following day, 28 May 1864, Sherman finally decided that this westward flanking movement was getting him nowhere. Short on rations, his lines stretched nearly to the breaking point trying to hold the entire five-mile line of battle from south of Dallas to northeast of Pickett's Mill, as well as the lines of communication necessary to protect the supply line back to the railroad north of Allatoona. He ordered a gradual shifting motion of the line back east toward

Kennesaw and Marietta and sent his cavalry to capture Allatoona Pass itself. Johnston soon learned of this movement and ordered an attack on the Union right, straight toward Dallas itself, but was repulsed with no positive effects on the Union movement, and at the cost of more than 600 casualties.

By 1 June, Sherman had begun massing his armies at Big Shanty (now called Kennesaw) and made preparations to strike straight for the Chattahoochee River. Between stood the twin peaks of Kennesaw Mountain and Johnston's entire combat force. Johnston initially arranged his 65,000 troops in a thin, ten-mile-long line of battle that stretched from Brushy Mountain on the east to Lost Mountain on the west, about three miles northwest of Kennesaw Mountain itself. This line was known as both the "Lost Mountain" and "First Kennesaw" line.

In the late morning of 14 June 1864, Johnston, accompanied by Hardee, Polk, and several other general officers, climbed to the crest of Pine Mountain, roughly in the center of the line. While observing their lines, they were spotted by a Union artillery battery, posted less than a half-mile away, which immediately opened fire. The first round scattered the distinguished crowd; the aging and slow General Leonidas Polk was struck directly in the chest by the second Parrott shot and killed instantly.

After heavy attacks on 14, 15, and 17 June, Johnston realized that his men were spread much too thin and withdrew quietly during the pitch black night and heavy rains of 18 June two miles to the southeast. There he heavily entrenched from the railroad to the right, up across Kennesaw Mountain, Little Kennesaw Mountain, and Pigeon Hill, and left over a low ridge later know as Cheatham Hill. This strong, compact six-mile-long "Kennesaw," or "Second Kennesaw," line was reinforced by artillery batteries placed on the heights and cavalry placed on both flanks. One Union officer noted that the natural barricade of the mountain seemed purposefully made to stop any attacking army. The sides facing the Union troops were steep and boulder-strewn, and most of the rest was covered with thick scrub. Confederate engineers cleared the peaks of trees and brush to serve as signal and artillery stations. The main entrenchments were at the proper military crests, with a series of screening entrenchments and fire pits before them at the mountain base.

Cannon were hauled by hand up the steep slopes, 100 men per gun pulling, tugging, and cursing all the way. Eventually, two four-gun batteries were established on Pigeon Hill, one four-gun battery on the north end of Big Kennesaw, another nearly on the peak, and nine guns atop Little Kennesaw. Before they were emplaced completely, firing erupted between them and newly arriving Union batteries. This was followed by a series of probing and skirmish actions by scattered Union infantry units.

Impatient as ever, Sherman soon saw that these probing actions were gaining nothing, so again he returned to his classic flanking moves. Hooker's XX and Schofield's XXIII Army Corps were sent on a sweeping movement to the south of the Kennesaw line to attempt to gain Marietta and cut off the Confederate line of retreat. Johnston's near supernatural ability to read Sherman's intentions came to his aid once again; through a pounding thunderstorm on the night of 21 June, Hood's entire corps marched from the far right of the line to the far left, consolidating and entrenching across the path of the approaching Union troops on Powder Springs Road, just west of Marietta.

As the Union troops probed and advanced down that road on the afternoon of 22 June, Hood suddenly decided to abandon his fairly strong defensive position and risk it all on a full-force assault. Hindman's division into the north and Stevenson's division on the left suddenly burst out of the thick woods into an open plain near the Kolb farm, straight into the massed rim of more than forty Union artillery pieces. The attack gained nothing, falling apart nearly before coming within rifle range of the hastily dug Union lines. The shattered remnants of Stevenson's division attempted to take refuge in a shallow creek bed, where they were continuously raked by artillery fire until able to pull back after dark.

With his probing actions indecisive and his flanking maneuver halted at Kolb farm, Sherman chose yet another tactic. Tiring of the constant way Johnston slipped out of his flanking attacks, and possibly hoping to destroy the Confederate Army of Tennessee in one huge battle, he issued the order for a direct assault on the entrenchments of the Kennesaw line itself, to begin at 8:00 A.M. on 27 June. McPherson was ordered to attack the southern side of the mountain, Thomas was ordered to attack south of the Dallas road in support of McPherson, and Schofield was directed to feint south of the Kolb farm area as a diversion.

At 9:00 A.M., three brigades of McPherson's corps stepped off, moving up into the steep slopes of Pigeon Hill, straight into the rocky fortifications. Surprisingly, some made it far enough to engage in hand-to-hand combat atop the entrenchments before being forced back under heavy artillery fire. Union losses in this futile attack were more than 850, with Confederate losses described as "about 250."

Thomas chose to attack a salient in the Confederate line nearly three miles south of Pigeon Hill, later famous as the Dead Angle. Believing that one mighty push would drive out the heavily entrenched Confederates of Cheatham's division, Thomas decided to use heavy infantry formations. The five attacking brigades each spread out across a 200-yard front (1,500 to 2,000 yards

The Atlanta railroad depot, 1864 (Photograph by George N. Barnard / *Library of Congress*)

was more nearly normal), with about ten yards between each brigade. The overwhelming fire from the Confederate line proved so intense that the ten-yard interval gradually closed until all five brigades ended up attacking as a single mass twelve ranks deep. An absolute slaughter ensued as every artillery piece and rifle within range concentrated on the 1,000-yard front line.

By nightfall, most Union units had been completely thrown back, those few left under some protection of the hilly terrain would stay within rock-throwing distance for the next six days and keep up a constant sniping harassment. The only gain of the entire day's action, ironically, was Schofield's diversionary attack to the south, which managed to get between Johnston's line and the Chattahoochee River while the Confederate forces were distracted by the main attack. Sherman was enraged over the failure to break the Confederate lines,

however, and seriously contemplated ordering further attacks the next day. Thomas brought him back to reality by informing him that "one or two more such assaults would use up this army." Sherman finally reported in a cable to Washington that night that his attack had failed and that he had suffered "about 3,000 casualties." Several reports dispute this figure, placing it closer to 7,000 or even 7,500. Confederate losses for the day were placed at just under 1,000.

After his stunning defeat at Kennesaw Mountain, Sherman required more than a week just to regroup and resupply his demoralized soldiers. On 1 July, he abandoned for good his frontal assault tactics on entrenchments and planned another flanking maneuver to the south and east, to try once again to bypass Johnston and gain Marietta. Johnston's scouts observed the huge army getting under way before any real progress could be made. With no real natural defensive barrier to help stop the numerically superior Union army, Johnston decided to abandon Marietta and fall back across the wide, shallow Chattahoochee River, burning or destroying whatever supplies and equipment Sherman might find useful along the way.

By the afternoon of 2 July, Johnston set up a new line of defense at the small town of Smyrna, just northwest of the Chattahoochee, while his main body crossed to the south bank. This line collapsed in less than a day of heavy skirmishing with forward elements of the Union line, and by the next afternoon Johnston pulled back to his last line of entrenchments north of the river.

Finding nearly all the ferries and pontoon bridges out due to the high water caused by weeks of heavy rains, and what bridges remaining either heavily defended or burned, Sherman was running out of options to find a crossing that would not result in losing most of his army in the muddy water. Garrard's 2d Division Cavalry (Brigadier General Washington Elliott's Cavalry Corps, Schofield's XXIII Army Corps) was sent about fifteen miles to the north and quickly captured the small town of Roswell, overlooking the Chattahoochee River. He found the bridge there burned, but discovered several spots nearby where the river could be safely forded. With Union major general George Stoneman's cavalry division ranging as far south as Sandtown, McPherson's corps feinting to the right, and Thomas's corps keeping the pressure on the river line, Schofield's corps was quickly moved up river on 8 July to find the best crossing site.

In the early afternoon of 9 July, finding a 300-yard-wide, relatively shallow spot over a submerged fish dam near Sope Creek (Soap Creek on some maps), Union colonel Daniel Cameron's 103d Ohio Infantry swam across to establish a beachhead. Encountering no opposition, Schofield then ordered a crossing in force at 3:30 that afternoon. Led by a combat amphibious assault by the 12th Kentucky Regiment under Union lieutenant colonel Laurence H. Rousseau, part of Colonel Robert K. Boyd's 3d (Kentucky) Brigade (the same brigade that had "withdrawn for rations" at Pickett's Mill), the crossing was an outstanding success. The only Confederates in the area were part of a small picket outpost, who got off only a single volley before running away.

By nightfall the entire division was across, and with the news of the Union on the south bank, Johnston decided that his only recourse was to retreat again. Abandoning the river line to Sherman, Johnston pulled his forces back south of Peachtree Creek, on the very doorstep of Atlanta itself. Without further resistance to his river crossing, Sherman paused only long enough to rebuild pontoon and railroad bridges before striking south again. On 11 July, McPherson was sent eastward toward Decatur and Stone Mountain, with orders to cut the railway between Atlanta and Augusta. Sherman's

greatest fear at this point was that Johnston would receive reinforcements by rail from Lee's Army of Northern Virginia. Thomas was sent south toward Peachtree Creek, with Schofield marching just to his right headed toward Buckhead.

Johnston carefully noted the Union approach and planned to wait until close contact was established and then attack the gap between Thomas and Schofield before they were deployed for the fight. Before he could carry out this attack, Jefferson Davis carried out one of the worst decisions made during the war and fired Johnston. Late in the afternoon of 17 July, Hood was promoted to general and given command of the entire Army of Tennessee.

The day after Hood took command, Union infantrymen of Palmer's XIV Army Corps advanced through heavy resistance mounted by Wheeler's cavalry to the northern banks of Peachtree Creek, near Howell Mill Road. At just about the same time, Garrard's cavalry, supported by McPherson's infantry, reached the Georgia Railroad and captured the railroad depot at Stone Mountain, fifteen miles east of Atlanta. On 19 July, three brigades of Palmer's XIV Army Corps forced a crossing of Peachtree Creek toward Moore's Mill, followed by other crossings under fire by elements of Howard's IV Army Corps near Peachtree Road and Hooker's XX Army Corps near Collier Road. By nightfall the Union forces formed a solid line of blue-coated infantry on the south banks of Peachtree Creek itself, facing due south toward the Confederate line arranged atop low hills about one-half mile away.

Pleased with the progress of his subordinates, Sherman ordered Thomas to cross Peachtree Creek and engage Hood, Schofield to capture Decatur, and McPherson to advance toward Atlanta, tearing up the railroad tracks along the way. Obsessed with detail, Sherman sent word on exactly how he wanted the tracks torn up: "Pile the ties into shape for a bonfire, put the rails across and when red hot in the middle, let a man at each end twist the bar so that its surface becomes spiral."

Hood had a reputation as a battlefield brawler, and he wasted little time going on the offensive. A general attack was ordered at about 1:00 P.M. on 20 July, intended to drive the dug-in Union infantry back across the creek and as far as the banks of the Chattahoochee River. Before the attack could commence, Hood ordered the entire line to shift a little under one mile to the east to protect his right flank from counterattack. Although this movement threw the whole line into disarray and caused a general confusion about where to advance, Hood ordered the attack to begin at 4:00 P.M.

At about 2:45 P.M., Confederate major general William W. Loring's division (Stewart's corps) stepped off, almost immediately encountering Union infantry and mistakenly initiating battle in the center of the line.

Confederate major general William B. Bate's division of Hardee's corps, ordered to begin the general assault on the extreme right of the Confederate lines, did not actually move out until nearly one-half hour later. The rest of the two-mile-long line followed in piecemeal, advancing more in small groups and masses rather than well-formed lines, a result of the uneven terrain and thick underbrush.

The only real success of the entire assault was made by Confederate brigadier general Thomas M. Scott's brigade (Stewart' corps) of mostly Alabama troops, who advanced through the Tanyard Branch and Collier Road vicinity, attacking, driving off, and capturing the flag of Union colonel Patrick H. Jones's 33d New Jersey Infantry Regiment (Geary's 2d Division, Hooker's XX Army Corps), as well as a four-gun artillery battery. Scott's men were soon forced to withdraw, as no other unit was able to break through to support them on either flank.

No other unit made even that little of a success, and the entire attack was over with all units back in their original positions by 6:00 P.M. that evening. The well-positioned Union forces had badly mauled the advancing Confederates. Although the numbers engaged were fairly even with 21,450 Federals to 18,450 Confederates, casualties were much more one-sided, 1,780 Union to 4,800 Confederate. Hood's first outing as an army commander was a unqualified disaster.

To add insult to injury, shortly before noon of 20 July, four 20-pounder Parrott rifles of Union captain Francis De Gress set up and began firing the first of thousands of artillery shells into the Gate City itself. The first shell exploded at the intersection of Ivy and East Ellis Streets, killing a young girl who had been walking with her parents past Frank P. Rice's lumber dealership on the northwest corner. Shelling would continue for several weeks at the rate of one round every fifteen minutes. The bombardment posed more as a harassment and reminder of the siege than it did an attempt at destruction.

Before the fighting even died down at Peachtree Creek, Sherman was massing his forces for the next assault. McPherson's three corps were set in motion down the Georgia Railroad to attack Atlanta from the east, while Thomas and Schofield were ordered to close up and keep as much pressure on the Confederates as possible. By late in the day on 20 July, forward elements of Union major general Frank P. Blair's XVII Army Corps engaged Wheeler's dismounted cavalry on a small hilltop two miles to the east of Atlanta. Heavy combat erupted as the two lines collided, until the cavalrymen were overwhelmed and withdrew about midnight.

Realizing the tactical importance of the small hill, in the early morning of 21 July Blair sent in Union brigadier general Mortimer D. Leggett's 3d Division and

Brigadier General Giles A. Smith's 4th Division against Cleburne's division, which had replaced the decimated cavalrymen. Cleburne's men spent the night reinforcing the hilltop position, but were unable to stop the Union assault. The Confederates withdrew slightly and then spent most of the rest of the day attempting to retake the hill. While the battle raged on, Blair ordered up his artillery and set the guns into newly reversed entrenchments, bringing Atlanta itself within good artillery range for the first time. In honor of his men's heroics, the hilltop was renamed Leggett's Hill, a name that the area still bears on some maps today.

Hood had no intention of pursuing the same sort of well-planned, but plodding and slow retreat that Johnston used. Instead he thought he saw an opportunity for offensive action against McPherson. Withdrawing Stewart's corps and the Georgia Militia to the strongly fortified positions in the outer ring of defenses around Atlanta, Hood ordered Hardee's corps on an all-night forced march. Moving due south down Peachtree Street through the middle of town (and panicking the civilians, who believe that their entire army was deserting them), they swung eastward toward Decatur, attempting to get behind Blair's corps lines before moving north into the line of battle. Cleburne's division withdrew with some difficulty from the action on Leggett's Hill and joined Hardee's march. At the same time, two divisions of Wheeler's cavalry were sent around the Union left flank, to attempt a strike at Federal supply wagons in Decatur.

Unknown to the Confederates, McPherson was worried that they would attempt this exact movement and had ordered his lines extended and turned to the south. Dodge's XVI Army Corps was ordered to Blair's left, facing southeast, where the men entrenched, as had become the norm. At McPherson's urging, Blair's men also heavily entrenched and blocked lanes of approach before them.

By the morning of 22 July, Hardee's men had trudged down the McDonough Road south of Atlanta and then turned to the northeast on the Fayetteville Road toward Decatur. Still trying to make up the time lost on the rest stops, Hardee ordered Cleburne's and Brigadier General George E. Maney's divisions to begin deploying to the left when they reached Bouldercrest Road, while Bate's and Major General William H. T. Walker's divisions continued on up the road before turning left on what is today called Wilkinson Drive. Both of these moves into line were short of their original goals.

Soon running into a large mill pond that their guides had repeatedly warned them about, Walker's and Bate's divisions wandered around in the thick forest for nearly an hour trying to sort themselves out and get into line of battle. As Walker roundly cursed their guides, grumbling that they must be "traitors" to allow him to get himself in such a fix, he raised his field glasses to try to figure out his next move. A nearby Union picket spotted Walker and killed him with a single well-aimed shot.

Walker's command was taken over by Brigadier General Hugh W. Mercer, and the planned dawn attack commenced at about 12:15 P.M. after more confusion and shifting of troops. On advancing to the planned line of departure, the Confederates discovered to their horror that, far from being in the Union rear, they were advancing straight into a heavily invested front-line position. Pressing forward under intense fire from Sweeney's 2d Division (Dodge's XVI Army Corps), they immediately were raked by fire from two well-sited artillery positions, one six-gun Napoleon battery (Lieutenant Andrew T. Blodgett's 1st Missouri Light Battery) and one six-gun three-inch ordnance rifle battery (Captain Jerome M. Burrows 14th Ohio Light Battery, noted as being replaced in command by Lieutenant Seith M. Laird in a few accounts).

About thirty minutes later, Cleburne's and Maney's divisions launched their attack to the left of the ongoing fight, straight into the bend of the Union line held by Giles Smith's 4th Division (Blair's XVII Army Corps). This attack was much more successful, driving the Union line all the way north to Leggett's Hill and capturing an entire infantry regiment (Lieutenant Colonel Addison H. Sander's 16th Iowa), as well as eight artillery pieces.

McPherson had been eating lunch with his staff and corps commanders less than a mile away when he heard the sudden crash of artillery fire. He hastily mounted his horse and rode south with a small group of officers to check on the situation, pausing atop a nearby hill. From there he could see that Sweeney's division was holding up well, but he could not see the situation on the other end of the line. Striking out immediately for the spot between the two Confederate assaults, he realized that his line was not continuous in that area and quickly ordered up more troops to fill the gap. Riding through the unmanned gap toward Giles Smith's position, his party suddenly burst out of the heavy forest into a clearing, coming face to face with the advancing 5th Confederate Regiment (Captain Richard Beard's Tennessee). The Confederates called on him to surrender, but attempting to escape, he wheeled his horse around, raised his hat in salute, and attempted to make the tree line. A single shot fired by Corporal Robert F. Coleman tore through McPherson's lungs, killing him instantly.

Hood finally realized that the Union left flank was engaged, not the rear as planned, and ordered Cheatham's corps out of the east Atlanta defense line and to assault the entrenched Union main line. At the same time, Maney's division was ordered to break off and move to Cleburne's left, where they could support

Cheatham's attack. Maney's division started their assault at about 3:30 P.M. Cheatham's corps moved out one-half hour later, possibly as a result of confusion over orders. Once again, Leggett's Hill was in the center of much of the action, but the repeated Confederate assaults failed to regain control of it.

The general assault found a weak spot at the position held by Union brigadier general Joseph Lightburn's 2d Brigade (Brigadier General Morgan L. Smith's 2d Division, Logan's XV Army Corps). Confederate brigadier general Arthur M. Manigault's brigade (Cheatham's corps) led the assault, pushing through the railroad cut (near the present-day Inman Park MARTA Station) and capturing a four-gun artillery battery that had been cutting them to pieces (De Gress's 1st Illinois Light Battery H, consisting of four 20-pounder Parrott rifles); it then turned left and battered four Ohio regiments (the 47th, 54th, 37th, and 53d, in turn). More Confederate units poured through the opening, capturing another two-gun artillery battery, and forced a total of four Union brigades to retreat from a nearly half-mile front.

Sherman, observing from his headquarters about three-fourths of a mile to the northwest, ordered Schofield to mass all his artillery (twenty guns) at the Confederate breach and ordered Logan to collect eight brigades to fill in the gap. Between the massed artillery and Logan's strong counterattack, the Confederates were soon forced back into their original positions at a heavy loss. Wheeler's cavalry strike at Decatur met with more success, driving back two regiments of infantry and capturing 225 prisoners and an artillery piece, but Wheeler was ordered back to the west to support Hardee before he could capture or destroy the Union supply train, his main goal.

The day was another unqualified disaster for the Confederate Army of Tennessee. Total casualties ran more than 5,000 (Sherman claimed more than 8,000, but this was no doubt exaggerated) for no gain other than twelve briefly captured artillery pieces that could not even be withdrawn in the retreat, as all the caisson horses had been killed in the action. The Union Army of the Tennessee fared little better, giving up no territory but losing 3,722 killed, wounded, or missing.

Four days after the indecisive battle of Atlanta, on 26 July Union major general Oliver O. Howard took over McPherson's Army of the Tennessee and immediately began moving to the west along the northern arc of Atlanta's defenses. The targets this time were the last two open railroads leading into the besieged city, the Macon and Western and the Atlanta and West Point.

Hood soon learned of the Union movement and decided that this would be a good opportunity to launch an offensive action. He sent his old corps, now under command of Lieutenant General Stephen D. Lee, along with Stewart's corps west down Lick Skillet Road (now Gordon Road) to confront Howard at the small cross-roads where Ezra Methodist Church stands and to arrive before the Union troops could reach the vital railway.

This was in itself not a bad plan, the only problem being that Howard's corps had already reached the cross-roads, was aware of Hood's intent, and was entrenching before Lee's corps ever left the city. Lee did not know this when his corps marched out of the Atlanta defenses about 10:00 A.M. on 28 July, with Brigadier General John

C. Brown's and Major General Henry D. Clayton's divisions leading the column line of march. Within a mile or so, Brown encountered elements of Confederate brigadier general William H. Jackson's cavalry division, who inform him of the entrenched Yankee lines ahead. Lee made a poor decision and ordered Brown's and Clayton's men to move straight ahead and assault without additional support.

Brown's division hastily formed in line of battle directly opposite three Union brigades and part of a

Federal encampment on Decatur Street, Atlanta, 1864 (Photograph by George N. Barnard / *Library of Congress*)

Shell damage to the Potter house, Atlanta, 1864
(Photograph by George N. Barnard / *Library of Congress*)

fourth of Morgan Smith's 2d Division (Logan's XV Army Corps) and then moved forward about 12:30 P.M. Clayton's division lagged a bit behind, moving through thick forest over to Brown's right flank. Clayton formed up and moved forward about 10 minutes later, also into the same four Union brigades. Both Confederate divisions were assaulting uphill into a barricaded, entrenched line of heavily supplied infantry (the Union troops had been issued 100 rounds per man before the battle, about 40 percent more than usual) and were being thrown into the headlong fight piecemeal as they arrived. In addition, the forest in this area was so thick that the assaulting Confederates could not see the Union entrenchment until they were nearly on them.

Only one unit managed to break through the Union barricade, Colonel William F. Brantley's Mississippi brigade on the extreme left of the Confederate line of assault, but it was pushed back by a strong counterattack before its troops could invest the trench lines. The rest of the Confederate line melted away under rifle fire so intense that "no mortal could stand," as put by Union colonel Hugo Wangelin (3d Brigade commander, Smith's 1st Division, Logan's corps).

Stewart's corps fared no better on their attempt. Leading the way was Confederate major general Edward C. Walthall's division over the same ground that Brown had charged through. Stumbling over the dead and wounded Confederates in the thick forest, his line was repulsed in quick order, and his dead and wounded lay side by side with Brown's. Sporadic skirmishing and sniper fire continued until dark, when the Confederates withdrew back into the Atlanta defenses, carrying as many wounded as the exhausted men were able to drag behind them.

For the third time in less than ten days, Hood had wrecked part of his once hardened and capable army by sending them against superior forces who were well-entrenched. Total casualty figures for the brief attack are difficult to assess accurately, as few Confederate records exist, but somewhere between 2,500 and 5,000 were killed, wounded, or missing. The Union lost about 600.

Both sides gained and lost something as a result of the ten-day, three-battle campaign around the Atlanta defenses. Sherman failed to take the city proper, but did inflict serious damage on the Confederate Army of Tennessee. Hood failed to cripple or even drive back any of the three Union grand armies before him, but he did manage to hold the city and two of the four railroads supplying it.

After the battle at Ezra Church, Sherman turned to his cavalry corps to try to cut Hood's supply line. On 27 July, McCook's 1st Division Cavalry with about 3,500 horsemen moved around the western flank of Atlanta's defenses, bound for Lovejoy Station about twenty-five miles south of the city. Later the same day, Garrard's 2d Division Cavalry and Stoneman's cavalry division moved around the eastern line of defense with about 5,000 horsemen toward the same destination. The plan was to tear up the last remaining railway supplying Atlanta, along with its accompanying telegraph line, and then proceed to the Macon and Andersonville prisoner-of-war camps to release the more than 30,000 Union prisoners.

Sherman did not have to wait long for word of his "great cavalry raid." By 30 July, McCook's division had been thoroughly routed near Newnan by two cavalry brigades under Wheeler's personal command, assisted by several infantry units. The next day, Stoneman's entire force was captured, killed, or scattered at Sunshine Church just north of Macon. Stoneman not only failed to liberate the Union prisoners at Macon and Andersonville, he suffered the ignobility of joining their ranks at Macon's Camp Oglethorpe.

The "great raid" was not only a spectacular Confederate victory, but so many cavalry horses were captured that an entire brigade was able to be mounted. Sherman, noted for his extravagant prose in victory, was somewhat more terse in defeat, writing: "On the whole the cavalry raid is not deemed a success."

Sherman grew increasingly more frustrated with his inability to pound or starve Hood's troops out of the city and ordered yet another attack on the single remaining railroad to try to force the Confederates out in the open where they could be finally destroyed. On 4 August, Schofield's XXIII and Palmer's XIV Army Corps were ordered to swing around to the southwest and strike toward the two remaining railroad tracks near East Point. Another squabble between officers—this time between Palmer and Schofield over who was the senior officer—delayed the movement for nearly two full days.

Hood got word on 5 August of the Union movement and ordered a new line of emplacements built along the Sandtown Road and staffed by Bate's division of Hardee's corps reinforced by a two-gun artillery battery, a brigade of the Georgia Militia, and Confederate brigadier general Lawrence S. Ross's Texas Cavalry Brigade.

At dawn on 6 August, Union brigadier general Jacob D. Cox's 3d Division (Schofield's XXIII Army Corps) advanced with a 2,500-man front against the now heavily entrenched Confederate left. This attack got within thirty yards of the Confederate line before being broken up with severe loss and thrown back. Several other multibrigade assaults were attempted with the same result, and nearly 400 casualties.

In the midst of all this action, still upset over his argument with Schofield, Union major general John M. Palmer tendered his resignation and quit his command. Brigadier General Richard W. Johnson hastily took command and ordered an immediate assault on the right of the Confederate line. They were no more successful, suffering 200 more casualties for no gain. Total Confederate losses for the day were about 200, included those captured in their forward skirmish positions in the early part of the battle. Sherman described the action as "a noisy but not bloody battle."

Frustrated with his inability to cut the rail lines, Sherman pondered his next move. A direct assault on the Atlanta fortifications was completely out of the question. An interlocking series of artillery batteries and infantry parapets ringed the city a little over a mile out from its center, reinforced by as many as four rows of abatis and long lines of chevaux-de-frise. In those works were the tired, hungry, and undersupplied but highly experienced Confederate Army of Tennessee supplemented by the Georgia State Line, Georgia Militia, and other irregular troops. Planned and constructed by Georgia's chief military engineer, Confederate captain Lemuel P. Grant, using slave labor from nearby plantations, the fortress city was "too strong to assault and too extensive to invest," according to Sherman's own chief of engineers, Captain Orlando M. Poe. Sherman decided simply to bombard the city into submission.

On 1 August, Sherman had ordered Schofield's artillery to increase their rate of fire, and after the disaster at Utoy Creek, he sent for large artillery guns and plenty of ammunition. Two 30-pounder Parrott rifles were brought in from Chattanooga, specifically to demolish buildings, and eight huge 4.5-inch siege guns were in place by 8 August. On 9 August, Sherman ordered every battery within range to open fire, "and make the inside of Atlanta too hot to be endured." That day alone more than 5,000 shells slammed into the city's heart.

Sherman kept the intense bombardment up for more than two weeks, gradually wearing away the strength and endurance of the hollow-eyed soldiers within the city

fortifications. Then, suddenly, on 25 August all the guns fell silent. Hood hoped for a moment that Sherman had given up and was withdrawing, but his hopes were dashed when word came of yet another Union flanking attempt. Thomas's entire Army of the Cumberland and Howard's Army of the Tennessee moved around the right of Atlanta and swept down on the Atlanta and West Point Railroad, nine miles southwest of East Point. Hood could not hope to muster any sort of force to stop them, but pulled nearly his entire army out of Atlanta to try to protect the last remaining railway, leaving Stewart's corps and Smith's Georgia Militia to hold the city lines.

Realizing that Sherman intended to strike at Jonesboro and cut the railway, after dark on 30 August, Hood ordered Hardee's and Lee's corps to move hastily to defend the small town. Encountering Union pickets about 3:00 A.M. and not wanting to risk a night battle, the two Confederate corps moved slightly to the east, not arriving in line at Jonesboro until just after noon on the 31st. Hood was almost frantic to defend his railroad, sending Hardee repeated messages to attack "as soon as you can get your troops up."

At 3:00 P.M. that afternoon the order came to fix bayonets and drive the Yankees from their trenches. The Confederate assault, two corps wide, advancing through open fields and against concentrated artillery cannister fire never made it closer than sixty yards at any point before withdrawing. Losses were staggeringly one-sided, at least 1,700 Confederate versus 179 Union soldiers killed or wounded.

At the same time, Schofield's Army of the Ohio, reinforced by Union Major General David S. Stanley's IV Army Corps, moved around the southern Atlanta defenses and struck the Macon & Western Railroad near Rough & Ready. Quickly overwhelming the small dismounted cavalry unit stationed there, the Union troops ripped up the tracks and moved north toward East Point.

At 6:00 P.M. that evening, Hood ordered Lee's corps back to help defend Atlanta against the new attack, leaving Hardee alone in Jonesboro facing three full Union corps. At midnight, Hardee sent a message by courier to Hood (the telegraph wire having been cut about 2:00 P.M.) advising that the attack had failed and Atlanta should be abandoned. Through the rest of the long hot night, Hardee's forces shifted around to cover the gaps left by Lee's departure and dug in as best they could. All knew that their real job was to hold the main Union armies long enough for Hood to get the rest of the forces out of Atlanta.

At 4:00 P.M. on 1 September the Union attack began, led by two brigades of Brigadier General William P. Carlin's 1st Division (Brevet Major General Jefferson C. Davis's XIV Army Corps). They were quickly followed by brigade after brigade, division after division, until three full corps were engaged in the assault. Amazingly, although one side of his line caved in and 865 prisoners and two full batteries of artillery were captured, Hardee managed to hold until the attack ended after nightfall. About midnight, he withdrew his three remaining divisions south to Lovejoy Station, leaving behind about 1,400 dead and wounded. The Union force fared little better, losing a total of 1,272, but at last taking and cutting the railway line they had sought for so long.

On the morning of 1 September, having received Hardee's dreadful message, Hood at long last ordered the evacuation of the doomed city. With the railway cut, it was impossible to take much in the way of supplies with them, so warehouses were ordered opened up for the civilians. Stewart's corps and Smith's Militia began marching out around 5:00 P.M., with French's divisional pickets acting as a rearguard and withdrawing about 11:00 P.M. Sappers and engineers hastily prepared the abandoned military supplies for destruction. About midnight, a thunderous roar announced the end for a large ammunition train that Hood was unable to withdraw. Sherman heard the blast fifteen miles away in his headquarters at Jonesboro and knew he now had the city.

On 3 September 1864, Sherman telegraphed Major General Henry W. Halleck in Washington: "So Atlanta is ours, and fairly won." Hood managed to slip away with what remained of his forces, more or less intact after blowing up his large ammunition train and abandoning warehouses full of supplies. No complete records exist, but somewhere nearly 30,000 starving and ill-equipped troops were left to carry out Hood's desperate plan to strike at the Union rear. Well over 81,000 troops were still available to Sherman, who decided not to follow and finish off the badly mauled Confederate force. Instead he would simply rest and resupply within the fortifications of Atlanta.

Between Dalton and the gates of Atlanta lie the graves of 4,423 Union and 3,044 Confederate soldiers. During the four-month campaign, 22,822 Union and 18,952 Confederates were wounded, and a total of 17,335 on both sides were captured or disappeared.

—*John E. McKay*

See also Atlanta Campaign; Dallas, Georgia, Battle of; Ezra Church; Jonesboro; Kennesaw Mountain; Peachtree Creek; Resaca, Battle of; Rocky Face Ridge, Battle of; Stoneman's Raid (July 1864); Utoy Creek.

For further reading:
Cannan, John. *The Atlanta Campaign, May–November, 1864* (1991).
Castel, Albert E. *Decision in the West: The Atlanta Campaign of 1864* (1992).
Crompton, James. "The Second Division of the 16th Corps in the Atlanta Campaign." In *The Atlanta Papers* (1980).
Evans, David. *Sherman's Horsemen: Union Cavalry Operations in the Atlanta Campaign* (1996).

ATLANTA, GEORGIA

Atlanta's importance as a railroad, industrial, and distribution center, and its symbolism as the South's "second capital," made the city a focal point during the Civil War. The city began inauspiciously as the small settlement known as Terminus. Incorporated in 1843 as Marthasville (named for the governor's daughter), the town changed its name again to Atlanta in 1847. Before the war, Atlanta remained important principally for its railroads. Four railroads converged in the city: the Georgia Railroad, the Atlanta & West Point, and the Macon & Western, in addition to the Western & Atlantic. By the late 1850s, calling itself the "Gate City of the South," Atlanta boasted the largest and grandest passenger depot in the region. Its population of 10,000 included many prosperous merchants, industrialists, and professionals who built fine homes, although the city had few paved streets and had problems with gambling and prostitution.

With its railroad and commercial interests, Atlanta did not support secession before 1860. In the presidential contest in that year, the city gave a majority of its votes to Unionist candidate John Bell. However, Abraham Lincoln's election moved public opinion toward secession, Atlanta fire-eaters burned the president-elect in effigy, and unionism gave way to support for Confederate nationhood. Several thousand Atlanta men joined the Confederate armies, while women volunteered their time with the Ladies' Soldiers' Relief Society or the Atlanta Hospital Association. Nevertheless, throughout the war, a minority of Atlantans continued to support the Union. Most of city's Unionists were merchants. They visited the city's prison, which housed three hundred Federal soldiers, and smuggled provisions to these men. Occasionally they acted as spies. Nervous Confederates, fearing plots to liberate slaves and prisoners, harassed and occasionally imprisoned Unionists.

The war hindered commerce in Atlanta, just as it did in other cities of the Confederacy. Early in the war, the city's merchants still managed to import some supplies from New York by way of Memphis and other towns along the Mississippi River. When Federal military success closed this commercial avenue, Atlanta's merchants hoped to import goods from Europe. Although several Atlantans founded blockade-running companies, this activity carried its own hazards.

While commerce foundered, industry flourished. Atlanta's wartime factories produced a wide range of consumer goods, ranging from saddles and plows to soap, buttons, and porcelain teeth. The city became best known as an ordnance center. Its factories manufactured a wide array of military goods, including knives, swords, cannon, pistols, and naval armor plate for the famous ironclad *Merrimack*. Atlanta's most important factory was the Confederate government arsenal, run by

Colonel Moses H. Wright. Opened in the spring of 1862, after arsonists burned an earlier Confederate facility in Nashville, the arsenal produced harnesses and saddles, percussion caps, rifle cartridges, and artillery shells. Employing nearly 5,500 men and women, it would be Atlanta's biggest employer of the nineteenth century. The city also housed the Quartermaster's Depot, commanded by Major G. W. Cunningham. It produced shoes, along with underclothing, shirts, pants, jackets, and hats for the Confederate army, hiring dozens of shoe-makers and tailors, along with three thousand seam-stresses. Atlanta's contributions to the war effort, along with the city's importance as a rail center, made it an obvious target for the Union military.

With its economic success the city's population grew to nearly 22,000. But Atlanta's situation began to decline even before the arrival of General William T. Sherman's army. The city's factories suffered from a lack of raw materials. Skilled labor was in short supply. With the city's rapid wartime population growth and lack of sanitation, Atlanta was not a very healthy place to live. A smallpox epidemic beginning in December 1862 afflicted at least 100 city residents. Atlantans suffered from the inflation that bedeviled the entire Confederate South. As the war stretched on, price gouging, food scarcities, and lawlessness increased. On 18 March 1863, a group of Confederate war widows, angered by the high cost of food, rioted by breaking into stores on Whitehall Street and stealing flour, bacon, and other items. The city marshal arrived quickly and reestablished order with no serious injuries. Similar riots occurred in other Georgia cities, as well as in the Confederate capital of Richmond. Although the city attempted to offer "poor relief" to its indigent residents through special grocery stores, free medical care, and paid burial, there was never enough money to help all of those in need.

Although city residents once considered themselves safe from Yankee invasion because they believed the Union army could never negotiate the north Georgia mountains, the Federal army shattered their compla-cency by breaking through Confederate lines at Chattanooga in November 1863. By May 1864, with Sherman pushing his way south, many Atlantans began to leave the city, seeking refuge in safer locations. Others stayed even when Sherman's bombardment of the city began on 20 July. They sought shelter in makeshift pits dug in back yards and covered with metal sheeting or railroad ties. Twenty civilians died in the six-week siege, including, ironically, a free African-American man who operated a barbershop in a local hotel and who was killed by a shell fragment. On 2 September 1864, after Sherman's army had flanked the Confederates south of the city, Mayor James Calhoun surrendered Atlanta. Sherman ordered the city's evacuation before beginning the systematic destruction of railroads and all war indus-

tries. The ensuing fires claimed between 4,000 and 5,000 buildings, including many residential structures.

In November 1864, after an occupation of two months, General Sherman and his army left Atlanta, with Savannah as their next goal. Like the ancient phoenix it adopted as its new symbol, the city of Atlanta would quickly begin to rise again, eventually establishing itself as the center of the postwar New South.

—*Wendy Hamand Venet*

See also Atlanta Campaign.
For further reading:
Dyer, Thomas G. *Secret Yankees: The Union Circle in Confederate Atlanta* (1999).
Rose, Michael. *Atlanta: A Portrait of the Civil War* (1999).
Russell, James Michael. *Atlanta 1847–1890: City Building in the Old South and the New* (1988).

AUGUR, CHRISTOPHER COLUMBUS
(1821–1898)
Union general

Born to Ammon Augur and Annis Wellman Augur in Kendall, New York, Christopher Augur moved to Michigan with his mother after his father's death. In 1839 he received an appointment to the U.S. Military Academy, from which he graduated in the class of 1843, sixteenth of thirty-nine. At the outbreak of the Mexican-American War, he fought in northern Mexico under Zachary Taylor and served as an aide to two of Taylor's generals. After the war, Augur served on garrison duty in the Pacific Northwest and fought in several of the Indian wars there. At the outbreak of the Civil War he was commandant of cadets at the U.S. Military Academy.

Promoted to brigadier general of volunteers in November 1861, Augur managed the outlying defenses of Washington, D.C. In March 1862, he was part of the initial advance south toward Richmond and led the force that captured Fredericksburg, Virginia, in April 1862. He occupied the town until July, when his division was made part of John Pope's Army of Virginia. He fought at Cedar Mountain on 9 August. At approxi-mately 7:00 P.M. he was severely wounded and had to leave the field. He was promoted major general of volun-teers for his bravery at Cedar Mountain.

Augur's injury prevented him from returning to duty until November 1862. His first assignment was to serve as Nathaniel P. Banks's second-in-command for Banks's Louisiana campaign. For the first four months of the campaign, Augur commanded the District of Baton Rouge in Banks's Department of the Gulf. In May 1863 Augur took command of the attack made on Port Hudson on 21 May and then oversaw the left of the siege works until the surrender. By that point, Augur's health, aggravated by his earlier wound, forced him to ask for a leave of absence. He was unable to exercise a field command for the remainder of the war.

From October 1863 until August 1866, Augur commanded the Department of Washington. Along with maintaining the defenses of the city, Augur engaged in a variety of activities during his command in Washington. During Ulysses S. Grant's campaign against Robert E. Lee that commenced in the spring of 1864 and lasted until Lee surrendered in April 1865, Augur was charged with equipping and moving Grant's replacement troops through Washington down to the front as quickly as possible. Augur managed this monumental task while also guarding the city during the summer of 1864 against Jubal Early's raid and remaining vigilant through the fall of 1864 and into the early months of 1865 against the activities of other Confederate raiders like John Singleton Mosby. During these hectic times, Philip Sheridan commended Augur for the assistance he rendered him during the latter's Shenandoah Valley campaign.

After the war, Augur's duties in Washington hardly tapered off. He was charged with keeping the streets cleared during the various troop reviews after the Confederate surrenders and was instructed to oversee the execution of Andersonville commandant Henry Wirz in November 1865.

When the remainder of the volunteers were mustered out of service in 1866, Augur became the colonel of the 12th Infantry. He was promoted to brigadier general in 1869. He served in the various Indian wars of the post–Civil War era and for a time in 1876 commanded the Department of the Gulf during the last days of Reconstruction. Augur retired at the rank of brigadier general in 1885. He died in the District of Columbia on 16 January 1898.

—*David S. Heidler and Jeanne T. Heidler*

See also Cedar Mountain, Battle of; Port Hudson Campaign; Washington, D.C.
For further reading:
Men of the Time; Being Biographies of Generals Halleck, Pope, Siegel, Corcoran, Prentiss, Kearney, Hatch and Augur (1862).

AVERASBORO (AVERASBOROUGH), BATTLE OF
(16 March 1865)

The battle near Averasboro, North Carolina, was the first of two engagements fought during the third stage of Union major general William T. Sherman's Carolinas campaign in 1865. This engagement, which was fought between the Black and Cape Fear rivers, represented the initial Confederate attempt to monitor the Federal advance northward from Fayetteville, North Carolina.

The arrival of General Sherman's two armies at Fayetteville, North Carolina, on 11 March 1865 signaled the beginning the third stage of the Federal raid northward through the Carolinas. Sherman now prepared to move overland to Goldsboro, North Carolina, where he expected to link up with additional reinforcements and supplies. Within a hundred miles of Sherman, Confederate general Joseph E. Johnston worked to concentrate his scattered forces to form an army to stop the Federal advance. One of those forces was the provisional corps of two divisions under the command of Lieutenant General William J. Hardee, which was encamped on the old Plank Road north of Fayetteville, North Carolina. General Hardee's corps consisted of garrison troops that were displaced by General Sherman's march through Georgia and South Carolina. As his troops rested near the Smith plantation, General Hardee soon received orders from General Johnston to conduct a delaying action to determine whether Goldsboro or Raleigh was Sherman's next objective. The information would be vital to Johnston, so that he would be able to organize an attack on one of the two Union columns. General Hardee deployed his forces in three positions to receive Sherman's advance. His first two lines were manned by brigades from Brigadier General William B. Taliaferro's division, and the third line was occupied by Major General Lafayette McLaws's division in front of the intersection of the Goldsboro and Raleigh roads.

On 15 March 1865, elements of General Sherman's left wing brushed into skirmishers of Colonel Alfred Rhett's brigade on the old Plank Road. This Union column consisted of four infantry divisions of both XIV and XX Army Corps under the command of Major General Henry Slocum and brevet Major General Judson Kilpatrick's 3d Cavalry Division. The initial contact came from General Kilpatrick's troopers pushing down the old Plank Road. They quickly discovered Rhett's brigade was entrenched and supported by artillery. A general engagement commenced on both sides of the road, during which Colonel Rhett was captured by Federal scouts. Rhett's brigade began to probe the Union cavalry, and soon Union infantry was brought up to reinforce General Kilpatrick's men.

The next morning (16 March 1865), General Kilpatrick again attempted to clear the road and soon found his troopers fighting with Confederate infantry supported by artillery fire. The Union situation became worse, when rebel infantry began to press Kilpatrick's flanks. General Slocum quickly ordered up the two divisions of XX Corps into line to reinforce the Federal line, and called up his artillery to shell the Confederates. While this pressure was maintained on Rhett's brigade, Colonel Henry Case's brigade from the 3d Division, XX Corps, swung around the Confederate right flank and unhinged the position. Rhett's brigade soon retreated northward after abandoning two cannon.

The survivors of Rhett's brigade fell back on Brigadier General Stephen Elliott's brigade, which was deployed a couple of miles to the north. With General Sherman now on the field, the Union commanders pushed forward to clear the road. With the deployment of another division from XIV Corps, General Elliott soon found his brigade pressed on three sides by Union forces. He quickly pulled his regiments back to General McLaws's position. General Slocum's advancing troops, who were attempting to probe the rebel flanks, quickly discovered this line. Unlike the first two positions, this line was anchored on both the Black and Cape Fear rivers by Confederate cavalry, and its center was reinforced with artillery and infantry. After several failed attempts to turn the position, the Federal infantry was soon settled into heavy skirmishing with McLaws's division until nightfall.

During the night of 16 March, General Hardee received orders to move his troops to the north and rejoin General Johnston's army near Smithfield, North Carolina. General Johnston now needed to get his army united, so that a plan could be developed to attack General Sherman. At the same time, Sherman prepared to send portions of XV Corps to assist Slocum's advance. By 17 March the Confederates had abandoned their defensive lines, and Sherman saw the opportunity to push his forces eastward to avoid any further Confederate contact.

—*William H. Brown*

See also Carolinas Campaign.
For further reading:
Barrett, John G. *The Civil War in North Carolina* (1963).
———. *Sherman's March through the Carolinas* (1956; reprint, 1996).
Long, E. B. *The Civil War Day By Day: An Almanac* (1971).
U.S. War Department. *War of the Rebellion: A Compilation of the Official Records of the Union and Confederate Armies* (1880–1901).

AVERELL, WILLIAM WOODS
(1832–1900)
Union general

William Woods Averell was born on 5 November 1832 in the small town of Cameron, New York. The son of a farmer and minor political figure, Averell began attending the U.S. Military Academy at West Point in December 1850. His academic career was less than stellar, and upon graduation in 1855 he ranked in the lower third of his class. Yet, Averell was a natural at horsemanship. It was as a horseman that he gained his prominence and enjoyed much success.

In 1857 Averell was sent to the New Mexico Territory, where his skills as a cavalryman were invaluable in scouting operations. In 1859, however, a serious leg wound sent him home to convalesce, and for the next two years he lived at his family's residence in Bath, New York. It was there that Averell learned of the attack on Fort Sumter in 1861.

Yearning for a return to military service, Averell presented himself for duty on 16 April 1861. He was ordered to Fort Arbuckle, situated west of Arkansas, to relay an order to the commander, who had lost communication with Washington, to destroy all property, retreat north, and prepare for war. This journey took Averell deep into Southern territory, but he survived it and returned to Washington to help muster volunteers. Eventually he was later assigned as assistant adjutant general to Colonel Andrew Porter.

After fighting at Bull Run, Averell moved briefly to the staff of the provost marshal in Washington, D.C. Since horsemanship was Averell's true passion, however, he was not happy serving as an administrative officer, and he soon sought a field appointment. On 7 October 1861, Averell's hope was realized when he assumed command of the 3d Pennsylvania Cavalry. By June 1862, he had transformed his unit of green cavalrymen into accomplished horsemen, and by August, Averell had attained the rank of brigadier general. The next two years revealed Averell to be an adept commander who was skilled at handling his men. He was moved into West Virginia to help aid in that infant state's separation from Virginia and to conduct raids against various strategic targets. Starting in August 1863 through May 1864, Averell's raids into western Virginia scored the most success in distracting Confederate forces in the region and harrying the Army of Northern Virginia's lines of supply out of east Tennessee.

In August 1864, Averell's command was placed under Philip Sheridan, who was about to start his destructive raid of the Shenandoah Valley. Averell would serve under Sheridan into September 1864, but after the battle of Fisher's Hill on 21–22 September 1864, Averell lost his command when Sheridan accused him of incompetence.

Averell's postwar career proved to be profitable. In October 1865, Averell became involved in the Averill Coal and Oil Company. In 1866, he learned that he was to receive the appointment of consul general to British North America at Montreal. In the fall of 1870, Averell's interest in the new mineral asphalt led by 1880 to his becoming president of The American Asphalt Company. Though the company split within two years, Averell was rewarded with nearly $700,000. Exhibiting a remarkable penchant for invention, Averell went on to design an underground electrical conduit for use in telegraphic, telephonic, and lighting.

In 1888, Averell was appointed assistant inspector general of Soldiers Homes. He died in 1900.

—*Chad A. Reisig*

William W. Averell (*seated*) (*Library of Congress*)

See also Averell's Raids; Fisher's Hill, Battle of.
For further reading:
Amato, Nicholas J., and Edward Eckert, eds. *Ten Years in the Saddle: The Memoir of William Woods Averell: 1851–1862* (1978).
Pond, George E. *The Shenandoah Valley in 1864* (1883).

AVERELL'S RAIDS
(August 1863–May 1864)

During the second half of 1863 and into the spring of 1864, Union operations in West Virginia were aimed at destroying railroads and depriving the Confederacy of valuable resources such as lead and salt

mines in southwestern Virginia. Four raids mounted or participated in by Brigadier General William W. Averell tried to accomplish these goals and achieved mixed results.

The first raid occurred in August 1863 and had as its principal purpose clearing out Confederate forces from the area around Huntersville so that a subsequent operation could be mounted against Staunton and the Virginia & Tennessee Railroad. Averell was also instructed to seize the Virginia Court of Appeals law library at Lewisburg. The library had been purchased for the western counties and was thus deemed the property of West Virginia. In any event, the new state's judges needed it to hold court.

Departing from Winchester on 5 August, Averell's command consisted of four companies of West Virginia cavalry, the 14th Pennsylvania Cavalry, three regiments of mounted infantry, Gibson's Independent Battalion, and a battery of artillery. After a short skirmish on 6 August with elements of John Imboden's command, the Union force arrived at Moorefield, where it stayed for two days. Although Averell was short of supplies, he headed south again on 9 August, but stopped in Petersburg until he could at least have his horses shod. Partially supplied on 17 August, but still lacking adequate ammunition, he elected to proceed. He pushed south toward Monterey, destroying a saltpeter works near Franklin en route. On 20 August, he entered Monterey and arrested the officers of the quarterly court in session there. He also heard of plans being hatched by Imboden and Major General Samuel Jones to counter the Federal raid.

The Confederate response to the raid was hampered by ignorance of Averell's real intentions. Major General Samuel Jones, the Commander of the Department of Western Virginia, persisted in the belief that the Union raid was directed at Staunton and the vital Virginia & Tennessee Railroad. He directed forces under his command to respond accordingly and requested from Robert E. Lee that detachments from the Army of Northern Virginia move to defend Staunton. Instead of heading toward Staunton, Averell in accordance with his orders pushed toward Huntersville, the only resistance being the annoyance of snipers lurking in the scrub. He skirmished on 22 August outside of Huntersville with elements of Colonel William "Mudwall" Jackson's scattered command, outflanking and forcing them to retire southeastward toward Warm Springs. The 8th West Virginia pursued, overran the Confederate bivouac at Camp Northwest, and destroyed it and its stores. Reinforced on 23 August by the 10th and part of the 2d West Virginia as well as another battery, Averell drove toward Warm Springs the next day to skirmish again with Jackson and force him eastward toward Millborough.

Averell hoped that his march toward Warm Springs, east of Huntersville and consequently in the direction of Staunton, had misled the Confederates into thinking that the town really was his objective. The next day, he compounded the ruse by sending the 10th West Virginia back to Huntersville while he resumed his southerly march toward Callaghan's, smashing another saltpeter works on the way at Jackson's River. From Callaghan's, Union scouts ranged east to Covington and as far south as Sweet Springs, capturing rebel wagons and torching another saltpeter facility.

Although Jackson would later claim that he had deduced Averell's actual objective to be Lewisburg and had tried to notify Jones of it, it was not until Averell showed up in Callaghan's that Jones came to a realistic conclusion about Union movements. He recalled Colonel George S. Patton, commanding the 1st Brigade, from his march toward Warm Springs and directed him to White Sulphur Springs, about halfway between Lewisburg and Callaghan's. Since Averell had run Jackson out of Pocahontas County, on 26 August he now turned to Lewisburg, moving over the difficult road from Callaghan's that crossed two mountain ranges in the space of ten miles. As his advanced parties were debouching from a long defile, they ran into Patton's soldiers who had executed a night march to reach White Sulphur Springs almost at the same time as Averell did. The two forces, growing to their full strengths with ensuing arrivals, stubbornly contested the ground for the remainder of the day and held their positions that night. The next morning, Averell attempted to renew the fight, but his dwindling ammunition prompted him to break off the attack at midmorning and fall back toward Huntersville in good order. By felling trees behind him on roads that ran through ravines, he was able to impede the Confederate pursuit. Jones's hope that John Imboden was moving down from Monterey with enough speed to cut off Averell at Huntersville also proved forlorn, so the Union raiders safely reached Beverly, northeast of Huntersville, by the end of the month. Averell's losses were a little more than 200, mostly from the engagement at White Sulphur Springs. Jackson had lost not more than 20 men in the skirmishing around Huntersville and Warm Springs, and Patton's losses at White Sulphur were about 200.

The Federal effort had been only half realized and ultimately pointless at that. Rebel forces soon reoccupied Pocahontas County with Jackson's command headquartered at Mill Point. Averell remained in Beverly until undertaking the second of his raids in November. This effort had as its objective the capture of Lewisburg with an operation that had Averell advancing south from Beverly while Brigadier General Alfred Duffié moved east from Charleston in the Kanawha Valley. Infantry would occupy Lewisburg while all mounted troops pushed forward by way of Union to the Dublin Depot of the Virginia & Tennessee Railroad. Nearby they would destroy the railroad's New River Bridge. On 1 November, Averell left Beverly on the Staunton Pike heading toward Bartow with two regiments of infantry, four mounted regiments, an independent battalion of cavalry, and two light batteries. Two days later, Duffié pulled out of Charleston commanding a detachment of Brigadier General Eliakim P. Scammon's Third Division consisting of two regiments of infantry, two mounted regiments, and a section of artillery.

Averell moved through Greenbank toward

Huntersville and approached Mill Point on 5 November, where he skirmished with Jackson's outposts. Badly outnumbered, Jackson judiciously withdrew to a formidable position on Droop Mountain over which ran the main Lewisburg road. From there Jackson called for reinforcements from Brigadier General John Echols who hurried up from Lewisburg. By the time Averell was moving on Jackson's position on the morning of 6 November, a fourteen-mile march had brought Echols into position and swelled the rebel numbers on the crest to about 1,700 men. They mounted a stout defense against the superior Union force, but the defensive advantages of mountainous terrain also proved treacherous, for Averell was able to mask his movements behind rolling hills and in deep ravines. Gradually aware of a Federal effort to turn his left and mindful of Duffié's column advancing from the west, Echols elected to withdraw rather than risk being surrounded. The four miles of road along the crest of Droop Mountain, however, proved perilous, and a general panic was only barely averted as the rebels began their retreat. Some of Echols's people ran, though, and it was this element of the withdrawal that apparently created a rumor that he had been routed after a catastrophic defeat that left the whole region open to Averell's designs. As a result, Major General Jones was in dread for two days and made no secret of it to Richmond.

Actually, Echols was in fairly good shape, except he was most alarmed over the chance that Duffié would cut off his retreat at Lewisburg. For his part, Duffié had been only lightly engaged in skirmishes along his route—one at Little Sewell Mountain on the same day as Droop Mountain and another just west of Lewisburg at Muddy Creek the following day. Realizing the need for haste if he was to bag Echols, he left his infantry at Little Sewell Mountain and raced toward Lewisburg, but when he arrived at midmorning on 7 November, the rebels had slipped the noose, passing through the town and heading farther south toward Union the previous night. Duffié later uncharitably claimed that, had Averell been less aggressive at Droop Mountain, Echols would not have been so rapid in his retreat, and the Kanawha column would have had time to close the trap at Lewisburg. The two men never got along afterward.

Averell arrived in Lewisburg late in the afternoon on 7 November to find the business of destroying Confederate stores and ordnance well under way. The question now was what to do next. Averell's orders left it to his discretion about the practicability of proceeding with his mission to the Virginia & Tennessee Railroad, and at the end of the following day he would exercise his option to break off the operation and go home. He and Duffié sallied forth with their troopers southward early on 8 November, but Echols had made a thorough job of blocking the roads with felled trees. And then the blue

troopers ran into Echols's rearguard at Second Creek about fifteen miles south of Lewisburg. Duffié declared that his people could not proceed. He had only a day's rations, and his infantry, able to make only ten miles a day, would be starving if they did not get home. Averell was loaded down with prisoners and materiel from Droop Mountain, so everybody went back to Lewisburg and from there parted ways, Duffié to the west, Averell's infantry north to Beverly, and Averell with his troopers to the east toward Callaghan's and the Valley of the South Branch.

Haste urged the Yankee troopers. By then, every Confederate in the region was alerted. John Imboden had left his headquarters near Bridgewater, Virginia, early on 5 November and raced toward Goshen. From there he had moved toward Covington on the assumption that Averell intended to destroy the forges and furnaces in the area or perhaps make for Staunton; and it was there, between Callaghan's and Covington, on 10 November that Averell brushed against Imboden's pickets before abruptly turning north and racing up Back Creek as fast as he could move. Imboden was content to watch him, still suspicious that he would strike east and do some more destruction somewhere, so Averell was able to reach Petersburg by 14 November and his destination at New Creek three days later. By then, Duffié had been back in Charleston four days, his only problem upon his return being the weather: five inches of new snow had blocked the roads across Little Sewell Mountain.

This second raid into Confederate-occupied West Virginia had not reached the railroad, but it had demonstrated the vulnerability of the region to swift incursion. Casualties for the raiders were rather light—a little more than a hundred, and most of those from the fight at Droop Mountain—yet they were as light for the defenders, in spite of Jones's initial alarm. Echols counted almost 300 of his command missing, but most of those had run during the brief panic of the retreat. What had to be more alarming to Richmond, however, was the ease with which Federal troopers could move through the region even when encountering organized Confederate resistance, and the reflexive response of Jones to cry for help from the overburdened Army of Northern Virginia the moment a bluecoat appeared south of Huntersville. The Federal perspective was also alloyed, for Averell had failed to exploit his rather easy advance to Lewisburg.

Nonetheless, Averell had barely returned to his lines when a third raid was planned for December. It would be the most ambitious and complicated yet, relying on two elaborate feints to draw attention away from the main objective, which was the Virginia & Tennessee Railroad bridge, either at Bonsack's Station or Salem, Virginia. On 8 December, Averell's entire command moved out of New Creek, headed toward Petersburg, and then to

Franklin and Monterey. He was accompanied by two regiments of infantry and artillery that left his column at Monterey to head east toward McDowell, Virginia, and from there not only guard Averell's line of retreat but also to threaten Staunton and tie down Imboden as well as Jubal Early and Fitzhugh Lee. In case the Confederates remained unimpressed by that menace, all of Brigadier General Jeremiah Sullivan's 1st Division Cavalry, two infantry regiments, and a battery would ride up the Shenandoah Valley from Harper's Ferry to occupy Harrisonburg and also threaten Staunton from the north. Simultaneous to Averell's sortie on 8 December, Brigadier General Scammon's 3d Division set forth from Charleston toward Lewisburg as the 28th Ohio Cavalry and two infantry regiments advanced from Beverly toward Droop Mountain to support Scammon's maneuver. From Lewisburg, Scammon was supposed to head south toward Union and then act as though he were threatening the New River Bridge some twenty-five miles south of Salem. All the activity aimed at perfectly plausible targets would, it was hoped, so confuse and distract the Confederate defenders that Averell would be able slip unmolested into the Roanoke region and do some major tearing up of the railroad there.

It was, as it turned out, wise for the Union plan to employ more than enough complications because some of them simply did not work. Scammon's part of the project was no help at all because skirmishes at Big Sewell Mountain and Meadow Bluff on 11 December apparently convinced him that Lewisburg was indefensible. Rather than joining the forces coming from Droop Mountain—where Jackson's tattered command had again been put to flight—and then demonstrating toward the New River Bridge, Scammon pulled back to the west. Only Alfred Duffié's cavalry and some artillery remained in Lewisburg, and that only briefly. Scammon, alarmed that guerrilla's were threatening his rear and gray regulars were increasing on his front, simply went home. When Colonel Augustus Moor leading the forces down from Droop Mountain tried to communicate with Scammon, he made the puzzling discovery that Confederates were still in Lewisburg and the alarming one that they were beginning to people the roads to his rear. He hastily headed back to Beverly, and the entire western part of the operation collapsed just as Averell was approaching his target.

It did not matter, although it would make Averell's escape adventurous. Yet Confederate resources were stretched so thin by the end of 1863, even the failures of this raid accounted for its principal success. The Federal threat to Staunton at first preoccupied the only significant forces in the region, so, as Averell came down a little-known road on Back Creek, he was able to surprise even Jackson's rear guard retreating from Droop Mountain. When he reached Callaghan's, he heard that

Federals were in Lewisburg—Scammon had not yet been spooked out of it—so he made a move east toward Covington in case anybody was watching before racing southwest to Sweet Springs. He then learned about Scammon's inexplicable retreat from Lewisburg and must have taken pause. Word was that Echols was near Union, but Averell took heart when a captured Rebel revealed that nobody knew that bluecoats were south of Lewisburg. He switched back to the southeast, moved through New Castle, and descended on Salem. His arrival there on 16 December was such a surprise to everyone, including the residents, that he found the town's considerable supply depot completely unguarded. Moreover, he was able to send parties out on the railroad miles to the east and west, destroying five bridges and tearing up sections of rails.

Averell had shelled a train of Confederates trying to get into Salem, so his hours of destroying rail lines and burning supplies in the town were borrowed ones. At 4:00 P.M. that afternoon, he headed back north along the same route of his advance, now concerned about getting out of the hornet's nest he had stirred up. Samuel Jones was advancing from the west and Fitzhugh Lee, out of his camp near Charlottesville two days earlier, was moving southward toward Averell's line of retreat. Jubal Early had raced out of Hanover Junction on 15 December and in forty-eight hours was in Millborough, from whence he would register an unanswered demand for Averell's surrender on the 20th. As perilous as this closing snare was, darkness and exhaustion were even more immediate enemies. Averell's people had been in the saddle for more than a day riding hard for the better part of a hundred miles, so he had to stop near Salem and give his men and animals some rest.

Rain began to fall hard and continued through the night of 16 December into the next day. Craig's Creek in Averell's front became a cataract, and he was barely able to get his wagons and artillery across it. By the time the bedraggled raiders reached New Castle on 18 December, both they and their sodden ammunition were almost useless. By now, Jones was closing on the Sweet Springs Road, and Fitz Lee was in Fincastle, a stone's throw from the Yankee raiders. At 9:00 P.M., Averell feinted toward Lee at Fincastle and then whirled on Jones with such fury that he drove his pickets back a dozen miles. The Yankee troopers then stoked up fires and promptly abandoned them to creep north toward Covington on a back road.

Now, the main obstacle to escape was Jackson's River, swollen and running fast with broken ice on its surface. The Confederates had made arrangements to burn the bridges should Averell try to use them, but the defense of them had been entrusted to hapless "Mudwall" Jackson, whose impediments to Averell's escape would prove completely ineffective. When Averell appeared, the bridge fires could not be set. Also a captured message from General Jones to Jubal Early revealed to Averell all the plans of his pursuers. As a sharp fight for control of the bridges developed, the Yankees crossed and burned them so quickly that Averell's rearguard was trapped on the south bank. Most of them swam the icy river. Gathering up at Callaghan's, the raiders raced northwest through frozen passes. When they camped at the northern base of Droop Mountain on 21 December, their clothes were in shreds and they had no rations. Finally, they rode into Beverly on Christmas Eve.

It had been an arduous journey that left Averell's people badly used and minus almost 200 casualties, but they had finally done extensive damage to the Virginia & Tennessee Railroad, although it was quickly repaired. Yet, the raid had revealed again the permeable nature of Confederate defenses in the region. As for the gray defenders, the principal casualty of this last Federal sortie was Samuel Jones's career. In spite of Jones's attempts to lay blame elsewhere and claim vigilance where none had really been demonstrated—Jones as late as 11:00 P.M. on 15 December suspected that Averell was heading toward Fincastle rather than Salem—both Jefferson Davis and Robert E. Lee became so disenchanted with Jones that he was replaced. In March 1864, Major General John C. Breckinridge would become the new commander of the Department of Western Virginia. Soon he too would have to face another and, as it happened, the final of Averell's West Virginia raids.

Jones's Federal counterpart, Brigadier General Benjamin F. Kelley, was replaced in March as well, a victim of Union failures to secure the upper valley and make any dent in southwestern Virginia. Major General Franz Sigel became the new commander of the Department of West Virginia, and one of the changes he made was to make Averell the commander of a unit designated as the 2d Cavalry Division composed of Duffié's brigade, the 14th Pennsylvania, the 8th Ohio, and the 1st, 5th, and 7th West Virginia. When Lieutenant General Ulysses S. Grant actively formulated a grand, coordinated campaign to end the war, it included another move on the Virginia & Tennessee Railroad with the goal of making it useless for the movement of men and supplies between East Tennessee and the Army of Northern Virginia. Ultimately this task fell to Brigadier General George C. Crook, nominally under Sigel, but virtually independent in his command of the Kanawha Valley. Crook devised a plan to take a column of 6,000 infantry to destroy the New River Bridge while Averell led his cavalry to Saltville. The main column of Union infantry marched along the Kanawha River and headed south toward Rocky Gap, fought at Cloyd's Mountain, captured Dublin, and destroyed the Virginia & Tennessee Railroad bridge at New River. Meanwhile, Averell's cavalry on 5 May moved out from Logan Court

House toward Wyoming Court House, skirmishing there with elements of the 8th Virginia Cavalry out of Saltville. Moving over rough and unmarked terrain through Abb's Valley, the Union troopers emerged to skirmish again with the 8th Virginia and then some Kentuckians near Tazewell Court House. As he approached Saltville, however, Averell despaired over news that the town had been fortified by Brigadier Generals John Morgan and W. E. "Grumble" Jones, a testament to the importance that Richmond assigned to the salt works there.

Electing to seek a more vulnerable target and keep Confederate forces from assailing Crook, Averell headed toward the lead works at Wytheville, but Morgan and Jones arrived there before him and assumed strong positions in Rocky Gap. Averell was fought to a standstill there on 10 May in a four-hour engagement that cost him 114 casualties. That night he withdrew toward Dublin, where he arrived next evening in a heavy rain that drenched his command and turned the New River, now bereft of its bridges thanks to Crook's work, into a nearly impassable torrent. Averell was just barely able to ford the river ahead of the pursuing Jones and Morgan. Reaching Christianburg, he received instructions from Crook to tear up as much of the Virginia & Tennessee Railroad as he could, but he soon learned of Confederates bearing in from the west by train. Heading north toward Crook's column, Averell led his troopers over some of the most terrifying terrain any could remember, especially since the rains had made the narrow mountain paths all the more perilous. Confederate attempts to block his progress proved fruitless, so he finally made it to Crook's column in Union on 15 May.

This last of Averell's raids in the region was much like the previous three. It had accomplished little of tangible strategic value except to prevent a concentration of Confederate strength against Crook's main initiative. Yet, Averell had shown a Federal presence in a region whose Unionist sympathies were vulnerable to unchallenged Confederate occupation. The raids also demonstrated Averell's uncanny talent for evasion that used terrain, rapid movement, and surprise to their best advantages. As spotty as his achievements in the mountains of West Virginia were, they had their moments of intrepid execution. Confederate soldiers did not like to hear that he was in the area. It was a compliment.

—*David S. Heidler and Jeanne T. Heidler*

See also Averell, William Woods; Cavalry, C.S.A; Cavalry, U.S.A.; Cloyd's Mountain, Virginia; Jones, Samuel; Kelley, Benjamin Franklin; West Virginia.

For further reading:
Duncan, Richard R. *Lee's Endangered Left: The Civil War in Western Virginia, Spring of 1864* (1998).
Eckert, Edward K., and Nicholas J. Amatos, eds. *Ten Years in the Saddle: Memoir of William Woods Averell, 1851–1862* (1978).

AYRES, ROMEYN BECK
(1825–1888)
Union general

Romeyn Ayres was born in East Creek, Montgomery County, New York. He received an appointment to the U.S. Military Academy and graduated twenty-second of thirty-eight in the class of 1847. Upon commissioning, he went to Mexico, where the fighting had ceased before his arrival. He served for the remainder of the year on garrison duty in Mexico before being sent to a variety of posts in the West and South before the Civil War. At the outbreak of that conflict, Ayres was a captain in the 5th Artillery.

Ayres's battery was attached to William T. Sherman's brigade at First Bull Run. Still a captain of artillery the following year, Ayres commanded the artillery of the 2d Division, IV Corps, at the siege of Yorktown and the battle of Williamsburg and was commended by Brigadier General Erasmus Keyes for his actions. Ayres participated in the raid up the Pamunkey River on 17 May 1862 and fought in the remaining actions of the Peninsula campaign.

During the late summer of 1862, Ayres participated in George McClellan's pursuit of Robert E. Lee, fighting at Crampton's Gap and Antietam. For the latter battle, he was commended by Colonel William H. Irwin. In November 1862, Ayres was promoted to brigadier general of volunteers and was made acting chief of artillery for the IV Corps, a position he occupied during the battle of Fredericksburg.

Because general officers seldom commanded artillery units, Ayres was moved to the infantry in early 1863. At Chancellorsville he commanded Sykes's division of the V Corps. Commanding the same division at Gettysburg,

Ayres fought on Little Round Top on the afternoon of 2 July. Ayres left the army shortly after the end of the battle to use his division to patrol the congressional districts of New York to prevent additional draft riots. In the fall of 1863 he fought at Bristoe Station and in the Mine Run campaign.

In March 1864 Ayres was given command of the 1st Brigade, 1st Division, V Corps. He crossed the Rapidan River on 4 May as part of Ulysses S. Grant's campaign against Robert E. Lee. At the beginning of the battle of the Wilderness the following day, Ayres noticed that the right flank of his brigade was unsupported by any other unit. Knowing that the Confederate corps under Richard Ewell was in position to attack him there, Ayres complained that he needed reinforcements on his flank. Before any action could be taken, he was attacked and his brigade decimated. He fought gamely with what he had, but was forced to withdraw. For his actions he was given command of the 2d Division, V Corps on 5 June. He continued in this command during the siege of Petersburg until he was wounded in January 1865. He returned to command in time to fight at Five Forks on 1 April and was commended for his actions there.

After the war, Ayres was promoted to lieutenant colonel in the regular army and served in garrisons in Arkansas, Louisiana, and Florida before being promoted to colonel of 2d Artillery in 1879. He died on active duty on 4 December 1888 at Fort Hamilton, New York. He was buried in Arlington National Cemetery.

—*David S. Heidler and Jeanne T. Heidler*

See also Five Forks; Wilderness, Battle of the.
For further reading:
Rhea, Gordon C. *The Battle of the Wilderness, May 5–6, 1864* (1994).
———. *The Battles for Spotsylvania Court House and the Road to Yellow Tavern, May 7–12, 1864* (1997).

B

BABCOCK, ORVILLE ELIAS
(1835–1884)
Union officer

An 1861 graduate of West Point who rose quickly in the ranks of Union officers during the Civil War, Orville E. Babcock is notable for his military success and for his close association with Ulysses S. Grant. Babcock served in a variety of capacities as a trusted aide. He was "a man in whom I have great confidence," Grant wrote later. After Grant became president, he demonstrated his confidence in Babcock by publicly defending him against charges of corruption, an act that reflected badly on Grant and his administration.

Orville Elias Babcock was born to Elias Babcock, Jr. and Clara Olmstead Babcock at Franklin, Vermont, on 25 December 1835. Upon graduation from West Point in 1861, the newly commissioned second lieutenant was given command of a company of engineers. In November 1861, he was assigned to the Army of the Potomac, and in April 1862, he was appointed a staff officer to General W. B. Franklin. Later that year, General George B. McClellan, commander of the Army of the Potomac, cited Babcock for work "splendidly done" and recommended that he be promoted. Babcock was subsequently cited for "meritorious service" in the defense of Knoxville and for "gallant conduct" at Fort Sanders, the battle of the Wilderness, and Petersburg. In 1864, Babcock was appointed acting chief for the Department of the Ohio and shortly thereafter joined General Grant's staff as an aide-de-camp.

In April 1865, when the Army of Northern Virginia moved west of Petersburg, Grant sent Babcock behind Confederate lines to deliver the terms of surrender to Robert E. Lee. Babcock reported that he discovered Lee about a half mile from Appomattox lying on the ground under an apple tree by the side of the road. One of Lee's staff officers took the summons from Babcock and handed it to Lee. After reading it, the general announced that he would accompany Babcock to meet with Grant, but Lee asked that Babcock first notify General George Meade of his decision to avoid any resumption of hostilities. Babcock agreed, asking Meade to hold back until he received orders from Grant. Lee and his secretary then rode with Babcock to Appomattox Court House, where Lee formally submitted his surrender to Grant.

On 6 June 1865, Orville Babcock was promoted to brigadier general by brevet. On 8 November 1866, Babcock married Annie Eliza Campbell at Galena, Illinois. After Grant's inauguration as president on 4 March 1869, Grant appointed Babcock his private secretary. In this capacity, Babcock became a friend of John McDonald, a supervisor of internal revenue at St. Louis. Because of their friendship, and because he and his wife had accepted expensive gifts from McDonald, Babcock was investigated and later indicted by a St. Louis grand jury for conspiracy to commit fraud. McDonald was indicted, along with other officials, as a member of the infamous Whiskey Ring. Grant shielded Babcock, protesting that Babcock was innocent of the charges, an act that caused much criticism of the president. In February 1876, Babcock was found not guilty and, for a short time, returned to his duties at the White House. But the publicity surrounding the affair, along with other scandals that were revealed, further tainted the Grant administration, and Babcock retired to private life, becoming superintendent of buildings and grounds for Washington, D.C. He later became chief engineer for lighthouse establishment in Florida, assuming responsibility for the construction of a lighthouse at Mosquito Inlet. However, on 2 June 1884, before construction could begin, Babcock was drowned when a shorebound schooner he was on overturned and sank. He was forty-nine.

—*James R. Belpedio*

See also Grant, Ulysses S.
For further reading:
Grant, Ulysses S. *Personal Memoirs of U.S. Grant* (1885).

BAGBY, GEORGE WILLIAM
(1828–1883)
Southern journalist

Born in Buckingham County, Virginia, to George Bagby and Virginia Young Evans Bagby, George William attended a variety of boarding schools and colleges before graduating in 1849 from the University of Pennsylvania Medical School. He practiced medicine only briefly, however, before entering the field of journalism. Before the Civil War he edited the Lynchburg

Virginian and the Lynchburg *Express*. Besides his editorial chores, Bagby also served as a Washington correspondent for a number of southern newspapers as well as writing numerous articles for the *Southern Literary Messenger*. For his correspondent work and the articles for the *Messenger*, Bagby was paid by the article, giving him the incentive to become one of the most prolific journalists in the South.

In 1860 Bagby took the position of editor of the *Southern Literary Messenger*. He served in that capacity for most of the war. Though Bagby wrote about the war in general, he was a Virginian, who when he was not reporting news from the front and the government, wrote primarily about Virginia for Virginians. Therefore his literary efforts were not read much beyond his own state. His most famous series during the war consisted of articles he penned under the name of Mozis Adduma, a homespun, comedic philosopher.

Because Bagby lived and worked in Richmond throughout the war, his insights were hungrily sought by a news-starved Confederacy. Therefore he served as a correspondent for several southern newspapers. He wrote for the Charleston *Mercury* under the pseudonym of "Hermes," for the Mobile *Register* as "Gamma," and the Columbus (Georgia) *Sun* as "Pan." Because of the many connections he cultivated within the Confederate government, he also wrote for newspapers in Richmond.

Bagby's reporting style was direct and often critical of the military and the Confederate government. His numerous confidential sources in the government kept him informed not only of troop movements, but also of important decisions made by President Jefferson Davis. Early in the war, Bagby became an outspoken critic of Davis and often of Davis's generals. His antagonism toward Davis's policies only grew as the war progressed. Eventually, he openly sided with Confederate vice president Alexander Stephens in the vice president's feud with Davis.

In his articles on the military, Bagby wrote mostly about the eastern theater. He became an ardent supporter of Robert E. Lee, although he was critical of the general's early actions in 1861 in what would become West Virginia. Bagby was effusive in his praise for J. E. B. Stuart when the flamboyant cavalry commander rode around George McClellan's army on the Peninsula in the spring of 1862, but was quick to criticize Stuart when the general was surprised at Brandy Station a year later. In the latter part of the war, Bagby rode the trenches outside Petersburg to observe the struggle there. The articles he wrote from the siege of that city were in high demand throughout the South.

Besides his journalistic endeavors, Bagby was technically in the Confederate army from 1861 until 1864, although his weak health kept him out of combat. He briefly served as a clerk on P. G. T. Beauregard's staff at First Bull Run, but apparently had no other serious military duties for the next three years. He left the army in 1864, the same year he resigned as the editor of the *Southern Literary Messenger*. In that year he became the associate editor of the Richmond *Whig*. His articles for the *Whig* were increasingly critical of President Davis's conduct of the war.

After the war, Bagby temporarily moved to New York City but soon returned to Virginia where he made his living as a lecturer, author, and editor. From 1870 to 1878, he also held the position of state librarian in Richmond. He became involved in Virginia politics and opposed reforms to the state government. In spite of failing eyesight, he remained a prolific author, although his works were seldom read outside his native state.

—*David S. Heidler and Jeanne T. Heidler*

See also Newspapers; *Southern Literary Messenger*.
For further reading:
Andrews, J. Cutler. *The South Reports the Civil War* (1970).
King, Joseph Leonard. *Dr. William Bagby: A Study of Virginia Literature* (1927).

BAILEY, JOSEPH
(1825–1867)
Union general

Born in Pennsville, Ohio, Joseph Bailey went with his family to Illinois while he was still a child. As an adult he moved to Wisconsin, where he became a civil engineer before the war. At the outbreak of the Civil War, Bailey was commissioned a captain in the 4th Wisconsin Cavalry.

After being mustered into federal service, the regiment went to Washington, D.C. Seeing little action in the early months of the war, Bailey and his regiment were sent to the Gulf of Mexico in the early months of 1862 to participate in the reduction of New Orleans. Once the city had fallen, Bailey became the acting chief defensive engineer for the city. In May 1863, Bailey was promoted to major; in July 1863, to lieutenant colonel. Though still a member of the 4th Wisconsin, Bailey served most of his time as an engineering officer.

As an engineer officer, Bailey was sent to Port Hudson in the summer of 1863, helping in the reduction of the town. In the spring of 1864, again on detached service from the 4th Wisconsin, Bailey accompanied the Nathaniel P. Banks's Red River expedition. Upon the retreat during this campaign, Banks and the fleet of thirty-three boats accompanying him discovered to their dismay that the water level of the river had fallen since their earlier passage and that the boats could not move over the shoaled areas. While most of the engineers on the trip believed the situation hopeless and that the boats would have to be destroyed, Bailey convinced the senior officers to allow him to construct wing dams to raise the water level at the shoals. Using several thousand soldiers as laborers, Bailey constructed the dams and was able to save the boats. For his actions, Congress voted Bailey its thanks, one of only fifteen officers to receive such an honor. In May 1864 Bailey was promoted colonel of the 4th Wisconsin.

He did not have the opportunity to enjoy his new command for he was again detached and made the commander of the Engineering Brigade of XIX Corps, Department of the Gulf. He commanded this brigade, made up almost entirely of African-American troops, in the Mobile Bay campaign of September 1864. Bailey was commended for his bravery and initiative in this campaign.

In October 1864, Bailey was the commander of the District of West Florida and then briefly commanded the District of Baton Rouge at the end of the year before finally being given command of a cavalry division in the Department of the Gulf. In November 1864 Bailey was promoted to brigadier general. Several times, however, in the last months of the war, Bailey's engineering skills gained him detached duty as an engineer.

In May 1865, Bailey fulfilled his last important military duty. As the commander of the 2d Brigade of the 2d Cavalry Division, Department of the Gulf, Bailey and his division were sent from Alabama to Baton Rouge. During this ride, Bailey and his men were to determine the extent, if any, of continued Confederate military activity in that area and the attitude of the civilian population. Bailey's determination was that there was no longer any military activity in the area and that the civilian morale was so low that they could present no threat to Union authority.

Bailey resigned his volunteer commission on 7 July 1865 and returned to civilian life. He moved to Missouri, where he became the sheriff of Vernon County in 1866. He was killed near Nevada, Missouri, by two miscreants he had arrested on 21 March 1867.

—*David S. Heidler and Jeanne T. Heidler*

See also Mobile Bay; Red River Campaign.
For further reading:
Cron, Frederick William. "Colonel Bailey's Red River Dams." In *The Military Engineer* (1937).

BAILEY, THEODORUS
(1805–1877)
Union naval officer

In his nearly fifty-year career in the U.S. Navy, Theodorus Bailey rose from midshipman to rear admiral and served in a wide variety of assignments before, during, and after the Civil War. He is perhaps best remembered for his role in the capture of New Orleans—and particularly as one of two officers sent to demand the city's surrender—and subsequently as commander of the one of the navy's wartime blockading squadrons.

Bailey was born near Plattsburgh, New York, on 12 April 1805 and was educated at Plattsburgh Academy. His father was a judge and his mother was prominent in local society. In addition, Bailey's uncle had served in both the U.S. House of Representatives and the Senate. These political and social connections enabled him to receive a midshipman's commission in January 1818.

The young officer first served on the *Cyane* off Africa and in the West Indies before being assigned to the Pacific Squadron's *Franklin* in 1821. During the next forty years he served on a number of ships and in different positions ashore. These included duty on board the schooner *Shark* in the West Indies, on the receiving ship *Fulton*, and aboard the warships *Natchez* and *Vincennes*. While serving on the latter vessel, Bailey rounded Cape Horn, stopped at various Pacific islands, and eventually circumnavigated the globe.

After recruiting duty and service at the New York Navy Yard, Bailey sailed on the USS *Constellation* in the East Indies Squadron. During the Mexican-American War he commanded the *Lexington* as it transported troops to California and conducted blockade duty. Having previously risen to the rank of lieutenant, Bailey was promoted to commander in 1849 and to captain six years later. Bailey would subsequently command the *St. Mary's* and serve in the Pacific Squadron until 1856, when he began a five-year leave of absence. His distinguished antebellum career had earned Bailey a reputation as one of the more experienced and capable officers in the U.S. Navy.

Upon the outbreak of the Civil War, Captain Bailey took command of the frigate *Colorado*, which was assigned to the West Gulf Blockading Squadron. His ship helped defend Union-occupied Fort Pickens near Pensacola, Florida, and Bailey organized an expedition to capture a Confederate privateer in Pensacola Bay. In the spring of 1862, after commanding the *Colorado* while it performed blockade duty near the mouth of the Mississippi, Bailey was selected by David Farragut to assist in the Union attack against Forts Jackson and St. Philip, below New Orleans. The *Colorado* drew too much water to cross over the bar at the mouth of the Mississippi, so Bailey transferred his flag to the gunboat *Cayuga*. He led Farragut's 1st Division during the 24 April 1862 attack that successfully breached a chain barrier across the river, passed the forts, and dueled with a small fleet of Confederate gunboats. His ships then bombarded the Southern batteries at Chalmette and, by the morning of 25 April, had reached New Orleans with the rest of Farragut's fleet. Early that afternoon, Farragut sent Bailey ashore to receive the city's surrender. A large, pro-Confederate crowd had assembled at the wharf and hurled insults at Bailey and another Union officer who had accompanied him when they stepped ashore. The two officers, "unguarded and alone, looking not to the right or to left, never frowning, never flinching, while the mob screamed in their ears," walked to City Hall, where they demanded the city's surrender. "It was one of the bravest deeds I ever saw done" commented a southern onlooker.

After the surrender of New Orleans, Farragut sent Bailey to Washington, D.C., to convey the reports of his operations against the city. In failing health, Bailey recuperated while in command of the naval station at Sackets Harbor, New York. In November 1862, Bailey received an appointment as acting rear admiral and was assigned to command of the East Gulf Blockading Squadron (EGBS), which was responsible for the blockade of Florida from Cape Canaveral on the Atlantic coast to St. Andrew's Bay in the Gulf of Mexico. The veteran officer remained in this position, with his headquarters at Key West, until August 1864. Florida's long, shallow coastline and its proximity to Cuba and the Bahamas presented a number of difficulties for the Union blockading fleet. While the EGBS could often maintain fewer than 20 ships on patrol, it still managed to capture or destroy 283 Confederate vessels attempting to run the blockade. Of these, 150 were taken during Bailey's tenure. The EGBS also conducted numerous raids along the coast to destroy rebel saltworks, provided supplies to Florida unionists, and assisted in the formation of a regiment known as the 2d Florida Union Cavalry.

Assigned in September 1864 to command of the Portsmouth Navy Yard, Bailey saw no further active service during the war. He was formally promoted to rear admiral in July 1866, and, in poor health, he retired three months later. In his retirement, the veteran naval officer lived in Washington, D.C., and served on a number of naval boards. He died on 10 February 1877.

—David J. Coles

See also Blockade of C.S.A.; New Orleans, Capture of.
For further reading:
Buker, George E. *Blockaders, Refugees, & Contrabands: Civil War on Florida's Gulf Coast, 1861–1865* (1993).
Coles, David J. "Unpretending Service: The *James L. Davis*, the *Tahoma*, and the East Gulf Blockading Squadron." *Florida Historical Quarterly* (1992).
Hearn, Chester G. *The Capture of New Orleans, 1862* (1995).
Katcher, Philip R.N. "Union Captain Theodorus Bailey Faced Down an Angry Southern Mob to Take Command of New Orleans." In *America's Civil War* (2000).

BAIRD, ABSALOM
(1824–1905)
Union general

Born to William Baird and Nancy Mitchell Baird in Washington, Pennsylvania, Absalom Baird was educated at Washington College, after which he accepted an appointment to the United States Military Academy in 1845. He graduated ninth of forty-three in the class of 1849. Upon graduation he was commissioned into the artillery and sent to Florida during the difficulties there that preceded the Third Seminole War. Upon leaving Florida, he returned to West Point where he served as an instructor. Following his stint at the Academy, Baird was transferred to the Department of Texas.

The outbreak of the Civil War found him in Washington, D.C., as a lieutenant, 1st Artillery, where he accepted the position of adjutant general to Brigadier General Daniel Tyler. He served in that capacity with Tyler's division at Blackburn's Ford on 18 July 1861 and a few days later at First Bull Run.

In November 1861 Baird was promoted to major and made assistant inspector general. In that job he was responsible for mustering into United States service many of the volunteers who made their way to Washington. In preparation for the Peninsula campaign in the spring of 1862, Baird became chief of staff and inspector general for IV Corps, Army of the Potomac, commanded by Erasmus Keyes.

Baird traveled to the Peninsula where he participated in the siege of Yorktown and the subsequent battle of Williamsburg. In the midst of the campaign, on 28 April 1862, he was promoted to brigadier general. Shortly thereafter he was transferred to the Army of the Ohio to take a field command.

In command of the 27th Brigade Baird was part of the force in June 1862 that took control of Cumberland Gap. He remained at Cumberland Gap through the summer. Following evacuation from that position in September, Baird was sent to the Army of Kentucky, where he commanded a brigade under Gordon Granger in the campaign against Braxton Bragg. He remained there, using his brigade to guard strategic points against Confederate cavalry, until February 1863 when he was sent to Nashville, Tennessee. Later in the spring he took command of a division in the Army of the Cumberland.

Baird commanded the reserve division in the Tullahoma campaign, after which he was given command of a division in the Army of the Cumberland's XIV Corps commanded by George H. Thomas. He commanded that division during the Chickamauga campaign, where he occupied a strategic point on the Horseshoe Ridge. His division suffered very heavy casualties on 19 September. The following day Baird and his depleted division held their ground against furious Confederate assaults and remained to guard the withdrawal of the remainder of the corps. The army's commander, William S. Rosecrans, and Thomas commended him for the gallantry he displayed during the battle, and Rosecrans recommended his promotion to major general of volunteers.

During the Chattanooga campaign in October–November 1863 Baird displayed the same courage and initiative that had won him recognition at Chickamauga. On 25 November 1863 Baird and his division participated in the attack on Missionary Ridge. Again George Thomas commended his courage, and Ulysses S. Grant recommended his promotion to major general of volunteers.

In early 1864 Baird commanded his division in north Georgia where he fought at the demonstration against Dalton, Georgia, 22–27 February. He continued to skirmish with Confederates in north Georgia through the early spring of 1864 and then led his division in the Atlanta campaign.

Baird fought in all the major engagements of the Atlanta campaign, especially distinguishing himself at Resaca, Kennesaw Mountain, and Peachtree Creek. Toward the end of the campaign at the battle of Jonesboro, Baird led a successful brigade charge against a heavily defended Confederate position. In 1896 he received the Medal of Honor for his actions in that battle.

After the fall of Atlanta, Baird led his division in pursuit of John Bell Hood before returning to Atlanta to participate in William T. Sherman's March to the Sea. He continued in command of his division through the Carolina campaign and was present at the surrender of Joseph Johnston. In June 1865 George Thomas again recommended Baird for promotion to major general of volunteers, but though he had been breveted to that rank in September 1864, none of the many recommendations for his actual promotion were acted on.

During the immediate postwar period, Baird served in the Freedmen's Bureau. Upon being mustered out of the volunteer army, he reverted to major and again took up the duties of an assistant adjutant general. Over the next nineteen years he served at a variety of posts in the role of inspector general, gradually rising in rank. In 1885 he became inspector general of the army at the rank of brigadier general. He traveled to France in 1887 to observe that country's army on maneuvers. He retired to his home in Relay, Maryland, a year later. Baird lived quietly in retirement, dying at home on 14 June 1905. His remains were interred at Arlington.

—*David S. Heidler and Jeanne T. Heidler*

See also Chickamauga; Jonesboro; Missionary Ridge.

For further reading:

Baird, John A. *Profile of a Hero: The Story of Absalom Baird, His Family, and the American Military Tradition* (1977).

Bowers, John. *Chickamauga and Chattanooga: The Battles That Doomed the Confederacy* (1994).

Cozzens, Peter. *This Terrible Sound: The Battle of Chickamauga* (1992).

BAKER, EDWARD DICKINSON
(1811–1861)
U.S. senator and officer

Edward Baker was born in London, England. His family moved to the United States in 1815, and Baker spent the next ten years of his life in Philadelphia before his family moved to Indiana and then Illinois. While still a teenager, Baker studied law and was admitted to the Illinois bar at the age of nineteen. At twenty-four, Baker moved to Springfield, Illinois, where he became over the next seventeen years a prominent attorney and political figure. During his time in Springfield, Baker became close friends with another rising young lawyer, Abraham Lincoln. Abraham and Mary Lincoln named their second son after their close friend Baker.

In his early political life, Baker was a Whig, although he did not always follow the party line. At the age of twenty-six, Baker entered the Illinois legislature and served two terms in the lower house before moving to the state senate in 1840. In 1844 he defeated his good friend Lincoln for the district's Whig nomination to the U.S. House of Representatives and won the election. While in the House beginning in 1845, Baker broke party ranks by supporting the expansionist policies of President James K. Polk.

At the outbreak of the Mexican-American War, Baker traveled from Washington to Illinois to raise a regiment. He became colonel of the regiment and took it to serve under Zachary Taylor in northern Mexico. Baker returned briefly to Congress at the end of 1846 and, wearing his uniform, urged the Congress to vote more funds for the maintenance of soldiers at the front.

Shortly after the beginning of 1847, Baker resigned his congressional seat and joined Winfield Scott's Mexico City campaign. From April through September 1847, Baker fought in all the major battles of the war and commanded a brigade at one point.

After the Mexican-American War, Baker returned to Illinois, where he moved to another congressional district and was elected to Congress. In 1851 Baker left Congress and the following year moved to California. Baker's Whig and then Republican affiliations meant that he would have little political future in heavily Democratic California. He became, however, a popular local attorney in San Francisco and, in spite of his politics, was much in demand as a public speaker.

His political future bleak in California, Baker accepted the invitation of Oregon Republicans to move to that state and run for the U.S. Senate in 1860. Baker did so and won the election. As senator-elect from Oregon and the only Republican senator from the West Coast, Baker made it a personal crusade to encourage those states, particularly California, to stay in the Union. Some people later credited him with saving the heavily Democratic state for the United States.

On his way to Washington after his visit to California, Baker stopped in Springfield to meet with President-elect Lincoln. Over the next several months, Baker made several stirring speeches urging support for the Union. He refused the offer of a brigadier general's commission because any commission at the general rank would require him to resign his Senate seat. Therefore, when offered the colonelcy of the 71st Pennsylvania (sometimes referred to as the 1st California because of Baker's ties to the West Coast), he accepted. Throughout the summer of 1861, Baker divided his time between training his regiment and serving in the U.S. Senate.

In August 1861, Baker commanded a brigade along the Potomac, though he remained at the rank of colonel. On 28 September 1861, Baker commanded his brigade at a skirmish near Munson's Hill, Virginia. A week earlier he had been offered a major general's commission but was apparently still considering it and had made no reply.

On 21 October, Baker's commander Brigadier General Charles P. Stone ordered Baker to demonstrate against Confederates across the Potomac near Poolesville. At Ball's Bluff, without careful reconnaissance, Baker moved across the river into a trap. He was killed, and most of his command were killed or captured. He had never replied to the offer of a major general's commission.

The president deeply mourned the loss of his friend, but the most lasting impact of the debacle was the persecution of Charles Stone. Many blamed Stone for the popular Baker's death. That Stone was a Democrat did not help his cause. He was called before the Committee on the Conduct of the War and eventually arrested without charge. He was imprisoned for 189 days and never held an important command for the remainder of the war.

—*David S. Heidler and Jeanne T. Heidler*

See also Ball's Bluff; California; Joint Committee on the Conduct of the War; Stone, Charles Pomeroy.
For further reading:
Blair, Harry C., and Rebecca Tarshis. *The Life of Colonel Edward D. Baker, Lincoln's Constant Ally, Together with Four of His Great Orations* (1960).
Farwell, Byron. *Ball's Bluff: A Small Battle and Its Long Shadow* (1990).

BAKER, LA FAYETTE CURRY
(1826–1868)
Union general

Born in Stafford, New York, the son of Remember Baker, La Fayette Curry Baker moved with his family to Michigan while still a child. As an adult, he traveled the country as a handyman, living for a time in San Francisco, where he claimed later to have served as one of the city's famous vigilantes. At the outbreak of the Civil War, Baker lived in New York, but quickly offered his services to the government in Washington as a spy.

U.S. commanding general Winfield Scott employed Baker in the summer of 1861, sending him to Richmond to spy on the Confederate government. While there, Baker apparently convinced Confederate officials that he would spy on the Federal government for them. His audacity won him a place in the Union government as a detective.

In the fall of 1861, Baker investigated suspected disloyal persons in Maryland, Pennsylvania, and New York. In October he traveled to Niagara Falls to prevent the movement of Confederates from across the border in Canada into the United States.

Over the next year, Baker engaged in a variety of spy and courier missions for the Union government. Given Baker's penchant for embellishing or even fabricating his role in most activities, it is still difficult to separate fact from fiction in his own writings.

The trust that high-ranking officials such as William Henry Seward and Edwin Stanton placed in Baker encouraged him to usurp power. In February 1862, Baker asked permission to arrest Senator Jesse Bright of Indiana should the Senate expel the contentious Democrat. It does seem certain that during the war—especially starting in 1862 when he was appointed special provost marshal for the War Department—Baker began to take bribes for looking the other way on certain matters. Consequently, he became one of the most corrupt government officials in Washington, which was no mean feat in a city known for widespread corruption.

On 5 May 1863, Baker received a colonel's commission with command of the 1st District of Columbia Cavalry. While still engaged in spy missions, Baker also patrolled the periphery of the city to detect Confederate raids. In October 1863, his regiment skirmished with John Singleton Mosby's Raiders near Fairfax Court House.

In July 1864, Baker traveled west to St. Louis to investigate suspected disloyal persons there. The city had experienced a rash of arson, and to make matters worse for the government, a counterfeit ring was apparently operating in the area. Baker reported back to Washington that he believed an organization existed in the western states bent on the overthrow of the Federal government by destroying Federal property and undermining the currency.

The following year, when Abraham Lincoln was assassinated, Baker was in New York. He received an urgent telegram from Secretary of War Stanton on 15 April asking him to return to Washington to apprehend the assassin. Baker took command of a 25-man contingent to track down the killer or killers and was personally in command when John Wilkes Booth was located and killed. Baker was promoted to brigadier general dating from 26 April, the date of Booth's death.

By that time, Baker's effective tracking of Booth and the apprehension of the other alleged conspirators could not blunt congressional alarm that Baker had become a power unto himself, and a corrupt one. For that reason, Congress reduced Baker's reward for the death of Booth and the capture of the other conspirators to $3,750 from

$17,500. Baker's fortunes continued to slide when he was fired by President Andrew Johnson.

Baker tried to exact some revenge on Johnson by testifying at the impeachment hearings, but could produce no evidence against the president. In 1867 Baker published his memoirs, but it is difficult to discern what is true in this very colorful account of his adventures. He died the following year on 3 July 1868 in Philadelphia, but by then he had provided an even more enduring and dubious legacy. During Johnson's impeachment controversy, Baker embarrassed the government by revealing the existence of the diary that had been taken from Booth after his capture. The small notebook, which had been in Stanton's possession, was now produced with several pages missing. Conspiracy theorists eventually would use the allegedly expurgated Booth diary to bolster their claims that the U.S. government was behind the Lincoln assassination.

—*David S. Heidler and Jeanne T. Heidler*

See also Espionage; Lincoln Assassination.
For further reading:
Mogelever, Jacob. *Death to Traitors; The Story of General Lafayette C. Baker, Lincoln's Forgotten Secret Service Chief* (1960).
Orrmont, Arthur. *Mr. Lincoln's Master Spy: Lafayette Baker* (1966).

BALDWIN, JOHN BROWN
(1820–1873)

Confederate officer and congressman

John Baldwin was born to Briscoe G. Baldwin and Martha Brown Baldwin near Staunton in Augusta County, Virginia, and educated at the Staunton Military Academy and the University of Virginia before studying law and opening a practice in Staunton. Besides practicing law, Baldwin was an active Whig in Virginia politics. He served one term in the Virginia House of Delegates.

As the sectional crisis intensified in 1860, Baldwin opposed secession. As a member of the Virginia convention, he voted against the ordinance of secession and served as delegate to Washington to confer with Abraham Lincoln regarding a peaceful solution to the crisis. When Virginia seceded after the Sumter crisis and Lincoln's subsequent call for volunteers, Baldwin offered his services to the state.

Appointed by Governor John Letcher to be inspector general of Virginia with the rank of colonel in May 1861, Baldwin's primary duty was the supervision of the mustering in of Virginia troops. Later in the summer, he was made the commander of the 52nd Virginia Infantry, which became part of the Confederate Army of Northwestern Virginia. Stationed at Alleghany Mountain, Baldwin complained bitterly in the fall about the difficulty of obtaining supplies in the area. He even

took the liberty of bypassing the military chain of command by writing directly to Secretary of War Judah Benjamin about his men's plight. Baldwin commanded the 52nd through the fall, seeing some action, but ill health led him to accept the candidacy from Augusta County for its seat in the Confederate Congress. Baldwin won the election and resigned his commission to take his seat.

Serving in the First and Second Confederate Congresses, Baldwin, although considering himself a strong supporter of the war effort and early on in his career there accepting most of the recommendations of President Jefferson Davis, increasingly came to object to what he saw as violations of states' rights and personal property rights by the Confederate government. In November 1862, he complained about the seizure of civilian flour by the army. Temporarily mollified by the explanation that the price paid for the flour in question had been agreed to by the millers and the officers on the scene, Baldwin remained for the most part an administration supporter during his first term in Congress.

Baldwin's second term, however, was another matter. He joined a growing chorus of critics who believed that the government was putting an unnecessary burden on the civilian population through excessive seizures of foodstuffs, and he also criticized the government for the repeated suspension of the writ of habeas corpus in certain areas. Still his main concern remained food, particularly in Virginia. He argued that the government could more efficiently use requisitioned slave labor in harvesting food rather than in building military fortifications, and he warned that if the government continued to take civilian food, riots and civil unrest would result.

After the war, Baldwin returned to Staunton and his practice, but also retained his interest in politics. He was elected by his district to the Virginia House of Delegates in 1865 and served as that body's speaker and the architect of its rules of procedure. He continued to be active in state and national politics, serving as a Virginia delegate to the 1868 Democratic National Convention. Increasingly poor health caused him to withdraw from public life, and he died near Staunton on 30 September 1873.

—*David S. Heidler and Jeanne T. Heidler*

See also Congress, C.S.A.; Habeas Corpus, Writ of (C.S.A.).
For further reading:
Curry, Charles. *John Brown Baldwin: Lawyer, Soldier, Statesman* (1928).

BALLOONS

Both Union and Confederate forces used balloons for observation and intelligence gathering during the early part of the Civil War. Ballooning was an established practice before the Civil War. A regular balloon unit, the Ier Compagnie d'Aerostiers, was created during the French Revolution, and balloons were used for military reconnaissance during the battle of Fleurus in 1794. President Washington attended a balloon ascent in 1793 by French aeronaut Jean Blanchard.

With clear signs of approaching hostilities, several individuals approached the U.S. War Department in early 1861, suggesting the formation of a balloon corps that would use their balloons for battlefield observations. Principal among these aspiring military aeronauts were Thaddeus Lowe, John Wise, and John La Mountain.

Thaddeus Sobieski Constantine Lowe became interested in using balloons for military intelligence gathering. Lowe had been ballooning for several years and on 20 April 1861, while practicing for an Atlantic crossing, set a distance record of more than 900 miles in nine hours when he left Cincinnati, Ohio, and ended near Unionville, South Carolina. After being jailed twice by Carolinians who thought he was a Yankee spy, Lowe luckily received aid from some local academic admirers and made his way by train back to Ohio.

Lowe had previously solicited the aid of the Smithsonian Institution in sponsoring him in his endeavors to cross the Atlantic. A committee of Philadelphians had written the secretary of the Smithsonian, Professor Joseph Henry, in December 1860 requesting "aid and advice" for Lowe in his attempt to cross the Atlantic.

On 5 June 1861, Lowe took his balloon, the *Enterprise*, to Washington and again solicited the aid of Professor Henry to convince the government of its military usefulness. Henry had several communications with President Lincoln, Secretary of War Simon Cameron, and several senior officers of the Topographical Engineers, recommending Lowe's balloon for military use. On 18 June 1861, with the help of Henry, Lowe demonstrated his balloon by lifting off from the Columbian Armory in Washington. The balloon was inflated with "street gas" from one of the gas mains on the armory grounds, and Lowe made several ascensions from the armory, the Smithsonian grounds, and the south lawn of the White House. Lowe was equipped with telegraphic equipment and an operator provided by the American Telegraph Company. Lowe telegraphed to President Lincoln:

Balloon Enterprise, June 1[8], 1861
To the President of the United States:
Sir;
This Point of observation commands an area nearly 50 miles in diameter. The city, with its girdle of encampments, presents a superb scene. I have pleasure in sending you this first dispatch ever telegraphed from an aerial station, and in acknowledging indebtedness for your encouragement for the

opportunity of demonstrating the availability of the science of aeronautics in the military service of the country.

On 21 June, Professor Henry sent a report of the trial to Secretary Cameron detailing the technical aspects. He included the facts that the balloon could stay inflated for three days, be towed by a few men over fields, be let up by ropes, and serve as a platform for telegraphic communications. Henry also commented that Lowe's balloon could only be used in a city where "street gas" could be obtained. Otherwise, it would require a device for generating gas if the balloon was to be deployed at a distance beyond that to which it could be towed. Henry also requested that Lowe be reimbursed $250 for his expenses to conduct the trials. The same day Henry filed his report, Captain A. W. Whipple, Topographical Engineers, directed Lowe by telegram to take his balloon to Arlington. Lowe complied and later moved the balloon to Falls Church where he made a number of observations. The balloon was also used to send several engineering officers aloft and some panoramic sketches were made of the surrounding countryside.

On 26 June, Lowe was distressed to hear that Whipple had decided to order a balloon from John Wise because Wise's estimate for construction was $200 less than that proposed by Lowe. Whipple indicated that Lowe might be retained to operate the balloon, but Lowe was indignant and told Whipple that he would not be willing to risk his life by using a machine "made by a person in whom I had no confidence."

John Wise was an experienced aeronaut from Lancaster, Pennsylvania, who had made his first flight in 1835. Wise received a contract from Whipple to provide a balloon for use by the Bureau of Topographical Engineers. Lowe attempted to obtain gas for his balloon to move it toward the impending battle on his own accord. When the director of the gas company informed Lowe that Wise's balloon was to be used instead, Lowe removed his balloon from the gas pipes. Major Albert Myer, chief signal officer of the army, transported the Wise balloon toward the battle with a detachment of twenty men from the 26th Pennsylvania Infantry. Due to Myer's impatience once he heard the sounds of the battle, the balloon was attached directly to a wagon and the mules whipped to a trot. The balloon soon became tangled in trees and was abandoned. Whipple later directed Lowe to move his balloon to Manassas where he made significant observations of troop positions after the battle.

Lowe's other significant competitor was John La Mountain from Troy, New York. La Mountain had teamed with John Wise in 1859 and had taken a trip in a balloon named the *Atlantic*, departing from St. Louis and landing near Henderson, New York, in less than

The balloon *Intrepid* being inflated during the battle of Fair Oaks, Virginia, 31 May 1862. (*National Archives*)

twenty-four hours. The feat had set a distance record for a nonstop flight, but it had also resulted in the end of the partnership between Wise and La Mountain.

La Mountain, like Lowe, had contacted the War Department offering his services as an aeronaut. La Mountain did not receive an initial response, but in June 1861 he was invited to demonstrate his balloon at Fort Monroe by Major General George Benjamin Butler. La Mountain made several flights from Fort Monroe in his balloon *Atlantic*, and after a flight on August 10 he reported to Butler:

I attained an altitude of 3,500 feet, and made observations as follows: About 5 or 6 miles northwest of Hampton I discovered an encampment of the enemy, but owing to the misty state of the atmosphere, caused by the recent rain, I was unable to form a correct idea of their numerical force, but should judge from 4,000 to 5,000. There were no vessels or encampments of any kind either at York or Back Rivers or at New Market Bridge.

La Mountain later made an ascent in his balloon from the Union ship *Fanny* at Hampton Roads to observe Confederate batteries on Sewell's Point, Virginia.

La Mountain continued making observations without an official sponsorship, but he entered into an acrimonious relationship with Lowe after Lowe was given an official position. The two battled in the media and through their various military champions. At one point, Lowe was directed by the Topographical Engineers to surrender one of his balloons for La Mountain's use. The dispute ended on 19 February 1862, when Major General McClellan ordered that La Mountain's services would no longer be used.

On 29 June 1861 Whipple wrote Lowe that he should repair his balloon and the Topographical Engineers would employ his services for $30 per day on the days that he went aloft. Lowe replied that he would serve for $10 per day if the army would instruct him to construct a new balloon designed specifically for military purposes. On 2 August Whipple complied and directed Lowe to construct a balloon that contained at least 25,000 cubic feet of gas, made of the "best India silk." Lowe completed construction of his new balloon on 28 August, and the balloon went aloft the next day. Lowe made observations of the Confederates building earthworks on Munson's Hill and Clark's Hill. Lowe's balloon quickly became popular with senior officers and several went aloft with Lowe, including Brigadier Generals Fitz John Porter and

Irvin McDowell. On 7 September Major General George McClellan went up and examined the enemy's works.

On 25 September, Lowe received an order for four more balloons and gas generators for use by the Army of the Potomac. Two of the balloons were to be smaller because Lowe had recommended smaller balloons for bad weather. He received $1,500 each for the larger ones and $1,200 for the smaller versions. They were constructed from silk and coated with varnish. The larger ones, *Intrepid* and *Union*, were filled with "coal gas" and the smaller ones, *Washington* and *Constitution*, were filled with hydrogen.

In March 1862 the responsibility for Lowe's balloons was transferred from the Topographical Engineers to the Quartermaster Department. Lowe was ordered to transport his balloons to Fort Monroe to support operations on the peninsula, and he shipped his balloon to Fort Monroe on the steamer *Hugh Jenkins*. Lowe's balloons were used frequently to make observations of the Confederates at Yorktown. Numerous general officers

Thaddeus S. Lowe observing the battle of Fair Oaks from the *Intrepid*. (*National Archives*)

and their staffs and guests, including the Comte de Paris, ascended in the balloons for observations. Brigadier General Fitz John Porter made over one hundred such flights. Lowe recalled in his report that Porter made one flight by himself aided on the ground by one of Lowe's assistants. Instead of the three or four ropes Lowe normally used, a single rope tethered the general. When that rope broke, Porter in free flight released all the gas in his eagerness to get down. The deflated balloon descended like a parachute, but the experience left Porter wary of future flights in Lowe's balloons.

Lowe frequently used the telegraph to relay his observations from the balloon without descending. On the morning of 4 May Lowe telegraphed McClellan that Yorktown had been evacuated by the Confederates. Lowe made numerous flights from the banks of the Chickahominy River and on several occasions took Brigadier General George Stoneman aloft for observations. Lowe and Stoneman could see Richmond from the Chickahominy and later learned that the citizens of Richmond had observed the balloon. A Richmond paper reported:

> The enemy are fast making their appearance on the banks of the Chickahominy. Yesterday they had a balloon in the air the whole day, it being witnessed by many of our citizens from the streets and house tops. They evidently discovered something of importance to them, for at about 4 P.M. a brisk cannonading was heard at Mechanicsville and the Yankees now occupy that place.

Lowe continued to make frequent flights during the Peninsula campaign. The Balloon Department's services were particularly noteworthy during the battle of Fair Oaks. At one point, Lowe attempted to ascend in the small balloon *Constitution*, but the weight of his telegraph equipment would not allow him to obtain the proper height. He descended and attempted to inflate the larger balloon *Intrepid*. Faced with losing more than an hour to inflating the large balloon, Lowe seized upon the idea of transferring gas from the *Constitution* to the *Intrepid*. After instructing soldiers to cut the bottom out of a camp kettle, Lowe used it to connect the two balloons and transferred the gas, thus allowing him to make a timely ascent to a sufficient height in the *Intrepid*.

The Confederates were less successful in their attempts to use balloons for observations. The first attempt was a hot air balloon constructed by a novice. A more successful attempt was the "Silk Dress Balloon." This balloon was constructed of multicolored bolts of dress silk. The only gas available for this balloon was in Richmond, so it had to be towed inflated to the battlefield. It was captured by a Federal gunship on 4 July 1862 while tethered to a barge on the James River. A second

"Silk Dress Balloon" was tethered over Richmond until it was lost in a storm.

During the Peninsula campaign, Lowe became ill in late June with malaria and remained incapacitated until early September. He continued to support the Army of the Potomac under its subsequent commanders performing numerous observations at Fredericksburg under Major General Ambrose Burnside. Lowe also played a significant role at Chancellorsville supporting Major General Joseph Hooker, but he never gained the favor with Burnside and Hooker that he had enjoyed with McClellan. A review of the correspondence by Hooker concerning the Balloon Corps during 1862 reveals a general mistrust of the service on his part. The demise of the Balloon Department began with its transfer from the Quartermaster Department to the Corps of Engineers. Captain C. E. Comstock, Corps of Engineers, was placed in control of the "Balloon Establishment" and became Lowe's immediate supervisor.

One of Comstock's first actions was to reduce Lowe's compensation from $10 to $6 per day. Lowe was incensed and protested in a letter to the chief of staff, Major General Daniel Butterfield, only to be rebuked for not using the chain of command, which meant sending his complaint through Comstock. Lowe had previously experienced difficulties in accounting for supplies and equipment and his civilian status had caused him difficulties in the Army of the Potomac. The pay reduction, and Comstock's dismissal of Lowe's father, who had worked for him since the Peninsula campaign, was the last straw. He served until the end of the battle of Chancellorsville and then resigned his position on 8 May 1863.

James and Ezra Allen, who had worked for Lowe as assistants, replaced him for a time. The Allens had similar difficulties with lack of authority and complained to Lowe in a letter shortly before the Balloon Department was disbanded:

> Since you left the army of the Potomac, we have endeavored as you requested, to make this branch of the service as efficient as possible, but to accomplish what was done when you were in charge is simply impossible under the present management, and I fear that things will soon be in such a condition that when an important observation is wanted, it cannot be had.

In July 1863 control of the Balloon Corps was offered to Colonel Albert Myer, Chief Signal Officer, but he declined it. The Balloon Corps was disbanded in August 1863. Balloons eventually reentered service in 1892 when the Signal Corps purchased a balloon for observation from a French company. It was christened the *General Myer* in honor of the first chief signal officer who happened to be the officer responsible for snagging the army's first balloon in the trees en route to the Bull Run battlefield.

—*Bill Cameron*

See also Lowe, Thaddeus.

For further reading:
Brown, J. Willard. *The Signal Corps, U.S.A. in the War of the Rebellion* (1896).
Evans, Charles M. "Air War Over Virginia." *Civil War Times* (1996).
Haydon, F. Stansbury. *Aeronautics in the Union and Confederate Armies with a Survey of Military Aeronautics Prior to 1861* (1941).
Lowe, T. S. C. "The Balloons with the Army of the Potomac." In *The Photographic History of the Civil War*, vol. 4 (1987).
———. "Report of Operations." Official Records, Series III, vol. I.
Raines, Rebecca Robbins. *Getting the Message Through, A Branch History of the U.S. Army Signal Corps* (1996).
Scheips, Paul J. "Union Signal Communications: Innovation and Conflict." *Civil War History* (1963).

BALL'S BLUFF, BATTLE OF
(21 October 1861)

Ball's Bluff was a small battle by the standards of the Civil War, but it had ramifications far beyond its size. It was only the second significant battle in the east, and received a great deal of attention in both North and South. Edward Baker, a senator from Oregon and close personal friend and political ally of President Lincoln, was killed during the battle and became a martyr to those who took a hard line against the Confederacy. Perhaps most importantly, the defeat spurred the creation of the Joint Committee on the Conduct of the War by Congress; the Committee became a persecutor of those who were considered to be soft on defeating the Confederacy and destroying slavery.

George McClellan took command of Union forces around Washington, D.C., in the wake of the defeat at Bull Run in July 1861. He immediately set about training and improving the state of his army. As the good campaigning weather of fall 1861 passed, however, he began to feel pressure to advance on the Rebel forces just across the Potomac River from Washington. Probes and raids by Yankee forces over the Potomac combined intelligence gathering with training. On 19 October McClellan ordered General George McCall to conduct a reconnaissance toward the village of Dranesville, Virginia, covering a topographical survey in the area. McClellan alerted neighboring commander General Charles P. Stone of the movement and told him to keep a vigilant watch on the town of Leesburg; if the Rebels evacuated it, he could move in. A "light demonstration" on Stone's part would help move them on.

Stone moved one brigade to the Potomac opposite Leesburg. When an inexperienced scouting party crossed into Virginia during the night of 20 October, it mistook

Death of Colonel Edward Baker at Ball's Bluff, from an 1862 engraving (*Library of Congress*)

shadows for an unguarded Confederate camp. Stone ordered Colonel Charles Devens and 300 men to make a dawn attack. If no other Confederate forces were found, Devens was to stay on the Virginia side and conduct a further reconnaissance. When Devens found no camp, he pushed on to Leesburg, which he found empty of enemy troops. Devens requested reinforcements so that he could hold Leesburg.

When Stone ordered additional troops to join Devens, only three boats were available to ferry soldiers to the Virginia side and so movement was slow. Colonel Edward Baker was ordered to take command of the larger force, totaling 1,640 men. Baker was an inexperienced soldier, but he was also an old Illinois friend of President Abraham Lincoln. Lincoln, in fact, had named his second son after Baker. After he had moved west, Baker was elected senator from Oregon. He had turned down a commission as brigadier general, because it would require his resignation from the Senate. An outspoken enemy of any who would compromise with the slaveholding South, he looked forward to an opportunity to prove his point in battle.

Baker ordered his men to form a line of battle in a clearing near the river. Immediately in the rear of his position was the 100-foot Ball's Bluff; a single narrow path led down to the Potomac. More experienced officers worried about a wooded ridge immediately in front of Baker's line. Confederates on that height would be able to shoot down at the Union soldiers in the clearing below.

Actually, Confederate units under the command of Colonel Nathan "Shanks" Evans were slowly arriving on the battlefield and exchanging shots with the Yankees. At 3:00 P.M. the Confederates launched a general assault on the four Union regiments at Ball's Bluff. Soon, Evans's 1,600 Rebel soldiers in wooded cover were pouring shot into Baker's forces in the open. For three and one-half hours, the Union soldiers held on. Baker was killed around 5:00 P.M. Unable to stand the fire and unable to retreat in an orderly manner, the Yankee formation began to crumble. Some leaped off the bluff in an attempt to reach the river, and many were killed or injured by the fall. Others climbed safely down Ball's Bluff, but the few boats were swamped by the numbers trying to regain the Maryland side. As the Confederates fired down from the top of the bluff, boats sank and scores drowned in the river. By 7:00 P.M. the battle was virtually over and most Federal survivors were prisoners.

Union losses totaled 49 killed, 158 wounded, and 714 captured or wounded. Confederate casualties amounted to 33 killed, 115 wounded, and one man missing. The obvious disparity in losses was clear to all and trumpeted by the Confederates, while the defeat having occurred so near to Washington ensured that newspaper reporters would quickly spread the news to the rest of the country.

The effects were quickly felt in the North. For Lincoln, Baker's death was a personal blow. When informed, Lincoln stood stunned and silent for several minutes. He walked slowly back to the executive mansion with bystanders noting tears rolling down his face. Baker was buried in a state funeral attended by the president, vice president, congressional leaders, and the Supreme Court. He immediately became a martyr to the cause of the Union, despite the fact that his inexperience had contributed to the disaster.

Nonetheless, the political establishment was intent on discovering darker motives for the disaster. Although many regular officers blamed Baker, Republicans who favored a hard war policy and the destruction of slavery blamed McClellan and Stone. On 20 December, Congress created the Joint Committee on the Conduct of the War. Representatives from both the Senate and the House of Representatives thus formed a permanent committee to inquire into and investigate how the war was being directed. Investigations were conducted in secret, and the committee was soon persecuting those suspected of having Southern sympathies.

Their first victim was General Charles P. Stone. Witnesses denounced Stone, alleging that he secretly communicated with unnamed Southerners and returned runaway slaves to their owners. He was also blamed for failing to reinforce Baker at Ball's Bluff. The Committee took their findings to Secretary of War Edwin M. Stanton, who ordered Stone relieved of command and arrested on 8 February 1862. Stone was never tried, but enough testimony was released to the newspapers to paint him as a traitor. Stone was released from prison in August 1862, and though he served again, his military career was virtually at an end. Stone's experience remained an example and warning to Union commanders throughout the remainder of the war.

—*Tim J. Watts*

See also Joint Committee on the Conduct of the War; Stone, Charles P.

For further reading:
Farwell, Byron. *Ball's Bluff: A Small Battle and Its Long Shadow* (1990).
Grimsley, Mark. "The Definition of Disaster." *Civil War Times Illustrated* (1989).
Holien, Kim Bernard. *Battle at Ball's Bluff* (1985).
Sears, Stephen W. "The Ordeal of General Stone." *MHQ: The Quarterly Journal of Military History* (1995).
Tap, Bruce. *Over Lincoln's Shoulder: The Committee on the Conduct of the War* (1998).

BALTIMORE, MARYLAND

The first disruptions in Baltimore associated with the Civil War began in October 1860, when the city's trade with its largest geographic market, the South, began a precipitous decline. Bankruptcies and massive unemployment followed Lincoln's election as president in November. Baltimore's voters had given 46 percent of their votes to the Democratic Party candidate, John Breckinridge, who was widely perceived as a secessionist. John Bell, of the Constitutional Union Party, hastily formed in May in Baltimore's First Presbyterian Church, had claimed 45 percent of the vote, and 6.5 percent went to Union Democrat Stephen Douglas. Supporters of President-elect Lincoln had numbered only 2.5 percent of the vote, but they held their first pro-Union meeting on 6 December.

Three of the city's four major newspapers—the *Baltimore Clipper*, the *Baltimore American*, and the *Baltimore Sun*—supported Unionist activity in the city, and on 7 January 1861, both the *Clipper* and the *American* published a list of Unionist Baltimoreans consisting of more than one thousand names. The *Baltimore Republican*, published by the father-and-son team of Beale and Francis Richardson, supported the secession of six states during January and early February, the formation of the Confederate States of America on 4 February, and Jefferson Davis's election as the Confederate president five days later. The loud intensity of Baltimore's prosecessionists was the main reason for Lincoln's clandestine passage in the middle of the night of 22 February through Baltimore on his way to Washington, D.C., to assume the presidency.

Baltimore's proximity to the nation's capital established the city's importance to the Union. Against the wishes of his military advisors, Lincoln insisted that the nation's government would remain in Washington, rather than withdraw to Philadelphia. Almost all railroad and telegraph traffic between Washington and points north passed through Baltimore. The city was a transportation and communication hub and, from Lincoln's point of view, a bottleneck that secessionists could not be allowed to control. Even the physical arrangement of the city's railroad depots compounded the problem. There was no through traffic, and different railroad companies owned the different depots. Most people coming from the north en route to Washington arrived at the Calvert Street Station or the Bolton Street Station in the north of the city or the President Street Station on the southeastern side of the city. They would then either have to walk or take the city's streetcars to the Camden Street Station on the southwestern side of Baltimore, which linked the city with Washington via the Baltimore & Ohio Railroad.

Baltimore's status during the war was determined by events between March and November 1861.

Baltimore under federal occupation, 28 July 1863 (*Library of Congress*)

Baltimoreans responded to the failure of the Washington Peace Conference, the firing on Fort Sumter, and Lincoln's call for volunteers in various ways. At first, both the *Sun* and the *American* took a pro-Union but antiwar stand, while prowar Unionists formed the so-called Minute Men and secessionists formed the National Volunteers. Both groups met more or less continuously, but news of Virginia's secession on 17 April tipped the balance in favor of secessionists. Lieutenant John Thompson Mason Barnes, commissioned by Confederate president Davis, had already been recruiting Baltimoreans for the Confederate army, and the trickle of men leaving on steamboats for Norfolk, Charleston, and Savannah now turned into a flood. Most of the University of Maryland's Medical School physicians resigned to join the Confederate army. People commonly carried South Carolina palmetto flags and talked of the need for a Southern rights convention in the city and for resistance to the passage of Union troops through Baltimore. In this atmosphere occurred the infamous riot of Friday, 19 April 1861, in which civilians attacked the 6th Massachusetts Regiment as it marched

from the President Street Station to the Camden Street Station, en route to Washington, D.C. Twenty-six men were killed and more than a hundred wounded in the riot. An estimated three to four hundred Unionist families left Baltimore over the following weekend. The prosecessionist Maryland Guard began actively drilling, a new secessionist newspaper, *The South*, edited by Thomas W. Hall, appeared on Monday, 22 April, as did Governor Thomas Hicks's announcement that he was convening a special session of the state legislature on the twenty-sixth. James Ryder Randall wrote the poem/song, "Maryland, My Maryland," that was soon being published throughout the South, and there was a run on the Savings Bank of Baltimore. On Wednesday, 24 April, John Thompson Mason, chief of the Baltimore customs house and the organizer of Baltimore's States Rights Party, led the attempt to elect secessionists to vacated seats in the legislature. On Saturday, 27 April, the day after the state legislature convened, Lincoln suspended the writ of habeas corpus in the region between Washington and Philadelphia.

The die was now cast. As Washington's back door to

the North, Baltimore would have to be kept in the Union. The first Union troops—in the beginning numbering only about 1,200 under General Benjamin Butler—arrived in Baltimore on 13 May to begin the military occupation of the city that would last throughout the war. More soldiers arrived and constructed fortifications. Homes vacated by Baltimoreans who had joined the Confederacy were confiscated and turned into hospitals, while additional, new hospitals were built. Baltimore increasingly resembled an armed camp. The Union naval ship, *Harriet Lane*, was docked at the Calvert Street wharf, its guns trained—like those of General Butler's men on Federal Hill overlooking Baltimore's inner harbor—on the city's business district. Although Butler's command lasted only three days, his actions were a harbinger of what would come: he confiscated weapons and searched private property; he arrested Baltimoreans on the charge of treason; and, as provost marshall, he forbade all expressions of support for, or sympathy with, secession. In late June, Baltimore's prosecessionist city marshall, George P. Kane, was arrested with three civilian members of the Police Board. Meanwhile, the Union Relief Association was established to furnish food, reading material, and entertainment to the growing Union army garrison that now numbered about 40,000 men.

All this activity intensified after the first battle of Bull Run in mid-July 1861 that made Washington vulnerable to Confederate attack. In a memorandum of 26 July, Lincoln instructed, "Let Baltimore be held as now, with a gentle but firm and certain hand." The firm and certain hand revealed itself to be less gentle as time wore on. The War Department began its censorship of the news under the 57th Article of War in August 1861, and on 11 September, Secretary of War Simon Cameron warned Governor Hicks that any act of secession by the Maryland legislature must be prevented. He threatened to arrest all or any of the members who supported secession. A week later, on 17 September, he acted on his own advice and ordered the arrest of Baltimore's mayor, George William Brown, and various members of the city council. Frank Key Howard and Thomas W. Hall, editors of the *Baltimore Exchange* and *The South*, respectively, were also arrested. Civilian government virtually ceased to operate in the city, but under military guidance, support for the Union was encouraged with less coercive measures. General John A. Dix informed Provost Marshall Dodge in November 1861 that Maryland could be controlled by force, but it would better to control it through opinion.

Union officials spent the remainder of the war doing that through censorship of the press and public opinion and through advancing such organizations as the Union League. The Federal government contracted with Baltimore's merchants and industrialists for a wide

variety of goods and services, all the while restricting political participation only to those loyal to the Union. Demonstrations of patriotism such as displaying the Union flag were required and on-going, and the threat of military arrest was ever present, but the war gradually changed Baltimore society as emancipation became increasingly central to its purpose. African-Americans were actively recruited beginning in July 1863 at the Bureau of Colored Troops, and by the end of the year many of Maryland's leading politicians publicly advocated emancipation. Maryland became the first slave state to abolish slavery and rewrite its constitution. When the last Union troops left Baltimore in July 1865, the city had become a very different commercial and social community from what it had been in 1860.

—*Gary L. Browne*

See also Baltimore Riot; Hicks, Thomas H.; Maryland; Washington Peace Conference.
For further reading:
Browne, Gary. *Baltimore in the Civil War* (1986).
Catton, William Bruce. "The Baltimore Business Community and the Secession Crisis, 1860–61" (Master's thesis, 1952).
Pruzan, Jeffrey S. "Shadows of Civil War Baltimore." *Civil War Illustrated* (1995).
Sheads, Scott S., and Daniel C. Toomey. *Baltimore During the Civil War* (1997).

BALTIMORE & OHIO RAILROAD

Geography and leadership account for the Baltimore & Ohio (B&O) Railroad's crucial role during the Civil War. Its Washington, D.C., branch was a single track running from Camden Station in Baltimore, Maryland, through the Washington junction (frequently called Relay), then through the Annapolis junction (a spur line to Maryland's state capitol), to its Washington, D.C., depot at New Jersey Avenue and Second Street, N.W. (now a corner of Capitol Park). It alone connected the nation's capital with the Northern states. The western portions of Maryland and Virginia were dependent upon the B&O to reach eastern markets. At the outbreak of the Civil War in 1861, the B&O comprised 236 locomotives, 128 coaches, 3,451 cars, and 513 miles of line, much of it in slave territory. The railroad was crucial to the Union and, hence, a target for destruction by Confederate forces.

This was the dilemma confronted by John Work Garrett, the railroad's president, who was not afraid to change his mind. Garrett assumed the presidency of the B&O in November 1858. He reorganized management to make the road more profitable and presided over its transportation of troops to capture John Brown and his raiders at Harper's Ferry a year later. In that context, he announced that the B&O was a "Southern line . . . and will prove the great bulwark of the border, and a sure agency for home defense." But directly following

President Lincoln's call for volunteers fourteen months later, Garrett immediately arranged transportation for them to Washington.

Beginning on 17 April 1861 Garrett supported the Union, which in turn protected his road from competitors, chiefly the Northern Central owned by Secretary of War Simon Cameron, who was determined to establish a through-line through Baltimore. If Garrett had not acted, the Northern Central would have replaced the B&O as the northern connection to the nation's capital. Furthermore, the B&O would not have made the same huge wartime profits that his competitors did.

These profits proved essential in keeping the road in operation when Confederate forces raided B&O property 143 times over the course of the war. In the words of Archibald W. Campbell, Unionist editor of Wheeling's newspaper, the *Intelligencer*, "This road [the B&O] in its geographical position, is to be deeply sympathized with. . . . At Harper's Ferry it is completely under military despotism, and every train has to run the gauntlet of cannon and armed espionage." In 1861 alone, for example, twenty-three railroad bridges were burned; 102 miles of telegraph wire were cut; thirty-six and one-half miles of track torn up, stolen, or destroyed; forty-two locomotives and 386 cars stolen or destroyed; and the company's depot, hotel on Queen Street, machine shop, stone bridge, and roundhouses at Martinsburg, Virginia, were destroyed. More destruction followed every year, especially when Robert E. Lee crossed into Maryland in 1862, when he crossed through Maryland into Pennsylvania in 1863, and when General Jubal Early raided the region in 1864. The list of losses is staggering, and the principal figure behind the B&O's ability to restore itself was William Prescott Smith, the master of transportation throughout the war.

Troops, animals, food for both, and military supplies of nearly every description were shipped over the road. The railroad seemed be in a state of permanent construction, not only because of damage from the Confederate forces, but because cars frequently had to be altered to carry the different kinds of freight. Also, their sequencing from point to point required meticulous planning. All the elements of modern management—planning, organizing, controlling, coordinating, and directing—that made the Civil War the first modern industrial war were present in Garrett and Smith's administration. Perhaps a single instance that made everyone recognize the new industrial way of war and the importance of the railroads to it was Secretary of War Edwin M. Stanton's bold decision to ship 20,000 troops and materiel from General George Gordon Meade's Army of the Potomac in the eastern theater to General William S. Rosecrans's Army of the Cumberland, then at Chattanooga, Tennessee, in the fall of 1863. Stanton called Garrett and Smith of the B&O, Samuel M. Felton of the Philadelphia, Wilmington & Baltimore Railroad, and Thomas A. Scott of the Pennsylvania Railroad to Washington, where they planned and executed the all-rail, 1,200-mile transfer of the troops from Virginia, north through Washington, D.C., west to Indiana, and south to Bridgeport, Alabama, on the Tennessee River, in approximately five days. Such experiences as this enabled Garrett and Smith to expand capacity quickly when circumstances required it.

In June and July 1865 the end of the war saw the B&O move 233,300 troops, 2,000 tons of baggage, and

The Baltimore & Ohio railroad line opposite Harper's Ferry, (West) Virginia (*Library of Congress*)

27,000 mules northward out of their Washington depot. From Baltimore to West Virginia they also transferred 96,796 troops and 9,896 animals.

Garrett always remembered Stonewall Jackson's destruction of the B&O's properties at Martinsburg, Virginia, in June 1861, and he admired how Confederate colonel Thomas R. Sharpe, with just thirty-five men comprising six machinists, ten teamsters, and twelve laborers, had moved fourteen of his big locomotives—including a Hayes Camal 198, a Mason locomotive, and a "dutch waggon"—over forty miles of dirt roads from Martinsburg to Strasburg, Virginia. When the indispensable William Prescott Smith died prematurely at age forty-seven in 1872, Garrett hired Sharpe to replace him as master of transportation.

—*Gary L. Browne*

See also Railroads, U.S.A.

For further reading:
Bain, William E. *B&O in the Civil War: From the Papers of Wm. Prescott Smith.* (1966).
Hungerford, Edward. *The Story of the Baltimore & Ohio Railroad, 1827–1927* (1928).
Lawrence W. Sagle Collection. The B&O Railroad Museum, Ellicott City, Maryland.
Stover, John F. *History of the Baltimore and Ohio Railroad* (1987).
Summers, Festus P. *The Baltimore and Ohio in the Civil War* (1939).
Turner, George Edgar. *Victory Rode the Rails* (1953).

BALTIMORE RIOT
(19 April 1861)

The Baltimore riot that began about 11 A.M. on Friday, 19 April 1861, pushed Baltimoreans so close to supporting Maryland's secession that Federal authorities took military action to prevent it going further, an action that changed the city forever by forcing it to support the Union.

Baltimore's identification with secession was well known. Just 2,294 of the city's voters—2.5 percent of the total vote—cast their votes for Abraham Lincoln in the November 1860 presidential election. Instead, 46 percent of Baltimore's voters had supported John Breckinridge, the South's Democratic Party candidate. The winter following had been a tense one. As Southern states cascaded into secession and formed the Confederate States of America during the winter and early spring, Baltimore's primary market was disrupted and the city's economy fell into bankruptcy and mass unemployment. Pro-Union and larger prosecession rallies vied with the Workingmen's Aid Association for the attention of the unemployed before Lincoln had even departed Illinois to assume the presidency.

Lincoln received a letter threatening him with assassination in Baltimore on his trip to Washington, D.C., Samuel Felton, president of the Philadelphia,

Wilmington & Baltimore Railroad, on which Lincoln was to ride to Baltimore, had heard of the plot and hired Allan Pinkerton, a detective already working for him, to investigate. Felton and Pinkerton had good reason to worry; there were no through railroads in Baltimore. All the railroads terminated in depots scattered around the city. Two of these, the Calvert Street Station and the Bolton Street Station, were in the northern part of the city. The President Street Station, the terminal for Felton's road, lay on the eastern side of the harbor, while the Camden Station, depot for the Baltimore & Ohio Railroad Company and the only link to Washington, lay on the western side of the harbor. Everyone traveling from Pennsylvania through Baltimore to Washington had to get off the train at one of the three depots and then travel by foot or streetcar to the Camden Station. Lincoln himself did so on the night of 22 February 1861. In disguise in the middle of the night, the president-elect traveled in a closed, horse-drawn streetcar from the President Street to the Camden Station, doing so against the advice of his military advisors. Lincoln had personal knowledge of the problem that Baltimore posed.

Trouble intensified during the next month and a half. Peace efforts failed, Fort Sumter was fired upon, Lincoln issued his call for volunteers on Monday, 15 April, and Virginia announced its secession the following Wednesday. The entire week of 15 through 19 April, punctuated by these last two events, marked a defining moment for Baltimore. On 13 April, Unionists organized themselves into "Minute Men" and secessionists into "National Volunteers." They were milling in the streets on the 15th when Lincoln's call for volunteers caused many of the Unionists to enlist. The Confederate army recruiting office in Marsh Market closed, and the National Volunteers both condemned Lincoln's resort to force and called on citizens to resist the passage of Union troops through Baltimore.

The news of Virginia's secession just as suddenly swung the pendulum the other way. Baltimore's secessionists called for a Southern rights convention, while many intent on enlisting in Confederate armies left in steamboats bound for Norfolk, Charleston, and Savannah. Other National Volunteer groups marched in the streets. Events on Thursday, 18 April, further polarized the city. Over 700 National Volunteers met in Monument Square in the morning and walked to Bolton Station, where Pennsylvania volunteers had arrived en route to Camden Station and ultimately, Washington, D.C. The Baltimoreans screamed insults at the Pennsylvanians and threw bricks and paving stones at them. Later that afternoon they tried—unsuccessfully, in the face of Unionist resistance—to raise a Confederate flag on Federal Hill. Finally, that evening they attended a Southern rights convention led by Thomas Parkin Scott whose main topic was resistance to Union invasion.

The Baltimoreans were ready the next morning when the 6th Massachusetts Regiment arrived at the President Street Station. The 6th Massachusetts was organized into eleven companies and had left Boston on Wednesday, 17 April. Samuel Felton had warned the regiment's commander, Colonel Edward Jones, to expect trouble, and Jones had ordered his men to march from the President Street Station along Pratt Street to the Camden Station with arms ready. They were not to fire unless fired upon, however, and then only after their officers had ordered them to do so.

The train arrived a little after 10 A.M. The men disembarked to board the Pratt Street streetcars that would take them the mile and a half to Camden Station. Baltimore's secessionists gathered to hurl insults and then bricks and paving stones. As the crowd grew larger, it became more violent. By the time the seventh of the eleven companies had reached Camden, sand had been dumped on the streetcar rails, and ship anchors dragged over them, all as the rain of cobblestones, bottles, and other things continued. Mayor George William Brown and City Marshall George P. Kane led Baltimore's entire police force of about fifty men to shield the remaining troops and escort them to Camden. They doubled their pace to a quick jog, but both sides began shooting. By the time the beleaguered soldiers had reached Camden Station, four of their number were dead and thirty-six wounded. Twelve Baltimoreans lay dead and over a hundred wounded. The rioters then turned on Baltimore's Unionists among Pratt Street's business establishments, looting and destroying property and stealing weapons.

From Camden, the troops proceeded to Washington, and all were gone by early afternoon when Mayor Brown and Governor Thomas H. Hicks called for a citywide meeting in Monument Square. A crowd of approximately 10,000 met about 3:30 P.M. There, Brown, Hicks, several members of the city council, and Severn Teackle Wallis, a prominent secessionist, assessed Baltimore's situation and agreed that the city must oppose any additional Union troops moving through its streets. Unionists began leaving the city that night, and over the weekend an estimated three hundred to four hundred families fled. City officials and volunteers cut telegraph wires and stopped the mails between Baltimore and Washington and points to the north. They also burned railroad bridges north of the city, stopped food and medical supplies from leaving Baltimore, raised money from the banks, and contracted for muskets and cannon from Confederate military forces in Virginia. Meanwhile, they overwhelmingly elected states' rights supporters to the special session of Maryland's legislature called by Governor Hicks. With secession threatening in Baltimore, Lincoln suspended the writ of habeas corpus a week later, which allowed the Union military to arrest and hold suspected Confederates.

Those arrests began shortly after Union troops arrived on 13 May. Over the next six months, all expressions of support for secession and the Confederacy were outlawed, and people expressing such opinions were arrested, regardless of office or standing. City officials such as City Marshall George P. Kane, Mayor Brown, and several members of the city council, as well as Federal office holders and even judges found themselves imprisoned in Fort McHenry. Prosecession newspapers were shut down, and their editors were also imprisoned. News was censored and churches were required to fly the Stars and Stripes. Thus was the city physically secured for the Union.

—*Gary L. Browne*

See also Hicks, Thomas H.; Maryland.
For further reading:
Brown, George William. *Baltimore and the Nineteenth of April: A Study of the War* (1887).
Clark, Charles B. "Baltimore and the Attack on the 6th Massachusetts Regiment, April 19, 1861." *Maryland Historical Magazine* (1961).
Ellenberger, Matthew. "Whigs in the Streets? Baltimore Republicanism in the Spring of 1861." *Maryland Historical Magazine* (1991).
Towers, Frank. "A Vociferous Army of Howling Wolves: Baltimore's Civil War Riot of April 19, 1861." *The Maryland Historian* (1992).

BANKS, NATHANIEL PRENTISS
(1816–1894)
Union general

The son of a cotton mill worker, Nathaniel Banks was born in Waltham, Massachusetts, in 1816, worked in the mills as a child, and later earned the nickname "the Bobbin Boy of Massachusetts" for his early trade. He never attended college but spent considerable time educating himself in languages, oratory, and the law. After being admitted to the bar in the late 1830s, Banks dabbled in newspaper work and in 1849 was elected to the state legislature as a Democrat. The 1851 Free-Soil–Democrat coalition that sent Charles Sumner to the U.S. Senate also made Banks Speaker of the Massachusetts House. An able politician and orator, Banks soon became a major force in state politics and in 1853 was elected to the U.S. Congress.

Never a loyal party member, Banks switched allegiance to the upstart Know-Nothings in 1854 and two years later was chosen Speaker of the U.S. House. In 1857, the Free-Soil Banks was elected governor of Massachusetts as a Republican over Know-Nothing incumbent Henry Gardner. A highly effective and popular executive, Banks left office in 1860 to become vice president of the Illinois Central Railroad, succeeding George B. McClellan. When the Civil War began, Banks returned to Massachusetts and, although he had no military experience, was commissioned a major general and sent to Maryland. Because Banks was a prominent antislavery Republican from a crucial Northern state, Lincoln could not afford to leave him out of the war effort. In so doing, Banks became the quintessential "political general"—politically connected but militarily incompetent.

More concerned with military pomp than preparation, Banks quickly developed a reputation as an ineffectual commander better suited for parade grounds than for battlefields. Confederate general Thomas "Stonewall" Jackson proved his greatest nemesis. During McClellan's Peninsula campaign in the spring of 1862, Lee sent Jackson to the Shenandoah Valley to threaten Washington, D.C., divert Federal troops, and prevent any reinforcement of McClellan. Banks, commanding a sizable army near Harper's Ferry, advanced down the valley but was visiting Washington when his troops defeated Jackson at the battle of Kernstown in late March. Upon his return to the field, Banks cautiously followed the Confederates farther into the valley. Jackson meanwhile defeated a small Federal force at McDowell in western Virginia, turned toward Banks, and routed his left flank at Front Royal on 23 May. In danger of being cut off, the Federal army quickly retreated to Winchester and was again attacked by Jackson on 25 May. Beaten and weary, Banks's troops fled across the Potomac River. Over a third of his army had been lost in the Valley campaign and so many supplies were captured by Jackson that the Confederates dubbed the Massachusetts general "Commissary Banks." In three months, Jackson had prevented McClellan's reinforcement by feigning a threat to Washington and soundly defeated the overmatched Banks.

The two met again during the Second Bull Run campaign of August 1862. Commanding a corps of John Pope's Army of Virginia, Banks boldly attacked Jackson's forces at the battle of Cedar Mountain and nearly defeated the larger Confederate army. Outnumbered and bloodied, his corps was forced to retreat toward Washington, where he took command of the city's defenses. Twice beaten, Banks was transferred to New Orleans in November 1862 to direct the Department of the Gulf, succeeding fellow Massachusetts political general Benjamin F. Butler. Banks would never again command troops in the East.

Although President Lincoln wanted to begin the reconstruction of Louisiana, General Banks continued his military operations and began moving north to help open the Mississippi River. While Grant targeted Vicksburg, Banks aimed at capturing Port Hudson, a well-defended bluff-fortress above Baton Rouge. To allow Admiral David Farragut's small flotilla passage north of the fortress, thereby helping isolate both

Nathaniel Banks (Photograph by Mathew Brady Studio / *Library of Congress*)

Vicksburg and Port Hudson, Banks's army planned to feign a land attack from the south. His attack was late, however, and the navy barely escaped total destruction as they scrambled past the fortress in mid-March 1863. In May and June, Banks surrounded the fort and began a series of unsuccessful bloody attacks on the entrenched Confederates. His force suffered 4,000 casualties and lost another 7,000 soldiers to disease. Five days after the Vicksburg surrender on 4 July, Port Hudson also capitulated, giving Banks his first victory as a military commander.

Banks's military exploits were not finished, however. In March 1864, he was given overall command of the Red River expedition, a land-sea operation aimed to gain wider control of Louisiana, Texas, and Arkansas. Supported heavily by Lincoln, the plan was strongly opposed by Banks, Grant, and Farragut. Driving toward Shreveport, Banks battled Confederate forces under General Richard Taylor at Sabine's Crossroads and

Pleasant Hill on 8 and 9 April, but was forced to retreat. As a result of low water levels on the Red River, the Union navy was nearly trapped and slowly moved south with the army. Banks ended his military career with this complete Union disaster, which could have been much worse.

Meanwhile, Banks the politician remained busy "reconstructing" Louisiana. Instead of helping write a new constitution, Banks simply kept the antebellum document and deleted the sections relating to slavery. In addition, he called for statewide elections for the winter of 1864 to bring Louisiana back into the Union as a loyal state. This move angered many Radical Republicans by not promoting the suffrage rights of ex-slaves or engineering the exclusion of the old planters who had dominated state government before 1860. Complicating matters, Banks used the army to force ex-slaves away from "vagrancy" and back into plantation work, sustaining the state economy and gaining allies among the influential planter elite. Radicals thought Banks's governing too conservative, and he left New Orleans in 1865 to return to Washington and help lobby for the moderates' Reconstruction program.

Mustered out of service in August 1865, Banks returned to his native Massachusetts and immediately returned to his political roots. Elected as a Republican to the U.S. Congress, he chaired the Committee on Military Affairs and served until a feud with President Grant and his advocacy of Horace Greeley's presidential campaign caused his defeat for reelection in 1872. Banks returned to Congress in 1874 as a Democrat, but switched again to the Republican Party in 1876 and retired from Congress two years later. After ten years as a U.S. Marshal, he was elected to Congress as a Republican in 1888 and served until his death in mid-1894 at the age of seventy-eight.

Twice a Republican, twice a Democrat, and once a Know-Nothing, Nathaniel Banks, the crafty politician, always pictured himself a president, but never moved above the governor's chair or the Congress. A powerful voice in antebellum Republican politics and in the Reconstruction debate, he was less successful as a military commander, clearly outgeneraled by the likes of Jackson, Lee, and even Richard Taylor. His appointment, however, served an important political purpose. As the first Republican Speaker of the House and an important antislavery leader from a crucial state, his generalship doubled as a necessary political alliance for a president desperately seeking to unite a divided North. Like the appointments of John McClernand and Benjamin F. Butler, Banks, the "political general," served as a leader of men on the battlefield and a leader of opinion at home.

—*Michael J. Connolly*

See also American Party; Bull Run, Second Battle of; Free Soil Party; Front Royal, Battle of; Kernstown, First Battle of; Port

Hudson Campaign; Red River Campaign; Winchester, First Battle of.

For further reading:
Donald, David Herbert. *Lincoln* (1995).
Harrington, Fred Harvey. *The Fighting Politician: Major General N.P. Banks* (1948; reprint, 1970).
Hattaway, Herman, and Archer Jones. *How the North Won: A Military History of the Civil War* (1983).
Hollandsworth, James G. *Pretense of Glory: The Life of General Nathaniel P. Banks* (1998).

BARKSDALE, ETHELBERT
(1824–1893)
Journalist and Confederate congressman

The brother of United States congressman and Confederate general William Barksdale, Ethelbert Barksdale was born in Smyrna, Tennessee, the youngest child of William and Nancy Hervey Lester Barksdale. Their parents deceased, the four Barksdale brothers settled in Yazoo County, Mississippi, in 1837. Ethelbert Barksdale first edited the *Yazoo City Democrat* (1845–1850), before taking the reins of the state Democratic Party organ, the *Jackson Mississippian* (1850–1861), later called the *Clarion* (1867–1882). In 1843 he married Alice, daughter of Claiborne and Dianna Boone Harris of Holmes County, Mississippi. They had three children: Harris, Edwin, and Ethel.

Barksdale was a strong proponent of states' rights during the Compromise of 1850 crisis and worked for the election of Jefferson Davis as the State Rights Democratic gubernatorial nominee in 1851, but was not an original secessionist. Walking out of the Democratic convention in 1860 with his fellow Southerners, he campaigned instead for John C. Breckinridge. After Lincoln's election, Barksdale favored secession.

In the Confederate Congress Barksdale was viewed as a nationalist and a supporter of the Davis administration on many controversial issues: suspending the writ of habeas corpus, imposing martial law, conscription, tax increases, using slaves in the army, and negotiations for peace. Between congressional sessions he functioned as the president's eyes and ears in Mississippi, reporting directly on military and political affairs.

During the postwar period Barksdale was at first a cooperationist, even advocating black enfranchisement, but soon was a vocal and vigorous foe of Reconstruction Governor Adelbert Ames, consistently advocating the governor's removal from office. Finally, Barksdale became best known as a champion of small farmers in their disputes with the conservatives who controlled the state Democratic Party after 1875. For example, one of his House speeches, published as a pamphlet in 1885, was entitled, "No Taxation to Create Sinecures for the Benefit of Privileged Classes."

A fellow editor described him as "by all odds the

ablest editor of the state, [who] dealt the Republicans more sledge-hammer blows than any editor of his time. His writing was heavy, strong and powerful." From his vantage point as editor of the *Mississippian* and *Clarion* for nearly three decades, Barksdale exercised considerable influence on party policies. He was equally effective as a debater in public forums and as a congressman, appreciated not only for his encyclopedic knowledge of state politics, but also for his sociability and his often sarcastic and sharp verbal skills. A contemporary recalled, "Some of his paragraphs were electric batteries, which produced a shock from which only those victims who were blessed with strong nerves and great recuperative powers could recover. In person he was small, and his manner was grave and dignified. He rarely laughed, and there was something in his smile which indicated more of malice than of mirth."

A delegate to Democratic national conventions in 1860, 1868, 1872, and 1880, Barksdale served on the national platform committee five times, was a presidential elector in 1876, president of the state electoral college, and chairman of the state executive committee, 1877–1879. In 1890 he was defeated in his run for Congress as the Alliance Party candidate, and likewise lost his bid for a Senate seat in 1890. After his retirement from Congress, he tended his Oak Valley plantation in Yazoo County and wrote occasionally on agricultural subjects for various newspapers. He died at Oak Valley and was buried in Greenwood Cemetery, Jackson.

—*Lynda Lasswell Crist*

See also Barksdale, William; Congress, C.S.A.

For further reading:

Barksdale, Ethelbert. "Reconstruction in Mississippi." In *Why the Solid South?* (1890).

Davis, Reuben. *Recollections of Mississippi and Mississippians* (1890).

Halsell, Willie D. "Democratic Dissensions in Mississippi, 1878–1882." *Journal of Mississippi History* (1940).

Henry, Robert Hiram. *Editors I Have Known since the Civil War* (1922).

Peterson, Owen. "Ethelbert Barksdale in the Democratic National Convention of 1860." *Journal of Mississippi History* (1952).

Yearns, Wilfred Buck. *The Confederate Congress* (1960).

BARKSDALE, WILLIAM E.

(1821–1863)

Confederate general

William E. Barksdale was born to William Barksdale and Nancy Hervey Lester Barksdale in Smyrna, Tennessee. After being educated in Tennessee, the young William moved to Mississippi where he studied and briefly practiced law. Not finding that profession to his liking, he turned to the newspaper business and became the editor of the Columbus (Mississippi) *Democrat*. He used his paper to espouse strong states' rights views.

When war with Mexico broke out in 1846, Barksdale became a captain in the 2d Mississippi Volunteers. After that war he entered politics and was elected to the United States House of Representatives in 1853. He served in that body until he resigned on the secession of Mississippi in January 1861. During his congressional career he urged United States expansion into Latin America. As the sectional crisis worsened in the country, he became a strong proponent of Southern secession.

In March 1861, rather than continue his political career in the Confederacy, he enlisted in state forces and became the quartermaster general of Mississippi. Shortly thereafter, craving a more active role in the upcoming conflict, Barksdale accepted a post as colonel of the 13th Mississippi Regiment. His brother was Confederate congressman, Ethelbert Barksdale.

Barksdale's regiment was sent to Virginia, where it participated in the battle of First Bull Run. Barksdale developed a reputation early in the war for being eager to fight, and was commended for his actions on the Potomac River in October 1861. He continued to command the 13th during the Peninsula campaign in the spring and summer of 1862. During the Seven Days' battles he assumed command of the 3d Brigade of Magruder's Division when his brigade commander, Brigadier General Richard Griffith, was mortally wounded on 29 June at Savage's Station. Two days later at the battle of Malvern Hill, Barksdale distinguished himself and the brigade that would quickly become known as Barksdale's Mississippi Brigade. Barksdale was promoted to brigadier general on 12 August 1862.

Barksdale and his brigade did not arrive on the field at the battle of Antietam, 17 September 1862, until about 9 A.M., after the fighting was well underway. Because of his men's forced march, many had fallen by the wayside from exhaustion, and Barksdale was forced to enter the fighting on the Confederate left with only part of his brigade. Nevertheless, he and his men distinguished themselves in the heavy fighting that morning.

A few months later, Barksdale requested and received the duty of delaying the Union movement across the Rappahannock River at Fredericksburg, Virginia. As the Union forces prepared to assemble their pontoon bridges across the river, Barksdale's brigade moved down into Fredericksburg from the heights above the town to slow the work of the bridge assemblers. Using the brick walls of the many structures near the waterside, Barksdale's men so harassed the Northern workmen that Union general Ambrose Burnside was forced to order a large contingent of men to cross in boats to dislodge the riflemen. Barksdale then fought a delaying action against the Federal troops through the streets of the city.

During the Chancellorsville campaign in April and

May 1863, Barksdale's brigade remained behind in Fredericksburg as part of the force intended to delay any Federal crossing from that quarter. When the crossing occurred, Barksdale and his men delayed the Federal advance against overwhelming odds.

As part of Longstreet's corps, Barksdale participated in the attack on the Federal left on the second day at Gettysburg (2 July 1863). Again eager to be a part of the fighting, Barksdale champed at the bit as Longstreet meticulously arranged his forces for the attack on the Round Tops. When Barksdale was finally sent in, witnesses claimed to have seen his flowing white hair from a great distance as he led his brigade into the Peach Orchard. There his conspicuous appearance made him an easy target for Federal riflemen, and he was shot in both legs and the chest. Because of his condition, his men had to leave him behind when they were pushed back by a Federal counterattack. Union forces captured the general, and he died the next morning from his wounds.

—*David S. Heidler and Jeanne T. Heidler*

See also Fredericksburg, Battle of; Gettysburg, Battle of.

For further reading:

Barksdale, John A. *Barksdale Family History and Genealogy* (1940).

Hawley, Steve Carl. *Brigadier General William Barksdale, C.S.A.: A Study in the Generalship of a Volunteer Officer* (Master's thesis, Texas A & M University 1992).

McKee, James Willette. "William Barksdale: The Intrepid Mississippian." (Ph.D. dissertation, 1973).

BARLOW, FRANCIS CHANNING
(1834–1896)
Union general

Born to David Hatch Barlow and Almira Penniman Barlow in Brooklyn, New York, Francis Channing Barlow moved with his family to Brookline, Massachusetts, when he was a small child. He graduated from Harvard before embarking on the practice of law in New York City. At the outbreak of the Civil War, Barlow enlisted as a private in a three-month regiment, the 12th New York Volunteers.

The regiment traveled to Washington, D. C., where it became a part of the capital's defenses. Shortly after arrival Barlow was promoted to the rank of first lieutenant. Upon the mustering out of the regiment in August 1861, Barlow returned home to New York to help raise a long-term regiment. In November 1861 he was commissioned lieutenant colonel in the 61st New York Regiment. Upon arrival in Washington, the regiment became a part of the Army of the Potomac.

In preparation for the Peninsula campaign, Barlow and his regiment were sent to Fort Monroe in March 1862. In April, at the commencement of the campaign,

Barlow was promoted to colonel of the regiment. He and his regiment fought in most of the engagements of the Peninsula campaign, and he especially distinguished himself at the battle of Seven Pines. In August he was given command of a brigade of XI Corps, which he commanded at the battle of Antietam. In that battle he was seriously wounded when struck in the groin by a ball from a Confederate case shot. He was forced to leave the field and recuperated for several months before resuming command of his brigade. During his convalescence he was promoted to brigadier general of volunteers.

Barlow was unable to return to active duty until early 1863. He took command of his old brigade in XI Corps, now under the command of Oliver O. Howard, in April. Unfortunately for Barlow, he resumed command just in time to be a part of the rout of Howard's corps at Chancellorsville in early May. He was given command of 1st Division, XI Corps, in the move north in June in pursuit of Robert E. Lee's Army of Northern Virginia.

On the first day of the battle of Gettysburg, 1 July 1863, XI Corps was rushed forward to support I Corps north and west of town. As Barlow positioned his men north of town, the Confederate corps of Richard Ewell slammed into his lines. Barlow was shot through the body, the bullet exiting his back near his spinal cord. His fleeing men, assuming he was dead, left him on the field as they fell back to Cemetery Hill. As the Confederates pursued, Barlow was discovered by Confederate brigadier general John B. Gordon. Gordon gave the still conscious Barlow some of his water and had him taken to a nearby house, where Confederate doctors tended his wounds. For a brief time, Barlow was paralyzed from his wound. At the end of the three-day battle, the Confederates could not transport even their own most seriously wounded soldiers, so like them, Barlow was left behind. His wife traveled from New York to nurse him, and after a number of months in the hospital and on convalescent leave, Barlow returned to duty.

Initially unable to accept a field command, Barlow was sent in December 1863 to Springfield, Illinois, to oversee the draft depot there. By spring he felt fit enough to return to the Army of the Potomac, and at the end of March 1864 was given command of 1st Division, II Corps, under Winfield Scott Hancock. He commanded his division at the Wilderness, and then at Spotsylvania he was hand-picked by Hancock to lead part of the assault on 12 May against the Bloody Angle. In the attack the Federals captured over 3,000 Confederate prisoners, two general officers, almost two dozen artillery pieces, and thirty stands of colors. Hancock recommended that Barlow receive a brevet promotion to major general for his actions in the offensive. Shortly thereafter George

Gordon Meade, commander of the Army of the Potomac, made a similar recommendation. In August 1864 Barlow received the brevet promotion to major general.

Barlow fought at Cold Harbor and in the early engagements around Petersburg in June and July 1864. In mid-August 1864 he led his division in the battle at Deep Bottom Run, but shortly after the battle was forced to take an extended sick leave. His health had never fully recovered, and he was allowed to take a trip to Europe in an attempt to recover his strength. He returned in time to take part in the final phases of the campaign against Lee. He commanded 2d Division, II Corps, in reserve at Sayler's Creek and then was part of the Union capture of the bridge over the Appomattox River at Farmville on 7 April that allowed the continued pursuit of Lee's army.

Following the war, Barlow was promoted to major general of volunteers and briefly commanded II Corps before resigning his commission in November 1865 to return to his law practice in New York. He quickly became involved in New York politics and was elected the state's secretary of state before the end of the year. Over the next decade he held a number of positions, including another term as secretary of state, state attorney general, and United States marshal. He was also one of the commissioners charged with investigating the presidential election of 1876. By that time he had all but retired from public life to devote himself to his law practice. He remained active in New York's legal circles until his death on 11 January 1896. His remains were returned to his childhood home of Brookline, Massachusetts, for burial.

—*David S. Heidler and Jeanne T. Heidler*

See also Farmville/High Bridge; Gettysburg, Battle of; Spotsylvania, Battle of.

For further reading:
Abbot, Edwin Hale. *Francis Channing Barlow* (1983).
New York State Monuments Commission. *In Memoriam. Francis Channing Barlow* (1923).

BARNARD, GEORGE NORMAN
(1819–1902)
Photographer

George N. Barnard, a well-known and respected photographer in nineteenth-century America, ranges among the most important of his profession, due to his artistic sophistication, originality, and technical expertise. During his remarkably long career he dealt with a great variety of themes, including portrait art, news photography, American landscape, and the life of African-Americans after 1865. He is most noted for his pictures of the Civil War, especially for those of General William T. Sherman's campaigns. Because only

a few published statements exist and even fewer personal documents have survived, knowledge of Barnard is fragmentary. Yet as biographer Keith Davis has shown, Barnard's life need not remain a mystery.

George Norman Barnard was born on 23 December 1819 in Coventry, Connecticut, a village about eighteen miles east of Hartford. Barnard started out to live the life of a farmer's child, but things changed after the death of his father in 1826, when the family moved to live with relatives in nearby towns. Barnard's adolescent years were spent in family businesses, creating or amplifying in him a strong faith in personal improvement and material social progress. The overall atmosphere of this formative period apparently was progressive and literate.

In 1845, two years after his marriage, George Barnard and his wife moved to Oswego, New York, where he became the town's first full-time daguerreotypist after a one-year interim in the hotel business. He had been introduced to the technique by friends several years before, and itinerant daguerreotypists in Oswego possibly rekindled his interest in photography and its business potential. With low prices and high quality images, Barnard made his gallery a success well into the 1850s, allowing him to lead an upper-middle-class life. Because of the complicated process, the majority of daguerreotypes were produced in studios, though there are a few notable exceptions. On the night of 5 July 1853, a mill on the east side of the Oswego River caught fire, and the blaze quickly spread to adjacent buildings. Barnard preserved the spectacle in at least two memorable views, perhaps the earliest news photographs taken in America.

In December 1853 Barnard moved his studio to Syracuse, New York, where he was increasingly involved with the New York State Daguerreian Association, a self-regulatory body dealing with mounting competitive pressure among the rapidly expanding group of professional daguerreotypists. Due to the poor economy, Barnard was at last forced to close his studio in 1857. He went to work for Edward Anthony and produced stereographs depicting urban views and landscapes for a new mass market. He was even sent to take photographs in Cuba in 1860. He also worked for Alexander Gardner and for Mathew Brady at his Washington gallery, where he earned notice in 1861 for his photographs of Abraham Lincoln's inauguration and his cartes-de-visite of prominent persons in the capital.

As many other daguerreotypists had done when the process became obsolete in the late 1850s, Barnard adopted a new technique called the collodion, or wet-plate process. His earliest known collodion photographs are of the Civil War, taken in 1862 on the battlegrounds of First Bull Run for either Anthony or Brady. The following year, however, he returned to the battlegrounds as official photographer of the Military

George Barnard's photographic equipment southeast of Atlanta in 1864, photograhed by Barnard himself (*National Archives*)

Division of the Mississippi and the campaigns of General William T. Sherman.

In late December 1863 Barnard began the work for which he is best known. He started to duplicate maps for the Topographical Branch of the Department of Engineers and photographed rail links, buildings, camps, and the area around Nashville. Later, when he accompanied Sherman on his advance on Atlanta, he recorded a unique series of images of war-torn Georgia and of the captured city of Atlanta being demolished by Union troops in November 1864. While in devastated Charleston in March 1865, he took pictures of the ruins of Fort Sumter and the burned district of the port city. Other images were taken in Columbia, South Carolina, in March or early April 1865, and afterwards in North Carolina.

After the war, Barnard published some of his wartime photographs in an expensive collectors' edition, the *Photographic Views of Sherman's Campaign* (1866), with a separately issued thirty-two-page booklet written by Theodore R. Davis to explain the scenes depicted. Barnard operated a studio in Charleston, South Carolina, together with Charles Quinby, and another in Chicago, though the latter was destroyed during the

great fire of 1871—a catastrophe whose destructive force Barnard systematically documented as soon as he could obtain new equipment and materials.

From 1873 onwards, Barnard concentrated on producing portraits in his gallery in Charleston and took hundreds of stereographs of outdoor scenes and posed artistic shots. In 1880 he sold the business and returned to Rochester, New York, where he adapted to yet another revolution in photographic technique, the dry-plate process. For several years, Barnard worked as a promoter of the new plates for George Eastman. He resumed studio work between 1884 and 1888 in Painesville, Ohio, and then retired. In late 1892 or early 1893, George Barnard moved to Cedarville, New York, where he died on 4 February 1902.

—*Angela Schwarz*

See also Brady, Mathew B.; O'Sullivan, Timothy; Photography.
For further reading:
Barnard, George N. *Photographic Views of Sherman's Campaign* (1977).
Davis, Keith F. *George N. Barnard: Photographer of Sherman's Campaign* (1990).
McCaslin, Richard B. *Portraits of Conflict. A Photographic History of South Carolina in the Civil War* (1994).

BARNARD, JOHN GROSS
(1815–1882)
Union general

Born to Robert Foster Barnard and Augusta Porter Barnard in Sheffield, Massachusetts, John Gross Barnard was educated locally before cousin John Buel Porter, John Quincy Adams's secretary of war, gained him an appointment to the U.S. Military Academy. Barnard graduated second of forty-three in the class of 1833.

Commissioned in the Corps of Engineers, Barnard spent the next twenty-five years engaged primarily in the construction of coastal defenses. Most of the country's coastal fortifications dated to the Revolutionary War era and, as a result, the Corps undertook a lengthy modernization effort. Barnard was an important part of this effort.

In addition, Barnard undertook to supervise the improvement of U.S. harbors and inland waterways. His most extensive project, which extended to the post–Civil War years, was the improvement of navigation near the mouth of the Mississippi River. He wrote extensively on the subject, and time would eventually bear out the logic of his approach.

During the Mexican-American War, Barnard served under Winfield Scott. Along with supervising the construction of fortifications, Barnard made reports on the various battles, especially those around Mexico City. In the pre–Civil War period, Barnard also served one year, 1855–1856, as superintendent of the U.S. Military Academy. He also wrote extensively about his various engineering assignments, a habit that would carry over into the post–Civil War period, and he wrote about his various interests in scientific pursuits. The latter interest would lead to his being one of the founding members of the National Academy of Sciences.

At the outbreak of the Civil War, Barnard's reputation as a superior military engineer led to his being brought to Washington, D.C., to improve the capital's defenses. His field experience, however, led Major General Irvin McDowell to ask for his services in the first major campaign of the war at Manassas Junction, Virginia. Barnard designed much of the campaign. Despite the Union defeat at First Bull Run—the plan's execution had not been very good—McDowell commended him for his efforts.

When George McClellan arrived in Washington to assume command of the Army of the Potomac, he made Barnard that army's chief engineer. As a result, on 23 September 1861 Barnard was promoted from major in the regular army to brigadier general of volunteers.

In the spring of 1862, Barnard traveled with the Army of the Potomac to the York Peninsula, where he directed the siege of Yorktown and supervised field works at

John G. Barnard (Photograph by Mathew Brady Studio / *Library of Congress*)

Williamsburg and the battles of the Seven Days. McClellan's dissatisfaction with Barnard led to his being relieved of duty as chief engineer, Army of the Potomac, on 14 August and returned to his former post as the chief engineer of Washington, D.C., charged with directing the defense of the city. He remained in this position, with some detached duty to surrounding areas, until June 1864.

During his time in Washington, Barnard served as an advisor to the War Department on more than the capital's defenses. Because of his wide prewar experience with fortifications, he made recommendations on the defense of other areas as well. In addition, Barnard traveled to outlying areas, such as Harper's Ferry, to recommend changes to enhance their defense.

During the spring of 1864, Ulysses S. Grant began consulting Barnard on the best approaches to Richmond. Grant formalized the relationship on 5 June 1864 when he made Barnard the chief engineer of the Armies in the Field. Barnard traveled to Grant's army, then near Cold Harbor, and for the remainder of the war, with brief interruptions, remained until Robert E. Lee's surrender.

Those interruptions were occasioned by the need for Barnard's presence elsewhere. For instance, later in the summer of 1864, Barnard returned to Washington to deal with the emergency of Jubal Early's raid on the outlying defenses of the capital. Later in 1864, Grant sent Barnard to Savannah, Georgia, to confer with William T. Sherman on the best northward approach for Sherman's army.

During the war, Barnard continued to write, primarily publishing his views on the various campaigns in which he had been involved. After the war, he remained in the Corps of Engineers, rising to the regular rank of colonel. He also continued his prolific writing on various engineering and scientific subjects. His activities in the Corps continued to revolve around coastal defense, and to that end he traveled to Europe to study the best ways to improve U.S. fortifications in the wake of the development of armored vessels and rifled navy artillery. He retired from the service in 1881 and died on 14 May 1882 in Detroit, Michigan.

—*David S. Heidler and Jeanne T. Heidler*

See also Peninsula Campaign; Petersburg Campaign; Washington, D.C.; Yorktown.

For further reading:
Abbot, Henry Larcom. *Biographical Memoir of John Gross Barnard, 1815–1882* (1905).

BARNES, JOSEPH K.
(1817–1883)
Union surgeon general

Born the son of Joseph Barnes in Philadelphia, Pennsylvania, Joseph K. Barnes was educated in Massachusetts and attended Harvard University before choosing a career in medicine. In 1838 he graduated from the medical school of the University of Pennsylvania. In 1840 he entered the U.S. Army as a member of the medical corps. Serving first in Florida in the latter phases of the Second Seminole War, Barnes was next attached to Zachary Taylor in the Mexican-American War when the Army of Observation became the Army of Occupation as it crossed the Rio Grande River. Barnes was next transferred to Winfield Scott's command and accompanied Scott's army on the Mexico City Campaign.

After the Mexican-American War, Barnes served in a variety of frontier posts and was in the Northwest when the Civil War erupted. He transferred to the Department of Kansas, where he served as medical director. In April 1862, Major Barnes moved to the Department of the Mississippi and then to Washington, D.C.

For the next year and one-half, Barnes performed his duties so diligently, attending the thousands of wounded soldiers sent to Washington, that he gained the attention of the Secretary of War, Edwin Stanton. Barnes was promoted to lieutenant colonel in February 1863 and colonel in August 1863. Stanton was not pleased with the performance of Surgeon General William A. Hammond and replaced him with Barnes in September 1863. Barnes held the title of acting surgeon general until August 1864, when he became surgeon general and was promoted to brigadier general.

In this last year of the war, Barnes faced a number of challenges. As the war ranged in various theaters, it was his job to learn of engagements as quickly as possible to arrange for the establishment of field hospitals. Along with this heavy responsibility came the necessity of caring for large numbers of Rebel prisoners as the Confederacy collapsed. Barnes's department had to minister to these men as well as injured Union soldiers.

During Barnes's tenure as surgeon general he recruited as many highly qualified physicians as possible and worked to preserve the experience and knowledge gained for the medical profession by the war. After the war, his work came to fruition with the publication of the *Medical and Surgical History of the War of the Rebellion*. He also established the library that would become the Army Medical Library.

Perhaps Barnes's most difficult duty came in the last days of the war when he had to minister to the mortally wounded Abraham Lincoln. After Lincoln died, Barnes went to Secretary of State William Henry Seward's home. As part of the same conspiracy, another assassin had seriously injured the secretary the previous evening.

After the war, Barnes remained surgeon general, serving in the position until his retirement in 1882. Before he left the job, he had the unenviable task of attending to President James Garfield when that president was mortally wounded by an assassin. Barnes died in Washington, D.C., on 5 April 1883.

—*David S. Heidler and Jeanne T. Heidler*

See also Lincoln Assassination; Medicine.

For further reading:
Brevet Major General Joseph K. Barnes, Surgeon General of the United States Army, 1864–1882 (1904).

BARRINGER, RUFUS
(1821–1895)
Confederate general

Born to Paul Barringer and Elizabeth Brandon Barringer at their family home, Poplar Grove, near Concord, North Carolina, Rufus Barringer graduated from the University of North Carolina, studied law, and became a prominent attorney in the state before the war. He also entered North Carolina politics as a Whig. As the sectional crisis worsened, Barringer opposed secession for his state and supported the Constitutional Union candidate, John Bell, for president in 1860. When North Carolina seceded, however, Barringer raised his own cavalry company, which eventually became a part of the Army of Northern Virginia.

Barringer fought at the Seven Days, Second Bull Run, Antietam, and Fredericksburg. He was seriously wounded in the battle of Brandy Station on 9 June 1863, which prevented him from participating in the Gettysburg campaign. He was promoted to major on 26 August 1863 and, in October of the same year, to lieutenant colonel. In June 1864 he received a promotion to brigadier general and commanded a brigade in the division of William Henry Fitzhugh (Rooney) Lee, R. E. Lee's son. Barringer's brigade consisted of all North Carolina cavalry regiments. He briefly commanded a division at the battle of Reams's Station, 25 August 1864.

In April 1865, again as part of Lee's cavalry division, Barringer's brigade guarded the retreat of the Army of Northern Virginia. At the battle of Sayler's Creek, 3 April 1865, Barringer's brigade was decimated, and he was captured near Namozine Church. He remained a prisoner of war at Fort Delaware until July 1865.

After the war, Barringer became active in the Republican Party in North Carolina. He also resumed his law practice and wrote extensively about the war.

—David S. Heidler and Jeanne T. Heidler

See also Reams's Station, Battle of; Sayler's Creek, Battle of.

For further reading:
Barringer, Rufus. *Civil War Diary of General Rufus Barringer, PACS from Concord, North Carolina, April 1 Through August 8, 1865 from a Photocopy of the Original Manuscript given by Osmond Long "Bugs" Barringer, Jr., to the Southern Historical Collection, University of North Carolina, Chapel Hill, North Carolina* (1998).
Trudeau, Noah Andre. *Out of the Storm; the End of the Civil War, April–June 1865* (1994).

BARRY, WILLIAM FARQUHAR
(1818–1879)
Union general

William Farquhar Barry was born in New York City on 18 August 1818. His father died when Barry was young, but his mother hired a tutor to enhance his education, and the bright boy entered West Point and graduated seventeenth in his class in 1838. He joined the 2d U.S. Artillery and saw his first service along the Canadian border. While engaged in this duty he married Kate McNight in 1840.

During the Mexican-American War, Barry traveled with the 2d Artillery to Mexico, became quite ill, and was assigned to staff work upon his recovery. After the conflict, Barry endured the humdrum peacetime army until he was promoted to captain in 1852. After service against the Seminoles in Florida and in strife-torn Kansas in 1857 and 1858, Barry was recalled to Washington to write a tactical manual for U.S. artillery units.

The outbreak of the Civil War found Barry helping to defend Fort Pickens as a major in the 5th U.S. Artillery. By July, Barry had traveled north to become Brigadier General Irvin McDowell's chief of artillery. He fought at Bull Run after being with McDowell's force for only three days.

Under McDowell's orders, Barry placed two of his batteries on Henry Hill, even though infantry did not properly support them. Although Barry did try to find infantry to bolster the position, his gunners were overrun by a Confederate attack that proved to be the turning point of the battle. Yet Barry's career was little harmed by this, for many Union officers were culpable for the debacle. In August 1861 he became a brigadier general of volunteers. Major General George B. McClellan then appointed him chief of artillery for the Peninsula campaign.

Considering the vaunted reputation of the Army of the Potomac's artillery, it is strange that Barry is not better known for his vital role in developing this arm. When Barry came to Washington in July 1861, he commanded thirty guns, 400 horses, and 650 men. By March 1862 McClellan had 520 cannon, 11,000 horses, and 12,500 gunners for his campaign—-an increase Barry did much to facilitate.

After operations on the peninsula, Barry received a transfer to Washington to become the inspector of artillery for the U.S. Army and the chief of artillery of the Washington defenses. Camp Barry, an artillery marshalling camp in this vicinity, was named in his honor. Barry also tirelessly served on boards dedicated to improving Federal ordnance and fortifications, and coauthored a book in 1863 on McClellan's engineer and artillery detachments during the Peninsula campaign.

Barry's good service gained him a lieutenant colonelcy in the regular army in August 1863. Fellow officers were impressed with the bearing and cultured nature of the tall, handsome artillery officer. One peer wrote that he found Barry to be a "gentleman of cultivated tastes and a soldier." Other fellow officers marveled at Barry's classical knowledge and his ability to play the flute.

In the spring of 1864 Barry again took to the field, this time in the western theater serving as Major General Ulysses S. Grant's chief of artillery. He maintained this position under Major General William T. Sherman after Grant's promotion. During Sherman's Atlanta campaign, Barry kept his scattered batteries in good repair and well supplied with ordnance.

Barry relished serving under the successful Sherman, and Sherman returned the sentiments. In his Atlanta campaign report, Sherman lauded Barry as an officer of "enlarged capacity and great experience, [who] has filled the office of chief of artillery to perfection." On 1 September 1864, Barry gained a brevet promotion to major general of volunteers and colonel in the regular army.

After Barry fought in the campaign to drive

Confederate general John B. Hood from northeast Georgia, he received the dual brevets of brigadier and major general in the regular service on 13 March 1865. The capable artillerist then participated in Sherman's rugged push from Savannah through the Carolinas that resulted in the Army of Tennessee's surrender on 26 April 1865.

On 11 December 1865 Barry was promoted to full colonel and rejoined the 2d U.S. Artillery. By 1866 he was again on duty along the Canadian border, this time monitoring the Fenian situation. In the fall of 1867 he transferred to Fort Monroe, Virginia, to run the military's artillery school, a post he held for ten years.

In 1877 Barry took command of Fort McHenry, dying there on 18 July 1879. The old soldier is buried with his wife in Buffalo's Forest Lawn Cemetery.

—*Dana B. Shoaf*

See also Artillery.

For further reading:

Barnard, John Gross, and William F. Barry. *Report of the Engineer and Artillery Operations of the Army of the Potomac, From its Organization to the Close of the Peninsula Campaign* (1863).

Hitchcock, Henry. *Marching With Sherman; Passages From the Letters and Campaign Diaries of Henry Hitchcock, Major and Assistant Adjutant General of Volunteers. November 1864–May 1865* (1927).

BARTLETT, JOSEPH JACKSON
(1834–1893)
Union general

Born in Binghamton, New York, Joseph Jackson Bartlett studied law as a young man and started to practice in 1858. Upon the outbreak of the Civil War he enlisted in the 27th New York Volunteers and was elected a company captain. Shortly thereafter, however, he was chosen one of the regiment's majors.

After traveling to Washington, D.C., the regiment was made a part of Irvin McDowell's expedition to dislodge the Confederates occupying Manassas Junction. In the resulting battle of First Bull Run, Bartlett assumed temporary command of the regiment when its commander was wounded. He was commended for his bravery and credited with keeping the regiment in the battle when panic threatened. In September 1861 he was promoted to colonel and commander of the regiment, which by then was a part of the Army of the Potomac.

During the Peninsula campaign the following spring and summer, Bartlett, still at the rank of colonel, was given command of a brigade. He led his brigade during the Seven Days' battles and was commended for his actions at Gaines' Mill.

During the Maryland campaign he commanded his brigade at Crampton's Pass on 14 September as part of

William B. Franklin's VI Corps. Finally, in October 1861 he received the long-awaited promotion to brigadier general, one month before his twenty-eighth birthday. His promotion was not confirmed by the Senate in the requisite amount of time and expired the following March. It was resubmitted for the next session and confirmed.

In the meantime, Bartlett fought at Fredericksburg against Stonewall Jackson's Corps on the Confederate right. In the subsequent Chancellorsville campaign in May 1863, Bartlett, as part of VI Corps, remained opposite Fredericksburg while the remainder of the Army of the Potomac moved to flank Robert E. Lee's position. The corps crossed the Rappahannock after the bulk of Lee's army had left its works, took Marye's Heights and moved toward Lee's army from Fredericksburg. Bartlett fought at Salem Church before retreating back across the river with the remainder of the army.

During the Gettysburg campaign, Bartlett continued to command 2d Brigade, 1st Division, VI Corps, but on the evening of 2 July was given command of an extra brigade along with his own. He commanded both brigades the following day in the effort to dislodge the Confederate forces from the areas at the foot of the Roundtops. Following the battle, Bartlett temporarily assumed command of 3d Division, VI Corps, although he was back in command of his brigade by early August 1863.

In early September 1863 Bartlett nearly fell into Confederate hands. Headquartered with his brigade at New Baltimore, Virginia, Bartlett was unaware that his rather exposed position was known to Confederate cavalry general J. E. B. Stuart. Stuart, determined to bag Bartlett as a trophy of war, sent a small raiding party to New Baltimore to capture the Union general. The Confederates arrived in the middle of the night, but made enough noise that Bartlett was alerted to their presence before they found him. He was forced to flee his headquarters in his underclothes, something Stuart made great fun of in his final report.

In November 1863 Bartlett was transferred to V Corps and temporarily given command of 1st Division. He commanded that division at Rappahannock Station on 7–8 November and during the Mine Run campaign. Then in January 1864 he took his men into quarters at Rappahannock Station. He remained there through February 1864.

During Ulysses S. Grant's campaign against Robert E. Lee in the spring of 1864, Bartlett reverted to brigade command. He led 3d Brigade, 1st Division, V Corps at the Wilderness, Spotsylvania, and Cold Harbor. In July 1864, in the early phases of the Siege of Petersburg, Bartlett again temporarily succeeded to the command of 1st Division but was back in command of his brigade by August. In that month he received a brevet promotion to major general of volunteers. He continued to command the same brigade throughout the siege of

Petersburg into the early stages of the Appomattox campaign. On 1 April 1865 he again was made commander of 1st Division, V Corps, which he commanded until the surrender of Lee. When Lee's men marched out on 12 April 1865, Bartlett commanded the Union detachment that accepted the stacked Confederate arms.

A week and a half after the surrender Bartlett was transferred to IX Corps, where he briefly commanded 2d Division. He remained in the army until mustered out with most of the volunteers in 1866.

Following the war Bartlett entered into a diplomatic and government career. He served from 1867 to 1869 as United States minister to Sweden and Norway. Upon his return, he resumed the practice of law before accepting an appointment as a deputy pension commissioner. In his later years, Bartlett lived in Baltimore, Maryland, where he died on 14 January 1893. His remains were interred at Arlington.

—*David S. Heidler and Jeanne T. Heidler*

See also Appomattox Court House.
For further reading:
Trudeau, Noah Andre. *The Last Citadel: Petersburg, Virginia, June 1864–April 1865* (1991).
———. *Out of the Storm: The End of the Civil War, April–June 1865* (1994).

BARTLETT, WILLIAM FRANCIS
(1840–1876)
Union general

Born in Haverhill, Massachusetts, William Francis Bartlett was educated locally before enrolling in Harvard in 1858. When he learned of the surrender of Fort Sumter in April 1861, he left school to enlist in the army as a private in a ninety-day unit, the 4th Massachusetts. After being mustered out at the expiration of the unit's term, Bartlett later in the summer joined the 20th Massachusetts Infantry and was elected his company's captain.

In the early fall of 1861, the 20th Massachusetts became a part of the Army of the Potomac. In October 1861 Bartlett led his company in the disastrous Union defeat at Ball's Bluff. In the spring of 1862, Bartlett and the 20th traveled to the York Peninsula in Virginia to participate in the Peninsula campaign. In the fighting during the siege of Yorktown, Bartlett was struck in the leg by enemy fire and lost the limb to amputation.

Bartlett returned home, where he recuperated and received his degree from Harvard that summer. Rather than return to the 20th upon his recovery, he opted instead to raise a regiment on his own, and in November 1862 he was commissioned the colonel of the 49th Massachusetts. Upon being mustered into Federal service, the 49th was sent to Louisiana to

become part of the Army of the Gulf under the command of Nathaniel P. Banks.

Bartlett led his regiment in the battles for and the siege of Port Hudson. During the fighting in the spring and summer of 1863 he received two wounds and as a result could not move about the battlefield except on horseback. Even though he presented quite a target for his Confederate opponents, Confederates later claimed that their admiration for Bartlett's bravery prevented them from firing at him.

After the Port Hudson campaign, Bartlett again, because of his wounds, was forced to temporarily return home. After recovering through the summer and fall of 1863, he began to raise yet another regiment for Federal service.

Bartlett became the colonel of the 57th Massachusetts just in time for Ulysses S. Grant's Virginia campaign against Robert E. Lee. The 57th became a part of IX Corps commanded by Ambrose Burnside. Commanding his regiment in the opening battle of the campaign at the Wilderness, Bartlett was again seriously wounded. In June 1864 he was promoted to brigadier general of volunteers, and when he returned to duty in July, he was given command of 1st brigade, 1st division, IX Corps. His division commander was James H. Ledlie.

In July, Bartlett led his brigade in some of the early engagements around Petersburg. As part of IX Corps, he was also involved in the planning of the tunnel under the Confederate works that would result in the battle of the Crater. On 30 July he led his brigade forward after the initial explosion but was slightly wounded and had his prosthetic leg shot off. Unable to retreat with his men, Bartlett was captured by the Confederates. Ambrose Burnside commended Bartlett for his bravery at the Crater.

Bartlett spent several months in Richmond's Libby Prison before a special exchange could be arranged. Upon his release he returned to his brigade. Before the war was over he commanded a division of IX Corps at age twenty-four. In March 1865 he received a brevet promotion to major general for gallantry. After Lee's surrender, Bartlett remained in the army until being mustered out with most of the volunteers in 1866.

After leaving the army, Bartlett accepted a position with the Tredegar Iron Works in Richmond. The company had been confiscated by the U.S. government. Within a few years, homesick and in very poor health due to his many wounds received during the war, Bartlett returned to Massachusetts and settled in Pittsfield. He never regained his health and died in Pittsfield at the age of thirty-six on 17 December 1876.

—*David S. Heidler and Jeanne T. Heidler*

See also Crater, Battle of the; Port Hudson; Wilderness, Battle of the.
For further reading:
Palfrey, Francis Winthrop. *Memoir of William Francis Bartlett* (1881).

BARTON, CLARA
(1821–1912)
Union relief worker

The Civil War was a proving ground for Clarissa Harlowe Barton. Named for Samuel Richardson's eighteenth-century fictional heroine whose filial bonds could not protect her from the world of men, the Massachusetts native spent the war years navigating the treacherous waters of independent relief work and looking for allies among soldiers and government officials. In the first year and a half of the war, Barton brought food and supplies to thousands wounded at Second Manassas, Antietam, and Fredericksburg, before the Army Medical Department and other philanthropists had coordinated relief efforts. So adept was Barton at arriving at the moment of greatest need that she became known as the Army of the Potomac's "angel of the battlefield," and soldiers named their daughters after her. She was also adept at promoting her battlefield stories; postwar audiences had little idea that the legendary woman of steel suffered acutely from depression and lack of confidence throughout the war.

As the youngest of five, whose older siblings held parental authority over her, Barton was traditionally reared to keep house and respect her elders. From her father Stephen, who had fought Indians in Michigan Territory and was fond of regaling his young daughter with tales of his prowess, Clara inherited a love of nation and things military. Before she was out of adolescence, she was a skilled marksman and rider, and proficient—thanks to her mother Sarah—in the domestic arts. Starting in her eleventh year, Barton nursed her brother David for two years after he was seriously injured in a fall. She worked briefly in the family's satinet mill, then found her calling as a teacher late in the 1830s. A charismatic educator, Clara and her brother Stephen helped bring educational reform to North Oxford, Massachusetts, in the 1840s.

Only five feet tall in adulthood, Clara was determined to overcome her family's diminutive expectations for her future. In 1850 she began studies at the Clinton (New York) Liberal Institute in the hope of becoming something more than a New England schoolmarm. After her mother's death in 1851, Barton moved to school chum Mary Norton's home in New Jersey and found work in Cedarville. When opportunity arose to open a free school in Bordentown, Clara became a principal and built the student body from six to six hundred pupils in just one year. Soon the community hired a man to assume Barton's position, believing a woman unsuited to such responsibility, and Barton resigned rather than accept demotion. By 1854 she had secured one of the first jobs open to women in the U.S. Civil Service, as a Patent Office copyist in Washington. The target of male clerks' ire because she earned a salary equal to theirs and greatly surpassed their productivity, Barton worked under stress until 1857 when the Buchanan administration terminated her. After three years of nursing her ailing father in Massachusetts, Barton returned to the Patent Office under the Lincoln administration, but at a reduced salary, which felt like a slap in the face to her.

Initially uneasy about the prospect of becoming a relief worker—Barton believed that her reputation would suffer if she cast her lot with soldiers—she solicited supplies from friends in North Oxford in 1861 and began distributing them among Massachusetts boys stationed in Washington. As she stockpiled goods in her three-room flat at Seventh and Pennsylvania, Barton was called away to her father's deathbed. It was he who encouraged her to engage more actively in work at the front. With the help of Colonel Daniel Rucker in the Quartermaster's Office, she got permission and the wagons to carry her supplies to Culpeper Court House and, after Second Bull Run in August 1862, to Fairfax Station. When, years later, Barton confessed that she had brought only five cups, two buckets, one kettle, four knives, and two lanterns to serve several thousand men, she was quick to add that she "was never caught so again."

Barely three weeks later, Barton and four teamsters raced with provisions toward Sharpsburg, Maryland, on the eve of the battle of Antietam. Working in a farmhouse on a line of wounded that extended for five miles, Barton stopped for only a catnap between Saturday and Tuesday. During this time she extracted a bullet from the cheek of a soldier and helped surgeon James Dunn (whom she had assisted at Second Bull Run) perform amputations without flinching. Here also bullets passed through the sleeve of her dress, killing a man she was tending. After six weeks of hard service, Barton developed typhoid and returned to Washington. By December, she was literally back in the saddle with IX Army Corps, as Ambrose Burnside tried to outflank Robert E. Lee at Fredericksburg. In bitter weather, with 12,000 dead and thousands more wounded, Barton completed her first and best year of the war. Never again would so much authority to act on soldiers' behalf be given to her. The Sanitary Commission, which had little tolerance for women in charge, effectively put Barton and countless other independent relief workers out of business by the end of 1862.

The year 1863 was a low point in Barton's nursing career. Assigned to the Sea Islands during the siege of Charleston, she felt like an intruder on turf already contested by Sanitary Commission agents, Freedmen's Relief workers, and uncooperative staff officers. Even the presence of Barton's brother David in the Quartermaster's Office did little to shield her from "surgeons bristling like porcupines" at the prospect of civilian help and female nurses who compromised Barton's claim to center stage. Two friendships from this period were significant: Abolitionist and woman's rights advocate Frances Dana Gage challenged Barton intellectually and provided unstinting moral support; and Colonel John Elwell, whom Barton called "whole, solid, and deep," became her cavalier and lover, joining her at dawn for horseback rides on the beach.

Barton left Port Royal on the last day of 1863, having celebrated her forty-second birthday on Christmas. Back in Washington, she sank into severe depression, alleviated somewhat by an invitation to join the Army of the Potomac at Belle Plain in late spring. She was on hand for the battles of the Wilderness in May 1864 and the slaughter of 7,000 Union troops at Cold Harbor in June. In late June Benjamin Butler invited Barton to join his men at Point of Rocks, Virginia. She told her friends that she had been appointed superintendent of nursing for Butler's Army of the James, but she exaggerated: she worked in a "flying" or mobile field hospital staffed by nurses of equal responsibility. Never easy about relinquishing her diva status, Barton sparred with New Yorker Adelaide Smith until a surgeon, fearing Barton's ultimatums, sent Smith packing. In the fall General Butler helped Barton secure the release of her brother Stephen from a Union prison camp in Norfolk; Stephen had established mills in North Carolina in 1856 and was reviled as a Northern sympathizer when the war began.

By early 1865 Barton began to hatch a new plan in conjunction with Union prisoners of war released to Annapolis. She was determined to create a bureau of missing soldiers, hoping to provide desperate mothers and wives with information about their sons and husbands. Having no funds for starting up—her Patent Office job had long since stagnated and she was never on a nursing payroll—she sought President Lincoln's help. After a protracted struggle during which Barton called on such men of influence as Butler, Senator Henry Wilson, and Secretary of War Edwin Stanton for help, she learned that Captain James Moore had been appointed head of the U.S. Burial Bureau. Again, a man had been chosen to do what Barton knew she could do better; the particular choice was galling because Moore had stolen her thunder during the July 1865 expedition to identify missing soldiers at Andersonville prison. These events, coupled with the deaths of Stephen and her twenty-four-year-old nephew, Irving Vassal, in the spring, devastated her.

By December, Barton felt friendless. "I make up my mind more and more," she wrote, "that I must be and do by myself and alone, of all that I have helped no one who has strength is ready to help me, my affairs are as bad as they can be." But as she had done before, she made new plans—this time to capitalize on her war exploits from the podium. From 1866 to 1868, Barton gave more than 300 lectures in towns across the East and Midwest, sometimes earning $100 for an appearance. Years later, after

Barton's genius for relief had been realized in the American Red Cross (ARC) and she had retired from twenty-three years at its head, she told a G.A.R. encampment celebrating the fiftieth anniversary of the firing on Fort Sumter, "Under the guns our love grew up, under the sod it shall remain." Though Barton's work with the Red Cross made hers a household name by the 1880s, she always retained her keenest sense of connection with the soldiers she had cared for during the war. She continued to honor them long after her ARC leadership had begun to founder and she retired to Glen Echo, Maryland, in 1904. Here Barton spent her last years, promoting disaster relief, women's suffrage, and pay equity until her death at age ninety-one.

—*Jane E. Schultz*

See also American Red Cross; Nurses; United States Sanitary Commission.

For further reading:

Barton, Clara. Collection. Manuscript Division, Library of Congress, Washington, D.C.

Burton, David H. *Clara Barton: In the Service of Humanity* (1995).

Norton, Mary. Papers. Perkins Library, Duke University, Durham, North Carolina.

Oates, Stephen. *A Woman of Valor: Clara Barton and the Civil War* (1994).

Pryor, Elizabeth Brown. *Clara Barton, Professional Angel* (1987).

BARTON, SETH MAXWELL
(1829–1900)
Confederate general

Born in Fredericksburg, Virginia, the son of Thomas Bowerbank Barton, Seth Barton was admitted to the United States Military Academy at West Point at the age of fifteen. He graduated twenty-eighth in a class of forty-three in 1849. After serving briefly in New York Harbor, Barton was transferred to New Mexico. For the next eleven years, he served in a variety of frontier posts, achieving the rank of captain before resigning his commission on 11 June 1861 while stationed at Fort Leavenworth, Kansas Territory.

Following his return to Virginia, Barton offered his services to the Confederate army and received a captain's commission. In July 1861 he was offered the position of lieutenant colonel of the 3d Arkansas Regiment and traveled to western Virginia where that regiment was serving. He fought at Cheat Mountain under Robert E. Lee in September 1861. Later in the year, his engineering talents came to the attention of Confederate general Stonewall Jackson, and from the end of 1861 to early 1862, Barton served as Jackson's chief engineer.

On 11 March 1862 Barton was promoted to brigadier general and transferred to east Tennessee to serve under

E. Kirby Smith. Barton's primary task in the spring and summer of 1862 was to prevent Union movement through the Cumberland Gap. In the fall his brigade moved into Tennessee with the remainder of Kirby Smith's army to participate in Braxton Bragg's Kentucky campaign. In December 1862 Barton and his brigade were transferred to the defenses of Vicksburg, Mississippi.

In the Vicksburg campaign, Barton and his brigade fought in most of the major engagements, including Chickasaw Bayou, Chickasaw Bluffs, and the battle of Champion's Hill, where Barton lost 42 percent of his brigade. Barton surrendered with Confederate forces at Vicksburg in July 1863 and was paroled with the bulk of that army. After being exchanged shortly thereafter, Barton was sent to Petersburg, Virginia, to take command of the late Lewis Armistead's brigade of George Pickett's division. In the Confederate attack on New Bern, North Carolina, in January 1864, Barton became embroiled in a dispute with Pickett about the failure of that campaign. Shortly after this dispute, Barton was transferred to Major Robert Ransom's division in Virginia. After fighting at the Wilderness and Drewry's Bluff, Barton was this time criticized as incompetent by his new commander. Ransom removed Barton from command of his brigade on 10 May.

Over the next several weeks, Barton repeatedly requested that a court of inquiry be convened on his behalf, but although one was scheduled for 7 June, it was canceled at the last minute. Even though Barton's subordinate officers signed a letter attesting to his fitness for command, he did not return to active service until the fall of 1864 and then only in temporary command of a brigade. He did not regain permanent command of a brigade until January 1865. Barton was captured with most of his brigade at Sayler's Creek on 6 April and imprisoned in Fort Warren until July 1865.

Virtually nothing is known of Barton's life after the war except that he died in Washington, D.C., in 1900.

—*David S. Heidler and Jeanne T. Heidler*

See also Ransom, Robert, Jr.; Sayler's Creek, Battle of.

BARTOW, FRANCIS STEBBINS
(1816–1861)

Confederate congressman and officer

Born to Theodosius Bartow and Frances Lloyd Stebbins Bartow in Savannah, Georgia, Francis Bartow was educated at Franklin College in Georgia and Yale Law School before returning to Georgia to become a practicing attorney. In the years before the outbreak of the Civil War, Bartow became a very influential lawyer and active Whig politician. He served as both a senator and representative in the Georgia legislature. As the sectional crisis intensified in the 1850s, Bartow became increasingly associated with strong states' rights factions in the state. Following the election of Abraham Lincoln to the presidency, Bartow was selected a delegate to the Georgia secession convention as an advocate for secession.

Following the secession of the state, Bartow represented Georgia as one of the provisional congressmen to Montgomery, Alabama, where the Confederate States of America was formed. In Montgomery, Bartow was part of the Howell Cobb faction and supported Cobb for president of the Confederacy. He was one of the signers for Georgia of the Confederate Constitution.

Bartow served on several committees of the provisional Confederate Congress, including the Flag Committee. On that committee, Bartow urged that the new Confederate flag not stray too far from the appearance of the United States flag. Bartow also served as the chairman of the Military Affairs Committee of the Provisional Confederate Congress. In this position, he often conferred with President Jefferson Davis on the military preparedness of the new nation and on the proper military response to the continued presence of United States troops on Confederate soil. Bartow was anxious that, should a conflict occur, the Confederate States Army should be properly organized and supplied so that it could react quickly. Therefore, he urged the Confederate Congress and Davis to organize the army before any conflict occurred. Once the organizational process began, Bartow was instrumental in the selection of gray as the color for Confederate uniforms.

Once the war broke out at Fort Sumter in April 1861, Bartow resigned from the Confederate Congress to join the Confederate army. Before the war, he had been a captain in the Oglethorpe Light Infantry militia unit in Savannah, Georgia, and pictured himself as somewhat of a military expert. He raised and accepted the colonelcy of the 8th Georgia Regiment in the spring of 1861 and participated almost immediately in the seizure of Fort McAllister. Shortly thereafter, Bartow's regiment was transferred to Virginia, where he took command of a brigade at Manassas.

Although never promoted to brigadier general, Bartow commanded his brigade at First Bull Run. He fought alongside Bernard Bee's brigade on the north side of the Warrenton Turnpike and retreated with that officer and his brigade to Henry House Hill after the Federal offensive. Along with Bee, Bartow led a counterattack against the Union forces and was killed in that action.

—*David S. Heidler and Jeanne T. Heidler*

See also Bull Run, First Battle of; Cobb, Howell; Congress, C.S.A.; Georgia.

For further reading:
Confederate States of America. Congress. *Proceedings of the Congress on the Announcement of the Death of Colonel Francis S. Bartow of the Army of the Confederate States, and Late a Delegate in the Congress, from the State of Georgia* (1861).

BATE, WILLIAM BRIMAGE
(1825–1905)
Confederate general

Born to James Henry Bate and Amanda Weathered Bate in Bledsoe's Lick, Tennessee, William Bate was educated in Tennessee before becoming a steamboat clerk as a young man. At the outset of the Mexican-American War in 1846, he enlisted in the 3d Tennessee Volunteers as a private and rose to the rank of first lieutenant by the end of the war two years later. Following the Mexican-American War he became a newspaper editor for the *Tenth Legion* in Gallatin, Tennessee. He also entered politics as an active member of the Democratic Party and served in the Tennessee legislature from 1849 to 1851. While engaged in politics, Bate studied law at Lebanon University and opened an office after graduation in 1852. Bate had a private practice from 1852 until 1854, when he received an appointment as the attorney general for the Nashville District. He remained active in Democratic politics and became a strong advocate of states' rights. In 1860 he was selected as a Breckinridge elector for the presidential election and upon Lincoln's election, he supported Tennessee's secession from the Union.

After Tennessee seceded, Bate enlisted as a private to serve in that rank until receiving a colonel's appointment in the 2d Tennessee Regiment. He led his regiment at Shiloh where he saw his younger brother, Captain Humphrey Bate, commander of one of the Second Tennessee's companies, killed. He himself was severely wounded in the left leg. When doctors proposed amputating the limb, Bate held a gun on them to prevent it. He kept the leg, but he never walked again without a crutch.

During his recuperation, Bate was stationed at Huntsville, Alabama. While there on 3 October 1862, he received a promotion to brigadier general. By the end of the year, he was again commanding his brigade. He fought at Stones River and then in the Tullahoma campaign at the end of June 1863, at Chickamauga in September 1863, and led a division at Missionary Ridge in November 1863. In 1863 he was courted as a potential governor of Tennessee, but refused to leave the field. On 23 February 1864, he was promoted to major general and commanded a division of Hardee's Corps in the Atlanta campaign. He was commended for his actions at Resaca.

Like most of the Confederate army, he went with John Bell Hood into Tennessee following the fall of Atlanta, and was commended for bravery for his actions at Franklin. He fought tenaciously at Nashville in December 1864 and then joined Lieutenant General Joseph E. Johnston in the Carolinas in early 1865. He surrendered what was left of his division at Greensboro, North Carolina, in April 1865.

Though barred from voting or running for office during Reconstruction, Bate remained active in Democratic politics in Tennessee. With the return to Democratic domination of the state, he was elected governor in 1882. He remained in that office until elected to the United States Senate in 1886. As a United States senator, Bate sponsored a bill, passed in 1893, that removed the last federal controls over local elections remaining from the Reconstruction period. Bate died in office as a U.S. Senator in Washington, D.C., in 1905.

Wounded three times during the war, Bate was known as something of a martinet, although one who could inspire his men to perform tremendous feats of bravery.

—*David S. Heidler and Jeanne T. Heidler*

See also Missionary Ridge; Nashville, Battle of; Resaca, Battle of.
For further reading:
Bate, William B. "The Campaign in Tennessee: Official Report of Major-General William B. Bate of the Operations of His Division at Franklin, Murfreesboro and Nashville." *Annals of the Army of Tennessee and Early Western History* (1878).
Marshall, Park. *A Life of William B. Bate, Citizen, Soldier and Statesman* (1908).

BATES, EDWARD
(1793–1869)
U.S. attorney general

Edward Bates was born on 4 September 1793 in Goochland County, Virginia, to Quaker parents. His family was thrust into debt when, during the Revolutionary War, the British destroyed their plantation, a situation not fully rectified when his father died in 1805. The responsibility for rearing Bates, the youngest of twelve children, was assumed by his older brother Frederick. Over his mother's objections, Bates volunteered for service in the War of 1812. In 1814 he departed for St. Louis, where Frederick had established a successful law practice.

Bates read law for two years under the guidance of Rufus Eaton and received his license in 1816. While his brother and Eaton made their fortunes settling land dispute cases, Bates accepted the less lucrative cases involving the personal and professional affairs of politicians and members of the business community of St. Louis. Bates cut his political teeth on the campaign for Missouri statehood, developing a resentment for federal interference in states' rights. In 1826 he was elected as a Whig to serve in the Twentieth Congress, where he opposed U.S. occupation of Oregon. Losing the race for reelection to the House, Bates returned to Missouri, hoping to capture a vacant U.S. Senate seat, but was defeated by Thomas Hart Benton, one of Missouri's leading Democrats. Bates returned to practicing law and became the state's most prominent Whig.

Bates gained national recognition as the presiding officer at the 1847 River and Harbor Commission convention held in Chicago. He advocated increased funding for a series of internal improvements to develop the western states. Thereafter his opinion was sought regarding national political issues. He became a leading opponent of the extension of slavery into the territories, yet believed that the federal government must not meddle with the "peculiar institution" in states where it was established legally.

Bates acted as president of the last Whig convention in 1856. He remained suspicious of the new Republican Party because of its strong abolitionist element, but his anti-Lecompton stance in 1858 enamored many Republicans to him. A "Bates for President" drive launched by conservative Republicans before the 1860 convention flattered him, but suspicion of his Southern roots, advocacy of states' rights, and support for Millard Fillmore's campaign in 1856 stymied his candidacy. When the Chicago convention rallied around Abraham Lincoln, Bates graciously accepted defeat and agreed to join the president-elect's cabinet. His status as the most prominent border state politician in the cabinet gave him influence in the early days of the administration. He advocated strengthening the military presence along the Mississippi, forethought that reaped great benefit to the Union army during the war. Bates cheered the president's removal of General John C. Frémont from command in Missouri and provided legal justification for Lincoln's controversial suspension of the writ of habeas corpus.

Bates's habitual equivocation, as seen during the *Trent* Affair, caused him problems within the cabinet. Initially he applauded the detention of the Confederate diplomats, but pressure from Secretary of State William H. Seward, who feared a war with Great Britain, compelled Bates to reverse his position. Bates's conservative opinions became increasingly unpopular among his Republican colleagues. He opposed the admission of West Virginia as a state, believing this action assailed the Constitution to expedite emancipation. He publicly disagreed with the president over having the freedmen serve in the Union army and increased his criticism of congressional plans for rapid emancipation of the slaves. Bates opined repeatedly that the radicals in Congress were attempting to undermine the power of the executive branch and urged the president to be more decisive. Bates believed that the army was abusing the "military necessity" doctrine and posed a threat to the rights of civilians in occupied Confederate territory. As his influence on the president waned, Bates scrapped more openly with his colleagues. Tired of feuding with fellow cabinet members and with his health impaired, Bates resigned on 30 November 1864. He hoped that the president would reward his service by naming him chief justice of the Supreme Court to replace the deceased

Roger Taney. Bates was bitterly disappointed when Salmon P. Chase was chosen instead.

Bates returned to Missouri where Radical Republicans dominated the state government. He objected to the new state constitution and lobbied for an end to the military influence in the government. Disheartened by the course of events in his state and the national Reconstruction policy fashioned by the Radical Republicans in Congress, Bates's health deteriorated further until his death on 25 March 1869.

—Jane Flaherty

See also Election of 1860; Habeas Corpus, Writ of (U.S.A.); Missouri; *Trent* Affair.

For further reading:

Beale, Howard K., ed. *The Diary of Edward Bates, 1859–1866* (1930; reprint, 1971).
Cain, Marvin R. *Lincoln's Attorney General: Edward Bates of Missouri* (1965).

BATON ROUGE, BATTLE OF
(5 August 1862)

The August 1862 engagement at Baton Rouge, Louisiana, marked a period of joint army-navy operations by both antagonists. The 3,200 Federal troops who occupied Baton Rouge had been landed there by Federal ships commanded by Rear Admiral David G. Farragut after the failed July 1862 attack on Vicksburg. U.S. brigadier general Thomas Williams concentrated his garrison on the city's eastern side, with a detachment on the north and gunboats on the river anchoring the western flank.

Major General Earl Van Dorn, Confederate commander at Vicksburg, sought to exploit Farragut's defeat by seizing Port Hudson, which lay 25 miles north of Baton Rouge and between Baton Rouge and Vicksburg. In 1862, Vicksburg was the key to the Confederacy's Mississippi River defense.

Van Dorn assigned Major General John C. Breckinridge to lead the attack with 4,000 men of the Vicksburg garrison. The CSS *Arkansas*, the last of the Confederate ironclads, was assigned to provide artillery support and to fight Union gunboats that supported the city's western flank.

On 4 August, on the eve of the battle, almost half of the city's garrison was hors de combat due to fever. Many of the sick left their beds to join the defense.

Breckinridge's force of almost equal strength was stricken by fever. Breckinridge divided his force into two units under Brigadier General Daniel Ruggles and Brigadier General Charles Clark.

The first shots were fired early on the morning of 5 August. While Confederate attackers threw themselves at the city's eastern defenses, a smaller artillery-supported detachment attacked the Federal north flank and was turned back. General Clark's men arrived and reinforced the initial Confederate attack, eventually pushing the Federal left flank toward the eastern defenders. Fog added to the confusion of the battle, and Federal troops were routed westward into the city, pursued by vengeful civilians.

General Williams fell while trying to put together a counterattack. Union naval artillery intervened to prevent Breckinridge from exploiting his advance. The exhausted Federal troops remained in the city for the next several days while Ruggles's troops fortified Port Hudson. Clark was wounded on the battlefield and captured. Two weeks after the battle, Federal troops evacuated the city and returned to New Orleans. Union casualties were approximately 400 killed, wounded, and missing; Confederate losses were approximately 450 dead, wounded, and missing.

The battle at Baton Rouge marked the end of the CSS *Arkansas*. Its commander, Captain Isaac Newton Brown, was away on sick leave, and his replacement, Lieutenant Henry Kennedy Stevens, received orders to weigh anchor and support Breckinridge's attack. Since repairs had not been completed, the orders were ill advised. In addition, the *Arkansas*'s experienced chief engineer was left ashore due to sickness.

The *Arkansas* was not ready for action when the fighting on land started. The ship's engines failed several times, including once while the *Arkansas* was in front of Federal ships. On 6 August, the drifting and unmaneuverable *Arkansas* was scuttled by fire and sank.

—*James V. Holton*

See also *Arkansas*, CSS; Breckinridge, John Cabell.
For further reading:
Luraghi, Raimondo. *A History of the Confederate Navy* (1996).

"BATTLE HYMN OF THE REPUBLIC"

The "Battle Hymn of The Republic" by Julia Ward Howe is more identified with the American Civil War than any other piece of music. Sung to the tune of an old Methodist camp meeting song, it drew upon the musical legacy of African-American spirituals as well as that of the Protestant "Second Great Awakening." In response to the hanging of John Brown in October 1859, anonymous admirers who shared his vision of slave liberation began using the old tune:

John Brown's body lies a-mouldering in the grave,
John Brown's body lies a-mouldering in the grave,
John Brown's body lies a-mouldering in the grave,
But his soul goes marching on.
Glory, glory, hallelujah!
Glory, glory, hallelujah!
Glory, glory, hallelujah!
His soul goes marching on.

Thrice acknowledging that "John Brown's Body lies a-mouldering in the grave," it closed with the ominous warning that his dream of slave liberation marched on. Easily learned and used, the song spread quickly through the antislavery movement, the Republican Party, and, in 1861, the volunteer units of the Federal army.

However, the song's very simplicity inspired not only many verses but also more elaborate and less repetitive lyrics. "The John Brown Song," for example, related that

He captured Harper's Ferry with his nineteen men so true,
They frightened old Virginia 'til she trembled through and through.
They hanged him for a traitor, they themselves the traitor crew,
But his truth is marching on.

With the outbreak of the war, the volunteer units of the Federal army, particularly those with antislavery leaderships, took up the refrain. Clearly, until the formal adoption of emancipation as a war goal in late 1862, the singing of these verses represented a musical appeal to expand the political and social purposes of the war.

In October 1861, the newly arrived 14th Massachusetts sang "John Brown's Body" as it slogged its way through Washington during a driving rainstorm. Its commander, Colonel William B. Greene, was a radical Transcendentalist who, unusually, had been to West Point and provided a vital link between New England abolitionist leaders and the emerging military hierarchy. Assigned to build and garrison the fortifications adjacent to Washington in northern Virginia, the regiment frequently hosted official and quasiofficial visitors with its singing of "John Brown's Body."

In November, Governor John Andrew of Massachusetts brought a party across the Potomac to visit the regiment at Fort Albany. Julia Ward Howe was among the visitors. On the way back, Andrew remarked to Julia Ward Howe that the song might better employ its lines. On her return to Washington, Howe penned "The Battle Hymn of the Republic":

Mine eyes have seen the glory of the coming of the Lord:
He is trampling out the vintage where the grapes of wrath are stored;
He hath loosed the fateful lightning of His terrible swift sword:
His truth is marching on.

The title alone spoke volumes. The "Battle Hymn of the Republic" sings of a faith that history represented the unfolding of the divine will for human justice, that the American republic represented such progress, and that the ordeal of civil strife remained part of this ultimately benevolent process. Like its author, it continued to be identified with the range of social reforms that emerged from the Civil War, ranging from black rights to women's suffrage and the labor movement. It has, in the process, remained one of the most popular of the nation's patriotic "hymns."

—*Mark A. Lause*

See also Brown, John; "Dixie"; Howe, Julia Ward; Music.
For further reading:
Crawford Richard, comp. *The Civil War Songbook* (1977).
Roe, Alfred S., and Charles Nutt. *History of the First Regiment of Heavy Artillery Massachusetts Volunteers, Formerly the Fourteenth Regiment of Infantry, 1861–1865* (1917).
Silber, Irwin. *Songs of the Civil War* (1960).
Silverman, Jerry. *Ballads and Songs of the Civil War* (1993).

BATTLES AND LEADERS OF THE CIVIL WAR

Published as a four-volume book set in 1887, although some of the material was originally printed in *The Century* magazine in the preceding years, *Battles and Leaders of the Civil War* compiled the written recollections from men who survived the war. The editors of the book edition note that the genesis of this material began with the publication of two opposing views on the John Brown raid. From November 1884 to November 1887, *The Century* published its Civil War series, and circulation soared from 127,000 to 225,000 in the first six months alone. The book version expanded the material taken from the magazine publications.

In the introduction to the book, the editors state that their chief motive was "strict fairness to the testimony of both sides" and that their chief endeavors were "to prove every important statement by the *Official Records* and other trustworthy documents, and to spare no pains in the interest of elucidation and accuracy." Both sides of the conflict were thus scrupulously represented. The book was also richly illustrated.

The material in *Battles and Leaders* helped inform a whole generation of Americans, particularly those born immediately after the Civil War, about the bloody conflict. Some participants even used the opportunity to clarify or defend a particular matter of controversy they may have been involved in during the war. For example, Major General Oliver O. Howard explains his perspective of the embarrassing rout and retreat of his regiment by General Thomas J. "Stonewall" Jackson during the battle of Chancellorsville. Howard ends his account with a tribute to his rival:

Stonewall Jackson was victorious. Even his enemies praise him; but, providentially for us, it was the last battle that he waged against American Union. For, in

bold planning, in energy of execution, which he had the power to diffuse, in indefatigable activity and moral ascendancy, Jackson stood head and shoulders above his conferees, and after his death General Lee could not replace him.

Another interesting recollection is that of General James Longstreet, which engendered extreme controversy in its assessment of Lee's performance at Gettysburg, especially in ordering Pickett's fateful charge. About his role in the decision, Longstreet writes:

It has been said that I should have exercised discretion and should not have sent Pickett on his charge. It has been urged that I had exercised discretion on previous occasions. It is true that at times when I saw a certainty of success in another direction, I did not follow the orders of my general, but that was when he is away, you have a right to exercise discretion; but if he sees everything that you see, you have no right to disregard his positive and repeated orders. I never exercised discretion after discussing with General Lee the points of his orders, *and* when, after discussion, he had ordered the execution of his policy. I had offered my objections to Pickett's battle and had been overruled, and I was in the immediate presence of the commanding general when the order was given for Pickett to advance.

That day at Gettysburg was one of the saddest of my life.

Responding to Longstreet's self-exculpatory explanation, Colonel William Allan, formerly of the C.S.A., answered what many perceived to be Longstreet's heretical criticism of the beloved Lee:

Pickett was overwhelmed not by troops in front but by those on his flanks, especially by those on his right flank.... Yet Longstreet did not use any part of Hood's and McLaw's divisions to support Pickett, or to make a diversion in his favor, or to occupy the troops on his flank which finally defeated him.... Longstreet, in a word, sent forward one-third of his corps to the attack, but the remainder of his troops did not cooperate. And yet he reproaches Lee for the result!

Allan here is opening the insinuation that Longstreet, sulking over Lee's disregard of his advice and other perceived grievances, sabotaged the assault by not doing all he could to support an action with which he did not agree.

This four-volume treasure (a one-volume edition, selected and edited by Ned Bradford, also exists) of personal accounts of the most important period of American history is a rich and valuable contribution to the understanding of the war. However, care must be taken in accepting all of its insights at face value, since by their very nature these accounts are personal and subjective.

—*James H. Meredith*

See also Chancellorsville, Battle of; Jackson, Thomas Jonathan; Longstreet, James.
For further reading:
Bradford, Ned, ed. *Battles and Leaders of the Civil War* (1957).
Johnson, Robert Underwood, and Clarence Clough Buel, eds. *Battles and Leaders of the Civil War: Being for the Most Part Contributions by Union and Confederate Officers* (1887–1888).

BAXTER SPRINGS, BATTLE OF
(6 October 1863)

Among the violent altercations that characterized the guerrilla fighting along the Kansas-Missouri border during the Civil War was the battle of Baxter Springs, Kansas, in early October 1863. The battle, perhaps more correctly classified as a massacre, came about as an unintended consequence of Confederate partisan William Clarke Quantrill's bloody attack on the town of Lawrence, Kansas, on 21 August 1863. After butchering some 150 innocent citizens and setting the town ablaze, Quantrill and his force of 450 Confederate partisans managed to evade Union military units for more than a month. By 1 October, however, Quantrill found it necessary to move his force south to evade Federal patrols and take refuge for the winter in Confederate-controlled Texas. During the journey, Quantrill's band happened upon a small Federal military post located along the Texas road at Baxter Springs in southeastern Kansas.

Quantrill thought the fort an easy target and decided to attack the isolated outpost. He divided his command into two columns and approached the fort from either side of the Texas road. The column approaching from the north, under the command of one of Quantrill's lieutenants, David Poole, soon encountered a unit of the 2d Kansas Colored Infantry on the road outside the fort. After a brief skirmish, Poole's partisans drove the Federals back into the log and earthen structure. Although the Union troops suffered heavy casualties during Poole's surprise attack, Quantrill lost the element of surprise and was forced to attempt a half-hearted siege. The small Union garrison, consisting of the remainder of the 2d Kansas Colored Infantry and two companies of the 3d Wisconsin Cavalry, was able to hold off Quantrill's assault, thanks mainly to their use of a light howitzer and the reluctance of Quantrill's men to assault a fortified position.

At approximately the same time, Union general James G. Blunt was approaching the post at Baxter Springs from the north. Blunt, who was in the process of transferring his headquarters from Fort Scott in Kansas to the recently occupied Fort Smith in Arkansas, was burdened by several wagons carrying his personal effects and accompanied by only a small detachment, comprised mostly of clerks, staff officers, and members of his regimental band. Unaware of Quantrill's presence in the area, Blunt's column stumbled onto the scene just as the Confederates were leaving the fort. Quantrill's partisans, who had adopted the habit of wearing blue coats and carrying a United States flag, were mistaken by Blunt for a detachment from the outpost sent to escort him. Blunt realized his mistake too late as Quantrill's partisans opened fire on the confused Union column at close range, scattering the Federals in all directions and touching off a chaotic melee. When the rout ended, seventy of Blunt's 100-man detachment had been killed, many of them ridden down and shot by the Confederates even as they tried to surrender, and all of his wagons and supplies had been captured. Blunt and the remaining third of his force managed to escape the massacre and then outrace the pursuing Confederates, eventually reaching the safety of Fort Smith to the southeast.

Disappointed at having failed to capture or kill Blunt, Quantrill and his command resumed their trek towards Texas, randomly attacking frontier homesteads and Indian villages along their path, while the humiliated Blunt was temporarily relieved of command by Union general John M. Schofield for his role in the fiasco. Blunt would later regain his command, but the stinging defeat he experienced at Baxter Springs remained a dark blot on his military resume.

—*Daniel P. Barr*

See also Blunt, James G.; Guerrilla Warfare; Kansas; Quantrill, William.
For further reading:
Castel, Albert E. *Civil War Kansas: Reaping the Whirlwind* (1958; reprint, 1997).
Josephy, Alvin M. *The Civil War in the American West* (1991).
Monaghan, Jay. *Civil War on the Western Border, 1854–1865* (1955).

BAYLOR, JOHN ROBERT
(1822–1894)

Confederate officer and politician;
governor of Arizona Territory

Born in Kentucky, John Robert Baylor moved west with his family when his father assumed the post of assistant surgeon with the 7th U.S. Infantry at Fort Gibson in Indian Territory. Baylor returned east, attending school in Cincinnati, but the pull of the West was strong. When word reached Cincinnati of the Texas Revolution in 1835, Baylor ran away and tried to make his way to war. A concerned traveler intervened, returning the thirteen-year-old boy to his school.

After the death of his father, Baylor, still keen for adventure, abandoned his formal education and settled on the farm of his uncle near LaGrange, Texas, in 1840. Baylor participated in some of the Texan campaigns against Mexico, but always just missed actual combat. In 1842, the restless Baylor returned to Fort Gibson, where he taught school at the Creek agency. A year later he fled to Texas after authorities implicated him as an accomplice in the murder of a trader.

After this traumatic event, the young drifter began to settle down. In 1844 in Marshall, Texas, Baylor married Emily Hanna, with whom he raised seven sons and three daughters. The couple moved back to Fayette County, Texas, near his uncle, where Baylor raised livestock. In the early 1850s, Baylor was admitted to the bar, served a successful term in the state legislature, and received appointment as agent to the Comanche Reservation on the Clear Fork of the Brazos River. Controversy plagued his time in that post, and the state removed him for financial irregularities and for his propensity to argue with his superiors. Baylor, along with his brother George Wythe Baylor, subsequently became one of the leading persecutors of the Indians, ultimately leading partisan groups that forced the reservation Indians to relocate to Indian Territory.

Baylor was active during the Texas secession crisis of 1861. A member of the Knights of the Golden Circle, he raised prosecession forces that helped bring about the surrender of the U.S. Army's Department of Texas to state authorities in February. Baylor received the rank of lieutenant colonel for his services and helped organize the 2d Texas Mounted Rifles in March and April. He led a battalion of that organization west along the San Antonio to San Diego mail route, seizing abandoned U.S. army posts along the way.

After arriving at Fort Bliss near present-day El Paso, Texas, Baylor launched what is arguably the first Confederate offensive of the war in July. With approximately 200 troops from his regiment, Baylor moved into Mesilla, New Mexico Territory, and later captured nearby Fort Fillmore along with most of the 7th U.S. Infantry. Shortly thereafter, he organized the Confederate Territory of Arizona, with himself as governor. On 15 December, Baylor advanced to the rank of colonel in the Confederate army.

Baylor suffered a rocky tenure in office. A shortage of revenue, and an abundance of troubles with Apaches and U.S. troops plagued him, as did poor relations with his superior, Confederate general Henry Hopkins Sibley, who arrived in Mesilla with his reinforcing army from Texas at the end of 1861. Early the next year, Baylor left Arizona, determined to raise an army of his own in Texas and return to the desert southwest and complete its conquest. He traveled through the South, building financial and political support for his scheme before laying it before the Confederate government in Richmond.

President Jefferson Davis cut short Baylor's ambitions. Although the Confederate Congress had conferred upon Baylor the rank of brigadier general, the Confederate executive stripped him of that rank, and his position as governor, because of controversy involving his treatment of Indians in Arizona. Refusing to be disgraced, Baylor returned to Texas and volunteered to fight in the battle of Galveston on 31 December 1862 as a private of artillery.

Baylor was not through serving the Confederacy. In 1863, he parlayed his battlefield exploits into a seat in the second Confederate Congress, where he served on the Patents and Indian Affairs committees. In March 1865, the rift between Davis and Baylor had partially healed. That month, with the Confederacy crumbling around them, the president again authorized Baylor to raise a brigade of mounted Texans to liberate Confederate Arizona and restored him to the rank of colonel. Baylor was on his way home to pursue this errand when the war ended.

Baylor moved his family to San Antonio after the war and in 1873 made a serious but unsuccessful run for the Democratic nomination for governor. He continued to be politically active until 1878, when at age fifty-six Baylor moved his family to a sizable ranch at Montell, Texas, northwest of Uvalde. He continued in his confrontational ways, reportedly killing a man over a livestock issue in the 1880s. He died at home on 6 February 1894.

—*Donald S. Frazier*

See also Sibley, Henry Hopkins; Texas.
For further reading:
Baylor, George Wythe. *John Robert Baylor* (1966).
Finch, L. Boyd. *Confederate Pathway to the Pacific: Major Sherod Hunter and Arizona Territory, C.S.A.* (1996).
Frazier, Donald S. *Blood and Treasure: Confederate Empire in the Southwest* (1995).
Thompson, Jerry Don. *Colonel John Robert Baylor* (1971).

BAYONET

The bayonet is a device attached to the barrel of muskets for close combat. Developed and widely used in European warfare, the bayonet was an important weapon on the battlefield.

The most widely used bayonets in the Civil War were socket and sword bayonets. The socket bayonet was developed to fit around the front of the muzzle to allow continuous firing until a bayonet charge was ordered. The socket bayonet was a steel weapon ranging from fourteen to eighteen inches long. The shaft was triangular in shape and projected to a point. The purpose of the socket bayonet was not to slash at an opponent, but to stab and thrust. The shape of the socket bayonet would produce holes rather than cuts, much like a spear. The drill maneuvers practiced by infantrymen focused on thrusting motions to impale opponents. Bayonet wounds could be ghastly. After stabbing the victim, drill procedure called for twisting the gun to enlarge the wound.

Sword bayonets were shaped much like their name suggests. These larger bayonets attached to the side of the barrel and extended up to two feet past the muzzle. Unlike the socket bayonet, sword bayonets were equipped with a handle and were shaped with a sharp edge. These weapons could be used for stabbing or cutting. However, sword bayonets were considerably larger than socket bayonets and many soldiers found them unwieldy. Civil War muskets were heavy pieces of equipment without the bayonet, and the extension of two feet of steel increased the difficulty of musket movement and aiming.

Sword bayonets and socket bayonets were not interchangeable. Certain muskets required particular bayonets. The popular Springfield and Enfield rifles required their own socket bayonets, whereas the Model 1841 rifle and 1855 rifle were fitted with sword bayonets.

The bayonet saw limited action in the Civil War compared with that in previous European wars. Bayonet charges were not common occurrences and bayonet wounds were very rare. Many field surgeons confessed to never treating bayonet wounds. But bayonets continued to be part of the soldier's armament.

Some officers have defended the use of the bayonet in the Civil War. The bayonet served a deeper purpose than creating horrible wounds. It could be used as a shock weapon. In infantry drill, the command "Charge, bayonet!" was answered by the forward thrust of the musket and a collective yell from the ranks. A line of bayonets would be an impressive sight to an opposing army. The gleam of the "cold steel" and the surge of a mass body of troops could unnerve an opponent. Therefore, the bayonet served as a psychological weapon to disrupt enemy formations without actual contact.

The bayonet could also be used for defensive measures. When the call for bayonets was issued in desperate situations, soldiers knew that they must hold. One classic case involved Colonel Joshua L. Chamberlain's 20th Maine on Little Round Top at the battle of Gettysburg in 1863. Without sufficient ammunition, or the option to fall back, Chamberlain's bayonet charge prevented a Confederate key flanking maneuver and contributed to the Union victory.

The use of the bayonet in the American Civil War was limited on the battlefield. Most soldiers found the bayonet to be a nuisance, just one more piece of equipment to carry. Soldiers got the most use out of their bayonets as camp tools, candle holders, or digging uten-

sils. It was also necessary in the practice of stacking arms. Stacking arms was the interlocking of bayonets to prop the muskets off the ground. The psychological effect of bayonets on the battlefield can only be speculated. The number of wounds from bayonets were minimal, yet the bayonet continued to be issued to soldiers in all armies well into the twentieth century as a tool for hand-to-hand combat.

—*Ian M. Spurgeon*

See also Rifles; Springfield Rifle.
For further reading:
Griffith, Paddy. *Battle Tactics of the Civil War* (1989).
Lord, Francis A. *Civil War Collector's Encyclopedia* (1995).
Wiley, Bell I. *The Life of Johnny Reb: The Common Soldier of the Confederacy* (1978; reprint, 1997).

BAYOU DE GLAIZE
(May 1864)
See Yellow Bayou, Louisiana

BAYOU TECHE, LOUSIANA
(January 1863)
See Irish Bend

BEALE, RICHARD LEE TURBEVILLE
(1819–1893)
Confederate general

Born in Westmoreland County on Virginia's Northern Neck to Robert Beale and Martha Felicia Turbeville Beale, Richard Beale graduated in 1838 from the University of Virginia. After studying law, he began a private practice in Hague, Virginia. Also active in state Democratic politics, Beale was elected to the United States House of Representatives in 1847. After one term, he refused to stand for a second. He continued to be active, however, in the state party, participating in state constitutional reform and serving in the state senate from 1858 to 1860.

On the secession of Virginia from the Union, Beale received a commission in a cavalry unit known as Lee's Light Horse. In July 1861 he was promoted to captain and later in the year to major. The unit's main job was to patrol northern Virginia, particularly along the Potomac River. He commanded Camp Lee in his home of Westmoreland County in fall 1861. In this capacity he became concerned for the loyalty of the poor of his county and wrote to the Confederate War Department that the government needed to court the loyalty of the people by ensuring that adequate supplies reached the region. In spring 1862 his unit became a part of the 9th Virginia Cavalry regiment, and in April 1862 Beale was promoted to lieutenant colonel. With the creation of the

Richard Lee Beale (*Library of Congress*)

for the retreating Army of Northern Virginia out of Pennsylvania. In September 1863 he was wounded in a small skirmish and spent several months convalescing.

By January 1864, Beale was back in command of the 9th patrolling eastern Virginia, looking for food and reconnoitering Northern movements. In early March a part of the 9th took up the pursuit of Colonel Ulric Dahlgren in his retreat after the failed Kilpatrick-Dahlgren raid. Dahlgren was killed and Beale forwarded to the Confederate government what would become the controversial Dahlgren papers outlining a plot to kill Jefferson Davis and his cabinet.

Beale received a promotion to brigadier general in August 1864, although misplacement of the paperwork delayed his confirmation in that rank until early 1865. Nevertheless, throughout the fall of 1864, he commanded a brigade as part of W. H. F. Lee's cavalry division until the surrender of the Army of Northern Virginia in April 1865.

Following the war, Beale returned to Westmoreland County, where he was a planter and lawyer. After Reconstruction he served one term in the United States House of Representatives before returning to his law practice. He also spent much of the latter part of his life writing a history of the 9th Virginia Regiment. He died in Hague, Virginia.

—*David S. Heidler and Jeanne T. Heidler*

See also Kilpatrick-Dahlgren Raid; Stoneman's Raid (April–May 1863).
For further reading:
Beale, Richard Lee Turbeville. *History of the Ninth Virginia Cavalry* (1899).

BEAN'S STATION, TENNESSEE, ENGAGEMENT AT
(15 December 1863)

On 4 December 1863, after his failure to drive Ambrose Burnside from Knoxville, James Longstreet withdrew eastward on the road running north of the Holston River. Three days later, elements of the Army of the Ohio under Major General John G. Parke moved out of Knoxville on the same route to follow the retreating Confederates. By 9 December, the Union infantry was at Rutledge some twenty miles northeast of Knoxville and the cavalry was another five miles beyond at Bean's Station. The best that Yankee reconnaissance could determine was that Longstreet was stopped somewhere between Bean's Station and Rogersville, at most about ten miles farther on the same road toward Kingsport. Longstreet had superior numbers, so the Federals waited and watched—or at least they tried to.

Longstreet's rear guard stood firm enough to fight a series of brisk skirmishes beginning on the afternoon of 9

Army of Northern Virginia, the 9th Virginia became a part of the cavalry division of that army that eventually became a separate corps under the command of J. E. B. Stuart.

As a member of the 9th Virginia, Beale fought in the Peninsula campaign, Second Bull Run, and Antietam. Though always praised by his commanders, Beale apparently chafed under the restrictions of taking orders from others and three times tried to resign from the army, requesting permission to raise a troop of independent rangers. Each time, his resignation was refused. In October 1862, he was promoted to colonel of the 9th Virginia.

As the Union army moved down from Sharpsburg, Maryland, in the fall of 1862, it became the job of the 9th to patrol the area north of the Rappahannock River to hinder the Army of the Potomac's progress. Beale fought at Fredericksburg and in April 1863 was a part of W. H. F. Lee's cavalry brigade that engaged Major General George Stoneman in his raid during the Chancellorsville campaign.

Beale fought at Brandy Station before the Gettysburg campaign, at Gettysburg, and was part of the rear guard

December and continuing for the next several days. From these encounters the Rebels determined that their pursuers were not nearly as strong as first suspected, especially since William Sherman was returning to Chattanooga and Gordon Granger's IV Corps was being held near Knoxville. Consequently, on 15 December Longstreet whirled and drove upon Bean's Station, pushed back the Union forces there, and took possession of the crossroads that led south to Morristown and north to Tazewell. Longstreet hoped to trap the Federal cavalry by sending two brigades of troopers under William E. "Grumble" Jones around the Clinch Mountains to Bean's Station Gap while William T. Martin took four brigades south of the Holston to pinch the Yankee retreat from the south.

Martin was late, and the Federal cavalry and mounted infantry absorbed the shock and fell back, taking 115 casualties. The Federal retreat finally stopped about ten miles outside Knoxville at Blain's Crossroads and was there reinforced with Granger's IV Corps and everybody else available. Longstreet did not press the attack, however. The weather was ghastly, and winter quarters beckoned, so he again turned toward the mountains, moving off as Federal cavalry rode out to nip at the edges of his tattered army. As late as 29 December, blue and gray troopers were still sparring on Mossy Creek near Dandridge while Longstreet slipped into the mountains.

—David S. Heidler and Jeanne T. Heidler

See also Longstreet, James; Nashville, Battle of; Nashville, Tennessee; Parke, John Grubb; Tennessee.
For further reading:
Sheridan, Don. *The Battle of Bean's Station: A Spirited Conflict, December 14–16, 1863* (1997).

BEATTY, SAMUEL
(1820–1885)
Union general

Born in Mifflin County, Pennsylvania, Samuel Beatty moved to Stark County, Ohio, with his family when he was a small boy. He was educated locally and as a young man helped with the family farm. At the outbreak of the Mexican-American War, Beatty helped to raise a volunteer company, becoming a lieutenant in the 3d Ohio. He returned to his farm at the end of the war. When the Civil War started, Beatty was the county sheriff in addition to running the family farm.

News of Fort Sumter prompted Beatty to raise a company for Federal service. He was elected captain, and his company became a part of the 19th Ohio Infantry. By the end of May 1861 he had been selected colonel of the regiment. Later in the year, the regiment became a part of the Army of the Ohio.

In the spring of 1862, Beatty led his regiment south into Tennessee as part of Don Carlos Buell's effort to join

Ulysses S. Grant at Pittsburg Landing. Arriving at Shiloh aboard the steamboat *Planet* the night of the first day of the battle, 6 April, Beatty and his men saw serious action the following day in the Union repulse of the Confederate forces. During the advance on Corinth, Mississippi, the following month, Beatty was given command of the 19th's brigade.

Beatty commanded the same brigade that fall in the campaign against Braxton Bragg in Kentucky and fought with distinction at Perryville. He continued in command of the same unit during the battle of Stones River in December 1862, but, still at the rank of colonel, he succeeded to command of the division when its commander, Horatio P. Van Cleve, was wounded on 31 December. He was promoted to brigadier general of volunteers in early 1863 with a date of rank of 29 November 1862. He had been recommended for the promotion by William Rosecrans for his performance at Stones River.

With the recovery of Van Cleve, Beatty reverted to command of his brigade and led them effectively during the Tullahoma campaign in June 1863. In July 1863, he and his brigade were stationed in Manchester, Tennessee, guarding the army's supply train. In September he moved to join his division for the Chickamauga campaign. Both Van Cleve and the corps commander, Thomas L. Crittenden, commended Beatty for his actions at Chickamauga even though the overall performance of XXI Corps was poor.

After Chickamauga, Beatty moved to the command of 3d Brigade, 3d Division (commanded by Thomas J. Wood), IV Corps (commanded by Gordon Granger), Army of the Cumberland. During the Chattanooga campaign, Beatty was again conspicuous for his bravery, particularly in the Union attack on Missionary Ridge. He was commended by Granger for his part in that attack.

After the Chattanooga campaign, Beatty remained in Tennessee, primarily leading his brigade in reconnaissance missions scouting Confederate positions. In the spring he began to prepare his brigade for the upcoming Atlanta campaign, but when the army was about to move, he became seriously ill and had to relinquish command. He was unable to return to duty until the following fall, and hence missed the entire campaign.

By the time Beatty resumed command of his brigade, it had returned to Tennessee to meet the threat of John Bell Hood's invasion. He fought at the battle of Franklin. After the battle, Wood became commander of IV Corps, and Beatty was given command of the division. He commanded the division through the Nashville campaign at the end of the year and was commended by Major General George Thomas for his actions in that campaign. After the battle, Beatty led his division in pursuit of what was left of Hood's army. He remained in command of the 3d Division until March 1865, when he returned to his brigade command.

In early April 1865, Beatty and his brigade were given what at the time seemed like a very important assignment. Having heard of Robert E. Lee's evacuation of his lines at Petersburg and the abandonment of Richmond, Union forces in Tennessee expected the Army of Northern Virginia to move west, perhaps into Tennessee, before turning toward Joseph Johnston's force in North Carolina. For that reason Beatty was ordered to take his brigade to Jonesborough, Tennessee, and to send scouts from there to determine Lee's movements. After learning of Lee's surrender to Grant, Beatty's superiors ordered him back to his headquarters at Greeneville, Tennessee.

In May 1865, George Thomas, commander of the Army of the Cumberland, wrote a special recommendation to the War Department urging that Beatty be promoted to major general of volunteers for his gallantry at Chickamauga, Chattanooga, Missionary Ridge, and Nashville and for the pursuit of Hood after the battle of Nashville. He received a brevet promotion to that rank instead.

After being mustered out of the volunteer service in 1866, Beatty returned to his farm in Ohio. He lived there quietly until his death on 26 May 1885.

—*David S. Heidler and Jeanne T. Heidler*

See also Chattanooga, Tennessee; Missionary Ridge; Nashville, Tennessee.

For further reading:
Cozzens, Peter. *The Shipwreck of Their Hopes: The Battles for Chattanooga* (1994).
Sword, Wiley. *Embrace an Angry Wind: The Confederacy's Last Hurrah—Spring Hill, Franklin, and Nashville* (1992).

BEAUREGARD, PIERRE GUSTAVE TOUTANT
(1818–1893)
Confederate general

Certainly the most recognized and admired Southern general at the outset of the war, and arguably the most flamboyant, Pierre Gustave Toutant Beauregard never fulfilled his military aspirations or the hopes placed upon him by the Confederate public and political leadership. Embodying the paradoxes and travails of the Confederate high command, he was seen by some as an expert strategist betrayed by political enemies and by others as a vainglorious, inept officer undeserving of the high charges he received.

The scion of a powerful family of French, Welsh, and Italian extraction, Beauregard was born in the parish of Saint-Pierre near New Orleans on 28 May 1818. He was educated in the language of his Gallic forbears at the French School of New York City. It was at this institution that he familiarized himself with the life and campaigns of Napoleon Bonaparte, whose demeanor and tactics he purported to emulate throughout his military career. Over his parents' objections, he was admitted to the U.S. Military Academy at West Point in 1834. He rapidly distinguished himself as a highly intelligent, poised, and reflective cadet of great promise. He graduated second in the class of 1838, which included future Confederate officers Richard S. Ewell and Jubal A. Early, as well as Irvin McDowell, whom he was to face on the field of battle. Like his idol Napoleon, Beauregard was interested in gunnery, so upon graduation he elected to serve in the Army Corps of Engineers. He spent a few months redesigning fortifications in Rhode Island and Florida and was then reassigned to his native Louisiana for topographic and hydrographic work.

Beauregard fastidiously worked on these projects until the outbreak of the Mexican-American War, when he was sent to Tampa, Florida, to rebuild fortifications. Upon completion of what he considered an inglorious task, he requested to be sent to Mexico. Along with, among others, Captain Robert E. Lee and Lieutenant George B. McClellan, he was assigned to General Winfield Scott's staff. An active member of this chosen retinue of elite artillerists and engineers, he played a significant part in the successful siege of Vera Cruz. He later saw action at the battles of Contreras and Churubusco and played no small role in the strategy that led to the storming of the Chapultepec citadel and concomitant capturing of Mexico City. Beauregard, however, believed that he did not receive adequate accolades for his service in Mexico, a complaint that would later echo in his diatribes against his commanders during the Civil War. Further embittered by the lack of opportunities offered by the peacetime army—he tried to no avail to secure promotions in the artillery and infantry—he returned to New Orleans to enhance the accessibility and navigability of the Mississippi River.

Between 1853 and 1860, he served as New Orleans's superintendent engineer of U.S. Customs' installations. During this period, he was also somewhat active in politics, writing much on behalf of Democratic candidate Franklin Pierce in the 1852 presidential election and running for mayor of New Orleans in 1858 against a more successful Know-Nothing candidate. In September 1841, he had married Marie Laure Villeré, who died while giving birth to their second child in March 1850. He then married Catherine Deslonde, also a Creole aristocrat and sister-in-law of U.S. senator and political power broker John Slidell.

On 23 January 1861, thanks in no small part to Slidell's support, Beauregard was appointed superintendent of West Point. However, only five days later, having publicly admitted that he would follow Louisiana if the state seceded from the Union, he was forced to leave his new assignment. He resigned his Federal commission on 20 February 1861 to receive a brigadier generalship in the Confederate army on 1 March. Ostensibly planning to become head of the Louisiana state army, he was handed his first disappointment of the war when this command was given to his nemesis-to-be, North Carolinian Braxton Bragg. Capitalizing on what he hoped to be a close advisorial relationship with President Jefferson Davis, Beauregard was then dispatched to Charleston, South Carolina, to coordinate the siege of Fort Sumter. He took command on 6 March in spite of the suspicions of South Carolinians toward a French-speaking Louisianian, and he skillfully marshaled the artillery resources made available to him. The first shot of the conflict was fired on 12 April 1861 with the fort surrendering on 14 April. Beauregard allowed Union troops under his erstwhile West Point artillery instructor Robert Anderson to evacuate Sumter with full military honors.

Beauregard was summoned to Montgomery and given a welcome befitting the "Hero of Sumter." He was also given the command of Confederate forces then mustered for the defense of the Mississippi River from Vicksburg to the Tennessee-Kentucky border. He kept this assignment for only a brief time, receiving orders to proceed to the new Confederate capital of Richmond, Virginia, on 28 May 1861. While he developed a good rapport with Robert E. Lee, at the time commander of state troops, the first signs of friction with Jefferson Davis rapidly appeared. Beauregard fully expected to dictate Confederate strategy, its centerpiece being the creation of a sizable army concentrated in northern Virginia and dedicated to a northward invasion of Maryland and capture of Washington. Judged unclear and unrealistic, his plan, however, was rejected by Davis, much to Beauregard's chagrin.

With Richmond apparently committed to a defensive strategy, Beauregard abandoned the initiative to his Federal opponent Irvin McDowell, who moved South in mid-July 1861. During the ensuing battle of First Bull Run on 21 July 1861, Beauregard showed much bravery under fire, but also inefficiency and poor tactical control of front-line units. Only McDowell's ineptitude and Joseph E. Johnston's composure were to save the day and ensure a Federal debacle. Nonetheless, Beauregard was promoted to general in the regular Confederate army on 31 August 1861. He hoped to return to Louisiana, but on 22 October he and his Army of the Potomac were placed under the control of Johnston, who had been made commander of the Department of Northern Virginia. By the time this area again became an object of military contention the following spring, Beauregard was no longer there.

In January 1862, Beauregard was transferred to the western theater of operations. He was placed under General Albert Sidney Johnston, who gave him command of the corps constituting his left wing, an assignment that Beauregard understood as giving him quasi-autonomy. Confronted with the Federal capture of Forts Pillow and Donelson, Beauregard again succumbed to his tendency for overreaching, Napoleonic plans, designing a major offensive into Tennessee and that could possibly lead to an advance on St. Louis. He took official command of his self-styled Army of the Mississippi on 5 March 1862 and planned to connect with Johnston's main body near Corinth, Mississippi.

What followed was a battle with Federal forces that was one of the bloodiest fights of the war, the battle of Shiloh on 6–7 April 1862. Supported by able division commanders such as Leonidas Polk, William J. Hardee, and John C. Breckinridge, Johnston pushed the Federals almost back into the Tennessee River, but he was fatally wounded during the first day of the battle. Beauregard then assumed command of the whole Confederate army. His attack the following day could not break reinforced Federal lines, and he ordered a general withdrawal, which raised the ire of his subordinates, especially Braxton Bragg. After he evacuated Corinth under questionable circumstances, Beauregard clearly found himself the object of Davis's enmity. When Beauregard relinquished command to Bragg in June 1862 for the duration of a sick leave, the move was motivated as much by politics as by his compromised health.

Strong political backing for Beauregard's return to the West could not persuade Davis to relent, so in September 1862, Beauregard returned to Charleston to assume command of the Confederacy's coastal defenses. Compensating for the scarcity of troops with technological innovations such as ironclads, floating mines, and even a prototype submarine, he managed to repulse several assaults on the Charleston fortifications of Forts Sumter and Moultrie in April 1863 and Battery Wagner in July 1863. He also spent much time providing unsolicited advice on the conduct of the war (for instance, in the form of a plan for a major campaign to recapture New Orleans), thus doing little to placate the Confederate political and military leadership. Beauregard seems to have been genuinely distressed by what he considered Davis's military and political blunders and even spoke of leaving the Confederacy to offer his services to European nations. The death of his second wife in March 1864 further disheartened him.

Yet his star was destined to shine anew. After the Confederate disasters in the summer of 1863, Beauregard, who had repulsed yet another round of assaults on Charleston in August, was perceived by some as a reliable, fighting, and technically undefeated commander. Such at least was the opinion of officers such as James Longstreet. In late April 1864, Beauregard was consequently dispatched to the Department of North Carolina, which included Virginia south of the

James River. He knew that the region would be subjected to a Federal offensive in support of Ulysses S. Grant's overland thrust toward Richmond, and it came in the form of Benjamin Butler's landing at Bermuda Hundred on 5 May 1864.

Adroitly mustering limited assets, Beauregard held the Richmond-Petersburg line and defeated Benjamin Butler's forces at Drewry's Bluff on 15–16 May, a victory for which he received little credit. He again assisted Robert E. Lee successfully in the defense of Petersburg on 15–18 June 1864. Yet, his expectation of being placed on equal footing with the Virginian never materialized. Instead, his command was then placed in the Army of Northern Virginia. When Grant's failure to destroy Confederate forces in the field turned the Overland campaign into the siege of Petersburg, Beauregard's claim of mastery in defensive warfare caused another quarrel with Davis and Bragg, by then Davis's principal military advisor, that even Lee could not resolve.

In the fall of 1864, Beauregard was therefore sent to Georgia. After the fall of Atlanta, the Confederacy's accelerating collapse necessitated the creation of a new Department of the West including Georgia and the Carolinas. With misgivings but having little choice, Davis gave the command to Beauregard. Davis forbade Beauregard, however, from taking the field, so the only army in the area remained under the command of John Bell Hood. Unable to reverse a rapidly deteriorating situation after Hood's debacle at Nashville on 15–16 December, Beauregard oversaw the evacuation and retreat of Southern troops from Columbia and Charleston in the early spring of 1865. As a final humiliation, he again had to relinquish command to Johnston on 22 February 1865. On 1 May, shortly after Johnston's surrender to William T. Sherman, Beauregard left for New Orleans, reaching his hometown on 21 May.

Pardoned by President Andrew Johnson, Beauregard spent time in Europe on behalf of the New Orleans, Jackson, and Great Northern Railroad Company of which he served as president. Like many other Confederate officers, he was considered for military command abroad, but negotiations with Brazil, Rumania, and Egypt fizzled. Beauregard remained negligibly involved in Democratic Party politics, but was mostly active in 1872 in the ill-fated Reform Party, which sought to integrate freed slaves into Southern political life and to lure them away from the Republican Party.

A fairly wealthy man, Beauregard lent his name and credit to numerous endeavors, not all of them successful. Along with former classmate Jubal Early, he was thus seriously criticized for his supervision of the questionable Louisiana lottery between 1877 and 1893. Under the influence of Thomas Jordan, his former chief-of-staff, he wrote and published articles on the war, generally in response to Joseph Johnston's published recollections, *Narrative of Military Operations* (1874). Beauregard assisted his long-time friend Alfred Roman in the 1884 publication *of Military Operations of General Beauregard*, a work of self-vindication that he saw as paramount in molding his historical reputation. In 1879 he was appointed adjutant general of Louisiana and in 1888 was elected commissioner of public works.

Beauregard died on 18 February 1893 of heart failure. Mourned by an imposing delegation of Confederate veterans led by Edmund Kirby Smith, he was buried in the Métairie Cemetery, a few paces away from an equestrian statue of Albert Sidney Johnston.

—*Laurent Ditmann*

See also Bermuda Hundred Campaign; Bull Run, First Battle of; Drewry's Bluff, Battle of; Fort Sumter, Bombardment of; Shiloh, Battle of.

For further reading:

Basso, Hamilton. *Beauregard, the Great Creole* (1933).

Williams, T. Harry. *P.G.T. Beauregard: Napoleon in Gray* (1955).

Woodworth, Steven E., ed. *Leadership and Command in the American Civil War* (1995).

BEDINI, GAETANO
(1806–1864)
Roman Catholic cardinal, diplomat

Born in Sinigaglia, Italy (the hometown of Pope Pius IX), in May 1806, Gaetano Bedini served as secretary to the papal nuncio in Vienna in the late 1830s and in 1845 was appointed papal representative to Brazil, where he gained fame for his aggressive defense of the rights of German immigrants. Two years later, he returned to Italy and was appointed papal governor of Bologna. When Austrian troops brutalized and executed Bolognese revolutionaries in 1849, European liberals condemned Governor Bedini as a reactionary even though his influence with the Austrian authorities was relatively limited. Pius IX appointed him titular archbishop of Thebes and papal nuncio to Brazil in 1852, but also asked him to travel to the United States and inspect the Church there. Besides investigating the feasibility of an American nuncio, Bedini was to help settle a wide variety of Church problems with parish trustees, public schools, and the growing specter of anti-Catholicism. An accomplished diplomat and politician, he seemed an excellent choice to arbitrate Church difficulties in the United States.

Unfortunately for Bedini, the ex-priest and Italian revolutionary Alessandro Gavazzi preempted his visit, toured America, and for months assailed the prelate as the "Bloody Butcher of Bologna." In particular, he held Bedini responsible for the 1849 death of Father Ugo Bossi. Bossi, a Barnabite father, ally of Italian nationalist

Giuseppe Garibaldi, and well-known radical priest, was captured outside Venice by Austrian troops and executed. According to Gavazzi, the antiliberal Bedini had Bossi killed, subjugated Italian liberty in 1849, and was about to do the same to the United States. Gavazzi maintained that the visit of the ex–papal governor was not a diplomatic mission, but part of a greater papist plan to institute Catholic monarchism in the United States.

Archbishop Bedini's seven-month visit was a disaster, punctuated with riots, an assassination attempt, and a dramatic increase in anti-Catholic feeling. Arriving in New York on 30 June 1853, he was welcomed by New York bishop John Hughes and traveled to Washington, D.C., where he met with President Franklin Pierce and attended Georgetown University's commencement. Joined again by Hughes, he visited Milwaukee, the Indian Territory, and Detroit, offering Mass and speaking with American Catholics. While in Detroit, press criticism of Bedini's use of a Great Lakes military steamer began to sour his visit. The Bishop's three-week hiatus in Canada did not dampen protests, and details emerged of a foiled assassination plot planned by Sardinian revolutionaries in New York. Although frightened for his life, he remained in the United States through the fall and was convinced by Bishop Hughes to make an extended tour of the Midwest and South.

The decision to stay was a huge mistake. Bedini was accosted by nativists in Pittsburgh, riots broke out as he visited Cincinnati during Christmas week, mobs jeered him in Wheeling, Virginia (now West Virginia), and he was forced to cancel a trip to New Orleans over rumors of more violence. In cities across the country, he was burned in effigy and denounced as an enemy of American republicanism. After a last visit to Washington, he secretly took a train to New York and began to plan his departure for Europe. New York officials could not guarantee his safety and begged him to leave the country quickly and quietly. On 4 February 1854, Bishop Bedini and his assistants quietly took a rowboat off Staten Island and boarded a ferry steamer captained by a U.S. Marshal deputy. As a mob searched in vain for the Catholic prelate on the docks, Bedini boarded a British bound ship far out in New York harbor.

The visit not only set back Vatican diplomatic initiatives to America—an apostolic delegate was not sent to the United States until 1893—but effectively ended Bedini's career as a diplomat. In 1856, he was made secretary of the Sacred Congregation of Propaganda Fide and five years later was appointed cardinal-archbishop of Viterbo-Toscanella. He died at that post on 6 September 1864.

By instigating U.S. anti-Catholicism, the ill-timed Bedini visit of 1853–1854 helped destroy the Jacksonian party system in place since the 1830s. His U.S. tour factored in the emergence of the nativist Know-Nothing Party, the overthrow of the Whigs, and the creation of a new national Republican Party in 1856.

—*Michael J. Connolly*

See also American Party; Catholics.
For further reading:

Billington, Ray Allen. *The Protestant Crusade 1800–1860: A Study of the Origins of American Nativism* (1938).
Connelly, James F. *The Visit of Archbishop Bedini to the United States of America* (1960).
Guilday, Peter. "Gaetano Bedini: An Episode in the Life of Archbishop John Hughes." *Historical Records and Studies* (1933).
Shaw, Richard. *Dagger John: The Unquiet Life and Times of Archbishop John Hughes of New York* (1977).

BEE, BARNARD ELLIOTT
(1824–1861)
Confederate general

The son of Barnard E. Bee, born in Charleston, South Carolina, moved as a boy with his family to Texas. His father became prominent in the government of the Republic of Texas. In spite of the elder Bee's citizenship in that foreign country, he was able to secure his son an at-large appointment to the United States Military Academy at West Point. Bee graduated thirty-third of the forty-one members in the class of 1845.

Bee fought in the Mexican-American War (1846–1848), in which he received two brevet promotions and was wounded once. After the war he served in several frontier posts, rising to the rank of captain in the 10th Infantry. Bee resigned his commission on 3 March 1861 and received a major's commission in the Confederate infantry. Shortly thereafter, he was promoted to lieutenant colonel in the 1st South Carolina Artillery. Along with several other Confederate officers, including Thomas J. Jackson, he received a promotion to brigadier general on 17 June 1861.

Dispatched to the Shenandoah Valley in Virginia to become a part of Major General Joseph E. Johnston's growing army at Winchester, Bee took command of Johnston's 3d Brigade. Bee accompanied Johnston to Manassas Junction on 20 July 1861 to join forces with P. G. T. Beauregard's army there.

When Union forces under Irvin McDowell began their attack the following day, Bee was sent with his brigade to reinforce the Confederate left. Convinced that the primary fighting of the day would be on the Confederate right, Bee was angry about being removed from the scene of battle. Little did he realize that McDowell's main attack not only would come on the left, but would be in progress as Bee put his men into position.

As the Union attack unfolded, Bee and the other Confederate commanders north of the Warrenton

Turnpike quickly found their positions untenable. As they began falling back, the green troops' retreat turned into a rout, and the entire Confederate left threatened to collapse.

In the meantime, Thomas J. Jackson's brigade, more recently arriving on the left, had taken up a position along a ridge line called Henry House Hill. His men remained on the protected side of the hill as the retreating Confederates streamed by them. Bee fought desperately to rally his men when he spotted Jackson's brigade in its protected position. Different versions exist of what he said, but in effect Bee exclaimed, "There stands Jackson like a stone wall!"—apparently to urge his men to emulate that brigade's example. At least one witness later claimed, however, that Bee was criticizing Jackson for not coming to the aid of the retreating Confederates. Whatever Bee meant, he was responsible for one of he most enduring nicknames in American military history.

Bee never had the chance to explain what he had meant that afternoon on that hill. After the Confederates had stemmed the tide of the Union attack, Bee led an attack of his own, directly into Union artillery fire. He was mortally wounded and died the next day. Beauregard's report of the battle lamented Bee's death.

—*David S. Heidler and Jeanne T. Heidler*

See also Bull Run, First Battle of; Jackson, Thomas J.

For further reading:

McKissick, J. Rion. *General Barnard Elliott Bee: An Address* (1939).

BEECHER, HENRY WARD
(1813–1887)
Religious leader

Henry Ward Beecher (*Library of Congress*)

The son of prominent minister Lyman Beecher and brother of author Harriet Beecher Stowe, Henry Ward Beecher became one of the most influential ministers of nineteenth-century America. Although never a radical abolitionist, he opposed slavery and advocated civil disobedience to the 1850 Fugitive Slave Law. He was an ardent supporter of the Union cause during the Civil War, yet promoted a moderate position on Reconstruction policy. On these issues and others, Beecher reflected Northern white middle-class attitudes even as he shaped them.

Henry Ward Beecher attended Amherst College, where he was known more for his athleticism and practical jokes than his scholarship. He followed his father's wishes and entered Lane Seminary in Cincinnati, Ohio, to prepare for the ministry upon graduation from Amherst, but had little attraction to the severe Calvinist religion of his father's church. His exposure to the militant abolitionist students whose activities caused a crisis between Lane—which his father headed—and the white

population of Cincinnati in 1835 and 1836 convinced him that persuasion, rather than militancy, was more suited to his temperament. He married Eunice White Bullard, whom he courted at Amherst in 1837 and accepted a call to a small Presbyterian Church in Lawrenceburg, Indiana, in that year.

Success in the frontier district parish brought him to the attention of the Second Presbyterian Church in Indianapolis, where he accepted a position in 1839. In Indianapolis he assisted in the creation of a school for the deaf and the blind and gave a series of lectures in 1843 published as *Lectures to Young Men*. In these immensely popular lectures he emphasized the maintenance of moral values with colorful examples of the types of sin to be avoided.

On the issue of slavery Beecher chose a course that condemned slavery itself as sinful but did not challenge prevailing racial attitudes. In this, as in other issues, he believed that the public mood should dictate a minister's response. Beecher's moderation and emphasis on ethical values attracted the notice of New York merchants, who established the Plymouth Church in Brooklyn specifically to attract Beecher to the pulpit. In 1847 Brooklyn was growing quickly due to immigration and the older residents embraced the new social imperatives of respectability and order as a method of distinguishing themselves from lower classes and immigrants. This environment was well suited to Beecher's favorite themes, which he further refined and popularized during his forty-year tenure at Plymouth Church. His sermons did not challenge his middle-class congregation but rather reaffirmed their values and opinions. Beecher's philosophy of reform was aimed toward the enhancement of the existing social order and strengthening the family. More radical abolitionists like Theodore Weld and William Lloyd Garrison did the initial work of linking abolition with moral sensibilities, and by 1848 Beecher saw that the moment had come to join the abolitionists' fight. His relentless advocacy of barring slavery from the territories, especially in Kansas during the 1850s, resulted in the label "Beecher's Bibles" being given to the Sharps rifles carried by antislavery proponents in that territory.

Beecher's sermons emphasized the moral degeneracy of slavery, both for the slave and the surrounding free society. This was always linked to its impact on his central tenets of a Victorian-era faith in virtue, industry, thrift, and order. Slavery's deleterious effects were often exemplified in these sermons by its depressing effect on white social and economic mobility. As the middle-class white Northerner became more incensed by the moral dilemma of slavery, Beecher found that he was swept along. By the time of the Civil War, Beecher believed that war would purify society by reestablishing norms of order and morality in American culture. Patriotism itself was the expression of this commitment to national regeneration as Beecher linked the destiny of the nation to God's will. The man who earlier avoided controversy and contention thus became a militant supporter of the Union war effort.

After the Civil War, Beecher's views on the newly freed slaves retreated to his old position of moral suasion. His public and vocal stand against Federal protection of freedmen's rights and desire to rely instead upon public opinion to encourage the former slave states to recognize political rights for freedmen gradually as they became educated, and even civilized, brought him severe public criticism. Alienating the public (through newspaper reprints of his comments), his congregation, and even his family with such views, it was clear that Beecher's practiced fingers momentarily slipped off the pulse of public opinion. This public humiliation would not be forgotten as he focused on moral reform as a foundation of social stability with more domestic issues and continued to refine his position as a national religious leader. One project was the publication of *Evolution and Religion* in 1885 within which he reconciled scientific Darwinism with God's role in the universe.

In 1874 editor Theodore Tilton's public accusation of adultery between his wife and Beecher challenged Henry Ward Beecher's reputation as a moral authority. At this moment, probably no one in America was more linked with morality than Beecher, and the trial itself created a crisis of confidence in the idea of middle-class moral values. The trial was a staple of the tabloid-style newspapers of the day and commanded national interest. Ultimately, the jury, and later his own church's investigatory committee, were unable to reach a verdict on the charge.

Beecher's enduring cultural significance came from his superior oratorical skills and brilliant ability to articulate the mood of the most influential segment of American society almost before they themselves recognized their own shifts in opinion. His ability to preach familiar and orthodox Protestant doctrines that appealed to a large variety of mainstream congregants, his delivery of these homely truths liberally sprinkled with humorous and pointed illustrations, and his amazing ability to create an atmosphere of intimate conversation to an audience of several thousand were his most remarkable achievements. Although the scandal in his last years sullied his reputation, his popularity remained largely untouched, as evidenced by the over forty thousand mourners who attended his wake after his death from a cerebral hemorrhage in 1887.

—*Gretchen A. Adams*

See also: Abolitionists; Religion.
For further reading:
Abbott, Lyman. *Henry Ward Beecher* (1904).
Clark, Clifford E., Jr. *Henry Ward Beecher: Spokesman for Middle-Class America* (1978).

BELKNAP, WILLIAM WORTH
(1829–1890)
Union general

William Worth Belknap was the son of Brevet Brigadier General William G. Belknap, a career army officer who earned distinction in the Mexican-American War and who died in 1848. Belknap studied law in New Jersey and became a practicing attorney in the District of Columbia in 1851.

Belknap went to Keokuk, Iowa, in 1853 as a law partner of Ralph P. Lowe, a future governor of the state. He was an ambitious citizen, active in local politics. He was elected, as a Democrat, to the Seventh General Assembly in 1857, the first Iowa Assembly to meet in the new capital of Des Moines, and the first to meet under the authority of the new state constitution of 1857.

Belknap confronted Southern secession as a "War Democrat" and during the winter of 1860–1861 actively recruited, and was elected captain, of a local company of volunteers prepared to offer their services to the Union in case of war.

The town of Keokuk served as Iowa's military assembly and mustering center during the summer and fall of 1861, and Belknap's company was sworn into service as Company B, 15th Iowa Volunteer Infantry, in September 1861. The rest of the regiment was organized and mustered into service throughout the fall and winter, becoming fully organized by the end of February 1862, with Belknap commissioned as major in November 1861.

Belknap, due to his family's military tradition, was familiar with military drill and tradition and served as the regimental drill master while the volunteers were encamped in Keokuk.

Despite being in service for many months, the regiment did not receive its first weapons, uniforms, or true military drill until March 1862, when it shipped out from Keokuk to Benton Barracks, Missouri. The regiment was not long at Benton Barracks. Few of the soldiers had time to learn how to use their new rifles before they were sent to St. Louis in preparation for joining General Ulysses S. Grant's army in Tennessee.

On the morning of 6 April 1862, the green troops were transported to Pittsburg Landing, Tennessee, just as the battle of Shiloh was beginning.

The first day of the Shiloh battle was a disaster for the Union forces. The 15th Iowa fought as hard, and suffered

as much, as most other regiments in the army—of 760 men engaged, the regiment lost 188 men killed, wounded, or missing. Belknap suffered a shoulder wound.

On 27 April 1862, the 15th Iowa became part of Marcellus M. Crocker's Iowa Brigade and served in that unit for the rest of the war.

In August 1862, Belknap was promoted to lieutenant colonel and on 3 and 4 October led the regiment at the battle of Corinth. The regiment lost 85 men and Belknap won praise from Colonel Crocker for his bravery and ability to lead his men.

Belknap was promoted to full colonel in April 1863 and, with the exception of a few months when he served as a staff officer of XVII Corps, led the 15th Iowa during the Vicksburg campaign. At the close of the year, with their original terms of service nearly complete, Belknap and three-fourths of the regiment chose to reenlist. After returning from their veteran's furlough, Belknap and the other veterans of the Iowa Brigade joined William Sherman's army as it advanced across Georgia to Atlanta. From Kennesaw Mountain to the battles for the city itself, Belknap and the Iowa Brigade participated in virtually every engagement of the Atlanta campaign.

Belknap's greatest battlefield moment came on 22 July in the battle of Atlanta. Confederate troops seemed to attack from every side, and the fighting was so fierce that the Iowa troops were forced to fight first on one side of their trenches and then on the other side. Belknap, a large, red-bearded man who was often described as looking like a Viking warrior in battle, took advantage of the close-quarters combat to leap over the earthworks and grab an Alabama colonel and private as personal prisoners. Sherman rewarded his gallantry by appointing him brigadier general in August 1864 and giving him command of the Iowa Brigade.

Belknap served under Sherman throughout the March to the Sea and campaigns through the Carolinas. By the spring of 1865 he was in command of XVII Corps of Sherman's army with the rank of brevet major general.

At the end of the war he was offered a commission in the regular army, but he turned the offer down and returned to Keokuk, Iowa, and reopened his law practice. His service in the war caused him to abandon the Democratic Party and become a Republican, and, in 1869, on the personal recommendation of General Sherman, President U.S. Grant appointed him secretary of war, a position he held until 1876.

Belknap's political career ended in disgrace, one part of the corruption scandals that plagued the Grant administration. In March 1876 he was accused of malfeasance in office, charged with accepting bribes from an Indian post trader seeking political favors. Belknap resigned his office, in part to protect the reputation of his wife, who was also implicated in the scandal. President Grant accepted the resignation, but, even though he was

William W. Belknap (*Library of Congress*)

no longer in office, Belknap was formally impeached and subjected to a Senate trial. He was acquitted by the Senate but never again held a position in the Grant administration.

After his trial he returned to civilian law practice in Philadelphia and Washington, D.C. He remained popular with veteran soldiers and often returned to Iowa to serve as the presiding officer of the annual postwar reunions of the Iowa Brigade.

—*Kenneth L. Lyftogt*

See also Atlanta Campaign; Kennesaw Mountain, Battle of; Shiloh, Battle of.

For further reading:

Brigham, Johnson. *Iowa: Its History and Its Foremost Citizens* (1916).

Gue, Benjamin F. *A History of Iowa* (1903).

Iowa Adjutant General's Office. *Roster and Record of Iowa Soldiers in the War of the Rebellion* (1910).

Lewis, Lloyd. *Sherman: Fighting Prophet* (1932).

Sage, Leland L. *A History of Iowa* (1974).

Stuart, Captain A.A. *Iowa Colonels and Regiments: Being a History of Iowa Regiments in the War of the Rebellion* (1891).

Throne, Mildred, ed. *The Civil War Diary of Cyrus F. Boyd: 15th Iowa Infantry, 1861–1863* (1977).

———. "Iowans and the Civil War." *Palimpsest* (1969).

BELL, JOHN
(1796–1869)
Tennessee Unionist

John Bell was born in Mill Creek, Tennessee, on 18 February 1796, the son of Samuel Bell, a farmer and blacksmith, and Margaret Edminston. He graduated from Cumberland College in Nashville in 1814 and soon set his sights on a career in law. In 1816 he began his practice in Franklin, Tennessee. A year later he won a seat in the state senate. After a single term, Bell returned to his law practice and his new bride, Sally Dickinson, whom he had married in 1818. The couple had five children before Sally's death in 1832.

In 1822 the Bell family settled in Nashville, where Bell steadily built his reputation as an able, hardworking lawyer. In 1827 he won the first of seven consecutive terms in the U.S. House of Representatives. Although Andrew Jackson had backed Bell's opponent in the race, Bell pledged his allegiance to the popular Tennessee general when he became president in 1828. Bell disapproved of Jackson's war on the U.S. National Bank, but broke openly with the president only after Jackson ordered the removal of federal deposits from the bank in 1833. In 1834, Bell challenged Jacksonian loyalist and home state rival, James K. Polk, for the House Speaker's chair. Bell won the speakership and the bitter enmity of Tennessee Jacksonians, who exulted when Polk reclaimed the Speaker's chair from Bell in 1835. Bell contested Polk unsuccessfully for the speaker-

ship again in 1837 and lost narrowly to Robert M. T. Hunter of Virginia in 1839.

In 1835 Bell threw himself behind the presidential candidacy of Tennessee senator Hugh Lawson White, who was one of three candidates of the fledgling Whig opposition to challenge Vice President Martin Van Buren in the 1836 election. White carried Tennessee and Georgia, but his candidacy had little influence outside the South, where Whig voters supported either William Henry Harrison or Daniel Webster. Against a divided opposition, Van Buren captured the White House, and Bell's breach with the Democratic Party was complete.

Bell labored diligently for Harrison's 1840 presidential campaign, although he had originally supported Henry Clay's claim to the Whig nomination. The Whigs' "log cabin and hard cider" campaign earned the party its first presidential victory. Bell was rewarded with an appointment as secretary of war. When Harrison died a month after taking office, Vice President John Tyler assumed the reins of the administration. Tyler soon alienated Whig leaders in Congress when he proved implacably opposed to the Whig economic program. In 1841, at Clay's strong urging, nearly the entire cabinet, including Bell, resigned in protest.

Bell was elected to the Tennessee legislature in 1847 and was soon elevated to the U.S. Senate. He quickly became embroiled in the controversy over the status of slavery in the new territories acquired by the United States in 1848 as a result of the Mexican-American War. Southerners were outraged by Northern attempts to exclude slavery from the new lands and particularly opposed the plan of President Zachary Taylor to admit California as a free state. Clay attempted to break the sectional impasse with his Compromise package, which tied the admission of California to several other pro-Southern conditions. Bell opposed Clay's plan and urged instead the division of Texas into at least two slave states to appease Southern interests. Clay's omnibus bill failed, but its provisions eventually passed the Senate one by one. Bell belatedly endorsed the Compromise, sensing its popularity at home.

Bell and the disintegrating Whig Party faced another sectional controversy in 1854. The Kansas-Nebraska Act repealed the line between slavery and freedom that had been established in the 1820 Missouri Compromise, theoretically opening up the Kansas and Nebraska territories to slavery's expansion. Northern Whigs were outraged, and Southern Whigs such as Bell initially opposed the bill, arguing that it would provoke sectional hostility without delivering tangible benefits to the South. Once opposition to the bill became equated with antislavery sentiment, however, Southerners then rushed to endorse it. In the end, Bell cast the only Southern vote in the Senate against the bill; only seven

Southern Whigs followed his lead in the House. In 1858, after a bloody battle between antislavery and proslavery settlers, Kansas sought admission to the Union as a slave state under the controversial Lecompton constitution. Again, Bell broke with his region in opposing admission and was denounced by Southern Democrats as a traitor.

Bell's unsuccessful efforts to quell sectional tensions and prevent the collapse of the Whig Party in the 1850s won him praise from Northerners and conservative ex-Whigs. In 1860, a group of former Whigs nominated Bell as the presidential candidate of a new Constitutional Union Party and selected Edward Everett of Massachusetts for the vice presidential slot. Reserved in demeanor, Bell lacked the charisma of an effective candidate for national office; he also was hobbled by his party's refusal to address the slavery controversy. His only hope was for the Republicans to lose enough states in the North, and for Southern Democrats to divide their votes between Stephen A. Douglas and John C. Breckinridge, so that the election would be thrown into the House of Representatives. In the end, however, Bell carried only Tennessee, Virginia, and Kentucky, and Lincoln swept the North to win decisive electoral victory.

As the momentum of secession moved rapidly forward after Lincoln's election, Bell was characteristically cautious. He refused an urgent request from Mississippi conservatives to visit that state, instead issuing a public statement urging moderation and denouncing secession as an illegitimate solution to the South's grievances. In a major speech to a Nashville audience in January 1861, Bell reiterated his belief that the Republicans posed no immediate danger to the South, although he expressed a hope that Tennessee and Kentucky would join forces in a "Central Confederacy" if the Union dissolved. Bell's speech helped stay secession furor in Tennessee—on 9 February, voters voted overwhelmingly against a secession convention. In April, Bell traveled to Washington to confer with the new president and returned convinced that Lincoln's policy would be conciliatory.

Lincoln's decision to resupply Fort Sumter and his subsequent call for 75,000 troops reignited secession sentiment in the South. Bell reluctantly accepted that Tennessee would side with the Confederacy. His reversal on secession outraged some of his conservative allies, who thought Bell had cowed to popular opinion, but Tennessee's overwhelming vote for secession in June 1861 proved that little could have been done to keep the state in the Union.

Bell had no direct involvement in the Southern war effort, although he was certainly affected by wartime dislocation and destruction of property. Union forces invaded middle Tennessee in early 1862, damaging Bell's extensive iron and coal works, which he had obtained through his second marriage to Jane Erwin Yeatman in 1835. As Union troops approached Nashville, Bell

moved his family southward to Alabama and then to Georgia. After the war, he returned to Tennessee and attempted to rebuild his mines and mills in Stewart County; there he lived out the final years of his life.

Unrelentingly, Bell clung to the belief that compromise was possible on the slavery issue and blamed extremists in both sections for escalating tensions. His unsuccessful efforts to hold the Union together epitomized the tragic failure of moderation as the nation hurtled toward civil war.

—*Susan Wyly-Jones*

See also Election of 1860.
For further reading:
Atkins, Jonathan M. *Parties, Politics, and the Sectional Conflict in Tennessee, 1832–1861* (1997).
Bergeron, Paul H. *Antebellum Politics in Tennessee* (1982).
Crofts, Daniel W. *Reluctant Confederates: Upper South Unionists in the Secession Crisis* (1989).
Parks, Joseph H. *John Bell of Tennessee* (1950).

BELLE ISLE
Confederate military prison

An island in the James River connected to Richmond by a footbridge, Belle Isle was used as a day resort by the people of Richmond before the war. During the early months of the war, the island was used to drill new troops for the Confederate army. Because of the difficulty of swimming the rapids around the island, it was deemed an ideal place to house prisoners in tents once other facilities in Richmond became overcrowded.

Until the Peninsula campaign of the spring and summer of 1862, the buildings used as prisons within the city were adequate for the needs of the army. However, by April 1862 the number of Federal soldiers housed in the city had seriously overtaxed the available facilities. Therefore a company of cavalry was allocated to serve as guards, and in June the first Federal soldiers were brought to the island.

Used only for privates and noncommissioned officers, Belle Isle was intended only as a holding facility until more adequate prisons were available. As a result no buildings were erected, and the first prisoners were issued tents for their shelter. The men were confined to a 6-acre site surrounded by an earthwork that they were not allowed to cross. The first commandant of the prison was Captain Norris Montgomery, who was considered rather lenient with the men. Captain Henry Wirz replaced him in August 1862 and revoked all the privileges granted by his predecessor. Part of the reason for Wirz's seeming cruelty was that the numbers of prisoners in the stockade had swollen to 5,000 in areas that had been designed for 3,000. Wirz believed that such overcrowding and his limited number of guards dictated that captives be kept closely confined. Soon after Wirz took command, however, an exchange agreement emptied the grounds, and the prison was closed in September 1862.

Belle Isle opened again briefly in January 1863 following the battle of Fredericksburg and then again in May 1863 in response to the surplus of prisoners from the battle of Chancellorsville. Then Lieutenant Virginius Bossieux commanded the camp. His tenure as commandant was characterized by some of the worst conditions endured there. During the summer Belle Isle's average occupancy was double its 3,000-man capacity, and there were only 300 tents, which at best could sleep ten men each. The remaining half of the men had to sleep in the open, sometimes in holes they dug to provide some shelter.

By fall 1863 conditions had worsened, with as many as 8,000 men sometimes confined in the small enclosure. Word naturally leaked North of these conditions, and the situation at Belle Isle soon became one of the major sources of Northern propaganda regarding Southern cruelty to prisoners. General Neal Dow, a prisoner of war at Libby Prison in Richmond, was allowed to go to Belle Isle to distribute blankets that had been sent by the United States government, and following that visit he was able to slip out a report to the North on the conditions there. However, his intelligence did little, if anything, to improve the conditions at the camp. During the extremely hard winter of 1863–1864, the camp continued to be overcrowded, and some nights as many as fourteen men froze to death.

Conditions at the camp made disease rampant. To add to the misery of the prisoners, their swelling numbers drove up the price of food in Richmond and consequently caused a cut in their rations. During early 1864 the average ration consisted of a square of cornbread and thin soup that the men complained was full of bugs.

At the same time that conditions at the camp worsened, concerns increased that its proximity to Richmond made the prison a target for Union raiders hoping to liberate the inmates. As a result, in February 1864 the process of gradually removing the prisoners and shipping them by rail to Andersonville and other prisons farther south began. By the end of March, Belle Isle was again empty.

With the beginning of Ulysses S. Grant's campaign against Robert E. Lee in May of 1864, however, the need for prison facilities in Richmond again grew. Belle Isle was opened again in June 1864, and 6,000 prisoners were put there. They remained through the summer of 1864, but fears of attempts to liberate them caused their shipment south in October and caused the closure of the camp. It never opened again.

—*David S. Heidler and Jeanne T. Heidler*

See also Prisoners of War; Prisons, C.S.A.

For further reading:
Abbott, Horace R. *My Escape from Belle Isle* (1889).
Coburn, Jacob Osborn. *Hell on Belle Isle: Diary of a Civil War POW: Journal of Sgt. Jacob Osborn Coburn* (1997).
Goss, Warren Lee. *The Soldier's Story of His Captivity at Andersonville, Belle Isle and Other Rebel Prisons* (1867).
Hesseltine, William B. *Civil War Prisons: A Study in War Psychology* (1930; reprint 1998).
Robinson, Daniel W. "Belle Isle: Prison in the James, 1862–1865" (Master's thesis, 1980).
Speer, Lonnie R. *Portals to Hell: Military Prisons of the Civil War* (1997).

BELMONT, BATTLE OF
(7 November 1861)

On 1 September 1861, Union brigadier general Ulysses S. Grant took command of the District of Southeast Missouri, with headquarters at Cairo, Illinois. Charged with overseeing Union operations in southeastern Missouri, his responsibilities increased when Confederate forces under Major General Leonidas Polk and Brigadier General Gideon Pillow invaded neutral Kentucky and captured Columbus, a key position atop the bluffs along the east bank of the Mississippi. Polk fortified Columbus and made it the anchor of the Confederacy's main defensive line in the west. Across from Columbus lay Belmont, Missouri, an old ferry landing occupied by a small Southern garrison and renamed Camp Johnston. Until the Federals seized Columbus (called "the Gibraltar of the West" by Confederates), a large stretch of the Mississippi River would remain under Confederate control. Strategically located across the river from Columbus, Belmont was, to Grant, a logical place from which to start the process of capturing the fortress, something he had longed to do since early September.

On the evening of 6 November 1861 three thousand Union troops boarded transports at Cairo and steamed downriver toward Belmont. Escorted by the Union gunboats *Tyler* and *Lexington*, Grant's expeditionary force consisted of two infantry brigades, two cavalry companies, and a battery of artillery. In conjunction with the attack on Belmont, Union major general Charles F. Smith at Paducah was to send a force to demonstrate against Columbus. Early on 7 November, Grant's troops disembarked at Hunter's Farm, three miles above Belmont, and marched toward the Confederate camp. Under the overall command of Confederate colonel James C. Tappan, Camp Johnston was occupied by one regiment of infantry, a cavalry battalion, and an artillery battery. Once the attack commenced, Polk, hearing the gunfire, sent four more infantry regiments (2,500 men) under Pillow across the river to defend the outpost. As this force arrived to even the odds, Grant pressed his attack. After heavy fighting in a cornfield

The battle of Belmont, from an undated engraving (*Library of Congress*)

west of the camp, Pillow's line collapsed. Although orderly at first, Pillow's retreat soon lapsed into chaos as panic gripped his men, some of whom found themselves under fire from different directions. Some Southern units lost all cohesion as Grant's men, smelling blood, advanced toward the camp. The Federals continued to drive the Confederates toward the river and finally captured Camp Johnston. With victory in their grasp and exhilarated by their first taste of combat, many pursuing Union soldiers laid down their arms and began looting the camp, despite the desperate pleas of their officers to remain in the ranks. As Pillow's men huddled along the bank or fled upriver, the Union pursuit lost momentum. Men fell out to ransack tents, musicians struck up the "Star-Spangled Banner," and politician-officers, including John A. McClernand, gave patriotic speeches to commemorate the occasion.

On the opposite bank, Smith's demonstration failed to convince Polk for very long that the Belmont attack was only a diversion for the main attack against Columbus. Once Polk concluded that Smith was not a threat, he ordered the Columbus guns to open on the Federals milling about Camp Johnston and dispatched more reinforcements (five regiments) under Brigadier General Frank Cheatham to rescue the beleaguered Pillow. Glimpsing transports loaded with Southern

soldiers heading his way, Grant ordered his men back to the boats, but it took time to get them reorganized and underway. Meanwhile, the Confederates, buttressed by Cheatham's arrival, began a dogged and deadly pursuit of Grant's retreating columns. Some Federal units had to cut their way out and Grant himself barely escaped capture. Under fire from the shoreline, the Union steamers finally slipped away and returned to Cairo. The Federals suffered 607 casualties (including 120 dead) out of approximately 2,500 engaged, while the Confederates suffered 641 casualties (including 105 dead) out of approximately 5,000 engaged.

Grant claimed victory at Belmont, although contemporaries and historians alike have questioned this assessment, especially since his chaotic retreat left the enemy in possession of the field and because the battle accomplished few worthwhile results. Despite Grant's hope that he would achieve much more with his attack, Belmont and Columbus remained in Confederate hands until Forts Henry and Donelson fell in February 1862. The capture of these two important points shattered the Confederacy's western defensive line, and not until then did Polk abandon the Confederate Gibraltar of the West.

—*William B. Feis*

See also Cheatham, Benjamin Franklin; Grant, Ulysses S.; McClernand, John A.; Pillow, Gideon; Polk, Leonidas.

For further reading:
Feis, William B. "Grant and the Belmont Campaign: A study in intelligence and command." In *The Art of Command in the Civil War.* Edited by Steven E. Woodworth (1998).
Hughes, Nathaniel Cheairs, Jr. *The Battle of Belmont: Grant Strikes South* (1991).

BENJAMIN, JUDAH PHILIP
(1811–1884)

U.S. senator; Confederate attorney general, secretary of war, and secretary of state

Judah Benjamin was raised the son of Sephardic Jews in Charleston, South Carolina. His education included a brief period when he attended Fayetteville Academy in North Carolina, and in 1825 Benjamin entered Yale College. For reasons not entirely clear, he left Yale two years later without graduating. Benjamin soon thereafter moved to New Orleans, a cosmopolitan city with a religiously diverse population that included a sizable Jewish community. He found employment as a clerk in a commercial house, and he supplemented his income by giving English lessons. It was in his capacity as a tutor that he met and fell in love with Natalie St. Martin, the daughter of a wealthy and prominent Catholic family. After their marriage in 1833, Judah and Natalie's relationship was at the least peculiar; Natalie was terribly unhappy, and soon she and their daughter, Ninette, moved to Paris. Although the marriage lasted for over fifty years, Natalie spent most of those years in France.

Meanwhile, Benjamin was admitted to the Louisiana bar, where he displayed considerable skill at forcefully and successfully representing his many clients. He was considered by many people to be New Orleans's finest attorney. One of the more significant cases with which Benjamin was associated involved a slave mutiny aboard the ship *Creole.* He was hired by a New Orleans insurance company to argue that the ship owners were not due remuneration because the mutiny occurred in international waters. Benjamin's arguments in this case are fascinating and might lead one to conclude that he opposed Southern slavery as a cruel and inhumane institution. It is important to remember, however, that Benjamin merely presented the most forceful argument he could muster as a well-paid advocate, and his briefs in no manner reflected his personal views regarding slavery. In fact, Benjamin's foremost ambition seems to have been to join the ranks of Louisiana's elite planter class. Indeed, his success at the bar afforded him sufficient income to purchase a sugar plantation of several hundred acres, complete with nearly 150 slaves.

As the successful owner of a sugar estate, Benjamin circulated in upper-crust planter society, and he began courting prominent individuals in hopes of gaining political office. No relationship proved more valuable than his friendship with John Slidell, a New Orleans Whig whose political machine virtually ran the state. In 1842 Benjamin was elected as a Whig representative to the state legislature, and in 1848 he was a presidential elector from Louisiana. Benjamin was elected by his fellow Whigs as a U.S. senator in 1852, but his affiliation with the Whig Party was short-lived; he joined the Democratic Party in 1856 as a staunch Buchanan supporter. Benjamin served in the U.S. Senate until 1860, and during that period he developed a strong friendship with Jefferson Davis of Mississippi. This relationship did not begin cordially; during one heated exchange between the two senators regarding military appropriations, tempers flared nearly to the point of a duel. Yet Davis quickly realized that he had insulted Benjamin without warrant and he apologized openly on the floor of the Senate. From that time on the two were close friends who deeply respected one another.

On New Years' Eve 1860, Benjamin addressed a packed gallery in the Senate to deliver his farewell speech. The secession crisis had earlier prompted South Carolinians to withdraw their state from the Union, and after a secession convention in Louisiana was similarly productive, Benjamin promptly tendered his resignation.

Judah P. Benjamin (*Library of Congress*)

His farewell speech, though rife with caustic invective for Northern extremists, nevertheless was as eloquent as it was forceful in imploring Northerners to allow the South to depart the Union in peace.

As President Jefferson Davis assembled his cabinet for the fledgling Confederate government, he turned at once to Judah Benjamin to fill the post of attorney general, a position that required him to be the Confederacy's chief prosecutor. Although his duties involved purely civilian affairs, Benjamin regularly offered his opinion on military matters. His counsel was sound in a time when reason seemed wanting in many quarters. Davis soon relied on his attorney general as his principal adviser. By the time the government relocated to Richmond, Virginia, in late spring 1861, Davis and Benjamin had developed a close relationship based on Benjamin's unswerving loyalty to the president and Davis's profound trust in Benjamin. No person, perhaps with the exception of his wife Varina, advised Jefferson Davis more closely than did Judah Benjamin.

Soon after the first battle of Bull Run, when the Davis administration suffered harsh criticism for not pursuing Union general Irvin McDowell's fleeing army, Davis requested Secretary of War Leroy Walker's resignation. Walker had not been an especially efficient administrator, and his removal opened the way for Davis to appoint Benjamin as his replacement. Although seemingly illogical to appoint a person, such as Benjamin, with absolutely no prior military experience to such a highly important post within the Confederacy's military, Davis needed an individual who would unquestionably carry out directives. The fact was that Jefferson Davis believed himself most fit to run the War Department, and he thus appointed Benjamin to avoid the inevitable conflicts that would arise if a career military officer had been named. Benjamin had an almost obsessive commitment to efficient office management, and his organizational skills were at once beneficial.

Benjamin was a tireless worker who regularly spent ten to fifteen hours each day at his desk or in conference with the president. He rarely complained, was a most congenial person, and was ever the optimist, even during the darkest days of the war. Benjamin's high, full cheeks gave him the appearance of wearing a perpetual smile and having a carefree disposition that Davis seemed to appreciate, especially as the Confederacy's fortunes grew bleak. Not everyone, though, appreciated Judah Benjamin, and soon after assuming his duties at the War Department he was involved in disputes with some of the Confederacy's leading generals. P. G. T. Beauregard, for example, sent a letter to Benjamin requesting that he be placed in command of all Confederate armies in the eastern theater. When Benjamin refused this request, Beauregard wrote a scathing letter to Davis in which he referred to the war secretary as that "functionary at his desk." Davis was eventually able to placate Beauregard's delicate ego, but many well-trained officers resented following directives from a nonmilitary head of the War Department. A second dispute arose between Benjamin and Thomas J. "Stonewall" Jackson when the secretary ordered Stonewall to regroup his dangerously scattered armies in the Shenandoah Valley. Jackson complied with the order, but he obviously resented the unwarranted intrusion. Jackson offered his resignation, and once again Davis had to heal a breach between a popular general and his most loyal secretary.

As these disputes became public, and as Union armies made considerable military gains in the western theater, Benjamin's once sound reputation quickly evaporated. Newspapers throughout the South expressed doubts about his ability to lead the War Department, and not a few shamelessly suggested that as a Jew, Benjamin's loyalty should not only be questioned but closely scrutinized. Such attacks displayed an inherent prejudice against Jews, and Benjamin was a convenient target for disgruntled generals, ambitious politicians, and discontented newspaper editors.

Verbal attacks against the war secretary reached a crescendo after the fall of Roanoke Island in February 1862. The 2,500 Confederate soldiers garrisoned there under General Henry Wise were running desperately short of supplies as a superior Union force threatened to overtake them. Wise sent several letters pleading for more men and materiel, but Benjamin simply had little to send; about all that he could do was hope that the island's meager defenses would hold until supplies could be obtained. On 8 February 1862 Union forces numbering over 19,000 men stormed ashore and successfully seized the Confederate stronghold. General Wise's son, Jennings, was among the Confederate dead at Roanoke, and Benjamin suffered tremendous criticism from throughout the South. Calls for his resignation were universal, as were demands that Davis dismiss Benjamin, should the latter refuse to step down.

Robert M. T. Hunter of Virginia resigned as Confederate secretary of state in March 1862 after having a heated exchange of words with Davis. With his war secretary under assault for the Roanoke debacle, Davis felt it wise to remove Benjamin from the War Department and to name him as Hunter's replacement. Many people could not understand Davis's unwillingness to fire Benjamin outright; some even began referring to Benjamin as Mr. Davis's "pet Jew." Nevertheless, as the newly appointed secretary of state, Benjamin was in a role far more suitable to his talents and skills. It was becoming ever more imperative that the Confederate government cajole England and France into granting the Richmond government full diplomatic recognition. Such a pronouncement would have lent considerable validity to the South's quest for independence and an aura of illegality to Lincoln's war against it. Benjamin thus redirected his energies away from creating an efficient war department and toward gaining recognition from England and France.

Confederate diplomacy to mid-1863 had been driven largely by the deluded belief among many within the Richmond government that England's demands for Southern cotton would force recognition and perhaps prompt British intervention in the war to break the Union blockade. By 1862, however, it was apparent that such reasoning had been fallacious and that European powers were not going to enter the war to save cotton. Many Southerners—Benjamin among them—became convinced that recognition was not granted because of the South's determination to hold onto slavery. England had abolished the institution in 1833, and sentiment there was clearly against the South's labor system. After the disaster at Gettysburg in July 1862, Benjamin reasoned that recognition would be possible only if the Confederacy abolished slavery and showed the Palmerston government in England that the war was being fought more for Southern independence than for slavery. The problem for Benjamin was that, for the present at least, President Davis was not interested in freeing the slaves or even in entertaining the subject.

By summer 1864, when Lee's haggard and increasingly weakened army was entrenched at Petersburg staving off Grant's massive forces, the Confederacy's dark fate seemed all but certain without some dramatic shift in foreign policy. Although Benjamin had already concluded that emancipation was the South's only hope for independence, it was not until Lincoln's reelection in November 1864 that Davis agreed to discuss emancipation options. Benjamin proposed that emancipation should occur in two stages: first, Duncan Kenner, a Louisiana congressman who had favored emancipation since early in the war, should be dispatched to Europe and offer a promise of emancipation in return for recognition. Once Kenner's mission was complete, Benjamin proposed that Davis should declare all slaves free.

The problem with Benjamin's daring plan were the political risks involved. After all, did the president of a confederacy have authority to abolish an institution fundamentally protected by state authority? Secondly, Davis was concerned whether the troops would fight if slavery were abolished. Would the troops remain with the armies or simply return home demoralized? These uncertainties led Davis to move slowly on the emancipation issue. He did, however, consent to secretly send Kenner to Europe with authority to bargain on terms that included emancipation. Benjamin and Kenner then planned the latter's mission to Europe. Unfortunately for the Confederacy, Kenner's mission was initiated far too late in the war to sway either Napoleon III in France or Lord Palmerston in Britain. On 2 April 1865, when Lee notified the government that his army was retreating from Petersburg and that Richmond would have to be evacuated, Benjamin hurriedly packed the State Department's papers. He joined his colleagues within the administration for the train ride to Danville, Virginia, with the hope that some miracle could save the Confederacy.

Abraham Lincoln was assassinated on 14 April 1865. It was soon discovered that two of the coconspirators had maintained close ties to Benjamin, and he was at once suspected of plotting to kill the U.S. president. Although Benjamin had had nothing to do with Lincoln's death, his ties to the Surratt family were undeniable, and he knew that in the highly emotional atmosphere generated by Lincoln's death, he most assuredly would be tried and hanged.

Benjamin thus resolved to flee the country for England. After a harrowing four-month escape that took him to Florida, Bimini, Nassau, Havana, and, finally, Southampton, Benjamin was safe in England and resolute about putting the war behind him. He decided to pursue a new career as an attorney at the British bar, and after but five months of studying the intricacies of English law, Benjamin was permitted to practice in English courts. Perhaps Benjamin's most noteworthy and far reaching accomplishment during this period was his writing of the *Treatise on the Law of Sale of Personal Property*, a well-received textbook that for many years remained the standard work on sales contracts. He continued to practice law in England with great success, and he visited Natalie and Ninette in France on occasion. Benjamin suffered a heart attack in 1882 and was forced into retirement. He died in Paris in 1884.

From 1865 until his death, Judah Benjamin rarely spoke of his services to the Confederacy, perhaps preferring to forget those terrible four years. Though he served in three high-level positions, Benjamin's most influential role was as Jefferson Davis's closest friend and adviser. It actually mattered little which position Benjamin held, for Davis would have relied similarly on his advice in whatever capacity. As the Confederacy's fortunes turned bleak with each military loss, and as criticism of the Richmond government reached fever pitch, it was often Judah Benjamin who bore the brunt of the verbal attacks. And he did so while maintaining his characteristic pleasant demeanor and optimism.

—*Robert Saunders, Jr.*

See also Davis, Jefferson; Diplomacy, C.S.A.; Jews.
For further reading:
Butler, Pierce. *Judah P. Benjamin* (1981).
Evans, Eli N. *Judah P. Benjamin, The Jewish Confederate* (1988).
Meade, Robert D. *Judah P. Benjamin, Confederate Statesman* (1975).

BENNETT HOUSE

Owned by James Bennett (frequently spelled Bennitt) and his wife Nancy, the unassuming Bennett farmhouse in Orange County, North Carolina (near present-day Durham), was the site of the largest surrender of the American Civil War, on 26 April 1865. Bennett, his wife, and three children lived on 325 acres, raising hogs and growing potatoes, corn, wheat, and oats. Bennett was also a resourceful entrepreneur, serving as a tailor, cobbler, and broker of horse feed, tobacco plugs, and distilled liquor. Before the surrender negotiations, Bennett and his wife had been directly touched by the war, as their sons and son-in-law died during the conflict.

In March 1865, 60,000 Federal troops under the command of General William Tecumseh Sherman entered North Carolina south of Fayetteville. In an effort to check Sherman's advance, Robert E. Lee called General Joseph E. Johnston out of his retirement in Lincolnton, North Carolina, and gave him command of what was left of the Army of Tennessee and the Department of South Carolina, Georgia, and Florida. The two forces clashed near the small town of Bentonville on 19 March in what proved to be the largest battle on North Carolina soil. Forced to withdraw his army, Johnston moved north to Smithfield, then through Raleigh and west to Hillsborough. Sherman followed slowly, entering the North Carolina capital on 13 April and establishing his headquarters in the governor's mansion.

When rumors of Lee's surrender at Appomattox filtered into the Confederate encampment at Hillsborough, Johnston knew that the end was in sight. Not only did he face the imminent threat of Sherman's seemingly unstoppable force, but now the massive Army of the Potomac could conceivably join in the pursuit. Johnston made his opinion known to President Jefferson Davis when the two conferred in Greensboro, and on 14 April the Confederate commander wrote to Sherman asking for "a temporary suspension of active operations." Sherman agreed, and the two generals and their escorts met on the Hillsborough Road on 17 April, midway between their opposing armies.

After exchanging cordial greetings, Johnston suggested that the two parties proceed to the nearby Bennett farmhouse. Bennett gave his pro forma permission for the generals to confer in his house while their respective staffs remained outside lounging against his rail fence and under the blooming cherry trees. Before discussing terms, Sherman informed Johnston of Lincoln's assassination and watched as "the perspiration came out in large drops" on the stunned general's forehead. Johnston responded that this was "the greatest possible calamity to the South" and was reassured by Sherman that he did not hold the Confederate military

responsible for the tragedy. Sherman was prepared to offer Johnston the same terms and conditions that were made by General Ulysses S. Grant to Lee eight days earlier. Johnston, however, wanted to go one step further and work out terms for a permanent peace. Sherman agreed to meet again the next day if Johnston could secure the approval of the Confederate politicos and be permitted to negotiate for all the Confederate armies remaining in the field.

At 2:00 in the afternoon on 18 April, Sherman and Johnston reconvened at the Bennett house, prepared to work out an agreement for peace. After some preliminary negotiating, both parties agreed to very broad terms that provided for demobilizing all Confederate armies, depositing arms in state arsenals, recognizing state governments, establishing new federal courts, and restoring political and civil rights as long as laws were obeyed. In short, the war was to cease followed by a general amnesty. President Davis readily agreed to such liberal terms, but the federal government rejected them outright and instructed General Grant to direct Sherman to renegotiate terms strictly along the lines of those established with Lee at Appomattox on 9 April.

Accordingly, on 26 April, Johnston and Sherman met at the Bennett house for the third and last time and signed an agreement that conformed to Grant's guidelines. The document effectively ended the war in the Carolinas, Georgia, and Florida and demobilized and disarmed the 89,270 men still under Johnston's overall command.

—*Alan C. Downs*

See also Bentonville, Battle of; Carolinas Campaign; Johnston, Joseph Eggleston; Sherman, William Tecumseh.

For further reading:

Barrett, John G. *The Civil War in North Carolina* (1963).
Marszalek, John F. *Sherman: A Soldier's Passion for Order* (1994).

BENNETT, JAMES GORDON
(1795–1872)
Journalist, editor, and publisher

James Gordon Bennett became a dominant force in newspaper publishing during the middle of the nineteenth century. The Civil War especially encouraged the innovative Bennett to take advantage of a climactic event that would allow him to beat a fierce competition. What set him apart from his rivals was his adherence to basic principles of journalism, not the least of which was "if it bleeds, it leads." He also saw the need to put out as complete a paper as possible. This meant that cultural events, books, music, theater, and human interest, would share with crime and politics. His editorial policy was daring and courageous, often to the point of being dangerous to himself. Bennett had no fear of being physically attacked by someone whose interests he had criticized in his paper. He knew full well too that the reading public was too prone to regard "yesterday's news" too literally; therefore, any contradictions in the paper required few retractions. His *New York Herald* covered commerce, shipping, and business generally, but it was the sensational story that challenged for readership. Bennett came to his perception of what a real newspaper should be by hard experience. This experience taught him that independence meant that he and his paper would be beholden to no one.

Bennett was born a Catholic in intensely Protestant Scotland. He received a classical education of Greek, Latin, mathematics, history, and the Bible, all of which, and especially the last, were reinforced at home. He was set on a path to the priesthood, which he rejected after four years at Blair's College in Aberdeen. For five years until 1819 he traveled throughout Scotland and decided to go to the Americas with $25 in his pocket.

He landed in Nova Scotia, but it was not the America he had read about in books such as Benjamin Franklin's *Autobiography*. His classical education fitted him for everything and nothing. He taught bookkeeping in Halifax but the suffocating English atmosphere pushed him south to Portland. He did some teaching and absorbed something of the independent outlook of the people. He moved on to Boston and was repelled by the arrogance and snobbishness of the city. To him Bostonians seemed to represent a nation within a nation and they preferred their own. Religion was also a problem in Boston, as it seemed too much like that of the rigid Scot Presbyterians. He worked in a bookshop and printery, a job that allowed him to read extensively. His employers found him to be a good worker, but customers commented on his speech, ungainly manners, and especially his disconcerting crossed eyes. He was assigned to the print shop as a proofreader where he astutely absorbed the craft of printing for a commercial market. He stayed until 1823, when he moved to New York.

In New York, Bennett again did proofreading and bookkeeping and was hired at $5 a week, translating Spanish and French news for the *Charleston (South Carolina) Courier*. He spent ten months in the South and was impressed with the culture and pride of the city and the intelligence of the people working with him. He was quick to discover, however, that ideas and wit were secondary to appearances. His withdrawn behavior prevented him from participating fully in social settings. New York seemed to be more suited to him.

After writing freelance articles and editorials for various papers, he became an editor for Mordecai Noah's *Enquirer*, concentrating on politics in Albany and Washington. When the paper joined with James Watson Webb's *Courier*, Bennett went along to write on both

politics and banking. His editorials targeted the recharter bill of Nicholas Biddle's Second National Bank. The *Courier and Enquirer* was a powerful and prosperous paper that changed its beliefs on the bank after President Andrew Jackson vetoed the recharter. Bennett suspected the bank's influence, so he left. He himself had played a duplicitous game with Biddle by requesting underwriting to allow him to buy into the paper while maintaining contacts with the Jackson people. Rebuffed by the bank, Bennett heaped scorn on the bank as a "vast and corrupt political machine...buying and selling votes...bribing officials and editors."

Bennett tried without success to buy a paper in both New York and Washington and found work as editor for a Democratic Party daily, the *Pennsylvanian* in Philadelphia. He lasted two years and again returned to New York, where he was intrigued by the newest paper in town, the *New York Sun*, which was a penny paper that was sold directly by carriers who swarmed the streets with the little dailies. It was a paper designed for the common people and proved to be successful. Bennett saw possibilities for a more sophisticated penny daily.

Horace Greeley, who had his own ups and downs with dailies and weekly papers until he got political underpinning for his *Tribune*, referred Bennett to two printers he knew. Bennett started his paper in a basement room at 20 Wall Street on a couple of planks laid across some barrels. He named it the *Herald* with the first issue appearing on 6 May 1835. He worked from eight in the morning until ten in the evening, doing everything, from the work of editor to that of distributor. He structured his time to fit every facet of the paper, an organizational impulse that was to sustain him throughout his career and make his paper the most dominant media force in the nation by 1865.

His sharp wit and acerbic language poked and prodded the pretentious, the politician, the reformers, business promoters, and usurious bankers. All became targets. He invented the idea of attribution to anonymous sources for stories of his own creation. He prowled the streets seeking story ideas. He described dead people in gruesome detail, a practice he used when reviewing photographic exhibitions by Mathew Brady of battlefield casualties. He printed personal interviews with question-answer confrontations. He followed fire engines and police wagons and even hearses to get a story. The *Herald* soon became the one paper bought by New Yorkers. His paper was constantly threatened with lawsuits for slander and libel, and he was often attacked. His former employer, Webb, beat him up two times, and each time Bennett greeted his reading public with a full accounting, much to the dismay of Webb. The pen was mightier than the sword. Words and ideas were his answer to physical threats. Critics were relentless and unprincipled in their attacks. The success of the paper enraged his enemies, especially his former associates Webb and Noah.

After Bennett's marriage in 1840, Webb and Noah questioned the chastity of the bride, and when a son was born, they challenged Bennett's fatherhood. Bennett filed a lawsuit, and Noah was assessed a $250 fine. The harassment continued, however, and Bennett's wife chose to spend much of her time in Paris or on cruises. Bennett hewed to the task of putting out the best paper with the most stories. Money was devoted to expansion and to hiring more journalists. He gave them bylines and underwrote expenses. He hired vessels to meet foreign shipping at sea before they got to port in order to get the story first. He employed translators and sent correspondents to cover European events such as the Crimean War.

His paper was a great concern to political parties because its policy could often become mercurial. Generally conservative in criticism of abolitionists and its calls for the hanging of John Brown, it nevertheless insisted on crushing the Confederacy once war began, much to the disappointment of Southerners, who had appreciated his empathy for their interests before the war. The paper generally supported Democrats, except it went for John Charles Frémont in 1856. It did not support Lincoln in either election, though Lincoln was an avid reader of the *Herald*, even going so far as to offer Bennett an ambassadorship to France—which was declined by Bennett. Bennett had as many as sixty-five correspondents in the combat zones of the Civil War and kept a battery of columnists in Washington at a cost of $200 a week. Circulation grew from 100,000 to 123,000 in the first six months of 1862. William Russell, who had set the standard for combat correspondents in the Crimean War while writing for the *London Times*, became subject for a *Herald* story, which crowed in 1861 that it had bettered Russell in "truthfulness, graphic power and bravery of its reporters."

Nothing was spared in reporting the war. Shaping stories for public consumption was standard. Only the enemy had deserters, shirkers, stragglers, and cowards. Combat always ended decisively and genius of leadership became a given in news articles. Some reporters had insinuated themselves within military units, and Union commanders were uncertain about their status. T. W. Knox, a reporter for the *Herald*, was court-martialed by General William Tecumseh Sherman as a suspected spy; other reporters were mobbed by soldiers and run out of camps in ball and chain. For $15 to $50 a week and all the danger and excitement required, the reporters fed the appetite for news. Lincoln's people's war was guaranteed to be public by Bennett and his *Herald*.

The competition was left far behind by the speed, depth, and breadth of the *Herald*'s war coverage. Dailies in other cities around the nation picked stories from the *Herald* to run in their own papers. Bennett had expended

almost $750,000 in telegraph costs to cover the war. He even donated a sloop outfitted with cannon in return for a commission as lieutenant for his son, James, Jr., who promptly resigned his commission two years later when the ship was taken out of service in 1864. By this time, he was being groomed to take over the firm, which had grown to a dozen editors and almost 500 employees.

Though never a champion of Lincoln, Bennett used the *Herald* to ennoble him after his death. The martyrdom of Lincoln was assured by the paper, and those involved in the conspiracy were condemned with all the vituperative power for which the *Herald* was noted.

James Gordon Bennett turned control of the paper over to his son in 1867. He was certainly unsure of the ability of his dilettante son to continue the progress that had been made. Staying on top of technology, insisting on a cash-and-carry advertising practice, and stressing broad coverage of stories with a personal side were *Herald* hallmarks that eventually the Joseph Pulitzers and the William Randolph Hearsts parlayed into successes of their own. Virtually alone, as his wife preferred to stay in Europe, Bennett, Sr. had a stroke that paralyzed him from the waist down, and on 1 June 1872 he died with no family in attendance. On his deathbed he renewed his Catholic faith, calling upon the archbishop to take his confession and administer the last sacrament. His wife died in Germany the following year, also alone.

The *Herald* continued as a viable but declining force, as it was running on inertia alone. The son was not a hands-on manager, and by 1877 he was an expatriate in Paris after an embarrassing social gaffe that made him unacceptable in polite society. He remained in Paris for forty years, though he continued to manage the paper via trans-Atlantic cable messages. He maintained an expensive lifestyle with a large estate and a yacht. He also created the *Paris Herald*, which he steadfastly kept publishing during World War I. He died in 1918, and two years later the *Herald* was sold to Whitelaw Reid and the *New York Tribune* with the stipulation that "*Herald*" would appear first on any masthead. The younger Bennett's underwriting of the British explorer Henry M. Stanley's expedition to find the English explorer David Livingstone was a dramatic stroke that even the father might have approved.

—*Jack J. Cardoso*

See also New York Tribune; Newspapers.
For further reading:
Carlson, Oliver. *The Man Who Made the News* (1942).
Crouthamel, James L. *Bennett's* New York Herald *and the Rise of the Popular Press* (1989).
Cutler, Andrew J. *The North Reports the Civil War* (1955).
Fermer, Douglas. *James Gordon Bennett and the* New York Herald: *A Study of Editorial Opinion in the Civil War Era, 1854–1867* (1986).
Herd, Harold. *Seven Editors* (1955; reprint, 1977).
Kluger, Richard. *The Paper: The Life and Death of the* New York Herald (1986).

Schudson, Michael. *Discovering the News: A Social History of American Newspapers* (1981).
Seitz, Don C. *The James Gordon Bennetts: Father and Son* (1928).
Tebbell, John, and Sarah Miles Watts. *The Press and the Presidency* (1985).

BENNING, HENRY LEWIS
(1814–1875)
Confederate general

Born to Pleasant Moon Benning and Matilda Meriwether White Benning in Columbia County, Georgia, Henry Lewis Benning graduated from Franklin College (later the University of Georgia) in 1834 and began immediately to study law. He became a prominent attorney in Columbus, Georgia, and was active in state Democratic politics. In 1850 Benning was selected one of the state's delegates to the Nashville Convention, where he distinguished himself as a strong proponent of states' rights. From 1853 to 1859 he served as a judge on Georgia's supreme court. In April 1860 Benning served as a delegate to the Democratic National Convention in Charleston, South Carolina, and when that body adjourned to Baltimore in June 1860, Benning served as the vice president of the convention.

After the election of Abraham Lincoln, Benning became an ardent supporter of secession and served as a delegate to Georgia's secession convention. Following Georgia's secession, the convention sent him to Virginia to urge that state's secession.

In August 1861 Benning received a commission as the colonel of the 17th Georgia Regiment. His regiment was placed in the brigade of Brigadier General Robert Toombs and moved north to Virginia with him in the spring of 1862. Benning's regiment fought in the Peninsula campaign, especially distinguishing itself at Malvern Hill.

When General Toombs temporarily took command of a division at Second Bull Run, Benning assumed command of the brigade there and continued in that command at Antietam in September 1862. As the commander of Toombs's brigade at Antietam, Benning's primary responsibility was to resist the crossing of Antietam Creek by Union general Ambrose Burnside's corps at what would become known as Burnside's Bridge. The brigade gained a great deal of distinction that day by delaying the movement of Burnside across the creek and allowing time for reinforcements to be brought to the Confederate right. Benning continued in command of the brigade at Fredericksburg but took little part in the battle because of the brigade's placement in the second line of battle.

On 17 January 1863 Benning was promoted to brigadier general and placed in command of a brigade in John Bell Hood's division. He remained with that division through 1863. At Gettysburg, Benning and his brigade saw their heaviest action on the Confederate right in the Devil's Den on 2 July 1863.

Following Gettysburg, Benning was part of Longstreet's corps that was detached for temporary duty with Bragg's Army of Tennessee. On the way south, Benning's brigade allegedly destroyed the newspaper office of the Raleigh *Standard* because it was not as loyal to the war effort as the brigade thought it should be. Benning was not present during the riot.

Once with Bragg's army, the brigade was soon engaged in the battle of Chickamauga. A few weeks later Benning and his men fought again at the failed Confederate night attack at Wauhatchie, Tennessee. By early 1864, however, Benning was sent back to the Virginia theater where his brigade was placed in the division of Major General Charles William Fields. At the battle of the Wilderness, Benning suffered such a severe wound in his arm that he had to leave the army until the spring of 1865. He returned to his brigade in time to command it in the last few engagements of the war and was present at the surrender at Appomattox.

After the war Benning returned to his law practice and died one of Columbus's most successful attorneys in 1875. Fort Benning, outside Columbus, Georgia, is named for him.

—*David S. Heidler and Jeanne T. Heidler*

See also Antietam, Battle of
For further reading:
Gardner, David Tytus. "Henry Lewis Benning: Confederate General" (Master's thesis, 1998).
Kerrison, Marie W. "Henry Lewis Benning: States' Rights Advocate and Soldier" (Master's thesis, 1937).

BENTONVILLE, BATTLE OF
(19–21 March 1865)

Fought 25 miles southwest of Goldsboro, North Carolina, the battle of Bentonville was the largest battle ever fought in the state and the only significant attempt to arrest Union general William Tecumseh Sherman's advance through the Carolinas in the spring of 1865. Sherman, having left Savannah, Georgia, with 60,000 troops in late January, moved north in two wings of approximately 30,000 men each. Facing little resistance as his army advanced through South Carolina, Sherman concluded that Confederate troops in the area were too widely scattered to pose any real threat to his operation. His goal was first to reach Goldsboro, North Carolina, and link up with Federal forces under Generals Alfred E. Terry and John M. Schofield advancing westward from the coast. Achieving that objective, Sherman would continue northward toward Petersburg, Virginia, to aid Ulysses

The battle of Bentonville, from an undated engraving (*Library of Congress*)

S. Grant and his effort to crush Robert E. Lee and the Army of Northern Virginia.

With the fall of Fort Fisher on 15 January and the subsequent evacuation of Wilmington, North Carolina, on 22 February, the last open port of the Confederacy and the last major supply line to Virginia were in Federal hands. Desperately hoping to forestall a juncture of Sherman and Grant, Lee called General Joseph E. Johnston out of retirement in Lincolnton, North Carolina, with instructions to "concentrate all available forces and drive back Sherman." While duty and honor swayed him to accept the charge, personally Johnston recognized the futility of the task. He embraced the command, he later wrote, in hopes of achieving "fair terms of peace."

On 8 March, Sherman's army entered North Carolina and concentrated on capturing Fayetteville. Confederate cavalry led by Lieutenant General Wade Hampton struck their Federal counterparts under Brigadier General Hugh Judson Kilpatrick at Monroe's Crossroads on 10 March but were eventually driven back. Federal troops entered Fayetteville on 11 March and destroyed the arsenal and mills located in and around the city. Leaving Fayetteville on 15 March, Sherman's next planned stop was Goldsboro, where he would find fresh troops and supplies and be linked by rail to the coast.

While Sherman's two wings continued moving northward, Johnston was busy assembling a fighting force out of four commands: the remnants of the Army of Tennessee under Lieutenant General Alexander P. Stewart; Major General Robert F. Hoke's division from the defense of the North Carolina coast; Lieutenant General William J. Hardee's corps from Georgia and South Carolina; and Hampton's cavalry. Lacking sufficient numbers to engage Sherman's entire army, Johnston's hope was to concentrate his disparate troops at Smithfield, situated roughly midway between Goldsboro and the state capital of Raleigh, and then move to strike one of Sherman's two wings at a point when each was beyond supporting distance of the other. Uncertainty over Sherman's destination led Johnston to deploy Hardee's 6,455 men near a road junction at Averasboro to determine if the Federal objective was Goldsboro or Raleigh. A brief but intense battle ensued on 16 March between Hardee's command and elements of the Federal left wing under Major General Henry W. Slocum. Although Hardee eventually withdrew that evening toward Smithfield, the indecisive battle served to slow Slocum's column, further separating it from Sherman's right wing, which was advancing under the command of Major General Oliver Otis Howard.

Johnston recognized that he now had the opportunity he had been looking for. Accordingly, on the evening of 18 March, the Confederate general began positioning his troops in the formation of a scythe-like trap across the Goldsboro Road at Willis Cole's plantation near the community of Bentonville. The following morning, lead elements of Brigadier General William P. Carlin's division of Slocum's XIV Corps encountered Confederate troops as they were deploying. Expecting light resistance, Carlin's men pressed on, only to discover entrenched Confederate troops concealed in the thick underbrush. Johnston launched an attack, smashing Carlin's division, but was finally halted by a Federal counterattack led by Brigadier General William Cogswell. The two forces grappled with each other well into the evening until Johnston ordered a withdrawal back to his original position at the Cole plantation around midnight.

Johnston's plan for the following day was to establish a strong defensive perimeter while he removed his wounded to Smithfield. The Confederate commander also hoped that the Federals would decide to attack, thereby giving Johnston a defensive advantage. On 20 March, while Johnston worked to extricate his wounded and waited for Sherman to attack, Howard's column began to arrive on the field. The union of his two wings gave Sherman close to 60,000 men, three times the number of Johnston's force before the battle. Yet Sherman chose to avoid a general engagement.

On 21 March, a Federal reconnaissance of the Confederate left led by Brigadier General Joseph A. Mower wound up penetrating well into the Confederate rear and threatening Johnston's only avenue of withdrawal: the bridge across flooded Mill Creek. Confederate infantry and cavalry managed to stem the advance and reestablish a perimeter, but Johnston knew that he could no longer afford to hold his ground at Bentonville. That night, guided by torchlight, the Confederate army abandoned its position and crossed over Mill Creek toward Smithfield. Sherman chose not to pursue, deciding instead to continue on to Goldsboro.

The battle of Bentonville cost Johnston 240 killed, 1,700 wounded, and 1,500 missing. Sherman's casualties were 194 killed, 1,112 wounded, and 221 missing. The message to Lee was clear. Ever mindful of the Confederate general-in-chief's earlier directive to "drive back Sherman," Johnston wrote on March 23, "I can do no more than annoy him."

—*Alan C. Downs*

See also Averasboro, Battle of; Carolinas Campaign; Johnston, Joseph Eggleston; Sherman, William Tecumseh.
For further reading:
Barrett, John G. *The Civil War in North Carolina* (1963).
Hughes, Nathaniel Cheairs, Jr. *Bentonville* (1996).

BERDAN, HIRAM
(1823–1893)
Union general

Born in Phelps, New York, Hiram Berdan was educated as an engineer. Before the outbreak of the Civil War he worked as a mechanical engineer, primarily in New York City. He was also a competitive recreational rifleman and had won the honor of calling himself the best shot in the country for fifteen years. In addition to his own competitive shooting, he also had developed his own method of teaching marksmanship.

When the war began, Berdan wrote the commanding general of the army, Winfield Scott, offering his services in organizing a regiment of sharpshooters for the U.S. Army. Berdan met with Scott and so impressed the old general with his confidence that Scott gave approval for Berdan to establish a recruiting and training camp outside New York City.

Berdan spent the summer and most of the fall at his encampment attracting young men from all over the country to become part of his elite regiment. In the fall he began using his own method to train them to become crack shots at great distances. By October, the War Department was becoming somewhat impatient with the time it was taking to prepare the men for duty, and began sending Berdan letters urging him to bring his regiment to Washington. He did so in November 1861, and the regiment was dubbed the 1st U.S. Sharpshooters, and Berdan was commissioned its colonel. While in camp outside Washington, Berdan and his men quickly gained a reputation for considering themselves more important than other units and for engaging in many unmilitary extracurricular activities. The medical department also expressed concern that their camp sanitary conditions were anything but optimal.

The regiment saw its first major actions during the Peninsula campaign the following spring. Berdan was commended for his and his men's actions during the siege of Yorktown and at Hanover Court House a month later. They fought in the Seven Days and, after the retreat to Harrison's Landing, were summoned back to Washington in August to become a part of John Pope's Army of Virginia.

At Second Bull Run, Berdan and his men were used as skirmishers but were accused after the battle of not moving out enough in front of the other units to be effective. Berdan weathered the criticism to fight with distinction at South Mountain in the Maryland campaign and to suffer heavy casualties at Antietam. Berdan and his sharpshooters were also particularly useful in the engagement at Blackford's Ford in the pursuit of Robert E. Lee after Antietam.

Under Ambrose Burnside before and during the

battle of Fredericksburg, Berdan and his men became dissatisfied with their situation. Before the battle, the supply situation caused shortages of rations and, more importantly to Berdan, ammunition. Attached to V Corps as they had been since the Peninsula campaign, the sharpshooters might have expected, like the rest of the corps, to be heavily engaged at Fredericksburg but were held in reserve during the heaviest fighting on 13 December. They did not cross the Rappahannock until 14 December and were then used to guard the retreat of the rest of the army.

Berdan and his men remained in camp for much of the winter of 1863. With Joseph Hooker's reorganization of the Army of the Potomac, they were moved to III Corps under Daniel Sickles. Before that occurred, there was some discussion between the War Department and the leadership of the Army of the Potomac about elevating Berdan to a larger command and promoting him to brigadier general. Such a plan was abandoned because of the fear that if Berdan did not command the sharpshooters, they would not be as effective. Instead he was given command of the 1st and 2d U.S. Sharpshooters, a group that increasingly became known as Berdan's Brigade.

During the battle of Chancellorsville, Berdan actually succeeded temporarily to a real brigade command when Sickles placed him in charge of 3d Brigade, 3d Division of the corps. This brigade included his sharpshooters. During the battle, Berdan and his men were heavily engaged, suffering heavy casualties. Again it fell to the sharpshooters to guard the retreat of much of the army.

In early June, back in command of the 1st and 2d Sharpshooters, Berdan scouted the movements of Lee's Army of Northern Virginia. Still a part of III Corps in the brigade commanded by Brigadier General J. H. Hobart Ward, Berdan's sharpshooters saw some of their heaviest fighting on the second day of the battle of Gettysburg. Initially charged with guarding the flanks of the division as it moved on orders from Sickles down off Cemetery Ridge, later in the day Berdan succeeded to the command of the brigade when Ward was elevated to division command. The following day the sharpshooters spent much of their time clearing Devil's Den of remaining Confederates.

In the fall, in pursuit of Lee's army, Berdan and his men were heavily engaged at Kelly's Ford on 7 November 1863 and then again in the Mine Run campaign. Berdan, however, by no means a modest man, had become increasingly dissatisfied with his role in the Army of the Potomac and perhaps with his failure to advance. The glory and fame he had sought with the formation of the sharpshooters had simply not been forthcoming. In early 1864 he resigned his commission and returned to his engineering career. The units that he had created continued to bear his name for the remainder of the war.

Back in civilian life, Berdan turned to inventing, particularly arms and related devices, using his wartime experience as his guide to what armies needed. He invented the Berdan breechloading rifle and then traveled to Europe to demonstrate it to foreign governments. Most were very favorably impressed. He also invented a range finder with six-mile accuracy and a mechanical artillery shell fuse that increased control over when a shell would explode. Along with these activities, Berdan also worked with veterans groups, especially survivors of his old units. He attended reunions of the sharpshooters and worked with them to have a monument to them erected at Gettysburg. Because some of the states had already established monuments to the sharpshooter companies that represented their states, it became impossible to raise the necessary money to build a monument to the two regiments. Berdan died in New York in 1893 with his dream unrealized.

—David S. Heidler and Jeanne T. Heidler

See also Chancellorsville, Battle of; Gettysburg, Battle of; Rifles; Sharpshooters.

For further reading:
Fahle, Michael L. *The Best the Union Could Muster: The True Story of Berdan's U.S. Sharpshooters at the Battle of Gettysburg* (1998).

Marcot, Roy M. *Civil War Chief of Sharpshooters Hiram Berdan: Military Commander and Firearms Inventor* (1989).

Sword, Wiley. *Sharpshooter: Hiram Berdan, His Famous Sharpshooters, and Their Sharps Rifles* (1988).

BERMUDA HUNDRED CAMPAIGN
(May–June 1864)

In 1864 General Ulysses S. Grant, general in chief of the Armies of the United States, devised a plan consisting of a two-pronged attack to crush the Confederate armies, thus drawing the Civil War to a close. This plan featured a drive on the Confederate capital of Richmond, Virginia, by Grant, while General William T. Sherman crushed the heart of the Confederacy in his now infamous March to the Sea. As a component of the overall assault on Richmond, Grant sanctioned a smaller campaign on the Southern capital via the James River. Brigadier General Benjamin F. Butler, a political general with relatively little field experience, was to lead this campaign as the commander of the newly formed Army of the James. Butler, former commander of the Department of Virginia and North Carolina, selected Bermuda Hundred Landing in Chesterfield County, Virginia, as his base of operations. Bermuda Hundred Landing, located at the confluence of the James and Appomattox rivers, was only sixteen miles to the south of Richmond and eight miles north of Petersburg. What ensued was the Bremuda Hundred campaign, which lasted from May to June of 1864.

The Army of the James was created in April 1864

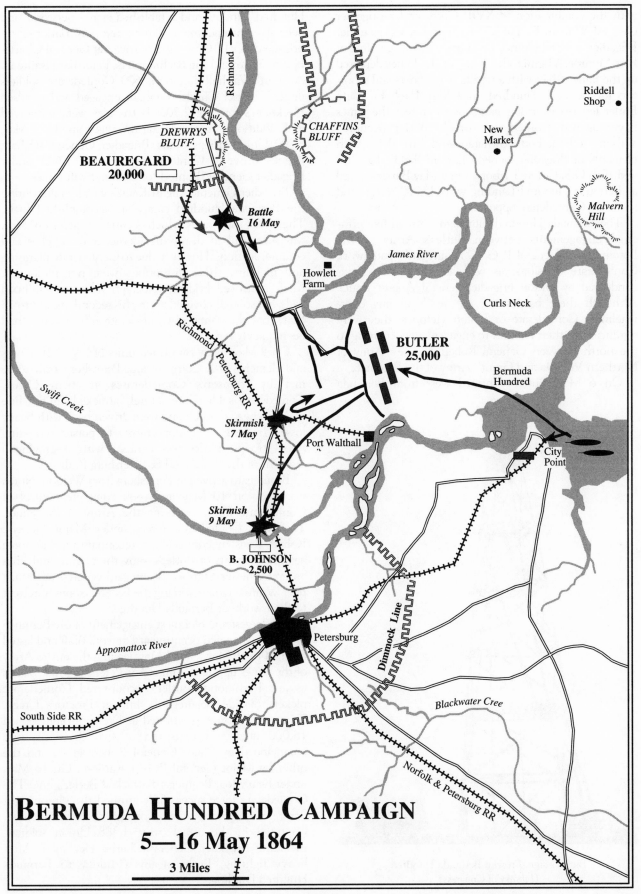

Richmond

DREWRYS
BLUFF

CHAFFINS
BLUFF

Riddell
Shop

New
Market

Malvern
Hill

BEAUREGARD
20,000

Battle
16 May

James River

Howlett
Farm

Curls Neck

BUTLER
25,000

Bermuda
Hundred

Richmond
Petersburg RR

Swift Creek

Skirmish
7 May

Port Walthall

City
Point

Skirmish
9 May

B. JOHNSON
2,500

Dimmock Line

Appomattox River

Petersburg

South Side RR

Blackwater Cree

Norfolk & Petersburg RR

BERMUDA HUNDRED CAMPAIGN
5—16 May 1864

3 Miles

with the combination of XVIII Corps under Brigadier General William F. "Baldy" Smith and X Corps under Brigadier General Quincy Gillmore. After assembling at Fort Monroe, Virginia, the Army of the James departed up the James River with a flotilla of gunboats and monitors for Bermuda Hundred on 4 May 1864. En route Butler left troops at key garrisons to protect the James River against Confederate attack. Butler occupied Wilson's Wharf, Fort Powhatan, and City Point with elements of Brigadier General Edward Wild's 1st, 7th, and 10th U.S. Colored Troops. On 5 May Butler arrived at Bermuda Hundred Landing with 30,000 troops and found no Confederate opposition.

The Bermuda Hundred campaign featured five principal engagements between Butler's Army of the Potomac and General P. G. T. Beauregard's patchwork Confederate divisions, as well as two cavalry raids conducted by Union brigadier general August Kautz. Although these battles did not result in any overwhelming Confederate or Union victories, they were significant in their relation to engagements occurring to the north between General Robert E. Lee's Army of Northern Virginia and Grant's Army of the Potomac.

On 6 May, Butler ventured west from Bermuda

Butler's signal tower, Bermuda Hundred
(*Library of Congress*)

Hundred Landing and established signal networks and defensive entrenchments. That afternoon, Butler sent a brigade of XVIII Corps under Brigadier General Charles Heckman toward the Richmond & Petersburg Railroad. At Port Walthall Junction, 600 Confederate soldiers under Colonel Charles Graham engaged and repulsed Heckman's force of 2,700. Both sides were reinforced with additional troops during the night and on 7 May, 8,000 Union troops under Brigadier General William Brooks drove a Confederate force of 2,600 under Brigadier General Bushrod Johnson to Swift Creek.

Brigadier General August Kautz's cavalry raids during the Bermuda Hundred campaign accomplished little. The first of these raids, which occurred from 5 to 10 May, was successful in disrupting Confederate supplies and communications. However, due to Confederate planning and mobility, these disruptions were not prolonged. Kautz destroyed bridges, telegraph lines, and railroad beds, but soon discovered during his second raid, 12 to 18 May, that the damaged Confederate infrastructure had been quickly repaired.

On 9 May Baldy Smith led units of his XVIII Corps and elements of X Corps towards Petersburg, only to be met by Johnson's Confederates at Swift Creek. Confederate soldiers prematurely attacked Smith's line at Arrowhead Church and were driven back with heavy losses. In spite of an opportunity to pursue retreating Rebel troops, Butler was content with destroying a segment of the Richmond & Petersburg Railroad.

Beauregard arrived at Petersburg from Weldon, North Carolina, on 10 May and took complete control of Confederate forces opposing the Army of the James. That day, Confederate forces under Major General Robert Ransom conducted a reconnaissance in force against elements of Butler's army threatening rail lines around Chester Station. Beauregard ordered an attack near Winfree House, forcing the Federal troops to retreat to their works at Bermuda Hundred.

The largest and bloodiest engagement of the Bermuda Hundred campaign occurred at Drewry's Bluff and lasted from 14 to 16 May. On 14 May, leading the entire Army of the James up the Richmond & Petersburg Railroad to assault Richmond, Butler encountered Confederate pickets outside Beauregard's line at Proctor's Creek. Beauregard's forces positioned at Drewry's Bluff totaled 18,000 men and consisted of two divisions, one commanded by Major General Robert Hoke and the other by Major General Robert Ransom. On 16 May, under heavy fog, Beauregard attacked Butler's line. The Confederate force successfully crushed the Union right flank, leaving many units disorganized and disoriented. Captured in the attack were 1,388 Union soldiers, including Brigadier General Charles Heckman. After heavy fighting, Butler again withdrew to Bermuda Hundred Landing.

Beauregard immediately pursued the Army of the James to its defensive lines at Bermuda Hundred. On 20 May, Confederates attacked the advanced Union positions at Ware Bottom Church and drove back the divisions of Adelbert Ames and Alfred Howe Terry. After considerable fighting throughout the day, Union forces regained their original positions, enabling the construction of the Howlett Line. This containment action bottled up the Army of the James, however, resulting in Butler's nickname, "Bottled-Up Ben." Troops remained at their respective lines until 16 June, when dawn broke and Federal troops found Beauregard had withdrawn his forces to protect Petersburg.

Butler's main objectives in the Bermuda Hundred campaign were to disrupt Confederate supply and communication networks, delay and detain Confederate reinforcements from joining Lee's Army of Northern Virginia, threaten Petersburg, and ultimately to aid in the assault on Richmond. While many of these objectives were in part accomplished, the lasting legacy of the Bermuda Hundred campaign rests with Butler's nickname of "Bottled-Up Ben." General Beauregard's construction of the Howlett Line effectively trapped Butler's larger Army of the James at Bermuda Hundred Landing, causing the campaign to be assessed overall as a stalemate.

—*Brock A. Magoon*

See also Army of the James; Butler, Benjamin Franklin; Drewry's Bluff; Kautz, August V.; Petersburg Campaign; Ware Bottom Church.

For further reading:

Humphreys, Andrew. *The Virginia Campaign of 1864 and 1865. The Army of the Potomac and the Army of the James* (1883).

Longacre, Edward G. *Army of Amateurs: General Benjamin F. Butler and the Army of the James, 1863–1865* (1997).

Robertson, William Glenn. *Back Door to Richmond: The Bermuda Hundred Campaign, April–June 1864* (1987).

Schiller, Herbert M. *The Bermuda Hundred Campaign* (1988).

BERRY, HIRAM GREGORY
(1824–1863)
Union general

Born to Jeremiah Berry and Frances Gregory Berry in Rockland, Maine, Berry was educated locally and worked at various jobs as a young man including carpentry. Eventually able to start his own business, Berry eventually went into banking and became a bank president. He was also interested in Maine Democratic politics and served in the Maine state legislature and as mayor of Rockland. He also served as an officer in the state militia.

At the outbreak of the Civil War, Berry raised, and became the colonel of, the 4th Maine Infantry. He led his regiment to Virginia, where he fought at First Bull Run in July 1861. The following year, as part of the

Army of the Potomac, Berry became a brigadier general in March and later in the spring participated in the Peninsula campaign. He led his brigade at the siege of Yorktown and the battles of Williamsburg, Seven Pines, and the Seven Days and was commended for his actions in most of these engagements. After this campaign, however, illness forced him to take an extended sick leave back to Maine. He returned to the Army of the Potomac in the fall of 1862 and was promoted to major general.

In spite of his promotion, Berry still commanded a brigade at Fredericksburg. Commended for his actions there, he even received praise for his brigade's discipline from Confederate major general A. P. Hill. In the engagement, Confederate artillery pinned down Berry's brigade and forced it to lie on the ground under Rebel batteries for two days.

In February 1863, Berry was given command of the 2d Division of the Daniel Sickles's Corps (III Corps). He led this division across the Rapidan River in the beginning days of the Chancellorsville campaign at the end of April 1863 and was partially responsible for re-forming Union lines on the morning of 3 May after the near disaster of Stonewall Jackson's charge of the evening before. In the midst of leading a countercharge against Confederate forces at 7:00 A.M. on 3 May, Berry was shot. He died approximately one-half hour later. His body was taken home for burial.

Though possessing virtually no military experience before the war, Berry earned the regard of superiors and subordinates for his integrity and ability to master the rudiments of military leadership.

—*David S. Heidler and Jeanne T. Heidler*

See also Chancellorsville, Battle of; Fredericksburg, Battle of.

For further reading:

Lemke, William. *A Pride of Lions: Joshua Chamberlain and Other Maine Civil War Heroes* (1997).

BERRYVILLE, VIRGINIA
(13 June 1863)

As Robert E. Lee began moving the Army of Northern Virginia behind the Blue Ridge to invade the North, he planned to have Richard Ewell's corps move on Major General Robert Milroy's 2d Division, VIII Corps, at Winchester, Virginia. To accompany that maneuver, he directed Ewell to detach Major General Robert E. Rodes's division and General Albert G. Jenkins's cavalry brigade to drive out Federal forces occupying Berryville. Rodes was then to cut Winchester's line of communication to Harper's Ferry by marching on Martinsburg.

The 3d Brigade under Colonel Andrew T. McReynolds had been in Berryville since late March, scouting from there to watch Snicker's and Ashby's Gaps through the Blue Ridge and Snicker's and Berry's Fords across the Shenandoah River. McReynolds was also guarding the line of communication to Harper's Ferry. His command consisted of the 6th Maryland Volunteer Infantry, 67th Pennsylvania Infantry, 1st New York Cavalry, and Captain F. W. Alexander's "Baltimore" Battery. His numbers were about 1,800, far inferior to those approaching him. Milroy had instructed McReynolds that if the 3d Brigade was needed at Winchester, about ten miles to the west, he would signal with four reports from the main fort's heavy guns.

Ewell on 10 June was near Brandy Station, where he had belatedly arrived to support Jeb Stuart the previous day. From Culpeper Court House, he proceeded by way of Gaines' Crossroads and Flint Hill to cross the branches of the Shenandoah near Front Royal. He reached Cedar Hill in two days and from there moved on to Winchester after detaching Rodes's division and some 1,600 of Jenkins's cavalry. From Cedar Hill, Rodes enlisted the service of John McCormack as guide and headed north on a back road toward Millwood. Jenkins meanwhile took the main road through Nineveh and White Post, also toward Millwood. The evening of 12 June found the division camped near Stone Bridge, and Rodes apparently expected Jenkins to be in Millwood screening the infantry's movements. Yet Jenkins did not reach Millwood on the night of the 12th, so when Rodes started toward Berryville the next morning, his advance was soon discovered, and McReynolds made arrangements to evacuate the town.

The problem was that Jenkins's cavalry potentially could cut the direct road to Winchester—precisely, in fact, what Rodes wanted it to do. With rebel forces not more than four miles away, McReynolds sent out his supply train northwest toward Bunker Hill escorted by a company of infantry and cavalry. He then sent the bulk of the 3d Brigade toward Summit Point, from where it would double back the twenty-three miles to Winchester. It was a substantial detour that more than doubled the distance the brigade would have to cover to reach Winchester, but it promised a better chance of avoiding the Confederate cavalry.

Avoiding Jenkins proved easier than either McReynolds or Rodes had expected. In fact, almost nothing went right for the Confederates. Once discovered, Rodes tried to hurry toward Berryville, but by the time he brought all his people up, he was meeting a determined resistance from what he deduced was McReynold's entire brigade. Actually it was only a rear guard of four Maryland infantry companies, part of Alexander's battery, and 150 troopers from the 1st New York. Their defensive positions were strong enough, however, to allow them to stall Rodes for almost an hour before they too moved off and revealed the ruse. Rodes sent Jenkins pounding after them, but the cavalry again

proved feckless. Only Major J. W. Sweeney's battalion found the retreating Federals at Opequon Creek, and his numbers were too small to accomplish anything other than a brief skirmish that left him badly wounded and from which he withdrew. The best Rodes could do was trudge after McReynolds toward Summit Point. As Ewell wryly observed, "Jenkins failed from some cause to overtake the enemy."

McReynolds reached Winchester about 9:00 P.M. Later that night, Milroy chose to move his division into the town's fortifications west of town where he planned to make a stand against the advancing Confederate column. Accordingly, the 3d Brigade took up positions in the Star Fort just north of the main bastion and awaited the arrival of Ewell's force looming from the south.

Later McReynolds would declare that the entire division, the 3d Brigade included, should have retreated to Harper's Ferry on 13 June rather than holing up at Winchester. Milroy's disastrous stand at Winchester seemed to bear out the claim, but that was hindsight. As a court of inquiry would later rule, the 3d Brigade might have been more imperiled had it moved independently from the main force.

—*David S. Heidler and Jeanne T. Heidler*

See also Jenkins, Albert Gallatin; Martinsburg, Virginia; Milroy, Robert H.; Winchester, Second Battle of.
For further reading:
Adams, Owen E. "Confederate Major General Robert E. Rodes: A Civil War Biography" (M.A. thesis, 1995).
Johnson, Freddie L., III. "Mountain Warrior: The Political and Military Career of Albert Gallatin Jenkins" (Thesis, 1993).
Steward, Michelle Lee. "Robert E. Rodes: Lee's Forgotten General" (M.A. thesis, 1997).

BIBB, HENRY
See Refugee Home Society

BICKERDYKE, MARY ANN BALL
(1817–1901)
Union Army nurse

She began with the war, knows all about cooking, and can cook forty things at once. I never saw such a worker; she stirs round the cookhouse with a big meat fork or ladle upraised, and looks as if she would annihilate them all." Thus Union nurse Mary Phinney von Olnhausen described Mary Ann "Mother" Bickerdyke when they met in North Carolina in 1865. Arguably the most influential nurse of the Civil War era, Bickerdyke loved common soldiers and gave their officers reasons to fear her wrath. Generals Ulysses S. Grant and William T. Sherman were known to defer to her wisdom in sanitary matters. Soldiers solicited her opinion about romantic prospects during the war and later asked her to testify in their behalf when they sought pensions. The respect and reverence her name inspired among patients were the result of her fearlessness before military authority and her success at putting the health and comfort of soldiers above all else.

Mary Ann Ball was born on a farm in central Ohio. Her mother died before she was two, and although her father remarried within several years, Ball spent her formative years living with grandparents and her maternal uncle's family. At age sixteen, she moved to Oberlin, where she claimed to have studied botanic medicine. Several years later she joined her uncle's family near Cincinnati and earned her keep by nursing cholera patients in a local hospital. Here she met and married English widower James Bickerdyke in 1847. The couple moved to Galesburg, Illinois, in 1856. However, by 1860 Mary Ann Bickerdyke had lived a life of transience, prematurely losing her mother, husband, and a daughter—a family portrait all too common in nineteenth-century America.

Supporting her remaining children by selling herbal remedies in Galesburg, Bickerdyke decided in June 1861 to help other mothers' sons by carrying church-donated supplies to typhoid patients in camp at Cairo. So abysmal were the conditions she encountered that she cleaned and cooked around the clock until the sick were made comfortable. This take-charge attitude, rendered even more effective when she could deputize others, characterized Bickerdyke's approach to work throughout the war. Matron of the Cairo hospital by the time wounded from the battle of Belmont arrived in November, Bickerdyke deferred only to her patients. When she suspected surgeons of pilfering delicacies meant for convalescents, she baked an emetic into a peach cobbler and left it on the counter for revenge. Bickerdyke also reported surgeons for graft, negligence, and drunkenness until they towed the line or were fired. Their appeals to higher authority, including to General Sherman, were fruitless. When another surgeon at Cairo wished to remove Bickerdyke early in 1862, she left it to a voice vote of the rank and file, who unanimously decided the referendum in her favor.

After the siege of Forts Henry and Donelson in February 1862, Bickerdyke and Mary Jane Safford, a diminutive Cairo resident who would go on to study medicine in Europe after the war, helped evacuate the wounded on hospital transports. When a Northern journalist publicized Bickerdyke's solitary late-night trip to the battlefield to ascertain if any of the fallen were still alive, she became a national celebrity. By the time the battle of Shiloh took place in April, the Sanitary Commission had made her its agent. At Savannah, Tennessee, in mid-April, she met Wisconsin governor Louis Harvey, who was so impressed with her that he left her five tons of unused supplies to distribute. After spending seven months in tent hospitals and proving her mettle to General Grant, Bickerdyke—now the Commission's hot commodity—was sent by Mary Livermore on a fund-raising tour of several Northern states.

Early in 1863 the Commission asked Bickerdyke to bring sanitary order to Union hospitals in Memphis. At this time, Superintendent of Nursing Dorothea Dix, fearing a competitor, wrote the powerful Western nurse "on the chance of opening a communication with you." As matron of the Gayoso, Bickerdyke imported washing machines, purchased with money from her speaking tour, and hired contraband women to do laundry. Unhappy with the unwholesome hospital cuisine, she collected a herd of livestock and a thousand chickens in Illinois and floated them down the Mississippi. From Memphis, she rejoined General Grant outside Vicksburg in July, then in September marched more than 400 miles to Chattanooga with Sherman's army. During the march, she put to work a fleet of black orderlies, who are said to have washed up to 2,000 pieces of laundry per day. The lone female nurse on hand for the battles of Missionary Ridge and Lookout Mountain in late November, Bickerdyke again made headlines when she burned defunct breastworks as kindling so that wounded soldiers would not freeze to death. When military police asked her under whose authority she had acted, she is reported to have said, "Under the authority of the Lord God Almighty. Have you got anything better than that?" Bickerdyke remained in the Chattanooga area for ten more months, aided by Eliza Chappell Porter who had shadowed her after Shiloh. Both women accompanied the XV Army Corps as it moved through Confederate territory toward Atlanta and attended soldiers at Resaca and Marietta. When Atlanta fell to Union forces in September, Bickerdyke and Porter began the two-month process of evacuating the sick and wounded to Northern hospitals. After a second speaking tour, Bickerdyke carried supplies meant for Sherman's troops outside Savannah, Georgia, to the needier troops returning from Andersonville prison to Wilmington, North Carolina, in early 1865.

After a brief trip to Washington for the Grand Review of the Union army in May, Mother Bickerdyke traveled to Camp Butler in Springfield, Illinois, where she helped in the mustering-out process and fought to have the barracks converted into soldiers' homes. In March 1866, she moved on to Chicago, collected her sons, and spent one year as matron of the Home for the Friendless. Working to raise money for soldiers' relief, she secured land in Kansas in the hope of helping veterans finance homes. Though the plan never materialized, Bickerdyke did open a boardinghouse in Salina, on the Kansas-Pacific Railroad line. By 1870, Bickerdyke was working in New York for the city board of missions and traveling periodically to Washington to testify in pension cases. In 1874, Bickerdyke moved back to Kansas to join her sons, but two years later, relocated to San Francisco for her health, where war friend and senator, General John Logan, helped get her a job at the U.S. Mint. The Woman's Relief Corps (WRC), established to aid aging nurses, took an interest in her in the 1880s, inviting her to speak at their functions. In 1886 one of the WRC's members, Margaret Burton Davis, published a one-dollar biography (*Mother Bickerdyke: The Woman Who Battled for the Boys in Blue*) to benefit the by-now legendary nurse. In the same year, Bickerdyke's service was honored with a $25 monthly pension—more than twice as much as nurses would receive when legislation was enacted in 1892. In 1887 she returned to Kansas to be with family as her health declined. While the spirit of sentimental reunion swept the United States, a Mother Bickerdyke Home and Hospital opened in Ellsworth, Kansas, in the 1890s. Bickerdyke died in nearby Bunker Hill several years later. The city of Galesburg dedicated a monument to her in 1906, where her likeness may still be seen in the courthouse square.

—*Jane E. Schultz*

See also Dix, Dorothea; Nurses; Women.

For further reading:

Baker, Nina Brown. *Cyclone in Calico: The Story of Mary Ann Bickerdyke* (1952).

Bickerdyke, Mary Ann Ball. Collection. Manuscript Division, Library of Congress, Washington, D.C.

Brockett, Linus P., and Mary C. Vaughan. *Woman's Work in the Civil War* (1867).

Holland, Mary Gardner. *Our Army Nurses* (1897).

Moore, Frank. *Women of the War: Their Heroism and Self-Sacrifice* (1866).

BICKLEY, GEORGE WASHINGTON LEIGH
(1819–1867)
Confederate officer

An antebellum adventurer with a dubious reputation, George W. L. Bickley was born in Louisa County, Virginia, in 1819. In 1851 he migrated from Tazewell County, Virginia, to Cincinnati, Ohio, where, after falsely claiming to be a graduate of the University of London medical school, he gained some measure of respectability as a physician, scholar, and journalist. Bickley married a wealthy widow and made liberal use of her fortune to finance a number of fruitless schemes. His wife, poorer but wiser, soon left him. Yet he saved himself from complete ruin by becoming the self-proclaimed champion of Southern expansionism.

With this venture, Bickley shrewdly manipulated the spirit of Manifest Destiny that swept the nation after the

Mexican-American War. Throughout the turbulent decade before the Civil War, American adventurers known as filibusters participated in illegal military expeditions that attempted to liberate Cuba or seize territory in Mexico and Central America. In 1854, Bickley founded the American Legion of the Knights of the Golden Circle, a secret paramilitary organization that sought to "regenerate Spanish America" through conquest and/or colonization by a "superior Anglo-American civilization." Seeking Southern support, President-General Bickley promised to restore the sectional balance of power by acquiring new territories for the expansion of slavery.

Little is known about the early activities of the organization. However the outbreak of civil war in Mexico in 1859, combined with Bickley's efforts to elude his creditors, sparked a major publicity campaign. Bickley toured several eastern cities before establishing his headquarters in Washington. Armed with a sixty-three page manifesto entitled *Rules, Regulations and Principles of the Knights of the Golden Circle*, Bickley vowed to "fight the battles of the South on Mexican soil." After a convention held at White Sulphur Springs, Virginia, on 8 August 1859, he prepared to take active operations. His followers were ordered in early 1860 to rendezvous in Texas for an advance into Mexico.

Both Texas governor Sam Houston and President James Buchanan had initially advocated U.S. intervention to restore order in Mexico. However, Houston was unwilling to lend support to Bickley's efforts to extend slavery south of the Rio Grande. On 21 March 1860, Houston issued a proclamation condemning the activities of the Knights. Houston's opposition coupled with Bickley's failure to deliver promised reinforcements led the Texas Knights to abandon the venture. Convinced that Bickley was a charlatan, they expelled him from the organization at a meeting in New Orleans in early April. Bickley promptly summoned a grand convention at Raleigh, North Carolina, on 7 May that reinstated him as head of the national organization.

On 18 July 1860, in an open letter published in the Richmond *Daily Whig*, Bickley called for another invasion of Mexico. Boasting that Mexico's liberal party would welcome the Knights as allies, he urged his followers to concentrate at Fort Ewen, Texas, on 15 September. The "Americanization" of Mexico, he assured Southerners, would silence abolitionists, remove the South's "bothersome" free black population, and cause cotton production to soar. Bickley established his headquarters in San Antonio on 10 October; however, the secession movement that swept the South after Abraham Lincoln's election to the presidency forced him to abandon his latest scheme. Although he did not abandon his dreams of empire, Bickley made the establishment of a Southern

Confederacy the next goal of his organization.

Bickley left Texas in late 1860 and spent the spring and summer of 1861 promoting secession in the crucial border state Kentucky. Vilified by Kentucky's pro-Union press, Bickley boasted in an open letter that more than 8,000 Kentucky "Knights" had rallied to his banner and threatened that the Confederate flag would soon fly over the state capitol. Publicly calling for volunteers on 29 June, he afterward established a recruiting camp just over the state line at Clarksville, Tennessee. However, Bickley was forced to disband his followers after a clash with Confederate leaders in the late summer of 1861.

The "General's" fortunes afterward sank like a stone. After his offer to raise a regiment of Kentucky cavalry was rejected by Confederate authorities in the fall of 1861, he repaired to the mountains of southwestern Virginia, where he spent the balance of 1862 in a futile effort to obtain authority from the governor to raise a mounted command. In a final plea for a commission, he boasted on 14 September 1862 that he had "built up practical secession and inaugurated the greatest war of modern times." Assigned to duty as surgeon in the Army of Tennessee, he deserted the Confederate cause on 6 July 1863. Making his way through the lines, he was arrested in Indiana shortly afterward and imprisoned by Federal authorities. Efforts to connect Bickley to Copperhead societies in the North proved futile and he was finally released on 14 October 1865. Sinking into obscurity, he reportedly died a broken man in Baltimore on 3 August 1867.

Although he sought to portray himself as a great filibuster chieftain, Bickley was a mere charlatan compared with bold adventurers such as William Walker. Furthermore, Bickley's Knights of the Golden Circle apparently had no connection with the similarly named secret, antiwar society that arose in the North during the Civil War. Rather, his organization was more properly connected with the sectional discord and expansionism that marked the 1850s. Yet, despite the farcical aspects of Bickley's career, his efforts to promote the extension of slavery and secession convinced many Northerners that he represented the South's true ambitions. In this respect, Bickley contributed significantly to the sectional crisis that led to war.

—*James M. Prichard*

See also Knights of the Golden Circle; Order of American Knights.

For further reading:
Crenshaw, Ollinger. "The Knights of the Golden Circle: The Career of George Bickley." *American Historical Review* (1941).
Klement, Frank J. *Dark Lanterns: Secret Political Societies, Conspiracies, and Treason Trials in the Civil War* (1984).
May, Robert E. *The Southern Dream of a Caribbean Empire, 1834–1861* (1973).

BIERCE, AMBROSE GWINETT
(1842–ca. 1913)
Union officer and author

Ambrose Bierce's sardonic and often macabre short stories based on his Civil War military experiences are classics of their genre. Born in Meigs County, Ohio, in 1842, Bierce was among the ten children of a poor farming family and purportedly educated himself from his parent's meager stock of books. When Bierce was six, his family relocated to Warsaw, Indiana. He was working in an Elkhart, Indiana, store when the Civil War began.

Eighteen-year-old Bierce enlisted as a private in the 9th Indiana infantry on 19 April 1861. The green regiment went to rugged western Virginia, where it participated in actions around Philippi. By July the regiment was back in Indiana and discharged. The 9th reorganized for three-year service with Bierce again in its ranks, this time as a sergeant. He soon became a sergeant major.

In early 1862 Bierce's regiment was placed in Brigadier General William B. Hazen's brigade of the Army of the Ohio. This began Bierce's friendly association with Hazen. While Bierce would excoriate other officers in his writings, he had only praise for Hazen.

Bierce fought at Shiloh—an experience he later recorded in the nonfiction "What I Saw of Shiloh"—and took part in the siege of Corinth. By December 1862 he had been promoted to second lieutenant. After fighting in the battle of Stones River, Bierce became a first lieutenant and joined Hazen's staff as a topographical engineer. In this capacity he saw service from Chickamauga to Missionary Ridge.

During the 1864 Atlanta campaign, Bierce's brigade experienced vicious fighting. At the battle of Pickett's Mill on 27 May, sheltered Confederates gunned down Hazen's men as they made a futile attack down a ravine. The engagement so outraged Bierce that he made it the subject of "The Crime at Pickett's Mill."

On 23 June near Kennesaw Mountain, Bierce was struck in the skull by a bullet. The round, wrote Hazen, "caused a very dangerous and complicated wound" and remained lodged in Bierce's head until surgically removed. Partially healed, Bierce returned to duty on the staff of Brigadier General Samuel Beatty to fight at Franklin and Nashville in the winter of 1864. In January 1865 Bierce, still in pain from his wound, asked for and received a discharge.

After the war, Bierce moved to San Francisco, where his newspaper writing career first blossomed. He married Mary Day in 1871, and they lived in England until 1876. While abroad, Bierce wrote for British publications. He returned to San Francisco to write for Bay City newsheets. By 1887 William Randolph Hearst had employed him as a writer for the *Examiner*, and Bierce authored a Sunday column entitled "Prattle." His acerbic writing style earned him the nicknames "Bitter Bierce," and the "Literary Dictator of the West Coast."

In 1891 Bierce published *Tales of Soldiers and Civilians*, a collection of short stories based on his military career. These gore-tinged writings shocked readers of the era. This passage, for example, is from "Chickamauga" and describes a woman killed by a stray round: "[T]he long dark hair in tangles and full of blood. The greater part of the forehead was torn away, and from the jagged hole the brain protruded ... a frothy mass of gray, crowned with crimson bubbles." The slain woman is found by her deaf-mute son, who in abject horror at the sight of his mangled mother, begins uttering screams described as "something between the chattering of an ape and the gobbling of a turkey." Clearly, Bierce had seen his share of carnage during the war.

Bierce was in Washington, D.C., by 1876, working for another newspaper. In 1906, he published the *Devil's Dictionary*, a collection of satiric phrases coined by the author.

Bierce's death is shrouded in mystery. Many believe that he died in Mexico in 1913 while helping to cover the exploits of Pancho Villa. Just before leaving, he wrote a letter to friends that predicted his death in a characteristically sarcastic manner. The missive ended: "Goodbye, if you hear of my being stood up against a Mexican stone wall and being shot to rags please know that I think it is a pretty good way to depart this life. It beats old age, disease, or falling down the stairs. To be a *gringo* in Mexico—ah, that is euthanasia!" Some historians contend, however, that Bierce died in an accident in the Grand Canyon.

Whatever caused his death, Ambrose Bierce ranks among the highest of those authors who based writings on their wartime experiences.

—*Dana B. Shoaf*

For further reading:
Joshi, S. J., and David E. Schultz. *Ambrose Bierce: A Sole Survivor/Bits of Autobiography* (1999).
McCann, William, ed. *Ambrose Bierce's Civil War* (1956).
Morris, Roy, Jr. *Ambrose Bierce: Alone in Bad Company* (1999).

BIG BETHEL, BATTLE OF
(10 June 1861)

Big Bethel is regarded by many as the first battle of the Civil War. Union major general Benjamin F. Butler, in charge of the Department of Virginia and North Carolina, established his headquarters early in the war at Fort Monroe, one of the few points in Virginia that remained in Federal hands. He soon occupied the nearby towns of Hampton and Newport News and began sending his men out into the surrounding countryside to look for Rebel troops. Colonel John B. Magruder

commanded the Confederate forces in the area. The nearest Confederate troops to Fort Monroe were only a few miles away. One outpost was at Bethel Church, and its nearby namesake, the village of Big Bethel; the other was at a smaller church known as Little Bethel.

After some minor skirmishes in early June 1861, Butler ordered a major attack against Little Bethel and Big Bethel. His men marched from their camps on the night of 9 June 1861. Under the command of Brigadier General Ebenezer Pierce, the Union force of about 4,400 men consisted of the 1st, 2d, 3d, 5th, and 7th New York Regiments; detachments from the 4th Massachusetts and the 1st Vermont; and an eleven-man detachment with two guns from the 2d U.S. Artillery. Pierce's men marched in two columns, one starting from Fort Monroe and the other from Newport News. The two columns were to unite near Little Bethel, and then attack the enemy there and at Big Bethel. Pierce's night march was plagued with bad luck and inept handling of his green troops. Near Little Bethel (which the Rebels had abandoned), the two Union columns mistook each other for the enemy and opened fire, causing twenty-one casualties.

The 1,400 Confederate troops near Big Bethel, under the command of Colonel Magruder, were Colonel Daniel H. Hill's 1st North Carolina Volunteers; 208 men of the 3d Virginia Infantry; Major E. B. Montague's Virginia Battalion; and Major George W. Randolph's Howitzer Battalion. They were deployed in earthworks around the road from Fort Monroe to Yorktown, at a bridge across the northwest branch of the Back River. The Confederate right, held by the 3d Virginia and one howitzer, was anchored on a hill south of the river. Most of the Confederates were entrenched north of the river. Thick woods and swamps protected much of their flanks.

The Rebel pickets were driven in about 8 A.M. on 10 June, and the main Union force marched into sight around 9 A.M. After two hours of skirmishing and artillery fire, Colonel Abram Duryee's 5th New York Zouaves and Colonel Frederick Townsend's 3d New York advanced toward the Confederate right. The Rebel troops holding the works had to abandon their position after a broken priming wire accidentally spiked their howitzer. The Zouaves rushed in to occupy the works. Instead of reinforcing the Zouaves, Townsend ordered a retreat when he saw what he thought was a body of enemy troops threatening his left. The "enemy" troops were only a company of Townsend's that been had separated from the main force. His mistake left the Zouaves unsupported. Colonel Hill ordered a counterattack, which drove the Yankees out of the captured works. Some of the Zouaves fell back from the Rebel works to a nearby building, from which they fired at the Confederates. Five men of the 1st North Carolina volunteered to charge the building and burn it. The Zouaves drove them back with a volley that mortally wounded Private Henry L. Wyatt.

Townsend and Duryee did not renew their attack. Major Theodore Winthrop led one last Union attack against the Rebel left north of the river. Leading part of the 1st Vermont and the 4th Massachusetts, Winthrop was shot dead. His death unnerved his men and squelched the attack.

After the repulse of Winthrop's charge, Pierce ordered a withdrawal. It was about 1 P.M. The retreat was disorganized and badly managed, but there was little pursuit and they returned safely to their camps.

The Union casualties were shocking for a country unprepared for war: eighteen dead, fifty-three wounded, and five missing. The Confederates lost only one man killed and seven wounded. A statue of the one dead Confederate, nineteen-year-old Private Henry L. Wyatt, stands today on the grounds of North Carolina's capitol in Raleigh. Wyatt was the first Southern soldier to die in a battle during the war. Wyatt's 1st North Carolina Volunteers, and its successor, the 11th North Carolina Infantry, proudly bore the nickname of the Bethel Regiment ever afterward.

The fight at Big Bethel brought shock and dismay to the North, and joy and confidence to the South. In terms of the number of troops involved and the strategic results, the battle was perhaps only a large skirmish that was soon overshadowed by the first battle of Bull Run. To many of the green soldiers of 1861, Big Bethel was their first battle, and it seemed for a time to have been a great one.

The site of the battle of Big Bethel today lies under the waters of the Big Bethel Reservoir, a man-made lake.

—*David A. Norris*

See also Bull Run, First Battle of; Butler, Benjamin F.; Zouaves.
For further reading:
Chapman, Craig S. *More Terrible Than Victory: North Carolina's Bloody Bethel Regiment 1861–65* (1998).
Hale, Edward. "The 'Bethel' Regiment." In *Histories of the Several Regiments and Battalions from North Carolina in the Great War 1861–65. Written by Members of their Respective Commands.* Edited by Walter Clark (1901).
U.S. War Department. *The War of the Rebellion: A Compilation of the Official Records of the Union and Confederate Armies.*

BIG BLACK RIVER, FIRST BATTLE OF
(17 May 1863)

On 16 May 1863, Ulysses S. Grant's army fought the largest and most significant battle of the Vicksburg campaign. The result of this Union victory at the battle of Champion's Hill was a Confederate retreat west in the direction of Vicksburg. Located twelve miles east of Vicksburg and ten miles west of the battlefield of Champion's Hill is the Big Black River. Upon reaching the Big Black River on the evening of 16 May, Lieutenant General John C.

Pemberton chose to defend a bridgehead on the east bank of the river. This action allowed a Confederate division, which became separated from Pemberton, to rejoin the army. Unbeknownst to Pemberton, Major General William W. Loring's "lost" division was marching in another direction, attempting to unite with the forces of General Joseph E. Johnston.

The Confederates built an entrenchment line in a north-south direction, across a one-mile neck of land formed by a loop in the river. The river and the bridges were to the rear, or west, of the Rebel position, which was anchored at each extremity near the river. The Rebels constructed a strong defense line of earth-covered cotton bales, with its flanks protected by the Big Black River. That evening Pemberton ordered General John Bowen to defend the bridgehead until the arrival of Loring's division. Under his command, Bowen had between 4,500 and 5,000 soldiers and eighteen artillery pieces rendered immobile when the horses were sent towards Vicksburg. He knew that he would soon be heavily outnumbered and that sooner or later would be forced to retreat to the safety of the west bank of the Big Black River, three-quarters of a mile to his rear.

Union general Eugene Carr's division of Major General John A. McClernand's XIII Corps resumed the pursuit of Pemberton's forces around 5:00 A.M. on the morning of 17 May. Within thirty minutes, McClernand's forces made contact with the Confederate position and halted to prepare for deployment. A frontal attack against such a fortified position would cost the Union many casualties. Not only because of the actual defenses, but because of the waist-deep bayou and marshy ground in front of the Confederate position. Flanking the Rebel position would be impossible because of the river at each end.

Brigadier General Michael Lawler's brigade did not fight in the previous day's battle and therefore did not share in the glory of the Union victory. Well-rested and ready for action, Lawler's brigade was at the spearhead of the Union advance. Lawler received orders from Carr, his division commander, to advance cautiously and reconnoiter the Rebel left. One of his regimental commanders reported back that a section where the Confederates had placed obstructions had been washed away by the recent heavy rains. Using this sheltered depression, a column of four abreast could reach the enemy's works relatively unnoticed.

Lawler ordered four regiments to take part in the attack on the Confederate left. He used the 21st and 23d Indiana in the lead, while having the 11th Wisconsin in close support and the 22d Iowa as a general reserve. As the 21st and 23d Indiana regiments were advancing over their respective avenues, he would use a diversionary force further to the south to confuse the defenders. The advance began around 9:00 A.M.

The attack on the Confederate left caught Bowen by

Big Black River Station, February 1864 (Photograph by William R. Pywell / *Library of Congress*)

surprise. The 23d Indiana charged out of the depression, through the marshy ground, and over the enemy's defensive works. They were able to break through the defense line and fired a deadly enfilading fire up and down the Confederate line causing the Rebels to scatter. As the 23d Indiana caused havoc on the Rebel left, the 21st Indiana and 11th Wisconsin charged across less concealed terrain to get to the defensive works. They had to leap into the stagnant bayou water in front of the Rebel position and make their way towards the breastworks. Upon reaching the Confederates, they too were able to create and exploit a breach in the defensive line.

Three Union regiments quickly exploited the breach and were able to roll up the Confederate line. The 22d Iowa, once through the opening, turned right and proceeded to push the Confederates toward the river, causing many either to flee or surrender. The 49th and 69th Indiana regiments turned to the South and rolled up the Confederate line, causing the center of the Rebel position to collapse. By 10:00 A.M. the Confederate defense was hopeless and Pemberton ordered a retreat to Vicksburg. Pemberton's forces did manage to destroy the bridges across the Big Black River, causing the Union army's pursuit to be delayed. Pemberton, still afraid that Grant would find a way to get between his forces and Vicksburg, ordered his army to retreat all the way to Vicksburg instead of establishing a line of defense in the hills west of the Big Black River. Now the path to Vicksburg would lay unhindered for Grant's army.

Elements of McClernand's Corps were the only Union forces engaged during the battle of Big Black River. The Union forces numbered around 10,000, while the Confederates numbered around 4,500. The casualties for the battle included 1,751 Confederates killed, wounded and captured and Union losses of 279 killed, wounded and missing. The Union also captured eighteen artillery pieces.

—*James L. Isemann*

See also Champion's Hill, Battle of; Pemberton, John Clifford; Vicksburg Campaign.

For further reading:

Arnold, James R. *Grant Wins the War: Decision at Vicksburg* (1997).

Miers, Earl Schenck. *The Web of Victory: Grant at Vicksburg* (1955; reprint; 1983).

Welcher, Frank J. *The Union Army, 1861–1865: Organization and Operations* (1989).

BIG BLACK RIVER, SECOND BATTLE OF

(February 1864)

See Meridian Campaign

BIGELOW, JOHN

(1817–1911)

U.S. consul general to Paris

For more than seven decades, as journalist, author, diplomat, and statesman, John Bigelow played a vital and virtually unparalleled role in American public life, enjoying considerable success in each of his chosen fields. Although only the controversial—and still debated—defeat of his close friend, Samuel Tilden, in the 1876 presidential race kept him from realizing the crowning achievement of serving as secretary of state, Bigelow came to be known as "First Citizen of the Republic." The historian Allan Nevins notes that Bigelow was "prominent in almost every great civic undertaking in New York in the last half-century of his life."

But Bigelow's place in history was best secured by his diplomatic service as American consul general in Paris during the Civil War, when he almost single-handedly blocked French intervention on behalf of the South and stymied Confederate plans to build a European-based naval fleet. Few members of the U.S. diplomatic service served their country as well as he.

Admitted to the New York bar in 1838, he fell in with a literary/political circle of prominent and soon-to-be-prominent men and began contributing essays to the *Democratic Review* and editorials to William Cullen Bryant's *New York Evening Post*. Taken by his obvious talent, Bryant in 1848 offered Bigelow a one-third share of the paper in hopes of grooming him as a possible successor. Over the next dozen years, Bigelow specialized in political journalism and his pieces on the free-soil and abolition movements attracted wide attention. He joined Bryant in helping to form the new Republican Party: in 1856, Bigelow wrote the official campaign biography of its first presidential candidate, John Frémont. Two years later, he covered the Illinois senatorial election for the *Evening Post*, and was greatly impressed by the Republican candidate, Abraham Lincoln.

Having made a considerable fortune at the *Evening Post*, Bigelow left the paper soon after the 1860 election, determined to spend his time on writing several biographies. But when he heard that the job of consul general at Paris was available, he lobbied intensely for it and beat out *New York Times* publisher Henry Raymond for the post. He arrived in France in August 1861.

Bigelow's assignment was critical: the South had three agents, led by William L. Yancey, already working in Paris to secure British and French support for the Confederate cause—specifically, military aid in breaking the Northern blockade, which, the Southerners declared, would resume the shipment of cotton to Europe. Bigelow was to head off such action—or any French and British intervention, for that matter—and to ensure that the European press remained favorable towards the North.

Arriving first in London, Bigelow used his formidable journalistic contacts to press home the argument that British military involvement on behalf of an aristocracy that practiced slavery would result in a social revolution in England. But British sentiment, fueled by the pro-Southern battle reports from William Russell of the *Times of London*, remained largely with the Confederates.

Similarly, in France government officials, with a few exceptions, greeted Bigelow coldly.

Bigelow's first success came in the wake of the *Trent* Affair, which enraged British public opinion against the North and in favor of immediate military intervention. Bigelow cannily wrote a studied defense of the American government's actions and arranged for it to appear in print. Because he was a diplomatic official, publishing it under his own name would have been considered a breach of protocol. So, Bigelow got General Winfield Scott to agree to sign it. The article, which was widely reprinted in both England and France, was later called "the most successful bit of propaganda in the whole war."

Almost immediately after, Bigelow was called on to counter another piece of Southern propaganda when charges appeared in the French press that the North had callously destroyed Charleston Harbor. Bigelow published letters in the French press demonstrating that no permanent damage had been done.

But the Northern blockade remained Bigelow's most formidable diplomatic obstacle. Thousands of British and French workers had been laid off because of its effects. Bigelow pressed Secretary of State William Seward to lift the blockade, citing the immense propaganda value that would result. "Such a proposal from our govt. would remove all pretext for recognizing the South," he wrote, and "would win for our govt. the esteem & gratitude of the continent." Happily for Bigelow's efforts, the Confederate government miscalculated: It arrogantly declared a virtual embargo, prohibiting its cotton from being sold to any nation that refused to recognize its legitimacy. Seward, through Bigelow, warned France that if it acceded to the South's demands, it might face a similar embargo on Northern wheat—and France had just suffered its worst grain harvest in three decades.

For the rest of the war, Bigelow found himself countering the propaganda efforts of John Slidell, one of the Confederate agents involved in the *Trent* Affair, and of Edwin de Leon, who came to Paris with $25,000 in Southern funds to be used "for the special purpose of enlightening public opinion." The Confederate agents' primary mission was arranging for French firms to build ships secretly—particularly ironclads and corvettes—with which the South might break the blockade. Bigelow tirelessly tracked down all the contracts and presented them to the French government, along with a vigorous diplomatic protest over the flagrant violation of neutrality laws. As a result of his efforts—which included bringing about a shift in French press opinion in favor of the North—the ships never sailed.

After the war, Bigelow rendered further service in Paris by preserving Franco-American friendship during the controversy over the Mexican emperor Maximilian's attempted empire building. Returning to the United States, Bigelow enlisted in the political career of his longtime friend, Samuel Tilden, serving as secretary of state for New York and then as principal advisor and strategist during the ill-fated 1876 campaign. He remained politically active for the remaining thirty-five years of his life, as a celebrated author—publishing biographies of Tilden and Benjamin Franklin—and as publicist for good-government causes. When Bigelow died in 1911, John Jay Chapman wrote that he "stands as a monument of old-fashioned sterling culture and accomplishment—a sort of beacon to the present age of ignorance and pretense, and to a 'land where all things are forgotten.'"

—*Eric Fettmann*

See also Blockade of C.S.A; Chicago *Tribune*; DeLeon, Edwin; Diplomacy, U.S.A.; Newspapers; Slidell, John; *Trent* Affair

For further reading:

Bigelow, John, Jr. *Retrospections of an Active Life* (1909).

Clapp, Margaret. *Forgotten First Citizen: John Bigelow* (1947).

Nevins, Allan. *The Evening Post: A Century of Journalism* (1922).

BIRNEY, DAVID BELL
(1825–1864)
Union general

Born in Huntsville, Alabama, the son of future abolitionist James G. Birney, David Bell Birney moved with his family while still a child to Cincinnati, Ohio. Birney was educated at Andover. Upon graduation, he lived briefly in Cincinnati before moving to Upper Saginaw, Michigan. He studied law there and practiced briefly before moving to Philadelphia, where he worked in business before admission to the Pennsylvania bar. Before the war, Birney became a prominent Philadelphia citizen and an officer in the local militia. At the outbreak of hostilities, Birney raised the 23d Pennsylvania. He led his regiment to Washington, where they patrolled along the Potomac River. Birney was promoted to brigadier general in February 1862.

Birney fought at the siege of Yorktown and at the battle of Williamsburg. Serving in Phil Kearny's division, Birney led his brigade at Seven Pines, where he was accused of not bringing his men up in time to participate in the battle. (A court-martial later exonerated him.) Birney fought in the Seven Days battles before returning to Washington, where Kearny's division became part of John Pope's Army of Virginia. At the battle of Chantilly on 1 September 1862, Birney took temporary command of the division when Kearny was killed.

Given command of the division though not yet the rank to go with it, Birney led his men at the battle of Fredericksburg, where they were trapped under Confederate artillery for two days after the battle was over. General George Stoneman commended Birney for his actions at Fredericksburg. At Chancellorsville,

David Bell Birney (*Library of Congress*)

Birney commanded the 1st Division of Daniel Sickles' corps (III Corps). After the battle, on 20 May 1863, Birney was promoted to major general.

Birney led his division forward into Pennsylvania in June 1863 and on the second day of the battle of Gettysburg took command of III Corps when Sickles was wounded. Birney too was wounded, but did not leave the field during the battle.

Back in command of his division at Bristoe Station and Mine Run, Birney again temporarily commanded III Corps in February 1864. After the reorganization of the Army of the Potomac, he commanded the 3d Division of Winfield Scott Hancock's corps (II Corps). Birney temporarily commanded the corps in July 1864, and in late July 1864 Birney was given command of X Corps.

At the time Birney took command of X Corps, he was already feeling the effects of malaria that he had contracted during the Petersburg campaign. After temporarily commanding the Army of the James in September 1864, his condition worsened. In early October he went home to recuperate, but the trip only exacerbated his illness. He died on 18 October 1864, only a week after returning home. His brother was Union brigadier general William Birney.

—*David S. Heidler and Jeanne T. Heidler*

See also Chantilly, Battle of; Fredericksburg, Battle of; Gettysburg, Battle of.
For further reading:
Davis, Oliver Wilson. *Life of David Bell Birney, Major-General United States Volunteers* (1867; reprint, 1987).

BIRNEY, WILLIAM
(1819–1907)
Union general

Born to James G. Birney and Agatha McDowell Birney in Madison County, Alabama, William Birney moved with his family to Cincinnati, Ohio, after his father rejected the institution of slavery and determined that he would work for its abolition. James G. Birney became an important advocate for abolition and no doubt influenced his son's views on the subject.

In Cincinnati, William Birney became an attorney. In the late 1840s Birney traveled to Europe and was in France during the revolutions of 1848. He was deeply affected by the events of that year and determined to stay to see the experiment in government to its conclusion. While there, he studied literature, taught in one of the nation's universities, and contributed articles for American newspapers about events in Europe. Enjoying the journalistic life, upon his return to the United States, Birney established the *Philadelphia Register*.

News of Fort Sumter motivated him to raise a New Jersey volunteer company that became a part of the 1st New Jersey. He commanded his company at First Bull Run. In September 1861, he was promoted to major in the 4th New Jersey. Birney was captured during the Peninsula campaign the following spring; upon his exchange in August 1862, he was promoted to lieutenant colonel of the 4th New Jersey.

At Fredericksburg on 13 December 1862, Birney and the 38th spent much of the day supporting some of the Federal batteries before advancing late in the day as part of John Reynolds's I Corps. In January 1863, Birney was promoted to colonel. He commanded his regiment at Chancellorsville, but since he and his men were detailed to guard the supply train, they saw no action during the battle.

Shortly after the battle of Chancellorsville, Birney's association with abolitionist causes brought about his promotion to brigadier general of volunteers and his appointment to recruit African-American soldiers. Through the summer of 1863 he was attached to the Department of Washington while recruiting his brigade. In the fall he moved his recruiting efforts to Benedict, Maryland, where he remained until early 1864. One of his sources for recruits was the slave prison in Baltimore.

In the spring of 1864, Birney was sent with his brigade to South Carolina. Shortly after his arrival, he was sent to command the District of Florida, headquartered at Jacksonville. From there he operated into the interior, destroying supplies, capturing Confederate soldiers on furlough, and destroying rail lines. Probably most active during July 1864, Birney skirmished with Confederates outside Jacksonville at Trout Creek in the middle of the month and made a raid on the railroad at Baldwin, Florida, from 23 to 28 July. During his time in Florida, a large part of the northeastern part of the state came firmly under Federal control. At the end of the month, however, he was recalled to Virginia to assume command of a brigade of the 3d Division, a largely African-American unit of X Corps of Benjamin F. Butler's Army of the James.

Upon assuming command of his brigade, Birney wasted no time before seeing action at Deep Bottom Run from 13 to 20 August. He was commended for his actions during that battle, and on 25 August he assumed command of the 3d Division. He continued to command this division through November 1864, and in December he assumed command of the 2d Division, XXV Corps under Godfrey Weitzel. Birney commanded this division through the last stages of the siege of Petersburg and the Appomattox campaign. He was present with his men at Robert E. Lee's surrender at Appomattox Court House. Toward the end of the war, in March 1865, Birney received a brevet promotion to major general of volunteers for his service during the conflict.

After the war, Birney did not remain in the volunteer service beyond the summer of 1865. Mustered out in August, he moved to Florida for several years, but, failing to make an adequate living there, he relocated to Washington, D.C. Initially he opened a private practice but eventually accepted an appointment as U.S. Attorney for the District. He also served as a correspondent on Washington affairs for the *New York Examiner*. In his later years, Birney also wrote extensively on such diverse topics as religion, political affairs, and his father. He retired to a house outside the capital at Forest Glen, Maryland, where he died on 14 August 1907.

—*David S. Heidler and Jeanne T. Heidler*
See also Florida; United States Colored Troops.
For further reading:
Birney, William. *General William Birney's Answer to Libels Clandestinely Circulated by James Shaw, Jr., Late Colonel of the Seventh U.S. Colored Troops* (1878).

BLACKFORD'S (BOTELER'S) FORD
(19–20 September 1862)

The Army of Northern Virginia retreated south after the battle of Antietam in September 1862 by crossing the Potomac at Blackford's (or Boteler's) Ford. By 19 September, two days after the battle, the Confederate army was back in Virginia and some forty-four guns of Lee's reserve artillery were covering the ford to prevent Federal pursuers from coming too close. The job was given to Brigadier General William N. Pendleton, Lee's chief of artillery, who was able to place all but eleven of the guns on points covering the ford. Lee instructed Pendleton to hold the ford through the nineteenth, if possible, to give his army time to put some distance between itself and the Army of the Potomac.

At 8:00 A.M. on 19 September, Union forces appeared on the bank opposite the ford. They were elements of Fitz John Porter's V Corps, and soon they had brought up about seventy pieces of artillery to pound the Confederate position. Pendleton had two brigades of infantry to help cover the ford, but he was to learn that their numbers had been much diminished by the battle at Antietam. Withering fire from Union sharpshooters presently joined the heavy artillery barrage as the riflemen moved to the banks of the Chesapeake and Ohio Canal. Pendleton not only saw his foremost artillery become impossible to man, he also found it hard to find 200 infantry to put forward to repel the Federal advance.

After a lull the Yankees renewed their attack in the late afternoon. Pendleton's ammunition was running low, so he weighed the choice of retiring against the risk of losing his guns. Trying to have it both ways, he instructed batteries to withdraw only if they could do so under cover. He hoped, forlornly as it happened, that the piecemeal retrograde would deceive the bluecoats at least until the day had passed. By sunset, though, the Confederates were being hard pressed, and by dark it became apparent that the Federal force meant to cross and assail his position. Just then, Pendleton's 200 infantry broke.

The river at Blackford's Ford was about 300 yards wide and only about three feet deep, so neither it nor the Confederates on the Virginia bank posed much trouble to the two Union brigades coming across. Under overall command of Brigadier General Charles Griffin, 2d Brigade, 1st Division, the party also included Colonel James Barnes's 1st Brigade. As the Yankees gained the crest of the high ground on the Virginia side, Pendleton worried that they might make a headlong rush that would likely see them capture the entire reserve artillery. He later claimed, however, that he could deduce from the range of their continuing barrage that such was unlikely—and it was. Only four Confederate guns fell to the Yankees. Nonetheless, at the time Pendleton was nearly frantic, so much so that he rushed to the rear and personally sought out Lee. Awakening the commanding general, Pendleton blurted out that all his guns had been taken. Lee told him to calm down; they would take stock of the situation the next morning.

At dawn the next day, 20 September, Lee told Stonewall Jackson to take care of the Union advance, so

Jackson sent A. P. Hill's Light Division toward Blackford's Ford. About a half mile from the river, Hill formed six brigades into two lines of battle, the first consisting of Dorsey Pender, Maxcy Gregg, and Edward L. Thomas. The second line contained the dead Lawrence O'Bryan Branch's brigade under the command of Colonel James Lane, James J. Archer's brigade, and Colonel John M. Brockenbrough commanding the wounded Charles M. Field's brigade. Gregg and Archer coordinated the two lines in an advance that was, in Hill's characteristic fashion, both unceremonious and grimly businesslike. It was hot work, for the Confederates moved into a nasty fire from the 70 guns across the river, as well as what remained of the two brigades atop the high ground on the Virginia side. Gregg easily collapsed the Federal right and center, but the left proved stubborn. In fact, Pender nearly got in trouble until Archer reinforced and extended his left flank to continue the push toward the river. The Federals commenced a general retreat, but confusion temporarily disorganized the maneuver, and the 118th Pennsylvania Regiment suffered heavy casualties. The regiment stumbled down the steep bluff to an exposed position on the river, where they were little more than targets for Confederate rifles above. Hill, hardened to such sights, nevertheless viewed this slaughter as remarkable; the Potomac, he said, was "blue with the floating bodies of our foe."

Casualties were about the same for blue and gray alike—almost 300 for Hill and little more than that for the Federals. After the carnage at Antietam earlier in the week, such losses possibly did not have the power to shock. Yet it was, as Hill noted, a stern lesson for the Army of the Potomac. The 118th Pennsylvania alone had lost 272 men, 3 officers included. That was what happened, Hill declared, when a retreating army was pressed too closely.

—*David S. Heidler and Jeanne T. Heidler*

See also Antietam, Battle of; Pendleton, William Nelson.
For further reading:
Lee, Susan Pendleton. *Memoirs of William Nelson Pendleton, D. D.* (1893).

BLACKWELL, ELIZABETH
(1821–1910)
Physician

In 1861, at the start of the Civil War, Dr. Elizabeth Blackwell led a group of elite white women in their efforts to found the Women's Central Relief Association (WCRA) in New York City, an institute that trained female nurses for the war. By September the WCRA had become one of the numerous local aid societies to come under the organizational banner of the U.S. Sanitary Commission (USSC). Many of the socially prominent women who were trained in nursing by Blackwell through the WCRA served temporarily as volunteers aboard hospital ships like the *Daniel Webster*, the *Ocean Queen*, and the *Spaulding*, and later as army nurses and relief workers. Through their experiences as volunteer nurses in the war, these women traversed the narrow confines of Victorian gender boundaries to work in the public sphere as was the custom for many white and a few free African-American women involved in antebellum reform. The women in the WCRA did so by emphasizing how gender traits associated with the feminine and domestic, such as the nurturing capacity of women, were well suited for nursing. Elizabeth Blackwell, their teacher, had already broken through one of the strongest barriers to women in the professions when she became the first woman to receive a degree from a U.S. medical school.

After being rejected by a number of major medical schools because of her sex, Elizabeth Blackwell was accepted by Geneva Medical College, a "country school" in upstate New York in 1847. Geneva was not being progressive in accepting a woman into their school. Her acceptance was a farcical gesture on the part of the faculty, who turned over to the student body—a reputedly "rude [and] boisterous" bunch—the decision of whether or not to admit Blackwell. Believing her application to be a hoax from a rival school, the students accepted it, expecting her to fail or be intimidated into leaving. Instead, she graduated in 1849 at the head of her class. Although this did not lead immediately to more liberal admission policies for women among existing medical schools, it did lead more women to take up the challenge.

Born in Bristol, England, in 1821, Blackwell moved with her family to New York in 1832 after a fire destroyed her father's business. When financial misfortune struck with the Panic of 1837 the family moved from New York City to Cincinnati, Ohio, that same year. Blackwell's father, Samuel, died in 1838 before he was able to recover financially, and left his wife and nine children practically destitute. With few other economic options available to them, Blackwell, her mother, and older sisters opened a school. Blackwell took other jobs teaching for several more years before she decided to go into the medical profession.

The source of Blackwell's interest in medicine and her ambition to get a medical degree against all odds are subjects of speculation, especially considering that she practiced medicine for only a short time before going into administration and then into public health and sanitation reform. Like her four sisters, none of whom ever married, Blackwell was emotionally and temperamentally unsuited for Victorian marriage. She may have sought a career in medicine as a means of caring for herself financially and thereby avoiding marriage, which in the absence of extenuating circumstances was expected of women in the antebellum era.

She also may have seen medicine as one of the most legitimate and credible avenues into social reform, an endeavor to which she was naturally drawn. Blackwell came from a family of reformers. Her father was a religious dissenter in England and became involved in both the abolitionist and temperance movements after he moved to the United States. Two brothers married women well known for their reform activism. Lucy Stone, noted abolitionist and women's rights and suffrage activist, and Antoinette Brown, one of the first women preachers to be ordained and have her own recognized ministry, were Elizabeth's sisters-in-law.

Whatever her motives for pursuing a medical degree, Blackwell recognized the need for women to have women doctors. A story she tells in her autobiography reveals, at least in part, one reason she chose to pursue the medical degree. Victorian etiquette and prudery too often made guarding their timidity a greater virtue for women than guarding their health. Male medical students in training received detailed instruction in how not to offend their female patients' modesty, including a reminder to keep the lights dim—even though such a practice could result in accidental mutilations of mothers and newborn infants. Dr. Charles D. Meigs, noted professor of women's medicine at Jefferson Medical College in Philadelphia, explained to his students the reason why they should never challenge their patients' timidity. His words attest to the strength of Victorian moral values. "It is perhaps best, upon the whole," Meigs wrote, "that this great degree of modesty should exist even to the extent of putting a bar to researches, without which no very clear and understandable notions can be obtained of the sexual disorders. I confess I am proud to say that in this country generally there are women who prefer to suffer the extremity of danger and pain rather than wave those scruples of delicacy which prevent their maladies from being explored. I say it is fully an evidence of the dominion of a fine morality in our society." Blackwell's consciousness of the cost of such standards was awakened when a friend who was apparently dying of uterine cancer told her, "If I could have been treated by a lady doctor, my worst sufferings would have been spared me." Accordingly, Blackwell saw women's entry into the medical profession as part of a "moral crusade," and she pursued the course until she broke a number of barriers to making this dream reality.

Blackwell's acceptance into, and completion of, medical school were only the beginning of her struggles. Finding a place to practice proved just as trying. After being barred from New York hospitals and dispensaries and then ostracized and ignored by male colleagues when she practiced in area clinics, Blackwell started a hospital, fully staffed by women to serve women and children only. Blackwell and her sister,

Emily, who had recently graduated from Cleveland Medical College in 1854 and finished postgraduate medical work in Europe, established the New York Infirmary for Women and Children in 1857. Dissatisfied with the caliber of training her staff of female physicians were receiving in the all-female medical schools most of them were forced to attend, Elizabeth and Emily founded the Medical College of the New York Infirmary for Women and Children in 1868. Thanks to the Blackwell sisters, who insisted that their college not merely meet but exceed existing standards of excellence in medical colleges, their school was ahead of its time with its higher-than-average standards of admission. The required entrance exam for applicants to the Medical College of the New York Infirmary was ten years ahead of a New York state requirement for medical schools. And the three-year program that the Blackwells' school required (as opposed to the customary two-year program) was the only one of its kind among medical colleges in the country. (Harvard's was not established until 1871.) As a final measure to ensure the competence of its graduates, the Blackwell sisters appointed an examining board of independent physicians. Elizabeth Blackwell returned to England in 1869 to help found the London School of Medical Medicine for Women, the first female medical college for women in Great Britain. She remained in England for the rest of her life.

In recent studies of Elizabeth Blackwell, feminists have noted some of the particularly progressive insights she held in spite of her opposition to openly feminist causes like the women's rights movement started in Seneca Falls, New York, in 1848. Blackwell's open and, among her peers, practically lone, criticism of "radical objectivity and scientific reductionism" in medicine was one that "foreshadow[ed] the maternalist strain of thinking among contemporary feminist philosophers and thinkers." Furthermore, given the trend in medicine at the end of the twentieth century toward holistic approaches that include homeopathic as well as allopathic treatments, Blackwell's perspective merits even more consideration. With regard to human sexuality, although Blackwell herself never married and apparently avoided intimate relationships with men altogether, she believed, unlike the majority of her Victorian male colleagues, that women had an even greater capacity for sexual passion than did men. Equally as consequential, she disagreed with the one-sex model of classical theory then prevalent that the male body was the norm. Agreeing with the scientific and resulting societal theory of complementarity to explain differences between the two sexes, Blackwell held nonetheless that it was the female, not the male, who was the norm upon which human sexuality was based.

—*Catherine O. Badura*

See also American Red Cross; Barton, Clara; Medicine; Nurses; United States Sanitary Commission.
For further reading:
Blackwell, Elizabeth. *Medicine and Society in America: Essays in Medical Sociology* (1972).
———. *Pioneer Work in Opening the Medical Profession to Women: Autobiographical Sketches by Dr. Elizabeth Blackwell* (1977).
Drachman, Virginia G. "The Loomis Trial: Social Mores and Obstetrics in the Mid-Nineteenth Century." In *Women and Health in America*, edited by Judith Walzer Leavitt (1984).
Krug, Kate. "Women Ovulate, Men Spermate: Elizabeth Blackwell as a Feminist Physiologist." *Journal of the History of Sexuality* (1996).
Monteiro, Lois A. "On Separate Roads: Florence Nightingale and Elizabeth Blackwell." *Signs: Journal of Women in Culture and Society* (1984).
Morantz-Sanchez, Regina. "Feminism, Professionalism, and Germs: The Thought of Mary Putnam Jacobi, and Elizabeth Blackwell." *American Quarterly* (1982).
———. "Feminist Theory and Historical Practice: Rereading Elizabeth Blackwell." *History and Theory* (1992).
Ross, Kristie. "Arranging a Doll's House: Refined Women as Union Nurses." In *Divided Houses: Gender and the Civil War*, edited by Catherine Clinton and Nina Silber (1992).
Rossi, Alice S. "The Blackwell Clan." In *The Feminist Papers: From Adams to de Beauvoir* (1973).
Scholten, Catherine M. "'On the Importance of the Obstetrick Art': Changing Customs of Childbirth in America, 1760–1825." In *Women and Health in America*, edited by Judith Walzer Leavitt (1984).
Wilson, Dorothy Clarke. *Lone Woman: The Story of Elizabeth Blackwell, the First Woman Doctor* (1970).

BLAINE, JAMES GILLESPIE
(1830–1893)
U.S. congressman

Born to Ephraim Lyon Blaine and Louise Gillespie Blaine in West Brownsville, Pennsylvania, James Gillespie Blaine was educated at Washington College. After graduation he tried school teaching but decided on the study of law instead. In 1854 he moved to Augusta, Maine, home to his wife's family, and began a career in journalism. As part owner and editor of the *Kennebec Journal* and editor for the *Portland Advertiser*, Blaine took a keen interest in politics. Although Blaine was originally a Whig, the passage of the Kansas-Nebraska Act in 1854 and Blaine's realization that Maine's population opposed the expansion of slavery caused him to identify with the new Republican Party, and he became a founding member of the party in Maine.

Blaine quickly became a party leader in the state. In 1856 he was selected one of the state's delegates to the Republican National Convention, where he unsuccessfully supported the nomination of John McLean of Ohio. Three years later he became chairman of the state party committee, a position he held for twenty-two years. In addition to his party activities, Blaine also served in the state legislature beginning with his election in 1858. In the same year, Blaine traveled to the Midwest, where he covered the congressional elections for his paper. There he witnessed one of the debates between Abraham Lincoln and Stephen Douglas and came away inspired by Lincoln. Even though he was not a delegate, in 1860 he went to the Republican National Convention in Chicago, where he worked behind the scenes to help Lincoln win the nomination. Afterwards he spent much of the summer campaigning for Lincoln. During the elections of 1860, Blaine was reelected to the lower house of Maine's legislature, and, after the legislature convened, he was chosen its speaker.

With the outbreak of the Civil War, in addition to his position in the legislature, Blaine served as the military agent for Governor Israel Washburn. In this capacity Blaine supervised recruitment and supplying of Maine's quota of volunteers. Ironically, when threatened with conscription later, Blaine hired a substitute rather than serve in the army.

In 1862, Blaine was elected to the U.S. House of Representatives. The first committees for the freshman congressman were the Committee on Post Offices and Post Roads and the Committee on Militia—not terribly inspiring assignments, but Blaine approached them with a sense of opportunity. He quickly gained a name for himself by pushing through legislation to authorize railroad cars for the U.S. Mail that allowed sorting en route and sped mail delivery. Blaine's first major speech in Congress also gained him a great deal of attention. In "The Ability of the American People to Suppress the Rebellion," Blaine delivered an inspirational call for greater efforts on the part of the people. The speech was subsequently printed in pamphlet form and distributed throughout the country.

Blaine as a congressman was careful to avoid issues that could make him dangerous political enemies. As a result, he seemed a friend to most members and was quite popular from the very beginning of his service. However, after his easy reelection in 1864, he inadvertently became embroiled in what would become a life-long feud with Representative Roscoe Conkling of New York. The quarrel between the two became one of the most bitter in congressional history. Out of it grew the two factions of the Republican Party during the Ulysses S. Grant administration known as the Stalwarts (Conkling) and the Half-Breeds (Blaine).

During the Lincoln administration, Blaine's activities in Congress showed him to be a strong supporter of the president. After Lincoln's death, however, Blaine fell more into the camp of the Radical Republicans, particularly on the issue of Reconstruction. Because he disagreed with some of the most extreme Radical proposals, however, he was seen primarily as a moderate by the end of Reconstruction. His ability to

work with all sides secured him election as Speaker of the House in 1869.

In 1876, Blaine was seen as a strong presidential candidate for the Republican Party. The exposure of some suspicious dealings with the Little Rock and Fort Smith Railroad put him under suspicion of corruption and ruined his chances for the nomination. Blaine, however, entered a new phase of his political career in 1876 when he was appointed to fill an unexpired term in the U.S. Senate. He served in the senate until he was appointed secretary of state by President James Garfield in 1881.

Blaine took a strong interest in foreign affairs during his brief tenure as secretary. The assassination of Garfield, bringing Conkling supporter Chester Arthur to the presidency, caused Blaine to resign at the end of the 1881. For the next few years, Blaine wrote what would be the first volume of his memoirs, *Twenty Years of Congress*. In 1884 he was somewhat vindicated in the party when he received the nomination for the presidency.

Blaine lost the election to Grover Cleveland and once again withdrew from public life. He completed his memoirs and traveled in Europe. In 1889 President Benjamin Harrison appointed him secretary of state. During the next three years, Blaine devoted himself to the foreign affairs of the United States, working most notably on cementing ties between the United States and Latin America. By the spring of 1892, however, he found himself increasingly at odds with the president and resigned his post in June 1892.

By the fall of 1892, Blaine's health began to fail. He became seriously ill and bedridden by early 1893 and died quietly in his sleep at his home in Washington, D.C., on 27 January 1893.

—*David S. Heidler and Jeanne T. Heidler*

See also Congress, U.S.A.; Conkling, Roscoe.
For further reading:
Blaine, James Gillespie. *Twenty Years of Congress* (1884–1886).
Russell, Charles Edward. *Blaine of Maine; His Life and Times* (1931).

BLAIR, AUSTIN
(1818–1894)

Governor of Michigan

Born to George Blair and Rhoda Blackman Mann Blair in Tompkins County, New York, Austin Blair attended Cazenovia Seminary and Hamilton College before enrolling in Union College, from which he graduated in 1837. Blair's parents were ardent abolitionists, and they no doubt influenced him along that same path as a young man. After his graduation from college, Blair studied law. After his admission to the bar in New York, he moved to Jackson, Michigan, where he established his practice in 1841.

In addition to his law practice, Blair took a strong

interest in Michigan Whig politics. In 1844 he was elected to the Michigan state legislature, where he was a strong supporter of African-American rights in the state. He served in the legislature until 1849 and there encouraged the passage of a law that would grant suffrage to African-American adult males and a Michigan personal liberty law designed to prevent the enforcement of federal fugitive slave legislation in the state.

Not finding the Whig Party in Michigan sufficiently antislavery in its official positions, Blair in 1848 joined the Free Soil Party. Six years later he participated in the meeting in Jackson that organized the Republican Party. The following year he was elected as a Republican to the Michigan state senate.

A strong supporter of William Henry Seward for the Republican presidential nomination in 1860, Blair chaired the Michigan delegation to the Republican National Convention in Chicago that year. When Abraham Lincoln was nominated instead, Blair pledged his support for the ticket and agreed to accept the state party's nomination for governor for the November election. He was elected governor and began his term in January 1861.

As governor of Michigan for most of the war (he was reelected for a second term in November 1862), Blair was a strong supporter of the Lincoln administration and worked tirelessly to raise troops and money for the war effort. After Lincoln's call for volunteers in April 1861, Blair convened a meeting of the state's leadership to address the most efficient methods possible for raising Michigan's quota. After this meeting, he called a special session of the state legislature for that body to appropriate the money to raise and equip ten regiments of Michigan volunteers. The state was in a rather precarious situation financially because of graft in the state treasury during the previous administration. Blair's quick response to the president's call and efficient recruiting methods gave Michigan the honor, however, of having its first recruited regiment reach Washington before any other volunteers.

Throughout the war, Blair corresponded frequently with the War Department regarding recruiting issues. Although he generally had little difficulty meeting the state's quotas during the war and enthusiastically approached those responsibilities, he had difficulties with the War Department bureaucracy in procuring the necessary arms for Michigan recruits before they left the state. He also received frequent and sometimes frantic requests from individual generals for additional troops in times of emergency. This was especially the case during the Confederate invasion of Kentucky in the late summer and fall of 1862 and in 1864 when rumors abounded that Confederates were amassing on the other side of the U.S.-Canadian border. Blair met all the requests that were within his power and gained the repu-

tation throughout his governorship as one of the staunchest supporters of the administration.

Along with his efforts to help raise troops and money for the war, Blair also took a very active interest in the activities of Michigan troops during the war. In the spring of 1862, after the battle of Shiloh, he traveled to Pittsburg Landing, Tennessee, to visit with the Michigan troops who had fought in that momentous battle and to encourage them in their future endeavors for the Union cause. He received frequent reports from Michigan officers regarding the behavior of Michigan troops in various engagements throughout the war. When those units were depleted by injuries and deaths, he worked tirelessly to recruit replacements so that Michigan units would not have to be combined with those of any other states.

In the spring of 1864 Blair traveled to Washington to confer with the president and the War Department about the progress of the war and Michigan's part in it. He came away satisfied that the end was in sight and that Michigan was still doing its part to bring about a successful conclusion to the war. Tired from his exertions during the conflict, he determined to retire from the governor's chair at the end of his second term.

After the war, Blair lived quietly while trying to reestablish his law practice. The call of politics proved too much, however, and he stood for a seat in the U.S. House of Representatives in the fall of 1866. Blair was elected and served three successive terms in Congress. A dispute with the party leadership in Michigan over the U.S. Senate nomination in 1871 caused Blair to join the reform wing of the party in 1872 and campaign for Horace Greeley for president. Blair returned to the regular party in the 1880s but never enjoyed much political success in his remaining years. Instead he devoted his time to his law practice and died quietly in retirement on 6 August 1894.

—*David S. Heidler and Jeanne T. Heidler*

See also Election of 1860; Republican Party.
For further reading:
Harris, Robert Charles. "Austin Blair of Michigan: A Political Biography" (Ph.D. dissertation, 1969).

BLAIR, FRANCIS PRESTON
(1791–1876)
Newspaper editor and presidential adviser

Francis Preston Blair was born in Abingdon, Virginia, the son of James Blair, attorney general of Kentucky, and Elizabeth Smith. Reared in Frankfort, Kentucky, Blair in 1811 graduated with honors from Transylvania University. In 1812 he married Eliza Gist, daughter of frontiersman Nathaniel Gist. For 64 years Eliza was Blair's equal partner in every endeavor. He enlisted in the army during the War of 1812 but had to be sent home from Indiana because of bleeding lungs.

As circuit court clerk of Franklin County from 1813 to 1830, Blair was deeply involved in local and state politics, and he coedited the *Argus*, a highly partisan local paper. After the depression of 1819, the Kentucky legislature passed controversial bankruptcy laws and created a bank to help debtors, which the state supreme court declared unconstitutional. The legislature then created a new supreme court that validated the same laws, and a bitter struggle ensued between the old and new courts. Blair served as clerk of the new court and president of the new bank. Ultimately, the old court won. In 1824 Blair supported Henry Clay for president, but in 1828 he helped Andrew Jackson carry Kentucky. In 1830 the grateful president made Blair editor of a new Washington paper dedicated to Jackson and his policies.

Blair's highly readable paper, *The Globe*, idealized democracy and made Jackson its symbol. Democratic Party newspapers nationwide reprinted Blair's editorials, and did much to spread the concept of America as a great experiment in democracy and a beacon of freedom for the world. Because the Bank of the United States exercised uncontrolled power over the American economy and enjoyed financial ties to various members of Congress and the Whig Party, Blair attacked the Bank as a threat to democracy and glorified both Jackson's veto of the bill renewing it and his transfer of the national treasury to state banks. When South Carolina tried to nullify the tariff laws, Blair portrayed this as an effort to destroy the national Union and pictured Jackson's threat of military force as a noble act of supreme wisdom. He was an adviser in Jackson's "kitchen cabinet," helped organize the Democratic Party into a national institution, and wielded great power in the dispensation of government jobs.

In 1840, when Martin Van Buren was defeated by Whig William Henry Harrison, *The Globe* opposed Whig efforts to recreate the Bank of the United States and raise tariffs. Harrison soon died, however, and his successor John Tyler vetoed the policies of the party that had elected him. Blair supported Tyler's vetoes and worked for the renomination and election of Van Buren in 1844.

In 1844 the major issue was the annexation of Texas, which had recently separated from Mexico. Many Northerners feared the addition of a vast new slave area, and Texas was claiming a huge section of Mexico that had never been part of Texas. Blair and Van Buren feared that annexation before a settlement of the Texas boundaries and an agreement between North and South with regard to slavery's extension would bring war with Mexico and eventually provoke an American civil war. This cost Van Buren the nomination, and even though the Democratic Party platform and its candidate, James K. Polk, advocated immediate annexation, Blair opposed it, although he did support Polk and win a $22,000 bet on his election. Polk, however, forced Blair to sell *The Globe* to a new editor more amenable to party discipline.

Blair retired to his Silver Spring plantation, but remained highly influential through his reputation and friendships. In 1848, although he owned a few slaves, he strongly supported Van Buren's free-soil presidential candidacy. He was certain that slavery should not go to the territories taken from Mexico and believed that Southern radicals led by John C. Calhoun were misrepresenting the issue to promote disunion. In 1850, like President Zachary Taylor, Blair opposed Henry Clay's compromise Omnibus Bill that tied the different slavery expansion issues into one bill, but approved the bills that finally passed one at a time. In 1852 he wrote pamphlets supporting the candidacy of Franklin Pierce, but was bitterly disappointed when Pierce gave much of the federal patronage to radical Southerners and promoted the Kansas-Nebraska Act, which repealed the Missouri Compromise and opened the western territories to slavery. He helped organize the new Republican Party that opposed the expansion of slavery, and when the abolitionist senator Charles Sumner was caned, Blair brought him to Silver Spring for recuperation. In 1856 Blair chaired the first Republican National Convention and was instrumental in securing the nomination of John C. Frémont for president. In a widely distributed pamphlet, "A Voice from the Grave of Jackson," he urged northwestern Democrats to vote for Frémont and argued that if Jackson were alive he would be a Republican.

Blair's son Montgomery was the attorney for Dred Scott when the Supreme Court ruled that the Missouri Compromise was unconstitutional, and his son Frank was a congressman from Missouri who made eloquent speeches advocating abolition and repatriation of the slaves to Latin America. Father and sons were influential delegates at the 1860 Republican Convention and were rewarded when Lincoln appointed Montgomery Blair postmaster general. Throughout Lincoln's presidency, Lincoln and Francis P. Blair were close friends and confidants. Blair argued passionately with Lincoln for reinforcing Fort Sumter, and Montgomery Blair was at first the only cabinet member opposed to its surrender. The Blairs persuaded Lincoln to make Frémont the western commander, and helped get Frémont relieved when he proved incompetent and rebellious. Frank Blair performed heroically as a general under Sherman, but returned to Congress briefly in 1864 to make speeches that destroyed Salmon P. Chase's effort to supplant Lincoln as the 1864 candidate. The Emancipation Proclamation did not apply to Maryland, but Blair immediately freed his slaves and supported the emancipation movement in Maryland.

By supporting Lincoln's cautious approach to abolition and reconstruction, the Blairs by 1864 had acquired numerous enemies. In September, at Blair's suggestion, his son Montgomery resigned from Lincoln's cabinet as part of the price for Frémont's withdrawal as a radical presidential candidate, but the Blairs and Lincolns remained close. In December 1864, with Lincoln's approval, Blair went to Richmond twice to implore Jefferson Davis to accept abolition and make peace. He brought back valuable information and his efforts led to a subsequent conference between Lincoln and Confederate vice president Alexander H. Stephens at Hampton Roads, Virginia. Blair's daughter Elizabeth Lee remained with Mary Lincoln almost night and day for a month after her tragic bereavement.

After the war, the Blairs favored an easy reconstruction process that would not threaten states' rights or white supremacy, and they soon broke with the Republicans. In 1868 Frank Blair was the Democratic vice presidential candidate and in 1871 he was elected to the Senate. In 1875, however, Frank died, and his broken-hearted father followed a year later on 18 October.

As a partisan editor, Blair exaggerated both the egalitarianism of the Democrats and the elitism of the Whigs, but by glorifying democracy as the national ideal and by identifying the immensely popular Jackson with a coherent democratic philosophy, he contributed to the national spirit that enabled Lincoln to save the Union in 1861. On the Texas issue he sacrificed personal advantage for principle, and he worked tirelessly and effectively to prevent the expansion of slavery and preserve the American Union. His Pennsylvania Avenue home in Washington, D.C., still serves as a guest house for visiting foreign dignitaries.

—*Elbert B. Smith*

See also Blair, Francis Preston, Jr.; Blair, Montgomery.
For further reading:
Laas, Virginia J., ed. *Wartime Washington: The Civil War Letters of Elizabeth Blair Lee* (1991).
Smith, Elbert B. *Francis Preston Blair* (1980).
Smith, William E. *The Francis Preston Blair Family in Politics* (1933; reprint, 1969).

BLAIR, FRANCIS PRESTON, JR.
(1821–1875)

Union general; U.S. congressman, senator, and vice presidential candidate.

The youngest and most spectacular son of Francis P. Blair, Francis Preston (Frank) Blair, Jr., was born at Lexington, Kentucky, on 19 February 1821. Extremely energetic, spoiled, and rebellious, he was expelled from Yale and the University of North Carolina for misconduct, and he finished at Princeton in 1841 without graduating because of a wild party during his final week. Through the intervention of Joseph Henry,

the degree was granted a year later. In 1842, after studying law at Transylvania University, Francis joined his brother Montgomery in St. Louis as another protege of Senator Thomas Hart Benton, who dubbed him the "Young Ajax." He was traveling in the Rocky Mountains when the Mexican-American War began and was at Bent's Fort in New Mexico when the area was conquered bloodlessly by General Stephen Kearny. Appointed by Kearny to be attorney general for the territory, he helped write a legal code and successfully prosecuted numerous criminals, as well as a handful of Mexican leaders convicted of treason for stirring up a final resistance.

In 1847 he married Apolline Alexander, who ultimately produced eight children and patiently endured his extravagance and constant financial misfortunes. In 1848 he established a free-soil newspaper in St. Louis and supported Martin Van Buren for president, despite the opposition of Benton. In 1849, when Blair was working for Benton's reelection, an assassin fired at him on a dark street. Serving in the Missouri legislature, 1852–1856, he vigorously opposed the extension of slavery, although he owned a handful of house servants, and in 1856 he supported the Republican John C. Frémont for president and was the only free-soil advocate elected to the U.S. Congress from a slave state. In Congress he urged the South to abolish slavery gradually, and argued that North and South should cooperate in a program of deportation and colonization of the slaves in Central America. In a widely published speech, "The Destiny of the Races on this Continent," he argued that while the Africans were a social and political burden to white society in the United States, they would raise the level of political life in Latin America because of their previous association with the democracy of the United States. Above all, he insisted, while slavery must go, miscegenation and the inevitable domination of the freedmen by whites would also threaten American democracy. Blair echoed the racial prejudice that dominated the thinking of most Americans, both North and South, but he at least recognized slavery and racial adjustment as national problems to be solved by sectional cooperation rather than merely a sin to be eliminated by the South with no assistance in the process.

Defeated by proslavery Democrats in 1858, Blair began organizing Union supporters in St. Louis. In 1860 he campaigned tirelessly for Lincoln and was again elected to Congress, where he became chairman of the Military Affairs Committee. Dividing his time between St. Louis and Washington, he and General Nathaniel Lyon organized Missouri's pro-Union forces and rescued the Federal arsenal that was being threatened by Confederate sympathizers.

His efforts were a major factor in keeping Missouri from seceding. He helped persuade Lincoln to make his long-time friend John C. Frémont the western commander with headquarters in St. Louis, but when the inexperienced Frémont proved ineffective, Blair contributed to and supported Lincoln's decision to relieve him.

In 1862 Blair recruited seven regiments in Missouri and was appointed brigadier general. Ulysses S. Grant and William T. Sherman were usually contemptuous of political generals, but Blair won their respect and high praise as a fearless and effective leader at Vicksburg and other battles. He was promoted to major general and was a top commander for Sherman on the latter's March through Georgia.

At one point in 1864 Blair resigned from the army long enough to make a blistering speech in Congress against the congressional radicals and the presidential ambitions of Treasury Secretary Salmon P. Chase. Having forced Chase to reaffirm his loyalty to Lincoln, Blair resumed his commission and rejoined Sherman in Georgia.

After the war, Blair supported Andrew Johnson's efforts to prevent a radical Reconstruction. He opposed black suffrage, the disfranchising of Southern whites, and the establishment of military governments in the Southern states. He failed to win control of the Missouri Republican Party from the radicals and switched back to the Democratic Party. In 1868 he was the Democratic candidate for vice president. Horatio Seymour, the presidential candidate, tried to soft-pedal the issue of Reconstruction, but Blair probably lost votes for the party by publicly demanding a complete reversal of the ongoing Reconstruction process.

In 1869 Blair forged an alliance between Missouri Democrats and liberal Republicans that won control of the Missouri state government. He was elected to the state legislature and in 1870 was chosen to fill an unexpired term in the U.S. Senate. In 1872, however, he was defeated for reelection. He was preparing for future battles, but suffered a stroke and did not recover. He learned to write painfully with his left hand, and continued his political efforts, but slowly lost ground and died on 9 July 1875.

Except for his widely shared racial attitudes, Frank Blair was a strong force for American democracy. His political campaigns invariably gave the voters clear-cut and unmistakable alternatives. Representing a slave-holding state, he fearlessly called for the abolition of slavery and the preservation of the Union. By keeping Missouri in the Union, supporting Lincoln against all comers, and serving with great military ability, he contributed significantly to the emergence of a better America, even though he opposed the developments his own efforts had helped make inevitable.

—*Elbert B. Smith*

See also Blair, Francis Preston; Blair, Montgomery; Election of 1864.

For further reading:
Laas, Virginia J., ed. *Wartime Washington: The Civil War Letters of Elizabeth Blair Lee* (1991).
Parrish, William E. *Frank Blair: Lincoln's Conservative* (1998).
Smith, Elbert B. *Francis Preston Blair* (1980).
Smith, William E. *The Francis Preston Blair Family in Politics* (1933; reprints 1969).

BLAIR, MONTGOMERY
(1813–1883)
U.S. postmaster general

Eldest son of Francis P. Blair and postmaster general in the cabinet of Abraham Lincoln, Montgomery Blair was born in Franklin County, Kentucky, on 10 May 1813, and grew to manhood thoroughly imbued with his father's democratic political principles. When his father moved to Washington in 1830 to edit Andrew Jackson's official party newspaper, Montgomery was enthralled by Jackson, who persuaded him to attend West Point. There he did well academically, but he disliked the academy intensely because of what he considered its favoritism, the low demands made upon its cadets, and the lazy and immoral habits of his fellow students.

He graduated in 1835 and served for a few months during the Second Seminole War in Florida, but then resigned from the army and studied law at Transylvania University. In 1837 he began practicing law in St. Louis as a protégé of Senator Thomas Hart Benton. His law practice and investments prospered, and he easily assumed the role of financial adviser to his father and brothers, none of whom possessed his business acumen. He served as U.S. district attorney for Missouri (1839–1841), mayor of St. Louis (1842–1843), and judge of the Court of Common Pleas (1845–1849). In 1848 he defied Benton and supported the Free Soil Party presidential candidacy of Martin Van Buren.

In 1844 his first wife, Elizabeth Buckner, died in childbirth, and in 1846 he married Mary Elizabeth Woodbury, daughter of former Treasury Secretary Levi Woodbury. In 1853 he moved back to the Washington area, where his law practice soon gained a national reputation. In 1857 he wrote a forty-page brief and argued brilliantly, though unsuccessfully, for Dred Scott's freedom in the famous Supreme Court case that resulted in a verdict denying either the Federal government or any territorial government the right to prevent slavery in any territory.

In 1856 Blair strongly supported the presidential campaign of John C. Frémont and the free-soil Republican Party. Earlier he had done much to straighten out Frémont's financial affairs. Frémont was defeated, but the Blairs played an important role in bringing former Jacksonian Democrats into the new party.

In 1860 the Blairs helped nominate Abraham Lincoln and were rewarded with Montgomery's appointment as postmaster general. Lincoln's immediate problem was how to retain the major Federal forts situated in the seceded Southern states. Fort Sumter, located in Charleston Harbor, was particularly vulnerable and highly symbolic. At first every cabinet member except Blair urged that Lincoln abandon it rather than risk a war. Blair, however, argued that only a show of firm strength could prevent a war, and cited the example of Jackson's victory over Nullification in 1832. He brought his brother-in-law, Gustavus Fox, a former naval officer, to Lincoln with an elaborate plan for reinforcing the fort. Lincoln agreed and Fox sailed for Charleston, but the Confederates attacked the fort before Fox's expedition could enter the harbor.

Lincoln's cabinet was bitterly divided between radicals like Chase and Stanton, who wanted immediate emancipation, and moderates like Blair, Welles, and Seward, who argued that the war must be won first by avoiding policies that might induce the border slave states to secede. The Blairs had originally persuaded Lincoln to give the western command to John C. Frémont, the radicals' favorite general, but they ultimately recommended his dismissal for incompetence and because, without authority, he had issued an emancipation proclamation for Missouri. When Lincoln relieved Frémont, the radicals were furious.

When the Union army was demoralized by the defeat of General John Pope at Second Bull Run, only Blair supported Lincoln's decision that George McClellan was the best hope for restoring morale. Blair considered McClellan the best commander from a political viewpoint, but ultimately agreed with Lincoln that McClellan lacked the aggressiveness needed for military success.

When Lincoln first informed his cabinet that an emancipation proclamation would be forthcoming, Blair approved, but urged a delay until after the upcoming elections. Lincoln did wait two more months, but, as Blair had feared, the proclamation cost the administration heavily in the northwestern state elections.

For Lincoln, Blair's supreme virtue was unselfish loyalty. In 1864 the Radical Republicans nominated Frémont for president, while the Democrats chose General McClellan and a platform calling for a negotiated peace. A Frémont vote large enough to give some key states to McClellan was a real possibility. Aware of the bitter personal animosity felt toward himself by Frémont and the radicals, Blair privately offered to resign if it would help induce Frémont to withdraw. Assuring Blair of his personal respect and gratitude, Lincoln accepted the offer, and Blair's resignation was an important part of Frémont's decision to withdraw. Blair's affection and support for Lincoln never wavered.

The office of postmaster general has usually been that of political manager, with subordinates actually managing the department. Montgomery Blair, however, took personal charge. He originated new practices such as requiring postage from the sender, free mail delivery, the sorting of mail on railway cars, the return-receipt system of accountability, and the money order system, which he developed as a means for soldiers to send and receive money. He organized a highly efficient postal system for the army and navy, and abolished the franking privilege for postmasters. In 1863 he sponsored the first International Postal Congress at Paris. The modern postal system was in large part his creation.

After the Civil War, Blair supported President Andrew Johnson's efforts to maintain Southern white supremacy and avoid harsh measures against the South. He agitated unsuccessfully for colonization of the freedmen. After the disputed presidential election of 1876, Blair established a newspaper to support Democrat Samuel J. Tilden's claim to the presidency, and represented Tilden before the electoral commission appointed to render the verdict. He was elected to the Maryland House of Delegates in 1878, but was defeated for Congress in 1882. He died on 27 July 1883.

—*Elbert B. Smith*

See also Blair, Francis Preston; Blair, Francis Preston, Jr.; Election of 1864.

For further reading:

Laas, Virginia J., ed. *Wartime Washington: The Civil War Letters of Elizabeth Blair Lee* (1991).
Monroney, Rita. *Montgomery Blair: Postmaster General* (1963).
Smith, Elbert B. *Francis Preston Blair* (1980).
Smith, William E. *The Francis Preston Blair Family In Politics* (1933; reprint, 1969).

BLAKELY, ALABAMA, BATTLE OF
(9 April 1865)

The Federal assault on Mobile, Alabama, began in August 1864 with David Farragut's victory in Mobile Bay. While that action effectively closed the port, the city itself remained in Confederate hands until the end of the war. Situated on the upper west side of Mobile Bay, the city of Mobile was protected on the west by heavy fortifications and across the bay to the east by Batteries Huger and Tracy and two fortifications, Spanish Fort and Fort Blakely.

In spring 1865, Ulysses S. Grant's coordinated offensive envisioned pressing the Confederacy at as many points as possible and thus a sizeable Federal army commanded by Major General E. R. S. Canby again seriously menaced Mobile. With the intention of reducing the Confederate forts on the east side of Mobile Bay and thus opening the Tensas and Alabama rivers, Canby hoped also to force Mobile's surrender.

Two columns would mount the attack. The main one moved by water and had Spanish Fort as its objective. The second, a smaller force under Major General Frederick Steele, moved out of Pensacola on 19 March, ultimately to head for Fort Blakely. First, however, Steele sent part of his command north to threaten Montgomery and Selma, while it covered cavalry units tearing up railroads. Steele had to cope with bad weather that plagued the early stages of the entire operation. Finally, low on supplies and sodden from heavy rains, his entire command turned west, reached Stockton, and from that place headed south to join operations on the east side of the bay.

On 1 April, Lieutenant Colonel Andrew B. Spurling's cavalry clashed with Confederates of the 46th Mississippi Infantry about five miles from Blakely at Sibley's Mills. Reinforced with additional cavalry and a regiment of African-American troops from Brigadier General John B. Hawkins's division, Spurling drove the Confederates out of their positions, losing only two men to the Confederate losses of seventy-five. One of the Federal casualties had been the result of a land mine exploding beneath a horse and rider. Steele compelled his prisoners "to dig up those remaining in this road." The next morning a Confederate attempt to retake the position failed when the African-American regiment resolutely held. The Confederates then withdrew into their works at Blakely.

By 5 April, an extended Federal line had invested both Blakely and Spanish Fort. The following day the siege at Blakely was pressed with skirmishing all along the Confederate works. The Union right was especially annoyed by enfilading barrages directed from the CSS *Nashville* stationed in the mouth of the Raft River. As for the defenders at Blakely, Brigadier General St. John R. Liddell knew that his 4,000 men could not long resist a force three times larger. When Spanish Fort fell on 8 April and Canby was able to shift guns and men from that place to Blakely, Liddell's cause became hopeless. He surveyed a Federal line of 45,000 men that was four miles long. On its right was Hawkins's division of African-Americans, then two brigades of Brigadier General Christopher C. Andrews's division spanning to James C. Veatch's division, which was linked to Kenner Garrard on the far left. A division of XIII Corps and two from XVI Corps supported the flanks, and an abundance of siege guns and field pieces were put into position.

Late on the afternoon of 9 April an assault conducted by 16,000 men got underway. It took twenty minutes to overwhelm the nine redoubts, rifle pits, and palisades that constituted the defenses of Fort Blakely. The bluecoats stumbled over broken ground obstructed by telegraph wire entanglements and made more treacherous by buried land mines. The action cost them more than 600 casualties, a hundred of whom were killed and thus

would never know that they had fallen the day Robert E. Lee surrendered at Appomattox. In the last desperate moments, Liddell led a tattered group of refugees to the shore of the bay as Lieutenant John W. Bennett brought in the *Nashville* to rescue as many Confederates as he could. Boats could only collect about 200 from the water, however, before Union sharpshooters drove them off. Liddell remained on shore and was captured along with more than 3,000 of his garrison.

Batteries Huger and Tracy were abandoned, and finally Federal troops occupied Mobile, one of the last cities of the Confederacy to fall. In less than a month, Richard Taylor would surrender those of the city's garrison who had escaped northward. They had the distinction of having tried to resist the last joint Federal operation of the American Civil War.

—*David S. Heidler and Jeanne T. Heidler*

See also Canby, Edward R. S.; Garrard, Kenner; Hawkins, John Parker; Mobile Bay; Mobile Campaign; Spanish Fort, Battle of; Steele, Frederick.

For further reading:

Hearn, Chester G. *Mobile Bay and the Mobile Campaign: The Last Great Battles of the Civil War* (1993).

Heyman, Max L. *Prudent Soldier: A Biography of Major General E. R. S. Canby, 1817–1873* (1959).

Maury, Dabney H. *Recollections of a Virginian in the Mexican, Indian, and Civil Wars* (1894).

Parker, Prescott A. *Story of the Tensaw: Blakely, Spanish Fort, Jackson Oaks, Fort Mims* (1922).

BLOCKADE OF THE C.S.A.

On 19 April 1861, President Abraham Lincoln announced a blockade of South Carolina, Georgia, Florida, Alabama, Mississippi, Louisiana, and Texas. Implementation began seven days later, as the Union navy began its blockading operations. On 27 April 1861, Lincoln extended the blockade to Virginia and North Carolina.

In implementing the blockade, the Union grappled with a fundamental contradiction. The North maintained throughout the war that the Confederate States of America did not exist—that the Federal government faced merely a domestic insurrection. If that was indeed the case, foreign governments had no justification for recognizing or aiding the Confederacy. But at the same time, if the Confederate States did not exist, could the Union legally blockade its own southern coastline? Secretary of the Navy Gideon Welles, taking such legal complications seriously, personally opposed initiating a blockade, favoring instead a policy of "closing" Southern ports, a traditional technique in times of domestic insurrection. Yet for practical military, political, and diplomatic advantages, President Lincoln and Secretary of State William H. Seward chose to ignore the legal technicalities of the issue and continued to maintain both positions—that the Confederate States did not in fact exist but that the Union could blockade the coastline anyway—throughout the war.

Lincoln's proclamation of the blockade created practical problems for both the Union and Confederate governments. With only a handful of ships available to blockade 3,000 miles of coastline, the Union faced the challenge of turning a paper blockade into a real one. At breakneck speed, therefore, Secretary of the Navy Gideon Welles proceeded to create a massive fleet by buying or commandeering virtually every vessel available—including ferry boats—and beginning a shipbuilding program that was to bear fruit later in the war. In addition, four blockading fleets were created: the North Atlantic, South Atlantic, East Gulf, and West Gulf blockading squadrons.

For the Confederacy, the problem was how to break a blockade without a fleet. The solution was to take advantage of the new technologies of naval warfare, such as rifled guns, armored vessels, commerce destruction, and submarine weapons.

Blockade running was triangular, with its three main corners at the South, the West Indies, and Europe (or sometimes even the North itself). Because of its proximity to the Confederacy, Nassau, Bahamas, was the headquarters of blockade-running operations. Other common destinations included Bermuda, St. Thomas, Havana, Jamaica, and Nova Scotia.

Nassau, in particular, grew wealthy because of the wartime trade with the Confederacy, in part because British colonial officials permitted blockade running to thrive, and indeed encouraged it. On rare occasions when the local government acted to stop a blockade runner, the action was half-hearted at best. The trade out of Nassau continued at full strength until the late fall of 1864, when Havana became the primary port and most of the trade began to head for Gulf ports. Major Confederate ports for blockade runners included Wilmington, North Carolina; Charleston, South Carolina; Savannah, Georgia; Mobile, Alabama; and, especially in the last year of the war when other ports had been closed, Galveston, Texas.

About 92 percent of all the attempts to run the blockade succeeded. (From a Northern perspective, then, the blockade was only about 8 percent effective.) However, the rate of success for blockade running declined significantly as the war progressed and the blockade itself became more effective. Some 300 steamers tested the blockade during four years of war. Of 1,300 attempts, 1,000 were successful. The average career of a blockade-running vessel was typically only about two round trips, but because of high profits there was always capital to construct new vessels. Innovative designs were developed for vessels constructed specifically for the purpose; a typical blockade runner was small and low with a shallow draft, equipped with collapsible

funnels, and capable of considerable speed. Whenever possible it used clean-burning anthracite coal

Although Secretary of the Navy Welles had originally opposed the blockade, he implemented the policy vigorously and encouraged aggressive naval actions that resulted in diplomatic conflicts. Union naval officers were sometimes overzealous in pursuing their blockading duty, and insensitive to issues of belligerent and neutral rights, so that Union naval interference with neutral shipping was a source of friction with both shippers and foreign governments. Not only zeal, but the vagueness of their instructions from Welles, frequently saw Union officers failing to observe the niceties of international law. They sometimes entered colonial ports without permission or sometimes hovered beyond the three-mile limit outside colonial ports, waiting for Confederate blockade runners or cruisers. Such practices in effect established an illegal blockade of a neutral port. In other instances, Union warships harassed or detained neutral ships suspected of having the Confederacy as their ultimate destination. Union warships often acted before checking the requirements of international law and occasionally fired on foreign merchant vessels, not all of which were carrying contraband to the Confederacy. The problem continued throughout the war, despite efforts after mid-1863 to be more scrupulous in observing neutral rights.

Enforcement of the blockade, in short, presented many practical challenges for the Union. The State Department had two goals, which occasionally conflicted with each other: halting or curtailing Confederate blockade running and cruiser activity, and avoiding diplomatic conflict with other nations. Thus, electing to institute and maintain a blockade was one thing, but making it work was another. One of the main difficulties was simply how to tell a blockade runner from a legitimate vessel. One method was the "rule-of-thumb" approach, a combination of intuition and physical and circumstantial evidence. Although it was not foolproof, captures under the "rule of thumb" usually stood the tests of prize courts.

Standard shipping regulations and new rules imposed by the United States in reaction to blockade running provided some basic standards for judging a voyage's legitimacy. Clues to illegal intentions included an incorrect type of license, the lack of appropriate papers (sometimes a vessel had been robbed of its papers), forged clearance papers, or papers whose evident purpose was to hide the origin or ultimate destination of a vessel. If a ship flew a Confederate flag there was no question, but if it flew a neutral flag, the Union navy had to determine if the flag itself was legitimate or simply an ensign hoisted temporarily to avoid capture. Such tasks fell, according to accepted international law, under the legitimate rights of a belligerent warship.

Despite the occasionally excessive energy with which Union squadrons enforced the blockade, their efforts were never enough to stem completely the flow of cotton out of the Confederacy or manufactured goods into it. Vessels broke the blockade throughout the war, but statistics suggest that the blockade became increasingly effective as the war progressed. In addition, the blockade's very existence probably dissuaded some shippers from even attempting to reach the Confederacy.

Successful blockade runners got Southern products to their international markets and brought in some of the materials that the South desperately needed. Typical cargoes on inward-bound runs were arms, ammunition, and other essential war products, in addition to luxury goods for wealthy Southerners. In exchange, Confederate traders were able to provide tobacco and, especially, cotton to other countries. In all, the trade was very profitable, and because Confederate cruisers and commerce raiders posed a more direct threat to Northern security, restricting those activities was more important to the Union war effort than was the ending of blockade running.

In the end, however, the blockade was significant for military, diplomatic, and economic reasons. Enforcing the blockade took Union warships away from other naval activity. Enforcement also made diplomatic conflict almost inevitable, particularly with Great Britain. In effect, the blockade and blockade running increased the difficulty of maintaining Anglo-American stability, the goal of both the United States and Great Britain throughout the war. From an economic perspective, the blockade—regardless of how many vessels did or did not manage to break it—choked the South. The Confederacy was not a self-sufficient nation and desperately needed the economic contacts with the outside world that the blockade made increasingly difficult. On the other hand, from the Northern perspective, the blockade contributed to economic woes by the disruption of normal shipping that characterized the war years.

—*Kenneth J. Blume*

See also Blockade Runners; Diplomacy, U.S.A.; Great Britain; Navy, U.S.A.; Prize Cases.

For further reading:
Bradlee, Francis B. C. *Blockade Running During the Civil War and the Effect of Land and Water Transportation on the Confederacy* (1925).
Dalzel, George W. *The Flight from the Flag: The Continuing Effect of the Civil War upon the American Carrying Trade* (1940).
Silverstone, Paul H. *Warships of the Civil War Navies* (1989).
Soley, James Russell. *The Blockade and the Cruisers* (1887).
Wise, Stephen R. *Lifeline of the Confederacy. Blockade Running During the Civil War* (1988).

BLOCKADE RUNNERS

Blockade runners were ships that attempted to elude the Union naval blockade of the South. The most successful and famous were swift, shallow-draft steamers, many of which were specially built in Britain. Lacking an industrial base, the South

was dependent on weapons, ammunition, machinery, cloth, medicine, and food run through the blockade. In Confederate soldiers' slang, "running the blockade" also referred to slipping in or out of camp without permission.

President Lincoln proclaimed a Union blockade of Southern ports on 19 April 1861, and the first capture of a blockade runner seems to have been made by the USS *Cumberland* off Virginia on 24 April. Yet until the Union could recall ships in foreign ports and buy or build new naval vessels, the blockade existed mostly on paper. An unofficial Southern boycott of cotton exports to Europe both failed to induce foreign intervention and lost the South valuable opportunities for importing necessities before the blockade tightened.

Early blockade runners were a motley collection of sloops, schooners, and small steamers that set out from many Southern ports. The racing yacht *America*, namesake of the America's Cup, was a blockade runner early in the war. Sailing vessels were soon replaced by steamships everywhere, except they retained some use in the Gulf of Mexico and as smuggling vessels on the East Coast. The first steam blockade runner to reach the South was the Fraser, Trenholm and Company's *Bermuda*, which entered Savannah from Liverpool on 18 September 1861. Her military cargo included four large seacoast guns. Much of the cargo was sold at auction. The *Bermuda* left Savannah on 29 October, and its cargo of 2,000 bales of cotton was sold in Britain at a fantastic profit.

Pointing to their great risks, owners of blockade runners such as the *Bermuda* charged tremendous prices. Cotton could be bought in the South and sold for ten times the cost in England. Freight charges and profits on outgoing cotton and incoming luxury merchandise could pay for a fine new steamer in one trip. Although private Southern and foreign firms owned many blockade runners, the Confederate government and the states of North Carolina and Georgia also bought their own ships. Major blockade-running firms included Fraser, Trenholm and Company and the related firm of John Fraser and Company, as well as Crenshaw and Collie and Company, and Edward Lawrence and Company. Yet many blockade runners were owned by small companies that held only one or two ships. Later in the war, the Confederacy regulated blockade running and required all vessels to reserve half their cargo space for government shipments at a set rate.

The South's major blockade-running ports were the Atlantic ports of Wilmington and Charleston, and the Gulf of Mexico ports of Mobile and Galveston. Other major ports were blocked or captured by Union forces early in the war. Some blockade runners used St. Mark's, Florida, and other minor ports. Charleston was the major port until the fall of Morris Island in summer 1863 exposed the harbor entrance to Union artillery fire. Most operations shifted to Wilmington for the rest of the

Wreck of the British-built blockade runner *Ruby*, run aground on Folly Island, South Carolina, 10–11 June 1863
(*Library of Congress*)

war. Wilmington, on the Cape Fear River, was admirably suited as a blockade-running port because Smith Island and the long and dangerous Frying Pan Shoals divided the mouth of the Cape Fear. Runners had two major approaches to the port, requiring the Union to maintain two separate blockading squadrons. Fort Fisher (the strongest fortification in the South) and other posts armed with long-range rifled guns kept the blockaders a considerable distance out to sea and saved many a blockade runner.

Blockade runners from Wilmington and Charleston typically tried to reach Nassau, Bahamas, or St. George, Bermuda. Goods brought from Europe in large deep-draft ships were transferred to fast shallow-draft vessels for the final dash to the South. Some trips were made to Halifax, Nova Scotia, during an outbreak of yellow fever in 1864. Blockade runners from the Gulf ports nearly always ran to Havana.

As the Union blockade tightened, blockade running companies began to purchase better ships. "Clyde steamers," modern coastal passenger boats built on Scotland's Clyde River, were popular by 1862. Companies soon built specially designed blockade runners. They usually were long, low, narrow-beamed and shallow-draft ships. They were painted dull white or light gray for camouflage, their masts were often hinged or set into sockets so they could be quickly lowered, and

the ships' boats were kept below the gunwales. They burned smokeless coal to avoid detection, and had special pipes for blowing off steam underwater. Staterooms were torn out and cargo space was expanded as much as possible. Outgoing runners might carry 600 to 800 bales of tightly pressed cotton, crammed into every space and piled high atop the decks. Although the Confederate government pressed for the importation of military supplies, medicines, food, and other necessities, private companies preferred to bring in highly profitable luxury items. Cigars, pepper, soap, laces, silks, and fine liquors and wines were popular imports.

Many crewmen were British or Irish, and the officers ranged from Confederate naval officers to British merchant ship or naval officers. Captured Confederates faced long spells in Northern prisons, but British subjects were usually released quickly. Pay rates reflected the high profits. Civilian captains could earn $5,000 in gold for a successful run from the Carolina ports, and even crewmen earned $250 or more per round trip. Officers could carry goods to sell on their own account. Confederate naval personnel on blockade runners received their regular monthly pay, but in gold.

Blockade runners usually departed on moonless nights. With their low profiles, smokeless coal, and camouflage paint, a blockade runner could slip by an

The USS *Fort Donelson* (the former Confederate blockade runner *Robert E. Lee*) at Norfolk, Virginia, December 1864
(*Library of Congress*)

enemy ship as little as a hundred yards away. Their speed enabled them to outrun nearly all pursuers except blockade runners that had been captured and put into Union service. Union sailors were eligible for prize money for capturing blockade runners. Some captured ships were added to the Union navy, while others were sold to private interests, which often put them back into blockade running. Under international law, a "neutral" blockade runner could not fire a shot in its defense without making its crew guilty of piracy and subject to hanging. Captures of blockade runners increased later in the war.

The Union navy's efficiency was increased by adding the swiftest blockade runners to its fleet. Pilots, needed to negotiate the intricate and dangerous shoals at Wilmington and Charleston, became scarce, as captured ones were never exchanged. Wilmington was lost to blockade running with the fall of Fort Fisher on 15 January 1865, and Charleston was evacuated on 17 February. Blockade running shifted to Galveston and the Gulf ports for a few final months. The last steam blockade runner to leave a Southern port, the *Lark*, left Galveston on 24 May 1865. President Johnson officially lifted the blockade on 23 June.

During the war, about 300 steamers attempted to run the blockade. Of these, 136 were captured and 85 were destroyed. Altogether about 1,000 out of 1,300 attempted runs were successful. The *Syren* held the

record with thirty-three successful round trips; the *Denbigh* with twenty-six was second. One of the last surviving blockade runners, the *Chicora*, operated as a Great Lakes excursion boat until 1919.

Supplies run through the blockade were crucial to the South's war effort. The Army of Northern Virginia was so dependent on imports of food and munitions through Wilmington that Lee said his army could not survive if that port fell. Blockade runners brought in about 60 percent of the South's modern small arms; a third of their lead; and two-thirds of their saltpeter necessary for gunpowder production. Uniforms, cloth, artillery pieces and ammunition, medicine, and great amounts of food also came through the blockade. Sales of cotton brought the Confederacy much-needed money and credit from Britain and France.

—David A. Norris

See also Blockade of C.S.A.

For further reading:
Hobart-Hampden, C. Augustus. *Never Caught: Personal Adventures Connected with Twelve Successful Trips in Blockade-Running During the American Civil War, 1863–4* (1900; reprint, 1967).
Taylor, Thomas E. *Running the Blockade* (1995).
Vandiver, Frank E., ed. *Confederate Blockade Running through Bermuda 1861-1865: Letters and Cargo Manifests* (1947).
Wilkinson, John. *The Narrative of a Blockade-Runner* (1877; reprint, 1984).
Wise, Stephen R. *Lifeline of the Confederacy Blockade Running During the Civil War* (1988).

BLUNT, JAMES GILPATRICK
(1826–1881)
Union general

Blunt was a leader of Union forces in the Trans-Mississippi and played a significant role in the battles of Old Fort Wayne, Cane Hill, Honey Springs, Prairie Grove, and Westport.

Blunt was born on 21 July 1826 in Trenton, Maine. Drawn to the sea at age fifteen, Blunt rose to the rank of captain in the merchant marine after five years. Eventually, Blunt moved to Columbus, Ohio, where he earned a degree from Starling Medical College in 1849. He set up a practice in New Madison, Ohio, before moving west and settling in Greeley, Kansas, in 1856. An ardent abolitionist, he aided John Brown in helping escaped slaves make their way to Canada. In Greeley, Blunt became active in Kansas politics. He participated in the Wyandotte Constitutional Convention in 1859, chairing the committee on militia.

Blunt's military career began as a Jayhawker, commanding cavalry in Senator James H. Lane's "Kansas Brigade." Blunt was commissioned a lieutenant colonel in the 3d Kansas Infantry in July 1861. After promotion to brigadier general of U.S. Volunteers on 8 April 1861, Blunt headed the Department of Kansas from 15 May to 19 September 1862 and defeated a mixed Confederate–Native American force under Colonel (later Brigadier General) Douglas H. Cooper at Old Fort Wayne, Indian Territory, in October 1862.

After Blunt's assignment to command of the 1st Division of the Army of the Frontier in October, he defeated Brigadier General John S. Marmaduke in a sharp action at Cane Hill, Arkansas, on 28 November 1862. Blunt, who was promoted to major general the day after his victory, vigorously pursued Marmaduke and dangerously isolated his command from the 2d and 3d Divisions of the Army of the Frontier that were located in Springfield, Missouri, more than 100 miles away. Confederate major general Thomas C. Hindman saw an opportunity for his I Corps, Army of the Trans-Mississippi, to crush Blunt's isolated division and then possibly invade Missouri and defeat the remainder of the Union army. Hindman's plans were foiled by the superhuman efforts of the 2d and 3d Divisions commanded by Brigadier General Francis J. Herron, who marched his troops a remarkable 110 miles in three days to reach Prairie Grove, Arkansas, to join Blunt. Hindman, fearful of Herron eight miles in his rear, ordered a night flanking march against him. Fighting erupted between Herron and Hindman on the afternoon of 7 December 1862. Hearing cannon fire, Blunt immediately marched to the sound of the guns. His timely arrival saved Herron's command. Tactically, the battle of Prairie Grove was a draw. Strategically,

however, the battle was a Union victory, as Confederate forces withdrew the next day over the Boston Mountains to Van Buren, Arkansas. Characteristically, Blunt aggressively hounded Hindman's forces to the Arkansas River and captured Van Buren shortly thereafter.

Blunt led the Army of the Frontier into Indian Territory in June 1863 and defeated a combined Indian-Confederate force led by Cooper at Honey Springs in early July. Blunt's military career suffered two successive jolts in October 1863, when William C. Quantrill's raiders surprised him and his headquarters staff outside Baxter Springs, Kansas. Because many of the Confederate bushwhackers were wearing captured blue uniforms, Blunt mistook them for Union soldiers. Blunt's group scattered and, of the roughly 100-man retinue, nearly 70 were hunted down and killed. Blunt managed to escape, but quarrels with his superior, Department of the Missouri head Brigadier General John M. Schofield, resulted in Blunt's being relieved of command.

Blunt's career seemed over as he bounced from one assignment to another until early 1864, when Major General Samuel R. Curtis was appointed to command the Department of Kansas. Curtis, who respected Blunt's military abilities and sympathized with his political leanings, placed him in command of the District of Southern Kansas. Blunt played a significant role under Curtis's command in the Army of the Border on 21–23 October 1864 during the battle of Westport, Missouri, which was part of Major General Sterling Price's Missouri Raid of 1864. After the Union victory, Blunt led an active pursuit of Price's forces. He mustered out of the service on 29 July 1865.

Blunt returned to Kansas after the war and resumed his medical practice. In 1869 he moved to Washington, D.C., where he became a solicitor of claims. Blunt, along with several others, was charged in 1873 by the Department of Justice with conspiracy to defraud the Cherokee Indians. The case was later dropped. Blunt was committed to a hospital for the mentally insane before he finally died on 27 July 1881. His remains were interred at Fort Leavenworth, Kansas.

For one who had no formal military training, Blunt was a remarkably successful army officer. He was aggressive to the point of recklessness, and at times this placed his command in precarious situations. While Blunt was aggressive, he was also lucky. At Prairie Grove, the remarkable march by Herron's troops rescued him from a difficult situation. Blunt may not have faced the top Confederate generals, but he deserves more credit than he is given. He served in the Trans-Mississippi, an under-staffed military backwater that Richmond seemed to abandon after the first year of the war. Blunt's aggressive personality and his politics sometimes made relations with his superiors difficult, but he did as well as could be expected with the resources and the men, including large numbers of African-Americans and Native Americans, allotted him.

—Terry L. Beckenbaugh

See also Baxter Springs; Cane Hill, Battle of; Honey Springs, Battle of; Prairie Grove, Battle of; Westport, Battle of.

For further reading:

Banasik, Michael E. *Embattled Arkansas: The Prairie Grove Campaign of 1862* (1996).

Castel, Albert E. *A Frontier State at War: Kansas, 1861–1865* (1958).

Josephy, Alvin M. *The Civil War in the American West* (1991).

Starr, Stephen Z. *Jennison's Jayhawkers: A Civil War Cavalry Regiment and Its Commander* (1973).

BONDS

The governments of both the Confederate States of America and the United States used bonds to finance their war efforts. The sale of bonds, which relies heavily on the investors' confidence in the strength of the government, fluctuated greatly depending on victories or defeats in the field.

Confederate States of America — The Confederacy's wealth was derived from land, the commodities produced on that land, and slaves. This financial structure, which lacks liquidity, proved to be incapable of meeting the sudden increase in expenses of a wartime economy. The Southerners had hoped that sales of their cotton and agricultural goods would provide ample fuel for the war machine, but the increasing effectiveness of the Union's blockade impeded trade; consequently, the flow of specie into Confederate coffers dwindled.

Within three weeks of the formation of the government, the Confederate Congress authorized the first sale of bonds. Dubbed the "bankers' loan," this initial issue represented $15 million worth of ten-year bonds that paid 8 percent interest. This loan was fully subscribed, primarily through sales to banks and other financial institutions. It became apparent to Secretary of the Treasury Christopher Memminger that the dearth of specie available in the Confederacy could stifle future bond sales, so another device would have to be employed.

In May 1861, the Confederate government unveiled a new issue of $50 million in bonds that sold for "specie, military stores, or from the proceeds of sales of raw produce or manufactured articles." This "produce loan" opened the bond market to planters who were cotton rich, but capital poor. The issue was expanded to $100 million in August, and another $250 million in April 1862, but sales of the bonds lagged. As the price of cotton rose, planters preferred to hold their cotton,

hoping for greater future profits, rather than exchange it for the fixed value of a bond.

As the fiscal problems of the Confederacy grew, Memminger decided to look abroad for money. A Confederate agent in France negotiated the Erlanger loan in March 1863, a $15 million bond issue that was sold in European cities. The bonds were convertible for discounted cotton. The initial enthusiasm for this loan soured after Confederate defeats in Vicksburg and Gettysburg. Undaunted, Memminger tried to launch another $250 million bond issue in England in April 1863. The "cotton loan" comprised twenty-year bonds that paid 6 percent interest and were redeemable in discounted cotton or coin. The British showed great interest in these bonds until the Union's financial agent in London, the highly regarded Robert J. Walker, spread the rumor that Confederate president Jefferson Davis had been involved in a failed bond issue during the 1840s in which hundreds of British investors had lost money. Thereafter, Confederate bonds sold poorly in Europe.

Desperate for revenue, in 1864 the Confederate government announced a funded loan called the "One Billion Dollar" issue. These bonds were redeemable in twenty years, paid 6 percent interest that was tax free, and would be funded with a 5 percent tax on all property and mandatory contributions from each of the Confederate states. To encourage sales, public auctions were held throughout the Confederacy, but few investors materialized. Most regarded the announcement of this loan as an admission of bankruptcy. The Confederate treasury collapsed months before Lee's surrender at Appomattox.

In total, bonds paid for 23 percent of the Confederate finances during the war. The total funded debt accumulated by the Confederate states amounted to $712 million. All the bonds purchased by investors lost their value with the dissolution of the Confederate government after the South's defeat. All state bonds issued during the war were repudiated as one provision of the Fourteenth Amendment and readmission to the United States.

United States — The Union government faced a similar crisis in meeting the immediate expenses of the war. Unlike the Confederate states, the North had a better financial infrastructure upon which Secretary of the Treasury Salmon P. Chase could draw.

Chase strove to keep interest rates low, fearing that a massive debt would be laid for future generations. In his first loan negotiations, Chase alienated the banking community with his demands for specie and inflexibility regarding the terms of the bonds. When the need for a second issue arose in February 1862, Chase requested a $500 million issue of bonds bearing 6 percent interest, redeemable after five years and payable in twenty years. By the following December, only $23.7 million of the "5–20s" had been sold. As the unpaid requisitions accumulated and bankers continued to rebuff the secretary's calls for support, Chase took the unconventional step of turning to a sales agent to market the bonds directly to the American people. Chase hired Jay Cooke, a Philadelphia banker and financier, in October 1862. Cooke established a nationwide marketing system and sold $400 million of the 5–20s by December 1863.

Cooke's success did not alleviate the Union's financial problems. In March 1863, a $900 million loan was approved, $300 for the current fiscal year and $600 for the following year. The bonds paid no more than 6 percent interest and were redeemable in 10 years and payable in 40 years. Sensitive to congressional criticism of his cozy relationship with Cooke, Chase did not employ Cooke's services to sell the "10–40s." Instead, he tried to sell the issue through the new national banking system. Only $73 million of this issue was sold. Chase was forced to use the 10–40s to pay requisitions as well as the salaries for the troops.

In March 1864, another issue of the 5–20s was floated; concerned about the mounting debt, Chase tried selling the new bonds at a 5 percent interest rate. This strategy failed. Three months later, Chase resigned his position as secretary and was replaced by William Pitt Fessenden, a fiscal conservative. Fessenden was shocked by the state of the Treasury and resolved to rectify the financial crisis. He rehired Cooke and raised interest rates; immediately bond sales improved and fresh money flowed into the Treasury.

At the end of the war, the Union's debt amounted to $2.7 billion. Both the interest on the bonds and their redeemable value were to be paid in gold according to a provision of the initial legislation authorizing the bonds. With the depreciation of the greenbacks during the war and the rise in the price of gold, the value of the North's war bonds increased sharply. Whether to honor the bonds in gold, as stipulated originally, or redeem them in greenbacks became one of the most divisive political issues in the immediate postwar years.

—Jane Flaherty

See also Chase, Salmon P.; Cooke, Jay; Diplomacy, C.S.A.; Fessenden, William Pitt; Financing, C.S.A.; Financing, U.S.A.; Greenbacks; Memminger, Christopher.

For further reading:

Dewey, Davis R. *Financial History of the United States* (1939).
Gentry, Judith Fenner. "A Confederate Success in Europe: The Erlanger Loan." *Journal of Southern History* (1970).
Richardson, Heather Cox. *The Greatest Nation of the Earth: Republican Economic Policies during the Civil War* (1997).
Schwab, John C. *The Confederate States of America, 1861–65; A Financial and Industrial History of the South during the Civil War* (1901; reprint, 1968).
Todd, Richard Cecil. *Confederate Finance* (1954).

BONHAM, MILLEDGE LUKE
(1813–1890)
Confederate general; congressman and governor of South Carolina

Milledge Luke Bonham was born to James Bonham and Sophia Smith Bonham in Edgefield District, South Carolina. He was educated locally and at South Carolina College before studying law and opening a practice near his childhood home. Along with his successful law practice, Bonham also displayed an early interest in politics and the military. He took a brigade of South Carolina troops to Florida and fought during the Second Seminole War. Upon his return, he remained active in the state militia. With the outbreak of the Mexican-American War, Bonham accepted a commission as a lieutenant colonel and fought under volunteer officer Brigadier General Franklin Pierce.

Between these two wars, Bonham served in the South Carolina legislature. After the Mexican-American War, Bonham served as solicitor for the district court of southern South Carolina until 1857. In that year, he was selected to fill the unexpired congressional term of his deceased cousin Preston Brooks, who was notorious for his caning of Massachusetts senator Charles Sumner. Bonham, who like his cousin was a strong supporter of states' rights, remained in Congress until Abraham Lincoln's election in the fall of 1860.

After the secession of South Carolina, Bonham traveled to Mississippi to arrange cooperation between that state and South Carolina. Returning home, Bonham, with the rank of major general, became the commander of all South Carolina troops. The arrival of P. G. T. Beauregard in Charleston signaled Confederate command of all troops besieging Fort Sumter and caused Bonham to place himself under Beauregard and accept the rank of brigadier general in the Confederate army.

After the surrender of Fort Sumter, Bonham led South Carolina troops north with Beauregard to Virginia. Bonham commanded his brigade first around Richmond before moving north to Fairfax and Alexandria and then to Manassas Junction. He commanded his brigade defending the center of the Confederate line at First Bull Run.

In November 1861, Bonham allowed his name to be put forward as a candidate for the Confederate Congress from South Carolina. Already in a dispute with the Jefferson Davis administration over its policy of using previous service in the U.S. Army to determine seniority in the Confederate army, Bonham was probably already contemplating leaving the army. Upon his election, he used the seniority dispute as an excuse to resign his commission on 27 January 1862.

In the Confederate Congress, Bonham held to his states' rights views, particularly regarding the removal of state troops to far away places within the Confederacy. However, realizing the need for a strong central government in time of war, Bonham believed that the government should be granted exceptional powers regarding economic issues. Later that year, Bonham was elected governor of South Carolina, necessitating his resignation from Congress in January 1863 to assume his new duties.

As governor of South Carolina, Bonham's early concerns centered on the coastal defense of the state, particularly at Charleston. He worked closely with the Confederate army there, especially during the summer of 1863 when the Federal forces launched a campaign to take the city. He vigorously requisitioned the use of slaves to construct defenses around the city.

At the end of his term as governor in January 1865, Bonham, in the midst of William T. Sherman's invasion of the state, again offered his services to the Confederate army. Given a commission as a brigadier general of cavalry under Joseph E. Johnston, Bonham led his brigades in Johnston's fighting retreat through the Carolinas and surrendered with that army in April 1865.

After his parole, Bonham returned to South Carolina and his law practice. He was elected to the South Carolina legislature and served two years there. In 1868 he represented South Carolina at the Democratic National Convention. After the end of Reconstruction, Bonham worked with Governor Wade Hampton to restore white South Carolinian control of the state. For the remainder of his life, Bonham served as a state railroad commissioner. He died suddenly of a stroke on 27 August 1890.

—*David S. Heidler and Jeanne T. Heidler*

See also Bull Run, First Battle of; South Carolina.

For further reading:
"Papers of Francis W. Pickens and Milledge L. Bonham, 1837–1920." Library of Congress.

BOONEVILLE, MISSISSIPPI, BATTLE OF
(1 July 1862)

The little-known battle of Booneville, Mississippi, resulted from three months of Union activity in north Mississippi after the narrow Union victory at Shiloh in April 1862. The brisk Union victory at Booneville caused Confederate major general Braxton Bragg to proceed with caution as he tried to retake the important railroad junction at Corinth, Mississippi. It was also at this battle that Union colonel Philip Sheridan began to earn his reputation for boldness, aggressiveness, and tenaciousness. His "brilliant affair of our cavalry" led Major General Henry W. Halleck to recommend him for promotion to brigadier general.

The little town of Booneville, roughly twenty miles south of Corinth, lay near the Corinth-Chattanooga railroad line. After the battle of Shiloh, Confederate

brigadier general P. T. G. Beauregard slowly withdrew to Tupelo, Mississippi. Bragg assumed overall command and made plans to retake the important railroad junction at Corinth. A Union cavalry brigade under the command of Brigadier General Washington L. Elliot sought to cut the line of retreat for Beauregard's army during the month after the battle of Shiloh. Although this expedition lasted only a few days, Federal forces destroyed part of the railroad, burned military stores, and captured 1,000 men. During this activity, Halleck learned that the enemy had released all its prisoners captured at Shiloh due to food shortages. This information encouraged Halleck to order Federal cavalry to advance. In late June, Halleck ordered a general movement south. Union scouts and Confederate deserters reported Bragg preparing an advance using Beauregard's army. Sheridan established a fortified position at Booneville on 28 June and braced for an attack.

Four thousand seven hundred troopers under the immediate command of Confederate brigadier general James R. Chalmers merged a few miles southwest of Booneville from the towns of Tupelo and Saltillo. Confederate scouts made contact with Sheridan's pickets three and a half miles southwest of Booneville. On 1 July Federal pickets fell back, straddling where the Tupelo and Saltillo roads converged. Federal forces repelled Chalmers's initial charge due to good positions and the new Colt revolving rifle. Sheridan's pickets could not hold their ground against Chalmers's lead elements and withdrew again toward a secondary position about one and a half miles closer to town. Sheridan's advance guard arrived to support his pickets shortly thereafter.

Confederate forces tried to turn the Federal left flank, but the arrival of Sheridan's main force thwarted this attempt. Despite overwhelming odds, Sheridan made the bold move of ordering Captain Russell Alexander Alger's 2d Michigan cavalry to attack the Southern rear. The 2d Iowa cavalry, commanded by Lieutenant Colonel Edward Hatch, supported the attack by engaging the Southern left flank and part of its rear. The remaining Federal troops fought a holding action until Chalmers sounded the retreat around 3:30 P.M. Sheridan rallied his troops and pursued Chalmers for four miles before swampy terrain and fatigue stopped the Federals.

The battle lasted roughly eight hours, from 8:30 A.M. to 3:30 P.M. Confederate records for the engagement are scarce; of the 4,700 Confederates participating, Sheridan counted no fewer than 65 dead. Of the 728 Federal troops involved, there were 41 casualties: 1 killed, 24 wounded, and 16 missing.

The actual battle of Booneville was a small affair. It was part of a larger effort on the part of the Confederacy to recapture Corinth, an important railroad junction in the northern part of the Confederacy. Chalmers's defeat caused Bragg to reevaluate his offensive plans, and gave time for Halleck to consolidate his forces for future operations. The battle was also a glimpse into the fighting abilities of Sheridan.

—*David P. Eldridge*

See also Corinth, Battle of; Corinth, Mississippi; Sheridan, Philip Henry.
For further reading:
Hutton, Paul A. *Phil Sheridan and His Army* (1985).
Robinson, Virgil, comp. *Booneville, Mississippi, in the Civil War: A Compilation of Information from Many Sources* (1998).
Sheridan, Philip. *Personal Memoirs of Philip Henry Sheridan, General of the U.S. Army. New and Enl. Ed. With an Account of his Life from 1871 to His Death, in 1888, by Brigadier-General Michael V. Sheridan* (1904).

BOONVILLE, MISSOURI, BATTLE OF
(17 June 1861)

After Union volunteers had secured St. Louis, Missouri, the prosecessionist governor of Missouri, Claiborne F. Jackson, called for 50,000 volunteers to form the so-called Missouri State Guard. Rather than encamping in or near the capital at Jefferson City, the Guard's commanding general, former Governor Sterling Price, decided to bivouac near Boonville, a village strategically situated on the Missouri River about fifty miles from Jefferson City. Jackson issued a call to the leaders of the militia districts to assemble their troops, and additional volunteers from the surrounding slave-holding counties swelled the numbers present to about 1,500 by 15 June 1861. Most of these men were poorly trained and armed. Also, most of their artillery was twenty miles farther south under Brigadier General Mosby Parsons.

Responding fast to the possibility that Jackson and Price might consolidate a stronger military force, Union general Nathaniel Lyon quickly and decisively moved about 2,000 soldiers upriver from his base in St. Louis, occupied Jefferson City on 15 June and, after leaving a detachment under Colonel Henry Boernstein in the city, attacked the militia in Camp Bacon near Boonville on 17 June. The Union forces moved by boat again, and much to Lyon's surprise they were allowed to land near the camp without meeting any opposition.

Jackson and his nephew, Colonel John S. Marmaduke, had formed a line of defense, but they had no artillery present to counter the two field pieces of Union captain James Totten, who quickly disposed of some sharpshooters in a house in his front. The Union infantry—most of Francis Blair's 1st Missouri and Company B, and Peter J. Osterhaus's 2d Missouri Rifle Battalion—drove the Missouri State Guard from the field in less than twenty minutes. Almost simultaneously, two companies from the 1st Missouri, covered by a steamboat with a field piece on board, took the camp

itself. Losses were comparatively light, with only three dead and about ten wounded on each side, and sixty Guardsmen captured. The Missouri State Guard was scattered, however, and many of its arms and provisions were lost.

The immediate military effect of the lightly won Union victory was that the remnants of Jackson's forces fled south. Sterling Price, who had been ill on his farm in Chariton at the time of the Boonville fight, evacuated Lexington, Missouri, and also moved south with another column of assembled militia and volunteers to unite with Confederate forces from Arkansas and Texas. The retreat of these prosecessionist Missouri forces not only returned the counties along the Missouri to Federal control for the duration of the war, but also seriously weakened the political authority of Claiborne Jackson. Many inhabitants of Missouri with pro-Southern leanings decided to remain submissive for the time being. The effect on Confederate recruiting efforts and in the long run on the morale of Missouri forces from the northern part of the state was negative.

Although a comparatively small engagement, the fight at Boonville received no small attention. Exaggerated claims about Union losses and Missouri State Guard resistance made the rounds in Southern papers; in New York a theater play, *The Battle of Boonville*, based on a report by a *New York Herald* correspondent who had accompanied Lyon, attracted a sizable audience.

—*Wolfgang Hochbruck*

For further reading:
Hinze, David C., and Karen Farnham. *The Battle of Carthage. Border War in Southwest Missouri* (1998).
Pollard, Edward A. *The Lost Cause: A New Southern History of the War of the Confederates* (1866).
Snead, Thomas L. "The First Year of the War in Missouri." In *Battles & Leaders of the Civil War*, vol. 1. (1956).

BOOTH, JOHN WILKES
(1838–1865)
Assassin of Abraham Lincoln

Born on 10 May 1838 near Bel Air, Harford County, Maryland, John Wilkes Booth was the son of Junius Brutus Booth and Mary Ann Holmes. Abandoning his wife, the elder Booth, a promising British actor, sailed for America with his young mistress, Mary Ann, in 1821. Junius Brutus Booth exploded onto the American stage and became one of the young republic's foremost actors. Plagued by alcoholism and fits of insanity, the "Mad Tragedian" died on tour in 1851.

Young John, who was raised on the remote family farm, Tudor Hall, received a sporadic education at local academies. Following in the footsteps of his late father and elder brother, Edwin, seventeen-year-old John made his stage debut on 14 August 1855 in Baltimore. An undisciplined but fiery performer, he subsequently appeared in popular plays and Shakespearean classics in Philadelphia and Richmond. The darkly handsome young actor made women swoon, while one contemporary claimed he possessed the same élan and oddness seen in his celebrated father.

Booth was widely regarded as a rising star by 1860, and he successfully toured the North and South as the nation drifted toward war. However, the young Marylander regarded himself primarily as a Southern actor, and he particularly sought the acclaim of Southern audiences. Unlike his father, who detested the institution, John defended slavery and denounced Northern abolitionists during the growing sectional crisis.

In the aftermath of the attempted insurrection at Harper's Ferry, Booth left the stage in Richmond, Virginia, and joined the Richmond Grays, a local militia unit. The uniformed actor was among the troops present when John Brown was executed on 2 December 1859. During the same period he also joined the Knights of the Golden Circle, a secret pro-Southern society that promoted secession and the expansion of slavery.

Yet, despite his devotion to the Southern cause, Booth did not take up arms with the outbreak of hostilities. Although he continued to pursue a career that took him through many Northern cities, Booth did not hesitate to denounce Lincoln and the Federal government openly. In late 1862, the fiery actor was arrested in St. Louis for declaring that he "wished the whole damn government would go to hell." He hinted to family members that he secretly assisted the Confederate cause by furnishing supplies and money, adding, "My soul, life and possessions are for the South."

By the fall of 1864, Booth had apparently grown weary of being a mere stage hero and armchair rebel. Unwilling to become just another soldier in the ranks, he sought the spotlight by leading a foray into Washington to capture President Lincoln. Booth was convinced that his masterstroke would either end the war or provide the Confederacy with a hostage to negotiate the release of all Confederate prisoners of war.

The actor-turned-conspirator continued to make theater appearances as he secretly put his grandiose plans in motion. After recruiting Samuel Arnold and Michael O'Laughlin, two old schoolmates and former Confederate soldiers, Booth traveled to Canada in October 1864. Historians have traditionally portrayed Booth as acting alone. At least one recent study, however, contends that Booth was already acting in concert with Rebel agents and that his kidnapping plot was supported by the Confederate secret service.

Booth subsequently returned to Washington and took up residence at the National Hotel. He then recruited John H. Surratt, whose widowed mother, Mary E. Surratt

John Wilkes Booth (*Library of Congress*)

ran a boarding house. By March 1865, his followers, who made Mrs. Surratt's rooms their headquarters, had grown to include David E. Herold, George A. Atzerodt, and a Confederate deserter named Lewis Paine (whose real name was Lewis Thornton Powell).

On 20 March, Booth's band of misfits prepared to kidnap Lincoln as he rode to a matinee performance for wounded soldiers at Campbell Hospital. Yet, the president attended another function, and Booth's dispirited followers, thinking the authorities knew of their plans, were thrown into a panic. Arnold, O'Laughlin, and Surratt promptly scattered, leaving Booth and the others to carry on alone.

The fall of Richmond and Lee's surrender at Appomattox forced Booth to abandon his original plans. On 11 April 1865, Booth was present when Lincoln gave what proved to be his last public address. The actor was enraged, however, by the president's references to limited black suffrage. "Now, by God, I'll put him through," he reportedly snarled.

Acting on his own accord, Booth apparently hatched a new plot in which he and his remaining followers would avenge the South by assassinating Lincoln, Vice President Andrew Johnson, and Secretary of State William H. Seward in one swift stroke. On the morning of 14 April 1865 Booth learned that Lincoln planned to attend the evening performance of *Our American Cousin*

at Ford's Theater. He quickly sought out his accomplices and prepared to strike that very night.

After carefully inspecting the scene of attack earlier in the day, Booth returned to Ford's Theater shortly after 10 P.M. and slipped into the presidential box. After firing one fatal bullet into the back of Lincoln's head, Booth stabbed the president's companion, a Union officer, and leapt over the balcony to the stage below. The desperate assassin reportedly shouted, "Sic semper tyrannis!", a Latin phrase meaning, "Thus always to tyrants!" Although he broke his left leg in the eleven-foot fall, Booth fled the theater, jumped on his horse, and escaped into the night.

As for the other conspirators, George Atzerodt lost his nerve and slunk away without making an attempt on the life of Vice President Johnson. Although Lewis Powell, alias Paine, brutally attacked Secretary of State Seward at his residence, he failed to inflict a fatal wound. David Herold overtook Booth somewhere outside Washington, and the pair fled through Maryland into Virginia.

On 26 April, Union cavalry surrounded the fugitives in a tobacco barn near Bowling Green in Caroline County, Virginia. Herold promptly surrendered, yet Booth, who vowed never to surrender, defiantly stood his ground until he fell mortally wounded. After initial interment at the Washington arsenal, his remains were exhumed in 1869 and buried in Green Mount Cemetery in Baltimore.

Many Southerners initially hailed Booth's "one mad act." In *The End of an Era*, John S. Wise of Virginia recalled that "among the thoughtless, the desperate, and the ignorant, it was hailed as a sort of retributive justice." A poetic tribute to Booth entitled "Our Brutus," sometimes attributed to Judge Alexander W. Terrell of Texas, reportedly circulated in the South after the assassin's death. Some of it was set to music in 1868, and in 1913 the *Confederate Veteran's Magazine* published a rendition of the poem.

However, as Lincoln's legend grew and many former Confederates came to recognize his death as a tragedy for the South, Booth was damned in the pages of American history as a misguided fanatic.

—*James M. Pritchard*

See also Lincoln Assassination.

For further reading:
Bryan, George S. *The Great American Myth: The True Story of Lincoln's Murder* (1990).
Kimmel, Stanley. *The Mad Booths of Maryland* (1940).
Rhodehamel, John, and Louise Taper, eds. *"Right or Wrong, God Judge Me": The Writings of John Wilkes Booth* (1997).
Smith, Gene. *American Gothic: The Story of America's Legendary Theatrical Family—Junius, Edwin and John Wilkes Booth* (1992).
Tidwell, William A., James O. Hall, and David Winfred Gaddy. *Come Retribution: The Confederate Secret Service and the Assassination of Lincoln* (1988).
Turner, Thomas Reed. *Beware the People Weeping: Public Opinion and the Assassination of Abraham Lincoln* (1982).

BORDER STATES

Border states were Southern in their sanctioning of slavery but were particularly ambivalent about the destruction of the Union. They charted courses characterized by shifting and contradictory allegiances.

The definition of a "border state" shifted somewhat during the course of the Civil War. By February 1861, seven slave states had seceded and formed the Confederacy, but eight had flatly declined to join them. From February into the late spring, North Carolina, Virginia, Tennessee, and Arkansas were considered border states along with Maryland, Kentucky, and Missouri, as well as Delaware, where the outcome was never in serious doubt. By June, when four more of these states seceded, the term came to refer rather narrowly to Maryland, Kentucky, and Missouri. Precisely in such areas did loyalists form their own Union Leagues.

Strategies for dealing with the border shifted accordingly. During that initial period from February into April 1861, the Unionists prevailed. The Confederates sought success by orienting to the existing political leadership in these states and by issuing dire warnings predicting their tyrannical "coercion" by the United States. In contrast, the Union, under both lame-duck Democratic president James Buchanan and incoming Republican president Abraham Lincoln, generally avoided any confrontation that would give substance to such fears of coercion that might push the border toward secession. The Lincoln administration amended this approach to take greater pains to avoid the further cession of Federal installations in areas now claiming to constitute the Confederacy. In this first phase, Unionist strategy successfully retained the loyalties of all eight slaveholding states that had not already seceded.

During the next phase, from April into September 1861, the Union and the Confederacy each obtained four of the eight slaveholding states that had not earlier seceded. The outbreak of open hostilities at Fort Sumter in Charleston Harbor and Lincoln's call for the states to supply the government with volunteer troops clearly presaged Federal "coercion." Given the imminence of an armed conflict, Southern state governments that had not wanted to secede would either have to do so anyway or render assistance to the U.S. authorities. Secession followed in Virginia (17 April), Arkansas (6 May), Tennessee (7 May), and North Carolina (20 May). Delaware, Maryland, Kentucky, and Missouri did not secede but did not necessarily embrace cooperation with the Federal authorities either.

Securing these border states imposed the most trying ordeal on the new Lincoln administration, elected with the weakest popular mandate of any presidency. However, the government succeeded through pragmatic approaches combining diverse strategies that varied considerably from state to state. Even afterward, though, its concern over the possible responses of these slave-holding states retarded the Federal expansion of its war goals to include emancipation.

Securing the nation's capital in the District of Columbia required a virtual military seizure of power in Maryland. In the weeks after the war's outbreak, secessionist officials sought to deny Federal transit to Washington, leading to attacks on Massachusetts volunteers passing through Baltimore (19 April) and resulting in a U.S. military occupation. With the suspension of the writ of habeas corpus (27 April), martial law largely superseded civilian authority in the state. This placed Maryland legislators under threat of immediate arrest when they voted to repudiate secession (29 April).

To a lesser extent, securing Washington also meant clearing the Confederates from the Potomac opposite Maryland. The Federals broke the Chesapeake blockade in small naval actions at Sewell's Point (18–19 May) and Aquia Creek (29 May–1 June), while also occupying the adjacent heights in Virginia at Arlington and Alexandria (24 May).

In the transmountain counties of western Virginia, differences over secession tapped a deep-seated tension between the local authorities and the tidewater political machines governing from Richmond. Just as Maryland straddled the rail lines north from Washington, the course of the Baltimore & Ohio between the capital and the Ohio valley passed through western Virginia. Virginians at Wheeling and other communities protested secession. When Federal troops, including Virginians, routed a Confederate force at Philippi (3 June), it marked the beginning of a successful Union campaign in the mountains. Under Washington's protection, an independent Unionist government of Virginia later established the new state of West Virginia.

In contrast to military occupation in Maryland or the fostering of local revolutionary movements in Virginia, the Lincoln administration simply left Kentucky alone. Badly divided between a Unionist legislature and a secessionist governor, the state authorities simply postponed a crisis by declaring Kentucky's neutrality (20 May). Because both sides sought to avoid toppling Kentucky into the enemy camp, they generally accepted this arrangement.

In Missouri, local federal officials gladly fostered the internal civil war that broke out in that state, as loyal citizens rose against the secessionist state government. Loyal citizens of St. Louis, mainly German immigrants, surrounded and forced the surrender of Camp Jackson (10 May), while secessionist units attacked Unionist encampments like Camp Cole (18 June) in the center of the state. When the de facto truce ended (11 June), Federal volunteers moved west from St. Louis into the interior against the state capital, Jefferson City. Union victory at Boonville (17 June) did not end the seces-

sionist threat, but it allowed for a state convention to reassemble (22 July), establishing a provisional military government. Despite decisive Confederate victories at Wilson's Creek (10 August) and Lexington (12–20 September), Federal reinforcements continued to pour into the state for some months. In the end, the Unionists wielded an unquestioned authority through much of the state.

Kentucky's neutrality broke when the Confederate forces moved north to occupy Columbus (3 September) in hopes of fortifying the Mississippi River, a movement that largely tipped the state toward the Union. Federal forces based at Cairo, Illinois, crossed to Paducah (6 September) as defenders of the state's sovereignty against rebel aggression and troops from both sides formed a long and very porous line of garrisons and outposts across the state.

Just as the opening of hostilities in western Virginia created dual governments in that nominally secessionist state, it had the same results in nominally loyal places. Claiming a quorum, the secessionists in the Missouri legislature reassembled at Neosho and voted for secession (28 October), ratifying the action later at Cassville (31 October). Placed in a similar position by the Federal army, pro-secessionist Kentucky officials, together with state militia officers, established their own legislature at Russellville and voted that state out of the Union (18 November).

It should also be noted that secession created the tumultuous conditions characteristic of the border state in some of the western territories. Although a territorial convention of transplanted Texans at Mesilla (16 March) also laid claim to much of present southern New Mexico and Arizona, the secessionist project simply stalled during these critical three months. Indian Territory, which later became Oklahoma, was occupied by the autonomous nation-states, the "Five Civilized Tribes." Their leaders early preferred neutrality, but Texas troops crossed the Red River in April to encourage the Choctaw and the Chickasaw to abrogate their treaties with the United States and make new treaties with the Confederacy that obligated every adult male to military service at the executive order of the president. The secessionists bypassed principal chiefs among the Creeks and Seminoles to make similar treaty arrangements with their internal rivals. The Cherokees managed to resist a treaty until August, but Confederate authority, on paper at least, extended to the Quapaws, Euchees, Delawares, Wichitas, Caddos, and even the Osage in Kansas. Their course, however, provoked little consistent concern in either Richmond or Washington, and rival factions allied to both sides emerged.

Militarily, the first year of the war centered on the fate of these border states. The struggle brought into play some of the principal commanders of the war. George B.

McClellan, Robert E. Lee, and Joseph Johnston first took their own troops into the fields of western Virginia. Operations to secure the river areas of Missouri and Kentucky shaped the early successes of Ulysses S. Grant and William T. Sherman. McClellan alternately denounced and assumed credit for the achievements of his subordinates, establishing his reputation for strong generalship early in the region. In contrast, Grant had a rather lackluster career in Missouri, although he was not so widely viewed as a failure as was Lee based on his losses in western Virginia.

By March 1862, however, Federal forces in the Virginia mountains had pushed beyond the trans-Allegheny counties that became West Virginia into the Shenandoah Valley. Union armies had pushed through Kentucky into Tennessee and through Missouri into Arkansas. That month, the Federals also turned back a bold Rebel effort in the New Mexico Territory.

Thereafter, Union authority was secure in these areas, though never so completely as in the North. Through eastern Maryland, an ongoing trafficking through the lines maintained its ties to the Confederacy; in the western part of the state, Confederate armies invaded at several points in the war. So, too, incursions by small Confederate columns and an ongoing guerrilla war continued to contest Union control in the interior of western Virginia. Kentucky and Missouri also experienced periodic invasions.

More innovatively, of course, the early military settlement of affairs in these states left a large number of secessionists behind Union lines, joined by growing numbers of captured and paroled Confederate prisoners. As the Federal armies pushed farther south, they required longer and increasingly vulnerable lines of supply going through such areas. From northern Virginia to Indian Territory, these border conditions inspired a unique type of hit-and-run guerrilla warfare that blurred lines between soldiers and civilians for both the combatants and their targets. The brutality of this fighting grew worse to the west, as did the vulnerability of civilian populations. In Missouri, civilians were as likely as not to be the targets of military operations, which left virtually no county records intact south of the Missouri River. Along the Missouri-Kansas border, entire towns were abandoned and burned, with thousands of desperate refugees camped among the charred ruins. Control changed hands so frequently in northwestern Arkansas, and especially in Indian Territory, that the areas became virtually depopulated.

Nevertheless, with even nominal Federal ascendancy, the authorities sought to maintain or develop loyal civilian mechanisms of power. The population generally took little active interest in the overthrow of the Union. In the end, the Confederacy simply faced a virtually impossible task even in those border states that joined it.

Most of the people of Kentucky and Missouri opposed secession, however much they dreaded or disliked Federal occupation. Neither North Carolina nor Arkansas held plebiscites on secession, even ones of dubious value like those held in Virginia and Tennessee. The military reversals in the war's first year quickly chilled the early war fever in such areas, and the Confederate imposition of conscription after spring 1862 failed to rekindle it.

In the end, the type of dual governments that first appeared along the border also pointed the course toward Federal victory and, ultimately, the reestablishment of loyal governments in the South. By November 1861, such competing governments vied in Virginia, Missouri, and Kentucky, as well as territorial administrations in the Southwest. By spring 1863, rival chiefs and grand councils contested for the loyalties of the divided Creek, Seminole, and Cherokee Nations. By the end of the war, Unionists in Louisiana, Tennessee, Arkansas, North Carolina, and Texas also formed governments allied to Washington.

—*Mark A. Lause*

See also Arkansas; Guerrilla Warfare; Indian Territory; Kentucky; Maryland; Missouri; West Virginia.
For further reading:
Coulter, E. Merton. *The Civil War and Readjustment in Kentucky* (1926).
Fellman, Michael. *Inside War: The Guerrilla Conflict in Missouri during the American Civil War* (1989).
Monaghan, Jay. *Civil War on the Western Border, 1854–1865* (1955).
Parrish, William E. *Turbulent Partnership: Missouri and the Union, 1861–1865* (1963).

BOTTS, JOHN MINOR
(1802–1869)
Virginia Unionist

I could not willingly take up arms against a Union that I have been taught and accustomed to adore, as indispensable to my own liberties, and I never will raise my hand against my native State, although her arm had ever been against me and mine." Written on 29 April 1861, John Minor Botts's letter to Attorney General Edward Bates revealed the anguish and conflict of conscience wrought by secession. Dismayed over his home state of Virginia's decision to secede, Botts implored Bates to call a National Convention and recognize the independence of those states that desired to leave the Union. It was the only way, Botts argued, to "save the unnecessary effusion of brothers' blood."

Botts earnestly believed that his plan would ultimately reunite the Union. After a trial separation, he hoped that the Southern states would understand the "hour of madness" that had rushed them to secession and, after reasoned deliberation, they would return to the

Union. To Botts, such a plan was exceedingly moderate compared with the threat of armed conflict. Botts's political career, in fact, revealed a consistently moderate course in the dispute between the North and South over slavery and its extension.

Born in Dumfries, Virginia, in 1802, Botts entered politics in 1831 as a Whig candidate for the Virginia legislature and was elected in 1833 to serve until 1839, when he entered Congress. He represented the Richmond District until 1843 and served again from 1847 to 1849. During his time in Washington, Botts was equally disdainful of abolitionists and those who attempted to usurp their constitutional right of petition through the 1836 "Gag Rule." He opposed the annexation of Texas and the Mexican-American War, but helped to bring the war to a successful conclusion by serving as the chairman of the Committee on Military Affairs. After leaving the House in 1849, he returned to Washington at the request of Henry Clay to help with the measures that led to the Compromise of 1850. Botts deplored both the repeal of the Missouri Compromise and the 1858 attempted statehood of Kansas under the Lecompton Constitution. In all of these actions, Botts displayed a sincere reverence for his duty to the nation and a respect for the spirit of political moderation and compromise.

John M. Botts was not, however, without passion. As the dispute between the North and South grew, he unleashed his ire at John C. Calhoun and radical, conspiratorial minded "Democratic bosses" who clamored for disunion. In a speech entitled "Union or Disunion," delivered before a crowd in Lynchburg, Virginia, on 18 October 1860, Botts argued that the Democratic Party had deliberately split its 1860 ticket between Stephen Douglas and John Breckinridge "to make the election of Lincoln sure, and thus get up agitation and excitement at the South." Moreover, Botts characterized Virginia governor Henry A. Wise as "The Unwise Henry A." for using John Brown's attack on Harper's Ferry to further the secession conspiracy.

Continuing the moderate course that had guided his path through the sectional dispute, Botts assured his listeners that Lincoln was not an abolitionist and that even if he were intent on usurping Southern rights he would first have to bypass Congress and the Supreme Court.

When Virginia ultimately called a convention to debate secession, Botts was nominated as a representative but, he argued, defeated by fraud. It was shortly after Virginia seceded that Botts wrote the letter to Attorney General Bates. When Bates refused to consider a National Convention, Botts retired to his farm near Culpeper Court House, unable to fight either the Union he revered or his home state. Still intent on proving a Democratic secession conspiracy, he began a book on

the causes of the war. Shortly thereafter, on 1 March 1862, Jefferson Davis declared martial law, and the next morning 100 soldiers under the command of a General Winder arrested Botts and searched for the manuscript, which had been given to the French Minister Count de Mercier for safekeeping. Incarcerated for eight weeks in a jail usually set aside for African-Americans, Botts was paroled only after a new Confederate secretary of war, Judah Benjamin, was appointed. Botts returned to his farm and waited out the end of the war.

In 1866, Botts published his "secret" work, *The Great Rebellion: Its Secret History, Rise, Progress, and Disastrous Failure.* That year he proposed a plan of reconstruction, which was rejected, and led the Virginia delegation to the Convention of Southern Loyalists held in Philadelphia. And though he criticized Jefferson Davis for his part in the secession conspiracy, and even called the Confederate president "the most unscrupulous despot since the days of Nero," Botts was among those who signed Davis's bail bond, proving again his ability to steer toward the moderate path.

—*Matthew S. Warshauer*

See also Civil Liberties, C.S.A.; Southern Unionism; Virginia.
For further reading:
Botts, John Minor. "Union or Disunion. The Union Cannot Be Dissolved. Mr. Lincoln Not an Abolitionist." Speech of the Hon. John M. Botts, Lynchburg, Virginia, October 18, 1860.
Lapidus, Robert D. "A Southern Enigma: The Unwavering Unionism of John Minor Botts" (M.A. thesis, 1972).
Webster, Clyde Cannon. "John Minor Botts: Anti-secessionist." Richmond College Historical Papers (1915).

BOUDINOT, ELIAS CORNELIUS
(1835–1890)
Cherokee Confederate officer and congressman

Born in the Cherokee Nation (present-day Georgia) to mixed-blood Cherokee leader Elias Boudinot, Elias Cornelius was just over four months old when his father signed the Treaty of New Echota, which would remove the Cherokees to Indian Territory. As a result of his action, three years later the elder Boudinot was assassinated. In turn, their white mother's family in New England raised his children.

Well educated in the east, Elias Cornelius returned to the west in the 1850s. He studied law in Fayetteville, Arkansas, where he eventually practiced law, engaged in civic activities, became active in the Democratic Party, and edited the *Fayetteville Arkansian*. Establishing himself as a notable supporter of Senator Robert Johnson, he was chosen as the first chairman of the Arkansas Democratic Central Committee. Quarrels within the Democratic Party in Arkansas between Robert Johnson and Representative Thomas Hindman led Boudinot to edit the *Little Rock True Democrat*.

When secession loomed, Boudinot considered himself a Unionist, as did many in northwest Arkansas. When his Unionist friend Judge David Walker was elected president of the Arkansas Secession Convention, Boudinot was chosen as secretary. The delegates initially opted against secession, but when fighting began they voted to secede.

After finishing his work for the secession convention, Boudinot joined his uncle Stand Watie, a leading Confederate supporter in the Cherokee Nation. Boudinot helped Watie raise a Cherokee Confederate regiment. They also put pressure on Principal Chief John Ross to sign a treaty of alliance with the Confederacy, which Ross did reluctantly.

When Ross led the Cherokee Nation into the Confederacy, Watie, Boudinot, who had been elected major, and the regiment had already seen action at the battle of Wilson's Creek in Missouri. Then in late 1861 in Indian Territory, Boudinot led his men against neutral-minded Creeks fleeing to Kansas in the battle of Chustenahlah. The following March he fought in the battle of Pea Ridge. In July, at the battle of Locust Grove, he again distinguished himself for bravery. By then, Boudinot had advanced to the rank of lieutenant colonel.

In mid-1862, Ross allowed himself to be captured and, with many followers, headed north with Federal troopers to Kansas, where he switched sides. The Southern Cherokees then elected Watie as principal chief and chose Boudinot as their delegate to the Confederate Congress.

Boudinot entered the Congress as one of the two youngest members. He had several close acquaintances in the Congress, including Robert Johnson. However, he did not have the right to vote and could speak only on Indian concerns. Boudinot nonetheless energetically engaged in pursuing Indian matters, and he eventually received the right to introduce legislation pertaining to Indian policy.

Concerned about the scarcity of Confederate soldiers in Indian Territory, Boudinot proposed that whites be offered Indian land if they enlisted in Cherokee forces. The idea of giving land to whites angered a majority of the Southern Cherokees. They rejected the proposal, and some sought to have Boudinot removed from the Congress. However, many endorsed his efforts to have the Indian Territory made a separate command. Boudinot also lobbied for Watie's promotion, and in May of 1864, Watie became a brigadier general. Thereafter, Boudinot turned his attention to the plight of Cherokee refugees and convinced the Congress to appropriate $100,000 for the Cherokee Nation.

With the defeat of the Confederacy, Boudinot played a significant role in representing the Cherokees in treaty negotiations. He and his fellow former Confederate Cherokees almost secured a treaty that would have split the Cherokee Nation between Southern and Union elements. However, a dying John Ross prevailed in getting a treaty that maintained tribal unity.

In the following years, Boudinot continued to be a controversial member of the Cherokee Nation. Although he served for a while on the official Cherokee delegation to Washington, D.C., he would venture on his own course—often at odds with a majority of his fellow Cherokees and other tribespeople in Indian Territory. He promoted opening unsettled parts of Indian Territory to white settlers, bringing in railroads, establishing federal courts, and making Cherokees citizens of the United States. In pursuing such goals, he spent most of his years after the Civil War as a lawyer, lobbyist, professional orator on Indian issues, and newspaperman.

Boudinot died in 1890 in Fort Smith, Arkansas, where he was practicing law and operating a farm in the Cherokee Nation.

—Thomas Burnell Colbert

See also Cherokee Indians; Ross, John; Watie, Stand.
For further reading:

Colbert, Thomas Burnell. "Prophet of Progress: The Life and Times of Elias Cornelius Boudinot" (Ph.D. dissertation, 1982).
Dale, Edward Everett, and Gaston Litton, eds. *Cherokee Cavaliers: Forty Years of Cherokee History as Told in the Correspondence of the Ridge-Watie-Boudinot Family* (1939).
Wilson, T. Paul. "Delegates of the Five Civilized Tribes to the Confederate Congress." *Chronicles of Oklahoma* (1975).
Wright, Marcus J. "Colonel Elias C. Boudinot." *Southern Bivouac* (1884).

BOUNTY SYSTEM

Bounties were payments made by the various governments of the Union and the Confederacy to induce men to enlist in the military. Even though volunteers initially supplied all the men needed on both sides, the tradition of using bounties was so strong that Congress passed a law only a month after Fort Sumter to enable the Federal government to pay a bounty of up to $300. The more hard-pressed Confederacy also passed an allocation for its bounty system in December 1861. The provision was for a $50 payment at the end of three years or more of service. As the need for men became more desperate in 1864, the Confederate bounty increased to $100. Yet the sum was in Confederate money, which in 1864 had little real value. Bounties in the Confederacy, therefore, never carried the weight they did in the North.

The U.S. Congress continued to adjust the bounty provisions throughout the war by specifying how much the bounty should be, when the bounty should be paid, and to whom it would devolve if the volunteer died in battle. In addition, states and local areas also added to the bounty pool. Local, state, and Federal agencies scraped together money by taxation, bond issues, and solicited donations. Because pay for soldiers throughout the war was low and sporadic, bounties enabled families at home to survive and added to the ability of returning soldiers to return to civilian life.

The draft changed the bounty system in both the North and the South. The Confederacy resorted to a draft in 1862. The Union also needed men that early, but the Lincoln administration was hesitant about instituting national conscription. Lincoln relied instead on allocating quotas to the states, a practice that shifted the burden of raising men to local areas. To forestall any move toward a national draft, states acted quickly. They subdivided their quotas regionally and increased their state bounties to encourage volunteers. In turn, the subdivided sections also increased their bounties. Theoretically, a volunteer might then benefit from three or four separate bounties when enlisting. Although the increased bounties helped in 1862, by 1863 none of these plans was sufficient and the Federal government instituted a draft.

Reactions to the draft were negative in both the Union and the Confederacy. The Northern draft gave the draftee five days after notice before reporting for induction. During those five days the draftee had the option of volunteering for the army and receiving a bounty. Being conscripted imparted a social stigma and carried no bounty, so it is surprising that some men actually remained drafted instead of volunteering.

As the availability of young, healthy men diminished and quotas increased, bounties from all sources soared dramatically. By January 1865, the *New York Tribune* quoted the local county bounty alone at $1,000. Such large sums enticed unscrupulous men to become bounty jumpers. They would claim bounties by volunteering, desert before reaching the front lines, and move onto the next locality to claim another and perhaps even larger bounty. Because a draftee/volunteer did not have to be a resident of the area, competition between counties and states became intense as draftable men shopped for the most lucrative bounties. Also, governments relied on brokers to provide eligible men, who were often garnered from some distance. Brokers from various states recruited immigrants disembarking from boats in New York and Boston to fill their quotas. These brokers took a cut of the bounty and added to an increasing corruption by intensifying competition for men and therefore enlarging the size of bounties. As the war progressed and bounties increased, indignation surfaced in the men who had earned earlier—and smaller—bounties. Resentment also arose in localities understandably envious of wealthier regions that could pay larger sums. Procedural differences further contributed to tensions.

Most historians agree that the draft worked during the Civil War. Yet the success of the draft must be balanced by the inducement proffered by bounty payments. And though bounties mainly accomplished what they were supposed to, both the immediate and long-term consequences of the system were negative. At the end of the war, Provost Marshall General James B. Fry wrote a report on the draft in which he castigated the bounty system as inviting corruption. His criticism was sufficient to ensure opposition to bounties in World War I.

—*Dorothy O. Pratt*

See also Conscription, C.S.A.; Conscription, U.S.A.; Pay, C.S.A.; Pay, U.S.A.

For further reading:
Geary, James W. *We Need Men: The Union Draft in the Civil War* (1991).
Moore, Albert B., ed. *Conscription and Conflict in the Confederacy Southern Classics Series* (1924; reprint, 1996).
Murdock, Eugene C. *One Million Men: The Civil War Draft in the North* (1971).

BOUTWELL, GEORGE SEWALL
(1818–1905)
Commissioner of internal revenue

George S. Boutwell distinguished himself as one of the Radical Republicans serving in the U.S. House of Representatives during the Civil War.

Boutwell began life humbly in Brookline, Massachusetts. During his teens he worked in a store in Lunenberg and attended school. He demonstrated an early interest in politics by writing commentaries for the local newspaper. In 1842 he commenced eight years of service in the Massachusetts legislature as a Democrat representing the town of Groton. Boutwell helped forge the union between antislavery Democrats and Free Soilers that overturned the Whig dominance of Massachusetts politics. This alliance supported his candidacy for governor in 1850 and Boutwell held two one-year terms. When he left the governorship, Boutwell studied law until 1862, when he was admitted to the bar.

Boutwell served on the Massachusetts Board of Education from 1855 to 1861, during which time he helped organize the Republican Party in the Bay State. Between 1862 and 1863, Boutwell was appointed to his first federal position, commissioner of internal revenue. In one year Boutwell organized the office that would soon supersede the Treasury Department in the number of employees. He wrote and published in 1863 *A Manual of the Direct and Excise Tax System of the United States*, which outlined how to comply with the complex new system.

Boutwell was elected to the House of Representatives during the turbulent years between 1863 and 1869. He became a secondary leader of the Radical Republicans behind the "tyrant" Thaddeus Stevens. He helped draft the Fourteenth and Fifteenth Amendments to the Constitution and lobbied extensively to counter the hesitancy many Republicans harbored about granting full suffrage for the freedmen. "Next to the restoration of the Union and the abolition of slavery, the recognition of universal suffrage is the most important result of the war," he wrote in his autobiography. Boutwell created an early draft of the Reconstruction plan that formed the basis of congressional Reconstruction. Boutwell was selected as chairman of the managers in President Andrew Johnson's impeachment trial.

In 1869 Boutwell accepted President Ulysses S. Grant's offer to become secretary of the treasury. He strove to reduce the massive public debt accumulated during the war, rid the department of corruption and its bloated payroll, and systematized the revenue collection apparatus. He is best remembered for thwarting the efforts of Jay Gould and James Fiske, Jr. to corner the gold market on "Black Friday," 24 September 1869, by releasing $4 million worth of the Treasury Department's gold to help stabilize its price. Boutwell's unabashed enthusiasm for the gold standard contributed to the "Crime of 1873" in which silver was demonetized for a brief period.

Boutwell represented Massachusetts in the Senate from 1873 to 1877. His most memorable contribution as a senator entailed chairing the committee that investigated the 1875 election in Mississippi in which the African-American vote was suppressed with astonishing brutality. The whole affair appalled Boutwell, who confided to his journals that he feared the outbreak of a second civil war if these outrages were allowed to continue.

After his failed reelection bid, Boutwell served in a variety of government positions, including chairman of the committee to revise the U.S. statutes and counsel for the government in defense of French citizens' claims for losses during the Civil War. Although Boutwell abhorred corruption, throughout his career he both dispensed and received the benefits of the patronage system that lay at the heart of the political baseness of the Gilded Age.

Late in the nineteenth century, Boutwell grew increasingly leery of the expansionist policies advocated by Republicans. He openly disagreed with President William McKinley's policy in the Philippines and eventually withdrew from the party. He served as president of the Anti-Imperialist League until his death in 1905.

—*Jane Flaherty*

See also Financing, U.S.A.; Lincoln's Reconstruction Policy; Radical Republicans; Wade-Davis Bill.

For further reading:
Benedict, Michael Les. *A Compromise of Principle: Congressional Republicans and Reconstruction* (1974).
Boutwell, George S. *Reminiscences of Sixty Years in Public Affairs* (1902; reprint, 1968).
Brown, Thomas H. *George Sewall Boutwell: Human Rights Advocate* (1989).

BOWEN, JOHN STEVENS
(1830–1863)
Confederate general

Born to William Parker Bowen and Ann Elizabeth Wilkins Bowen in Savannah, Georgia, Bowen attended the United States Military Academy, from which he graduated thirteenth of fifty-one in the class of 1853. He served in various frontier posts as a mounted rifleman until 1856, when he resigned his commission. Shortly afterward he moved to St. Louis, Missouri, where he worked as an architect until the outbreak of the Civil War. During his years in St. Louis he was a neighbor and friendly acquaintance of Ulysses S. Grant.

At the outbreak of the war, Bowen went with the Missouri militia forces that supported the Confederacy. Captured by Union forces under the command of Nathaniel Lyon at Camp Jackson, Bowen received his parole, but was later accused of violating it by accepting a commission as colonel of the 1st Missouri Confederate regiment on 11 June 1861. He served under Brigadier General Daniel M. Frost early in the war, before taking his regiment to Kentucky, where he served under Leonidas Polk.

Bowen was promoted to brigadier general on 14 March 1862 and commanded a brigade under John C. Breckinridge at Shiloh. He was wounded the first day there and did not see any further serious actions until the battle of Corinth in October 1862. As a result of that engagement Bowen entered into a dispute with Earl Van Dorn about that officer's movements during and following the battle. Van Dorn was vindicated in the subsequent investigation.

From the beginning of the Vicksburg campaign, Bowen was very active as one of General John C. Pemberton's best subordinates. On 1 May 1863 he held Port Gibson for almost 24 hours against three times his number and then destroyed key bridges in his retreat. For his actions at Port Gibson, Bowen was promoted to major general.

Bowen commanded a division in the battles outside Vicksburg and withdrew with the rest of Pemberton's army at the beginning of the siege. During the siege Bowen became seriously ill with dysentery, but continued in command and participated in the surrender negotiations. Some hope arose among the senior Confederate leadership in Vicksburg that Bowen's prewar acquaintance with General Grant would facilitate talks and perhaps lead to a lenient surrender, but Grant refused even to meet with Bowen.

Following the Confederates surrender, Bowen, like most of the officers received a parole, although there was some opposition because of his supposed violation of parole back in 1861. It probably mattered little to

Bowen; the dysentery he contracted during the siege had so weakened him that he died on 13 July 1863.

—*David S. Heidler and Jeanne T. Heidler*

See also Port Gibson.

For further reading:

"Proceedings of a Court of inquiry: Held at Abbeville, Mississippi on Charges Preferred by Brigadier General John S. Bowen, P.A.C.S., against Major General Earl Van Doren, P.A.C.S., from 15th to 22nd November, 1862." *Mobile (Alabama) Daily Register* (1862).

BOYCE, WILLIAM WATERS
(1818–1890)
Confederate congressman

Born to Robert Boyce and Lydia Waters Boyce in Charleston, South Carolina, William Waters Boyce was educated in local schools before attending South Carolina College and then studying law at the University of Virginia. He began his law practice in 1839 in Winnsboro, South Carolina, where he also owned a small plantation. Through the 1840s, Boyce became increasingly interested in South Carolina politics as a staunch defender of states' rights. In 1850 he was elected to represent his district in the state legislature partly because of his strong stance against the Compromise of 1850 and support for Southern rights. Two years later, he was elected to the U.S. House of Representatives again as a strong proponent of states' rights.

In Congress Boyce made numerous speeches on Southern rights and those issues that he believed threatened those rights. Very vocal on the issues of slavery in the territories, the protective tariff, and the acquisition of Cuba, Boyce also frequently expanded his speeches into lengthy pamphlets for distribution at home, no doubt wanting to assure his constituents and other Southerners as to his vigilance in protecting their rights.

While certainly not a fire-eater, Boyce believed that the election of Abraham Lincoln in 1860 justified Southern secession and supported that move for South Carolina. Before the convention met in that state, he was one of the prominent South Carolinians who wrote to President James Buchanan that the Federal forts in South Carolina would not be attacked until after secession and then only if a negotiated settlement could not be reached. After the war, he claimed that he had expected during the first weeks after secession that a compromise would be reached and that the seceded states would reenter the Union. Whether that statement was merely an effort to gain the good graces of the conquering government cannot be determined, but Boyce did not hesitate to accept a seat in the Provisional Confederate Congress in February 1861 and actively participate in the formation of the Confederate States of America.

During the creation of the Confederate government, Boyce served on several committees including the Drafting Committee of the executive portion of the Confederate Constitution; the Postal Committee; and after the selection of Jefferson Davis as provisional president, the Inauguration Committee. During that selection process, however, Boyce had endorsed the candidacy of Howell Cobb for president. Boyce's opposition to Jefferson Davis would continue for the remainder of the Confederacy's existence.

In the fall of 1861, Boyce was elected to the first regular Confederate Congress. From the beginning of that Congress's first session, Boyce became one of the most vocal critics of the method by which the Davis administration conducted the war. Initially Boyce supported a strong aggressive military policy and voted for spending measures that he believed would bring about such a policy. At the same time, however, he opposed the conscription measures taken by the Confederate Congress in early 1862 and strongly advocated steps be taken to improve local defense.

In committee work both in the First and Second Confederate Congresses, Boyce was very active, serving on the Currency, Ways and Means, and Naval Affairs Committees. He used these forums to become increasingly critical of Davis and to advocate that Congress take a more active role in directing the military affairs of the country. He recommended that the Confederate Congress create the position of commanding general of the army so that Davis would have less direct impact on military policy.

By the end of 1863, Boyce increasingly came to see the military situation as hopeless and began advocating opening negotiations with the United States. Davis's increasing use of the power to suspend the writ of habeas corpus alarmed him, not only because he did not trust Davis, but also because he feared that the independent Confederacy would become a dictatorship. His vocal advocacy of peace in 1864 began to wear on his constituents, who had not felt the full brunt of the war as yet and still believed that victory was possible. He became increasingly unpopular at home as well as with the Davis administration. He remained in his congressional seat until the end of the war, but was increasingly seen by other representatives as somewhat of a crank.

After the war, Boyce returned to Winnsboro, where he was greeted with less than enthusiasm by some of his neighbors. He had lost most of his property, but sought to rebuild his political fortunes by courting the Republican government in Washington. In July 1865, he wrote to Secretary of State William Henry Seward asserting his loyalty to the U.S. government and claiming that he had wanted compromise in 1860 and 1861 and that he had opposed Jefferson Davis throughout the war. Boyce asked

Seward that if he were elected to the U.S. Congress he be allowed to take his seat.

Boyce was being optimistic about his political chances in South Carolina; his peace efforts in the latter part of the war had made him unpopular throughout the state. Once he determined that, he moved to Washington, D.C., in 1866 and opened a law practice there. Over the next twenty years he developed a prosperous practice and was able to retire to an estate he purchased in Fairfax County, Virginia. He died there on 3 February 1890. His remains were taken back to Winnsboro for burial.

—*David S. Heidler and Jeanne T. Heidler*

See also Congress, C.S.A.

For further reading:

Taylor, Rosser Howard, ed. "The Boyce-Hammond Correspondence." *Journal of Southern History* (1937).

BOYD, MARIA ISABELLA "BELLE"
(1843–1900)
Confederate spy

Probably the most famous among the hundreds of women who performed espionage and resistance activity on behalf of the armies of the Civil War, Belle Boyd was born near Martinsburg, Virginia (now West Virginia), in 1843. By the time the war broke out, the teenaged Boyd had developed a bold and uncompromising stance in favor of her native South and had dedicated herself to doing whatever she could to serve the Confederate cause. Boyd began her career as a pro-Southern activist by shooting and killing a Yankee soldier who, as part of the Union forces occupying Martinsburg in July 1861, tried to hoist a Union flag above the Boyd family home. Although they did not arrest her for shooting the soldier, Union officials reportedly scolded Boyd roundly and temporarily placed a guard at her door to prevent similar demonstrations of her secessionism in the future.

Boyd responded to such cautions with disdain and soon began a regular routine of gathering and transmitting information to Confederate authorities on Union fortifications, troop movements, and battle plans. Considered extremely attractive and beguiling to men, Boyd made shrewd use of all her charms to serve the Southern cause. Even in her own time, a legend developed that Boyd could compel even apparently invulnerable men in blue to disclose precious military secrets. Indeed, some accused her of prostituting herself, literally, for the sake of the Confederacy. Although Boyd herself wrote candidly in her memoir, *Belle Boyd in Camp and Prison*, about her ability to entice enemy soldiers into revealing important information, she denied this baser charge with vehemence, and indeed, the evidence fails to support convincingly any such claim against her.

The espionage work for which Boyd is best known was her timely delivery of crucial information to General Thomas J. "Stonewall" Jackson during his May 1862 campaign to hold Virginia's Shenandoah Valley for the South. The previous March, frustrated by their inability to control Boyd's behavior, Federal officials in Martinsburg had sent Boyd about forty miles south to Front Royal, Virginia. There Boyd regularly eavesdropped on conversations and solicited information from Federal soldiers and officers as yet unfamiliar with either her face or her reputation. By the end of May, she had compiled a cache of information that she then transmitted personally on 23 May to Jackson's headquarters several miles outside of town. When he later recalled Boyd's daring horseback ride to convey the information she had collected, Confederate major Henry Kyd Douglas spoke nostalgically of the "romantic maiden" who had heeded "neither weeds nor fences . . . as she came on" to inform him that Union general Nathaniel Banks's forces were sufficiently few in number as to permit Jackson's easy victory over them, should Jackson move quickly. Tradition has it that the information Boyd brought that day was instrumental in allowing Jackson to drive Banks's forces back across the Potomac towards Washington, and Jackson's brief written statement acknowledging Boyd's courage and expressing his gratitude became one of her most treasured possessions.

Boyd did not avoid arrest for the entire course of the war. Indeed, twice before the events at Front Royal Boyd had been taken into custody, but only very briefly, in part because enduring traditions of chivalry made it difficult to hold her, and also, more practically, because of the dearth of prison facilities for women on either side during the war. Some weeks after her Front Royal adventure, however, Federal officials reached a breaking point over the troublesome Boyd, who seemed to be able to travel with complete freedom and to gather masses of important information, regardless of her growing reputation or repeated admonitions to cease and desist. Thus, when Boyd was captured again in late July 1862 following an expedition to carry dispatches, Federal officials held her for about a month at the Old Capitol Prison in Washington, D.C. There she earned the respect and admiration of many of her fellow inmates and even her jailers for her unrelenting dedication to the South.

Released at the end of August, Boyd resumed her espionage work, only to be arrested again the following summer and imprisoned for three months. Upon her next release, Boyd decided to exchange the work she had been performing for a new job of bearing dispatches from the Confederacy to its supporters in England. Accordingly, in May 1864 she boarded a blockade runner called the *Greyhound* and set sail for Europe. Before it had fairly got out to sea, however, the *Greyhound*—and its most famous passenger—were captured, and Boyd's spying career was finally brought to a close.

After the war Boyd took her wartime story to the stage, performing in England and America, and supplementing her theater performances with lectures to veterans' gatherings across America. Boyd also wrote her memoirs, married three times, bore three children, and collapsed for a brief period of time in a mental hospital in Stockton, California. She died in 1900 in Kilbourne, Wisconsin, apparently from a heart attack.

—*Elizabeth D. Leonard*

See also Espionage; Shenandoah Valley Campaign; Women.
For further reading:
Davis, Curtis Carroll, ed. *Belle Boyd in Camp and Prison, Written by Herself* (1968).
Douglas, Henry Kyd. *I Rode With Stonewall Being Chiefly the War Experiences of the Youngest Member of Jackson's Staff from the John Brown Raid to the Hanging of Mrs. Surratt* (1940).
Leonard, Elizabeth D. *All the Daring of the Soldier: Women of the Civil War Armies* (1999).
Scarborough, Ruth. *Belle Boyd: Siren of the South* (1983).
Sigaud, Louis. *Belle Boyd: Confederate Spy* (1944).

BRADFORD, AUGUSTUS WILLIAMSON
(1806–1881)
Governor of Maryland

Born to Samuel Bradford and Jane Bond Bradford in Bel Air, Maryland, Augustus Williamson Bradford was educated locally before enrolling in St. Mary's College. He graduated from that institution in 1824 after which he studied law and began his practice in Bel Air. Over the next two decades he divided his time between Bel Air and Baltimore. Along with his law practice, Bradford also became involved in Maryland Whig politics, though he became somewhat disillusioned with politics when Henry Clay was defeated for the presidency in 1844. While still respected in Maryland political circles, Bradford spent most of the time before the outbreak of the Civil War building his legal practice.

During the secession crisis in early 1861, Governor Thomas Hicks asked Bradford to represent the state at the Washington Peace Conference. An ardent supporter of the Union, Bradford at the meetings of the conference spoke strongly in favor of its preservation. Upon his return home, his name was mentioned increasingly as a candidate for governor on the state's new Union Party ticket. Bradford won the election handily, though accusations would be made later that Democratic voters had been intimidated into staying away from the polls. Although he was a demonstrated supporter of the Union, Bradford nevertheless tried without success to prevent the use of U.S. troops at polling places during future elections.

Governor Bradford had one of the most difficult jobs of any U.S. governor during the war. As the governor of a border state with strong support for the Confederacy (his son William Bradford enlisted in the Confederate army), Bradford, a very principled person, had to walk a fine line between support for the Union and violation of the Maryland citizens' civil rights. In frequent contact with the U.S. attorney general's office and sometimes directly with the president, Bradford worked for the release of members of the state legislature who had been imprisoned early in the war for expressing secessionists views and the prevention the use of troops in the domestic concerns of the state. At the same time, Bradford realized that conscription would be unpopular in a state as divided as Maryland and requested that the War Department supply troops whenever a draft was held.

The defense of Maryland increasingly became a concern in the late summer of 1862 and would remain a focus of Bradford's efforts until the fall of 1864. During each emergency, beginning with Robert E. Lee's invasion in September 1862, Bradford summoned state forces and called for extra volunteers to protect the threatened areas. Because many of the Southern sympathizers in the state viewed such activity as helping the U.S. Army, Bradford had to resort to a state draft on several occasions to meet the defensive demands of the state. During the last of the Confederate invasions in the summer of 1864, Bradford's home outside Baltimore was burned by a party of Confederate raiders, and all the contents of the house were destroyed. Bradford was singled out for this action because of his support for the Union and because Union general David Hunter had destroyed Virginia governor John Letcher's home the previous spring.

Bradford's efforts to keep as many citizens loyal to the Union as possible were complicated early in the war by the increasing numbers of runaway slaves after the commencement of hostilities. These slaves naturally saw the war as an opportunity to gain their freedom, but the reluctance of neighboring states to enforce the Fugitive Slave Act once the war started made it difficult for Bradford to convince the state's slave owners that the war was not about slavery. When many of the slaves also began taking refuge in Washington, D.C., and Federal officers there took no effort to return them to the state, Bradford's job became even more difficult. Ultimately Bradford, who did not own slaves, saw the inevitability of emancipation and used his influence to bring about the end of the institution in Maryland in a new constitution in 1864.

After leaving the governor's chair in 1866, Bradford served several years as the surveyor of Baltimore's port. After leaving that position in 1869, Bradford spent most of his time in his law practice. Disapproving of the direction of the Republican Party, of which he was now a member, during the first Ulysses S. Grant administration, Bradford joined the reform wing of the party and was chosen an elector for Horace Greeley in the presidential election of 1872. After that election, Bradford took little interest in public life and lived quietly outside Baltimore until his death on 1 March 1881.

—*David S. Heidler and Jeanne T. Heidler*

See also Maryland; Civil Liberties, U.S.A.
For further reading:
Cottom, Robert I., Jr., and Mary Ellen Hayward. *Maryland in the Civil War: A House Divided* (1994).

BRADLEY, AMY MORRIS
(1823–1904)
Union army nurse

Amy Morris Bradley was like other successful relief workers in her organizational genius and understanding of how to cut red tape without breaching military etiquette—a code of conduct she referred to as her "peace method." When she left the service in 1865, she had worked as a transport nurse, brought order to Alexandria's Convalescent Camp "Misery," helped hundreds of soldiers obtain discharges and back pay, and won praise from surgeons, hospital administrators, and soldiers as a woman "possessed of superior executive ability."

With a history of respiratory illnesses and weighing just over a hundred pounds, this native of East Vassalboro, Maine, was an unlikely candidate for war service when she arrived at Camp Franklin, Virginia, in September 1861. As a young child, Bradley lost her mother and was raised by her married sisters. At sixteen, she went to work teaching, a career she parlayed into administrative positions in the 1840s. By 1850 she was suffering from acute bronchitis and resigned her job in the hope of recovering in a brother's Charleston home. When Bradley returned to New England in 1851 and fell ill again, doctors advised her to relocate permanently. In 1853 she jumped at an opportunity to work in Central America as a governess. She moved to San Jose in November, and in a matter of months, had opened Costa Rica's first international school. Its principal until 1857, the thirty-eight-year-old spinster, now fluent in Spanish, accepted a job translating documents for a glass company in East Cambridge, Massachusetts.

From East Cambridge, she wrote to the 3d Maine Volunteers in 1861, asking for a position as a nurse. Regimental surgeons G. S. Palmer and George E. Brickett attempted to dissuade her, but Bradley insisted that she was equal to the rigors of camp life and started as matron on 1 September. With hard physical labor, Bradley's health actually improved; she would always prefer work in the field to that in poorly ventilated general hospitals. So adept was she in bringing order to the regimental hospital that by late fall, General Henry Slocum gave her charge of medical arrangements for his brigade. Near Camp Franklin she fitted out the Powell and Octagon houses to accommodate sick and wounded men. After the brigade left for Centreville in the spring, the hospitals were closed. After several weeks of transience Bradley went to Washington to seek employment with the Sanitary Commission, which was then equipping hospital boats in anticipation of McClellan's spring campaigns.

In retrospect, Bradley's move from the Army of the Potomac to the Sanitary Commission was not fortunate. Although commissioners like Frederick Knapp enthusiastically enlisted her aid, Bradley was snubbed by elite transport workers, who believed—erroneously—that she drew a salary. After conducting 1,000 wounded from Fortress Monroe to New York on the *Ocean Queen*, Bradley was left to manage the cleanup, a formidable task of flushing the decks of mud and effluvia and laundering bloody uniforms left behind. From the battle of Fair Oaks in May 1862, until McClellan's forces vacated the Peninsula at the end of the summer, Bradley served as custodial supervisor on seven ships, while "the Aristocracy of the Commission"—New York blue bloods like Katharine Wormeley, Georgeanna Woolsey, and Ellie (Mrs. George Templeton) Strong—managed to secure more desirable assignments. On board the *Knickerbocker* in June, Bradley met Michigan's Annie Etheridge, whose sterling work ethic and lack of pretense were more to Bradley's liking.

No sooner had Bradley helped evacuate men from the Peninsula to Aquia Creek than she was summoned to Washington to revive the Soldiers' Home on North Capitol, a facility that offered soldiers a free bed and food when they made the transition from the hospital to their regiments. After putting the home in order—accomplished chiefly through hiring three women to do the cooking, laundry, and chamber work—Bradley began to seek other venues for her organizational zeal. By December 1862 she began to clean up the dismal Convalescent Camp in Alexandria by establishing a hospital, bath house, cook house, and regular laundry service. Bradley also put into place procedures to help soldiers obtain back pay and discharge papers and to rescind desertion charges if they had been hospitalized. In a year's time, nearly 112,000 men went through the camp, hundreds of whom Bradley personally escorted through the military bureaucracy.

Early in 1864 the government sent inmates of the camp to area hospitals and reorganized it as Camp Distribution (later Rendezvous of Distribution). So grateful to Bradley were the convalescents, that a delegation honored her with a gold watch. Without its sick and wounded, Camp Distribution now served as a way station for soldiers awaiting assignment to new regiments. In the interest of disseminating information about furloughs, medical discharges, and sanitary procedures, Bradley created the *Soldiers' Journal* in February 1864, which ultimately boasted 20,000 subscribers, including President Lincoln and General Grant. For eighteen months, the journal was published weekly at five cents per copy; its profits of over $2,000 went to an orphanage after the war. On her last day of service in August 1865, Bradley was nearly killed when a driver lost control of her carriage and left her to fend for herself from the back seat. The irony of spending four years exposed to bullets and disease only to be killed by a runaway horse was not lost on Bradley, who managed to stop the animal before it vaulted over a cliff.

Bradley traveled to Wilmington, North Carolina, in late summer, where she turned her attention back to school administration. Under the auspices of the Soldiers' Memorial Association, she opened a free school, which became the seed for Wilmington's public schools later in the century. Bradley maintained her roles as teacher and administrator until her retirement in 1891. She died thirteen years later at the age of eighty.

—*Jane E. Schultz*

See also Etheridge, Annie; Nurses.
For further reading:
Bradley, Amy Morris. Diaries and Letterbooks. Perkins Library, Duke University.
Brockett, Linus P., and Mary C. Vaughan. *Woman's Work in the Civil War* (1867).
Cashman, Diane Cobb. *Headstrong: The Biography of Amy Morris Bradley* (1990).
Moore, Frank. *Women of the War: Their Heroism and Self-Sacrifice* (1866).

BRADY, MATHEW B.
(ca. 1823–1896)
Photographer

Little is known about Mathew Brady's early life except that he was born in Warren County, New York, to Andrew and Julia Brady around 1823. Afflicted with an eye inflammation as a teen, Brady

Brady's photographic outfit near Petersburg, Virginia, *ca.* 1864 (*Library of Congress*)

Mathew Brady (*center, in hat*) and troops under fire before Petersburg, Virginia, 21 June 1864
(Photograph by Mathew Brady Studios / *National Archives*)

traveled to Albany and Saratoga in search of a cure. During his time in Saratoga, Brady probably met portrait painter William Page. Through this acquaintance, he most likely met Samuel F. B. Morse, who in the 1830s was experimenting with the new medium of daguerreotypy, an early form of photography. As Morse was offering lessons in the new art at the time, most scholars believe that this is where Brady first learned what was to become his trade.

In 1843 Brady was living in New York City and manufacturing cases to house daguerreotypes, jewelry, and painted miniature portraits. By April 1844 Brady had opened his first studio, the Daguerrean Miniature Gallery, on Broadway. In October of the same year, he exhibited his work at the American Institute's annual fair and won the premium (or highest) award, which he won again in 1845, 1846, 1849, and 1857.

Shortly thereafter, Brady began his lifelong endeavor of collecting images of notable Americans. He opened a studio in Washington, D.C., in 1849 so that he could obtain portraits of the important political personages in the city. To this end, he made daguerreotypes of Henry Clay, Daniel Webster, John C. Calhoun, Zachary Taylor, and Millard Fillmore. In 1850 Brady published his collection in a book entitled *The Gallery of Illustrious Americans*, which sold for $15 a copy. At around the same date, Brady married Juliette Handy.

Brady's work continued to win the praise of others working with daguerreotypy. In 1851 he won a medal at the Fair of All Nations in London, England, and in 1854 he won a bronze medal at the New York Industrial Exhibition at the Crystal Palace for his daguerreotypes.

By 1858 Brady had two studios on Broadway, the largest with twenty-six employees. One of these employees was a Scottish immigrant named Alexander Gardner. When Brady decided to open a new studio in Washington, D.C., to replace the earlier studio that had eventually failed, the photographer chose Gardner to manage it. Brady's National Photographic Art Gallery, on Pennsylvania Avenue, enabled him to acquire photographs of the politicians in the city, including presidential candidates Stephen A. Douglas and Abraham Lincoln, as well as all the members of the House of Representatives, some of whom would become notable for their roles in the Confederate cause.

By the outbreak of the Civil War, Brady's business was near its peak. The advent of carte de visite cameras enabled a photographer to take multiple pictures simultaneously. Exposed on paper and mounted on card stock, these new photographs provided inexpensive likenesses for a wider portion of the public and thus expanded Brady's business in both New York and Washington. At the same time, his photographers were in the field with the Union army, recording the events of the war.

Brady's photographic gallery, at the corner of Broadway and Tenth Street, New York
(*Frank Leslie's Illustrated Newspaper* / *Library of Congress*)

Engravings based on Alexander Gardner's photographs of the aftermath of Antietam were the first graphic images of battlefield dead and were published in *Harper's Weekly*. The original photographs, on display at Brady's New York studio, caused an outcry of horror among his patrons.

Throughout his career, though he had many wealthy and influential friends and was able to amass property and investments, Brady could not manage his finances. Constantly in debt, he managed to procure loans on his good name and artistic talent. By the end of the Civil War, however, Brady was in serious financial difficulty. The photographic medium that he helped make popular, the carte de visite, undermined the attraction of his New York and Washington galleries. Now that the images of famous personages could be reproduced in quantity and sold to the public, individuals could collect their own small portrait galleries.

At the end of the war, Brady negotiated to sell his massive archive of photographs to the prestigious New York Historical Society. The profits of the sale were intended to pay off his outstanding debts. To his great disappointment, the deal fell through. In 1870, Brady then traveled to Washington to try to sell his collection to the federal government. His debts too large to ignore,

in 1872 Brady sold his opulent New York studio and filed for bankruptcy. Finally, in 1875 the U.S. Congress bought the title to the Brady collection for $25,000. The embattled photographer was then able to pay off his debts.

Brady remained in Washington and worked with his nephew Levin Handy, also a photographer. Though his enthusiasm for the art had waned, Brady continued to take portraits of notable people, though he no longer pursued them with as much vigor as he had twenty years earlier.

After his wife's death in 1887, Brady's health deteriorated, exacerbated by alcohol and depression. He managed to open his last studio in 1890 in Washington, where, instead of his portraits, he was the main attraction. As the only survivor of the many photographers who recorded the Civil War, Brady became popular among journalists interested in the great upheaval of the previous generation. Regaining some of his interest in the promotion of his work, he began compiling a slide lecture of his old photographs. In 1895, a traffic accident aborted his plans and left him with a broken leg. He never fully recovered from the injury and died a year later, on 16 January 1896 in New York.

Brady was ever popular with the former soldiers of the

"Brady, the Photographer, Returned from Bull Run,"
22 July 1861 (*Library of Congress*)

Civil War and with the New York art world, and his funeral was financed by artists and the veterans of the New York 7th Regiment Veterans Association. He was buried beside his wife in Congressional Cemetery in Washington, D.C.

—*Heidi Campbell-Shoaf*

See also Photography.
For further reading:
Panzer, Mary. *Mathew Brady and the Image of History* (1994).
Sullivan, George. *Mathew Brady: His Life and Photographs* (1994).

BRAGG, BRAXTON
(1817–1876)
Confederate general

The acerbic, easily agitated Confederate commander Braxton Bragg, who was probably the most ill-suited general to lead a large army in the war, was born in Warrenton, North Carolina, on 21 March 1817.

Bragg's brother, Thomas, would serve as Confederate attorney general. A strict disciplinarian in an army that caviled at strict discipline, few other commanders earned such severe rebukes from his subordinates than Bragg. Although he never proved himself competent in leading a large force, he was given this responsibility in several key campaigns. Even counting the one major victory he could claim at Chickamauga, he mismanaged them all.

He graduated fifth of fifty in his 1837 class at West Point and served in both the Second Seminole War and the Mexican-American War. Serving under General Zachary Taylor in Mexico, he was promoted three times for extraordinary service, yet two assassination attempts were reportedly made on his life by fellow soldiers, an early indication of his ability to make enemies. He later served with Colonel Albert Sidney Johnston in his Utah expedition before Bragg resigned his commission as a brevet lieutenant colonel in 1856. In the time between then and the beginning of the Civil War, Bragg lived as a sugar planter in Louisiana. In 1861, he was appointed brigadier general and was assigned to coastal defense in Pensacola, Florida, where he quickly took charge of various navy assets and fortifications. Subsequently, he was given command over the whole Gulf Coast defense and was promoted to major general before he and his troops were sent to reinforce General Albert Sidney Johnston in Corinth, Mississippi. Before the battle of Shiloh, Bragg served as Johnston's chief of staff, helping to organize an army almost in shambles. During the battle, Bragg acted gallantly as he directed attacks at the center of the conflict; he had two horses shot out from under him. After Johnston's death on the battlefield, Bragg was elevated to second in command by General P. G. T. Beauregard, whose subsequent ill health led him to depart the army and leave Bragg in command. Bragg quickly began establishing strict discipline for his troops and reorganizing the damaged army. Eventually abandoning Corinth, Mississippi, he shifted his command to Chattanooga, Tennessee.

From Chattanooga, Bragg began planning and organizing an offensive north through central Tennessee into Kentucky. During these preparations, Bragg applied what became a habit of purging officers he thought inferior. He also began exhibiting the effects of stress, a condition that tended to further diminish his ineffectiveness as a commander. Nonetheless, when Bragg advanced, he pushed Union general Don Carlos Buell out of Tennessee without fighting a battle. By 15 September, Bragg's men were marching to Munfordville, Kentucky, and received the surrender of the Union garrison there. Although he was now in a position to break Buell's lines of communication, Bragg allowed Buell to reach Louisville. His efforts to recruit Kentuckians for the rebel cause proved unsuccessful as well. As the Confederate invasion of Kentucky turned into a muddle, its fortunes were finally settled at the battle of Perryville, where a stalemate forced the Confederates south. The failure of the Kentucky invasion revealed Bragg's inability to control army operations, even to the point that he began to run out of provisions. Moreover, his failure in Kentucky caused considerable disappointment throughout the Confederacy, so in October he was summoned to Richmond to answer critics in the government. President Jefferson Davis allowed him to keep his job, however, which would prove to be one of the most crucial mistakes of his presidency.

By Christmas 1862, Bragg's army was encamped in Murfreesboro, Tennessee, where from Nashville the new Union commander General William S. Rosecrans would oppose it. Rosecrans was under pressure to advance on Bragg, so on 31 December, the armies were in place for battle near Stones River. Lacking the strength and the imagination to exploit the success of an early Confederate assault, Bragg managed only a series of attacks against a firm Union line during the next two days. Bragg had thought Rosecrans would retreat to fortifications in Nashville, but when the Federals remained in place, it was the Confederate army that retreated as rain threatened to put Stones River out of its banks. Rosecrans did not follow, but the campaign was a strategic defeat for Bragg, and it left his army badly mauled. Total casualties from the battle were staggering at almost 25,000 men.

Historians have generally been critical of Bragg for his lack of imagination at Stones River. Although his experience at Shiloh and Perryville had made him aware of the futility of such frontal assaults, he persisted in them at Stones River. Bragg's tactical management of battles hence followed a distinctive and deadly pattern. Initial success would occur, often in spite of Bragg's muddled understanding of the tactical picture, and then that success would lose momentum until Bragg was unable to deliver a final decisive blow.

After Stones River, Bragg retreated to Tullahoma and awaited Rosecrans's inevitable advance, although the Federal force would not begin another campaign until June. Because Bragg was preparing to send reinforcements to embattled Vicksburg, Rosecrans finally accelerated his offensive. A demonstration against one of Bragg's divisions at Shelbyville set the stage for General George H. Thomas to attack another at Manchester. With other Union forces moving to outflank his positions around Tullahoma, Bragg ignominiously retreated to Chattanooga, giving up central Tennessee without fighting a battle for it.

In mid-August 1863, Rosecrans again tried to beguile Bragg into giving up ground without a fight. Dividing his Army of the Cumberland into three parts, Rosecrans threw Bragg into a confused belief that he was about to be outflanked again. Fearful that he would be separated

from the important city of Atlanta, Bragg gave up Chattanooga without a fight, but he soon discovered that Rosecrans had kept the Union army divided. Bragg concentrated his own forces to attack the most exposed part of Rosecrans's scattered advance. Yet when he failed to destroy the Union army piecemeal, Rosecrans recognized his peril and quickly regrouped. On 18 September, the Union and Confederate armies faced one another across Chickamauga Creek, unaware of the other's exact location. Bragg wanted to get between Rosecrans and Chattanooga, and the endeavor brought on a full-scale engagement at Chickamauga. Again early success gave way to a series of stalled attacks, this time against George H. Thomas's stubborn stand on Snodgrass Hill. Although Rosecrans despondently retreated to Chattanooga, there was some irony in that Bragg's objective of reclaiming that city had resulted in driving the Federal army into it. Furthermore, while Bragg could claim the field at Chickamauga with a sound defeat of the enemy, he had done nothing to make his victory meaningful. Instead, he had allowed the shattered Union forces to limp away and dig in.

It was a mistake that was compounded later by his poor troop placement around Chattanooga. Also, his chronic inability to get along with subordinates, especially the more talented ones, finally reached a critical level after Chickamauga. Jefferson Davis tried to intervene in October with a personal visit to Bragg's headquarters, but the beleaguered president tried to placate everyone, with the result that the situation was only worsened. On the other side, Ulysses S. Grant had acted decisively to replace Rosecrans with Thomas. The stage was set in November 1863 for Bragg's final humiliation.

On 23 November, Thomas began breaking Bragg's siege of Chattanooga by advancing on Orchard Knob, a rise below Missionary Ridge where most Confederate forces were in place. Sherman attacked Bragg's right, and General Joseph Hooker assailed Confederates on Lookout Mountain. When the center of the Union attack spontaneously charged up Missionary Ridge and routed the Confederates there, Bragg had to flee the city's environs. He barely made it into Dalton, Georgia. While reliable Patrick Cleburne fended off Federal attempts to destroy the retreating army, Bragg reformed his shattered force the best he could. As Rosecrans had similarly done after the battle of Chickamauga, Bragg braced himself for the consequence of this last dismal failure.

Davis accepted Bragg's resignation and replaced him with General Joseph E. Johnston. Bragg's days of field command were over, but his military career continued when his loyal friend President Davis brought him to Richmond as his military adviser. By then, the Confederacy's military fortunes were to enter such a rapid decline that Bragg's influence for good or ill in this new position would be hard to calculate. Some would insist, however, that he again blundered by letting the Union capture the last remaining open Confederate port at Wilmington, North Carolina. Fleeing with the Davis party upon the evacuation of Richmond, Bragg and his wife were captured in Georgia. After the war, he pursued a career in civil engineering and became a railroad executive. He died in Galveston, Texas, in 1876 and was buried in Mobile, Alabama.

Bragg's reputation has never recovered from the series of tactical blunders he began during his 1862 invasion of Kentucky and concluded with his mismanagement at Chattanooga the following year. Unable to cultivate talent on his staff and with a penchant for alienating his most gifted subordinates, Bragg was audacious when he should have been careful and timid when he should have been bold. Certainly as much as any individual, he was responsible for Confederate defeat.

—*James H. Meredith*

See also Army of Mississippi; Buell, Don Carlos; Chattanooga Campaign; Chickamauga, Battle of; Davis, Jefferson; Kentucky; Munfordville, Battle of; Perryville, Battle of; Rosecrans, William Starke; Shiloh, Battle of; Stones River, Battle of; Tullahoma Campaign.
For further reading:
Buell, Thomas B. *The Warrior Generals: Combat Leadership in the Civil War* (1997).
Coffey, David. *John Bell Hood and the Struggle for Atlanta* (1998).
McWhiney, Grady. *Braxton Bragg and Confederate Defeat* (1969).
Snow, William P. *Lee and His Generals* (1982).

BRAGG, EDWARD STUYVESANT
(1827–1912)
Union general

Born to Joel Bragg and Margaretha Kohl Bragg in Unadilla, New York, Edward Bragg was educated locally and at what would become Hobart College before reading law and being admitted to the bar in 1848. Two years later he moved to Fond du Lac, Wisconsin, where he became a prominent attorney and Democratic leader.

In the election of 1860, Bragg supported the presidential candidacy of Stephen Douglas and traveled to Charleston, South Carolina, in the spring of 1860 as a Wisconsin delegate to the Democratic National Convention. Upon the election of Abraham Lincoln in the fall of 1860 and the outbreak of the Civil War in the spring of 1861, Bragg organized a company and became a captain in the 6th Wisconsin Infantry. The 6th Wisconsin would become one of the regiments composing the famous Iron Brigade. Bragg was promoted major in September 1861.

For the first year of the war, the 6th did garrison duty in Washington, D.C. During that time, in June 1862, Bragg was promoted to lieutenant colonel. In July 1862 the 6th became part of John Pope's Army of Virginia and

marched out of the city. It saw its first action at Cedar Mountain in August 1862. By the end of the month, Bragg was in temporary command of the regiment after its colonel was injured at Gainesville, Virginia, on 28 August during the Second Bull Run campaign.

Bragg continued to command the 6th at South Mountain and Antietam and fought at Fredericksburg. He was promoted colonel and commander of the regiment in March 1863 and led those troops into battle as part of I Corps under the command of John Reynolds at Chancellorsville. Because of illness, Bragg did not participate in the Gettysburg campaign.

The following fall, however, still part of I Corps, the regiment and the Iron Brigade fought at Bristoe Station and the Mine Run campaign. During the spring of 1864, Bragg led the 6th in the opening stages of Ulysses S. Grant's campaign against Robert E. Lee. At the Wilderness, Bragg assumed command of the Iron Brigade, and a month later he was recommended for promotion to brigadier general by George Gordon Meade and was promoted on 25 June 1864. Bragg led his men in the attempt to cut the Weldon Railroad at Globe Tavern in August 1864 and Hatcher's Run in October 1864.

Bragg took a short leave of absence in January 1865 and in February 1865 went with what was left of his brigade to Baltimore to help with the organization and transport of new troops. He would see no major action for the remainder of the war and was mustered out of the volunteers in October 1865.

After the war, Bragg returned to Wisconsin, his law practice, and Democratic politics. He served in the state legislature and was elected to the U.S. House of Representatives in 1876. As a delegate to the 1884 Democratic National Convention, Bragg coined the phrase, in referring to the nomination of Grover Cleveland, "We love him for the enemies he has made!" Later in life Bragg served as consul general to Hong Kong during the Theodore Roosevelt administration. Bragg died on 20 June 1912 at home in Fond du Lac, Wisconsin.

—*David S. Heidler and Jeanne T. Heidler*

See also Globe Tavern; Hatcher's Run; Iron Brigade.
For further reading:
Farnum, George R. "Edward S. Bragg: Soldier, Lawyer and Diplomat." *American Bar Association Journal* (1944).

BRAGG, THOMAS
(1810–1872)
Confederate attorney general

Born in Warrenton, North Carolina, to Thomas Bragg and Margaret Crossland Bragg, the younger Bragg was educated locally before being sent as a youth to a military school in Connecticut.

Upon his return to North Carolina, Bragg studied law and began his own practice in 1833. Over the years before the outbreak of the Civil War, Bragg became one of the most respected attorneys in the state. During this time Bragg also became active in North Carolina Democratic politics. He was slow to advance in party circles, however, because he lived in a largely Whig area of the state. He served two terms in the state legislature in the 1840s before gaining the attention of state Democratic leaders and won the governorship of the state in 1854. He won reelection in 1856. Judged a very able governor by his contemporaries, Bragg was also viewed as a moderate on secession. Although he believed that secession was a perfectly legitimate response to violations of Southern rights, Bragg did not believe that that remedy was the best solution for the South. His excellent handling of state affairs during his four years in office caused his election to the United States Senate in 1859.

In the Senate, Bragg continued his moderate stand regarding secession and affirmed his strong belief in the limited powers of the federal government. Although he still did not believe that secession was in the best interest of the South or of North Carolina, he supported his state when it seceded in May 1861. For a brief time he served as an assistant to Governor John W. Ellis, until the governor's death in July 1861. In November 1861 he accepted appointment by Confederate president Jefferson Davis as Confederate attorney general.

During his brief tenure as attorney general, Bragg was considered a close adviser of Jefferson Davis. Bragg worked hard to protect civilian rights and to insist that the military adequately compensate civilians for requisitioned supplies. He received numerous requests for the release of civilian prisoners. Confederate policies were becoming increasingly unpopular in Bragg's native state of North Carolina, so in March 1862 Bragg resigned his cabinet post and returned home to act as a spokesman for the Confederate government against the increasingly strong peace movement in North Carolina.

Over the next few years Bragg worked tirelessly to offset the criticisms leveled at Jefferson Davis by states' right advocates such as Governor Zebulon Vance. Some people in the state credited him with moderating some of Vance's extremist views. In March 1864 Bragg became the North Carolina commissioner for the Confederate law suspending the writ of habeas corpus, an onerous duty in a fractious state. From 1864 to 1865, Bragg edited the North Carolina *State Journal.*

Following the war, Bragg returned to his legal practice. In 1870, the legislature hired him as one of its attorneys in the impeachment of Governor William Holden. He died in Raleigh two years later. Bragg was the brother of Confederate general Braxton Bragg.

—*David S. Heidler and Jeanne T. Heidler*

See also North Carolina.

For further reading:
Bragg, Thomas. Thomas Bragg Diary, 1861–1862. Southern Historical Collection of the University of North Carolina Library at Chapel Hill.
Cowper, Pulaski. *Sketch of the Life of Governor Thomas Bragg: To which is Appended an Account of First Joint Discussion Between Gov. Thomas Bragg and Hon. John A. Gilmer, at Murphy, Cherokee County, in 1856* (1891).
Peele, W. J. *Lives of Distinguished North Carolinians with Illustrations and Speeches* (1898).
Snow, William Parker. *Lee and His Generals* (1982).

BRAMLETTE, THOMAS ELLIOTT
(1817–1875)
Union officer; Kentucky governor

Thomas Elliott Bramlette was born on 3 January 1817 to Colonel Ambrose S. and Sarah Bramlette in Cumberland (now Clinton) County, Kentucky. After education in the common schools, he studied law and was admitted to the bar in 1837. That year he married Sallie Travis with whom he had two children. After her death in 1872, he married Mrs. Mary E. Graham Adams in 1874. Bramlette was elected to the Kentucky House of Representatives in 1841 but did not seek reelection. Appointed commonwealth attorney in 1848, he resigned in 1850 and moved to Columbia, Kentucky. In 1856 he won election as a judge of the Sixth Judicial District.

A staunch Unionist Democrat, Bramlette resigned his judgeship in 1861 to raise and command the 3d Kentucky Volunteer Infantry Regiment. When he resigned in 1862 over a command dispute, Lincoln appointed him United States district attorney for Kentucky, and he moved to Louisville. Commissioned a major general in 1863, he was raising a division when the Union Democrats nominated him for the governorship. He won easily over Charles A. Wickliffe. In his 1 September 1863 inaugural address, Bramlette promised to make every effort to preserve the Union and the Constitution, but soon he demonstrated that even a strong Unionist could differ with the administration's policies.

While the Emancipation Proclamation did not apply to Kentucky, Bramlette accused Lincoln of breaking his promise not to interfere with slavery in the states that had it. His protests increased when the Union moved to enlist black soldiers. He threatened to use force to halt enlistments in Kentucky, but he led a delegation to Washington that got some concessions from Lincoln. The black soldiers, and later their families, gained freedom by military service, and before the war ended some 71 percent of Kentucky's African-Americans had become free.

Bramlette clashed frequently with overzealous military commanders who violated civil rights and interfered with elections. In a scathing 3 September 1864 letter to Lincoln, Bramlette complained that "We are dealt with, as though Kentucky was a rebellious and conquered province. . . . I am opposed to your reelection and regard a change of policy as essential to the salvation of the country." The governor helped the Democratic presidential candidate, George B. McClellan, carry Kentucky by a wide margin in 1864. He was much incensed in 1864 when Major General Stephen Gano Burbridge expelled Lieutenant Governor Richard T. Jacob to the Confederacy. Lincoln, who had not been consulted, allowed Jacob to return to Kentucky.

Toward the end of the war Bramlette was bedeviled by increased guerrilla activities in his state. On 4 January 1864 he issued a drastic proclamation that held Rebel sympathizers responsible for guerrilla raids, but later he quarreled with General Stephen Gano Burbridge for excessive enforcement of the orders. Bramlette helped secure Burbridge's reassignment in early 1865, but his differences continued with Major General John M. Palmer.

Lincoln could not persuade Kentucky to accept some form of gradual compensated emancipation, but Bramlette saw that slavery was doomed. He recommended that the legislature ratify the Thirteenth Amendment, provided that adequate compensation was paid to owners of slaves. Both Houses rejected his advice.

After Lincoln's assassination, Bramlette set aside a day for state mourning and admitted in a public address that the president had been correct in his views. The Democrats carried the state elections easily in August 1865, and in December Bramlette eased the return of former Confederates by promising a general pardon to those indicted in state courts. He furiously opposed the introduction of the Freedmen's Bureau into the state. While the legislature conferred some civil rights upon the new freedmen, Bramlette successfully opposed ratification of the Fourteenth and Fifteenth Amendments. (In 1976 Kentucky ratified the Civil War Amendments.)

When he left office in 1867, Bramlette lauded the state's prosperity and called for an end to sectional hatred. By then Kentucky had become part of the solid Democratic South. Bramlette resumed his law practice in Louisville, where he was active in civic affairs. After a brief illness he died there on 12 January 1875.

—*Lowell H. Harrison*

See also Kentucky.
For further reading:
Basler, Roy P., ed. *The Collected Works of Abraham Lincoln* (1953–1955).
Clift, G. Glenn. *Governors of Kentucky, 1792–1942* (1942).
Coulter, E. Merton. *The Civil War and Readjustment in Kentucky* (1926).
Webb, Ross A. Thomas Elliott Bramlette. In *Kentucky's Governors, 1792–1985* (1985).

BRANCH, LAWRENCE O'BRYAN
(1820–1862)
Confederate general

Born to Joseph Branch and Susan Simpson O'Bryan Branch, Lawrence O'Bryan Branch was brought up by his uncle John Branch, who was governor of North Carolina. His wealthy uncle saw that Lawrence was well educated (for example, his tutor was future secretary of the treasury and chief justice of the Supreme Court Salmon P. Chase). Lawrence attended the University of North Carolina before transferring to Princeton, from which he graduated in 1838. He studied law and dabbled in journalism in Tennessee before moving to Florida. He fought briefly in the Second Seminole War and practiced law in Florida before moving back to North Carolina in 1848.

In North Carolina Branch managed his plantations and became active in railroad promotion in the state. He served for three years as the president of the Raleigh & Gaston Railroad and became active in the 1850s in North Carolina politics. An active Democrat, he was chosen as a Franklin Pierce elector in the election of 1852 and in 1854 was himself elected to the United States House of Representatives. He served in that body until the secession of North Carolina. He was considered to be a moderate supporter of states' rights but not an advocate of secession. He served on the Committee on Territories, where he advocated the distribution of moneys from the sale of public lands to the states. He strongly supported the policies of President James Buchanan but refused an appointment as secretary of the treasury upon Georgian Howell Cobb's resignation in January 1861. After the firing on Fort Sumter and the subsequent call by President Abraham Lincoln for Federal volunteers, Branch changed his views regarding North Carolina's secession and advocated the state's departure from the Union.

After North Carolina's seceded, Branch offered his services to the state as a private, but the governor appointed him the quartermaster and paymaster general of North Carolina. He resigned this position shortly, however, to accept a commission as the colonel of the 33d North Carolina Regiment. In November 1861 he was made a brigadier general in the Confederate army, commanding forces around New Bern, North Carolina. Upon the assault on this position in March 1862 by an overwhelming Federal force under Ambrose Burnside, Branch successfully led his men in retreat to the York Peninsula.

In June 1862 Branch was transferred to Stonewall Jackson's corps. He commanded a brigade of A. P. Hill's division, Jackson's corps at the battles of the Seven Days', Cedar Run, Second Bull Run, and Ox Hill before moving with his brigade as part of Robert E. Lee's first invasion of Northern territory in September 1862. As part of Jackson's corps, Branch led his men to Harper's Ferry and participated in the taking of that Union position before moving with Hill's division to Sharpsburg to link up with the remainder of Lee's army as it prepared for an assault by George McClellan. In the resulting battle of Antietam, Branch arrived late with the remainder of Hill's division, which had been left behind by Jackson to mop up in Harper's Ferry. Branch did not arrive on the battlefield until late in the day on 17 September 1862. Hill's arrival had caused a retreat by the Union left. Riding ahead of his men to exhort them to pursue more rapidly, Branch was shot in the head and killed instantly.

—*David S. Heidler and Jeanne T. Heidler*

See also Harper's Ferry; New Bern, Battle of.
For further reading:
Brawley, James S. "The Public and Military Career of Lawrence O'Bryan Branch" (Master's thesis, 1951).

BRANDY STATION, BATTLE OF
(9 June 1863)

The largest cavalry clash of the Civil War, the battle of Brandy Station took place as Robert E. Lee began to move his army north for the invasion of Pennsylvania in 1863. Although the battle was technically a Confederate victory, it demonstrated how much the Union cavalry had closed the gap against its Southern counterpart since the beginning of the war.

After his brilliant victory at Chancellorsville in May 1863, Lee began to plan another invasion of the North. By the end of the month, he began to draw his forces together near Culpeper for a march northward. Lee placed General J. E. B. Stuart and his formidable cavalry at Brandy Station, just east of Culpeper, to screen the rest of Lee's army as it began to head to the Blue Ridge Mountains on its way to Pennsylvania. On 5 June, Stuart staged a grand review to boost morale and show

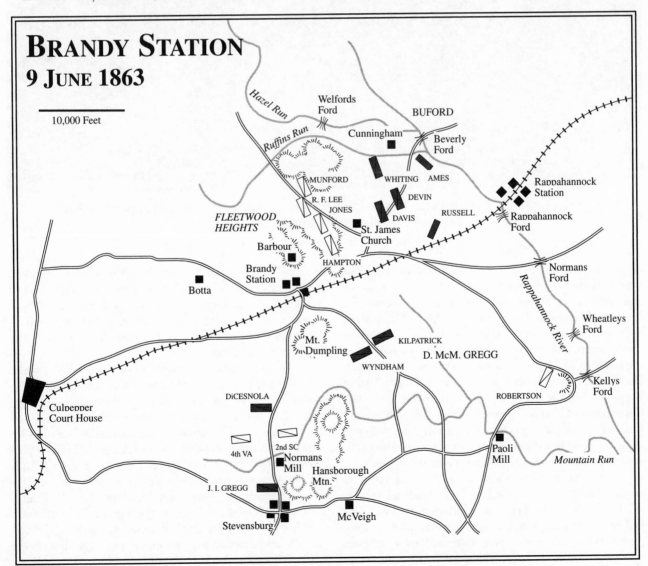

Unidentified woman with officers of the 1st Brigade, Horse Artillery, at their Brandy Station headquarters, February 1864
(*Library of Congress*)

off his dashing troops. Lee could not attend, so Stuart staged another review on 8 June.

Unknown to Stuart, uninvited guests had observed his second pompous display. General Alfred Pleasonton, with some 8,000 cavalry troops and 3,000 supporting infantrymen, lurked across the Rappahannock River. On the morning of 9 June, Pleasonton struck across the river. He formed his division into two wings. General John Buford's brigade crossed Beverly Ford on the Rappahannock, while General David Gregg breached Kelly's Ford six miles downstream later that day. Buford's troops opened the battle when they struck Confederate cavalry pickets in an early morning haze on 9 June.

Stuart's distracted troops were caught completely off guard. Buford's troops pressed on the Confederates under W. H. F. "Rooney" Lee, son of Robert E. Lee. The Federals nearly captured a light artillery unit as they pushed the Confederates away from the Rappahannock. Around 10:00 A.M., Wade Hampton finally counterat-

tacked for Stuart and turned back the Yankee offensive. Generals Rooney Lee and "Grumble" Jones also attacked Buford's forces from other sides. The battle surged back and forth around St. James Church. Buford began to concentrate on the Confederate left, around the Cunningham farm.

Around noon, the second part of Pleasonton's cavalry joined the attack. David Gregg's forces, delayed by the slow arrival of one division, stormed across Kelly's Ford around noon and came in directly behind the Confederates. The attack was potentially disastrous for Stuart's cavalry, and they were in danger of being routed by the upstart Union troopers. Gregg entered Brandy Station, sweeping Confederate pickets from his path. He was heading for Fleetwood Hill, just outside Brandy Station. This elevation was the key to the battlefield. Whoever controlled this hill possessed a great advantage.

A single heroic act may have saved the day for the Confederates. At the bottom of Fleetwood Hill sat

Rufus Ingalls and officers at the Army of the Potomac headquarters, Brandy Station, April 1864
(Photograph by Timothy O'Sullivan / *Library of Congress*)

Lieutenant John Carter with a six-pound cannon, left there for want of ammunition. Major Henry McClellan, Stuart's aide, frantically signaled Carter to bring the gun to the crest of Fleetwood Hill. Carter quickly unlimbered the gun and hauled it to the top of the hill where he packed it with bits of metal and substandard shells. There was enough powder for only one shot.

Meanwhile, Gregg was leading his troops towards Fleetwood Hill. As his forces began to ride up the hill, Carter fired the one blast his cannon had. It hit nothing, but it stopped the Yankees in their tracks. Colonel Percy Wyndham, the leader of the Federal column, suspected that the shot came from a line of guns set just over the top of the hill. He paused his men to wait for Gregg and the rest of the force. The ploy bought critical time for the Confederates. McClellan summoned part of Jones's brigade toward Fleetwood Hill. A frantic, hand-to-hand struggle for the hill ensued. The two sides literally charged through each other, and the summit of the hill changed hands numerous times.

Five miles south of Brandy Station yet another battle was raging. Colonel Alfred Duffié had split from Gregg's wing to cover the Union left flank. He encountered two regiments from Hampton's division and soundly defeated the rebels. Duffié then rode toward Brandy Station on a route that would have brought him directly into the Confederate rear. The move might have won the battle for the Union, but Duffié received an order to rejoin Gregg. This forced his men to backtrack several miles, and it effectively took them out of the action. They were the only division in Pleasonton's cavalry that could not embroider "Brandy Station" on its flag.

Back at Fleetwood Hill, the action continued. Buford's men, pinned down by the triple Confederate attack earlier, now surged ahead when the Confederates had to turn their attention toward Gregg's attack from

A canvas pontoon boat (50th New York Engineers) at Brandy Station, winter 1863–1864
(Photograph by Timothy O'Sullivan / *Library of Congress*)

the far right. This Union advance only fueled the chaos of the battle. The day saw many spectacular cavalry charges and saber fights as well as intense combat by dismounted troops. Fighting continued until the late afternoon, and the Confederates finally controlled Fleetwood Hill. Both sides were exhausted.

The Union cavalry evacuated the battlefield by the early evening after an intense ten-hour engagement. Because the Confederates held the field, Stuart could call it a victory. The Confederates inflicted some 935 casualties while sustaining 525. But most observers realized what had happened. The Union cavalry had surprised the Southerners and matched them blow for blow for the first time during the war. It removed the sense of inferiority that had haunted the Federal troopers in previous engagements. The huge psychological advantage that the Confederate cavalry had enjoyed throughout the war was lost in a single day. With a new sense of confidence, the Union cavalry fought well in succeeding battles. At Gettysburg, it fought Stuart's troops to a standstill as the Confederates tried to disrupt Union lines from the rear. Stuart's troops held Brandy Station, but were embarrassed by the tremendous difficulty they had in breaking even.

—*Richard D. Loosbrock*

See also Buford, John; Cavalry, C.S.A.; Cavalry, U.S.A.; Gregg, David M.; Hampton, Wade; Lee, William Henry Fitzhugh; Pleasonton, Alfred; Stuart, J. E. B.
For further reading:
Carter, Samuel, III. *The Last Cavaliers: Confederate and Union Cavalry in the Civil War* (1979).
Downey, Fairfax Davis. *Clash of Cavalry: The Battle of Brandy Station, June 9, 1863* (1959).
Nofi, Albert A. *The Gettysburg Campaign: June and July, 1863* (1986).

BRANNAN, JOHN MILTON
(1819–1892)
Union general

Born in Washington, D.C., John Milton Brannan as a teenager worked as a messenger in the House of Representatives. He became popular with the representatives and used his influence to secure an appointment to the U.S. Military Academy. He gradu-

John M. Brannan (*Library of Congress*)

ated twenty-third of fifty-two in the class of 1841. Commissioned a second lieutenant of artillery, Brannan served at several posts before the outbreak of the Mexican-American War. During that conflict, he was a member of the 1st Artillery and participated in Winfield Scott's Mexico City campaign. Brannan was wounded at Belen Gate and was brevetted to captain during the war.

After the Mexican-American War, Brannan served at a variety of frontier posts and fought briefly in Florida during the Third Seminole War. As tensions escalated between North and South in the early months of 1861, Brannan commanded Fort Taylor at Key West, Florida, as a captain of the 1st Artillery. He had only forty-four men at the post, and after Florida seceded in January 1861, he became increasingly concerned about secessionists trying to take the fort.

Brannan continued unmolested at the fort for the remainder of the year, during which he was made brigadier general of volunteers in September 1861. On 11 January 1862 the Department of Key West was created, which included all of Florida north from Key West to Cape Canaveral on the east coast and the Appalachicola River on the west coast. He remained in command there until August 1862, when he received command of the District of Beaufort, South Carolina.

On 3 September 1862, he received temporary command of the Department of the South headquartered at Hilton Head, South Carolina.

From Beaufort and the area around Hilton Head, Brannan organized an expedition down the coast at the end of September directed at St. John's Bluff near Jacksonville, Florida. A few weeks later, on 22–23 October, Brannan commanded an expedition against the plantations near Pocotaligo, South Carolina.

In the spring of 1863, Brannan was transferred to the Army of the Cumberland. He initially commanded the 1st Division of XXI Corps before being transferred to command the 3d Division of XIV Corps, commanded by Major General George Thomas. In this command he fought in the Tullahoma campaign and in September 1863 at Chickamauga.

At Chickamauga, the 3d, commanded by Brannan, engaged in one of the preliminary skirmishes with Nathan Bedford Forrest's cavalry on 19 September, and then on the 20th Brannan and the 3d Division served as one of the bulwarks of the defense of Horseshoe Ridge on the extreme left of Thomas's corps. Brannan retreated with the remainder of the corps in the late afternoon.

On 10 October 1863, Brannan was relieved of command of the 3d Division and became the chief of artillery for the Army of the Cumberland. He served in that capacity during the Chattanooga campaign and at Missionary Ridge. The following spring he became the chief of artillery for the Atlanta campaign. In all the engagements of that campaign through the surrender of the city, Brannan commanded the Union artillery.

With the commencement of William T. Sherman's March to the Sea, Brannan reverted to the command of the artillery for the Army of the Cumberland and returned to Tennessee, where for the remainder of the year he lent his expertise in combating John Bell Hood's campaign there.

After the war, Brannan returned to the rank of major in the 1st Artillery. For a short time after the war, Brannan commanded the Department of Georgia that included Fort Pulaski, the place of imprisonment for many high-ranking former Confederates. He was promoted to lieutenant colonel in 1877 and colonel in 1881. During his postwar service, he was stationed at a variety of posts in New York, Florida, and Pennsylvania. He retired in 1882 and died on 16 December 1892 in New York City.

—*David S. Heidler and Jeanne T. Heidler*

See also Atlanta Campaign; Chickamauga, Battle of; Florida; Jacksonville, Florida.
For further reading:
Bowers, John. *Chickamauga and Chattanooga; The Battles That Doomed the Confederacy* (1994).
Cozzens, Peter. *This Terrible Sound; The Battle of Chickamauga* (1992).

BRATTON, JOHN
(1831–1898)
Confederate general

General John Bratton of South Carolina was one of only a few men who enlisted in the Confederate army as a private, rose to the rank of brigadier general, and fought in both Eastern and Western theaters of action. Born in Winnsboro, South Carolina, to Dr. John Bratton and his second wife Isabella on 7 March 1831, the future general spent his formative years in the Palmetto State. As an adult John Bratton followed in his father's footsteps. He pursued a career in medicine. After graduating from South Carolina College in 1850 Bratton attended Charleston College for his medical training. He started his own practice in Winnsboro in 1853 and continued in that profession until the Civil War broke out in 1861.

When the Civil War started, John Bratton volunteered in Summerville, South Carolina, for twelve months. The doctor became a 30-year-old private in what later became the 6th South Carolina Infantry Regiment. On 25 June 1861, only twelve days after enlisting, Bratton was appointed second lieutenant. The 6th South Carolina moved in mid-July 1861 from Charleston to Richmond, Virginia. Arriving on 21 July, Bratton and his comrades marched immediately to the Manassas battlefield, which they reached in the afternoon of the battle. Although not engaged the sights of war impressed the new lieutenant. The regiment saw no action during the rest of 1861 and the end of the year found Bratton at Centreville, Virginia.

The next year was far more eventful for both the regiment and Bratton, starting with his appointment as colonel of the unit in April. He held the rank of colonel until promoted brigadier general in May 1864. In early 1862 the 6th South Carolina was part of General Richard H. Anderson's brigade of General James Longstreet's Second Division in the Army of Northern Virginia. Bratton commanded the regiment in the engagements at Williamsburg and Seven Pines, where he was wounded in the left arm and captured by Federal forces on 31 May 1862. Following his capture Colonel Bratton was transported to Fort Monroe, Virginia, where he stayed until exchanged on 31 August 1862. He rejoined the regiment in October.

Winter set in and Federal general Ambrose Burnside determined to launch a December attack on the Confederate army at Fredericksburg. Ostensibly part of General Micah Jenkins's brigade of General George Pickett's division in General James Longstreet's I Corps, Colonel Bratton's regiment was placed at various points in the Confederate line in the days leading up to the battle. The 6th South Carolina was in the center of Longstreet's corps for several days before being moved to the flank. Here it served to connect Longstreet's and General Thomas J. Jackson's corps. During the battle Bratton's men saw no action, which he described in a letter to his wife on 16 December: "We were not called upon to do anything but stand a little shelling, by which we lost one man wounded."

Though his participation in the battle of Fredericksburg was scant, John Bratton was recommended for promotion to brigadier general in January 1863. The recommendation came from General Micah Jenkins, passed through General Richard Anderson and General Longstreet before Robert E. Lee forwarded it to the Confederate War Department for approval. Unfortunately for Bratton there were no openings available, so the recommendation was denied.

In the fall of 1863 Bratton's 6th South Carolina, still in Micah Jenkins's Brigade, accompanied Longstreet's Corps to the West. General Jenkins's brigade did not arrive in time to fight in the battle of Chickamauga, however. During the battle General John B. Hood was seriously wounded and Longstreet put Jenkins in command of Hood's division. Colonel Bratton was then elevated to command Jenkins's Brigade. In this capacity Bratton led a night attack on Federal forces at Wauhatchie on 28–29 October, 1863. In this engagement Bratton had the 1st, 2d, 5th, and 6th South Carolina Regiments and Hampton's Legion at his disposal. Opposing him were the 109th and 111th Pennsylvania Regiments along with the 137th and 149th New York Regiments, commanded by General John W. Geary. After a fight of several hours the Confederates were forced to withdraw, and Bratton reported 356 casualties.

Colonel Bratton returned to Virginia when General Longstreet was ordered to rejoin General Lee's army. When Micah Jenkins was killed on 6 May 1864 during the battle of the Wilderness, Bratton was promoted to brigadier general. He led the brigade through the rest of the war, suffering a shoulder wound in October 1864. At Appomattox, Bratton's brigade was the largest in the Army of Northern Virginia, numbering about 1,500 effectives.

Following the war John Bratton entered politics. In 1866 he was elected to the South Carolina state legislature and served one term. Ten years later he chaired the South Carolina delegation that attended the Democratic National Convention. In 1884 Bratton was elected to the U.S. House of Representatives and served one term. His final act in South Carolina politics was his defeat in the gubernatorial election in 1890 at the hands of Ben "Pitchfork" Tillman. General John Bratton died on 12 January 1898 in Winnsboro, South Carolina, and is buried there.

—*Christopher C. Meyers*

See also Wauhatchie, Battle of.

For further reading:
Bratton, John. Letters. Southern Historical Society Collection, University of North Carolina at Chapel Hill.
Freeman, Douglas Southall. *Lee's Lieutenants: A Study in Command* (1942–1944).
Pickenpaugh, Roger. *Rescue By Rail: Troop Transfer and the Civil War in the West, 1863* (1998).

BRECKINRIDGE, JOHN CABELL
(1821–1875)

Confederate general and secretary of war

Born on 16 January 1821, near Lexington, Kentucky, John Cabell Breckinridge grew to maturity in a family that expected greatness. The only son of the six children of Mary Clay Smith and Joseph Cabell Breckinridge, he learned early that his paternal grandfather had been a U.S. senator and attorney general under Thomas Jefferson and was the man who in the 1790s introduced the Kentucky Resolutions stressing states' rights. Breckinridge's father died when the boy was only two, but in his thirty-five years had been speaker of the Kentucky House and then the commonwealth's secretary of state. John's grandfather, on his mother's side, had been president of the College of New Jersey at Princeton and had married a daughter of a signer of the Declaration of Independence. When John C. Breckinridge attended Centre College, where he received his degree in 1838, his brother-in-law served as the school's president. Breckinridge's favorite uncle held the Presbyterian Church's highest national office and won accolades as the father of the public school system in Kentucky. In short, almost everywhere young John turned, he had powerful examples of family achievement, models of leadership, and useful supporting allies.

A college graduate before the age of eighteen, Breckinridge spent part of a year as a resident graduate at Princeton and then enrolled in legal classes at Transylvania University, where he received his law degree in 1841. He moved to Iowa to practice his profession, but in two years returned to his home state and married Mary Cyrene Burch in December 1843. That happy union produced six children over the next decade. His wife's family ties added to Breckinridge's network and included cousin George W. Johnson, later the first governor of Confederate Kentucky.

In June 1847, as a young attorney Breckinridge gave an eloquent and powerful speech concerning the Mexican-American War, then raging. Soon the handsome, witty, charming, and charismatic Breckinridge won wide acclaim. He followed that with service in the conflict, as a major, but saw no real action in Mexico. However, the experience did give him insight into battle and war, and the costs.

Returning to Kentucky after the war, Breckinridge soon entered the political world and was repeatedly successful. Although his closest influences had been Whig, he soon joined the Democratic Party, as part of its Young America. At age twenty-eight, he won a seat in the Kentucky legislature; in 1851, at age thirty, he went to the United States House Representatives and won reelection by defeating a former Kentucky governor. In 1856, he ran for national office as the vice presidential candidate with James Buchanan, and on election became the youngest in the nation's history to serve in that position. Before the unhappy term ended, the state legislature selected him to be U.S. senator, beginning in March 1861.

But the presidency beckoned as well before then. During the 1850s, Breckinridge had fashioned a political philosophy based on a belief in a limited government with a strict interpretation of the Constitution. Regarding slavery, for instance, though he held a few slaves at various times, he apparently did not by 1860, and yet he defended the institution, supported the *Dred Scott* decision, and argued for the constitutional right to hold slaves as property. But he remained far removed from the fire-eating secessionists. That moderate stance brought him the presidential nomination for the Southern Democrats in 1860, after the Northern branch selected Stephen A. Douglas. With John Bell leading the Constitutional Unionists, and Abraham Lincoln (whose wife Breckinridge had known back in Lexington) heading the Republicans, Breckinridge found himself in a four-candidate race. Viewed in the North as the slaveholder's candidate, Breckinridge tried to show his moderation and wide appeal, but found only limited success. His support indicated, in fact, that his greatest allies in the South came from rural Democratic areas more than from slaveholding ones. But in 1861, as vice president, he had the duty to announce Lincoln elected with 170 electoral votes to his own 72, with Bell and Douglas dividing the other 51. At age forty, Breckinridge had suffered his first and only political defeat.

As a senator, Breckinridge followed a somewhat strange course over the next months. He stressed the right of secession, saw state after Southern state leave the Union, and watched as Kentucky declared neutrality. Had he joined the Confederacy early, he might have been an important figure in its political circles. Breckinridge had widespread appeal and support. As it was, he remained in Washington, attacked the Republicans for what he stressed were their unconstitutional actions, and called for a peaceful separation. But as the fighting continued, his obvious Southern sympathies became evident, and politicians termed him a traitor in their midst. Throwing off neutrality, Kentucky declared itself Union in September 1861. That same month, fearing arrest, Breckinridge left the commonwealth and joined the Confederate army: "I exchange, with proud satisfaction, a term of six years in the Senate of the United States for the musket of a soldier." The most prominent Kentuckian to fight for the South, he would not be able to return to his native state for more than seven years.

Made a brigadier general in November 1861, despite his lack of combat experience and West Point training, Breckinridge first led what became known as the famous Orphan Brigade. While never a military strategist, he did prove a successful general overall. Displaying some of the characteristics that made people follow him in politics, Breckinridge seemed a natural leader. He showed courage and coolness during battles, inspired the troops at key times, and impressed them as a man who cared. And he did. A humane person, Breckinridge never became reconciled to the killing that war brought.

During the conflict, Breckinridge served as a subordinate commander in six major battles—Shiloh, Stone's River, Chickamauga, Chattanooga, Cold Harbor, and Winchester—and as an independent commander at Port Hudson and in southwest Virginia and the Shenandoah Valley. In his first major battle, as a division commander at Shiloh in April 1862, he made mistakes, as did so many officers leading large numbers of soldiers in battles beyond the scope of anything they had seen. His unit, however, did fight well, with terrible losses—368 killed, 1,682 wounded, 165 missing, a total of 34.7 percent of the force.

Promoted to major general after that fight, Breckinridge led troops toward Baton Rouge in an attempt to retake the city. Despite malaria and heat prostration, his men drove the Union troops back, but gunboats prevented further advances. He did occupy Port Hudson, which would remain a key Confederate post after that. That attack took Breckinridge away from the army, now led by Braxton Bragg, that invaded Kentucky in the fall of 1862. Ordered to join that campaign, he learned of the defeat at Perryville before reentering Kentucky. Disappointed, some thirty-miles from his home state, he turned back.

A long conflict then began between Breckinridge and Bragg. The commanding general blamed the Kentuckian for not having joined him sooner; the popular Breckinridge had little regard for Bragg as a leader, or man. When Bragg ordered the execution of a Kentuckian deserter who had gone home to help his starving family and had been retaken as he returned to the army, Breckinridge had protested in vain and had grown physically ill at the killing. Soon those disagreements grew.

At Stones River in December 1862 and January 1863, Breckinridge did not initially move his unit into place, as per General Bragg's plan, as quickly as he should have.

Nor did others. In an attempt to break Union lines, Bragg then ordered Breckinridge to attack a well-defended Federal position. Anticipating huge losses in an assault that few thought could succeed, the Kentuckian vehemently protested, but carried out the orders. The bloody repulse had the expected effect and Breckinridge saw many of his men, and personal friends, die. Bragg's report, critical of Breckinridge's role in the battle, brought Breckinridge to request a court of inquiry, but none resulted.

In the battle of Chickamauga in September 1863, Breckinridge's division fought well, suffered losses of nearly a third of the unit, and contributed to the Confederate victory. However, two months later as a corps commander at Chattanooga, Breckinridge was ordered to send a portion of his troops to another part of the battlefield and his thinned ranks proved little match for the sizable Union forces before him. That battle ended Bragg's career in the West, but, as usual, he blamed others for the defeat, particularly Breckinridge, charging him with drunkenness. As William C. Davis and other authors have noted, although Breckinridge certainly enjoyed one of Kentucky's best-known products, the charges of overindulgence do not withstand scrutiny and are not supported by others.

After several months of leave in late 1863 and early 1864, Breckinridge became commander of the almost forgotten Western Department of Virginia theater. There he generally did well under difficult circumstances. His worst moment of the war may have come in October 1864 at the battle of Saltville, where—without his knowledge—Confederates began massacring the African-American Union soldiers they encountered. By the time he ordered that to end, the worst of the military murders had already occurred. On the other hand, his victory at the battle of New Market in May 1864 had been his finest day as a general. Outnumbered and forced to use the Virginia Military Institute cadets from his reserves, Breckinridge handled his artillery well, made hard decisions, and won a complete victory, inflicting considerable Union losses. Confederates praised him as a "New Jackson in the Valley." Transferred to the east, his division fought at Cold Harbor in June, and then he joined Jubal Early in his advance on Washington. Breckinridge got close enough to see the Capitol dome, then a retreat followed. The ensuing battle of Winchester proved to be his last military battle.

On 6 February 1865, Confederate president Jefferson Davis made Breckinridge the last, as it turned out, Confederate secretary of war. Breckinridge's efforts in that office showed the strengths that he might have brought to the government had he been made a part of it earlier. Confident enough to challenge Davis, Breckinridge operated as a powerful secretary, relieving General Lucius Northrop as commissary general, devising a better supply plan, advising on strategy, and working closely with General Robert E. Lee. But by then, the cause was lost and within months the armies were surrendering.

Breckinridge supervised the evacuation of Richmond, advised General Joseph E. Johnston regarding his negotiations with General William T. Sherman, and, perhaps most important, presented President Davis with his thoughts on how to proceed. As debate raged on whether to continue to fight, in some guerrilla-type warfare, the secretary of war advanced arguments made earlier, that the Confederacy "should not disband like bandits" but rather should surrender with dignity and respect: "this had been a magnificent epic; in God's name, let it not terminate in a farce." Breckinridge realized the reality—the war was over and the killing should stop. For him personally, however, flight was his future. Fearing arrest as a traitor, Breckinridge made a tortuous and somewhat heroic escape through Florida, to Cuba, and then to Europe. Over the next few years, he remained in exile, traveling, waiting. Then, with a pardon from the president, Breckinridge and his family returned to the United States, arriving back in Lexington in March 1869.

Over the next six years, Breckinridge served as a defense and corporate attorney, as well as president of both a railroad company and an insurance company. In one of his few public stances, he denounced the Ku Klux Klan and supported the admission of black testimony in the courts. On 17 May 1875, at the age of fifty-four, John Cabell Breckinridge died. Although he had achieved in many different areas, the war had dictated that his bright promise remained not fully realized.

—*James C. Klotter*

See also Early's Washington Raid; Election of 1860; Kentucky; New Market, Battle of; Orphan Brigade.

For further reading:

Davis, William C. *Breckinridge: Statesman, Soldier, Symbol* (1974).

Heck, Frank H. *Proud Kentuckian: John C. Breckinridge, 1821–1875* (1976).

Klotter, James C. *The Breckinridges of Kentucky, 1760–1981* (1986).

BRECKINRIDGE, ROBERT JEFFERSON
(1800–1871)

Presbyterian minister and abolitionist

Born on 8 March 1800, Robert J. Breckinridge was the son of Mary Breckinridge and John Breckinridge, the legislator who in 1798 introduced what came be known as the Kentucky Resolutions. Robert attended Princeton and Yale and graduated from Union College in New York in 1819. In 1823 he married his cousin, Ann Sophonisba Preston,

with whom he would have eleven children. By 1825, Breckinridge had began his life's work as a Kentucky politician-farmer. When his wife died, he married another cousin, the widow Virginia Hart Shelby, and they had three more children.

In 1832 Breckinridge was ordained in the Presbyterian Church and served in Baltimore, Maryland, and Lexington, Kentucky. After a stormy year as president of Jefferson College in Pennsylvania, he returned to Kentucky, where he took the appointment of superintendent of public instruction. Under his reforms, Kentucky school attendance increased almost tenfold in four years. He found his niche as a professor at Danville Theological Seminary in Kentucky, where he published his two largest theological works.

Breckinridge was an active stump speaker, never hesitating to support his controversial stances on compensated emancipation and colonization, Know-Nothingism, and Unionism. He led the drive for the 1833 Non-Importation Law, which limited the number of slaves imported into Kentucky. In the 1840s he went from Clay Whiggism to the American Party, where he complained about the effects of immigrants and the Catholic faith on the morals of native white Americans. He helped form the Friends of Emancipation, a society whose members promised to free their slaves' children when the children reached the age of twenty-one.

On the steps of the courthouse in Lexington, Kentucky, on 4 January 1861, Breckinridge gave a powerful speech, "The Day of National Humiliation," which verbalized the Unionist beliefs of many in the border states. On 4 July of that year, his eldest son, Robert Jr., led the Ashland Rifles out of Lexington to form the first organized Kentucky volunteers for the C.S.A. A few months later, his nephew, John C. Breckinridge, former vice president of the United States, left to become a Confederate brigadier general. A year later his second son, Willie, left to join the South, as did two sons-in-law. Two of his youngest sons and three other sons-in-law joined the U.S. Army, thus exemplifying the horrors of "the Brothers' War."

When President Abraham Lincoln issued his Preliminary Emancipation Proclamation in 1862, Breckinridge objected strenuously. He believed it unconstitutional and even immoral, but most importantly, it undermined the Unionist cause in Kentucky that he espoused. The president's decision to use African-American troops Breckinridge saw as even more dangerous. However, upon the threat of Kentucky governor Thomas E. Bramlette's issuing a nullification proclamation of the federal draft of African-Americans, Breckinridge led a caucus that persuaded the governor to issue a more moderate message to Kentuckians and to persuade them to accept the U.S. recruiting efforts. Ultimately, even though the

Emancipation Proclamation never affected Kentucky, more than 23,000 black Kentuckians earned their freedom by joining the Union forces.

Though committed to public support for the Union, Breckinridge continued in his role as a slave owner. In July 1864 he went to the Federal headquarters at Camp Nelson, Kentucky, and demanded that General Speed Fry return to him seventeen women and children who had run away from his farm to join their male relatives stationed at the camp.

That summer, as Kentucky's Union Democratic Party split, Breckinridge led those who were "Unconditional Unionists." He stumped across the state, openly opposing such conservative Union Democrats as Governor Bramlette, Lieutenant Governor Richard Jacob, and *Louisville Journal* editor George Prentice. Unconditional Unionist delegates chose Breckinridge to represent them at the 1864 Baltimore convention, where he served as temporary chairman. The Kentucky delegation then called upon President Lincoln, who had just been renominated, and, with Breckinridge as their spokesperson, they protested especially against the military power of Governor Bramlette and also against the draft in Kentucky for home defense.

Between 20 and 25 July 1864, the Unconditional Unionists gave to the military the names of their political competitors to be arrested for treason and thereby secured their own election. In early October, over the course of two weeks while convalescing after a fall from his horse, Breckinridge met with elite groups of Unionists, including the military commander of Kentucky, General Stephen G. Burbridge. These meetings became widely known, and Breckinridge was labeled as the leader of a "Secret Inquisition." According to a Kentucky newspaper, Burbridge's local advisors used him "as a mere instrument to satiate their own cravings for human blood."

As the war drew to a close, Breckinridge feared the continued vigilantism and guerrilla warfare. By 1865 he reversed his position on black troops and advocated stationing more blacks in the state. This stance, along with his past association with the hated General Burbridge and President Lincoln, made him extremely unpopular.

The Union lost Kentucky after the Civil War. Breckinridge watched in dismay as the various parts of the Republican platform were rejected. He envisioned doom and destruction for his state and nation. He could not even halt the split in the Kentucky Synod of the Presbyterian Church in 1866.

Breckinridge's second wife had died in 1859, and at the age of sixty-eight Breckinridge married the young widow Margaret Faulkner White in 1868. He resigned from the Danville Theological Seminary as a result of ill health in October 1869, and he died two years later on 27 December 1871.

—*Randolph Hollingsworth*

See also Kentucky.
For further reading:
Collins, Lewis. *Collins' Historical Sketches of Kentucky: History of Kentucky* (1874; reprint, 1966).
Gilliam, William D., Jr. "Robert J. Breckinridge." *Register of the Kentucky Historical Society* (1971).
Howard, Victor B. *Black Liberation in Kentucky: Emancipation and Freedom, 1862–1884* (1983).
Kelley, Ruth E. "Robert Jefferson Breckinridge: His Political Influence and Leadership during 1849 and the Civil War" (M.A. thesis, 1948).
Klotter, James C. *The Breckinridges of Kentucky, 1760–1981* (1986).

BRENTWOOD, TENNESSEE
(25 March 1863)

As Ulysses S. Grant commenced plans to move on Vicksburg during early 1863, farther to the east Union and Confederate forces clashed around Nashville and the outlying region. South of Nashville, about halfway to Franklin, Lieutenant Colonel Edward Bloodgood guarded the Harpeth River Bridge of the Nashville & Columbia Railroad. Bloodgood had about 520 men of the 22nd Wisconsin Infantry camped to protect the forks of the Wilson and Franklin pikes as well as a nearby rail facility. He had placed 230 men of the 19th Michigan Infantry under Captain E. B. Bassett at a stockade a mile and a half south of Brentwood near the railroad bridge. Nathan Bedford Forrest moved upon this place early on 25 March to capture the garrison and its supplies, as well as destroy the Harpeth River Bridge.

Forrest intended to reduce both the stockade and Brentwood simultaneously by sending Colonel James W. Starnes's 2d Brigade to cross the Harpeth six miles east of Franklin. Starnes was to cut the telegraph and tear up the railroad before moving on the stockade. Meanwhile, Forrest would accompany Brigadier General Frank C. Armstrong's 1st Brigade with the 10th Tennessee Cavalry attached to assail Bloodgood at Brentwood.

Everything got underway before dawn on 25 March, and brushes with Union pickets over a wide area alerted the Federals that something was afoot. Telegraphed warnings to Bloodgood, however, were blocked when the Confederates cut the wires. Bloodgood would not know about the large force bearing down on him until it arrived. Forrest was having his own troubles. He had difficulty getting his artillery across the Harpeth and consequently was late in arriving at Brentwood. Alone near the stockade and increasingly bewildered about what might have gone wrong, Starnes finally moved around to the Hillsborough Pike. News of Starnes's presence had been enough, however, to convince Bloodgood that the stockade was under attack and the bridge was being wrecked. He tried to advance to help Bassett, but he promptly ran into Forrest who had finally arrived. It was now between 7 and 8 A.M. Forrest had posted a squadron of the 10th Tennessee to watch his rear and another to cut any Federal retreat toward Nashville, while watching out for Federal reinforcements from that direction. He then took ten companies of the 10th to the right while Armstrong took his brigade and the artillery to the left.

Bloodgood's desperation was not alleviated when he discovered his telegraph dead. He tried to send couriers for help, but only one got out, and Forrest captured him. Soon Bloodgood had a note demanding his surrender, to which he replied that Forrest would have to come in and get him. It was an empty boast, of course—the Confederate force outnumbered his ten to one—but he hoped that a little time would allow him to get away toward Nashville. Bloodgood did not have even a little time, however. Six companies of the 10th Tennessee had already dismounted to begin the attack when Bloodgood found that the road to Nashville was blocked. He surrendered. It had all taken about half an hour.

While the business went on of gathering up prisoners and materiel and destroying what they could not carry, Forrest swung south with the 4th Mississippi Cavalry, 10th Tennessee Cavalry, and artillery to finish the job at the stockade on the Harpeth. It was even shorter work. One round from the Confederate artillery convinced Bassett to capitulate. Forrest counted more than 200 prisoners from the stockade including eleven wagons and three ambulances. He demolished the railroad bridge, destroyed what he could not carry, and moved away with what he could toward Hillsborough. For good and precautionary measure, he hurled skirmishers toward Nashville to drive in pickets there to within three miles of the city.

By now the Federal command was alert to what was going on. Gordon Granger sent Brigadier General Green Clay Smith with about 700 troopers of the 2d Michigan, 9th Pennsylvania, 4th Kentucky, and 6th Kentucky to relieve Brentwood. Arriving early in the afternoon, Smith found the smoldering wreckage that always marked a finished Forrest project. The Federal cavalry was game, though, so Smith rode in hard pursuit of the scattered Confederates lumbering off to the west laden with their prisoners, wagons, and mules. He found the rear of them three and a half miles outside of Brentwood. It was Starnes, and suddenly there was a nasty little fight as Smith's troopers fell upon him with a will. Starnes was driven back about six miles, abandoning wagons, mules, and supplies along the way, before making a stand near the Little Harpeth River. Forrest reappeared to move on Smith's left while Brigadier General John A. Wharton's cavalry brigade circled to the right. All the Yankees could do was fall back to Brentwood. They had reclaimed some men and materiel, but Forrest was free to proceed toward Spring Hill, while most of his 700 prisoners, still in hand, were escorted to Columbia.

The cavalry action on the Little Harpeth provided something for the Federals to praise in an otherwise discouraging episode. For their part, Bloodgood and Bassett came under harsh criticism for what was regarded as their unseemly haste in surrendering. Granger noted that had these "milk and water soldiers" held out for even an hour, Union cavalry might have arrived in time to cut up Forrest.

—David S. Heidler and Jeanne T. Heidler

For further reading:
Fulcher, Richard Carlton. Brentwood, Tennessee: The Civil War Years (1993).

BREVET RANK

Brevet rank was usually an honorary rank awarded to an officer for valor in battle or for meritorious service. The tradition of brevet rank began in the British army before the Revolutionary War, and this tradition was continued in the U.S. Army. In the years after the Revolutionary War, Congress wrote legislation that specified the circumstances under which brevet ranks could be awarded and defined the actual amount of authority that brevet ranks gave to the awardee. In general, brevet ranks were higher than the individual's official rank, but held none of the authority or the pay of that higher rank.

The Civil War created a situation in which the awarding of brevet ranks became very commonplace. More than 1,700 officers and at least one enlisted man were awarded brevet ranks during the war, the majority of these ranks being awarded at the end of the war as a gesture of thanks. Unfortunately, the awarding of brevet ranks became so commonplace and overused that it was often difficult to determine the legitimate rank of an officer. An officer could simultaneously hold a state militia rank, a rank in the U.S. Volunteers, a rank in the U.S. Army, and a brevet rank. Though the regulations of the Confederate army provided for the awarding of brevet ranks, there is no evidence of a brevet rank ever being awarded.

After the Civil War, the awarding of brevet ranks became less and less common, though several were awarded during the Spanish-American War. The last brevet rank to be awarded by the United States was given to Tasker H. Bliss in 1918. Bliss, who held the rank of lieutenant general in the U.S. Army, was awarded the brevet rank of full general in order for him to be considered an equal of the European delegates at the Paris Peace Conference.

—Alexander M. Bielakowski

For further reading:
Boatner, Mark Mayo III. Army Lore and the Customs of the Service (1954).
———. Military Customs and Traditions (1956).

BRICE'S CROSS ROADS/GUNTOWN, BATTLE OF
(10 June 1864)

On 10 June 1864, Confederate forces under Major General Nathan Bedford Forrest routed a numerically superior Union force commanded by Brigadier General Samuel D. Sturgis at the northeastern Mississippi battle of Brice's Cross Roads (also known as Guntown and Tishomingo Creek). Although the Union's goal of preventing Forrest from disrupting General William Tecumseh Sherman's supply line in middle Tennessee was achieved, the battle also stands as the foremost victory in Forrest's notorious career. Confederate forces inflicted heavy casualties and captured sixteen pieces of artillery and significant supplies.

As Sherman moved into northern Georgia, he grew increasingly concerned about the vulnerability of his supply and communication lines in middle Tennessee. In late May 1864, Sherman instructed Union forces in Memphis to hunt down and defeat Forrest's cavalry. Major General Cadwallader C. Washburn, Union commander at Memphis, planned and organized an effort to carry out an attack 100 or more miles into northern Mississippi. At the heart of this plan was chief of cavalry General Sturgis. Sturgis's force included three brigades of infantry led by Colonel William L. McMillen totalling 5,000 men, two brigades of cavalry commanded by Brigadier General Benjamin H. Grierson totalling 3,300 troops, twenty-two pieces of artillery, and 250 wagons loaded with three weeks of food and ammunition. An African-American division held additional motivation to punish Forrest. The 55th and 59th U.S. Colored Troops had pledged to revenge Forrest's horrific and cowardly massacre of several dozen black soldiers after they had surrendered at Fort Pillow, Tennessee, only eight weeks before. Union troops departed Memphis on 1 June and immediately encountered the first of seven days of rain storms and the start of many miles of muddy roads. Progress was slow and exhausting. In one week, Sturgis had covered only fifty miles as they arrived at the small town of Ripley.

Sherman was correct in anticipating Forrest's intention of attacking middle Tennessee. Forrest was camped at the Tennessee River in northern Alabama preparing for such an assault. He quickly returned to Mississippi when he received word of Sturgis's move into Mississippi. Forrest positioned his 4,800 men along the Mobile & Ohio Railroad so that he could respond to a Union advance on either Corinth or Tupelo. On 8 June, when he received a report that Sturgis was advancing toward Tupelo, Forrest selected the spot for the field of fight to be at the intersection of two roads, a place known to locals as Brice's Cross Roads. The narrow road (muddy from heavy rain), dense woods, and thick brush was just the terrain Forrest needed to execute his aggressive plan. His strategy called for fighting the numerically superior Union forces in two phases. The Union cavalry, moving ahead of the infantry, would be destroyed first. As fighting broke out, Union infantry would rush in the June heat to the battle, arrive exhausted, and be an easy target for Confederates. Forrest and his men executed this plan to perfection.

At 5:30 A.M. Grierson's 3,300 cavalry troopers rode out of camp and advanced southeastward along Ripley Road. An hour and a half later, Colonel William L. McMillen and 5,000 soldiers followed. By 10:00 A.M. fighting between dismounted cavalry units had begun. In heavy fighting, the outnumbered rebels charged several times, and on each occasion they were repulsed. The intense June heat became a factor as Federal cavalry were near collapse and Union infantry arrived exhausted from their five-mile race to join the fight. The battle was unfolding according to Forrest's plan.

After a brief lull in fighting, Forrest organized his men for a series of coordinated assaults. At 1:30 P.M., Colonel Tyree H. Bell's 2,800 men hit the Union right. Yankee soldiers halted this attack and mounted a brief counterattack. The next rebel advance, this time on the Union left, was stopped as well. The fight was now six hours old, when Forrest sent his right, his left, and a small group at the Union rear, forward at once. This massive assault crushed Union lines and brought a complete collapse. The Union retreat quickly became a scene of chaos and slaughter as overturned wagons clogged the escape route and Confederate cannons took aim at the panicked mob. Led primarily by black Union troops, a brief, but spirited attempt to hold off Forrest's advance failed, and Union soldiers rushed desperately from advancing rebels.

The Confederate pursuit continued into the night and the next day. Greatly fatigued and embarrassed, Union forces reached the safety of Memphis on 13 June. A tally sheet provides clear evidence of the magnitude of Forrest's victory. Federal losses included 223 killed, 394 wounded, 1,623 captured, 16 pieces of artillery, 176 wagons, and a significant amount of ammunition and arms. Forrest's loses were 96 killed and 396 wounded. After the battle of Brice's Cross Roads, Union frustration with its inability to destroy General Forrest grew. In August 1864, an even larger Union force under General Andrew J. Smith failed to defeat the illusive target. But Forrest was never able to slow Sherman's advance through Georgia with a successful attack on his Tennessee supply lines.

—*Bruce D. Mactavish*

See also Forrest, Nathan Bedford; Sturgis, Samuel Davis; United States Colored Troops.

For further reading:
Bearss, Edwin C. *Forrest at Brice's Cross Roads and in North Mississippi in 1864* (1979).
Wills, Brian Steel. *A Battle from the Start: The Life of Nathan Bedford Forrest* (1992).

BRIGHT, JESSE DAVID
(1812–1875)
U.S. senator

Born to David Graham Bright and Rachel Bright in Norwich, New York, Jesse David Bright moved to Madison, Indiana, with his family when he was a small child. He was educated locally in New York and Indiana. As a young man, he became active in Indiana Democratic politics. He rose quickly in state party circles, serving first as a probate judge, then as a marshal of the district court and as a state senator, and then as lieutenant governor by the age of thirty-one. His wide political experience at such a young age gave him a great deal of influence over the pro-Southern wing of the Indiana Democratic Party. This influence brought him election in 1845 by the state legislature as U.S. senator from Indiana. During Bright's time in the Senate, he purchased a farm in Kentucky and owned a few slaves who worked on that farm.

In the U.S. Senate, Bright was a strong proponent of national expansion and accommodation of Southern concerns regarding the territories. He also used the organization skills he had honed in Indiana politics, using patronage and other methods, to build a large bloc of support. He quickly became a powerful member of the Senate. In 1850 he served on the committee that drew up the proposals that would become the Compromise of 1850, and in 1854 he was a very influential supporter of the Kansas-Nebraska Bill. During the maneuvering before the Democratic National Convention in 1856, Bright became a strong supporter of the candidacy of James Buchanan and worked with a number of other prominent Democrats to secure Buchanan's nomination and then election. Bright was naturally a strong supporter of the administration and opponent of the Stephen Douglas faction of the Democratic Party on such issues as the Lecompton Constitution for Kansas. Douglas's break with Buchanan on this issue caused the president's supporters such as Bright to begin planning early to block Douglas's nomination for the presidency in 1860.

The Democratic Convention in Charleston promised to be the most contentious in party history, and Bright and other Buchanan administration operatives certainly contributed to the acrimony by doing everything within their power to block the nomination of Stephen Douglas. This combination with opposition to Douglas of most Southern delegations succeeded in blocking the Little Giant's nomination in Charleston and forced the convention to Baltimore, where it became irreparably divided.

With the election of Abraham Lincoln in the fall of 1860 and the subsequent secession of the lower South, Bright became a part of the Democratic opposition to the Lincoln administration in Congress. Over the years, Bright's rather highhanded political maneuvering and obvious sympathy for the South had offended many of his colleagues in the Senate. In the spring of 1861, those enemies found the ammunition they needed to attack Bright's loyalty to the Union. In March, Bright wrote a letter of introduction for an acquaintance who was traveling to Montgomery, Alabama. The letter was addressed to Jefferson Davis and referred to Davis as the president of the Confederated States. To Bright's enemies, this form of address in effect recognized the legitimacy of Davis's title. As a Kentucky slave owner and strong supporter of the previous administration, Bright's loyalty was already suspect, but this action proved to be too much for some of the other senators.

Over the summer and fall of 1861, this opposition to Bright became organized and in early 1862 brought charges against Bright in the Senate with the goal of bringing about his expulsion. Bright tried to defend himself by arguing that the letter had been written before a war had erupted, but after almost three weeks of debate, the Senate voted on 5 February, 32 to 14 to expel Bright from the Senate. His expulsion was attributed by many to the fact that he had made so many political enemies among Republicans and some Democrats. Some War Democrats, though, fretted that the action might embolden Republicans to take similar actions against other Democrats.

Two days before Bright was expelled from the Senate, Lincoln administration special security agent Lafayette Baker wrote to Secretary of State William Henry Seward suggesting that Bright would probably move to the Confederacy after his expulsion and that he should probably be arrested before he could leave. Seward refused to act on the suggestion. Upon his return home, Bright tried to secure reelection, but even to most Indiana Democrats he had become too much of a political liability. After sixteen years in the U.S. Senate and as one of the nation's leading behind-the-scenes political operatives, Bright went to his farm in Kentucky in disgrace. He lived there quietly until after the war, when he again entered public life.

Bright remained in Kentucky after the war, returning briefly to politics as a member of the Kentucky state legislature. He also became active in Kentucky business activities including the growing coal mining industry there. In the last year of his life he moved to Baltimore, Maryland, where he died on 20 May 1875.

—*David S. Heidler and Jeanne T. Heidler*

See also Congress, U.S.A.; Democratic Party; Election of 1860.

For further reading:
Smith, Vickey Dee. "The Expulsion of Jesse D. Bright from the United States Senate" (M.A. thesis, 1974).

Thornbrough, Emma Lou. *Indiana in the Civil War Era, 1850–1880* (1965).

Van Der Weele, Wayne J. "Jesse David Bright: Master Politician from the Old Northwest" (Ph.D. dissertation, 1958).

BRIGHT, JOHN
(1811–1889)
British statesmen

The most prominent of Britain's parliamentary radicals, John Bright waged a public battle against British intervention in the American Civil War. Linking the abolition of slavery to the rights of labor in this public campaign, he sought to mobilize British working-class support for the North. Although historians continue to debate whether he succeeded in this respect, Bright's campaign seems to have forged an alliance between radicalism and trade union leaders that proved highly significant for British politics after the Civil War.

Born at Rochdale in Lancashire on 16 November 1811, John was the second child of Jacob Bright, a cotton mill owner, and Martha Wood. As a Quaker, John obtained his education at a variety of schools associated with the Society of Friends in Lancashire and Yorkshire. His education completed by 1827, John assisted his father in overseeing the family cotton mill business.

Bright first entered local politics in the 1830s, when he became involved in a dispute that started when Dissenters in Rochdale sought to prevent the Church of England from imposing a compulsory rate on the town. Bright took a leading role in opposing the rate and achieved some local prominence. Shortly thereafter, he joined the Anti-Corn Law League, which sought to abolish the tariffs that protected domestic agriculture. Bright's activities on behalf of the League, a powerful pressure group, made him a household name throughout Britain and associated him with Richard Cobden, with whom he would form a long-lasting political partnership.

In 1847, a year after the repeal of the Corn Laws, Bright won a seat in the House of Commons representing Manchester. Associated with the parliamentary radicals in the Commons, he pushed for free trade, reductions in public expenditures, extension of suffrage, and a less aggressive foreign policy. He vigorously opposed the Crimean War, a stance that cost him a great deal of popularity. In the late 1850s he launched a public campaign to extend the franchise, but met with little response. He did play a major role, however, in backing the free trade treaty that Cobden negotiated with France in 1860.

Bright had long admired the United States as a shining example of what a middle-class democracy could accomplish. Bright believed that if Britain enjoyed a greater degree of social and political democracy, Britons would come to possess the liberty and prosperity that seemed to characterize the United States. In fact, he and Cobden referred so frequently to America in their speeches that they became known in the House of Commons as the "members for the United States."

With the outbreak of the American Civil War in 1861, Bright immediately threw his support behind the North. As a Quaker, he had a strong moral objection to slavery and believed (well before most Britons) that a Northern victory would culminate in the destruction of that "peculiar institution." He also supported the North because he believed it represented the best part of the American experiment. In his eyes, Northern democracy had safeguarded the liberty that allowed people to live up to their potential.

Nominally committed to supporting Lord Palmerston's coalition government, Bright and his fellow radicals took the lead in attempting to prevent the administration from intervening in the conflict. They knew that Palmerston was ill disposed toward the United States, and they feared that his tendency toward aggressive foreign policy moves might culminate in war. Bright, however, did not have much of a following in the House of Commons, nor did he exert much influence on the Cabinet. Consequently, he took his message to the public in an attempt to educate British opinion on the American conflict.

During the *Trent* Affair, Bright publicly argued that instead of sending an ultimatum, Britain should take its case against the United States before international arbitration. He and Cobden urged moderation upon the North. Bright also deployed what influence he could upon Charles Villiers and Thomas Milner-Gibson, the two radicals in the Cabinet.

With the peaceful resolution of the *Trent* Affair, Bright sought to achieve two related ends. First, he wanted to prevent the British government from offering its good offices to mediate the conflict, because such a move could only benefit the South. Second, he sought at all costs to prevent the government from officially recognizing the Confederacy. In pursuit of these objectives, he frequently spoke about the war in public, appealing mainly to working-class audiences. Perhaps his most important tactic consisted of linking the cause of abolition to the rights of labor. Historians have long disputed the effectiveness of Bright's oratory in attracting British working-class support for the North. It seems clear, however, that a number of important labor leaders entered radical politics during the Civil War because of their opposition to slavery. During the conflict, then, Bright began forming the basis of the alliance between radicalism and trade unionism that eventually played a large role in the politics that led up to the extension of the franchise in 1867.

Because of his wholehearted support of the Union, his politics, and his reputation as the representative of the working man, Bright won the gratitude of the North.

Although his activities may not have played a pivotal role in preventing the British government from intervening in the conflict, they provided comfort for Northerners who came to see that not all Britons proved hostile to the United States.

After the war ended, Bright took advantage of the alliance between labor and radicalism that he had formed and pressed again for the extension of suffrage. Although the Liberal reform act of 1866 failed and the government fell, Bright had popularized reform to such an extent that the Conservatives, who subsequently came to office, felt compelled to introduce a sweeping reform measure to expand suffrage in Britain.

When the Liberals returned to power in 1868, Bright joined the Cabinet as president of the Board of Trade, but resigned after suffering a breakdown in 1870. He returned to the Cabinet as the chancellor of the Duchy of Lancaster in 1873, holding the post until the administration fell in 1874. He held the office again from 1880 until 1882, when he resigned because he opposed Gladstone's Irish Home Rule bill.

In May 1888 Bright fell ill, suffering from a combination of diabetes and Bright's disease. After lingering for some months, he died at One Ash, the family home in Rochdale, on 27 March 1889.

—*Hubert F. Dubrulle*

See also Diplomacy, U.S.A.; Great Britain; Palmerston, Viscount; *Trent* Affair.

For further reading:

Ausubel, Herman. *John Bright, Victorian Reformer* (1966).
Read, Donald. *Cobden and Bright: A Victorian Political Partnership* (1967).
Robbins, Keith. *John Bright* (1979).
Trevelyan, George Macaulay. *The Life of John Bright* (1913).

BRISTOE STATION, BATTLE OF
(14 October 1863)

The Bristoe campaign began 10 October 1863. General Robert E. Lee had learned that the Army of the Potomac's 6th and 7th Corps were headed west to participate in the Chattanooga campaign. Though outnumbered almost two to one, Lee auda-

The Army of the Potomac near Bristoe Station, October 1863 (*Library of Congress*)

ciously decided to interpose his troops between the Federal army and Washington, analogous to what he had done at Second Bull Run.

By 13 October, the Confederates, moving north, had passed Warrenton, west of Manassas Junction. However, the Army of the Potomac, commanded by Major General George G. Meade, who had intercepted Confederate signals, was already retreating up the Orange & Alexandria Railroad, intending to mass at Centreville.

The battle of Bristoe Station was actually two battles on the same day, 14 October 1863, with the first occurring near Auburn, just northeast of Bristoe. As the Union 2d Corps, commanded by Major General Gouverneur K. Warren, attempted to cross Cedar Run, it was attacked by ex-U.S. congressman and now Confederate colonel Thomas Ruffin's 1st North Carolina Cavalry. Warren faced a dilemma: "to halt was to await annihilation, and to move as prescribed" took him into a valley, "above which loomed Confederates."

Brigadier General Alexander Hays, Warren's 3d Division commander, sent out skirmishers who repulsed Ruffin's cavalry and mortally wounded Ruffin. Then, along with Brigadier General John C. Caldwell's division, Hays's men drove away the remainder of Lieutenant General J. E. B. Stuart's cavalrymen. With St. Stephens Road now open, the Union 2d Corps hurried toward Bristoe Station to catch up with Major General George Sykes's 5th Corps.

Lee, acutely aware of a golden opportunity to cut Meade's army into pieces and destroy it piecemeal, advanced Lieutenant General A. P. Hill's corps up the Warrenton Turnpike. Hill spied Sykes's 5th Corps waiting to ford Broad Run, a swift-moving stream just east of Bristoe. Mistakenly thinking that this was the rear of the whole Union column, Hill smelled blood and moved in for the kill. He impetuously ordered a coordinated attack by Brigadier General Henry Heth's Division and Major William T. Poague's artillery battalion on the unsuspecting Union corps.

The initial shelling forced Sykes's men to clamber wildly across Broad Run. Encouraged, Heth ordered the brigades of Brigadier Generals John Walker, William W. Kirkland, and John R. Cooke to attack around 4 P.M. To Hill's and Heth's surprise, however, Warren's 2d Corps was waiting to cross the stream, with Hays's column in the lead. Realizing that Heth's Division was now in danger from a rear attack, Hill halted Cooke's men and sent out two companies of the 27th North Carolina as skirmishers to test the Union strength.

Warren's corps, the smallest of the Union troops and greatly outnumbered, headed for an opening extending on both sides of the railroad tracks that rose to a gentle hill occupied by two lines of Heth's Confederates. Then it was a race for a deep cut by the far side of the railroad, where the embankment facing the Confederates could serve as a breastwork.

The Union troops quickly occupied the cut, repulsed the first Confederate attack, and prepared for the second line. It came with what a Union captain labeled a "mad rush." Yet the Union fire, lasting possibly twenty minutes, forced many of Heth's men to huddle behind a house. With nowhere to go, the Confederates began to retreat toward the hill from whence they had come, all the while ducking Union fire. Union skirmishers were immediately ordered after them, capturing those who had tried to find safety in the small house and then their guns, which were left unprotected during the withdrawal.

The battle of Bristoe Station would be refought in accounts thereafter, with Hill and Lieutenant General Richard Ewell blamed for failing to annihilate the Union 2d Corps. The main criticisms were that not only had Hill and Ewell outnumbered Warren, Hill also had enjoyed plenty of time to survey the land from the high ground above Bristoe, which was near Ewell's prewar home. A melancholy Lee could only say to Hill that dreary night, "Bury these poor men, and let us say no more about it." Bury they did, for the Confederates had suffered approximately 1,400 casualties, "roughly one man lost every two seconds of the engagement." By contrast, the Union II Corps lost a total of 546 killed, wounded, and missing, with almost 40 percent of the casualties sustained by Hays's division.

Although Lee had failed to cut off Meade's withdrawal, and the battle would be considered insignificant, the Army of Northern Virginia had temporarily destroyed a key railroad and had forced the Army of the Potomac back 40 miles.

—*Wayne Mahood*

See also Caldwell, John C.; Hays, Alexander; Hill, Ambrose Powell; Warren, Gouverneur K.

For further reading:

Fleming, George T., ed. *The Life and Letters of Alexander Hays* (1919).

Henderson, William D. *The Road to Bristoe Station: Campaigning With Lee and Meade, August 1–October 20, 1863* (1987).

Robertson, James I., Jr. *A.P. Hill: The Story of a Confederate Warrior* (1987).

Walker, Francis. *History of the Second Army Corps of the Army of the Potomac* (1891).

BROOKE, JOHN MERCER
(1826–1906)

Confederate naval officer; ordnance designer

John Mercer Brooke's father, George Mercer Brooke, entered the U.S. Army in 1808 and ended the War of 1812 as a major with the brevet rank of colonel. In 1824 he constructed Fort Brooke on the site of present-day Tampa, Florida. There, on 18 December 1826, John Mercer Brooke was born.

Young Brooke joined the U.S. Navy as a midshipman in 1841 and graduated from the Naval Academy in 1847. Promoted to lieutenant in 1855, Brooke's intellectual curiosity and scientific bent led to useful inventions, including deep-sea sounding leads that eventually made possible the laying of an Atlantic cable. Later he led major explorations of the north Pacific and the coast of Japan. He also escorted the first Japanese diplomatic mission to the United States.

On 20 April 1861, three days after the secession of Virginia, Brooke resigned his commission in the U.S. Navy. His wife and close friends seem to have been the key factors in the decision. Future admiral David Dixon Porter stated that he only regretted the loss of two men from the U.S. Navy: Catesby ap R. Jones and Brooke.

Commissioned a lieutenant in the Virginia navy on 23 April, Brooke was made naval aide to the commander of Virginia forces, General Robert E. Lee. When it was clear that Virginia would be linked to the Confederacy, Brooke applied for a commission in the Confederate navy. On 2 May 1861 Confederate secretary of the navy Stephen R. Mallory informed him that he had been granted a commission as a lieutenant.

In a June meeting with Mallory, Brooke assured the secretary that the South could build its own ironclads. Mallory then transferred Brooke to the naval ordnance office, where he supervised work on armor and guns for the CSS *Virginia*, the former USS *Merrimack*. Scuttled by the Federals when they abandoned the Gosport (Norfolk) Navy Yard, she had been raised and was undergoing conversion into an ironclad.

Brooke's ordnance achievements were remarkable, particularly given his lack of experience in what he undertook. Brooke was responsible for the *Virginia's* slanted armor casemate, subsequently copied in other Confederate ironclads, as well as the idea of her bow and stern extensions under water. Yet friction between Brooke and constructor John D. Porter, who claimed credit for the *Virginia's* design, contributed to Brooke's subsequent lack of interest in the ironclad program. Promoted to commander in September 1862, Brooke in March 1863 was named chief of the Confederate Bureau of Ordnance and Hydrography, which post he held until the end of the war.

Brooke designed a variety of guns for the Confederacy, including 8- and 9-inch smoothbores, 10- and 11-inch double-banded smoothbores, and the 11-inch triple-banded smoothbore. He is, however, best known for his double- and triple-banded rifled guns, produced in 6.4-inch, 7-inch, and 8-inch bore sizes. They were probably the finest rifled navy guns on either side in the war. As with his Union counterpart, John A. Dahlgren, Brooke understood that a hemisphere offered the strongest cap for a cylindrical pressure vessel. He also

understood, as did Union founder Robert P. Parrott, the gain in strength afforded by a wrought-iron band around the breech of a cast-iron gun.

Brooke-designed guns are identified, with few exceptions, by a fully hemispheric breech contour; layers of welded-on reinforcing bands; a plain tapered chase extending from the reinforcing bands to the muzzle; unturned rough exteriors; and, save in the smoothbores, 7-groove rifling of right-hand twist.

After the war Brooke joined the Virginia Military Institute faculty as professor of astronomy, meteorology, and geography. He served in that position from 1865 until 1899. Brooke died in Lexington, Virginia, on 14 December 1906.

—*Spencer C. Tucker*

See also Dahlgren, John Adolph Bernard; Mallory, Stephen R.; Ordnance, Naval; *Virginia*, CSS.

For further reading:

Brooke, George M., Jr. *John M. Brooke. Naval Scientist and Educator* (1980).
Brooke, John M. "The *Virginia* or *Merrimack*: Her Real Projector." *Southern Historical Society Papers* (1891).
Olmstead, Edwin, Wayne Stark, and Spencer Tucker. *The Big Guns. Civil War Siege, Seacoast and Naval Cannon* (1997).

BROOKE, JOHN RUTTER
(1838–1926)
Union general

John Brooke was born on his family's farm near Pottstown, Pennsylvania. He received his early education at local schools, but this sturdy six-foot-tall farm boy was described as "not especially fond of books, uncouth in manner, and participating but seldom in the social doings of the young people of the neighborhood" and his stentorian voice was characterized as "uninviting by reason of its depth and brusqueness." Brooke was sent away to schools in New Jersey and West Chester, Pennsylvania, and then he went west and lived for a time with an uncle who served in the army. He then returned to the farm and was essentially managing it when war began in 1861.

When a local militia company was reorganized, Brooke was selected as its captain. This company joined the 4th Pennsylvania and served for three months. Brooke then returned home, obtained a colonel's commission from Governor Andrew G. Curtin, and organized the 53d Pennsylvania, becoming its colonel.

Brooke's regiment was assigned to the 1st Division, II Army Corps, and went to the Peninsula with the Army of the Potomac. The 53d first engaged the enemy at Fair Oaks on 1 June 1862, suffering heavy casualties. After fighting at Gaines's Mill and the Peach Orchard during the Seven Days' battles, Brooke's regiment went north when the army withdrew from the Peninsula. Brooke's men fought at Antietam and then at Fredericksburg, where the 53d again sustained heavy losses.

Brooke was then placed in command of the 4th Brigade, 1st Division, II Corps, and ably directed his men at Chancellorsville and Gettysburg. After leading his brigade through the wheatfield at Gettysburg on 2 July 1863, Brooke was wounded in the ankle and assisted off the field. He returned to active duty the following spring, after commanding a convalescent camp at Harrisburg. During the 1864 Virginia campaign, Brooke's men were actively engaged in the Wilderness, Spotsylvania, and Cold Harbor. In this latter battle, on 3 June, Brooke was seriously wounded and incapacitated for any further active duty. Promoted to brigadier general effective from 12 May 1864 and then to major general on 1 August, Brooke sat on courts-martial until the spring of 1865, when he received command of a division in Winfield S. Hancock's new corps, which occupied the Shenandoah Valley.

After returning home in 1865, Brooke accepted a commission as lieutenant colonel in the regular army and was assigned to the 37th Infantry, which was stationed in New Mexico. Brooke thereafter served in the army until his retirement in 1902. He was successively promoted to major general and served in a number of various posts, including stints in Colorado, Mississippi, Louisiana, Alabama, Montana, Massachusetts, and New York. Brooke also was in command of the Departments of the Platte, Dakota, and Missouri.

When war with Spain was declared in 1898, Brooke took command of both I Army Corps and Camp Thomas on the Chickamauga battlefield. He accompanied the expedition to Puerto Rico, where he remained as military governor after the end of hostilities. Brooke then was transferred to Cuba and served as governor of the island until 1900, when he was placed in command of the Department of the East.

Reaching the mandatory retirement age in 1902, Brooke left the army. The general was twice married; his first wife died during childbirth in 1867, and he remarried ten years later. He died in 1926 and is buried in Arlington National Cemetery.

—*Richard A. Sauers*

See also: Cold Harbor.

For further reading:

Auge, M. *Lives of the Eminent Dead and Biographical Notices of Prominent Living Citizens of Montgomery County, Pa.* (1879).
"General John R. Brooke." *Philadelphia Public Ledger* (1898).
"Major General John R. Brooke." *New York Herald* (1898).

BROOKS, PRESTON SMITH
(1819–1857)

U.S. congressman

Preston Brooks was born on 6 August 1819 in Edgefield, South Carolina. He attended South Carolina College but left without a degree in 1839. In 1842 he was admitted to the South Carolina bar, where he practiced law until he was called to public service shortly thereafter. During 1842–1844 he served as aide-de-camp to South Carolina governor James Henry Hammond. When Hammond's term as governor expired in 1844, Brooks ran for and won a seat in the South Carolina house, where he served only a single two-year term. He returned to public service in 1853, when he was elected to the U.S. House of Representatives.

A man of unquestioned loyalty but limited judgment, Brooks's public career was marked from its earliest days by violence. Brooks engaged in an argument with Louis Wigfall in 1840 over Hammond's gubernatorial bid. Wigfall, who supported Hammond's opponent, had already fought two duels with members of Brooks's family, killing one of Brooks's relatives. Soon enough Brooks and Wigfall were fighting a duel of their own. Both missed their first shots, but Brooks's second shot struck Wigfall's leg as Wigfall seriously wounded Brooks in the hip. Brooks carried the bullet and required the use of a cane for the remainder of his life.

As a representative of South Carolina in Congress, Brooks was said to have possessed great but underutilized oratorical skills. Although his oratory may have been exceptional, it was his temper that has made him most remembered to history. It was during this time that the Senate took up the issue of Kansas. Massachusetts senator and ardent abolitionist Charles Sumner on 19 and 20 May 1856 delivered a two-day long speech entitled, "The Crime against Kansas," in which he denounced the old and infirm Senator Andrew P. Butler of South Carolina. Butler, who was Preston Brooks's cousin, was ill and absent from the proceedings. Brooks took it upon himself to defend his cousin's honor. Claiming later that he waited two days for an apology, Brooks searched out Sumner on 22 May 1856 and found him seated at his desk on the floor of the Senate shortly after it had recessed for the day. After the briefest exchange, Brooks began to beat Sumner on the head with a gutta-percha cane until it was in splinters. Only then was he restrained. During the attack, Sumner had been held fast by his desk bolted to the floor until he managed to wrench it loose and collapse. Sumner's recovery would take several years, while Brooks was lionized by Southerners as a hero and defender of liberty.

In dealing with what amounted to a case of battery, Congress had to act on behalf of Sumner. An investigating committee from the House voted in favor of expelling Brooks, but a vote along party lines saved him from the necessary two-thirds majority. After taking the floor of the House to explain his reasons for the attack, Brooks resigned his seat and returned to South Carolina. His constituents immediately returned him to the House of Representatives.

The Brooks-Sumner incident further expanded the already gaping sectional rift, illustrating to Southerners that Northerners were cowardly abolitionists and to Northerners that Southerners were violent hatemongers. Within a month of the attack, Massachusetts representative Anson Burlingame spoke to the House to label Brooks a coward who lacked the ethics of fairness. Brooks responded by challenging Burlingame to a duel. In accordance with the *code duello*, Burlingame chose the location, selecting the Canadian side of Niagara Falls so that Brooks would have to travel through the heart of the North. When Brooks refused to go, it was triumphantly reported throughout the North as evidence of his cowardice. Nonetheless, during the months that followed the attack on Sumner, Brooks received countless canes from Southerners with laudatory notes and inscriptions encouraging future beatings.

Brooks would not live to see the war that he had a small role in foreshadowing. Within a year of the beating incident, he died at Brown's Hotel in Washington on 27 January 1857. Although obviously possessing a temper, Brooks was said to have been a kind and gentle man capable of great generosity. Evidently during the months after the attack, Brooks understood the detrimental effects for the South caused by his reckless attack on Sumner.

—*Brian D. McKnight*

See also Butler, Andrew Pickens; Kansas-Nebraska Act; Sumner, Charles.

For further reading:

Campbell, J.E. "Sumner, Brooks, Burlingame, or the Last of the Great Challenges." *Ohio Archaeological and Historical Society* (1925).

Heidler, David S. *Pulling the Temple Down: The Fire-eaters and the Destruction of the Union* (1994).

Nevins, Allan. *Ordeal of the Union* (1947).

Walther, Eric H. *The Fire-eaters* (1992).

BROOKS, WILLIAM THOMAS HARBAUGH
(1821–1870)

Union general

Born in New Lisbon, Ohio, William Thomas Harbaugh Brooks received an appointment to the U.S. Military Academy in 1837 at age sixteen. He graduated forty-sixth of fifty-two in the class of 1841. Commissioned into the 3d U.S. Infantry, Brooks was sent immediately to Florida, where he fought in the final phases of the Second Seminole War. The end of that conflict saw him bouncing from post to post before the outbreak of the Mexican-American War had him traveling to Texas to serve in Zachary Taylor's Army of Occupation. After serving in northern Mexico under Taylor, Brooks was transferred to Winfield Scott's army and participated in the Mexico City campaign. He served under Captain Robert E. Lee during that campaign. During the Mexican-American War, Brooks received two brevet promotions for bravery.

After the end of that conflict, Brooks joined the staff of Brigadier General David E. Twiggs. He served as that officer's adjutant general and then as Twiggs's aide-de-camp while Twiggs commanded the Department of Texas. At the end of the 1850s, Brooks served in New Mexico, where he engaged in campaigns against the Navajo Indians. During that time, he contracted a series of illnesses that would plague him for the remainder of his life.

At the outbreak of the Civil War, Brooks was a captain in the 3d U.S. Infantry. His extensive military experience, however, gained him rapid advancement, and in September 1861 he became brigadier general of volunteers. Commanding a brigade in William F. Smith's division, Army of the Potomac, Brooks saw little action in the fall of 1861 and the winter of 1861–1862. In early 1862, however, he privately complained to friends about the arrest of Charles P. Stone for the Ball's Bluff fiasco. Word of Brooks's complaints reached some Radical Republicans, who marked him as a potential disloyal officer.

During the spring of 1862, Brooks led his brigade in the Peninsula campaign. He distinguished himself during the siege of Yorktown, the battle of Williamsburg, and the Seven Days. In the latter series of engagements, Brooks was wounded at the battle of Savage's Station. In command of the same brigade, 2d Division, VI Corps, Brooks fought in the Maryland campaign at Crampton's Gap on 14 September and at Antietam on 17 September 1862. In the latter engagement he marched his men to the battlefield from Crampton's Gap the morning of the battle and brought them immediately into the fray. He was wounded during the battle.

After Antietam, Brooks and his division were headquartered at Hagerstown, Maryland. While there on 18 October, he was given command of 1st Division, VI Corps. He commanded that division in the battle of Fredericksburg. Like so many officers in the Army of the Potomac, Brooks disapproved of the battle plan for Fredericksburg and believed the results of the battle vindicated his judgment. The subsequent attempt to flank Robert E. Lee's position in the infamous Mud March only further confirmed him in the opinion that Ambrose Burnside was unfit for command. Brooks, like other officers (Joseph Hooker most conspicuous among them), made no secret of his disdain for Burnside. Before his dismissal as commander of the Army of the Potomac, Burnside dismissed Brooks from the army for complaining about government policy. Burnside took this action at the same time that he tried to dismiss Hooker for similar offenses. The dismissals had to have the final approval of the president, and Abraham Lincoln, who was about to appoint Hooker as Burnside's successor, declined to approve the dismissals. However, again Brooks had criticized policy and was again marked as a potential troublemaker.

Brooks continued to command his division in the Chancellorsville campaign, but in late May 1863 he was transferred to the Department of the Monongahela, headquartered in Pittsburgh, Pennsylvania. Ironically one of Brooks's first duties was to cooperate with Ambrose Burnside's Army of the Ohio in the repulse of John Hunt Morgan's Ohio Raid. For the most part, however, Brooks confined himself to recruiting duty, primarily recruiting three-month units used for emergencies like the Morgan raid. Brooks had been promoted in June 1863 to major general of volunteers, but the Senate never approved the promotion, and it expired the following spring.

In April 1864, Brooks was ordered back east to assume command of the 1st Division, XVIII Corps. He fought with his division at Drewry's Bluff and Cold Harbor. On 18 June he was given command of X Corps, Army of the James. His health, however, was deteriorating quickly, and he did not know then whether he would be able to continue in a field command. Brooks also was in the middle of a dispute with the commanding general of the U.S. Army, Ulysses S. Grant. When Brooks's promotion to major general had expired, he had expected to have his name resubmitted, as had happened with officers in similar circumstances. Neither Grant nor the president had raised the issue, and Brooks was angry. When Grant refused to address his concerns in July 1864, Brooks resigned both his volunteer and regular commissions, and Grant accepted.

After the war, Brooks moved to Huntsville, Alabama, where he bought a farm. During his few remaining years, he made many friends among his former enemies, and became one of the most well-liked men in the community. His death on 19 July 1870 was mourned greatly by his new friends, who buried him in the local cemetery.

—*David S. Heidler and Jeanne T. Heidler*

See also Burnside, Ambrose; Crampton's Gap.

For further reading:

Gallagher, Gary W., ed. *The Fredericksburg Campaign: Decision on the Rappahannock* (1995).
Trudeau, Noah Andre. *Bloody Roads South: The Wilderness to Cold Harbor, May–June 1864* (1989).

BROUGH, JOHN
(1811–1865)
Governor of Ohio

Born to John Brough, an English immigrant, and Jane Garnet Brough in Marietta, Ohio, the younger John Brough received a local education, but the death of his parents when he was a child led him to enter the printing trade and eventually journalism. He used his skills in this area to work his way through Ohio University. He studied law after graduation and became active in Ohio Democratic politics. He served in the lower house of the state legislature where he demonstrated great administrative abilities as the chairman of the banking and currency committee. This experience led to his appointment as state auditor. During his time in office, he removed many of the abuses within the state tax system.

Returning to the newspaper business in the 1840s and his law practice, he used the profits from both to invest in railroad projects. He served as the president of several railroad companies in the years before the outbreak of the Civil War.

Unlike many Ohio Democrats, Brough was a strong supporter of a vigorous prosecution of the war. He used his influence with the state's railroads to speed the movement of troops and equipment. The growth of opposition in his state, led by such Copperheads as Clement Vallandigham, caused Brough to begin speaking out publicly about the need for support from all citizens. These speaking engagements became so popular and influential that the Republican Party of Ohio approached Brough in 1863 to run for governor. He agreed and won an overwhelming victory over Vallandigham.

Brough began his term as governor in January 1864 and immediately demonstrated his strong support for the war effort by a renewed push for recruiting in the state and his insistence that officers of state forces be promoted based on merit. Somewhat discouraged by the lackluster recruiting in the state, he wrote to the War Department within two months of taking office, suggesting that bounties be suspended as useless and that the draft be increased.

While Brough advocated widespread conscription, he was also tremendously concerned about the physical condition of Ohio troops. He worked tirelessly to improve military hospitals in the state and wrote to the War Department frequently urging better and more numerous supplies for Ohio troops. He also worked diligently to obtain federal reimbursement to the state for the damage done during the summer of 1863 by the raid conducted by John Hunt Morgan.

Along with these activities Brough took an active interest in the war in all theaters. He frequently corresponded with Ohio officers regarding the performance of Ohio troops in battle and the state of the war throughout the country. In addition, he proposed and entertained creative solutions to various problems facing the state, including recruiting. One of the major impediments to recruiting by 1864 was the shortage of men to work the many farms in the state. For that reason, he was intrigued by a proposal put forth by Major General George Thomas that Confederate deserters be sent to states such as Ohio to work as agricultural laborers. He also suggested to Secretary of War Edwin Stanton that federal recruiting be conducted in occupied areas of the South to take advantage of what he believed to be the large loyal population there.

The military readiness and defense of Ohio were also among Brough's major concerns. Morgan's raid in 1863 left the state shaken and left many people, including Brough, convinced that, given the opportunity, Confederate raiders would raid again. To protect against such a possibility, Brough increased the efficiency of home guard units. At the same time, he proposed to the War Department that new recruits and draftees be retained in border fortifications, freeing more veteran troops to move to the various fronts. He also took Stanton's advice in the summer of 1864 to establish regular patrols of the Ohio River by state recruited boats.

During his first year in office, Brough returned a large measure of efficiency to the state government and the state's military preparations. Yet, he also offended a large number of defenders of the status quo and those people who had made a great deal of money or gained advancement because of the war. Because of what he deemed the emergency nature of the situation, he also was less than politic in some of his dealings with important people in the state. Because of this mounting opposition and his failing health, he decided not to seek reelection in 1865. As it happened, he would have been unable to serve a second term. He died on 29 August 1865, four months before his term expired.

—David S. Heidler and Jeanne T. Heidler

See also Vallandigham, Clement.

For further reading:
Reid, Whitelaw. *Ohio in the War: Her Statesmen, Her Generals, and Soldiers* (1868).

BROWN, ALBERT GALLATIN
(1813–1880)

Confederate congressman

Born in Chester District, South Carolina, on 31 May 1813, Albert Gallatin Brown moved to Copiah County, Mississippi, when he was ten years old. He attended Mississippi College and Jefferson College. He was admitted to the bar, but in 1835 he began an impressive political career. Before the Civil War, Brown served as a state legislator, state circuit court judge, governor for two terms, and congressman (1839–1841, 1847–1853). He represented Mississippi in the U.S. Senate from 1854 until 14 January 1861, when he withdrew upon the secession of his state.

A Democrat, Brown was a strict constructionist and an opponent of banks. The Compromise of 1850 and the rise of the Republican Party after 1854 made him a fervent Southern nationalist, and his rhetoric became increasingly belligerent. He defended slavery as a blessing for all whites and blacks and advocated the acquisition of Cuba and the admission of Kansas as a slave state. Brown consistently protected the interests of nonslaveholders and advocated fair taxation and free public education. He

was successful in influencing the yeomen farmers' "triple prejudices against large slaveholders, against [blacks], but most of all, against the North."

With Lincoln's election, Brown urged the immediate secession of the slave states. After his resignation from the Senate, he organized a company in the 18th Mississippi Infantry and participated in First Bull Run. Brown was cited for bravery at Ball's Bluff in October 1861. Mississippi then elected Brown to the Confederate Senate, and he took his seat on 18 February 1862. As chair of the Committee on Naval Affairs, Brown worked well with Secretary Stephen R. Mallory.

Brown's commitment to Southern nationalism never wavered during the war. The preservation of the Confederacy took precedence over states' rights. He encouraged government intervention to reduce cotton and tobacco production and to increase foodstuffs. An ardent defender of conscription, Brown opposed practically all exemption and substitute laws. He railed against the rich and speculators who both avoided service and undermined the war effort. He favored suspending the writ of habeas corpus so the government could better enforce the draft and preserve the nation. Never a defeatist, Brown rejected pursuing all peace negotiations and in February 1865 proposed legislation emancipating slave soldiers if they proved loyal. To him, Southern nationhood ultimately was much more important than slavery.

After the war, Brown returned to farming and occasionally practiced law. Although mostly retired from politics, he unsuccessfully urged Mississippi Democrats to educate and incorporate African-Americans into the party. He criticized white violence against blacks but to no avail. He died at his farm near Terry in Hinds County on 12 June 1880 and is buried in Jackson.

—M. Philip Lucas

See also Congress, C.S.A.; Conscription, C.S.A.; Mallory, Stephen R.; Mississippi.

For further reading:
Alexander, Thomas Benjamin, and Richard E. Beringer. *The Anatomy of the Confederate Congress; A Study of the Influences of Member Characteristics on Legislative Voting Behavior, 1861–1865* (1972).
Rable, George C. *The Confederate Republic: A Revolution against Politics* (1994).
Ranck, James Byrne. *Albert Gallatin Brown: Radical Southern Nationalist* (1937).

BROWN, ISAAC NEWTON
(1817–1889)

Confederate naval officer

Born in Livingston County, Kentucky, the son of Samuel Brown, Isaac Newton Brown moved to Mississippi when he was a child. He entered the U.S. Navy as a cadet at the age of seventeen. He served his first years in the navy in the West Indies and on the rivers of Florida during the Second Seminole War. He received his full commission in 1840. During the Mexican-American War, Brown served in the Gulf of Mexico and during the siege of Vera Cruz. After the war, he served on Pacific station, made a trip to Australia, and made two circumnavigations of the world. When not on sea duty, he served a stint at the U.S. Naval Observatory and doing coastal surveys. Immediately preceding the outbreak of the Civil War, Brown was executive officer on the USS *Niagara*, the ship that took the first Japanese ministry back to Japan. When Brown and the *Niagara* returned to the United States, the Confederate States of America had been formed.

Brown resigned his lieutenant's commission and offered his services to the Confederacy. He was commissioned a lieutenant in the Confederate States Navy in June 1861 and in the fall of 1861 was sent west to aid in the defense of the Mississippi and other western rivers. Before leaving the East, however, Brown arranged for the shipment of fifty guns from the Norfolk shipyard. He also made preparations to have material shipped west with which he could construct mines to defend many of the western rivers. With the limited Confederate ship-building capabilities, Brown believed that mines would be an integral part of Confederate river defense.

Upon arrival in the West, Brown's work converting private vessels to ironclads was interrupted in early 1862 when he was hurriedly sent to Nashville to prepare boats to protect the Cumberland River. All of these preparations came too late, however, to prevent U.S. Army and Navy forces from taking Forts Henry and Donelson and bringing about the evacuation of Nashville.

Brown was then sent to New Orleans, where, until Union forces took possession of the city, he supervised construction of gunboats. He left with his workers at the approach of the Federals and traveled up the Mississippi to Vicksburg. On 9 May 1862, Brown took command of the Confederate ironclad ram, CSS *Arkansas*. The vessel was used in defense of Vicksburg through the summer of 1862, especially on 15 July 1862, when he defeated a larger Union force. For his actions on that day he was promoted to commander on 25 August 1862. At that time, Brown was on an extended sick leave, and in his absence the *Arkansas* was destroyed by its crew to prevent its capture after running aground.

Upon his return to duty, Brown, now without a ship, supervised the mining of western rivers, particularly concentrating on the Yazoo. His efforts were responsible for the destruction of two Federal ironclad boats. He also supervised shipbuilding during this time at Yazoo City. In command of a land force comprising a mix of sailors and soldiers, Brown participated in the defense of Vicksburg in the spring and early summer of 1863.

Not present at the surrender of Vicksburg, having been sent east, Brown assumed command in early 1864

of the CSS *Charleston* at Charleston, South Carolina. He served there until the Federal army occupied Charleston. The government in Richmond then sent him west again to take command of what naval forces remained. During his overland journey, he heard of the collapse of the Confederacy and surrendered himself to Federal authorities at Montgomery, Alabama. Brown was paroled on 22 May 1865 and allowed to return to his plantation in Mississippi. For the remainder of his life, Brown lived quietly at his home in Mississippi and on land he acquired in Corsicana, Texas, after the war.

—*David S. Heidler and Jeanne T. Heidler*

See also *Arkansas*, CSS; Navy, C.S.A.

For further reading:

Carroll, John M., ed. *Register of Officers of the Confederate States Navy, 1861–1865* (1983).

Gretchell, Charles Munro. "Defender of the Inland Waters: The Military Career of Isaac Newton Brown, Commander, Confederate States Navy, 1861–1865" (M.A. thesis, 1978).

Luraghi, Raimondo. *A History of the Confederate Navy* (1996).

Scharf, J. Thomas. *History of the Confederate States Navy: From Its Organization to the Surrender of Its Last Vessel* (1877; reprint, 1996).

BROWN, JOHN
(1800–1859)
Abolitionist

Born in Torrington, Connecticut, and raised in Ohio, John Brown was the third of six children of Owen and Ruth Mills Brown. The Brown family held deep religious convictions and solid antislavery beliefs. Owen Brown provided his children with a strong Calvinist foundation, and he raised them in an environment in which slavery was considered unacceptable and unjust. It was from his father that John Brown inherited his abhorrence of slavery and his commitment to religion.

In 1820, Brown married Dianthe Lusk in Hudson, Ohio. Six years later, the couple sold their farm and moved to Pennsylvania, where Brown opened his own tannery, the first of his many failed business ventures. Brown farmed, operated a tannery, raised sheep, drove cattle, served as a wool company agent, and was involved in land speculation at various times in his life, but he was wholly unsuccessful in all of these pursuits. He experienced serious financial problems by age thirty-one and declared bankruptcy at age forty-two. By the time he was fifty-six, he had accumulated in six states a string of twenty failed businesses, which ultimately contributed to the filing of twenty-one lawsuits against him.

Although Brown had always opposed slavery, he was not committed to the cause until he attended an abolitionist meeting in Cleveland in 1837. Upon the conclusion of this meeting, Brown swore that he would dedicate his life to the abolition of slavery. Nonconformist and radical in his approach, Brown never joined an antislavery society, he demanded immediate emancipation for slaves, and he was not averse to the use of violence. His commitment to the destruction of slavery was unwavering.

By 1848, Brown had grown increasingly militant in his opposition to slavery. The previous year when he first met Frederick Douglass, Brown revealed to Douglass his plan for freeing the slaves. Brown believed that the Alleghany Mountains were the "hills to freedom" and that they were the best place from which to launch an attack on slavery. Brown told Douglass that he hoped to start an insurrection with twenty-five of his own men who would quickly be joined by slaves. After the meeting, Douglass wrote in his newspaper, the *North Star*, that Brown, "though a white gentleman, [was] in sympathy, a black man, and as deeply interested in [the black] cause, as though his own soul had been pierced with the iron of slavery."

In 1855, after a temporary move to Kansas, Brown continued his fight against slavery. The passage of the Kansas-Nebraska Act in 1854 had drawn several of Brown's sons to the newly organized Kansas Territory. After living in Kansas for a few months, the sons informed Brown of the tension that existed between proslavery and antislavery forces in the area. Subsequently, Brown left his wife and younger children in New York and traveled with his son Oliver and his son-in-law Henry Thompson to join the others in Kansas. Years later, Brown admitted that he had moved to Kansas to fight, not to settle permanently.

In May 1856, as tensions in Kansas continued to rise, Brown, five of his sons, and Thompson joined the Pottawatomie Rifles in the free-soil defense of Lawrence, Kansas. By the time the group reached Lawrence, however, proslavery forces had already sacked the town and U.S. troops had restored order. Brown was furious with the proslavery forces and the failure of the Lawrence men to defend their town. Consequently, he persuaded several men to accompany him to Pottawatomie Creek. Brown, determined to exact revenge, wanted to "sweep the creek of all proslavery men." Armed with broadswords, the party approached three houses in the area and killed five men, including John Doyle and two of his sons, Allen Wilkinson and William Sherman. Throughout the rest of his life, Brown remained vague about his role at Pottawatomie. He was never legally punished for the crimes.

The Pottawatomie massacre of 24–25 May 1856 helped trigger guerrilla warfare in Kansas that lasted throughout the fall. Coupled with the recent sack of Lawrence on 21 May and the caning of Charles Sumner on the floor of the Senate on 22 May, the massacre led many in Kansas to believe that the Civil War had begun. At this time, John Brown made the fight to end slavery his full-time career. Throughout the remainder of the

An early portrait of John Brown (*Library of Congress*)

year, Brown and his sons fought in Kansas and Missouri. In August, Brown organized a company of "Kansas Regulars" and headed for Osawatomie, Kansas. On 30 August, proslavery Border Ruffians from Missouri raided free-state Osawatomie. In the process, they burned and looted the town and killed Brown's son Frederick. After the battle of Osawatomie, Brown vowed, "I will die fighting for this cause. There will be no more peace in this land until slavery is done for." Henceforth, this symbol of the antislavery crusade was known as "Old Osawatomie Brown."

In October 1856, Brown returned to the East, where he soon began a speaking tour to raise money for his military company. By this time, Brown had nearly finalized his plans for a future attack on the federal arsenal at Harper's Ferry, Virginia. He lacked only the money necessary to carry out the plan.

In 1858, Brown briefly returned to Kansas and launched an invasion of Missouri in which a slave owner was killed and eleven slaves were freed. After the invasion, Brown continued his speaking tour, although there was a $200 bounty on his head.

On Sunday, 16 October 1859, John Brown led his men in the failed attack on Harper's Ferry. Less than thirty-six hours later, a company of U.S. Marines under the leadership of Colonel Robert E. Lee and Lieutenant J. E. B. Stuart halted the assault and killed ten of Brown's men, including his sons Oliver and Watson. Brown was seriously wounded and captured. On 2 November, he was convicted of treason, murder, and insurrection, and he was sentenced to death. On 2 December 1859, John Brown, who had failed at almost everything he had tried, and who believed that as an abolitionist he had carried out the will of God, was hanged in Charlestown, Virginia. He died convinced that he was "worth inconceivably more to hang than for any other purpose."

—*Jennifer L. Bertolet*

See also Abolitionist Movement; Abolitionists; Harper's Ferry; Kansas.

For further reading:

Abels, Jules. *Man on Fire: John Brown and the Cause of Liberty* (1971).

Oates, Stephen B. *To Purge This Land with Blood: A Biography of John Brown* (1970).

Villard, Oswald Garrison. *John Brown 1800–1859: A Biography Fifty Years After* (1910; reprint, 1966).

BROWN, JOHN CALVIN
(1827–1889)
Confederate general

Born in Giles County, Tennessee, to Duncan Brown and Margaret Smith Brown, the younger Brown graduated from Jackson College, studied law upon graduation and quickly became a prominent attorney in Pulaski, Tennessee. Before the war, Brown was more devoted to his law practice than politics, although he was a member of the Whig Party. He opposed secession and served as an elector for John Bell's Constitutional Union Party candidacy for president in the 1860 elections. However, upon the secession of Tennessee after Fort Sumter was fired upon, Brown enlisted in the Confederate army as a private.

Brown served at that rank only briefly before being named colonel of the 3d Tennessee Infantry in May 1861. In early 1862 he temporarily commanded a brigade at Fort Donelson and was part of the ill-fated garrison there that surrendered in February 1862. Exchanged in August 1862, he was promptly promoted to brigadier general.

Brown commanded his brigade at Perryville in October 1862 and was wounded there. A year later while commanding a brigade of Major General Alexander P. Stewart's division at Chickamauga, he received a second wound. Within two months, he was again leading his brigade, and at Missionary Ridge his actions merited commendation for bravery. Brown commanded a division of John Bell Hood's corps during the Atlanta campaign and again received notice for his actions at Dalton. On 4 August 1864,his acting divisional command became official with his promotion to major general.

Brown accompanied Hood's army as it moved into Tennessee in the fall of 1864. An exploding shell severely wounded him at Franklin, an event that threatened to remove him permanently from the war. After a slow convalescence, he joined Joseph E. Johnston's army in North Carolina on 2 April, just weeks before Johnston's surrender. Brown was paroled from Greensboro, North Carolina.

Following the war, Brown resumed his lucrative law practice and became a prominent businessman. In 1870 and 1872, he was elected governor of Tennessee. He died in Red Boiling Springs, Tennessee, in 1889.

—*David S. Heidler and Jeanne T. Heidler*

See also Fort Donelson.

For further reading:

Butler, Margaret. "The Life of John C. Brown" (Master's thesis, 1936).

BROWN, JOSEPH EMERSON
(1821–1894)
Georgia governor

Joseph E. Brown, governor of Georgia throughout the Civil War, was a brilliant politician whose career revealed the social and ideological fault lines within the Confederacy. Displaying acute political instincts, Brown registered the discontents of Southern society and then channeled them to advance his public career. Although not a constructive statesman, Brown was a sensitive barometer of trouble and a vigorous, resourceful foe of President Jefferson Davis and the policies of the Confederate central government.

Brown burst onto the political scene in 1857 when the convention of Georgia's Democratic Party deadlocked. Nominated as a dark horse candidate for governor, he defeated Benjamin H. Hill of the American Party and thereafter held onto center stage in Georgia politics until his retirement from the U.S. Senate in 1890. In his first term as governor, Brown showed a perceptive grasp of class issues in politics. Though he was rapidly becoming rich, Brown's background was that of a country lawyer, and he took strong Jacksonian stands against the banks, which appealed to rural voters. In his second term he emphasized military preparedness and states' rights, anticipating the effective appeals that he soon would make to the elite.

Throughout the Civil War Brown stressed two powerful political themes: strict adherence to states' rights and social equity in the sacrifices made by Georgia's people. As the champion of states' rights and state sovereignty, Brown repeatedly lambasted the Davis administration and appealed to an increasingly disaffected elite. As an innovator in social welfare policies, Brown demonstrated concern for the suffering of the common people and brought them tangible measures of relief. In both ways his actions advanced his renown and strengthened his position, even as the fortunes of the Confederacy declined.

Brown signaled his extreme states' rights views even before Georgia joined the Confederacy. As soon as the state seceded from the United States, he sent a representative abroad with instructions to seek diplomatic recognition from Queen Victoria, Napoleon III, and the king of Belgium. More strong steps were soon to follow. He jealously kept all his state's guns under his own control and threatened to disarm Georgia volunteers when they left the state to fight for the Confederacy. Next he began a practice of offering the Confederacy "skeleton" regiments—units that had a full complement of officers (appointed by Brown up through the level of colonel) but only a scattering of enlisted men. To win the favor of Georgia's voters, he frequently insisted that units of the army actually were militia and therefore entitled to elect their officers.

In the conscription law Brown found his preeminent states' rights cause. The governor objected almost immediately to the Confederate Congress's first conscription law, passed in April 1862, and thus became a leader of opposition to the Davis administration. Denying the necessity of the law, he demanded a long list of exemptions, denounced conscription as a power to "destroy the civil government of each State," and ordered his state's enrolling officers not to cooperate with Confederate officials. A few weeks later he sent President Davis a long attack on the law, calling conscription "subversive of [Georgia's] sovereignty, and at war with all the principles for the support of which Georgia entered into this revolution." Among his turgid arguments was the assertion that the Confederacy could not draft the militia of the states, which he defined as "the whole arms-bearing population of the State who are not enlisted in the regular armies of the Confederacy."

This letter prompted an exchange on constitutional theories, in which Brown took delight in pillorying Jefferson Davis as more of a broad constructionist than Alexander Hamilton. When the Confederate Congress passed a second conscription act in September 1862, Brown thundered that this law "strikes down" Georgia's "sovereignty at a single blow," destroyed the state's militia, and left his citizens defenseless against any slave uprising. These protests undermined unity and support for the central government. Even Jefferson Davis admitted publicly that "unexpected criticism" had "impaired" the government's efforts to raise an army, and other politicians and newspapers took up the cry against the administration. Eventually Brown allowed conscription to go forward, as court cases repeatedly upheld the authority of Congress, but his actions kept more than 8,000 Georgians out of the army and weakened support for the cause.

As he became the champion for states' rights theo-

rists, Brown also won gratitude from thousands of ordinary citizens by ministering to their needs. When shortages of salt foreshadowed the greater suffering that would follow, Governor Brown ordered seizures of salt throughout his state and sold this vital preservative at bargain prices to soldiers' wives and destitute widows. To supply the common people and his state's troops, Brown also found funds to manufacture salt in Virginia. With impressive energy he arranged the manufacture of cotton cards, so that people could make cloth, and bought blankets, shoes, and other supplies for soldiers. He fought to suppress the distilling of scarce grain and from the legislature obtained appropriations as large as $10 million for relief. At times he denounced conscription officers as dragging off hundreds of men who left helpless families behind them. In all of his efforts he put the poorest citizens, ordinary soldiers, and their families first. Arguing that "the poor have generally paid their part . . . in military service, exposure, fatigue and blood, the rich, who have been in a much greater degree exempt from these, should meet the money demands of the Government," he won the gratitude and support of the poor.

Reelected twice during the Civil War, Brown took his opposition to the Confederate government to a new level in the spring of 1864. Resentment of the suspension of the writ of habeas corpus and a yearning for peace were growing in Georgia. In concert with Alexander and Linton Stephens, Brown assailed the central government and promoted the idea of peace negotiations. First Brown addressed a special session of the state legislature, condemned the Congress for authorizing Jefferson Davis to make "illegal and unconstitutional arrests," and asserted that only negotiations could end the fighting. Linton Stephens and his more prominent brother followed with vigorous denunciations of the suspension of the writ and other essential war measures. Their supporters then introduced resolutions calling on the people to act "through their state organizations and popular assemblies" to end the war. All these proposals tapped strong emotions in war-weary Georgia, but others were dismayed at the prospect of Confederate disunity and state-initiated disintegration. Supporters of the government managed to pass resolutions supporting Jefferson Davis and the war effort along with the peace resolutions.

Joe Brown ended his Confederate career as he had started it—a foe of the central government and a hindrance to its war effort, but a popular politician who knew how to appeal to both rich and poor. His shrewdness and insight kept him in high political office through a checkered, but long and successful, postwar career.

—*Paul D. Escott*

See also Georgia
For further reading:
Candler, Allen D., ed. *The Confederate Records of the State of Georgia* (1910).

Escott, Paul D. *After Secession: Jefferson Davis and the Failure of Confederate Nationalism* (1977).

Hill, Louise Biles. *Joseph E. Brown and the Confederacy* (1939).

Parks, Joseph H. *Joseph E. Brown of Georgia* (1977).

Richardson, James D., comp. *A Compilation of the Messages and Papers of the Confederacy* (1906).

U.S. War Department. *The War of the Rebellion: A Compilation of the Official Records of the Union and Confederate Armies* (1880–1901).

Yearns, W. Buck. *The Confederate Governors* (1985).

BROWN, WILLIAM WELLS
(ca. 1814–1884)
African-American abolitionist and author

William Wells Brown was born near Lexington, Kentucky. In a narrative of his life as a slave, he wrote about his enslaved mother, Elizabeth, who told him that she was a daughter of Daniel Boone and a slave lover. She told him his father was a white slave owner, George W. Higgins. The family moved to St. Louis, where Brown was hired out because of his embarrassing resemblance to his master's white nephew. In 1830 Brown worked for the abolitionist Elijah P. Lovejoy at the St. Louis *Times*. Later he was sold to a merchant and then to a riverboat captain.

Brown escaped in 1834 to Ohio, where a Quaker by the name of Wells Brown helped him. After reaching Cleveland, Brown became part of the antislavery movement, attended Black National Conventions, and began teaching himself to read and write. He married Elizabeth (Betsey) Schooner in that same year. Of their three children only two survived, Clarissa (born in 1836) and Josephine (born in 1839). Brown's most successful business venture was stewarding for lake steamers, and he eventually settled his young family in Buffalo, New York. In one year he helped sixty fugitives reach Canada.

In 1847 Brown and his wife separated and he moved to Boston with his two daughters. There he published his story of his life as a slave, *Narrative of William W. Brown, a Fugitive Slave*, first published in 1847 and expanded the next year to sell 8,000 copies in two years.

He went as one of several American representatives to the World Peace Congress in Paris in 1849. There he established his renown as a nonviolent Garrisonian by emphasizing the role of the threat and use of violence by slave owners. He asserted, "The dissemination of the principles of peace would be the means of emancipation." He remained in Europe for the next five years, researching in the archives of England and France and also visiting the West Indies. He also helped to found and run in 1852 the London newspaper *The Anti-Slavery Advocate*.

Out of this period in his life came the first novel published by an African-American. Published in 1853, *Clotel; or, the President's Daughter: A Narrative of Slave Life in the United States* was a politically charged narrative of slave life in the Southern states. By putting at the center of this novel the black offspring of President Thomas Jefferson, Brown put in print what the Hemmings family alleged for so many years.

Although he wrote many plays, only one was published: *The Escape; or, A Leap for Freedom*, published in Boston in 1858. The five-act drama is generally acknowledged to be the first play published by an African-American author. The other plays he presented as dramatic readings in place of the usual antislavery lecture while on tours. His journalist talent can be found in his contributions to the *London Daily News*; *The Liberator*; Frederick Douglass' paper; and *The National Anti-Slavery Standard*. His most important books were history books written during and after the Civil War.

After the election of Abraham Lincoln and as the secession crisis grew, Brown continued making his money from his antislavery publications, even serializing a revised portion of his novel *Clotel* under the name of "Miranda; or The Beautiful Quadroon" in the *Weekly Anglo-African* (1 December 1860–6 March 1861). He discouraged black enlistments until blacks had won equality of treatment in the military. In September 1862, President Lincoln issued his preliminary Emancipation Proclamation and few Northern blacks rejoiced; many saw the move as a cautious war measure, even callous rather than humanitarian in motive. Brown said at that time, "The colored people of the country rejoice in what Mr. Lincoln has done for them, but they all wish that General Frémont had been in his place." (U.S. general John C. Frémont had on 30 August 1861 established martial law in Missouri and freed the slaves of all traitors.)

At a meeting of black activists held in Liberty Hall, New Bedford, on 18 February 1863, Brown gave an address that reversed his position. He described at length the heroic heritage of black Americans and how they had already made progress in the integration of America. He said they "had poets and preachers; it was time to have a hero on the battlefield....The time had come...for the black man to vindicate his own character." In March, President Lincoln sent Adjutant General Lorenzo Thomas to the Mississippi Valley with the authority to raise black troops. Brown joined Massachusetts governor John Andrews's "Black Committee" that worked to encourage and recruit black men into the 54th and 55th Massachusetts Infantry and the 5th Massachusetts Cavalry. General Orders No. 143, dated 22 May 1863, established the Bureau for Colored Troops with the authority to supervise organizing black units and examine candidates seeking commissions in them. This was a milestone in the history of blacks in the Civil War: they now fought officially for the United States and not just for a state or individual. However, in Massachusetts, only whites could join the militia and no blacks could be commissioned as officers. "Equality first, guns afterward," posited Brown.

That year, while living in Cambridgeport, Massachusetts, Brown published *The Black Man*, a set of historical and literary essays that traced the African origins of black Americans. This publication was a heroic effort to explode current myths of blacks' "natural inferiority." Brown included fifty-three biographical sketches of artists, teachers, actors, poets, preachers, lawyers, rebel slave leaders, and rulers of Haiti and Liberia. He showed that he had fully broken with the nonviolence of Garrisonianism by portraying Nat Turner as the model for black action needed in the South during the Civil War. This book went through ten printings in three years.

In the summer of 1863, whites in New York City rioted ostensibly in protest of the draft, but from 13 to 17 July they expressed their frustrations and hatred against Americans of African descent. More than eleven African-American citizens were killed, hundreds wounded, thousands left homeless and destitute. Brown was there recruiting blacks for the Massachusetts regiments and recorded the heroic efforts of men and women during those violent times.

In October 1864 in Syracuse, New York, Brown attended the National Convention of Colored Citizens of the United States, organized by Frederick Douglass. There he helped draft "Declarations of Wrong and Rights." He also revised his novel *Clotel* that year and reissued it under the name *Clotelle: A Tale of Southern States*, adding more dramatic scenes and references to actual newspaper accounts and historical facts of the horrors of slavery in the South. Clotelle was the name of his two-year-old daughter; he had married in 1860 Annie Elizabeth Gray. Also in 1864 Brown began treating patients in the Boston area, and thereafter he added M.D. after his name.

In 1867 he published *The Negro in the American Rebellion; His Heroism and His Fidelity*. He wanted to give historical proof of what African-American men had contributed to the building of the nation that debated whether to give them basic civil rights. Though the book began with the deeds of the military man of African descent in the American Revolution and continued with the War of 1812, more than half of the book was devoted to the last two years of the Civil War. It was the first published historical analysis of the black role in the Civil War. It was not a popular book and did not sell well; many copies were burned in the great Boston fire of 1872.

After the war, Brown continued to give lectures on black history, but he redirected his abolitionist energies toward temperance work and medicine. In 1880 he published his last and most popular book, *My Southern Home; or The South and Its People*. He urged black self-respect, hard work, and self-improvement, recom-

mending emigration from the South. He foreshadowed W. E. B. DuBois's *Souls of Black Folks* (1903) when he appealed to his fellow African-Americans: "Don't be ashamed to show your colors, and to own them." Brown died on 6 November 1884 in Chelsea, Massachusetts, from a tumor of the bladder and was buried in an unmarked grave.

—*Randolph Hollingsworth*

See also Abolitionist Movement; African-American Soldiers, C.S.A.; Douglass, Frederick; Emancipation Proclamation; Garrison, William Lloyd; Underground Railroad; United States Colored Troops.

For further reading:

Brown, Josephine. *Biography of an American Bondman, by His Daughter* (1856).

Brown, William Wells. *The Black Man: His Antecedents, His Genius, and His Achievements* (1863).

———. *My Southern Home; or The South and Its People* (1880).

———. *The Negro in the American Rebellion* (1867).

Candela, Gregory L. "William Wells Brown." In *Afro-American Writers before the Harlem Renaissance*, vol. 50 of *Dictionary of Literary Biography* (1986).

Dunnigan, Alice Allison. *The Fascinating Story of Black Kentuckians: Their Heritage and Traditions* (1982).

Farrison, William Edward. *William Wells Brown: Author and Reformer* (1969).

Lucas, Marion B. *From Slavery to Segregation, 1760–1891. A History of Blacks in Kentucky*, vol. 1 (1992).

Mabee, Carleton. *Black Freedom: The Nonviolent Abolitionists from 1830 through the Civil War* (1970).

BROWNING, ORVILLE HICKMAN
(1806–1881)
Union politician

Orville H. Browning was a friend and political associate of Abraham Lincoln. Browning's increasingly conservative wartime views, however, conflicted with Lincoln's emancipation policy and other administration war measures, and in the postwar years Browning drifted away from the Republican Party that he had helped to shape in antebellum Illinois. His diary and correspondence are important primary sources for Civil War–era history.

Browning, like Lincoln, was a native Kentuckian, born on 10 February 1806 near Cynthiana in Harrison County. He attended Augusta College and then read law with an uncle. He passed the bar and moved to Quincy, Illinois, in 1831. The next year he served briefly as a militiaman in the Black Hawk War. He married in 1836 and entered politics the same year, winning election to the state senate as a Whig. In 1843 he lost a race for the U.S. Congress to Democrat Stephen A. Douglas. In 1850 and 1852 he was again unsuccessful in congressional elections. During these prewar years Browning gained a reputation as an able attorney and influential public figure, though he was sometimes considered aloof and somewhat conceited. He was noted for his stately manner and his old style ruffled shirts and cuffs.

Browning believed slavery was wrong in the abstract, and he opposed its extension beyond the states where it already existed. He was not sure, however, that there was any better system for relations between the races in America. He favored proposals to colonize freed blacks outside the country. In 1845 he became the vice president of the Illinois Colonization Society. Throughout his life he never abandoned a common belief of his time that blacks were inferior to whites.

The Kansas-Nebraska Act of 1854 roused his anger. He joined the newly formed Republican Party, and in 1856 and 1858 he drafted state party platforms that helped attract like-minded conservatives to the Illinois Republican banner. In the presidential election of 1860 Browning actually favored the Missouri conservative Edward Bates, but as an Illinois delegate to the Chicago convention he did his part to help his friend Lincoln obtain the nomination. Lincoln followed Browning's suggestion to soften some strident language in his first inaugural address, replacing a threat to "reclaim" captured Federal property with a less bellicose resolution to "hold, occupy and possess" Federal positions. Browning let Lincoln know of his desire to become a U.S. Supreme Court justice, but with the sudden death of Stephen Douglas in June 1861, the Republican governor of Illinois, Richard Yates, appointed Browning to finish Douglas's term in the U.S. Senate.

The onset of a shooting war radicalized Browning for a time. As a senator, he declared the North should treat the seceded states as conquered territories; he voted for the First Confiscation Act; he supported General John C. Frémont's proclamation freeing the slaves in Missouri; he defended the administration against criticism for arbitrary arrests of Northern citizens; and he voted to emancipate slaves in Washington, D.C.

By late spring 1862, however, Browning began reverting to his characteristic conservatism. First, he opposed the Second Confiscation Act. Then he broke unequivocally with the Radical Republicans by condemning Lincoln's preliminary Emancipation Proclamation as unconstitutional and unwise. He persisted in admonishing Lincoln to abandon emancipation right up until the policy officially took effect on 1 January 1863. Browning became so alienated by the course of events that in the 1864 presidential election he refrained from supporting Lincoln's reelection. Though his political relations with Lincoln became strained, the two men and their wives maintained cordial personal relations. The Brownings had been of particular comfort to the grieving Lincolns on the death of their son Willie in 1862, and Browning served as a pallbearer at the president's funeral.

Democrats won control of the Illinois legislature in

the 1862 elections, so Browning did not retain his U.S. Senate seat. He remained in Washington, however, where as a lobbyist he used his connections with Lincoln and other government leaders to obtain favors for his clients. During the last months of the war he was apparently involved in a failed scheme to make money trading in Confederate commodities.

After the war, Browning was a strong critic of the Radical Republicans in Congress and their reconstruction policies. He even participated in an unsuccessful attempt to form a new conservative political party. President Andrew Johnson appointed him secretary of the interior in 1866. Browning stood by the president in his impeachment battle with Congress, serving in a dual capacity as attorney general during the impeachment trial. When President Grant took office in 1869, Browning returned to Illinois where he prospered as an attorney for the Chicago, Burlington & Quincy Railroad. He also finally reached the Supreme Court— but in the capacity of an attorney arguing for railroad interests in one of the Granger cases. He died in Quincy on 10 August 1881 at the age of seventy-five.

—Byron Andreasen

For further reading:
Baxter, Maurice. *Orville H. Browning: Lincoln's Friend and Critic* (1957).

BROWNLOW, WILLIAM GANNAWAY
(1805–1877)

Tennessee Unionist

Born 25 August 1805 in Wythe County, Virginia, William Brownlow came of age with, and helped to shape, the evangelical world of the antebellum South. A Unionist, his religion and politics illustrate the complexity of Southern proslavery and secession views. Orphaned at age eleven, Brownlow worked for ten years as a carpenter and laborer before being converted to evangelical Christianity at a camp meeting. With no formal education, he became a circuit rider for the Methodist Episcopal Church, preaching repentance and damnation in western Virginia, North Carolina, and eastern Tennessee. He married in 1836 and settled in Elizabethton, Tennessee.

A man of fiery temper and fiercely committed to religious and political truth, Brownlow found an outlet for his contentious personality through editing a newspaper, the *Whig*, which he published in Knoxville from 1849 to 1862. Despite the convention that ministers were not to meddle in partisan politics, Brownlow was a vocal champion of Henry Clay and the Whig Party's program of economic development. He loathed Democrats and increasingly focused his political vitriol on Andrew Johnson, the leading Democrat in eastern Tennessee.

Brownlow also represented the truth of evangelical

Christianity as he understood it. He wrote book-length diatribes denouncing Catholicism as contrary to scripture and, during the 1850s, defended the Methodist Church from charges leveled against it by James Robinson Graves, a Baptist editor in Nashville, Tennessee. Graves characterized Methodism as "a great iron wheel" because its polity rolled over congregational liberty. Brownlow responded with two tomes, *The Great Iron Wheel Examined; or its False Spokes Extracted* and *The Little Iron Wheel Enlarged: or Elder Graves*.

Brownlow also loathed abolitionism. He referred to Harriet Beecher Stowe as "ugly as Original Sin." He considered abolitionism as contrary to the Bible and to the Constitution, which made slaves "a lawful species of property." He concluded that "those who feed and clothe them well, and instruct them in religion, are better friends to them than those who set them at liberty." In these exchanges, Brownlow relied on ad hominem arguments and liberal interpretation of scripture. He pointed out that the biblical Cain had nullified God's law in slaying Abel, and suggested that throughout the Bible, nullification equaled sin.

Apart from a personal devotion to his deity, Brownlow's special loyalty was to the Union. During the secession crisis, he urged people to pray for "grace to perceive the right path, which. . . leads from the camps of Southern mad-caps and Northern fanatics." He rejected the notion that secession was an appropriate remedy for Lincoln's election and counseled moderation. At the same time, Brownlow displayed a United States flag over his house and announced that he would support secession and join the Democratic Party only "when man forgets to be selfish, or Democrats lose their inclination to steal." He pledged that he would "fight the Secession leaders until Hell freezes over, and then fight them on the ice."

Brownlow's pro-Union invective had a supportive audience in eastern Tennessee, but it also invited the ire of the Confederate government. Anxious to avoid provocation, it did not move against Brownlow or other Unionists until Brownlow's increasingly vehement editorials in his newspaper, the Knoxville *Whig*, became impossible to ignore. After a brief incarceration, Brownlow was permitted to flee to the North, where he published an account of his experiences during the early days of secession and civil war.

Lionized in the North as the embodiment of the quintessential loyal Southerner, Brownlow toured Northern cities before returning to Tennessee behind the Union army. He resumed publishing his newspaper in November 1863. He labored alongside Andrew Johnson, his antebellum archfoe, to obtain Tennessee's restoration to the Union. Brownlow supported Johnson's efforts, and quasi-legal machinations, to get some sort of approval for the abolition of slavery and a government organized along the lines of Lincoln's Proclamation of Amnesty and Reconstruction. When Johnson became Lincoln's vice president, Brownlow succeeded Johnson as wartime Reconstruction governor.

Conservative Unionists abandoned Brownlow at this point because they feared that wartime Reconstruction would lead to the political equality of freedmen. They hoped to regain control of their state and to keep former slaves out of politics. Brownlow had initially supported this position, but rather than lose office, he supported Federal efforts to register black voters, courted their support, and won reelection in 1867. Although he doubtless recognized that the forces of Redemption and the Ku Klux Klan would be ultimately irresistible, Brownlow had the legislature elect him to the United States Senate in 1868, and he served out his full term. He died on 29 April 1877.

—*Edward R. Crowther*

For further reading:
Brownlow, William G. *Sketches of the Rise, Progress, and Decline of Secession; with a Narrative of Personal Adventures among the Rebels* (1862).
Coulter, E. Merton. *William G. Brownlow: Fighting Parson of the Southern Highlands* (1937).
Harris, William C. *With Charity for All: Lincoln and the Restoration of the Union* (1997).

BROWNSVILLE, TEXAS

Sixty-five miles up the Rio Grande from its mouth on the Gulf of Mexico, Brownsville was the site of one of the first Confederate successes in the war when the small Union garrison evacuated nearby Fort Brown after a show of force by Texas troops in early 1861. Brownsville became a significant trading center because of its proximity to Matamoros, Mexico, just across the river. Although the president of Mexico, Benito Juarez, favored the Union, the governor of Tamaulipas Province, Santiago Vidaurri, maintained friendly relations with Confederate Texans. As a result, as other Confederate ports were shut down by the Union blockade and as the Mississippi was closed to Confederate traffic, Brownsville became the center of a bustling trade between Southern cotton growers and English, French, and even Yankee merchants. Confederate and Texas authorities tried without effect to control the indiscriminate trade between Southerners and Northerners. From late 1861 until the end of the war, thousands of ox-drawn wagons laden with cotton wound their way through south Texas to Brownsville from as far away as Louisiana and Arkansas. A Texan who served as a teamster on one of those wagons recalled years later that the trail stretching north from Brownsville "became a broad thorofare along which continuously moved two vast unending trains of wagons"—one southbound, piled high with cotton; and

Confederates evacuating the town of Brownsville (*Harper's Weekly* / *Library of Congress*)

the other northbound, crammed with military and civilian supplies. By mid-1863 the Brownsville *Flag* could announce that "the town is crowded with merchants and traders from all parts of the world, and the side-walks are blocked up with goods." Northern traders eagerly bought all the cotton they could get from Mexican intermediaries acting on behalf of Texas cotton speculators; Southerners then used the profits to buy "all manner of explosive and destructive things" to sell to the Confederate military. Because of its economic prosperity, which benefitted not only the few men who became millionaires trading in cotton, but also skilled and manual laborers, the town's wartime population swelled to 25,000, while Matamoros soared to 40,000 and the makeshift town of Bagdad on the Rio Grande to 15,000. The cotton trade naturally attracted the attention of the United States government, which mounted the Rio Grande campaign to shut it down. Brownsville served as the headquarters of the Union 8th Corps when it occupied parts of the Rio Grande Valley and Texas Gulf Coast between November 1863 and July 1864. Union troops in occupied Brownsville set up housekeeping in the courthouse and other public buildings, published their own newspaper, the *Loyal National Union Journal*, held the occasional review or military ball, and enjoyed

the illicit attractions of both Brownsville and Matamoros. Brownsville also served as "capital" to the new provisional governor of Texas, the former Congressman and Texas Unionist Brigadier General A. J. Hamilton. Along with other well-known Unionist refugees like former U.S. District Court Judge Thomas H. DuVal and Hamilton's former law partner John Hancock, Hamilton attempted to establish a government loyal to the United States. They established a chapter of the Union League, a national Republican organization, and recruited a few hundred troops for the Union's 1st and 2d Texas Cavalry.

Brownsville was also the scene of much intrigue related to Mexican politics, after Mexico itself was thrown into civil war by the French invasion of 1862. Competing armies fought on behalf of the French, for the Mexican president, Juarez, or for powerful borderland opportunists like Juan Cortinas, a Mexican-Texan rancher who in 1859 had briefly occupied Brownsville during a dispute with local law officers. Matamoros changed hands several times during the course of the war; the defeated factions would often retreat across the river to Brownsville to lick their wounds and plan their next attack. Union troops actually crossed over to Matamoros during the fighting one night in 1864 to protect the U.S. consulate. When much of the Federal occupation force was transferred to Louisiana in the summer of 1864, Confederate troops under Colonel John "Rip" Ford began pushing Union detachments out of the Rio Grande Valley in June and July. Skirmishes at Ebonal on 22 July and on the outskirts of Brownsville on 25 July convinced the disorganized Yankees to evacuate the city on 29 July. It remained a Confederate stronghold in south Texas for the remainder of the war. The Rebel force, again under the command of Ford, that won the last land battle of the Civil War at Palmito Ranch rode out of Fort Brown. The city and its neighboring fort were finally reoccupied by Union soldiers in late May 1865.

—*James Marten*

See also Blockade of C.S.A.; Hamilton, Andrew Jackson; Matamoros, Mexico; Palmito Ranch, Battle of; Rio Grande Campaign.

For further reading:
Daddysmith, James W. *The Matamoros Trade: Confederate Commerce, Diplomacy, and Intrigue* (1984).
Hunter, John Warren. "The Fall of Brownsville on the Rio Grande, November 1863" (n.d.).
Kerby, Robert L. *Kirby Smith's Confederacy: The Trans-Mississippi South, 1863–1865* (1972).
Marten, James. "For the Army, the People, and Abraham Lincoln: A Yankee Newspaper in Occupied Texas." *Civil War History* (1993).

BRYANT, WILLIAM CULLEN
(1794–1878)
Poet

William Cullen Bryant was born on 3 November 1794 in Cummington, Massachusetts, the son of Peter Bryant, a physician, and Sarah Snell. Bryant's early start with books came from his parents. He attended Williams College in Williamstown, Massachusetts, from 1810 to 1811. He then studied law privately, was admitted to the bar in 1815, and practiced law in Plainfield and Great Barrington for ten years. Moving to New York in 1825, he became associate editor of the *New York Evening Post* from 1826 to 1829 and editor-in-chief from 1829 to 1878. In 1836, he became half-owner of the journal.

An ardent believer in human rights and liberty, Bryant, speaking on 4 July 1820 at Stockbridge, Massachusetts, had already evinced an abhorrence of slavery. He found reprehensible the Missouri Compromise of 1820, which extended slavery in the Louisiana Purchase territory south of latitude 36°30' and in Missouri, north of the line. In 1836, angered by antiabolition violence in Cincinnati to stop James G. Birney from publishing his abolitionist newspaper, Bryant defended the right to bring the slavery issue into the public arena. He became outraged again in 1837

when Reverend Elijah P. Lovejoy, editor of an antislavery paper in Alton, Illinois, was murdered by a mob.

Bryant wove the Civil War into his poetry. "The Antiquity of Freedom" (1842), was a forerunner of his later verses: "...nor yet, O Freedom! close thy lids/In slumber; for thine enemy [Tyranny] never sleeps,/And thou must watch and combat till the day/Of the new earth and heaven." In April 1844, Bryant's articles raised the issue whether Texas should join the Union as a slave-holding territory from which other states could be created. Sincerely devoted to the Wilmot Proviso (1846), which would have barred slavery in any territory acquired from Mexico, Bryant urged Congress in 1847 to prohibit slavery expansion into New Mexico and California. In the presidential election of 1848, antislavery Democrats, antislavery Whigs, and the Liberty Party combined to nominate a "Free Soil" ticket, headed by Martin Van Buren, who now had approved of the exclusion of slavery from new territories. Bryant supported Van Buren, but the Free Soilers did not win a single state. Bryant's *Evening Post*, a Free-Soil Democratic newspaper, objected to the Compromise of 1850 that, by abandoning the Wilmot Proviso, opened the Mexican cession to slavery. Though the Democratic Convention of 1852 expressed its loyalty to the Compromise of 1850, Bryant, wanting to remain affiliated with Democratic Free Soilers, accepted their presidential nominee, Franklin Pierce.

The Kansas-Nebraska Act of 1854, which repealed the prohibition of slavery north of 36°30' in the Louisiana Purchase territory, caused Bryant to work industriously on the formation of the Republican Party, which stood for resisting the extension of slavery. In 1856, he threw the increasingly influential *Evening Post* solidly behind their presidential candidate, John C. Frémont. Bryant, who had written many editorials denouncing the Kansas-Nebraska Act, called attention in 1856 to the violence of slaveholders attempting to establish their control over free-state Kansas. He also reprimanded newly elected President James Buchanan for his proslavery policy, believing that Buchanan was contributing greatly to the disruption of the Democratic Party. And in 1857, when Chief Justice Roger B. Taney ruled that Congress never had the right to exclude slavery from a territory, Bryant complained that the "peculiar institution" had become a Federal institution.

In late 1858, Bryant sensed the emergence of Abraham Lincoln as a prominent national figure and, with other leading New York Republicans, brought about his historic visit to the Cooper Institute on 27 February 1860. Bryant introduced the speaker, praising him for his involvement in the Frémont campaign of 1856. After Lincoln's nomination for the presidency three months later, Bryant unhesitatingly and vigorously supported his candidacy, committing the *Evening Post* to work strenuously to elect him.

The restoration of the Union became the *Evening Post*'s editorial policy and, throughout the war, the editors rejected any compromise with the South. Bryant, who in a 12 November 1860 editorial declared that peaceable secession was an "absurdity," advised the president-elect in his letter of 25 December 1860 to be resolute on the questions of slavery and secession. In "Not Yet" (July 1861), Bryant expressed optimism: "Shall traitors lay that greatness low?/No,/and of Hope and Blessing, No!" In "Our Country's Call," written shortly thereafter (1861), he implored workaday men to take up arms: "…we/Must beat the banded traitors back."

A diligent advocate of immediate and universal emancipation by 1862 in editorials and in speeches at abolitionist rallies, Bryant arguably had rebuked Lincoln for rescinding General Frémont's proclamation of 31 August 1861, which had freed the slaves of rebellious Missourians. Later, in a speech on 2 October 1863, Bryant made a particularly robust statement opposing the president's policy of gradual emancipation. Further, arguably questioning Lincoln's leadership, he visited the president in August 1862, counseling him to pursue the war forcefully if the Union cause was not to be lost. Immediately after the horrendous Union defeat at Fredericksburg, Bryant in his editorial of 18 December 1862, asked with a sense of hopelessness, "How long is such intolerable and wicked blundering to continue? What does the President wait for?"

To counteract the growing peace movement in the North fueled by the Copperhead press, Bryant in 1863 helped direct an organized effort aimed to rally public support for continuing the war. In his 6 September 1864 editorial, "No Negotiations With the Rebel Government," he insisted on no peace without the abolition of slavery. In that same month, Bryant became confident of Lincoln's reelection, and his paper firmly supported the chief executive. In "The Death of Lincoln" (April 1865), the sorrowful Bryant wrote of the president's compassion and strength: "Oh, slow to smite and swift to spare,/Gentle and merciful and just:/Who, in the fear of God, didst bear/the sword of power, a nation's trust!" A year later, in "Death of Slavery" (May 1866), he recalled the cruelties imposed on the slaves and, addressing the slaveholders, exclaimed: "Well was thy doom deserved…."

Bryant, who was a founder and devoted worker for the National Freedmen's Relief Association (1863), declared in his Cooper Institute address of 26 February 1864 that the major challenge of reconstruction was to provide assistance to the four million slaves in their transition to freedom. Generally in agreement with Johnson's views on reconstruction, he strongly favored a conciliatory policy after the war: for example, his readiness to accept state approval (rather than a congressional act) for the abolition of slavery. Bryant insisted, however, on federal protection of the freed people's civil rights and on their omission from the population count (to determine representation in Congress) until they were granted the right of suffrage. In 1868 he supported Grant's candidacy for the presidency; but only reluctantly, because of the administration's policies, did he support Grant's reelection campaign. Bryant, a civic leader in New York City, was an early supporter of public parks (one in Manhattan was renamed Bryant Park in 1884) and a participant in the formation of the Metropolitan Museum of Art in 1870. Bryant died in New York City on 12 June 1878.

—*Bernard Hirschhorn*

See also Abolitionist Movement; Free Soil Party.
For further reading:
Brown, Charles H. *William Cullen Bryant: A Biography* (1971).
Bryant, William Cullen II, and Thomas G. Voss, eds. *The Letters of William Cullen Bryant* (1984, 1992).
McDowell, Tremaine. *William Cullen Bryant: Representative Selections with Introduction, Bibliography and Notes* (1935).
McLean, Jr., Albert F. *William Cullen Bryant* (1989).
Nevins, Allan. *The Evening Post: A Century of Journalism* (1922).

BUCHANAN, FRANKLIN
(1800–1874)
Confederate admiral

After a distinguished forty-five-year career in the U.S. Navy, Franklin Buchanan went south in 1861 and commanded both of the Confederate Navy's famous ironclads—the CSS *Virginia* (nee *Merrimack)* and the CSS *Tennessee*—in the process earning the distinction of being the Confederacy's only full admiral.

Buchanan was born at Auchentorlie, a family estate near Baltimore, on 17 September 1800, the fifth child and third son of Dr. George Buchanan, a physician, and Laetitia McKean, the daughter of a prominent Philadelphia family. He obtained a U.S. Navy midshipman's warrant at the age of fourteen during the War of 1812, but the war ended before he could report for duty. Most of his early naval service was in the Mediterranean on the frigate *Java* and the ship-of-the-line *Franklin*, and in the Caribbean where the U.S. Navy pursued pirates and slavers in smaller craft. Promoted to lieutenant on 13 January 1825 and to commander on 8 September 1841, Buchanan obtained his first command in September 1842 as captain of the sloop *Vincennes*. He married the former Ann Catherine (Nannie) Lloyd, a member of a prominent family on Maryland's Eastern Shore, with whom he had nine children.

Highlights of Buchanan's pre–Civil War career include his role as the founding superintendent of the U.S. Naval Academy in 1845–1846, and his command of the sloop *Germantown* in the War with Mexico (1847–1848) in which capacity he twice led shore expe-

Franklin Buchanan (*Library of Congress*)

ditions to capture Mexican fortifications. In 1853–1854, he was the captain of Matthew C. Perry's flagship during the expedition to Japan and conducted the negotiations that eventually led to a rapprochement between the U.S. and Japan.

Promoted to captain in 1855, Buchanan was posted to the command of the Washington Navy Yard in 1859. He was there on 19 April 1861 when a Massachusetts regiment passing through Baltimore on its way to Washington in anticipation of civil war was assailed by a civilian mob.

The troops opened fire, and when it was over four soldiers and twelve civilians lay dead. This event provoked Buchanan to tender his resignation from the Navy in the full expectation that Maryland would soon secede and join the Confederacy. When that did not happen, he sought to recall his resignation. But Secretary of the navy Gideon Welles did not want half-hearted patriots in his navy and informed Buchanan that his name was to be struck from the Navy list.

Buchanan's sympathies for the South derived in part from his close association with his slave-holding in-laws, the Lloyds of Wye House. Even so, he delayed several weeks before deciding to join the Confederacy. Not until after the battle of Bull Run (21 July 1861) did he leave his home on Maryland's Eastern Shore and cross the Potomac to offer his services to the Confederate navy. Serving briefly in an administrative capacity as Chief of the Bureau of Orders and Detail, he was posted in February 1862 to the command of the newly reconstituted ironclad steamer *Virginia*, created from the scorched hull of the frigate *Merrimack*.

On 8 March 1862, Buchanan led the *Virginia* out of its Gosport Navy Yard berth and down the Elizabeth River into Hampton Roads on its maiden voyage. He immediately attacked the two U.S. Navy warships lying off Newport News Point, sinking the sloop *Cumberland* with his iron ram, and shelling the frigate *Congress* into submission. Irritated when Federal troops on shore fired at the boarding party that was attempting to secure the surrendered *Congress*, Buchanan took up a musket himself and fired back. His bravado made him a target for the Federal troops as well, and he received a serious wound through his upper thigh. That wound kept him from being in command when the *Virginia* dueled the *Monitor* the next day.

Promoted to the rank of full admiral, Buchanan's next command after he recovered from his wound was in Mobile Bay. There the Confederacy could not convert existing ships into ironclads; it had to construct them from the raw materials. This proved a daunting task.

Nevertheless, after months of effort, marred by difficulties in obtaining iron plate and engine parts, guns and a crew, Buchanan could finally boast in May 1864 that a fully armed and manned ironclad floated in Mobile Bay, the CSS *Tennessee*.

On 5 August, the Federal fleet offshore under the command of Rear Admiral David G. Farragut, got underway with the clear intention of fighting its way into Mobile Bay. Buchanan conned the *Tennessee* into the channel off Fort Morgan and prepared to attack the Federal warships one by one as they entered. The first of them, however, the ironclad monitor *Tecumseh*, struck a mine and exploded spectacularly, going to the bottom in just 25 seconds and taking 93 men with it. Farragut's other ships steamed into the bay and Buchanan moved forward to engage. The slow speed of his ironclad (6 knots) made it impossible for him to use his ram, but he engaged in a furious gun duel with the entire Federal fleet as his own vessel was rammed three times by three different Federal warships. He was again wounded when flying debris from a Federal shell smashed his leg. Not long thereafter, it became evident that he would have to surrender: with the *Tennessee's* steering chains cut, the vessel could no longer maneuver, several of her guns were out of order, and she could not effectively defend itself.

Buchanan was a prisoner of war in Fort Lafayette (New York) for several months before he was exchanged in April of 1865. He arrived back in Mobile just as the war ended. After the war, Buchanan served for a year as president of Maryland Agricultural College (later the University of Maryland) and as secretary for the Life Assurance Association of America. He died quietly at his home, the Rest, on Maryland's Eastern Shore on 11 May 1874 survived by his wife and nine children.

—*Craig L. Symonds*

See also Farragut, David Glasgow; Mobile Bay; *Monitor* versus *Virginia*; Navy, C.S.A.; *Tecumseh*, USS; *Tennessee*, CSS.

For further reading:

Brown, John William. "Franklin Buchanan, Naval Leader" (M.A. thesis, 1948).

Lewis, Charles Lee. *Admiral Franklin Buchanan, Fearless Man of Action* (1929).

Still, William N., Jr. "The Confederate States Navy at Mobile, 1861 to August 1864." *Alabama Historical Quarterly* (1968).

Symonds, Craig L. *Confederate Admiral: The Life and Wars of Franklin Buchanan* (1999).

Walter, Francis X. *The Naval Battle of Mobile Bay, August 5, 1864; & Franklin Buchanan on the* Tennessee, *A Portrait of the Admiral of the Confederate Fleet in Mobile Bay* (1993).

BUCHANAN, JAMES
(1791–1868)

Fifteenth president of the United States

Born near Memersburg, Pennsylvania, James Buchanan graduated from Dickinson College in 1809, studied law at Lancaster, and amassed a large fortune. In 1819 his fiancee died suddenly, and he vowed to remain a bachelor. This may have affected his political outlook, because in Washington later he shared bachelor quarters with Southerners who became his closest friends.

After 1824 he became a Jacksonian Democrat. As a U.S. representative (1821–1831) and senator (1834–1845), he voted with the Southern planters against tariffs, federal support for homesteads, river and harbor improvements, and land grants for schools. He was minister to Russia in 1832–1833. As Polk's secretary of state (1845–1849), he advocated limited annexations during the Mexican War, but later opposed the peace treaty because it did not annex enough territory. While minister to England (1852–1857), he coauthored the Ostend Manifesto, which urged the annexation of Cuba, by force if necessary, to prevent Cuba's abolition of slavery.

As president from 1857–1861, Buchanan alienated many Northerners and strengthened the new free-soil Republican Party by advocating proslavery policies. In 1857 he influenced and urged compliance with the Supreme Court's *Dred Scott* decision, which declared the Missouri Compromise limitation on western slavery to be unconstitutional. When a small pro-Southern minority in Kansas wrote the Lecompton Constitution approving slavery, Buchanan unsuccessfully pressured Congress to admit Kansas as a slave state.

During 1857–1858 the United States suffered a brief recession for which Buchanan offered no solutions. This helped cause the off-year elections of 1858 to go heavily Republican, which angry Southerners interpreted as opposition to slavery. Senator Stephen A. Douglas was the only Democrat strong enough to maintain the party coalition of South and northwest, but Buchanan disliked Douglas and gave the political patronage in the northwest to the senator's proslavery enemies.

At the Democratic Presidential Convention in 1860, the only candidate with a significant following in both North and South was Douglas, who was clearly no enemy of slavery. Supported by the president, however, the radical Southerners countered the moderation of Douglas with the "Alabama Platform," demanding Federal protection for slavery in all territories. No Northern delegate could support this principle and it was defeated. As a result, seven Southern states bolted the convention and later nominated Vice President John C. Breckinridge, while the Northern Democrats nominated Douglas. The Buchanan White House served as campaign headquarters for Breckinridge, and the Democratic split helped elect Lincoln with less than 40 percent of the popular vote.

With Lincoln elected and seven Southern states preparing to secede, Buchanan's annual message blamed the crisis entirely upon the North. He denounced secession as unconstitutional, but defended the reasons for secession, announced his unwillingness to coerce seceding states, and asked for Northern concessions that every Southerner knew would never be granted. This probably influenced those Southerners still debating secession. He also strongly supported various efforts to frame an acceptable compromise. Even without the seceded Southerners, Congress did pass a thirteenth amendment denying Congress any right to deal with slavery, but the battle of Fort Sumter intervened before it could be ratified.

Despite his personal sympathies, Buchanan rejected Southern demands for the Federal Forts Pickens, Taylor, and Sumter. He strengthened the first two and they remained intact. Sumter, however, was inside Charleston Harbor and very vulnerable. The army's chief, General Winfield Scott, urged Buchanan to strengthen the forts, pointed out that no forces were available for doing it, announced that a Union that could be preserved only by force was not worth saving, and suggested that the United States should be divided into four separate nations. When Buchanan ordered the warship *Brooklyn* to reinforce Sumter, Scott persuaded him to substitute the unarmed sidewheeler *Star of the West*. Confederate guns repulsed the ship and Scott later blamed Buchanan for not sending the *Brooklyn*, although the decision had been made by Scott. Four ships prepared to defend Sumter were already assembled in New York when Lincoln took office. To his credit, Buchanan handed the fort to Lincoln intact.

While the sectional conflict dominated Buchanan's attention, he also advocated very aggressive foreign policies, most of which were prevented by Congress. He sent an army against the Utah Mormons, and only skilled intervention by Thomas L. Kane prevented serious bloodshed. He offered to buy Alaska for the Mormons, but the Russians refused his tentative $10 million offer. He successfully opposed British expansion in Central America and won a dispute over the U.S-Canadian border in Puget Sound. In trying to stop the African slave trade, the British were searching suspicious-looking vessels. The United States was committed by treaty to assist this effort, but Buchanan ordered every available vessel to protect American ships from search or detention. When William Walker invaded Nicaragua with a Southern army, he was arrested by Commodore Paulding and an American fleet. Buchanan, however, ordered Walker released and reprimanded Paulding for invading Nicaraguan territory.

When France threatened Mexico, Buchanan asked Congress for money to buy northern Mexico, and he later asked for authority to invade Mexico to obtain "indemnity for the past and security for the future." In 1859 his congressional friends tried to get $30 million to buy Cuba. When a Paraguayan sniper killed an American sailor, Buchanan sent nineteen warships carrying 200 guns and 2,500 men to seek redress. Paraguay paid $10,000, apologized, and signed a useless trade treaty. Perhaps Buchanan was merely trying to unite the North and South against some common enemy, but his proposals indicated a readiness to annex everything from the Rio Grande to Colombia.

In retirement, Buchanan was unfairly harassed by charges that he had sacrificed Fort Sumter and sabotaged war efforts. Congress abolished his franking privileges and his portrait was removed from the Capitol. Buchanan, however, supported the war and opposed the peace plank in the 1864 Democratic presidential platform. He opposed the Emancipation Proclamation, however, and wanted to allow the Confederates to "return to the Union just as they were when they left it." He published letters that demolished General Scott's false charges, and his well-documented 1868 memoirs established his innocence of wrongdoing, but his belief that Northern fanatics had provoked the war unnecessarily remained strong. He died on 1 June 1868.

—*Elbert B. Smith*

See also Democratic Party; Election of 1856.
For further reading:
Auchampaugh, Philip G. *James Buchanan and His Cabinet on the Eve of Secession* (1926).

Buchanan, James. *Mr. Buchanan's Administration on the Eve of the Rebellion* (1866).
Curtis, George T. *Life of James Buchanan* (1883).
Klein, Philip Shriver. *President James Buchanan: A Biography* (1962).
Moore, John Bassett. *The Works of James Buchanan: Comprising His Speeches, State Papers, and Private Correspondence.* (1908–1911; reprint, 1960).
Smith, Elbert B. *The Presidency of James Buchanan* (1975).

BUCHANAN, ROBERT CHRISTIE
(1811–1878)
Union officer

Although best remembered as a military martinet, Robert C. Buchanan was in reality an officer of distinguished accomplishments in forty years of service. He was born in Baltimore on 1 March 1811, to an established old Maryland family; his mother's sister was Mrs. John Quincy Adams. He graduated from West Point in 1830, was assigned to the 4th Infantry Regiment, saw service in the Black Hawk War, and fought at the battle of Lake Okeechobee in the Second Seminole War.

In 1845 Buchanan's regiment went to Texas with Zachary Taylor's Army of Observation, and Buchanan, by now a captain, fought in the engagements at Palo Alto and Resaca de la Palma in May 1846, winning a brevet promotion to major, and at the battle of Monterrey, Mexico, that September. In November 1846 he was selected to lead the Baltimore and Washington Battalion of Volunteers and held that position until the volunteers were mustered out of service in May 1847. Returning to the 4th Infantry, Buchanan marched to Mexico City with Winfield Scott's army, participating in the battles at Churubusco, Molino del Rey (for which he was breveted to lieutenant colonel), and Chapultepec. After the war he served on the frontier and in California, where he commanded Fort Humboldt in 1854 and the District of Southern Oregon and Northern California in 1856. In 1855 he was made a major in the 4th Infantry.

Buchanan was promoted to lieutenant colonel of his regiment in September 1861 and commanded it in the defenses of Washington, D.C., from November 1861 to March 1862, at which time it was made a part of the Army of the Potomac. In May 1862, still a lieutenant colonel, Buchanan became commander of one of the two regular brigades making up Sykes's division of Fitz John Porter's V Corps. Buchanan led the brigade until March 1863, fighting in McClellan's Peninsula campaign, being promoted by brevet to colonel for his part in the engagement at Gaines' Mill, the Seven Days' battles, the Second Bull Run campaign, the Maryland campaign of 1862, and the battle of Fredericksburg. In November 1862 he received a recess appointment as brigadier general of U.S. Volunteers, but when Congress convened the following March, he was not confirmed and the commission expired.

Buchanan saw no more field duty. He was briefly commander of Fort Delaware, then chief of recruiting in New Jersey for a year. He was promoted to colonel of the 1st Infantry in February 1864 and commanded his regiment in the garrison at New Orleans from November 1864 to August 1865. At war's end he received the regular army brevet promotions of brigadier general for the battle of Malvern Hill and major general for participation in Second Bull Run and Fredericksburg.

For two years following the war, Buchanan served on commissions and with the Freedman's Bureau. From March 1868 to March 1869 he commanded in Louisiana, overseeing and administering the volatile mix of Reconstruction politics in that state. He then returned to command of his regiment and retired from active duty in December 1870. He died in Washington on 29 November 1878.

Buchanan was the quintessential regular army officer. He administered evenhanded discipline in the ranks, while instilling respect, and his men affectionately called him "Old Buck." To civilians, his imperious manner suggested arrogance and the local settlers of northern California referred to him as "Jesus Christ Jr." It has been implied that Buchanan's strict attitude drove the despondent Ulysses S. Grant, who served under him at Fort Humboldt, out of the service in 1854. Yet John R. Kenly wrote that Buchanan had "a remarkable equanimity of temperament," suitable for dealing with a volunteer compound. Aside from his meritorious conduct on the field of battle, Buchanan's finest hour was in Louisiana in 1868 where by his "wisdom, firmness and moderation," he prevented bloodshed, restored order, and ended military rule. Joseph G. Dawson wrote of Buchanan that he was "perhaps the most objective and fair-minded commander to serve in the state during the post-war years."

—*Russell K. Brown*

See also Freedmen's Bureau; Louisiana.
For further reading:
Coffman, Edward M. *The Old Army: A Portrait of the American Army in Peacetime, 1784–1898* (1986).
Cullum, George W. *Biographical Register of the Officers and Graduates of the U.S. Military Academy at West Point, New York, from its Establishment, in 1802, to 1890; With the Early History of the United States Military Academy* (1891).
Dawson, Joseph G., III. *Army Generals and Reconstruction: Louisiana, 1862–1877* (1994).
Kenly, John R. *Memoirs of a Maryland Volunteer* (1873).

BUCK AND BALL

The buck and ball was a cartridge or other loading consisting of one standard caliber round ball topped by three smaller buckshot. In rare instances, cartridges topped with four buckshot have been observed. Although sometimes used in shotguns and caliber 0.58 and 0.577 rifled muskets, buck and ball was most commonly used as a caliber 0.69 smoothbore musket loading. In effect a miniature grapeshot load, buck and ball was capable of inflicting horrendous wounds in all four weapons at close range. Its scatter effect, however, rendered the buck and ball most effective in extending the killing range of the notoriously inaccurate caliber 0.69 smoothbores to approximately 200 yards. Although phased out by many frontline units by midwar, buck and ball cartridges have been recovered in Confederate campsites that date from late April 1865.

—*Jeff Kinard*

See also Minié Ball; Rifles; Smoothbores; Springfield Rifle.
For further reading:
Lord, Francis A. *Civil War Collector's Encyclopedia* (1995).
McKee, W. Reid, and M. E. Mason, Jr. *Civil War Projectiles II: Small Arms & Artillery* (1980).

BUCKINGHAM, WILLIAM ALFRED
(1804–1875)
Governor of Connecticut

Born to Samuel Buckingham and Joanna Matson Buckingham in Lebanon, Connecticut, William Alfred Buckingham was educated locally. As a young man, he taught school for a while before learning the surveying trade and then entering the dry goods business. He eventually purchased his own store in Norwich, Connecticut. Using his profits from the store to invest in a variety of enterprises, Buckingham ultimately became a wealthy man when he became involved in the infant rubber industry.

Buckingham was active in Connecticut politics. He served two terms as the mayor of Norwich, the first time as a Whig and the second as a Republican. He received the Republican nomination for governor in 1858. He was elected for the first of eight one-year terms as a moderate Republican.

With the election of Abraham Lincoln as president in 1860, Buckingham became a strong supporter of the administration. Even before the outbreak of the Civil War, he wrote to Lincoln offering his support in the crisis. He began the early stages of military mobilization of the state as early as January 1861, but at the same time believed it incumbent upon him to pursue all avenues for peace and sent representatives from the state to the Washington Peace Conference. He made it clear before these delegates departed, however, that there could be no compromise on the issue of slavery in the territories.

Once the war began, Buckingham worked tirelessly to recruit Connecticut's quota of volunteers for Federal service. In fact, the recruitment of Federal soldiers would occupy much of his time for the next four years. Along with recruitment, Buckingham also selected the commanders of the regiments that were raised in the state. Initially some of his appointments were criticized as not representing a geographic balance in the state. As a result, he appointed war committees throughout the state to make recommendations to him, thus ending much of the criticism. Ultimately Connecticut, largely due to Buckingham's efforts, furnished one of the largest per capita percentages of volunteers of all Union states.

Once Connecticut citizens were recruited for Federal service, Buckingham believed it his duty to see to their welfare as best he could. He traveled to recruiting camps to inspect the facilities and talk with the soldiers about their needs. He also traveled to the fronts to meet with the Connecticut soldiers who had seen action during the war. He corresponded frequently with Connecticut officers to learn not only about the performance of Connecticut troops in battle but also to determine their needs while serving away from home. As part of his efforts to protect the welfare of Connecticut soldiers, Buckingham also expanded the hospital facilities of the state and worked to bring home seriously wounded men so that they might recover near their families.

Besides his concern for the interests of Connecticut troops, Buckingham also took an active interest in the military affairs of the entire Union. He wrote to the president and the War Department, offering advice about what he viewed as the vital military interests of the country and where the military could most usefully be deployed. Unlike many of his eastern counterparts, he believed that the West held part of the key to Confederate defeat. He urged the president to put resources into the conquest of Texas so that the loyal people of that state could be used to help the Union while the Confederacy would be deprived of the food resources of that area.

While engaging in all of these activities, Buckingham also had to stand for reelection every year. Doing so no doubt provided some distractions from his primary duties, especially because he was not even free from criticism within his own party. Not considered radical enough by some Connecticut Republicans, these men criticized Buckingham for not urging African-American recruitment with the Federal government. Democrats also criticized him, though for other reasons. That he was forced to use a draft to meet some Federal quotas gave Democrats some ammunition among those voters who did not wholeheartedly support the war effort. Buckingham's strongest Democratic challenger during the war was the popular Thomas H. Seymour, but the governor was able to weather all threats to his position and retained the governorship through the war.

Buckingham was considered one of the most loyal of the Northern war governors and certainly one of the hardest working. In 1866 he considered his job done, and he declined to run for reelection for a ninth term.

He lived quietly for two years before accepting election to the U.S. Senate. He brought to the Senate the same work habits and dedication to his constituents and the nation that had made him such a popular governor. He died in office on 5 February 1875.

—*David S. Heidler and Jeanne T. Heidler*

See also Seymour, Thomas.
For further reading:
Niven, John. *Connecticut for the Union: The Role of the State in the Civil War* (1965).

BUCKNER, SIMON BOLIVAR
(1823–1914)
Confederate general; governor of Kentucky

Simon Bolivar Buckner, the longest surviving Confederate general of lieutenant general rank, was born 1 April 1823 at the family estate in Hart County, Kentucky. Both parents, Aylett Hartswell and Elizabeth Ann (Morehead) Buckner, were of Virginia ancestry. The boy attended schools in Greenville and Hopkinsville, then received an appointment to West Point in 1840. Six feet tall, handsome, possessed of a powerful physique, he graduated eleventh in a class of twenty-five in 1844. After routine garrison duty, he taught at West Point in 1845 and 1846 before joining the American army in Mexico, where General Winfield Scott became his hero. Buckner resumed teaching at West Point after the Mexican-American War but left because he objected to compulsory Sunday chapel. On 2 May 1850, he married Mary Jane Kingsbury, daughter of an army officer who had extensive real estate investments in Chicago. Buckner resigned his commission in 1855 and joined his father-in-law in business until 1858, when he returned to Kentucky.

Buckner reorganized the moribund Kentucky militia and became its inspector general in 1860. As the Civil War started, Governor Beriah Magoffin used Buckner in efforts to secure acceptance of Kentucky's neutrality from Union and Confederate officials. In August 1861 Buckner refused a Union commission as brigadier general; he accepted that rank in the Confederate army in September. When Kentucky's unusual neutrality ended in early September, Buckner occupied Bowling Green and probed northward. A fatal error by Albert Sidney Johnston who did not withdraw troops from Fort Donelson, and a comedy of command errors led to Buckner surrendering Donelson and its troops to his friend Ulysses S. Grant on 16 February 1862.

Exchanged in August 1862, Buckner was promoted to major general and assigned to Braxton Bragg's army. He commanded a division in William J. Hardee's corps during the summer 1862 invasion of Kentucky. At Munfordville, Union colonel John R. Wilder sought Buckner's advice on whether he should surrender some

4,000 troops. At Perryville on 8 October 1862 Buckner's division made gains against the Union left flank, but the Confederates soon withdrew from the state. In December 1862 Buckner assumed command of the Department of the Gulf, but in May 1863, he was shifted to the Department of East Tennessee, which in August became part of Bragg's Department of Tennessee. Buckner led a corps at Chickamauga, but, disgusted with Bragg's leadership, he participated in efforts to get Bragg removed from command. Bragg reduced Buckner to divisional command and ordered him to East Tennessee, but Buckner's illness blocked that transfer.

In February 1864 Buckner took command of John Bell Hood's division and again was assigned to the Department of East Tennessee. Then he learned on 2 May 1864 that he had been transferred to the Trans-Mississippi Department. General Edmund Kirby Smith secured Buckner's promotion to lieutenant general and gave him command of the District of West Louisiana; on 19 April 1865 he was assigned the enlarged District of Arkansas. Buckner became Kirby Smith's chief of staff on 9 May 1865, and it was he who surrendered the Trans-Mississippi Department on 26 May.

Buckner was a competent, dependable general who never attained great military success. His active involvement in the anti-Bragg cabal hurt his reputation in administrative circles.

Ordered to remain in New Orleans, Buckner wrote for a newspaper, became a commission merchant, then president of an insurance company. He was allowed to return home in early 1868, and litigation recovered much of his prewar property. His wife died in 1874. In 1885 he married twenty-eight-year-old Delia Claiborne. Their son, Simon Bolivar Buckner, Jr., was born in 1886.

Elected governor of Kentucky as a Democrat in 1887, Buckner gave the state an honest, efficient administration. The conservative legislature usually checked his occasionally liberal policies. When Treasurer James W. "Honest Dick" Tate absconded with the state's funds in 1888, Buckner loaned the state enough money to keep it solvent until taxes were collected. At the end of his term Buckner retired to a quiet life at Glen Lily, near Munfordville. Threatened with blindness, he memorized five of Shakespeare's plays so he could "read Shakespeare in the dark." Cataract operations were successful. In 1895, he failed in a bid to be elected U.S. Senator. Unable to accept William Jennings Bryan's money policies, Buckner ran for vice president in 1896 on the Gold Democrat ticket with Union general John M. Palmer.

Buckner enjoyed attending Confederate encampments, and in 1909 he made a nostalgic trip to Mexican War battlefields. He was delighted when his son was admitted to West Point in 1904. The Sage of Glen Lily died at home on 8 January 1914 and was buried in Frankfort.

—*Lowell H. Harrison*

See also Bragg, Braxton; Fort Donelson; Kentucky; Smith, Edmund Kirby.
For further reading:
Connelly, Thomas L. *Army of the Heartland: The Army of Tennessee, 1861–1862* (1967).
———. *Autumn of Glory: The Army of Tennessee, 1862–1865* (1971).
Harrison, Lowell H. "Simon Bolivar Buckner." In *Kentucky's Governors, 1792–1985*, edited by Lowell H. Harrison (1985).
Hewitt, Lawrence L. "Simon Bolivar Buckner." In *The Confederate General*, edited by William C. Davis (1991).
Stickles, Arndt M. *Simon Bolivar Buckner: Borderland Knight* (1940).

BUELL, DON CARLOS
(1818–1898)
Union general

Born on 23 March 1818, Don Carlos Buell spent the first years of his life on a small farm in Lowell, Ohio, on the Muskingum River. His father died when Buell was young, and the boy was sent to live with his uncle in Lawrenceburg, Indiana. In 1837 he was appointed to West Point and graduated in 1841, ranking thirty-second of fifty-two, which caused him to be appointed to the 3d Infantry. He served briefly in the Second Seminole War. In 1843 he was court-martialed for severely reprimanding a private, but was acquitted. He served gallantly in the Mexican-American War, participating in numerous campaigns and battles, including the battle of Churubusco, and won brevets to captain and major. Severely wounded at Churubusco, he was soon transferred from line to staff duties, serving in the adjutant general's department for the next thirteen years. He was posted in several military departments, including those in Texas, Missouri, Utah, and New York.

In 1859 Secretary of War John B. Floyd assigned Buell to the War Department, and the following year he sent Buell on a secret mission to observe the mood in Charleston, South Carolina, and the condition of Robert Anderson's garrison in Fort Moultrie. After a brief stay, Buell was convinced that the military situation was so pressing that he left instructions with Anderson to move his garrison to Fort Sumter if Anderson had tangible evidence that South Carolina would threaten his force. He was afterwards sent to San Francisco, where he spent the remainder of the Great Secession winter as well as the spring and summer of 1861. Prior to his departure from Washington, he was commissioned brigadier general of volunteers on 17 May 1861. In September 1861, at the urging of George B. McClellan, Buell was assigned to the Army of the Potomac. In November, McClellan appointed Buell to replace William T. Sherman as commander of the newly designated Department of the Ohio, whose army was headquartered in Louisville, Kentucky.

It was McClellan's intention for Buell to lead the Army of the Ohio into eastern Tennessee to liberate the loyal residents in that region from Confederate oppression. Because of the lack of roads and with winter fast approaching, Buell urged an alternative advance over the Cumberland and Tennessee rivers or over the railroad to Nashville. Despite the opposition of civil and military superiors, the river campaign was carried out with only slight modification and resulted in the river victories at Fort Henry and Fort Donelson in February 1862. Ulysses S. Grant's victories enabled Buell to march overland unopposed to Nashville, which surrendered on 26 February 1862. In the campaign to Corinth, Mississippi, that March and April, Buell arrived at Pittsburg Landing and helped turn what was almost certain defeat into victory by counterattacking the second day at the battle of Shiloh. Buell then served under Henry W. Halleck (appointed overall commander of the West in March 1862) in the campaign to take Corinth, an operation that lasted until 30 May 1862, when Confederate commander P. G. T. Beauregard abandoned the railroad junction.

In June 1862 Halleck ordered Buell east toward Chattanooga, Tennessee, with instructions to repair the Memphis & Charleston Railroad as he advanced. Buell's army was continually harassed by Confederate cavalrymen John Hunt Morgan and Nathan Bedford Forrest. In August Confederate commander Braxton Bragg reached Chattanooga before Buell and then took his army into Kentucky, hoping to entice Kentuckians to join the Confederacy. In September, Buell marched his army into Kentucky and reached Louisville in late September before Bragg. On 8 October 1862 part of the Army of the Ohio engaged Bragg's army in the bloody but indecisive battle of Perryville. Bragg gave up the field to Buell and retired into eastern Kentucky and Tennessee, but Buell pursued too slowly. As a result, Lincoln removed him from command and replaced him with William S. Rosecrans.

Critics accused Buell of being out of touch with the Union's war aims and of being too sympathetic with the Southern cause. Shortly after being relieved, Buell demanded a trial to clear his reputation. Secretary of War Edwin M. Stanton agreed and after five months of testimony the court acquitted Buell of any wrongdoing or mismanagement of his army. Although Grant recommended that Buell be restored to duty, the Lincoln administration concluded that the commander was too much of a political liability, particularly because Buell refused to fight a war for emancipation. He resigned his commission in June 1864.

After the war Buell spent his life in Kentucky operating an ironworks and a coal mine. In 1885 President Grover Cleveland patronized the veteran with a short-term civil service position as a government pension agent.

During the war Buell ignored political considerations. He was reserved in manner and was thought to be unfriendly to the administration. Though he was an administrator and organizer of ability, his political liabilities and refusal to wage anything but a limited war proved too costly for the administration. He died on 19 November 1898 in Airdrie near Paradise, Kentucky, and was buried in Bellefontaine Cemetery, St. Louis.

—Stephen D. Engle

See also Corinth, Mississippi; Fort Sumter; Perryville/Chaplin Hills, Battle of; Shiloh, Battle of.
For further reading:
Chumney, James. "Gentleman General: Don Carlos Buell" (Ph.D. dissertation, 1964).
Engle, Stephen D. *Don Carlos Buell: Most Promising of All* (1999).

BUFORD, ABRAHAM
(1820–1884)
Confederate general

Born to William B. Buford and Frances Walker Kirtley Buford in Woodford County, Kentucky, Abraham Buford attended Centre College briefly before receiving an appointment to the United States Military Academy at West Point. He graduated fifty-first of a class of fifty-two in 1841. As a member of the 1st Dragoons upon graduation, Buford served in a variety of frontier posts before being promoted to first lieutenant at the beginning of the Mexican War in 1846. He received a brevet promotion to captain for his actions at the battle of Buena Vista in February 1847. Following that war, he was stationed in New Mexico before being transferred to the army's cavalry school at Carlisle, Pennsylvania. He resigned his commission in 1854 to return to Kentucky and pursue the family business of cattle and horse breeding.

Upon the outbreak of the Civil War and after much soul searching, Buford decided to side with the Confederacy. In 1862 he offered his military services to the Confederate army. On 2 September 1862 he accepted a commission as a brigadier general and joined Braxton Bragg's Kentucky campaign. During Bragg's retreat from Kentucky, Buford's Kentucky cavalry brigade guarded the army's withdrawal to Knoxville, Tennessee. Buford commanded his brigade at the battle of Stones River. Shortly after Stones River, Buford's brigade was placed under the command of Major General William W. Loring. As part of Loring's division, Buford participated in the Vicksburg campaign. He remained in Loring's division until spring 1864 when he received command of one of Nathan Bedford Forrest's cavalry divisions. At Tupelo in July 1864 his division was considered the most heavily engaged of all Confederate divisions present. He was wounded late in the year and did not return to active service until the war was almost over.

After the war, he returned to Kentucky and became one of the nation's most important breeders of thoroughbred horses. By the 1870s, personal and financial tragedies began to take their toll. His only son died in 1872 and his wife shortly thereafter. His business interests suffered and bankruptcy lost him his home. He committed suicide in Indiana in 1884. His cousin was Union general John Buford.

—*David S. Heidler and Jeanne T. Heidler*
See also Tupelo, Battle of.

BUFORD, JOHN
(1826–1863)
Union general

John Buford was born on 4 March 1826, in Woodford County, Kentucky, but migrated with his family to Rock Island, Illinois. He was born into a prominent family. Both his grandfather and great-uncle had been officers in Virginia regiments during the American Revolution. His father was a prominent Democratic politician in Illinois and a political opponent to Whig politician Abraham Lincoln. After attending Knox College in Galesburg, Illinois, for one year, Buford entered the U.S. Military Academy at West Point, New York, and graduated near the middle of his class in 1848. Such had become something of a family tradition. His half-brother Napoleon Bonaparte Buford, who would become a Union major general, entered West Point in 1827; his cousin Abraham Buford, who would become a Confederate brigadier general, did so in 1841. Buford was commissioned a second lieutenant in the 1st Dragoon Regiment. A year later he was transferred to the 2d Dragoon Regiment, where he spent the remainder of his prewar career. He fought against the Sioux, helped to keep the peace in Kansas, served in Texas and the Southwest, and participated in the abortive Mormon War in 1858.

When the Civil War began, Buford was a captain in the 2d Dragoon Regiment. Promoted to major on 12 November 1861, he was given the position of assistant inspector general of the defenses of Washington, D.C. After Major General John Pope arrived in Washington to take command of the newly formed Army of the Virginia in June 1862, however, Buford was promoted to brigadier general of volunteers on 27 July 1862 and given command of the Cavalry Brigade, II Corps, Army of the Virginia. Buford rightly recognized that the main roles of cavalry in the Civil War would be as mounted infantry and as reconnaissance for higher commands. He used his own cavalry for these two purposes expertly during the war.

During the battle of Second Bull Run, Buford performed well before being wounded in the knee during the Army of the Potomac's withdrawal and was initially reported as killed in action by Union newspapers. After recovering from his wounds, Buford became the chief of cavalry of the Army to the Potomac under Major General George B. McClellan during the Maryland campaign and under Major General Ambrose E. Burnside at the battle of Fredericksburg. After Major General Joseph Hooker's appointment as commander of the Army of the Potomac, the cavalry was reorganized and Buford found himself in command of the Reserve Brigade, Cavalry Corps. With Major General George Stoneman in command of the newly formed Cavalry Corps, Army of the Potomac, Buford was one of only a few people to receive any praise for their actions during Stoneman's unsuccessful raids in the Chancellorsville campaign.

During the battle of Gettysburg, Buford gained his greatest fame and performed his greatest feat of the Civil War. On 1 July 1863, Buford, who had been promoted to major general of volunteers on 1 June 1863 and was now commanding the 1st Division of the Cavalry Corps, encountered elements of the Army of Northern Virginia outside Gettysburg, Pennsylvania. With only one man per yard of ground, Buford ordered his men to dismount to oppose the advance of Confederate lieutenant general A. P. Hill's III Corps along the Chambersburg Pike toward Gettysburg. This delaying action allowed Union major general John Reynolds to deploy his I Corps to meet the Confederates outside Gettysburg, therefore, denying them the defensive value of the town itself.

In the autumn of 1863, Buford was stricken with typhoid fever and went on sick leave in November 1863. Already weakened by his years of hard campaigning, which included a poor diet, exposure, lack of sleep, and too much stress, he died on 16 December 1863 and was buried at West Point. His promotion to major general in the regular army was presented to him on his deathbed, though it was backdated to the first day of the battle of Gettysburg.

—*Alexander M. Bielakowski*

See also Buford, Abraham; Cavalry, U.S.A.; Gettysburg, Battle of.
For further reading:
Longacre, Edward G. *Cavalry at Gettysburg: A Tactical Study of Mounted Operations during the Civil War's Pivotal Campaign 9 June–14 July 1863* (1986).
———. *General John Buford: A Military Biography* (1995).
———. *Mounted Raids of the Civil War* (1975).

BUFORD, NAPOLEON BONAPARTE
(1807–1883)
Union general

Born to John Buford and Nancy Hickman Buford in Woodford, Kentucky, Napoleon Bonaparte Buford was educated locally before receiving an appointment to the United States Military Academy in 1823. He graduated sixth of thirty-eight in the class of 1827.

Buford was commissioned an artillery officer and served at a variety of posts in the east and on the frontier over the next four years. In 1831 he was granted a leave of absence to study law at Harvard. Following his studies there, he returned briefly to West Point as an instructor before resigning his commission in 1835.

Upon leaving the army, Buford worked for a while as an engineer in Kentucky and then moved to Illinois, where he became involved in a variety of business enterprises, including banking. At the outbreak of the Civil War Buford raised a regiment of volunteers and became its colonel when it was mustered into Federal service as the 27th Illinois.

Buford and the 27th were placed under the command of Brigadier General Ulysses S. Grant headquartered at Cairo, Illinois. Buford led his regiment in its first major action under Grant at Belmont, Missouri, on 7 November 1861. He distinguished himself in the battle and was commended for his bravery in action. Due to the negligence of senior officers, he and his men were almost captured, but Buford was able to extricate them from the field. For the remainder of the year Buford and his regiment served in garrison duty in Cairo.

In early 1862 Buford and the 27th were transferred to the command of John Pope and the Army of the Mississippi. Buford participated in the occupation of Columbus, Kentucky, in early March and temporarily commanded the garrison there until called to command the so-called Flotilla Brigade in Pope's assault on Island No. 10. Buford's brigade was transported aboard Andrew Foote's gunboats. During the siege, Buford led his brigade on a raid to Union City, Tennessee, which netted Pope's army some much-needed supplies. For this action he would later in the spring be promoted to brigadier general of volunteers.

Following the surrender of Island No. 10, Buford briefly commanded the fortifications there. Later in the spring, after his promotion to brigadier general, Buford commanded a brigade in the advance on Corinth. During the late summer Buford came under the command of William Rosecrans at Corinth. He participated in the defense of the town in the fall of 1862, but on the second day of the battle fell dangerously ill from sunstroke and had to be hospitalized. His immediate superior, Brigadier General Charles S. Hamilton, commended Buford for his actions at Corinth. Once he was able to assume desk duty, Buford was sent east to serve on court-martial duty.

Upon his arrival in Washington, Buford was made a member of the court that heard the case of Fitz John Porter. Like some other members of the court, Buford had ties to the case in that he had served under Porter's accuser, John Pope, in the west. This duty done in early 1863, Buford, whose health was still precarious, was sent to command the garrison at Cairo, Illinois. Buford

remained in command at Cairo through summer of 1863. During that time, one of his primary responsibilities was to direct the various recruited and drafted units to points throughout the Western theater. During the summer of 1863 these routine duties were interrupted when a raid by Confederate John Hunt Morgan threatened southern Illinois. Buford saw to the defense of the area as best he good with his limited garrison and the raw recruits stationed there.

In September 1863, Buford was sent to Helena, Arkansas, to command the District of Eastern Arkansas. He commanded this post until February 1865. During that year and a half, Buford experienced everything from the boredom of a remote post to periodic raids and sabotage by Confederate forces and sympathizers. To deal with the raids he knew that he needed cavalry, but it was difficult to persuade other nearby commanders to relinquish any. When he finally received some cavalry support in the spring of 1864, it was not nearly as much as he had requested.

Besides Buford's problems acquiring the cavalry he needed, he complained that most of the new troops he received were African-American recruits. The previous year Buford, while still in Cairo, had been accused of not doing enough to help refugee former slaves because he disagreed with abolition. He denied the charges, arguing that he had expended a great deal of his resources helping the unfortunate refugees. In 1864 when he complained about having to rely on African-American soldiers, he explained that the reason he preferred white soldiers was that they were generally better trained and less subject to bushwhackers in the area who resented the presence of African-Americans in uniform.

Receiving no satisfactory answer to these complaints and suffering ever-failing health, Buford became very dissatisfied with his assignment. In addition, feeling ignored by his superiors, he found himself occupied more and more with annoying administrative duties. Along with protecting his position, he had to supervise the sale of cotton being shipped north from occupied areas, to prevent smuggling, and to oversee the food and shelter needs of an ever-increasing number of refugee slaves. In dealing with the latter situation, he silenced his critics by creating a model program for providing for the immediate and long-term needs of the former slaves. By early 1865, however, he no longer felt physically able to continue and requested to be relieved. His request was granted in early March 1865, after which he was brevetted a major general of volunteers. After being relieved, Buford was granted a leave of absence until mustered out of the army in August 1865.

Following the war, Buford engaged in a variety of business activities in Colorado and Illinois. He retired to Chicago, where he died on 28 March 1883. He was the older half-brother of Union general John Buford, who died during the war.

—*David S. Heidler and Jeanne T. Heidler*

See also Arkansas; Belmont, Battle of.

For further reading:
Hughes, Nathaniel Cheairs, Jr. *The Battle of Belmont: Grant Strikes South* (1991).

BULL RUN, FIRST BATTLE OF
(21 July 1861)

Manassas Junction, Virginia, was the magnet that attracted the armies of North and South to the banks of Bull Run in July 1861. There two railroads, the Manassas Gap and the Orange & Alexandria, connected thirty miles southwest of Washington, D.C. The Orange & Alexandria was a natural line of advance for a Union army marching southward from Washington, while the Manassas Gap was important because Confederate forces in northern Virginia were divided. Eleven thousand men under Joseph E. Johnston guarded the Shenandoah Valley, while Pierre G. T. Beauregard had 22,000 men at Manassas, Centreville, and Fairfax Court House. The Manassas Gap linked these two armies and made it possible for the South to concentrate its forces wherever the threat was greatest.

The commanding general of the Union army, Winfield Scott, opposed an offensive into Virginia. Such a move, Scott feared, would only exacerbate sectional tensions. He also had little faith in the ninety-day volunteers that had been gathering around Washington since April. President Abraham Lincoln, however, believed a quick offensive against Manassas was worth a try and ordered Union general Irvin McDowell to organize a 35,000-man army for an operation against Manassas. McDowell shared Scott's apprehensions over the reliability of his untrained army, but received little sympathy from Lincoln, who admonished, "You are green it is true, but they are green also."

On 16 July, McDowell's army began its march out of Washington, but did not reach Fairfax Court House until the evening of the seventeenth, giving the Rebels time to evacuate their advanced outpost there. McDowell's lead division, under Daniel Tyler, reached Centreville the following day and found Beauregard had already evacuated the town to concentrate behind Bull Run. Tyler then pushed on toward the Bull Run crossings, provoking a sharp skirmish at Blackburn's Ford, in which the Confederates thrashed Tyler's force and forced it to withdraw back to Centreville.

Beauregard's army was now positioned in an eight-mile line that was strong on the right, where the Orange & Alexandria Railroad crossed Bull Run and a series of fords—Mitchell's, Blackburn's, and McLean's—provided convenient crossing points.

Alone at the far left was Nathan G. Evans's brigade overlooking a stone bridge where the Warrenton Turnpike crossed Bull Run.

After the setback at Blackburn's Ford and reconnaissances demonstrated that Beauregard's right was too strong to be attacked, McDowell learned that Sudley Ford, a few miles upstream from the stone bridge, was weakly defended and offered a convenient route around the Confederate left. So on 20 July he drew up a battle plan that called for Tyler to march his division west along the Warrenton Turnpike from Centreville toward the stone bridge, followed by David Hunter's and Samuel Heintzelman's divisions. Tyler would make a demonstration at the bridge to make Beauregard think the main attack would come there, while Heintzelman and Hunter turned north and moved to Sudley Ford. There they would cross the run at 7:00 and then march south along the Manassas-Sudley Road to crush Beauregard's left and rear.

It was a good plan. However, its success, like McDowell's entire campaign, depended upon whether Robert Patterson's army in the Valley could prevent Johnston from reinforcing Beauregard. Unfortunately for McDowell, Patterson failed, and on 19 July units from Johnston's army began boarding railroad cars bound for Manassas.

To make matters worse for McDowell, his plan began unraveling from the minute he awoke his men at 2:00 A.M. on 21 July. First, it took an hour for Tyler to get on the road toward the stone bridge. His division then marched at a snail's pace through the pitch black night until it finally reached the stone bridge at 5:30 A.M. Yet the flanking force had only just begun moving north toward Sudley Ford. At 6 A.M. Tyler began his demonstration by firing an artillery shell across Bull Run; Hunter's lead brigade under Union general Ambrose Burnside was three miles from Sudley Ford. To make matters worse, Burnside found the road leading to their crossing point was little more than a cart path. Not until 9:30 A.M.—over two hours behind schedule—did the 13,000-man Union flanking force begin crossing Bull Run.

By 8 A.M. Evans had begun to suspect that Tyler's force at the stone bridge was in fact a feint, a suspicion that was confirmed by a warning from a Confederate signal station: "Look out for your left, you are turned." Leaving 200 men to watch Tyler, Evans led 900 men north to Matthews Hill. By midmorning, the Confederate force on Matthews Hill had swelled to 2,800 with the arrival of Francis Bartow's and Barnard Bee's brigades. Their goal was simply to slow down the Federal army and buy time for Beauregard and Johnston to shift forces north to save the Confederate flank.

They bought an hour and a half. By 11:30 A.M. McDowell's flanking force had crushed the Confederate

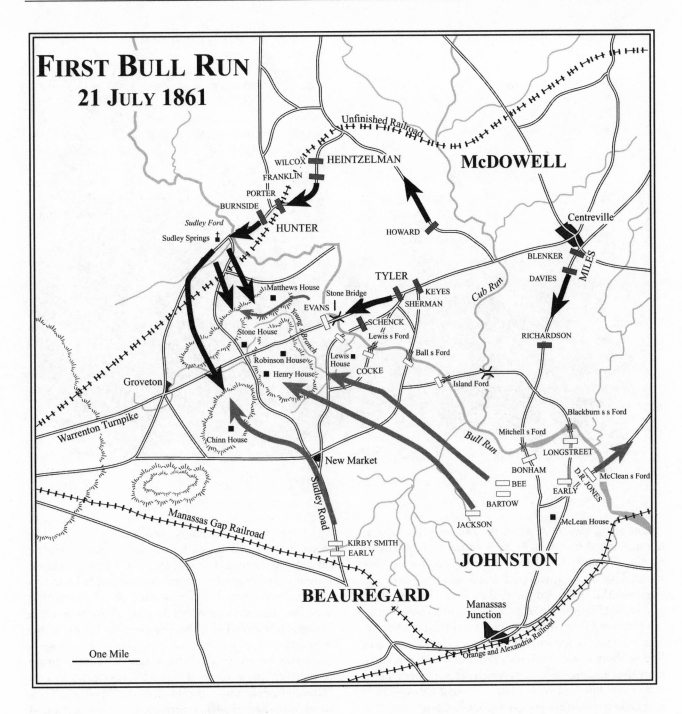

FIRST BULL RUN
21 JULY 1861

Unfinished Railroad

McDOWELL

WILCOX HEINTZELMAN
FRANKLIN
PORTER
BURNSIDE
Sudley Ford
Sudley Springs   HUNTER

Centreville

HOWARD

BLENKER   MILES

DAVIES

Cub Run

Matthews House
Stone Bridge   KEYES
TYLER   SHERMAN
EVANS
SCHENCK
Stone House   Lewis s Ford

RICHARDSON

Young s Branch
Robinson House   Lewis
House   Ball s Ford
Henry House   COCKE

Groveton

Island Ford

Blackburn s Ford

Mitchell s Ford
LONGSTREET
BONHAM
Chinn House   BEE   EARLY   McClean s Ford
DR. JONES

Warrenton Turnpike
New Market

Bull Run

BARTOW

JACKSON   McLean House

Manassas Gap Railroad

Sudley Road

KIRBY SMITH
EARLY

JOHNSTON

BEAUREGARD
Manassas
Junction

One Mile

Orange and Alexandria Railroad

line on Matthews Hill and sent the Rebels fleeing southward. "Victory! Victory!" an ecstatic McDowell shouted to his men on Matthews Hill. "The day is ours."

This was not how Beauregard had expected the battle to develop. He had massed his forces on the right so he could attack McDowell's left and rear and won the approval of Johnston, who had arrived at Manassas on 19 July to assume overall command, for the scheme. Yet, the complex and confusing orders Beauregard issued for the operation and the crisis on Matthews Hill compelled the Southern commanders to abandon this plan and begin shifting forces northward.

Henry Hill, approximately a mile and a half south of Matthews Hill and six miles north of Manassas Junction, would be the key to the battle. If McDowell could capture it, his victory would be complete. But instead of immediately pushing his 18,000 men southward to drive the beaten and disorganized remnants of Evans's, Bartow's, and Bee's commands off Henry Hill, McDowell decided to have only James B. Ricketts's and Charles Griffin's batteries fire at the hill from Dogan's Ridge.

Beauregard and Johnston took full advantage of McDowell's generosity and began moving reinforcements to Henry Hill. The most important to arrive,

First Battle of Bull Run, 21 July 1861 (*Library of Congress*)

Thomas J. Jackson's brigade, reached the hill around noon. Upon his arrival, Jackson ordered his five regiments of infantry to take cover on the reverse slope of Henry Hill and began rounding up artillery pieces. By the time McDowell decided that he would have to fight for Henry Hill, Jackson had thirteen guns in position.

At around 2 P.M. McDowell ordered the batteries on Dogan's Ridge to Henry Hill so they could blast Jackson's line at short range. Ricketts arrived on the hill shortly thereafter and placed his guns south of the Henry House, with three hundred yards of open ground between him and Jackson. Griffin's battery then arrived on Ricketts's left and a massive duel commenced between their eleven guns and Jackson's artillery.

The Confederates got the better of the exchange. The Federals were now within range of Jackson's smoothbore cannon, which they had not been on Dogan's Ridge, and began taking significant casualties. At the same time, the Confederate line was now too close for the rifled Federal guns to be effective and most of their shells sailed harmlessly over the heads of the Confederates. To make matters worse, McDowell's efforts to push up infantry support to Ricketts and Griffin were unsuccessful, while Jackson's line grew stronger by the minute.

Then, as the guns roared, a legend was born that would fire Southern hearts for years to come. As he rallied his troops behind Jackson's line, General Barnard Bee beseeched them to "follow me back to where the fighting is." When they asked where that was, Bee dramatically pointed to his left and shouted, "Yonder stands Jackson like a stone wall; let's go to his assistance."

As this was going on, Griffin concluded that a change of tactics was necessary if the Federals were going to break the Confederate line. He then took two guns back to the Sudley Road, turned south, swung around Ricketts's guns, and positioned them on a slight rise to Ricketts's right. From here, Griffin hoped to hit Jackson's line with a destructive enfilade fire.

At approximately 3 P.M. Griffin observed an unidentified force moving toward his new position from the right. Although a number of men in this force were wearing blue uniforms, Griffin deduced that it was hostile and ordered his men to load their guns with canister. Just then, McDowell's chief of artillery, William Barry, told Griffin: "Don't fire there. Those are your battery support." Griffin disagreed. "They are Confederates," he protested, "as certain as the world." Barry was adamant:

View of the battlefield, First Battle of Bull Run, July 1861 (*Library of Congress*)

"I know they are your battery support." Griffin reluctantly yielded to the judgment of his superior.

The unidentified force was in fact Confederate William Smith's battalion of Virginia troops. Seventy yards from Griffin's position they stopped, lowered their muskets, and fired a devastating volley at the Federal gunners. Smith and Arthur Cummings's 33d Virginia Infantry Regiment then charged and captured Griffin's guns. Sensing the tide had turned, Jackson then ordered two of his regiments to charge Ricketts's battery. Soon Ricketts's guns were in Rebel hands as well.

Just then McDowell finally managed to get infantry up to his beleaguered artillerymen and a desperate struggle ensued in which the guns changed hands several times. The Federal effort was fatally compromised, however, by McDowell's failure to commit fully

his superior numbers and the fact that, although McDowell managed to get fifteen regiments into the battle, not once did more than two join the fight together. Finally, at around 4 P.M. a spirited charge by two regiments from Confederate colonel Phillip St. George Cocke's brigade pushed the last Union forces off Henry Hill.

As the battle raged on Henry Hill, McDowell ordered Oliver O. Howard's brigade to Chinn Ridge. If Howard could seize the ridge, he would be on the western flank of Henry Hill and in an ideal position from which to deliver a decisive stroke against the Confederate line. Just then, however, Arnold Elzey's and Jubal Early's brigades, the last Confederate reinforcements from the Shenandoah Valley, reached the battlefield. At 4 P.M. they arrived on Chinn Ridge and crushed Howard's

Federal soldiers at Confederate forticifications near Manassas, March 1862
(Photograph by George Barnard / *Library of Congress*)

command. Beauregard then ordered his entire line forward. This convinced McDowell that his army had had enough for one day, and at 4:30 P.M. the Federal retreat began.

With their army "more disorganized by victory than that of the United States by defeat," the Confederate high command was unable to organize an effective pursuit. The Federals were thus able to recross Bull Run well enough, but then a Confederate artillery shell capsized a wagon on the Cub Run Bridge, creating a bottleneck on their line of retreat. Whatever order had existed until then evaporated as panic gripped the exhausted Union troops and the civilians who had come out to Centreville to watch the battle. The retreat degenerated into a chaotic flight back to Washington, and what had been a closely fought battle became a decisive Southern victory. Altogether, nearly 900 men had been killed and over 2,700 wounded, numbers that would pale in comparison to later battles, but nonetheless shocked a nation that had naively expected a relatively bloodless war.

Southerners had anticipated that one victory such as Bull Run would persuade the North to abandon the effort to restore the Union by force. Lincoln, however, made it clear after the battle that he would continue the fight by organizing new armies for the long war to come.

Thirteen months later the men in blue and gray would meet again in battle on the plains of Manassas.

—*Ethan S. Rafuse*

See also Bartow, Francis S.; Beauregard, P. G. T.; Bee, Barnard; Jackson, Thomas J.; Johnston, Joseph E.; McDowell, Irvin.
For further reading:
Davis, William C. *Battle at Bull Run: A History of the First Major Campaign of the Civil War* (1977).
Freeman, Douglas Southall. *Lee's Lieutenants: A Study in Command*, vol. 1 (1942–1944).
Hennessy, John. *The First Battle of Manassas: An End to Innocence July 18–21, 1861* (1989).
Johnson, Robert Underwood, and Clarence Clough Buel, eds. *Battles and Leaders of the Civil War: Being for the Most Part Contributions by Union and Confederate Officers* (1887–1888).
U.S. War Department. *War of the Rebellion: A Compilation of the Official Records of the Union and Confederate Armies* (1880–1901).

BULL RUN, SECOND BATTLE OF
(29–30 August 1862)

Following the end of the Peninsula campaign, General Robert E. Lee sent Stonewall Jackson north with 24,000 men to watch the new Federal Army of Virginia, led by Major General John Pope. Consisting of three corps (commanded by generals Franz Sigel, Nathaniel P. Banks, and Irvin McDowell), Pope's

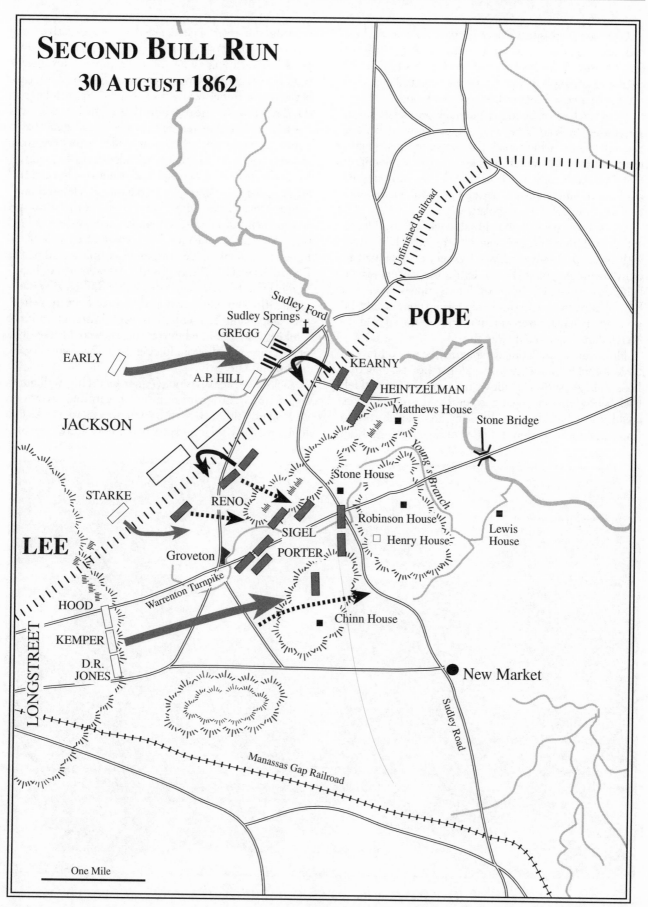

SECOND BULL RUN
30 AUGUST 1862

Unfinished Railroad

POPE

Sudley Ford

Sudley Springs

GREGG

EARLY

A.P. HILL

KEARNY

HEINTZELMAN

Matthews House

Stone Bridge

JACKSON

Stone House

Young's Branch

STARKE

RENO

Robinson House

Lewis House

SIGEL

Henry House

LEE

PORTER

Groveton

Warrenton Turnpike

Chinn House

HOOD

KEMPER

D.R. JONES

LONGSTREET

New Market

Sudley Road

Manassas Gap Railroad

One Mile

51,000 men were spread over northern Virginia. Pope had received orders to await the transfer of the Army of the Potomac from the Peninsula to join his forces; the combined strength would total well over 100,000 men and prove a new threat to Lee and Richmond.

From his base at Gordonsville, Jackson moved north across the Rapidan River on 9 August toward Banks's Second Corps, which had reached Culpeper. Banks reacted swiftly and attacked Jackson at Cedar Mountain that day. After some hard fighting, Banks was repulsed but Union reinforcements negated Jackson's victory and he withdrew across the Rapidan.

Once Lee knew of the initial stages of the Union withdrawal from the Peninsula, he sent James Longstreet with most of his corps to join Jackson. Lee planned to cross the Rapidan on Pope's left while cavalry struck behind the enemy lines to burn bridges over the Rappahannock River. If all went well, Pope would be isolated from reinforcements and defeated before McClellan's troops could join him.

However, as the Confederate army began to move, a Union cavalry force captured dispatches that alerted Pope to Lee's plans. He quickly ordered a retreat and fell back behind the Rappahannock on 18 August before Lee could react. Pope deployed his army from Kelly's Ford to Rappahannock Station to prevent Lee's troops from crossing the river. Lee decided to move upriver and attempt to turn Pope's right. Accordingly, Jackson's divisions began sidling along the river, probing for a weak spot. Fighting took place at Freeman's Ford on 22 August before some Rebels crossed at Sulphur Springs later in the day. However, heavy rains that night led to a rapid rise in the river, threatening the Rebels on the east bank. Southern workmen built a new bridge across the river, allowing the isolated force to withdraw on 24 August.

By this time, the Pennsylvania Reserves division had arrived to join Pope, as had Samuel P. Heintzelman's Third Army Corps. The Union Fifth Army Corps was not far behind. Lee, in a quandary, decided on a bold plan. Jackson would take his corps and move beyond Pope's right flank while Longstreet skirmished along the Rappahannock. Jackson would sweep down on Pope's supply line, the Orange & Alexandria Railroad. By interdicting this rail line, Lee hoped to force Pope away from the Rappahannock and back toward Washington. If the Yankees were not lured into battle, they could at least be driven into Washington, freeing the ravaged countryside in time for harvest.

Jackson's three divisions (Ambrose P. Hill, William B. Taliaferro, and Richard S. Ewell) began their march on 25 August. Although their column was spotted by Union lookouts, the Rebels moved with celerity and Pope failed

Second Battle of Bull Run, 29 August 1862 (*Library of Congress*)

Men of Company C, 41st New York Infantry, at Manassas (Photograph by Timothy O'Sullivan / *Library of Congress*)

to grasp the significance of the route of march. Jackson's column headed to Salem, then through Thoroughfare Gap across the Bull Run Mountains to Gainesville. Late on 26 August, Confederate horsemen captured Bristoe Station, then, followed by infantry, moved north along the railroad to Manassas Junction, the site of Pope's massive supply depot. Easily scattering the few defenders, Jackson's men took possession of the junction after dark.

Although surprised by the enemy in his rear, Pope realized that Lee's army was separated in two parts. If he moved quickly, his men could overwhelm Jackson before Longstreet could arrive. Early on 27 August, Pope abandoned the Rappahannock and turned his army toward Manassas. After repelling the attack of a New Jersey brigade from the Union Sixth Army Corps, moving from Alexandria, Jackson's men destroyed whatever supplies they could not take with them. In the meantime, Joseph Hooker's division of the Third Army Corps encountered Ewell's Division at Kettle Run, near Bristoe Station. Ewell managed to hold off the attacking Yankees before rejoining Jackson at Manassas later in the day.

Jackson was aware that Lee and Longstreet were at Salem that night. After his men burned the Union supplies, he withdrew to a position he selected near the old Manassas battlefield of July 1861. Throughout the night and into the morning of 28 August, Jackson's men abandoned Manassas Junction and moved into position behind an unfinished railroad cut north of the Warrenton Turnpike. Hidden by the embankment and wooded terrain, Jackson's tired soldiers settled down to await events. Stonewall hoped to avoid detection until Longstreet's men arrived via Thoroughfare Gap, ten miles to the west. If, perchance, Union troops continued to block the way, Jackson could still withdraw northward.

Throughout the day on 28 August, Union troops converged on Manassas Junction, only to find Jackson gone. The Union division of James B. Ricketts moved to Thoroughfare Gap, encountering the van of Longstreet's column already moving through the gap. Ricketts deployed and contested the enemy advance, but was outnumbered and forced to withdraw. Meanwhile, Pope was confused and issued contradictory orders to his troops

Soldiers with damaged rolling stock of the Orange & Alexandria Railroad, Manassas Junction, August 1862
(Photograph by Timothy O'Sullivan / *Library of Congress*)

as he attempted to locate the enemy. Wrongfully believing that Jackson had moved toward Centreville, Pope issued orders for his scattered divisions to move in that direction.

Rufus King's division of McDowell's corps moved along the Warrenton Turnpike across the front of Jackson's hidden corps. Jackson spied the Yankee column and decided to attack in order to expose his position to Pope's view, knowing that Longstreet would join him the next day. The Confederates moved forward as the day was drawing to a close and attacked John Gibbon's brigade at the Brawner Farm. Both sides fed troops into the savage close fighting that continued well after dark. The bloody stalemate resulted in heavy casualties for both sides before King withdrew his bloodied division.

Pope, thinking that King had encountered a retreating Jackson, issued attack orders for his converging divisions. Franz Sigel's First Corps of the Army of Virginia moved into position on Jackson's front on 29 August and began a series of piecemeal assaults on the railroad cut. John Reynolds's Pennsylvania Reserves soon joined the fray. As Major General Fitz John Porter's Fifth Army Corps, Army of the Potomac, marched

toward the field, Pope issued orders for Porter to move west to take position between Jackson and Longstreet. But Pope did not know that even as Sigel launched his first attacks, Longstreet was already beginning to deploy on Jackson's right. Porter's skirmishers encountered these new arrivals; the Union general halted his movement and spent most of the day vacillating.

Meanwhile, Heintzelman's corps reached the field and joined in the attacks on Jackson's line. Troops from Major General Jesse L. Reno's Ninth Army Corps came onto the field, as did McDowell's two divisions. Pope failed to coordinate their attacks, and, as a result, although individual Union brigades briefly gained ground and pierced Jackson's line, each attack was eventually repulsed. By the end of 29 August, Jackson held his position and Longstreet was deployed to his right, extending the Confederate line south of the Warrenton Turnpike. Lee wanted Longstreet to attack, but the general demurred, claiming that he faced an unknown number of Yankees to his front and right. The day ended with Longstreet launching a limited advance to discover what lay in his front. His men encountered King's divi-

Pontoon bridge across Bull Run, 1862 (*National Archives*)

sion and some confused fighting took place after dark until Longstreet recalled his brigades, which returned to their original positions.

At daylight on 30 August, Pope still believed that the enemy was retreating, even though he knew Longstreet was on the field. Skirmishing along Jackson's front revealed that the enemy was yet on the field, and Pope spent the morning undecided what to do. Finally, with the skirmishing along Jackson's front providing all the evidence that the enemy was still there, Pope decided to launch a massive attack on Jackson. Porter was to mass his corps on the left and assail the enemy line.

Porter began his attack shortly after 3:00 P.M. His men, though brave, were unable to pierce the enemy line. Enfiladed by Longstreet's artillery, the attackers were repelled at every point and Porter withdrew. With the repulse of Pope's largest attack, Lee ordered Longstreet forward. His divisions surged ahead, thrashing Colonel G. K. Warren's small brigade, then mauling a brigade of Pennsylvania Reserves. The oncoming Rebels rolled forward and met the next Union line on Chinn Ridge, where a mixed force of troops from two corps managed to hold long enough for another line to take position on Henry House Hill.

By this time, Pope had ordered a retreat by the entire army. Throughout the late afternoon and evening hours, the Federals fell back across Bull Run and headed toward Centreville. Longstreet's men seized Henry House Hill after the Yankees withdrew, but with their organization disrupted and darkness coming on, further pursuit was not possible. Pope continued to retreat to the Washington defenses. On 1 September, Jackson's troops collided with the retreating Union armies at Chantilly. In a confused battle in the rain, Jackson was repelled and the campaign soon ended. The Union army suffered a loss of 16,054 officers and men—1,724 killed, 8,372 wounded, and 5,958 missing. Lee reported a loss of 1,481 killed, 7,627 wounded, and only 89 missing, a total of 9,197.

—*Richard A. Sauers*

See also Army of Virginia; Pope, John
For further reading:
Gaff, Alan D. *Brave Men's Tears: The Iron Brigade at Brawner Farm* (1985).
Hennessy, John J. *Return to Bull Run: The Campaign and Battle of Second Manassas* (1993).
———. "The Second Battle of Manassas." *Blue & Gray Magazine* (1992).
Kelly, Dennis. "Second Manassas: The Battle and Campaign." *Civil War Times Illustrated* (1983).

BULLOCH, JAMES DUNWODY
(1823–1901)
Confederate diplomat

Born into a prominent Georgia family, James Dunwody Bulloch was the son of James Stephens Bulloch and Hester Amarinthia Elliott Bulloch. The younger Bulloch's sister, Martha Bulloch, married Theodore Roosevelt, Sr., and became the mother of future president Theodore Roosevelt.

Born and reared in Savannah, Georgia, James Bulloch developed an interest in the sea at an early age. At age 16 he accepted a midshipman's berth in the U.S. Navy. He served on several vessels, including the USS *United States*, USS *Decatur*, and USS *Delaware*, and on several stations, including Latin America, the Mediterranean, and the Pacific, before receiving his first command with the mail steamship *Georgia*. The U.S. government engaged in this activity to give young officers experience commanding steam vessels, but Bulloch, like so many others, used this experience to find civilian employment as a steamer captain and left the service in 1854.

With Georgia's secession, Bulloch returned home to provide naval assistance to his native state. The start of the Civil War caused Bulloch to offer his services to Confederate secretary of the navy, Stephen Mallory. Given the rank of commander, Bulloch hoped to command a Confederate warship, but his expertise in commanding various types of vessels caused the Confederate government to detail him to Europe, where he was charged with procuring ships for the new nation.

Over the next four years, Bulloch became an invaluable Confederate agent, contracting for numerous ships, but also involved in the acquisition of other essential supplies for the Confederacy and arranging for their transport through the Union blockade. By July 1861, Bulloch had already purchased in Great Britain ten ships suitable for commerce raiding and was being watched closely by U.S. agents in Europe.

After seeing the purchase and beginning of the construction of what would become the CSS *Florida* and CSS *Alabama*, Bulloch purchased a large number of war supplies and personally escorted them back through the blockade and then returned to Great Britain in February 1862.

When pressure from U.S. diplomats made it increasingly difficult for Bulloch to purchase ships and supplies in Great Britain, Bulloch moved his operation to France in early 1863. Receiving regular payments from the Confederate treasury to finance his operation, as late as the fall of 1863, Bulloch was still shipping necessary items back to the Confederacy and working to outfit commerce raiders. His tireless efforts during the war exceeded those of all other Confederate purchasing agents and have been credited with prolonging the war.

After the war, Bulloch, believing he could not expect a pardon from the U.S. government and having grown fond of his European surroundings decided to live in Liverpool and go into the shipping business there. He was often consulted in his adopted home on matters of maritime law. In his spare time, he wrote about some of his activities during the war in what became *The Secret Service of the Confederate States in Europe*. He died in Liverpool, England, on 7 January 1901.

—*David S. Heidler and Jeanne T. Heidler*

See also Diplomacy, C.S.A.; Navy, C.S.A.

For further reading:
Nuckols, Jack Randall. "A Confederate Agent in Europe: The Life and Career of Commander James Dunwody Bulloch" (M.A. thesis, 1982).
Young, Michael T. "A Study of the Activities of James Dunwody Bulloch: Confederate Naval Agent in Great Britain" (M.A. thesis, 1968).

BUMMERS

The term *bummers* is a derisive term describing foragers operating out of Major General William T. Sherman's Army of Georgia and Army of the Tennessee during the Savannah campaign of 1864 (March to the Sea) and the Carolinas campaign. Many times, this term is a negative one referring to the abuses of this foraging system on the populations of Georgia, South Carolina, and North Carolina. This word *bummer* still brings out strong emotional feelings in the Southern United States relating to the conduct of the war by General Sherman.

Bummer is a reference to the detailed soldier who goes out independently to obtain food for his parent unit. Knowing that his columns would be cut off from supply during the march to Savannah, Georgia, General Sherman ordered his two armies to institute a system of obtaining food from the countryside to enable the columns to continue to advance without any concern over wagon-based or rail-based supply. In Special Order 120 on 9 November 1864, Sherman established the guidelines for foraging. Sherman desired that brigade commanders would organize foraging parties, which would consist of officers commanding a detachment of soldiers from each regiment of the brigade. This detachment would leave the camps in the morning to forage along the skirts of the columns and obtain enough food to keep the wagons filled for at least ten days. General Sherman desired these forager detachments to move out on foot and return to the camps with horses and mules.

Despite Sherman's intentions, the art of foraging took on a life of its own. The system of foraging would become more decentralized with more detachments ranging across the countryside. Soon, these detachments would become permanently mounted with horses and mules from Southern farms, and detachments would start to travel farther from their parent units to find food. By the time of the Carolinas campaign, many of these detachments were also operating as a form of cavalry by screening columns and racing ahead to capture important locations. The greater mobility gave rise to competition between detachments for choice locations for forage. Many foraging parties would race each other to the nearest town to secure it for their own unit. A classic example was the intense rivalry between the forager detachments of XIV and XX Army Corps in South Carolina. In some cases, these ad hoc units would fight each other more than the Confederate cavalry and militia units.

The greatest problem with these forager detachments was the different levels of discipline found in these units. Some detachments were tightly controlled by both divisional and brigade-level officers in an attempt to control any abuses. On the other hand, some detachments were allowed to range freely over the country and take items that were not considered forage. In addition, a number of soldiers took the opportunity to leave their regiments to conduct their own forage trips. It was to these unauthorized foragers that the term *bummer* originally applied. These bummers, along with army deserters and Confederate cavalry units foraging in the same area, had a truly devastating effect on the civilian populations of Georgia, South Carolina, and North Carolina.

A week into the Savannah campaign, many corps and divisional commanders were issuing orders to curb the destruction of mainly abandoned homes along the march route. This destruction of abandoned houses increased tenfold during the march through South Carolina. In addition to abandoned homes, occupied dwellings would be in danger of destruction, especially if Union soldiers were killed in the area. Confederate cavalry and civilians began to attack forager detachments, and in many cases no quarter was given to the Union soldiers. Detachments started to limit their foraging areas to routes where they could get support from the main columns in case of an attack. By mid-February 1865, correspondence was began between Union and Confederate generals to curb the killing of Union soldiers, but no resolution was ever made.

By the time General Sherman's two armies were entering North Carolina in March 1865, most forager detachments were led by a permanently assigned officer with a select group of noncommissioned officers and privates. This system provided more forage for the column and also ensured more control over the actions of the detachment. By the time of the occupation of Goldsboro, North Carolina, on 24 March 1865, the foraging system was discontinued in Sherman's two armies. By this point, the Union armies faced an organized Confederate army with superbly led cavalry. Any detachments going out would find themselves almost constantly open to Confederate cavalry attacks. Finally, a supply line was opened to New Bern, North Carolina, and Sherman's forces did not need a foraging system to keep the army fed.

—*William H. Brown*

See also Carolinas Campaign; Sherman, William Tecumseh; Sherman's March to the Sea.

For further reading:
Barrett, John G. *Sherman's March through the Carolinas* (1956).
Faust, Patricia. *Historical Times Illustrated Encyclopedia of the Civil War* (1986).
Glatthaar, Joseph T. *The March to the Sea and Beyond: Sherman's Troops in the Savannah and Carolinas Campaigns* (1985).
Grimsley, Mark. *The Hard Hand of War: Union Military Policy Toward Southern Civilians, 1861–1865* (1995).
Marszalek. John F. *Sherman: A Soldier's Passion for Order* (1994).

BURBRIDGE, STEPHEN GANO
(1831–1894)
Union general

Born on 31 August 1831 in Scott County, Kentucky, Stephen G. Burbridge was the son of Captain Robert Burbridge, a War of 1812 veteran, and Eliza Ann Barnes. After completing studies at Georgetown College from 1845 to 1847, he attended the Frankfort (Kentucky) Military Institute. Young Burbridge subsequently studied law but chose the life of a merchant and farmer.

With the outbreak of the war, Burbridge left his Logan County farm and raised the 26th Kentucky Infantry for the Union cause. Commissioned colonel on 27 August 1861, he was too ill to command at Shiloh. Promoted to brigadier general of volunteers on 9 June 1862, he subsequently served ably at Chickasaw Bayou, Arkansas Post, and the Vicksburg campaign.

On 15 February 1864, Burbridge was placed in temporary command of the District of Kentucky. At the request of Governor Thomas Bramlette and other prominent Kentuckians, the command became permanent on 14 March. Although largely Unionist in sentiment, Kentucky bitterly opposed any measure that threatened the existence of slavery. Within this volatile political climate, the new commander was forced to contend with the frequent threat of guerrilla depredations and large-scale enemy cavalry raids

Burbridge served ably in the field and was breveted major general of volunteers on 4 July 1864 for shattering John Hunt Morgan's command during the noted raider's last foray into the state. Although Burbridge's advance into southwestern Virginia was halted at Saltville on 2 October 1864, he subsequently participated in Major General George Stoneman's successful raid into the vital region from 10 to 21 December 1864. Although a slave owner, Burbridge vigorously supported the organization of black troops in the state. Praised for his efforts by Adjutant General Lorenzo Thomas, Burbridge was hailed by the men of the 5th and 6th U.S. Colored Cavalry regiments as the "pioneer of freedom for the slaves of Kentucky."

After Lincoln's 5 July 1864 proclamation declaring martial law and suspending the writ of habeas corpus in Kentucky, Burbridge assumed extensive civil and military powers. In his zeal to crush dissent, he ordered the arbitrary arrest of "disloyal" citizens, including several prominent critics of the Lincoln administration, and suppressed those newspapers he considered "rebel sheets." Burbridge's bayonets also controlled the polls during state elections and the presidential contest of 1864. While praised by Kentucky "radicals," conservative Unionists loudly condemned him as a tyrant. Governor Bramlette became his bitter foe and in late 1864 bombarded Lincoln, Grant, and Sherman with demands for Burbridge's removal.

Burbridge's extreme measures to rout out the guerrilla menace proved the most controversial aspect of his career. Issued on 16 July 1864, his General Orders No. 59 decreed that four guerrilla prisoners would henceforth be publicly executed for every Unionist murdered by irregulars. Scores of men fell before his firing squads in the months that followed. Historians have overlooked that Confederate forces operating in Kentucky frequently shot Union irregulars out of hand. However, it is undeniable that the victims of Burbridge's policy were executed without trial for crimes they did not commit. Outraged Kentuckians damned Burbridge as a butcher—a charge that would haunt him for the rest of his days.

Burbridge's bitter feud with Bramlette and his alienation of Kentucky's conservative majority cost him the support of both Grant and Lincoln. After a conference between the president and a delegation of prominent Kentuckians in Washington, Burbridge was relieved of command on 23 February 1865. Although initially ordered to report to General George H. Thomas at Nashville, Burbridge spent the remainder of the war without a command. He subsequently resigned his commission on 1 December 1865.

Burbridge remained a controversial figure for years after the conflict. Vilified by Kentucky's Democratic press as a "despot" and "butcher," he was frequently forced to defend his war record publicly. Although warmly defended by many wartime comrades and Republican leaders, Burbridge failed to obtain any further military position or government office. Virtually ostracized, he lamented in 1867 that "my services to my country have caused me to be exiled from my home." He afterward left Kentucky and established a successful legal practice in Washington, D.C. He retired from the legal profession in 1879 and accepted a position with a Philadelphia real estate firm. He died in Brooklyn, New York, on 2 December 1894 and was buried in Arlington National Cemetery.

A victim of partisan politics both during and after the conflict, Burbridge claimed, rightly in most cases, that he merely followed the orders of his superiors. Nevertheless, he never shrank from carrying out ruthless measures nor did he exhibit the judgment and skill necessary to command in a politically turbulent district. He remains to this day one of the most controversial figures in Kentucky history.

—*James M. Prichard*

See also Bramlette, Thomas E; Kentucky; Morgan, John Hunt; Morgan's Raids.

For further reading:

Coulter, E. Merton. *The Civil War and Readjustment in Kentucky* (1926).

Falaise, Louis De. "General Stephen Gano Burbridge's Command in Kentucky." *Register of the Kentucky Historical Society* (1971).

Louisville *Commercial* (9 January 1882; 5 February 1882).

Louisville *Courier-Journal* (7 and 8 December 1894).

BURNETT, HENRY LAWRENCE
(1838–1916)
Union general

Born to Henry Burnett and Nancy Jones Burnett in Youngstown, Ohio, Henry Lawrence Burnett was educated at Chester Academy before embarking on the study of law. He opened a practice in Warren, Ohio, in 1859. Upon the firing on Fort Sumter, Burnett addressed Union meetings in and around Warren trying to encourage support for the Union and recruiting for the U.S. Army. When he was criticized for not being in the army himself, he enlisted in a volunteer regiment that became the 2d Ohio Cavalry. In August 1861 he was elected captain of his company.

In the fall of 1861 the 2d Ohio was sent to Missouri, where it saw considerable action. The following year Burnett's regiment served in Kansas and during the repulse of Braxton Bragg from Kentucky. As part of the Army of the Ohio, Burnett and the regiment participated in the engagements of that force through the summer of 1863. In August of that year, Burnett was promoted to major and was chosen by the army's commander, Ambrose Burnside, to serve as the judge advocate for the Army of the Ohio. Burnside, frustrated in dealings with potentially disloyal persons like Clement Vallandigham, sought to regularize the procedures for dealing with civilian political prisoners. During his early time in his position, Burnett gained a great deal of experience in trying political prisoners, experience that would stand him in good stead for the remainder of the war and beyond.

In 1864, Indiana governor Oliver P. Morton requested assistance from the army in prosecuting suspected disloyal persons. Burnett was sent to the governor's assistance to prosecute before military tribunals alleged members of the Knights of the Golden Circle. Burnett also traveled to Illinois, where he successfully prosecuted individuals involved in a conspiracy to free the Confederate prisoners at Camp Douglas outside Chicago. He also investigated and prosecuted individuals involved in attempts to incite draft riots in the Midwest.

Burnett's growing experience made him a valuable member of the legal team that prepared the military prosecution of Lamdin P. Milligan at the end of 1864. He offered one of the opinions that it was perfectly justified to try the case in a military court even though the civil courts of Indiana were functioning. Of course it would be the very fact that the civil courts were operational that brought about the overturning by the Supreme Court of Milligan's conviction in *Ex parte Milligan* after the war.

In early 1865, Burnett was transferred to Washington, D.C., to work directly under Joseph Holt in the judge advocate general's office. In March he was brevetted to colonel and later the same month to brigadier general. With the Lincoln assassination in April 1865, Burnett would see his greatest responsibility.

As assistant judge advocate to Holt, Burnett was given the responsibility of conducting much of the investigation of the assassination and collecting evidence against those suspected of being involved in the conspiracy. During one point in his investigation, his experience with the Knights of the Golden Circle and his conviction that the group was involved in so many conspiracies convinced him that that group had masterminded the Lincoln assassination. He later changed his view somewhat to believe that Confederate government officials had planned the assassination.

During the trial, Burnett served as Holt's special assistant. His primary duty was to organize the evidence against the defendants for presentation to the panel of military judges. Although he did not openly disagree with Holt, Burnett questioned some of his chief's methods, particularly the strict secrecy regarding much of the trial. Burnett wrote privately to Secretary of War Edwin Stanton complaining of some of his misgivings but was instructed by Stanton that he was to be governed in all aspects of the trial by Holt.

With the trials complete, Burnett was mustered out of the volunteer service. He returned to Ohio, where he practiced law in Cincinnati. He moved to New York City in 1869, where he entered into partnership with a number of prominent attorneys and soon gained a reputation as one of the most important corporate lawyers in the nation. At different times during his career, he represented the Erie Railroad, British concerns in the Emma Mine case, and the Rutland Railroad Company. He was also very active in behind-the-scenes activities of the Republican Party and served as an unofficial advisor to William McKinley. When McKinley became president he appointed Burnett one of New York's federal district attorneys. In his later life, Burnett wrote extensively while living much of the time on his estate near Goshen, New York. He died in New York City on 4 January 1916 from complications of pneumonia.

—*David S. Heidler and Jeanne T. Heidler*

See also Ex parte Milligan; Knights of the Golden Circle; Lincoln Assassination.
For further reading:
Burnett, Henry Lawrence. "Assassination of President Lincoln and the Trials of the Assassins." In *History of the Ohio Society of New York, 1885–1905* (1906).
———. "The Controversy between President Johnson and Judge Holt." In *Some Incidents in the Trial of President Lincoln's Assassins* (1891).
Turner, Thomas Reed. *Beware the People Weeping; Public Opinion and the Assassination of Abraham Lincoln* (1982).

BURNS, ANTHONY
(ca. 1834–1862)
Fugitive slave

No single event galvanized the antislavery contingent in Boston and Massachusetts like the capture and return of Anthony Burns. On 24 May 1854, as Burns, an escaped slave, walked home from work, a deputy marshal arrested him, detaining him in Boston's municipal courthouse. This event was explosive because it coincided with passage of the Kansas-Nebraska Act, repealing the 1820 Missouri Compromise prohibiting slavery in certain areas of the country. Northerners, particularly abolitionists, interpreted the Kansas-Nebraska Act as another assault on freedom, another victory for Southern slaveholders' power.

As word spread, members of Boston's Vigilance Committee organized a meeting for 26 May at Faneuil Hall. Thousands clamored to listen to fiery orations by abolitionists. Some decided to attempt to free Burns. After gathering axes, a battering ram, pistols, and knives, a crowd of 500 milled around the courthouse. When the door burst, Reverand Thomas Wentworth Higginson and another stormed in, grappling with deputies. In the melee a deputy was fatally stabbed. Burns remained behind bars. Though state and federal governments would attempt to prosecute the rowdies, no convictions resulted.

While attorneys Richard H. Dana and Charles M. Ellis labored to prevent their client's return to slavery, others raised money to purchase Burns from his owner, Virginian Charles F. Suttle, who requested $1,200. When the parties met to conclude the sale, U.S. district attorney Benjamin F. Hallett, forbid it, declaring that the Fugitive Slave Law had to be obeyed. This 1850 law required special U.S. commissioners to conduct hearings, grant arrest warrants, and issue documents returning slaves to owners. Hallett feared that, if Burns were sold, the federal government would not reimburse Boston for debts incurred in apprehending and confining Burns.

Newspaper accounts of Burns put his age between twenty and thirty years. Not even Burns knew his exact age, but his tombstone bears the date 31 May 1834. He was the youngest of thirteen children, and his owner, Suttle, hired him out to various employers. Burns enjoyed a measure of independence, running errands and working in a grocery store, a tavern, and a sawmill. He underwent religious conversion and preached to slaves, ministering and performing marriages. In 1854, Burns worked for a Richmond apothecary who permitted Burns to find other odd jobs. Burns found work along the docks and stowed aboard a Boston-bound ship, landing in February. Later, the scarcely literate Burns penned a letter to his brother in Virginia that was intercepted by Suttle, who rushed to Boston.

After hearings and motions, the commissioner ruled on 2 June that Suttle owned Burns and ordered the fugitive returned to Virginia. That afternoon an estimated 50,000 people lined the streets waiting to catch a glimpse of Burns. Businesses closed and people hung black shawls and fabric out of windows and hoisted over the street a large black coffin bearing the word "Liberty." Surrounded by sixty volunteer guards and marine and infantry companies, Burns walked to the ship returning him to the South. He was transported to Norfolk, Jamestown, and finally Richmond, where he was kept handcuffed and chained at the ankles in a six- by eight-foot room for four months.

In November, Suttle sold Burns to a North Carolina slave owner for $905. In 1855, Boston acquaintances purchased Burns's freedom from his new owner for $1,300. Burns spoke in Northern cities about his travails and later enrolled at Oberlin College and Cincinnati's Fairmont Theological Seminary. Burns moved to St. Catherine's, Ontario, in late 1860 to minister at the black Baptist church there. After a brief tenure, he died of tuberculosis on 27 July 1862.

In the sensational case's wake, Massachusetts's voters shunned the Democratic and Whig parties in fall elections in 1854. The nascent Know-Nothing, or American, Party triumphed in the gubernatorial election as well as in the state house and in congressional races. Democrats lost because voters identified the party with Stephen Douglas's Kansas-Nebraska Act and President Franklin Pierce's eagerness to enforce the Fugitive Slave Law. Although the Know-Nothing Party espoused anti-Catholic and anti-immigrant policies, it did pass the most comprehensive Personal Liberty Law, hoping to prevent another incident like the Burns case. Burns was the last fugitive slave returned from Boston.

—*Kathleen R. Zebley*

See also Abolitionist Movement; Abolitionists; Dana, Richard Henry; Emerson, Ralph Waldo; Fugitive Slave Act; Higginson,

Thomas Wentworth; Parker, Theodore; Personal Liberty Laws; Thoreau, Henry David.

For further reading:
Maginnes, David R. "The Case of the Court House Rioters in the Rendition of the Fugitive Slave Anthony Burns, 1854." *Journal of Negro History* (1971).
Pease, Jane H., and William H. Pease. *The Fugitive Slave Law and Anthony Burns: A Problem in Law Enforcement* (1975).
Shapiro, Samuel. "The Rendition of Anthony Burns." *Journal of Negro History* (1959).
Von Frank, Albert J. *The Trials of Anthony Burns: Freedom and Slavery in Emerson's Boston* (1998).

BURNS, JOHN LAWRENCE
(1793–1872)
Gettysburg citizen

Enshrined as the "hero of Gettysburg" in American popular mythology, John Burns remains one of the most famous human-interest stories of the Civil War. Born John Lawrence Burns in Burlington, New Jersey, on 5 September 1793, he was the son of an immigrant from Aberdeenshire, Scotland. Although Burns was a cobbler by trade, it appears that his true aspirations were always for a military life. Burns was said to have served in the army during the War of 1812, having fought in the battle of Lundy's Lane, and was "in camp in

John Burns at his home following the battle of Gettysburg
(*Library of Congress*)

preparation for the Mexican War," being at that time a resident of Gettysburg, Pennsylvania. When the Civil War broke out, he tried twice to join local volunteer units, but was rejected because of his age. Supposedly, he managed to circumvent this obstacle by finding work for a while as a Union wagoneer in Washington.

In the lapses between wars, local records indicate that Burns played a visible part in the public life of the community. In 1853 he was appointed the Gettysburg borough constable, winning election to the office in 1855 under the Know-Nothing ticket. He was again appointed constable in 1856 when the leading vote candidate declined the position. The following year Burns won victory as an anti-Buchanan candidate by a single vote. Not on the ballot in 1858 and 1859, he was defeated in 1860 when he ran as an independent Democrat. When he ran as constable for the last time in 1862, he was listed as a Union Party candidate.

The record of his political activities before the battle of Gettysburg suggests that Burns was essentially a Democrat and a nationalist who had little use for abolitionist sentiment or the pro-Southern posture advocated by the Democratic Party in the 1850s. Given this political sentiment and his prior military experience, it is not surprising that, when the war reached Gettysburg in July 1863, Burns went out to meet it.

Over the years Burns's story has become so riddled with myth and legend that it has become almost impossible to discern fact from fiction. The fact remains, however, that on 1 July 1863, the first day of the battle, Burns, dressed in civilian clothes and armed with an antiquated musket, left his home on the west side of town and joined the Union troops on McPherson's Ridge. According to eyewitnesses, Burns approached Major Thomas Chamberlain of the 150th Pennsylvania Infantry, offering his assistance. Accepted into the unit, he engaged the enemy for a while on the skirmish line about fifty yards ahead of where his monument stands today. Soon afterward he moved into the ranks of the 7th Wisconsin Infantry. During a lull in the fighting, Lieutenant A. D. Rood, Company K, led him to Colonel John B. Callis, who, fearing the old man's capture and execution as a guerilla or bushwhacker, had him sworn in as a volunteer soldier, thus dispelling the myth that Burns was the only civilian per se to fight in the battle. By the time the day's fighting was done and outflanked Union forces had retreated back through Gettysburg to take up a defensive position on Cemetery Hill, Burns had been wounded at least three times, in the arm and calf of the leg. Left behind in the retreat, Burns was caught by the Confederates, who bandaged his wounds and carried him to his home.

News of Burns's participation in the battle quickly spread through the ranks. On 5 July he was visited at his home by the lieutenant who had met and encouraged him at the firing line and had taken him before Colonel Callis of the 7th Wisconsin. After the battle, Burns was serenaded by army bands. Even Abraham Lincoln sought him out after delivering his Gettysburg speech, and they attended church together. Burns also profited financially from his 1 July adventures. He was awarded a pension by a special act of Congress, and he received thousands of dollars in contributions from all over after the battle. After selling his home to the Springs Hotel Company as a potential tourist attraction, his last days were spent near a little farm that he owned at Bonneauville, Pennsylvania, where he died on 4 February 1872.

—*Samantha Jane Gaul*

See also Gettysburg, Battle of.
For further reading:
Burns, John, File. Adams County Historical Society.
Burns, John, Vertical File V8-28. Library, Gettysburg National Military Park.
Coco, Gregory A. *On the Bloodstained Field: 130 Human Interest Stories of the Campaign and Battle of Gettysburg* (1987).
Craven, Wayne. *The Sculptures at Gettysburg* (1982).
Johnston, John W. *The True Story of John Burns* (1916).
The National Cyclopaedia of American Biography (1921).
Patterson, John S. "John Burns and Jennie Wade: The Hero and Heroine of Gettysburg?" Paper Presented at American Folklore Society Meeting, Philadelphia (1989).
Pennsylvania at Gettysburg: Ceremonies at the Dedication of the Monuments Erected by the Commonwealth of Pennsylvania to Major General George C. Meade, Major General Winfield S. Hancock, Major General John F. Reynolds and to Mark the Positions of the Pennsylvania Commands Engaged in the Battle (1904).
Presbyterian Church, Gettysburg, Pennsylvania. *Presentation and Unveiling of the Memorial Tablets Commemorating the Lincoln and Burns Event (November 19, 1863) Held at the Presbyterian Church, Gettysburg, Pa., Nov. 19th, 1914* (1916).
Sifakis, Stewart. *Who Was Who in the Civil War* (1988).

BURNSIDE, AMBROSE EVERETT
(1824–1881)
Union general

Born in Indiana, Ambrose Burnside received his early education at Liberty Seminary before being apprenticed to a tailor after his mother died. Always interested in the military, Burnside secured an appointment to West Point and graduated eighteenth of twenty in the class of 1847. Commissioned a lieutenant in the artillery, Burnside was sent to Mexico, where the shooting had stopped before his arrival in Vera Cruz.

Burnside was assigned to Captain Braxton Bragg's battery of the 3d Artillery, which was then stationed at Fort Adams, Newport, Rhode Island. In 1849, the battery was transferred to the New Mexico territory, where Burnside was slightly wounded during a skirmish with Apache warriors.

After a brief assignment to Jefferson Barracks, St. Louis, Burnside was part of the survey party of the U.S.-

Mexican boundary. In 1852, he was sent to Fort Adams, where he married Mary Bishop Richmond and worked on perfecting a breech-loading carbine that he had invented. Burnside resigned from military service in 1852 to devote his full energies to developing this weapon. Although government boards liked the carbine, Secretary of War John B. Floyd essentially demanded a bribe to secure a contract. Personally honest, Burnside rejected the offer and his firm went bankrupt. The disillusioned Burnside went west in search of work and was hired by his friend, George B. McClellan, to a position in the Illinois Central Railroad. In 1861, Burnside was the rail line's treasurer, with an office in New York.

Burnside was commissioned colonel of the 1st Rhode Island and led a brigade at First Bull Run, where he committed his troops piecemeal and did not provide outstanding service. However, Burnside was promoted to brigadier general of volunteers on 6 August and placed in command of the training of provisional brigades of the new Army of the Potomac. A simple, honest man, Burnside stood six feet tall, his face adorned by magnificent muttonchop whiskers. "The very beau ideal of a soldier," wrote one newspaper correspondent.

In the fall of 1861, McClellan assigned Burnside to command the Coast Division, a three-brigade unit assigned to conduct coastal operations in support of the Army of the Potomac. Burnside assembled 15,000 men and a motley array of gunboats and transport vessels at Annapolis, Maryland. In early January, the fleet put to sea and arrived at Hatteras Inlet, North Carolina, where it sustained few casualties while riding out two major storms. Finally, the fleet, supported by naval warships, headed north and attacked Roanoke Island on 7–8 February 1862. Overwhelmed by Federal troops and ships, the 2,500-troop garrison was cornered and forced to surrender.

After wiping out the small North Carolina naval squadron at Elizabeth City on 10 February, Burnside moved most of his infantry toward Newbern, fighting with Southern defenders on 14 March a pitched battle that resulted in another victory. After capturing the city, Burnside dispatched a brigade to besiege Fort Macon, guarding Beaufort harbor. After a day's bombardment, the fort surrendered on 26 April. Thereafter, Burnside's troops conducted raids along the Carolina coast and waited for further orders, hampered by lack of reinforcements.

As a result of the failure of the Peninsula campaign, Burnside brought many of his troops to reinforce McClellan. Now promoted to major general (to rank from 18 March), Burnside was placed in command of the new IX Army Corps, which went to Fredericksburg to reinforce John Pope's Army of Virginia. Burnside remained in Fredericksburg directing troop movements and was not involved in the defeat at Second Manassas.

The general, in command of both his IX Corps and Joseph Hooker's I Corps, moved with the reorganized army and fought at South Mountain on 14 September and at Antietam on 17 September 1862. In the war's bloodiest day, Burnside was ordered to seize the lower stone bridge over Antietam Creek. A series of assaults finally carried "Burnside's Bridge," but it was too late in the day and, even though IX Corps advanced, Southern reinforcements blunted its late afternoon attack on Lee's right flank.

On 10 November, despite his protestations, Burnside replaced McClellan in command of the army. He devised a plan to move the army quickly to Fredericksburg and outflank Lee, but a series of mishaps forced the army to remain opposite the city while waiting for pontoon bridges. The delay allowed Lee time to entrench his army behind the city, and Burnside, doggedly pursuing his original plan, crossed his army and fought a battle on 13 December, suffering more than 12,000 casualties in failed assaults. As a result of this defeat and the January 1863 Mud March, several officers literally revolted, and Burnside was removed from army command.

Lincoln, still respecting the general, assigned Burnside to command of the Department of the Ohio. The general became involved in political imbroglios when he suppressed newspapers suspected of sedition and arrested Ohio politician Clement Vallandigham on charges of treason. Burnside supervised the extension of Union power into eastern Tennessee, culminating with the capture of Knoxville and then a successful November 1863 defense against James Longstreet's Confederates.

In the spring of 1864, IX Corps was brought back to Virginia and took part in Grant's offensive against Lee. Burnside initially reported directly to Grant because he outranked Meade, but when events proved this system too clumsy, Burnside consented to serve under Meade for the good of the service. The general's last combat action occurred on 30 July, when he supervised the debacle at the Crater. Meade and Burnside got into a heated argument that day and, as a result of the defeat, a court of inquiry made Burnside the scapegoat. Having gone on leave after the Crater fiasco, the general resigned from the service in April 1865.

After the war, the affable Burnside returned to Rhode Island and was thrice elected governor. During the Franco-Prussian War, Burnside served as a mediator in an effort to end the hostilities. From 1878 until his death in 1881, Burnside served as a U.S. senator from Rhode Island. He is buried in Swan Point Cemetery, Providence, Rhode Island.

—*Richard A. Sauers*

See also Antietam, Battle of; Crater, Battle of the; Fredericksburg, Battle of; Mud March; Vallandigham, Clement L.
For further reading:
Marvel, William. *Burnside* (1991).
Poore, Ben Perley. *The Life and Public Services of Ambrose E. Burnside, Soldier-Citizen-Statesman* (1882).
Sauers, Richard A. *"A Succession of Honorable Victories": The Burnside Expedition in North Carolina* (1996).

BUTLER, ANDREW PICKENS
(1796–1857)
U.S. senator

Born on 18 November 1796 to Revolutionary War veteran William Butler and Behethland Foote Moore, Andrew Pickens Butler grew up in the revolutionary tradition of independence. His mother's midnight ride to warn American troops, in a fashion similar to that of Paul Revere, had brought about the meeting between her and William Butler. After receiving his early education at Moses Waddell's academy in Abbeville District, the same school that had produced Senators John C. Calhoun and George McDuffie, Andrew Butler went on to South Carolina College, where he graduated in 1817. During the two years after his graduation, Butler studied law and was admitted to the South Carolina bar in 1819. He settled in Edgewood at "Stonelands," and his practice thrived. His reputation grew, aiding his election in 1824 to the South Carolina lower house, where he served until 1831. In 1832 he was elected to the South Carolina senate. Butler was a moderate by antebellum South Carolina standards, but he nevertheless successfully aligned himself with Calhoun and became an outspoken proponent of nullification. The year 1833 proved to be one of change for Butler. He resigned his newly gained seat in the Senate upon his election as judge of the court of general sessions and common pleas.

By 1846, Butler was growing bored with judicial work. He resigned his judgeship and his position as trustee of South Carolina College, a position that he had held since 1829, and chose to serve out the remainder of retiring George McDuffie's U.S. Senate term. Running unopposed in 1848, Butler was elected on his own and was reelected in 1854. Serving the early part of his term alongside of John C. Calhoun, Butler benefited from Calhoun's friendship and influence. Although he could never rival Calhoun in the Senate, Butler was not intimidated by the elder statesman and vigorously attacked some of his more radical work. Yet Butler, noted for his skill in debate, was a devoted servant to his slaveholding constituency, opposing the admission of California and supporting the Fugitive Slave Act. Perhaps he is most remembered for his part in igniting the infamous Brooks-Sumner incident in the U.S. Senate. Butler's impassioned speech on the Kansas question apparently helped to provoke Charles Sumner to make his "The Crime against Kansas" speech in 1856. Sumner verbally attacked several Southern politicians, including Butler, then absent from the Senate as a result of illness. On 22 May 1856, Preston Brooks, Butler's cousin and a member of Congress, sought to defend his family's honor by thrashing Sumner with a cane on the floor of the Senate. Butler, who had been suffering from ill health for some

time, died just over a year later on 25 May 1857 at his home in Edgefield.

While Andrew Pickens Butler enjoyed a hugely successful public life, his personal life was filled with misfortune. He lost his first wife, Susan Anne Simkins, only months after their marriage. In 1832, he married Harriet Hayne, who died after their second year of marriage, leaving Butler to raise their infant daughter Nancy, who later married Confederate general Johnson Hagood. Throughout the turbulent years of Butler's personal life, his mother was his most trusted companion, helping to raise Nancy and keeping house for him until her death in 1851.

—Brian D. McKnight

See also Brooks, Preston Smith; Sumner, Charles
For further reading:
Aldrich, Alfred P. Memoir of Judge Andrew Pickens Butler (1878).
Perry, Benjamin Franklin. Reminiscences of Public Men (1883).

BUTLER, BENJAMIN FRANKLIN
(1818–1893)
Union general

The general perhaps reviled the most by Confederates was born in Deerfield, New Hampshire, on 5 November 1818 to Captain John Butler and Charlotte Ellison Butler. Only five months old when his father died of yellow fever, Benjamin and his siblings lived with relatives until they moved to Lowell, Massachusetts, where his mother began keeping a boardinghouse in 1828. Graduating from Lowell high school in 1834, Butler matriculated at Waterville College in Maine (now Colby College). Contrary to his mother's hopes of a career for him in the ministry, Benjamin was intrigued by the physical sciences and he disdained the college's religious atmosphere. Butler's fervent wish to attend West Point went unfulfilled. However, before graduating in 1838, he watched attorney Jeremiah Mason argue a case, moving Butler to study law, and in 1840 he was admitted to the bar.

The young lawyer joined the Masonic Order and enlisted in the Lowell City Guards. Many of his cases were police court cases, and he specialized in criminal law, winning a high percentage of verdicts. By the 1850s, the five-foot-four, redheaded, barrel-chested, and cross-eyed native of New Hampshire boasted New England's largest criminal practice.

Butler pursued other interests with the same zeal as he pursued law. He pressed for reforms in police court procedures and in currency and banking, and he sought ten-hour days for factory workers. Interest in reform and Democratic politics led him to win a seat in the Massachusetts state house in 1853 and in the state senate in 1859. He lobbied to reduce the usual fourteen-hour workday to a ten-hour day, whereupon corporations voluntarily moved to eleven hours. Butler's reputation spread in law, politics, and business when he purchased a majority interest in the Middlesex Corporation, Lowell's first woolen mill.

While Butler refused to endorse the Fugitive Slave Law, his maverick streak led him to agree with fellow "Hunker" Democrats that the Constitution protected slavery. Butler further enraged Massachusetts Democrats at the Charleston Democratic Convention in 1860 by casting 57 ballots in favor of Jefferson Davis for president, instead of Stephen Douglas. The convention splintered and some delegates agreed to meet in Baltimore. Democrats who refused to support Douglas nominated John C. Breckinridge for president. Butler had vested personal interests because he was selected as candidate for Massachusetts governor on the Breckinridge ticket.

After Republican Abraham Lincoln's election as president in 1860, South Carolina seceded and several Southern states followed. Alarmed by looming civil war, Butler joined a political foe, Republican Massachusetts governor John Andrew, to urge preparations for war. Militia brigadier general Butler informed the governor that the state militia needed woolen overcoats, and Andrew placed the order with Butler's Middlesex Company. Setting aside previous squabbles, Andrew and other politicians recognized Butler's value; namely, this faithful Democratic operative placed his country above party loyalty, regarding secession as treason, and he might entice other Democrats to support the Union.

Brigadier General Butler led the 8th Massachusetts Militia to Maryland, where a tense situation held. Maryland's proximity to Washington meant that it must remain Unionist so that the nation's capital was not exposed. Butler's bold proclamations quelled any thought Marylanders had of seceding, but irritated General in Chief Winfield Scott. Butler vowed to arrest all Maryland legislators if they passed an ordinance of secession. Furthermore, Butler confiscated Maryland's great seal; thus, if state leaders passed a secession ordinance, they could not affix a seal making it legal. On 25 April 1861, Winfield Scott ordered Butler to command the Department of Annapolis and keep open the rail line between Annapolis and Washington. With characteristic impetuousness, Butler occupied Baltimore without Scott's knowledge, and Scott ordered the Massachusetts general to Fort Monroe. Lincoln softened the blow by making Butler the first major general of volunteers.

Initially dismayed at his new assignment, Butler turned to innovative spying techniques and war machines. Learning of a volunteer balloonist, Butler used the man's services to spy on Confederate troops, camps, and ships. Butler was also the first to use the new Gatling guns. Butler established a precedent when he classified as contraband slaves who escaped to Federal lines for safety. He employed former slaves on fortifications, refusing to return them to their Southern owners.

Still, Butler longed for active military engagement and his chance came when he acquired maps of Richmond through a private source. In June 1861, Butler believed he could lead an invasion by way of the James River and seize the Confederate capital. On his own initiative, Butler aimed for Big Bethel, heading straight for disaster. His own confused colonels fired on comrades; Confederate batteries opened up, shooting many Federal soldiers at close range, and Butler's men beat a hasty retreat. This failure forced Lincoln to relieve Butler of his command at Fort Monroe and in the Senate almost cost Butler his commission.

Butler turned his attention to recruiting young Democrats in New England into the army. He kept a high profile, shuttling between Massachusetts and Washington, hoping for a new opportunity to showcase his skills. When troops were to join Admiral David Farragut and Comander David Dixon Porter in attacking New Orleans, Butler accompanied as army commander.

On 1 May 1862, Farragut transferred command of New Orleans to Butler. His troops subdued the largely pro-Confederate population of 168,000, which greeted soldiers with jeers and wishes that yellow fever would wipe them out. Butler declared that citizens had to respect the Federal government and remove signs of Confederate allegiance. When gambler William Mumford tore down the U.S. flag and dragged it through the streets, Butler hung him. What is less known is that in later years Butler assisted Mumford's widow in finding employment. Butler ordered that civil officers, attorneys, and even clergy take oaths of allegiance to the Union. Butler's most infamous act, General Order No. 28, proclaimed that any woman who insulted Federal troops would "be treated as a woman of the town plying her avocation." This threat served its purpose and Butler never had to enforce it.

Butler's New Orleans tenure proved controversial, especially concerning business transactions with his brother, Colonel Andrew Jackson Butler. General Butler fined merchants and entrepreneurs not engaging in trade. Washington and New Orleans officials grew suspicious as Andrew Butler gained trade permits allowing steamboats through enemy lines to sell contraband items such as salt and medicine, returning with cotton and sugar, which fetched premium prices in New York. Although General Butler cannot be directly linked to violating the law, the affair appeared unseemly when coupled with rumors of the confiscation of private property and the stealing of silver spoons, charges the general never could put to rest.

Butler's iron-fisted civic control prevented the usual outbreak of yellow fever. Butler ordered ships arriving from infected ports quarantined. He enforced rules of cleanliness and organized wagons to pick up and dispose of refuse. Still, this could not redeem the man Jefferson Davis branded a felon and outlaw deserving execution. Lincoln and Secretary of State William Henry Seward received numerous complaints from foreign consuls stationed in New Orleans about Butler's behavior. In late 1862, Lincoln removed Butler, replacing him with Nathaniel Banks.

Butler returned to Lowell, remaining away from the war for almost a year. In November 1863, he assumed command of the Departments of Virginia and North Carolina and busied himself with trying to exchange military prisoners. In May 1864, he attempted to prove his leadership qualities by assisting Ulysses S. Grant's assault toward Richmond. Butler was to lead troops from Fort Monroe along the James, marching toward Richmond's rear. Butler's Army of the James was to prevent Confederate soldiers from bolstering Lee's army. On 5 May, Butler and 12,000 soldiers occupied City Point and Bermuda Hundred. Eight days later, Butler assaulted enemy lines at Drewry's Bluff, but was quickly repulsed. On 16 May, rebel general P. G. T. Beauregard pushed Butler's men back to the Bermuda Hundred neck and cut Union soldiers off from the city and railroads. Butler's troops had nowhere to go and gradually they were detailed to assist Grant. Again, Butler's quest for military greatness evaporated.

After this debacle, Butler returned to administrative duties, cleaning up Norfolk to prevent yellow fever outbreaks. Treasury Secretary Salmon P. Chase noticed Butler's political value and offered Butler the post of vice president on his ticket. Lincoln sought him too, to replace Hannibal Hamlin. Butler flatly refused both offers, preferring to continue as major general. Instead, on election day in 1864, Butler and several thousand troops in ferry boats surrounded Manhattan and prepared to squelch any riots such as the ones in 1863.

As commander of the Virginia and North Carolina military department, Butler wished to seize Wilmington, North Carolina closing the Confederate port. His strategy involved detonating 300 tons of powder aboard a tugboat positioned near Fort Fisher, guarding the city's entrance. With the fort neutralized, Federals would land and capture it. Butler proposed this scheme in the fall of 1864 and coordinated the attack with the navy, which only added to the confusion in December 1864. Unbeknown to Butler, the navy ordered the explosion, doing minimal damage to the fort. When Butler learned of it, he landed his troops, only to watch them repulsed. In early January 1865, Lincoln removed Butler from command. Butler later learned of the successful second expedition to Fort Fisher.

After the war ended, Butler returned to politics in 1866, now as a congressman. In Washington he champi-

oned controversial causes such as civil rights, assistance for freed people and impoverished whites, women's suffrage, greenback currency, and eight-hour workdays for government workers, and he chaired the House Committee on Reconstruction.

Never far from the spotlight, Butler served as a prosecutor in President Andrew Johnson's impeachment trial and vociferously argued for conviction only to be outraged by the not-guilty verdict of the Senate. Butler shepherded the Ku Klux Klan Bill through Congress, goading colleagues to vote for the bill by waving the bloody shirt of a carpetbagger savagely beaten in Mississippi. The bill, passed in April 1871, was one of Butler's most prized accomplishments.

Butler served three consecutive terms in Congress from 1867 to 1875, losing in 1874 but elected in 1876 for a final term. In 1878, disillusioned with the Republican Party, he returned to his Democratic roots. Still, one office had repeatedly eluded him: the post of governor of Massachusetts. In 1881, the Democratic and National Greenback and Labor state conventions nominated Butler and he was elected in 1882, serving only one term. Butler's defeat for reelection permitted him to accept the 1884 presidential nomination of both the Anti-Monopoly and Greenback Parties. His last political battle failed and Butler faded away. He continued his legal practice and wrote his memoirs in 1891. Two years later, on 11 January 1893, Butler died in Washington.

—*Kathleen R. Zebley*

See also Army of the James; Bermuda Hundred Campaign; Drewry's Bluff; Election of 1864; Fort Fisher.

For further reading:
Butler, Benjamin F. *Autobiography and Personal Reminiscences of Major-General Benjamin F. Butler* (1892).
Capers, Gerald M., Jr. "Confederates and Yankees in Occupied New Orleans, 1862–1865." *Journal of Southern History* (1964).
Holzman, Robert S. "Ben Butler in the Civil War." *New England Quarterly* (1957).
———. *Stormy Ben Butler* (1961).
Trefousse, Hans Louis. *Ben Butler: The South Called Him Beast!* (1957).
West, Richard S., Jr. *Lincoln's Scapegoat General: A Life of Benjamin F. Butler, 1818–1893* (1965).

BUTLER, MATTHEW CALBRAITH
(1836–1909)

Confederate general

Born in Greenville, South Carolina, the son of William Butler and Jane Tweedy Perry Butler, the younger Butler grew up in a privileged, well-connected family (his uncle was Senator Andrew Pickens Butler). After attending college, Butler studied law, and after admission to the bar he began what would become a prominent practice in Edgefield. He married the daughter of Governor Francis W. Pickens, further cementing his position in South Carolina society. Butler also became involved in South Carolina politics and was elected to the state legislature in 1860.

On the formation of the Confederacy, however, Butler resigned from the legislature to become the captain of the Edgefield Hussars. In May 1861, he accepted a commission in Hampton Legion. The Legion traveled to Virginia where it took part in the battle of First Bull Run. Shortly thereafter, Butler was promoted to major for his actions at Bull Run.

Butler continued with the Legion in the Peninsula campaign and for his actions there, particularly at the battle of Williamsburg in May 1862, was promoted to colonel of the 2d South Carolina Cavalry Regiment. He commanded the regiment at the battles of Second Bull Run and Antietam in Virginia, and the cavalry raid on Chambersburg, Pennsylvania, in October 1862. Following the battle of Fredericksburg, Butler led the 2d South Carolina in the Confederate cavalry raid on the Federal position at Occoquan, Virginia, and was able to make off with much-needed supplies for the Army of Northern Virginia.

In June 1863 severe wounds inflicted on him at the battle of Brandy Station cost Butler his right foot to amputation. His slow convalescence kept him from the Gettysburg campaign. He returned to the Army of Northern Virginia in September 1863, and at the same time was promoted to brigadier general.

In the spring of 1864, Butler commanded a brigade of Hampton's division and was cited for his bravery at the battles of the Wilderness and Spotsylvania Court House. His exploits won him promotion to major general in September 1864. In January 1865, as the winter fighting in Virginia ground to a halt, Butler's division was detached to the Carolinas to aid in the campaign against Union general William T. Sherman. Butler participated in all of Joseph Johnston's delaying actions and was involved in the preliminary negotiations for the surrender of Johnston's army.

Following the surrender, Butler returned to his law practice in Edgefield, South Carolina. He also reentered politics and became very active in trying to return the Democratic Party to power. He served in the state legislature and from 1876 until 1894 was United States Senator from South Carolina. When the Spanish-American War broke out in 1898 he received an appointment as a major general of volunteers and served on the settlement commission in Cuba after the war ended. He then became a prominent businessman and died in Washington, D.C., in 1909.

—*David S. Heidler and Jeanne T. Heidler*

See also Butler, Andrew P.; South Carolina.

For further reading:

Brooks, Ulysses Robert. *Butler and His Cavalry in the War of Secession* (1909).
Cumming, Joseph B. *True Lovers: Remarks Made by Joseph B.*

Cumming, Introducing General Matthew Calbraith Butler, Orator of the Day, On the Occasion of Decorating Confederate Soldiers' Graves at the Augusta Cemetery, Memorial Day, 1895 (1895).

BUTLER'S PROCLAMATION
(15 May 1862)

A lawyer and politician in his native Massachusetts, Brigadier General Benjamin F. Butler took command of the city of New Orleans on 1 May 1862. Only recently taken by Federal troops, the city's sentiments were divided, and Butler's abrasive nature did nothing to close the chasm. In the first days of his command, he further alienated the hostile New Orleans populace by confiscating an entire hotel when its pro-Southern proprietor refused to serve him breakfast.

Particularly troublesome to Butler's forces were the women of New Orleans. Determined to do all they could to oppose the Union general's authority, the city's women protested in a number of ways. Butler's men were insulted, spat upon, and even showered with the contents of second-story chamber pots. For more than two weeks he and his troops endured the insults. Understanding that arresting the women would only fill the jails and further anger the perpetrators, he sought an alternative. Butler settled on a method of controlling them in his Order No. 28, also referred to as "the Woman Order." Issued on 15 May, his order stated:

> As the officers and soldiers of the United States have been subject to repeated insults from the women (calling themselves ladies) of New Orleans, in return for the most scrupulous non-interference and courtesy on our part, it is ordered that hereafter when any female shall, by word, gesture, or movement, insult or show contempt for any officer or soldier of the United States, she shall be regarded and held liable to be treated as a woman of the town plying her avocation.

Butler's order further evidenced the perceived callous disrespect Federal men had for women and sent shock waves throughout the entire nation. Northerners and Southerners alike were outraged that the Union commander was not protecting the women of New Orleans. The British press even interpreted the order as authorization for Federal troops to rape.

Although Butler's Order No. 28 made him increasingly unpopular, it was effective in curbing overt acts of insult on his troops. The remainder of Butler's time in New Orleans continued to be stormy, and he was removed from command in December 1862. Still with some political power, he continued to be a thorn in the side of Abraham Lincoln's administration until Lincoln could afford to relieve himself of Butler toward the end of the war.

—*Brian D. McKnight*

See also Butler, Benjamin Franklin; New Orleans.

For further reading:
Butler, Benjamin F. *Private and Official Correspondence of Benjamin F. Butler* (1917).
Hearn, Chester G. *When the Devil Came Down to Dixie: Ben Butler in New Orleans* (1997).

BUTTERFIELD, DANIEL
(1831–1901)
Union general

Born to John Butterfield and Malinda Harriet Baker Butterfield in Utica, New York, Daniel Butterfield was educated locally and at Union College before entering the business world. He used his father's connections to become superintendent of the American Express Company's eastern division. Before entering into business, Butterfield had traveled the country, particularly the South, and had come to the conclusion that conflict was inevitable over the issue of slavery. In the years before the Civil War he was active in the New York militia, becoming the colonel of the 12th New York Militia.

At the outbreak of the war with the firing on Fort Sumter, Butterfield was on a business trip in Washington, D.C., and briefly became the first sergeant of the Clay Guards, a makeshift citizens' militia organized in the event of a Southern attack on the city. With the threat ended, he returned to New York City to prepare the 12th for induction into Federal service, an event that was accomplished on 2 May 1861. Butterfield was commissioned the regiment's colonel. Leaving Washington on 24 May 1861, the 12th New York Militia became the first Union regiment to enter the state of Virginia.

Butterfield and the 12th spent the first months of the war serving in western Virginia under Major General Robert Patterson at Martinsburg. In fall 1861 Butterfield was summoned back to Washington, where he was promoted to brigadier general of volunteers. He received a regular commission as a lieutenant colonel on 14 May. Butterfield was given command of a brigade in the Army of the Potomac and became a part of the Peninsula campaign in the spring of 1862. With the organization of the army into corps, his brigade became a part of Fitz John Porter's V Corps.

During the early phases of the Peninsula campaign, Butterfield led his brigade during the siege of Yorktown and even commanded the Federal operations on 27–28 April as general of the trenches. During the Seven Days' battles, Butterfield distinguished himself, especially at the battle of Gaines' Mill, where he personally seized a fallen regimental flag to rally his men and succeeded in leading them forward. He was seriously wounded in the engagement and in 1892 received the Medal of Honor for his actions on that day.

Butterfield returned to duty in time for the Second Bull Run campaign, where he once again served under Fitz John Porter. He fought at Antietam, and a month later was given command of a division of V Corps. He became the corps commander when Fitz John Porter was relieved in November 1862 to face the court-martial that would eventually remove him from the army. Butterfield commanded V Corps in the battle of Fredericksburg, leading it against the stone wall at the base of Marye's Heights. Butterfield had been promoted to major general with a date of rank of 29 November 1862.

With Ambrose Burnside's replacement by Joseph Hooker as commander of the Army of the Potomac at the end of January 1863, Butterfield became Hooker's chief of staff. In this role, he handled routine communications between Hooker and the other generals and aided the reorganization of the Army of the Potomac from Burnside's grand divisions to strictly an organization composed of corps. One of the most famous things that Butterfield did as chief of staff of the Army of the Potomac was to design the corps badges that Hooker envisioned to increase unit pride among the men, an idea originated by the late Phil Kearny.

Daniel Butterfield (*Library of Congress*)

Butterfield served as Hooker's chief of staff during the chaotic battle of Chancellorsville and remained in that position under Hooker's successor, George Gordon Meade. On 3 July 1863 Butterfield was seriously wounded during the artillery duel that preceded Pickett's Charge at Gettysburg. Following the battle he became involved in a heated dispute with Meade over whether Meade had seriously contemplated retreat on 2 July 1863. Butterfield said he had; Meade said he had not. As a result of the dispute, Butterfield transferred to the Army of the Cumberland to serve under his old commander, Joseph Hooker, who commanded XX Corps.

At Chattanooga, Butterfield became Hooker's chief of staff, a position he held during the battle of Lookout Mountain through the following spring and the commencement of the Atlanta campaign. Early in that campaign, however, Butterfield was given command of the 3d Division of Hooker's corps. He commanded that division through the early engagements of the campaign, but became seriously ill in early July 1864 and had to leave his command. He never sufficiently recovered to hold another field command in the war but did sit on court-martial duty.

Following the war Butterfield remained in the army, supervising recruiting in New York City and commanding the harbor forces there. He resigned his commission in 1870 when promised an appointment by President Ulysses S. Grant as New York City's U.S. subtreasurer. He left that position to return to the business world. At various times for the remainder of his life, he had interests in the railroad, steamboat, hotel, and banking industries. He was also quite active in veterans organizations and causes, organizing a number of reunions and parades of veterans, including the funeral of William T. Sherman. He became famous after the war for having composed "Taps" while the Army of the Potomac was encamped at Harrison's Landing, Virginia, during the summer of 1862. He died on 17 July 1901 at Cold Spring, New York.

—*David S. Heidler and Jeanne T. Heidler*

See also Fredericksburg, Battle of; Gaines' Mill, Battle of; Music.

For further reading:
Butterfield, Julia Lorrilard Safford. *A Biographical Memorial of General Daniel Butterfield including Many Addresses and Military Writings* (1904).

BUTTERNUTS
See Uniforms, Ensignia, and Equipment

BUZZARD ROOST
(February 1864)
See Dalton, Georgia, First Battle of

C

CADWALADER, GEORGE
(1806–1879)
Union general

George Cadwalader was born in Philadelphia on 16 May 1806, one of three sons of General Thomas Cadwalader and Mary Biddle Cadwalader. He attended the University of Pennsylvania, where he read law, and was admitted to the bar. His progenitors were among the first families of the Penn land grant and were familiars of statesmen and presidents. As was the case with many of the Northern participants in the Civil War, Cadwalader had close family connections in the South. His wife, Frances (also known as Fanny) Butler Mease, whom he married in 1830, was a granddaughter of U.S. senator Pierce Butler of South Carolina.

Cast in this mold, by 1826 he was a member of the already significant 1st City Troop (1st Troop, Philadelphia City Cavalry) and was captain of the Philadelphia Greys in 1832. Cadwalader was commissioned brigadier general of the 1st Brigade, 1st Division, Pennsylvania militia, and commanded forces in the streets during the divisive nativist riots that erupted from the activities of the American, or Know-Nothing, Party in 1844. After spending a few years administering to his private affairs, Cadwalader returned to public duty at the beginning of the Mexican-American War and was commissioned a brigadier general of volunteers in the regular army in March 1847. Brevetted major general for gallantry in the Chapultepec fighting, he also served briefly as the governor of the state of Toluca. Philadelphia welcomed him as a hero in 1848 on his return.

Cadwalader practiced estate law, maintained his military interests, and became a trustee of the Mutual Assurance Company, an early underwriter of policies against domestic loss due to fire, and popularly known in Philadelphia as the Green Tree. He would become chairman of that board and continue to serve in that capacity until his death.

At the outbreak of the Civil War, Cadwalader, then fifty-five, was appointed a major general of volunteers and commanded the whole of the 1st Division under General Robert Patterson, chief commander of the Pennsylvania troops. In this capacity Cadwalader also served on boards of inquiry, in garrison commands, as advisor to the president and the secretary of war, and on various military commissions.

The lawyer-general became embroiled in the constitutional challenges that characterized the early part of the war. In an attempt to deal with the Copperheads, or Peace Democrats, on 27 April 1861 Lincoln had issued a proclamation that suspended the writ of habeas corpus covering the line from Philadelphia to Washington. It allowed the army to imprison anyone who threatened its operations and keep them in jail as long as they were deemed a threat. No judge could demand the release of the prisoners so the civil courts could try them.

In a matter of weeks, scores of individuals were arrested and transported to military prisons. One of these men was John Merryman, lieutenant of a secessionist drill company at Cockeysville, Maryland. Caught burning railroad bridges and recruiting for the South, he was imprisoned in Fort McHenry in Baltimore. The day after the incident, Chief Justice Roger B. Taney issued a writ of habeas corpus, which ordered that Merryman be tried before a regular court or released. Taney had it served on Cadwalader, who was commander at Fort McHenry. When Cadwalader refused to accept the writ, Taney believed that he had no alternative but to rule that the chief executive had acted unlawfully. Citing Cadwalader for contempt of court, Taney then wrote an opinion about the section of the U.S. Constitution that allows the suspension of habeas corpus, arguing that Congress, not the president, had the power to suspend habeas corpus. However, unable to make an argument for broad presidential war powers, Lincoln merely ignored Taney's opinion and adhered to the writ's suspension throughout the Civil War. The man at the center of the controversy, John Merryman, was nearly forgotten in the public debate. Later, he was released from imprisonment.

From August 1863 until the end of the war, General Cadwalader commanded the post at Philadelphia. With the end of hostilities, Cadwalader gave his resignation on 1 July 1865 and again returned to private life, devoting himself to his private interests. Cadwalader died at home on 3 February 1879 and was buried in Christ Church Cemetery with honors.

—Samantha Jane Gaul

See also Merryman, John.
For further reading:
Baltzell, E. Digby. *Philadelphia Gentlemen* (1979).
Burt, Nathaniel. *The Perennial Philadelphians* (1975).
Garvan, Anthony N. B., and Carol A. Wojtowicz. *Catalogue of the Green Tree Collection* (1977).
Leffingwell, Edward G. "'A Fine Animal': Portraits of General George Cadwalader of Philadelphia" (M.A. thesis, 1984).
Taylor, Frank H. *Philadelphia in the Civil War, 1861–1865* (1913).
Warner, Ezra J. *Generals in Blue, Lives of Confederate Generals* (1959; reprint, 1964).
Weigley, Russell F., ed. *Philadelphia, A 300-Year History* (1982).

CAIRO, U.S.S.

While the most famous ironclad warships of the Civil War fought in coastal operations, many smaller ironclads performed distinguished service on southern rivers. Subject to ambushes along narrow river channels, ironclads proved invaluable in saving their crews from hostile fire. Early in the war, both sides of the conflict constructed makeshift armored vessels using wood, thin metal shielding, or even bales of cotton. In January 1862, however, the Union unveiled its first class of purpose-designed riverine ironclads constructed at Mound City, Illinois.

Often referred to as the City class, the seven ironclads (*Cairo, Carondelet, Cincinnati, Louisville, Mound City, Pittsburgh,* and *St. Louis*) were designed by Samuel B. Pook and constructed under the direction of James B. Eads. Essentially armored rafts fitted with a bow ram, the *Cairo* and its sister ships were propelled by a stern paddle wheel, although the two and a half inches of armor plate also covered the paddle wheel, making the ships appear to be propeller driven. Unfortunately, the heavy armor limited "Pook's Turtles," as the ships became known, to a top speed of only five knots. The ships were armed with thirteen guns (four on each broadside, three facing forward, and two firing to the rear).

The *Cairo* enjoyed an active but unfortunately brief career. Like its sister ships, the *Cairo*'s construction was funded by the Union army, and the vessels operated under army control until transferred to the navy's new Mississippi Squadron in the summer of 1862. The *Cairo* itself took part in only three major engagements. The first, in May 1862, found the *Cairo* providing gunfire support for the Federal assault on Fort Pillow, Tennessee. Surprised by a force of eight Confederate rams, the *Cairo* assisted other Union warships in driving off the attackers. The Union suffered severe damage to two gunboats, but the *Cairo* itself was undamaged. One month later, as part of the wider Union effort to capture Memphis, Tennessee, the *Cairo* and other Union

The USS *Cairo* (*Library of Congress*)

gunboats destroyed the only significant Confederate naval force on the Mississippi River.

In December 1862, the *Cairo*, under the command of Lieutenant Commander Thomas O. Selfridge, moved into the Yazoo River to support Union assaults on Vicksburg, Mississippi. Union forces under the command of General William T. Sherman attempted to approach Vicksburg through its northern waterways, and navy gunboats were instrumental in forcing the advance upriver. Ignoring warnings of Confederate torpedoes (underwater mines) in the area, Selfridge rashly ordered the *Cairo* past other Union warships acting as minesweepers to respond to Confederate fire from the shore. Before the *Cairo* could return fire, two torpedoes, detonated by Confederate troops hidden ashore, exploded in rapid succession and the Union ship immediately began to list to port. Nothing could be done to save the ship, which sank in six fathoms of water. Fortunately, the *Cairo*'s stout armor absorbed most of the blast, the ship sank slowly, and the entire crew escaped without loss of life. The *Cairo* earned the dubious distinction of become the first ship to be sunk by an electrically detonated torpedo.

Immediate salvage of the wreck was minimal, essentially limited to the ship's guns. Buried in a sandy grave, the *Cairo* remained forgotten until the National Park Service began a search for the wreck in 1956. The *Cairo* was raised from the Yazoo River in 1965 and after extensive restoration was installed at the Vicksburg National Military Park in 1977 as a permanent exhibit alongside a museum featuring artifacts collected from the wreck site.

—*Steven J. Ramold*

See also *Carondelet*; Eads, James B.; Fort Pillow, Massacre; Ironclads; Navy, U.S.A.; Pook's "Turtles"; Riverine Warfare, U.S.N.; Vicksburg Campaign; Yazoo Expedition.

For further reading:
Canney, Donald L. *The Old Steam Navy. Volume Two: The Ironclads, 1842–1885* (1993).
Fowler, William M., Jr. *Under Two Flags: The American Navy in the Civil War* (1990).
Selfridge, Thomas O. *Memoirs of Thomas O. Selfridge, Jr., Rear Admiral, U.S.N.* (1900).
Silverstone, Paul H. *Warships of the Civil War Navies* (1989).

CALDWELL, JOHN CURTIS
(1833–1912)

Union general

Born in Lowell, Vermont, John Curtis Caldwell was educated at Amherst College before embarking on a career in education. Not long before the outbreak of the Civil War, he had accepted a position as a principal at Washington Academy in Maine, and so it was in that state that he helped to raise a volunteer regiment for Federal service. In November 1861, he was commissioned colonel of the 11th Maine Volunteers.

John Curtis Caldwell (*Library of Congress*)

The regiment departed Maine for Washington, D.C., on 13 November 1861.

Upon arrival in Washington, Caldwell and his regiment became a part of the defenses of Washington. They remained there until May 1862, when the 11th became a part of the Army of the Potomac and were sent to the York Peninsula in Virginia. After the battle of Seven Pines, in which their brigade commander, Oliver O. Howard, was seriously wounded, Caldwell was given command of the 1st Brigade, 1st Division, of II Corps, which was commanded by Edwin Sumner. He commanded that brigade through the Seven Days' campaign.

During the Maryland campaign, Caldwell continued in command of his brigade, of which the 11th Maine was a part. Briefly during the battle of Antietam, he assumed command of the 1st Division when its commander, Israel B. Richardson, fell mortally wounded. However, after directing the operations of the division for a short time against the Bloody Lane, Caldwell was superseded in command by Winfield Scott Hancock, who had been sent personally by George McClellan to take command of the division. Corps commander Sumner commended Caldwell for his actions in the battle.

Hancock remained in command of the division after Antietam, and in October he directed the reconnaissance activities of Caldwell and his brigade out of Harper's Ferry. In one such mission from 16 to 17

October 1862, Caldwell and his men scouted the area between Harper's Ferry and Charles Town and skirmished heavily with Confederate forces there. The following month, Caldwell led his men in the Army of the Potomac's move toward the Rappahannock River.

In the battle of Fredericksburg, Caldwell led his brigade against the heavily defended Confederate position on Marye's Heights. Very early in the advance, the brigade came under heavy fire, and Caldwell had difficulty rallying his men for the offensive. While in the midst of trying to turn a fleeing regiment, he was struck in the side by a Confederate bullet. He remained in command, however, and continued to urge his men on. As they pushed forward, he was hit again, this time in the left shoulder, and was forced to leave the field. Hancock commended Caldwell for his bravery in the battle.

Returning to duty in February 1863, Caldwell commanded his brigade in the battle of Chancellorsville, after which he was given command of the division when Hancock was elevated to II Corps commander. In the battle of Gettysburg, although Hancock had been sent ahead by George Gordon Meade to assess the situation in Gettysburg, the remainder of the corps, including Caldwell and his division, did not arrive on the field until early on 2 July. When Hancock was wounded the next day, Caldwell temporarily assumed command of the corps. He returned to his division when Gouverneur K. Warren assumed command of the corps. Periodically for the remainder of the year, Caldwell would assume command of the corps when Warren was away from headquarters.

In October 1863, Warren commended Caldwell for the thankless job he had done in guarding the corps' advance at Bristoe Station and then guarding the corps' retreat. Late in the year, Caldwell commanded his men in the Mine Run campaign. In early 1864, he led his men in demonstrations along the Rapidan River.

In March 1864, during the reorganization of the Army of the Potomac in anticipation of Ulysses S. Grant's campaign against Robert E. Lee, Caldwell was unceremoniously relieved of his divisional command and sent to Washington to serve on military boards. He engaged in that type of duty for the remainder of the war. In April 1865 he was selected as one of the officers to escort Abraham Lincoln's body back to Springfield, Illinois. Caldwell remained in the army until being mustered out of the volunteer service in 1866.

After the war, Caldwell returned to Maine, where he practiced law briefly. After serving as the adjutant general for the state, he embarked on a diplomatic career when he was appointed consul to Valparaiso, Chile. In 1874 he was appointed U.S. minister to Uruguay. He returned to the United States in 1882. He lived in Kansas for more than a decade before accepting another diplomatic post in 1897 as consul to Costa Rica. He

remained there for twelve years before retiring in 1909. He died on 31 August 1912 in Calais, Maine.

—*David S. Heidler and Jeanne T. Heidler*

See also Antietam, Battle of; Bristoe Station, Battle of; Fredericksburg, Battle of.

For further reading:
Brady, Robert. *The Story of One Regiment: The Eleventh Maine Infantry Volunteers in the War of the Rebellion* (1896).
Maxfield, Albert. *Roster and Statistical Record of Company D of the Eleventh Regiment Maine Infantry Volunteers: With a Sketch of Its Services in the War of the Rebellion* (1890).

CALHOUN, JOHN CALDWELL
(1782–1850)
U.S. senator, cabinet member, presidential candidate

John Caldwell Calhoun was born in 1782 near Abbeville, South Carolina. Calhoun's educational opportunities were limited, although they were advanced by the occasional tutelage offered by his brother-in-law, Reverend Moses Waddel. After his parents' death and a period of self-education, Calhoun entered Yale College, studying under the arch-Federalist Dr. Timothy Dwight. He proceeded to study law for two years under Judge Tapping Reeve at the Litchfield Law School, the most prominent institution devoted to legal training during this period. Returning to his native South Carolina to practice law, a pursuit he considered "both dry and laborious," Calhoun was married and served two terms in the South Carolina legislature before being elected to the U.S. House of Representatives in 1811. As a congressman, Calhoun continued to embody republican principles and acquired a reputation as a moral statesman who regarded republicanism and patriotism as synonymous: he supported the War of 1812; he revised James Madison's original national bank proposal and backed limited internal improvements; and he continued to praise a free economy and a regime founded on "reason and equity" that was surrounded by a world of "fraud, violence or accident."

As many have noted, Calhoun supported "national" legislation during his early career, encouraging scholars to inappropriately divide his life into stages based on his perceived degree of attachment to a centralized political order. The rising protectionist spirit in America would also affirm Calhoun's wisdom in supporting the 1816 tariff, even though he held subsequent tariffs in disdain. In 1817, President Monroe asked Calhoun to assume the helm at the War Department, where he served until 1825.

Calhoun was generally considered too philosophical for such a practical post, but he accepted the appointment out of a republican sense of duty. In the course of two terms in office, Calhoun completely reorganized and revitalized the War Department and its staff, resolved its financial problems resulting from the War of 1812, and demonstrated a new, more compassionate approach to Native American affairs. Calhoun also began reforming West Point through a new spirit of openness in terms of admissions and administrative procedures. Calhoun has been described as the ablest war secretary the government had before Jefferson Davis in 1853.

A broad spectrum of supporters encouraged Calhoun's candidacy for president in 1824 against his fellow cabinet members William H. Crawford and John Quincy Adams, Speaker of the House Henry Clay, and war hero and newly elected senator Andrew Jackson. Initially entering the presidential field, Calhoun realized he lacked adequate support and withdrew after Pennsylvania nominated Andrew Jackson. Accepting the vice-presidential nomination, Calhoun was elected by a large majority. The results in the presidential contest between Jackson and Adams were inconclusive in terms of the electoral and popular vote, and the election was thrown into the House of Representatives, where Jackson's nemesis Clay served as speaker. In an unusual series of events, Clay came to Adams's aid, with the House vote securing the election for Adams. The president-elect proceeded to appoint Clay secretary of state. Many Americans considered the supposed arrangement between Clay and Adams a "corrupt bargain." Calhoun believed the "corrupt bargain" had disrupted the balance between preserving liberty and assuming power explicitly reserved to the people; "improperly acquired" power would doubtless be "improperly used," he opined. Calhoun and either Adams or his representative engaged in a pseudonymous debate about the sources of political power. Calhoun began to separate himself from what he considered to be Adams's abuses of office, and he supported General Andrew Jackson in 1828. It was as part of this ticket, later known as the Democratic Party, that Calhoun was elected vice president in 1828.

The falling apart of the political union between Calhoun and Jackson is one of the most remarkable events in American politics. Calhoun had hoped Jackson would assume the republican political mantle, but his expectations were not fulfilled. Several controversies were ignited that raised questions about the corruptibility of the administration. The most important of these concerned Mrs. Margaret Eaton, wife of Jackson's dear friend and secretary of war, John H. Eaton. Out of a sense of propriety, Mrs. Calhoun and most ladies in Washington refused to receive her into their homes. After John Eaton made the controversy public, Calhoun was forced to respond; he stated that his wife's actions amounted to a moral stance and not an act of snobbery, as it had been called.

As a result of the dispute with Jackson over the protective tariff, Calhoun resigned as vice president and was elected to the Senate. In an attempt to moderate the crisis posed by tariff-related concerns and the "Force Bill" in 1832, Calhoun questioned the prospect of preserving the union by force, and not relying on the "harmonious aggregate of the States." Up to this point in his career as a statesman, Calhoun had made few statements regarding slavery. Troubled by the increasing influence of abolitionism and the rise of sectional conflict, Calhoun would devote the remainder of his life to defending the South and attempting to avoid conflict. Retiring from the Senate in 1843, he unsuccessfully pursued the presidency for the last time. In 1844, Calhoun was appointed secretary of state.

Returning to the Senate in 1845, Calhoun served as a thoughtful critic of the war with Mexico, and he suggested that the conflict would encourage disharmony between the North and South. In 1844, Calhoun had helped contain the truly revolutionary Bluffton movement, composed of his fellow South Carolinians. Many leading South Carolina politicians threatened drastic responses to a troublesome new tariff and the questionable status of Texas. Calhoun's success at moderating the conflict demonstrated both his restraint in a crisis situation and his lack of control over the politicians often described as "Calhounites" due to their intimate ties to the statesman.

Published after his death, Calhoun's two treatises on political theory and American constitutionalism, *Disquisition* and *Discourse*, demonstrate his hope that America could avoid the pending conflict. Calhoun's persistent concern about the unequal treatment of the South would, he feared, lead to increased regional tensions and to civil war. His last years were spent attempting to unify the South and avoid strife. On 31 March 1850, Calhoun died in Washington, D.C. In death, Calhoun became a source of inspiration for the Confederate government, its leaders, and the South. Calhoun's understanding, albeit imperfect, of restraint within political order remains one of the most important characteristics of his political thought and his achievement as a statesman. In Calhoun's interpretation, the interposing and amending power of the states implicit in the Constitution could only augment authentic popular rule by allowing for a greater diffusion of authority. Calhoun's purpose was the preservation of the original balance of authority and the fortification of the American political system against the obstacles it faced.

—*H. Lee Cheek, Jr.*

See also South Carolina.
For further reading:
Wilson, Clyde N. *John C. Calhoun: A Bibliography* (1990).
Wiltse, Charles M. *John C. Calhoun: Sectionalist, 1840–1850* (1951).

CALIFORNIA

California's request for admission to the Union in 1850 contributed substantially to the sectional crisis that led to the Civil War. Bitter arguments over its slave or free status paralyzed the Congress and brought the Union to the brink of dissolution in 1850. The compromise that was eventually hammered out preserved the free state status that had been the desire of the majority at California's constitutional convention in 1849. Nonetheless, pro-Southern sympathies continued to fester in southern California and made their political will felt through the state Democratic Party. In particular, California's Tennessee-born senator William M. Gwin, through the California Fugitive Slave Act of 1851, made efforts to have fugitive slaves returned who had fled to the state before the advent of statehood.

As the sectional crisis escalated in the 1850s, California's emerging political establishment took note, but regional issues seemed to be predominant. The anti-slavery Republican Party did well in California when local hero John C. Frémont was its standard bearer in 1856, but Abraham Lincoln's candidacy drew considerable opposition from a variety of the state's residents and Lincoln carried the state only narrowly in the election of 1860.

The secession crisis of the winter of 1860–1861 found Californians on both sides of the issue. Newspapers such as the *Bulletin* and *Alta California* in San Francisco and the *Bee and Union* in Sacramento were staunch supporters of the Union. Secession sentiment found its voice in such papers as *The San Francisco Herald, Marysville Gazette*, the *Los Angeles Star*, and the *Sonora Democrat*. Politicians ranged on both sides of the issue. Still others such as Representative John C. Burch and Governor John B. Welles called for the creation of a Pacific Republic, and a flag-raising ceremony in Stockton in 1861 seemed to be the high-water mark of this impulse. The state legislature passed a resolution on 17 May 1861 (the anniversary of the convocation of the Constitutional Convention) that the "people of California are devoted to the Constitution and Union now in an hour of trial and peril." In the elections of 1861, a coalition of War Democrats and Republicans elected California's first Republican governor, the staunchly pro-Unionist Leland Stanford. Although Stanford was careful to distance himself from support of antislavery politics, his strong support of the Union guaranteed California's loyalty.

Much early scholarship on Civil War California suggests that the state was a hotbed of Southern sympathy and that there were serious dangers that the state would bolt the Union. The presence of future Confederate general Albert Sidney Johnston at the presidio in San Francisco, the existence of pro-Confederate societies such as the Knights of the Golden Circle and the Committee of Thirty, and "plots" to use armed schooners such as the *Chapman* as a privateer under Confederate letters of marque led many to believe that a serious possibility existed of California secessionists detaching the southland from the Union. Indeed, pockets of disloyalty existed, and concerns about a Confederate invasion of the lower part of the state appear to have flourished for a time. However, more recent scholarship has challenged this view and suggested that there never was a serious possibility that California would leave the Union. Indeed, estimates suggest that only 7 percent of California's population came from the seceded states. Further, historians such as Ronald Woolsey have suggested that anti-Union sensibilities among southern Californians stemmed not from an affection for the Confederacy, but out of a constellation of local and regional issues related to concerns about states' rights, economic issues, frustration with efforts at reform, and the intricacies of party politics.

Unionist sentiment was strong and well entrenched throughout the state. A leading apostle of Unionist sentiment and a major support for the U.S. Sanitary Commission was Unitarian minister Thomas Starr King. King's eloquence praised the Union cause and mobilized hundreds of Californians to donate to the agency. In all, California sent about 15,000 men to the Union army, including two regiments of cavalry and eight of infantry. Some of these men served in Massachusetts and Washington Territory. The California Battalion, headed by Lincoln's friend Edward D. Baker, saw service in other venues. The deployment of Federal troops to other locations in the East gave local California militia an opportunity to protect the Indian frontier.

California gold, about $15 million in all, shored up the Federal treasuries during the war and helped to stabilize U.S. currency. This gift, more than the various volunteers, was California's most important gift to the Union cause.

The Civil War had important implications for California that would help to reshape its destiny. The enactment of the Transcontinental Railroad Bill providing for the construction of a major railroad line across the country with Sacramento as its western terminus had significant implications for the state. Pro-Unionist politicians, such as Leland Stanford, and other loyal Californians, such as Collis P. Huntington, would benefit dramatically from the new line, and these bands of steel would ensure California's linkage to the larger republic. The onset of the Civil War found California to be a remote province of a vast nation. The politics of the war left it with a new political configuration and the origins of the economic base that would provide for its future economic dominance.

—*Steven M. Avella*

See also: Baker, Edward Dickinson.
For further reading:
Gilbert, Benjamin F. "California and the Civil War, Bibliographical Essay." *California Historical Society Quarterly* (1961).

———. "The Confederate Minority in California." *California Historical Society Quarterly* (1941).

Hunt, Aurora. *The Army of the Pacific, 1860–1866* (1951).

Lewis, Oscar. *The War in the Far West: 1861–1865* (1961).

McAffee, Ward M. "California's House Divided." *Civil War History* (1987).

Posner, Russell M. "Thomas Starr King and the Mercy Million." *California Historical Society Quarterly* (1964).

Stanley, Gerald. "Civil War Politics in California." *Southern California Quarterly* (1982).

———. "Slavery and the Origins of the Republican Party in California." *Southern California Quarterly* (1978).

Woolsey, Ronald C. "Disunion or Dissent?" *Southern California Quarterly* (1984).

———. "The Politics of a Lost Cause." *California History* (1991).

CAMERON, JAMES
(1801–1861)
Union colonel

James Cameron, a younger brother of Simon Cameron (Lincoln's first secretary of war), was born in Maytown, Lancaster County, Pennsylvania. After a rudimentary education, James was apprenticed to Simon, who was then in the publishing business. By 1827, James had settled in Williamsport, where he became copublisher of the Lycoming *Gazette*. In 1829, he returned to Lancaster, where he took control of *The Political Sentinel*, which he owned while studying law in the office of James

Simon Cameron (*Library of Congress*)

Buchanan. In 1839, Cameron was appointed superintendent of motive power on the Columbia Railroad. Four years later, he was named deputy attorney general of the mayor's court in Lancaster.

When the Northern Central Railroad began construction of a line along the West Branch of the Susquehanna River, Cameron secured a management position in the company. During this time, he purchased a farm just south of Milton. Today, his mansion is owned by the Milton Historical Society.

When war erupted in 1861, Cameron, thanks to his brother Simon's influence, received a colonel's commission and was assigned to the 79th New York. As part of Colonel William T. Sherman's brigade, the 79th took part in First Bull Run on 21 July. Colonel Cameron was the inspiration of bravery to his raw recruits, personally leading a series of charges up the slope of Henry House Hill, trying to save the abandoned Union batteries in position there. During one of these attacks, Cameron was hit in the chest and instantly killed. His men carried the body to the rear, but abandoned it when the Union army began its disorganized retreat.

Cameron's body was buried on the field and remained there until Union occupation of the area in March 1862. At that time, it was identified by the peculiar buckskin shirt the colonel had worn under his uniform. The bones were disinterred, placed in a proper casket, and taken to the Cameron Family Plot in the Lewisburg, Pennsylvania, Cemetery. There, on 18 March, it was buried with full military honors, attended by a host of dignitaries. In 1874, the city of Sunbury erected its Civil War monument, surmounted by a lifesized figure of the colonel.

—*Richard A. Sauers*

See also Bull Run, First Battle of, Cameron, Simon.
For further reading:
Barto, William N. "James Cameron First Northern Colonel To Die In Civil War." *Milton Standard* (1964).
"Biographical Annals." *The Miltonian* (1889).
De Fontaine, F. G. "Death of Colonel Cameron." *Philadelphia Weekly Times* (1883).
"Obsequies of the Late Colonel Cameron." *Philadelphia Daily Evening Bulletin* (1862).

CAMERON, SIMON
(1799–1889)
U.S. secretary of war

Born in Maytown, Pennsylvania, to Charles Cameron and Martha Pfoutz Cameron, Simon Cameron was educated locally before being apprenticed to a journalist in Harrisburg, Pennsylvania. During the 1820s he worked at various newspapers in Pennsylvania and Washington, D.C., and for a time was a part owner of one. In addition to his brief journalism career, Cameron also took an early interest in national and Pennsylvania politics. An early supporter of John C. Calhoun, Cameron supported the South Carolinian in the state convention of 1824. A staunch supporter of the protective tariff for American industry, Cameron turned against Calhoun later in the decade.

In the meantime, Cameron, in addition to his political interests, was diversifying his business activities, investing in a wide range of enterprises, including canals, railroads, and iron. He always saw his political activities as being tied to his business interests and supported candidates who he believed would advance his economic status. In 1832 he led the Pennsylvania delegation to the Democratic National Convention in Baltimore.

Until 1837, when he served as a delegate to the Pennsylvania Constitutional Convention, Cameron devoted most of his time to his business interests. By then he had become somewhat of a protégé of powerful Pennsylvania Democrat James Buchanan and, through Buchanan's efforts, in 1837 Cameron was appointed commissioner to the Winnebago Indians. Accused of using his position to cheat the Indians out of part of their treaty payments, Cameron was replaced shortly after assuming the position. The charges were never substantiated, but the incident damaged his chances for political office for a time.

In the mid-1840s, Cameron began courting the Whig Party in Pennsylvania in the hopes of gaining that minority party's support for his bid to become a U.S. senator. Such efforts succeeded in gaining him election in 1845, but it caused many of his fellow Democrats, including Buchanan, to doubt his loyalty to the party.

In the Senate, serving the unexpired term of James Buchanan, who had been appointed secretary of state, Cameron gave a glimpse of the master political manipulator he was to become. His occasional support, however, for Whig measures made him suspect in Democratic eyes, and his membership in the Democratic Party made support for him in the state legislature (in which by that time the Whigs had gained a majority) an impossibility. Therefore, in 1849 he returned home a private citizen.

After returning to Pennsylvania, Cameron worked to create a political machine to control Pennsylvania politics. He hoped to exert sufficient control to challenge the power of his old friend James Buchanan. In 1852 he worked for Lewis Cass's nomination for the presidency in opposition to Buchanan, an effort that was partially responsible for the Democratic nomination of Franklin Pierce. By the mid-1850s, aspiring Democratic candidates were seeking Cameron's support in election bids to even minor offices.

In 1855 Cameron ran again for the Senate, this time courting the support of the American Party (the "Know-Nothings"), but he once again fell short. After this failure, he aligned himself more with the American Party, which allowed him by 1856 to quickly make the transition to the new Republican Party organization in the state. He worked hard, though unsuccessfully, for John C. Frémont's presidential candidacy in 1856 in opposition to the Democratic nominee, James Buchanan. These efforts paid off among Republicans and his old American Party allies when they combined in January 1857 to elect Cameron to the U.S. Senate. This election went a long way toward increasing Cameron's power within Pennsylvania.

One of the biggest issues Cameron championed in the Senate was the protective tariff, especially in the midst of the economic crisis that began in 1857. He also pushed for less government spending. His popularity with the rank-and-file workers of his home state because of these stands may have had some influence on his decision to seek the Republican nomination for president in 1860.

As an early move in this direction, supporters established Cameron clubs in Pennsylvania and, with less success, in other states. The biggest obstacle to his success became his lack of support outside Pennsylvania. At the Republican National Convention in Chicago, Cameron operatives ultimately made a deal with Abraham Lincoln's managers that if the Cameron people would throw their votes to Lincoln on the second ballot, Lincoln would offer Cameron a cabinet post.

Once he was elected, Lincoln was not so sure about the arrangement. He knew the stories of Cameron's political dealings and allegations of corruption, but he also knew how important it would be to have the support of Pennsylvania for his administration. On 31 December 1860, Lincoln sent a message stating that he would offer Cameron either Treasury or War. Cameron made the message public, but Lincoln quickly had second thoughts. However, the need for Pennsylvania support, especially in light of the growing secession crisis, caused Lincoln to reconsider yet again, and Cameron was formally nominated secretary of the War Department on 5 March 1861.

Cameron assumed control of an antiquated War Department that did not have a fraction of the bureaucracy needed to manage the coming conflict. Despite his previous business experience, Cameron approached his monumental undertaking tentatively. When Secretary of State William Henry Seward stepped in to try to bring some order, Cameron became angry.

To complicate Cameron's ever-mounting difficulties, he also had to deal with thousands of office seekers. As a thoroughgoing practitioner of the spoils system, he should have been prepared, and he did become quite famous for rewarding his friends with lucrative jobs.

On military situations, beginning with the Fort Sumter crisis, Cameron showed little if any leadership. During the cabinet discussions regarding whether or not Fort Sumter should be resupplied, Cameron tended to support Seward's and General Winfield Scott's position that the fort should be evacuated. Other than expressing that view, he took little interest in the matter.

Once the war began and states began answering their quotas for the 75,000 volunteers Lincoln had called for, Cameron's office found it impossible to keep up with the paperwork of processing the volunteers. When it came to putting these soldiers in the field, Cameron showed little interest in military strategy and had difficulties dealing with the egos of his generals. He seemed to be at a loss to handle the legal difficulties posed by the actions of generals like Benjamin Butler and John C. Frémont when these officers tried to confiscate or free the slaves in their districts.

Cameron's War Department is most famous for the corruption that ran rampant as a result of the proliferation of government contracts. Undoubtedly the primary reason for the mismanagement of these contracts was that Cameron and his staff were too overwhelmed with the amount of paperwork involved to oversee properly the administration of government contracts. As a result, many soldiers were issued inferior weapons, inadequate clothing, and bad food, often at terribly inflated prices.

Although many of these problems did not become nationally known until after Cameron left the cabinet, the president was aware of many of the complaints. Then, to compound Lincoln's growing disappointment with his secretary, Cameron in his annual report of December 1861 advocated the use of former slaves as soldiers, a complete diversion from Lincoln's stated policy on the matter. Putting such a statement in his report without consulting Lincoln was bad enough, but then Cameron made the report public before Lincoln had even seen it. The president forced Cameron to change the report, omitting the recommendation regarding arming former slaves, and then pushed the secretary into accepting the nomination to the recently vacated ministership to Russia. To salve Cameron's political dignity, Lincoln did it in such a way as to make it appear that Cameron had wanted to leave the cabinet.

During the previous few months, Cameron had been associated more and more with the ranks of the Radical Republicans, a circumstance that eased his confirmation as minister to Russia. In the meantime, however, his political enemies were working steadily at investigating his administration of the War Department. The results of the investigation brought about his censure by the House of Representatives before he left for Russia.

Even though he was publicly defended by the president, Cameron left for Russia in May 1862 under a cloud. Almost as soon as he arrived in Russia he began asking for a furlough. Part of his reason for wanting to come home so soon was his wife's poor health, but he also undoubtedly wanted to be in Pennsylvania for the elections of 1862. When he received permission to return home, he did so immediately and, while still holding his diplomatic post, stood as a candidate for the U.S. Senate. Even after losing his bid, he showed no desire to return to Russia. President Lincoln finally extracted a resignation from him in February 1863. To add insult to injury, shortly after his resignation Cameron was accused of bribery in the late Senate race, and the state lower house concluded that the charges were true. He was never prosecuted in the case.

Although he no longer held a political position, Cameron still remained active in Pennsylvania politics. He worked behind the scenes for his candidates, and, beginning at the end of 1863, he started efforts on behalf of Lincoln's renomination. These efforts, along with his exertions for Lincoln's reelection, brought him back into the president's good graces and increased his ability to mete out patronage positions in Pennsylvania.

For the next few years, including the first two after the end of the war, Cameron concerned himself primarily with strengthening his Pennsylvania political machine. Initially he supported the efforts of Lincoln's successor, Andrew Johnson, but he broke with the president as Johnson's popularity declined. In early 1867, Cameron reentered the national political arena when he was elected from Pennsylvania to the U.S. Senate.

In the Senate, Cameron again joined the ranks of the Radicals, strongly supporting the impeachment and unsuccessful effort to remove Andrew Johnson from office. He also worked for the nomination and election of Ulysses S. Grant as president in the election of 1868. Throughout Grant's eight years in office, Cameron's biggest challenge was to retain control of the Pennsylvania machine he had created and to squelch the growing reform movement in the state. One of the ways he sought to perpetuate his legacy was to gradually move his son, J. Donald Cameron, into his position of leadership. He achieved part of that goal in May 1876, when his son was named secretary of war. In early 1877, Cameron resigned his Senate seat and arranged for his son to win the special election to fill the seat.

In retirement Cameron traveled, worked on his country estate, and remained interested in Pennsylvania politics. He died on his estate, "Donegal," outside Maytown, Pennsylvania, on 26 June 1889.

—*David S. Heidler and Jeanne T. Heidler*

See also Lincoln, Abraham; Pennsylvania; Seward, William Henry.

For further reading:
Bradley, Erwin Stanley. *Simon Cameron; Lincoln's Secretary of War, A Political Biography* (1966).

CAMP CHASE
Union prison

After the fall of Fort Sumter, thousands of Northerners responded to President Abraham Lincoln's call for volunteers. Columbus, located near the geographic center of Ohio, was a logical rendezvous point for the state's soldiers and in short order became overcrowded with raw recruits. Responding to the crisis, Governor William Dennison leased a 165-acre tract located four miles west of the city. The camp of instruction—soon turned over to the War Department—was originally styled Camp Jackson, but on 20 June 1861 it was renamed in honor of one of Ohio's most notable public figures, Treasury Secretary Salmon P. Chase.

Camp Chase performed a multitude of roles during the Civil War. As a point of muster and instructional camp, it harbored such notables as James Garfield, Rutherford B. Hayes, and William McKinley. It also saw service from 1861 to 1863 as a detention site where paroled Federal soldiers awaited exchange before returning to active service. In addition, it was a mustering-out post for soldiers whose enlistment terms had expired. But its lasting image is that of a stockade for Confederate military and political prisoners, a purpose for which it was not officially designed.

The first prisoners, twenty-three in number, arrived at Camp Chase on 5 July 1861, but were soon returned to their homes in Virginia's Kanawha Valley. More and more captives arrived in the following months, until by November nearly 300 were held within the camp's wooden ramparts. By April 1862 the number swelled into the thousands after the Confederate surrenders of Fort Donelson and Island Number 10. To meet the growing numbers, three separate stockades were constructed, each adjoining one another at the camp's southeastern edge on fewer than thirteen acres of land.

Discipline in the prison's early months, however, could not be characterized as severe. Captured Confederate officers were permitted to wear their swords and sidearms, retained the services of their African-American body servants, and were often seen wandering the streets of Columbus in full uniform. Such transgressions resulted in the transfer of most officers to the Johnson's Island prison facility on Lake Erie and a necessary tightening of rules within the camp itself.

By 1863 conditions in Camp Chase had deteriorated substantially. Nearly 8,000 prisoners and approximately 4,000 Federal soldiers awaiting parole jammed the 130-acre facility. Poor drainage turned camp streets into muddy quagmires. Sanitation was typically substandard, with typhoid fever and dysentery common. Smallpox also swept through the stockade, killing nearly 500 prisoners in one month alone.

In mid-1863 Federal authorities suspended the parole system, or cartel, in response to the Confederate refusal to exchange captured black soldiers and alleged Rebel parole violations. Public opinion too came to demand harsh treatment for Confederate prisoners, especially as reports of wretched conditions at Southern stockades reached Northern domiciles. By 1864 food, clothing, and

blankets were withheld from the captives, and purchases from camp sutlers were prohibited. Under these trying conditions, several escape attempts occurred—some successful—and a conspiracy to free the camp's prisoners was foiled.

As the war drew to a close, the number of prisoners at Camp Chase plummeted from a wartime high of nearly 9,000 to 3,400 by the end of May 1865. By July all remaining captives were finally released. After the war, the camp was destroyed, leaving only a cemetery containing the graves of 2,260 Confederate prisoners. In all, some 25,000 Confederate captives passed through Camp Chase's gates, as well as over 150,000 Federal soldiers.

—*Christopher S. Stowe*

See also Johnson's Island; Prisons, U.S.A.

For further reading:

Hesseltine, William Best. *Civil War Prisons: A Study in War Psychology* (1930).

King, John H. *Three Hundred Days in a Yankee Prison; Reminiscences of War Life, Captivity, Imprisonment at Camp Chase* (1904).

Knauss, William H. *The Story of Camp Chase, A History of the Prison and Its Cemetery, Together with Other Cemeteries Where Confederate Prisoners Are Buried, Etc* (1906).

McCormick, Robert W. "About Six Acres of Land: Camp Chase, Civil War Prison." *Timeline* (1994).

Shriver, Philip R. *Ohio's Military Prisons in the Civil War* (1964).

CAMP DOUGLAS, ILLINOIS
Union prison

Built in southeastern Chicago in the early fall of 1861 as a training depot for Union soldiers, Camp Douglas (named for Stephen A. Douglas, who had died in June 1861) was converted to a Union prison in 1862. Surrounded by a six-foot-high stockade fence, the barracks of very flimsy construction were originally intended for the new recruits to occupy for only a short time. Located on low, swampy ground, the camp was not a particularly healthy place even for the Union soldiers who originally occupied it. Because of the topography, sewage disposal was never adequate, and water quality was very poor.

Since the camp was not built as a prison, security there was rather poor when the first prisoners from the surrender of Fort Donelson began arriving in late February 1862. The citizens of Chicago were alarmed at the few guards provided and the resulting large number of escapes. There is no evidence, however, that any of the escapees ever harmed any local citizens.

When those first prisoners arrived, the camp still housed recruits preparing for active duty. As a result, when the prison population ballooned to 4,372 Confederate privates and noncommissioned officers at the end of February 1862, the commander of the camp, Colonel James Mulligan, was at somewhat of a loss as to how to handle the overflow. To compound these difficulties, Chicago in winter is cold in the best of circumstances, but Camp Douglas was in a particularly exposed position, and the camp's one water pump frequently froze. As a result of these conditions, about 13 percent of the original Fort Donelson prisoners died.

Relief and philanthropic organizations in Chicago and surrounding areas learned of the plight of the prisoners and began taking up collections of money and goods to ease the men's suffering. These efforts, however, caused much grumbling among the Union soldiers at the camp, who often took the relief supplies for themselves.

By the end of spring 1862, the camp housed 8,962 prisoners. The stables had to be used to handle the overflow, and escapes increased. Some of the men were aided by Southern sympathizers in Chicago. As a result of the escapes and the conditions at the camp, it quickly gained a very bad reputation not only among the prisoners but also to U.S. Commissary General of Prisoners Colonel William Hoffman and to the U.S. Sanitary Commission.

Mulligan, no doubt a bad administrator, was nevertheless hampered by a very poor budget that did not allow him to improve the drainage situation at the camp. His successor, Colonel Joseph H. Tucker, who assumed command in June 1862, was an equally poor administrator, but like Mulligan pleaded for the funds to improve the sewers and to build more barracks.

Tucker became so frustrated with the number of escapes during the summer of 1862, and the obvious help the escapees were receiving from people in the community, that he declared martial law in the area around the camp. Twenty-five prisoners escaped on 23 July, and although most were eventually recaptured, Tucker responded by arresting some of the local citizens he suspected of being involved.

Because of the prisoner cartel negotiated in the summer of 1862, Tucker's problems seemed to be over. He began to prepare to release his prisoners at the end of August and to transport them to the parole point of Cairo, Illinois. If the prisoners took an oath of allegiance they could be released immediately. Almost 1,000 did so, and more than 200 of those men were recruited into the Union army. The remainder, with the exception of those too ill to travel, were shipped out in September.

In the fall of 1862, Camp Douglas returned to the function of a training camp for recruits. Very soon, however, it took on a new role as a camp for Federal troops paroled after their capture by Thomas J. "Stonewall" Jackson at Harper's Ferry. About 8,000 of these Union soldiers had to remain at Camp Douglas until they were officially exchanged. These men, serving under the command of Brigadier General Daniel Tyler, had to endure the same bad conditions that the Confederate prisoners had lived through the previous winter, spring, and summer and as a result became mutinous. Tyler had to bring in regular

Federal troops to quell the riots. Luckily for everyone, exchanges were completed, and the parolees left the camp by the end of November 1862.

On 6 January 1863, Brigadier General Jacob Ammen assumed command of Camp Douglas. Shortly thereafter, he began receiving Confederate prisoners from the battle of Stones River. There were about 1,500 in the first batch to arrive. Soon another large group arrived from the surrender of Fort Hindman. Conditions at the camp were no better than before. Ammen was better at administration and security than his predecessors, but without additional funds, he could do little about the sanitation and overcrowding. As a result, smallpox and other diseases were rampant. Fortunately for the prisoners, another exchange was arranged, and all but the sick were gone by 3 April. Not so fortunately for the civilian population along their route to the exchange point at City Point, Virginia, the prisoners took smallpox with them, and it spread to several Northern cities through which the prisoners passed.

Since the Union intended to resume using the camp for new recruits, efforts were made in the spring and summer to improve the sewage system at the camp. By August, with the improvements not yet complete, Union victories throughout the summer forced the Union government to begin using the camp for a prison once again. The new commander for the camp was Colonel Charles V. De Land. Unfortunately for the hapless De Land, not only were conditions still very poor, but some of his new prisoners included members of John Hunt Morgan's infamous raiders. These men proved especially adept at finding ways out of the camp, and under De Land's command there were more than 150 escapes from Camp Douglas.

Partly due to De Land's problems, General William W. Orme assumed command of Camp Douglas on 23 December 1863. Orme tried to bring order to the prison ration and clothing allotment system and to improve security. Barracks were moved away from the stockade and were elevated off the ground to prevent tunneling. These efforts were somewhat successful, and escapes decreased.

In May 1864, Colonel Benjamin J. Sweet assumed command of a more orderly and cleaner Camp Douglas. Sweet was a very strict disciplinarian who increased punishments and cut rations. As a result, escape attempts increased. Throughout the end of 1864, rumors abounded of various conspiracies to free the prisoners. Some of the rumors had Confederate raiders coming out of Canada; others centered around Copperhead groups in the Midwest planning an attack on the camp. Sweet used the rumors as an excuse to round up Southern sympathizers in the Chicago area and imprison them at Camp Douglas. No attack was ever made.

With the war over, orders were received on 8 May

1865 to administer the oath of allegiance to the prisoners and to make arrangements for them to receive transportation to their homes. It took several weeks to process the prisoners, and by the end of July 1865 one of the most infamous Northern prisons was closed.

—*David S. Heidler and Jeanne T. Heidler*

See also Ammen, Jacob; Prisoners of War; Prisons, C. S. A.
For further reading:
Levy, George. *To Die in Chicago: Confederate Prisoners at Camp Douglas, 1862–1865* (1994).

CAMP JACKSON MASSACRE
(10 May 1861)

Missouri governor Claiborne Fox Jackson not only refused to provide the state's quota of four infantry regiments toward Lincoln's call for 75,000 volunteers, but also designed to break his state out of the Union. The state convention did not follow him, but secessionist "Minute Men" started arming all over the state. Unionists also took matters into their own hands. Politician Francis Preston Blair and Captain Nathaniel Lyon, the recently appointed commander of the St. Louis Arsenal, were in the forefront of the Unionist response, and the large group of veteran revolutionaries from Europe, notably those of the German Turner and Schuetzen-Vereine, were also involved. In 1848 and 1849, these revolutionaries had overthrown local and state authorities to advance grand national aspirations and democratic ideas in their native lands. In 1861, they were prepared to do so again in their adoptive country. Franz Sigel, Henry Boernstein, Dr. Adam Hammer, and Peter Osterhaus were pivotal characters among these revolutionists.

After forming the required Union regiments (including a battery of artillery that was attached to the 3d Regiment, "Lyon's Fahnenwacht") and five more regiments of Reserves (later referred to as Home Guards), the pro-Union forces in St. Louis proved much stronger than the secessionist element. Almost 80 percent of their number were German, with the balance drawn from the Anglo-American, French, Czech, and Hungarian population in St. Louis and adjacent counties.

Early in May, Governor Jackson called the militia into camp. This was his right, but many pro-Union officers had already left the ranks, and the secessionist leanings of the rest were well known, so Unionists in St. Louis feared an attempt to seize the local arsenal. The Missouri Volunteer Militia assembled in Camp Jackson on the fringe of St. Louis under the command of Brigadier General Daniel M. Frost. While most of the arms in the arsenal had been shipped to Illinois for safekeeping, other weapons arrived at Camp Jackson. Some came out of the arsenal in Liberty, Missouri, that had been seized by secessionists. A particular shipment, supposedly of heavy arms,

was used by Lyon to justify a move against Camp Jackson on 10 May 1861. Apparently stories about Nathaniel Lyon in woman's clothing conducting a reconnaissance of the camp before making this decision are not true.

On the morning of the 10th, many of the Union men still marched in shirtsleeves because no regulation uniforms had been issued. There was also a dearth of cartridge boxes, and most belts were condemned material from the Mexican-American War. Still, the Union regiments far outnumbered the state militia, and they were definitely better armed. Frost's militia—numbering between 800 and 1,200, according to varying sources—were divided into two regiments commanded by John Knapp and John S. Bowen.

About 3 P.M., the Unionists surrounded Camp Jackson, and Lyon sent a note to Frost demanding his surrender. Frost complied, his men were disarmed, and preparations were made to march them away from the camp. Several companies from Sigel's 3d Missouri occupied the camp. Meanwhile, a crowd (including William T. Sherman, still a civilian) had gathered, mostly out of curiosity. Some members of the crowd, however, were armed and meant to disrupt the capture of the camp. Before the column got under way, an altercation between Union soldiers and the mob, joined by some militia who had escaped from the camp, flared into violence.

It remains uncertain what precisely happened in the ensuing Camp Jackson massacre. Some soldiers, unnerved by verbal abuse and pelted with debris, started firing. Boernstein's 2d Missouri appears to have done most of the shooting, yet one of the first victims struck by a bullet was Captain Constantin Blandovski of Sigel's regiment. According to local newspapers, twenty-eight civilians were killed, including a woman and a 14-year-old girl. At least two soldiers were also killed. After the shooting had ceased, the captured militia were marched to the arsenal and incarcerated there. Soon they were allowed to take the oath of allegiance and go home, but many went to join the secessionist forces being assembled by Governor Jackson instead.

The Camp Jackson incident forcibly consolidated the Union position in St. Louis and subdued the secessionist element, but its overall effect was negative. The reaction of pro-Southern newspapers was predictable, but even the Union press exaggerated the scale of the violence, probably out of anti-German feelings. The result was to drive many wavering advocates of compromise such as Sterling Price into the secessionist camp. The murder of several German and Unionist citizens in St. Louis and the massacre of a Home Guard company in Cole County can also be attributed to feelings aroused by the incident.

Some evidence suggests that Camp Jackson was on the verge of being dismantled at the time of Lyon's attack. Ordnance captured from the camp certainly indicates that the assembled "Minute Men" were no immediate threat to the Union cause. The operation may have been unnecessary, and its bloodshed was even more tragic for this reason.

—*Wolfgang Hochbruck*

See also Jackson, Claiborne Fox; Lyon, Nathaniel; Missouri; Osterhaus, Peter; Price, Sterling; Sigel, Franz.

For further reading:
Boernstein, Henry. *Memoirs of a Nobody* (1997).
Rombauer, Robert J. *The Union Cause in St. Louis in 1861* (1909).
Rowan, Steven. "The Second Baden Revolution: Missouri 1861." In *1848/49 and the United States* (in press).
Winter, William. *The Civil War in St. Louis* (1995).

CAMP MORTON
Union prison

After President Abraham Lincoln's call for volunteers on 15 April 1861, Governor Oliver P. Morton of Indiana set aside the Indiana State Fairgrounds, which had been erected at Indianapolis in 1852, to serve as a recruitment and training camp for Indiana's volunteers. At that time the fairgrounds were informally given the name Camp Morton, a designation that would become official when the camp was later converted to a prisoner-of-war camp. The camp remained a training facility until the end of the year.

In early 1862 Camp Morton was converted into a prison for captured Confederates. The conversion consisted of placing a fence around the exhibition buildings that would be used to house the prisoners. Because most of these halls had been used as livestock exhibit buildings in the days when the grounds housed the fair, they contained no floors and thin walls. The poor living conditions in the barracks, however, were belied by the pleasant appearance of the fairground buildings at the entrance to the camp. When the first prisoners arrived from the engagements at Forts Henry and Donelson at the end of February, nothing had been done to make these buildings more fit for human habitation. Throughout Camp Morton's existence as a prisoner-of-war camp, it would have the reputation as one of the more uncomfortable and unhealthy of the Union prisons. Even as late at the end of 1863, some of the barracks still had no stoves for heat and none of the buildings had floors. In late 1864 new hospital buildings were erected, but this came too late for many of the sick and wounded prisoners.

The first commandant at Camp Morton, Colonel Richard Owen, did what he could to alleviate the suffering of the prisoners there, but the poor facilities and the bad drainage at the site still caused a great deal of illness at the camp. Because of the poor conditions, bad water, and cold barracks, the prison suffered about 20 percent fatalities from disease. Those conditions also

led to numerous escape attempts and about 150 successful escapes. The most common means of escape at Camp Morton was through tunneling, a practice facilitated by the lack of floors in the buildings. Commandants relied on informers among the Confederate prisoners to alert them to such plans. The largest escape attempt occurred on the night of 14 July 1862 when over fifty men tried to escape through a tunnel. Most were either killed or captured.

By the fall of 1862 the prisoners at Camp Morton had been exchanged, and the camp reverted to a training facility. With the breakdown of the exchange agreement, however, the camp was reconverted into a prison in early 1863. It remained open until the end of the war. Over the last two years of its use as a prison it was commanded successively by Colonel James Biddle and then by Colonel Ambrose A. Stevens.

When Camp Morton was reopened in 1863, it was originally to be used as a camp for wounded Confederate prisoners. The demand for space soon brought thousands more prisoners there than the camp was equipped for. Over the winters of 1863–1864 and 1864–1865, overcrowding and extremely cold weather caused the deaths of many prisoners.

Winter was not the only tense time at Camp Morton, however. In the summer of 1864 there were several threats of prisoner revolts. In June the rations were cut, including the complete elimination of coffee from the ration list. Extra artillery was sent to the camp and trained on the barracks and exercise yards to prevent a concentration of prisoners.

The bad conditions at Camp Morton probably facilitated the efforts of Major General John Pope in early 1865 to recruit Confederate prisoners for federal service on the frontier. Those who refused to join Pope in the West remained, though many were released in May 1865 to make their way home. Most of the remaining prisoners were those too sick or wounded to travel, and in June 1865 they were transferred to other facilities so that Camp Morton could close.

—*David S. Heidler and Jeanne T. Heidler*

See also Prisoners of War; Prisons, C.S.A.

For further reading:
Little, Robert Henry. *A Year of Starvation Amid Plenty, or, How a Confederate Soldier Suffered from Hunger and Cruelty in a Prison of War During the Awful Days of the Sixties* (1966).
Speer, Lonnie R. *Portals to Hell: Military Prisons of the Civil War* (1997).
Winslow, Hattie Lou. *Camp Morton, 1861–1865: Indianapolis Prison Camp* (1995).

CAMP NELSON, KENTUCKY

A Federal supply depot and major recruitment center for African-American troops in Jessamine County, Kentucky, Camp Nelson was established by order of Major General Ambrose Burnside in June

1863 to serve as a supply depot for the Army of the Ohio to support its campaign in eastern Tennessee to capture Knoxville. Later in the war, the camp supported Union troops and operations in eastern and central Kentucky and southwestern Virginia.

Lieutenant Colonel J. H. Simpson was placed in charge of selecting the site and beginning construction. He located the camp on the Lexington-Danville Turnpike approximately five miles south of the county seat town of Nicholasville in an area protected by the steep palisades of the Kentucky River. Located north of the Kentucky River and thus able to use the palisade as a natural defensive barrier, the new camp replaced Camp Dick Robinson, which was south of the river. The camp was named for Major General William Nelson, who had established Camp Dick Robinson, the first Union recruiting camp in the state.

In addition to serving as a quartermaster depot, the camp also housed a military hospital, a prison, repair shops, and a bakery. Large-scale workshops built wagons and ambulances, as well as harness. There were also repair facilities. At its peak the camp covered 4,000 acres and had approximately 300 buildings. The camp was served by an elaborate water system that pumped water from the river into a half-million-gallon reservoir and then distributed the water throughout the camp through pipes. There were extensive defensive works, including Fort Bramlette, eight named earthen fortifications connected by trenches and breastworks. On three sides, however, Camp Nelson was protected by the 4,000-foot palisades that rose from the Kentucky River and Hickman Creek; the earthworks were only on its north.

Several Kentucky and Tennessee regiments were organized and trained at Camp Nelson. The number of troops garrisoned there varied between 3,000 and 8,000 and the number of civilian employees exceeded 2,000. Soon after Camp Nelson was established, it attracted large numbers of African-Americans. More than 10,000 enlisted in the Union army and formed all or part of eight regiments. Three other regiments of U.S. Colored Troops, as the African-American soldiers were designated, trained at Camp Nelson. Many of these men escaped slavery with their families, who followed them to Camp Nelson. A refugee camp was established near the present community of Hall. Its population exceeded 3,000 at times. Not all commanders of the camp were sympathetic to the freedmen and conditions at the camp were often hard. In November 1864, 102 refugees died of disease and exposure after Brigadier General Speed S. Fry ordered all of the refugees expelled from the camp.

Fry's action caused tremendous controversy and led directly to Congress's granting freedom to the families of African-American soldiers. A refugee home, with ninety-seven cottages, more than fifty tents, and a number of other buildings, including a school, was estab-

lished. The home was administered jointly by the U.S. Army and the American Missionary Association. The American Missionary Association sent Reverend John G. Fee to serve as minister and administrator. Fee established a church and a school and organized the refugee camp into the community of Hall. When Camp Nelson was closed and abandoned by the army in June 1866, the Freedmen's Bureau took over responsibility for the refugee camp. Ariel Academy was established and operated into the twentieth century. After the war, Fee founded Berea College to provide racially integrated higher education in Kentucky.

When the camp was abandoned, nearly all of the buildings, except those in Hall and at the camp cemetery, were sold for their lumber and taken down. The camp's cemetery, established the year that Camp Nelson was organized, was designated as a national cemetery in 1868. In addition to some 1,600 soldiers from Camp Nelson, including 600 African-Americans, more than 2,200 other Union casualties from Perryville, Richmond, and Covington were reburied there when military cemeteries were consolidated.

—*William H. Mulligan, Jr.*

See also Fry, Speed S.; United States Colored Troops.
For further reading:
Lucas, Marion B. "Camp Nelson, Kentucky during the Civil War: Cradle of Liberty or Refugee Death Camp." *The Filson Club History Quarterly* (1989).
———. *From Slavery to Segregation. A History of Blacks in Kentucky*, vol. 1 (1992).
McBride, W. Stephen. "Civil War Material Culture and Camp Life in Central Kentucky: Archeological Investigations at Camp Nelson." In *Look to the Earth: Historical Archeology and the American Civil War* (1994).
Sears, Richard D. "A Practical Recognition of the Brotherhood of Man"; John G. Fee and the Camp Nelson Experience (1986).
Smith, John David. "The Recruitment of Negro Soldiers in Kentucky, 1863–1865." *Register of the Kentucky Historical Society* (1974).

CAMPBELL, JOHN ARCHIBALD
(1811–1889)

U.S. Supreme Court associate justice; Confederate assistant secretary of war

John Archibald Campbell was born in Washington, Georgia. In 1837 he moved to Mobile, Alabama, where he opened a law practice specializing in land dispute cases. Campbell was an especially gifted attorney, and his arguments in court led to wide acclaim as Alabama's preeminent advocate. His opinions on issues of the day were often solicited by such prominent people as John C. Calhoun, who was becoming acutely protective of states' rights. Campbell was likewise a staunch defender of states' rights, yet his perception of the Union was far less radical than Calhoun's, and he generally understood the Union as representing a governmental system of shared powers between federal and state authority. Campbell believed that a proper balance between the relative powers of the federal and the state governments must be recognized and always observed. Yet he and many others were perplexed about where that line should be drawn. In any event, he believed that purely local concerns were beyond the reach of the national government. Believing that slavery was a "purely local concern," he thus was of the opinion that it could never be abolished by federal authority. This did not mean, however, that Campbell was an especially enthusiastic defender of slavery. Actually, his views on the South's "peculiar institution" were moderate and in some respects revolutionary: though he despised radical abolitionists, whom he felt would rid the South of slavery without the least concern for Southern rights, Campbell believed that slavery was an outmoded and inefficient system that was economically detrimental. He proposed that slaveowners recognize the need to replace slavery with free labor and that states enact a number of reforms to facilitate slavery's demise. Campbell recognized that his views differed significantly from slavery's mainstream defenders, but he felt that abolition was inevitable and that Southerners needed to prepare the slaves to become productive, law-abiding citizens upon gaining their freedom. Any attempt, however, by the Federal government to abolish slavery was, to Campbell, a gross violation of states' rights philosophy and the Constitution.

Campbell was one of eight delegates to represent Alabama at a convention in Nashville in 1850. The purpose of this Nashville Convention was to protest the impending Compromise of 1850, but Campbell sought a moderate response instead of a radical ultimatum that threatened to destroy the Union. In 1853 President Franklin Pierce nominated Campbell to fill a vacancy on the U.S. Supreme Court. Although Campbell had never served as a judge, he had often proved his mastery of the law while arguing cases before the Supreme Court.

Campbell's jurisprudence well complemented a Court that largely sought a structure of shared power between the federal and state governments. Yet, the Taney Court has best been remembered for its fateful decision in the Dred Scott case of 1857. Due largely to the gravity of the case, Campbell issued a separate, but concurring opinion. Despite charges of radicalism hurled by antislavery elements, his ruling fundamentally was an exegesis on the relative constitutional powers of the state and Federal governments and not an attempt to protect Southern institutions in the territories. Campbell recognized that Congress had previously established several precedents in which the Federal government had assumed the authority to legislate concerning the status of slavery in U.S. territories. But these actions, he argued, had been predicated on a fundamental misinterpretation of the Constitution that established far too much power for the Federal government. As a Supreme Court justice, Campbell was determined that the Court firmly establish that the Federal government had absolutely no jurisdiction over slavery, either in the states or in Federal territories. Slavery was purely a local concern, and Congress could neither facilitate its expansion nor abrogate its existence, in Campbell's view.

With Lincoln's election to the presidency prompting the secession crisis, Campbell advised his fellow Southerners to move slowly and not take precipitous acts. However, one by one the states of the Deep South seceded, and Campbell blamed radicals in both sections of the nation for bringing about the Union's destruction. He hoped that moderates would see the danger and seize an opportunity to restore the Union and repair the ill feelings between the sections, and he was genuinely alarmed when hostilities threatened to erupt over the possession of Federal properties, particularly Fort Sumter in Charleston harbor.

Consequently, Campbell began holding secret communications with Secretary of State William Seward, who informed the justice that Lincoln would soon withdraw all Federal forces from Sumter. Campbell then relayed this information to the Montgomery government, always believing that Seward had been telling the truth. Weeks passed, however, and the Federal troops at Sumter showed no signs of leaving. After several more exchanges between Campbell and Seward, the former was again convinced that Sumter would be evacuated. But, as it unfolded, the Sumter crisis was not being controlled by Seward, and his promises to Campbell that Lincoln intended to abandon the fort were groundless. Campbell was soon convinced that the secretary of state had duped him, and he greeted the opening of hostilities when Confederates bombarded the fort in April 1861 with dismay. Campbell remained in Washington until late May, when he resigned his seat on the Supreme Court and returned to Alabama. In the fall of 1862 Campbell moved to Richmond, and the recently appointed Confederate secretary of war, George Randolph, invited him to become the War Department's assistant secretary.

Campbell was hardly enthusiastic about his new post, and he accepted the position solely, as he explained, to be of some use in bringing about a negotiated end to the struggle. His duties at the Confederate War Department involved promoting the efficient operation and communication among the nine bureaus that made up the department. His primary task was to advise the secretary on a number of important legal matters that concerned conscription, exemptions, confiscations, and passports to cross enemy lines. Campbell's rather thankless role as assistant secretary was mundane, routine, and completely devoid of authority over troop movement, supplies, or military strategy. He ordered no one into battle, requisitioned no supplies, and moved no troops. He was, in so many respects, a mere functionary, albeit a rather important one.

Campbell had always opposed the war, and he sought ways in which the two governments could end hostilities. Yet neither side was willing to enter into discussions until late in the war, when the Confederacy's chances for survival were especially bleak. Many Southerners were suggesting that the South seek an honorable end to the war, and this peace movement was growing steadily with each successive loss on the battlefield. Confederate president Jefferson Davis finally agreed to peace talks between representatives of both governments, and Campbell, along with R. M. T. Hunter and Alexander Stephens, was selected to meet with Lincoln and Seward at Hampton Roads, Virginia, for a conference in which the ending of hostilities could be discussed. However, this meeting was destined to be unproductive. Lincoln asserted that discussions could be held to reunite the nation, but Davis preconditioned such talks singularly on the South's peaceful departure from the Union. Campbell, Hunter, and Stephens—all peace advocates—were thus hamstrung in their efforts at making the conference successful. Campbell had earlier concluded that the South's military losses had so weakened its position that any hope of independence had long since faded. His main purpose in attending the conference was determining what type of Reconstruction Lincoln had in store for the defeated South. Nevertheless, as the meeting had been predicated on diametrically opposing objectives, it was productive of little else except cordial talks by the attendees.

Campbell returned to Richmond after the Hampton Roads conference dejected at its failure to end the war. Yet he was determined to convince as many high-level Confederate government officials as possible that the South should seek to end the fighting and reenter the Union quickly. In March 1865, after querying the heads of the Confederate War Department's nine bureaus, Campbell drafted a lengthy report to Secretary John Breckinridge, detailing the South's bleak situation. The message from Campbell's report was painfully clear: it was time for the South to end the fighting in any way possible. Campbell's report was indeed persuasive, but it failed to convince President Davis that the South was defeated. Instead, the Confederate president tried to rally Southerners to continue the fight. Davis's efforts were of little avail; Richmond was evacuated on 2 April and Lee surrendered just one week later. Campbell, though saddened by the South's defeat, was nonetheless relieved that the nation's horrifying nightmare had finally ended. His focus thus shifted to Reconstruction, hoping that the process of rebuilding the nation would not mean that the Southern people would needlessly suffer at the hands of vengeful Northern generals and politicians.

When the Confederate government evacuated Richmond on 2 April 1865, Campbell effectively resigned his post that day and decided that he would not leave with the government. Instead, he chose to surrender himself to Federal troops in the hope of speaking with Lincoln about Reconstruction. Lincoln visited Richmond on the fourth, and when he learned that Campbell wanted to meet, arranged an interview for the following morning aboard the *River Queen* docked at City Point. Lincoln's thoughts on Reconstruction were by no means clear, yet he asked Campbell to summon a meeting of the Virginia legislature so that Lee's army could be dismissed and Virginia returned to the Union. Lincoln's suggestion to Campbell was astonishing in its implications: the president had inadvertently recognized the validity of secession by requesting that Virginia legislators—many of whom had voted to secede in 1861— restore their state to the Union. Evidently, with his strong desire to avoid yet another bloody battle between Lee and Grant, Lincoln failed to realize that if Virginia legislators could vote to restore their relationship to the Union, by implication they likewise retained the option to destroy that relationship again.

Campbell began arrangements for the legislature to meet, but soon he received an order from Lincoln contravening his earlier permission. Upon the president's return to Washington, Secretary of War Edwin Stanton apparently convinced Lincoln that his permission for the legislature to meet had been a serious error. Campbell remained in Richmond, hopeful that Lincoln's promises of leniency would be kept, but he soon learned the dreadful news that the president had been assassinated.

On 22 May 1865, five weeks after the Lincoln assassination, Campbell was arrested at his home in Richmond. The reasons for his arrest are unclear, but at the time there was some indication that he may have been involved in a Confederate conspiracy to kill the president. A young lieutenant from Alabama had written Jefferson Davis in December 1864 offering to assassinate Lincoln, and the letter was forwarded to the Confederate War Department. Campbell endorsed the letter—as he did with all written communications—and forwarded it to the attorney general's office. This routine endorsement seemed to indicate complicity in the offer, and federal officials who believed the assassination was planned in Richmond were quick to arrest anyone who was remotely associated with Lincoln's death. Campbell remained imprisoned at Fort Pulaski, Georgia, until October 1865, when he was finally paroled by President Johnson.

Impoverished and virtually without property, Campbell eventually moved to New Orleans, where he established a new law practice. He was readmitted to argue cases before the U.S. Supreme Court in 1867, and within a few years had rebuilt his reputation and wealth. He was involved in several significant cases of the late nineteenth century, including the *Slaughterhouse Cases*, in which the Supreme Court was asked for the first time for an interpretation of the Fourteenth Amendment. Campbell continued to practice law until his retirement in 1885. He died in Baltimore, Maryland, in 1889.

—*Robert Saunders, Jr.*

See also Dred Scott Case; Fort Sumter; Hampton Roads Peace Conference; Lincoln Assassination; Secession.

For further reading:

Connor, Henry Groves. *John Archibald Campbell, Associate Justice of the United States Supreme Court, 1853–1861* (1920).
Mann, Justine Staib. "The Political and Constitutional Thought of John Archibald Campbell" (Ph.D. dissertation, 1966).
Saunders, Robert, Jr. *John Archibald Campbell: Southern Moderate, 1811–1889* (1997).

CAMPBELL'S STATION, TENNESSEE, BATTLE OF
(16 November 1863)

The battle of Campbell's Station, Tennessee, was the first major engagement of the 1863 Knoxville campaign. On 4 November, General James Longstreet left Chattanooga with approximately 15,000 men, including two divisions, two artillery battalions, and General Joseph Wheeler's cavalry, to crush the Union forces under General Ambrose Burnside's command. Before crossing the Tennessee River near Loudon on 14 November, Longstreet dispatched Wheeler's cavalry for operations near Knoxville south of the Holston River. Easily outnumbered, as his forces in the area, including IX Corps and the 2d Division of XXIII Corps, totaled 5,000, General Burnside decided to allow Longstreet to cross the Tennessee River unopposed. Burnside's strategy was to maintain contact with the opposing force without entering a serious engagement, while withdrawing toward his defenses in Knoxville and luring the Confederate troops away from Chattanooga.

Early on the morning of 15 November with the Confederate forces to his west and separated by a bend in the Tennessee River, Burnside began to evacuate his forces to Knoxville. The Federal forces moved along the East Tennessee & Georgia Railroad, while the Southern troops traveled along a parallel route, the Kingston Road. Both armies stopped near Lenoir, where they were separated by only one and a half miles. Burnside realized that, if he continued along the railroad and Longstreet followed the Kingston Road toward Knoxville, he would slowly be squeezed into a trap with the Confederates on one side and the river on his other. To escape, Burnside had to get ahead of Longstreet by reaching the strategic road junction at Campbell's Station first. To prevent Burnside's escape, Longstreet split his force, sending one division commanded by General Micah Jenkins on his right to pursue Burnside, while General Lafayette

McLaws's division would march ahead on his left to capture the junction at Campbell's Station.

Early in the morning of 16 November, Burnside began the almost ten-mile march from Lenoir to Campbell's Station. Heavy rains and mud slowed the march. Eventually, General Burnside ordered his extra wagons to be abandoned and destroyed, using his horses to pull what few artillery pieces he had. Although this move gave Burnside more mobility, it also benefited the Confederates, who found many of the wagons still intact and gained much needed supplies.

While his main forces were delayed in the mud, Burnside ordered Colonel John F. Hartranft's IX Corp to run ahead of the column and secure the road junction at Campbell's Station. Hartranft's mounted troops arrived at the strategic crossroads first, beating the advancing Confederate forces under General McLaws by less than an hour. Once Hartranft's forces reached the crossroads, he marched down the Kingston Road to give the Union troops and wagon trains plenty of room to maneuver through the junction toward Knoxville. McLaws's approaching troops tried to prevent passage of the Union forces and wagon trains through the road junction, but they were too few. As Burnside's troops moved through the junction, they occupied defensive positions, with the 1st Division, IX Corps, on the Union right; the 2d Division, IX Corps, on the Union left; and XXIII Corps in reserve. Burnside planned to fight a delaying action to buy time for Captain Orlando Poe of the Corps of Engineers to strengthen the defenses of Knoxville.

As the Confederates reached the crossroads in force, General Longstreet ordered McLaws to send a cavalry diversion to the north around the Union right. At the same time, Longstreet dispatched General Evander M. Law from Jenkins's division with two brigades around the Federal left to attack in their rear. Law's attack, however, did not come off as planned. He delayed. When he did move, he attacked the front, rather than the rear, of the Union left. Some officers charged that Law, who was jealous of Jenkins's command of John Bell Hood's division, had deliberately delayed the attack to prevent Jenkins from receiving the credit. Burnside's troops repulsed attacks from both Law on their left and McLaws on their right before withdrawing under cover of artillery. The ensuing darkness prevented the Confederates from mounting a counteroffensive, and the battle ended as night fell.

As night fell, Burnside continued his withdraw to the defenses of Knoxville. The battle for the strategic crossroads had cost the Union 318 killed and wounded, while the Confederates had lost 174 men. The battle had spared Burnside's forces an early defeat and bought the Federal forces occupying Knoxville time to prepare for the upcoming siege. For General Longstreet, the battle was a disappointment. If Wheeler's cavalry had been present or McLaws had reached the crossroad minutes earlier,

Longstreet would have won his campaign at the start. The discord that manifested itself in the Law-Jenkins feud did not bode well, as it foreshadowed problems in command that would plague Longstreet's campaign.

—*William Hartley*

See also Knoxville Campaign.

For further reading:
Fink, Harold S. "The East Tennessee Campaign and the Battle of Knoxville in 1863." *East Tennessee Historical Society's Publications* (1957).
Longstreet, James. *From Manassas to Appomattox: Memoirs of the Civil War in America* (1896; reprint, 1960).
Seymour, Digby Gordon. *Divided Loyalties: Fort Sanders and the Civil War in East Tennessee* (1982).
Wert, Jeffry D. *General James Longstreet: The Confederacy's Most Controversial Soldier—A Biography* (1993).

CANBY, EDWARD RICHARD SPRIGG
(1817–1873)
Union general

Although Edward R. S. Canby's failed to attain the notoriety of such Union generals as William Tecumseh Sherman or Ulysses S. Grant, his Civil War career was nearly as noteworthy and arguably as successful. He was born in 1817 at Piatt's Landing, Kentucky, but moved to Crawfordsville, Indiana, with his family the following year. While studying at Wabash College in 1835, Canby was appointed to West Point, where he graduated thirtieth in a class of thirty-one in 1839. Shortly after graduation, Canby was assigned to a regiment assisting in the removal of the last bands of Cherokee Indians from Georgia to the Oklahoma Indian Territory. Canby then saw action in Florida during the Second Seminole War, but it was during the Mexican War that his star truly began to rise. He participated in most of the major engagements of that conflict, from the siege of Veracruz to the fighting in and around Mexico City, and was breveted twice during the war for meritorious conduct. Following the cessation of hostilities with Mexico, Canby continued to serve in the army, occupying a number of positions, ranging from frontier garrison duty to service in the so-called Mormon War. He eventually earned a promotion to major and was assigned to various posts in the New Mexico Territory.

The outbreak of the Civil War found Canby in command of Fort Defiance, New Mexico, where he was assigned the task of keeping a close watch on hostile bands of Navajo Indians in the region. A proven frontier commander, Canby was immediately promoted to colonel and placed in command of the entire Department of New Mexico, with explicit orders to defend the territory against a suspected invasion by a Confederate army under the command of Henry Hopkins Sibley. Despite being defeated by Sibley at the

Edward R. S. Canby (*Library of Congress*)

battle of Val Verde on 21 February 1862, Canby's troops managed to hold nearby Fort Craig, which contributed to the Confederate leader's decision to turn his attention towards the Colorado gold fields rather than Sante Fe. Canby regrouped his beleaguered troops and gave pursuit, eventually catching and defeating the Confederates at Glorieta Pass, New Mexico, on 28 March and again at Peralta, New Mexico, on 15 April. Although Canby's forces inflicted heavy casualties on Sibley's army during the two battles, Canby was unable to capture his adversary, and Sibley's ravaged command eventually managed to escape the territory.

Although some detractors criticized Canby for failing to capture Sibley's command, he was breveted a brigadier general in the regular army for his service in defending the New Mexico Territory. Canby was then transferred to the eastern department, where he served as an assistant adjutant general in Washington for a year and later participated in the suppression of draft riots in New York City during the summer of 1863. Canby returned to the field in May 1864 as a newly promoted major general in command of the Military Division of Western Mississippi, which was in severe disarray in the wake of the disastrous Red River campaign. Canby reorganized the division, and also was instrumental in planning and implementing the Union assault on Mobile, Alabama, in April 1865, which led to the fall of the city on 12 April and also the capture of Montgomery on 27 April. Following Mobile, Canby was again promoted, this time to the command of the Departments of the Gulf and Arkansas, although his successes in Alabama did not garner the public praise they might have, had they not come on the heels of Robert E. Lee's surrender at Appomattox Court House on 9 April. Despite the overshadowing of his accomplishments, as well as his being severely wounded by Confederate guerrilla forces during the Mobile campaign, Canby continued at his post for the remainder of 1865, and eventually accepted the surrender of the last remaining Confederate field armies under Generals Edmund Kirby Smith and Richard Taylor.

Following the war, Canby continued his military career with the permanent rank of brigadier general in the regular service. He served on an advisory staff in Washington and on Reconstruction duty in the South before returning to the west in 1870. Canby finished out his career in the Pacific Northwest as commander of the Department of the Columbia and later the Division of the Pacific. It was while serving in this capacity that Canby was attacked and killed by a group of Modoc Indians under the leadership of the northern California war chief Captain Jack during a meeting to renew peace negotiations on 11 April 1873.

—Daniel P. Barr

For further reading:
Frazier, Donald S. *Blood and Treasure: Confederate Empire in the Southwest* (1995).
Hall, Martin H. *Sibley's New Mexico Campaign* (1960).
Heyman, Max L. *Prudent Soldier: A Biography of Major General E. R. S. Canby, 1817–1873* (1959).
Josephy, Alvin M. *The Civil War in the American West* (1991).

CANE HILL, BATTLE OF
(28 November 1862)

In the fall of 1862, Union brigadier general James G. Blunt's division of the Army of the Frontier was camped near Maysville in the extreme northwestern corner of Arkansas. Seventy miles to the south at Fort Smith on the Arkansas River was Confederate major general Thomas C. Hindman and a sizable army. Hindman ordered Brigadier General John S. Marmaduke to take his cavalry division over the Boston Mountains and harass Blunt. If Marmaduke succeeded in fixing Blunt in place, Hindman intended to move north with the remainder of his army and attack Blunt's isolated division. The nearest Union reinforcements were seventy miles away near Springfield, Missouri.

Blunt refused to cooperate by remaining inert. When he learned that a Confederate force was slowly winding through the mountains in his direction, he advanced thirty-five miles in two days and struck the vanguard of Marmaduke's column near the village of Boonsboro, later known as Cane Hill. Surprised and outnumbered about 5,000 to 2,000, Marmaduke retreated. Brigadier General Joseph O. Shelby's cavalry brigade formed the rear guard and fought a series of delaying actions that allowed the rest of the division and its train to withdraw into the Boston Mountains. The battle was actually a nine-hour running fight that swirled steadily southward across twelve miles of rolling terrain. The fighting ended when the Confederates reached the safety of the narrow mountain passes. As was generally the case in mounted engagements, losses were comparatively light for the numbers involved: there were at least forty-one Union and forty-five Confederate casualties.

The next day Marmaduke rejoined Hindman on the Arkansas River. Blunt returned to Cane Hill and remained there, despite being more than one hundred miles south of the nearest supporting force and only thirty miles north of Hindman's army. Shrugging off Marmaduke's tactical defeat at Cane Hill, Hindman believed that Blunt had played into his hands by moving deeper into Arkansas. He set in motion a second operation to destroy Blunt that resulted in the battle of Prairie Grove on 7 December 1862.

—William L. Shea

See also Blunt, James G.; Hindman, Thomas C.; Shelby, Joseph O.

For further reading:
Banasik, Michael E. *Embattled Arkansas: The Prairie Grove Campaign of 1862* (1996).
Scott, Kim Allen, and Stephen Burgess. "Pursuing an Elusive Quarry: The Battle of Cane Hill, Arkansas." *Arkansas Historical Quarterly* (1997).

CANNON, WILLIAM
(1809–1865)
Unionist, Delaware governor

Born in Bridgeville, Delaware, to Josiah and Nancy Cannon on 15 March 1809, William Cannon received an elementary-school education but never attended high school. Cannon entered into a career in business and demonstrated considerable ability for commercial ventures. Cannon became wealthy as a merchant and landowner and maintained a special interest in the production of fruit. Within a few years, he married Margaret N. B. Laws.

As part of a family devoted to the Democratic Party, Cannon retained an keen interest in politics. Cannon was active in promoting the welfare of his native Sussex County, and he encouraged the construction of the Delaware Railroad into the area.

As a Democrat, he was won sequential elections to the Delaware house of representatives in 1844 and 1846 and served as state treasurer in 1851. Within a decade, Cannon had established himself as a prominent politician in Delaware. In 1861, he was selected as one of his state's five delegates to the Peace Conference in Washington. He supported the Crittenden Compromise as well as other measures to ameliorate tensions between regions. When all measures dedicated to preserving the Union appeared to fail, Cannon began to support the Republican Party. It is possible that in addition to his defense of union, he was also disappointed with the Democratic Party's inability to facilitate his ambition to become governor.

In November 1862, he was the Union Party's candidate for governor. While the Democrats won a majority in the state legislature, Cannon was elected by a small majority and was inaugurated in January 1863. His opponent protested the presence of Federal troops at polling booths during the election and suggested the Lincoln administration's decree to send troops was an attempt to help Cannon. Upon taking office, Cannon appointed Nathaniel B. Smithers as secretary of state. Smithers was a confidant who would have a great influence on Cannon and perhaps serve as his chief political advisor and speech writer during the remainder of his life. From the earliest moments of his governorship, Cannon was an ardent supporter of preserving the federal union. In his inaugural address he urged more federal control and proclaimed his steadfast support for the union.

Throughout his governorship, Cannon was at odds with the legislature, which was under the control of the Democratic Party. At one point, the legislature passed a law intended to outlaw federal arrests within the confines of Delaware. Cannon responded by failing to recognize the act. He suggested that following the order would weaken the state's devotion to the union. On 1 March 1865, Cannon died in office, having served just over two years. He was succeeded by Gove Saulsbury, the presiding officer of the Delaware Senate and a Democratic stalwart.

—*Lee Cheek*

For further reading:
Hancock, Harold Bell. *Delaware During the Civil War* (1961).
Journal of the House of Representatives of the State of Delaware (1863–1865).
Munroe, John A. *History of Delaware* (1993).

CAREY, HENRY CHARLES
(1793–1879)

Publisher, writer, and political economist

Henry C. Carey emerged as the leading advocate of the American free laborer in the years immediately preceding the Civil War. Through his texts on political economy, numerous pamphlets, and newspaper articles, Carey promoted the policies of high tariffs and an abundant money supply as the means for "elevating and equalizing the condition of man throughout the world." The oldest son of Irish political refugee and protectionist Mathew Carey, Carey inherited his father's deep disdain for the British rigid class system and free trade policies.

Born and raised in Philadelphia, Carey began working in his father's publishing house at the age of nine. He eschewed formal education, preferring to read and work. By the age of twenty-four he became a partner in Carey, Lea & Carey, one of the leading publishing houses in the country. In 1835, he wrote his first treatise, *Essay on the Rate of Wages*, in which he celebrated U.S. exceptionalism and advocated free trade.

After his first book, Carey left the publishing business and became a full-time political economist. He published his three-volume *Principles of Political Economy* in 1837. He countered the primary theses of the two pillars of economic theory of this period, David Ricardo and Thomas R. Malthus. Carey rejected Ricardo's belief that land lost value and productive capacity over time; instead, Carey posited that the labor expended to make land arable and fecund increased its value and, ultimately, the wealth of the nation. Similarly, Carey countered Malthus's dark predictions that population increases led to a decrease in the quality of life. Instead, Carey believed that the economy of the United States was boundless and would continue to grow. Carey's optimism for continued U.S. prosperity was based on his faith in democratic government, the guaranteed right of private ownership of property, low taxes, and the high U.S. wages, contrasted with those in Europe.

The economic downturn of 1837 forced Carey to reappraise many of his tenets. Over the next several years he examined the tariff history of the United States and concluded that high tariffs correlated with periods of prosperity. In 1848, he published his revised views on tariffs in *Past, Present, and Future*, and renounced his free trade stance. He collaborated with *New York Tribune* editor Horace Greeley, writing a plethora of articles and editorials on the virtues of protective tariffs. Carey proclaimed high tariffs as the best means for protecting the wages of U.S. employees by decreasing the competition that they faced from goods produced abroad by lower paid workers. Carey revealed his distrust for merchants and financiers, instead extolling the virtues of producers, including farmers, laborers, and manufacturers. He believed that producers, working together "in harmony" in small towns throughout the country, formed the basis for future prosperity.

Carey's conversion to protectionism came at an inopportune moment. The positive effects of the Walker Tariff of 1846, the discovery of gold deposits in California, and the beginnings of the industrial boom combined to create a decade of prosperity. Carey continued writing and speaking, but his ideas did not generate popular support until the economic downturn of 1857. The displacement of workers caused by this recession, coming on the heels of the passage of the low tariff of 1857, suddenly made Carey's message seem prophetic.

Carey's ideas were embraced by the Whig element of the new Republican Party. The Republicans took Carey's theme that protecting and encouraging agriculture, industry, and regional commerce could ensure the nation's prosperity and incorporated these ideas into their successful 1860 campaign. Carey's protectionist message resonated most successfully in Pennsylvania, a traditionally Democratic state whose iron industry had been convulsed by the 1857 downturn. Lincoln won in Pennsylvania, one of the few states where the tariff represented the main issue in the campaign.

However, Carey's influence on the new administration was tempered. He approved of the higher tariffs, eight-hour workday for government employees, and open immigration policies adopted by the Republican administration, but vehemently disapproved of the internal taxation legislation initiated during the Civil War and the postbellum contraction of the currency. Carey declared his support for the Greenback Party in the 1872 election.

Carey's antipathy for the British, high taxes, and the increasing influence of financiers on government officials increased his disillusionment with the Republicans throughout the 1870s. After his death, many of his ideas were discounted as superficial, but during his lifetime Carey's influence was tangible.

—*Jane Flaherty*

See also Greeley, Horace.
For further reading:
Carey, Henry C. *The Harmony of Interests: Agriculture, Manufactures, and Commercial* (1851; reprint, 1976).
Conkin, Paul K. *Prophets of Prosperity: America's First Political Economists* (1980).
Huston, James L. "A Political Response to Industrialism: The Republican Embrace of Protectionist Labor Doctrines." *Journal of American History* (1983).
Smith, George W. *Henry C. Carey and the American Sectional Conflict* (1951).

CARLIN, WILLIAM PASSMORE
(1829–1903)
Union general

William Passmore Carlin was born on 24 November 1829 in Richwoods near Carrollton, Illinois. Carlin's father was the county clerk for Greene County, and his uncle was governor of Illinois in 1838. Carlin received his appointment to the U.S. Military Academy through a competitive examination. In 1850, he graduated twentieth in a class of forty-three. Carlin entered the 6th U.S. Infantry, where he became a brevet lieutenant. He participated with his unit in campaigns against the Cheyenne and the Sioux and in the Mormon expedition of 1858. By 1860, Carlin had attained the rank of captain.

With the coming of the Civil War, Carlin was appointed colonel of the 38th Illinois Volunteers in August 1861. Colonel Carlin and his regiment were sent to Missouri and Arkansas and operated against guerrillas. By mid-1862, Carlin received command of a brigade and was assigned to Major General Don Carlos Buell's Union army during the Confederate invasion of Kentucky. Carlin distinguished himself in the battle of Perryville, Kentucky, and received a promotion to brigadier general.

Later in 1862, Carlin and his brigade were assigned to Brigadier General Jefferson C. Davis's division in the right wing of the Army of the Cumberland. This marked the beginning of the rocky relationship between General Carlin and General Davis that haunted Carlin's career throughout the war. Carlin and his men were engaged in the fierce fighting at Stones River, Tennessee, on 31 December 1862. In the summer of 1863, Carlin participated with Davis's division in the Tullahoma campaign. During the battle of Chickamauga, Georgia, in September 1863, Carlin's brigade was nearly destroyed during the retreat of Davis's division. Carlin accused Davis of directing artillery fire on his troops. The feud became so destructive that Major General George Thomas sought to separate the officers by assigning them to two different divisions during the reorganization of the Army of the Cumberland in late 1863.

Now with the 1st Division, XIV Army Corps, General Carlin's brigade served through the Chattanooga campaign of November 1863. In 1864, illness, business dealings, and the strain of campaigning forced Carlin to request several furloughs. He served with his brigade through the Atlanta campaign in 1864 and eventually rose to command of the 1st Division by August 1864. By that time, Davis was in command of XIV Corps. Throughout the Savannah campaign and during the first stages of the Carolinas campaign, there was a underlying tension in the relationship between the two generals. During the final march to Goldsboro, North Carolina, problems again started to rise between the two officers. On 17 March 1865, General Carlin was not able to effect a rapid crossing of the Black River and held up the army's advance for a day. His division was finally assigned the head of the column on 19 March 1865, and Carlin's division stumbled into prepared Confederate positions along the Goldsboro Road. After several unsuccessful probes, General Carlin's three brigades were assaulted by elements of General Joseph E. Johnston's Confederate army. Carlin's men were routed off the field, and for a time Carlin was separated from his men. When he and his division were reunited, they were assigned a reserve role for the remainder of the fighting. Upon arriving in Goldsboro, North Carolina, Carlin applied for a leave of absence due to exhaustion and sickness. Carlin left his division so that he could travel north, and his division was assigned to another officer.

General Carlin returned to the army on 1 May 1865. He was assigned to command a division in the Department of West Virginia until August 1865, when he was mustered out of volunteer service. Afterward, he remained with the regular army, where he was reduced to the rank of major. He served with the 16th Infantry and spent several months in the Freeman's Bureau for Tennessee from 1866 to 1872. In July 1872, Carlin was promoted to lieutenant colonel and was assigned to the 17th Infantry. In April 1882, Carlin received a promotion to colonel and was given command of the 4th Infantry. Through the efforts of several individuals, Carlin received a final promotion to brigadier general on 17 May 1893. On 24 November 1893, the day that he retired from active service in the U.S. Army, General Carlin was awarded the Medal of Honor for his actions in the battle of Bentonville, North Carolina. Carlin moved back to Carrollton, Illinois, and became active in the local chapter of the Grand Army of the Republic. While traveling back from Spokane, Washington, Carlin died in his sleep on 4 October 1903. His body was taken back to Carrollton for burial.

—*William H. Brown*

See also Bentonville, Battle of; Chickamauga, Battle of; Davis, Jefferson Columbus.

For further reading:
Faust, Patricia. *Historical Times Illustrated Encyclopedia of the Civil War* (1986).
Girardi, Robert I., and Nathaniel C. Hughes, Jr., eds. *The Memoirs of Brigadier General William Passmore Carlin USA* (1999).
Heitman, Francis B. *Historical Register and Dictionary of the United States Army* (1903).
U.S. War Department. *The War of the Rebellion: A Compilation of the Official Records of the Union and Confederate Armies* (1880–1901).
Warner, Ezra J. *Generals in Blue* (1964).

CARLISLE, PENNSYLVANIA

Settled by Scots-Irish and German settlers in the 1700s, Carlisle, Pennsylvania, was a well-established legal, farming, and merchants' community by the middle nineteenth century. The county seat of Cumberland County, the town was home to Dickinson College and host to the Carlisle Barracks, the first officer's training college of the army established by George Washington. The presence of the barracks created a more cosmopolitan atmosphere in the town than in other southern Pennsylvania communities. Army officers from the South and New England settled there with their families while studying at the college.

The town and county were traditionally Democratic and, because of economic ties to Maryland and Virginia as well as to other Pennsylvania towns, viewed the rise of the Republican Party with suspicion. By 1860, however, the sectional crisis had split Carlisle residents according to their political allegiance. Abraham Lincoln received 425 votes to Breckinridge's 406, and the county handed the victory to the Republicans with only a 386-vote majority (3,593 to 3,207). During the secession crisis, Carlisle newspapers maintained a general tone of noncoercion toward the Southern states.

The attack on Fort Sumter erased all thoughts of peaceful secession or compromise. Carlisle residents responded enthusiastically to Lincoln's call for 75,000 volunteers and later contributed to numerous three-year regiments. The 11th, 36th, 78th, and 87th Pennsylvania Infantry regiments all contained large numbers of Carlisle men and fought with the Army of the Potomac in nearly all of its major campaigns.

Alarmed by Robert E. Lee's first invasion of the North, which was stopped at Antietam Creek in September 1862, Carlisle again felt the threat of enemy occupation in June 1863. Situated at the crossroads of several important highways, and home to the Army Barracks, the town was certain to be a target of Lee's second invasion. In the early evening of 27 June, elements of Fitzhugh Lee's cavalry approached Carlisle from the direction of York and occupied the Barracks, which was systematically burned to the ground in the next few days. Surprised by the sudden appearance of Confederate cavalry, citizens went into a panic and were calmed only by the presence of several companies of the 37th New York Infantry, who refused to vacate the town. Seeing no other alternative, the Confederate Horse Artillery opened fire and shelled the town from hills west of the community. Under a flag of truce, the Confederates ceased the bombardment and demanded an unconditional surrender of the town. When leading citizens refused, the shelling resumed and continued for several hours. Mrs. R. K. Hitner wrote, "the shelling commenced, not allowing us five minutes to reach a place of safety, though word was sent that our end of town must be vacated. Up town we ran amid the firing, seeing and hearing shells bursting and whizzing all around and about us—such horrors we never experienced. The old and sick, carried from their beds through the fiery shower, little children snatched from their slumbers—it was a terrible sight."

The bombardment ended only when the Confederate cavalry ran out of ammunition and departed, vowing to return and "finish the job." Despite the long period of shelling, not one Carlisle resident was killed, and the town sustained only minor damage. Most citizens either fled to the countryside after the bombardment or hunkered down in their basements. Two men from the

37th New York were wounded, one mortally. The regiment evacuated the town late on 27 June and was replaced by Confederate infantry of General Robert E. Rodes's division the next day. Carlisle residents offered no further resistance to the Confederates, who occupied the town, demanded 1,500 rations, burned the barracks, and then departed on 1 July to join the bulk of the Army of Northern Virginia concentrating at Gettysburg.

—*Christian B. Keller*

See also Gettysburg, Battle of; Pennsylvania.

For further reading:

Coddington, Edwin B. *The Gettysburg Campaign: A Study in Command* (1968).

Hitner, Mrs. R.K., to Mrs. David Hastings. Letter, Carlisle Barracks Collection (1863).

Landis, Merkel. "Civil War Times in Carlisle." Address delivered at the Hamilton Library, Carlisle, Pennsylvania (1931).

CARNEGIE, ANDREW
(1835–1919)
Industrialist

Andrew Carnegie was born in Dunfermline, Scotland, on 25 November 1835. He was the eldest of the two sons of Margaret (Morrison) and William Carnegie, a linen weaver and a Chartist supporter. At age eight, young Andrew attended the one-room school of Mr. Robert Martin. His four years at Martin's school constituted his only formal education. When the introduction of mechanized looms led to a great decline in the handloom business of his father, the Carnegies in 1848 left Scotland for America.

Living with his family in Allegheny, across the river from Pittsburgh, Carnegie held several jobs and began to learn the ways of the business and industrial world. In 1852 Thomas Scott, who was the superintendent of the western division of the Pennsylvania Railroad offered Carnegie $35 a month to serve as his telegrapher and personal secretary. During the 1850s the perceptive Carnegie became associated with the managerial revolution that affected the operations of U.S. railroads. Under Scott, he contributed in numerous ways to the leadership of the Pennsylvania Railroad and was named in 1859 to succeed Scott as head of its western division.

During the Civil War, Carnegie supported the cause of the Union. Similar to his father, who died in 1855, he was a proponent of social equality. Carnegie in fact became an abolitionist and in 1856 wrote several antislavery editorials for Horace Greeley's *New York Tribune*. Moreover, as a result of his admiration for, and sympathy with, its principles, Carnegie in 1856 joined the Republican Party. After the Civil War broke out, Thomas Scott was named assistant secretary of war in charge of military transportation and wisely brought Carnegie to Washington, where he was to supervise telegraphic communications for Union troops in the Washington area. Heading a railroad crew in late April 1861, Carnegie went to Annapolis Junction to repair telegraph lines; he then directed a train that carried General Benjamin Butler's troops and wounded to Washington. Prior to its arrival, Carnegie received a gash to his face while trying to fix wires that had been cut by the Rebels. Upon his arrival in the nation's capital, he was praised for his gallant feats.

Carnegie in other ways was active during the Civil War. In early May 1861 he brought David Strouse and other competent telegraph operators to Washington to promote the cause of the Union. By recruiting Strouse and other operators, Carnegie helped to establish the United States Military Telegraphers Corps. During the battle of Bull Run in July 1861, he tried to keep open telegraph stations between Alexandria and Fairfax, but met with only partial success. After the Union defeat at Bull Run, Carnegie, who had provided assistance to wounded soldiers, suffered sunstroke. In autumn 1861 he went back to Pittsburgh to perform his duties with the Pennsylvania Railroad.

Carnegie prospered in his business activities during the remaining years of the war. With William Coleman in 1861 Carnegie assisted in the formation of the Columbia Oil Company; he invested $11,000 in this company and ultimately made from his investment over $1 million. In 1862 he organized the Keystone Bridge Company, a firm that built the first iron bridges in the nation. Two years later he established the Cyclops Iron Company. Carnegie in 1865 purchased the Kloman Company and formed the Union Mills, a firm that dominated the production of iron products for the railroads. That same year, he ended his employment with the Pennsylvania Railroad and devoted his full attention to the building of his business empire.

After the Civil War, the industrial and humanitarian achievements of Carnegie were especially impressive. During the early 1870s he built the Edgar Thomson Works, the most efficiently operated steel plant in the world and one that embodied the effectively functioning Bessemer converter. By the 1880s, Carnegie acquired 50 percent interest in the Frick Coke Company and purchased the Duquesne Steelworks and Hartman Steel. Consisting of such carefully selected partners as Henry C. Frick and Charles M. Schwab, Carnegie Steel functioned as a private partnership, rather than as a public corporation. This firm greatly expanded because Carnegie insisted that profits be plowed back into it. By adhering to tenets of cost reduction, of consolidation, and of verticality, Carnegie amassed a fortune in the steel business.

However, Carnegie did encounter severe problems with labor during the 1892 Homestead Strike. Unable to negotiate a contract with the members of the

Amalgamated Association of Iron and Steel Workers in late June of that year, Frick became involved in a violent strike at this plant; he employed Pinkerton detectives to protect nonunion workers and was himself nearly assassinated. Following settlement of the Homestead Strike, Carnegie distanced himself from Frick, but was viewed both by his workers and the public as a perfidious industrialist. Consequently, Carnegie, who had published the "Gospel of Wealth" three years before the eruption of the Homestead Strike and who thought that capitalists should perceive themselves as the trustees of wealth and act to return it, wanted by the late 1890s to spend more time with charitable causes and less time with his business interests.

After J. P. Morgan bought him out in March 1901 and established the United States Steel Corporation, Carnegie devoted his energy to philanthropic projects. He funded, among other things, public libraries, the Carnegie Institute of Technology in Pittsburgh, and the Carnegie Corporation of New York. His career, consequently, revealed the conflict between his father's egalitarianism and his mother's realism. Carnegie, who had married Louise Whitfield in April 1887, died on 11 August 1919 in Lenox, Massachusetts, and was buried in Tarrytown, New York.

—*William Weisberger*

For further reading:
Carnegie, Andrew. *The Autobiography of Andrew Carnegie* (1920).
Hendrick, Burton J. *The Life of Andrew Carnegie* (1932).
Josephson, Matthew. *The Robber Barons* (1962).
Livesay, Harold C. *Andrew Carnegie and the Rise of Big Business* (1975).
Thomas, Benjamin P., and Harold M. Hyman. *Stanton: The Life and Times of Lincoln's Secretary of War* (1962).
Wall, Joseph Frazier. *Andrew Carnegie* (1970).

CARNIFEX FERRY, BATTLE OF
(10 September 1861)

The battle of Carnifex Ferry was small but significant. The last in a series of battles in mountainous western Virginia during the summer of 1861, Carnifex Ferry pitted Union troops commanded by Brigadier General William S. Rosecrans against Confederate forces led by Brigadier General John B. Floyd.

The battle was staged near the Gauley River in Nicholas County, Virginia (now West Virginia). Federal strategy throughout the western Virginia campaign of 1861 aimed at controlling the Baltimore & Ohio Railroad and river transportation within the region, but the battle also was pivotal due to the pending 24 October vote for statehood for western Virginia. The vote was a critical event for control of the area including access to the Ohio River.

Preceding the clash at Carnifex Ferry and after the Union victory at the battle of Rich Mountain on 10 July,

the two armies had a series of minor skirmishes. Several occurred near Hawks Nest, where Union troops under Brigadier General Jacob Dolson Cox repeatedly clashed with Confederates led by Brigadier General Henry Alexander Wise. The mutual personal antagonism of Floyd and Wise, both ex-governors of Virginia, kept the Confederates from a united effort.

The battle of Cross Lanes near Carnifex Ferry on 26 August resulted in a rout of the Federals commanded by Colonel E. B. Tyler of the 7th Ohio Volunteer Infantry. Floyd established his command on the bluffs overlooking Carnifex Ferry, one of the few places where large numbers could cross the river, and named it Camp Gauley. He protected his position by the construction of entrenchments. At the end of August, Floyd had about 2,000 troops at Camp Gauley with approximately 6,000 more in the area. Wise received orders to bring his troops up from the Gauley River area, but due to transportation difficulties and his own obstinacy, only a portion of his troops arrived in time for the battle on 10 September.

Beginning 31 August, Union forces advanced south from Clarksburgh with plans to attack the Confederate force. More than 6,000 troops with Colonel William H. Lytle and the 10th Ohio of Brigadier General Henry W. Benham's brigade in advance marched toward Camp Gauley. Starting in the early hours of the morning of 10 September, they made their final march from Summersville, south to the heavily wooded area around Carnifex Ferry. Scouts reported that breastworks near a clearing close to the road and the Patteson house indicated the presence of Confederate forces. General Benham, ignoring the intelligence, ordered Lytle and his men to push forward. As Benham with the 1st Brigade and the 10th Ohio approached, Floyd's forces fired. Having blundered into Floyd's entire army, Benham sent word back to Rosecrans asking for help. Fighting began about 3:00 P.M. and lasted the remainder of the day. By nightfall, the Union forces had 158 casualties, whereas the Confederates counted 20. Colonel John W. Lowe (12th Ohio) became the first field grade officer from Ohio killed during the war. Colonel Lytle received a serious leg wound that took him out of action for four months. At nightfall the Confederates still held their position on top of the bluff.

During the night of 10 September, General Floyd decided to abandon Camp Gauley to the larger Union force. He ordered his troops to retreat down the steep road to the ferry and escaped south to Greenbrier County, where General Robert E. Lee waited for them.

Both Rosecrans and Floyd claimed victory. Although not decisive in outcome, Carnifex Ferry holds significance because the Union forces retained firm control of the Kanawha Valley and most of western Virginia. Shortly afterward, the residents of western Virginia voted in favor of separation from Virginia and becoming a new state.

Although a minor battle, Carnifex Ferry is interesting for the large number of present or future general officers who participated (fifteen Union and five Confederate) and for the presence in the 23d Ohio of two future presidents of the United States (Rutherford B. Hayes and William McKinley).

—Ruth C. Carter

See also Floyd, John Buchanan; Rich Mountain, Battle of; Rosecrans, William Starke; Wise, Henry Alexander.

For further reading:

Carter, Ruth C. *For Honor, Glory and Union: The Mexican and Civil War Letters of Brigadier General William Haines Lytle* (1999).

Cohen, Stan B. *The Civil War in West Virginia: A Pictorial History* (1976).

Lamers, William M. *The Edge of Glory: A Biography of General William S. Rosecrans, U.S.A.* (1999).

Lowry, Terry. *September Blood: The Battle of Carnifex Ferry* (1985).

CAROLINAS CAMPAIGN
(1 February–23 March 1865)

Having completed his March to the Sea and rested briefly, Union general William T. Sherman marched out of Savannah on 1 February, 1865, his army of 60,000 accustomed to

destructive war by its systematic depredations in Georgia. His proximate goal was to devastate Confederate resources in his path and punish South Carolina for its leadership in secession; his ultimate goal was to advance through North Carolina into Virginia and direct his forces at the rear of Lee's army, serving as an anvil to Grant's hammer. At first, his opponents were hopeful that the terrain would frustrate his purposes. In the wettest season the region had experienced in years, he had to negotiate flooded swamps by the score and cross nine swollen rivers with all their tributaries. In the face of harassing fire from the Southern troops, his engineers, commanding hastily improvised "pioneer" battalions composed of soldiers and freedpersons, accomplished daily projects of draining water, clearing brush, and building bridges, roads, and causeways. Despite the obstacles of enemy and environment, his armies made a pace of about ten miles a day, all the while achieving in their ravages a level of ferocity and thoroughness never approached in Georgia. Like their commander, the Union troops sincerely felt South Carolina must be taught an unforgettable lesson and gave full rein to their fury, leaving little in their trail but ashes. The civilian population of South Carolina suffered horribly.

At the outset, Sherman had disposed his infantry in

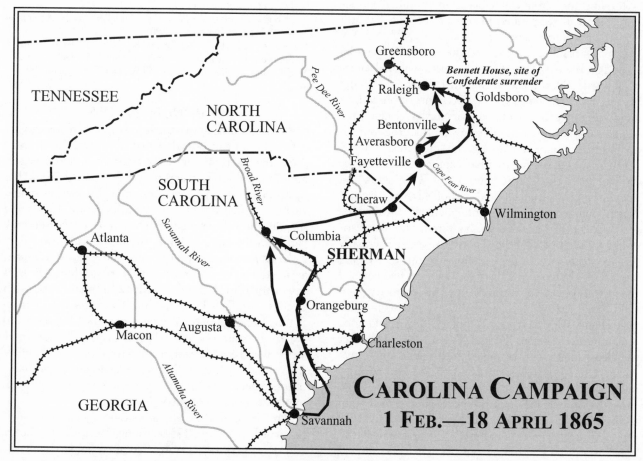

CAROLINA CAMPAIGN 1 FEB.—18 APRIL 1865

four parallel corps marching in column and spread over a front of thirty miles with the cavalry a separate column on the left. His enemies, under the overall command of General Joseph E. Johnston, had severely limited forces at their disposal and could only guess at his intentions. The two easternmost columns, XV and XVII Corps, seemed bound for Charleston to avenge Fort Sumter; the two westernmost columns, XIV and XX Corps, for Augusta and its munitions factories. Each of those cities had been garrisoned with about 10,000 troops scraped together with some difficulty. A small rebel cavalry force under General Joseph Wheeler could do little more than observe his progress. At the Edisto River, it became evident that Sherman intended for his columns to converge on Columbia, South Carolina's capital, which had been left almost undefended and could muster only token resistance before falling on 17 February. In the confusion of the city's capture, a fire started from bales of cotton being burned by the defenders and, with the assistance of some of Sherman's troops and a gale-force wind, burned about a third of the city. Though an investigation seven years after the war established that Sherman did not intend or order the burning of the city and acted to bring the conflagration to an end as quickly as possible, the Columbia firestorm forever cemented among Southerners Sherman's reputation for ruthlessness.

Moving north from Columbia against minimal opposition, Sherman reorganized his troops, forming XV and XVII Corps into a single column, with XIV and XX Corps in a parallel column, and the cavalry keeping its station on the left. The orgy of destruction abated somewhat at the North Carolina border, Sherman having perhaps been chastened by press accounts of his actions and feeling that the poor farmers of North Carolina were less culpable in the matter of secession than the well-to-do South Carolinian planters and fire-eaters. On 22 February, a Union army that had captured Fort Fisher in January drove the Confederates out of Wilmington and marched under General John A. Schofield toward central North Carolina to link up with Sherman. Meanwhile, the defenders of Augusta and Charleston, who had abandoned those cities and headed north to contest Sherman's passage through North Carolina, began converging around Goldsboro. On 15 March, Sherman had reached the vicinity of Fayetteville and turned his advance toward the capital, Raleigh. Johnston's plight was desperate; his only chance was to attack XIV and XX Corps and hope to shatter them before XV and XVII Corps could cover the dozen miles that separated the Union army's two wings. On 19 March, Johnston attacked the advance units of Sherman's left at Bentonville with about 17,000 troops and achieved some initial success. The Union troops were quick to dig in, however, and held off repeated attacks throughout the day. Sherman was able to concentrate and smash the Confederate left. He allowed

Johnston to retreat rather than press his advantage, and on 23 March he reached Goldsboro and was joined by Schofield. His army was resting and refitting for the invasion of Virginia when news of Lee's surrender reached it. General Johnston surrendered all Confederate forces in the vicinity to Sherman on 26 April.

—Joseph M. McCarthy

See also Bentonville, Battle of; Columbia, South Carolina; North Carolina; South Carolina.

For further reading:

Angley, Wilson, et al. *Sherman's March through North Carolina: A Chronology* (1996).
Barnard, George N. *Photographic Views of Sherman's Campaign* (1977).
Barrett, John G. *Sherman's March through the Carolinas* (1956; reprint, 1996).
Davis, Burke. *Sherman's March: The First Full-Length Narration of General William T. Sherman's Devastating March through Georgia and the Carolinas* (1988).
Glatthaar, Joseph T. *The March to the Sea and Beyond: Sherman's Troops in the Savannah and Carolinas Campaigns* (1985).
Hitchcock, Henry. *Marching with Sherman: Passages from the Letters and Campaign Diaries of Henry Hitchcock, Major and Assistant Adjutant General of Volunteers. November 1864–May 1865* (1995).
Lucas, Marion B. *Sherman and the Burning of Columbia* (1976).
Miller, William J., ed. *The Peninsula Campaign of 1862: From Yorktown to the Seven Days* (1993–1996).
Nichols, George Ward. *The Story of the Great March from the Diary of a Staff Officer* (1972).
Osborn, Thomas. *The Fiery Trail: A Union Officer's Account of Sherman's Last Campaign* (1986).
Royster, Charles. *The Destructive War: William Tecumseh Sherman, Stonewall Jackson, and the Americans* (1991).
Sherman, William T. *Memoirs of William T. Sherman* (1990).

CARONDELET, USS

The *Carondelet* was the lead ship in a revolutionary class of gunboats designed to control the rivers of the western states. As the first armored vessels built in the Western Hemisphere, the *Carondelet* and her sisters began their service soon after the war began and guaranteed freedom of movement for Union troops and supplies throughout the war. The *Carondelet* herself took part in every major action in the west except two.

Desperate for fighting vessels, the U.S. government awarded a contract for seven gunboats to James B. Eads in August 1861. In his shipyard at Carondelet, just south of St. Louis, Eads built his ships to a design by Samuel Pook. Due to her unusual appearance, the *Carondelet* and her sisters were known as "Pook's Turtles." Eads drove 4,000 men day and night, seven days a week, to complete the vessels in 100 days. Eads was even forced to pay many of the expenses out of his own pocket when the government was slow to cover costs.

The basic design was a modified rectangular flat-bottomed river scow, 175 feet long, 50 feet in the beam, and drawing 6 feet of water. Nominal displacement was

512 tons. The gun deck was covered by a pyramidal casemate, with sloping sides to deflect shot. The front of the casemate was armored with 2.5 inches of iron plate, backed with 24 inches of oak planking. Similar plates extended 32 feet back on either side to protect the engines and boilers. The sides and stern of the casemate consisted of only 5 inches of oak, as it was intended that only the front would be turned toward the enemy. A paddle wheel was located at the stern in a deep swallowtail and was covered to protect it from Confederate shot. The *Carondelet* carried thirteen guns of varying sizes, changing throughout the war as newer weapons became available.

The *Carondelet* was commissioned on 10 January 1862, under the command of Henry Walke. Walke was a senior naval officer who viewed his assignment to the river forces as a demotion. A man with something to prove, Walke soon displayed his initiative and willingness to take chances. The *Carondelet* bombarded Fort Henry on 6 February, and, after the fort's surrender, traveled up the Tennessee River to destroy railroad bridges leading to Memphis. On 13 February, Walke and the *Carondelet* began a bombardment of Fort Donelson on the Cumberland River in support of General Ulysses S. Grant. The following day was nearly a disaster for the *Carondelet*. Defensive fire from Fort Donelson disabled her sister ships *Louisville*, *Pittsburgh*, and *St. Louis*. The *Carondelet* herself suffered severe casualties, partly from the explosion of one of her own guns. Walke still refused to break off the action until warned that several hits below the waterline had started leaks threatening the ship. Grant was forced to capture Fort Donelson by a more conventional siege.

Following repairs, the *Carondelet* returned to the Mississippi River to support General John Pope in his siege of Island No. 10. Batteries on the island prevented Union vessels from moving downriver, but Pope could not cross the Mississippi and capture Island No. 10 until gunboats could support him. Only Walke believed that it was possible to run an ironclad past the island. Following careful preparation and taking advantage of a storm, Walke attempted to run down the river on 4 April. The *Carondelet* was halfway through the danger zone when she was discovered by the Rebels. At least sixty guns fired at her, but no hits were scored. Three days later, her sister ship, the *Pittsburgh*, joined the *Carondelet* at New Madrid downriver from Island No. 10. Together, the two ironclads chased off the Confederate gunboats and ensured a safe crossing by Pope's troops. Seven thousand Confederate soldiers and 100 cannon were quickly captured.

The *Carondelet* continued to support Union army operations. In June 1862 she was among the fleet that destroyed a squadron of Confederate gunboats at Memphis. By July the fleet of river gunboats and ironclads were just above Vicksburg, where they were joined by Admiral David G. Farragut's fleet, conquerors of New Orleans. On 15 July, the *Carondelet* and two other vessels were sent up the Yazoo River to investigate rumors that the Confederate ironclad *Arkansas* was coming down to the Mississippi. Contact was made, and in a running fight the *Carondelet* was badly damaged and forced ashore. The *Arkansas* was also damaged, particularly in the funnel, and forced to take shelter at Vicksburg. The *Arkansas* later was blown up by her own crew when her engines failed.

After being repaired, the *Carondelet* and the other ironclads were busy seeking dry land for Grant's army to launch an assault on Vicksburg. In April 1863 Grant took his army down the west bank of the Mississippi. The *Carondelet* with other gunboats ran down the river past the batteries of Vicksburg. They protected the army's crossing of the Mississippi south of Vicksburg, and kept up the blockade while Grant's army laid siege to the city. When Vicksburg fell on 4 July, the Mississippi was free of Confederate forces.

The *Carondelet* spent most of the rest of the war patrolling the Mississippi's tributaries, looking for Rebel raiders. Her participation in the Red River expedition of early 1864 was undistinguished, but she supported Thomas's forces in the battle of Bell's Mill in December 1864. She was decommissioned in June 1865, and sold to a civilian buyer before the end of the year. The *Carondelet* was not the most powerful ironclad in the western states during the Civil War, but she was in the right place at the right time to help ensure a Union victory.

—*Tim J. Watts*

For further reading:
Branch, Mary Emerson. "A Story behind the Story of the *Arkansas* and the *Carondelet*." *Missouri Historical Review* (1985).
Gosnell, H. A. *Guns on the Western Waters: The Story of the River Gunboats in the Civil War* (1949).
Huffstot, Robert D. "The *Carondelet*." *Civil War Times Illustrated* (1967).
Melville, Phillips. "The *Carondelet* Runs the Gauntlet." *American Heritage* (1959).
Smith, Myron J., Jr., and Thomas Addison. "Notes on the fate of USS *Carondelet*." *Nautical Research Journal* (1974).

CARR, EUGENE ASA
(1830–1910)
Union general

Carr was a prominent figure in the Trans-Mississippi during the Civil War and a veteran of the Wilson's Creek, Pea Ridge, and the Vicksburg campaigns. He is better known for his long years fighting Indians in the West, where he earned the respectful sobriquet "War Eagle" from his Native American opponents.

Carr was born in 1830 in Boston Corner, Erie County, New York, into a family with deep roots in the New

World. His ancestors crossed the Atlantic shortly after the *Mayflower* and played a prominent role in the settling of Rhode Island. Carr graduated from West Point in 1850, the start of a distinguished forty-three–year career in the U.S. Army. Commissioned a brevet second lieutenant in the regiment of 3d Mounted Rifles (later the 3d Cavalry), Carr received the first of many wounds while fighting Indians in Texas in 1854. He received a promotion to captain in the 1st Cavalry in 1858, and was stationed at Fort Washita in Indian Territory on the eve of the Civil War.

Carr was transferred to the 4th U.S. Cavalry in August 1861, and fought with this unit at Wilson's Creek, Missouri, on 10 August. Shortly after Wilson's Creek, Carr accepted a commission as colonel of the 3d Illinois Cavalry. In command of the 4th Division of the Army of the Southwest under Brigadier General Samuel R. Curtis, Carr played a significant role in the crucial battle of Pea Ridge, Arkansas, on 7–8 March 1862. Major General Earl Van Dorn's Confederate Army of the West attempted to outflank Curtis and cut the Federals from their lines of communication. Carr's division, outnumbered by Confederate forces around Elkhorn Tavern, stubbornly held its ground and in the process gained valuable time for the remainder of the army to turn and face the Confederates. During the fighting around Elkhorn Tavern on 7 March, Carr was wounded three times. For his brave and skillful leadership in the battle, Carr received the Medal of Honor. He was promoted to brigadier general of U.S. volunteers on 7 March 1862.

Upon Curtis's promotion to head the District of the Missouri, Carr was made commander of the Army of Southwestern Missouri in October 1862. Carr became ill (probably suffering from malaria) and was transferred to command of the District of St. Louis and then the 2d Division of the Army of Southeast Missouri from February to March 1863. He was then transferred to the 14th Division of XIII Corps, Army of the Tennessee, with which he saw action at Port Gibson, Louisiana; Champion's Hill and Big Black River, Mississippi; and the siege of Vicksburg. After the fall of Vicksburg on 4 July 1863, Carr led the left wing of XVI Corps of the Army of the Tennessee before he returned to the Trans-Mississippi to command a cavalry division in the Camden expedition, the Arkansas portion of the ill-fated Red River campaign of 1864.

In his final act of the Civil War, Carr commanded the 3d Division of XVI Corps in an attack led by Major General Edward R. S. Canby on Mobile, Alabama. Carr mustered out of the U.S. volunteers on 15 January 1866. Although he held the rank of brevet major general in both the U.S. Army and the U.S. volunteers, he reverted to his prewar rank of major of the 5th U.S. Cavalry. After the war, Carr saw much action against Indians in the West, moving up through the ranks until he was

appointed brigadier general in 1893. Carr retired in 1893 more famous for his exploits as an Indian fighter than for his heroics in the Civil War. He died on 2 December 1910 and was buried at West Point, New York.

Carr was an aggressive and talented leader who deserved a higher rank during the Civil War. His stubborn delaying action on the first day at Pea Ridge highlighted an impressive Civil War record. Greatly respected by his men, Carr was impatient with what he believed were incompetent superiors, and he did not hesitate to say so. This placed him in hot water with his superiors at times, but his demonstrated abilities kept his career on track. Carr's legacy has been diminished by his service in the low-profile Trans-Mississippi and western theaters, but that should in no way diminish his reputation.

—*Terry L. Beckenbaugh*

See also Mobile Campaign; Pea Ridge, Battle of; Vicksburg Campaign; Wilson's Creek, Missouri.

For further reading:

Josephy, Alvin M. *The Civil War in the American West* (1991).
King, James T. *War Eagle: A Life of General Eugene A. Carr* (1963).
Shea, William L., and Earl J. Hess. *Pea Ridge: Civil War Campaign in the West* (1992).

CARRICK'S FORD
(13 July 1861)

Confederate colonel John Pegram's surrender to George B. McClellan after the battle of Rich Mountain compelled General Robert S. Garnett to abandon his positions on Laurel Hill and retreat toward the Cheat River and northwestern Virginia. Brigadier General Thomas A. Morris mounted a Federal pursuit composed of three infantry regiments and artillery with Captain H. W. Benham in overall command. They hoped to cut off Garnett's flight.

Such was no small task. Torrential rain and the Confederate's felling of trees in Benham's path had made the daunting terrain of deep valleys and steep mountains all but impassable. Nonetheless, both blue and gray troops, unseasoned as they were, gamely slogged on. It began to rain again at dawn on 13 July and by midmorning the drizzle had become a lashing downpour that would continue into the afternoon. The Confederates managed to cross the Cheat River except for the 1st Georgia and 23d Virginia Infantry regiments, along with a section of artillery and some cavalry. Garnett's wagon train also lagged behind, especially slowed by the rain-choked roads. Near Kaler's Ford, Benham found this rear guard, drove in its pickets, and unlimbered his artillery. The inexperienced Georgians and Virginians commenced as skillful a retrograde as they could manage, falling back in good order some three and a half miles toward Carrick's Ford before taking a

The battle of Carrick's Ford, 13 July 1861 (*Library of Congress*)

stand, doing so there more or less because they had to. The problem was the river, swollen deep at Carrick's, and the wagons, several of which were lost in the crossing. Colonel William B. Taliaferro commanding the 23d Virginia got across and gained high ground on the right bank, though. After offering up a cheer for Jefferson Davis—it was early enough in the war for such gestures—they opened fire on Benham's skirmishers appearing on the other side.

The Federals soon were replying with a heavy fire of their own, but their artillery could not find the range of the enemy. Three Confederate guns and musketry held off the bluecoats for more than an hour. With his ammunition nearly exhausted, Taliaferro again had the 23d retreat, this time in enough confusion to leave wounded on the field. Soon the regiment met Garnett, who placed ten sharpshooters pulled from its ranks at a bend in the road. He sent the remainder of the men toward the main column, while he remained with the detachment to discourage too close a Federal pursuit. When Benham's advance pressed in close, Garnett was giving the order to retire when a bullet struck down the man next to him. Just that quickly, another killed Garnett. He was the war's first general officer to fall in combat.

Exhaustion and the weather prevented a continued Federal pursuit of the fleeing Confederates. The 23d Virginia had left only about thirty of their number dead

at the engagement around Carrick's Ford, but the episode made for a grim conclusion to a sobering campaign. It all had been a significant strategic setback and a profound psychological blow for the new Confederacy, the one because it dimmed the political fortunes in the region and the other because Garnett's death gave pause to those who had blustered about a gloriously short and bloodless war.

For his part, McClellan was exultant over the general success of his first campaign. Neither he nor the nation that would soon lionize him could know that it was to be the zenith of his military exploits. Moreover, the failure to smash anything other than Garnett's rear guard at Carrick's Ford contributed in part to McClellan's growing fixation with minute detail and a tendency to avoid delegating authority. The pitfalls of such an attitude would not become apparent right away, and for the time being, the man the newspapers soon dubbed an American Napoleon could bask in his success and pass judgment on his enemies. Contemplating the dead Garnett, McClellan curtly observed, "Such is the fate of traitors."

—*David S. Heidler and Jeanne T. Heidler*

See also Garnett, Robert S.; McClellan, George B.; Rich Mountain, Battle of; Taliaferro, William Booth; West Virginia.
For further reading:
McClellan, George B. *McClellan's Own Story: The War for the*

Union, the Soldiers Who Fought It, the Civilians Who Directed It, and His Relations to It and to Them (1887).

Newell, Clayton R. *Lee vs. McClellan: The First Campaigns* (1996).

Thomas, Joseph W. "The Campaigns of Generals McClellan and Rosecrans in Western Virginia, 1861–62." *West Virginia History* (1944).

CARRINGTON, HENRY BEEBE
(1824–1912)
Union general

Born in 1824, Henry Beebe Carrington was a Connecticut Yankee transplanted to Ohio. While a young man, he heard John Brown speak and became an ardent abolitionist. After attending Yale University, Carrington taught school and was practicing law in Ohio when he assisted in organizing the Republican Party there. A close friend of Ohio governor Salmon P. Chase, he organized the Ohio state militia in 1857. He accomplished this task so well that Ohio sent nine militia companies across the Ohio River to protect the western counties of Virginia so volunteers there could be organized.

In May 1861 Carrington was named colonel of the Ohio 18th U.S. Infantry. He was later made adjutant general of Ohio and placed in charge of the regular army camp in that state. In August of 1862, Indiana governor Oliver Morton requested his services in Indiana, and he was made chief mustering officer and post commander in Indianapolis. He was promoted to brigadier general of United States Volunteers in November 1862, and made commander of the District of Indiana, Department of the Ohio, in March 1863.

While in Indiana, Carrington caused controversy by investigating and putting on trial members of the Sons of Liberty and other allegedly disloyal groups. When he arrived in Indiana, political warfare between the adherents of the Lincoln administration and their opponents was beginning in earnest. The Republican Party's favorite political target, the elusive Knights of the Golden Circle, was blamed for every military and political reversal, and Carrington endorsed the view wholeheartedly. He blamed appalling desertion rates on treasonable secret societies, and in his long report of March 1863, he declared that the situation in Indiana bordered on open revolt. Yet he grossly exaggerated membership in these secret societies for political purposes, seizing upon minor and irrelevant incidents to accuse Democrats of treasonous activities.

Carrington's motives seem to have been a dread of active field service and a desire for promotion. By attributing the danger in Indiana solely to secret organizations that only he understood, he could keep his safe and comfortable position in Indianapolis and still obtain promotions often denied desk-bound warriors.

Carrington frequently clashed with Indiana civil authorities over his arbitrary arrests, Draconian displays of military force, and deprivations of civil rights. His imprudence and rashness in dealing with Indiana's heated political situation eventually got him relieved of command in April 1863. He was so unpopular in the state by this time, especially among Democrats, that he was known derisively as the "Hero of the Home Brigade." Though Democrats labeled him a coward, he served Governor Morton ably in the field of political warfare, for which he was well suited. The Supreme Court would later overturn many of Carrington's actions in Indiana, but at the time Lincoln upheld him and he enjoyed considerable support from Indiana Republicans. He was also credited with energetic leadership in stimulating enlistments in the state.

Carrington was hardly a warrior, though. When given a force to chase Confederate raider John Hunt Morgan out of the state in July 1863, Carrington fortified his courage with so much liquor that he fell off his horse. Meanwhile, he could not shake his fixation with the supposed enemy in his midst. From July 1863 until May 1864, Carrington was on detached duty in Indiana and hired a corps of detectives to infiltrate the Sons of Liberty and other suspected disloyal organizations. These spies worked with an evident determination to discover the treason they were being paid to find. Their reports, however, consisted of unfounded rumors circulating in the Union press and offered no evidence of illegal or treasonous conduct by the groups. Thus knowing every move the secret societies made, Carrington and Morton had no reason to fear them as a menace to domestic peace. Yet Morton held up the societies as strawmen and made great political capital out of exposing alleged plots and trying putative traitors. Finally, such behavior became too much even for Carrington. As the fall 1864 elections approached, Morton was eager to start the military trials of arrested Copperhead "conspirators." To Carrington's credit, he denied the legality of military trials while the civil courts were open and functioning freely. Morton broke with Carrington over the issue and had him replaced.

Mustered out of the Volunteers in August 1865, Carrington was sent west, where he built Fort Kearny. He fought in the Red Cloud War in which he was severely wounded, but he later established friendly relations with important Indian chiefs. He taught military science at Wabash College before retiring in 1870.

Carrington pursued a literary career and wrote *The Battles of the American Revolution* in 1876. He also wrote many other works on international, military, and Indian affairs. He died in 1912.

—*Ron Hamilton*

See also Copperheads; Morton, Oliver Perry; Order of American Knights; Sons of Liberty.
For further reading:
Fesler, Mayo. "Secret Political Societies in the North during the Civil War." *Indiana Magazine of History* (1918).

Stampp, Kenneth. *Indiana Politics during the Civil War* (1949).
Terrell, W. H. H. *Indiana in the War of the Rebellion: Report of the Adjutant General of Indiana*, vol. 1 (1960).
Tredway, G. R. *Democratic Opposition to the Lincoln Administration in Indiana* (1973).

CARROLL, ANNA ELLA
(1815–1894)
Pamphleteer

Anna Ella Carroll, daughter of Maryland governor Thomas King Carroll, political pamphleteer for the American (Know-Nothing) Party, and paid lobbyist for various interests in 1850s Washington, is better known for her claim to have devised the so-called Tennessee Plan for the Union army than for her pamphlets that laid out the presidential rationale for using the army to enforce Federal laws within the Southern states.

Little is known of Carroll's life prior to midcentury. Never married, she made her living as a lobbyist for various interests and politicians, using her connections with Maryland, New York, and Washington politicians to promise patronage positions to all who would hire her to write on their behalf. (Her enemies declared her to be a confidence woman as well, who "borrowed" money and never repaid it.) One of a number of women active in partisan politics rather than social reform movements and acquainted with innumerable politicians who enjoyed the attention of a bright, flatteringly attentive female listener, Carroll wrote campaign literature for Millard Fillmore's 1856 presidential campaign as the Know-Nothing candidate, and promoted the candidacies of William Henry Seward, John Minor Botts, and Thurlow Weed. The outbreak of war found her writing in support of Maryland governor Thomas Hicks's attempts to prevent any meeting of Maryland legislators to stave off a vote for secession.

Living in Washington throughout most of the war, Carroll approached the War Department in 1861 after a trip to St. Louis, where she visited a riverboat captain, Charles Scott, and discussed the apparent difficulty the Union was having invading the South. According to a letter Carroll wrote to the Washington, D.C., *National Intelligencer* shortly after the Confederate surrender in 1865, Scott pointed out the strategic value of using the Tennessee and Cumberland rivers, which flowed north, instead of the Mississippi River, to invade the Confederacy via Tennessee. Gunboats damaged by Confederate fire would float northward, back into Union territory, and the Tennessee was navigable clear to Alabama, providing excellent ingress to the heart of the Confederacy. Neither river was strongly fortified and control of them would relieve Union loyalists, particularly those in eastern Tennessee.

Carroll took Scott's information, drew up a map, and presented it to the War Department's assistant secretary,

Thomas Scott, in November 1861. She was no doubt gratified to see the Union invade Tennessee up the rivers she had suggested the following February, with victorious battles at Forts Henry and Donelson. Carroll did not realize that her plan duplicated one published in the *New York Times* earlier in November 1861. It also resembled the overall strategy undertaken by the Union army commanded by Generals Henry Halleck and Ulysses Grant, the latter of whom had captured Smithville and Paducah at the mouths of the rivers that fall and was waiting for Union gunboats before venturing farther inland.

Carroll depended upon her writing to make her living, and shortly after the war, she began petitioning Congress for money and recognition of her efforts at writing military strategy. Carroll had made a verbal agreement with Assistant Secretary Scott to write for the War Department in the summer of 1861. The agreement stemmed from Carroll's pamphlets supporting Lincoln's actions in the early days of the war. The most important of these, *Reply to Breckinridge* (1861), detailed arguments by Lincoln and Attorney General Edward Bates that, as commander in chief, Lincoln could use the armed forces to perform his duties as chief enforcement officer of the United States. In other words, he could call for volunteers, suspend the writ of habeas corpus, institute a naval blockade, and use the army to put down a domestic rebellion, a legal fiction he employed throughout the war.

Carroll's pamphlets were so clearly written and so accessible that Secretary of State William Henry Seward, who knew Carroll from the early 1850s, when she promoted his presidential candidacy for the Whig Party, ordered them printed up and laid on every desk in Congress. The legal rationale Carroll described was later delineated by notable lawyer Horace Binney and published more widely, but Carroll did provide the earliest explication of Lincoln's actions in the critical first months of the war.

Later pamphlets Carroll wrote criticized the president's actions, particularly regarding the Union's confiscation of slaves as contraband of war. She also promoted colonization efforts by Aaron Columbus Burr, illegitimate son of Aaron Burr, and suggested in a letter to the *New York Times* that, as peaceful coexistence between blacks and whites seemed unlikely, colonization in a friendly Central American colony might be the best answer to preserve the black community of ex-slaves. Such suggestions came to naught, and Carroll returned to petitioning the president, Thomas Scott, and finally Congress for payment for the creation of the Tennessee Plan as a task more likely to be compensated.

Carroll's claim was alive for years. From 1865 until her death in 1894, Carroll filed petitions, wrote pamphlets, and begged for letters of confirmation from men such as Grant, Cassius Clay, Benjamin Wade, and

Secretary of War Edwin Stanton. Her cause was adopted by the suffragists Susan B. Anthony, Sarah Ellen Blackwell, and Elizabeth Cady Stanton, and they held subscription drives to raise money for her as she aged and grew infirm. She became a symbol of the military's disregard for both civilians and women when it came to the work of the war, and her invention of evidence to support her claim was disregarded by readers who took her evidence at face value. Her role as a symbol continues to the present with continual appearances of Carroll in Civil War historiography as an unsung female hero or a romanticized player in the politics of the period. Her legal acumen, widely respected by politicians, including Lincoln, holds less appeal than her legendary status as military strategist.

Carroll lived her last years in Washington, D.C., entertaining occasional visitors curious about her declared status by supporters as the "Woman who saved the Union." She was cared for by her sister Mary and lived mostly on money from subscriptions provided by suffragists. Carroll died of kidney failure in Washington on 19 February 1894. Ironically, her gravestone is as inaccurate as much of the rest that is known about her, and is misdated 1893.

—*Janet L. Coryell*

See also American Party; Anthony, Susan B.; Stanton, Elizabeth Cady; Women.

For further reading:

Carroll, Anna Ella. *Reply to the Speech of Hon. J. C. Breckinridge* (1861).
———. *The War Powers of the General Government* (1861).
Coryell, Janet L. *Neither Heroine nor Fool: Anna Ella Carroll of Maryland* (1990).
Greenbie, Sydney, and Marjorie Greenbie. *Anna Ella Carroll and Abraham Lincoln: A Biography* (1952).
Williams, Kenneth P. "The Tennessee River Campaign and Anna Ella Carroll." *Indiana Magazine of History* (1950).

CARROLL, SAMUEL SPRIGG
(1832–1893)
Union general

The son of William Thomas Carroll, clerk of the Supreme Court, and a member of the famous Carroll family of Maryland, Samuel Sprigg Carroll was born in Washington, D.C. He was educated locally before receiving an appointment to the U.S. Military Academy. He graduated forty-fourth of forty-nine in the class of 1856. Carroll served at various frontier posts before returning for duty at West Point in 1860. He left the academy in November 1861 and a month later was named colonel of the 8th Ohio. Carroll served with his regiment in western Virginia until the following summer.

Carroll and the 8th Ohio fought in the Shenandoah Valley campaign against Thomas J. "Stonewall" Jackson in the spring of 1862. He commanded a brigade under James Shields for most of that campaign, particularly at

Kernstown and Port Republic. Carroll continued to command the brigade under James B. Ricketts in the Army of Virginia at Cedar Mountain but was wounded a few days later in a skirmish on the Rapidan River. He was unable to rejoin his command until after the battle of Antietam.

In the battle of Fredericksburg, Carroll commanded a brigade of III Corps. In the spring he moved to the command of a brigade in Darius Couch's II Corps and commanded that brigade at Chancellorsville and Gettysburg. He was commended by his division commander, Brigadier General Alexander Hays, for his actions at Gettysburg on 2 July. Carroll continued to command his brigade during the Bristoe Station and Mine Run campaigns in the fall of 1863 through the early spring of 1864.

It would be during the early phases of Ulysses S. Grant's campaign against Robert E. Lee in May 1864 that Carroll gained the serious attention of higher-ranking officers. Commanding his brigade in the division of Brigadier General John Gibbon, Carroll fought in the late afternoon of 5 May in the battle of the Wilderness. The following day, Carroll received a serious wound in the arm but refused to leave the field and continued to lead his men later in the day when his brigade was placed in reserve. Four days later at Spotsylvania Court House, leading a frontal assault on Confederate works, Carroll was again wounded in the right arm and suffered severe casualties to his brigade. While temporarily in command of Gibbon's division three days later on 13 May in another charge, Carroll was shot again, this time in the left arm, and the wound shattered much of the bone in the arm. He had to be carried from the field. For Carroll's actions during these battles, George Gordon Meade, commander of the Army of the Potomac, recommended Carroll for promotion to brigadier general. When the promotion occurred, Carroll's date of rank was 12 May 1864.

Carroll's wounds required a long recuperation. Although he was able to serve on light duty such as courts-martial during the fall, he was unable to accept a field command until December 1864. Given command of the 2d Division, Department of West Virginia, under Winfield Scott Hancock, Carroll operated primarily in the Shenandoah Valley against independent Confederate cavalry commands like that of John Singleton Mosby. In April 1865 he was given command of the 4th Provisional Division, Army of the Shenandoah.

After the war, Carroll chose to remain in the army, although he found it increasingly difficult, given his wartime wounds, to hold an active command. He retired in 1869 at the rank of major general, the rank accorded him due to the wounds he had suffered during the war. Unable to lead a very active life in retirement, Carroll lived quietly in Washington and at one of the family homes in Maryland on the city's outskirts. He died on 28 January 1893 in Montgomery County, Maryland.

—*David S. Heidler and Jeanne T. Heidler*

See also Spotsylvania, Battle of; Wilderness, Battle of the.
For further reading:
Matter, William D. If It Takes All Summer; the Battle of Spotsylvania (1988).
Rhea, Gordon C. The Battle of the Wilderness, May 5–6, 1864 (1994).
Rhea, Gordon C. The Battles for Spotsylvania Court House and the Road to Yellow Tavern May 7–12, 1864 (1997).

CARSON, CHRISTOPHER HOUSTON "KIT"
(1809–1868)
Union general; federal Indian agent

Arguably the greatest frontier legend in U.S. history, Christopher H. "Kit" Carson was born on Christmas Eve, 1809, in Madison County, Kentucky, but spent the majority of his childhood years in the Boone's Lick district of western Missouri. He was apprenticed to a saddle and harness maker at age fourteen, but quickly traded in an artisan's life for the open trail, taking passage on a wagon train and eventually reaching New Mexico Territory in 1826. By his twentieth birthday, Carson had established himself in Sante Fe as an able fur trapper and scout, whose travels took him throughout the Far West from the Rocky Mountains to the Pacific Ocean. Like many mountain men of the era, Carson came into close contact with the Indians of the region, but unlike many of his contemporaries, Carson enjoyed a relatively amicable relationship with the native inhabitants of the region. He was reported to be self-restrained and temperate toward the local Indians, and he eventually married into both the Arapaho and Cheyenne tribes.

Carson's national reputation was launched in 1842, when he met John C. Frémont while on a trip to Missouri and was hired as a guide and scout for Frémont's western explorations. It was Carson who was largely responsible for leading Frémont's expeditions throughout the expanses of the Great Basin and the mountains of the West. Frémont's highly publicized and widely read reports of his travels portrayed Carson as the epitome of a heroic frontiersman, earning the young guide national notoriety and instant fame.

Carson enhanced his reputation during the Mexican-American War, when he successfully guided General Stephen Kearny's expedition from New Mexico Territory to California and helped Kearny repress a local challenge to U.S. authority in the region. Carson spent the last year of the war as a personal courier of President James K. Polk, carrying messages to and from Polk to his commanders in the Far West.

After the war, Carson returned to New Mexico Territory, where he began a successful career as a rancher and where he was appointed Federal Indian agent for northern New Mexico Territory in 1853. Carson was still serving as Indian agent when the Civil War broke out, and, like the majority of New Mexico Territory residents, Carson could not escape military entanglement in the burgeoning conflict between the North and the South. In 1861, he resigned his commission as Indian agent in order to help organize the 1st New Mexico Volunteer Infantry, to which he was appointed as a lieutenant colonel. Carson's volunteers saw action in 1862 at the battle of Val Verde, New Mexico, and again at Glorieta Pass, New Mexico, which were important steps in preventing Confederate occupation of the New Mexico Territory.

However, the majority of Carson's military efforts during the Civil War were directed at the Indians of the territory, including the Mescaleros and Kiowas, although his most notable campaigns took place against the Navajo. Although Carson, who preferred discussion and moderation to compulsion, had garnered a reputation for being a sympathetic and reasonable Indian agent in the years preceding the Civil War, his policies toward the Navajo occupying the New Mexico Territory were decidedly harsh. When bands of Navajo refused to be confined to government reservations in 1863, Carson engaged in a brutal economic war in which he led troops on punitive raids into Navajo territory, burning crops and villages and capturing or slaughtering livestock and horses. Without adequate shelter or provisions, the Navajo were left at the mercy of regional Indian rivals, including the Utes, Puebloes, and Hopis, who joined Carson's marauding units to take full advantage of the Navajo's weakened condition and wreak vengeance on their traditional enemy. In 1864 the vast majority of the Navajo in the New Mexico Territory surrendered to Carson. He then forced some 8,000 ravaged Navajo men, women, and children to endure a 300-mile forced march—what became known as "the long walk"—from their homes in present-day Arizona to the government reservation at Fort Sumner, New Mexico.

Despite being breveted a brigadier general in 1865 for his successful prosecution of the Navajo campaign and cited for meritorious service in conducting Indian affairs in the region, Carson was reduced to his original rank of lieutenant colonel shortly thereafter when his regiment was downsized. Two years later, he was mustered out of the service with his volunteer unit and resumed his career as a rancher. In 1868 Carson moved his family to Boggsville, Colorado, in the hopes of expanding his ranching interests, but died shortly thereafter at nearby Fort Lyon on 23 May 1868.

—Daniel P. Barr

See also Frémont, John Charles; Glorieta Pass, Battle of; Val Verde, New Mexico, Battle of.
For further reading:
Carson, Christopher H. Kit Carson's Autobiography (1935).
Carter, Harvey Lewis. Dear Old Kit: The Historical Christopher Carson (1968).

Gordon-McCutchan, R.C., ed. *Kit Carson: Indian Fighter or Indian Killer?* (1996).

Guild, Thelma S. *Kit Carson: A Pattern for Heroes* (1984).

Trafzer, Clifford E. *The Kit Carson Campaign: The Last Great Navajo War* (1982).

CARTHAGE, BATTLE OF
(5 July 1861)

Carthage, a small city in southwestern Missouri, can claim the sad honor of having been the site of the first large-scale land battle of the Civil War, more than two weeks before First Bull Run. Far from the capitals and big cities, with no reporters from the big newspapers at hand, it pitted a motley crowd of some 6,000 pro-Confederate Missouri State Guardsmen, one third purportedly without firearms, against an equally motley array of Union volunteers, who were predominantly German. Federal forces consisted of nine companies of the 3d Missouri Infantry and six of the 5th Missouri Infantry, plus an artillery battalion, divided into two four-gun batteries. Most of the Missouri State Guard volunteers had only some militia experience, and some had no military training at all. Several of the German officers were veterans of the European revolutions of 1848–1849, and their troops had received some training in St. Louis. The overall commander of the Union forces was Colonel Franz Sigel, the commanding officers of the infantry regiments were Anselm Albert and Friedrich Salomon, and the chief of artillery was Franz Backhoff, as well as a number of company and battery officers could be included in this group.

Following their defeat at Boonville, Missouri, in June 1861, prosecessionist forces commanded by Missouri governor Claiborne Jackson and Confederate general Sterling Price withdrew into the southwestern corner of the state to link up with each other and join with forces from Texas and Arkansas. They also could protect important lead mines in the region.

At the same time, Colonel Sigel's column of the Union expedition into southwestern Missouri, which had been organized by Brigadier General Thomas Sweeny, moved overland from the railhead at Rolla to occupy Springfield on 23 June and Neosho on 1 July, with the object of heading off the State Guard. On 5 July the opposing forces met several miles north of Carthage. After an initial exchange of fire, Sigel realized his dangerous situation. The Missouri State Guard, many of whom were mounted, outnumbered the Federals, who were already exhausted from long marches. Their grey "Forty-eighter"-style uniforms were in rags, and no cavalry was available to support them or to guard their flanks. As the pro-Confederate State Guard threatened to flank and surround Sigel's approximately 1,000 men, a battle ensued in which the Union forces kept moving back in the direction of Carthage, repeatedly repulsing charges by the State Guard. Backhoff's cannoneers outgunned those of Hiram Bledsoe and Henry Guibor on the other side, and apart from some bitter fighting at Dry Fork Creek, the State Guard apparently did not press its numerical advantage. Some reports stated that Sigel's column marched in a moving, open-square formation of infantry and wagons, with gun sections "leap-frogging" to guard front, sides, and rear simultaneously.

There was no fighting for awhile as the State Guard stayed out of reach. Some troops tried to execute an intelligent pincer movement into Sigel's back at Buck Branch. There was, however, a lack of generalship among the State Guard in decisive moments, even though several generals—John B. Clark, Monroe M. Parsons, James S. Rains, and William Y. Slack—were present, with Governor Jackson nominally having the overall command. Thus Union lieutenant colonel Franz Hassendeubel's 3d Missouri Battalion scattered the guardsmen blocking their path at Buck Branch. Sigel's column withdrew through the town of Carthage and by nightfall had managed to extract itself from danger.

In the end neither side won, although each claimed it had, and with some justification. Sigel's outnumbered command inflicted higher casualties than it suffered and, after a day of hard fighting, managed an orderly withdrawal. The badly equipped and badly led Missouri State Guard drove their adversaries from the field, proving an ability to fight under adverse conditions. Psychologically, the advantage was on the secessionist side: with reinforcements arriving from Arkansas (capturing a company Sigel had left in Neosho on the day of the battle), the pro-Confederate forces were able to consolidate and train their commands while using the lead mines. Meanwhile, Union forces held Springfield and waited for General Nathaniel Lyon's column to come up, and it was more than a month before forces clashed again at Wilson's Creek.

—*Wolfgang Hochbruck*

For further reading:

Hinze David C., and Karen Farnham. *The Battle of Carthage. Border War in Southwest Missouri* (1998).

Snead, Thomas L. "The First Year of the War in Missouri." In *Battles and Leaders of the Civil War*, vol. 1. (1956).

Steele, Phillip W., and Steve Cottrell. *Civil War in the Ozarks* (1993).

CARUTHERS, ROBERT LOONEY
(1800–1882)

*Confederate governor of Tennessee;
U.S. representative*

Robert Looney Caruthers was born in Smith County, Tennessee, near Carthage on 31 July 1800. Caruthers escaped his impoverished upbringing, completing studies at Washington College in his home state. After his admittance to the bar, he practiced law and served as the clerk of Tennessee's House of Representatives (1823–1824) and labored as the clerk of Smith County's Chancery Court.

In 1826, Caruthers's move to Lebanon, Tennessee, proved a fortuitous one in terms of his political career. The young lawyer caught the eye of Governor Sam Houston, who tapped Caruthers as the attorney general of the 6th Judicial District, which he served from 1827 to 1832. After he resigned this position, Caruthers campaigned and won election to a seat in the state's House of Representatives. Caruthers's association with national politics proved short-lived. Elected as a Whig in 1841, Caruthers served in the House of Representatives until 1843, declining reelection.

When Caruthers returned to Lebanon, he focused his energies on the establishment of Cumberland University. He held the office of president of the Board of Trustees from 1842 to his death in 1882. In 1847, Caruthers helped create the department of law, making Cumberland the first university-affiliated law school in the state. This was quite an innovation and addition to the school, as only fifteen university law schools were operating in the United States at this time. Caruthers's knowledge of law and his reputation as an articulate, skilled attorney won him an appointment to fill a vacancy on the Tennessee Supreme Court in 1852. Two years later, Caruthers won election to the court and served until the outbreak of the Civil War.

As Southern states seceded and linked their futures to the Confederacy, the states of the upper South attempted to resolve the crisis. In January 1861, Tennessee's General Assembly elected Caruthers as a delegate from the 5th Congressional District to the Peace Convention at Washington, D.C. Caruthers opposed secession, but did not believe the federal government had the right to interfere with slavery.

The convention failed to reconcile the North and the South, and this (coupled with the firing on Fort Sumter and President Abraham Lincoln's summons for troops to quell the rebellion) propelled Tennessee voters to secede from the Union. Caruthers brought his leadership experience to the Provisional Congress of the Confederate States.

By early 1862, the Union army occupied the western and middle sections of the Volunteer State, and Governor Isham Harris and the state's Confederate government had fled Nashville. President Lincoln selected Senator Andrew Johnson as military governor of Union-occupied Tennessee. Still, Harris maintained a façade of power, and in 1863 called for a convention and a subsequent election for the offices of governor and Confederate congressmen. In a convention and an election that were irregular and specious, Caruthers was elected governor and Confederate congressmen were selected. Although the congressmen took office in Richmond, Caruthers never assumed the office.

After the war, Caruthers continued his law practice, and in 1868 accepted the position of professor of law at Cumberland University. His devotion to the school was evident in his donation of land and financing of a law building that was named in his honor. The law school produced two U.S. Supreme Court justices, Howell Jackson and Horace Lurton, and Secretary of State Cordell Hull. The law school remained there from 1878 to 1962 until declining enrollment and financial concerns prompted its move to the campus of Howard College (now Samford University) in Birmingham, Alabama.

After a long career in law, politics, and education, Judge Caruthers died on 2 October 1882.

—*Kathleen R. Zebley*

See also Tennessee.
For further reading:
Burns, Frank. *Wilson County* (1983).
Caldwell, Joshua W. *Sketches of the Bench and Bar of Tennessee* (1898).
Longum, David J., and Howard P. Walthall. *From Maverick to Mainstream: Cumberland School of Law, 1847–1997* (1997).
McBride, Robert M., and Dan M. Robinson. *Biographical Directory of the Tennessee General Assembly* (1975).

CASEY, SILAS
(1807–1882)
Union general

Born in East Greenwich, Rhode Island, Silas Casey received an appointment to the U.S. Military Academy at age fifteen. He graduated thirty-ninth of forty-one in the class of 1826. After receiving his commission, Casey served along the Great Lakes until the outbreak of the Second Seminole War brought his transfer to Florida. By the end of that conflict, Casey had reached the rank of captain. During the Mexican-American War, Casey served in Winfield Scott's Mexico City campaign, in which he earned two brevet promotions and was wounded twice. After the war, Casey was transferred to the Pacific Northwest, where he would spend most of the years before the outbreak of the Civil War. In 1855 he became the lieutenant colonel of the newly created 9th Infantry and its colonel in early 1861. In the same year, System of Infantry Tactics, for which he was primarily responsible, was published. It became more popularly known as "Casey's Tactics" and was adopted as the standard infantry manual by the U.S. Army in 1862.

At the outbreak of the Civil War, Casey commanded Fort Steilacoom in the Washington Territory. He was recalled from the northwest and was made brigadier general of volunteers in August 1861. Casey initially commanded a brigade in the Army of the Potomac, but his considerable experience led him to be tapped for extra duties in the fall of 1861. For example, he managed the military details of the Washington funeral of

Silas Casey (*Library of Congress*)

President Abraham Lincoln's friend Colonel Edward Baker.

In the spring of 1862, Casey was given command of a division in Erasmus Keyes's IV Corps for the upcoming Peninsula campaign. He commanded his division in the siege of Yorktown, the battle of Williamsburg, and the preliminary skirmishes before Seven Pines. On 31 May at Seven Pines, Casey's division was the first to be struck when Joseph Johnston attacked south of the Chickahominy River. Casey fought bravely but was pushed back by the Confederate onslaught. He was later quietly criticized by the commander of the Army of the Potomac, George B. McClellan, for being caught unawares, which greatly angered Casey. Despite his defeat, Casey was promoted to major general of volunteers for his actions at Seven Pines. Casey also led his division in the Seven Days'.

When McClellan's army was recalled from the peninsula in August 1862, Casey was transferred to Washington to supervise the training procedures for new recruits. At the end of the year he was placed in command of the provisional division of the Department of Washington. During the next few months, his primary duty was trying to combat the various Confederate raids against the Federal outposts south of the city. Since he

was in the Washington area, Casey was also tapped for various other duties, particularly courts-martial. From late 1862 to early 1863, he served as a member of the court-martial of Fitz John Porter.

In May 1863, Casey received appointment to the board that would occupy him for much of the remainder of the war. He became the president of the board that examined officers for fitness to command African-American troops. Casey took a strong interest in this new task and even published *Infantry Tactics for Colored Troops* to aid the new officers in their task. He remained president of the examination board until July 1865.

Casey stayed in the army after the war, reverting to the rank of colonel of the 9th Infantry. Physical infirmities led him to request retirement in 1868. He lived most of his retirement years in Brooklyn, New York, where he died on 22 January 1882. His remains were interred near his family's home in Rhode Island.

—*David S. Heidler and Jeanne T. Heidler*

See also Fair Oaks/Seven Pines; United States Colored Troops; Washington, D.C.

For further reading:

Cornish, Dudley Taylor. *The Sable Arm: Negro Troops in the Union Army, 1861–1865* (1966).

West Pointers and Early Washington: The Contributions of U.S. Military Academy Graduates to the Development of the Washington Territory, From the Oregon Trail to the Civil War, 1834–1862 (1992).

CASS, LEWIS
(1782–1866)
Antebellum Democratic politician

Lewis Cass, the "Father of Popular Sovereignty," was born in Exeter, New Hampshire. He attended Phillips Exeter Academy (one of his schoolmates was Daniel Webster) and moved with his family to Ohio, where his father, a Revolutionary War veteran, had received bounty lands. Lewis studied law under Return Jonathan Meigs and won a seat in the legislature in 1806. A staunch supporter of President Thomas Jefferson during the Aaron Burr conspiracy, Cass was appointed federal marshal for Ohio. He also served as a brigadier general in the militia at the outbreak of the War of 1812. Cass was included in General William Hull's ignominious surrender of Fort Detroit to the British and, after his release on parole, joined General William Henry Harrison at the battle of the Thames. With the Northwest thus secure for the remainder of the war, Harrison appointed Cass governor of Michigan Territory. Cass held that post for eighteen years, as Michigan grew to the threshold of statehood. Governor Cass was a true Democrat, believing in the ability and right of the people to govern themselves; and he was a champion of spread-eagle expansionism, convinced it was U.S. destiny to extend the blessing of liberty throughout the continent.

Lewis Cass (*Library of Congress*)

In 1831, Cass succeeded John H. Eaton as Andrew Jackson's secretary of war. The ethnocentrism and paternalism of the antebellum era were reflected in Cass's support of Indian removal to west of the Mississippi River as a humanitarian relocation. Cass also reinforced the Charleston harbor fortifications during the nullification crisis, a harbinger of the sectional conflict that led to the Civil War. After serving as minister to France, and quarreling with the provisions of the Webster-Ashburton Treaty pertaining to the African slave trade, Cass was elected to the U.S. Senate from Michigan. He became James K. Polk's administration's most strident congressional proponent for an aggressive prosecution of the Mexican-American War and rejoiced at the vast land cession that ended the conflict. He remained a senator until replaced by Zachariah Chandler in 1857, resigning briefly after his nomination for the presidency in 1848.

To ensure the preservation of the Union in the face of increasing sectional tensions, Cass worked assiduously for political compromise. His letter to Alfred O. P. Nicholson, dated 24 December 1847, was a nationally recognized effort to use the ideal of self-government to repudiate the Wilmot Proviso. As the Father of Popular Sovereignty, Cass denied that Congress had the authority to regulate slavery in the territories. Cass opposed slavery, in the abstract, yet blithely accepted black bondage as a condition of maintaining the republic. He objected to being labeled a "doughface" (a Northern man with Southern principles), but Cass was an accommodating constitutionalist who evolved into a Northern apologist for the "peculiar institution." Slavery was a political question to him, not a moral one; and Popular Sovereignty was an attempt to remove the explosive issue of slavery expansion from the halls of Congress.

Cass joined chairman Henry Clay on the Committee of Thirteen, which drafted the legislation that emerged as the Compromise of 1850. That landmark settlement implicitly adopted Popular Sovereignty regarding slavery and the territories, but within half a dozen years the doctrine was repudiated. Cass personally regretted the introduction of Stephen A. Douglas's Kansas-Nebraska Bill, because it reopened the sectional debate, but he eventually supported it as a Democratic Party measure. Cass despaired when the inflamed political atmosphere was stoked by "Bleeding Kansas" and the *Dred Scot* case, which he endorsed.

Cass served as James Buchanan's secretary of state, and repudiated the Popular Sovereignty principle during the debate over the admission of Kansas to the Union. The Buchanan administration endorsed the proslavery Lecompton Constitution, despite the demonstrated free-state majority in Kansas and Douglas's defiance. The Cass creed no longer functioned as a viable ideological bridge between Democrats.

Cass concurred with most of Buchanan's positions regarding the secession crisis, but he resigned from the cabinet in December 1860, after the president decided not to reinforce military posts in the South. The attack on Fort Sumter galvanized the old warrior. The discarded symbol of antebellum nationalism and political moderation, Cass enthusiastically addressed several Union recruitment rallies and contributed to the equipping of volunteer regiments. He also supported Abraham Lincoln's administration during the *Trent* Affair. He cabled Secretary of State William Henry Seward, recommending he take the opportunity to commit Great Britain to the American position on the right-of-search issue by releasing the Confederate agents seized from the British ship.

As the Civil War dragged on, Cass's health deteriorated. Although he lamented the "fatal error" made by the North in raising "that abominable Negro question," he contended that Southerners bore the "major responsibility for their insane attempt to break up the government." His heart remained "set upon the integrity of the Union, and…the restoration of the Seceding States to the Supremacy of the Constitution." He ended a lifetime of public service as he commenced it: defending the

United States against foreign and domestic assault. It is fitting that Lewis Cass survived the Civil War he labored so futilely to prevent.

—*Willard Carl Klunder*

See also Buchanan, James; Popular Sovereignty.
For further reading:
Dunbar, Willis Frederick. *Lewis Cass* (1970).
Klunder, Willard Carl. *Lewis Cass and the Politics of Moderation* (1996).
Smith, William L.G. *The Life and Times of Lewis Cass* (1856).
Woodford, Frank B. *Lewis Cass: The Last Jeffersonian* (1950).

Young, William T. *Sketch of the Life and Public Services of General Lewis Cass* (1852).

CASTLE THUNDER
Confederate prison

Although also the name of a prisoner-of-war facility in Petersburg, Virginia, Castle Thunder in Richmond was by far the more infamous of the two prisons bearing the same name. During the summer

Castle Thunder from Cary Street, 1865 (*Library of Congress*)

of 1862 the Confederate government acquired the Gleanor's Tobacco Factory, Palmer's Factory, and Whitlock's Warehouse, all on the same block, to convert into a prison for deserters and political prisoners. A high fence and watchtowers connected the three buildings before the prison was opened in August 1862.

The original capacity for the buildings was set at 1,400, but like most Civil War prisons, that number was quickly exceeded. Also, because of the Peninsula campaign during the earlier part of the summer, the use of the prison for only political prisoners and deserters was abandoned. Confederate deserters and male political prisoners were housed in one building, women and African-American prisoners in another, and Federal deserters and prisoners of war in the third. A brick wall in the back of the compound was used for executions, these consisting mainly of the Confederate deserters who were convicted by court-martial. Many times these men were sentenced to lashings instead, and these punishments were usually carried out in the back of the compound as well. There were reports that guards would occasionally deliver unauthorized lashings, especially of deserters, before their trials.

Captain George W. Alexander was selected the prison's commandant and remained in that position throughout the war. Alexander quickly gained a reputation for brutality, often using his large dog, Nero, to intimidate the inmates. His and his guards' alleged mistreatment of prisoners led in the spring of 1863 to an investigation by the Confederate Congress. After testimony from both sides, Alexander was exonerated, though there continued to be evidence until the end of the war that prisoners were mistreated.

Part of the problem that arose in Castle Thunder was endemic to Civil War prisons. Unexpected overcrowding, food and medicine shortages in the Confederacy, and the filth and diseases that usually accompanied such circumstances, made for a miserable experience for all prisoners. Dysentery was prevalent, and epidemics of such diseases as small pox only added to the horrors of prison life. By January 1863 Castle Thunder was at twice its expected capacity, at 3,000 prisoners.

Occasionally, the prisoners' distress was alleviated by supplies sent in by the United States government, but such packages became fewer as the war dragged on. Some of the overcrowding was eliminated when Federal deserters were transferred to other prisons later in the war. Their spaces were quickly filled, however, when it was determined to place Confederate soldiers accused of crimes such as theft or murder in Castle Thunder. Complaints arose during the summer of 1864 that such a policy not only removed those men from the front where they were desperately needed, but also effectively removed other men who were needed to guard them.

As one of the few facilities in the Confederacy with a specific area set aside for women prisoners, Castle Thunder also gained a certain notoriety. Most of the women were political prisoners, but there were a few who had been captured while disguising themselves as men in the Union army. The most famous woman prisoner was the Union physician, Dr. Mary Walker, who was captured in north Georgia in April 1864 and transferred to Castle Thunder because of the paucity of facilities for women prisoners in the Confederacy. She was kept there until August 1864, when she was exchanged after spending her months in prison writing letters to newspapers complaining about the conditions and the rations at the prison.

As it became apparent in March 1865 that the Union capture of Richmond was likely, Alexander began making arrangements to move the prisoners out of the city. On 3 April 1865 the prisoners were evacuated to Danville, Virginia. During the destruction of much of Richmond that ensued, Castle Thunder remained standing, and as a consequence was used as a prison by the Federal occupation forces. It was returned to its original owners after the occupation, but was destroyed by fire in 1879.

—*David S. Heidler and Jeanne T. Heidler*

See also Prisoners of War; Prisons, C.S.A.

For further reading:

Fischer, Ronald W. "A Comparative Study of Two Civil War Prisons: Old Capitol Prison and Castle Thunder Prison" (M.A. thesis, 1994).

Speer, Lonnie R. *Portals to Hell: Military Prisons of the Civil War* (1997).

CASUALTIES

A casualty is defined as a loss of a man due to injury, sickness, death, captivity, or desertion. During the Civil War, a total of 2.9 million men served the Union, but this number is deceptive, because many of these men enlisted for only three months or were called up only briefly for emergency circumstances. Approximately, 1.5 million men actually enlisted to serve for "three years or the duration," but even this number can be misleading, as the Union never had that many men under arms at any one time. Of these men 630,000 became casualties during the war, and 360,000 were killed in action or died of disease. The Confederate total of men is even more difficult to determine because they did not keep as complete records. It appears that 1.2 million men served the Confederacy during the war, but as in the case of the Union, this number is deceptive and represents all the men who served the Confederacy, no matter how short their term of service. Approximately 800,000 of these men actually enlisted for the "three years or the duration" of the war. Of these men, 340,000 became casualties during the war, and 250,000 were killed in action or died of disease.

In the Union army during the Civil War, only four regiments suffered more than 70 percent casualties in a single battle. The highest of these losses was the 1st Minnesota Infantry Regiment, which suffered 82 percent casualties out of 262 men engaged at the battle of Gettysburg. The highest number of total casualties (rather than percentage of casualties) suffered by a Union regiment during a single battle was the 1st Maine Heavy Artillery Regiment at the battle of Petersburg. The 1st Maine suffered 67 percent casualties out of 950 men engaged.

In the Confederate army during the Civil War, the highest percentage of casualties suffered by one regiment in a single battle was the 1st Texas Infantry Regiment, which suffered 82 percent casualties out of 226 men engaged at the battle of Antietam. The highest number of total casualties (rather than percentage of casualties) suffered by a Confederate regiment during a single battle was the 26th North Carolina Infantry Regiment at the battle of Gettysburg. The 26th North Carolina suffered 72 percent casualties out of 820 men engaged.

The costliest battle of the Civil War for both sides appears to have been the battle of Gettysburg. During that battle, the Union suffered 23,000 casualties with 3,000 men killed (the greatest loss for the Union in a single battle during the war). During the same battle, the Confederacy suffered 20,000 casualties with 2,500 men killed. Though Gettysburg was a very costly battle for the Confederacy, the worst casualties suffered by the Confederacy in a single battle occurred during the Seven Days' battles. During the Seven Days', the Confederacy lost 20,500 men as casualties with 3,500 men killed. The costliest single day of the Civil War for both sides was the battle of Antietam (17 September 1862). During the battle of Antietam, the Union suffered 12,000 casualties with 2,100 killed, while the Confederacy suffered 14,000 casualties with 2,700 killed.

—*Alexander M. Bielakowski*

See also Disease.

For further reading:

Fox, William F. *Regimental Losses in the American Civil War, 1861–1865* (1889).

Livermore, Thomas L. *Numbers and Losses in the Civil War in America, 1861–1865* (1996).

Phisterer, Frederick. *Statistical Record: A Treasury of Information about the U.S. Civil War* (1996).

CATHOLICS

While the Civil War divided a number of denominations as well as the nation, the Roman Catholic Church sought to maintain neutrality by sacrificing political unity to achieve religious unity.

By 1860 Catholics were the majority religion of the North. Southern Catholics were a minority in a culture dominated by evangelical orthodoxy. Southern Catholics tended to concentrate in the cities as well as in southern Maryland and the Kentucky bluegrass region. In addition, there were approximately 100,000 Catholic slaves in the South, with Louisiana accounting for 62,000 alone. Catholics represented a variety of ethnic groups, notably the Irish, but also French Louisianans and German farmers.

Before the outbreak of war, the Church avoided the impending crisis as much as possible. In the decrees and pastoral letters issued from the First Plenary Council at Baltimore in 1852, there was no mention of slavery, abolition, or sectional differences. Even sixteen days after the surrender of Fort Sumter, the Third Provincial Council of Cincinnati issued a pastoral letter that noted concern over the country's welfare but underscored the bishops' reluctance to enter the political arena.

Southern Catholics mirrored the society in which they lived and upheld slavery as a necessary evil. Bishop John England of Charleston said he personally was opposed to slavery but recognized it as being compatible with man's law and divine will. Shortly before becoming bishop of Savannah, Augustin Verot assailed the evils of the slave trade, but reiterated the paternalistic view of slavery as being both a duty and a burden through which heathen Africans might be brought to salvation. Nonetheless, in 1858 Bishop William Henry Elder of Natchez noted that few slaves of Catholic masters received special spiritual instruction.

Catholic laity, orders, and clergy all owned slaves. Some, such as Chief Justice Roger B. Taney, provided for the manumission of theirs. Brother Joseph Mobberly of the Society of Jesus helped run a Jesuit plantation in Maryland and did much to see to the slaves' spiritual welfare, but he was relieved of his duties because of his harsh treatment of the slaves. The Jesuit order sold all their slaves in 1836.

Catholics remained aloof from the abolitionist movement. Even though Pope Gregory XVI condemned the slave trade in 1839, no official doctrine condemned slavery as such. Northern Catholics also saw abolitionism as a New England Protestant movement aligned with nativism and other anti-Catholic movements and chose not to involve themselves.

With the outbreak of hostilities, Catholics tended to side with the local majority. On both sides, Catholic bishops blessed battle flags and prayed for victory. Exceptions did occur, such as when German Catholics in Texas opposed secession. What was important for the Church was that Catholic soldiers fight bravely and honor their faith, regardless which side they were on. Such comportment would serve as the basis of judgment on the Church. One hundred forty-five thousand Irish Catholics served in the Union army and were the most visible Catholic group. Indeed, as the war wore on, the Union actively recruited Irish immigrants to join the army.

Catholics did more than fight. Some priests became

chaplains or "Holy Joes." Most served for only a short time, as bishops would recall men to meet the needs of the local parish. Also, many Protestant officers refused to accept Catholics as chaplains. Still, Catholic chaplains sought to hold religious services, administer sacraments, and hear confessions. Priests and Catholic sisters working in hospitals sought to sustain Catholic identity and interest, especially among the dying. In particular, nearly 500 sisters of twenty or more orders served as nurses, earning the gratitude and praise of those they helped.

In the South, Catholics took on unique roles. Father John Bannon, the "fighting chaplain" of a Missouri Irish company, went to Rome as an emissary to try to persuade the papacy to extend recognition to the Confederacy. He reported to President Davis that he believed his mission to be successful, but later events proved him wrong. The Confederacy was acutely aware of Union efforts to recruit the Irish. To counter this effort, the Confederates sent Lieutenant James L. Capston and later Bannon to Ireland to dissuade Irish from going to the United States and enlisting, but many Irishmen found the $500 cash inducements too difficult to resist. Bishop Patrick Lynch of Charleston traveled to Rome to request that the Pope oppose recruitment of the Irish to fight for the Union.

The fate of the freed slaves was an issue for Catholics in a number of ways. In the North, Irish Catholics rioted against blacks in New York City in 1863, underscoring a fear that they would lose their jobs to freedmen. In the South, Bishop William Elder of Natchez sought to attend to the spiritual needs of the emancipated slaves, but he avoided supplying their material needs as he feared alienating planters and being labeled a secret abolitionist. Elder later sought to counter the Protestant influence of New England teachers educating the emancipated slaves by trying to secure the services of the black nuns of the Oblate Sisters of Providence, but he was unable to do so. At the same time Bishop Verot called for education of freedmen and their inclusion in the Catholic Church. At the Second Plenary Council in Baltimore in 1866, however, Church leaders from both North and South talked of cooperation to rebuild the Church in the South, but none offered a missionary plan for ex-slaves. Greater unity was achieved in rebuilding Catholic property destroyed during the war. However the Church turned its attention from Reconstruction to meeting the needs of the new wave of immigrants entering the country.

—*Daniel Liestman*

See also Chaplains; Churches; Jews; Religion; Sister Nurses.
For further reading:

Blied, Benjamin J. *Catholics and the Civil War: Essays* (1945; reprint, 1992).
Hausfeld, Eric Edward. "Catholic Involvement in Civil War Diplomacy" (M.A. thesis, 1965).
Holland, Timothy J. "The Catholic Church and the Negro in the United States prior to the Civil War" (Ph.D. dissertation, 1950).
Murphy, Robert Joseph. "The Catholic Church in the United States during the Civil War Period: 1852–1866." *Records of the American Catholic Historical Society* (1928).

CATLETT'S STATION, BATTLE OF
(14 October 1863)

Also known as Auburn, Auburn Ford, and Auburn Mills, Virginia, Catlett's Station was the stage for a battle in the Bristoe campaign, which has generally been viewed as one of military maneuverings. In an attempt to advance on Washington D.C., General Robert E. Lee took advantage of the relative inactivity of the days after the Gettysburg campaign. As Lee advanced, Major General George G. Meade and the Army of the Potomac withdrew. As only skirmishes resulted, Lee attempted to outflank the Union forces, sending Major Lieutenant Ambrose P. Hill to the west and Lieutenant General Richard S. Ewell to follow the Federal withdrawal north along the Orange & Alexandria Railroad.

Fronting the advancing Confederate infantry, Major General J. E. B. Stuart, riding with Captain William McGregor, commander of the horse artillery, found himself to the side of the Union forces who were making their way to Manassas. On the night of 13 October 1863, moving along the railroad line, the Union troops stopped at Auburn, near Catlett's Station. It was here that Stuart decided to make a reconnaissance of the Union forces. Within a safe distance, Stuart leisurely inspected the Federal forces who had stopped their march. What he did not expect was that a similar mass of troops was approaching within a few hundred yards of Stuart's rear. Realizing that his cavalry was surrounded by two corps of Federal infantry, he found his situation extremely critical.

Quickly he concealed his men in the nearby woods, close enough to the Union troops that their conversations could actually be heard. The Confederate cavalry remained silent and still throughout the night with only a few brave men dashing out among Federal forces and through their lines in order to inform Lee of the possibly disastrous situation of the cavalry. At dawn on 14 October, a dense fog descended on the area, further concealing Stuart's location in the woods. To Stuart's rear, one brigade of Union infantry stopped to camp on a nearby hill, within a quarter mile, just opposite the Confederate cavalry. When firing was heard in the distance off of the Warrenton Road, Stuart ordered McGregor's troops to charge out and open fire upon the encamped Union soldiers, muskets at rest and coffee pots in hand. After the initial confusion of the Confederate firing, the Union troops, under the command of Brigadier General Joshua Owen and Colonel Thomas Smyth, gathered their weapons to receive the charge of

Brigadier General James Gordon's cavalry. Gordon's charge was repulsed, after which, however, the Union forces, still unorganized, scattered and retreated. Stuart initially found himself outnumbered and disadvantaged; however, Lee, updated on Stuart's position throughout the night, sent a brigade of infantry to reinforce the cavalry. By this time, though, the Union forces had gathered themselves in retreat to join together with the main body of the Army of the Potomac.

It was Stuart's resourcefulness and ability to command and influence his troops that allowed him to escape near disaster. The encounter was not completely void of tragedy, however; the Confederates lost Colonel Thomas Ruffin of the 1st North Carolina cavalry. Taking twenty-eight prisoners, the Federals lost eleven men with forty-two others wounded. Although a minor skirmish, both forces met later in the day further down the road at Bristoe Station, a major and particularly bloody battle of the Bristoe campaign, which cost the South 1,300 lives and put an end to this military offensive.

—*Andrew Paul Bielakowski*

See also Bristoe Station, Battle of; Stuart, James Ewell Brown.
For further reading:
Blackford, W.W. *War Years with Jeb Stuart* (1945; reprint, 1993).
Garnett, T.S. *Riding with Stuart: Reminiscences of an Aide-de-Camp* (1994).
Hill, D.H., Jr. *North Carolina*. Vol. 4 of *Confederate Military History* (1899).

CATRON, JOHN
(ca. 1780s–1865)

U.S. Supreme Court associate justice

John Catron was born Pennsylvania, with some sources listing 1781 and others 1786 as his year of birth. He became an associate justice and chief justice of the Tennessee Court of Errors and Appeals and an associate justice of the United States Supreme Court. The scion of an immigrant German-Swiss family, Catron grew up in poor circumstances on a Virginia farm, then migrated to Tennessee.

After a campaign under General Andrew Jackson, Catron, who apparently was self-taught, commenced a career at the bar. Wartime popularity brought an appointment as state's attorney for his region of Tennessee. In 1818, Catron moved to Nashville, where he benefitted from the Panic of 1819. He mastered the complicated situation of Tennessee land titles; because he favored longtime possessors over actual title holders, the legislature named him to a spot on the state's highest court in 1824. There, Catron helped establish the view of state police powers that endured until the constitutional revolution of 1937: Laws must apply to all members of society alike, Catron wrote, not favor some chosen few.

Marrying a relative of James K. Polk, Catron became one of the leading Tennessee Jacksonians. Catron's 1829 newspaper series against the Bank of the United States won Jacksonians' plaudits. In 1832 he drew up nationalist resolutions supportive of Jackson's Nullification Proclamation to be adopted at a public meeting chaired by Governor William Carroll. The meeting unanimously adopted the resolutions, which denied the rights of nullification and secession. Catron privately hinted to Jackson that he would endorse the use of force to support Jackson's principles.

With Jackson's popularity in Tennessee waning, a constitutional convention abolished Catron's court. Returning to private practice, Catron spent the bulk of his time running the Jacksonian *Nashville Union*. Catron's support for the 1836 presidential campaign of Martin Van Buren earned him a nomination to the United States Supreme Court. His appointment, one of the last matters to which Jackson attended as president, won confirmation on 8 March 1837, at the start of Van Buren's term, by a Senate vote of twenty-eight to fifteen. Catron remained in correspondence with Jackson until Old Hickory's death, as well as serving as an advisor to Presidents Polk and James Buchanan.

Catron's most notorious judicial endeavor came in connection with the epochal case of *Scott v. Sanford* (U.S. 1857), best known as the *Dred Scott* case. Entering into correspondence with the president-elect shortly before inauguration day, Catron requested Buchanan's assistance in persuading Buchanan's fellow Pennsylvanian, Justice Robert C. Grier, to join the anti-Scott majority. Buchanan's intervention succeeded.

Catron concurred separately in Chief Justice Roger B. Taney's majority opinion. He held that Taney's decision to review the plea in abatement was mistaken, and he believed that Taney's discussion of the question of African-American citizenship was entirely dictum. In other words, Catron believed, though he did not publicly say, that Taney's attempt to rule Federal citizenship for blacks unconstitutional itself violated the provision of Article III that the Federal courts have jurisdiction only over "cases and controversies" properly brought before them.

Catron also maintained that domiciling a slave in a free state freed him, sojourning there temporarily did not, and returning him to slave territory negated whatever claim to freedom he might have had as a result of his journey. Catron further disagreed with Taney's insistence that Congress had no jurisdiction over the territories, but he agreed that slavery was legal in the territories under the state land cessions. The Northwest Ordinance made slavery illegal in Virginia's old lands north of the Ohio, and Congress could not undo that, so Congress could not outlaw slavery in North Carolina's and Georgia's cessions to Ohio's south. Besides, the Louisiana Purchase treaty included a guarantee that Frenchmen and Spaniards would continue in the "enjoyment of their liberty, property, and the religion which they profess." For Catron, this provision meant that slavery, legal under the pre-1803 dispensation, could not be banned in the former Louisiana Territory.

His last argument for the Missouri Compromise's invalidity was John Calhoun's old argument about the states' common stake in the territories: the states owned the territories in common, so whatever was property in any of the states could be taken into the territories. This classically Jacksonian attention to the rights of states in the Federal system had figured in other aspects of Catron's performance as a Supreme Court justice. For example, in *Cooley v. Board of Wardens* (U.S. 1852), Catron joined the majority in holding that states had authority to regulate local aspects of interstate commerce insofar as they were not governed by congressional legislation.

When secession came, Catron remained at his post. He rode circuit in those parts of his circuit that were not behind Confederate lines, and he cooperated in the Union military effort by way of his stingy stewardship of the writ of habeas corpus. He lived to see the Union victorious, then died in Nashville on 30 May 1865, leaving no children.

—*Constantine Gutzman*

See also Dred Scott Case; Supreme Court, U.S.
For further reading:
Fehrenbacher, Don E. *The Dred Scott Case: Its Significance in American Law and Politics* (1978).
Gilman, Howard. *The Constitution Besieged: The Rise and Demise of Lochner Era Police Powers Jurisprudence* (1993).

CAVALRY, C.S.A.

One of the most romantic aspects of the American Civil War in general and the Confederacy in particular was the cavalry. Ranging in assessment from effective for screening, scouting, and raiding to foolish for supposedly being unwilling to endure combat, the Confederate cavalry produced some of the most colorful characters in the war. At least for the first half of the war, these Southern horsemen also uniformly outperformed their opponents.

Yet the dramatic images of charging horsemen and flashing sabers were rare. It became common for cavalrymen to use the animals to reach a battlefield, and then fight dismounted. Every fourth man would hold the horses while the others advanced on foot. The horseholders remained in the rear, usually the safest part of the battlefield. Should the need arise, the horses could be brought up or the men fall back to them, mount, and ride off.

As any good cavalryman would attest, care and maintenance of his horse was paramount. This was particularly true of Confederate troopers, who had to supply their own mounts. They were entitled to receive the value of the horse at the time they were mustered into the service if the animal was killed in combat. Worn-out mounts had to be replaced as well, particularly after a raid deep behind Union lines, or other arduous service. However, remounts for most of the Southern troopers became more difficult to obtain as the war progressed, and loss of a horse might mean a transfer from the cavalry.

Despite the later difficulties, several factors account for the initial advantage the Confederate cavalry arm enjoyed over its Union counterpart. One was the exposure most Southerners had to horses, as well as the quality of the animals themselves. A second factor was the organization of the Southern cavalry as independent units. At full strength a cavalry regiment would consist of ten companies of between sixty and eighty men. These regiments could cooperate with other elements of the army or operate independently. Third was the capability of its leadership. James Ewell Brown "Jeb" Stuart, Nathan Bedford Forrest, and others demonstrated the highest aptitude for mounted service.

Jeb Stuart won a reputation as a daring cavalier by literally riding rings around his opponents. Twice he rode around Union general George B. McClellan's army. In the first instance, he found the Federal flank near Richmond "in the air" or unsupported. His report of that fact to Robert E. Lee caused the Confederate general to plan a strike against that exposed flank, launching the Seven Days' campaign. In the second instance, Stuart circled McClellan's force on a raid in October 1862 that took him as far north as Chambersburg, Pennsylvania.

Forrest launched similarly spectacular cavalry operations and produced significant results in the Western theater of the war. His raid on the Union garrison at Murfreesboro, Tennessee, netted him approximately 1,200 prisoners in July 1862, while an expedition against the Union supply center at Johnsonville, Tennessee, resulted in the destruction of millions of dollars worth of supplies in November 1864. In defensive operations, Forrest proved just as effective as he had been in conducting raids. In April and May 1863 he pursued and captured Abel Streight's raiders, while throughout the summer of 1864 he thwarted repeated Union expeditions into the heart of Mississippi, highlighted by the brilliant tactical victory at Brice's Cross Roads on 10 June.

John Hunt Morgan inflicted significant damage, and garnered his share of headlines, on raids into Kentucky in 1862 and 1863, although it was a raid beyond that state into Indiana and Ohio in July 1863 that led to his capture and incarceration in the Ohio State Penitentiary. Even so, Morgan delighted Southerners by escaping from the prison and returning to the South. His daring escape added to his earlier fame as "The Francis Marion of the War."

Indeed, from the earliest days of the war, the Confederate cavalry generated attention and respect from friends and foes alike. At First Manassas or Bull Run, fear of the "Black Horse" cavalry encouraged a rout of panicky Union troops at the end of that battle. But for all of the cavalry service's glamour, the fighting at Brandy Station, Virginia, on 9 June 1863 was the closest the Civil War came to having a classic cavalry confrontation. By no coincidence, it was also the largest cavalry battle of the war. Repeated charges and countercharges on that bloody field marked a fight in which some 17,000 mounted troopers on both sides clashed with each other. Although Stuart claimed the victory, the Federals emerged from the fight with renewed confidence in their own developing capabilities.

By the time Jeb Stuart met his end at Yellow Tavern, north of Richmond, on 11 May 1864, the Confederate cavalry's best days were past. Wade Hampton's "Beefsteak Raid" in September 1864 was one of the cavalry's last great exploits in the east.

In the Western theater, Confederate cavalry commanders like Forrest, John Hunt Morgan, Earl Van Dorn, and Joseph Wheeler launched cavalry raids that were often as destructive of Union supply lines as they were daring. They could be strategically effective as well. In December 1862, Forrest and Van Dorn so thoroughly destroyed the rail lines in western Tennessee and the forward Union depot at Holly Springs in northeastern Mississippi that their actions halted Ulysses S. Grant's initial overland advance against Vicksburg. But the Confederates failed to accomplish a similar result against William T. Sherman in 1864. Even so, Sherman worried that Southern cavalry raiders would smash his extended supply lines while he closed in on Atlanta, Georgia. However, when Forrest finally turned on those lines, it was too late; Atlanta had already fallen.

Even in the midst of a war, debates raged over the relative significance of given cavalry leaders or of the cavalry commands in the respective theaters of war. Stationed briefly with Braxton Bragg's army, Lieutenant General James Longstreet wrote to tell Stuart that his experiences in both arenas led him to consider the eastern cavalry superior to the western cavalry. And Confederate lieutenant general Daniel Harvey Hill, who had made himself unpopular in Virginia by saying that he "had not seen a dead man with spurs on," revised his thinking after watching Forrest's dismounted troopers advance on foot into combat at Chickamauga, Georgia.

Confederate cavalry functioned effectively in the Trans-Mississippi as well. Not strapped by the shortages in horseflesh that plagued the rest of the Confederacy, they launched raids, fought dismounted in major actions like Pea Ridge, scouted enemy movements, and screened friendly forces. Although the leaders generally proved less capable or popular than some of the Confederate cavalry leaders in the other theaters, they performed quite well. John Marmaduke and Joseph Shelby led or participated in several cavalry raids in Arkansas and Missouri.

Despite its romance and valor, at no point was it really likely for the Confederate cavalry alone to alter the course of the Civil War. Nevertheless, the cavalry arm proved remarkably successful at conducting raids, scouting expeditions, and screening operations that certainly helped to extend the war. In the end, it was a lack of numbers and resources, and the improvement in their opponent's organization and skills, that prevented the Confederate cavalry from being as effective a force as it had been for most of the conflict. Nevertheless, while the cavalry forces that surrendered at the end of the war were but shadows of themselves, the fact and the fiction of the exploits of the Southern horsemen were just beginning to grow.

—*Brian S. Wills*

See also Brandy Station, Battle of; Forrest, Nathan Bedford; Morgan, John Hunt; Stuart, James Ewell Brown.

For further reading:
Oates, Stephen B. *Confederate Cavalry West of the River* (1961).
Ramage, James A. *Rebel Raider: The Life of John Hunt Morgan* (1986).
Thomas, Emory M. *Bold Dragoon: The Life of J.E.B. Stuart* (1988).
Wills, Brian Steel. *A Battle from the Start: The Life of Nathan Bedford Forrest* (1992).

CAVALRY, U.S.A.

Between 1861 and 1865 the Union cavalry developed from a dispersed and ill-used force into a united and immensely powerful combat arm that significantly assisted the Northern victory. Lincoln's original 1861 call for volunteers did not include cavalry. Belief in a short war, coupled with the vast expense of equipping cavalry and the correlating lack of immediate combat readiness, supported the decision. The regular army's five mounted regiments, with the addition of a sixth in May 1861, were expected to be sufficient.

Defeat at Bull Run in July 1861 ended official opposition to volunteer cavalry, and despite initial hesitation, the Union fielded 258 regiments and 170 companies of mounted soldiers of varied enlistment terms. A standard Union cavalry regiment on paper numbered 1,200 officers and troopers, composed of five squadrons of two troops each with 100 men per troop led by a captain, a first lieutenant, and two second lieutenants. Each regiment was commanded by a colonel, a lieutenant colonel, and three majors, in addition to two surgeons, an adjutant, a quartermaster, and a commissary. The noncommissioned staff consisted of a sergeant-major, quartermaster, and commissary sergeants, as well as a saddler and chief farrier or blacksmith.

In 1863 the troop organization was given elastic strength varying from 82 to 100 men, and the supernumerary second lieutenant was discarded. A regimental veterinary sergeant was authorized, although few such positions were filled by competent individuals. The

Dismounted parade of the 7th New York Cavalry in camp, 1862 (*National Archives*)

squadron organization was also dropped and four troop battalions were implemented when units were on detached service. Although the cavalry suffered proportionally fewer casualties than the infantry, it was engaged more frequently in combat; 10,596 Union troopers were killed and 26,490 were wounded throughout the war.

Troopers were equipped with saddles designed by George B. McClellan that were fashioned to be comfortable on horses' backs and withers. The saddle had attachment eyes to strap on necessary accouterments and was padded by indigo blue woolen saddle blankets. Some officers, however, preferred nonregulation French or English flat saddles with iron stirrups. Troopers were provided single-reined bridles with curb bits. Officers usually had double-reined bridles. Regulars eschewed the use of martingales (straps that led from the harness through the forelegs to prevent rearing), although volunteers often employed them. Union cavalrymen were armed with Colt revolvers, sabers, and, originally, single-shot carbines, which were later exchanged for Henry or Spencer repeating weapons. Fully caparisoned, the cavalry horse's load, exclusive of the rider, hovered near 110 pounds; with the trooper and his weapons, the total burden ranged between 255 and 270 pounds.

Union cavalry skill and power developed slowly during the first two years of war. Throughout 1862, while Confederates operated in a body under daring commanders, Union cavalrymen suffered from organiza-

tional handicaps. Regiments were parceled out to infantry commands for use as vedettes, couriers, orderlies, and escorts. Such duty prevented concerted action and continually diminished cavalry strength. Lack of a centralized command structure further debilitated cavalry field effectiveness and subjected Union troopers to conflicting orders and purposes. These problems were only corrected in stages as successive Federal army commanders learned to mass their cavalry and employ it effectively.

In the East, Union cavalrymen endured repeated humiliations by J. E. B. Stuart's Rebel cavalry, although promising commanders such as George Bayard and John Buford emerged. When Major General Joseph Hooker took command of the Army of the Potomac in early 1863, reformation of his forty cavalry regiments became a priority. Hooker created a unified cavalry corps commanded by Major General George H. Stoneman organized into divisions and brigades with attached batteries of horse artillery. The corps had its first real test in a massive raid behind Lee's lines during the Chancellorsville campaign. The expedition's barren results and politics in the high command resulted in Stoneman's replacement by Alfred Pleasonton.

On 9 June 1863 Pleasonton hurled 9,000 cavalrymen against a like number of Confederates at Brandy Station. The battle was the war's largest cavalry engagement, and although Stuart retained possession of the battlefield, the audacity, determination, and skill exhibited by

A Union cavalry charge near Culpeper, Virginia, 14 September 1863 (*Library of Congress*)

Union troopers swelled Federal confidence, while giving Confederate pride a significant jolt. Additional cavalry probing actions at Middleburg, Aldie, and Upperville further displayed the rising skill, professionalism, and élan of the Union cavalry corps. On 1 July, at Gettysburg, Buford's two brigades delayed Confederate infantry long enough for Union infantry to concentrate on the scene. On 3 July opposing cavalries clashed fiercely east of the main battlefield. The Union cavalry corps firmly repulsed all Rebel attacks and spearheaded the pursuit of Lee's beaten army after the battle.

In the west Union cavalry suffered from similar organizational and leadership problems. Each western military department had its own cavalry division, and some mounted units were shared among several armies, further complicating concentrated action. Failure to employ cavalry efficiently meant Union armies in the west with extended supply lines were open to attack by intrepid Confederate cavalry raiders such as John H. Morgan, Nathan B. Forrest, and Joseph Wheeler.

By 1863 western cavalry forces had improved in effectiveness. General Ulysses S. Grant used cavalry to assist his Vicksburg campaign by sending Brigadier General Benjamin H. Grierson and 1,700 troopers on a diversionary raid through Mississippi. The raiders reached Baton Rouge, Louisiana, on 2 May after sixteen days of spreading alarm and confusion behind Confederate lines. A similar disruptive raid through Alabama and Georgia

attempted by General Abel D. Streight from William S. Rosecrans's army in Tennessee ended in disaster and capture. The following year, however, William T. Sherman used his combined armies' cavalry forces as an important component in his Georgia campaign, despite difficult terrain. Not until December 1864 was a concerted western cavalry corps formed, consisting of seven divisions led by Brigadier General James Harrison Wilson. When John Bell Hood's Confederates suffered a staggering winter defeat at Nashville, Wilson's horsemen turned their retreat into an unmitigated rout.

The Union cavalry displayed tremendous advances in strength and military effectiveness during the war's final year and was greatly assisted by Northern industrial and agricultural resources. In horses alone, a conservative estimate would have the loyal states supplying 451,180 cavalry mounts, exclusive of those captured. The formation of a Cavalry Bureau in July 1863 was designed to improve the cavalry's field organization and efficiency. In addition, the bureau administered several nationwide remount and horse-recruiting depots to restore broken-down army animals. Giesboro Point, the largest of these facilities, situated on the Potomac River near Washington, could accommodate over 30,000 animals; however, an insurmountable shortage of competent veterinarians limited the number of horses that could be successfully tended.

In the east during 1864 the cavalry reached a new

level of success under the energetic leadership of Philip H. Sheridan and aggressive subordinate commanders like Wesley Merritt, George A. Custer, and David M. Gregg. In combat Union horsemen used mounted charges, dismounted attacks, and combinations of both to attack and defend against the Confederates. During dismounted combat, every fourth trooper held the horses in the rear of the firing line. Employment of such tactics, coupled with repeating carbines, allowed Union troopers to best Rebel cavalry repeatedly and prevail against Confederate infantry.

Sheridan used the Army of the Potomac's cavalry corps of three divisions containing 12,424 men plus twelve batteries of horse artillery to strike vigorously at the enemy's industrial and agricultural resources. In May and June 1864 Sheridan conducted two massive raids, resulting in severe engagements at Yellow Tavern, Trevilian's Station, and Meadow Bridge. In August, the 1st and 3d Cavalry Divisions were transferred to help secure the Shenandoah Valley, and Union cavalrymen played a skillful and decisive role in attaining victories at Opequon, Cedar Creek, Waynesboro, and Tom's Brook.

The war's final months witnessed several campaigns that amply illustrated Union cavalry dominance. In the west the cavalry corps of the Division of the Mississippi under James H. Wilson swept through Alabama, torching Rebel property and capturing the fortified cites of Selma, Montgomery, and Columbus. George Stoneman twice struck from eastern Tennessee, raiding into southwestern Virginia and North Carolina and wrecking railroads, as well as destroying lead and salt manufactories—movements intended to coincide with and assist Sherman's northward advance.

In Virginia the Union cavalry's stellar fighting abilities and tireless activity prevented prolongation of the war by smashing Lee's flank at Five Forks, harrying retreating Rebel columns, and finally blocking Lee's escape routes to compel him to surrender at Appomattox Court House. War's end found Union horseman to be the finest battle-hardened cavalry in the world, and in recognition of excellent service assisting the Union victory, the cavalry corps led the final review of armies in Washington in May 1865.

—*David J. Gerleman*

See also Averell's Raids; Cavalry, C.S.A.; Chambersburg Raid; Forrest, Nathan Bedford; Forrest's Raids; Pleasonton, Alfred; Stoneman, George; Stoneman's Raid (April–May 1863); Stoneman's Raid (July 1864); Stoneman's Raid (December 1864–January 1865); Stoneman's Raid (March–April 1865); Stuart, J. E. B.; Stuart's Dumfries Raid; Stuart's First Ride Around McClellan; Wheeler, Joseph; Wheeler's Raid (August–September 1864); Wheeler's Raid (October 1863); Wilson, James H.; Wilson's Selma Raid.

For further reading:
Davis, Sidney Morris. *Common Soldier—Uncommon War: Life as a Cavalryman in the Civil War* (1994).
Evans, David. *Sherman's Horsemen: Union Cavalry Operations in the Atlanta Campaign* (1996).
Keenan, Jerry. *Wilson's Cavalry Corps; Union Campaigns in the Western Theatre, October 1864 through Spring 1865* (1998).
Longacre, Edward G. *Lincoln's Cavalrymen: A History of the Mounted Forces of the Army of the Potomac* (1999).
Starr, Stephen Z. *The Union Cavalry in the Civil War* (1979–1985).

CEDAR CREEK, BATTLE OF
(19 October 1864)

Brigadier General Philip Sheridan's campaign in the Shenandoah Valley had by October 1864 handed Jubal Early's Valley Army two stinging defeats at Winchester and Fisher's Hill and had routed his cavalry at Tom's Brook. Sheridan also laid waste to the potential harvest in the valley to deprive Robert E. Lee of valuable sustenance. Confident that he had destroyed both the valley's bounty and Early's spirit, Sheridan planned to quit the Shenandoah and join Ulysses S. Grant's lines at Petersburg. He even began detaching elements of VI Corps, sending them toward Ashby's Gap, while he departed for a strategy conference in Washington. Sheridan was so sure that nothing would happen in the valley that he dismissed as a ruse intelligence that Longstreet was moving to Early's assistance. He did, however, recall the detachments.

Sheridan was right about the burnt-up valley and Longstreet, but he had missed the mark on Early completely. True, Early's Valley Army was bedraggled, but it was made up of hardened veterans unused to defeat. Also Sheridan's devastation had been so thorough that Early had a problem feeding his people. He could move down the valley toward the retiring Union army or toward supplies at Staunton. Before the disaster at Tom's Brook, his diminished force had been reinforced, not by Longstreet but by Thomas Rosser's cavalry and the return of Joseph Kershaw's infantry division. All this considered, Early elected to close on the Federal position.

Sheridan's Army of the Shenandoah sat along Cedar Creek, a meandering stream that stretched westward from the north branch of the Shenandoah River and away from hulking Massanutten Mountain. The position was not a good one, but Brigadier General Horatio Wright, whom Sheridan had left in charge, was mainly worried about the most vulnerable point of the Federal configuration on the right flank. There Wright's three divisions sat behind Cedar Creek with level, open ground inviting an attack from the west. Cavalry under George A. Custer and Wesley Merritt covered this approach, but the position remained a cause for concern. To Wright's left sat William Emory's two divisions, and to his left, across the Valley Pike, rested George Crook's two divisions, anchored by the Shenandoah, here a

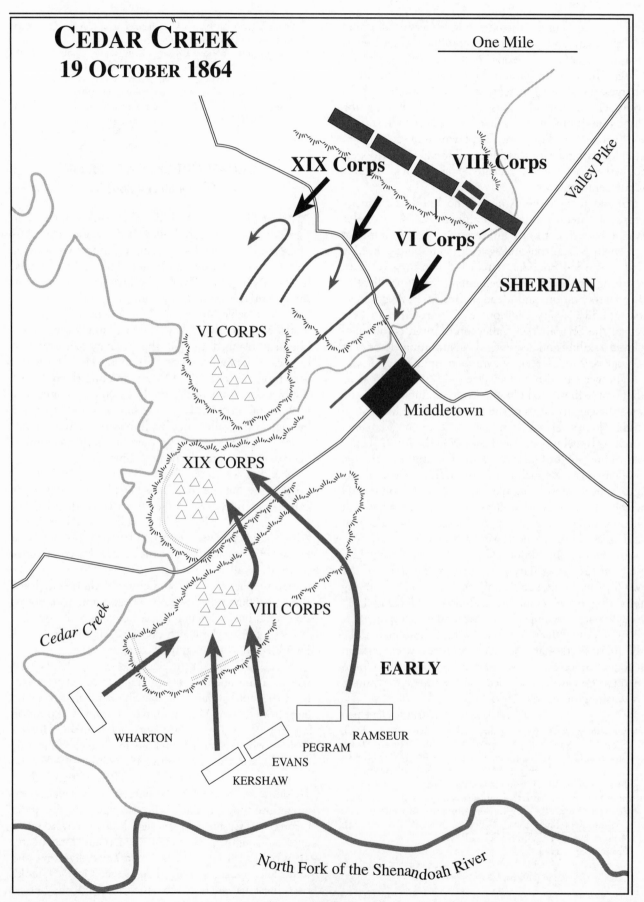

CEDAR CREEK
19 OCTOBER 1864

One Mile

XIX Corps

VIII Corps

VI Corps

SHERIDAN

Valley Pike

VI CORPS

Middletown

XIX CORPS

VIII CORPS

EARLY

Cedar Creek

WHARTON

RAMSEUR

PEGRAM

EVANS

KERSHAW

North Fork of the Shenandoah River

The battle of Cedar Creek, 19 October 1864 (*Library of Congress*)

wider stream than Cedar Creek. Crook was actually the weakest part of the line, but he could feel secure in the shadow of Massanutten Mountain's sheer face. In any event, Wright did not expect any trouble, even after it became apparent that Early was in his front.

After probing about a bit—a sharp skirmish at Hupp's Hill on 18 October produced about 200 casualties on each side—Early had his cartographer Jedediah Hotchkiss and John B. Gordon scale Massanutten Mountain to survey the Federal deployment. They returned with a plan to exploit the Union position in an unexpected way. Gordon would move three divisions across the Shenandoah River to traverse the north face of Massanutten Mountain above Cedar Creek. He would then recross the river and assail Crook on the Federal left. Meanwhile, Kershaw would cross Cedar Creek farther upstream, while Wharton advanced on the Valley Pike. After Crook was destroyed, the remainder of the bluecoats could be cut up in detail. Early agreed and just that quickly everything was set in motion.

The plan was an emulation of the sweeping flanking maneuver that Stonewall Jackson had employed so brilliantly at Chancellorsville in May 1863. At that battle,

Lee had frozen Joseph Hooker into place while Jackson had swung around to Hooker's unprotected right flank and had nearly hammered the Union army to pieces. Chancellorsville had taken too long to develop, however, and darkness had helped prevent Hooker's complete annihilation. At Cedar Creek the terrain was more daunting than the distance, but Early had everybody moving shortly after midnight. He would have the entire next day to annihilate Phil Sheridan. Early even planned to send cavalry to capture Sheridan, who was thought to be at his headquarters in Belle Grove.

The weather helped at first. A moon just past full guided the Confederates along their way. Also, a local inhabitant's guidance on a route across the north face of Massanutten sped the deployment. At dawn, everyone was in place, and as simultaneously as anything happened in this war, Gordon and Kershaw plunged across the creek, just as John Wharton's horse artillery opened on the Union center. In a half hour, Crook's VIII Corps on the Union left had collapsed, fled, or fallen prisoner. Confederate success was so complete and rapid, in fact, that unit cohesion broke down as regiments jumbled up and got out of order with others. Many also paused to plunder the Union camps, so any urgency of pursuit to press their initial advantage was lost.

Visibility became a problem as well. A lowering fog made it impossible to see more than a few yards, so the general flight of the Union army remained unexploited. Stephen Ramseur and John Pegram had folded up VIII Corps and shooed it back toward Middletown, but the commingling of their divisions and the fog gave them pause. So they sat for an hour, which gave Federal officers time to gather their wits and their panicked men, putting both in order. A small knot of resistance formed by elements of Brigadier General George Getty's division of VI Corps eventually anchored itself on the hill at Middletown's village cemetery. In the fog these men did a good job of persuading Early, Pegram, Ramseur, and Wharton—who actually tried to dislodge Getty—that they were the entire VI Corps. The bulk of VI Corps actually was rearward, establishing with elements of the shattered XIX Corps a line to resist the next Confederate onslaught.

That onslaught never came, for even after the sun burned off the fog, Jubal Early hesitated. Gordon would later intimate that Early had shown unsettling signs of lethargy for several days, and possibly the ugly failures of the previous weeks had undone him. In any case, by 10:30 A.M. Early was acting as though the battle was done and victory was his. When Gordon urged him to press forward, Early told the crestfallen Gordon that the Yankees were beaten and would retire soon enough.

General Philip Sheridan at the battle of Cedar Creek
(*Library of Congress*)

Gordon reminded Early that VI Corps of the Army of the Shenandoah was the most hard-bitten of a hardened lot and that it would have to be driven from the field. Yet Early insisted that the bluecoats in the distance were whipped and soon would be moving on. "My heart went into my boots," Gordon said later, for he believed that this lost opportunity would rank as one of the most colossal mistakes of the war. The fight at Cedar Creek would not be another Chancellorsville; it would be the first day at Gettysburg.

Just after the battle, Jubal Early bluntly declared, "The Yankees got whipped and we got scared." But that observation was only partly right and, as far as the Yankees were concerned, wholly temporary. Sheridan had returned from Washington, but he had not yet rejoined the army when the guns began to sound at Cedar Creek. Riding toward the battle from Winchester, he met stragglers, whom he successfully exhorted to join him, and then set forth with urgency on a pounding twelve-mile gallop that would later fall into the lore as "Sheridan's Ride." By the time he arrived at the hastily constructed line gathered around VI Corps, Wright had matters well enough in hand to have Sheridan thinking on the offense. When he learned what he already suspected—that Longstreet had not joined Early—he was committed to reversing this reverse. Rather than going away, as Early had predicted, Sheridan began carefully preparing a counterattack.

He took his time, so an eerie silence fell over the now sunny field as the two armies shifted here and there. Some Confederate maneuvers were unfortunate, for they stretched their lines thin and created a gap at Gordon's position. Suddenly, at 4:00 P.M. Sheridan struck, hurling XIX Corps into that gap and following it with George A. Custer's cavalry. It collapsed Gordon's division and soon had Kershaw in full retreat as well. At the center, Ramseur's people stood against VI Corps for an hour and a half. As Ramseur was mounting his third horse to resume rallying his men, a bullet tore through his lungs. The wound would kill him.

When it became clear that cavalry were gaining their rear, Wharton and Pegram also broke with little order. Everybody was streaming toward Fisher's Hill, when a bridge blocked by an abandoned wagon stalled the retreat and added to the panic. For a while, it was a headlong race in which the only advantage lay in outrunning the blue infantry.

Early briefly contemplated making a stand at Fisher's Hill, but soon abandoned that idea and the position. On 20 October he continued a general withdrawal toward New Market, his army having suffered a third major defeat and leaving the Shenandoah Valley completely in the hands of the Federals. Sheridan had lost more than 5,500 of his nearly 31,000-man army, but he had finally won the day and would enjoy a steadily increasing celebrity. Early's Valley Army was devastated by this last disaster, suffering almost 3,000 casualties and losing virtually all of its artillery in the headlong flight from the field. Early himself was roundly criticized from nearly all quarters for the mishandling of the campaign in general, and especially for the defeat that capped its conclusion. Cedar Creek provided telling omens for the collapsing Confederacy, for it was not only a tale of missed opportunity; it was also a sign of a formerly aggressive commander's ebbing resolve upon the most crucial occasion.

—*David S. Heidler and Jeanne T. Heidler*

See also Early, Jubal; Fishers Hill, Battle of; Gordon, John B.; Pegram, John; Ramseur, Stephen; Shenandoah Valley Campaign (August 1864–March 1865); Sheridan, Philip H.; Tom's Brook, Virginia.

For further reading:
Collier, Mark C. *The Night Attack and Exploitation Portion of the Battle of Cedar Creek (Or Belle Grove), Oct. 19, 1864* (1997).
Gordon, John B. *Reminiscences of the Civil War* (1903).
Mahr, Theodore C. *The Battle of Cedar Creek: Showdown in the Shenandoah, October 1–30, 1864: Early's Valley Campaign* (1992).

CEDAR MOUNTAIN, BATTLE OF
(9 August 1862)

Mismanaged on both sides, the battle of Cedar Mountain (the location also known as Slaughter Mountain, Cedar Run, Cedar Run Mountain, and Southwest Mountain), Virginia, caused the Confederate army nearly to suffer a humiliating defeat from a Union army half its size.

Early in 1862, Brigadier General John Pope received recognition for Union military victories in the west. For such successes, he was called east and given command of the newly created Union Army of Virginia on 26 June 1862. The fragmented Army of Virginia was reorganized to consist of the Mountain Department, Department of the Shenandoah, and the Department of the Rappahannock. Positioned around Culpeper, Virginia, Pope's mission was to protect Washington, D.C., guard the Shenandoah Valley, and move east to Charlottesville to pose a threat to General Robert E. Lee in order to draw Lee's attention away from Major General George McClellan's advancing armies.

In mid-July, Lee sent Major General Stonewall Jackson northwest to protect the rail junction at Gordonsville and to watch the movements of the Union army. On 7 August, informed of the cavalry and infantry, unknown in number, Lee sent Jackson and his three divisions north to Orange Court House, taking advantage of McClellan's inactivity. Meanwhile, Pope planned an advance south to the Rapidan River, east of the Blue Ridge Mountains. Upon hearing of the Confederate advance, Pope deployed his troops in an effort to cover a wide expanse from Madison Court House to Culpeper. To the south of Culpeper, however, north of the Rapidan River, Jackson's large army of 24,000 men, doubling that of Pope's, lay in wait, intending to strike quickly and destroy the first Union corps to arrive.

Jackson's plan was to subdue the first corps, placing his forces in perfect position to defeat the other two, one at a time, as they approached. Brigadier General Nathaniel Banks's division of Pope's Union forces, fronted by cavalry, struck first, however. By midmorning on 9 August 1862 at Cedar Run, eight miles south of Culpeper, the Confederates encountered Pope's cavalry. Jackson took most of the afternoon to deploy his troops. The Confederate forces met the Union troops at 4:00 P.M., allowing enough time for the Union forces to arrive, following three miles behind Banks. Experiencing gaps in formation, the two Confederate divisions under Major General Richard S. Ewell and Brigadier General Charles S. Winder still moved forward experiencing little opposition initially, though Winder, commanding the left, was mortally wounded by a Union shell. Soon

The battle of Cedar Mountain, 9 August 1862 (*Library of Congress*)

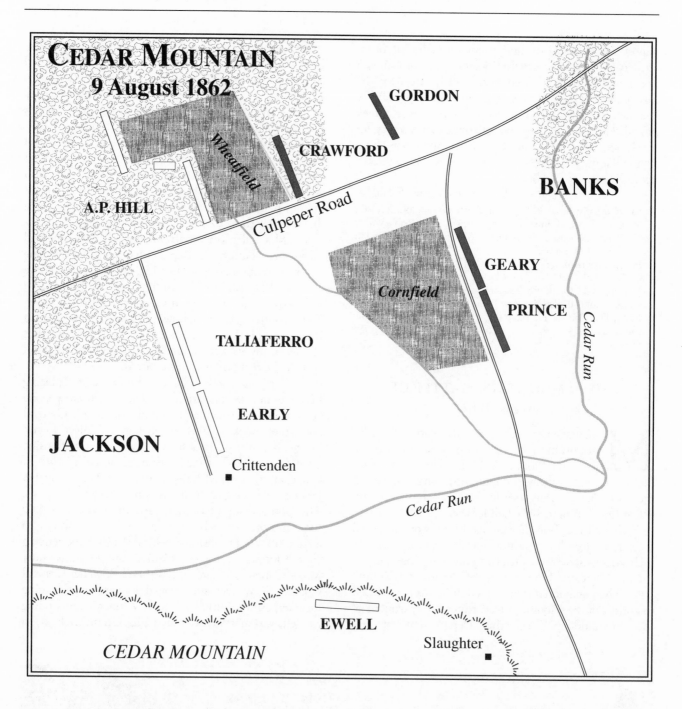

after the Confederate advance, however, Banks's troops furiously drove on to Winder's exposed left. This tremendous assault caused the Confederate army's left side to give way, devastated by the Union charge.

Alarmed at seeing his left side collapse, Jackson immediately rode into the nearby forest to rally his troops and lead them into battle. Although Banks used almost all of his 9,000 troops in the initial assault, Ewell's right side was pushed back but held its ground. In the early evening, the Union advance was stopped as the third Confederate division arrived under the command of Major General Ambrose P. Hill. The gaps caused by the Union assault were eventually mended by Hill's

12,000 men and allowed for a Confederate counterattack. Although Union reinforcements were on their way from Culpeper, they arrived much too late to allow the Federals to continue on. Still fighting hard, the outnumbered Union forces stubbornly withdrew from the field at around 6:30 P.M. Although Jackson ordered Hill to follow, artillery fire, exhaustion, and darkness put an end to the Confederate pursuit. Federal reinforcements under Brigadier General James B. Ricketts arrived in the night to halt the Confederate advance, seven miles south of Culpeper. Sometime after 11:00 P.M., Jackson, unwilling to risk any more lives in his advance, ordered his men to halt and set up camp for the night.

The Cedar Mountain battlefield, August 1862 (Photograph by Timothy O'Sullivan / *Library of Congress*)

The battle cost the Federals 314 killed, 1,445 wounded, and 622 missing, totaling 2,381 men of the 8,000 engaged. The Confederates, employing 16,800 men, suffered 1,341 casualties, not to mention the loss of Winder, greatly diminishing the value of this Confederate victory. Although Jackson claimed a victory, driving Pope from the field, he had grossly miscalculated. His drawn-out and calculated march allowed for Pope to position the rest of his men, behind Banks's initial charge. Banks, outnumbered, could have quite possibly overcome the staggering odds; however, he erred in not leaving a reserve when attacking and not requesting reinforcements from Pope.

—*Andrew Paul Bielakowski*

See also Army of Virginia; Banks, Nathaniel Prentiss; Hill, Ambrose Powell; Jackson, Thomas Jonathan; Pope, John; Winder, Charles S.

For further reading:

Krick, Robert K. *Stonewall Jackson at Cedar Mountain* (1990).
Stackpole, Edward J. *From Cedar Mountain to Antietam* (1993).

CENTRALIA MASSACRE
(27 September 1864)

In September 1864, guerrilla activity in Missouri markedly increased as a result of excitement over Confederate general Sterling Price's expected invasion of the state. Confederate officers roamed the state to fill the ranks of Price's army. Many bushwhackers, however, cared little about the larger war effort and just perpetuated the violence that had enveloped Missouri for several years. On the night of 26 September, more than 200 veteran guerrillas assembled about four miles south of Centralia, a small town in the north central part of the state. John Thrailkill, Dave Poole, George Todd, and the notoriously violent William "Bloody Bill" Anderson led the combined bands. The next morning, Anderson and thirty of his men left the camp and rode into Centralia to find news of Price and check the stocks of the local stores. The tiny town, which consisted of only two hotels, two stores, a schoolhouse, and a few homes, had been alerted to the guerrillas' presence only minutes before.

Anderson's men began terrorizing the citizenry, demanding anything that caught their eye. A whiskey barrel was found and soon emptied, adding drunken enthusiasm to the atmosphere. When a stagecoach from nearby Columbia arrived, its luckless occupants were quickly robbed of their valuables. Among the passengers was William S. Rollins, a well-known Unionist congressman, who escaped certain death by lying about his identity and then hiding out in a hotel. About an hour and a half after the destruction had begun, a northbound train from St. Louis appeared. The engineer spotted the bushwhackers and attempted to run by the station at full steam but the unknowing brakeman brought it to a squealing halt, thus delivering 125 civilian passengers and 23 unarmed Union soldiers into the guerrillas' grasp.

After robbing the civilian passengers, the guerrillas turned their attention to the Union soldiers, who were separated from the rest and stripped of their uniforms. On Anderson's order, the guerrillas began firing into the crowd of pleading men, executing them in plain sight of the horrified onlookers. Within a few minutes, all the soldiers had been killed except Sergeant Thomas M. Goodman, who Anderson hoped to exchange for a recently captured member of his company. After the train was set afire and headed down the track under steam, Anderson and his mob departed, leaving twenty-two soldiers and a civilian (an unfortunate German immigrant dressed in blue that day) dead at the railroad station.

Major A. V. E. Johnston and three companies of the green 39th Missouri had been in the field since 10:00 P.M. the previous night following rumors of the guerrillas' whereabouts. The regiment had been organized only two weeks before and consisted primarily of inexperienced farm boys armed with Enfield muskets and mounted on plow horses and mules. Johnston's troops entered Centralia around 3 P.M. on the afternoon of the 27th, having seen smoke rising from a distance. After hearing of the morning's violence, Johnston left 35 men in Centralia and followed the guerrilla's trail south with about 120 troopers. They followed the bushwhackers' pickets into an open field near Young's Creek, south of town.

The guerrilla chieftains were ready for the Federals' arrival and lured them toward a horseshoe-shaped trap outlining the field into which they rode. Upon seeing the guerrillas arrayed in a line across the opposite end of the field, Johnston dismounted his troops and sent the horses to the rear with every fifth man. The militia fixed bayonets and prepared to receive the mounted charge on foot. On Anderson's signal, the trap closed and the bushwhackers attacked the panicking young troopers from three sides. The first rush by Anderson's men from the base of the "horseshoe" galloped through Johnston's horrified line and continued toward the horseholders who broke and fled in terror.

The fighting lasted only a few minutes and ended in the complete annihilation of Johnston and his little command. The guerrillas then moved among the fallen bodies, mutilating many and even scalping some. They chased down the fleeing horseholders and slaughtered them, following one all the way into Centralia. There some of the troops left behind by Johnston were killed as well. That night, the guerrillas broke into smaller groups and returned to the brush to avoid Federal retribution. The day's toll of death and destruction marked one of the most brutal events in Missouri's Civil War. One month later, Union troops shot and killed Anderson outside Albany, Missouri, when he attempted an attack similar to the one made on Johnston and his men.

—*Ronald G. Machoian*

See also Anderson, William "Bloody Bill"; Guerrilla Warfare; Missouri; Todd, George.
For further reading:
Barton, O.S. *Three Years with Quantrill: A True Story Told by His Scout John McCorkle* (1992).
Brownlee, Richard S. *Gray Ghosts of the Confederacy: Guerilla Warfare in the West, 1861–1865* (1958).
Castel, Albert E., and Thomas Goodrich. *Bloody Bill Anderson: The Short, Savage Life of a Civil War Guerrilla* (1998).
Goodrich, Thomas. *Black Flag: Guerrilla Warfare on the Western Border, 1861–1865* (1995).
Rodermyre, Edgar T. *History of Centralia, Missouri* (1936).
War of the Rebellion: A Compilation of the Official Records of the Union and Confederate Armies (1893).

CHALMERS, JAMES RONALD
(1831–1898)
Confederate general

Born in Halifax County, Virginia, to Joseph Williams Chalmers and Fannie Henderson Chalmers, the younger Chalmers moved to Tennessee and then Mississippi as a child with his family. He graduated from South Carolina College in 1851 and after studying law began his practice in Mississippi. In 1858 he became state district attorney for the 7th District. A strong Democrat, Chalmers advocated secession in 1860 and was elected to the Mississippi Secession

Convention. He was selected the chairman of the Military Affairs Committee of that body.

At the formation of the Confederate States of America, Chalmers received a captain's commission in March 1861 and was appointed the colonel of the 9th Mississippi Regiment in April 1861. Stationed initially at Pensacola, Chalmers participated in the night raid on Santa Rosa Island on 8–9 October 1861. Chalmers was promoted to brigadier general on 13 February 1862, at which point he and his brigade, known as the "Pensacola Brigade," moved north to join Confederate forces in northern Mississippi.

Moving between Iuka and Corinth in an effort to determine Federal movements before the commencement of the Shiloh campaign, Chalmers's brigade scouted Union flanks at Pittsburg Landing during the first few days of April. During the battle of Shiloh, Chalmers commanded his brigade as part of Major General Jones Withers's division and was commended for his bravery during the two-day battle.

After Shiloh, Chalmers temporarily moved to the cavalry, but at his request returned to his brigade in July 1862. In that capacity, he moved north as part of Braxton Bragg's Kentucky campaign in the late summer of 1862. He led the attack that resulted in the successful Confederate siege of Munfordville, Kentucky. In what would become the Perryville campaign, he briefly earned the wrath of his commander, Bragg, by engaging in an unauthorized attack on a Federal position. He redeemed himself in the upcoming campaigns in the fall and winter of 1862, distinguishing himself as a brigade commander under Leonidas Polk at Stones River where Chalmers was wounded.

After that battle, Chalmers transferred permanently to the Confederate cavalry. In April 1863 he became the commander of the Military District of Mississippi serving under Nathan Bedford Forrest. During the Vicksburg campaign, Chalmers operated in northern and eastern Mississippi in attempt to harass Northern movements. After the fall of Vicksburg, Chalmers destroyed rail lines and foraged for the remaining Confederate troops in the state.

By 1864 Chalmers commanded one of Forrest's divisions, though he did not always get along with his temperamental commander. Chalmers commanded the lead elements of Forrest's attack on Fort Pillow and was present during the controversial attack on and killing of much of the African-American garrison. He continued under Forrest at the battle of Tupelo, 14–15 July 1864, after which Chalmers led his division in John Bell Hood's Tennessee campaign of the fall of 1864. By early 1865, Chalmers commanded all Confederate cavalry in Mississippi. He surrendered in May 1865.

After the war, Chalmers returned to his law practice and to Mississippi politics. He served in the state senate and three terms as a U.S. congressman. He retired from politics in 1888 and began practicing law in Memphis, Tennessee, where he died.

—David S. Heidler and Jeanne T. Heidler

See also Fort Pillow; Santa Rosa Island, Battle of; Tupelo, Battle of.

CHAMBERLAIN, JOSHUA LAWRENCE
(1828–1914)
Union general

Joshua Lawrence Chamberlain left his college professorship in 1862 to become lieutenant colonel in the 20th Maine, Army of the Potomac. He became a hero at Gettysburg when he helped save Little Round Top for the Union, suffered a near-fatal wound at Petersburg, and after the war served four terms as governor of Maine. His remarkable bravery and fearless battlefield conduct earned him lasting distinction.

When the war began Chamberlain was a professor of rhetoric at Bowdoin College in Brunswick, Maine. In 1861, the college's administration offered the charismatic and highly respected Chamberlain the chair of modern European languages. The position came with lifetime tenure and a two-year sabbatical for study in Europe, the college to continue his salary and pay his expenses. Chamberlain gave up the trip, but he did use his leave to accept a commission as lieutenant colonel of the 20th Maine.

The 20th Maine joined the Army of the Potomac in September 1862. It arrived just in time for the battle of Antietam, although the green regiment, newly trained, was held in reserve behind Union lines. Chamberlain and his men received their baptism of fire at Fredericksburg in December. They were involved in one of the many futile attacks launched against the Confederates entrenched on Marye's Heights. Chamberlain spent the night pinned down by Confederate fire, using dead Union soldiers for cover.

While quarantined because of an outbreak of smallpox, the regiment missed the next major engagement at Chancellorsville. Chamberlain, however, was promoted to colonel and commander of the regiment in May 1863, and his exploits at Gettysburg would make him famous. The 20th Maine, part of Colonel Strong Vincent's brigade, was held in reserve below Little Round Top. Only a few Federal signalmen occupied the small peak at the southern end of the Union line, but they spotted Confederates advancing up the hill. An urgent order from Gouverneur K. Warren brought Chamberlain and his men to the summit of Little Round Top. Vincent's four brigades reached the summit just ahead of the Confederates with Chamberlain's unit holding the left side of the makeshift Union line. William Oates's 15th Alabama assailed Chamberlain's regiment and nearly turned the Union flank, but the Maine men held. Chamberlain suffered several minor wounds, and the unit took heavy losses in close fighting, but his bold counterattack secured the critical Federal position. Chamberlain's bravery at Gettysburg later earned him the Medal of Honor.

He was also given command of a brigade, although with no promotion in rank. From 1863 to the summer of 1864 he alternated between commanding a regiment and a brigade. A stint on court-martial duty in the spring of 1864 kept Chamberlain out of the massive engagements in Virginia. He returned to his comrades in time for the battle of Cold Harbor, but the 20th Maine played no part in the disastrous Union assault at that place. After the defeat at Cold Harbor, the Army of the Potomac swung farther south and attempted to capture the rail center at Petersburg, and it was near there that Chamberlain led his brigade against a Confederate breastwork called Rives's Salient. He suffered a severe pelvic wound that caused so much internal damage that doctors at a field hospital pronounced the wound mortal. When the news reached Chamberlain's division commander G. K. Warren, he recommended that as a tribute Chamberlain be promoted before he died. U. S. Grant, recalling other times when Chamberlain had been passed over for promotion, immediately signed the order. Two weeks after being wounded—a time during which he barely clung to life—Chamberlain signed his acceptance of the commission that made him a brigadier general.

Incredibly, he began to recover. He spent the rest of 1864 convalescing in Annapolis, Maryland, and his home in Brunswick. He never completely recovered, however, and would suffer pain from his wounds for the rest of his life. Nevertheless, Chamberlain chose to return to the Army of the Potomac in February 1865, as the army began its final campaign against Robert E. Lee and the Army of Northern Virginia. His brigade played a key role in the battles of White Oak Road and Five Forks during Lee's desperate attempt to escape Petersburg. Chamberlain was wounded again, but he achieved distinction when he single-handedly reversed a Union retreat. He was able to remain in the field and was present at Appomattox Court-House. Grant, aware of Chamberlain's reputation as a brave and inspiring battlefield commander, selected him to conduct the formal infantry surrender ceremonies. Just before mustering out of the service, Chamberlain was breveted to major general.

Chamberlain returned to Maine a decorated hero, wounded six times. In 1866 he became the governor of Maine by the largest margin in that state's history, and he was reelected for three more one-year terms. When he left politics in 1870 he was the unanimous choice to become president of Bowdoin College, the institution that only reluctantly had let him go to war. At Bowdoin he instituted a drill system and military science program for all students, feeling that military training was a bene-ficial augmentation of academic study and that future wars were inevitable. Within a year, a major uprising of students forced Chamberlain to threaten expulsion for anyone who refused to drill. Although he broke this student strike, the college first made the program voluntary and then abolished it within a decade.

After stepping down as Bowdoin's president in 1883, Chamberlain spent his remaining years in various business ventures and participating in veteran's organizations. In his final days he attended the fiftieth anniversary of Gettysburg and penned a book, published posthumously as *The Passing of the Armies*. This memoir is an account of the war's closing months and is considered one of the best personal narratives of the war. He died on 24 February 1914 from an infection in the hip wound suffered at Petersburg.

—*Richard D. Loosbrock*

See also Appomattox Court House; Gettysburg, Battle of; Petersburg Campaign.

For further reading:

Linderman, Gerald F. *Embattled Courage: The Experience of Combat in the Civil War* (1987).

Nesbitt, Mark. *Through Blood and Fire: Selected Civil War Papers of Major General Joshua Lawrence Chamberlain* (1996).

Trulock, Alice Rains. *In the Hands of Providence: Joshua L. Chamberlain and the American Civil War* (1992).

CHAMBERSBURG, BURNING OF
(July 1864)

Chambersburg, Pennsylvania, gained national notoriety when Confederate raiders under the command of General John McCausland torched it on 30 July 1864. Home to some 5,200 residents, the town lay about twenty miles north of the Mason-Dixon Line. In October 1862, Jeb Stuart's Cavalry had briefly occupied the town, which surrendered without resistance. Between 15 June and 2 July 1863, residents had faced a more substantial Confederate presence while General Robert E. Lee used Chambersburg as a concentration point for the Confederate army. Residents were largely spared full-scale looting and destruction by Lee's General Orders No. 72 and 73, which forbade injury to private property. A year later, Chambersburg was the military headquarters for the Union Department of the Susquehanna, with thousands of Northern soldiers stationed near town.

The Chambersburg raid was most directly inspired by General David Hunter's unprovoked burning of homes of three prominent Southern sympathizers in West Virginia. In return, Confederates would burn Northern homes. On 28 July, General Jubal Early put Brigadier General John McCausland in charge of a cavalry detachment that was to occupy Chambersburg and demanded $500,000 in greenbacks or $100,000 in gold as compensation for the houses that Hunter had ordered destroyed. Early and McCausland had used this strategy a few weeks earlier, raising $200,000 from Frederick, Maryland, residents. Reaching Franklin County on 29 June, McCausland found his progress slowed by a small regiment of Union cavalry, buying time for trains to leave Chambersburg with supplies, equipment, and most of the borough's cash reserves. The first Confederates arrived at Chambersburg at dawn on June 30 and swiftly occupied the town.

Chambersburg's citizens were summoned to the town center, presented with Early's demands, and given a deadline of three to six hours (depending on account) in which to produce the cash, or the town would be "laid in ashes." When the citizens refused and the deadline expired, McCausland ordered his men to fire the town. Accounts of the burning vary widely. Chambersburg residents described violent, drunken Confederates and mass looting, while Confederates tended to report a more orderly operation, although marred by a few soldiers bent on revenge or spurred on by liquor. At least one colonel refused to carry out the order to burn and was arrested, but charges were dropped the next day. No one died in the fire, but more than 550 structures were destroyed, leaving 3,000 people homeless. A state commission, set up after the war to handle property claims, estimated total damage to real and personal property at $1,628,431.

Until their deaths, McCausland and Early defended the burning as a necessary act. McCausland's raid, however, did little more than provide Confederates with a modicum of revenge while doing nothing to advance Confederate strategic and military aims. It actually hurt the Confederacy, causing Ulysses S. Grant to bring Union forces in the valley under the unified command of General Philip Sheridan. Sheridan took decisive control of the area by the end of 1864, and Chambersburg was prospering again within two years of the raid.

—*Anne Sarah Rubin*

See also Chambersburg Raid; Early, Jubal A.; Early's Washington Raid; Hunter, David; McCausland, John; Pennsylvania;

For further reading:

Alexander, Ted, et al. *Southern Revenge! Civil War History of Chambersburg, Pennsylvania* (1989).

Hoke, Jacob. *Historical Reminiscences of the War or Incidents which Transpired in and about Chambersburg during the War of the Rebellion* (1884).

Schenck, Reverend B. S. *The Burning of Chambersburg, Pennsylvania* (1864).

Smith, Everard H. "Chambersburg: Anatomy of a Confederate Reprisal." *The American Historical Review* (1991).

CHAMBERSBURG RAID
(9–12 October 1862)

One of Major General J. E. B. Stuart's most famous raids, the Chambersburg Raid became known as his "second ride around McClellan." Stuart handpicked 600 men each from the brigades of W. H. F. Lee, Wade Hampton, and W. E. "Grumble" Jones, and a four-gun detachment under Major John Pelham. Their objectives were to learn what they could of McClellan's army in Maryland; destroy the Cumberland Valley Railroad bridge over Conococheague Creek near Chambersburg, Pennsylvania; capture government officials to exchange for Southern prisoners; and capture horses and mules.

Crossing the Potomac at McCoy's Ford at dawn on 10 October, they narrowly missed six regiments of Federal infantry under Major General Jacob Cox. Rain hampered Union army signal stations, and when the raiders reached Chambersburg around 7:00 P.M., some prominent citizens surrendered the town. Stuart left Chambersburg early the next morning. A detail left behind under Colonel M. C. Butler destroyed 5,000 muskets and other weapons and burned the railroad depots, machine shops, and much rolling stock, although they could not burn the iron railroad bridge.

Believing that Cox's regiments would be waiting for him if he returned the way he had come, Stuart decided to ride east, then south, again taking his men around McClellan's army. The route would be twice as long but would surprise the enemy. At Cashtown, Stuart turned south and entered Maryland near Emmitsburg, where Southern sympathizers greeted him. Local troopers guided Stuart along back roads to avoid detection, and the men rode day and night, sometimes dozing in the saddle. After midnight, Stuart and a small party took a side-trip to visit a young woman he had met during the Antietam campaign, rejoining the column about 7:00 A.M.

Stuart had reports that Brigadier General George Stoneman and several thousand men were ahead of them, guarding the Potomac fords. A local officer recommended that Stuart use White's Ford, three miles below the mouth of the Monocacy. W. H. F. Lee's brigade was in the advance as the Rebels neared the ford, where 200 Union infantrymen blocked their way. Lee bluffed, demanding their surrender, and the Union soldiers abandoned their position as Lee began to attack. Pelham's guns kept them back while Stuart's men forded the river. Helped by the Union commanders' slow reactions, Stuart's force had safely slipped through a region guarded by more than 100,000 of McClellan's men.

Lee considered the raid "eminently successful." Stuart had brought the war to Northern territory and embarrassed the Union army. The raid contributed to Lincoln's dissatisfaction with McClellan and hastened the president's replacement of him as commander of the Army of the Potomac.

—*David A. Norris*

See also Stuart, J. E. B.; Stuart's Dumfries Raid; Stuart's First Ride around McClellan.

For further reading:

Blackford, W. W. *War Years With Jeb Stuart* (1945; reprint, 1993).

Freeman, Douglas Southall. *Lee's Lieutenants: A Study in Command* (1942–1944).
McClellan, Henry B. *The Life and Campaigns of Major General J. E. B. Stuart, Commander of the Cavalry of the Army of Northern Virginia* (1885).
Thomas, Emory. *Bold Dragoon: The Life of J. E. B. Stuart* (1988).

CHAMPION'S HILL, BATTLE OF
(16 May 1863)

General Ulysses S. Grant, commanding the Federal Army of the Tennessee, had accomplished the dangerous feat of running his army past the Confederate fortress at Vicksburg on the Mississippi River in April 1863. Grant was now in a position to move upon the rebel bastion. However, he knew that Confederate General Joseph E. Johnston was organizing an army at Jackson, the capital of Mississippi. If Grant moved immediately on Vicksburg, he might find himself trapped between two enemy armies. Therefore, the Federals marched toward Jackson to eliminate that threat while also preventing the two Confederate armies from uniting.

On 14 May, two of Grant's three corps, commanded by Generals William T. Sherman and James B. McPherson, attacked and defeated Johnston's Confederates at Jackson. While Sherman's XV Corps remained in Jackson, McPherson's XVII Corps joined General John A. McClernand's XIII Corps and headed west. On 16 May the decisive battle of the entire Vicksburg campaign was fought at a place about halfway between Jackson and Vicksburg.

The Confederates, commanded by General John C. Pemberton, occupied a height that was variously called Midway Hill or Champion's Hill. The name Midway Hill was used because it was about halfway between Jackson and Vicksburg. Champion's Hill was the more common name and was derived from the owner's name. The hill was about 60 to 70 feet high and the Vicksburg and Clinton Road ran over its crest. To the south of the hill (or left from the position of the approaching Federal army), the terrain was severely broken, cut up with ravines, hills, and tangled woods. This land was virtually impassable for an invading army. On the north side of the hill, the terrain was more accessible to an attacking force. Open and undulating fields dominated this terrain, which was the primary site of the engagement.

The Federal forces, numbering approximately 30,000 men, advanced on Champion's Hill in three columns. On the left was General Andrew J. Smith's division of McClernand's XIII Corps. Because of the nature of the terrain, Smith's men played only a minor role in the battle. In the center was General Peter Osterhaus's division of McClernand's corps. These men also had virtually no role in the battle because of the terrain. The battle would be fought almost entirely on the right of the Federal line. On the right were General Alvin P. Hovey's division of McClernand's corps and Generals John A. Logan and Marcellus M. Crocker's divisions of McPherson's XVII Corps. Also on the right were Generals Grant and McPherson.

Opposing this formidable array of blue-clad troopers were approximately 20,000 Confederates under General Pemberton. Confronting the left and center of the Federal line were the divisions of Generals John S. Bowen and William W. Loring, while General Carter L. Stevenson's division bore the brunt of the attack from the Union right.

The battle on the right commenced at about 10:30 A.M. when General Hovey threw out skirmishers. Logan's division was positioned on Hovey's right and Crocker constituted the reserve. By 11:00 A.M. the fighting started in earnest. The Federal line advanced up the slope of Champion's Hill against a withering Confederate fire. For several hours the combatants clashed and the crossroads on the hill changed hands three times. At approximately 2:30 P.M. General Hovey brought out his artillery, placing his heavy guns between his troops and Logan's men. This bombardment succeeded and Logan's division followed with a bayonet charge. By 3:00 P.M. the battle was over.

The Confederates, who suffered some 3,800 casualties, beat a hasty retreat toward Vicksburg. The Federals suffered about 2,400 casualties and followed closely behind the withdrawing enemy. The battle of Champion's Hill was a significant engagement, the most important of the entire Vicksburg campaign. It prevented a junction between Generals Johnston and Pemberton and opened the way to Vicksburg.

—*Christopher C. Meyers*

See also Jackson, Mississippi; Pemberton, John C.
For further reading:
Bearss, Edwin C. *The Campaign for Vicksburg* (1985–1986).
Miers, Earl Schenck. *The Web of Victory: Grant at Vicksburg* (1955; reprint, 1983).

CHANCELLORSVILLE, BATTLE OF
(2–3 May 1863)

A brick tavern and family residence at the intersection of the Orange Turnpike and Orange Plank Road, Chancellorsville lent its name to one of the most important battles of the Civil War. Situated at the strategic intersection of five roads in the heavily wooded region north of Fredericksburg, Virginia, Chancellorsville evolved as one of Robert E. Lee and Lieutenant General Thomas J. "Stonewall" Jackson's greatest triumphs.

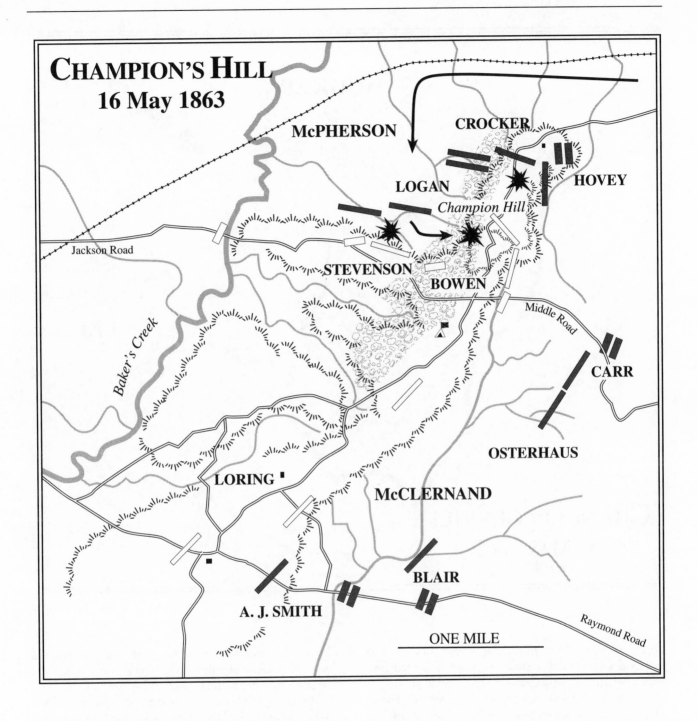

CHAMPION'S HILL
16 May 1863

McPHERSON

CROCKER

LOGAN

Champion Hill

HOVEY

Jackson Road

STEVENSON

BOWEN

Baker's Creek

Middle Road

CARR

OSTERHAUS

LORING

McCLERNAND

BLAIR

A. J. SMITH

ONE MILE

Raymond Road

Since assuming command of the Army of the Potomac in January 1863, Union major general Joseph "Fighting Joe" Hooker focused his efforts on rebuilding his army after the previous December's debacle at Fredericksburg. His army of 130,000 shouldered the finest weapons, wore the best uniforms, and ate the highest quality rations the United States could supply. His army included over 11,000 cavalry in a newly organized corps and 496 modern, rifled artillery pieces. With new equipment and daily drilling, Hooker considered the Army of the Potomac the finest army in the world. He also created an efficient intelligence service and integrated a tactical

cover and deception operation into his plans to dislodge Lee from the trenches at Fredericksburg.

Through an adroit use of spies, line crossers, Confederate deserters, Union sympathizers, and intercepted Confederate semaphore messages, Hooker learned of the Confederate weakness around Fredericksburg. He received numerous reports of how thin Lee's line was along the Rappahannock River. Frequent updates from the Confederate side of the river allowed Hooker to formulate a plan that initially deceived Lee and allowed the Union general to steal a march around the Confederate left flank. Hooker, unlike

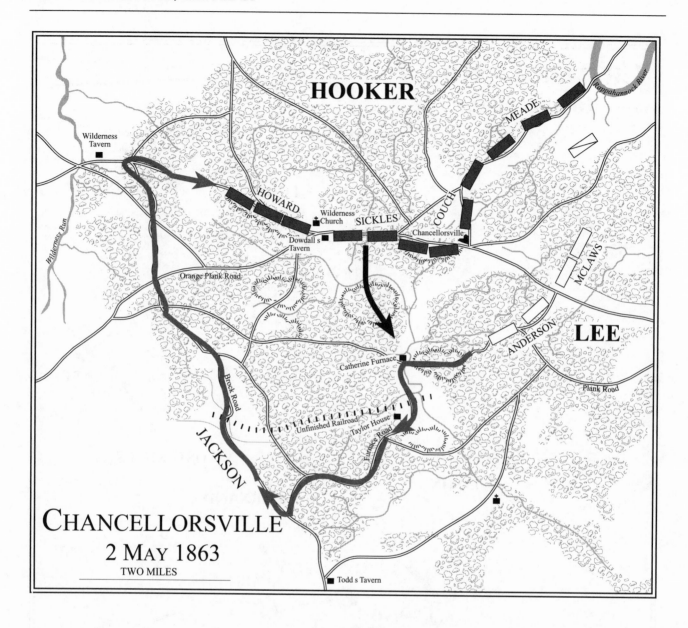

HOOKER

MEADE

Rappahannock River

Wilderness
Tavern

Wilderness Run

HOWARD

Wilderness
Church

SICKLES

COUCH

Chancellorsville

Dowdall's
Tavern

MCLAWS

Orange Plank Road

ANDERSON

LEE

Catherine Furnace

Plank Road

Brock Road

Unfinished Railroad

Taylor House

Furnace Road

JACKSON

CHANCELLORSVILLE
2 MAY 1863
TWO MILES

Todd's Tavern

most Union generals in similar circumstances, also possessed a remarkably accurate estimate of Confederate troop strength before undertaking the campaign.

Across the Rappahannock, spread along the river's edge for almost twenty-five miles, Lee's Army of Northern Virginia numbered about 60,000 effectives. Just off a hard winter, Lee's men resembled scarecrows more than soldiers. Tattered remnants of uniforms covered their malnourished frames and many lacked adequate footgear. They subsisted on a few ounces of cornmeal and bacon a day, the bacon rancid as often as not.

The gaunt Confederate horses and mules suffered from lack of fodder as well. A single rail line ran to the rear of the Confederate line at Fredericksburg and proved insufficient to supply Lee's army. As a result he sent over 400 artillery horses to winter pasture farther south. Due to supply shortages and to counter a Federal

threat to southeast Virginia, Lee had dispatched Lieutenant General James Longstreet's Corps to Suffolk, Virginia, thus depriving himself of his largest corps.

Hooker's well-conceived strategy consisted of three major maneuvers. First, he would send his cavalry, commanded by Major General George Stoneman, far upriver with the double mission of drawing Lee's cavalry screen away from the Confederate left flank and then raiding deep into Virginia to disrupt Lee's supply line from Richmond. Second, he directed Major General John Sedgwick, with I and VI Corps, to deploy across from Fredericksburg and by strong demonstrations to divert Lee's attention from the main Union attack. If Lee weakened his line, Sedgwick was to cross the Rappahannock below Fredericksburg to become the left wing of a double envelopment, crushing Lee's retreating army. Major General Daniel Sickles's III Corps would

Union artillery before Chancellorsville, 1863 (*Library of Congress*)

remain on Stafford Heights across from Fredericksburg to command the city with its long-range artillery. Third, Hooker planned to march upriver with Major Generals George G. Meade's V, Oliver O. Howard's XI, and Henry W. Slocum's XII Corps. This force would rapidly cross the Rappahannock and crash down on Lee's unprotected left flank. Hooker believed that whether Lee chose to remain and fight or retreat toward Richmond, Hooker could destroy the Army of Northern Virginia with his superior force.

During mid-April Hooker set his plan in motion. He directed both cavalry and infantry demonstrations at all the major crossing sites in the vicinity of Fredericksburg. Lee believed that Hooker's main thrust would come from the north. Yet with all the Union activity, he could not afford to redeploy his troops until he was sure of the main point of attack. Hooker had further convoluted the situation with false messages indicating Stoneman's ultimate objective was the Shenandoah Valley. In all, his deceptions allowed Hooker to steal a march on Lee, something seldom, if ever, accomplished by Union generals. In fact, Hooker's turning movement on Lee is arguably the greatest intelligence coup of the Civil War.

On 28 April Stoneman's cavalry, hampered by inclement weather and muddy roads, finally initiated the campaign by crossing the Rappahannock and riding behind Lee's lines. Hooker's plan, however, began to unravel when Major General J. E. B. Stuart countered Stoneman's raid with a small detachment of Confederate cavalry. Discerning that Stoneman's purported thrust

toward the valley was a ruse, Stuart rapidly realigned his horsemen along the river to screen Lee's left flank. Stoneman's harried command would ride through the Virginia woods for a week without accomplishing either the diversion of Confederate cavalry or the disruption of Lee's railroad to the south.

On 29 April, Hooker pushed through Stuart's cavalry screen at Kelly's Ford north of Fredericksburg and then moved across the Rapidan River at Germanna and Ely's Fords. While Hooker's troops fought their way through Stuart's small but slashing cavalry attacks and the almost impenetrable wilderness around Chancellorsville, Sedgwick threw two pontoon bridges across the Rappahannock River in front of Jackson's positions south of Fredericksburg. Both Lee and Jackson wanted to destroy one of the Union wings, but they disagreed about which one to attack. Lee decided to wait for the situation to develop further before committing himself to a pitched battle. He did, nonetheless, order Major General Richard Anderson to move his division toward Chancellorsville to confront any Yankee advance toward Fredericksburg.

On 30 April, when Hooker unaccountably halted his advance and consolidated his position, he lost the initiative and allowed Lee time to maneuver against him. In part, Hooker's hesitation and his fading confidence resulted from his advance elements meeting stronger resistance than he had expected. Actually, he could have easily broken the thin Confederate line and advanced on both the Orange Turnpike and Plank Road. Historians still debate whether Hooker was drunk during

Confederates killed in Sedgwick's assault on Marye's Heights at Fredericksburg, 3 May 1863,
during the Chancellorsville campaign (Photograph by Andrew J. Russell / *National Archives*)

the campaign. Known for his high consumption of alcohol, Hooker supposedly swore off liquor for the campaign, but some contemporary evidence indicated that he returned to his bottle for liquid courage when confronted by the determined Confederates.

When Stuart's patrols and prisoners confirmed the large Federal force advancing from the north, Lee realized that the main attack was at Chancellorsville and Sedgwick's river crossing was only a diversion. Lee immediately ordered Major General Jubal Early, with less than 10,000 effectives, to defend Fredericksburg from the trenches along Marye's Heights. Lee would shift most of his army to meet Hooker's advance. From Early's left, Lee immediately sent two brigades from Major General Lafayette McLaws's division to support Anderson near Zion Church Ridge east of Chancellorsville. Lee then directed Jackson to withdraw his men from their defensive line and move toward Chancellorsville. He also ordered Stuart to ascertain the size and locations of the Union force struggling through the underbrush around Chancellorsville.

Early on the morning of 1 May, Jackson donned a new

uniform and led his corps to engage the Yankees east of Chancellorsville. When he arrived at the Confederate lines about 8 A.M., he promptly organized an attack with its axis of advance westward along both the Orange Turnpike and Plank Road. About 11:30 A.M. the Confederate skirmishers encountered the Union advance guard plodding east on the same roads. Without adequate cavalry support, the surprised Federal brigades grudgingly gave way to the advancing Rebel infantrymen. Lee soon arrived on the battlefield and assumed command from Jackson.

Utilizing an unfinished railroad bed graded through the thickets, Lee's infantry turned the Union right and forced Hooker to bend his southern flank almost 90 degrees to meet the threat. By sundown, stiffening Federal resistance halted Lee's advance through the darkening woods. Even though Sickles's and Darius Couch's corps had crossed the Rappahannock to reinforce him, Hooker unaccountably—and against his corps commanders' advice—ordered his men to return to their positions of the previous night.

Seeking an opening for a morning attack, Lee

dispatched several of his staff officers to evaluate the Federal line, while he and Jackson sat at a campfire awaiting a report from Stuart. Upon their return, members of Lee's staff adjudged the Union defenses too formidable for a frontal assault. Stuart and a local Confederate sympathizer, Charles C. Welford, on the other hand, arrived with much more decisive intelligence. Fitzhugh Lee's cavalry had discovered Hooker's unprotected right flank dangling in the wilderness, and Welford offered to lead the Confederates around Catherine's Furnace and westward along little-known forest trails to exploit the situation. Lee had discovered Hooker's weakness.

With this information Jackson, with Lee's concurrence, formulated a plan that ignored most of the basic principles of war. His audacious plan called for Lee to hold Hooker in place with only 15,000 troops, while Jackson looped to the west with approximately 30,000 soldiers to attack the unprotected Union flank.

At 4 A.M. on 2 May, Lee held a final conference with Jackson and then ordered the day's operations to commence. Jackson led the divisions of Robert Rodes, R. E. Colston, A. P. Hill, J. J. Archer, E. L. Thomas, and finally his artillery on a twelve-mile circuitous march through the heat of the day. To cover Jackson's movements, Lee committed both Anderson's and McLaws's divisions in lines of skirmishers to make Hooker think it was a major assault. When one of Sickles's divisions, situated on the high ground of Hazel Grove about one mile south of Chancellorsville, reported Confederate troops moving south near Catherine's Furnace, Hooker thought it was evidence of Lee retreating. Oliver O. Howard, deployed on the Union right, reported that he had also seen this maneuver, but he was preparing for an attack from the west. Howard was counting on the tangled wilderness and only 700 men to defend his right flank. Unconcerned, Hooker turned his attention to Lee's bothersome attacks east of the Chancellorsville crossroads. To put more pressure on what he mistakenly thought to be a retreating army, he ordered Sedgwick to attack the Confederate positions at Fredericksburg.

Jackson's advance units did not arrive on a high wooded ridge west of Howard's XI Corps until midafternoon. Jackson's assault was delayed by his desire to gain the best position on the Federal right flank. As his brigades arrived Jackson arrayed them in an attack formation almost two miles long. In the fading daylight

Wounded soldiers being tended in the field after the battle of Chancellorsville, 2 May 1863 (*National Archives*)

Jackson quietly ordered his division commanders to commence their attacks.

As Howard's men prepared their supper, a hoard of screaming Confederate infantrymen burst from the woods and routed the astonished Yankees. Jackson's men irresistibly surged forward for over two miles before gathering darkness, loss of unit cohesion in the woods, and increasing Federal resistance finally halted their advance. When Jackson returned from a personal reconnaissance ahead of his disjointed units about 9 P.M., troops from the 18th North Carolina Infantry mistook his party in the darkness for Union cavalry and fired on it. Several of his staff fell wounded, and Jackson was hit in three places. Early the next day surgeons amputated his shattered left arm. He began a normal recovery but developed pneumonia and died on 10 May. Lee and the Confederacy lost one of their most aggressive generals, a loss that would be sorely felt at Gettysburg two months later.

Stuart assumed temporary command of Jackson's corps after Jackson and his senior infantry officers fell wounded. During the night, Stuart prepared to resume the attack and drive on Chancellorsville. Confederate artillery officers identified the high ground at Hazel Grove as key to the battle, and Stuart planned to seize it at dawn. Hooker abandoned this decisive terrain before Stuart ordered his men forward, however, and Rebel artillerymen rushed to occupy the commanding terrain. Desperate fighting in the woods between Hazel Grove and Chancellorsville exacted more casualties on 3 May than had Jackson's flank attack.

Concentrated Confederate cannon fire from Hazel Grove added to Union casualties and disorder. A shell struck the column on which Hooker was leaning at Chancellor's Tavern and further addled the already disconcerted general. After a shot of brandy, Hooker ordered a general withdrawal to the north. With his separated command linked together, Lee rode triumphantly to Chancellorsville Cross Roads among his cheering men.

The situation at Fredericksburg, however, demanded Lee's immediate attention. Sedgwick, after three bloody assaults, had broken through Early's positions at Marye's Heights and the Federals were advancing on Lee's rear. The Confederate commander quickly disengaged McLaws's Division and ordered him east to meet Sedgwick. McLaws failed to react with alacrity, but General Willcox's men halted the Union troops at Salem Church, four miles west of Fredericksburg. Lee arrived on the morning of 4 May to coordinate an attack that regained Marye's Heights and forced Sedgwick to retire across the Rappahannock that night.

On 5–6 May Hooker, against most of his subordinates' advice, abandoned his line north of Chancellorsville and retreated across the Rappahannock. At any point during the campaign either of Hooker's wings outnumbered their opponents and could have achieved his primary goal of

driving Lee back toward Richmond if Hooker had followed his original plan. Yet Hooker's vaunted intelligence operation broke down at the crucial moment. The absence of Stoneman's cavalry meant that Hooker was deprived of intelligence about Confederate strength and positions; with such information he may well have won the battle.

Lee suffered about 13,000 casualties to Hooker's 18,000. Yet the most portentous casualty was Stonewall Jackson, whose death on 10 May required that Lee reorganize the Army of Northern Virginia. While the spectacular victory at Chancellorsville presented Lee with an opportunity to invade the North, it would not be the same army that did so. He and his men would carry an effusive confidence into battle at Gettysburg. There awaited the grim discovery that they were not invincible.

—*Stanley S. McGowen*

See also Fredericksburg, Second Battle of; Hooker, Joseph; Howard, Oliver O.; Jackson, Thomas J.; Lee, Robert E.; Mud March; Salem Church, Battle of; Stoneman, George.

For further reading:
Fishel, Edwin, C. *The Secret War for the Union* (1996).
Furgurson, Ernest B. *Chancellorsville, 1863: The Souls of the Brave* (1992).
Gallagher, Gary W., ed. *Chancellorsville: The Battle and Its Aftermath* (1996).
Robertson, James I., Jr. *Stonewall Jackson: The Man, the Soldier, the Legend* (1997).
Sears, Stephen W. *Chancellorsville* (1996).

CHANDLER, ZACHARIAH
(1813–1879)
U.S. senator and cabinet officer

Zachariah Chandler was born in Bedford, New Hampshire, on 10 September 1813. The son of Samuel Chandler and Margaret Orr, Chandler came from a long line of Puritan stock, descending from a William Chandler, who emigrated to New England during the Great Migration of the late 1630s. Chandler was educated in Bedford schools until he was 15. He then attended academies in nearby Pembroke and Derry, graduating when he was 16 years old. After graduation, he taught school for one year in the Piscataquog or "Squog" district. In 1833 Chandler began working as a clerk for the firm of Kendrick and Foster in nearby Nashua. Later that year, he decided to move to Michigan territory with brother-in-law, Franklin Moore. Using $1,000 that Chandler had received from his father, Chandler and Moore began a dry goods business in the small town of Detroit.

Chandler quickly rose to prominence in Detroit. An energetic and ambitious businessman, Chandler dissolved his partnership with Moore in 1836 and struck out on his own. Supplying farmers who came to Detroit for market, Chandler quickly accelerated his business operations, eventually expanding into wholesale dry goods, which he supplied throughout the interior of Michigan. Chandler invested profits from his business into real estate, toll roads, and railroads. At the time of his death, he had a personal estate of $2 million. At age 31, Chandler married Letitia Grace Douglass, a wealthy New Yorker. The Chandlers had one daughter, Minnie, who was born in 1848.

Chandler took an interest in local politics shortly after arriving in Detroit; however, he did not run for office until 1850. In that year, he was elected as a Whig delegate to the Michigan Constitutional Convention. In 1851, he was nominated as the Whig mayoral candidate for the city of Detroit and defeated Democratic candidate John R. Williams. In 1852, Chandler was the Whig candidate for governor of Michigan, but was defeated by Democrat Robert McClelland. In the aftermath of the Kansas-Nebraska Act, Chandler was one of the leading Michigan Whigs favoring fusion with disgruntled Democrats and Free Soilers. He played an active role in the July 1854 Republican Convention at Jackson, Michigan, and in 1856 was elected as a delegate to the Republican National Convention in Philadelphia. Although as the first Republican gubernatorial nominee he was overlooked in favor of Kinsley S. Bingham, Chandler was regarded as a strong senatorial candidate to contest the seat of Lewis Cass in 1857. As a result of Republican electoral victory in Michigan in 1856, the Michigan legislature chose Chandler as its U.S. senator in March 1857.

Chandler was elected to three successive terms in the U.S. Senate. His skillful use of patronage allowed him to dominate Michigan politics for almost twenty years. As a U.S. senator, Chandler applied the same vigor and ambition that had characterized his business career. Throughout his senatorial career, he advocated protective tariffs, internal improvements, and other measures generally supportive of business, principles that were in accordance with his Whig background. In foreign policy, Chandler was a persistent Anglophobe who spoke frequently of annexing Canada. Consistent with his Republican principles, Chandler supported antislavery measures and spoke out frequently against slavery and the South.

During the secession crisis, Chandler was outspoken in his demand that newly elected President Abraham Lincoln make no compromises with any of the seceded states. "Without a little blood-letting," Chandler wrote Michigan governor Austin Blair, "this Union will not…be worth a rush." Throughout the war, Chandler advocated harsh, rigorous measures, including emancipation, the arming of black troops, and confiscation of rebel property. As a member of the powerful Committee on the Conduct of the War, Chandler was a persistent critic of Democratic generals that the Committee deemed too cautious and timid. Perhaps his most controversial act as a member of the committee was a highly charged and partisan speech delivered in the Senate in July 1862 criticizing then commander of the Army of the Potomac, George B. McClellan. Although Chandler and other Radical Republicans disagreed with Lincoln on the pivotal issue of Reconstruction, Chandler played an important role in unifying the Republican Party in the 1864 presidential election. While a number of party radicals were tempted to support the third-party candidacy of John C. Frémont, Chandler help arrange a deal whereby Frémont withdrew his candidacy in exchange for the resignation of Postmaster General Montgomery Blair. Because Blair was a conservative Republican who was hated by many radicals, his removal from the cabinet helped convince many Radical Republicans to support Lincoln in the presidential election.

After the war, Chandler became a forceful advocate of Radical Reconstruction and a bitter opponent of his former Senate colleague, President Andrew Johnson. A proponent of impeachment, Chandler was outspoken in his denunciation of Johnson and his Republican colleagues who voted to acquit Johnson. While some Republicans became disillusioned with the administration of Ulysses Grant and tired of Radical Reconstruction, Chandler became a loyal supporter of Grant, who continued to favor Radical Reconstruction. When disillusioned Republicans united with Democrats to nominate Horace Greeley to oppose Grant's reelection in 1872, Chandler had nothing but contempt for his former colleagues.

In 1875 Chandler was defeated in his quest for a fourth successive Senate term. He was appointed as Secretary of the Interior in the last days of the Grant administration and was also appointed national chair of the 1876 Republican presidential campaign. Despite his lack of enthusiasm for presidential nominee Rutherford B. Hayes, Chandler applied his usual energy to the campaign, even contributing personal funds. Denied an appointment to Hayes's cabinet, Chandler finally retired to his farm near Lansing, Michigan. In 1879, however, Chandler came out of retirement when Senator Isaac Christiancy resigned his Senate seat, and Chandler was chosen to complete the term. It would prove to be a brief return. While campaigning for the Republican Party in October 1879, Chandler suffered a stroke in his hotel room in Chicago and died on 31 October 1879. In a political career that spanned over twenty years, Chandler began as a Whig, turned into a Radical Republican reformer, and ended his career as a Republican stalwart.

—*Bruce Tap*

See also Johnson, Andrew; Radical Republicans; Republican Party.
For further reading:
The Detroit Post and Tribune. *Zachariah Chandler: An Outline of His Life and Public Service* (1880).

George, Sister Mary Karl. *Zachariah Chandler: A Political Biography* (1969).

Harris, Wilmer C. *Public Life of Zachariah Chandler, 1851–1875* (1917).

CHANTILLY, BATTLE OF
(1 September 1862)

Robert E. Lee was not a completely satisfied man on the morning of 31 August 1862. Although Lee had just won a spectacular victory at the Second Bull Run, John Pope's army still retained its organization and a great deal of fighting spirit as it regrouped in a strong defensive position at Centreville. However, Lee still had room to maneuver before he ran up against the powerful defenses of Washington and was determined to make the most of it. He ordered Thomas J. "Stonewall" Jackson to take his command north along the Gum Springs Road to the Little River Turnpike. From there, he was to march eastward just past the tiny hamlet of Germantown where the turnpike intersected Pope's line of communications along the Warrenton Turnpike. James Longstreet's command would maneuver in front of Centreville to hold Pope there and then follow Jackson.

Shortly after noon on 31 August, Jackson's men, screened by J. E. B. Stuart's cavalry, began their march. After a ten-mile hike through heavy rain, they reached Pleasant Valley Church on the Little River Turnpike several miles west of Germantown and bivouacked there for the night. Stuart's cavalry, however, reached Germantown by the early evening and could see Federal wagons moving along the Warrenton Turnpike. Stuart decided to have a little fun and ordered his two cannon to fire on them, causing "commotion, up-setting, collisions, and smash-ups," before heading back down the Little River Turnpike to make camp north of where it intersected the Ox Road at Ox Hill.

As this was going on, Pope was sticking to General-in-Chief Henry Halleck's instructions not to abandon Centreville. On the morning of 1 September, however, evidence of the Confederate flanking march arrived. Pope responded by ordering Joseph Hooker to take a division to Germantown and block the Confederate line of march to Fairfax. Hooker reached Germantown at around 2:30 P.M. and posted his men on high ground east of where the Little River Turnpike crossed Difficult Run. By that time, Pope had finally decided to abandon Centreville and was retreating east along the Warrenton Turnpike with Jesse Reno's IX Corps leading the way.

Jackson reached Ox Hill at about the same time Hooker arrived at Germantown. He then pushed Stuart, supported by infantry and artillery, east along Little River

Turnpike toward Fairfax. Stuart encountered Hooker's line and reported to Jackson that it was too strong to be attacked successfully with the force on hand. So Jackson decided to halt operations at around 4 P.M. and wait for Longstreet to arrive before determining what to do next.

Just then, Isaac I. Stevens, commander of the lead division of Reno's corps, rode up to a knoll north of the Warrenton Turnpike and caught a glimpse of the skirmish line Jackson had pushed south to watch Pope's line of retreat. As storm clouds rolled in from the southwest, Stevens then ordered his division into line and led it north toward Ox Hill.

At approximately 5:00 P.M. the battle of Chantilly, or Ox Hill, began—as did what one participant would describe as "one of the wildest rainstorms I ever witnessed." As lightning and thunder crashed, the wind howled, and a torrential downpour drenched the combatants, Stevens's division smashed into the Confederate line north of the Reid house and caused a Louisiana brigade to break and run. Then, however, a bullet struck Stevens in the head, killing him instantly. Devastated by the loss of their leader, the Federals became dispirited and before long were falling back. A brigade from Philip Kearny's division of Samuel Heintzelman's corps arrived on the battlefield and pushed forward into a cornfield north of the Reid house where a desperate hand-to-hand struggle ensued. Learning of a possible gap in the Federal line, Kearny rode forward into the cornfield for a personal reconnaissance. There he encountered an unidentified force that turned out to be Confederate and demanded his surrender. Kearny refused and attempted to escape, but he was cut down by a Confederate bullet.

Shortly after Kearny fell, the battle wound down as officers and men on both sides recognized the futility of continuing the fight in the darkness and rain. By 6:30 the battle was over. Jackson had lost approximately 500 of the 15,000 men he had on hand; about 700 of the 6,000 Federals engaged became casualties. Later that night Pope's army began arriving at Fairfax Court House. Lee had run out of room to maneuver in Virginia. His next move would take the war across the Potomac into Maryland.

—*Ethan S. Rafuse*

See also Kearny, Philip.
For further reading:
Harsh, Joseph L. *Confederate Tide Rising: Robert E. Lee and the Making of Southern Strategy, 1861–1862* (1998).
Hennessy, John J. *Return to Bull Run: The Campaign and Battle of Second Manassas* (1993).
Smith, Robert Ross. "Ox Hill: The Most Neglected Battle of the Civil War, 1 September 1862." In *Fairfax County and the War Between the States* (1961).
U.S. War Department. *The War of the Rebellion: A Compilation of the Official Records of the Union and Confederate Armies* (1880–1901).

General Kearny's charge at Chantilly, 1 September 1862 (*Library of Congress*)

CHAPLAINS

At the outbreak of the Civil War, neither side had an official policy regarding chaplains. In May 1861 the U.S. War Department issued General Orders 15 and 16, which provided for the appointment of "regularly ordained" ministers of a "Christian denomination" to become chaplains by vote of the regimental officers. Union chaplains received little guidance. Congress and the War Department left responsibilities to the chaplain and the denomination. Army regulations only required reporting on the moral and religious state of the troops and making suggestions for improving social conditions. It was not until 1864 that holding regular services was required. In the absence of specific duties, Union chaplains relied on *The Army Chaplain, His Office, Duties, and Responsibilities, and the Means of Aiding Him* by the Reverend William Young Brown. It outlined some of the most necessary traits for chaplains, foremost of which was "ardent piety." In addition, Brown said that they needed to have proficiency as teachers, as well as resolution, energy, good health, and courage. U.S. Army chaplains received $100 a month. Approximately 2,300 served the Union army as chaplains.

Chaplains from all major denominations served the Confederate army. Although the Confederate Congress passed Bill 102 authorizing the president to appoint chaplains, Jefferson Davis deferred to his commanders. As a result, units such as Thomas "Stonewall" Jackson's II Corps were especially well served. Still, the common practice was that most were elected by troops or selected by officers. In the Confederacy an estimated 640 men served as chaplains. Confederate chaplains started out earning $85 a month, but this was soon cut to $50. In 1862 the amount was raised to $80. Some Confederate units and denominations increased their chaplains' salary by subscription. Confederate army regulations made little mention of the duties of chaplains, and like their Union brethren, Confederate chaplains received little direction. Most relied on James O. Andrew's *Letter to the Chaplains in the Army*. The thin missive by the retired Methodist bishop urged the chaplains to work faithfully and not be discouraged. Chaplains' associations formed to discuss matters of mutual concern and to petition the Confederate Congress to prohibit parades, inspections, and other activities on the Sabbath. In addition to the military chaplaincy, the Confederate army recognized

Chaplains of the 9th Corps at Petersburg, Virginia, October 1864 (*Library of Congress*)

other religious workers. Although they had no military standing, army missionaries, army evangelists, and colporteurs often served as chaplains. Whatever their background, Confederate chaplains were largely credited with the revivals that swept army camps during the war.

Chaplains in both armies shared similar activities. They worked alone or with local clergy to hold religious service. They also held prayer meetings, conducted baptisms, distributed tracts, and oversaw moral order and temperance. Sermons focused on loyalty, courage, and the righteousness of their respective cause. Chaplains also wrote letters on behalf of sick, wounded, or illiterate soldiers and also tended camp libraries. In battle they went to the front lines to offer encouragement to stragglers, aid for the wounded, and last rites for the dying. Two Union chaplains received the Medal of Honor for single-handedly rescuing wounded soldiers under fire. After battle, chaplains served the field hospitals and also wrote letters to families of the recently deceased. If captured, they served as ordinary prisoners, though they often led religious services in the prisoner camps.

Chaplains on both sides sought to keep morale high, though as the war wore on for the Confederacy, increasing numbers of troops ignored the chaplains exhortations to fight bravely. Many chaplains began to adopt the theme of the lost cause and a God who deserted the Confederacy—all of which did nothing to improve morale. In the Union army, chaplains also worked to assist and teach former slaves. They also looked after freedmen serving in the army, some even serving as chaplains of the black regiments.

Although the chaplaincy was predominantly Protestant, Roman Catholics and Jews also had chaplains. As Protestants tended to view the army as a strong opportunity for evangelism, Catholics feared that they would "steal souls" from the Catholic ranks. In that light, Catholics began having priests become chaplains in the North and to a lesser degree in the South. Still, the Federal army had only forty priests, commonly called "Holy Joes," who served an estimated 200,000 Catholics in uniform, the majority Irish. Most priests served only short times because their bishops commonly recalled them to meet local diocese needs. Further inhibiting the influence of Catholics was the reluctance and often refusal of Protestant officers to accept priests as chaplains. As a consequence, Catholic chaplains served predominantly Catholic regiments. Even here, ethnicity was an issue; it was difficult to find and place qualified Irish priests with Irish units and German-speaking priests with German units. Still Catholic chaplains made their presence known, taking confessions before battle and working to improve the general moral order of the army camps.

Jewish chaplains also participated. In July 1861 as Clement Vallandigham's bill to allow ordained rabbis to become chaplains was going down to defeat, the 5th Pennsylvania Cavalry elected one of their own, Michael Allen, a Philadelphia Hebrew teacher, to be regimental chaplain where his messages were accepted by both Jew and gentile. When a Young Men's Christian Association worker challenged Allen's appointment, Allen resigned. Rabbi Arnold Fischel, an ordained rabbi, was then appointed, but Secretary of War Edwin Stanton denied the nomination and Fischel, an experienced lobbyist, spent the next year on Capitol Hill pushing his cause. In July 1862, Congress changed the law to read "religious denominations" rather than "Christian denomination." The first Jewish regimental chaplain was Ferdinand Leopold Samer, a German, who served the mostly German-speaking 54th New York Volunteers. Samer was also the first Jewish chaplain to be wounded as well as the first Jewish chaplain to be absent without leave. After being severely wounded at Gettysburg, he left the hospital for home before the arrival of his discharge papers. Although Jews were allowed to serve in the Confederate chaplaincy, none is known to have done so, even though some 3,000 Jews fought for the Confederacy.

Others served too. The Confederacy had the first African-American chaplain. A Tennessee regiment called on a pious slave known as "Uncle Lewis" to conduct religious services. He was a source of pride to the unit and was credited for leading three revivals. In addition, Unaguskie, served as chaplain of a Confederate Cherokee battalion.

The chaplaincy on both sides was exclusively male although the 1st Wisconsin Heavy Artillery unanimously elected Ella E. Gibson chaplain. She was an ordained minister of the Religio-Philosophical Society of St. Charles, Illinois. Lincoln passed the appointment to Stanton with the notation, "This lady would be appointed Chaplain..., only that she is a woman. The president has not legally anything to do with such a question, but has no objection to her appointment." Stanton, not wanting to set a precedent, however, declined to recognize the appointment.

In the postwar literature, works such as A Narrative of the Great Revival Which Prevailed in the Southern Armies during the Late Civil War between the States of the Federal Union and Christ in the Camp did much to promote the concept of muscular Christianity so much in vogue in the late nineteenth century. Images of strong and masculine Protestant chaplains were created to offset a growing popular mind set of religion seeming to be feminine. Especially in the South, many were portrayed as "fighting chaplains" who excelled in fighting both Satan and Yankees. Only more recently has scholarship turned to examining other aspects of this topic, notably diversity.

—Daniel Liestman

See also Chaplains, African-American; Religion.
For further reading:
Armstrong, Warren B. For Courageous Fighting and Confident Dying: Union Chaplains in the Civil War (1998).
Bennett, William W. A Narrative of the Great Revival Which Prevailed in the Southern Armies during the Late Civil War between the States of the Federal Union (1877).
Brown, William Young. The Army Chaplain, His Office, Duties, and Responsibilities, and the Means of Aiding Him (1863).
Faust, Drew Gilpin. "Christian Soldiers: The Meaning of Revivalism in the Confederate Army." Journal of Southern History (1987).
Jones, J. William. Christ in the Camp (1887).
Miller, Randall M., Harry S. Stout, and Charles Reagan Wilson, eds. Religion and the American Civil War (1998).
Pitts, Charles F. Chaplains in Gray (1957).
Robinson-Durso, Pamela. "Chaplains in the Confederate Army." Journal of Church and State (1991).
Slomovitz, Albert I. The Fighting Rabbis: Jewish Military Chaplains and American History (1999).
Wiley, Bell Irwin. "'Holy Joes' of the Sixties: A Study of Civil War Chaplains." Huntington Library Quarterly (1953).

CHAPLAINS, AFRICAN-AMERICAN

When the Civil War began the United States Army had only twenty-six chaplains on duty. These clergymen, who were all white, served as post chaplains and were not attached to any particular regiment. The outbreak of hostilities led to a tremendous increase in the size of the chaplaincy to match the increased number of regular and volunteer Union army forces. The army also began to assign chaplains to serve in individual regiments. Unfortunately, those changes led to a great deal of confusion over commissioning, uniforms, and pay. They also resulted in the admission of many totally unfit men, who hurt the reputation of the chaplaincy. Congressional legislation passed in July 1862, followed by Army General Order 91, successfully rid the army of undesirables and helped to form a thoroughly professionalized chaplaincy by the end of 1862.

Black chaplains did not enter service with the Union army until after the Emancipation Proclamation in 1863. The delay proved fortunate, for by then the professionalization of the chaplaincy had occurred. African-American chaplains were consequently spared the problems of the war's early years. The higher standards required of the chaplaincy meant that fewer black clergymen qualified, but they ensured that the men who did so were the best in the African-American community.

Henry McNeal Turner was the first African-American to serve as an army chaplain in Federal service. Turner was born free in South Carolina and became an African Methodist Episcopal (A.M.E.) Church minister in 1853. By the start of the Civil War, he was pastor of the Israel A.M.E. Church in Washington, D.C., which provided him the opportunity to meet influential Republican politicians. Turner impressed these leaders early on in the war when he helped organize African-American civilians into construction brigades to strengthen Washington's defenses. He also helped to recruit large numbers of African-American troops after Congress authorized their enlistment. Thanks to his powerful political friends, Turner was made chaplain of the 1st United States Colored Troops (U.S.C.T.) on 10 September 1863. Chaplain Turner immediately faced discrimination from whites, however. While on board the steamer *Manhattan*, a white steward refused to permit Turner to enter the dining facility through the front entrance, even threatening him with a knife. The steward was arrested and brought up on charges, but that was not the end of the challenges that faced the new chaplain. Although Congress had authorized chaplains' salaries set at $1,200 per year, army paymasters defiantly interpreted the regulations to mean that black chaplains should be paid the same rate as black common laborers. The matter finally made its way up to President Abraham Lincoln, who referred the matter to his attorney general. He ruled that black chaplains should be paid the same as white ones.

Other black ministers, such as Chaplain William Hunter of the 4th U.S.C.T. soon followed Turner into service. Hunter fought to get fair treatment for the men in his unit who had been promised at their enlistment the same pay as white troops but instead were paid less. He wrote letters and pushed the issue until Congress finally rectified the pay difference in 1864. The Reverend William J. Hodges enlisted in the 36th U.S.C.T. with the hope of becoming that regiment's chaplain. Instead, the officers named David Stevens chaplain, and Hodges rose to the rank of sergeant major. Francis Boyd thought he, too, could become chaplain of the 109th U.S.C.T. by first enlisting in that unit. When no opportunity came, Boyd skipped the chain of command and wrote directly to General Benjamin Butler. Successfully convincing Butler of his qualifications, Boyd was appointed chaplain. His victory was short-lived, however, for the 109th's commander was highly irritated that Boyd had gone over his head and worked against the new chaplain at every turn. After three months, he succeeded in having Boyd stripped of his commission and returned to the rank of private.

Garland White was more successful. A former slave of Georgia senator Robert Toombs, he had escaped to Canada where he became an A.M.E. pastor. Once the Civil War began, he commenced an intensive letter-writing campaign to the secretary of war, urging that he be appointed a chaplain. When that tactic did not work, he moved his family to Ohio and began recruitment duty. Eventually he enlisted in the 28th U.S.C.T. and served as the regiment's unofficial chaplain. The unit's commander recommended that White's role be made official, but the request was refused because regulations required that no chaplain's position could be filled until the regiment reached full strength. White's patient persistence finally paid off and on 25 October 1864 he was commissioned as the 28th's chaplain. He was part of the lead element that entered Richmond in 1865 when an elderly black lady approached troops of the 28th asking to see if a man named Garland White was among them. When the woman was brought to Chaplain White, he discovered that she was his mother; he had not seen her since being sold to Robert Toombs as a small boy.

Being an army chaplain also had its dangers. Turner contracted smallpox and later was hospitalized after being thrown from his horse in a skirmish. Samuel Harrison of the 54th Massachusetts contracted malaria shortly after his arrival in South Carolina and was discharged after only four months on duty. Some duties were simply unpleasant. Jeremiah Asher of the 6th U.S.C.T. was appalled at the sight of five hundred wounded troops at a Portsmouth, Virginia hospital, many without arms and legs. Nevertheless, he provided ministry to the men as best he could. George LeVere of the 20th U.S.C.T. had the unenviable task of spending three hours providing comfort to a condemned soldier who was then executed by firing squad. LeVere remarked that it was the saddest spectacle he had ever witnessed.

Some duties were more rewarding. African-American chaplains served as recruiters, and the black troops they enlisted obviously took pride in serving their country and helping to free their people. Many black chaplains also served as educators to their illiterate troops. The chaplain of the 62d U.S.C.T. proudly noted that more than 200 troopers had learned to read by the end of their enlistments. Another chaplain wrote that he hoped every soldier in his regiment would become literate by the end of the war.

For all chaplains, white or black, the primary mission was to proclaim the Christian gospel, and in this role the uniqueness of the black chaplains truly stands out. White chaplains who served in all-black units—such as George N. Carruthers—often had difficulty relating to the men. Carruthers criticized his black troops' custom of worship, noting that it consisted "more in emotional exercises than a conscientious performance of duty and trust in God." Another white chaplain, Thomas Stevenson of the 114th U.S.C.T., also complained, stating that black worship was "narrow and superficial...and often preposterously absurd." These men did not know that black troops' religion was a blend of their African heritage, slave experience, and evangelical Protestant Christianity that had merged to create something very different from white practices. African-American Christianity had been forged by slaves meeting secretly at night in places they called hush harbors. There they created what scholars have called the Invisible Institution. Services possessed the same external forms of the white masters' evangelical faith, but they were inherently different because of a strong and persistent element of black folk religion. Blacks shouted during worship services, sang a new type of song called the spiritual, believed in spirit possession, and were generally much more vocal and lively. Black funerals were different, too. Just as they had in Africa, blacks broke up the possessions of the dead and placed them on top of the grave to help release the spirit of the deceased.

Most white army chaplains failed to understand the faith of these black troops. But it was African-American Christianity that helped blacks deal with everyday life in a brutal form of slavery that was degrading, based on race, and permanent. Slavery severely damaged the African religious and cultural heritage of the slaves, but African-American Christianity helped blacks survive by developing a new, coherent worldview. The message black chaplains preached was one of hope, salvation, and dignity, all of which served to boost the morale of the troops.

The Union army utilized the services of 2,300 chaplains during the Civil War. One hundred thirty-three of these men served in the all-black regiments. Of these 133 clergymen, 14 were African-American. That number may seem small, but the impact the black chaplains made was significant far beyond their numbers through their work as recruiters, teachers, role models, and proclaimers of the message of African-American Christianity.

—*Alan K. Lamm*

See also African-American Soldiers; Chaplains; Religion.
For further reading:
Angell, Stephen Ward. *Bishop Henry McNeal Turner and Afro-American Religion in the South* (1992).
Honeywell, Roy J. *Chaplains of the United States Army* (1958).
McPherson, James. *The Negro's Civil War: How American Blacks Felt and Acted during the War for the Union* (1965).
Norton, Herman A. *Struggling for Recognition: The United States Army Chaplaincy, 1791–1865* (1977).
Raboteau, Albert J. *Slave Religion: The "Invisible Institution" in the Antebellum South* (1978).

CHARLESTON (ILLINOIS) RIOT
(28 March 1864)

Resentments centered on opposition to Lincoln administration war policies and verbal and physical abuse directed against Democrats in central Illinois exploded in a spasm of violence on 28 March 1864. When it ended, nine men lay dead or dying and twelve were wounded on the courthouse square in Charleston, Illinois. Located about 120 miles southeast of the state capital at Springfield, Charleston, the Coles County seat, was a community atop the cultural fault line that stretched across the center of the state. Along this uneven border, residents with Southern antecedents confronted those with New England or mid-Atlantic state backgrounds in cultural, political, and social conflict. The confrontational atmosphere that evolved on the Civil War Northern home front only heightened these tensions. Democrats, often termed Copperheads by Republicans, increasingly spoke out against what they perceived as suppression of free speech and conversion of the war from one to preserve the Union to a crusade to free the slaves. Large numbers of Democrats from the area served in the Union army, however, as the level of voluntary enlistments negated any need to impose conscription in Charleston or elsewhere in Coles County.

Tensions had been building in Coles and Edgar, a neighboring county to the East, for at least a year before the bloody confrontation in Charleston. Both counties were in the Seventh Congressional District, which in November 1862 sent a Democratic opponent of the Lincoln administration, John Rice Eden of Sullivan, to Washington. A supporter of appropriations for troops and equipment, Eden, like other downstate Illinois Democrats, was outspoken against perceived violations of free speech and press by Union supporters. Two months after Eden's election, an attempt by Coles County critics of the war's direction to hold a peace meeting was disrupted by Republicans. A few weeks later, they successfully staged a meeting, passing resolutions calling for an armistice, opposition to unconditional emancipation, and declaring that habeas corpus "must and shall be maintained." Democratic passions were further inflamed when an area judge was arrested by Indiana troops who crossed state lines after the jurist refused to allow four army deserters to be returned to the Hoosier state. Only a last-minute release order from a Federal judge kept the Democratic jurist from being transported to and tried in Indiana.

In Mattoon, Coles County's most populous community and, according to the Democratic *Chicago Times*, the "most fanatical, intolerant, mobocratic hole of abolitionism in this part of the State," Democrats staged a rally for free speech and peace on 1 August 1863, attracting a crowd estimated between 3,000 and 12,000. A number of speakers, including Eden, urged Democrats to maintain their rights and continue opposition to Lincoln's war aims at the ballot box, in the courts, and, if necessary, Eden proclaimed, "in another way." The next month, Eden's congressional colleague, James C. Robinson, who represented the district south of Charleston, told a rally that a government conspiracy

Clashes between soldiers and civilians erupted in several Northern cities, including Charleston, Illinois, during the course of the Civil War. (*Corbis*)

was afoot to keep Democrats from voting. As citizens it was their duty, Robinson said, to go to the polls, even if they had to "wade through blood knee deep to the ballot box." Days later, a Democratic newspaper in Shelbyville, seat of Shelby County directly west of Coles, said that if all other alternatives failed, Democrats retained the "inalienable right of revolution." Historian Jean Baker has linked such language with an antebellum Democratic tradition of republicanism, which triggered powerful fundamental associations and ideals among party members.

Further dry tinder was added when, in January 1864, members of the 54th Illinois Infantry began an extended leave in Mattoon. Idle soldiers occupied themselves by drinking and attacking Democrats in the streets of the city. Among their victims were a prominent local physician and the judge who had been arrested by Indiana troops. On 30 January 1864, members of the 54th fatally shot a Democrat who attempted to flee rather than take

the "loyalty oath" they administered. On 16 February 1864 a street altercation between Democrats and soldiers in the Edgar county seat of Paris resulted in severe wounds for one Democrat. Six days later, another confrontation in Paris left one Democrat dead and two soldiers wounded. In March soldiers attacked Democrats on the streets of Charleston in two separate incidents, one involving members of the O'Hair family prominent in Democratic politics in Coles and Edgar counties.

On 28 March Charleston's square filled with soldiers and Democrats, many of the latter farmers who were in town for a party rally to be addressed by Eden. As tensions mounted and whiskey flowed during the day, the rally was canceled and Eden moved about the square urging Democrats to return home peacefully. Hopes for peace were shattered when David Nelson Wells, a young Democrat from Edgar County, became involved in a dispute with Oliver Sallee, a soldier, outside the courthouse. Shots were exchanged and both men fell mortally wounded. Suddenly, firing became general as Democrats retrieved weapons from wagons and under their coats, directing their fire at the soldiers, many of whom were unarmed. Leading the Democrats was Coles County Sheriff John O'Hair, a Democrat elected in 1862. After about one minute, the firing ceased and O'Hair led the Democrats out of the city. Moments later, a suspected rioter was captured by the soldiers and fatally shot as he attempted to flee. The same bullet also took the life of a Republican bystander. The final toll was six Union soldiers, a Republican bystander, and two Democrats killed, and twelve men wounded. With the exception of the New York City Draft Riots, Charleston's affray resulted in the bloodiest toll for a civil disturbance on the Northern home front, surpassing casualties in Chicago and Boston.

Most of the leading Democrats, including Sheriff O'Hair, were not captured. In the panic that followed the riot more than fifty Democrats were arrested. Twenty-nine were held by the military and transported to Springfield, where thirteen were released. Those remaining were transferred to a Federal prison at Fort Delaware, where they were held without trial until released on Lincoln's orders seven months later. Although a local grand jury indicted Sheriff O'Hair, who eventually returned to Coles County, and fourteen others, only two men, both minor figures, stood trial. The trial was moved to Effingham, about forty miles southwest of Charleston, and in November 1864 both defendants were acquitted.

—*Robert D. Sampson*

See also Copperheads; New York City Draft Riots; Peace Democrats; Riots, C.S.A.; Riots, U.S.A.

For further reading:
Coleman, Charles Hubert, and Paul B. Spence. "The Charleston Riot, March 28, 1864." *Journal of the Illinois State Historical Society* (1940).
Sampson, Robert D. "'Pretty Damned Warm Times': The 1864 Charleston Riot and 'The Inalienable Right of Revolution.'" *Illinois Historical Journal* (1996).

CHARLESTON MERCURY

As the most passionate supporter first of slavery and then of the formation of the Confederacy (a position it first advocated nearly three decades before the Civil War began), it was altogether appropriate that the Charleston *Mercury* would publish the first official notice of the initial act of secession: a broadside extra published immediately following the South Carolina legislature's passage of the secession resolution, proclaiming "The Union Is Dissolved!"

Founded in 1822, the *Mercury* quickly became the most extreme opponent of abolition and a fierce advocate of nullification. Yet despite its political zealotry, it was widely respected in the North and looked to as the

most authoritative voice of the secession movement. Its wartime editor, Robert Barnwell Rhett Jr., was the son of John C. Calhoun's eventual successor in the U.S. Senate. Indeed, the elder Rhett, who for most of the previous decade had advocated a Southern Confederacy, vied with Jefferson Davis for the Confederate presidency. Passed over by the Confederate Congress even for a cabinet appointment, Rhett—although a strong proponent of civil war as a means of guaranteeing the disintegration of the Union—became a fierce critic of Davis's administration, and the *Mercury*, under his son's editorship, was recognized as Rhett's mouthpiece.

The Harvard-educated younger Rhett assumed editorial control in 1857. By time the war began, the paper's circulation had quadrupled, mostly because of the vituperative editorials that Rhett and his brother Edmund composed and that were widely credited as instrumental in pushing South Carolina towards secession. Nineteenth-century journalism historian Frederic Hudson wrote that the *Mercury* was "a paper of remarkable ability and not surpassed by any other southern paper in the support of its peculiar political views." Abraham Lincoln recognized its importance and subscribed to it long before he was elected president. Others in the North, however, tried to belittle Rhett's influence. A *New York Tribune* correspondent dismissed him as "a well-known wealthy agitator" whose slogan was "I'd rather rule in Hell than serve in Heaven" and insisted that the *Mercury*'s circulation was no more than 550 daily, half of which were exchanges with other papers.

Yet there was no denying that Rhett's *Mercury*, more than any other paper, incited the South to fever pitch. During the secession crisis of 1860, when Charles Dana, then with the *New York Tribune*, sent correspondent Charles Brigham to Charleston as a secret correspondent, the *Mercury* called for his lynching. Brigham, in turn, took to taunting Rhett in print: "If the *Mercury* is really curious as to my whereabouts," he wrote, "let him look into one of the big guns of Fort Sumter. He may find me there." Following Lincoln's election, the *Mercury* declared that the only remedy "for the crisis which is at hand (is) disunion—the separation of South Carolina, whether alone or with others, from the Union which can only be a badge of infamy to her!"

In January 1861 the paper tried to undermine Lincoln's support in the North by printing what it said was an exchange of correspondence during the previous month in which "the abolition president" declared that John Brown did not deserve to be executed, having committed at worst "a gross misdemeanor" at Harper's Ferry, and adding that he did not consider the Supreme Court's *Dred Scott* decision binding because "it is hostile to the advancement of Republican principles." The *Illinois Daily State Journal* promptly denounced the letter as "a gross forgery," but not until it had been reprinted widely.

Despite their devotion to the Southern cause, Rhett and the *Mercury* relentlessly denounced Confederate president Jefferson Davis's "imbecility" and the arbitrary nature of his administration, including "star chamber" meetings of its Congress and suspension of the right of habeas corpus. Rhett also criticized what he regarded as the gross incompetence of most of the South's generals. In this respect, the *Mercury* was a counterpoint to its rival, the pro-Davis *Charleston Daily Courier*.

A contemporary account contrasted the two papers: "The *Courier* is practical and the *Mercury* speculative. The *Courier* deals with the present and the past, and the *Mercury* more with the future. The *Courier* is content to meet events as they occur, and the *Mercury* anticipates them. There is more diffusion in the *Courier*, and more compactness in the *Mercury*. The *Courier* is pleased to hold on the even tenor of its way; the *Mercury* is bold, dashing, presumptive, and prophetic"

During the siege of Charleston, the *Mercury* continued to publish on schedule, although it was quickly reduced to a single-page edition. On the 589th day of the siege, the *Mercury*'s pages were filled with an account of the burning of Charleston by fleeing Confederate troops.

For all its criticism of the South's military performance, the *Mercury* was responsible for coining the legend of one notable general. It was to Leonidas W. Sprat, the paper's correspondent at the battle of First Bull Run, that an aide to General Barnard Bee told how the mortally wounded commander had observed his colleague, Thomas J. Jackson, and declared, "There is Jackson standing like a stone wall. Let us determine to die here, and we will conquer."

Following the Union occupation of Charleston, the *Mercury* was shut down. Rhett had hoped to shift publication to Augusta, Georgia, but his press and equipment were destroyed at Charlotte Junction and he took refuge in Alabama. The *Mercury*'s presses remained silent until November 1866, when publication resumed under editor Rhett. But despite seeming financial success, the paper closed for good two years later. In his farewell editorial, the younger Rhett, defiant to the end, vowed to "take my place among [the South's] ruined children—better so than to be the proudest and most honored of her successful enemies—and to wait, hoping, praying, expecting the bright coming of her final deliverance, the independence and prosperity of the South."

—*Eric Fettmann*

See also Newspapers; Rhett, Robert Barnwell.

For further reading:

Andrews, J. Cutler. *The South Reports the Civil War* (1970).
Britton, James C. "Images of the Future in the *Charleston Mercury*, 1848–1860" (M.A. thesis, 1980).
Davis, Lee Wright. "Robert Barnwell Rhett, Jr., and the *Charleston Mercury*, 1861–1865" (Honors thesis, 1977).
Harper, Robert S. *Lincoln and the Press* (1951).
Hudson, Frederic. *Journalism in the United States from 1690 to 1872* (1873; reprint, 1968).
Segars, Ernest B. "A Study of the *Charleston* (S.C.) *Mercury* during Robert Barnwell Rhett, Senior's, Tenure as an Editorial Writer, 1861–1863" (M. A. thesis, 1974).
Starr, Louis M. *Bohemian Brigade: Civil War Newsmen in Action* (1954; reprint, 1987).

CHARLESTON, SOUTH CAROLINA

See Carolinas Campaign; Fort Sumter, Bombardment of ; Secessionville, Battle of; South Carolina

CHASE, SALMON PORTLAND
(1808–1873)

Secretary of the treasury; chief justice of the U.S. Supreme Court

Salmon Portland Chase came to the office of secretary of the treasury primarily because his Republican Party denied him the office he wanted most—the presidency. Chase's career was one that combined antislavery principle and political ambition. In appointing him to the treasury position, Abraham Lincoln knew that Chase would be a capable cabinet officer, but he also knew that Chase's desire to be chief executive would be unceasing, and as a member of the administration the president could more easily keep tabs on his political intrigues. Lincoln would be correct on all of these assumptions, and in 1864, in accepting Chase's fourth effort to resign, the president again realized that Chase was too reliable and principled a leader to lose. Thus, once safely reelected, Lincoln appointed Chase to be chief justice of the United States, effectively removing him from politics and hopefully ensuring the constitutional changes that had come with the Civil War.

Chase's early rise in politics began as a Cincinnati attorney. Born in New Hampshire, he had lived briefly in Ohio as a boy under the stern and watchful eye of his uncle, Episcopal Bishop Philander Chase. After teaching school briefly and reading law under former attorney general William Wirt in Washington, D.C., Chase settled in Cincinnati in 1830 at the age of twenty-two. There, as an elitist Whig, he became interested in reform and, through his brother-in-law William Colby, abolitionism. He soon attained local prominence in his unsuccessful defense of fugitive slaves. Chase used the argument that residence in free territory made the fugitive a free person, but only rarely was he able to persuade the courts to accept his reasoning. He nevertheless gained notoriety in Cincinnati as the "Attorney General for Runaway Negroes." Abandoning the conservative Whig Party, he joined with the newly formed Liberty

Salmon P. Chase (*Library of Congress*)

Party in 1841 as a supporter of presidential candidate James G. Birney. His conversion to antislavery politics and principle had been a remarkably swift one, yet was genuine, for he rejected the refusal of the two-party system to embrace reform and resolved to work toward the goal of eliminating or at least containing slavery.

By 1844, Chase sought to broaden the third-party's appeal with a more prominent candidate than Birney, and in 1848, Chase led Liberty supporters into a coalition with the more moderate antislavery Free Soil Party. The following year, Free Soilers in the Ohio legislature engineered Chase's election to the U.S. Senate along with a partial repeal of Ohio's racist black laws, but it was a victory that revealed that Chase appeared willing to go to extreme lengths to secure his own election at the expense of the third-party's independence. In the Senate, Chase opposed the expansion of slavery and the proslavery components of the Compromise of 1850. He also revealed his growing political ambition and assumed a prominent role among those promoting the new Republican Party.

In 1856, Chase mounted his first challenge for a presidential nomination. Elected in 1855 and 1857 to be governor of Ohio, he saw that office as a stepping stone to the presidency. His best opportunity came in 1860, but poor management by his political lieutenants and a

reputation for antislavery radicalism and political intrigue eliminated him. In addition, his cold and aloof manner kept people at arm's length as did his morally righteous attitude. His role in politics before 1860 had left too many enemies. Yet he loyally campaigned for Lincoln who then rewarded him by naming him treasury secretary. It was a position of unprecedented difficulty, given the expense and duration of the war.

Chase has received mixed reviews for his role in the Treasury, but the consensus of historians views his achievements as significant. Chase, as well as most Union leaders, initially assumed it would be a war of a few months that could be financed through traditional methods of borrowing and higher tariffs and taxes. As the prospect of a quick Confederate surrender faded, bolder and more imaginative financial tactics emerged. Chase reluctantly accepted greenbacks as legal tender to help raise needed revenue and in 1863 and 1864 championed a national banking system with the aid of Ohio senator John Sherman. Under the new system, nationally supervised banking associations issued bank notes guaranteed by the federal government. The result was a more secure currency in a time of economic volatility.

The sale of bonds was an added element that meant heavy government borrowing and brought great controversy. Chase made Philadelphia banker Jay Cooke a special treasury agent, a position that gave Cooke a commission for the sale of government bonds. Cooke's efforts realized more than $500 million of desperately needed revenue for the war effort, a result that meant stability for the government and charges of favoritism against both Chase and his friend Cooke. Yet Cooke produced the desired results and managed the loans well. The Union war debt, while enormous, compared favorably with later wars and especially with that of the beleaguered Confederacy.

Equally controversial were Chase's efforts to control and regulate trade, especially in Union-held areas of the South. Speculators sought to profit from trade in cotton and other products scarce in the North. Treasury agents were understaffed and subject to bribery as bureaucratic regulations expanded. Chase appointed political allies who could use their positions to advance his candidacy for 1864, but who also did a creditable job in controlling illegal trade. Overall, the results reflected credit on the economic integrity of the secretary but exposed him to charges of political manipulation.

Chase made little effort to confine his attention to financial issues, using his position in the cabinet to try to persuade the cautious president to a more advanced policy on slavery and civil rights. He complained bitterly when Lincoln rescinded the orders of Generals John C. Frémont and David Hunter freeing slaves within their commands, and he urged General Benjamin F. Butler to do the same within his New Orleans command. Chase rarely appreciated or understood the pressures that Lincoln faced from the many conservative forces, which compelled him to move slowly. Chase rejoiced when Lincoln finally responded with his preliminary proclamation of emancipation in September 1862. Clearly the pressure of Chase and Republican senators such as Charles Sumner of Massachusetts was a factor in the president's change. Chase and Sumner also urged the use of black troops in Union armies, and again the president responded with a policy that encouraged former slaves to aid the Union cause militarily. Chase's efforts on behalf of black suffrage brought more limited immediate acceptance, but again Lincoln appeared to be moving in Chase's direction. Despite his often contentious relationship with Lincoln, Chase could feel justly proud that he had helped to advance the cause of racial equality.

The president was less receptive to Chase's efforts to advise him on military and political matters, including the appointment of high officers and the movement of Union armies. In December 1862, when Chase tried to force Lincoln's hand and secure the removal of Secretary of State William H. Seward from office, the president skillfully outmaneuvered him and exposed his amateurish efforts at a meeting with cabinet and Senate leaders. Chase appeared oblivious to the fact that he could not compete with a master politician of Lincoln's ability. Still feeling himself uniquely qualified for the presidency, Chase urged supporters within and outside the Treasury to forward his candidacy. Always denying such an interest, Chase convinced few of his loyalty to the administration.

As 1864 approached, congressional supporters clumsily tried to mount a Chase movement, but they served only to point further suspicion on the secretary himself. Clearly Republican leaders and voters preferred Lincoln's steady course of moderation to the uncertainties of a Chase presidency. Again, the skillful Lincoln outmaneuvered his secretary and easily won renomination. Lincoln now felt secure enough to accept Chase's resignation over a patronage dispute involving the New York collectorship. Still the party loyalist and opportunist, the former treasury secretary campaigned vigorously for Lincoln's reelection knowing that the imminent death of Chief Justice Roger Taney could give him a new role of influence. Lincoln reluctantly agreed, realizing that the constitutional changes regarding finances and racial policy of the war years might be solidified by a Court under Chase's leadership even though Chase would continue to seek political advantage.

Indeed Chase continued to reveal both political ambition and commitment to racial equality after the war during his years as chief justice. Not always in agreement with Republican leaders in Congress, he nonetheless avoided an open confrontation between the Supreme Court and Congress. Although he opposed efforts to establish military rule in the defeated states of the Confederacy, he endorsed legislation that granted civil and political rights to African-Americans. He clashed over Senate efforts to deny him a prominent role in the impeachment trial of Andrew Johnson in 1868, and, when Republicans chose Ulysses S. Grant as their candidate for president, Chase sought a Democratic nomination instead. His efforts, in part engineered by his ambitious daughter Kate Chase Sprague, failed partly because Democrats rejected his policies of racial equality. Yet he could rejoice in the ratification in 1870 of the Fifteenth Amendment, which granted suffrage to black men.

If ability and desire were the sole criteria in choosing a president, Salmon P. Chase was more qualified than many who have occupied the White House. Yet his ambition was not matched by political savvy. Try as he might, he could never convince enough politicians of either party that his advanced racial views or his controversial ambition could win the voters' approval. His arrogant, stuffy, and pompous nature further alienated party leaders and voters alike. When Lincoln considered Chase for chief justice, Ohio senator Benjamin Wade caustically commented: "Chase is a good man, but his theology is unsound. He thinks there is a fourth person in the Trinity." Yet, if denied what he sought most, Chase is also remembered for his stern commitment to racial justice and equality. His moral courage was at least as great as his unending ambition to be president. His Civil War record was thus one of controversy, frustration, and achievement.

—*Frederick J. Blue*

See also Cooke, Jay; Financing, U.S.A.; Lincoln, Abraham; Republican Party.
For further reading:
Blue, Frederick J. *Salmon P. Chase: A Life in Politics* (1987).
Burlingame, Michael, and John R. Turner Ettlinger, eds. *Inside Lincoln's White House: The Complete Civil Diary of John Hay* (1997).
Donald, David Herbert, ed. *Inside Lincoln's Cabinet: The Civil War Diaries of Salmon P. Chase* (1954).
Niven, John. *Salmon P. Chase: A Biography* (1995).
———, ed. *The Salmon P. Chase Papers* (1993–1998).

CHATTAHOOCHEE RIVER, GEORGIA, OPERATIONS AROUND
(5–17 July 1864)

In early May 1864, Major General William T. Sherman began the Atlanta campaign by putting the Armies of the Cumberland, Tennessee, and Ohio in motion with the hope of eventually campaigning across the state of Georgia. By early July, the three armies neared the Chattahoochee River. Less than two weeks later, they had pushed the Confederate forces to a position south of the river and only a few miles from Atlanta. When the Confederate troops abandoned their defenses along the north side of the river, Sherman's army achieved one of the major goals of the campaign, namely, the taking of the territory from the Tennessee to the Chattahoochee rivers.

On 4 July, Union forces staged demonstrations in and around Nickajack Creek and Turner's Ferry. In general, they pushed back the Confederate defenders, although units of the Georgia Militia offered stiff resistance around Turner's Ferry. That night, however, the Confederate forces, commanded by General Joseph E. Johnston, withdrew to positions just on the north side of the Chattahoochee to avoid being flanked by Sherman's troops. Once their retreat had been discovered, the Union soldiers pursued the Confederates all the way to the river.

The Confederates had heavily fortified their defenses around the bridges and roads traversing the Chattahoochee. Specifically, Johnston had ordered the construction of a system surrounding the railroad bridge, pontoon bridges, and roads associated with Pace's, Montgomery's, and Turner's ferries and composed of redoubts connected by infantry and artillery parapets. According to Captain Orlando M. Poe, Sherman's chief engineer, the defenses around the railroad bridge were "by far the strongest we had yet encountered." The Union leadership doubted if these defenses could be successfully assaulted. Even if possible, they believed that many would die in the effort. So, they decided to take the position by flanking it. This would necessitate the crossing of the Chattahoochee.

All day on the 5th, heavy skirmishing occurred between the two armies. This only strengthened Sherman's resolve to cross the river before the Confederates could strengthen their defenses. He, therefore, ordered Major General John M. Schofield's Army of the Ohio to cross the river on the eastern end, while the remainder of the army created a diversion to the west. At daylight on the 8th, Schofield managed to get his army across the river at the mouth of Soap Creek without the rebels' knowledge. By that evening, Union engineers had laid a bridge. A few miles to the south of Soap Creek, Major General Oliver O. Howard's IV Corps of the Army of the Tennessee, built a bridge at Power's Ferry. Still further to the south, Union troops saved a pontoon bridge set ablaze by retreating Confederates at Pace's Ferry. Thus, by the 9th, Sherman's troops had secured three crossings over the Chattahoochee.

Johnston's retreat to the north side of the Chattahoochee greatly concerned Confederate president Jefferson Davis. He feared that Johnston had boxed himself in by placing the river at his back. Crossing the river, in Davis's opinion, was not a good option since it would allow Sherman to cut communications with Alabama and capture points important to the Confederacy. Nonetheless, in light of the Union crossing, Johnston abandoned his position and retreated across the river during the night of the 9th. By the next morning, Sherman could claim that the Union forces were the "undisputed masters north and west of the Chattahoochee."

At this point began what Sherman called "the real game for Atlanta." For the next several days, Sherman strengthened his positions along the Chattahoochee, gathered supplies, and allowed the soldiers to rest. On 17 July, however, the entire army advanced and crossed the river between Roswell and Power's Ferry; Atlanta lay only eight miles away from the Union forces.

Johnston, in the meantime, had adopted a defensive strategy due to his being outnumbered. He planned to wait for an opportunity to attack. While planning the defense of Atlanta late on the night of the 17th, he received a telegram relieving him of command. The secretary of war cited Johnston's inability to stop the Union advance, as well as the general's lack of confidence in his ability to ever do so; Johnston later disputed these charges. Command was given to Lieutenant General John Bell Hood, one of Johnston's corps commanders. His former commander told Hood that his plans had been to attack the Federal army as it was crossing Peachtree Creek. Two days later, on 20 July, Hood attacked Sherman in the battle of Peachtree Creek.

—*Scott M. Langston*

See also Atlanta Campaign; Peachtree Creek, Battle of.
For further reading:
Castel, Albert E. *Decision in the West: The Atlanta Campaign of 1864* (1992).
Hedley, F.Y. *Marching through Georgia: Pen-Pictures of Everyday Life* (1884).
Johnson, Robert Underwood, and Clarence Clough Buel, eds. *Battles and Leaders of the Civil War: Being for the Most Part Contributions by Union and Confederate Officers* (1887–1888).
Kerkiss, Sydney C., comp. *The Atlanta Papers* (1980).
The War of the Rebellion: A Compilation of the Official Records of the Union and Confederate Armies (1880–1901).

CHATTANOOGA CAMPAIGN
(November 1863)

After the stunning 20 September 1863 defeat of his Army of the Cumberland in the valley south of Chattanooga, Tennessee, along Chickamauga Creek, Union general William Rosecrans personified the collective mood of his forces: He was despondent. After craftily maneuvering the Confederates out of Chattanooga in August, Rosecrans was now a defeated man. Routed and (except for the dogged performance of General George Thomas on Snodgrass Hill during the battle) almost completely defeated by the Confederate force of General Braxton Bragg, Rosecrans's army straggled back to Chattanooga, hunkered down as best they could, and awaited their fate. Without ever realizing that time would eventually prove to be more on the Union's side than on his, Bragg, having allowed his defeated enemy to vacate the field at Chickamauga, dispersed his army into siege formation around the city of Chattanooga and attempted to starve the Union army into submission. The Confederates' primary defensive position was maintained atop Missionary Ridge, east of Chattanooga.

At the time, it would have been hard to say which commander was in the better position. Although Bragg seemed to have the upper hand, having dramatically defeated Union forces on the field and now in the possession of the high ground around his enemy, he did not have enough troops to completely circumvent the city, so the Union soldiers were never entirely cut off from some reinforcements. The newly formed Cracker Line kept the Union modestly supplied. And as time would later tell, Bragg never deployed his troops as efficiently as he could have. For his part, Rosecrans, in shock over his shattering defeat, would not have the opportunity to recover his reputation and the morale of his army: he was relieved of command by General Ulysses S. Grant, who had been given command of all forces in the Western theater of operations. Grant replaced Rosecrans with the "Rock of Chickamauga," General Thomas. In his

memoirs, Grant described the abject situation he found the Army of Cumberland in when he first visited Chattanooga soon after assuming overall command:

We crossed to the north side of the river, and, moving to the north of detached spurs of hills, reached the Tennessee at Brown's Ferry, some three miles below Lookout Mountain, unobserved by the enemy. Here we left our horses back from the river and approached by foot. There was a picket station of the enemy on the opposite side, of about twenty men, in full view, and we were within easy range. They did not fire upon us nor seem to be disturbed by our presence. They must have seen that we were all commissioned officers. But, I suppose, they looked upon the garrison of Chattanooga as prisoners of war, feeding or starving themselves, and thought it would be inhuman to kill any of them except in self-defen[s]e.

His army utterly demoralized, Grant quickly set about regaining the fighting spirit of his soldiers. Chattanooga was a vital rail and river transportation center, a strategic embarkation point for any offensive operations into

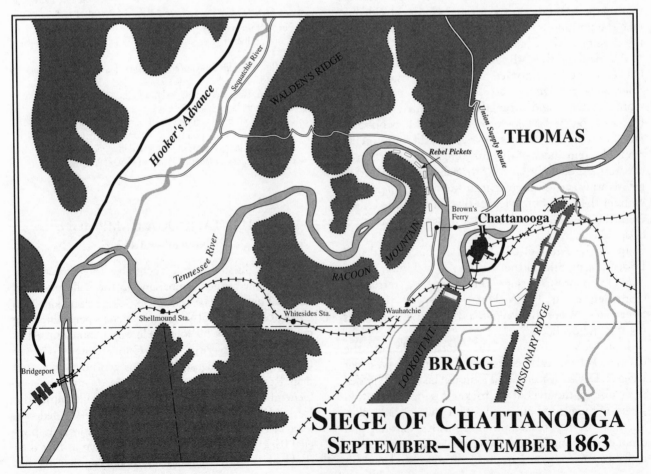

SIEGE OF CHATTANOOGA
SEPTEMBER–NOVEMBER 1863

General Sherman's headquarters at Chattanooga (*Library of Congress*)

Georgia and other Deep South territories. The complete loss of this city would have been a serious setback for Union forces.

Whereas Lincoln and Grant acted decisively in restoring effective leadership among their forces, Davis and Bragg did just the opposite. Bragg's most important subordinates, Nathan Bedford Forrest and James Longstreet, were allowed to leave Bragg's immediate command because they had openly questioned Bragg's abilities. Although he remained with Bragg, another of the Confederacy's finest officers, General Patrick Cleburne, had also alienated himself from the acerbic Bragg. On a visit to Bragg's command in October, Davis attempted to restore order in the ranks by objurgating the subordinates rather than firing Bragg, which would have been the wisest course of action. Thus, by scattering Bragg's angry, proud (and more competent) subordinates, Davis not only diluted Bragg's troop strength, he drained the Army of Tennessee of its most talented leaders as well. In the end it would prove a fateful decision.

By 15 November, when Grant finally had General William T. Sherman at his side, the Union forces were ready to fight their way out of the siege. With the Confederates spread out all over Missionary Ridge, Grant's basic strategy was to have Sherman's forces attack the northern flank and for General Joseph

Hooker's troops to clear the Confederate forces around Lookout Mountain in the south and then move toward the Rossville Gap, which was on the southern end of Missionary Ridge. Grant also devised that, to keep Bragg from freely reinforcing his flanks, he would have General George Thomas first capture Orchard Knob and then feign an attack at the center of Missionary Ridge, a position that was considered impregnable. As simple as this plan seemed at the time, in reality it would prove far more complicated to implement.

Sherman's forces, which started on the opposite side of the Tennessee River from the other Union forces, had difficulty against stubborn Confederate resistance led by General Cleburne. Anything that could have gone wrong did go wrong for Sherman, including missing the boat that was to take him back to his army from a conference with Grant. Rain and poor logistical planning delayed Sherman's expected attack from 20 November to the 23d, and when his forces did attack, they lacked their usual ferocity. According to Thomas B. Buell,

Sherman delayed. He seemed lethargic, with no sense of urgency. His lead divisions remained idle while the remaining two crossed during the remainder of the finest division, Cleburne's, to the right wing. Sherman could have used his first two divisions at daybreak to capture the objective, a rail-

Confederate prisoners at the Chattanooga depot, 1864 (*Library of Congress*)

road tunnel about a mile down the ridge, because it was undefended. When Sherman finally got underway at one o'clock, Cleburne was already there, entrenching and prepared to fight.

With Cleburne burrowing in at Tunnel Hill, Sherman seemed to be stumbling around, seemingly unaware even of the terrain ahead of him. He soon became defensive-minded when he was supposed to be responsible for the bulk of the offensive.

Grant did not seem to have a clue about the goings-on with his favorite soldier and was not completely aware of the activities of Hooker as well. He ordered that both Sherman and Thomas attack at dawn on the 25th, with the latter either taking the rifle pits at the base of Missionary Ridge or moving left to help Sherman. Grant never intended Thomas's men to attack the center of the Confederate line directly ahead because the thinking was that they would be slaughtered trying to capture the high ground. Sherman found the fighting at Tunnel Hill no more successful than the day before, and his advance was once again stalled. However, the fierceness of the

conflict forced Bragg to drain reserves from his center to relieve the pressure on Cleburne.

Grant and Thomas were waiting at Orchard Knob, hoping to hear that Hooker had been successful on Lookout Mountain and was on his way to help dislodge the Confederates from their perch on Missionary Ridge. Although Hooker had experienced an easy victory on Lookout Mountain, his troops were severely delayed in returning because retreating Confederate general Carter L. Stevenson had burned the bridge over Chattanooga Creek. Hooker's victory in the "Battle above the Clouds" had been much easier than he had ever imagined, so much so that he actually made it more difficult than it needed to be. Although he was victorious, Hooker's overcautious behavior added more delay and confusion to the overall campaign. Seemingly stalled on all fronts and frustrated by delay after delay, Grant was uncharacteristically indecisive until he ordered his troops to take only the rifle pits at the foot of Missionary Ridge, although such an action would place the Union soldiers in a precarious position from Confederate guns above. When Thomas's men took the rifle pits, overrunning the severely outnumbered Confederates, they indeed found life hellish and so spontaneously attacked up the steep ridge as a matter of survival.

Their own assault took the Union high command by complete surprise; Grant muttered that there would be hell to pay if the advance ended in disaster, but of course it did not. The attack moved forward unevenly as the Union troops ran up the slope with the Confederate defenders' guns seemingly stunned into silence. As the blue line streamed up the hill, the gray one fled in desperation and fear. Bragg could only watch in disbelief as the center of his line broke. With his headquarters on the top of the ridge threatened, Bragg hurriedly had to escape to the rear of his army in Dalton. The troops of Confederate generals William J. Hardee and John C. Breckinridge had been soundly defeated, so Cleburne's forces, the only ones on the gray side to have stopped the enemy during the engagement, then had to fight a rearguard retreat in order to save the Confederate army from complete demolition.

On the 26th, Cleburne moved his division through the city of Ringgold, organized a defense-in-depth position between the White Oak Mountains and Taylor Ridge, and waited for Hooker to advance. Surprised by Cleburne's concealed position, the Union forces were soon pinned down and stopped in their tracks. When Grant arrived on the scene, he immediately called off Hooker's movement through Ringgold Gap because he was far more concerned about activities with General Ambrose Burnside's Union forces in Nashville that were being threatened by Confederate general Longstreet's offensive. Longstreet's campaign had been planned as a way to relieve the shaky command situation Davis had found when he visited Bragg before the battle of Chattanooga; it turned out to be a political decision that backfired. It is clear that Longstreet's leadership during the battle would have helped immensely.

Although the Confederates were soundly defeated, largely due to their misalignment but also due to their being utterly demoralized by Bragg's incompetence, they managed not to disintegrate. They eventually were able to reorganize among the hills around Dalton, situated on the rail line that ran into their main supply base in Atlanta. Bragg, whose nerves on a good day seemed to have been bad, now faced the profound defeat of an army that just several months before had celebrated a remarkable victory at Chickamauga and the siege of Chattanooga. To his credit, he immediately requested his dismissal as commander of Confederate forces in Georgia, and Davis obviously had no other choice but to accept. Acting on advice from Lee, the Confederate president brought General Joseph Johnston out of retirement and sent him to reorganize and prepare the Confederate forces for the inevitable defense of Atlanta.

The relief of the Chattanooga siege would prove to be one of the decisive events of the later stages of the war. Sherman, who soon became commander of an army when Grant was promoted to greater responsibility and sent to the eastern front, would use it as his supply base on his march to Atlanta and eventually the sea. Johnston, for his part, spent the winter of 1864 devising defensive strategies to stop the determined Sherman. The casualties for this Chattanooga campaign were approximately 5,400 for the Union and 6,900 for the Confederates.

—*James H. Meredith*

See also Bragg, Braxton; Chattanooga, Tennessee; Cleburne, Patrick Ronayne; Lookout Mountain, Battle of; Missionary Ridge, Battle of; Sherman, William Tecumseh; Thomas George Henry.

For further reading:
Bowers, John. *Chickamauga and Chattanooga: The Battles That Doomed the Confederacy* (1994).
Buell, Thomas B. *The Warrior Generals: Combat Leadership in the Civil War* (1997).
Cozzens, Peter. *The Shipwreck of Their Hopes: The Battles for Chattanooga* (1994).
Grant, Ulysses S. *Personal Memoirs of U. S. Grant* (1885).
McDonough, James L. *Chattanooga—A Death Grip on the Confederacy* (1984).
Roland, Charles P. "Chattanooga-Ringgold Campaign: November 1863." *The Civil War Battlefield Guide* (1998).
Sword, Wiley. *Mountains Touched with Fire: Chattanooga Besieged, 1863* (1995).

CHATTANOOGA, TENNESSEE

As the Tennessee River winds through the southern Appalachian Mountains, it makes a large horseshoe bend. The town of Chattanooga sits inside this bend and between two ridges that form the Chattanooga Valley. Lookout Mountain, rising almost 1,800 feet above the river, overlooks the town's southwestern edge. Supposedly, the name "Chattanooga" derives from the Creek phrase for "rock that comes to a point," which aptly describes the narrowing of the mountain as it nears the city. To the southeast stands another formidable natural barrier, Missionary Ridge. About one-third as high as Lookout Mountain, Missionary Ridge runs fifteen miles south from just above Chattanooga to Rossville, Georgia.

Before 1850, the town's 2,500 inhabitants made their living largely from the river. Unfortunately, gorges and water hazards just below Chattanooga make large-scale riverborne commerce from Middle and West Tennessee upstream to Knoxville nearly impossible. Incorporated in 1839, Chattanooga remained a relatively small port during most of the antebellum period. However, Tennesseans rapidly accelerated railroad construction in the 1850s, and Chattanooga's unique geographical location among the mountains and on the river proved ideal for business. In less than a decade, Chattanooga became a major Southern transportation hub. Four railroad lines

A U.S. military train at the Chattanooga depot, 1864 (*Library of Congress*)

eventually passed through Chattanooga: one line connecting the Midwest to the lower South via Nashville, a second linking the Mississippi at Memphis with Charleston, a third running to Atlanta, and a fourth uniting Richmond with the Deep South via Knoxville.

The surrounding area benefited immensely from the railroads, and Chattanooga's population just before the war swelled to about 5,000 residents. When compared with other Tennessee urban areas such as Nashville, which held 40,000 people, Chattanooga curiously remained a relatively small town. Several large deposits

of iron, lead, coal, and copper were also mined within proximity, adding to its economic attractiveness. The availability of easily accessible transportation routes and abundant natural resources spawned industrial growth in northern Alabama and Georgia throughout the 1850s. By 1860, Chattanooga itself boasted two major iron works, making Tennessee the nation's third highest iron-producing region behind Pennsylvania and New York.

As Tennessee flirted with secession, Chattanooga's residents became deeply divided. A few days after leaving the U.S. Senate in January 1861, Jefferson Davis stayed in

Federal engineers constructing a temporary bridge across the Tennessee River at Chattanooga, March 1864 (*National Archives*)

Chattanooga for one night while en route back to Mississippi. Local citizens, mostly former Whigs who still hoped a compromise could be reached, gathered outside Davis's hotel, the Crutchfield House. They prodded Davis into giving an oration on current events to the assembled crowd. Despite the future Confederate president's rather moderate tone, one of the hotel's proprietors and a staunch Unionist, William Crutchfield, addressed the same crowd after the weary Davis had retired, denouncing him as a traitor. Informed of Crutchfield's charges, Davis returned, challenging his accuser to a duel. Thomas Crutchfield, William's brother and a Southern sympathizer, intervened and forcibly removed his sibling from the lobby to defuse the situation. Reports of this incident spread quickly across the South and served to polarize further the opposing factions.

Hamilton County, like most of East Tennessee, voted against secession in the Tennessee special elections of 1861, but the results reflected a peculiar pattern. The majority of the secessionist support had come from the urban districts, which had been recently settled by Georgians and Alabamians. Unionist support came from the rural districts that had been established by Northern settlers in the early 1800s. During the war, each side in the county took turns persecuting and confiscating the property of the other, control depending upon which army currently held the town. The destruction and near

starvation inflicted by the war's shifting tides only worsened the suffering and deepened the animosities.

Initially, residents thought that their isolated mountain location would shield them from the ravages of war, but it was precisely Chattanooga's location that made the town a primary target. The residents failed to realize that Chattanooga's new railroads now made it the gateway to the South, and any army that occupied the city would hold a decided advantage over its enemy. For the Union, capturing Chattanooga would divide the Confederacy geographically and deprive the Army of Northern Virginia of vital foodstuffs and war materials produced in the lower South. Furthermore, Chattanooga's railroads gave Union forces the ability to leave the rivers and rely principally upon trains for supply as they pushed south toward Atlanta. The importance of Chattanooga to the Confederate war effort then ensured that the city would not be surrendered without a fight.

In August 1863, the Army of Tennessee retreated from Tullahoma to Chattanooga, but left the city when the Army of the Cumberland appeared on the Chickamauga Creek southwest of the city. The two armies clashed at Chickamauga in September 1862, and Federal forces, routed by the Confederates, retreated into Chattanooga to regroup. For two months, the Confederates laid siege to the city, preventing any supplies from entering. During the siege, Union troops destroyed buildings for firewood and confiscated animals, including horses, for food. Ulysses S. Grant eventually broke the siege in late November 1863 by launching daring assaults on Confederate-held Lookout Mountain and Missionary Ridge. General William T. Sherman subsequently used Chattanooga as a logistical base during the Atlanta campaign and infamous March to the Sea.

As the Union army advanced southward, thousands of freed slaves began streaming into Chattanooga. Their presence placed an additional burden upon a white population already struggling to recover from the havoc wrought by battle and the Federal occupation. Violence between blacks and whites erupted throughout Chattanooga, and Union authorities were barely able to maintain any semblance of order. The Freedmen's Bureau finally arrived in 1865 and restored a measure of stability to the city.

Ironically, Chattanooga's wartime experience stimulated rather than hindered its economic growth. Many Union soldiers returned to the area after the war and brought large amounts of Northern capital to rebuild the city's damaged infrastructure. New iron factories and several additional trunk lines were built. Freedmen and returning Confederate soldiers provided the newly constructed factories and mines with an abundant supply of cheap labor. By 1877, Chattanooga had become a major Southern manufacturing center.

—*Derek W. Frisby*

See also Chattanooga Campaign.
For further reading:
Cozzens, Peter. *The Shipwreck of Their Hopes: The Battles for Chattanooga* (1994).
Goven, Gilbert E., and James W. Livingood. *The Chattanooga Country, 1540–1962: From Tomahawk to TVA* (1963).
McDonough, James Lee. *Chattanooga—A Death Grip on the Confederacy* (1984).
Wilson, John. *Chattanooga's Story* (1980).
Woodworth, Steven E. *Six Armies in Tennessee: The Chickamauga and Chattanooga Campaigns* (1998).

CHEAT MOUNTAIN, VIRGINIA
(10–14 September 1861)

Confederate fortunes in the mountainous western counties of Virginia had turned decidedly dark during the summer of 1861. The defeat at Rich Mountain, followed by General Robert Garnett's death at Carrick's Ford, had so alarmed Richmond that on 28 July Robert E. Lee departed the capital to supervise a campaign seeking to reverse the gains Major General George McClellan had made in the region. McClellan's successes had won him the foremost Union command. Conversely, Lee's record in those same mountains, starting with the abortive affair at Cheat Mountain, would only diminish his reputation.

Some things Lee could not control. The weather was inordinately wet—it had rained every day in August—and it had dampened the soldiers' spirits almost as much as the military setbacks had. It had also made them sickly. They perhaps felt—and rightly so—that their commanders were only marginally competent, and when those commanders were experienced, they could be querulous. Lee had replaced the fallen Garnett as commander of the Army of the Northwest with William Wing Loring, an officer who had outranked Lee in the United States Army before secession and who apparently now resented the arrival of his nominal superior. Lee took pains to preserve Loring's good will, even to the point of establishing a separate headquarters at Valley Mountain and framing his orders in the form of suggestions. Whether authorities in Richmond endorsed this deference or not, Lee was habituated to it and characteristically sought to preserve amiability with courtesy. The result was an odd command structure that had Lee acting more in the role of brotherly counselor than dominant general. It was a bad arrangement for several reasons. For one, although he wielded at best a modified authority, Lee would bear all the blame when things went wrong.

Officially Loring was in command, but Lee found him reluctant to mount any sort of campaign. Weighing the Confederate situation against Union strength, there was some wisdom in that caution, but Lee knew that morale both in the mountains and elsewhere could not endure prolonged inaction. Consequently, he urged Loring to make a concerted move on a Federal fortification atop the crest of Cheat Mountain. Loring instead devised a plan to attack Federal troops near Huttonsville, thus to isolate the Cheat Mountain garrison, which he apparently believed to be very formidable.

Actually, Colonel Nathan Kimball had only about 300 men of the 14th Indiana Infantry on Cheat Mountain. The real strength of Brigadier General Joseph J. Reynolds's 1st Brigade was along the Staunton-Parkersburg pike and westward near Elkwater. Lee agreed to Loring's plan, although he continued to scout for ways to fall upon the fort atop Cheat. When Colonel Albert Rust, commanding the 3d Arkansas Infantry, reported he had found just such a route, Lee and Loring revised the plan. Added now to Loring's march down the Tygart River Valley toward Huttonsville was a surprise attack on Cheat Mountain by Rust's 1,600 Arkansans. Another column would cut off Kimball's line of retreat and H. R. Jackson's brigade would poise on Cheat's first summit to occupy the ridge, once Rust had reduced the Federal fort. Loring made the orders formal on 8 September, and the following day Lee issued what was styled a special order, but actually and admittedly was an exhortation. "The eyes of the country are upon you," he proclaimed.

Curiously, no Federal eyes were. Confederate forces began moving into position on 11 September and continued their maneuvers undetected. Lee followed the column marching down the Tygart Valley as rain again began to fall and the air took on a noticeable chill. Yet operations appeared on schedule and slated for success. Everything hinged on Rust surprising Kimball's Cheat Mountain garrison, for the sound of his guns would signal everyone else to attack. On the cold, wet dawn of 12 September, however, no sound of combat carried from Cheat Mountain. Rust had made the arduous march and had arrived on the perimeter of Cheat's fort on time—in spite of the rain, he noted—but then he captured a few Union pickets who blithely informed him that Kimball's garrison numbered between 4,000 to 5,000 men. Rust conducted a personal reconnaissance and had neither the experience nor anyone who did to expose this for the lie it was. His prisoners cheerfully began to relate how Confederate plans were common knowledge and that the telegraph was summoning Federal reinforcements for a crushing blow in the Tygart Valley. Already fearful of slaughtering his regiment with an attack on the Cheat Mountain fort, Rust now presumed the entire campaign was a doomed enterprise. Without firing a shot, he withdrew. By then, Reynolds was sending reinforcements to Kimball. Never having heard Rust's guns, the main column sat idle in the valley. Finally judging all surprise lost, it too fell back. The battle never happened, though skirmishes resulted in a few casualties and prisoners for each side.

The main casualty for the time being was Lee's reputation. On 14 September, he described the campaign as a "forced reconnaissance" and promised that it had revealed enemy weaknesses that would be exploited "at such time and in such manner as General Loring shall direct." Yet nothing could put a good face on the miscarriage. Rust more bluntly observed, "The expedition against Cheat Mountain failed." When news reached Lee that his aide Colonel John A. Washington had been killed by a sniper's bullet while conducting a reconnaissance, his desolation was nearly complete.

—*David S. Heidler and Jeanne T. Heidler*

See also Carrick's Ford; Kimball, Nathan; Lee, Robert E.; Loring, William Wing; Reynolds, Joseph Jones; Rich Mountain, Battle of; West Virginia.

For further reading:
Zinn, Jack. *R. E. Lee's Cheat Mountain Campaign* (1974).

CHEATHAM, BENJAMIN FRANKLIN
(1820–1886)
Confederate general

Benjamin Franklin Cheatham achieved fame as a leader in the Confederate Army of Tennessee. His term as commander in the Western theater included many of the area's most important battles. The quality of Cheatham's leadership during the Civil War remains unclear, but his importance is unquestioned.

Born at Nashville, Tennessee, on 20 October 1820, Cheatham came from a distinguished political family. Several of his father's relatives held political offices at the state level. His maternal ties included James Robertson, the patriarch of one of Tennessee's "first families" and an important member of the first political movements in the state. Several of Cheatham's relatives also had served in the military, including his father, Leonard, who fought with Andrew Jackson in the War of 1812.

Military service became important to Cheatham as a young man. In the early 1840s, he joined a local militia company, the Nashville Blues, and received promotion to first lieutenant before resigning his commission after five years of service. His experience with the Nashville militia proved important when the United States declared war on Mexico in 1846. Cheatham returned to his old militia company as a captain. He served with distinction at the head of Tennessee's "Bloody First" Regiment at the battle of Monterrey. After returning to Nashville for a rest, the members of the newly organized 3d Tennessee Regiment selected Cheatham as their colonel. He hoped that further service would elevate him to brigadier general, but the war ended without his realizing that goal.

Between 1849 and 1853, Cheatham spent his time in California supplying the gold-seekers with merchandise from his store and food and lodging from his hotel-restaurant. His return to Tennessee brought not only a resumption of farming activities, but involvement in political life. He was appointed a major general in the Tennessee militia. President James Buchanan considered him for the posts of governor of the Utah Territory and consul to Aspinwall (now Colón), Panama, but Cheatham was never offered the first and turned down the second. He also ran unsuccessfully for mayor of Nashville.

When Tennessee seceded from the Union in 1861, Governor Isham G. Harris appointed Cheatham to the position of brigadier general in the new Provisional Army of Tennessee. In July, Cheatham retained the same position when the Army of Tennessee joined the Confederacy. He participated in the battle of Belmont in late 1861. In April 1862, Cheatham, now a major general, led the 2d Division during the fighting at Shiloh. He was subsequently involved in the major battles that took place in Tennessee.

In the fall and winter of 1862, Cheatham led divisions at the battles of Perryville in Kentucky and Stones River in middle Tennessee. He faced controversy after Stones River when several reports alleged that he appeared intoxicated. The issue of Cheatham's alleged inebriation disappeared, however, as the Confederate

Benjamin F. Cheatham (*Library of Congress*)

army moved toward Tullahoma and then Chickamauga. Cheatham's soldiers performed admirably in defensive maneuvers at Chickamauga. Yet contention among Confederate commander Braxton Bragg and several Confederate leaders, including Leonidas Polk, Cheatham's superior and mentor, led Cheatham to resign his command. He eventually changed his mind about his resignation, but not before the Confederate forces lost Lookout Mountain. Cheatham rejoined the army in time to witness the loss of Missionary Ridge.

After the Atlanta campaign and the battle of Kennesaw Mountain, Cheatham received a promotion to corps commander when William J. Hardee left the army as a result of conflicts with Bragg. The new corps commander moved with John Bell Hood's army into middle Tennessee. Cheatham experienced his lowest point of the war when Hood accused him of failing to attack Federal troops at Spring Hill in late November 1864. The Federal soldiers escaped and helped bolster the Union defense at the battle of Franklin, which resulted in a Confederate defeat. Historians have debated whether Cheatham erred in allowing the Federal troops to escape. The blame likely lies with Hood, Cheatham, and at least one subordinate officer, John C. Brown. Cheatham's reputation never recovered from this accusation.

After the battle of Nashville, Cheatham served the rest of the war as a division commander in North Carolina under Joseph E. Johnston. After the war, he ran unsuccessfully for a congressional seat in 1872, losing to Horace Maynard. In 1874, Cheatham accepted the post of superintendent of state prisons in Tennessee, and in 1885 he became the postmaster in Nashville. He died the next year on 4 September, a man who had defended his military reputation to the end.

—*Mark R. Cheathem*

See also Franklin, Battle of; Nashville, Battle of.
For further reading:
Connelly, Thomas L. *Army of the Heartland: The Army of Tennessee, 1861–1862* (1967).
———. *Autumn of Glory: The Army of Tennessee, 1863–1865* (1971).
Losson, Christopher. *Tennessee's Forgotten Warriors: Frank Cheatham and His Confederate Division* (1989).

CHEROKEE INDIANS

At the outbreak of the American Civil War, the approximately 17,000 members of the Cherokee Nation lived in the northeastern section of Indian Territory, north of the Arkansas River. As was true for most nations living within the boundaries of Indian Territory, the Cherokees split over the issue of allegiances. The division of the Cherokees, however, had deep roots stemming from the factionalism created by the differences of opinion over the wisdom of standing up to the U.S. government and its removal policies of the 1830s. The split was also linked to the differing attitudes toward slavery and slaveholding among native people, some of whom were full-bloods who retained their traditional customs, while other mixed-bloods were more culturally akin to Southern whites. For example, before their removal, many Cherokees living in northern Georgia and Alabama adopted the institution of slavery. As removal became a reality, Cherokee slaveholders took their slaves with them and established laws similar to the slave codes in existence throughout much of the South. The retention of slaves (used primarily in Indian Territory for stock herding and salt making, as well as the more typical agricultural purposes) allowed the elites in Cherokee society to preserve their preeminence. Many mixed-bloods became affluent planters living like white planters elsewhere in the South. During the 1850s, however, non-slaveholding Cherokees grew more vocal in their opposition to the institution and found support among Protestant missionaries, who often had direct ties to the abolitionist movement in the northeast.

On 17 May 1861, Principal Chief John Ross issued a proclamation reminding the Cherokees of their obligations arising under the treaties with the United States. Foremost among Ross's concerns was fear that any course other than neutrality would provide a pretext for Federal military operations in Cherokee country. Ross also declared to the Cherokee National Council that he personally preferred that their treaties with the United States remain in effect because they provided for annuities on which the Cherokees depended for the operation of their schools, press, and government. In opposition to Ross, Stand Watie, a Georgian by birth and the lone survivor of the Cherokee leaders who formally supported removal, organized the Knights of the Golden Circle in Indian Territory. The Knights were generally a secret organization of supporters of Southern rights and the expansion of slavery. Watie and his followers actively worked to bring the Cherokees into the Confederate fold. Another secret society called the Keetowahs (or Pins) opposed the efforts of the Knights and endorsed maintaining the established treaties with the United States. Violence broke out between the two groups at Webbers Falls in the summer of 1861 over the raising of a Confederate flag.

Eager to formally bring the Cherokees into the Confederacy, Special Commissioner Albert Pike of the Confederate Bureau of Indian Affairs met with Ross at his stately mansion at Park Hill near Tahlequah. There Ross officially informed Pike of his plans to honor the treaties with the United States but to remain neutral in the impending war. More than likely, Ross was nevertheless well aware of the growing support for Stand Watie and feared that he might lose his place as principal chief at the hands of Confederate authorities eager to see Watie assume the position. On the other hand, if Ross chose to listen to Pike and break the treaties with the United States, the Cherokees stood to lose millions of dollars held in trust in Washington and to alienate all the full-blood Keetowahs who kept Ross in office.

The immense pressure manifesting itself upon the shoulders of the principal chief throughout the late summer of 1861 persuaded Ross to support a formal treaty of recognition and association with the Confederacy. The other major Indian nations in the territory had signed treaties. Stand Watie was gaining power as he organized his regiment of mixed-bloods and headed toward the northeastern border with Kansas to guard against a possible Federal invasion. There was also a rumor that Watie was going to establish a separate Cherokee government and ally with the Confederacy if Ross continued on his path of neutrality. Ross was also well aware of recent Confederate victories at Manassas and Wilson's Creek, which could be signals of imminent victory for the South.

Consequently, at a 21 August assembly at Tahlequah, John Ross won approval from the council to open negotiations with the Confederate Bureau of Indian Affairs through its special agent, Pike. For his part, Pike offered the Cherokees a treaty that included protection from invasion, the continuation of annuity payments, respect for Cherokee titles to their lands, the purchase of Cherokee neutral lands on the Kansas border at the price

they wanted, the right to maintain the institution of slavery, and representation in the Confederate Congress. Ross signed the treaty of alliance on 7 October and offered Pike the services of a regiment of home guards composed mostly of Keetowahs and commanded by Colonel John Drew, a Ross devotee.

Although Article 41 of their treaty with the Confederate States called for the Cherokees to furnish a regiment of ten companies of mounted men, with two reserve companies to serve in the armies of the Confederacy for twelve months, the only units of substance to be organized were in fact established before the alliance: Stand Watie's company of mixed-bloods and Colonel Drew's regiment of Keetowahs. Watie's command participated in the battle of Pea Ridge on 7 March 1862 and served as a home guard unit operating against bands of Indians from various nations who remained loyal to the Union.

In the summer of 1862, Union troops marched on Tahlequah and captured John Ross. The principal chief went to Washington, where he argued that he had had no choice but to sign a treaty with Pike. Ross then issued a proclamation of Cherokee loyalty to the Union and watched as three of his sons enlisted into the Union military.

With Ross in Washington, Stand Watie used the opportunity to declare himself the new principal chief of the Cherokee Nation and proceeded to consolidate his power. Thus the division of the Cherokees in Indian Territory was complete. For the remainder of the war, supporters of each faction still living in the territory staged hit-and-run campaigns against the other. Families were murdered, homes vandalized, crops burned, and livestock butchered.

The bitter, partisan experience of the Cherokee Nation in Indian Territory, however, was not shared by the Eastern Band Cherokees living in the Smoky Mountains of western North Carolina and eastern Tennessee. Although these Cherokees were not particularly swayed to the Confederate cause, their agent, William H. Thomas, was very much a Southern sympathizer. Thomas put together a regiment of 400 Cherokees who were to be used primarily as a home guard. Thomas's legion, as the group came to be called, also served as enforcers of Confederate conscription, as watchmen for possible Union invasion, and as counterespionage agents. As the war progressed, two companies of the legion were transferred to Virginia in 1864, and a few Eastern Band Cherokees were on hand at the evacuation of Richmond. Thomas and approximately 600 of his men surrendered on 9 May 1865 in Waynesville, North Carolina. They were the last sizable Confederate force to surrender east of the Mississippi River.

—*Alan C. Downs*

See also Pea Ridge, Battle of; Pike, Albert; Ross, John; Thomas, William Holland; Watie, Stand.

For further reading:

Gaines, W. Craig. *The Confederate Cherokees: John Drew's Regiment of Mounted Rifles* (1989).

Hauptman, Laurence M. *Between Two Fires: American Indians in the Civil War* (1995).

Josephy, Alvin M. *The Civil War in the American West* (1991).

CHESAPEAKE AFFAIR

Hijackers disguised as passengers seized the SS *Chesapeake*, bound from New York City for Portland, Maine, in the dark hours of 8 December 1863 off Cape Cod. John Braine, a Kentuckian vengeful from wrongful imprisonment by Union authorities, wanted to man a privateer. Once in control, Braine and his men entered New Brunswick waters and at Grand Manaan Island, picked up coal and their commander, Vernon Locke, of Shelburne County, Nova Scotia. Most of the passengers and crew were put off in a small boat. They rowed for Saint John and raised the alarm. Telegraph messages from the local American consul alerted the Washington government, and a hue and cry erupted the next day.

Meanwhile, Locke sold cargo at Shelburne, New Dublin, and Mahone Bay, Nova Scotia, to raise money. He renamed the *Chesapeake* the *Retribution* to fit an old letter of marque he carried from the Confederate government. On 14 December, he anchored at Petite Riviere and Braine fled to avoid arrest by authorities at Liverpool. Locke hid the *Chesapeake* in the Le Harve River as a Union gunboat entered Lunenburg harbor. Later, Locke steamed for Sambro, near Halifax, to rendezvous with a coaler Braine had contracted, but Union warships blockaded both ships, and on 16 December Union boarding parties took control of them. Some of the crew fled, but several, including Nova Scotians, were captured. The senior Union officer present ordered the capture legalized in Halifax to satisfy the demands of neutrality.

When the *Chesapeake* entered Halifax under a prize crew, and Union warships followed with prisoners in irons, the affair entered a critical phase for Anglo-American relations, with the potential to reprise the near disaster of the *Trent* crisis of 1862. Colonial authorities issued warrants to arrest Braine and Locke. They also accused the United States of violating British neutrality. Many Haligonians had strong anti-Union sympathies, which actually were more anti-Yankee and pro-British than pro-Confederate. When U.S. officers, under instructions by Secretary of the Navy Gideon Welles, brought their prisoners to the Queen's Wharf for transfer, a pro-Confederate crowd tussled with British authorities, and the raiders escaped.

Overall, the British and American governments were determined to avoid a clash. William Henry Seward officially disavowed and apologized for the seizures at Sambro and promised to censure those responsible. Lord Lyons, the British minister to Washington, pointedly accepted these reassurances. Public opinion as expressed in Northern and Provincial newspapers remained calm, colonial authorities moved to apply the letter of the law, and the *Chesapeake* affair slumbered in a slow legal aftermath that ran from late December 1863 to March 1864.

The trials of the hijackers in Saint John, and the later disposition of the *Chesapeake* herself, were well covered by the maritime and Northern press. New Brunswick's courts found against the hijackers tried there, but an appeal got them released in March 1864 under a writ of habeas corpus. They promptly decamped to escape rearrest under new warrants. Lincoln's government was relieved because these men had been mostly British subjects. If they had been extradited and tried in the North, diplomatic tension would have been revived. At Halifax, Judge Alexander Stewart of the Vice Admiralty Court impounded and returned the *Chesapeake*'s goods, and declared the ship herself a victim of pirates. On 19 March 1864 the vessel steamed under Union naval escort for Portland and its owners. Haligonians accused of abetting the escapees, however, received only reprimands and fines.

The *Chesapeake* issue thus ended as British and American officials had hoped. Confederate secretary of war Judah P. Benjamin sent University of Virginia law professor J. P. Holcombe to Halifax in an effort to turn events to the South's advantage, but it was all over when he arrived. Even so, the affair had echoes. Rumors swirled of further plots and Union authorities took steps to defend against future hijackings of coastal steamers. Seward ordered that anyone bound to the British provinces would need a passport and warships were stationed to check passengers' credentials at sea. The governor of Maine demanded federal protection and rumors and alarms excited the borderland towns of Calais and St. Stephen from time to time.

Overall, the *Chesapeake* affair revealed how deeply the maritime British colonies had become intertwined with the Civil War by late 1863. Many Haligonians welcomed and feted Confederates, whether they were passing through or were sojourners. The mercantile community profited from the demands for supplies and carriers even as the local population freely ventilated anti-Yankee prejudices and debated the motives and justice of the Union and Confederate causes. Those differences became academic after Appomattox, but both Confederate and Union veterans lie buried in the city, mute testimony to Halifax's status as a maritime nexus for one part of the American Civil War.

—*Reginald C. Stuart*

See also Diplomacy, C.S.A.; Diplomacy, U.S.A.; Great Britain; Holcombe, James; Privateers.

For further reading:

Cox, George. "Sidelights on the *Chesapeake* Affair, 1863–64." *Royal Nova Scotia Historical Society, Collections* (1951).

Jones, Francis I. "Treason and Piracy in Civil War Halifax: The Second *Chesapeake* Affair Revisited." *Dalhousie Review* (1991–1992).

Marquis, Greg. *In Armageddon's Shadow: The Civil War and Canada's Maritime Provinces* (1998).

McDonald, Ronald H. "Second *Chesapeake* Affair." *Dalhousie Review* (1974–1975).

Smith, Philip Mason. *Confederates Down East: Confederate Operations in and around Maine* (1985).

CHESNUT, JAMES
(1815–1885)
Confederate congressman and general

Born to James Chesnut and Mary Cox Chesnut in Camden, South Carolina, the younger Chesnut was educated at Princeton University and studied law upon his return to South Carolina. After opening a practice in Camden, Chesnut became involved in South Carolina politics. Between 1840 and 1858, he served terms in both houses of the South Carolina legislature. He also represented the state in 1850 at the Nashville Convention. In 1858, he was selected to fill the unexpired term of the late Josiah J. Evans in the U.S. Senate. Chesnut remained in that body until the election of Abraham Lincoln as president in November 1860.

An ardent secessionist, Chesnut believed that an early exit from the national legislature might start a stampede of states out of the Union. At home he worked feverishly to bring about the secession of his own state, serving as a member of the secession convention and one of the authors of the ordinance of secession. After other gulf states followed South Carolina out of the union in early 1861, Chesnut was selected to represent his state to the Provisional Confederate Congress in Montgomery, Alabama. He traveled there with his wife, Mary Boykin Chesnut, the future author of *A Diary from Dixie*.

In Montgomery, Chesnut pushed for unity within the Southern Confederacy and believed that one of the best ways to achieve such unity was to discourage South Carolina dominance of the proceedings and encourage a distribution of offices among citizens of all member states. As a result, he opposed the selection of any South Carolinian for president or vice president of the Confederacy. Some of his most important work was on the committee that drafted the Confederate Constitution.

As the crisis over Fort Sumter worsened in the spring of 1861, Chesnut returned home and offered his services as a voluntary aide to the Confederate commander in Charleston, P. G. T. Beauregard. Chesnut was one of a group of Beauregard aides who negotiated with Major Robert Anderson before the bombardment began on Fort Sumter. Privately Chesnut expressed sympathy for Anderson's predicament. Chesnut sent the note to Anderson at 3:20 A.M. on 12 April warning him that the firing would commence in approximately one hour.

After the surrender of Fort Sumter, Beauregard was sent to Virginia. In June 1861, Chesnut made arrangements to join him, leaving his home in early June and arriving in Richmond on 12 June. During the first part of the summer, Chesnut, because of his legal training, served as judge advocate on Beauregard's staff at the rank of colonel. On 13 July Beauregard sent Chesnut to Richmond with a suggestion for President Jefferson Davis that Beauregard's and Joseph Johnston's armies join at Manassas Junction to meet the potential Union attack there. During the ensuing battle of Bull Run on 21 July, Chesnut served as Beauregard's aide.

In August, Chesnut was back in the Confederate Congress, but longed for the military life. Because he was a friend of President Davis from their days in the U.S. Senate together, he was pestered for jobs. Chesnut also found himself in the middle of a growing feud between the president and Beauregard, the one his friend and president, the other his former military commander. He tried to use his influence over both to mediate the dispute, but was increasingly frustrated in his efforts. In January 1862 he received appointment as the chief of the Military Department of the Executive Council of South Carolina. He held that position for most of the remainder of 1862. One of his primary duties was to review requests for exemptions from military service, a task not at all to his liking. In the late fall of 1862, he resigned this post to accept a position as a military adviser to President Davis, again with the rank of colonel.

Serving directly under Davis for the next eighteen months, Chesnut conducted inspections of military forces as far away as the western Confederate armies. He also traveled to Chattanooga in August 1863 to meet with Braxton Bragg on Davis's behalf (and perhaps to determine if the mounting criticism of Bragg was justified). In the fall campaigns of 1863, Chesnut served as Bragg's aide. Still it was not the active command he desired, and in April 1864 he accepted the command of all reserve forces in South Carolina at the rank of brigadier general.

Headquartered at Columbia, Chesnut watched and waited with growing dread as William T. Sherman began his campaign in neighboring Georgia. There was little he could do, however, but wait. When Sherman brought his army into South Carolina in early 1865, Chesnut placed his reserves under the command of Joseph E. Johnston. Chesnut remained behind with the militia when Johnston and Sherman moved into North Carolina and remained in command in South Carolina until the end of the war.

After the war, Chesnut returned to his law practice but never regained the fortune he had accumulated before the war. He remained active in South Carolina Democratic politics, though his citizenship was not restored until the end of Reconstruction. He died at his home near Camden on 1 February 1885.

—*David S. Heidler and Jeanne T. Heidler*

See also Chesnut, Mary Boykin; Davis, Jefferson; South Carolina.

For further reading:
Chesnut, James. *James Chesnut, Jr., Papers, 1779–1872, Camden, Kershaw District, South Carolina* (1986).
Woodward, C. Vann, ed. *Mary Chesnut's Civil War* (1981).

CHESNUT, MARY BOYKIN
(1823–1886)
Southern diarist

Mary Boykin Chesnut began her diary, "I do not allow myself vain regrets or sad foreboding. This southern confederacy must be supported now by calm determination—and cool brains. We have risked all, and we must play our best for the stake is life or death." This opening set the tone for the life of one of the best personal representations of the Confederacy during the Civil War. Blessed with an amazing wit and intelligence, Chesnut was both politically and socially astute, and therefore quite capable to offer commentary on the events she saw around her.

Born on 31 March 1823 into an aristocratic family in Statesburg, South Carolina, Chesnut received all the benefits her family background afforded her. She was educated at an exclusive boarding school in Charleston, yet she was also well groomed in the domestic arts. Married at seventeen to James Chesnut, she left her childhood behind to move in with her husband's parents at his family plantation, Mulberry, near Camden, South Carolina. However, she was given little to do; her mother-in-law retained control over the household. Further complicating her situation was her inability to bear children, and the first twenty years of her marriage offered few outlets for her frustration.

Chesnut's fortunes changed in 1858 with the election of her husband to the U.S. Senate. The couple moved to Washington, D.C., where she became acquainted with many of the prominent politicians of the day including Jefferson and Varina Davis. Chesnut began to keep her diary in 1861, after James resigned his seat in the Senate in protest over the election of Abraham Lincoln as president. However, the commentary in her diary reflects both her centrality and her marginality as a Southern woman. She operated within the structure of Southern society, staunchly supporting the war, and enjoying the privilege of a slave society, yet she also criticized social conventions. Although she harbored an aversion to slavery, her allegiance to her class and social standing were much stronger. She was hardly an abolitionist, and her antislavery opinions were, as she termed it, "narrowly self-interested." Her quarrel with the slave system was that it "threatened and degraded her position as a woman." In fact, she criticized Harriet Beecher Stowe's *Uncle Tom's Cabin* for taking "an extraordinary freak of nature and presenting it as a specimen of a class—a common type." She argued that Southern women of her class "hate[d] slavery worse than Mrs. Stowe."

Chesnut used her diary to criticize both slavery and Yankee "interference" and also to record personal information. In 1862, James received a commission as an aide to President of the Confederacy Jefferson Davis, and the Chesnuts moved to Richmond, Virginia. During these years, Chesnut's diary was filled with comments in praise of General Robert E. Lee and her distress concerning the long casualty lists. She noted, "Think of all these young lives sacrificed!" The war, however, took its toll on James, and the couple moved back to South Carolina in April 1864. Chesnut noted, "We are at sea. Our boat has sprung a leak." Nevertheless, as it became apparent that the South was fighting a losing battle, Chesnut was forced to retreat once again, this time to Lincolntown, North Carolina. She wrote, "We had as much right to fight to get out as they had a right to fight to keep us in. If they try to play the masters—anywhere upon the habitable globe I will go, never to see a Yankee. And if I die on the way, so much the better." For Mary Chesnut, the war resulted in the resumption of Northern patriarchy, and upon return to Camden, South Carolina, discovery of the destruction of Mulberry by Union forces. Deeply in debt, the Chesnuts faced new challenges in the postbellum era, complications they had never had to face as members of the elite.

Mary Boykin Chesnut's diary provides not only a glimpse into the life and experiences of a privileged Southern woman, but also a look at one who defied the Southern stereotype. Her diary, however, underwent numerous revisions. At her death in 1886, she left behind many versions of the diary; entire sections between 1862 and 1864 are completely missing and may have been destroyed during the war. Chesnut had begun to revise her diary after the war, but she was forced to stop in the mid-1870s, only to resume in 1881. She continued this task until 1885 and the death of both her husband and her mother, and she never returned to the project. She died in 1886.

Historians need to remember that, as Chesnut worked on her revisions, she was aware of the South's postbellum attitudes toward slavery, and this may explain some of her ambivalence on the subject of slavery.

—*Jennifer Harrison*

See also Chesnut, James; Women.

For further reading:
DeCredico, Mary A. *Mary Boykin Chesnut: A Confederate Woman's Life* (1996).
McDonald, Kendra Lynne. "The Creation of History and Myth in Mary Boykin Miller Chesnut's Civil War Narrative" (Ph.D. dissertation, 1996).
Muhlenfeld, Elisabeth. *Mary Boykin Chesnut: A Biography* (1981).
Williams, Ben Ames, ed. *Mary Boykin Chesnut: A Diary from Dixie* (1949).
Woodward, C. Vann, and Elisabeth Muhlenfeld. *The Private Mary Chesnut: The Unpublished Civil War Diaries* (1984).

CHEYENNE INDIANS

With the coming of the Civil War, factions among the Cheyenne pursued multiple strategies to preserve their homeland. In particular, strategies for both accommodation and resistance matured during the turbulent 1850s, intensified throughout the Civil War years, and culminated under Reconstruction politics. Even though they avoided direct involvement in the sectional battles that divided the Union, the Cheyenne nation faced a war of another kind.

The Cheyenne migrated to the midlatitude grasslands during the eighteenth century, developing small-scale agriculture in the river valleys of the region. They also began to expand their political economy by exploiting the buffalo herds and the trading corridors between the Missouri River and the Rocky Mountains. Although the Northern and Southern Cheyenne were geographically split by the Platte River and the Oregon Trail, they shared a linguistic and cultural system. They also concluded an alliance with the Arapaho to drive out common enemies. By the 1860s the Cheyenne numbered approximately 3,500 in population. They were recognized among their neighbors not only for their power in war but also by their prosperity in peace.

Meanwhile, the character of the region began to change. The eventual depletion of the buffalo herds and the recurring epidemics of disease exacted a heavy toll in Cheyenne country. Although the Fort Laramie Treaty of 1851 recognized extensive territorial claims, the Cheyenne were unable to arrest the colonization of Kansas and Nebraska after 1854 and the Colorado gold rush of 1859. With the order of things collapsing, the United States Indian Bureau demanded new treaties and a greater presence for the Federal army as peace keepers—a role the bluecoats were ill prepared to fulfill. Accommodating the Federal government's demands, pacifist leaders Black Kettle, Left Hand, and Lean Bear signed the Treaty of Fort Wise in 1861. They relinquished all the hunting grounds assigned by the Fort Laramie Treaty for a reservation along the upper Arkansas River, where they were promised land allotments, annuities, and security.

Militant war parties called dog soldiers repudiated the peace accord. Originally a military society, they eschewed trade and farming but continued hunting buffalo. Carrying war medicines into battle, they traditionally fought in intertribal conflicts and adapted a fierce lifestyle to fight new enemies. Young men who joined the resistance movement lived off the booty captured from overland trails, trading posts, and frontier settlements. By 1864 the Cheyenne and Arapaho warriors were joined by cohorts from the Lakota, Comanche, and Kiowa. Together, the bands terrorized settler parties, plundered freighters, and raided ranches. Of course, their actions undermined the strategies for accommodation that were being advocated by Cheyenne peace factions.

The violence escalated into the Cheyenne-Arapaho war of 1864–1865. Among the Federal forces called to fight, the 1st Colorado Cavalry fell upon a number of Cheyenne camps, recovering some livestock but also attacking innocent village people and killing pacifist leaders. Among those killed was Lean Bear, who was shot while riding forward from his camp with papers he had received during a visit to Washington, D.C. The cavalry attacks culminated on 29 November 1864, when volunteers sworn into Federal service were led by John Chivington against the camp of Black Kettle along Sand Creek in Colorado. At least 163 men, women, and children were massacred during the attack, although Black Kettle escaped with his life.

Thereafter, Plains Indians from the Canadian border to the Red River followed a warpath for revenge. Indeed, Tall Bull became one of the most prominent dog soldiers committed to resistance. Roman Nose, a militant from the Elk Scrapper society of the Cheyenne, also refused to meet with Federal agents whom he blamed for the atrocities against his people. In January 1865, 1,000 Cheyenne and Sioux warriors attacked Julesburg, Colorado, where they pillaged the store, plundered the warehouses, and defeated a company from the 7th Iowa Cavalry.

With the Treaty of the Little Arkansas on 14 October 1865, the war ended for most Cheyenne south of the Platte River. Signed with war-weary bands, the Treaty of Medicine Lodge in 1867 assigned them to a 5-million-acre reservation between the Cimarron and Arkansas rivers in Indian Territory. Some of the most militant dog soldiers, nonetheless, joined with their kinsmen among the Sioux bands and refused to submit. In the northern plains they fought in the Powder River war from 1865 to 1866. During 1868, 700 warriors clashed with Federal patrols at the battle of Beecher Island in Colorado. Following a nine-day siege wherein Roman Nose died, black troops of the 10th U.S. Cavalry rescued the Federal command there.

The end of the Civil War enabled William T. Sherman and Philip Sheridan to expand Federal military control over the Cheyenne and their confederates. When George A. Custer led the 7th U.S. Cavalry in a winter campaign in 1868, Black Kettle was killed at the Washita River, where he had been promised a reservation. In 1869 President Ulysses S. Grant declared that the reservations were part and parcel of a Federal peace policy to move the Indians toward "civilization and ultimate citizenship." As the U.S. government began a long and difficult process for reconstructing the Union, the Cheyenne nation continued its struggle for self-determination.

—*Brad D. Lookingbill*

See also Chivington, John M.; Sand Creek Massacre.

For further reading:
Carlson, Paul H. *The Plains Indians* (1998).
Grinnell, George Bird. *The Fighting Cheyennes* (1915; reprint, 1955).
Josephy, Alvin M. *The Civil War in the American West* (1991).
Moore, John H. *The Cheyenne* (1996).
Stands in Timber, John, and Margot Liberty. *Cheyenne Memories* (1967).

CHICAGO TRIBUNE

Still a relatively young newspaper and voice in the rapidly growing Midwest, the *Chicago Tribune* was the first metropolitan newspaper to endorse Abraham Lincoln for president and was largely responsible for Lincoln's early political popularity. It provided extensive coverage of the Civil War, fielding as many as twenty-seven battlefield correspondents and suffering the first wartime correspondent casualty in U.S. history. It also took on the near monopoly of the New York press on American public opinion during the war. Capitalizing on its connections with President Lincoln and the Republican Party, the *Tribune* emerged from the war as the most influential newspaper in the Midwest but not the most popular in its own hometown of Chicago.

The *Chicago Tribune* began as a weekly literary supplement called *Gem of the Prairie* in 1847, but it became more visible in a crowded field of competitors in Chicago in September 1855 when attorney and newspaperman Joseph Medill, political activist Charles Ray, and three other partners bought and merged it with several other newspapers. Medill was a leading advocate of the newly founded Republican Party and was said to have suggested the name of the new political organization. He was an abolitionist and deeply impressed by the antislavery views and imposing physical appearance of Abraham Lincoln. Medill and other *Tribune* reporters followed the future president, reporting and transcribing all the speeches during Lincoln's unsuccessful senatorial bid in 1858 except for one, delivered on 29 May 1858. That speech so mesmerized Medill and other reporters present that they failed to write it down, and it has since been known as Lincoln's "Lost Speech." The *Tribune* did provide extensive coverage and a full text of Lincoln's

famous "House Divided" speech two weeks later. Medill became so friendly with Lincoln in the late 1850s that he later claimed to have snapped "Dammit, Abe, get your feet off my desk!" when Lincoln made a visit to the *Tribune* editorial room. Lincoln reportedly flared briefly at Medill and then removed his boots.

In the face of strident opposition from almost every other newspaper in the country, the *Tribune* championed Lincoln for president at the Republican Party's second national convention, held in Chicago in May 1860. That the convention was even held in Chicago was a minor miracle, the result of tireless boosterism by the *Tribune* and other newspapers for the young, upstart city. The *Tribune* published a special convention edition that included a political biography of Lincoln written by co-owner John Scripps and provided extensive convention coverage, encouraging local Lincoln supporters to yell whenever their candidate's name was mentioned. "Without attempting, therefore, to convey an idea of the delirious cheers, the Babel of joy and excitement, we may mention that strong men wept like children, that two candidates for gubernatorial chairs of their respective states, who looked to the nomination of Honest Old Abe to carry the Republican cause at home through the storm, sank down in excess of joy," the *Tribune* reported after Lincoln's nomination on 19 May 1860. Recognizing the threats for succession being made by the South in the wake of Lincoln's victory, the *Tribune* reiterated an opposition to disunion that had earned it a radical reputation before the war.

The Civil War, along with the purchase of the competing *Chicago Democrat* in 1861, made the *Tribune* one of Chicago's most popular papers. The newspaper published 36,000 copies of its report on the battle of First Bull Run, the largest run in its history up to that time, and it averaged about 40,000 copies daily at the height of the war in 1864. The paper specialized in western war coverage, calling for military action in the West as early as 1861. When it criticized General John C. Frémont's decision to free slaves and declare martial law in the West a year before Lincoln's Emancipation Proclamation, other Chicago and antislavery newspapers including the *New York Tribune* attacked it. Medill and Ray responded on 3 October 1861 that a newspaper was still a "watchman on the walls" even during wartime and that military men should not be exempt from editorial criticism. Albert Holmes Bodman was probably the paper's best war correspondent. As adept at poker and cotton running as he was at obtaining battlefield information, the irrepressible Bodman returned to Chicago with a nest egg of $22,000 after covering the war for only five months at a weekly salary of $16. Another *Tribune* correspondent, Irving Carson, crossed Confederate lines on scouting missions for Illinois resident General Ulysses S. Grant, until he was decapitated by a six-pound cannonball on 6 April 1862 as he stood within six feet of Grant while covering the battle of Shiloh. Carson was the first U.S. newspaper correspondent to be killed in battle.

Even with its connections to Lincoln, the *Chicago Tribune* never equaled the influence of the *New York Tribune* and other New York newspapers during the war, but it provided the first significant Midwestern contribution to national political discourse. The Northern victory cemented the *Tribune's* reputation as a newspaper of influence and prestige in the nation at large, but it took much for it to become the most popular in Chicago. In the immediate years after the Civil War, Chicagoans were evenly split in their reading loyalties between the *Tribune* and Wilbur F. Storey's fiery *Chicago Times*, and both had about the same circulation.

—*Richard Digby-Junger*

See also Election of 1860; Medill, Joseph; Newspapers; War Correspondents.

For further reading:
Andreas, Alfred T. *History of Chicago from the Earliest Period to the Present Time* (1884).
Kinsley, Philip. The Chicago Tribune: *Its First Hundred Years* (1943).
Strevey, Tracy E. "Joseph Medill and the *Chicago Tribune* in the Nomination and Election of Lincoln." *Papers in Illinois History and Transactions for the Year 1938* (1939).
Wendt, Lloyd. Chicago Tribune: *The Rise of a Great American Newspaper* (1979).

CHICKAMAUGA, BATTLE OF
(19–20 September 1863)

The battle of Chickamauga was the culmination of a month-long game of cat and mouse between Major General William S. Rosecrans's Federal Army of the Cumberland and General Braxton Bragg's Confederate Army of Tennessee. Played out in the sparsely settled, heavily timbered valleys of north Georgia, Rosecrans tried to duplicate his success of late June 1863, when with spectacular maneuver he had pried Bragg out of his positions around Tullahoma, Tennessee, with virtually no losses and no major battle.

This campaign would be different. Bragg's loss of a considerable chunk of Tennessee without a fight had dismayed the government in Richmond, even though to some extent the Tullahoma disaster had been of Richmond's own making: Bragg's army was diminished by two infantry and one cavalry division in May and early June 1863 when President Jefferson Davis ordered troops sent to Mississippi to save Vicksburg. That effort proved in vain, and Bragg's weakened army was forced to retreat before an active opponent in his front. Richmond now sent troops back to Bragg as best it could. Not only were the original detachments returned from Mississippi, they brought additional men with them. A corps was moved down from east Tennessee, and on 9 September, two divisions of James Longstreet's I Corps of the Army of

Northern Virginia began boarding trains in Virginia for the trip west. That Davis was sending veterans from General Robert E. Lee's vaunted army was proof that Richmond viewed Bragg's situation as a serious emergency.

Rosecrans's Federals had crossed the Tennessee River downstream from Chattanooga on 2 September. The crossings were largely undetected and hence went unopposed because Confederates had been deceived into thinking Rosecrans would come across the river north of the town. Bragg now found Union troops south of him in force, and to avoid being trapped in the city he again retreated. This time, however, he was determined not to go without a fight. Once Rosecrans was over the Tennessee River, the mountainous terrain forced him to spread out widely, so his army was moving in three isolated columns. Clearly, these widely scattered Federal forces offered Bragg an opportunity to destroy his opponent in detail, but Rosecrans, acting on misinformation from Confederate deserters, persisted in the belief that Bragg's army was demoralized and in full retreat.

Bragg's first significant attempt to trap and crush one of the Federal columns was aimed at General James S. Negley's division on 9 September. Negley had pushed into an isolated mountain valley called McLemore's Cove that morning, and Bragg quickly concentrated troops under Confederate Generals Thomas C. Hindman and D. H. Hill to attack Negley from two directions, trapping him there.

Unfortunately for him, Bragg lacked the respect of his subordinates by September 1863 and a casual disregard for his orders had become commonplace. Much of this festering situation was Bragg's fault—he had alienated subordinates by recriminating them after the battles of Perryville and Murfreesboro. Yet it hardly reflects well on his officers that virtually none of them felt compelled to obey his direct orders. Neither Hindman nor Hill (who as a recent arrival did not even have the excuse of prior service with Bragg) chose to attack on the morning of 10 September, and Bragg waited in vain to hear the opening guns. Negley escaped the next day.

On 13 September, Bragg tried again. General Thomas L. Crittenden's 21st Corps, which Rosecrans had ordered out of Chattanooga to pursue Bragg, was alone at Lee and Gordon's Mill on West Chickamauga Creek about a dozen miles south of Chattanooga. Bragg ordered a strong force under General Leonidas Polk to attack. Polk ignored the order, however, and demanded more troops, insisting that it was he who was about to be attacked. Time again slipped away, time that Rosecrans used to collect his scattered forces.

The morning of 18 September found the two armies facing each other across West Chickamauga Creek near Lee and Gordon's Mill. Bragg now conceived a third plan: he would shift troops northward, interpose them between Rosecrans and Chattanooga, and attack southward to drive the Federals back into the mountains and destruc-

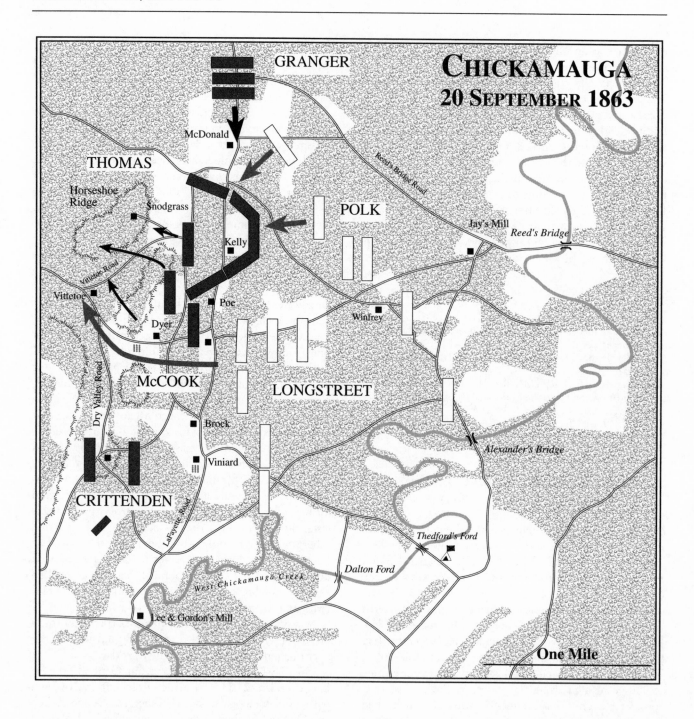

CHICKAMAUGA
20 SEPTEMBER 1863

GRANGER

McDonald

THOMAS

Horseshoe
Ridge

Snodgrass

Reed's Bridge Road

POLK

Jay's Mill

Reed's Bridge

Kelly

Vittetoe Road

Poe

Winfrey

Vittetoe

Dyer

McCOOK

LONGSTREET

Dry Valley Road

Alexander's Bridge

Brock

Viniard

CRITTENDEN

LaFayette Road

Thedford's Ford

Dalton Ford

West Chickamauga Creek

Lee & Gordon's Mill

One Mile

tion. Meanwhile, the two armies sparred on the afternoon of 18 September. Union cavalry opposed Confederate crossings at Reed's and Alexander's bridges in skirmishes that greatly slowed the rebel advance and thus delayed Bragg's plan until the next morning. Rosecrans, now aware that Bragg was trying to flank him to the north, moved General George H. Thomas's XIV Corps in a difficult night march to counter the rebel move.

The next morning, Thomas started the battle of Chickamauga when he sent a division forward to strike at what he thought was an isolated Confederate brigade west of the creek. The division ran into Confederate

dismounted cavalry under Nathan B. Forrest, and a sharp engagement resulted. This brush with Federal forces alarmed Bragg, who thought he was well north of Rosecrans. He canceled an advance by three corps and instead committed reinforcements piecemeal to Forrest. As the men of Major General W. H. T. Walker's Confederate Reserve Corps escalated the battle, Thomas in turn put another Union division into the fight.

The pattern of piecemeal escalation continued throughout the day, spreading the fighting from north to south as both armies steadily hurled troops into action. Had Bragg stuck to his original plan and sent the three

The battle of Chickamauga, from a battlefield sketch (*Library of Congress*)

corps forward first thing in the morning, he might have shattered Rosecrans' army by exploiting the mile-wide gap between Thomas's corps and the rest of the Union army to the south around Lee and Gordon's Mill. However, as the day wore on, Rosecrans shifted division after division northward, closing the gap. The last gasp of the day's fighting came after nightfall, when Patrick Cleburne's Confederate division attacked, causing much sound and fury but little real damage to the Federal position.

That afternoon, Longstreet had finally arrived at Catoosa Station from Virginia after an arduous nine-day train trip. Lacking a guide to take him to the battlefield, he did not arrive at Bragg's headquarters until 11:00 P.M. Bragg immediately took the risky step of completely reorganizing his army into two wings, giving Longstreet one of them, containing more than half the Confederate force. The task confronting Longstreet was daunting, for he was unfamiliar with the setting and did not know the disposition of his command in it. Two-thirds of these men he had never commanded before.

With unhappy consequences for the rebels, Bragg made Leonidas Polk the commander of the other wing. Bragg ordered Polk's wing, including D. H. Hill's corps, to open the battle at dawn by attacking Thomas on the Union left. Longstreet's attack to the south would support this effort once Polk's men were fully engaged. The delay at least would give Longstreet a little time to get his people sorted out and in position. Yet, in what would become an infamous controversy after the war, Polk never sent proper attack orders to Hill. For his part, Hill did little to seek out either of his superior officers. The result was that at dawn on 20 September, when Bragg expected to hear the roar of battle, all was quiet.

Bragg sought out both Hill and Polk, and when they could not provide explanations for the delay, he finally ordered every available divisional commander into action at once. By then, it was 9:00 A.M., and the result was another round of piecemeal attacks similar to the previous day's fighting. A brief crisis on the Federal north flank occurred when rebel forces nearly gained the

Federal rear and possession of the critical Lafayette Road. But the Union line there under Thomas repulsed the Confederates and then held firm. By midday, the contest had produced nothing except longer casualty lists.

Fate and James Longstreet were about to change that, however. Rosecrans had become obsessed with Thomas's defensive efforts to the point of neglecting the rest of his line. At about 10:30, a Union staff officer brought word that one Union division was out of place, leaving a gap in the line. Actually, no gap existed, but Rosecrans had lost track of where everybody was. Reacting impetuously, he ordered General Thomas J. Wood to move his division at once. Any other division commander might have waited to question the order, but only recently Rosecrans had publicly admonished Wood for failing to obey an order promptly. When Wood received this one, he carried it out at once, well knowing it would create a gap rather than close an imaginary one.

At that instant and at that place, Longstreet launched his attack on the Federal right. Arrayed in a dense column six brigades deep, Longstreet's troops moved directly toward the newly created gap and smashed through the Union line with ease. Almost instantly, the right side of the Union line dissolved into chaos. Despite several determined stands, within an hour much of Rosecrans's army was in full retreat toward Chattanooga with Rosecrans

himself caught up in the withdrawal, leaving Thomas as the ranking commander. In fact, George H. Thomas's beleaguered corps, now alone on the battlefield, was about to be enveloped by Longstreet's unimpeded advance.

Two things saved Thomas from destruction. First, Colonel John T. Wilder's mounted infantry brigade launched a daring attack on Longstreet's flank and temporarily halted the Rebel onslaught. Second, a combination of fragmented Federal forces rallied on Snodgrass Hill to the right and rear of Thomas's bending line. Soon they were reinforced by the timely arrival of General Gordon Granger's Reserve Corps. By 1:00 P.M., these men had built a scratch Federal line to protect Thomas's right flank. Longstreet spent the rest of the day trying to break that line, but it managed to hold until evening, thus gaining George H. Thomas the enduring nickname "The Rock of Chickamauga." Thomas's stubborn resistance allowed the remainder of the Union army to withdraw successfully. That night, Thomas himself pulled back to Rossville, and by the next day the entire Union force had retreated to Chattanooga.

Chickamauga was one of the bloodier battles of the war with each side losing about 28 percent of their number. Approximately 58,000 Federals suffered 16,179 casualties. Confederate casualties are less precise, but accounted for approximately 18,500 of the 68,000 troops involved.

Battle of Chickamauga as depicted by Currier & Ives (*Library of Congress*)

Lee & Gordon's Mills on the Chickamauga battlefield, 1863 (*National Archives*)

Bragg's subordinates were unhappy that he did not order an aggressive pursuit, and ultimately Chickamauga proved in D. H. Hill's words a "barren victory." The rebels besieged the Union army in Chattanooga for a month, a siege ultimately broken with the arrival of Ulysses S. Grant and fresh troops. The Army of Tennessee then fell back into the north Georgia mountains to await the next Federal move—the drive toward Atlanta.

—*Dave Powell*

See also Army of Kentucky; Bragg, Braxton; Chattanooga Campaign; Chattanooga, Tennessee; Granger, Gordon; Rosecrans, William S.; Thomas, George H.

For further reading:

Cozzens, Peter. *This Terrible Sound: The Battle of Chickamauga* (1992).

Tucker, Glenn. *Chickamauga: Bloody Battle in the West* (1961; reprint, 1981).

Woodworth, Steven E. *A Deep Steady Thunder* (1998).

CHICKASAW BLUFFS, BATTLE OF
(27–29 December 1862)

This engagement, also known as the battle of Chickasaw Bayou or the battle of Walnut Hills, proved to be a Confederate victory. The battle prevented Union general William T. Sherman's Yazoo expedition from capturing Vicksburg and brought about

an end to General Ulysses S. Grant's first attempt to capture the Confederate river stronghold.

After the battle of Corinth in October 1862, Grant continued to move southward toward Vicksburg. Grant proceeded down the Mississippi Central Railroad from his forward supply base at Holly Springs. Grant's plan involved his force of 40,000 engaging the Confederate forces responsible for defending Vicksburg, while Sherman's surprise movement down the Mississippi River would easily defeat the skeleton force left to defend Vicksburg.

Grant encountered some problems during his movement into the heart of Mississippi. Cavalry leaders Generals Nathan Bedford Forrest and Earl Van Dorn caused trouble in Cavalry rear. Forrest with 2,000 men tore up nearly fifty miles of railroad track and telegraph lines, while inflicting 2,000 casualties on the Union forces and capturing or destroying a large quantity of supplies and equipment. Van Dorn inflicted an even greater loss, when his force of 3,500 swung behind Grant's army to capture the weakly defended Union forward supply base at Holly Springs.

The Holly Springs fiasco happened the same day that Sherman's Yazoo expedition left Memphis. Grant, realizing the vulnerability of his position with a force of 20,000 Confederates in front of him and his supply line compromised, called off his advance on Vicksburg. He attempted to get word to Sherman that he had to cancel his advance, but the disabled telegraph wires prevented the message from getting through. This support in which Sherman needed to keep the Confederate defenders around Vicksburg at a minimum did not materialize, and with Grant's retreat, Confederates headed back to run the Vicksburg defenses.

Sherman's Yazoo expedition left Memphis on 20 December 1862 and the following day arrived at Helena, Arkansas, to pick up the remaining troops that would complete his invasion force. The Yazoo expedition, around 32,000 strong, was divided into four divisions: Andrew J. Smith commanded the 1st Division, Morgan L. Smith led the 2d Division, George W. Morgan commanded the 3d Division, and Frederick Steele led the 4th Division. On 26 December, the Yazoo expedition and the accompanying U.S. Navy vessels turned up the Yazoo River and three of the four divisions disembarked on the left bank of the Yazoo about ten miles upstream, or about six miles north of Vicksburg.

Sherman's advance on the city became even more difficult. The Chickasaw Bluffs, offering an excellent defensive position, were between Sherman's force and Vicksburg. This location was made more defensible because the land between the bluffs and the Yazoo River was largely bottomland, comprised mostly of swamps and quagmires, made worse by continuing rainfall. Only a few roads or causeways could be used to transport the troops effectively, and these acted as focal points for the Confederate artillery, adding to the difficulty in approaching the Chickasaw Bluffs.

The Confederate forces were mainly spread between a forward line of rifle pits at the base of the Chickasaw Bluffs. The Confederates anchored the nearly four-mile-long line in a way that it could not be turned. The eastern terminus, or right end, of the rebel forward position ended at the broad Chickasaw Bayou; the western end abutted the left bank of the Mississippi River. Behind this forward line was the main Confederate position, becoming increasingly well entrenched and running along the crest of the bluffs. From this position, the rebel artillery could cover the open ground below. All of the routes through the bottomland led to the Confederate defensive positions around Chickasaw Bluffs. The terrain through which the Union army had to advance and fight had a decisive impact on battle.

Over the next two days, 27 and 28 December, as the Union forces were advancing slowly southward toward the Chickasaw Bluffs and skirmishing with Confederate picket forces, the rebels acquired more and more reinforcements, raising their numbers from 6,000 to well over 12,000. On 28 December, the forces under Sherman, notably Steele's 4th Division, came under such heavy fire that they were unable to advance on Walnut Hills to the east and later reembarked and returned to the center to support Morgan's 3d Division. On the same

day, Morgan's forces drove the Confederates back in front of them, but were stopped by artillery fire.

However, the major fighting took place on 29 December. Sherman's plan of attack was relatively simple. He was determined to break through the Confederate center, and to do so required diversionary fire from Admiral David D. Porter's gunboats as well as feints against the enemy's flanks. The main part of the attack focused on the center. The attack got under way around noon after Morgan's troops completed the needed preparations for the attack. Morgan's and Steele's 3d and 4th Divisions were in the center on the move on the Chickasaw Bluffs. The only success, limited as it was, came from Frank Blair's brigade of Steele's division. They advanced on the Confederate rifle pits and chased the Rebels up the bluffs. The Confederate's heavy fire from their main line forced Blair's men to retreat back to the Confederate forward rifle pits. There they came under devastating fire from above. The fire was so intense that Blair's brigade was not able to leave until under the cover of darkness. The rest of the brigades of Morgan's and Steele's divisions were decimated when being caught in the open by heavy fire. By nightfall, Sherman's forces had made no significant progress in removing the Confederate's from the bluffs.

Although Sherman wanted to renew the attack, he thought better of it. The strength of the enemy position, coupled with the deteriorating weather conditions, forced him to call off all the attacks on Vicksburg and return to Milliken's Bend, Louisiana. The Union lost a total of 1,776 men, while the Confederates sustained 207 casualties. Sherman failed in his first independent command and his assault should never have been attempted, even if he had received word of Grant's cancellation of his advance. A frontal assault over open ground against entrenched troops proved to be suicidal; unfortunately Sherman would not be the last to learn this important lesson. The end result of the failed Vicksburg campaign was that Grant no longer attempted an overland route to Vicksburg in which his supply line would be vulnerable. Instead, he relied on the Mississippi River as a base of operations against the Confederate stronghold and incorporated lessons learned from his previous campaign into his strategy.

—*James L. Isemann*

See also Sherman, William Tecumseh; Steele, Frederick; Yazoo Expedition.

For further reading:

Arnold, James R. *Grant Wins the War: Decision at Vicksburg* (1997).

Miers, Earl Schenck. *The Web of Victory: Grant at Vicksburg* (1955; reprint, 1983).

Welcher, Frank J. *The Union Army, 1861–1865: Organization and Operations.* (1989).

CHICKASAW INDIANS

Removed from their Mississippi homeland in the 1830s, most Chickasaw Indians lived in the south-central portion of Indian Territory (later Oklahoma) on the eve of the Civil War. The other major southeastern Indian groups resided around the Chickasaws: the Choctaws to the east, the Creeks and Seminoles bordering them to the north, and the Cherokees located still farther north. The firestorm of secession and the Civil War struck the Indian Territory as harshly as anywhere else in the country.

As soon as the Confederacy came into being, efforts began to recruit the Chickasaws and other groups in Indian Territory into an alliance with it. Confederate officials, especially those from Texas and Arkansas, coveted the Indian Territory as an important source of livestock and food and as a strategically important location from which to launch attacks to the north and west. The Chickasaws and their Choctaw neighbors overwhelmingly supported the Confederacy throughout the war, with the Chickasaws adopting a resolution calling for independence from the United States and alliance with the Confederate States on 25 May 1861. They signed a formal treaty with the Confederates on 12 July.

The reasons the Chickasaws championed the Confederate cause were varied. Out of a total population of less than 5,000, about 200 Chickasaw slaveholders owned approximately 1,000 slaves, and many of these slaveholders held prominent positions in the Chickasaw National Government. Many Chickasaw slaveholders raised cotton and were connected to the greater "King Cotton" economy throughout the South. Federal Indian agents among the Chickasaws held strong Southern sympathies—the Choctaw-Chickasaw agent in 1861 was Mississippian Douglas H. Cooper. Furthermore, the Chickasaws, and other Indians removed from the southeast earlier in the century, retained animosity towards the government that had forced them to abandon their ancestral homes. Depredations committed by whites and corruption among U.S. officials responsible for managing Chickasaw funds also contributed to ill feelings toward the United States.

In late July 1861 Douglas Cooper began organizing a fighting force made up of Chickasaw and Choctaw volunteers, with Choctaw leader Tandy Walker as his second-in-command. Chickasaw men enthusiastically joined Cooper's First Regiment of Mounted Rifles, and several other cavalry and infantry regiments were formed in Indian Territory as well. Chronically short of supplies, the Chickasaw mission in the war was largely defensive. Chickasaws saw their first action in November 1861 against Creeks and Seminoles who were attempting to remain neutral. Except for a brief foray into southwest Missouri in 1862 (where at the battle of Newtonia Chickasaw soldiers were credited with winning the skirmish) and an interception of Union forces in western Arkansas during April 1864, Chickasaws fought mostly along the Arkansas River-Canadian River defensive line within Indian Territory. By 1863 Union armies occupied Indian Territory north of this line.

Little fighting took place within the Chickasaw Nation itself, but after 1863 a severe refugee problem arose there. Thousands of pro-Confederate Cherokees, Creeks, Seminoles, and their families fled southward away from Union armies. These newcomers seriously strained food resources and other rations. This refugee crisis resulted in deprivation for everyone in Chickasaw country, a situation that was not relieved until the end of the war.

The Civil War disrupted and permanently changed many aspects of Chickasaw life. Schools, courts, and government buildings became hospitals and barracks during the war, and the Chickasaw National Government met only irregularly. Much of the land was ruined by troop encampments and abandonment. Nearly all of the moveable property, crops, and livestock had been consumed, and marauding parties of armed men confiscated much that was left. Diseases, especially smallpox, devastated Chickasaws and other Indian peoples who had little immunity. Nevertheless, the Chickasaws held out until the very end; Chickasaw governor Winchester Colbert did not formally surrender until 14 July 1865, three months after Lee's surrender to Grant.

The postwar world looked dramatically different. Nearly 200 Chickasaw soldiers died in the war, about 4 percent of the population. Chickasaw slaves gained their freedom and the cotton economy they had supported fell apart. The United States required the Chickasaws to grant their ex-slaves forty acres of land each or $100 if they wanted to move out of Chickasaw territory. Finally, the United States ordered the Chickasaws to pay reparations to the small number of pro-Union Chickasaws who had fled during the war.

Chickasaws supported the Confederacy from principles and experiences that told them it was the best course to take, but the decision brought tremendous hardship when it became clear that the United States would win the war.
—*Greg O'Brien*

See also Cherokee Indians; Choctaw Indians; Creek Indians; Seminole Indians.
For further reading:
Abel, Annie Heloise. *The American Indian as Participant in the Civil War* (1970).
Gibson, Arrell. *The Chickasaws* (1971).
Hauptman, Laurence M. *Between Two Fires: American Indians in the Civil War* (1995).
Littlefield, Daniel F., Jr. *The Chickasaw Freedmen: A People without a Country* (1980).

CHINESE-AMERICAN SOLDIERS

In 1860, according to a U.S. Census Bureau report, all the 34,933 Chinese in the United States lived in California. It seemed that no Chinese participated in the American Civil War. However, recent research has revealed at least three Chinese volunteers in the Union army and one Chinese in the Union navy.

Hong Neok Woo, who came to the United States on board a U.S. warship, lived in Lancaster, Pennsylvania, for nine years and became a citizen on 22 September 1860. On 29 June 1863, he joined the 50th Infantry of the Pennsylvania Volunteers. After the battle of Gettysburg, Woo was honorably discharged along with his company on 15 August 1863. Woo later returned to China and worked for U.S. missionaries in Shanghai.

Joseph Pierce at age ten was bought by a captain Peck in Canton, China, and brought to Kensington, Connecticut. The Peck family named him "Pierce" after then President Franklin Pierce. In August 1862, at age twenty, Pierce joined the 14th Infantry of the Connecticut Volunteers. The 14th Infantry took part in thirty-four battles and suffered heavy casualties (234 survived to be discharged in 1865, as opposed to the 1,015 who formed the unit in 1862). Pierce received a promotion from private to corporal on 1 November 1863, and he was honorably discharged on 31 May 1865 in Alexandria, Virginia. After the war, he married Martha Morgan and lived in Meridan, Connecticut, until his death on 3 January 1916.

Antonio Dardell as a boy was bought by a sea captain and brought to Connecticut. He joined the 27th Infantry of the Connecticut Volunteers at New Haven in October 1862. The 27th Infantry suffered heavy casualties in the three battles it fought. On 27 July 1863, Dardell was honorably discharged in New Haven along with the 27th Infantry. After the war, he married Mary Payne and lived in New Haven. On 17 March 1882, he became a naturalized citizen. He died on 18 January 1933, and was buried in Madison, Connecticut.

Tsui Kuo Ying, Chinese minister to the United States, wrote in his diary in 1891 that there was a Chinese named Ah Mei in Chicago. Ah Mei studied in a military school for several years and served in the U.S. Navy during the Civil War. After the war, he became a U.S. citizen and was permitted to vote in important elections. The name and story have not been confirmed. However, in 1865 there was a Chinese in Chicago who sent letters to relatives in China. The census also shows that there was a Chinese in Chicago in 1870.

The stories of Hong Neok Woo, Joseph Pierce, Antonio Dardell, and Ah Mei demonstrate the patriotism of these Chinese-Americans who contributed to the war against slavery and helped save the Union.

—*Qingsong Zhang*

For further reading:
Zhang, Qingsong. *Mei guo Bai Nian Pal Hua Nei Mu.* [*A History of Chinese Exclusion in the United States*] (1998).

CHIVINGTON, JOHN MILTON
(1821–1894)
Union officer

Born in Warren County, Ohio, on 21 February 1821, John Chivington had public school education before entering the family lumber business at age eighteen. Chivington reached a turning point in his life in October 1842. Converted at a Methodist meeting, he soon became a minister.

As it did to many of his contemporaries, the West beckoned him. Chivington served Methodist congregations in Illinois, Missouri, and, finally, the Kansas-Nebraska Conference. Standing six feet four and a half inches, with a strong voice and "commanding presence," Chivington preached his pro-Union, antislavery beliefs wherever he preached. Described as a man of "energy, ability, and force of character," Chivington thrived under the pressures of work in the West. In 1860, he became presiding elder for the new Rocky Mountain Conference, an outgrowth of the 1859 gold rush. Chivington proved an ideal choice. He knew frontier folk and western conditions, relished hard work and travel, and had long displayed strong leadership abilities. He needed all these traits in his far-flung district. His success was graphically shown by the fact that within one year the Conference jumped from one preacher and twenty-seven members to seventeen preachers and 348 members. Colorado's only newspaper, the *Rocky Mountain News*, hailed his efforts because churches, a positive sign of civilization, had arrived.

Meanwhile, the nation was pulling apart. Initially, the region benefited because not until Southerners left Congress would Colorado be organized as a free territory. For Chivington, the outbreak of the Civil War proved agonizing because he was torn between his church and his country. The latter won, and Chivington ended his active role in the Methodist church.

Like an Old Testament prophet/warrior, Chivington enthusiastically answered his country's call. He helped recruit, organize, and train the 1st Regiment of Colorado volunteers. That needed to be done quickly because Coloradans were apprehensive about their present and future. They saw themselves isolated, with unfriendly neighbors, and separated by a month's travel from the pro-Union states. Washington neither would nor could be of much help.

Colorado was threatened in the winter of 1861–1862 by Confederate forces under General Henry Hopkins Sibley marching northward up the Rio Grande from Texas. Colorado gold could aid the South. Union forces under General Edward R. S. Canby skirmished and withdrew to Fort Union, New Mexico, where Canby ordered the 1st Colorado to join him. These volunteers proved their worth, marching 400 miles in thirteen days.

The two small armies fought at Apache Canyon and Glorieta Pass on 26–28 March. The struggle was undecided until Chivington led troops that swept around the Confederate rear and captured and destroyed Sibley's wagon train. The "fighting parson's" bold move ended the Confederate hope of conquering the Southwest. Chivington came back to Colorado a hero.

After the New Mexico campaign, Colonel Chivington in 1862 was appointed military commander of Colorado Territory. Hampered by insufficient troops, lack of supplies, and continuing rumors of threats to outlying ranches and stage stations, Chivington worked hard to defend settlements and keep the essential and vulnerable overland trails open.

The Sioux outbreak in Minnesota in 1862, driving many of those angry Indians out on the plains, made the situation even worse. In the spring of 1863, warfare broke out, closing the trails. Travel stopped, mail arrived via San Francisco, stage stations were destroyed, and outlying farms and ranches were attacked. Because of all this, Colorado's cost of living rose alarmingly and Coloradans blamed the Indians. Neither Chivington nor Washington had the ability to stop the warfare. Patrols and a few small garrisons did not stem the attacks. Coloradans' anger and frustration mounted. That magnified the racism, misunderstanding, and fears that they had brought with them about their plains and mountain neighbors. With the coming of winter, the plains warriors withdrew, and the trails reopened. Colorado's mining had declined, however, and people already were leaving for the new promised land of Montana. It was either grow or die in nineteenth-century America. Matters worsened.

The relief from raiding and warfare proved only temporary; in the spring of 1864, it started again. The plains people's grievances had not been answered either. Their land and way of life were disappearing under the onslaught of white settlement. All the feelings of Coloradans from the previous year were intensified. Such warfare could not continue or Colorado faced a bleak future. Chivington and Governor John Evans responded, raising the 3d Colorado. The territory and Chivington had started down the road to Sand Creek.

The attack on the Cheyenne and Arapaho village by the 3d Colorado on 29 November 1864, and its aftermath, marked the end of Chivington's military career. Under mounting criticism over the attack, Chivington resigned. The Sand Creek controversy followed him throughout the rest of his life.

Chivington resigned from the army in 1865 and moved away from Colorado. He eventually returned in the 1880s and found Coloradans' attitude sympathetic toward his actions at Sand Creek. He spent his remaining years in the state and died in Denver on 4 October 1894.

—*Duane A. Smith*

See also Glorieta Pass, Battle of; Sand Creek Massacre.
For further reading:
Craig, Reginald S. *The Fighting Parson* (1959).
Josephy, Alvin, M. *The Civil War in the American West* (1991).
Roberts, Gary L. "Sand Creek: Tragedy and Symbol" (Ph.D. dissertation, 1984).
Smith, Duane A. *The Birth of Colorado: A Civil War Perspective* (1989).

CHOCTAW INDIANS

During the Civil War, most Choctaws lived in the Western Choctaw Nation in what is now southeastern Oklahoma. A few who had not been relocated by the federal government in the 1830s remained in their traditional Mississippi homeland.

Before the outbreak of war, the slaveholding Western Choctaws leaned heavily toward the Southern cause. Douglas H. Cooper, the tribe's government agent, was an active Southern sympathizer and influenced many Choctaws. He also threatened that, if they did not go with the South, they risked having property confiscated. In the same vein, white supporters of slavery from Arkansas and Texas mounted an effective, if not intimidating, propaganda campaign to persuade the Choctaws to side with them. Finally, as Union troops withdrew from Fort Washita in May 1861, many Choctaws believed that the U.S. government had abandoned them. Not all shared these sentiments, however. Peter Pitchlynn, a tribal leader, remained convinced that the tribe must remain loyal to the Union. Not a strong supporter of slavery personally, Pitchlynn argued that the tribe would lose its annuities if it broke with the United States. He also advocated neutrality as a possibility.

Nonetheless, the Choctaws held a secessionist meeting at their capital of Doakesville on 1 June 1861. At the urging of Robert M. Jones, a Choctaw with large slaveholdings, Principal Chief George Hudson appointed a committee to meet with the Confederacy to plan for the raising of a Choctaw regiment for the Confederate army. On 14 June, the Choctaw National Council declared the Choctaw Nation "free and independent of the United States." On 12 July, the Choctaw Nation signed a treaty of alliance with the Confederate States of America. The agreement guaranteed the nation a degree of independence greater than it had with the United States. The Confederacy also assumed all financial obligations of the federal government. Promised representation in the Confederate Congress, the Choctaws and other Indian tribes were seated but limited to one nonvoting delegate per tribe.

The first Indian regiment put into Confederate service was the 1st Choctaw and Chickasaw Regiment under the command of Douglas H. Cooper, by then a

Confederate colonel. Eventually the Western Choctaw formed five additional units. Most of their service was as home guards, but they did participate in several significant engagements. In November and December 1861, Choctaws fought in battles that forced neutral Indians into Kansas. In March 1862, Choctaws covered the Confederate retreat from Pea Ridge, and in July and August 1863, they unsuccessfully opposed the Federal march on Fort Smith and were later defeated at the battles of Honey Springs and Perryville.

Taking the measure of the Choctaws' weakened condition, Federal troops in late 1863 launched an invasion of the tribe's nation. In February 1864, Colonel William A. Phillips stopped his Union column near Fort Washita and sent a message to the Choctaws inviting them to surrender in return for amnesty or face destruction. Phillips, however, did not attack. Instead he turned his column south to Texas. Although Western Choctaw troops continued to engage in a number of raids, their military power was all but broken.

Initially the war had little impact on the Mississippi Choctaw. As the conflict progressed, however, the Confederacy began organizing them. The 1st Mississippi Choctaw Infantry was formed in late 1862. Commanded by Major J. W. Pearce, the entire unit was captured in March 1863 at Camp Moore Louisiana. The 1st Battalion of Choctaws for the Confederacy was then organized in February 1863 under General Arnold Spann. Other than being involved in a battle near Ponchatoula, Louisiana, and rescuing twenty-three survivors of a Confederate troop train, which plunged into the Chunky River, it saw little action.

The war affected the Choctaws in nonmilitary ways. Although the Confederacy promised to maintain federal annuities, it only did so in depreciated currency. The tribe thus found it difficult to finance its own government and was forced to close several schools. Compounding the problem was the widespread rustling of Choctaw herds. Cattle thieves commonly sold the stolen livestock to Union army contractors. This and a serious drought resulted in food shortages. By 1862, the Choctaws were also supporting 6,000 Confederate Indian refugees. Initially, the Choctaws were able to utilize a food distribution system to support the influx, but as the problem became more acute, the tribe began restricting corn to its own people. Even with such measures in place, food shortages continued. Refugees also formed gangs that stole food and property.

Given their deteriorating situation, the Choctaws elected Peter Pitchlynn principal chief in the hope that his connections with the government in Washington would serve the tribe well. Although he continued a pretense of loyalty to the Confederacy, he was instrumental in securing favorable surrender terms. After Appomattox, the Choctaw and other tribes met at Camp

Napoleon on the Washita River to consider the future. Although some thought the war could be continued west of the Mississippi, the predominant sentiment was that further resistance was futile. This set the stage for the formal surrender of the Choctaw on 19 June 1865.

Unlike other tribes, Choctaw troops were allowed to return home rather than being paroled. In addition, they were given the protection of the United States. Pitchlynn called for a grand council of tribes formerly allied with the Confederacy to meet on 1 September 1865 at Armstrong Academy where a federal commission would meet with them to write a final and permanent peace. When the conference failed to occur, all sides agreed to meet again at Fort Smith. Choctaws arrived late to the peace talks and balked at a federal demand that they cede their land for resettlement of Kansas tribes. Unable to reach an agreement, the Choctaws sent a five-member delegation to Washington, D.C. The result of the visit was a treaty signed on 28 April 1866 that was more favorable than most accorded to other "rebel" tribes.

The agreement encouraged, but did not require, Choctaws to adopt former slaves and included $300,000 to facilitate their adoption or relocation. The accord also provided for limited settlement of Kansas tribes. In addition, the Choctaws agreed to railroad rights-of-way, the creation of local U.S. courts, and adjudication of loyal Indian claims. In return for these concessions, the United States agreed to resume annuities and restore pre-1861 trust funds. The Choctaws ratified the treaty on 21 December 1866.

Although the Choctaws sided overwhelming with the Confederacy, eleven tribal members joined the Union army, notably Captain Nathaniel Krebbs, who fought the 1st Choctaw and Chickasaw Mounted Rifles Regiment on several occasions.

—*Daniel Liestman*

See also Chickasaw Indians; Kansas.

For further reading:

Abel, Annie Heloise. *The American Indian in the Civil War, 1862–1865* (1992).
Baird, W. David. *Peter Pitchlynn: Chief of the Choctaws* (1972).
Bonnifield, Paul. "The Choctaw Nation on the Eve of the Civil War." *Journal of the West* (1973).
Fischer, LeRoy H. *The Civil War in Indian Territory* (1974).
Holcomb, Raymond L. *The Civil War in the Choctaw Nation* (1997).

CHURCHES

In 1865 more than 25 percent of Americans held church membership, and perhaps half of the population regularly attended worship services. These churches both shaped and reflected popular beliefs and attitudes, providing a vocabulary for believers to comprehend life's events. Churches helped to create the moral climate for fratricide and molded the zeal with which the Civil War was fought. They interpreted its occurrence as a divine manifestation of, at least initially, uncertain direction. Until the outcome was clear, they labored to convert the soldiers at the front and to continue their programs of worship and watch care on the home front.

Large Protestant denominations had served as one major bulwark of the growing republic in the antebellum period. As moral institutions, churches found themselves mired in debates about the rectitude of slavery, specifically on questions of appointing slaveholders to ecclesiastical and missionary offices. Beginning in 1837 and continuing to early 1861, these national organizations divided over these questions along sectional lines, with Northern Christians holding that the sin of slaveholding disqualified a person from ministerial office and, in some cases, from church membership. Southern churches strongly disagreed, holding that the Bible specifically recognized the master-slave relationship.

Churches crafted powerful moral apologies for their anti- and proslavery positions, which linked the cadences of the Bible and theories of scriptural interpretation into compelling arguments affirming either the abolition or the continuation of slavery. Increasingly, these justifications embraced all aspects of moral economy, and Northerners and Southerners came to view the institutions and attitudes of their respective sections as having Jehovah's sanction and likewise perceived the structures and beliefs in the other sections as infidelity. Antebellum churches helped cloak the sectional debate and the outbreak of civil war in a moral language of theological certainty that made compromise increasingly unacceptable.

When the Civil War erupted in 1861, churches that had not already done so severed their remaining intersectional ecclesiastical bonds, with the Roman Catholics and the Old School Presbyterians each declaring their sectional loyalties. Denominations passed resolutions affirming their support for their section's armies and governments, and, despite the large numbers of church members who joined the armies, marshalled large numbers of individuals who went to the front as evangelists and colporteurs. In the North, the Roman Catholic Sisters of Charity sent scores of well-trained nurses to work in army hospitals, while other churches raised money for, and supported the efforts of, the United States Sanitary Commission. Northern and Southern churches provided chaplains for the various armies and conducted large-scale missionary and revival meetings among the troops. Churches supported Bible societies that labored to provide each soldier with a prayer book, a testament, or a Bible. They operated religious presses that produced special religious newspapers for the troops. Although the presence of camp followers, dice, playing cards, and alcohol among the soldiers indicated that the evangelistic efforts by churches did not eradicate vice in the army, these ecclesiastical efforts did do much to soften

Log church built by the 50th New York Engineers at Poplar Grove, Virginia, March 1865 (Photograph by Timothy O'Sullivan / *Library of Congress*)

some of the immoral tendencies of young male behavior. And abundant testimony exists that soldiers took quite seriously the teachings of Christianity, especially on the eve of battle, an event that promised for many a quick trip to the Judgment Seat.

Churches underwent significant transformations themselves during the war. In the antebellum era, denominations had defined themselves in strict doctrinal terms and often had little to do with groups who adhered to different creeds. The denominations themselves were often divided into conservative and reform wings that were estranged from one another. In both North and South during the Civil War, these groups came together within and across denominational lines to support ecumenical efforts among the soldiers and out of a belief that God Almighty was deciding the sectional questions that had divided the nation. In the North especially, the Civil War bridged the chasm between abolitionist and conservative Christians, who found in the Emancipation Proclamation and in the need for industrial power to crush secession a vital link connecting elements of practical and ideal conduct. This bridge led to conservative funding for the American Missionary Association, which had been founded by abolitionists in 1846. It began in 1862 establishing schools and conducting church services for former slaves who were in areas of the South now controlled by Union armies. The war years provided the experiential foundation and new theological assumptions that led many

Northern churches to embrace the social gospel by the close of the nineteenth century.

Southern churches, especially their denominational leadership, supported the Confederate war effort. Defeats, however, led many ministers to express a belief that God was chastening the South for failing to discharge its full duty to Southern slaves. Laws restricting slave literacy—meaning slaves could not legally learn to read the Bible—and the lack of legal recognition for slave marriages were two salient features in Southern society that church leaders targeted for structural reform. Methodist bishop George Foster Pierce told the Georgia legislature that it would be preferable to end slavery than operate it in a manner that jeopardized the souls of slaves.

Historians still debate whether the concerns of Southern churches hastened the Confederate defeat or prolonged resistance. Likely, one may find evidence to argue both sides of the question, but clearly the activities of evangelical missionary societies in the Army of Northern Virginia seemed to have boosted morale in the trenches around Petersburg in 1864 and 1865, suggesting that the doings of churches may have had different effects behind the lines than at the front.

On the whole, churches provided moral succor to their respective societies. They comforted the bereaved and reminded them that their love ones had died in a just cause. They exhorted their congregations on the home front to show courage in crisis, because God, they believed, was working directly in human history through the Civil War. They rallied the troops to bravery in battle and to moral conduct in the army camps. And they affirmed to their respective societies that the Civil War was a holy contest in which divine will would be revealed. At war's end, Northern churches affirmed that the United States, having been baptized in blood and purged of slavery, enjoyed Jehovah's special blessing. Unbowed, Southern churches still affirmed Southern righteousness and interpreted the Confederate defeat as God's peculiar way of disciplining his chosen people.

—*Edward R. Crowther*

See also Catholics; Chaplains; Chaplains, African-American; Jews; Sister Nurses; United States Sanitary Commission.

For further reading:

Miller, Randall M., Harry S. Stout, and Charles Reagan Wilson, eds. *Religion and the American Civil War* (1998).

Moorhead, James H. *American Apocalypse: Yankee Protestants and the Civil War, 1860–1869* (1978).

Silver, James. *Confederate Morale and Church Propaganda* (1957).

CINCINNATI, SIEGE OF
(September 1862)

The siege of Cincinnati never took place, but the threat of an invasion frightened residents and resulted in military assignments and construction

during August and early September 1862. General Edmund Kirby Smith moved his forces into north-central Kentucky's bluegrass region during August with the hope of inducing local residents to take up arms for the Confederate cause. Few responded despite the enthusiastic reception that greeted Smith's arrival at Lexington and also that of John Hunt Morgan who arrived via Glasgow and Danville. At the same time, Confederate general Braxton Bragg was moving into Kentucky while General Don Carlos Buell and his Union forces were still in Nashville. The presence of so many Rebel forces with few Federal troops seemingly gave the Confederates a real opportunity to threaten Cincinnati and the Kentucky towns of Newport and Covington along the Ohio River.

Cincinnati, the nation's fifth largest city in 1860 with a population of 161,044 and known as the Queen City of the West, was a key communication center for points south and west. In the antebellum era, much of Cincinnati's commerce depended on the South. Confederates reasoned that, if they could reach Cincinnati, it would mean a tremendous psychological as well as tangible victory. Little in the way of military obstacles stood in their paths except a few siege guns near Covington and the Ohio River.

Alert to the movement of the Confederates closer to their city, the members of the Cincinnati City Council considered how best to defend the city. The council pledged to meet any expenses that the military might require during the emergency. Ohio's governor David Tod ordered all loyal men in the surrounding counties to arm themselves, form companies, and proceed to Cincinnati. At the same time, Major General Lewis Wallace, an Indiana native, received orders to assume command of the defense of Cincinnati and its Kentucky suburbs. After consulting with the mayors of Newport, Covington, and Cincinnati, Wallace declared martial law on 2 September. The proclamation of martial law appeared in the next morning's newspapers, two days before the beginning of the Confederate advance.

Cincinnati's residents obeyed the martial law order enthusiastically. While schools and businesses closed and streetcars stopped running, all able-bodied men reported for labor or military service. Thousands of citizen soldiers drilled in hastily organized companies organized by wards. Families buried their valuables or shipped them out of town. Fortifications behind Newport and Covington were strengthened, and overnight the construction of a pontoon bridge from coal barges across the Ohio enabled the transport of troops, artillery, and lumber for barracks. Mount Adams, Price Hill, and other strategic points within Cincinnati were fortified as secondary defenses.

Surrounding rural districts heeded the governor's call and hastened to support Cincinnati with large numbers of men, soon known as the Squirrel Hunters because of their long rifles. They ate at the Fifth Street market house and slept in warehouses, halls, and other available large buildings. Kirby Smith's delay at Lexington for a day or two eliminated his chance of invading Cincinnati. Just days after the proclamation of martial law, the city and its patriotic men along with the Squirrel Hunters had ensured the safety of the city. Later the citizens wondered if the situation really had warranted such severe measures.

Two days after martial law began, it ended with the exceptions that businesses had to close at 4:00 P.M. and drilling would continue in the evenings. Yet both black and white citizens continued their services; a black brigade provided labor on the fortifications while white citizens, 3,000 per day, continued their work with the spade. Militia organizations and reserve regiments continued drilling while the women of the town supplied a steady stream of provisions including coffee, ice water, sandwiches, and peaches. Some households even kept food tables outside on their porches for the home guard and citizens on guard duty or drilling. The need to join in Cincinnati's defense had brought its citizens together.

From 3 to 10 September, the trenches were staffed every night and some scouting of the front took place. Engineers had given shape to hasty fortifications, now remembered, in part, through the names of the northern Kentucky communities of Fort Wright, Fort Mitchel, and Fort Thomas. When Kirby Smith's force moved toward Cincinnati, Governor Tod responded to Major General Wright's request for help by asking the military committees of northern Ohio to send immediately all available armed men to Cincinnati. A few skirmishes occurred and again business was suspended. Events went no further. Governor Tod acted to check his call for volunteers, so many had responded.

Due to Buell's advance into Kentucky along with Smith's awareness of Cincinnati's defense preparations, General Bragg ordered Smith away from the northern advance toward Cincinnati to provide support for his army. By 12 September, General Wallace learned that Smith had retreated. Citizens rejoiced. Governor Tod announced the safety of Cincinnati and offered congratulations. The Squirrel Hunters received official commendation from the Ohio Senate and House of Representatives, and General Wallace on leaving the city paid tribute to its spirited citizens with an elegant and graceful farewell address.

Although Cincinnati was never invaded, the threat was real. Citizens, black and white, men and women, rallied in support despite the disruption brought by the curtailment of normal daily activities. Men throughout Ohio and nearby joined in the effort to defend Cincinnati, the region's dominant community. Except for raids, the threatened siege of Cincinnati, was the closest that a major Northern city in the West came to invasion during the Civil War.

—*Ruth C. Carter*

See also Smith, Edmund Kirby; Tod, David.

For further reading:

Reid, Whitelaw. "Siege of Cincinnati." In *Ohio in the War: Her Statesmen, Her Generals, and Soldiers* (1868).
Smith, David M. "The Defense of Cincinnati: The Battle That Never Was" (Website, 1999).
Tucker, Louis L. "The Siege of Cincinnati by a Pearl Street Rifle." *Historical and Philosophical Society of Ohio Bulletin* (1962).
Wallace, Lew. *Lew Wallace: An Autobiography* (1906).

CITY POINT, VIRGINIA

Located on a peninsula of the south bank of the James River where the Appomattox River comes into the James, City Point was the terminus for the City Point Railroad that connected Petersburg, Virginia, to the James River. As early as 1 April 1864, Union major general Benjamin Butler recognized the location's possible importance in supplying an army operating against Richmond from the south. Lieutenant General Ulysses S. Grant gave Butler instructions to seize it and begin operations against Richmond so as to divide Robert E. Lee's army in preparation for Grant's campaign from the north.

Because of the buildup of Federal troops at Fort Monroe and the reported visit of Grant to Butler there in early April, Lee anticipated a move on City Pont during the second week of April 1864. As a result, he instructed that defenses south of Richmond and at Petersburg be strengthened.

Butler started up the James with the Army of the James at about dawn on 5 May 1864. The first action of his men occurred when Brigadier General Edward Wild and his African-American brigade took possession of Wilson's Wharf on the north bank of the James because the high ground overlooking the wharf commanded the channel. They faced no resistance. The remainder of the army continued upriver aboard their transports.

A brigade of Brigadier General Edward Hincks's African-American division commanded by Colonel Samuel Duncan was assigned the job of being the first to land at City Point. At the wharf, the men saw a soldier exchange ship unloading recently exchanged Confederate prisoners. They also saw Confederate signalers on a bluff overlooking the wharf sending messages to another signal station in the direction of Petersburg. As a result, the troops landed quickly and hurried up the bluff, where they captured the signalmen at approximately 4:00 P.M. The Federal troops immediately lowered the Confederate flag and raised the U.S. flag. They then signaled the remainder of the army still in the river that City Point had been secured.

Wharves at City Point after the explosion of ordnance barges, 4 August 1864 (*Library of Congress*)

City Point was a very small town with virtually no businesses and few homes. Hincks took the largest house for his headquarters and began securing the defenses of the town toward Petersburg, with Federal gunboats protecting him on the river side. The remainder of the army moved up the river to unload at Bermuda Hundred Landing a few miles up the James River.

In addition to Bermuda Hundred, City Point became over the next few weeks another threatened point of invasion into the interior toward Petersburg. Major General George Pickett, the Confederate commander south of Richmond, knew that he did not have the resources to deal with threats from both positions. On 9 May he had to try when Hincks moved out of City Point along the Appomattox River to divide Confederate attention in the midst of Butler's advance from Bermuda Hundred. Hincks withdrew back to City Point at the end of the day.

During the next two weeks, City Point became the base for cavalry raids against the railroads around Petersburg. However, the failure of Butler's Bermuda Hundred campaign caused Grant at the end of May to order that troops be withdrawn down the James and that City Point be the farthest point on the river held by Federal troops.

In June 1864, City Point became the main supply base for Grant's entire army during what would become the siege of Petersburg. Supplying an army of over 100,000, the expanded wharves of the once sleepy little tobacco port became one of the busiest ports in the country. Throughout the campaign, City Point also remained the primary communication point between Grant and the rest of the nation, particularly Washington. It was also the arrival and embarkation point for President Abraham Lincoln when he visited Grant during the next year.

—*David S. Heidler and Jeanne T. Heidler*

See also Bermuda Hundred Campaign; Butler, Benjamin Franklin; Hinks, Edward; Pickett, George.
For further reading:
Robertson, William Glenn. *Back Door to Richmond; The Bermuda Hundred Campaign, April–June 1864* (1987).

CIVIL LIBERTIES, C.S.A.

The Confederate Constitution held the same guarantees for personal liberties as the amended U.S. Constitution. At his inauguration as president of the Confederacy in February 1861, Jefferson Davis stressed that point. He knew that backing for secession had not been solid, especially among plain folk. Many remained strongly pro-Union. Even after Lincoln's call for an invasion of the South, signs of disloyalty to the Confederacy persisted. In May, an Alabama friend warned Davis that there were many small farmers insisting that they would "fight for no rich man's slaves." Davis was well aware of his precarious position. He needed to maintain what support there was for the new government, and he intended to tread lightly where civil liberties were concerned.

Nevertheless, by early 1862, largely from fear of internal dissent, Congress and the Davis administration were imposing restrictions on civil liberties. In January, Congress made it unlawful for the press to publish news of military operations. But Davis was reluctant to enforce the act because it might alienate newspaper editors. In the North, many editors, aligned as they were with one political party or the other, usually remained silent when the government shut down rival newspapers. The Confederacy's lack of a party system meant that Southern editors tended to support each other on freedom of the press issues. Confederate authorities closed only one paper, the ardently pro-Union *Knoxville Whig*, edited by William G. Brownlow. Davis was not always so restrained.

In February, Congress authorized Davis to declare martial law and suspend habeas corpus. Soon after, it allowed generals in the field on their own authority to impose martial law. Civilians could now be arrested and held without charge. Even when they were charged, they could be tried in military courts. Richmond was one of the first cities that Davis placed under martial law. Its military governor, General John H. Winder, was soon rounding up civilians he considered dangerous. Among them was the Reverend Alden Bosserman, who had publicly prayed for Confederate defeat. Another was John Minor Botts, a former U.S. congressional representative. His crime had been openly declaring neutrality. Arrests of civilians became so frequent that the second floor of Richmond's Castle Thunder military prison was reserved for them.

In April, Davis asked for military conscription and Congress enacted the law for it. For non-slaveholding whites, it meant that they would be forced to fight for the "rich man's slaves" whether they wanted to or not. Even more galling was that men of wealth could avoid the draft by hiring a substitute or paying the government an exemption fee. And there was the infamous twenty-slave law, which virtually excused planters from the draft outright. From that point on, for an ever-increasing number of Southerners the conflict was a rich man's war. That seemed especially evident in the newspapers. One advertisement for a substitute offered "a good price" payable "in cash, land, or negro property." Another read: "WIFE WANTED—by a young man of good habits, plenty of money, good looking and legally exempt from Confederate service."

Reaction to conscription in general and the twenty-slave law in particular was swift and direct. When several draft evaders in Randolph County, Alabama, were arrested, an angry mob attacked the jail and set the prisoners free. Near Buena Vista, Georgia, a band of draft dodgers armed themselves and swore that they would die before being forced into Confederate service. Even Vice President Alexander H. Stephens called conscription, martial law, and habeas corpus restrictions dangerous violations of the Confederate Constitution that did little more than undermine public support. Governor Joseph E. Brown of Georgia, claiming states' rights, also opposed the Confederate draft, but declared one himself for the state militia. Planters easily avoided Brown's draft by bribing state enrolling officers or using their influence in local courts to have themselves declared exempt. One way or another, men of wealth had little trouble avoiding military duty, state or Confederate. That fact reinforced the sentiment among the general Southern population of its being a rich man's war.

Like conscription, the Confederacy's confiscation of private property, or impressment, turned many Southerners against the government. Not only did many Southerners have an aversion to the government's taking what it wanted at will, but they knew that impressment agents frequently sold goods on the open market and pocketed the proceeds. James Bush headed a committee of citizens in Early County, Georgia, who warned that corruption among impressment officials was so widespread that it would "ultimately alienate the affections of the people from the government." Sometimes the abuse did not end with simple corruption. Letters poured into government offices complaining of impressment gangs who shot up livestock and tore down fences. One victim remarked that they did more harm than the Yankees.

Though no member of any class held impressment in high regard, and many argued that it was unconstitutional, the common people were concerned that the wealthy did not contribute their fair share. With planters devoting much of their acreage to cotton, impressment fell heaviest on the general population. They were mostly subsistence farmers who tended to grow more produce, which was what the army needed. It seemed that only when their farms were stripped bare did impressment agents turn to the plantations. Even then, planters were reluctant to part with their surplus. Some used political connections to avoid impressment. Others simply hid their supplies. One soldier recalled how planters "would hide their wagons under straw piles, and carry off their horses....Some of these men [are] rich—worth fifty thousand dollars."

As reluctant as planters were to hand over produce and livestock, they were even more unwilling to part with their slaves. The government confiscated slaves for work on entrenchments and other fortifications, but paid slaveholders for their services. And if a slave died under impressment, the owner was paid $2,500. Widows and orphans of deceased soldiers enjoyed nowhere near that compensation for their loss. Still, planters complained vigorously. If they had some political influence, they could often avoid having their slaves taken at all. Alabama planter John Horry Dent went through the state's governor to have his slaves excused from work on fortifications at Mobile. When the city fell to Union forces in August 1864, however, Dent condemned its defenders for lacking resolution and courage.

Planters' unwillingness to materially support the war only reinforced the attitude of its being a rich man's war. Though there were questions about impressment's constitutionality, the issue for most Southerners was much larger. A cause that sustained corruption and planter profits at the expense of the lives and liberties of the general population could hardly sustain widespread support. And it did not. In the end, desertion and disaffection among Southerners contributed decisively to Confederate defeat.

—*David Williams*

See also Brownlow, William G.; Castle Thunder; Class Conflict, C.S.A.; Conscription, C.S.A.; Constitution, C.S.A.; Desertion; Impressment.

For further reading:

Escott, Paul D. *After Secession: Jefferson Davis and the Failure of Confederate Nationalism* (1977).

Mathis, Robert Neil. "Freedom of the Press in the Confederacy: A Reality." *Historian* (1975).

Moore, Albert B. *Conscription and Conflict in the Confederacy, Southern Classics Series* (1924; reprint, 1996).

Neely, Mark E., Jr. *Southern Rights: Political Prisoners and the Myth of Confederate Constitutionalism* (1999).

Robbins, John B. "The Confederacy and the Writ of Habeas Corpus." *Georgia Historical Quarterly* (1971).

Robinson, William M., Jr. *Justice in Gray: A History of the Judicial System of the Confederate States of America* (1941).

Tatum, Georgia Lee. *Disloyalty in the Confederacy* (1934; reprint, 1970).

Williams, David. *Rich Man's War: Class, Caste, and Confederate Defeat in the Lower Chattahoochee Valley* (1998).

CIVIL LIBERTIES, U.S.A.

The Lincoln administration's first violations of civil liberties came shortly after the war began. In several regions, mainly the border states, Lincoln suspended the writ of habeas corpus, which had been a constitutional protection of citizens against imprisonment without charge or trial. A number of pro-Confederate Marylanders, including Baltimore's mayor and the archsecessionist John Merryman, were thrown in jail without a warrant only weeks after the firing on Fort Sumter. Supreme Court Chief Justice Roger Taney, responding to the arrests with *Ex parte Merryman*, insisted that Lincoln had no constitutional authority to suspend the writ. Lincoln ignored the decision but made arrests sparingly, hoping that the mere threat of arbitrary imprisonment would be enough to keep dissenters at bay.

Such threats proved less effective as the war became increasingly unpopular. Deserters became a problem for the army and it was increasingly difficult to find recruits to take their places. By September 1862, Lincoln felt compelled to announced his preliminary Emancipation Proclamation and accept the services of black troops. It was not a position most white Northerners were eager to support, and opposition to the war rose dramatically. Even less popular than emancipation was military conscription, which went into effect early the next year. Northerners, especially those of the working class, already feared an influx of blacks from the South if slavery were to be abolished. For them, it would certainly mean greater job competition and perhaps lower wages. Now many would be forced to fight for slavery's end against their will. Even those who supported emancipation saw deep contradictions in holding a military draft during a war that was, at least in part, for liberty.

Opponents of Lincoln's policies became increasingly vocal in the wake of emancipation and the draft. Lincoln responded with more than words. Anticipating the firestorm of hostility, Lincoln suspended the writ of habeas corpus throughout the North just days after he announced emancipation. He defined treason very loosely as overt or implied, and in some areas, often far from the battle lines, allowed civilians to be tried by military courts. Even silence was no protection for dissenters. Said Lincoln, "The man who stands by and says nothing when the peril of his government is discussed cannot be misunderstood. If not hindered he is sure to help the enemy." Freedom of speech was trampled underfoot as Lincoln moved against dissenters. A number of newspapers critical to his administration, such as the *New York World* and the *Philadelphia Evening Journal*, were forced to suspend operations. Others, like the German-language antiwar paper *National Zeitung*, were denied use of the postal service. Thousands upon thousands of Lincoln's critics were arrested without warrant. Persons suspected of treason were sometimes tortured, a violation of the Constitution's protection against cruel and unusual punishment. Some were handcuffed and suspended by their wrists. Others were hosed down with painful jets of water. One man was subjected to this water torture for two hours until it finally broke his skin. Secretary of State William H. Seward, and probably Lincoln himself, knew of the torture. But no directives against such treatment ever came from the administration.

In trying to suppress dissent, Lincoln and other Republicans were often motivated more by politics than by patriotism. They tended to paint their opponents with a broad brush of treason, and people sometimes suffered arrest and worse for no other crime than being a Democrat. The antiwar or Peace Democrats were special Republican targets. As a sign of protest against Lincoln's suppression of civil liberties, Peace Democrats wore pennies with the head of "Liberty" emblazoned on them. This practice gave rise to the term "Copperheads," though Republicans equated them with the poisonous snake of that name. Most outspoken of the Copperheads was Clement L. Vallandigham of Ohio. A congressman at the war's beginning, he opposed every war measure Lincoln pursued and was especially critical of Lincoln's record on civil liberties. Vallandigham was on a collision course with the administration.

The inevitable clash came in 1863 when General Ambrose Burnside issued General Order No. 38. Burnside commanded a military district covering the states of Ohio, Indiana, Illinois, Michigan, and that part of Kentucky east of the Tennessee River. Though the region encompassed no battlefront, his order made clear that anyone who so much as implied treasonable sentiments would be tried not in a civil court but before a military commission. Vallandigham, running for his party's nomination to the governor's seat, decided to challenge Burnside's order directly. On 1 May he delivered an antiwar speech at Mt. Vernon, Ohio, in violation of General Order No. 38, calling the order itself unconstitutional. Vallandigham was arrested a few days later and put on trial for treason. Even prosecution witnesses said Vallandigham had denounced violent resistance to the law, saying that voters should use the ballot box to affect change. He was nevertheless convicted of treason and banished to the Confederacy. Vallandigham quickly moved to Canada and continued his antiwar efforts from exile.

Reaction to the Vallandigham case was more critical than most Republicans had expected. In some cases it was violent. The day after Vallandigham's arrest, a mob of outraged Democrats in Dayton, Ohio, attacked the Republican newspaper office and burned it to the ground. There were even Republicans who thought that arresting Vallandigham went too far. Horace Greeley, while supporting some limits on freedom of speech and the press, saw more loyal dissent than treason in Vallandigham. George William Curtis, a strong supporter of Lincoln's policies from the beginning, also opposed the arrest. And Joel Parker, the Harvard law professor who had written a strong defense of Lincoln in

the *Merryman* case, now called his administration a military despotism.

Stung by the Vallandigham backlash and rising anti-administration sentiment, Lincoln and the Republicans toned down their partisan rhetoric. Civil liberties still suffered, but now victims were selected more carefully. And, afraid of losing power altogether in the 1864 elections, Republicans sought an alliance with Democrats who supported the war. Together they formed the Union Party, nominating Lincoln for a second term and Democrat Andrew Johnson of Tennessee as his running mate. Even with backing from the War Democrats, Lincoln carried the November election by only 10 percent of the popular vote.

Trials by military commission continued in the months after Appomattox, mostly in the South. Finally, in the spring of 1866, the Supreme Court declared such trials unconstitutional where civil courts were in operation. Chastising Lincoln's wartime policies, the court ruled that neither civil courts nor the writ of habeas corpus could be suspended in areas not under martial law and that martial law could be declared only in an area of actual combat.

—*David Williams*

See also Conscription, U.S.A.; Copperheads; *Ex parte Merryman*; *Ex parte Milligan*; Habeas Corpus, Writ of (U.S.A.); Supreme Court, U.S.; Taney, Roger B.; Vallandigham, Clement L.

For further reading:
Hyman, Harold M. *"A More Perfect Union": The Impact of the Civil War and Reconstruction on the Constitution* (1973).
Klement, Frank. *The Limits of Dissent: Clement Vallandigham and the Civil War* (1970).
———. *Dark Lanterns: Secret Political Societies, Conspiracies, and Treason Trials in the Civil War* (1984).
Neely, Mark E., Jr. *The Fate of Liberty: Abraham Lincoln and Civil Liberties* (1991).
Paludan, Phillip S. *A Covenant with Death: The Constitution, Law and Equality in the Civil War Era* (1975).
———. *A People's Contest: The Union and the Civil War, 1861–1865* (1988).
Randall, James G. *Constitutional Problems under Lincoln* (1951).

CLARK, CHARLES
(1811–1877)
Confederate general; governor of Mississippi

Born outside Cincinnati, Ohio, and educated in Kentucky, Clark, as a young man, moved to Mississippi, where he taught school and read law. After admission to the bar, he practiced law and became active in Mississippi Whig politics. From 1838 until 1844 he served in the state legislature. Upon the outbreak of the Mexican-American War, he raised a state regiment, but apparently never saw combat. After the war, Clark returned to state politics and, during the sectional controversies that resulted in the Compromise of 1850, remained true to his Whig affiliation and supported the compromise measures put forth by Henry Clay.

As the sectional crisis heated up again in the late 1850s, however, Clark began to rethink his Unionist sentiments, switched to the Democratic Party, and became an advocate for secession. From 1856 to 1861 he again served in the state legislature and in 1860 served as a state delegate to the Democratic National Convention in Charleston, South Carolina. Clark was defeated by a moderate in his bid to attend the state secession convention, but upon Mississippi's withdrawal, he was chosen as one of the four brigadier generals of state forces. He quickly rose to the rank of major general of state troops. On 22 May 1861, Clark accepted a commission as a brigadier general in the Confederate army and was mustered into service in Pensacola, Florida. Sent to Virginia, he had no more than arrived before receiving orders to report to Kentucky.

On 1 November 1861, Clark took command of the Mississippi brigade under Albert Sidney Johnston in Kentucky. On his way to Kentucky, Clark stopped briefly in east Tennessee to aid in the suppression of a revolt of Unionists there. After Clark had arrived in Kentucky, his brigade was placed in William J. Hardee's Central Army of Kentucky as part of John B. Floyd's division. By March, however, Clark had assumed command of the 1st Division within Leonidas Polk's corps.

Clark commanded the 1st Division at Shiloh, where he received a wound in the hip. After his recovery, he and his division served in John C. Breckinridge's corps and participated in the Confederate offensive against Baton Rouge on 5 August 1862. Clark commanded the right in the failed attack and was so severely wounded that his men could not move him from the field when they retreated. As a result, Union forces captured and sent him to New Orleans for medical treatment. His commander, Breckinridge, tried to have money and clothing sent to him behind Union lines to make his captivity more comfortable, and his wife came to New Orleans to nurse him. Nevertheless, he failed to regain the full use of his legs and had to use crutches for the rest of his life.

Released from federal confinement in February 1863, Clark returned to Mississippi. As a result of his lack of mobility and bad health, he resigned his commission in October 1863 and was elected governor of Mississippi. He remained in that position until the end of the war.

As governor, Clark was active in communicating with Confederate military officials regarding the defense of the state. He protested the impressment of slaves into Confederate service, but he enthusiastically provided state troops whenever called for by Confederate officers. When Clark heard that Confederate forces in Mississippi

had surrendered to the Union in May 1865, he called the legislature into special session to deal with the crisis. In this brief session, Clark delivered to the legislature an address in which he expressed horror and regret at the assassination of Abraham Lincoln. Shortly after this address, Union military forces arrested and sent him to Fort Pulaski, Georgia, where he remained imprisoned until October 1865.

Clark returned to his plantation and law practice in Mississippi. Toward the end of and immediately after Reconstruction, he again became active in Mississippi politics. He died in December 1877.

—*David S. Heidler and Jeanne T. Heidler*

See also Baton Rouge, Battle of; Mississippi.

CLARK, HENRY TOOLE
(1808–1874)
Confederate governor of North Carolina

Henry Toole Clark was born in Edgecombe County, North Carolina, in 1808. His father, James West Clark, was a former congressman. Young Clark entered the University of North Carolina at the age of fourteen and graduated in 1826. Clark read law in Raleigh and was admitted to the bar, although he rarely practiced. He spent several years running his family's plantation and business affairs.

In 1850, Clark entered public life as colonel of the 21st Regiment of North Carolina Militia. In the same year, he was elected to the state senate as a Democrat. He remained in the senate until the outbreak of the Civil War, and he was elected speaker of the senate in 1858 and in 1860.

Clark's post as speaker led him to the governor's office. By June 1861, Governor John Ellis was in such poor health that Clark was serving as acting governor before he officially took office upon Ellis's death on 7 July 1861. North Carolina had no lieutenant governor then, and the speaker of the senate was next in line of succession to the governor. Clark's term as governor lasted until his original term as senator was up, at the time of the elections in August 1862. Clark continued to preside as speaker of the senate while he was governor.

Clark was blamed by many when Union forces captured Hatteras Inlet, New Bern, and other strategic sites in eastern North Carolina in late 1861 and early 1862. The disasters were largely beyond his control, because nearly all of North Carolina's soldiers were being sent to Virginia, leaving few troops besides raw recruits and militia. His appeals to Richmond for more troops never yielded enough help.

Clark generally cooperated with the Davis administration. He tried to remain above politics and to avoid controversy if possible. While he was not a dynamic leader, nearly everyone acknowledged his honesty and good character. His greatest talents were not as a political leader, but as an administrator. He worked diligently and efficiently to recruit and supply his state's Confederate troops. North Carolina's soldiers were generally the best uniformed and equipped in the Confederacy, and much of the credit is due to the work of Clark and Brigadier General James G. Martin, the state's adjutant general. Clark's actions included encouraging state contracts with firms to manufacture gunpowder and arms; soliciting civilian donations of clothing, food, and medical supplies; and dispatching an agent to buy arms in Europe in the fall of 1861. One of Clark's innovations was an agreement with the Confederate quartermaster department that North Carolina would clothe its own troops and receive commutation money from the Confederate government in exchange.

Clark could not avoid becoming embroiled in political controversy; the opposition Conservatives (mainly former Whigs) identified him with the recent military defeats in the state and the increasingly unpopular policies of the Davis administration. Clark's own faction, the Confederate Party (mainly former Democrats), did not nominate him to run for governor at the end of his term.

Clark returned to his home near Tarboro after leaving office. On 20 July 1863, he was nearly captured during a Union cavalry raid on Tarboro. Clark was just about to take his daily horseback ride when the enemy troops came into sight. They pursued, but were unable to catch him, though Union soldiers did plunder and vandalize his house. The *State Journal* of Raleigh reported on 12 August 1863 that Clark's house was "shamefully abused. [The raiders] ransacked the house from top to bottom, breaking open trunks, chests, and drawers." Later that day, the Union soldiers set fire to the town bridge as they withdrew. Clark was reportedly one of the first volunteers to begin fighting the fire.

Clark was elected to the state senate for a final term in 1866, but thereafter he played little role in state politics. He spent much of his later life studying North Carolina history and sharing his knowledge with other historians. Clark died on 17 April 1874.

Clark's plantation just outside Tarboro was called Hilma, a name created by joining the first letters of his children's names. Clark's home was sold after his death and, in 1899, his plantation became one of the first golf courses in North Carolina.

—*David A. Norris*

See also North Carolina.
For further reading:
Barrett, John G. *The Civil War in North Carolina* (1963).
Mercer, Garry Carnell. "The Administration of Governor Henry Toole Clark, 1861–1862" (M.A. thesis, 1965).
Powell, William S., ed. *Dictionary of North Carolina Biography* (1979–1994).
"Tarboro" *Southerner* (27 February 1908).

CLASS CONFLICT, C.S.A.

Class animosities that surfaced in the Confederacy had been building for some time. Wealth was largely synonymous with slaveholding in the antebellum South, and three-fourths of Southern whites owned no slaves. By the 1850s, despite their racist fears, resentment among nonslaveholders toward the slave system was on the rise. That resentment was most forcefully expressed by Hinton Rowan Helper, son of a slaveless North Carolina farmer. Helper argued in *The Impending Crisis of the South,* published in 1857, that slavery kept most white Southerners locked in poverty. Such class-based discontent was beginning to spread panic among slaveholders. One planter asked nervously, "If the poor whites realized that slavery kept them poor, would they not vote it down?" When Lincoln was elected in 1860, promising only to restrict slavery's expansion, slaveholders thought that his position could encourage the development of a Southern antislavery movement. A slavery defender warned that, with Lincoln in the White House, poor farmers might one day soon have an "Abolition party" in the South. Driven largely by that fear, slaveholders and their political allies forced their way out of the Union state by state. Most Southerners had, in fact, opposed immediate secession. A leading South Carolina secessionist admitted that popular support for leaving the Union was weak. "But whoever waited for the common people when a great move was to be made—We must make the move and force them to follow."

Though there was some initial enthusiasm for the Richmond government after Lincoln's call for invasion, it was not enough to sustain a war effort. As early as the fall of 1861 it was difficult to get volunteers for the army, and desertion was already becoming a problem. The Confederacy's response served only to highlight class disparities. In April 1862, it enacted a military draft that wealthy men could avoid by hiring a substitute or paying an exemption fee. Even worse, slaveholders with twenty or more slaves were automatically exempt from the draft. Said Private Sam Watkins of this twenty-slave law: "It gave us the blues…and there was raised the howl of 'rich man's war, poor man's fight.'" What the planters wanted, said one Alabama farmer, was "to git you pupt up and go to fight for their infurnal negroes and after you do there fighting you may kiss there hine parts for o they care."

Cotton overproduction was another source of class resentment. Though cotton growing declined during the war, planters never devoted enough land to food production. When citizens in Cuthbert, Georgia, criticized Robert Toombs for raising too much cotton, he publicly insisted that he would grow as much as he pleased. An indignant local newspaper editor shot back: "We believe Toombs, because he is rich, does pretty much what he wants…if he were a poor man he would be hanged."

Confederate class conflict as parodied in *Frank Leslie's Illustrated Newspaper* (*Library of Congress*)

Toombs was far from alone. With prices on the rise, many cotton producers and dealers were getting richer than ever. Some openly bragged that the longer the war went on the more money they made.

The inevitable result of cotton overproduction was a severe food shortage that hit women especially hard. Planters had promised to keep soldiers' families fed, but they never grew enough food to meet the need. Much of what food they did produce was sold to speculators, who priced it far beyond the reach of most of the general population. While poor families with absent fathers and husbands faced hunger, wealthy Southerners enjoyed a lifestyle hardly touched by the war. As late as March 1865, one woman described a meal at the Cook House in Columbus, Georgia, where the table was so heavy with food that it actually groaned. Such class disparities were clearly reflected in the wartime illustration shown here, and they were the major source of Southern disunity.

Desperate to avoid starvation, many women turned to theft and violence. As early as 1862, food riots began breaking out all over the South. Major urban centers such as Richmond and Mobile saw the biggest riots. In Georgia alone there were food riots in all the larger cities—Atlanta, Columbus, Macon, Augusta, and Savannah. Even small towns, such as Georgia's Thomasville and Marietta, and North Carolina's High Point and Salisbury, saw food riots. Congress responded in February 1864 by reducing the twenty-slave exemption to fifteen and mandating that exempt slaveholders

provide food at reduced prices to soldiers' families. The act helped ease food shortages and class tensions in Virginia but had little impact in the Deep South. There, planters ignored the ill-enforced law and kept growing too much cotton. The result was continued hunger and rioting through the rest of the war. In Valdosta, Georgia, a band of armed women raided the government depot and made off with a wagonload of bacon. In neighboring Miller County, a mob of fifty soldiers' wives stole a hundred sacks of corn from Colquitt's depot.

It seemed increasingly obvious to husbands that their wives were fighting a rich man's war, which made the desertion problem even worse. One Confederate officer wrote home to his wife: "I can see that discontent is growing rapidley [sic] in the ranks and I fear that unless something is done…we will have no army. The laws that have been passed generally protect the rich, and the poor begin to say it is the rich man's war and the poor man's fight, and they will not stand it." Desertion became so serious by the summer of 1863 that Jefferson Davis was begging absentees to return. If only they would, he insisted, the Confederacy could match Union armies man for man. But they did not return. A year later, Davis publicly admitted that two-thirds of Confederate soldiers were absent—most of them without leave. Many deserters joined with draft dodgers and other anti-Confederates to form guerrilla bands, sometimes called "tory" or "layout" gangs. They attacked government supply trains, burned bridges, raided local plantations, and harassed impressment agents and conscript officers. So violent did this internal civil war become that on 24 November 1863, the *Confederate Union* of Milledgeville, Georgia, wrote: "We are fighting each other harder than we ever fought the enemy." Tory gangs were most numerous in the southern hill country and pine barrens, where they all but eliminated Confederate control by 1864. The Red River Valley of Texas and Louisiana served as a haven for those resisting the Confederacy, as did the Okefenokee Swamp in south Georgia.

On 5 April 1865, only days before the Confederacy's collapse, an editorial appeared in Georgia's *Early County News* that read in part, "This has been a rich man's war and a poor man's fight. It is true there a few wealthy men in the army, but nine tenths of them hold positions, always get out of the way when they think a fight is coming on, and treat the privates like dogs....there seems to be no chance to get this class to carry muskets." Such attitudes had long since undermined support for the Richmond government, and they had a decisive impact on Confederate defeat.

—David Williams

See also Conscription, C.S.A.; Desertion; Impressment; Riots, C.S.A.; Tax-in-Kind.

For further reading:

Bailey, Fred A. *Class and Tennessee's Confederate Generation* (1987).

Baker, Robin E. "Class Conflict and Political Upheaval: The Transformation of North Carolina Politics during the Civil War." *North Carolina Historical Review* (1992).

Barney, William. *The Secessionist Impulse* (1974).

Blair, William. *Virginia's Private War: Feeding Body and Soul in the Confederacy, 1861–1865* (1998).

Durrill, Wayne K. *War of Another Kind: A Southern Community in the Great Rebellion* (1990).

Escott, Paul D. *Many Excellent People: Power and Privilege in North Carolina, 1850–1900* (1985).

Moneyhon, Carl H. "Disloyalty and Class Consciousness in Southwestern Arkansas, 1852–1865." *Arkansas Historical Quarterly* (1993).

Neely, Mark E., Jr. *Southern Rights: Political Prisoners and the Myth of Confederate Constitutionalism* (1999).

Williams, David. *Rich Man's War: Class, Caste, and Confederate Defeat in the Lower Chattahoochee Valley* (1998).

Williams, Teresa C. "'The Women Rising': Class and Gender in Civil War Georgia" (M.A. thesis, 1999).

CLASS CONFLICT, U.S.A.

Expressions of Northern class conflict during the Civil War, like those in the South, reflected not only the immediate inequities that the lower class population endured but also deep-seated animosities that had been there for years. The workers' struggle in the industrial North for decent living and working conditions was decades old. Strikes were common. So was violent repression, often at the hands of government forces. Workers tried to strengthen their position by coming together in unions. Some went further and formed their own political parties. During the Lynn, Massachusetts, strike of 1860, the largest before the Civil War, disaffected laborers founded a Workingmen's Party that carried the city elections that year.

During the first months of the secession crisis, support for or opposition to war broke down mainly along class lines. Most Northerners, especially those of the lower classes, seemed willing to let secession stand rather than resort to arms. It was primarily business elites having economic ties to the South who pressured Lincoln for war. He came under intense lobbying from financial backers and other industrialists to keep the cotton states in the Union. How else could they guarantee continued access to Southern markets and cheap cotton? Reflecting those fears, the *Boston Herald* warned on 12 November 1861 that an independent Confederacy would "impose a heavy tax upon the manufactures of the North, and an export tax upon the cotton used by northern manufacturers. In this way she would seek to cripple the North."

Such arguments carried little weight with the working class. Most of them had nothing against slavery in the South, just its extension. They certainly had no desire to put their lives in danger trying to keep the cotton states in the Union by force. One newspaper in Rochester, New York, reported on the difficulty that officers had getting recruits, despite the availability of unemployed, able-bodied men by the thousands. "We hear a great deal of talk," said the editors of the *Rochester Union*, "among the ardent platform Republicans about coercing the secessionists of the south by means of Northern soldiers, but the indications are that the fighting is to be done mostly with the tongue."

Only after the Confederacy's bombardment of Fort Sumter fired enough nationalistic fervor was Lincoln able to get the volunteers he needed to combat secession. But that fervor quickly died down after the Union defeat at Bull Run. The flow of recruits slowed to a trickle, and desertion was a constant drain on the army's personnel. By late 1862, Lincoln found it necessary to do what he had resisted for more than a year—announce an Emancipation Proclamation and accept the services of black volunteers. Most white Northerners were similarly resistant, even hostile, to emancipation. Though racism was a motivation, it was strongly bolstered by economic concerns. The working classes feared a wave of black migration from the South, which might mean greater job competition and lower wages.

Anxiety among the common people rose to a fever pitch in 1863 when Congress enacted military conscription. Now they would be forced to fight in a war many did not want for an objective they did not support. Even worse, men of wealth could avoid the draft by hiring a substitute or paying a $300 commutation fee. For many

The Albany Contractors who have "influence" at Washington, and   Their Victim.

Union class conflict, from an 1861 *Harper's Weekly* cartoon (*Library of Congress*)

workers, $300 was a year's wage. One labor leader demanded the commutation fee be repealed so wealthy men could fight their own war. But they did not. Contemporary and future captains of industry had no desire to captain troops in the field. John D. Rockefeller, Andrew Carnegie, J. P. Morgan, Philip Armour, Jay Gould, and James Mellon all bought their way out of military service. Mellon's father told him he could be a patriot without risking his own life. There were, he said, plenty of other lives worth much less.

In the summer of 1863, draft protesters in New York and other cities distributed "Song of the Conscripts," a parody of the patriotic recruiting song "We Are Coming Father Abraham." One verse went:

We're coming, Father Abraham, three hundred thousand more,
We leave our homes and firesides with bleeding hearts and sore,
Since poverty has been our crime, we bow to thy decree,
We are the poor and have no wealth to purchase liberty.

The cry of "rich man's war" swept the North that summer, and the country faced the worst riots in its history. Mobs of working class New Yorkers, men and women, roamed the streets shouting, "kill the niggers,"

and went after well-dressed gentlemen too, calling them "$300 men." They torched the draft office, razed pro-Lincoln newspapers, looted and destroyed the homes of prominent Republicans and abolitionists (including the composer of "We Are Coming Father Abraham"), burned an orphan's home for black children, and lynched at least a dozen blacks. In all, more than 100 people lost their lives during the furious rampage. Federal troops straight from the battle of Gettysburg rushed in to stop the carnage. There were similar antidraft riots in Boston, Newark, Toledo, Chicago, St. Paul, Milwaukee, and numerous other towns.

Working people also resented that the war was making rich men richer, often through graft and corruption. Military contracts frequently went to suppliers who cut costs by producing poor quality goods. Inferior wool, called "shoddy," that fell apart soon after delivery was so common that the term soon came to describe any defective equipment. The wartime illustration shown here reflects the indignation that was so widespread. Even more galling to working people was that corporate profits were soaring and prices with them, but wages lagged far behind. Labor strikes were often their result. Railroad workers in New York, riggers in Boston, and coal miners in Pennsylvania were among the laboring multitudes who fought for economic justice. Capitalists struck back hard, with government forces on their side. Lincoln's army beat down striking workers in, among other places,

Rutland, Vermont; St. Louis, Missouri; Cold Springs, New York; and Tioga County, Pennsylvania.

There was widespread resentment of such heavy-handed methods. But unlike the South, the North had a well-financed party system that channeled most lower class anger into the electoral process. Strange political bedfellows developed as Democrats and Republicans alike used the rhetoric of labor and patriotism to denigrate their opponents and garner support. In Lynn, where the Workingman's Party had been so strong, the Republicans were in control by 1863. At the national level, Republicans and War Democrats joined forces in 1864 to form the Union Party, nominating Lincoln for president and Democrat Andrew Johnson of Tennessee as his running mate. Resistance by the lower class hampered the North's war effort to some degree, but a combination of political manipulation and brute force kept class conflict from having a decisive impact.

—*David Williams*

See also Conscription, U.S.A.; Election of 1864; New York City Draft Riots; Riots, U.S.A.

For further reading:
Bernstein, Iver. *The New York City Draft Riots: Their Significance for American Society and Politics in the Age of the Civil War* (1990).
Dawley, Alan. *Class and Community: The Industrial Revolution in Lynn* (1976).
Fite, Emerson. *Social and Industrial Conditions in the North during the Civil War* (1910).
Palladino, Grace. *Another Civil War: Labor, Capital, and the State in the Anthracite Regions of Pennsylvania, 1840–68* (1990).
Paludan, Phillip S. *"A People's Contest": The Union and Civil War, 1861–65* (1988).
Sharkey, Robert P. *Money, Class and Party: An Economic Study of Civil War and Reconstruction* (1959).

CLAY, CASSIUS MARCELLUS
(1810–1903)
Emancipationist, diplomat

Cassius Marcellus Clay, one of Kentucky's most colorful personalities, was born in Madison County on 19 October 1810. His father, General Green Clay, was a wealthy landholder and slaveholder and a powerful politician. His mother, Sallie Lewis Clay, came from a prominent Virginia family. Clay attended local schools, the Madison Seminary, and St. Joseph's College in Bardstown. He entered Transylvania University in 1828 but transferred to Yale College in 1831. There he became acquainted with several New England notables, and he became concerned with the slavery question. In December 1831 he wrote his brother Brutus that "all the slave holding states must soon be free!" A William Lloyd Garrison speech influenced his thinking, but Cassius Clay never accepted abolitionism, and he defended slavery as being constitutional.

After returning to the White Hall estate in 1832, Clay completed a law degree at Transylvania. He was elected to the state house in 1835, lost in 1836, and won again in 1837 as a Whig. That was his last elective office because his mild antislavery views attracted opposition. Later he freed the slaves belonging to him, but kept those belonging to the estate; Clay was attacked by both antislavery and proslavery advocates. Six feet or more tall and of powerful physique, Clay became noted for violent encounters with opponents. A bowie knife was his favorite weapon. In 1833 he married Mary Anne Warfield, daughter of a prominent family, and they had ten children, two of whom died as infants.

In opposing slavery, Clay stressed its adverse economic effect upon individuals and the state. Although he considered slavery evil, he refused to stress anything more than gradual emancipation. When some local editors refused to print his frequent epistles, Clay began editing *The True American* in Lexington in 1845. Anticipating adverse reaction, he armed the building for defense but, while he was ill with typhoid fever, a Committee of Sixty shipped his press to Cincinnati.

Clay regained some popularity by going to the Mexican-American War as captain of a cavalry company, although he had opposed Texas annexation because it would allow slavery to expand. Back in Kentucky, he was severely wounded on 15 June 1849 when attacked by several men, but he managed to kill Cyrus Turner with his knife. Despite Clay's efforts, no antislavery man was elected to the 1849 constitutional convention, and the institution remained firmly fixed in Kentucky's constitution. Clay ran for governor in 1851 for an Emancipation Party. Although badly beaten, he was convinced that he had helped destroy the state Whig Party. Clay turned to the Republican Party as it emerged in the 1850s. A slaveholder who opposed slavery and an effective public speaker, Clay was an exotic figure who attracted considerable attention in the North. One of his listeners at Springfield, Illinois, on 10 July 1854 was Abraham Lincoln. With characteristic modesty, Clay claimed to have influenced Lincoln's views on slavery.

Initially, Clay supported abolitionist John G. Fee and his associates in building an antislavery community at Berea. Clay and Fee were the odd couple of the state antislavery movement. The moderate emancipationist was noted for his violent encounters; the determined abolitionist was a pacifist who prayed for mobs who dragged him from his pulpit. But Clay did not protect the Bereans when they were forced to leave in December 1859.

Clay supported John C. Frémont for president in 1856, served on the Republican National Committee, and backed Lincoln in 1860. Clay received 101 votes for vice president, but factional and sectional reasons doomed him to defeat. Clay expected to be rewarded for his efforts, possibly as secretary of war, but after being passed over for top positions he accepted the ministry to Russia. When he arrived in defenseless Washington in mid-April 1861, Clay organized Clay's battalion to help secure the city until troops arrived.

A popular figure in Russia, Clay returned to the United States in 1862 to make room for Simon Cameron. Commissioned a major general, Clay was unable to secure what he thought was a suitable command. When Lincoln sent him to Kentucky to report on the situation there, Clay assured the president that loyalists were in firm control of the state, but he reported erroneously that Kentucky would accept compensated emancipation. Back in Russia during 1863–1869, Clay claimed credit for expediting the purchase of Alaska. After his return home, Clay received an "adopted" son from Russia. Active in the Liberal Republican movement, Clay's dislike of the Radical Republicans drove him into the Democratic Party. Clay favored black voting, but rejected a social revolution for the new freemen.

After a long separation, Clay divorced his wife in 1878. He continued to be outspoken in his declining years, but eccentric behavior, such as marrying a fifteen-year-old farm girl in 1894 and refusing to pay taxes, tarnished his reputation. This legendary Kentuckian died at White Hall on 22 July 1903 during a violent storm. He was buried in Richmond, Kentucky.

—*Lowell H. Harrison*

See also Diplomacy, U.S.A.; Kentucky.

For further reading:

Clay, Cassius Marcellus. *Life of Cassius Marcellus Clay: Memoirs, Writings and Speeches* (1886).

Richardson, H. Edward. *Cassius Marcellus Clay: Firebrand for Freedom* (1976).

Robertson, James Rood. *A Kentuckian at the Court of the Tsars: The Ministry of Cassius Marcellus Clay to Russia* (1935).

Smiley, David L. *Lion of White Hall: The Life of Cassius Marcellus Clay* (1962).

CLAY, CLEMENT CLAIBORNE, JR.
(1816–1882)

U.S. senator; Confederate senator

Clement Claiborne Clay, Jr., was born 13 December 1816 to Clement Comer and Susanna Claiborne Withers Clay in Huntsville, Alabama. He graduated from the University of Alabama in 1835, studied law at the University of Virginia, and was admitted to the bar in 1839. In 1843, he married Virginia Caroline Tunstall and the couple made their home with the Clays in Huntsville. Politically a Jacksonian Democrat and disciple of John C. Calhoun's states' rights doctrine, Clay gained modest success in state politics, elected to successive terms in the legislature in 1842 and

1844. He also practiced law and was a judge in Madison County from 1846 to 1848. In 1853, Clay was elected to the U.S. Senate, where he opposed government land acts, veterans' pensions, and federal expenditures on internal improvements. During the debate over Kansas's admission to the Union, the Alabama senator supported the proslavery Lecompton Constitution and saw the incident as proof of the South's waning influence in Congress. In the years that followed, Clay pursued sectional interests, opposing both Douglas Democrats and Republicans. In the presidential election of 1860, Clay supported John C. Breckenridge and upon Alabama's secession he resigned his seat in the Senate.

The secession crisis took a toll on Clay's precarious health, and he spent 1861 seeking relief for his asthma, hiring out his slaves, and tending to his unstable finances. When the Alabama legislature met in November, he was elected to the Confederate Senate on the tenth ballot. Arriving in Richmond the following February 1862, Clay continued to support fiscally conservative legislation as he had throughout his career and closely allied himself with Jefferson Davis and his administration. But when Clay opposed a bill to increase soldiers' pay, both his conservatism and ties to the administration raised criticism among his constituents. From April to September of 1862, northern Alabama had been occupied by the Union army, and when the Confederacy regained the area, disaffection festered over conscription, deteriorating economic conditions, and the government's ineffectiveness. Vulnerable to these criticisms as the political climate in his home stated shifted, Clay lost his bid for reelection. But his steadfast support for Davis earned him an appointment as secret envoy to Canada in April 1864.

From his post at St. Catherines, Ontario, Clay worked with other agents and Clement L. Vallandigham to encourage Peace Democrats during the presidential campaign of 1864. He met with Horace Greeley at Niagara Falls to discuss conditions for peace, but Clay lacked the authority to negotiate. Clay also orchestrated the Confederate raid on St. Albans, Vermont. But when the raiders were later captured and tried, Clay's participation was exposed and he was forced to leave Canada for violation of neutrality laws. Returning to the Confederacy, he joined his wife as a refugee and arrived in Richmond as the Confederate government was retreating. Clay then started west, intending to flee to Mexico, but when Andrew Johnson ordered his arrest for conspiracy in the assassination of Abraham Lincoln, the former senator and agent surrendered to Federal forces. For the next year, Clay was imprisoned with Jefferson Davis at Fort Monroe, during which time Virginia Clay worked tirelessly among federal officeholders to secure her husband's release. After numerous interviews with Andrew Johnson and letters of support from Ulysses S.

Grant and Thaddeus Stevens, her efforts succeeded in obtaining Clay's release in April 1866.

When Clement and Virginia Clay returned to Alabama, they found that occupation, emancipation, and unsettled debts had destroyed their family's wealth. Their difficulties were compounded because Clement had never been financially independent from his family and his father's estate was encumbered by debts. As a result, the former senator settled in a modest farmhouse on his land outside Huntsville, where he struggled unsuccessfully with free labor and declining cotton prices and liquidated family lands and railroad stock to meet debts. He also failed in an attempt to sell insurance. With his finances and health destroyed by war, and struggling at times with alcohol, Clay withdrew from public affairs, declining to enter politics after his pardon in 1880. During the same period, Virginia Clay spent more time away from her husband and their reduced circumstances, participating in society through the charity of friends and seeking loans to relieve the couple's troubled finances. On 3 January 1882, Clement Claiborne Clay died at his farmhouse, ending a life in which a once-powerful and honored scion of an elite Southern family was broken by the revolutionary forces of the Civil War.

—*Christine Dee*

See also Clay-Clopton, Virginia Caroline Tunstall.
For further reading:
Alexander, Thomas Benjamin, and Richard E. Beringer. *The Anatomy of the Confederate Congress; A Study of the Influences of Member Characteristics on Legislative Voting Behavior, 1861–1865* (1972).
Bleser, Carol K., and Frederick M. Heath. "The Clays of Alabama; The Impact of the Civil War on a Southern Marriage." In *In Joy and Sorrow: Women, Family and Marriage in the Victorian South, 1830–1900* (1991).
Clay Family Papers. In *Records of Antebellum Southern Plantations* at Duke University Library.
Clay-Clopton, Virginia Tunstall. *A Belle of the Fifties: Memoirs of Mrs. Clay of Alabama, Covering Social and Political Life in Washington and the South, 1853–66; Put into Narrative Form by Ada Sterling* (1905; reprint, 1999).
Nuermberger, Ruth K. *The Clays of Alabama: A Planter-Lawyer-Politician Family* (1958).
Thornton, J. Mills III. *Politics and Power in a Slave Society: Alabama, 1800–1860* (1978).
Tidwell, William A. *April '65: Confederate Covert Action in the American Civil War* (1995).

CLAY, HENRY
(1777–1852)
American statesman

Born in Hanover County, Virginia, on 12 April 1777, Henry Clay moved to Lexington, Kentucky, in 1798. He had been admitted to the Virginia bar the previous year, and soon he was enjoying a prosperous legal career as a trial lawyer specializing in criminal cases. He entered politics as a Democratic-Republican in 1803, serving three years in the Kentucky legislature, after which he was appointed to fill vacated U.S. Senate seats in 1806 and again in 1810. When the second Senate term expired in 1811, he won election in his own right to the United States House of Representatives. Attesting both to his popularity and to the high rate of turnover in House membership, he was elected Speaker in his freshman term.

Although Clay nurtured presidential ambitions, it was in the national legislature that he won his greatest laurels and made his most effective contributions to the growing republic. He occupied the Speaker's chair in the House off and on for the next fifteen years, thus to hold the record for the longest service in that office during the nineteenth century. The power of the speakership was due to Clay's personality and innovations, and it could be said that he was the creator of the position as it functions to the present day. Clay, however, was hardly a martinet. Instead, his penchant for tact and conciliation made him an effective political negotiator and influential power broker even when he did not wield the appointive power of the speakership. His talents, well applied during several national crises involving slavery and sectionalism, would earn him the appellation "The Great Compromiser."

During Clay's initial service in the House, he headed the War Hawks, a faction of the Republican Party that urged war with Great Britain to protect United States neutral rights during the Napoleonic Wars. Named a commissioner on the peace delegation that negotiated the Treaty of Ghent ending the War of 1812, he returned to Congress in 1815 and again became Speaker of the House. He wanted in 1817 to become President James Monroe's secretary of state, the position many saw as the anteroom to the presidency, but John Quincy Adams received the appointment. Clay was embittered by the slight and unattractively sought to embarrass the Monroe administration at every opportunity. He even abandoned his expansionism to criticize Andrew Jackson's 1818 invasion of Spanish Florida.

Clay, however, helped to resolve the potentially dangerous national crisis that loomed in 1819 when the Missouri Territory applied for statehood. The entrance into the Union of a slave state would have upset the sectional balance between the free North and the slave South. When Northerners tried to place restrictions on slavery in Missouri as a condition of its admission, Southerners caviled. An ugly debate ensued that paralyzed Congress and foreshadowed how divisive the slavery issue would become. Clay was instrumental in securing the passage of the Missouri Compromise in 1820 that arranged for Maine's admission as a free state to balance that of Missouri. The compromise also established the parallel of 36 degrees 30 minutes of latitude as slavery's northernmost boundary in the area of the

Louisiana Purchase. This uneasy arrangement quieted the sectional controversy for the time, but its real and ongoing importance was the attempt to restrict slavery with the Missouri Compromise Line, thus to prevent the need for acrimonious debate in the future.

Although Clay owned slaves, he did not approve of slavery as an institution because he thought it at variance with American ideals of liberty. Yet he also believed that debates about slavery distracted the country from its real destiny of territorial expansion, economic growth, and internal improvements. As a nationalist who favored promoting American business through protective tariffs and encouraging economic stability through the functions of a national bank, Clay's broad interpretation of federal authority ran counter to the growing popularity of Jacksonian Democracy. Advocating limited government, supporters of Andrew Jackson were disappointed in their attempt to elect Jackson president in 1824. When Jackson achieved only a plurality over a field of three other candidates, Clay included, the contest was thrown into the House of Representatives. There Clay's enormous influence proved pivotal in electing John Quincy Adams. Adams named Clay secretary of state, prompting Jacksonians to denounce Clay's support for Adams as first bought and now paid for with a "Corrupt Bargain." The charge was incessantly repeated and helped to frustrate the Adams administration, including Clay's state department, from achieving anything significant. Jackson was overwhelmingly elected in 1828, and Clay seemed repudiated as a national leader.

In 1831 Kentucky sent him to the Senate, however, and from that vantage he would be a key player in ending another sectional crisis when the nullification movement flared in 1832. Many Southerners believed high tariffs were contrived to benefit Northern industries at the expense of Southern agriculture. South Carolina "nullifiers" finally responded by announcing that no tariffs would be collected in their ports after 1 March 1833. Jackson's promise to enforce the law, with force if necessary, had the potential of setting off civil war. Clay worked with fellow senators, including John C. Calhoun, to arrange a compromise tariff reduction that allowed Jackson and South Carolina to back away from the crisis with everyone claiming victory.

Clay's political disappointments continued, though. Jackson soundly defeated him in the 1832 presidential election. As leader of the Whig Party, he became a tenacious contender for the presidency in the 1840s, but gained the party's nomination only in 1844. The Democrat James K. Polk won the election that year. Clay's personal life was tragically affected by his son's death in the Mexican-American War, a conflict that he and other Whigs, such as freshman congressman Abraham Lincoln, opposed. Nearly destroyed with grief,

he retired to Lexington, but returned to the Senate in 1849 to help avert yet another sectional crisis.

Clay was indispensable in resolving the controversies that broke over the Union in 1850. This latest and most serious assault on national harmony was a direct result of the acquisition of western territory from Mexico. California's desire to be admitted to the Union as a free state enraged Southerners as much as the Southern demand for a more stringent fugitive slave law alarmed Northerners. Added to these troublesome questions was a move to abolish the slave trade in the District of Columbia, a border dispute between slave state Texas and the territory of New Mexico, and the question of whether the remainder of the Mexican cession (New Mexico and Utah) would be organized as free or slave territory. Clay dubbed these "the five bleeding wounds" and predicted that if they were not mended, the Union would die. In helping to design the Omnibus Bill that as the Compromise of 1850 would try to resolve all five controversies at once, he adhered to the nationalist principles that had guided him from the outset of his career. The preservation of the Union was foremost, so he had no qualms about including a fugitive slave law in the package as an incentive to Southerners to accept the essentially pro-Northern balance of the bargain.

Clay's age and health worked against him in 1850 as much as Congress and President Zachary Taylor's resistance to compromise did. Having set the wheels of conciliation in motion in such way as to garner Daniel Webster's invaluable support, Clay succumbed to exhaustion and left the realization of this last meaningful compromise to others.

He died two years later, two years after John C. Calhoun and only a few months before Daniel Webster. The three were venerated as the Great Triumvirate, and their passing marked the end of an era in American politics. With them died the foremost living memories of the Constitution as a process of concessions and temporary settlements. The new generation of politicians coming to power would ultimately find concessions impossible and would demand that settlements be permanent. Clay had predicted that the Compromise of 1850 would, like the Missouri Compromise, quell the slavery debate for another thirty years. When he died on 29 June 1852, the Union had less than a decade before slavery would provoke the secession crisis that led to the Civil War. One of the reasons was that Clay and men like him were no more.

—*David S. Heidler and Jeanne T. Heidler*

See also Calhoun, John Caldwell; Fugitive Slave Act; Webster, Daniel

For further reading:

Eaton, Clement. *Henry Clay and the Art of American Politics* (1962).

Mayo, Bernard. *Henry Clay* (1937).

Poage, George R. *Henry Clay and the Whig Party* (1965).

Remini, Robert V. *Henry Clay: Statesman for the Union* (1991).
Van Deusen, Glyndon G. *The Life of Henry Clay* (1979).

CLAY-CLOPTON, VIRGINIA CAROLINE TUNSTALL
(1825–1915)
Author and suffragist

Virginia Caroline Tunstall was born in North Carolina on 16 January 1825, the daughter of Peyton Randolph Tunstall and Ann Arrington Tunstall, and was raised by maternal relatives in Tuscaloosa, Alabama. She graduated in 1840 from the Female Academy in Nashville and returned to Tuscaloosa, where her vivacity, along with her family's status, made her popular and attracted the attention of Clement Claiborne Clay, Jr. After a brief courtship, the couple married in 1843, and Virginia Clay accompanied her husband to his family's home in Huntsville, Alabama, where she resided for the next decade.

During the ensuing years, Clay only briefly occupied a home of her own, as her husband failed to profit from his law practice and her property was insufficient for their support. But when her husband was elected to the U.S. Senate in 1853, Clay achieved independence from her in-laws, accompanying her husband to Washington, D.C. Shortly after her arrival in the capital, she gave birth to a stillborn daughter. Thereafter childless, Clay played a leading role in society that would have been impossible for most women with families. Her circle included President Franklin Pierce, Jefferson Davis and Varina Davis, and James and Mary Chesnut. During this time, Clay also served as surrogate mother for numerous female relatives, orchestrating their entrance into the elite society she presided over.

As sectional tensions mounted, Clay continued to lead Washington society, but in 1860, political tensions had damaged her husband's precarious health, forcing the Clays to leave Washington. The couple returned to Huntsville, summering in the mountains and traveling to Louisiana to relieve Clement's asthma. By January 1861, the Clays returned to Washington as Alabama seceded from the Union. As a staunch advocate of states' rights and immediate secession, Clement Clay resigned his Senate seat, and the couple returned to Huntsville. When her husband was elected to the Confederate Senate in 1861, Clay accompanied him to Richmond in February 1862. This marked the beginning of her life as a war refugee, for Huntsville was occupied by Federal forces in April 1862. For most of the war, Clay lived among friends and relatives in Georgia and South Carolina, at times visiting her husband in Richmond and participating in society at the Confederate capital. Elitist and extravagant, Virginia Clay neither participated in wartime charities nor economized, but instead devoted her time to socializing and maintaining family relationships. After Lincoln's assassination, her husband was imprisoned for alleged conspiracy, and Clay traveled between Huntsville and Washington, intervening with President Andrew Johnson and other leading politicians on her husband's behalf. In May 1866, her efforts succeeded and her husband was released.

Returning to their home, the Clays found the family's wealth destroyed and their political influence reduced. In the years that followed, Clay adapted better to postwar changes than did her husband. While her husband struggled to secure a living from their modest farm, she maintained relationships, participated in society through the charity of friends, and secured loans to improve their finances. While her penchant for society remained intact, her self-reliance increased after the war, and she became the stronger spouse while her husband collapsed financially and emotionally. Capitalizing on her husband's past influence, she participated in Democratic politics. She also preferred her own apartment in Huntsville to the isolation of the farm where her husband resided. But despite these changes, the Clays marriage remained intimate and committed and when Clement died in 1882, Virginia eulogized him lovingly. In 1887, she married Alabama Supreme Court justice David Clopton, a former colleague of Clement C. Clay, Jr. and moved to Montgomery until her second husband's death 1892.

Virginia Clay-Clopton, as she referred to herself, returned to the farm outside Huntsville and remained involved in politics. Convinced of women's talents for politics and the necessity of women's achieving economic independence, she joined the campaign for women's suffrage, serving as president of the Alabama Equal Suffrage Association from 1896 through 1900. She was equally committed to preserving the antebellum and Confederate memories and began writing her memoirs in 1900. *A Belle of the Fifties*, edited by New York journalist Ada Sterling, was published in 1904 and joined a growing genre of Southern women's wartime memoirs. But sales proved disappointing, largely because *Belle* was quickly eclipsed by Mary Boykin Chesnut's *Diary from Dixie*. Although it has taken almost a century, *Belle* has become valued for its insight into both the antebellum lives of elite Southerners and one woman's attempt to memorialize that world in the postwar decades. Virginia Clay-Clopton died in 1915, yet her life and memoirs testify to the war's impact on women's lives and how women's voices have transformed our understanding of the Civil War.

—*Christine Dee*

See also Chesnut, Mary Boykin; Clay, Clement Claiborne, Jr.
For further reading:
Bleser, Carol K., and Frederick M. Heath. "The Clays of

Alabama; The Impact of the Civil War on a Southern Marriage." In *In Joy and Sorrow: Women, Family and Marriage in the Victorian South, 1830–1900* (1991).

Clay Family Papers. In *Records of Antebellum Southern Plantations* at Duke University Library.

Clay-Clopton, Virginia. *A Belle of the Fifties: Memoirs of Mrs. Clay of Alabama, Covering Social and Political Life in Washington and the South, 1853–66; Put into Narrative Form by Ada Sterling* (1905).

Nuermberger, Ruth K. *The Clays of Alabama: A Planter-Lawyer-Politician Family* (1958).

Wiley, Bell Irvin. *Confederate Women.* No. 38 of *Contributions in American History* (1975).

CLAYTON, HENRY DELAMAR
(1827–1889)
Confederate general

Born in Pulaski County, Georgia, the son of Nelson Clayton and Sara Carruthers Clayton, the younger Clayton graduated from Emory and Henry College in Virginia and began the study of law in Alabama. He began the practice of law in Clayton, Alabama, in 1849 and became involved in Alabama Democratic politics. As a member of the Alabama legislature, he was a strong proponent of states' rights.

At the formation of the Confederate States of America, Clayton enlisted in the Confederate army as a private and was sent to Pensacola, Florida. He did not remain a private for long. At the end of March 1861, Clayton was made the colonel of the 1st Alabama Regiment. The following year, Clayton raised and assumed command of the 39th Alabama Infantry and moved his regiment north to join Braxton Bragg in Kentucky.

Not arriving in time to participate at Perryville, Clayton commanded his regiment at Stones River, where he was seriously wounded. After a lengthy recuperation, Clayton was promoted to brigadier general in April 1863 and took command of the unit known as the Alabama brigade. He commanded this unit at Chickamauga in September 1863 as part of Alexander P. Stewart's division.

Upon Stewart's promotion to lieutenant general the following year and his assumption of the command of Leonidas Polk's corps, Clay assumed command of Stewart's division. In July 1864 he received a promotion to major general. Having already fought in the early phases of the Atlanta campaign, Clayton distinguished himself in the latter stages in the battles around that city.

After the fall of Atlanta, Clayton and his division moved north with General John Bell Hood into Tennessee. Though his division did not take part in the battle of Franklin, Clayton and his men were conspicuous in their bravery at Nashville in December 1864. Clayton and his division were commended for their devotion to duty in guarding the retreat from Nashville.

In early 1865, Clayton joined Joseph E. Johnston in the Carolinas and surrendered with Johnston's army in April 1865.

After the war, Clayton returned to Alabama, where he returned to his life as a planter and attorney. Beginning in 1866, he served for almost twenty years as an Alabama circuit judge before retiring to accept the position as the president of the University of Alabama. He died in that position at Tuscaloosa.

—*David S. Heidler and Jeanne T. Heidler*

See also Nashville, Battle of.

For further reading:
Williams, Margaret. "Henry D. Clayton: His Congressional Career" (M.A. thesis, 1942).

CLAYTON, POWELL
(1833–1914)
Union cavalry commander

Powell Clayton was born in Bethel County, Pennsylvania, in August 1833. He was educated at the Partridge Military Academy in Bristol, Pennsylvania, and later studied civil engineering in Wilmington, Delaware. In 1855 Clayton moved to Leavenworth, Kansas, and, four years later, he was elected city engineer and surveyor.

Politically, Clayton was a pro-Union Democrat who voted for Stephen A. Douglas for president in 1860. One biographer, writing of Clayton in 1861, noted that his "weather-beaten face, receding hairline, and unkempt mustache and goatee made him appear older than his twenty-seven years."

At the outbreak of the Civil War, Clayton joined the Union army and was made captain of Company E of the 1st Kansas Infantry. His company took part in the battle of Wilson's Creek near Springfield, Missouri, on 10 August 1861. Clayton fought bravely but failed to hear a crucial command to retreat and continued to advance his company while the rest of the regiment was retiring. He literally had to fight his way off the battlefield, and his company suffered more casualties than any other unit involved in the battle. Despite this stumbling start, Clayton soon developed a reputation for courage and coolness under fire. The *Leavenworth Daily Times* referred to him as "one of the bravest, most energetic and dashing officers in the service."

After Wilson's Creek, Clayton was promoted to lieutenant colonel and given command of the 5th Kansas Cavalry. The 5th Kansas moved into Arkansas as part of the Union force that occupied Helena in July 1862. When Confederate forces attacked Helena in July 1863, Clayton's command completely thwarted the northernmost wing of the three-pronged Confederate advance and contributed to the decisive Union victory. In the late summer of 1863, the 5th Kansas participated in the campaign to capture the

Arkansas state capital at Little Rock. The city fell to Union forces on 10 September 1863.

That month, Clayton and about 550 men from the 5th Kansas and the 1st Indiana Cavalry were ordered to Pine Bluff, Arkansas, to protect the town and its cotton from Rebel raiders and to pacify the surrounding countryside. Clayton made a favorable impression on many of the local citizens. One resident with a pronounced dislike for Federal soldiers nonetheless wrote to her son, "He [Clayton] is a very gentlemanly man and by his humane and obliging manner has quite won the people." Along with defending the town, Clayton had to provide for large numbers of former slaves who flooded into Pine Bluff after the Federal occupation.

In late October, 2,000 Confederates under Brigadier General John S. Marmaduke attacked Pine Bluff. Alerted to the Rebel advance, Clayton put about 300 of the former slaves to work barricading the courthouse square with cotton bales from a nearby warehouse and posted sharpshooters in adjacent houses and buildings to cover all avenues of approach. The Confederate attack began around 9:00 A.M. but, despite repeated attempts, the Rebels were unable to penetrate the Union defenses. Around 2:00 P.M. Marmaduke ordered a retreat. "The Federals," he wrote in his official report, "fought like devils." A Federal soldier at Pine Bluff noted, "Colonel Clayton rode master-spirit of the storm; his commanding figure and conspicuous uniform were seen whenever danger threatened, calmly issuing orders, and encouraging his men; he remained in the saddle throughout this action, and it is one of the strange anomalies of war that he was not killed."

The battle of Pine Bluff was the last major Civil War action for Clayton. Apart from occasional skirmishes and operations against guerrillas, he spent the rest of the war in Pine Bluff, preparing for another Confederate attack that never came. A few months before the war ended, President Lincoln promoted him to brigadier general.

While he was still the Federal commander at Pine Bluff, Clayton purchased a cotton plantation near the town, and in December 1865 he married Adaline McGraw, the daughter of a steamboat captain who had served as an officer in the Confederate army. In 1867, Clayton helped found the Arkansas Republican Party, and the following year, with many former Confederates disfranchised, he was elected governor. His tenure as governor (July 1868–March 1871) was one of the most turbulent and controversial in the state's history.

Clayton later served as U.S. senator from Arkansas and U.S. ambassador to Mexico, and he was a Republican National Committee representative from Arkansas for forty years. Powell Clayton died in Washington, D.C., on 25 August 1914.

—*Thomas A. DeBlack*

See also Arkansas.

For further reading:
Brown, A. D. "The Battle of Pine Bluff: The Yankee View." *Jefferson County (Arkansas) Historical Quarterly* (1989).
Burnside, William H. *The Honorable Powell Clayton* (1991).
Christ, Mark K., ed. *Rugged and Sublime: The Civil War in Arkansas* (1994).
Leslie, James W., ed. "Arabella Lanktree Wilson's Civil War Letter." *Arkansas Historical Quarterly* (1988).

CLEBURNE, PATRICK RONAYNE
(1828–1864)
Confederate general

One of the more interesting and tragic figures of the Civil War, Pat Cleburne earned a fame that derived from four circumstances: his Irish birth, his remarkable effectiveness as a division commander in the Army of Tennessee, his proposal in January 1864 that the South free its slaves and incorporate them into the Confederate army, and his dramatic death in the ill-fated charge at Franklin, Tennessee, on 30 November 1864.

Cleburne was born on 16 March 1828 near Ballincollig in County Cork, Ireland. His father was a Protestant country physician and his mother was the daughter of a prominent Irish Protestant family. His mother died when he was only 19 months old, but not long afterward his tutor became his stepmother and the woman he called "Mamma" all his life. From age twelve to fifteen, Cleburne attended the private Greenfield School, but after his father died in 1843, the family could no longer afford the school fees and he took a job as an apothecary's assistant in Mallow. Later he traveled to Dublin to seek admission to the Apothecaries College. Rejected, he joined the British army.

Cleburne spent two and one-half years in Her Majesty's 41st Regiment. It was an unhappy duty. Instead of journeying to exotic far away places, the regiment was assigned to constabulary duty to keep the peace in an Ireland ravaged by the potato famine. At age twenty-one, Cleburne inherited a small legacy from his father's estate and he used it to buy his way out of the army. He and his siblings then took passage to the United States and arrived in New Orleans on Christmas Day 1849.

The Cleburne siblings scattered to various parts of America. After a brief sojourn in Cincinnati, Cleburne settled in Helena, Arkansas, where he managed a drug store and later became a lawyer. When Arkansas seceded and war appeared imminent, Cleburne joined the local militia company and was elected its captain. When, after the outbreak of war, that company was amalgamated with nine others to form a regiment, Cleburne was elected its colonel, and when that regiment was brigaded together with three others under the overall command of the professional soldier William J. Hardee, that officer recommended Cleburne for command of the brigade.

Cleburne saw his first important action in the battle

of Shiloh on 6–7 April 1862. His brigade was in the front rank during the surprise morning attack on 6 April. Despite horrific casualties, he pressed his command forward until nightfall, when his remaining troops bivouacked on the battlefield. The next morning, Ulysses S. Grant's counterattack forced Cleburne's brigade back along with the rest of the army to its starting point. Of the 2,750 men in his six regiments, 1,043 were killed, wounded, or missing—losses of 38 percent. Cleburne's leadership in this, his first battle, was marked more by enthusiasm than judgment, but he absorbed several valuable lessons that he subsequently applied in other battles. In particular, these included using artillery with the advance and developing a specialized group of sharpshooters.

During the Confederate invasion of Kentucky in late summer, Cleburne commanded a small division consisting of his own brigade plus that of Preston Smith. His division led the advance northward from Knoxville, Tennessee, to Richmond, Kentucky, where Cleburne's small division played the central role in defeating and pursuing a disorganized Federal division on 29–30 August 1862. While preparing the attack, Cleburne was wounded in the face. A minié ball pierced his left cheek, smashed several teeth, and exited through his mouth. He recovered in time to participate on 8 October 1862 in the battle of Perryville, where again his command broke the enemy line, though this time the Federals did not abandon the battlefield. In both of these fights, Cleburne demonstrated his ability to apply practical lessons of combat by making effective use of both artillery and sharpshooters.

Promoted to major general and the permanent command of a division in November, Cleburne embarked on a series of remarkable battlefield performances. In the battle of Stones River (or Murfreesboro) on 31 December 1862–2 January 1863, his division routed the Union right wing and drove it four miles back onto the Nashville Pike. In the battle of Chickamauga on 19–20 September 1863, his division assailed with such ferocity an entrenched force significantly stronger than his own that the Federal commander, William S. Rosecrans, pulled forces from other parts of the field to reinforce the position on Cleburne's front. That opened the way for the successful Confederate counterattack that won the day.

Cleburne's military prowess was most evident in the battles for Chattanooga. On the north end of Missionary Ridge on 25 November 1863, Cleburne's single reinforced division hurled back repeated attacks by William T. Sherman's four divisions in what was supposed to be the major Federal effort that day. Failing to move Cleburne off Tunnel Hill, Sherman asked Grant for support, and Grant authorized a feint by George Thomas's corps in what became the charge up Missionary Ridge. After the rest of the Confederate army broke, Cleburne was assigned the task of defending the rear guard,

Patrick Cleburne (*Library of Congress*)

including the army's wagon trains. In that role, Cleburne's division beat off a concerted attack by Joseph Hooker's Corps at Ringgold Gap on 27 November 1863. Twice in three days, therefore, Cleburne's division saved the Army of Tennessee from destruction.

Though Cleburne's own prestige was at an all time high in the winter of 1863–1864, the Confederacy itself faced a bleak future. In an effort to solve the Confederacy's desperate problem of personnel shortages, Cleburne in January 1864 asked for a meeting of the army's senior officers. At that meeting he formally proposed that the Confederacy abolish slavery and recruit black troops for the Confederate army. He argued that, along with generating a potential half million new soldiers, such a step would pave the way for recognition by Britain and France and strip the Lincoln administration of a moral issue. The horrified reaction of most of those present showed him that this was an issue whose time had not yet come, and all present were ordered to keep the proposal a secret.

Cleburne remained an active and effective division commander in the campaign for Atlanta during May–July 1864, winning important tactical victories at Kennesaw Mountain on 27 June and the battle of Atlanta (or Bald Hill) on 22 July. In the battle of Jonesboro on 31 August–1 September 1864, he commanded a corps in battle for the only time in the war. None of those battles was a clear Confederate victory, however, and on 1 September 1864 John Bell Hood was forced to evacuate Atlanta.

Cleburne's division took the lead again during Hood's desperate invasion of Tennessee in the fall of 1864. Hood held him partly responsible for the "escape" of the enemy at Spring Hill on 29 November 1864, and both Hood and Cleburne may have conceived of the charge at Franklin the next day to be an opportunity for Cleburne to atone. In that attack, Cleburne's division held the position of dubious honor in the center of the Confederate line as it swept forward across two and one-half miles of open ground against well-prepared entrenchments. About fifty yards from the Federal line, Cleburne fell with a bullet in his chest, one of six Confederate generals to die in that assault.

—*Craig L. Symonds*

See also Atlanta Campaign; Chattanooga Campaign; Chickamauga, Battle of; Franklin, Battle of; Jonesboro, Battle of; Kennesaw Mountain, Battle of; Richmond, Kentucky, Battle of; Shiloh, Battle of; Stones River, Battle of.

For further reading:
Symonds, Craig L. *Stonewall of the West: Patrick Cleburne and the Civil War* (1997).

CLINGMAN, THOMAS LANIER
(1812–1897)

Confederate general

Thomas L. Clingman, one of North Carolina's leading public figures of the nineteenth century, was born in Huntsville, North Carolina. Because his father died when Clingman was only four years old, his mother and his father's brother raised him. Clingman excelled at the University of North Carolina, graduating first in his class in 1832. Afterward he studied law under the direction of William A. Graham, one of the state's leading Whig politicians, who encouraged the younger man's boundless political ambition.

Clingman served a term in the state house of commons in the 1830s and won election to the state senate in 1840. He warmly advocated the Whig program of internal improvements, particularly turnpikes and railroads. These were popular measures among the small farmers of western North Carolina who desired superior access to eastern markets. Clingman established himself as a leading proponent of the interests of the western part of North Carolina partly by emphasizing that, as he saw it, eastern interests took precedence in the minds of other party leaders. In 1843 he capitalized on his newfound stature by defeating a popular Whig incumbent for election to the U.S. House of Representatives. For the next two decades, as he was elected repeatedly to Congress, Clingman became firmly established as one of the state's most influential political leaders.

Clingman won a reputation in Washington for his fiery speeches and his considerable skill at both crafting legislation and guiding it to passage. He also made considerable waves by breaking ranks with every other Southern congressman and voting against the "gag rule" prohibiting debate on the issue of slavery. Clingman argued that this rule played into the hands of abolitionists by making them appear to be persecuted. Clingman's characteristically iconoclastic stance, which Whigs applauded in both his home state and the North, outraged Southern Democrats. He further enraged Democrats with his bitterly partisan speeches denouncing them.

William L. Yancey of Alabama responded to one of Clingman's verbal attacks with a congressional speech in which he personally insulted Clingman, causing the North Carolinian to challenge him to a duel. Because Yancey was an expert shot and Clingman had never fired a pistol, the odds seemed to favor the Alabama congressman overwhelmingly. The duel that followed resulted in plenty of publicity, although both men missed their targets.

Despite his position of influence in the Whig Party, Clingman became increasingly unhappy with the party's failure to gratify his desire for a seat in the Senate. In 1848, he cooperated with Democrats in an unsuccessful effort to replace Whig senator George E. Badger. Thereafter, Clingman gradually began moving toward the Democratic Party, bringing many of his western supporters with him. Clingman's defection clearly played a leading role in the collapse of the state's Whig Party organization soon after, although historians continue to debate whether it was the decisive factor.

During the 1850s, in response to the intensifying sectional crisis, Clingman became a vociferous supporter of Southern rights. During the presidential campaign of 1856, he issued a public letter in which he advocated secession in the event of the election of Republican John C. Frémont. Clingman also gained much attention in the 1850s as a result of engaging in a controversy with his old University of North Carolina professor Elisha Mitchell. The argument concerned the question of which man had first identified and climbed the highest mountain east of the Mississippi, now officially designated as Mount Mitchell. This complicated disagreement eventually led to Mitchell's accidentally plummeting to his death, a tragedy that many Whigs blamed on Clingman.

In 1858, North Carolina Democrats finally gratified Clingman's long-standing ambition and elevated him to the U.S. Senate to complete the term of Asa Biggs, who had recently resigned. In 1860, Clingman won election to a full six-year term; however, North Carolina's secession cut his term short in April 1861. Clingman, a strong supporter of secession, immediately resigned when North Carolina seceded.

Deciding that his staunch public advocacy of Southern independence made it necessary for him to fight for the cause personally, Clingman joined the Confederate army. He was elected colonel of the 25th North Carolina Infantry Regiment in August 1861 and received a promotion to brigadier general the next May. His appointment and promotion were purely political, for he had no military experience. His brigade saw its first action at a skirmish near Goldsboro in December 1862, when Clingman particularly distinguished himself by his personal courage. Early in 1863, however, while stationed in South Carolina, the brigade earned a reputation for low morale, high desertion rates, and general unreliability. Nevertheless, Clingman and his men performed well after being summoned to reinforce Robert E. Lee's Army of Northern Virginia in 1864. Clingman's brigade participated in the Confederate victories at Drewry's Bluff, Cold Harbor, Petersburg, and Weldon Railroad. Clingman was wounded in the leg during the latter battle, effectively ending his active service. Although he displayed no exceptional strategic or tactical abilities, his wartime service was not undistinguished.

Clingman did not return to political prominence after the war. Former Whigs in North Carolina continued to detest him, and his willingness to break ranks with Democratic leaders proved unacceptable during the bitter Reconstruction period. On one occasion, a conflict with a Democratic editor left Clingman severely beaten in the face with his own cane. Clingman did make a mark in the postwar years by his efforts to prove the feasibility of the use of zircon as an electric conductor and to promote the use of tobacco for medicinal purposes. He squandered much of his personal fortune pursuing these largely illusory goals.

Clingman increasingly regretted his failure to marry, although his belated efforts to court several wealthy widows suggest financial as much as romantic motives. He never adjusted successfully to his fall from public prominence and continued to live in Washington while Congress was in session long after he ceased to have any influence there, eventually drawing increasing ridicule from unfriendly reporters. Always eccentric—he had a lifelong habit of talking to himself and was egocentric even by the standards of antebellum Southern statesmen—Clingman's mental health entered a sharp state of decline in the last few years of his life. He died in Morganton, North Carolina.

—*Michael Thomas Smith*

See also North Carolina.

For further reading:
Inscoe, John C. "Thomas Clingman, Mountain Whiggery, and the Southern Cause." *Civil War History* (1987).
Jeffrey, Thomas E. *Thomas Lanier Clingman: Fire Eater from the Carolina Mountains* (1998).
Kruman, Marc W. "Thomas L. Clingman and the Whig Party: A Reconsideration." *North Carolina Historical Review* (1987).

CLOYD'S MOUNTAIN, BATTLE OF
(9 May 1864)

As Lieutenant General Ulysses S. Grant mounted his overland campaign against Robert E. Lee in the spring of 1864, he intended to deprive Lee of the support and sustenance that customarily flowed to the Army of Northern Virginia from east Tennessee and the Shenandoah Valley. As part of this design Brigadier General George R. Crook had the task of destroying the Virginia & Tennessee Railroad's bridge over the New River near Dublin. The railroad's bridges had been a target of several raids in the latter part of 1863, but this Federal assault on this bridge was to be the most coordinated and menacing so far. Major General Franz Sigel's advance up the Shenandoah Valley coincided with Crook's move toward Dublin, for instance, to cause the diversion of the meager Confederate defenses of the area away from the railroad bridge to the Shenandoah breadbasket.

Nonetheless, Crook had a formidable task. Daunting terrain and worse weather made his progress out of the Kanawha Valley a logistical ordeal. Setting forth from Gauley Bridge with 6,500 men and twelve artillery pieces on 2 May, he was to be followed out of Logan's Court House three days later by Brigadier General William W. Averell's 2,000-man cavalry brigade. By moving on Saltville, Averell would form yet another distraction from both Crook's column and its real purpose. Crook labored over the cragged country, marching along the Kanawha River before heading south toward Rocky Gap. By 8 May, he was near Shannon's Bridge, less than ten miles from his objective, when he discovered a Confederate force, the first real resistance he had encountered, in his front.

The multiple Union movements in the region had worked to draw away and scatter Confederate resources. Lawyer-turned-cavalry-commander Brigadier General Alfred G. Jenkins had just been placed in command of forces in southwestern Virginia when the elaborate ballet of Federal offensives was put into motion. Suddenly aware of Crook's approach, Jenkins began a desperate effort to cobble together some defenses. He barely recalled a brigade on its way to fight Sigel in the Shenandoah Valley. Jenkins's best efforts could muster less than 2,500 men, mostly home guards, and a few field pieces. Yet he was doubtless encouraged by the high ground he could occupy, and even at the last minute a few extra men were trickling into place.

The ground was near Cloyd's Mountain, extending into James Cloyd's nearby farm. Here heavily forested hills framed a wide meadow, part of the course of Back Creek. The Confederate position, enhanced by hastily constructed earthworks and log fortifications, was strong enough to give Crook pause when he looked it over on the morning of 9 May, but it was only a pause. "They may whip us," Crook commented, "but I guess not." The artillery traded shots for most of the morning before Crook directed his assault against the Confederate right. After making considerable progress, the Union advance composed of West Virginia and Ohio troops stalled just in front of the gray line and became vulnerable targets for Confederate muskets.

Meanwhile, Jenkins responded to the pressure on his right by reinforcing it from other parts of his line. A charge into the right center section of that line jarred the Confederates until they stiffened and a vicious melee ensued. The fighting nearly caused the Federals to falter, when Colonel Rutherford B. Hayes led his 1st Brigade of Ohioans into the fray and broke the Virginians. When Crook committed reinforcements the day was his. Bluecoats overran Confederate batteries, and Jenkins himself fell wounded, his left arm mutilated. Command then devolved on Brigadier General John McCausland, who put up a spirited resistance until extracting his spent forces before they, like the wounded they left behind them, fell to capture. Jenkins was among that number. Union surgeons tried to save his life by cutting off his shattered arm, but in less than two weeks he was dead. He was thirty-three.

Cloyd's Mountain was the war's fiercest contest fought in that region. Although it lasted only about an hour, the combat claimed 688 Union casualties and more than 538 Confederates. After the battle, only five miles of undefended country stood between George Crook and Dublin, and by evening the next day the Virginia & Tennessee Railroad's New River Bridge was a smoldering ruin.

—David S. Heidler and Jeanne T. Heidler

See also Averell's Raids; Crook, George; Hayes, Rutherford B.; Jenkins, Albert G.; McCausland, John; West Virginia.
For further reading:
Broun, Thomas L. "Cloyd's Mountain Battle." *Southern Historical Society Papers* (1909).
Cook, Roy Bird. "Albert Gallatin Jenkins—A Confederate Portrait." *West Virginia Review* (1934).
Duncan, Richard R. *Lee's Endangered Left: The Civil War in Western Virginia, Spring of 1864* (1998).
Johnson, Flora Smith. "The War Record of Albert Gallatin Jenkins, C.S.A." *West Virginia History* (1947).
Johnson, Freddie L., III. "Mountain Warrior: The Political and Military Career of Albert Gallatin Jenkins" Master's thesis, Kent State University, (1993).
McManus, Howard Rollins. *The Battle of Cloyd's Mountain: The Virginia and Tennessee Railroad Raid* (1989).
Schmitt, Martin F., ed. *General George Crook: His Autobiography* (1960).

COBB, HOWELL
(1815–1868)
Confederate general, congressman

Born at the family plantation, Cherry Hill, in Jefferson County, Georgia, to John Addison Cobb and Sara Rootes Cobb, Howell Cobb moved with his family to Athens, Georgia, when he was a child. He was educated at what would become the University of Georgia, and, after graduating at the age of nineteen, he studied law. Cobb began his practice in 1836 and in 1837 was appointed solicitor general for Georgia's Western Circuit. In addition to the law, Cobb also took a strong interest in state Democratic politics and in 1842 was elected to the U.S. House of Representatives. In Congress, Cobb quickly gained a reputation as a moderate, and it was his ability to deal with all sides that earned him election as speaker of the House in 1849.

Cobb was a strong supporter of the Compromise of 1850. He knew, however, that strong states' rights sentiment within the Georgia Democratic Party led many in the state to oppose it. Therefore, after the passage of the separate bills of the compromise package in September 1850, Cobb returned to Georgia to campaign for the people's support of the measure. Governor George Towns had called a convention to consider Georgia's response to the compromise, and Cobb and fellow unionists Alexander Stephens and Robert Toombs succeeded in persuading enough Georgians to accept the compromise that the elected convention had no desire to take drastic action.

The regular Democratic Party in Georgia, dominated by a states' rights element, turned against Cobb, causing him to briefly become affiliated with the new Union Party in the state. Cobb was elected governor in 1851 but found he could accomplish little without regular Democratic support. As a result, in 1853 he returned to the Democratic Party. Cobb now found himself not trusted by either group, and he failed in his attempt to be elected to the Senate. In 1855, Cobb returned to the House of Representatives.

During the 1856 presidential election, Cobb campaigned enthusiastically for his old friend James Buchanan. He was rewarded with an appointment as secretary of the treasury. By 1859 he was very interested in gaining the nomination to the presidency in 1860. His supporters in the Georgia legislature called for a convention to select delegates to the Democratic National Convention to be held in Charleston, South Carolina, in the spring of 1860. They called for the Georgia convention to meet on 8 December, not giving most areas of the state time to arrange for the selection of delegates. As a result, the convention was dominated by Cobb people who agreed to put his name in nomination in Charleston. Other Democrats were outraged and insisted that another convention be held in March 1860. When this one met, it refused to endorse Cobb's candidacy for the presidency.

After the breakup of the Democratic Party at Charleston and subsequently at Baltimore, Cobb campaigned for John C. Breckinridge for president. The former unionist Cobb also urged Georgia's secession should the Republican Abraham Lincoln be elected. After the election, Cobb wrote a lengthy address to the people of Georgia that was printed in pamphlet form, urging the state to immediate secession. On 8 December 1860, he submitted his letter of resignation to Buchanan and returned to Georgia.

Upon returning home, Cobb went on a speaking tour trying to influence the election of the delegates to the upcoming Georgia secession convention. He was battling strong unionist feeling in the state, and even after the delegates were selected, Cobb worked with strong secessionists to try to secure enough votes for immediate secession. The Georgia convention voted for immediate secession and then selected ten delegates to the convention that had been called to meet in Montgomery, Alabama, to form the Confederate States of America. Cobb and his brother Thomas R. R. Cobb were selected as delegates.

Once this provisional congress convened in February 1861, Howell Cobb was unanimously selected its president. While he was mentioned frequently as a possible candidate for provisional president of the Confederacy, especially by his brother, Cobb was still not trusted by a lot of Southern Democrats. The honor of course went to Jefferson Davis, and against the opposition of Cobb, former unionists and fellow Georgian Alexander Stephens was selected provisional vice president.

Cobb remained in the Provisional Congress, where he urged military preparation and a strong show of force against the Federal forts in Confederate territory. During his brief period in Congress, he showed himself to be a strong supporter of a central government and a defender of the policies of Jefferson Davis.

Cobb decided even before Congress adjourned from special session on 21 May 1861 that he would raise a regiment of Georgians and offer his military services to the Confederacy. Two of his sons were already in the Confederate army, and a third would join before the end of the year. In June, President Davis gave Cobb permission to raise his regiment, and Cobb began recruiting in Georgia. He canvassed the state for enlistees for several weeks, but the Provisional Congress was due to convene on 20 July and he had to leave the last of the recruiting to his officers. The regiment arrived in Richmond in August, and Cobb divided his time between the new military life and his congressional duties. By the end of the month, the regiment was mustered into service as the 16th Georgia Infantry.

After the adjournment of Congress, Cobb was sent with his regiment to Yorktown, Virginia, in October 1861 to become part of the command of John Bankhead Magruder's Army of the Peninsula. Cobb and his regiment spent most of their time working on the defenses of the York Peninsula. In November, Cobb had to leave his regiment periodically to attend the last session of the Provisional Congress. One of the main topics of discussion was the seizure of James Mason and John Slidell

from the H.M.S. *Trent*. Cobb hoped that this violation of British neutrality might bring Great Britain into the war on the side of the Confederacy. Other than speculate, however, all Cobb could do was hope and make arrangements to prepare his men to spend the winter on the York Peninsula.

During the winter of 1861–1862, Cobb fulfilled his final duties as president of the Provisional Congress and turned his gavel over to the incoming speaker of the regular Confederate Congress in February 1862. During the previous few months he had despaired that it would not be the short war he had expected, and he was determined to serve the Confederacy in the military rather than through politics for the duration of the conflict.

Also in February 1862, Cobb was promoted to brigadier general and was given command of Magruder's 2d Brigade. In March, Cobb was charged with manning the defenses of Suffolk, Virginia, and was then sent to North Carolina to protect the railroad approaches out of that state into Virginia. The beginning of the Union landings presaging George McClellan's Peninsula campaign quickly brought about Cobb's recall to Yorktown to help with Magruder's defense of the lower peninsula. Magruder commended Cobb for his actions during the siege of Yorktown.

Cobb and his brigade were withdrawn back toward Richmond beginning on 4 May. Cobb's 2d Brigade did not participate in the battle of Seven Pines on 31 May. At the end of June, however, Cobb and his men were heavily involved in the latter phases of the Seven Days', particularly the disastrous charges at Malvern Hill. The 2d suffered almost 33 percent casualties at that engagement on 1 July.

In the meantime, Cobb's health had begun to fail. He tried to remain with his brigade, but his efforts were hampered by his assignment by Lee to handle negotiations with the Union army for a prisoner exchange. He finally had to abandon the effort and take a leave for health reasons. He returned to Georgia to rest.

Upon Cobb's return to Virginia in August 1862, his brigade was watching what was left of McClellan's army at Harrison's Landing. Shortly Cobb received orders to move his men north to join with the remainder of the Army of Northern Virginia. Cobb and his men did not arrive soon enough to participate in the battle of Second Bull Run, but they did join the army at Frederick, Maryland, in the early phase of Lee's first invasion of the North.

As part of Major General Lafayette McLaws's division, Cobb's brigade was sent from Frederick to participate in the taking of Harper's Ferry. On 14 September, sent by McLaws to defend Crampton's Gap at South Mountain against the Federal attempt to relieve Harper's Ferry, Cobb's brigade was part of the force that was overwhelmed by an attacking Union corps and forced back into Pleasant Valley. Though much reduced in strength, Cobb's brigade then fought under McLaws at Antietam on the Confederate left.

Sharp words were exchanged between Cobb and McLaws over the behavior of Cobb's brigade at Crampton's Gap, and while the rift was eventually smoothed over, Cobb's poor health caused him to request another leave in October 1862. He returned home, from where he requested a transfer to an area closer to home. He request was granted, and he was assigned to the command of General P. G. T. Beauregard at Charleston, South Carolina.

Beauregard gave him command of the District of Middle Florida, headquartered at Quincy. Cobb left for his new assignment in December 1862. Cobb worked hard, especially to strengthen the defenses of the Apalachicola River, but his efforts were hampered by the citizens of the area, who openly collaborated with Union forces in the Gulf of Mexico. Cobb's experience in Florida was very frustrating. He could never secure requested reinforcements to man more than 100 miles of coastline, and he received very little cooperation from the local population. Luckily, no Union offensive occurred during Cobb's time in command there. Cobb's frustrations in Florida were only exacerbated by news in December 1862 that his brother Thomas had been killed at Fredericksburg.

In September 1863, Cobb was transferred to Atlanta, Georgia, to supervise recruiting of Georgia troops. What should have been a welcome assignment that would put him closer to home and family proved very unpleasant because of Cobb's dislike for Georgia governor Joseph Brown. Cobb's support for the Davis administration and Brown's antipathy toward it, however, made Cobb's presence in Georgia important to secure the release of Georgia troops to Confederate service. Cobb was also charged with organizing troops for Georgia's defense. Officially Cobb held the title of commander of the Georgia Guard. By giving Cobb this authority, the Confederate War Department hoped to wrest control of Georgia troops from Brown.

Concerned primarily with Georgia's defense, Cobb worked diligently to arm and equip the Georgia Guard. He also diplomatically avoided as many altercations with Brown as possible. In the fall of 1863 he was promoted to major general. Shortly thereafter, following his defeat at Chattanooga, General Braxton Bragg fell back into north Georgia. Since Cobb's Georgia Guard technically fell under Bragg's command, when Cobb learned that Bragg was to be replaced, Cobb went to Richmond to advise President Davis regarding the new commander. Cobb enthusiastically supported Davis's decision to replace Bragg with General Joseph E. Johnston.

In February 1864, the enlistments of the Georgia Guard expired, temporarily leaving Cobb without a command. He spent the next two months traveling around the state making speeches trying to stir up support for the Confederate government and encourage enlistments. In March he was made commander of the Georgia Reserve Force.

Cobb began organizing his new command in Macon in April 1864. The unit was to consist of able-bodied men between seventeen and eighteen years and between forty-five and fifty years old. Once organized, the men were to return home to be prepared to be called out on a moment's notice.

From the very beginning, Cobb had to do battle with Confederate military authorities, who wanted to get their hands on his new command, and with Governor Brown, who tried to exempt large numbers of men from serving in the Reserve. He surmounted these obstacles and commanded his troops in protection of middle Georgia against Federal raiders during the Atlanta campaign in the summer of 1864. He repulsed an attack by Brigadier General George Stoneman in a skirmish called East Macon on 30 July 1864.

With the fall of Atlanta in early September, the threat of raids increased, and Cobb responded as best he could. When Union general William T. Sherman started on his March to the Sea in November, the Reserve was fully activated. There was little these units could do to stop Sherman's march, and, after the fall of Savannah, Cobb had to concern himself with maintaining order in the state. In early 1865, he moved his headquarters to Augusta and waited.

As the Confederacy's military situation began its collapse in early spring, Cobb began receiving conflicting orders about where to send his few troops. The biggest threat he saw to Georgia, however, was the movement of Federal troops east through Alabama toward Georgia. As a result, he moved what men he had toward Columbus, Georgia. Arriving too late to mount an effective defense, he evacuated to Macon on 17 April and a few days later surrendered to Brigadier General James Wilson.

Cobb was paroled but was arrested about a month later for his part in the secession of Georgia and the formation of the Confederacy. President Andrew Johnson pardoned Cobb, however, before he was imprisoned.

After his release from arrest, Cobb settled in Macon, where he resumed the practice of law. While he did not hold political office after the war, he did speak out against the increasing restrictions of Reconstruction. In the fall of 1868 he took a vacation with his family to New York and died suddenly in New York City on 9 October 1868.

—*David S. Heidler and Jeanne T. Heidler*

See also Cobb, Thomas Reade Rootes; Congress, C.S.A.; Crampton's Gap; Georgia.

For further reading:
Montgomery, Horace. *Howell Cobb's Confederate Career* (1959).
Reid, Randy L. "Howell Cobb of Georgia: A Biography" (Ph.D. dissertation, 1995).

COBB, THOMAS READE ROOTES
(1823–1862)
Confederate congressman and general

Born to Joseph Addison Cobb and Sarah Robinson Rootes Cobb, Thomas R. R. Cobb was the brother of Howell Cobb. Thomas Cobb graduated from the University of Georgia and studied law before opening a practice in Athens, Georgia. Over the years he became a recognized authority in Georgia on constitutional law. Before the Civil War, Cobb worked for both the state legislature, where he codified the state's laws, and for the state supreme court. He also wrote extensively, particularly on the legality of slavery. His two most famous works were *Inquiry into the Law of Negro Slavery* and *A Historical Sketch of Slavery from the Earliest Periods*.

A strong advocate of states' rights, Cobb was prompted by Abraham Lincoln's election in November 1860 to advocate the immediate secession of Georgia by the legislature. When the legislature called for a convention instead, Cobb was elected to that body. In the convention Cobb was a strong advocate of secession. Alexander Stephens later wrote that Cobb was one of the major figures responsible for Georgia leaving the union. After secession, he was the driving force behind the revision of the state Constitution. That task accomplished, Cobb and his brother Howell were sent as delegates to the Provisional Confederate Congress in Montgomery, Alabama.

In Montgomery, Cobb's most important activity was his service on the committee to draft a permanent Confederate constitution. He also worked behind the scenes to try to secure the election of his brother Howell as provisional president.

Impatient with the political activity in Congress by the summer of 1861, Cobb resigned his seat to raise a cavalry legion that would bear his name as Cobb's Legion. Commissioned colonel, Cobb commanded the legion at the siege of Yorktown in the opening phases of the Peninsula campaign as part of his brother Howell's brigade. He fought under James E. B. Stuart during the Seven Days' battles. Continuing with the Army of Northern Virginia throughout the summer campaigns at Second Bull Run and Antietam, Cobb was recommended for promotion by Robert E. Lee on 27 October 1862. The promotion to brigadier general became effective 1 November 1862.

At Fredericksburg, Cobb and his brigade were placed on Marye's Heights in front of the Marye House.

Defending his position against repeated assaults on 13 December, during one of the later attacks Cobb was struck by an enemy bullet in the thigh and bled to death before he could receive medical attention.

Certainly not a brilliant general, Cobb exhibited an unquestioned bravery that inspired his troops. In Georgia politics, he had never enjoyed prominence before the secession crisis, but he skillfully used obvious oratorical and legal abilities to influence the actions of his state.

—*David S. Heidler and Jeanne T. Heidler*

See also Congress, C.S.A.; Constitution, C.S.A.; Fredericksburg, First Battle of; Georgia.
For further reading:
McCash, William B. *Thomas R. R. Cobb; The Making of a Southern Nationalist* (1983).

COBURN, ABNER
(1803–1885)
Governor of Maine

Born to Eleazar Coburn and Mary Weston Coburn in Canaan, Maine, Abner Coburn was educated locally. As a young man he taught school briefly before entering the timber business with his father and brother. By the time of his father's death, the company had become one of the richest in the state and owned more timberland than any other. Coburn's wealth led him by the 1850s to invest in a variety of other enterprises including railroads. By mid-decade he had become the president of the Maine Central Railroad.

While engaging in his various business pursuits, Coburn also took an active interest in Maine politics. Beginning his political career as a Whig, Coburn served in the state legislature. With the demise of the Whig Party, Coburn was a driving force in organizing the new Republican Party in Maine. He would maintain a leadership position within the state's party for the remainder of his life.

In 1860 Coburn was seen as a strong possibility to be the Republicans' candidate for governor. He failed to gain the nomination, but used his influence for the first two years of the war to urge support for the war effort. In 1862 he received the party's nomination and won the election. He took office in early 1863 when Union forces, especially in the Eastern theater, were not faring well. The war in many Northern states, including Maine, was becoming less popular and recruiting more difficult.

While Coburn spent much of his early months in office trying to fill Federal recruiting quotas, he faced considerable opposition in some parts of the state. When Congress enacted Federal conscription in the spring of 1863, Coburn faced the task of convincing his state's citizens of the wisdom of this new policy. Those areas of the state that had already supplied a large number of recruits to the Union army did not believe it was fair that their percentage of draftees would be the same as those areas that had not supplied as many men. Throughout the summer of 1863 Coburn tried to fill the Federal draft quota, while also keeping an already unhappy population calm. He repeatedly requested of conscription officials that they work more closely with him and keep him informed about policies and quotas quickly so that he could prevent rumors from starting among the general population.

In addition to his almost ceaseless work on filling conscription and recruiting quotas, Coburn was asked during the summer of 1863 to provide temporary 100-day troops to meet the emergency of Robert E. Lee's invasion of Pennsylvania and to recruit state troops to guard prisoners placed at Fort Preble. By fall he was nearly at his wit's end. It was then that he learned that most of the recruits and draftees were not being placed in veteran Maine regiments that had been depleted by combat but instead were being formed into new units. He argued that state pride was at stake and that many people had been following the exploits of these older units with tremendous pride in the accomplishments of their fellow citizens. To allow those units to disappear for want of replacements was a big mistake if the government wanted to continued to gain volunteers from Maine.

By the end of his one-year term, Coburn was tired and discouraged in his dealings with the Federal government. One of his last official acts was to request an extension on fulfilling the state's recruiting quota because it was almost filled. He had not even received the Republican Party's nomination for a second term, partly because he had antagonized the leadership in Washington and partly as the result of an effort by Republicans to court the War Democrats in the state. Consequently there had been a fusion in the ticket. Coburn left office in early 1864 and returned to his business activities.

Coburn continued to support the war effort and the Republican Party. After the war, while remaining active in party affairs, he devoted much of his time to civic pursuits and philanthropy. He was especially interested in improving educational opportunities in Maine and donated large sums of money to higher educational institutions in the state. In 1884 at the age of eighty-one, Coburn was selected one of the state's Republican electors. He died on 4 January 1885 as a result of a stroke suffered at one of the meetings of this group. In his will he left much of his considerable fortune to charitable groups.

—*David S. Heidler and Jeanne T. Heidler*

See also Conscription, U. S. A.

For further reading:
Fogg, Clara Newhall. *Abner Coburn* (1924).
Williams, Charles Evarts. *The Life of Abner Coburn: A Review of the Public and Private Career of the Late Ex-Governor of Maine* (1885).

COLD HARBOR, BATTLE OF
(3 June 1864)

In 1864 as the armies of Ulysses S. Grant and Robert E. Lee collided violently in Grant's drive toward Richmond, Grant made the biggest mistake of his military career when he ordered a frontal assault on entrenched Confederates at Cold Harbor, Virginia. The results were staggering casualties for the Union and a significant turning point in the war. The battle was the starkest example of how battlefield tactics and military thinking could tragically miss the measure of the war's weaponry.

Cold Harbor was only one awful battle in a horrifying campaign. In the spring of 1864, the Army of the Potomac embarked on yet another attempt to defeat Lee and take Richmond. It had become a sickening pattern for the North. Nearly a half-dozen times in the previous three years the Army of the Potomac entered Virginia to fight and conquer Lee, and each time it had failed. When the army limped away from these defeats, Abraham Lincoln usually replaced its commanding general. The army would then rest and retool before launching another attempt.

The 1864 campaign would be different. Grant, now commander of all Union forces, would accompany the Army of the Potomac while George G. Meade remained its official commander. Grant understood that his objective was not so much Richmond as it was Lee's army. In the opening battle of this epic campaign, Lee defeated Grant in the battle of the Wilderness on 5–7 May, but Grant, unlike his predecessors, did not retreat. Instead, he slid his army to Lee's right, and the two armies clashed again at Spotsylvania Court House on 10–12 May. As Grant again tried to turn Lee's flank to envelop the Confederates and reach Richmond, the campaign became a race.

From Spotsylvania, Grant continued to wheel south around Lee's right flank. Since the Confederates had the advantage of interior lines, the Federals could not outmarch them. On 30 May, a Confederate attack at Bethesda Church failed to slow down the Union advance. The following day, part of Union general Philip Sheridan's command arrived at Cold Harbor, a small tavern less than ten miles from Richmond. Finding Confederate troops under Fitzhugh Lee already in possession of the strategic crossroads, Sheridan's forces ejected the Confederates in a light action that left the crossroads in Federal hands. On 1 June, Lee failed to retake the intersection, but more troops from each side were gathering, with Federal forces outnumbering the Confederates. To exploit the advantage, Meade suggested an attack, and Grant agreed. Late on the afternoon of 1 June, Union troops assaulted the Confederate line to score some modest gains before the Confederates

Firing mortars at Cold Harbor, from a battlefield sketch by Alfred R. Waud (*Library of Congress*)

finally held. The Union lost 2,200 troops. It was an ominous indication of things to come.

Grant prepared a major attack for 2 June that would comprise a frontal assault all along the Confederate line but most heavily against its flanks. The Confederate right would be the focus because these men had fought on the previous day, and Grant was speculating that they had not had time to fortify their line. Grant also knew that Lee's right was being reinforced at the expense of his left, so there would have to be a weakness somewhere. A complete frontal assault would find it, break Lee's line, and give him no room to regroup. Yet the planned dawn attack never happened because Winfield Scott Hancock's corps was late after getting lost the previous evening and marching several extra miles to get into position. Grant rescheduled the attack for the morning of 3 June.

The delay proved tragic for Federal forces. The Confederates now had an extra day to dig trenches and construct fortifications. Just how dramatically warfare had changed would be amply illustrated by this campaign and especially this battle. The powerful and accurate Springfield rifle had made close-order linear assaults across open fields impossible. Trenches offered huge advantages for defending infantry. With proper artillery support, entrenched troops could not be dislodged. Previous battles had offered commanders a chance to learn this lesson. At

Fredericksburg, Confederates in shallow trenches and behind a stone wall thwarted numerous Union charges. At Gettysburg, Union troops entrenched on Culp's Hill easily repulsed repeated Confederate attacks. And at Spotsylvania, just three weeks before Cold Harbor, Union attacks in fog and rain had scored only moderate successes against Confederate trenches.

These lessons did not help the Union at Cold Harbor. Just why Grant chose to attack, especially after Lee's men had been given a full day to dig in, is puzzling. Between Spotsylvania and Cold Harbor, Grant had probed entrenched Confederate positions along the North Anna River and had decided against an attack. By early June, however, he apparently believed that, if his army could break through to pin the Confederates against the Chickahominy River, he would have a chance to destroy Lee. Perhaps after weeks of flanking and inconclusive fighting, Grant had decided the time had come for a decisive battle.

The Union army spent 2 June wearing itself out by shifting men back and forth, while the Confederates built a masterful system of entrenchments. Mistakes multiplied throughout the Union chain of command. Grant left many details of the assault to his corps commanders, and no one at any level conducted a proper study of the terrain to assess its disadvantages. That evening, a sense of fatalism settled in over the Army of the Potomac. Veterans knew what a frontal assault against the Confederate breastworks would mean. Horace Porter, one of Grant's staff, noticed men calmly pinning their names and addresses on their coats so their bodies could be identified.

At dawn on the morning of 3 June, Hancock's, Horatio Wright's, and W. F. Smith's corps began to move forward. They moved at the same time but terrain and lack of coordination made their line so ragged that the coming battle would actually resemble dozens of small attacks, with brigades and even regiments operating alone. In one part of the line, a division broke to avoid a thick swamp, an obstacle a proper survey by Federal officers would have revealed. As wave after wave of Union troops charged straight into withering Confederate fire, most Federals fell in the open fields, never coming close to the entrenchments. Union general Francis Barlow's division did break the Confederate line at one point, but the zigzag pattern of the trenches allowed Confederates to enfilade the spot with artillery, and the Federal penetration quickly recoiled under savage fire.

The attacks could not continue under such a murderous barrage. Within a half hour, Union troops were heading back to their lines while some of Barlow's shattered command remained cowering in holes hastily dug in the open area before the breastworks. First reports of the engagement were misleading enough to encourage Grant to continue the assault, but the order to do so found commanders so stunned by the carnage that no other attacks occurred. The toll was indeed staggering and sobered the most battle-hardened veterans. The Union lost some 7,000 men, while the Confederates suffered a relatively light 1,500 casualties. Grant would later say that this and his 22 May 1863 assault at Vicksburg were his most regretted decisions of the war.

Firing continued throughout the day, and for several more days the two sides continued sniping at each other. Meanwhile, Lee and Grant's attempts for a truce to collect their wounded fell into confusion about precise terms, stalling an agreement until 7 June. By then, most of the wounded Union soldiers in front of the Confederate breastworks had either died or been rescued by comrades. On 12 June, the Army of the Potomac began another march, this time toward the rail center of Petersburg south of Richmond. The waltz of the two

The battle of Cold Harbor, by Alfred R. Waud (*Library of Congress*)

Collecting the remains of soldiers killed in battle at Cold Harbor, 1864 (Photograph by John Reekie / *Library of Congress*)

great armies had taken them all the way around the Confederate capital.

Grant and other Union officers came under bitter criticism for the attack at Cold Harbor specifically and for the bloody campaign in general. Grant's aggressive campaign against Lee produced almost 50,000 casualties in slightly more than a month and had only reached the same spot that George McClellan occupied two years before. If in doing so, Grant was applying pressure that Lee could not long withstand, the question remained if Grant's own army could persist in that pressure. Cold Harbor changed the Army of the Potomac, making it wary of future assaults on entrenched troops, infecting it with what amounted to "Cold Harbor Syndrome." At Petersburg few such attacks were made. Instead, each army settled into the trenches it would occupy for nine months. The Civil War had become a very different type of war. The ghost of Cold Harbor became the siege of Petersburg.

—*Richard D. Loosbrock*

See also Grant, Ulysses Simpson; Hancock, Winfield Scott; Lee, Fitzhugh; Lee, Robert Edward; Meade, George Gordon; Smith, William Farrar; Wright, Horatio Gouverneur.

For further reading:

Catton, Bruce. *Grant Takes Command* (1968).

———. *A Stillness at Appomattox* (1953).

Trudeau, Noah Andre. *Bloody Roads South: The Wilderness to Cold Harbor, May–June 1864* (1989).

COLFAX, SCHUYLER
(1823–1885)
Speaker of the U.S. House of Representatives

A fierce abolitionist journalist and politician before the war, "Smiler" Colfax was a Radical Republican and Speaker of the U.S. House during the impeachment of President Andrew Johnson in 1868 and was forced out of office after one term as

Ulysses S. Grant's vice president when his name surfaced in the Crédit Mobilier scandal.

Colfax was born in New York City on 23 March 1823, six months after his Wall Street banker father died of tuberculosis. He, his mother, and his stepfather moved to Indiana in 1836, where his stepfather became involved in local politics. Young Schuyler was encouraged to study law, but he began contributing to Horace Greeley's *New York Tribune* in 1839 and showed inclinations both as a journalist and politician. At the age of twenty-two in 1845, Colfax borrowed money to buy half-interest in a struggling South Bend weekly, which was renamed the *St. Joseph Valley Register*. The paper became one of the leading Whig voices in Indiana. Colfax edited the *Register*, largely in absentia, for nineteen years, advocating local development, banking reform, railroad construction, and abolitionism. He argued that the motto of the North should be "Not another inch of slave territory!"

Colfax was elected to Congress in 1854 as a Whig, but aligned himself with the new Republican Party. He denounced Stephen A. Douglas's plan to permit slavery in Kansas, delivering a stirring speech in the House on 21 June 1856. The Republican Party circulated more than a million copies of the speech in brochure form. At the same time, Colfax opposed reforms that would have protected the property rights of married women, widows, and orphans.

Abraham Lincoln received only lukewarm support from Colfax in Lincoln's 1858 Illinois senatorial campaign, and Colfax did not attend the Republican Party National Convention in Chicago in 1860. Upon Lincoln's nomination, however, Colfax campaigned enthusiastically for the Illinois attorney in Illinois, Iowa, Missouri, and Michigan. When the Civil War began in 1861, Colfax joined others in predicting that the war would not last for long. He helped prepare Indiana to send its men to battle, but did not volunteer for the Union army, a fact used against him in future political campaigns. His first wife, whom he had married in 1844, was often ill and died in 1863.

Colfax was elected Speaker of the House on 5 December 1863, resigning as editor of his newspaper, and remained in the powerful position until he assumed the vice presidency in 1869. He was a political ally of Radical Republican Thaddeus Stevens, and he acted as a publicist for Stevens, introducing many of Stevens's ideas in congressional speeches. Capitol correspondents nicknamed him "Smiler" for his suave, always smiling personality, which became biting whenever politics were involved. Colfax considered 1 February 1865, the day he signed the House resolution for the Thirteenth Amendment, outlawing slavery, the happiest day of his life. He was also a friend of President Lincoln. He was with Lincoln in January 1863, not long after the public

release of the Emancipation Proclamation, when Lincoln and his wife were surrounded in their carriage by an angry mob outside a Washington theater. Declining an invitation to join the president at Ford's Theater, Colfax was also the last public figure to shake Lincoln's hand the night Lincoln was assassinated in April 1865.

Colfax worked with Stevens and other Radical Republicans to develop plans for reconstruction. He tried to avoid a public split with President Andrew Johnson, but he voted against Johnson when the House impeached the president in February 1868 and was surprised when the Senate failed to convict him. The popular Colfax campaigned for the nomination to be Ulysses S. Grant's vice president, and the pair was elected on 3 November 1868 on the strength of some 700,000 popular votes from the newly enfranchised African-American population. The *New York Tribune* noted that the new federal government had a record number of journalists, including Colfax and new Speaker James G. Blaine.

Colfax knew that being vice president would mark the end of his active political career. He presided over the Senate but never became part of the Republican leadership. The highlight of his term was a speech he made on 10 May 1869 at Promontory, Utah, when the first transcontinental railroad was completed. Colfax was interested in a second term in 1872, but he was accused of accepting a bribe from Crédit Mobilier, a construction company secretly owned by the directors of the Union Pacific Railroad. There was evidence that a check for $500 had been deposited in his bank account at the time the bribe was said to have been made. Colfax was not renominated and he returned to South Bend, Indiana, in 1873 at the age of 50.

Remarried in 1868, Colfax spent his final years as a public orator, earning more than his vice presidential salary. He spoke about his travels, his memories of Abraham Lincoln, and temperance. A lifelong teetotaler, no alcoholic beverages were ever served at Colfax's parties or receptions. On 13 January 1885, Colfax was changing trains at Mankato, Minnesota, when to reach another station he had to walk nearly a mile in a temperature thirty degrees below zero. He collapsed and died of a heart attack. He was identified by papers he carried.

—*Richard Digby-Junger*

See also Congress, U.S.A.; Radical Republicans.

For further reading:

Furlong, Patrick J., and Ann Leonard. "Schuyler Colfax, 1823–1885." In *The Vice Presidents: A Biographical Dictionary* (1998).

Hollister, O.J. *Life of Schuyler Colfax* (1886).

Smith, Willard H. *Schuyler Colfax: The Changing Fortunes of a Political Idol* (1952).

COLQUITT, ALFRED HOLT
(1824–1894)
Confederate general

Alfred Holt Colquitt, member of a prominent Georgia political family, had a varied Civil War career in which he rose in rank from captain to brigadier general. While in command of a brigade in the Army of Northern Virginia during 1862–1863, he generally performed well, with the notable exception of the battle of Chancellorsville. Transferred to South Carolina and later to Florida, he would earn redemption at the February 1864 battle of Olustee, where he took field command of a small force that won a decisive Confederate victory. Colquitt would earn his greatest fame, however, in the postwar years, serving two terms as governor of Georgia followed by two terms in the U.S. Senate.

Alfred Colquitt was born in Monroe, Georgia on 20 April 1824. His father, Walter T. Colquitt, had served as U.S. Senator and member of the House of Representatives. After graduating from Princeton in 1844, Colquitt studied law and two years later he earned admission to the Georgia bar. During the Mexican War he served as a staff officer with the rank of major. After that war Colquitt turned to politics, winning election to the U.S. House of Representatives in 1852. Because of concerns over the health of his wife, the former Dorothy Tarver, he did not seek reelection. Following Dorothy's death in 1855, Colquitt married her sister, Sarah. He returned to politics in 1859 and won a seat in the Georgia Senate. An ardent secessionist, Colquitt served as presidential elector for John C. Breckinridge and was a member of the Georgia Secession Convention in 1861.

Upon the outbreak of hostilities, Colquitt was commissioned a captain in the 6th Georgia Infantry. In May 1861 he was elected colonel of the regiment, and he shortly thereafter rose to command a brigade on the Virginia Peninsula. Colquitt participated in the defense of Richmond in the spring of 1862, and on 1 September of that year he received a commission to the grade of brigadier general. Over the next eight months Colquitt led his brigade of Georgians and Alabamians through the Antietam, Fredericksburg, and Chancellorsville campaigns.

Before Chancellorsville, Colquitt's performance had been solid, if not spectacular. His most distinguished service took place at Turner's Gap and Antietam. In the latter action his brigade suffered terrific casualties while defending the Cornfield and Bloody Lane. The 6th Georgia, for example, lost more than 200 men in the fighting, with only twenty-four soldiers escaping unscathed. At Chancellorsville, however, Colquitt's hesitation during Thomas "Stonewall" Jackson's 2 May attack, in the mistaken belief that Union troops were massing on his flank, slowed the Confederate onslaught and led to criticism of his abilities. Douglas Southall

Freeman wrote that Colquitt showed "doubtful achievement" at Chancellorsville and, "concerning him, the question fundamentally was one of judgment." After Chancellorsville, Colquitt and his depleted brigade of Georgians were transferred first to North Carolina, and then to Charleston. Colquitt participated in the defenses of that city during the summer and fall of 1863.

In early 1864, Colquitt received orders to move his brigade to Florida, to help repulse a Federal invasion of that state. Forced to march overland through parts of south Georgia and north Florida, Colquitt's veterans arrived in Lake City only days before they would face a Union advance from Jacksonville. On 20 February 1864, Colquitt's brigade was entrenched near Olustee Station, about thirteen miles east of Lake City. It was part of a small army of about 5,000–5,500 men under the command of Brigadier General Joseph Finegan that faced a similar-sized force of Federals led by Brigadier General Truman Seymour. After skirmishing developed east of the Confederate defenses, Finegan ordered Colquitt to advance with part of his brigade and join the fighting. The Georgian remained in tactical command for most of the engagement, with Finegan remaining at the main Confederate defense line until late in the battle. "I in common with the entire command," Colquitt would later write, "understand that Genl Finegan was not on the field of Olustee at all." The Southern forces won a decisive victory at Olustee, driving the Federals back to their Jacksonville defenses and inflicting casualties that approached 40 percent of the Union force.

Colquitt and his brigade subsequently returned to Virginia, where they participated in defending against Grant's Overland campaign and the opening portion of the siege of Petersburg. Transferred again to North Carolina, Colquitt was ordered to Fort Fisher, but the fort capitulated before he could assume command. He remained in North Carolina until the surrender.

After the war, Colquitt returned to Georgia where he practiced law and reentered politics. The Bourbon Democrat was elected governor in 1876 and 1880, and later served two terms in the United States Senate. Colquitt, along with Joseph Brown and John Gordon, composed part of the great triumvirate of Georgia postwar politics. The "Hero of Olustee" died on 26 March 1894 and was buried in Macon.

—David J. Coles

See also Olustee, Battle of
For further reading:
Coleman, Kenneth. "The Administration of Alfred H. Colquitt as Governor of Georgia" (M. A. thesis, 1940).
Davis, William C., ed. *The Confederate General* (1991).
Evans, Clement A., ed. *Confederate Military History: A Library of Confederate States History* (1899; reprint, 1987).
Freeman, Douglas Southall. *Lee's Lieutenants: A Study in Command* (1942–1944).

COLT, SAMUEL
(1814–1862)
Inventor

Samuel Colt, who was born on 19 July 1814 in Hartford Connecticut, is best known as the inventor of the most popular and widely used revolvers (in both the Union and Confederate armed forces) during the Civil War. From a young age, Colt displayed a talent for invention. His first major successful experiment was a demonstration of an explosive mine, which unfortunately showered spectators with mud and debris. After this incident Colt was sent to Amherst Academy, but was forced to leave after another of his experiments caused a fire on school property.

After leaving Amherst, Colt became apprenticed as a sailor. On a voyage to India in 1830, Colt conceived of the idea that would eventually become his revolver design, and he carved a wooden model of the design on the return trip. Colt perfected his famous revolver by 1835 and had obtained United States, British, and European patents on it by the following year. Without any great demand for a rapid-fire weapon during peacetime, however, Colt's company went bankrupt in 1842. The Mexican War changed his circumstances quickly and, by the outbreak of the Civil War, the Colt Patent Arms Manufacturing Company dominated the revolver market. His manufacturing plant, which had opened in Hartford in 1855, became the largest privately owned armory in the world. Colt was innovative in both his use of advanced manufacturing methods, such as the use of interchangeable parts and a production line, and his progressive treatment of his assembly-line employees.

Undoubtedly, the most famous of Colt's many revolver designs were the 0.36-caliber Colt Navy and the 0.44-caliber Colt Army. These two revolvers were essentially an identical design that was chambered in two different calibers. The 6-shot Colt revolver could be loaded with paper or linen prepackaged cartridges or simply with loose gunpowder and a lead ball. The cartridges or powder and balls were loaded into the front chambers of the revolver's cylinder, while the rear of each chamber had to be capped with a percussion cap to fire the weapon. While this system may seem horribly awkward by modern standards, it was the height of technology during the Civil War. About 200,000 Colt revolvers were produced during the Civil War era. The U.S. government purchased approximately 127,000 of these, while the remainder were probably purchased privately by many soldiers.

Along with his successful revolvers, Colt also produced the Colt-Root Model 1855 repeating rifle. The Colt repeating rifle, the design of which was based on Colt's revolver, was produced in a wide range of styles and calibers (0.40 through 0.64). During the war approx-imately 4,700 Colt repeating rifles were delivered to the U.S. government. The apparent reason for the relatively small number of rifles ordered relates directly to the greatest problem of the rifle itself—a dangerous tendency for more than one of the rifle's rounds to discharge at one time. This problem cost numerous soldiers a hand, an arm, or even in a few cases, their lives. As a result, the 1st U.S. Sharpshooter Regiment, which had originally been issued Colt repeating rifles, was resupplied with Sharps' rifles. The Colt repeating rifles that were issued during the Civil War were generally issued to Michigan and Ohio regiments. In fact, the 21st Ohio Infantry Regiment, which was instrumental in stopping Confederate lieutenant general James Longstreet's I Corps' breakthrough at Chickamauga did so with Colt repeating rifles.

In 1850 Connecticut governor Thomas H. Seymour had Colt commissioned a lieutenant colonel in the Connecticut State Militia. Thus, it was no surprise that Colt was authorized to form the 1st Connecticut Revolving Rifles Regiment at the outbreak of the Civil War. Due to administrative problems, however, the regiment never saw active service. Unfortunately, as the Civil War approached, the workaholic Colt's health began to deteriorate and he finally succumbed to rheumatic fever on 10 January 1862.

—*Alexander M. Bielakowski*

See also Rifles.
For further reading:
Hosley, William. *Colt: The Making of an American Legend* (1996).
Rohan, Jack. *Yankee Arms Maker: The Incredible Career of Samuel Colt* (1935).
Wilson, R. L. *Colt: An American Legend* (1986).

COLUMBIA, SOUTH CAROLINA, BURNING OF
(17 February 1865)

On 14 February 1865, William Tecumseh Sherman's army left Orangeburg, South Carolina, headed for the state capital of Columbia. The army stopped south of the city on 15 February. While waiting to proceed, many of the officers and men probably reflected on the especial distaste they felt for the state of South Carolina, which they viewed as the instigator of the war. Sherman's marchers had already been more destructive in South Carolina than they had been in Georgia, burning many of the towns in their path to Columbia. Many of the soldiers bragged that they would burn Columbia too when they entered that city.

During the night of 15 February, Confederate soldiers shelled the Union encampments, which further infuriated Sherman and his men. The following morning the army moved forward to the Congaree River, from where they could see Columbia and Lieutenant General Wade Hampton's Confederate cavalry patrolling the streets. All the bridges across the Congaree had been destroyed, so Sherman sent XV Corps under Major General Oliver O. Howard north to move on the town from that direction. Sherman ordered Howard before the latter departed to destroy any public property, railroad property, and manufacturing concerns in the city but not to destroy private property. On the night of 16 February, Howard's engineers built a pontoon bridge across the Broad River and prepared to enter the city the following morning.

Columbia was full of people who had fled ahead of Sherman's army. Now many of these people were trying to get out of town any way they could. By the night of the 16th they knew that there was no Confederate force large enough to do them any good close enough to defend the town. The chaos of the fleeing people also made it relatively easy on the nights of 15 and 16 February for Southern looters to start to work on the abandoned houses and businesses. To add to the chaos, on the 16th Confederate gunpowder at the railroad depot accidentally ignited and exploded during the morning.

Hampton knew that there was nothing he could do, so he told Mayor T. J. Goodwin that the military was pulling out on the morning of 17 February and that Goodwin should surrender. Lieutenant General P. G. T. Beauregard was in town as well, and that night he and Hampton conferred. One of the biggest topics of discussion was the presence of many bales of cotton in the streets of the town. Hampton had planned to have it removed outside the city for burning, but now there was no time. Both he and Beauregard agreed that it would be too dangerous to the town to burn it in the streets because of the danger of fire spreading to buildings, so they decided to leave it.

On the morning of 17 February, Hampton sent the mayor and his entourage north out of the city to surrender and began pulling his men out. Howard's corps was already crossing the Broad River. The mayor found the lead elements of this corps and offered his surrender. Word was sent back to Sherman, who had ridden to the Broad, and he authorized the acceptance of the surrender. He instructed Howard to proceed with the occupation of the city.

As the first Union troops entered Columbia, they discovered that the town contained a great deal of alcohol and immediately began consuming it. Barrels of whiskey and wine were brought out into the streets, and each group of soldiers who entered the city had its pick of some of the best alcohol Columbia had to offer. A situation quickly developed in which the few sober soldiers could not control the drunk ones.

During the late morning, Sherman entered the city

General Sherman's entry into Columbia, 17 February 1865
(*Library of Congress*)

with the remainder of XV Corps. By that time it was noticed that some of the cotton the Confederates had left in the streets was on fire. Sherman later contended that the retreating Confederate soldiers had set the fires, and some witnesses confirmed that at least some of the early fires were set by Confederates, but when the wind fanned the flames and they started spreading to nearby buildings, many of the Union soldiers tried to prevent people from extinguishing the flames. There were also witnesses who saw some of the drunken soldiers set fires to cotton and to buildings. Some of those who did not go so far as to set fires cut fire hoses and impeded fire engines trying to reach the fires.

At the same time, some of the Federal soldiers tried to help put out fires, and later that afternoon Sherman promised the mayor additional help and assured him that the Union army would not destroy the town. While this promise was being made, the flames spread through the town. Under cover of darkness, some soldiers began setting new fires in different parts of the city. Many of the buildings of South Carolina College were set on fire, including a Confederate military hospital with many disabled soldiers inside. Those fires were extinguished. The Washington Street Methodist Church was then set ablaze because soldiers thought that it was the Baptist church that had housed the first meeting of the South Carolina Secession Convention before it moved to Charleston. Many private homes were looted and then burned.

While this devastation continued, some soldiers and officers still tried to prevent any further destruction and

The burning of Columbia (*Library of Congress*)

worked very hard to protect civilians from harm. A fresh, sober division was brought into town during the early morning hours of 18 February to restore order and to fight fires. Sherman even left his headquarters to help fight some of the fires. Dawn brought an end to arson but also a clear view of the tremendous destruction. At least one-third of the town had been completely destroyed and many other parts seriously damaged. After destroying some of the public property that had survived the fires, the Union army left the city on 20 February. Sherman left behind some food for the destitute people of the city.

After the war, some of the property owners of Columbia unsuccessfully tried to sue for damages to their property. In 1873 a commission investigated the fires and exonerated the officers on both sides. No real blame was assigned.

—*David S. Heidler and Jeanne T. Heidler*

See also Carolinas Campaign; Sherman, William Tecumseh.

For further reading:

Barrett, John G. *Sherman's March Through the Carolinas* (1956; reprint 1996).

Glatthaar, Joseph T. *The March to the Sea and Beyond: Sherman's Troops in the Savannah and Carolinas Campaigns* (1985).

COLUMBUS, KENTUCKY

Columbus, Kentucky, was a strategic point on the Mississippi River for both the Union and the Confederacy. In 1861 Columbus, Kentucky, was the northern terminus of the Mobile & Ohio Railroad and an important transshipment point for rail and river traffic. Steamboats called regularly to connect with the railhead. In addition, ferries carried trains between Columbus and Cairo, Illinois. The community was, therefore, a key link in movement of goods and passengers on the Mississippi. In addition, Columbus was the site of the first high bluffs along the river downstream from Cairo.

At the beginning of September 1861, Confederate general Leonidas Polk broke the stalemate over Kentucky's self-proclaimed neutrality in the national crisis that followed secession and the first battle of Manassas (Bull Run) by occupying Columbus and Hickman, Kentucky, another river port nearer the Tennessee border. Polk focused the largest part of his force at Columbus, and it became the western anchor of the Confederate defense line that spread across southern Kentucky, through Bowling Green, to the Cumberland Gap. The high bluffs made Columbus a logical point to try to control the Mississippi, and its rail and water transportation links allowed it to be supplied easily. Within two months the garrison grew to some 13,000 troops and more than 10,000 slaves who constructed extensive earth works. Fort DeRussy, as the Confederate fortification was named, had more than 140 cannon and presented a formidable obstacle to Union movement on the river. There were earthworks with cannon atop the bluff and water-level river batteries. In addition, an anchor was strung across the river, supported on pontoons and protected by torpedoes set to explode on contact. "The Gibraltar of the West" as it was known, was one of the most heavily fortified places on the continent. Polk and his troops were also rallying points for the pro-Confederate citizens in the Jackson Purchase region of Kentucky, and several Confederate regiments were raised in the area.

After Polk occupied Columbus, Federal general U. S. Grant, who was at Fort Defiance outside Cairo, moved quickly to occupy Paducah and Smithland, Kentucky. Paducah was the major city in far western Kentucky and controlled the confluence of the Tennessee and Ohio rivers. Smithland controlled the confluence of the Tennessee and Cumberland rivers. Grant observed Polk's activities closely and periodically sent gunboats down the river and troops on demonstrations to test the strength of the Confederate fortifications. In November, when Polk established a camp on the Missouri side of the Mississippi at Belmont and appeared to be extending a defensive line across southern Missouri, Grant moved quickly to stop this expansion by moving against the Confederate camp at Belmont.

Grant's troops overran the Confederate camp at Belmont, forcing a rapid withdrawal, but the cannon from Columbus quickly forced the Federal troops to withdraw in extreme disorder and Grant nearly saw his victory turn into disaster. The battle of Belmont was Grant's first action as a combat commander and it ended with the Confederates in control of the river and confident of the strength of their position.

While Grant continued to probe the defenses of Columbus by land and river, his attention quickly shifted to the Cumberland and Tennessee rivers. In February of 1862 his troops and the gunboats of Navy Flag Officer Andrew Foote captured Forts Henry and Donelson, establishing Union control of those two rivers. The capture of Forts Henry and Donelson, combined with the decimation, due to disease, of the Confederate garrison at Camp Beauregard in western Graves County, Kentucky, left Columbus exposed to attack overland from the east. Rather than wait for that attack, Polk withdrew his forces during the last days of February and the first of March, leaving nearly all the cannon and large caches of supplies. When the first attacking Union troops arrived on 2 March 1862, they rode right into the fort and seized it without opposition.

Union troops occupied Columbus for the remainder of the war. Fort DeRussy was renamed Fort Halleck. Columbus also served as a district headquarters for the Union army and was an important staging area for the Vicksburg campaign. Troops from Illinois, Ohio, and the upper Midwest transferred from riverboats to rail at Columbus. The commissary corps, quartermaster corps, and transportation corps all had district headquarters at Columbus in addition to the overall district headquarters and Fort Halleck. Although it is almost impossible to estimate the number of troops at Columbus at any one time because of their constant movement, it can be said that it was a large and active center of Federal activity. Units from Columbus patrolled the Jackson Purchase and established garrisons in other communities to protect railroad bridges, crossroads, and other strategic locations. Although Columbus was never directly attacked, the Purchase remained staunchly pro-Confederate, perhaps even becoming more so as the war continued. Confederate guerrillas and Nathan Bedford Forrest's cavalry frequently attacked patrols, supply trains, and railroad bridges. Federal officers and troops thought of themselves as being in enemy territory and at some peril, even though Kentucky never seceded and remained a Union state. They frequently delayed sending troops south to the Vicksburg campaign to provide additional resources to use against Forrest and the guerrillas. This was a source of considerable annoyance to U. S. Grant, who sent many strongly worded telegrams to Columbus to get troops moving south and frequently changed district commanders.

Early in the Federal occupation, slaves began coming to Columbus, both from the Purchase and from surrounding states, seeking freedom and the protection of the Federal army. The lack of a clear policy on how to treat escaped slaves caused a great deal of confusion at Columbus. Once the policy decision was made that they not be returned to their masters, commanders at Columbus had to provide for them. A colony of some 1,000 contrabands, as the former slaves were known at the time, was established on Island No. 10, some miles down river from Columbus after the Confederates abandoned it. Other former slaves were used as casual labor on the fortifications at Columbus and in loading and unloading riverboats and trains. Some were sent to Cairo and as far away as St. Louis in response to requests for labor from Federal commanders. By 1863 African-Americans were being enlisted into the Union army at Columbus and throughout the Jackson Purchase, although due to opposition to black military service by Kentucky's political leaders they were often credited to the District of Memphis or another Tennessee location until 1864. The 4th U.S. Heavy Artillery Colored was largely raised in the Columbus area and was headquartered there for most of the war. Units from the 4th served all over the Jackson Purchase guarding railroad bridges, crossroads, and courthouses, as well as at Columbus.

As the war in the western theater wound down, activity at Columbus slowed, although pickets were still posted daily through July 1865. The Freedmen's Bureau had a district office in Columbus that was active in helping establish schools and churches for the freed people, as well as locating African-American veterans who were due back pay and other benefits. Fort Halleck was deactivated, and the ordnance and other materiel left behind was removed by the Quartermaster General Corps in 1867–1868. The military cemetery was relocated to Mound City, Illinois, in the 1870s. In 1934 the largest part of the fortifications became Columbus-Belmont State Park.

—*William H. Mulligan, Jr.*

See also Kentucky.

For further reading:
Hughes, Nathaniel Cheairs, Jr. *The Battle of the Belmont: Grant Strikes South* (1991).
Mullen, Jay Carlton. "The Turning of Columbus." *Register of the Kentucky Historical Society* (1966).
U.S. War Department. *The War of the Rebellion: A Compilation of the Official Records of the Union and Confederate Armies* (1880–1901).
Whitesell, Hunter B. "Military Operations in the Jackson Purchase Area of Kentucky, 1862–1865." *Register of the Kentucky Historical Society* (1965).
Whitesell, Robert D. "Military and Naval Activity between Cairo and Columbus." *Register of the Kentucky Historical Society* (1963).

COMMISSARY

The term *commissary* is the shortened version of "commissary of subsistence," which referred to the staff officer or staff function that had the responsibility to procure, store, and issue food to the troops. The ultimate responsibility of this logistical mission fell to the Union or Confederate subsistence departments, each headed by a "commissary general of subsistence."

Organized in 1818, the U.S. Army Subsistence Department had an authorized strength of only twelve officers when the Civil War began. Secession brought the immediate resignation of four officers, a loss of one-third of the department. Congress remedied the situation by passing legislation in August 1861 that added twelve more officer positions, for a total of twenty-four. This was still too small a corps to oversee the procurement and issuance of food for hundreds of thousands of men, so a year and a half later the department again was modestly enlarged to twenty-nine officers. When Fort Sumter fell, the head of the Subsistence Department was Colonel George Gibson, an old man who had been an invalid for many years. Running the day-to-day operations of the department was Lieutenant Colonel Joseph P. Taylor (brother of Zachary Taylor and uncle of Confederate general Richard Taylor), who became the commissary general of subsistence when Gibson died in September 1861.

The Confederate Subsistence Department was created by act of the Confederate Congress that was signed into law on 26 February 1861. Appointed initially as the acting commissary general of subsistence, Lucius B. Northrop eventually received the full appointment and remained the commissary general of the Confederacy until February 1865. His department, like its Union counterpart, was undermanned for such a herculean task. The legislation creating the Confederate Subsistence Department authorized a commissary general with the rank of colonel, six to eight staff officers ranging in rank from lieutenant colonel to captain, and a few clerks. Northrop's abrasive personality only made a difficult situation even worse.

Unlike European wars, in which troops were generally expected to live off of the land in wartime, most food for the Union forces was purchased in the major metropolitan areas of the North and then packed and shipped to field depots. From there, the foodstuffs were issued to the commissary officers of the field armies and then transported to the troops. The exception to this procedure was the procurement of flour and beef, both commodities usually being purchased in the areas were the armies were operating. Much of the fresh beef was transported with the armies in herds and then slaughtered as needed.

The Confederates also tried stockpiling commissary supplies in centralized locations, such as Richmond. Since the Confederate armies normally were operating in their own territory, however, it did not always make sense to ship commodities to a distant warehouse only to have those same commodities shipped back to the areas of operation. Complicating matters for the Confederate commissary of subsistence was rising inflation, civilian hoarding, breakdowns in the transportation system, lack of salt and other preservatives, packaging shortages (kegs, sacks, cans, etc.), and Union victories in (or occupation of) important flour- and meat-producing regions. As the war progressed, these problems intensified, making it more and more difficult for Confederate commissary officers to provide an adequate ration of food for their soldiers.

For most of the war, the daily food allowance for Union soldiers was, by regulation, "twelve ounces of pork or bacon, or, one pound of salt or fresh beef; one pound and six ounces of soft bread or flour, or one pound and four ounces of corn meal; and to every one hundred rations, fifteen pounds of beans or peas, and ten pounds of rice or hominy; ten pounds of coffee, or, eight pounds of roasted (or roasted and ground) coffee, or, one pound and eight ounces of tea; fifteen pounds of sugar; four quarts of vinegar;…three pounds and twelve ounces of salt; four ounces of pepper; thirty pounds of potatoes, when practicable, and one quart of molasses." These rations were issued in camp; while on the march a

Commissary Department, Army of the Potomac, at Brandy Station, Virginia, February 1864
(Photograph by Timothy O'Sullivan / *National Archives*)

soldier's daily issue was one pound of hard bread, three-fourths of a pound of salt pork or one and a quarter pounds of fresh meat, and sugar, salt, and coffee. To prevent scurvy, commissary offices issued small quantities of dried fruit, potatoes, or kraut whenever possible. When periods of prolonged hunger did occur in the Union armies, it usually was not due to actual food shortages but because the armies had outdistanced their supply lines, or because of bureaucratic foul-ups.

The Confederate Subsistence Department at the beginning of the conflict used the exact same ration allocation—at least on paper—as its Union counterpart, but procurement and distribution problems forced Commissary General Northrop to curtail the daily ration. In reality, cornmeal became the staple of the Confederate soldier's diet, supplemented by whatever other foodstuffs were issued by the commissary department or appropriated by the soldiers themselves. At the end of the war, Northrop admitted that, from 1863 on, it had been "impossible to provide the ration set up by army regulations, and that the issue had been steadily declining."

Field armies of the Union and the Confederacy usually had one field-grade officer as their chief commissary of subsistence. These men were assisted by officers and enlisted men filling similar staff positions all the way from corps down to regimental level. The staff officers in the echelons below army level—normally "acting commissaries,"—consolidated requests from their subordinate units, ensured the paperwork was filled out properly, and forwarded the requests to the next higher command. When the requests were filled, these men ensured that the correct amounts of rations were picked up, transported, and issued to their subordinate commands. For example, the chief commissary of subsistence for the 1st Division, V Corps, Union Army of the Potomac, would have provided staff supervision for the requisitioning, transportation, and issue of food for the three brigades assigned to his division. The brigade chief commissaries had similar responsibilities and provided staff supervision of the regimental quartermasters (who, in most instances, also served as the commissary officer) and who were assisted by their commissary sergeants. At the company level of organization, infantry companies were authorized one commissary sergeant. Company quartermaster sergeants usually fulfilled the commissary duties in cavalry troops and artillery batteries.

—*Mark Snell*

See also Northrop, Lucius Bellinger.
For further reading:
Creveld, Martin Van. *Supplying War: Logistics from Wallenstein to Patton* (1977).
Goff, Richard D. *Confederate Supply* (1969).
Risch, Erna. *Quartermaster Support of the Army: A History of the corps, 1775–1939* (1989).

Wiley, Bell. *The Life of Billy Yank: The Common Soldier of the Union* (1952; reprint, 1993).

———. *The Life of Johnny Reb: The Common Soldier of the Confederacy* (1943; reprint, 1978).

COMSTOCK, CYRUS BALLOU
(1831–1910)
Union general

Born in Massachusetts, Cyrus Ballou Comstock received an appointment to the U.S. Military Academy in 1851. He graduated first of thirty-four in the class of 1855. After receiving his commission in the Corps of Engineers, Comstock served on a variety of engineering projects before returning to West Point as an instructor. At the outbreak of the Civil War he was called to Washington, D.C., to aid the chief engineer in preparing the capital's defenses. With the creation of the Army of the Potomac, Comstock was appointed to the position of assistant to the chief engineer, Army of the Potomac, working directly under John Gross Barnard.

Comstock traveled with the Army of the Potomac to the York Peninsula in the spring of 1862 and served as first lieutenant of engineers and Barnard's assistant during the early engagements of the Peninsula campaign. In early June after the battle of Seven Pines, Comstock was named the chief engineer of Edwin Sumner's II Corps. He served in that capacity for the remainder of the Peninsula campaign through the Seven Days.

During the Maryland campaign, Comstock commanded, still at the rank of first lieutenant, a battalion of engineers. He and his men operated both at South Mountain and the battle of Antietam. In November, after the change of command of the Army of the Potomac from George B. McClellan to Ambrose Burnside, Comstock was named chief engineer of the Army of the Potomac. His biggest challenge in this new position of responsibility was to supervise the movement of the pontoon bridges ordered by Burnside to span the Rappahannock River at Fredericksburg. The constant delays out of Washington and then the transport of the pontoons to Fredericksburg made Comstock's task a complicated one.

In the spring of 1863, Comstock was finally promoted to captain, but with Joseph Hooker's reorganization of the Army of the Potomac was reduced to commanding an engineering battalion in the Chancellorsville campaign. In that campaign he supervised the movement to and erection of pontoon bridges at Kelly's Ford in the flanking maneuver of Robert E. Lee's Army of Northern Virginia. During the Army of the Potomac's retreat he accomplished the same task at United States Ford. After the end of the campaign, Comstock was transferred to the Army of the Tennessee to aid with the siege of Vicksburg, Mississippi.

Arriving outside Vicksburg in June 1863, Comstock brought his considerable wartime experience to bear on the erection of siege works outside the city. On 1 July he had so impressed Ulysses S. Grant that the commanding general made him chief engineer of the Army of the Tennessee. Comstock held that position through the capitulation of Vicksburg and most of the fall of 1863. In November he was promoted to lieutenant colonel and became assistant inspector general of the Division of the Mississippi, headquartered at St. Louis.

In the early months of 1864, Comstock held the same position as a member of Grant's staff and traveled around the theater with the commanding general. In March, when Grant went east to assume command of all U.S. forces, Comstock became his senior aide-de-camp. Comstock served in this position for the remainder of the war with the exception of several special missions that he conducted for Grant away from the Virginia theater.

As Grant's aide-de-camp, Comstock performed a variety of duties, including passing on the general in chief's orders to corps commanders, acting as courier during battles, and acting a chief engineer for specific offensives. He was especially active during the Wilderness campaign, moving between different corps directing the commanders to the positions desired by Grant. His chief commended him for his gallantry during that campaign.

During the Federal attack on Fort Harrison outside Richmond in September 1864, Comstock was assigned by Grant to direct many of the Union preparations and was again commended by Grant for his actions in the battle. At the end of 1864, after the first attempt on Fort Fisher, North Carolina, directed by Benjamin F. Butler, failed, Grant assigned Comstock as chief engineer for the second attempt to be made in January 1865. Again, after the successful campaign against this Confederate stronghold, Grant praised Comstock's skill and dedication. Alfred Terry, commander of the expedition, also commended Comstock for his role in the campaign.

Returning to Virginia and Grant's staff, Comstock remained through much of the final phases of the siege of Petersburg. In March, however, Grant sent his trusted aide to Mobile, Alabama, to assist Edward R. S. Canby in the campaign against Mobile. As a result, Comstock was not present at Lee's surrender in April 1865. He returned at the end of April and remained Grant's aide until 1866. On 6 June 1865, Grant wrote to the War Department recommending Comstock for brevet promotions in the regular army to major for his actions in the siege of Vicksburg, to lieutenant colonel for his bravery during the battle of the Wilderness, to colonel for the attack on Fort Harrison, and to brigadier general for the Fort Fisher campaign. All of these recommendations were acted upon, with the addition of a brevet promotion to major general for his role in the Mobile campaign.

After the war, after leaving Grant's staff, Comstock returned to the Corps of Engineers. He remained in the army, serving in a variety of places as an engineering officer until being forced to retire because of age in 1895 at the rank of colonel.

—David S. Heidler and Jeanne T. Heidler

See also Fort Fisher; Fredericksburg, Battle of.

For further reading:
Comstock, Cyrus Ballou. *The Diary of Cyrus B. Comstock* (1987).

CONFEDERATE DIASPORA

To the farthest place from the United States, if it takes me to the middle of China." With these words, Judah P. Benjamin, Confederate secretary of state, described a journey taken by numerous Southerners in 1865. Nearly 8,000 men, women, and children entered a diaspora that required residence in Mexico, Brazil, Venezuela, Peru, Jamaica, Canada, England, and even Egypt.

Several factors motivated these self-exiles. Some, like Benjamin, feared persecution by vindictive "Yankees." He warned other prominent politicians to "risk death" in their escape efforts rather than accept "the savage cruelty" of Northern retribution. Federal law allowed the death penalty for treason, and though few expected large-scale executions, confusion and uncertainty persuaded some to leave the country.

Others could not stand to live under the U.S. flag, which Henry Derrick called "that hated emblem of cursed tyranny." "Any other country would be better than this," agreed David McCorkle. Then there was Jo Shelby, who not only refused to live in the Union but even considered a continuation of the Civil War from Mexico. Samuel H. Lockett expressed a more common reason to seek fortune elsewhere. Like all former Confederate officers, he was barred from duty with the U.S. military, while civilian jobs for men with such talents were rare. As Lockett put it, "It is awful to be poor." For most Confederate exiles, new opportunity, rather than fear of punishment, was the motivation for their exodus.

The vast majority moved to several nations in Latin America. For some, like Benjamin, or John C. Breckinridge, places such as Cuba were simply a stopover on the way to Canada or England. Many more Southerners saw Mexico or Brazil as a new home. The former refuge quickly turned sour, while the latter became the only successful Confederate "colony."

Mexico, which attracted the largest contingent of Southerners, was in the midst of a vicious war. On one side was the empire of Maximilian, a puppet government backed by France. President Benito Juárez led a powerful opposition supported by Washington. Thus it is not surprising that Southern refugees sided with Maximilian.

They even named their principal colony Carlota, after the emperor's wife. Many indicated their allegiance with offers to join the Imperial Army. In August 1865, Jo Shelby and several hundred troopers rode into Mexico City with the hope of forming a complete unit of ex-Confederates.

With nearly 3,000 ex-Union veterans serving in Republican forces, the stage seemed set for a small-scale continuation of the Civil War. Maximilian wisely figured this could result in direct U.S. intervention and refused to accept Shelby's command. Individuals, such as General John Magruder, did join the Imperial forces, but by 1867 the war ended with a complete victory for Juárez. As allies of the despised Imperialists, most Southerners now returned home.

A different story unfolded in Brazil, where a stable government invited ex-Confederates to establish colonies. In places such as New Texas, small communities attempted to transplant cotton, watermelon, and other Southern crops. The largest colony formed at Vila Santa Bárbara, in São Paulo State. The city later became Americana, while its residents were dubbed "Os Confederados." Between 1866 and 1868, numerous families moved there. Although many went home after a few years, about 500 stayed. Descendants of the original settlers maintain Southern traditions to this day, even including a Sons of Confederate Veterans Camp.

While the largest number of émigrés went to Brazil and Mexico, some famous personalities traveled much farther. Benjamin ended up in England, where he reentered the legal profession, but died in Paris in 1884, never having returned to the United States. John R. Tucker became an admiral in the Peruvian navy and gained additional fame as an Amazonian explorer. Even more exotic was the postwar career of William Wing Loring. Hired as a mercenary by the khedive of Egypt, Loring won the aristocratic title of pasha, fought a gun battle with the nephew of Benjamin Butler, and participated as second-in-command for the ill-fated Gura campaign in 1876. Like most émigrés though, he finally returned home, probably sharing the feelings of the Lockett family, who were "…very happy at being back again among white people…where there are no nasty Arabs, and fleas, and flies, and lice, and bed bugs, and dirt."

—John P. Dunn

See also Benjamin, Judah Philip; Breckinridge, John Cabell; Mexico; Shelby, Joseph Orville.

For further reading:
Hanna, Alfred J., and Kathryn Abby Hanna. *Confederate Exiles in Venezuela* (1960).
Hesseltine, William B., and Hazel C. Wolf. *The Blue and Grey on the Nile* (1961).
Rolle, Andrew F. *The Lost Cause: The Confederate Exodus to Mexico* (1965).
Sutherland, David. "Exiles, Emigrants, and Sojourners. The Post Civil War Confederate Exodus in Perspective." *Civil War History* (1985).

Werlich, David P. *Admiral of the Amazon: John Randolph Tucker, His Confederate Colleagues, and Peru* (1990).

CONFISCATION ACTS
(6 August 1861 and 17 July 1862)

The Confiscation Acts were proposed by Senator Lyman Trumbull (Republican, Illinois) and passed by Congress to confiscate property used to aid the rebellion and property of those who supported the Confederacy. However, neither President Abraham Lincoln nor Attorney General Edward Bates vigorously implemented either law. The acts did represent the wish of many in the North to attack slavery and pushed Lincoln to embrace emancipation but failed to have a major impact on Reconstruction.

Congress passed the first act after General Ben Butler's admission, in May 1861, of fugitive slaves into Union lines as contrabands. It authorized the president to seize any property used to aid the insurrection and terminated the claims of masters over those persons (slaves) employed to assist the Confederate military. The act, however, failed to define the status of slaves whose owners forfeited their claims to them. The proceedings were to be adjudicated in district and circuit courts with pertinent jurisdiction, that is, where the property prevailed or had been seized. This meant, in August 1861, that most property subject to confiscation was inside the Confederacy. Discussion in Congress over the first act was brief. Only Democrats and border-state Republicans in the House opposed the bill, while only one Republican voted with Senate Democrats against it.

General John C. Frémont offered a more direct attack upon those who supported the rebellion. In September 1861 he proclaimed rebel property seized and slaves freed in Missouri. When Frémont declined to change the proclamation to conform to the first act, Lincoln revoked it, in part to prevent Kentucky and other border states from joining the Confederacy. Many in the North protested the president's action and urged Congress to legislate against the rebels' property and slavery. Most Union generals, however, were reluctant to enforce the first act or encourage fugitive slaves to enter their lines. Nonetheless, slaves continued to arrive, and some were put to work on behalf of the Union.

Lincoln's 3 December message to Congress noted the pressure for more vigorous measures against the South but urged that the war not degenerate "into a violent and remorseless struggle." Trumbull introduced his second act on 5 December. It called for the "absolute and complete forfeiture forever" of all property that belonged to those who supported the rebellion. Over the next seven months, Congress debated a variety of confiscation proposals at considerable length. Supporters of sweeping confiscation argued that forfeiture could extend beyond the life of the offender because the property itself was made guilty by the rebel's support of the rebellion. Confiscation was therefore not a bill of attainder and not unconstitutional. The use of *in rem* proceedings would allow forfeiture of property without the owner's presence, and confiscation could be accomplished more expeditiously. Most Republicans were for moderate confiscation, to be executed by the president only for military purposes and only for the life of the rebel. They argued that property could not be guilty and that the *in rem* proceedings were unconstitutional. Confiscation could not extend beyond the offender's life and therefore could not be the basis for Reconstruction. Most Republicans agreed that slaves could be emancipated through confiscation, although almost no one expressed interest in their status after slavery other than to provide for their colonization outside the United States.

Moderates prevailed in the final confiscation bill. It provided confiscation and punishment for six classes of rebels, broad executive authority (including the power to pardon), the opportunity for rebels to swear allegiance and avoid confiscation, the liberation of slaves in Union controlled areas, and the colonization of willing freed slaves. The bill did not explicitly allow for forfeiture beyond the offender's life. The act also did not free slaves unless courts found their owners to be rebels, and the military had no power to adjudicate the matter of ownership. Nor did the act affect slaves of nonrebels or those who swore allegiance to the North. Only two Republicans in the House and two in the Senate joined Democrats to oppose the second act.

Lincoln had indicated that he favored less severe measures against the South. In March 1862 he had urged gradual emancipation upon the border states and reiterated this plea when Congress passed the second act. He had also revoked General David Hunter's April proclamation that freed the slaves in Georgia, Florida, and South Carolina. Moderates dispatched Senator William Pitt Fessenden of Maine to ask the president how to avoid a veto of the second act. The result was a joint resolution, subsequently passed by Congress, that guaranteed that confiscation of rebels' slaves would only be prospective and that no forfeiture of real property would extend beyond the life of the offender. This weakened an already drastically modified version of Trumbull's original bill and guaranteed that no land would be available for freed slaves or Northern soldiers and that Reconstruction would be limited. Like the first, the Second Confiscation Act was not very well crafted. Nor did Congress provide any funds for its implementation, thereby deterring local officials from enforcing it vigorously.

Lincoln signed the law on 17 July, but also sent his veto message to Congress. Although the president supported confiscation for military purposes, he worried that "a justly discriminating application of it, would be very difficult," if not impossible. His chief concern was that confiscation should not extend beyond the life of the offender. Yet Lincoln realized the importance of attacking slavery, which was a central part of confiscation. Within two weeks, he presented his preliminary Emancipation Proclamation to the cabinet and issued another proclamation, invoking the sixth section of the second act, warning all persons "to cease participating in, aiding, countenancing, or abetting the existing rebellion." He also authorized the recruitment of "free Negroes" and slaves into the military and the seizure of any property for military purposes.

Administration of the First Confiscation Act by Virginia-born Attorney General Bates, a moderate from Missouri, was strict but limited, reflecting Lincoln's concerns. Not until January 1863 did the president actually authorize the attorney general to enforce the first act. Nor did Bates produce a policy on how to implement the act; instead he urged local officials to read the act themselves and carefully pursue only that property that had been used to assist the Confederacy. The small amounts of property confiscated under the first act reflected both the conservative influence of Bates and the difficulty of finding such property in the North.

Bates's enforcement of the second act was no more vigorous. This again followed the president's example. In late August 1962, Horace Greeley, New York *Tribune* editor, had expressed disappointment at the lax enforcement of the second act. Lincoln replied that he would "save" the Union "in the shortest way under the Constitution." Lincoln said, "[I would do] *less* whenever I shall believe what I am doing hurts the cause, and I shall do *more* whenever I shall believe" it will help restore the Union. For Bates, this meant never urging vigorous enforcement of the second act. Instead, he asked district attorneys to take few risks, keep expenses down, prevent injustice to property owners, and limit embarrassment to the government.

On 13 November 1862 Lincoln charged Bates with direction to seize, prosecute, and condemn property under the second act. But he omitted any reference to slaves, thereby leaving the emancipation provisions to the military, which generally ignored them. Lincoln's orders also allowed Bates to control confiscation and deny local officials any latitude in the execution of the second act. Bates expected them to execute the law vigilantly, but with care to "avoid hasty and improvident seizures." District attorneys also proved reluctant to prosecute cases unless they were guaranteed expenses, which Bates rarely granted. Bates's greatest contribution to the confiscation effort was passing along information about property liable to seizure. Although his administration of the second act was honest and careful, it lacked any conviction that the law was just or good.

Military officers, the first to encounter property of any sort in the South, were the best potential enforcers of the Confiscation Acts. Several commanders suggested that they would be vigorous in the prosecution of the second act, but not much confiscation occurred by the military. General Benjamin Butler in New Orleans, for example, threatened confiscation and thereby persuaded a majority in New Orleans to pledge allegiance to the Union. In 1864, General Lew Wallace issued two orders for the confiscation of property in Maryland, but Bates objected because they interfered with his authority. Ultimately nothing was confiscated. In the end, few commanders showed much interest in confiscation, despite some prodding by Secretary of War Edwin Stanton, and that suited Bates, who wished to control administration of the acts.

Treasury Department officials, who followed in the military's path, also could have been effective agents of confiscation. They saw confiscable property before marshals or district attorneys appeared in most areas and could have prevented property title transfers, which often protected it from confiscation. But their responsibilities lay in collecting captured and abandoned property. Moreover, the three treasury secretaries during the war encouraged officials to cooperate with the attorney general. The inability to profit from handling confiscable property also deterred the treasury officials from expanding their opportunities. As a result, except in New Orleans, little confiscation took place in concert with treasury officers.

New Orleans realized the second largest amount of money from confiscated property, largely because it remained in Union control for such a long period and was the wealthiest city in the South. Even so, only $60,000 from the sale of confiscated property was collected there, which was almost one-fifth of the final total. Virginia proved to be the most vulnerable area for confiscation, but most of this occurred after the war.

On 8 December 1863, Lincoln offered a pardon to most participants in the rebellion, and this exercise seriously undercut confiscation for the remainder of the war. Proponents of confiscation failed to object to the pardoning process provided for in the second act, but by early 1864 some moved to repeal the joint resolution to allow confiscation beyond the life of the offender. It was even argued that Lincoln, having read the views of William Whiting, legal adviser to the War Department, now believed that forfeiture could extend beyond the life of the guilty party because confiscation did not rest upon treasonous behavior. But the various efforts over the following year to revoke the resolution failed.

By January 1865, Lincoln favored confiscation for only the most prominent rebels. According to Alexander Stephens, Lincoln even assured the South he would be lenient in his use of confiscation. President Johnson also wanted to spare the South a harsh Reconstruction based on widespread confiscation. But, unlike Lincoln, Johnson used confiscation to punish more classes of rebels, as his May 1865 pardon proclamation indicated. He focused particularly on those with property valued at over $20,000, many of whom were in Virginia. Those excluded from pardons had to request them personally from the president. In the end, most rebels were able to escape confiscation, but not before Attorney General Joshua Speed had four months in which to implement the second act with some vigor. By September, however, Johnson directed the Freedmen's Bureau to return property that was to have been rented to freedmen and suspended enforcement of the second act. The irony is that the second act was well executed only after the war ended and only for four months. Oliver Otis Howard, director of the Freedmen's Bureau, tried to circumvent Johnson's wish to restore land to former rebels, but he failed.

Contrary to predictions from both opponents and supporters of confiscation, the courts liberally interpreted both the first and second act. They granted Congress the benefit of the doubt on most procedural questions and accepted the constitutional argument for confiscation.

—John Syrett

See also Bates, Edward; Butler, Benjamin F.; Congress, U.S.A.; Frémont, John C.; Howard, Oliver O.; Hunter, David; Speed, Joshua; Trumbull, Lyman.

For further reading:

Basler, Roy P., ed. *The Collected Works of Abraham Lincoln* (1953–1955).

Belz, Herman. *Abraham Lincoln, Constitutionalism, and Equal Rights in the Civil War Era* (1998).

Curry, Leonard P. *Blueprint for America: Nonmilitary Legislation of First Civil War Congress* (1968).

Randall, James G. *Constitutional Problems under Lincoln* (1951).

CONGRESS, C.S.A.

Shortly after the first seven Confederate states had seceded, their state legislatures sent delegates to Montgomery, Alabama, to lay the foundations for a new nation. The delegates wanted to establish a government as quickly as possible, while secessionist sentiment was still high, and so they adopted a provisional constitution with only one day's discussion. Upon adoption of the provisional constitution, the convention became the provisional Confederate Congress. When Arkansas, Tennessee, North Carolina, and Virginia seceded after the conflict at Fort Sumter, their representatives to the provisional Congress were also chosen by the state legislatures. As such, the provisional Confederate Congress had no members chosen by popular vote.

The Provisional Congress remained in office until 17 February 1862. The task of organizing the new Confederate government took most of their attention for their first months in office. They spent their first month writing a permanent constitution, which essen-

tially mirrored the U.S. Constitution except that it explicitly protected slavery and affirmed the sovereignty of the states. Once the permanent constitution had been adopted, the provisional Congress acquired a legal code by adopting all U.S. laws consistent with the Confederate Constitution. They elected Jefferson Davis as provisional president and Alexander Stephens as provisional vice-president and then established a bureaucracy, including a postal system and judiciary, that mirrored that of the United States. The Congress arranged to have its laws published both in book form and in the largest newspaper in each Confederate state. Most rules of legislative procedure were carried over from the U.S. Congress.

Once the government had been established, the Confederate Congress had to turn to the task of preparing the new nation for a war. They initially hoped to finance the war with a low tariff, and to field a relatively small army numbering only 100,000 men, but the firing on Fort Sumter changed their plans. On 16 May 1861, the Confederate Congress authorized the issue of $20 million in Treasury notes and $50 million in bonds. They also gave the president the power to accept as many volunteers as presented themselves for duty, and placed all telegraph operations under his control. They also established a fairly high 15 percent tariff that stayed in place for the duration of the war. These measures set the Confederacy on a course that would eventually undermine their economy, essentially leaving the government unable to meet its financial obligations by the end of the war.

The first elections in the Confederacy were held in November 1861. Each state had the same representation as under the U.S. government, and the same election procedures were used. There was very little campaigning; while a few districts had heated debates over local issues, there was little discussion of national policy. Candidates usually announced themselves in newspapers and did little else. Voters tended to support the same men they had before the war, and the membership of the first elected Confederate Congress was essentially the same as that of the provisional Congress.

When the First Confederate Congress met on 18 February16 1862, the primary issue they had to be concerned with was maintaining the Confederate army. Most soldiers had enlisted for one year, which was almost up. It was clear that many soldiers were tired of war and wished to return home. Faced with the possibility of losing half of his army, President Jefferson Davis asked the Confederate Congress to approve conscription of all able-bodied men between the ages of eighteen and thirty-five. The Congress complied, though they granted exemptions to a long list of occupations that were deemed more important to the home front than the army. As the war wore on, the Congress was compelled to extend the

The Confederate Capitol at Richmond, Virginia, 1865 (*Library of Congress*)

conscription age to forty-five and then fifty, and to reduce the number of exempt professions dramatically.

Financial issues were a recurring item on the Confederate Congress's agenda. Early in their first session, Treasury Secretary Christopher Memminger asked for an issue of both treasury notes and bonds, and the Congress agreed to the request. However, the Confederate government proved unable to sell as many

bonds as were issued, and so late in 1862 Congress enacted a law that forced people to buy bonds by slowly reducing the value of currency. In April 1863, the Congress levied its first taxes on citizens. Property, income, licenses, business, and agricultural products were among the taxed items.

Supplying the Confederate army was also an ongoing concern for the Confederate Congress. Early in the war, it became a matter of practice for army agents to do whatever was needed to acquire what the army needed, including taking things by force. In March 1863 the Confederate Congress essentially legalized this practice by passing the Impressment Act, which permitted material supplies and agricultural products to be seized, as long as a "fair" price was paid, to be determined by a system of arbitration. In February of the next year, the Congress enacted even stricter rules, ordering that no staple crops could be exported and that no luxury goods could be imported.

In many instances, then, the Confederate Congress found itself in the position of having to violate the principles of state sovereignty and a weak federal government upon which the Confederacy had been founded. Most of the time, at least for the first several years of the war, Confederate congressmen and the citizens of the Confederacy were willing to accept the Congress's actions on these occasions as necessary compromises to allow them to keep up the war effort. The debate became heated, however, in February 1864, when Congress considered whether to suspend the writ of habeas corpus. Suspending the writ allowed prisoners to be held indefinitely in prison without being charged with a crime, and was essentially geared toward silencing internal opposition to the war. The Confederate Congress actually suspended the writ three times, with the first instance occurring in February 1862, but their discussions in February 1864 were the most difficult and vitriolic. President Jefferson Davis was being roundly attacked in the press and by the electorate, and he felt that it was imperative that he continue to have the power to imprison people at will. His entire annual message to Congress on 4 February 1864 was a long plea for a renewal of his authority to suspend the writ. After much acrimony, the Congress consented, but it would prove to be the last time. When the bill came up for renewal in August of that year, it was defeated.

If the debate over the writ reflected some of the chinks in the Confederate armor, so did developments within the Congress. When forming the Confederate Constitution, Congress had hoped to have no political parties. However, 90 percent of those men who served in the Confederate government had been officeholders at some point in the United States government, and old habits often died hard. By 1864, the first clear developments had appeared within the legislature, between members from "exterior" and "interior" districts. Exterior districts were those occupied by U.S. troops, and sole legislation passed by the Confederate Congress had little impact there. Congressmen from those districts tended to vote in favor of legislation that could help their states escape Union control. Interior districts were still under the control of the Confederate government, and congressmen from those districts tended to focus on local

concerns and on legislation designed to sustain the national government.

By November 1863, the Confederacy had a full party system. Past politics became openly important for the first time in three years, and voting was much more issue-driven. The primary concerns for a congressman were his former party, his position on whether the war should be ended, and his position on Jefferson Davis's performance. When the second Congress finally met in May 1864, party sentiment was so strong that it was difficult to enact meaningful legislation. Most Congressmen focused on attacking the president, or arguing over whether the Confederate government should try to reach a peace settlement with the enemy.

The second session of 1864 would be the Confederate Congress's last. Once again, the legislature was essentially stalemated, at a time when the Confederate economy and the armies in the field were in dire straits. Many Congressmen became so frustrated that they left Richmond and went home. By March 1865, shortly before the end of the session, desperation had set in. On 13 March, less than a month before the end of the war, the remaining congressmen passed a bill allowing the conscription of slaves into the Confederate army. For many Confederate citizens, it was the culmination of four years of Congress violating the principles upon which the nation had been founded.

—*Christopher Bates*

See also Conscription, C.S.A.; Davis, Jefferson.

For further reading:

Alexander, Thomas B., and Richard E. Beringer. *The Anatomy of the Confederate Congress; A Study of the Influences of Member Characteristics on Legislative Voting Behavior, 1861–1865.* (1972).

Yearns, W. Buck. *The Confederate Congress* (1960).

CONGRESS, U.S.A.

By the time the founders of the United States gathered to write a constitution to replace the Articles of Confederation, the North and South had already developed into distinctly different places. The rocky soil and harsh climate that was typical of many Northern states meant that agriculture was not especially profitable, and so the North had begun to develop a commercial economy based on trade and industrial production. The South, of course, had a slave-based economy that had a profound impact on other aspects of Southern life—social structure, culture, value system, and so forth.

The sectional differences that developed between the North and the South had origins in the Constitutional Convention. To count the South's slaves toward its population for purposes of determining apportionment in the House of Representatives led to the adoption of the three-fifths rule, a measure that would prove increasingly annoying to the North. The goal of the founders, however, was to mute the sectional issue as much as possible by creating a balance in the Congress between the North and the South. From the beginning, however, there were indications that the effort was probably futile. In 1793, less than six years after the adoption of the Constitution, Congress was compelled to address Southern complaints that escaped slaves were able to move freely throughout the North without fear of capture. After much debate, Congress passed the Fugitive Slave Act, which empowered federal marshals and magistrates to return runaway slaves to their owners. Many Northern states passed laws almost immediately trying to block enforcement of the act. Less than a decade had elapsed since the adoption of the Constitution, and already Congress was having difficulty addressing sectional issues in a way that was satisfactory to both sides.

A few decades later, mediating sectional difficulties returned to the top of Congress's agenda. Thomas Jefferson's decision to negotiate the purchase of Louisiana added a substantial amount of territory to the young nation, and both Northerners and Southerners wanted to claim it as part of their region. In 1819, Missouri petitioned for entry into the Union as a slave state, which threatened to upset the balance of power between slave and nonslave states in the Senate. Representative James Tallmadge offered a bill that would have allowed Missouri into the Union with the stipulation that slavery be restricted there. Not surprisingly, the bill passed the Northern-controlled House but not the Senate. Finally, a compromise temporarily postponed the issue. The Missouri Compromise of 1820 admitted Missouri as a slave state and Maine as a free state, and stipulated that no slavery would be permitted in the Louisiana purchase north of 36° 30' latitude.

The Missouri Compromise was the first of several sectional sectional compromises, but as time passed, keeping harmony became a much more complicated and difficult thing to do. Debates over the tariff, Texas's request to be admitted as a state, the acquisition of additional land in the Mexican-American War, and the rapid growth of the state of California after gold was discovered there all inspired lengthy and acrimonious sectional debate in the halls of Congress. In 1850, Henry Clay put together his final and most difficult compromise agreement. The Compromise of 1850 admitted California as a free state, while New Mexico and Utah were organized as territories with the fate of slavery there to be decided by the voters, a system known as popular sovereignty. In addition, the slave trade in Washington, D.C., was ended and a new, stronger Fugitive Slave Law replaced the old one of 1793. Neither the North nor the South was really satisfied with the agreement, and as it happened the Compromise of 1850 was only a temporary truce.

As Clay and the leaders of his generation passed from the scene, the magnetic and forceful Stephen A. Douglas, the "Little Giant," succeeded them. Douglas was a strong advocate of popular sovereignty, and he wanted to extend it to all territories, not just New Mexico and Utah. The Kansas-Nebraska Act of 1854 extended popular sovereignty to those two territories. It essentially repeated the Missouri Compromise, opening the possibility that slavery could exist in every state in the Union. Many congressional leaders were violently angry, and some of them joined together to publish an article in *The National Era* entitled "An Appeal to the Independent Democrats," in which they condemned Douglas and the Kansas-Nebraska Act. Congress's power to keep peace between the sections was quickly fading.

The situation quickly began to deteriorate. In 1855, there was open, armed conflict in Kansas and Missouri. Congress proved unable to take action to stop the fighting in "Bleeding Kansas." In 1856, Senator Charles Sumner made a vitriolic antislavery speech in the Senate, and shortly thereafter he was beaten with a cane by South Carolina representative Preston Brooks. With the election of Abraham Lincoln as president in 1860, the seven states of the lower South seceded. The Senate, led by John Crittenden of Kentucky, made a last-ditch attempt to save the Union, but by then there was no middle ground upon which North and South could agree. The congressmen from the states that had seceded resigned.

While Southerners were organizing the Confederate Congress, Northern congressmen were organizing rallies to stir war fever, to show support for the president, and to call for aggressive military action against the South. After the outbreak of hsotilities, and at Lincoln's request, Congress met in special session beginning on 4 July 1861. The president asked for and received congressional approval of several war measures he had already taken, most notably calling for volunteers. This pattern would repeat itself many times throughout the war as Lincoln, who interpreted his powers broadly, would take action and then get retroactive congressional approval.

The 37th Congress met for its regular session at the end of 1861. The special session in July had been brief and was called strictly to deal with war matters. The regular session, however, provided an opportunity to the Republicans that they were ready to seize. Most of the Democrats in the Congress had been from Southern states, and all of the Southern Democrats from seceded states except for Andrew Johnson had resigned, leaving the Republicans with an overwhelming majority. They quickly passed several bills that had been a part of the 1860 platform: the Homestead Act granted 160 acres of public land to any settler after five years' improvement; the Morrill Act gave land to states to establish colleges and universities; and the Pacific Railroad Act provided funds for a transcontinental railroad. Of course, the 37th

Congress also had to be concerned with matters relating to the war, and in that area it passed several ground-breaking measures, including the nation's first income tax and approving the issue of "Greenback" currency.

Relations between Lincoln and the Congress had been cordial early in the war, but they were increasingly at odds as the war wore on. The remaining Democrats in Congress had been fairly silent for the first year, but they eventually organized into two very vocal factions. The War Democrats were concerned only with reunion and did not support any measures aimed at ending slavery or aiding the freed slaves, while the Peace Democrats pushed for peace at any cost, including disunion. The Republicans also divided into factions. The moderate Republicans tended to support the president, but the increasingly prominent Radical Republicans were very critical of the president, focusing especially on his caution in emancipating the slaves and his Reconstruction plans. The Radicals were also the driving force behind the Committee on the Conduct of the War, which investigated whatever the Radicals wanted to investigate, and in the balance did more harm than good.

The Committee on the Conduct of the War was a way for congressional Republicans to vent their frustrations with the president's conduct of the war. However, as time passed, their focus was increasingly on his Reconstruction plans. At about the same time that Lincoln issued the Emancipation Proclamation, the occupation of Southern lands made it necessary for the administration to begin formulating some sort of reconstruction policy, a clear process by which states would be removed from the control of the Confederate government and be put under the control of the federal government. Congress began to debate the issue in 1862 but had reached no agreements by the end of 1863, by which time there were large amounts of Southern territory under federal control. So Lincoln decided to take action, and in December of 1863 he issued a general proclamation of amnesty and reconstruction. Lincoln's Reconstruction plan came to be known as the Ten Percent Plan. It required that Southerners wishing to rejoin the Union swear an oath of future allegiance to the United States. When 10 percent of the number of people who had voted in the elections of 1860 had done so, they would constitute an electorate that would create a new state government.

Many members of Congress, especially the Radicals, did not like Lincoln's nondoctrinaire approach. The Wade-Davis Bill, passed in July 1864, was much more stringent than Lincoln's plan. It required that 50 percent take the oath of future loyalty for the state to be readmitted. Further, once the state was readmitted, the only people who could vote were those who took an ironclad oath, guaranteeing future loyalty and swearing that they had not assisted the Confederacy in any way. Since almost everyone had assisted the Confederacy, this provision would have essentially excluded everybody. The bill also ruled out any role for the president and the military in Reconstruction. Finally, the bill restricted the vote to whites. Lincoln pocket-vetoed the bill, and Wade and Davis issued an angry manifesto attacking the president and his policies.

Congress also spent considerable time bickering about the problem of what to do about the slaves who were freed. Most Republicans felt that the government would have to take an active role in helping the South make the transition away from a slave-based economy. In March 1865, after nearly two years of debate, Congress established the Freedmen's Bureau. This marked the first time in American history that the federal government assumed responsibility for the social welfare of individuals.

The Freedmen's Bureau would enjoy many successes and would play an important role in the years after the war, but at the time the Civil War ended it was by no means clear what its role would be or how much it would achieve. And beyond the vaguely defined act creating the bureau, Congress had made no decisions as to how Reconstruction would proceed by the time it adjourned in March 1865, not to reconvene until December. Meanwhile, President Lincoln's plan for Reconstruction had been only mildly successful and had come under a great deal of criticism. As such, when Lincoln was assassinated in April 1865, there were no successfully reconstructed states and there was no clear Reconstruction policy. The task of finding a balance between the practicality of Lincoln and the consistency sought by Congress fell to Lincoln's successor, Andrew Johnson.

Andrew Johnson's Reconstruction plan proved to be a failure. The difficult task of rebuilding the Union would have brought the executive and legislature into serious conflict regardless of who was president. Congress was already wary of the extraordinary powers that Lincoln had wielded during the war and was on record as resistant to the idea of his wielding such broad authority during the rigors of reunion. Lincoln's astute political instincts had allowed him to avoid catastrophic confrontations with Congress, but Johnson lacked such talent. The inevitable result was a costly battle between the president and legislature over control of Reconstruction that was marked by Johnson's increasing political impotence and ultimately his impeachment.

During the increasing sectional tensions that preceded secession and war, Congress had labored to solve problems through the traditional methods of compromise and accommodation. Yet it failed finally to avert the crisis for the same reasons that all other national institutions failed to avoid rapture. When the war broke out, the country faced a national emergency of the first order that required a decisive and praid action, so the role of Congress was necessarily diminished by its tendency to deliberate over questions and delay in resolving them. Congressional frustration over the legislature's marginalization by a talented and popular president took on several forms, most notably the formation of the Committee on the Conduct of the War. Yet for all such frustrations, the legislative branch forged a productive partnership with the Lincoln administration that only occasionally broke into quarrels and in the main was a contributing factor in Northern victory.

—*Christopher Bates*

See also Brooks, Preston Smith; Joint Committee on the Conduct of the War; Douglas, Stephen Arnold; Kansas-Nebraska Act; Peace Democrats; Radical Republicans; Sumner, Charles; Wade-Davis Bill; War Democrats.

For further reading:

Bogue, Allan G. *The Congressman's War* (1989).

Boykin, Edward. *Congress and the Civil War* (1955).

Hyman, Harold. *The Radical Republicans and Reconstruction, 1861–1870* (1967).

Stampp, Kenneth. *The Era of Reconstruction* (1965).

Williams, T. Harry. *Lincoln and the Radicals* (1941).

CONKLING, ROSCOE
(1829–1888)
United States congressman

Born in Albany, New York, Roscoe Conkling was the son of Eliza Cockburn and Alfred Conkling, a prominent Whig congressman, diplomat, and lawyer. Conkling decided to become a lawyer, like his father, and in 1850 he moved to Utica, where he began his political and legal careers at the same time, accepting an appointment as district attorney. In 1854, he helped to found the Republican Party in New York, and the next year he married Julia Seymour, sister of New York's Democratic governor, Horatio Seymour. In 1858 he was elected to the House of Representatives, where he would serve for most of the next decade before being elected to the Senate in 1867.

In large part, Conkling owed his quick rise up the political ladder to his magnetic personality. He was handsome, and in good physical shape, and he possessed tremendous self-confidence. Conkling certainly did not build his career around his legislative accomplishments. He occasionally took a strong stand on some issues, opposing the issuance of Greenback currency and speaking out against Radical Reconstruction, but he rarely took the lead and throughout his career he was never associated with a major piece of legislation. His efforts were instead geared toward maintaining party machinery and solidifying his power base. Senate colleague John Sherman noted that "he never interests himself in anything but personal antagonisms."

As Conkling's career progressed, his grip on New York politics became increasingly tight. Many political bosses of the era based their power on patronage and personal alliances, but Conkling, who was somewhat aloof and had few close personal friends, preferred instead to focus on making trouble for those who dared cross him. Senator James A. Garfield, one of Conkling's main targets, described him as "a great fighter, inspired more by his hates than his loves." When James G. Blaine publicly made fun of Conkling's "turkey-gobbler strut," Conkling refused to speak to Blaine ever again, and the two became bitter enemies. Conkling also maintained ongoing feuds with most of the other leading political figures of his day, including Carl Schurz, Horace Greeley, George William Curtis, James A. Garfield, and Rutherford B. Hayes. Conkling even had difficulty maintaining cordial relations with his family. His relationship with his wife became strained and remote, and she rarely accompanied him to Washington. This eventually led to a highly publicized love affair with Kate Chase Sprague that caused Conkling some amount of embarrassment. Conkling also cut his daughter and only child, Bessie, off after she married a man he did not like.

The only person with whom Conkling seems to have had a close personal and professional relationship was Ulysses S. Grant. The two men had a great deal of respect and affection for one another. When Grant became president, he allowed Conkling to take responsibility for all government appointments made in the state of New York, cementing the Senator's power over the Republican Party there. At this point, Conkling was at the height of his power. When Chief Justice Salmon P. Chase died, Grant offered the job to Conkling, who refused, believing that he would succeed Grant as president.

The 1876 Republican convention proved to be the great disappointment of Conkling's political life. The convention was split between his followers and those of Blaine. To break the deadlock, the convention turned to a third candidate, Rutherford B. Hayes. After Hayes's nomination and election, Conkling had to satisfy himself with leading the antiadministration faction in Congress, known as the "Stalwarts." Conkling did everything he could to frustrate the president's agenda and to otherwise create legislative gridlock. In one highly publicized event, Conkling caused several of Hayes's nominees for patronage positions in New York to be rejected by the Senate.

At the Republican convention of 1880, Conkling led the movement to renominate Ulysses S. Grant for a third term. While he did not succeed in that, he did manage to get New Yorker Chester Arthur nominated for the vice-presidency and to keep his rivals James G. Blaine and John Sherman from securing the presidential nomination. The eventual presidential nominee, Ohioan James A. Garfield, was not entirely acceptable to

Conkling, but he eventually gave his support, believing that Garfield would give him control over New York patronage.

After being elected, however, Garfield gave the post of secretary of state to his fellow Ohioan Blaine. Several other appointments made it increasingly clear to Conkling that he was an outsider as far as the president was concerned. Outraged, he broke with Garfield and became an outspoken critic of the administration. In May of 1881, Garfield named William H. Robertson as his choice for collector of the Port of New York, the most lucrative patronage position in the country. As he had done to Hayes's first nominee for the position, Conkling tried to have Robertson rejected. Garfield refused to back down, insisting that the right to make appointments without undue Senate interference was an important presidential prerogative. Some senators were unwilling to alienate the new president, others were aware that the public largely agreed with Garfield's position, and many had tired of Conkling's constant troublemaking. Whatever the case, Conkling was defeated, and on 14 May 1881 he resigned from the Senate. He hoped to be vindicated by being reelected, but he had lost control of New York politics, and he was defeated. Conkling spent his final years in private law practice, dying in New York City in 1888.

—*Christopher Bates*

See also Blaine, James Gillespie.
For further reading:
Burlingame, Sara Lee. "The Making of a Spoilsman: The Life and Career of Roscoe Conkling from 1829 to 1873" (Ph.D. dissertation, 1974).
Conkling, Alfred R. *The Life and Letters of Roscoe Conkling, Orator, Statesman, Advocate* (1889).

CONNOR, PATRICK EDWARD
(1820–1891)
Union general

Patrick E. Connor, originally born in County Kerry, Ireland, emigrated with his family to New York City at the age of twelve. Connor's pre–Civil War career was split between military service and civilian business pursuits. He enlisted for a five-year term with a dragoon company of the U.S. Army in 1838, during which time he saw action in Florida during the Second Seminole War and served garrison duty in the Iowa Territory. After the expiration of his enlistment, Connor briefly returned to New York City to pursue business interests, but a failed mercantile enterprise prompted his move to Texas in 1846. Upon his arrival, tense relations with Mexico prompted Connor to enlist in the Texas Volunteers, with whom he eventually earned the rank of captain. During the Mexican-American War, he distinguished himself in numerous engagements along the

Texas-Mexico border, including Palo Alto and Resaca de Palma, before being wounded in the fighting at Buena Vista.

His injuries forced Connor to resign his commission in 1847 and return to his civilian pursuits, which shortly thereafter swept him westward with the burgeoning tide of the California Gold Rush. In California, Connor was active in mining, construction, and other mercantile pursuits, and also joined a militant vigilante group known as the California Rangers. Their primary purpose was to hunt down outlaws, bandits, and cattle thieves. Connor won local distinction with this group in 1853 when he captured and executed the notorious bandit Joaquin Murieta. He parlayed his fame into a successful business and political career in the city of Stockton, becoming one the town's most prominent leaders and wealthiest residents.

The outbreak of the Civil War provided Connor with an opportunity to renew his military career, although his hopes for a prominent command in the East were never realized. He joined the Union army in 1861 and was appointed colonel of the 3d California Volunteer Infantry. Connor's command was instructed to move into the Utah territory to secure the lines of communication with the East and also to protect the overland trails from Indian and Confederate aggression. While serving in Utah, Connor became a staunch opponent of the Mormon church and, in particular, Brigham Young, whom he considered a traitor and secessionist in his own right. In 1862, Connor established Camp Douglas on a bluff to the east of Salt Lake City, with an eye toward keeping a tight rein on the Mormons as well as guarding the overland passage to California.

Despite his distrust of the Mormons and strong personal dislike for Brigham Young, Connor was vigilant in his pursuit of Indian groups that threatened the western travel routes. In January 1863 he led 300 men in a victorious attack against a mixed force of 250 northwestern Shoshone and Bannock Indians in the battle of Bear Creek (present-day Franklin, Idaho). As a reward for subduing this group of Indians, Connor was commissioned a brigadier general in the U.S. Volunteers. In 1865 he was placed in charge of the Powder River expedition, a largely futile campaign intended to pursue and punish hostile bands of the Sioux, Arapaho, and Northern Cheyenne inhabiting the region of present-day Wyoming. The expedition produced few tangible results, although Connor did engage and defeat a small contingent of Arapaho along the Tongue River in August 1865.

Although relations with the Indian tribes of the region remained mostly amicable for the duration of the Civil War, tensions with the local Mormons continued to run high during Connor's tenure in Utah. This was partly due to Connor's efforts to diminish Mormon influence in Utah by offering favorable terms for any non-Mormon emigrants to the region, especially miners. After his appointment as commander of the District of the Plains in 1865, Connor increased his pressure on the Mormons by establishing an army-run newspaper, the *Union Vidette*, which actively criticized Brigham Young and opposed the Mormon-controlled *Deseret News.*

The aftermath of the Civil War saw the end of Connor's military career, as he was mustered out of service at the rank of brevet major general on 30 April 1866. After his discharge, Connor remained in the region, where he began a successful career as a miner and real estate developer in Utah and Nevada. He also founded a specifically non-Mormon political party in Utah, the Liberal Party, and ran repeatedly for high political offices. However, his continued opposition to the Mormon government of Utah and failed political campaigns reversed his early financial successes and resulted in foreclosure on the majority of his mining and real estate holdings. Despite a long and active civil and military career, Connor died in 1891 a relatively poor and obscure man.

—*Daniel P. Barr*

See also California; Young, Brigham.

For further reading:

Colton, Ray Charles. *The Civil War in the Western Territories: Arizona, Colorado, New Mexico, and Utah* (1959).

Long, E. B. *Saints and the Union: Utah Territory during the Civil War* (1981).

Madsen, Brigham D. *Glory Hunter: A Biography of Patrick Edward Connor* (1990).

Rogers, Fred B. *Soldiers of the Overland* (1938).

Varley, James F. *Brigham and the Brigadier: General Patrick Connor and His California Volunteers in Utah and along the Overland Trail* (1989).

CONSCRIPTION, C.S.A.

By the spring of 1862, the twelve-month voluntary enlistments of Confederate soldiers made at the outset of the war were beginning to expire. Disillusionment with military life and news of hardships on the home front led many of these soldiers not to reenlist, and Confederate leaders quickly realized that a continued reliance on voluntary enlistment would not keep the army adequately staffed. In response, the Congress of the Confederate States of America passed the first of three conscription acts on 16 April 1862 and began the first national military draft in U.S. history.

The first Conscription Act extended the enlistments of all twelve-month volunteers still in service for three years or until the end of the war and required all white males between the ages of eighteen and thirty-five to serve for a similar term. Numerous exemptions based on occupation were a feature of the act. Someone not otherwise exempted could hire a substitute to take his place. As an incentive, the act allowed all men who volunteered for duty before 15 May 1862 to organize their own regiments or reorganize existing ones and elect their own officers.

They would also receive a $50 bounty. Failure to volunteer by the deadline would result in a forfeiture of the bounty, loss of the right to enlist in a regiment of one's own choosing, and loss of the right to choose one's officers.

President Jefferson Davis emphasized conscription as the only fair method of consolidating control of Southern troops, distributing the burden of military service equally among the Southern states, and developing a unified system of military discipline. Many criticized the policy, however, as a usurpation of states' rights. Governors Joseph E. Brown of Georgia and Zebulon Vance of North Carolina were vocal critics, but following key decisions in the supreme courts of several Southern states, chiefly Virginia, North Carolina, and Georgia, upholding conscription as a constitutionally held power of the Confederate government, most states reluctantly recognized the act. Ideological differences, however, over control of conscription efforts, definitions of procedure, and primacy of Confederate over state conscription efforts continued throughout the war.

The Confederate Congress passed a second conscription act on 11 October 1862 that expanded the eligible ages to include white males between thirty-five and forty-five. It continued the use of substitutes and statutory exemptions, although the latter were in an amended form that expanded the list of exempted positions and tightened eligibility requirements. A third conscription act, passed on 17 February 1864, expanded the age limits to include men as young as seventeen and as old as fifty.

Built into the acts were exemption clauses that only added to the controversial nature of conscription. While this policy naturally exempted the mentally or physically disabled from military duty, it reserved most exemptions for those deemed essential to the social, political, and economic stability of the South: state and Confederate employees, politicians, contractors, overseers, shoemakers, tanners, blacksmiths, wagon makers, millers, mill engineers, millwrights, and employees of wool and cotton factories and paper mills. In the Second Conscription Act, planters with twenty or more slaves were automatically exempted under the infamous "Twenty-Negro Law." Also, the cost of a substitute was always high and ultimately enormous. Ranging from $300 in the beginning of the war to several thousand dollars by the end of it, the hiring of a substitute was beyond all but the wealthiest class of citizens.

The existence of multiple organizations charged with overseeing enlistment also added to the confusing hodgepodge of eligibilities and exemptions. West of the Mississippi River, the head of the Trans-Mississippi Department controlled enlistment efforts and answered directly to the War Department. East of the Mississippi River, the newly formed Bureau of Conscription in the Office of the Adjutant General directed recruitment. But not long after the bureau's creation, the Confederate inspector general attempted to consolidate conscription efforts under army command and directed each field commander to assign recruitment officers to draft new soldiers from the surrounding countryside. General Braxton Bragg initiated one such enlistment drive in northern Alabama under the command of Brigadier General Gideon J. Pillow that openly competed with the more timid civilian efforts in the region.

Conscription never enjoyed popular support in the Confederacy. Poor whites, angered by the socioeconomic bias built into the three acts, used conscription as a reason for desertion or failing to appear for service. Armed bands of deserters and layouts (men who refused to be enlisted) seized control of whole counties and actively fought conscription efforts by assassinating conscription agents and waging guerrilla warfare against both Confederate and state troops sent to arrest them. The largest of these deserter counties existed along the Appalachian Mountains in north Georgia, western North and South Carolina, and eastern Tennessee.

The three conscription acts point to the great disparity in war expectations between the wealthy planter and yeoman farmer. Only those white Southern males with the socioeconomic power to gain the exempted government positions, pay the required exemption fees, or hire substitutes at exorbitant prices could avoid military service. Exemption policies only accentuated those differences and led to a burgeoning black market. Enlistment agents profited from the sale of forged exemption documents. Competition for government offices increased, and new, extraneous offices offered shelter from military service to the sons of the planter elite.

While conscription did help consolidate military power under Confederate control, it did little to ensure popular support for the war effort. Corruption among enlistment officials, coupled with a rapid increase in public opposition, violent uprisings, and Confederate military defeats led to a breakdown in conscription efforts in the last six months of the war. Attempts to arrest deserter gangs and reluctant conscripts ceased in many areas, and Confederate officials had to consider the efficacy of enlisting the one remaining captive source of soldiers, the Southern slave population.

—*David Carlson*

See also Brown, Joseph E.; Conscription, U.S.A; Vance, Zebulon.

For further reading:
Moore, Albert B., ed. *Conscription and Conflict in the Confederacy, Southern Classics Series* (1924; reprint, 1996).

CONSCRIPTION, U.S.A.

The first national draft in U.S. history was authorized by President Abraham Lincoln when he signed the Enrollment Act on 3 March 1863. Before this legislation, the Federal Militia Act of 1862 had given the president authority to draft 300,000 men, but widespread opposition and increased volunteering provoked by the measure suspended its implementation. Governors made every effort to induce volunteer enlistments after Lincoln issued two new calls for troops from the states in the summer of 1862, going as far as to offer outstanding bounties to get a sufficiency of men under arms.

By the end of 1862, however, the number of volunteers in the North had sharply declined. Military service entailed significant personal sacrifices if one had a family, ran a farm, or had a business. At the same time, wartime industries attracted many workers with wages substantially higher than a soldier's meager pay. Furthermore, there was a growing agitation against the war throughout the country, led by the Peace Democrats and other antiadministration forces. All of these forces combined greatly discouraged volunteering in the latter part of 1862.

With the decline in volunteering, governors were not very successful in meeting federal requisitions for using state militias, and a new method had to be employed to meet the personnel needs for the Union armies. Congress's answer to this problem was to pass a national conscription law known as "An Act for Enrolling and Calling Out the National Forces, and For Other Purposes," otherwise known as the Enrollment Act. In final form, the Enrollment Act consisted of thirty-eight sections. Upon the request of the president, males twenty to forty-five were to be drafted first, followed by all married men between the ages of thirty-six to forty-six. Males seventeen to twenty could serve with the permission of a parent or guardian. The need for men was first apportioned to each individual congressional district. Names were then procured through a laborious house-to-house enrollment conducted by government agents. Finally, a lottery in each congressional district determined who would go to war. If the proper number of men had volunteered in a given district, the draft would not apply there. Thus, it was in the interest of government authorities in the counties and cities to recruit men as vigorously as they could to keep the draft from affecting people in their area. The draft stirred recruiting drives all over the country and resulted in a great many men going into the army who probably would not have enlisted if left to their own devices.

The following drafts were held:

15 June 1863: 100,000 (6 months)
17 October 1863: 500,000 (3 years)
14 March 1864: 200,000 (3 years)
23 April 1864: 85,000 (100 days)
18 July 1864: 500,000 (1, 2, and 3 years)
19 December 1864: 300,000 (1, 2, and 3 years)

This legislation also created the bureaucracy necessary to implement the Federal draft. Administering the draft became the responsibility of the Provost Marshal General's Office of the War Department. The country was divided into 185 congressional districts, with each congressional district becoming a draft district headed by a provost marshal whose responsibility was registering and calling up draftees. His broad authority also included the right to arrest and detain all persons resisting the draft or discouraging enlistments. To further implement this authority, the Enrollment Act also established military commissions and invested these bodies with the power to try civilians suspected of spying and, where appropriate, to impose the death penalty.

The most controversial aspect of the Enrollment Act was its provision for various exemptions, however. All men called to service could legally avoid it by obtaining one of a number of exemptions, the most common involving physical or mental disability. Also, any son responsible for taking care of aged or infirm parents, a brother whose siblings were orphaned under the age of twelve, and a father of motherless children who were less than twelve years old were all exempt from the draft.

Whether able to secure an exemption or not, however, all drafted men were guaranteed two other means of legally avoiding military service—substitution and commutation. A conscript who possessed the means could either pay a $300 exemption fee or provide a substitute. Congress deliberately inserted these provisions to soften the impact of a potentially unpopular law on a war-weary public. These exemptions nonetheless gave rise to a charge that the Civil War was "a rich man's war and a poor man's fight."

With some modifications, including the repeal of commutation in March 1864, the Enrollment Act remained in effect until the close of the war, but not without encountering major dispute along the way. All across the country, insurgent citizens protested against the federal draft. In Columbia County, Pennsylvania, enrollment officers encountered severe problems in trying to register men. One soldier sent in to round up deserters was killed, resulting in the arrest of more than forty men who were later imprisoned at Fort Mifflin. Likewise, in the town of Berkeley, in Luzerne County, Pennsylvania, citizens rioted in protest against the military draft and subsided only after the militia had fired upon them, with four or five of the insurgents left dead in the streets. Nor was this spirit of dissent confined entirely to Pennsylvania. For five days in New York City, mobs roamed throughout the city in protest of the draft. Those riots resulted in more than a thousand deaths. Likewise, similar riots took place in the West, most notably in the town of Port Washington, Wisconsin.

All in all, the conscription act was radical in that it allowed the Federal government to replace the states as the primary agency for personnel mobilization. Likewise, although the implementation of the draft itself was largely a failure in many states, with only 6 percent of Union troops being draftees, it did manage to stimulate volunteering for the remainder of the war.

—*Samantha Jane Gaul*

For further reading:

Earnhart, Hugh G. "Commutation; Democratic or Undemocratic?" *Civil War History* (1966).

Geary, James W. "Civil War Conscription in the North: A Historiographical Review." *Civil War History* (1986).

———. *We Need Men: The Union Draft and the Civil War* (1991).

Itter, William August. "Conscription in Pennsylvania during the Civil War" (Ph.D. dissertation, 1941).

Leach, Jack Franklin. *Conscription in the United States: Historical Background* (1960).

Levine, Peter. "Draft Evasion in the North during the Civil War, 1863–1865." *Journal of American History* (1981).

Murdock, Eugene C. *One Million Men: The Civil War Draft in the North* (1971).

———. *Patriotism Limited, 1862–1865: The Civil War Draft and the Bounty System* (1967).

Paludan, Phillip S. *"A People's Contest": The Union and the Civil War, 1861–1865* (1988).

Sterling, Robert E. "Civil War Draft Resistance in the Middle West" (Ph.D. dissertation, 1974).

CONSTITUTION, C.S.A.

The controversies that led to the secession crisis of 1860–1861 gained momentum from the widely held Southern presumption that the primary and explicitly stated reason for having enacted the U.S. Constitution—to form a more perfect union—was being perverted by the political aggressions of the North. Discontented Southerners had no quarrel with the Constitution itself; indeed, they were in the habit of brandishing its principles like a talisman. Countless declamations reverently hailed the Constitution while condemning what the Union had become. In 1861, having decided that they could no longer live within the Union created by the U.S. Constitution, these Southerners sought to form a more perfect union of their own, but they did so by framing a document very much like the one from which they had fled.

After the secession of the seven Deep South states (South Carolina, Georgia, Florida, Alabama, Mississippi, Louisiana, and Texas), a convention met in Montgomery, Alabama, to establish a Southern government. Convening on 4 February 1861 and calling itself the Provisional Congress of the Confederate States of America, it consisted of representatives from South Carolina, Georgia, Alabama, Mississippi, Florida, and Louisiana, which amounted to only six of the fifteen slave states and did not include the recently seceded Texas. The states represented had selected delegates in varied ways, but each had been consistent in limiting its delegation to match the number of its former U.S. congressional delegation. On the matter of the Constitution, each state would have a single vote. In four days, the Congress unanimously adopted a Provisional Constitution that almost exactly replicated that of the United States. The Provisional Congress then put a twelve-man committee, headed by Robert Barnwell Rhett, to work on conceiving a permanent document.

Montgomery was considerably animated by this drama unfolding in what was actually a sleepy southern town. Office-seekers as well as delegates crowded the hotels and eateries, and entertainments filled the nights. In this atmosphere, for the next five weeks, the Montgomery convention would frame a constitution, going about it in a curiously deliberate and thorough way, as though the peace following secession was a permanent fixture and no urgency required any preparations for war.

What the convention did regard as urgent was the need to write a permanent instrument of government, establish an executive, and provide the provisional legislature with authority until regular congressional elections could be held. The appointment of provisional executive officers—Jefferson Davis as president and Alexander H. Stephens as vice president—was managed with some facility, and some delegates believed that writing the Constitution would prove just as easy, especially because framing the new document would require little originality. Georgia and Alabama delegates, for instance, had been instructed to move for the adoption of the U.S. Constitution without alteration. Although that did not happen, and the business of writing the document would be more complicated and contentious than anyone had thought, the permanent Constitution that emerged from committee on 28 February and was adopted on 11 March did closely resemble the U.S. Constitution, even in its wording. The principal differences were its emphasis on states' rights, protecting slavery, and correcting what were regarded as defects in the processes of government.

A paramount concern with states' rights was reflected throughout the document, beginning with the preamble. Rather than forming a "more perfect union," the states were acting in their "sovereign and independent" capacities to create "a permanent federal government." Officers of the Confederate government could be impeached by a state legislature. Yet the supremacy of the states was not absolute in the new document. State officers had to take an oath to uphold the Confederate Constitution, and the national government's laws and treaties were to take precedence over state constitutions and statutes. Likewise, the limitations on states in the U.S. Constitution were copied into the Confederate Constitution. No state could independently ally or confederate with another state or power. States could not coin money or pass any bill of attainder or ex post facto

law. They could not impair the obligation of contracts, grant any title of nobility, keep troops or warships in time of peace, or engage in war except in case of invasion or imminent danger. Although the Confederate Constitution did not mention the right of secession, it can be inferred that the delegates believed that each state retained such a right. They were, after all, recently on record asserting that the absence of a specific right of secession in the U.S. Constitution did not impair the Southern states' power to secede from the Union.

States' rights also accounted for the main differences between Article III of the Confederate Constitution that created the judiciary and the provisions for a judiciary in Article III of the U.S. Constitution. The jurisdiction of Confederate courts did not include cases arising from diversity of citizenship, nor did the Confederate Constitution draw a distinction between cases of law and equity. The Confederate Constitution allowed for the establishment of a Supreme Court, yet the Confederacy never actually formed one.

The maintenance of slavery was specifically addressed in several places in the Confederate Constitution. For instance, it stated that no national law impinging on "the right of property in negro slaves" could be adopted. Recalling the considerable problems that slave questions had created in the Union's western territories, the delegates insisted that slavery be acknowledged and preserved by the Confederate Congress and by territorial governments in any such areas acquired by the Confederacy. The *Dred Scott* decision was institutionalized in the document as well, with the stipulation that citizens of states could take their slaves into such territories. Also reciprocal citizenship guarantees among the states assured the property rights of slaveholders in any and all states, regardless of a state's position on slavery. Advocates of reviving a legalized foreign slave trade, however, were rebuffed.

The Confederate Constitution sought to correct problems with government procedures that practice had revealed in the workings of the U.S. government. The more conspicuous of these changes included the modification of the amending process to provide for the proposal of amendments by a convention of the states. Congress had no authority to propose amendments, and ratification would be accomplished by either two-thirds of the state legislatures or by a similar number of state conventions. To cure the ills of patronage and to stop special interests from raiding the treasury and wrecking budgets, Congress could not appropriate money except by a two-thirds vote of both houses. Exceptions were clearly defined. Each appropriation bill had to register its amount and describe its intention. The president was given the authority to veto individual items in an appropriation bill, thus introducing the concept of a line-item veto. To prevent dubious initiatives from hiding in complicated legislation, each bill could address only one subject that had to be clearly indicated in the bill's title. Cabinet officers in the executive branch could take seats in either house of Congress with the pertinent body's permission. The president was to serve a six-year term and could not succeed himself, thus eliminating both the powers derived from extended incumbency and the weaknesses caused by lame duck status.

With the adoption of the permanent Constitution on 11 March 1861, the Confederate government emerged as a full-grown entity, at least in its form if not its substance. The accomplishment occasioned complaints from only a few quarters. The *Charleston Mercury* grumbled that the Confederacy's version of the U.S. Constitution merely planted the same sectional seeds that had blossomed in the American republic, but that was the voice of Rhett's disappointment regarding the exclusion of an African slave trade and the refusal to exclude free states preemptively from the Confederacy. George Fitzhugh described the Federal Constitution as "the most absurd and contradictory paper ever penned by practical men," yet it was a grumble from someone many viewed as a chronic malcontent. The Gulf states had removed themselves from the Union, but the majority of those states' citizens had not removed themselves from the American political tradition, as they understood it. "They will find it easier," muttered South Carolina planter David Gavin, "to destroy a government than to make one." But Southern secessionists had not really destroyed a government so much as they were in the process of transferring national authority from Washington (where they felt it had been corrupted) to Montgomery (where it presumably would remain incorruptible).

The similarity of the Confederate Constitution to that of the Union did not reveal a lack of imagination on the part of the delegates at Montgomery. The necessity of maintaining order in a potentially revolutionary setting made the virtually wholesale adoption of the U.S. Constitution a certainty. The delegates in Montgomery had the task of hastily satisfying the normal sentimental, cultural, and political memory of Americans who happened to be Southerners. The Confederacy would keep much of the American status quo: the Confederate seal would memorialize George Washington, just as the Confederate Constitution would emulate the government over which he had presided.

Ironically, the very things that made the South less devoted to the Union created the need for some binding tie within the new Southern one. The Southerner had a legal conception of national identity, so the Union for most Southerners had always appeared in tandem with its Constitution. The necessity for a national identity of some kind made the South embrace not just the U.S. Constitution but also the concept of constitutionalism as the natural order of things.

—*David S. Heidler and Jeanne T. Heidler*

See also Courts, C.S.A.
For further reading:
Davis, William C. *"A Government of Our Own:" The Making of the Confederacy* (1994).
Fehrenbacher, Don E. *Constitutions and Constitutionalism in the Slaveholding South* (1989).
Lee, Charles. *The Confederate Constitution* (1963).
Nieman, Donald. "Republicanism, the Confederate Constitution, and the American Constitutional Tradition." In *An Uncertain Tradition: Constitutionalism and the History of the South* (1989).

CONSTITUTIONAL UNION PARTY
(1860)

The Constitutional Union Party originated in the late 1850s as a response to the increasing sectionalism that pervaded the United States' two major political parties, the Republicans and the Democrats. Supporters emphasized the need for unconditional support for the Constitution and the preservation of the Union, regardless of ideological inclinations on other issues, particularly that of slavery. Although short-lived, the existence of the party demonstrated that there were still Americans who sought a political solution to the acrimonious divisiveness present in the country.

The late 1840s and 1850s witnessed the introduction of several new political parties. Each party highlighted a concern of Americans. The Know-Nothings put forth an "America First" slogan with its anti-immigrant, anti-Catholic platform. Others, like the Republican and the Free-Soil parties, viewed slavery as the greatest threat to American unity. As each new party appeared, however, it increasingly included members who argued for their positions without considering compromise.

This lack of compromise spawned a reaction towards moderation for some Americans. When President James Buchanan unwisely accepted the illegal proslavery Lecompton Constitution for Kansas in 1858, members of all the major parties of the 1850s—Republicans, Know-Nothings, Northern Democrats, former Whigs—called for the president to disavow the proslavery constitution that the state had drawn up under questionable circumstances.

Buchanan's failure to respond favorably presented an opportunity for a new political party to emerge. Some dissatisfied members of the Democrats and the former members of the Whig and Know-Nothing Parties organized a Unionist Party at the state level. As tensions heightened between the North and South, the Unionist leaders at the state level organized a national campaign for the presidency and named themselves the Constitutional Union Party.

On 9 May, Constitutional Union delegates from twenty-one of the thirty-three states met in Baltimore, Maryland, to select their presidential and vice-presidential candidates for the 1860 election. According to one scholar, most of the attendees "were or appeared to be venerable gentlemen representing a generation of almost forgotten politicians; most of them had retired from public life involuntarily rather than by choice." The rhetoric of the speeches reinforces this characterization of an alienated generation. Patriotic statements poured forth from the podium, all hearkening back to a more glorious past when citizens placed the nation above party or sectional interests.

When it came time to make a choice for leadership, the names of the most prominent candidates—John J. Crittenden of Kentucky, Sam Houston of Texas, and John Bell of Tennessee, among others—reflected moderation. Crittenden was the logical choice to lead the party, but he declined to submit his name. Houston's supporters pressed hard for his nomination, but his association with the Democratic Party doomed any chance of receiving the votes of the numerous former Whigs. When the votes were cast on the second ballot, Bell received the nomination. His running mate was lifetime politician Edward Everett of Massachusetts, a devoted compromiser.

Bell appeared a strong compromise candidate. Originally a Jacksonian Democrat in the late 1820s, Bell chose to enter the Whig Party in the 1830s. In the 1840s and 1850s, he served as United States senator throughout the period of sectional discord following the Mexican War. Although a slaveowner, Bell opposed his region when he voted against the Kansas-Nebraska Act of 1854 and the admission of Kansas as a slave state in 1858.

The Constitutional Union Party's platform stated that political parties normally used the platform to "mislead and deceive the people"; therefore, its members promised simply to "recognize no political principle other than the Constitution of the Country, the Union of the States, and the Enforcement of the Laws." While this statement provided the core of the platform, the rest of the document echoed the patriotic fervor of the convention.

The 1860 contest, however, was not such an election. From the opening days, it became obvious that moderation would not win the presidency. In reality, two elections took place. The first was in the Northern states, where Republican nominee Abraham Lincoln opposed Northern Democrat Stephen A. Douglas. In the Southern states, Bell and Southern Democrat John C. Breckinridge contested for votes. The result was expected: Lincoln won the presidency by a majority of the electoral and a plurality of the popular votes. Bell accumulated thirty-nine electoral and 588,879 popular votes. Kentucky, Tennessee, and Virginia—all border states—supported the Constitutional Union Party with their electoral votes.

The Constitutional Union Party fell apart after the election. Although some supporters continued the crusade, the Civil War came, and moderation disappeared by military force.

—*Mark R. Cheathem*

See also Bell, John; Election of 1860; Everett, Edward.
For further reading:
Morison, Elting. Election of 1860. In *History of American Presidential Elections, 1789–1968*. Edited by Arthur M. Schlesinger, Jr. (1971).
Nash, Howard P. *Third Parties in American Politics* (1959).
Parks, Joseph H. *John Bell of Tennessee* (1950).
Stabler, John Burgess. "A History of the Constitutional Union Party: A Tragic Failure" (Ph.D. dissertation, 1954).

CONTRABANDS

Warriors throughout history have considered all goods and property seized during a conflict to be contraband, if such items can aid and abet the enemy's ability to continue to make war. The Civil War is a unique conflict because the assets that were considered contraband often included human beings. As Southern plantations were liberated by advancing Union forces, many slaves sought self-emancipation by rushing toward the advancing Union lines. The question of what to do with these individuals, ostensibly the chattel property of Confederate sympathizers, and also the status of these liberated persons were perplexing issues that often faced Union commanders in the field. The mixed signals and miscues between the Lincoln administration and the U.S. Army suggest that no clear policy regarding former slaves as contraband had been developed at the onset of the Civil War and that the formulation of such policy was a work in progress during the first months of the conflict.

Abraham Lincoln did not issue the Emancipation Proclamation until 22 September 1862. Before then, a carefully crafted veil of discomfiture shrouded the question of emancipation. Faced with the dilemma of keeping the proslavery border states of Missouri, Kentucky, Maryland, and Delaware in the Union, the Lincoln administration believed that any rash action toward wholesale emancipation might drive these states toward secession, thus augmenting the Confederacy and extending its ability and resources to make war. In this world of high stakes politics all decisions regarding the status of slaves as contraband of war were viewed as profound decisions that could affect the conduct of the war.

On 24 May 1861, only six weeks after the opening shots were fired at Fort Sumter, Union general Benjamin F. Butler reported to authorities in the War Department that he had put a group of fugitive slaves to work at Fortress Monroe, Virginia. In his dispatch, Butler described the fugitives as "contraband of war," and stated that some were employed on construction projects while others picked cotton. Although the fugitive slaves were not considered to be legally emancipated, they were effectively free, and they did receive a small wage (usually twenty-five cents per day plus rations) from the Federal Treasury for the labor that they performed for the Union

Escaped slaves camped near Culpeper, Virginia, November 1863 (Photograph by Timothy O'Sullivan / *Library of Congress*)

forces. Nevertheless, among Northern abolitionists the catch phrase "contraband of war" became almost synonymous with emancipation. Slaves liberated in this fashion were often referred to simply as contrabands. This practice became increasingly common after Congress passed the first Confiscation Act on 6 August 1861. This measure authorized the freeing of slaves in areas that were already under Union army control and who had previously been employed to aid the Confederate cause.

Even with these policies in place, President Lincoln still proceeded very cautiously on the issue of emancipation. In September 1861, Lincoln ordered General John C. Frémont to revise a proclamation of martial law that he had issued. Frémont's initial proclamation had freed the slaves of all disloyal slaveholders in Missouri. In December 1861, Lincoln convinced Secretary of War

Simon Cameron to delete several controversial passages in his annual report to Congress. It was Cameron's wish to urge emancipation as a wartime necessity and to advocate the use of former slaves as military laborers and as soldiers. Shortly after Cameron submitted the revised report, Lincoln removed him from the War Department by naming him minister to Russia.

For many former slaves, their role as "contraband of war" was a part of the transition from slavery to freedom. The role of emancipation and contrabands was always closely linked, and when freedom finally came to the slaves in the South, Union lines swelled as tens of thousands of the newly free joined the camps and eventually the ranks of their liberators. Coping with the demands of vast contraband camps that were teeming with displaced persons was a taxing obligation to the War Department and represents one of the first social welfare efforts sponsored by the U.S. government. The provision of basic supplies of food, shelter, and clothing; the furnishing of rudimentary health services; and the establishment of schools were not skills traditionally associated with the military, but as the war progressed the efforts to assist the wards of the government in the contraband camps became more systematic. Not surprisingly, when Congress created the Bureau of Refugees, Freedmen, and Abandoned Lands in March 1865, the agency was placed under the auspices of the War Department and General Oliver O. Howard was appointed its first director.

—*Junius P. Rodriguez*

See also Border States; Butler, Benjamin F.; Emancipation Proclamation; Frémont, John C.; Howard, Oliver O.

For further reading:

Buker, George E. *Blockaders, Refugees, and Contrabands: Civil War on Florida's Gulf Coast, 1861–1865* (1993).

Eaton, John. *Grant, Lincoln, and the Freedmen: Reminiscences of the Civil War, with Special Reference to the Work for the Contrabands and Freedmen of the Mississippi Valley* (1907).

Swint, Henry L., ed. *Dear Ones at Home: Letters from Contraband Camps* (1966).

COOK, PHILIP
(1817–1894)
Confederate general

Born to Philip Cook and Martha Wooten Cook in Twiggs County, Georgia, the younger Philip Cook was educated at Oglethorpe University and the Law School of the University of Virginia. Before going away to law school, however, Cook fought briefly as part of a Georgia volunteer unit in the Second Seminole War. After receiving his law degree, Cook settled in Oglethorpe, Georgia, where he practiced law. Upon the outbreak of the Civil War, Cook enlisted as a private in a company of volunteers organized in Macon County. He and the company traveled to Virginia, where they were incorporated into the 4th Georgia Regiment.

The 4th Georgia was headquartered at Portsmouth, Virginia. After the officers of the regiment learned of Cook's education, he was made the adjutant for the entire regiment and was promoted to lieutenant. He remained in that position through the Peninsula campaign of the spring and early summer of 1862. In the Seven Days' during that campaign, he was wounded in the Confederate assault on Malvern Hill. After the Peninsula campaign, Cook was promoted to lieutenant colonel in the 4th Georgia. He held that rank through the battle of Second Bull Run and the Maryland campaign. At Antietam, Cook and his men fought in some of the bloodiest fighting of the war as part of the force that tried to defend Bloody Lane. After the battle of Antietam, when the regiment's commander George

Pierce Doles, was elevated to the command of the Georgia brigade, Cook became the commander of the 4th Georgia.

As part of the rear elements of Thomas J. "Stonewall" Jackson's corps on the Confederate right at Fredericksburg in December 1862, Cook and his regiment did not see heavy action. Chancellorsville in May 1863 would be another matter. In Jackson's attack on Joseph Hooker's flank, Cook was hit by a Union bullet that broke his leg. He was out of action for several months and returned home to Georgia to recover. During his convalescence, Cook was elected and served briefly as a state senator.

Back in command of the 4th Georgia in the late fall of 1863, Cook commanded the regiment in the Mine Run campaign at the end of the year. In the spring of 1864, Cook commanded his regiment during the opening phases of Union general Ulysses S. Grant's campaign against Robert E. Lee. In the early stages of the battle of Cold Harbor in early June, George Doles was killed at Bethesda Church, and Cook succeeded to the command of the Georgia Brigade. In August 1864 he was promoted to brigadier general and was sent with his brigade to become a part of Jubal Early's army in the Shenandoah Valley.

Cook led his Georgia Brigade in all the major battles of Early's campaign against Philip Sheridan and particularly distinguished himself at Cedar Creek. He returned with his brigade to the Army of Northern Virginia in the trenches of Petersburg in early 1865. In the Confederate assault on Fort Stedman on 25 March 1865, Cook was again seriously wounded. He was taken to one of the Confederate hospitals in Petersburg, where he was recovering when Union forces captured the town on 3 April. He was made a Federal prisoner of war.

After the war, Cook returned to Georgia, where he opened a law practice in Americus. He remained an active attorney there until 1880, but in the meantime he had also become active in Georgia state politics, an interest that he had not demonstrated before the war. He served in the state constitutional convention in 1865, and he served five terms in the U.S. House of Representatives. After his time in Congress, he retired briefly from public life but was prevailed upon to become the state's secretary of state in 1890. He died in that office on 20 May 1894.

—*David S. Heidler and Jeanne T. Heidler*

See also Antietam, Battle of; Fort Stedman; Petersburg Campaign; Shenandoah Valley Campaign.

For further reading:

Stackpole, Edward J. *Sheridan in the Shenandoah: Jubal Early's Nemesis* (1992).

Thomas, Henry W. *History of the Doles-Cook Brigade Army of Northern Virginia, C.S.A.* (1903; reprint, 1988).

Trudeau, Noah Andre. *The Last Citadel: Petersburg, Virginia, June 1864–April 1865* (1991).

COOKE, JAY
(1821–1905)
Union financier

The second son of Eleutheros Cooke, a lawyer and congressman, and his wife, Martha, Jay Cooke was born on 10 August 1821 and reared in Sandusky, Ohio. An ambitious person, Cooke left school at age fourteen to work in the Sandusky dry goods and hardware store of Hubbard and Leiter. In 1836 he went to St. Louis to work for a wholesale firm. After the Panic of 1837 brought an end to this business, Cooke found employment the next year with the Washington Packet & Transportation Company, and in 1839 ended up in Philadelphia. That year he was hired by E. W. Clarke & Company, a prominent investment firm in the Quaker City. The self-confident Cooke sold discounted bank notes and marketed with great success stocks and bonds of local companies. In 1843 he became a partner in this firm and the next year married Dorothea Elizabeth Allen. Between 1846 and 1848, Cooke sold Mexican War bonds for the Clarke firm. As a result of effective advertising in Philadelphia newspapers and of the complex operations of the Treasury's depository system, Cooke, along with other members of his firm, derived great profits from the sale of these government obligations. After the Clarke Company folded during the Panic of 1857, Cooke, who had made a small fortune with this firm, went into temporary retirement and waited for a favorable moment to establish his own investment company.

In January 1861 he opened in Philadelphia the investment firm of Jay Cooke & Company, and became the leading financier to support the cause of the Union. His firm offered stocks, bills of exchange, commercial paper, and government notes and bonds. In 1861 Cooke helped to sell for Pennsylvania $3 million of state bonds. Cooke emphasized to potential buyers the importance of patriotism, and met with great success in marketing both small and large denominations of this issue.

Cooke also attracted the attention of individuals in Washington, D.C. The close ties between his younger brother, Henry David Cooke, and Salmon Chase, the former governor and senator of Ohio who had been appointed in 1861 as Lincoln's secretary of the Treasury, greatly enhanced the opportunities of Cooke's firm to engage in business with the federal government.

After opening an office in Washington in February 1862, Cooke was named in October of that year as a Treasury agent to assist in the distribution of $500 million worth of Treasury bonds—the largest offering of bonds in American history up to that point. Cooke proved to be quite capable in offering the so-called 5-20 bond. This was a bond with a 6 percent coupon that could be paid in five years, but was required to be paid in twenty. Cooke developed a viable marketing strategy to sell these bonds; he advertised the 5-20s in newspapers and on billboards and also used bankers and insurance agents in small towns to sell them. By January 1864 Cooke had succeeded in selling the entire amount of this government bond issue, amounting to about $360 million, from which he received a small commission of about $200,000.

Before the end of the Civil War, Cooke assisted in the distribution of another Treasury issue. William P. Fessenden, who replaced Chase as Treasury secretary in June 1864, named Cooke in late January 1865 as the Treasury's fiscal agent for the offering of the 7-30 bond. These were three-year notes that paid 7.3 percent interest. Cooke also effectively marketed this issue. He especially relied upon working-men's savings banks to sell $600 million worth of this Treasury obligation within less than six months.

After the war, Cooke engaged in the Treasury's refunding activities but also encountered severe financial difficulties of his own during the early 1870s. To expand his business, Cooke had established a branch bank in New York in 1866 and one in London in 1870. George S. Boutwell, who served as secretary of the Treasury under President Ulysses S. Grant, authorized Jay Cooke & Company in 1871 to head American and European syndicates for the selling of ten-year Treasury bonds with a coupon of 5 percent. With support especially from J. & W. Seligman & Company, the syndicates of Cooke quickly sold about $133 million of this issue between June and August of that year. However, Cooke's efforts during the early 1870s to sell securities for the Northern Pacific Railroad were not marked by success. As a result of depositors withdrawing funds from his bank in August 1873, Cooke on 18 September 1873 was forced to close the doors of his firm, and thus brought about the Panic of 1873.

The career of Cooke proved important to the outcome of the Civil War and to American financial history. He is best remembered for his patriotic service to the Union's cause and for his effectiveness as a financial marketer. Cooke, who lived in a mansion in Chelten Hills, Pennsylvania, was a religious and a charitable man; he was active in the American Sunday School Union and made donations to Dartmouth, Princeton, and Kenyon Colleges. Cooke died on 16 February 1905 in Ogontz, Pennsylvania.

—*William Weisberger*

See also Chase, Salmon P.; Fessenden, William Pitt.
For further reading:
Carosso, Vincent P. *The Morgans: Private International Bankers, 1854–1913* (1987).
Geisst, Charles R. *Wall Street: A History* (1997).
Larson, Henrietta M. *Jay Cooke: Private Banker* (1936).
Niven, John. *Salmon P. Chase: A Biography* (1995).
Oberholtzer, Ellis P. *Jay Cooke: Financier of the Civil War* (1907).

Sobel, Robert. *Panic on Wall Street: A History of America's Financial Disasters* (1968).

COOKE, JOHN ESTEN
(1830–1886)
Southern novelist

Born into an old Virginian family on 30 November 1830, John Esten Cooke oscillated for years between a career in the law and the avocation of writing. His talent pointed him toward writing, and ultimately he felt most at home with that calling. His achievement in placing stories in the *Southern Literary Messenger* and *Harper's* and the success of several books he published before the Civil War settled him finally upon a career as an author. *The Virginia Comedians* (1854) was a set of stories set in the late colonial period. With his richly detailed descriptions, Cooke here anticipated the postwar local color school of fiction.

In his early writing career, Cooke was remarkably critical of the "aristocracy" and silent about slavery. His Democratic posture and his belief in progress cast him as an antebellum Southern liberal, yet Cooke became an ardent secessionist and joined Confederate forces after Virginia's secession. Throughout the war, he served as a staff officer in the Army of Northern Virginia, coming into close contact with Robert E. Lee, Thomas J. "Stonewall" Jackson, William N. Pendleton, J. E. B. Stuart, and Turner Ashby. These last two he notably depicted in his novels as the epitome of Southern and particularly Virginian chivalry.

His 1863 *Life of Stonewall Jackson* was a resounding success. The volume was pirated by a New York publishing company and republished in London. In the United States, until it was banned, it was a bestseller. Republished in 1866 in New York as *Stonewall Jackson: A Military Biography*, it appears responsible for at least some of persistent myths about Jackson. Portions of the work appeared with some editing in Cooke's novel *Surry of Eagle's Nest* (1866). For the next decade, Cooke would rework and reincorporate historical and fictional characters from the Jackson biography and *Surry* in such works as *Wearing of the Gray* (1867), *Hilt to Hilt* (1869), *Hammer and Rapier* (1870), and a sequel to the events in *Surry* entitled *Mohun: The Last Days of Lee and His Paladins* (1869). After producing a 600-page *Life of General Robert E. Lee* the year after Lee's death in 1870, Cooke reverted to romance writing.

Apart from some slurs against foreigners in the Union armies, Cooke's portrayal of Yankees was typical in that the Union armies and their leaders are described as plodding and unimaginative. The depiction, however, is largely devoid of hatred. One of Surry's brothers even fights for the Union. Essentially wicked characters such as Fenwick (also in *Surry*) exhibit no sectional or personal loyalties, and gentlemanly bearing and courage such as that of Turner Ashby are depicted as ideal qualities that transcend defeat and death.

In *The Wearing of the Gray*, a volume of romanticized but ostensibly historical personal portraits, Cooke opined that the war was not so much an "official transaction" as it was a dramatic set of events. When he was accused of perpetuating "Confederate lies," Cooke noted in a letter to G. W. Bagby in 1879 that the so-called lies were both popular and financially rewarding. The charge that he wrote lies was unfair in any case: Cooke related legends and myths, sometimes drawing on material already in a Southern oral tradition. In some respects, his works were the descendants of the historical fiction of Sir Walter Scott, but his descriptions of Southern heroes as knightly figures met the emotional needs of readers North and South after the experience of a completely unsentimental and brutal modern war.

Cooke in his later years acknowledged that the school of realism evinced by William Dean Howells had brought sentimental fiction into disfavor, though he declined to complain, conceding "that fiction should faithfully reflect life, and…[I] am now too old to learn my trade anew." Cooke died on 27 September 1886, but evidence of his influence can be detected in the work of John Fox, Mary Johnston, and in such celebrated Southern classics as William Faulkner's *Sartoris*.

—*Wolfgang Hochbruck*

See also *Southern Literary Messenger*.

For further reading:
Bratton, Mary Jo. "John Esten Cooke and His 'Confederate Lies.'" *Southern Literary Journal* (1981).
Brumm, Ursula. "Definitions of Southern Identity in the Civil War Novels of John Esten Cooke" In *Rewriting the South* (1993).
Cooke, John Esten. *Surry of Eagle's Nest* (1866).
Davidson, James Wood. *The Living Writers of the South* (1869).
Moses, Montrose. *The Literature of the South* (1910).

COOKE, PHILIP ST. GEORGE
(1809–1895)
Union general

The youngest of three sons, Philip St. George Cooke was born at Leesburg, Virginia, to Dr. Stephen and Catherine Esten Cooke. He gained appointment as a plebe to West Point under the name of Philip St. George through a clerical error made when he entered the academy. Graduating in 1827, Cooke was commissioned second lieutenant in the 6th Infantry Regiment in Missouri. He served the next six years at various western stations and on expeditions into Indian country.

Cooke served in the Black Hawk War of 1832 and the

following year was commissioned first lieutenant of the newly organized 1st Dragoons. On 31 May 1835 while stationed at Fort Leavenworth he was promoted to captain. It was from this frontier post that Cook made many inroads into the West, including one in 1845, when his command reached the South Pass of the Rocky Mountains, covering a record distance of 2,200 miles in ninety-nine days.

During the Mexican-American War, while under the command of General Stephen Watts Kearny's Army of the West, Cooke participated in the conquest of New Mexico and California, an operation achieved by hard marching rather than by fighting. At Bent's Fort (Colorado) on the Arkansas River, Cooke was ordered to advance ahead of the main force on to Santa Fe, with the intention of negotiating its surrender. With only an escort, his action resulted in the collapse of Mexican resistance before any real negotiation. It is important to note that, although initially his escort consisted of only twelve men, reinforcements from the main force, including a battalion of mostly Mormon enlistments, had been proceeding forward to join him. Cooke was placed in command of this battalion, and with the field commission of lieutenant colonel he was sent forward into California. Although his initial impression of these troops was not favorable, when he was reassigned nine months later there was no doubt that his efforts had turned them into an efficient organization.

In the years before the Civil War, Cooke was again on the frontier with escort duty or duties that placed him in the occasional skirmish with Apache and Sioux Indians. Promotions in the regular army were to major of the 2d Dragoons in 1847, lieutenant colonel in 1853, and colonel in 1858. In 1857 to 1858 Cooke took part in the Utah expedition. He also wrote a treatise for a new system of cavalry tactics for the army that would serve as the foundation for training the Union cavalry during the war. His final duty before the war was that of an army observer of the Italian war from 1859 to 1860.

At the outbreak of the Civil War in 1861, Cooke's family was divided over the competing loyalties of state and Union. Two daughters and his only son John R. Cooke followed Virginia into the war, as did his son-in-law, James Ewell Brown "Jeb" Stuart, with both becoming general officers in the Confederate army. This breach in the family was to last for many years after the war, as it left only a daughter, her husband, and Cooke's wife, Rachel Hertzog Cooke, in adherence to the Union. As for Cooke, the military commands on both sides believed that he too would follow Virginia into the Confederacy, but his loyalty to the Union was unshakable, and when a letter from a Confederate general was secretly delivered to him in Washington, he promptly handed it over to the War Department.

Because of his prewar rank of colonel, Cooke was appointed a brigadier general in the regular army on 12 November 1861. However, despite his record and experience in an army that was short of officers at the start of the war, he was placed in the rear. Commanding a cavalry brigade within Washington, D.C., and a cavalry reserve division with the Army of the Potomac during the Peninsula campaign of 1862 was his only actual field service during the war. It can only be surmised that the considerations of his origins and the divided loyalties of his family took precedence over his abilities as an officer or the needs of the Union army. For the rest of the war, Cooke commanded the district of Baton Rouge for a time, was employed on court-martial duties, and later was general superintendent of recruiting for the regular army.

After the close of hostilities in 1865, Cooke was breveted major general in the regular army. Besides his duties on boards of promotion, retirement, and tactics, he commanded successively the departments of the Platte, the Cumberland, and the Lakes. After fifty-six years of service to the army, Cooke retired from active service in 1873. He died in Detroit, Michigan, on 20 March 1895 and was buried in Elmwood Cemetery.

Cooke, a person with a good sense of humor and a stern disciplinarian with a high sense of honor and sincere religious feeling, authored other books besides his *Cavalry Tactics*. He published *Scenes and Adventures in the Army* and *The Conquest of New Mexico and California*. The former is his autobiography, which provides a picture of the West from 1827, the period of his first commission, to 1845. The book is interspersed with reflections on subjects of every conceivable nature. The second work is considered the more important of the two because it is strictly a historical narrative largely made up of extracts from the diary he kept at the time. Philip St. George Cooke was the uncle of the novelist John Esten Cooke.

—*Frank E. Deserino*

See also Cavalry, U.S.A.; Cooke, John Esten; Mormons; Stuart, James E. B.; Stuart's Ride around McClellan.
For further reading:
Cooke, Philip St. George. *Cavalry Tactics: or, Regulations for the Instruction, Formations, and Movements of the Cavalry of the Army and Volunteers of the United States* (1862).
———. *The Conquest of New Mexico and California: An Historical and Personal Narrative* (1878).
———. *Scenes and Adventures in the Army; or, Romance of Military Life* (ca. 1857).
———. *William Henry Chase Whiting, and François Xavier Aubry. Exploring Southwestern Trails, 1846–1854* (1974).
Cullum, George W. *Biographical Register of the Officers and Graduates of the U.S. Military Academy at West Point, New York, from Its Establishment, in 1802, to 1890; With the Early History of the United States Military Academy* (1891; reprint, 1940).
Tyler, Daniel. *A Concise History of the Mormon Battalion in the Mexican War, 1846–1847* (1964).
U.S. War Department. *The War of the Rebellion: A Compilation of the Official Records of the Union and Confederate Armies* (1880–1901).

COOPER, SAMUEL
(1798–1876)
Adjutant general, U.S. Army and C.S. Army

Samuel Cooper was born in upstate New York, the younger son of Mary Horton Cooper and Samuel Cooper, a Revolutionary War officer. At age fourteen he followed his brother to the United States Military Academy and was graduated as a second lieutenant, light artillery, in 1815. He was posted to various garrisons in New England, Florida, Virginia, and New York, including a tour as aide to the general in chief, Alexander Macomb, from 1828 to 1836. Also in 1836, Cooper authored *A Concise System of Instructions and Regulations for the Militia and Volunteers of the United States*. During the next twenty-five years he was exclusively a staff officer, seeing field action only once, with William J. Worth in the Second Seminole Wars. For meritorious conduct in helping to conduct the Mexican-American War Cooper was breveted colonel. In July 1852 he was named adjutant general, remaining at that post until March 1861, when he resigned to offer his services to the Confederacy.

Although a Northerner by birth, Cooper was married in 1827 to Sarah Maria Mason, descendant of a prominent Virginia family and the sister of United States Senator and Confederate diplomat James M. Mason. (Another Mason sibling was married to Robert E. Lee's brother Sidney S. Lee.) By marriage, therefore, Cooper had acquired considerable property in Fairfax County, Virginia. Additionally, he had worked closely with, and had become an ally and confidant of, Jefferson Davis, secretary of war in the Franklin Pierce administration (1853–1857). As president of the Confederate States in 1861, Davis immediately named Cooper adjutant and inspector general, describing his old friend as "a man as pure in heart as he was sound in judgment." Davis certainly valued Cooper's counsel and experience, as well as his "high literary culture." In 1877 the ex-president testified that "I never, in four years of constant consultation, saw Cooper manifest prejudice, or knew him to seek favors for a friend, or to withhold what was just from one to whom he bore reverse relations. This rare virtue—this supremacy of judgment over feeling—impressed me as being so exceptional, that I have often mentioned it."

In June 1861 Cooper was confirmed at the rank of senior general in Confederate service. His was the controlling hand in the administration of the fledgling army and his vast knowledge of military protocol, procedures, and personnel was invaluable. Prized by his superiors, the secretaries of war, Cooper was sometimes criticized for his legalistic rulings and slowness in rendering decisions, but all admired his uniform dignity and courtesy. Although he did not wield much influence in formulating strategy, he remained the Confederacy's consummate bureaucrat, even after the government was forced to flee Richmond in April 1865. He took his duties seriously to the end, turning over the vast archives of the Confederate War Department to Union authorities, thereby saving them for future generations. At the age of sixty-seven, having rendered five decades of distinguished military service, he retired to his ruined estate, dying there impoverished and all but forgotten.

—*Lynda Lasswell Crist*

See also Army Organization C.S.A.; Davis, Jefferson; Strategy, C.S.A.

For further reading:
Davis, Jefferson. *Rise and Fall of the Confederate Government* (1881).
Gow, June I. "Theory and Practice in Confederate Military Administration." *Military Affairs* (1975).
Jones, Archer. *Confederate Strategy from Shiloh to Vicksburg* (1961).
Jones, J. B. *A Rebel War Clerk's Diary at the Confederate States Captial* (1866).
Lee, Fitzhugh. "Sketch of the Late General S. Cooper." *Southern Historical Society Papers* (1877).
Younger, Edward, ed. *Inside the Confederate Government: The Diary of Robert Garlick Hill Kean* (1957; reprint, 1974).

COOPERATIONISTS

In the winter of 1860–1861, cooperationist was the label applied to Southerners who opposed immediate secession from the Union. Cooperationists favored coordinated action between the Southern states, calling for a Southern convention to resolve the issue of secession in the aftermath of Lincoln's election. The cooperationists were a complex and shifting coalition of politicians who sometimes differed on fundamental goals. While some leaders of the cooperation movement viewed it as the best way to achieve a South unified behind secession, others used the idea of cooperationism as a tactic to slow, or perhaps end, the secession movement in the South. During the secession winter of 1860–1861, cooperationists were generally stronger in the upcountry than in the plantation districts, and cooperationist leaders were more likely to be Whigs than Democrats.

In the lower Southern states, a significant minority of whites wished for some sort of cooperative action preceding secession to ensure unity among at least the Deep-South states. Of the seven Deep-South states that led secession before Fort Sumter, only South Carolina lacked a significant cooperationist opposition to immediate state secession. But the cooperationists disagreed among themselves. Some supported cooperative secession and argued that a united South could present a stronger united front if it acted in concert, rather than as individual states. For them, the disagreement with immediate secessionists was over tactics, not on the ultimate goal of Southern independence.

Other, more moderate cooperationists wished to

present some sort of ultimatum to the North. They demanded a convention of Southern states to draw up a list of demands to present to the incoming Lincoln administration, including protection of slavery in the territories, enforcement of the Fugitive Slave Law, and guarantee for slavery in the District of Columbia. If the Republicans rejected these demands, then a unified South could secede. Since Lincoln seemed unlikely to agree to these concessions and most Southerners did not trust him in any case, this position commanded little support in the secession conventions in the winter of 1860–1861.

The most conservative group of cooperationists could be described as conditional Unionists. They asked Southerners to give Lincoln a chance to prove that his intentions were moderate. Only if the president committed an "overt act" against slavery should the South resort to secession. While the ranks of the conditional Unionists included prominent men such as Georgia's Alexander Stephens, the future vice president of the Confederacy, they were disorganized in their efforts to stop immediate secession and failed to check the passions unleashed by the election of Lincoln. Cooperationists such as Stephens and the Alabama leader Jeremiah Clemens believed that secession would produce a long and bloody war. A small number of these cooperationists, including Clemens, voiced doubts about whether secession was constitutional.

Cooperationists exhibited considerable strength in all of the initial Confederate states except South Carolina and Texas, polling at least 40 percent in the election of delegates to secession conventions in Georgia, Alabama, Florida, Louisiana, and Mississippi. Nevertheless, when immediate secessionists carried the secession conventions, dissension was muted. A few cooperationists demanded popular referenda on secession, but, of the original seven Confederate states, only Texas held such an election. With very few exceptions, cooperationist leaders pledged their loyalty to the new Confederacy.

The election of delegates to the secession conventions seemed to confirm the fear held by some secessionists that non-slaveholding whites had little stake in a contest for the freedom of planters to own slaves. In many states, particularly Alabama, a split emerged between upcountry districts, which supported cooperationist delegates, and plantation-belt counties, which elected immediate secessionists. While cooperationism did not necessarily mean outright Unionism, the fact that districts that held few slaves supported cooperationists worried leaders who favored immediate secession. These men consciously worked to bring non-slaveholders into the secessionist fold, and in 1861 they experienced a remarkable degree of success in using the issues of protecting state sovereignty and constitutional liberties to win over non-slaveholders.

—*Wallace Hettle*

See also Stephens, Alexander Hamilton; Unionists.
For further reading:
Barney, William. *The Secessionist Impulse* (1974).
Freehling, William, and Craig Simpson, eds. *Secession Debated: Georgia's Showdown in 1860* (1992).
Johnson, Michael P. *Toward a Patriarchal Republic: The Secession of Georgia* (1977).
McPherson, James M. *Battle Cry of Freedom: The Civil War Era* (1988).
Potter, David M. *The Impending Crisis, 1848–1861* (1976).
Thornton, J. Mills, III. *Politics and Power in a Slave Society: Alabama, 1800–1860* (1978).

COPPERHEADS

The term Copperhead was used in a pejorative sense during the Civil War to discredit Democratic opponents of the Lincoln administration and the war. Republicans charged that Democratic dissenters with their attacks on the Union war effort were like venomous copperhead snakes. To gain partisan advantage at the polls, Republicans claimed that the Democratic Party constituted a disloyal opposition whose antiwar policies constituted a "civil war within a civil war." Throughout the war, administration officials, Union army officers, and congressional Republicans linked leading opposition Democrats to alleged secret societies formed in the North to aid the Confederacy and disrupt the Union war effort. These secret societies included the Knights of the Golden Circle, the Order of American Knights, and the Sons of Liberty. Complete with accounts of elaborate rituals, the existence of secret societies was largely the creation of Republican politicians to gain partisan advantage at the polls. The stereotype of Democratic disloyalty during the war allowed many Republican politicians to "wave the bloody shirt" on the campaign trail after the war.

Although secret societies did exist and some prominent Democratic political figures did have connections with them, most historians dismiss the notion of the Democratic Party as a disloyal opposition as exaggerated and misleading. Copperheads, in most cases, were simply Democrats who had serious questions about the way the war was being waged and the impact that the war was having on Northern society. Steeped in Jacksonian ideology that stressed states' rights, limited government, and antimonopolistic ideas, Copperheads were conservative, negrophobic, and fiercely independent.

While the firing on Fort Sumter temporarily united Democrats and Republicans in putting down secession, as the war dragged on, the action of Lincoln and the Republican-dominated Congress convinced many Democrats that their way of life was being threatened. In the lower Midwest, the closing of the Mississippi River forced numerous farmers to rely on railroad transportation to get their products to market. A rapid increase in railroad rates led to the charge that eastern capitalists were using the war to exploit the agrarian interests of the Northwest. Lincoln's conscription, the arrest and imprisonment of Democratic critics, and suspension of the writ of habeas corpus led to the charge that the war was superseding and circumventing the Constitution. Democratic critics charged that President Lincoln was a tyrant who trampled the Constitution in his effort to subdue the South.

Probably the greatest single issue prompting the rise of Copperheadism was the Republican policy on slavery, culminating in Lincoln's preliminary Emancipation Proclamation of 23 September 1862. Fiercely antiblack, many Democrats charged that their support for the war was compromised by fighting to abolish the institution of slavery. Claiming that emancipation was unconstitutional, Copperheads argued that it would have pernicious effects on Northern society. Charging that miscegenation would result, Copperheads played upon racial prejudices in numerous Civil War elections, sometimes very skillfully. Spurning Republican measures on race as too "radical," Copperheads coined the phrase "The Constitution as it is, the Union as it was, and the niggers where they are" to qualify their support for the war.

Copperheadism was also strong among certain ethnic groups such as German-Americans and Irish-Americans. Distrusting the Republican Party because of its previous connections with the Know-Nothings, many of these groups were wary of a Republican-dominated national government, associating Republican rule with New England puritan fanaticism. Ethnic opposition to the war expressed itself in antidraft violence, most prominently in the New York City draft riots of July 1863.

Although Copperheads emerged in every Northern state, there were several figures who provided key leadership. The most prominent Northern Copperhead was undoubtedly Ohio congressman Clement L. Vallandigham, who was arrested in 1863 for denouncing administration policies and banished to the Confederacy. Returning to Ohio in the summer of 1863, Vallandigham waged an unsuccessful campaign for governor of Ohio. Other prominent Copperhead political leaders included William A. Richardson of Illinois, Edward G. Ryan of Wisconsin, Samuel S. Cox and Alexander Long of Ohio, Daniel W. Voorhees of Indiana, Fernando Wood of New York, and George Woodward of Pennsylvania. A number of journalists, too, played important roles in fostering Democratic dissent against Republican war policies. Prominent Copperhead newspaper editors included Charles H. Lanphier, editor of the *Illinois State Register* (Springfield), Marcus Mills "Brick" Pomeroy, editor of the Lacrosse (Wisconsin) *Democratic*, Samuel Medary, editor of the *Crisis* (Columbus, Ohio), and Dennis Mahoney, the feisty editor of the Dubuque (Iowa) *Herald* whose criticism of the administration led to his arrest and imprisonment in Washington for a time.

The appeal of Northern Copperheadism was closely tied to Union war fortunes. Copperheadism gained widespread support in the aftermath of the preliminary Emancipation Proclamation, leading to substantial Democratic gains in the election of 1862. The disastrous defeats of the Army of Potomac at Fredericksburg in December 1862 and at Chancellorsville in May 1863 led to the so-called high tide of Copperheadism in the summer of 1863. Conversely, Union victories at Gettysburg and Vicksburg in July 1863 quelled the rise of Copperhead support and led to the eventual defeat of Copperhead gubernatorial candidates Clement Vallandigham in Ohio and George Woodward in Pennsylvania. The Union military situation in the summer of 1864 led to a temporary revitalization of Northern Copperheadism. Peace advocates within the Democratic Party dominated the committee that drafted the party's platform, adopting a plank that denounced the war as a failure. However, two prominent factors conspired to defeat the Copperheads. First, Democratic presidential candidate General George B. McClellan repudiated the peace plank. Second, the improving Union military situation—particularly with the fall of Atlanta—made Union military fortunes seem much more promising. The triumph of the Republican Party in the 1864 elections and the victory of Union arms in April 1865 also signified the triumph of Republican ideas on government, economics, and race over the conservative, individualistic, agrarian ideology of the Copperheads.

—*Bruce Tap*

See also American Party; Cox, Samuel S.; Knights of the Golden Circle; New York City Draft Riots; Order of American Knights; Sons of Liberty; Vallandigham, Clement L.; Wood, Fernando; Woodward, George W.

For further reading:
Curry, Richard O. "Copperheadism and Continuity: The Anatomy of a Stereotype." *Journal of Negro History* (1972).
Klement, Frank L. *The Copperheads in the Middle West* (1972).
———. *Dark Lanterns: Secret Political Societies, Conspiracies, and Treason Trials in the Civil War* (1984).
Silbey, Joel H. *"A Respectable Minority": The Democratic Party in the Civil War Era, 1860–1868* (1977).

CORINTH, BATTLE OF
(3–4 October 1862)

In late summer of 1862, Corinth, Mississippi, with its rail crossing of the Memphis & Charleston and Mobile & Ohio lines, remained the focal point for both Federal and Confederate forces in the Western theater. Shortly after the battle of Iuka, Mississippi, on 19 September 1862, Confederate generals Earl Van Dorn and Sterling Price met to discuss a joint attack upon Corinth. The two generals decided to combine their forces, with Van Dorn being the senior commander;

march their 22,000 men northward to Pocahontas, Tennessee; and make Federal general William S. Rosecrans believe they were going to attack Bolivar, Tennessee. They wanted to make a surprise attack on Corinth before Rosecrans could assemble troops from outlying areas.

Meanwhile, Federal general Ulysses S. Grant had moved his headquarters from Corinth to Jackson, Tennessee, leaving Rosecrans in total control of the railroad town. Rosecrans continued building the city's inner defenses. He posted troops in outlying areas, but close enough for their recall in case of necessity. Receiving contradictory intelligence, Rosecrans was not sure whether the Confederates would attack Bolivar or Corinth. He was confident in the formidability of his defensive works around Corinth and doubted that the enemy would attack troops securely placed behind these lines. Rosecrans believed that if the enemy forces did not strike the other cities, they would attempt to force the Federals away from the works at Corinth to draw the battle into the "open country" around the city. Rosecrans prepared to defend Corinth. He positioned three of his divisions: General Thomas McKean's on the right; General Thomas Davies in the center; and General Charles Hamilton on the right midway between the inner fortifications and the old Beauregard line, breastworks Beauregard had built in the spring during the seige of the city. A fourth division, commanded by General David Stanley, was held in reserve.

On the morning of 3 October 1862, after marching ten miles from Chewalla to Corinth, Van Dorn positioned his three divisions for the attack on Rosecrans and his 23,000 men in Corinth. General Mansfield Lovell's division was on the right; Price's Army of the West, on the left. They had to traverse felled timber and the Beauregard line located about two miles from Corinth. Lovell's division advanced upon a ridge outside the city near the Memphis & Charleston railroad line. Once the Confederates reached the summit, the Federal soldiers, under the leadership of General John McArthur from McKean's division, fled down the east side of the hill to Battery F, leaving a 24-pound Parrot gun, the "Lady Richardson."

About the same time this action was taking place, Brigadier Generals Dabney H. Maury and Louis Hébert, under a hail of rifle and cannon fire, slowly advanced through the fallen timber and reached the open ground inside the Beauregard line. The outnumbered Federals retreated slowly. After midday, Price called a break, because of the intense heat and the soldiers' lack of water.

Around 3:00 P.M., the Federals, under Davies, made a stand on the "White House" ridge about a mile from the railroad intersection. The Confederates took the ridge and were poised to capture the city, and the Federals retreated behind Batteries Robinett and Williams. Although Van Dorn wanted to pursue, Price, realizing

that his men were exhausted, insisted that they wait until the morning. During the night, both commanders repositioned their forces.

The next morning, Maury's artillery began shelling the city at around 4:00 A.M. Most rounds passed over the heads of the waiting Federals. At dawn Batteries Robinett, Williams, and Phillips bombarded the Confederates, who ceased firing.

Hébert, who should have begun his advance after Maury's bombardment, reported sick. Price assigned the Confederate left to General Martin Green, who was confused about what action he should take. An hour later, two of Green's brigades charged Battery Powell and began fighting their way to the railroad. They engaged the Federals in hand-to-hand, house-to-house combat within the city. The heaviest fighting took place near the Tishomingo Hotel.

Simultaneously, Maury's men became engaged in fierce battle at Battery Robinett. Despite grape and canister raining down upon them, Confederate troops led by Colonel William P. Rogers made three assaults on the battery. Rogers, whose horse had been shot from under him, grabbed his regimental flag from the fallen color bearer and climbed to the top of the parapet. He was shot and fell backward into the ditch. The Confederates could only retreat.

At the crossroads, the Federals pushed the scattered and exhausted Confederates out of the city. Meanwhile, Lovell, on the Confederate right, did not advance. Without his support, the Confederate attack could not be successful. The second day of battle was over by 1:00 P.M. Rosecrans reported Federal losses at 315 killed, 1,812 wounded, and 232 taken prisoner or missing. Confederate losses were 1,423 killed, 5,692 wounded, and 2,268 taken prisoner.

—*Kristy Armstrong White*

See also Corinth, Mississippi; Corinth, Siege of; Lovell, Mansfield; Maury, Dabney Herndon; Price, Sterling; Rosecrans, William S.; Van Dorn, Earl.

For further reading:

Cockrell, Monroe F., ed. *The Lost Account of the Battle of Corinth and the Court Martial of General Earl Van Dorn* (1955).
Cozzens, Peter. *The Darkest Days of the War: The Battles of Iuka and Corinth* (1997).
Rogers, Margaret G. *Civil War Corinth, 1861–1865* (1989).
Rosecrans, William. "The Battle of Corinth." In *Battles and Leaders of the Civil War* (1887).

CORINTH, MISSISSIPPI

Corinth, located in the northeast portion of Mississippi, was a young town when the Civil War entered its confines. In 1854 the leaders of Tishomingo County made a momentous decision. They invited the Mobile & Ohio and Memphis & Charleston rail companies to run lines through the county. The next year, when surveys were completed, it was determined that the lines would cross at a right angle on a section of property belonging to William Lasley. A town quickly emerged and was named Cross City. Only a few months later, the editor of the local newspaper decided that "Cross City" did not befit the emerging city. The name was changed to Corinth.

Corinth flourished throughout the remainder of the 1850s, but with the election of Abraham Lincoln and Mississippi's secession, war was close at hand. Many men from Tishomingo County served in the Confederacy and, as early as 1861, Corinth served as an assembly point for Confederate soldiers traveling by rail to various points in Florida, Alabama, Kentucky, and Virginia.

In the spring of 1862, Corinth became the focal point in the Civil War's Western theater. Both Northern and Southern leaders recognized the necessity of holding the city because of its valuable rail crossings. Corinth was also in proximity to ports on the Tennessee River, including Hamburg, Eastport, and Pittsburg Landing. Whoever controlled Corinth held an important logistical key to the entire lower Mississippi Valley.

The fall of Forts Henry and Donelson in February 1862 began a series of events leading to the Federal and Confederate advances on Corinth. The Confederates, under the leadership of General Albert S. Johnston, saw their trans-Appalachian defense line broken with the capture of these forts by Union general Ulysses S. Grant. They fell back on Corinth as the new anchor of their defense of the Lower South.

Federal general Henry W. Halleck set his sights on the same target. Early April 1862, the Federal army under Ulysses S. Grant camped at Pittsburg Landing, Tennessee, twenty-two miles northeast of Corinth. Johnston decided to take the offensive to prevent the massing of Federal forces, and he made a surprise attack upon the encamped Federal soldiers on the banks of the Tennessee River. Although the Confederates made a strong showing on the first day of the battle of Shiloh, they experienced a terrible loss when Johnston was killed. Taking his place as commander, General P. G. T. Beauregard immediately halted the attack late in the first day. Meanwhile, Grant received reinforcements, and on the second day of battle, the massed Federal troops pushed Beauregard off the battlefield. The Confederate army fell back toward Corinth.

While the Confederates were caring for their sick and wounded and improving the system of fortifications in Corinth, Halleck arrived at Shiloh, called for reinforcements, and began a march on the city. Because it entrenched every day, the Federal army took more than a month to travel the twenty-two miles from Shiloh to Corinth. Meanwhile, Beauregard knew that the Federal army was closing in on Corinth. He devised a plan to evacuate the city. By 30 May, as the Confederates were making their way southward on the Mobile & Ohio rail-road, the Federals marched into an empty city, thus beginning the occupation of Corinth.

The Confederate army, after the evacuation of Corinth, underwent significant change. They set up headquarters in Tupelo, where Beauregard suddenly absented himself because of illness. However, he failed to ask permission from his superiors to leave, and General Braxton Bragg was named to succeed him in command. By the middle of June, Bragg decided to move the bulk of his army toward Chattanooga for an invasion of Tennessee and Kentucky. The remaining Confederate forces in Mississippi were left under the commands of Generals Earl Van Dorn and Sterling Price.

It would not be until the fall of 1862 that the area again experienced fierce battles. In late September, Rosecrans engaged Price at Iuka, a small town on the Memphis & Charleston line twenty miles east of Corinth. Rosecrans was able to drive Price to the southwest of Iuka, where he joined forces with Van Dorn to make a combined attack on Corinth on 3 October. The Confederates made a two-day attack against the strongly fortified city, but could not take possession. They had no choice but to retreat.

The closely fought battles of Iuka and Corinth significantly affected both the Federal and Confederate armies. They were the last major Confederate offensive in north Mississippi. Likewise, victories in these battles enabled Grant to turn his attention toward Vicksburg. Because of the Confederate failure to take control in the Western theater of the war (and Lee's failure at the battle of Antietam), Confederate politicians lost all hope of receiving diplomatic recognition as an independent country from European leaders. Moreover, these battles seriously affected the careers of several officers. Van Dorn's failure at Corinth ruined his chances of ever leading an army again. On the contrary, Rosecrans gained much from his victories. He received higher rank and replaced General Don Carlos Buell as commander of the Army of the Cumberland.

Military activity in Corinth, however, did not end in 1862. Although the Federal army remained strongly ensconced in the area, many skirmishes took place between them and the Confederates throughout 1863. When the Federal army marched to Mobile, Alabama, in January 1864, the Confederate infantry and its artillery also evacuated the state, leaving its defenses in the hands of Confederate cavalry and bands of guerrillas. Confederate general Nathan Bedford Forrest, commander of the cavalry in northeast Mississippi, began repairing the Mobile & Ohio and Memphis & Charleston Railroads to strengthen Confederate communications and supply lines.

During early 1865, much skirmishing occurred in the area because many Federals spent the winter camped at Eastport along the Tennessee River. Finally, on 4 May 1865, the Civil War in Mississippi ended when

The battle of Corinth, 4 October 1862, from a Currier & Ives lithograph (*Library of Congess*)

Confederate general Richard Taylor surrendered to Federal general Edward S. Canby.

—*Kristy Armstrong White*

See also Corinth, Battle of; Corinth, Siege of; Mississippi.
For further reading:
Alcorn County Historical Association. *The History of Alcorn County Mississippi* (1983).
Cozzens, Peter. *The Darkest Days of the War: The Battles of Iuka and Corinth* (1997).
Rogers, Margaret G. *Civil War Corinth, 1861–1865* (1989).

CORINTH, SIEGE OF
(30 April–30 May 1862)

The Confederate army, commanded by General P. G. T. Beauregard after the death of General Albert Sidney Johnston at the battle of Shiloh, returned to Corinth, Mississippi. More than ever, Confederate leaders realized the significance of holding Corinth and its rail crossing, which afforded the army with reinforcements and supplies. Beauregard said that if he lost the city, he would lose the entire cause. Anticipating Federal pursuit, Beauregard ordered the construction of breastworks on the east and north sides of Corinth. Rifle pits were built to guard the roads from Shiloh that crossed the breastworks. Beauregard sent brigades to scout outlying areas.

Meanwhile, Federal general Henry W. Halleck, commander of the Western Department, arrived at Shiloh on 11 April 1862 and appointed General Ulysses S. Grant his second-in-command and gave leadership of the Army of the Tennessee to General George H. Thomas. Grant, though stripped of his army, was still the commander of the District of West Tennessee. With the Army of the Tennessee, General Don Carlos Buell's Army of the Ohio waited at Shiloh until the Army of the Mississippi under General John Pope could join them. On 30 April 1862, Halleck with three armies consisting of 120,000 men, the largest military force ever assembled in the United States, began the twenty-two–mile trek southward to Corinth. Despite the size of his force, Halleck worried about another surprise attack and kept his army compact, entrenched daily, and ordered his commanders to avoid general engagements. However, almost thirty skirmishes occurred during the advance, the most notable of these being at Farmington, the Russell house, and the Serratt house—all located within five miles of the Beauregard line.

On 25 May 1862, Beauregard conferred with his generals. Knowing that the Federal army was closing in on Corinth, he pointed out their lack of siege guns. Although General Earl Van Dorn's Army of the Trans-Mississippi with its seasoned troops had reinforced Beauregard, the army reported only 53,000 effectives. Moreover, the men remained weak from losses at Shiloh and from illnesses caused by poor food and inadequate sources of clean water in the Corinth area. Outnumbered two-to-one, Beauregard made the decision to save the Confederate army by evacuating the city as quickly and stealthily as possible because he feared that, if the Confederates waited any longer, they would either have to surrender or retreat under more inopportune circumstances.

Beauregard then executed a clever plan. A few days before 30 May 1862, soldiers replaced light artillery with "Quaker guns," logs painted black to give the appearance of real artillery. Trains moving southward took the sick, the wounded, and supplies toward safety. When the empty cars returned, Beauregard had the soldiers cheer as though they were welcoming reinforcements. He even had the men cook three days' rations as if they were preparing for battle. It was not until 29 May 1862 that many soldiers realized they were actually leaving town, not marching off to a new fight. Early on the morning of 30 May 1862, a detail burned or destroyed army stores and provisions that they had been unable to take with them. The Confederates hastily completed the evacuation.

Later that day, Halleck's armies marched into a deserted town. He ordered only a limited pursuit of the Confederate army. Halleck's purpose was to hold Corinth rather than bring on a full-fledged battle. Like many of his West Point counterparts, Halleck, a student of Swiss military strategist Antoine Henri Jomini, used the common-sense principles of Jominian theory to guide his actions. He believed that the capture of geographic location was more important that destroying the enemy. Within weeks, Halleck dispersed his armies throughout west Tennessee and north Mississippi, leaving only four divisions around Corinth to guard the railroad.

—*Kristy Armstrong White*

See also Corinth, Battle of; Corinth, Mississippi; Halleck, Henry W.; Mississippi.

For further reading:

Bettersworth, John K. *Mississippi: A History* (1959).
Cozzens, Peter. *The Darkest Days of the War: The Battles of Iuka and Corinth* (1997).
Force, Manning Ferguson. *From Fort Henry to Corinth* (1881; reprint, 1992).
Rogers, Margaret G. *Civil War Corinth, 1861–1865* (1989).

CORSE, JOHN MURRAY
(1835–1893)
Union general

Born at Pittsburgh, Pennsylvania, on 27 April 1835, John Murray Corse was the son of John Lockwood and Sarah Murray Corse. In 1842, the Corse family moved to Burlington, the capital of Iowa Territory, where John L. Corse owned a book and stationery store and served as mayor for six terms. John Murray Corse attended West Point from 1853 to 1855, quitting to become his father's business partner and read law. After he was admitted to the bar, Corse immersed himself in politics and was the Democratic nominee for Iowa secretary of state in 1860, losing the election.

On 13 July 1861, he was appointed major of the 6th Iowa Infantry. Corse served as inspector general on Brigadier General John Pope's staff at New Madrid and Island No. 10. By 21 May 1862, Corse advanced to the rank of lieutenant colonel of the 6th Iowa, commanding his regiment and being recognized for bravery at Corinth in October 1862. He was promoted to colonel on 29 March 1863, commanding his regiment in Mississippi. Because of his leadership at Vicksburg, Corse was named brigadier general of volunteers on 11 August 1863. He gained the confidence of the highest officers and the respect of the men under his command. Known for his moral lectures to his troops, Corse also had the reputation of being consistent and dependable in action. During the last week of August, he commanded the 4th Brigade, 4th Division, XV Corps of the Army of the Tennessee. He then commanded the division in the battles around Chattanooga. Wounded at Missionary Ridge on 25 November 1863, he returned to Burlington to recover.

By February 1864, Corse was ready to return to action. He rejoined the army for the Atlanta campaign, acting as General William T. Sherman's inspector general until 26 July 1864, when he replaced Brigadier General Thomas W. Sweeny, who was arrested after hitting General Grenville Dodge. Corse led the 14th Division, XV Corps, during the battles for Atlanta. By early October, Sherman planned to place Union troops between Confederate forces under General John B. Hood and crucial railroads. From Kennesaw Mountain, he signaled Corse, who was at Rome, Georgia, to move troops to Allatoona Pass to protect supplies there. Corse loaded 2,000 troops aboard rail cars, and they reached Allatoona shortly after midnight on 5 October, joining 890 troops under the command of Lieutenant Colonel John Tourtellotte. Corse and Tourtellotte ordered their men into position in trenches and two redoubts along a ridge above the railroad. Corse prepared for combat in a redoubt west of the railroad, and Tourtellotte stayed in a fort that was east of the tracks.

Confederate major general Samuel Gibbs French's division attacked at 7:30 that morning. The Confederate troops outnumbered the Union forces three to two and quickly cut communications lines. As Confederate troops surrounded the fort that morning, French demanded an unconditional surrender within five minutes "to avoid a needless effusion of blood" and promised that the Federals would be treated well as prisoners of war. Corse responded that "we are prepared for the 'needless effusion of blood' whenever it is agreeable to you."

During the ensuing assault, Corse lost a third of his command, but resisted the enemy attack. At 1:00 P.M., a minié ball struck Corse's ear, stunning him. Half an hour later, French suddenly withdrew his forces because he acquired incorrect intelligence stating that Union relief forces would arrive soon. From Kennesaw Mountain, Sherman watched the battle smoke and signaled, "Hold on to Allatoona to the last. I will help you." He told subordinates, "If Corse is there, he will hold out; I know the man." One of his staff officers saw a signal flag message: "We hold out. Corse here." Corse maintained his command, signaling, "I am short of a cheekbone, and one ear, but am able to whip all hell yet." Actually, Corse, who was often overly dramatic, suffered only a scratch but wore a bandage to call attention to his wound.

Regimental reports printed tributes to Corse's leadership. Sherman later praised Corse and his "handsome defense" in a general order, stressing that the preservation of Allatoona was crucial for the success of the March to the Sea, and Corse was brevetted major general. Inspired by Corse's bravery, Reverend Philip P. Bliss wrote the hymn "Hold the Fort" that included the stanza, "Faith is strong in their Commander/Gallant General Corse." The popularity of this hymn in the North caused the defense of the Allatoona supply depots to become more famous than other significant battles.

Corse joined Sherman during the advance to Savannah and led his division in the Carolinas campaign. After the war, he commanded the District of Minnesota, but disliked frontier tasks of guarding settlers from Sioux attacks. Mustered out of service on 30 April 1866, Corse served as a collector of internal revenue in Chicago, Illinois, then was employed by railroad and bridge construction firms. He settled in Massachusetts, where he was active in politics as the chairman of the state Democratic Committee. During President Grover Cleveland's first administration, Corse was Boston's postmaster. Corse married twice: in 1856 to Ellen Edwards Prince and in 1882 to Frances McNeil, niece of Franklin Pierce. Corse accompanied Sherman's remains to St. Louis in 1891. Corse died on 27 April 1893, at Winchester, Massachusetts, and was buried in an elaborate brick chapel in Burlington's Aspen Grove Cemetery. A statue of Corse stands in that city's Crapo Park.

—*Elizabeth D. Schafer*

See also Georgia, Battle of; Atlanta Campaign.

For further reading:
Castel, Albert. *Decision in the West: The Atlanta Campaign of 1864* (1992).
Salter, William. "Major-General John M. Corse." *Annals of Iowa* (1895).
Sherman, William T. *Memoirs of General William T. Sherman* (1990).
Swisher, Jacob A. *Iowa in Times of War* (1943).
Wright, Henry H. *A History of the Sixth Iowa Infantry* (1923).

COTTON

In the decades before the Civil War, the development of the cotton industry fueled the economic growth and westward expansion of the American South and played a major role in the rapid growth of the American economy overall.

Until the 1790s, the South grew and exported a relatively small amount of cotton. Rice, tobacco, and sugar cane were the most lucrative crops raised in the American South. The growth of the British textile industry, however, fueled the demand for cotton. Southern planters grew high-quality Sea Islands cotton, a long-staple cotton, along the coasts of South Carolina and Georgia. The fiber of this long-staple cotton could be separated from the seeds with relative ease, but because the warmer interior climate was not conducive to the growth of Sea Islands cotton, this variety of cotton could only be grown within forty miles of the coast. As a result, the production of Sea Islands cotton was limited.

American planters also grew Uplands cotton, a short-staple variety. Although inferior in quality to the long-staple Sea Islands cotton, Uplands cotton could be grown successfully in the South's warm interior. Until the nineteenth century, however, planters raised very little short-staple cotton. The task of separating the fiber from the seeds was time consuming. A full day's labor from a skilled field hand yielded only a single pound of seed-free fiber. The amount of labor required to process Uplands cotton did not make its cultivation a profitable venture.

In 1792 the United States exported 140,000 pounds of cotton. By 1811, however, that number soared to 64 million pounds. This dramatic growth is attributed to the invention of the cotton gin by Northerner Eli Whitney in 1793. A relatively simple machine, the cotton gin allowed field hands to separate the fiber of short-staple cotton from its seeds quickly and easily. The cotton gin immediately increased output fifty times, and later models further improved on this. Short-staple cotton could be profitably grown throughout the South and growers could meet the British demand for cotton.

By 1840 the South produced 60 percent of the world's cotton. By the time the Civil War broke out, cotton comprised half of all American exports. European nations imported a great deal of Southern cotton, but Great Britain was the South's top consumer, purchasing half of all it produced to sustain its booming textile industry. In fact, 80 percent of England's supply of cotton came from the American South.

As it became apparent that secession from the Union lay on the South's horizon, Southerners realized the benefits that might be had from England's dependence on their cotton. Southerners believed that if the cotton trade were interrupted, textile manufacturers and indeed, Great Britain itself, would face economic hardship. In 1858 Senator James Hammond of South Carolina speculated that if Britain's supply of cotton were cut off, "Old England would topple headlong and carry the whole civilized world with her." Others held similar ideas and speculated that if sectional tensions led to civil war, England would intervene on the South's behalf rather than risk suffering the catastrophic economic loss that could result from the interruption of trade. As secession grew near, this concept of "King Cotton" diplomacy gave Southerners confidence that they would gain England's economic and military support if civil war erupted.

In 1861 after the Civil War began, the Confederacy, to facilitate recognition and support from England, placed an informal embargo on cotton exported to Europe. Later, Southern planters cut cotton production in order to cultivate more food crops. By 1863, desperate for cash to help finance the war, Southerners ended their embargo and attempted to resume cotton sales to Europe. By then, however, those Southern ports that had not been seized by Union forces were subject to Union naval blockades, which effectively prevented the South from exporting goods.

The South overestimated the power of King Cotton. Britain suffered little from the interruption of trade. The 1860 cotton crop had been especially bountiful, and when the Civil War began in 1861, British warehouses were overstocked with cotton purchased in the years before the war erupted. By late 1862 when stocks did dwindle, the British textile industry felt the pinch of the cotton shortage, but the growth of other industries helped offset the ill effects. Furthermore, England now turned increasingly to Egypt and India for supplies of cotton. The South had placed too much faith in King Cotton and England never intervened in the Civil War on the side of the Confederate States.

—*Alicia E. Rodriquez*

See also Diplomacy, C.S.A.; Financing, C.S.A.

For further reading:
Bruchey, Stuart. *Cotton and the Growth of the American Economy: 1790–1860* (1967).
Hummel, Jeffrey Rogers. *Emancipating Slaves, Enslaving Men: A History of the American Civil War* (1996).
McPherson, James. *Ordeal By Fire: The Civil War and Reconstruction* (1992).
Owsley, Frank L. *King Cotton Diplomacy: Foreign Relations of the Confederate States of America* (1959).

COUCH, DARIUS NASH
(1822–1897)
Union general

Born in Putnam County, New York, the son of Jonathan Couch, Darius Couch was educated locally before receiving an appointment to the U.S. Military Academy. He graduated thirteenth of fifty-nine from the distinguished class of 1846. He went to

Mexico with most of his classmates and served under Zachary Taylor in northern Mexico, earning commendation for his conduct at the battle of Buena Vista in February 1847.

After the Mexican-American War, Couch served at a variety of posts and took a year's leave from 1853 to 1854 to conduct a scientific mission for the Smithsonian in northern Mexico. He returned to duty for one year before resigning his commission to work for his wife's family in Taunton, Massachusetts.

At the outbreak of the Civil War, Couch raised a regiment of Massachusetts troops and became the colonel of the 7th Massachusetts. Couch and his regiment arrived in Washington just before the battle of First Bull Run, but took no part in the battle. In August 1861, Couch was promoted to brigadier general of volunteers. The promotion may have come because of the intercession of his West Point classmate, George McClellan, now commander of the Army of the Potomac.

During the Peninsula campaign of the following spring, Couch commanded the 1st Division of Erasmus Keyes's IV Corps. Couch fought with distinction at Williamsburg, Seven Pines, and Malvern Hill. After the end of the campaign in early July 1862, his health began to fail. He believed that he had contracted tropical diseases while in Mexico years before and that these illnesses had permanently weakened his system. He submitted his resignation to McClellan, but rather than accept the resignation, McClellan had his old friend promoted to major general.

Couch did not see action again until the Antietam campaign of September 1862. As part of VI Corps, Couch and his division were sent to Harper's Ferry to attempt the relief of the garrison there. On this expedition, Couch fought at Crampton's Gap in an attempt to reach Harper's Ferry. After the battle of Antietam, Couch took command of II Corps and was sent by McClellan to reoccupy Harper's Ferry.

After the dismissal of McClellan, Couch remained in command of II Corps, and he led the corps at Fredericksburg in December 1862. After the debacle at Fredericksburg, Couch opposed the appointment of Joseph Hooker to replace Ambrose Burnside. In the spring of 1863, as Hooker's plan unfolded for the coming campaign, Couch argued against it. The Union defeat at Chancellorsville confirmed Couch in his opinion of Hooker, and he asked to be relieved from command of II Corps and from association with the Army of the Potomac. He was immediately transferred to command of the Department of the Susquehanna, which consisted primarily of the Pennsylvania militia.

During the Gettysburg campaign, Couch cooperated with Governor Andrew Curtin and the new commander of the Army of the Potomac, George Gordon Meade, in mobilizing the Pennsylvania militia to guard railroad

Darius Couch (*Library of Congress*)

bridges and scout Confederate positions. After the battle, Couch worked diligently to round up Confederate stragglers. Meade commended him for his cooperation during the campaign.

During the fall of 1863, Couch used the militia to keep order in the wake of the unpopular draft levy for the state, and the following spring and summer he kept watch on the lower Shenandoah Valley in an attempt to prevent Confederate raids into Pennsylvania.

On 23 November 1864, Couch was transferred to the Army of the Cumberland. He commanded the 2d Division of the XXIII Corps under Major General John Schofield and fought at the battle of Nashville, where he escaped serious injury when his horse was shot from under him. In January 1865, he took temporary command of the corps when Schofield went to Louisville, Kentucky, to arrange transportation for the corps to Annapolis, Maryland.

In February 1865, Couch was given command of the 2d and 3d Divisions of the corps in preparation for a landing on the North Carolina coast. The expedition was planned to cooperate with William T. Sherman as he moved up through the Carolinas. From March through April 1865, XXIII Corps operated in the coastal area of

North Carolina, using New Bern as a base. The entire campaign took its toll on Couch's health, and again citing that as his reason, he submitted his resignation on 8 May 1865. It was accepted on 26 May.

Returning to Massachusetts, Couch's Democratic affiliation cost him the governor's election in 1866. After several business ventures in Massachusetts and Virginia, Couch settled in Norwalk, Connecticut. He held several positions in the state militia and died in Norwalk on 12 February 1897. He was taken back to Taunton, Massachusetts, for burial.

—*David S. Heidler and Jeanne T. Heidler*

See also Gettysburg, Battle of; Hooker, Joseph; McClellan, George.

For further reading:

Kennedy, Edward F. *Lieutenant Darius Nash Couch in the Mexican War* (1977).

Smith, William Farrus. *In Memorium of General Darius Nash Couch: Read Before the Association of the Graduates of the United States Military Academy, June 10, 1897* (1897).

COURTS, C.S.A.

Article III of the Confederate Constitution established the nation's judicial system, which, like that of the United States, would function within a prescribed jurisdiction along with extant state courts. The Confederacy's court system was manifested at the district level, with each state constituting one or more districts. The district courts were given jurisdiction embracing the equivalent of both U.S. district and circuit courts, an innovation that eliminated jurisdictional ambiguities caused by the redundancy of U.S. district and circuit court levels. The Confederacy also operated an admiralty court in Key West as well as territorial courts in Arizona and what was designated as Indian Country, the southern regions of present-day Oklahoma.

Texas, Virginia, Tennessee, and Arkansas were deemed either too large or their terrain too daunting to compose a single district, so, under an amendment of 21 May 1861, Congress was allowed to create more than one district in those states. The districts were subdivided into divisions. As finally formed, the system consisted of eighteen districts: Eastern Virginia, Western Virginia, North Carolina, South Carolina, Georgia, Florida, Alabama, Eastern Tennessee, Middle Tennessee, Western Tennessee, Mississippi, Missouri, Kentucky (unorganized), Louisiana, Eastern Arkansas, Western Arkansas, Eastern Texas, and Western Texas. District judges were appointed by the president and approved by Congress.

It is frequently asserted that the Confederacy never established a Supreme Court, yet the distinction should be made between the establishment of a high court and the actual physical formation of one. In fact, a Confederate Supreme Court was authorized by both the provisional and permanent Constitutions and was established by Congress in the Judiciary Act of 16 March 1861. Under this legislation, the Supreme Court was to hold an annual session in the capital, and its bench would consist of all district court judges, a majority of whom in assembly would form a quorum. The peculiarity of district judges acting as members of the Supreme Court was a contrivance of the Provisional Constitution that persisted in the Judiciary Act of 1861. Presumably such a practice would impart regularity and uniformity to the body of Confederate jurisprudence. By the summer of 1861, however, the vast expanse of the Confederacy stretching from Virginia to west Texas made the composition of the Supreme Court bench implausible from a geographical standpoint. District judges attending Supreme Court sessions would have left their regions unattended for lengthy periods as they traveled to and from Richmond and conducted the Court's business in between. For this reason, President Jefferson Davis signed a bill on 31 July 1861 to suspend the January 1862 session of the Supreme Court until Congress could reconstitute it under the permanent Constitution's more liberal instructions about its membership. The Court technically did not cease to exist under this legislation—its opening session was merely postponed—yet actually the Court had never physically existed at all, a fact that made its reorganization the subject of subsequent legislative initiatives to "establish" the Court.

The First Congress of the Confederacy did not address reconstituting the Court until March and April of 1862. The House bill died in the Judiciary Committee, and the Senate bill, which would have established an office of chief justice and three associate justices, was tabled. Again in September the Senate took up the matter and again tabled it. The 1863 debates on this matter saw opposition emerge from those unwilling to erect a central legal authority that might impinge on the states' legal sovereignty. Apprehension about who Jefferson Davis would appoint to its bench also undermined support for a Supreme Court. And finally, the personal hostility between the bill's sponsor, Judiciary Committee Chairman Benjamin H. Hill, and its principal opponent, William Lowndes Yancey, doomed the initiative in that session. Congress took up the matter again in 1864 and finally tabled it for the last time in March 1865. The plan was to take it up again in November 1865, but by then, the Confederacy had ceased to be. The establishment of a Confederate Supreme Court, like much else in the Southern republic, had foundered on political and personal conflicts within Congress.

The opinions of the district courts were never officially reported, a practice that continued the one established by the U.S. district courts before the war. Confederate district court decisions were infrequently published as pamphlets, but usually they appeared in the newspapers, where partial or inaccurate information went uncorrected.

The courts ruled on a wide range of matters as authorized under the Judiciary Act, including the sequestration of enemy alien property, criminal cases, petitions from conscripts either to release them from service or remand them to the military, prize cases, and cases pertinent to the constitutionality of law. In matters of sequestration, copyright, and patents, the district courts held exclusive jurisdiction, but they were mutual in jurisdiction with the state courts concerning the deportation or naturalization of aliens and cases of law and equity where the dispute equaled or exceeded $5,000 in potential judgment. In the absence of a Supreme Court, the district courts also served appellate functions, including those on writs of error and alleged violations of civil liberties, such as the denial of habeas corpus privileges.

State courts continued to function as they had before the war, with the only difference being that they acknowledged the Confederate States of America as the sovereign authority. When they were formally reported, state court opinions appeared in the official reports of the states, a record of normal civil proceedings mixed with actions initiated by Confederate authorities trying to enforce conscription and taxation.

When the war ended with Confederate defeat, this entire Southern judicial system became just another manifestation of rebellion and thus was regarded as illegitimate in the eyes of the U.S. government. As the Supreme Court would remark in the 1869 case of *Hickman v. Jones*, "they were as if they were not." Yet in an 1873 ruling in *Horn v. Lockhart*, the Court would declare that there was no reason to dispute the authoritative nature of either judicial or legislative decisions in the former Confederacy "where they were not hostile in their purpose or mode of enforcement to the authority of the National government." Accordingly, rulings by Confederate courts were given the same weight and authority as the customary acts of civil government insofar as they did not promote insurrection or abet war. The U.S. government, out of practical necessity, decided that although the Confederate courts had not officially existed, the substance and consequences of their rulings did.

—*David S. Heidler and Jeanne T. Heidler*

See also Benjamin, Judah P.; Civil Liberties, C.S.A.; Conscription, C.S.A.; Constitution, C.S.A.; Impressment.

For further reading:

Neely, Mark E., Jr. *Southern Rights: Political Prisoners and the Myth of Confederate Constitutionalism* (1999).
Robinson, William M., Jr. *Justice in Gray: A History of the Judicial System of the Confederate States of America* (1941).

COURTS, U.S.A.

Under Article III of the U.S. Constitution, a federal court system was established with the creation of the Supreme Court and the sanction for Congress to establish lower courts. The Judiciary Act of 1789 set the number of justices for the Supreme Court and three levels of a federal judicial structure. Each state would have a district court. Circuit courts would consist of a district judge and two justices of the Supreme Court, the latter of whom would act as itinerants traveling the circuit. Supreme Court justices complained about the rigors and distractions of circuit riding, but with the exception of a brief period after passage of the Judiciary Act of 1801, the regimen officially remained in place throughout the remainder of the 19th century. Thus, it was not until after the Civil War when the Judiciary Act of 1869 established a separate judicial cadre for the circuit courts that the justices enjoyed some relief from this chore, and they continued to ride the circuit off and on until 1891 with the passage of the Circuit Court of Appeals Act. Even so, Congress did not formally abolish the circuit chores of the justices until 1911.

The activities of federal courts during the Civil War were of peripheral importance, exceptions being a few prominent decisions at the Supreme Court level. Part of the reason for that lay in the extraordinary burdens the crisis of war placed on constitutional processes—burdens that were most expeditiously addressed by the political system and the military. Yet in the setting of the lower federal courts, the marginality of the judiciary resulted from procedural limitations as well. Those restrictions were long-standing, having been set by Congress at the birth of the republic. At the time of the Civil War, state courts still had the task of deciding contentious questions between state and federal law, and appeals arising from such decisions were made directly to the Supreme Court. The consequence was a general diminution of federal judicial presence and activity during the war, especially when Congress authorized the Lincoln administration to suspend the privilege of the writ of habeas corpus and establish military commissions. Such protections the judicial system was able to offer citizens detained and tried under these extraordinary conditions were rare and mostly ineffectual. In any event, the lower court referrals either to the president (as in the case of John Merryman) or to the high court (as in the case of Lambdin P. Milligan) point to the impotence of the lower courts during the exceptional crisis of the Civil War.

—*David S. Heidler and Jeanne T. Heidler*

See also Ex parte Merryman; Ex parte Milligan; Supreme Court, U.S.

COVERT ACTION, CONFEDERATE

Although the term covert action had not yet been invented, the Confederacy spent about $1.5 million in gold on projects that today could be characterized in those words. Basically, an action is covert whenever its perpetrator or inspiration is hidden, although the action itself, and its consequences, may not be concealed. To the Confederates, such activities were covered by the term secret service.

The use of gold for secret service purposes of all kinds was carefully controlled by Confederate president Jefferson Davis and his secretary of state, Judah Benjamin. Each project was personally approved by Davis, and Benjamin monitored its execution.

Attacked and blockaded by an enemy with vastly superior resources, the Confederates searched for new ways to frustrate that enemy and achieve their independence. Initially, their clandestine efforts were directed primarily at the collection of information, but they rapidly learned that diplomacy alone could not achieve their objectives abroad.

A major effort was undertaken to buy weapons, ships, and other equipment abroad. To facilitate this effort, the export firm of Fraser, Trenholm, and Company of Liverpool, England, was appointed as the financial agent of the Confederacy. Although much of the procurement work had to be done in a clandestine manner, and James D. Bulloch, the Confederate in charge of ship procurement in Britain, regarded it as secret service, it was hardly covert action in the modern sense. Part of the Confederate effort in Britain, however, was devoted to propaganda, and a newspaper, the *Index*, was established as a Confederate mouthpiece in England. These activities would fit the modern definition of covert action.

Another covert action project involved the appointment of Father John B. Bannon as Confederate agent in Ireland, charged with the mission of frustrating the Union campaign to recruit Irish men for the Union army. The Irish-born Father Bannon, a chaplain of Missouri troops in the Confederate army, was persuaded to undertake the mission in September 1863. Although he worked hard at his mission, he was not successful in stopping the flow of recruits to the North.

The development of the concept of covert action was stimulated by the writings of Bernard Janin Sage, a Louisiana planter, who had served on a merchant ship in his youth. Sage was interested in the promotion of privateering at sea, and from that beginning he progressed to the promotion of irregular warfare on land as well as sea. He has received little recognition for his efforts, but he gave an important impetus to thinking about covert action, as well as other kinds of irregular warfare.

The largest true Confederate covert action project began in June 1863, when General Robert E. Lee persuaded Confederate president Jefferson Davis that the will to fight of the Northern people was the true target of the Confederacy. Lee also pointed out that, in view of the disparity in resources, the North could not be defeated by action on the battlefield alone. The people of the North needed to be persuaded that victory on the battlefield was not worth the effort.

Davis decided that it would be necessary to launch a new and drastic campaign of action to influence the population of the North, and chose as the main target the defeat of Abraham Lincoln in the election of 1864. He persuaded the Confederate Congress to pass legislation authorizing this new campaign and to appropriate money to finance it. This was finally achieved on 15 February 1864, when the Confederate Congress appropriated $5 million for secret service involving sabotage and attacks on targets behind enemy lines, as well as efforts to support antiwar politicians at the ballot box.

After some delay in finding a suitable chief for the operation, Jacob Thompson of Mississippi, a former secretary of the interior during the administration of U.S. president Buchanan, was chosen. He was given $1 million in secret service gold and sent to Canada as Confederate commissioner in April 1864. He was accompanied by Clement C. Clay, who also held the title of commissioner and represented the Confederate War Department. As Thompson had the money, it was clear that he was the senior of the two.

Thompson set up his quarters in Toronto and proceeded to establish contact with a number of antiwar politicians in the North. Clay set up operations in St. Catharines, near Niagara, a central point from which one could move west to Windsor for access to Detroit and east to Montreal for access to New York and New England. Together these operatives created a staff made up of diverse elements, including Confederate personnel already in secret service such as P. C. Martin in Montreal and Larry MacDonald in Toronto, Confederate soldiers who had escaped from Union prison camps, and a number of pro-Confederate civilians, particularly from Kentucky. These provided a pool of talent from which to recruit needed personnel. A few additional military personnel, such as Captain Thomas C. Hines of General John Hunt Morgan's cavalry, were provided by the Confederacy as the need arose.

Another member of the Confederate team was George Nicholas Sanders of Kentucky and New York. He had been active in Democratic Party politics for years, and was friendly to the Radical Republican element in a number of the European monarchies. Sanders was particularly fond of the chaos theory, which held that the removal of a few key officials by capture or assassination would disrupt normal government and provide an opportunity for antigovernment groups to seize power.

The Confederate operation in Canada tried to induce pro-Confederate Copperheads in the North to revolt, first at the time of the Democratic Party's convention in Chicago in August, and then at the time of the election. They also sponsored raids and sabotage to prove to the people of the North that the Lincoln administration was incapable of protecting them. The most notable of these raids took place in October 1864 at St. Albans, Vermont, where the Confederates seized over $200,000 in U.S. currency.

The Confederate efforts, however, were not enough to overcome the effect of Northern victories on the battlefield, and Lincoln easily won reelection in November 1864.

In 1864 the Confederates launched a parallel operation to capture President Abraham Lincoln as a hostage. John Wilkes Booth was recruited to play a leading role in this effort, and in October 1864 he spent several days in Canada in consultation with Sanders. This operation, like the broader campaign, ended in failure, and Booth unilaterally resorted to assassination.

One Confederate operation never took place, but is notable for the amount of money involved. Early in the summer of 1864 dissident Poles, suffering under the rule of the Russian Tsar, offered to raise a brigade of Polish troops to fight for the Confederacy. Jefferson Davis approved the idea and $250,000 in secret service gold was earmarked for this purpose. The money was sent to Colin J. McCrae, Confederate financial agent in Europe, but Confederate fortunes on the battlefield turned for the worse with the fall of Atlanta to General William T. Sherman, and the Poles apparently cooled to the idea. McCrae reported in December 1864 that he had not been approached by the Poles, and that the money was still under his control. Presumably it was still unspent when the war ended in 1865.

After the war Judah Benjamin wrote to all Confederate agents abroad and requested that they turn in to him any secret service funds that they might have left over. How much was turned in is not known, but there were reports of Confederate money being available to defend Confederates tried for wartime activities.

The Confederate covert action effort suffered from a lack of uniform understanding of its objectives by the diverse personnel employed, and from their lack of experience in clandestine operations, paltry training, and loose organization and discipline. In spite of these difficulties, the efforts of the Confederates involved in covert action had a major effect on public opinion in the North. If Confederate fortunes on the battlefield had remained favorable, covert action might have helped the Confederacy achieve independence.

—*William A. Tidwell*

See also Benjamin, Judah P.; Bulloch, James D.; Clay, Clement C.; Hines, Thomas H.; St. Albans, Vermont, Raid; Thompson, Jacob.

For further reading:
Bakeless, John. *Spies of the Confederacy* (1970).
Kinchen, Oscar A. *Confederate Operations in Canada and the North* (1970).
Tidwell, William A. *April '65: Confederate Covert Action in the American Civil War* (1995).
Tidwell, William A., James O. Hall, and David Winfred Gaddy. *Come Retribution: The Confederate Secret Service and the Assassination of Abraham Lincoln* (1988).

COVERT OPERATIONS, U.S.A.

During the Civil War, the Lincoln administration employed covert operations to frustrate Confederate activities in Europe, influence domestic and foreign public opinion, and, in at least one instance, possibly meddle in crucial New England elections. Such activities can be distinguished from espionage or covert activity that served to advance military missions, such as the work of Andrews's Raiders or the Kilpatrick-Dahlgren Raid on Richmond in 1864. The ostensible instrument of secret government endeavors, the U.S. Secret Service, was established on 23 July 1860, under the authority of the Treasury Department, but its only defined duties were then as now protecting the president and protecting the integrity of the currency by tracking down counterfeiters. It would not have a designated chief until after the war. Detective Allan Pinkerton worked for the army, especially for George McClellan, and he is sometimes mistakenly considered to have been the representative of a more solidly established government agency than he actually was. Lafayette C. Baker operated under Edwin M. Stanton's War Department as the chief of detectives, and he conducted operations that were secretly authorized by the president and the secretary.

Truly covert operations, however, were beyond the scrutiny of Congress. They were always funded in irregular or private ways and that, along with their purpose, always required that the administration maintain a way to exercise plausible deniability. In this regard, such covert operations were distinguishable from those conducted by the Secret Service, although the degree to which they were distinguishable remains a source of debate. The very nature of clandestine activity continues to veil its details for historians as much as it did for contemporaries. Not until the end of the 1950s, with Edwin C. Fishel's accidental discovery of the operational files of the Army of the Potomac's Bureau of Military Information, could an authoritative account of Union military intelligence be assembled.

It is known that Secretary of State William H. Seward directed secret enterprises throughout the war. He arranged to have them funded by nondescript government appropriations or frequently by private sources. They were carried out in both foreign and domestic settings and involved a makeshift, but relatively sophisticated, network of agents and informants. In Europe, Henry Shelton Sanford directed covert efforts to sway popular sentiment away from the Confederacy and toward the Union by bribing journalists and subsidizing newspapers. In addition to such ideological projects, Sanford also tried to obstruct Confederate efforts to procure ships, arms, and financial assistance from private firms.

Seward's State Department provided Sanford with his cover by appointing him U.S. minister to Belgium, and under that designation he arrived in Paris in 1861. Soon, however, he was ranging the continent, eventually establishing contacts as far away as Spain, Italy, and Prussia. In London, he worked to counter the activities of Confederate purchasing agent James D. Bulloch, a man Sanford considered so menacing that he proposed contriving a way to have the resourceful Confederate arrested. Through a helpful contact at Scotland Yard, Sanford fashioned a web of agents all over England. These operatives reported on cargoes moving out of British ports and infiltrated factories to advise Sanford of manufacturing arrangements that might be tied to the Confederacy. His secret payroll included business officials who revealed the terms of Confederate contracts, British postal workers who provided him with regular reports about correspondence to Confederate agents, and telegraph operators who shunted Confederate messages to him.

It was expensive work, especially when Sanford aggressively moved to thwart Southern manufacturing contracts by outbidding Confederate emissaries. Money was either inconsistently available or in short supply, and although Seward placed a secret fund of a million dollars at Sanford's disposal, the diplomat-agent spent about $15,000 of his own money secretly advancing the cause of the Union. Subsidizing European newspapers and bribing individual journalists was such an expensive proposition that Seward occasionally balked at the price. Instead, he enlisted prominent Americans to travel abroad and use what influence they could to accomplish the propaganda war more frugally. In Paris, U.S. Consul General John Bigelow was one such operative. Bigelow's experience as editor of the *New York Evening Post* made him all the more effective in dealing with newsmen. New York Republican Thurlow Weed performed similar service in persuading British newspapers to support the Union cause, especially when helped by Sanford's slush fund. Seward also recruited clerics to the cause, dispatching Archbishop John Hughes and covering his $5,000 in expenses to perform a wide range of sensitive tasks. Hughes reportedly met privately with Napoleon III in addition to encouraging Irish immigration to replenish the ranks of the Union army. Episcopal bishop Charles McIlvaine performed comparable work among British Anglicans. Meanwhile, impromptu mass meetings that emphasized the detestable immorality of slavery were spurred among the British working class by a host of nondescript operatives whose specialty was staging spontaneity.

Propaganda efforts marked the bulk of domestic operations conducted by Seward and his agents. In addition to waging a campaign of disinformation by planting false stories with a friendly press, the administration used direct payment through bribes and the more subtle compensation of patronage to control unfriendly newspapers and contrary journalists. Thurlow Weed successfully convinced James Gordon Bennett to alter the antagonistic stance of his *New York Herald*, a mission apparently accomplished by the administration's offer to make Bennett's son a revenue agent. There was at least one plan seriously considered by Seward and Lincoln to suborn Confederate newspapers, and in the propaganda war within the Confederacy, the clergy was again enlisted. Methodist minister James F. Jaquess, who was also a colonel in the Union army, was apparently put into contact with the administration through his superior officer, Brigadier General James A. Garfield, with the view of having Jaquess use his contacts within the Southern branch of the church. It is not clear what Lincoln expected Jaquess to accomplish as he traveled throughout the South in 1863. Possibly he was to seek out peace sentiments within his Southern brethren, but he might have been attempting to sow discontent among Southern clergy. In any event, Lincoln several times remarked that the government could have no connection with the traveling minister and that Jaquess was placing himself in some peril in undertaking his journey, observations that suggest that some people in Washington deemed him a spy.

The Lincoln administration undertook some covert activity within the Union beyond that necessary to infiltrate Copperhead groups and foil subversive conspiracies, certainly a legitimate enterprise of the state. One instance possibly involved attempts to influence the important 1863 congressional elections in New Hampshire and Connecticut, where Peace Democrats mounted a stiff campaign playing on antiadministration sentiments. The actual operation is still shrouded in shadows, but it is evident that Thurlow Weed was commissioned by Seward to make sure that Republicans won these contests. Weed accordingly raised at least $15,000 from private sources in the New York business community. How he used the money is unclear, but the Peace Democrats were narrowly defeated in the February elections.

The Civil War is often described as straddling the line that separates the last of the old wars and the first of the modern ones. Yet, in the use of covert operations, the Lincoln administration did not break new ground so much as it followed a tradition established by the founders during the American Revolution. Lincoln, the canny westerner, and Seward, the wily New Yorker, certainly understood the compelling need of extralegal activity in the face of high national peril. In the extraordinary crisis of the Union, it was part of a guiding attitude that Lincoln described as necessary to disenthrall the government from the routines of ordinary functions. Then, he said, they would save their country.

—*David S. Heidler and Jeanne T. Heidler*

See also Baker, La Fayette Curry; Copperheads; Covert Action, Confederate; Espionage; Peace Democrats.

For further reading:

Fishel, Edwin C. *The Secret War for the Union* (1996).
Klement, Frank L. *Dark Lanterns: Secret Political Societies, Conspiracies, and Treason Trials in the Civil War* (1984).
Mogelever, Jacob. *Death to Traitors; the Story of General Lafayette C. Baker, Lincoln's Forgotten Secret Service Chief* (1960).
O'Toole, G. J. A. *Honorable Treachery: The History of U. S. Intelligence, Espionage, and Covert Action from the American Revolution to the CIA* (1991).
Richardson, Albert D. *The Secret Service, the Field, the Dungeon and the Escape* (1865).

COX, JACOB DOLSON
(1828–1900)
Union general, lawyer, politician, and educator

Jacob Dolson Cox was born on 27 October 1828 in Montreal, Canada, the son of Thedia Kenyon and Jacob Dolson Cox, Sr., a builder who was working in the United States at the time. The family, of German extraction, returned to New York City, where young Jacob was raised. He apprenticed himself to read law in 1842 but moved to Ohio in 1846 to prepare for a college degree and graduated from Oberlin College in 1851. In 1849 he married Helen Finney, the daughter of the Reverend Charles G. Finney, Oberlin's president; the couple raised eight children. Cox moved the family to Warren, Ohio, to work as a high school principal and superintendent, resumed his law studies part-time, and passed the Ohio bar examination in 1853.

Cox was surrounded by abolitionist sentiment in the Western Reserve, among his wife's family, and at Oberlin College. He supported the antislavery Whigs and Free Soil Party and in 1855 served as a delegate from Warren to the first Ohio Republican Party Convention in Columbus. He was elected to the Ohio Senate in 1859 and joined Senators James A. Garfield and James Monroe to form the "Radical Triumvirate" and worked with outgoing Governor Salmon P. Chase and new Governor William Dennison to promote legislation friendly to the Union. Cox and Garfield began the study of military science, especially the works of Jomini, and secured commissions as brigadier generals of the Ohio militia.

With the outbreak of war in April 1861, Cox became a brigadier general of Ohio Volunteers and served under George McClellan in a force that moved into what is now West Virginia through the route of the Kanawha River. In July 1861 Cox advanced his army first to Charleston, then to Gauley Bridge and fought Virginia troops under Henry Wise at Scary Creek. Throughout the winter of 1861–1862, Cox held the Kanawha Valley against repeated Confederate skirmishes. In the spring of 1862, Cox joined a Union advance into Virginia under General John C. Frémont, but Union reverses in the Shenandoah Valley stopped the offensive and forced Cox to retreat to fortified positions near Princeton in western Virginia.

Cox's troops, known as the Kanawha Division, traveled back to the Ohio River and from Parkersburg rushed to Washington, D.C., in August 1862 to take up defensive positions in forts around the capital. In September Cox's troops joined the Army of the Potomac's movement to South Mountain and fought at Monocacy Bridge. His troops fought at Antietam on the Union left at the stone bridge.

After Antietam, Cox returned to western Virginia to clear out remaining rebel positions and in the spring of 1863 joined Ambrose Burnside's campaign in East Tennessee. Cox commanded the 3d Division of the XXIII Corps in battles throughout the spring and summer of 1864 in north Georgia including Rocky Face, Resaca, New Hope Church, Kennesaw Mountain, Chattahoochee, Atlanta, Jonesboro, and Lovejoy.

Cox returned to Tennessee in November of 1864 to meet the threat of John Bell Hood's invasion. Cox's men protected the Union retreat from Pulaski, skirmished at Spring Hill, and were at the center of the furious fighting near the Carter House at the battle of Franklin. Cox and his division also saw action at the battle of Nashville in December. These engagements finally won him promotion to major general.

Cox spent the last months of the war fighting in North Carolina. His forces captured Fort Anderson, fought at Town Creek, and helped force Confederate forces out of Wilmington.

Cox moved up the coast to New Bern and set out to rebuild the railroad to Kingston so William Tecumseh Sherman's forces could be supplied when they reached Goldsboro. Cox's troops fought Bragg's forces near Kingston and occupied the town and then took Goldsboro and moved on Raleigh. Cox was in charge of western North Carolina after the surrender of Johnston and then was given command of the District of the Ohio to muster out and discharge the army.

Cox was nominated and elected governor of Ohio on the Republican ticket in 1865. But during the campaign the issue of black suffrage surfaced to split his party and undermine his effectiveness as governor. Cox had come to believe that the nation was not yet ready for equality of black and white, based on his observations during the Civil War. Cox believed in setting up a district for the freed people encompassing parts of several southeastern states. These views outraged his former Radical and abolitionist friends and supporters. He also tried to mediate between Andrew Johnson and his Radical critics, though Cox's sympathies clearly lay with Johnson. The suffrage question for African-Americans living in Ohio was also contentious during Cox's administration. Legislative gridlock caused by these divisions rendered his administration ineffective, and he lacked the support necessary for renomination in 1867.

Cox moved to Cincinnati to practice law after his term expired and then served as secretary of the interior

in the cabinet of President Ulysses S. Grant in 1869. Disgust at the corrupt practices of his party and administration led to Cox's resignation in 1870 and to his joining the Liberal Republicans in 1872. He moved to Toledo to assume the presidency of the Toledo, Wabash & Western Railroad in 1873 and was elected to Congress in 1876 as a reformer. When he chose not to run again in 1878, his political career was finished. He returned to Cincinnati as a lawyer and became dean of the Cincinnati Law School and president of the University of Cincinnati. He also served as a trustee of Oberlin College, where he retired in 1897 to write his memoirs. He died on 4 August 1900.

—Gregory R. Zieren

See also Atlanta Campaign; Franklin, Battle of.
For further reading:
Cox, Jacob Dolson. *Military Reminiscences of the Civil War* (1900).
Phillip, Hazel Spencer. *The Governors of Ohio* (1954).
Reid, Whitelaw. *Ohio in the War: Her Statesmen, Generals and Soldiers* (1868).
Roseboom, Eugene H. "The Civil War Era: 1850–1873." Vol. 4 of *The History of the State of Ohio* (1944).

COX, SAMUEL SULLIVAN
(1824–1889)
U.S. congressman

Born the son of Ezekiel Taylor Cox in Zanesville, Ohio, Samuel Sullivan Cox was educated at Ohio University and Brown University, from which he graduated in 1846. Cox, who had excelled in school, had a literary bent as well as a love of travel. He wrote a book about his travels to Europe entitled *A Buckeye Abroad*, which was very popular. Shortly afterward in the early 1850s he followed his father into the newspaper business as the editor of the Ohio Statesman and gained the nickname "Sunset" Cox by using somewhat flowery language to describe a sunset. At the same time he became interested in Ohio Democratic politics, and his actions on behalf of the Franklin Pierce presidential campaign in 1854 earned Cox an appointment as a member of the U.S. legation in Peru. He was forced by ill health to resign the position before actually arriving in Peru.

In 1856 Cox accepted the Democratic nomination for Congress from his district and won the election. Taking his seat in 1857, Cox began a thirty-year congressional career, interrupted only by a four-year stint during the first years of Reconstruction and a short period as U.S. minister to Turkey. Cox came into Congress during the turbulent debates over Kansas and the Lecompton Constitution. He opposed the admission of Kansas under that document.

While in Congress over the next few years, Cox advocated what he considered any reasonable accommodation of Southern demands and worked hard to reach a compromise during the secession crisis of the winter of 1860–1861. At the same time, however, the prospect of war between the sections had him doing what he could to prepare his own state for hostilities. As early as December 1860, he wrote to the War Department requesting that Ohio be sent arms and ammunition from the federal government under the provisions of the Militia Act of 1808. The department informed him that under that law the state could be supplied with arms but that it would have to provide its own ammunition.

During the war, Cox was associated with the so-called Peace Democrats, who advocated a negotiated end to the war. He, however, never failed to vote in favor of any military appropriations that would help the troops in the field. His advocacy of peace and negotiations with the Confederacy could not help but make him suspect in Republican eyes and his friendship with notorious Copperhead Clement Vallandigham encouraged those suspicions. In 1863 Cox testified for Vallandigham, asserting that he did not believe Vallandigham to be disloyal and that he did not believe that Vallandigham had ever encouraged others to be so. Cox believed that Vallandigham had never done anything but encourage citizens to express their displeasure with the conduct of the war through their votes. Cox also stated that he himself had actually made some of the statements that were attributed to Vallandigham and interpreted as being disloyal.

In spite of some people's suspicions of Cox's loyalty, he remained active in Congress throughout most of the war, serving as a senior member of the House Committee on Foreign Affairs among others. On that committee he worked tirelessly at the end of 1861 to avert war with Great Britain over the *Trent* Affair. He also consulted with President Abraham Lincoln on a variety of issues that he hoped would ease tensions between the United States and the Confederacy. Of particular interest to him were prisoner-of-war status for captured Confederate sailors and protection of private property in occupied portions of the Confederacy.

Still, in spite of his best efforts to work with the Republican administration, Cox's activism within the Democratic Party and association with the opposition made such cooperation difficult. In 1864 he was accused of trying to persuade home-guard units in Ohio from going to the front, an accusation that was never substantiated. During the election of that year, he served as an Ohio delegate to the Democratic National Convention and offered a seconding speech for the nomination of George B. McClellan. He, along with McClellan, was defeated in November.

After leaving Congress in early 1865, Cox moved to New York City, from where he would later again serve in Congress. He returned to Congress in 1869 and became a voice for reform for the next two decades. He strongly supported civil service reform and the development and

admission of western states. After a brief stint as minister to Turkey from 1885 to 1886, he returned to Congress and died in office on 10 September 1889. During his life, he had been known as an honorable though somewhat independent congressman. He wrote extensively about his experiences in Congress and his travel abroad, publishing over half a dozen books in his lifetime.

—*David S. Heidler and Jeanne T. Heidler*

See also Congress, U.S.A.; Peace Democrats.
For further reading:
Cox, William Van Zandt. *Life of Samuel Sullivan Cox* (1899).
Lindsey, David. *"Sunset" Cox, Irrepressible Democrat* (1959).

CRAMPTON'S GAP, BATTLE OF
(14 September 1862)

The battle of Crampton's Gap (or Crampton's Pass) near Burkittsville, Maryland, was fought on 14 September 1862 between a small force of Confederate defenders, from the division of Lafayette McLaws, and the two divisions of the Army of the Potomac's VI Army Corps, commanded by Major General William B. Franklin. It was part of the larger offensive known collectively as the battles of South Mountain, during the Maryland campaign of 1862.

When the discovery of the Army of Northern Virginia's Special Orders No. 191 on 13 September gave Major General George McClellan the exact intentions and whereabouts of the divided Confederate army, he sent orders to General Franklin to take Crampton's Gap in South Mountain and then go to the defense of the Union garrison at Harper's Ferry, which at that time was under siege by Thomas J. "Stonewall" Jackson's command. McClellan's overall intent was to move swiftly against Lee's divided force and defeat each element before the Confederates could regroup. While Franklin's men attacked Crampton's Gap, the other elements of the Army of the Potomac would storm Turner's Gap and Fox's Gap, located about eight miles to the north of Crampton's Gap in the same mountain range.

McClellan organized the Army of the Potomac into three wings for the operation: the right, center, and left wings. The right wing would attack at Turner's Gap and Fox's Gap. The center wing would be held in reserve. Franklin commanded the left wing, composed of his own two divisions (commanded by Major Generals Henry Slocum and William F. "Baldy" Smith) and Major General Darius Couch's division from IV Corps. The left wing had the most important assignment. Franklin was ordered to seize Crampton's Gap, then move across the mountain into Pleasant Valley and cut off or destroy McLaws's command. Most of McLaws's force occupied Maryland Heights, overlooking the town of Harper's Ferry across the Potomac River. His command formed part of Stonewall Jackson's three-pronged attack on Harper's Ferry.

The VI Corps marched at first light on 14 September, passing over Catoctin Mountain and halting on the other side at the outskirts of the village of Jefferson to wait for Couch's division. After determining that Couch would not arrive for at least several more hours, around 10:00 A.M., Franklin decided to push VI Corps forward to Burkittsville, ten miles to the northwest of Jefferson. The head of VI Corps' column arrived at a point about two miles in front of Burkittsville around noon.

The Confederate defenders waiting for Franklin included Colonel Thomas Munford's understrength cavalry brigade—two regiments and a horse artillery battery—and the diminished infantry brigade of Colonel William Mahone, also much reduced in manpower and under the temporary command of Colonel William Parham. Attached to Parham's command was the 10th Georgia Infantry Regiment from Brigadier General Paul Semmes's brigade. On the other side of South Mountain at the far southwest edge of Pleasant Valley lay Brigadier General Howell Cobb's infantry brigade, ready to come to Munford's aid. All told, the Confederate force that initially would battle Franklin's corps—Munford, Parham, and the 10th Georgia—came to a total of no more than 1,000 men.

Even though the Confederates were vastly outnumbered—Franklin had approximately 12,800 soldiers in his two divisions—Munford and Parham took advantage of the man-made and natural obstacles confronting their antagonists. Parham's infantrymen were stretched out along a road that skirted the base of the mountain, and his men took cover behind a stone wall. Munford dismounted his cavalry regiments and posted one of them, the 2d Virginia, behind a single stone wall to the south of the road that led up to Crampton's Gap. He placed his other regiment, the 12th Virginia Cavalry, to the far left of the line, separate from the main force, to guard against a flank attack. The infantry regiments were positioned to the left of the 2d Cavalry. The 10th Georgia Infantry occupied the extreme left of the main Confederate defensive line. Halfway up Crampton's Gap, Munford sited a battery of horse artillery and a section of field artillery. About three quarters of a mile south of Crampton's Gap, a narrow road ascended South Mountain at a place called Brownsville Pass. There McLaws had instructed Brigadier General Paul Semmes to see to its defense. Semmes sent one infantry regiment and one battery of artillery.

From the outskirts of Burkittsville, Franklin surveyed the terrain and the dispositions of the enemy. He concluded that the position could be carried only by infantry attack, and directed General Slocum to advance through the village of Burkittsville and attack the Confederate right. Slocum picked the brigade of Colonel

Joseph Bartlett to lead the assault. Sometime between 2:30 and 4:00 P.M., Bartlett deployed his skirmishers and began the attack. (The exact time that the attack commenced is vague. Bartlett stated that the offensive started at 4:00, two of his regimental commanders reported that it began at 3:30, while yet another claimed it started at 2:30.)

It seems apparent that neither Franklin nor his subordinate commanders initially realized the paucity of the force opposing them, given the excellent cover and concealment that the stone walls, heavy woods, and rock outcroppings provided the defenders, who also took advantage of the rapid and steep ascent of South Mountain to improve their chances of success against the Union force. As Bartlett sent his skirmishers forward, General Smith was ordered to move two of his brigades through town to protect Slocum's flank. Smith retained his other brigade as a reserve.

Once the battle started up the mountain and into the woods, Franklin could no longer see its progress. The fighting continued for several hours against a determined foe who had been ordered to hold to the last man. Just as Parham and Munford's line was collapsing, Howell Cobb's 1,300-man brigade streamed down the mountain to bolster the defenses. Now, with the added punch of Cobb's brigade, the fighting rapidly intensified to a crescendo. As Slocum's men were pushing the Confederates up the steep and rugged slopes toward Crampton's Gap, Smith's soldiers succeeded in getting around the Southerners' already crumbling right flank and took many prisoners. By this point in the battle, all but one of the VI Corps' brigades had been engaged in the fighting. Couch still had not arrived and would not show up for several more hours.

As the sun was setting, Slocum's men clawed their way up South Mountain, virtually annihilating Cobb's brigade along the way. Cobb tried to organize a hasty defense at the top of the pass, but superior numbers and the irresistible momentum of the Union advance sent the last remnants of the Confederate force fleeing down the other side of South Mountain. The battle of Crampton's Gap ended just before dusk. Union casualties came to 533, while the Confederates lost approximately 800 men.

Although Franklin had completed the first part of the mission, he failed to follow up his success. When Crampton's Gap finally fell, there was not enough daylight remaining to continue into Pleasant Valley, so the push to Harper's Ferry would have to wait until 15 September. Around 10 P.M. on 14 September, Couch and his division finally arrived, giving Franklin a fresh division of more than 7,000 men that he could use for the next day's operation. Smith's division, of which only two brigades had been employed during the fighting at Crampton's Gap, also was ready for action. It was imperative that Franklin bring as much force to bear as he could muster, and do it as early as possible, so that once the battle commenced the Union commander at Harper's Ferry would hear the fighting, signaling that friendly forces were coming to his relief.

Franklin made two critical errors in judgment on 15 September. First, he did not have his command in position to attack McLaws at first light. Second, he overestimated the size of the Confederate force facing him. Even though his own command greatly outnumbered McLaws's force, Franklin believed otherwise. Instead of attacking he requested reinforcements from McClellan. His decision was an unfortunate mistake, not only for the Harper's Ferry garrison, but one that Franklin would regret for the rest of his life, even though he would never admit it outright. Franklin's poor generalship on the morning of 15 September 1862 negated the Crampton's Gap victory and contributed to the fall of Harper's Ferry, which surrendered at 7:15 A.M. Two days later, the bloody battle of Antietam was fought near Sharpsburg, Maryland, but Franklin and VI Corps played a very small role.

—*Mark Snell*

See also Antietam, Battle of; Cobb, Howell; Franklin, William Buel; McLaws, Lafayette; South Mountain, Battle of.

For further reading:
Reese, Timothy. *Sealed with Their Lives: The Battle for Crampton's Gap* (1998).
Sears, Stephen. *Landscape Turned Red: The Battle of Antietam* (1983).
Snell, Mark A. *William B. Franklin: A Biography* (in press).

CRATER, BATTLE OF THE
(30 July 1864)

The battle of the Crater, also called the battle of the Mine, was an effort initiated by the Federal troops at Petersburg to overcome the city's Confederate defenses. Because Petersburg was an important transportation hub, with five railroads connecting it to rivers and seaports, the city played a strategic role in getting supplies to Lee's army in the South, particularly after the fall of Vicksburg. Grant's strategy was to capture Petersburg to cut off Confederate supply lines, weaken the defenses around the Confederate capital, and capture Richmond, which was just seventy miles away.

The initial unsuccessful Federal assault on Petersburg, from 15 to 18 June 1864, resulted in a prolonged siege that lasted nearly ten months. The stalemate that ensued after 18 June led to suggestions on how to end it. Former coal miners of the 48th Pennsylvania Infantry and their commander, Lieutenant Colonel Henry Pleasants, who was a mining engineer before the war, suggested that a tunnel be constructed under Confederate trenches and that explosives be placed in

strategic locations to blow up Confederate fortifications above the ground. General Robert Potter, commander of the 2d Division, IX Army Corps, Army of the Potomac, took the idea to the corps commander, General Ambrose Burnside, in a formal proposal on 24 June. Burnside was receptive to the idea and General George G. Meade, Commander of the Army of the Potomac, initially approved it.

The 48th Pennsylvania's position in the trenches was in proximity to Elliott's Salient, a Confederate redoubt that was just 400 feet from the Union's outposts. Tunneling began on 25 June and was completed on 23 July. Four days later, the placing of the powder charge was finished. The main shaft of the tunnel ran 511 feet to a point twenty feet under the Confederate battery in the salient. Two lateral galleries with a total length of seventy-five feet were run under the enemy trenches. The tunnel averaged five feet in height. It was four and a half feet wide at the bottom and about two feet at the top. It was ventilated by a system whereby fire in a chimney near the entrance drew stale air out of the tunnel while fresh air was brought in through a wooden tube along the tunnel floor. The tube entered from under an airtight door at the entrance and ran to the end of the tunnel where the men were digging. The powder charge consisted of 320 kegs of gunpowder, totaling 8,000 pounds. A thirty-eight-foot section of the main tunnel was then filled with dirt and a fuse was improvised. All of this was done with few supplies from headquarters.

The plan of attack after the tunnel, or "mine," explosion occurred perhaps posed the biggest challenge. This part of the operation involved the black troops of the 4th Division, IX Corps, Army of the Potomac. The division was composed of the 19th, 23d, 27th, 28th, 29th, 30th, 31st, 39th, and 43d U.S. Colored Troops (USCT). The black 4th Division, commanded by Brigadier General Edward Ferrero, numbered 4,300 men assigned to two brigades led by Colonel Joshua Sigfried and Colonel Henry Goddard Thomas.

According to a report by Colonel Thomas, commander of the 2d Brigade, Burnside had decided that Ferrero's black troops would lead the assault because they were new, enthusiastic, filled with hope, and "not yet rendered doubtful by reverses or chilled by defeat." Moreover, the black troops were eager to prove themselves in battle. According to the official reports of various high-ranking commanders, the black troops drilled and practiced maneuvers for weeks in preparation for leading the attack after the explosion. Yet there are contrary published letters by the soldiers of the 4th Division. Writing from camp on 26 July 1864, Sergeant Major McCoslin of the 29th Infantry USCT, 4th Division informed readers of *The Christian Recorder*: "Our regiment is not in good fighting trim at present, on account of an insufficiency of officers. In other respects

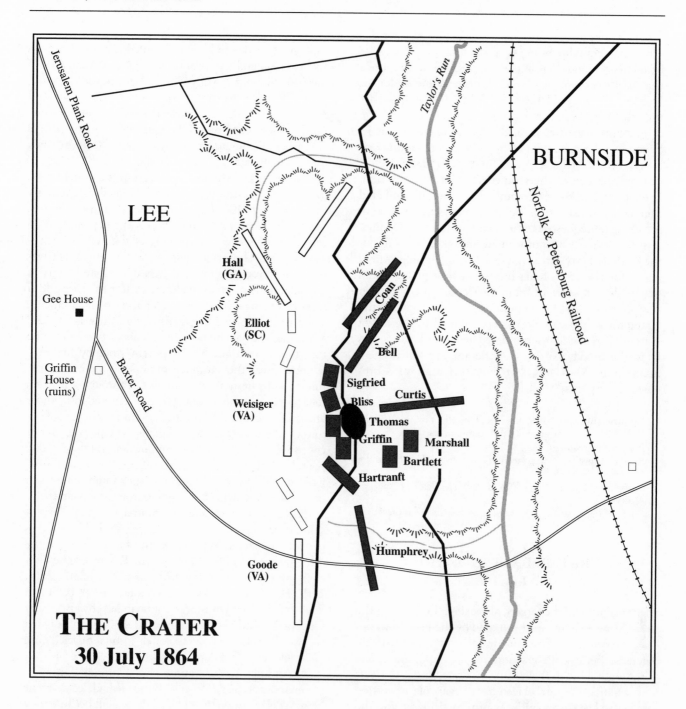

Jerusalem Plank Road

Taylor's Run

BURNSIDE

LEE

Norfolk & Petersburg Railroad

Hall
(GA)

Coan

Gee House

Elliot
(SC)

Bell

Griffin
House
(ruins)

Baxter Road

Sigfried
Bliss   Curtis

Weisiger
(VA)   Thomas
              Griffin   Marshall
                            Bartlett
              Hartranft

Humphrey

Goode
(VA)

**THE CRATER
30 July 1864**

they are all right. We are expecting every day to be sent to the front; but it is ordered otherwise, probably for the best. Our regiment has built two forts and about three miles of breastworks, which shows that we are not idle, and that we are learning to make fortifications, whether we learn to fight or not."

McCoslin's report on the military training of the black soldiers was corroborated in later years by Captain R. K. Beecham, who after leaving his regiment (2d Wisconsin) joined the 23d USCT in Petersburg, where he claimed to have served every day from 22 June 1864 until after the battle of the Crater. He wrote in a 20 August 1902 letter that appeared in The *National Tribune:* "I am prepared to

say from actual knowledge derived from personal experience with the Fourth Division that the only duty assigned to the said division for more than a month before the battle of the Mine was work upon our trenches and fortifications. The Fourth Division during all that time was drilled especially in the use of pick and shovel, and in no other manner. Of this fact I do not complain. My complaint is, that while the Fourth Division worked ceaselessly, heroically, day and night, on the trenches to the neglect of every soldierly preparation for the battle, it has been falsely and persistently reported to have received special preparation for a particular battle."

Just a few hours before the explosion was to take place,

Burnside informed the black troops and their commanders that they would not lead the attack. General Meade reportedly changed his mind about the use of the black division because "they were a new division and had never been under fire, while this was an operation requiring the very best troops." Meade also argued that, if the attack failed, the Union would be criticized for sacrificing black troops to the cannons of the enemy. Mainly for the latter reason, General Ulysses S. Grant agreed to Meade's decision. However, Burnside relentlessly attempted to persuade Meade to permit the black troops to lead the assault. Meade would not be moved. Finally, Burnside chose one of the white divisions by lot to lead the assault. Brigadier General James H. Ledlie commanded the 1st Division; Brigadier General Robert Potter commanded the 2d Division; and Brigadier General Orlando B. Willcox commanded the 3d Division. Straws were put into a hat from which each commander drew. The luck of the draw fell to Ledlie, who was considered the least able to do the job successfully.

At about 3:00 A.M. on 30 July, Pleasants entered the mine or tunnel and lit the fuse, which was expected to burn thirty minutes. However, when the explosion did not occur, around 4:15 A.M. Pleasants sent two men into the tunnel to investigate. The fuse had gone out. It was relit. At about 4:44 A.M., the four tons of gunpowder went off. The explosion made a crater from 150 to 200 feet long, sixty feet wide, and thirty feet deep. A Confederate battery and most of a regiment were blown up by the explosion. Ledlie's division entered the crater, but failed to advance promptly to the ridge (Cemetery Hill) beyond the crater. "Had they done this," reported Grant, "I have every reason to believe that Petersburg would have fallen." Grant further stated in his report on the battle that "other troops were immediately pushed forward but the time consumed in getting them up enabled the enemy to rally from his surprise (which had been complete) and get forces to this point for its defense. The captured line thus held being untenable, and of no advantage to us, the troops were withdrawn, but not without heavy loss. Thus terminated in disaster what promised to be the most successful assault of the campaign." In a hearing before the Committee on the Conduct of the War, Grant testified that "General Burnside wanted to put his colored division in front, and I believe if he had done so it would have been a success. Still I agreed with General Meade as to his objections to that plan…it would then be said…that we were shoving these people ahead to get killed because we did not care anything about them."

The official report put the Union dead at 504. In addition, 1,881 were wounded, and 1,413 were reported missing. On the Confederate side, it is estimated that at least 361 were killed, 727 wounded, and 403 missing.

Blame for the Union's failure to win the battle and capture Petersburg fell on Burnside, Ledlie, Ferrero, Bliss, and Willcox; but the Official Court of Inquiry placed most of the blame on Burnside and Ledlie. Shortly after the battle, both men were given leaves that ended with their resignations. The Joint Congressional Committee on the Conduct of the War later found that Meade was responsible for the loss of the battle because it was he who reversed Burnside's plan to use the fresh black soldiers to lead the attack. The only fault found in Burnside by the committee was the method that he used to select an alternative division to take the lead after Meade decided not to use the black division.

—*Dorothy L. Drinkard*

See also Burnside Ambrose E.; Petersburg Campaign.
For further reading:
Cavanaugh, Michael A., and William Marvel. *The Petersburg Campaign: The Battle of the Crater, "The Horrid Pit," June 25–August 6, 1864* (1989).
Drinkard, Dorothy L. *Illinois Freedom Fighters: A Civil War Saga of the 29th Infantry United States Colored Troops* (1998).
Trudeau, Noah Andre. *The Last Citadel: Petersburg, Virginia, June 1864–April 1865* (1991).

CRAWFORD, SAMUEL J.
(1835–1913)
Union officer; governor of Kansas

Samuel J. Crawford was a tough frontier soldier whose courageous battlefield exploits propelled him to two terms as governor of Kansas. While commanding the 2d Kansas Colored Infantry Regiment, he replied in kind after Confederate troops murdered black prisoners of war. He followed a similar course as governor when Indian raids devastated western Kansas.

Crawford was born near Bedford, Indiana, on 10 April 1835. Intent on a legal career, in 1857 he enrolled in the law school of Cincinnati College, where he graduated the following year. Crawford moved to Kansas in early 1859, entering local politics as a Republican. His neighbors elected him to the state legislature on 6 December 1859, but he did not take his seat until Kansas formally entered the Union in 1861.

Soon after the start of the Civil War, Crawford left the legislature and became a captain in the 2d Kansas Volunteer Infantry, a ninety-day regiment. The 2d Kansas fought at Wilson's Creek on 10 August 1861 and mustered out on 31 October, but Crawford was not ready to quit soldiering.

Seeking a new regiment, Crawford helped form the 2d Kansas Cavalry and was mustered in as a captain on 15 April 1862. While campaigning in northwest Arkansas later that year, Crawford attracted the notice of Brigadier General James G. Blunt, another Kansan. Captain Crawford's military credo was: "When in trouble, charge!" He won citations for the bravery and tactical initiative he displayed between 22 October and 7 December at Old Fort Wayne, Cane Hill, and Prairie Grove. Impressed by Crawford's performance, the other company officers of the 2d Kansas Cavalry petitioned to have him named their colonel, but Governor Charles Robinson refused.

Unable to gain promotion any other way, Crawford accepted Blunt's offer to command the 2d Kansas Colored Infantry (later the 83d U.S. Colored Infantry), a new regiment that assembled at Fort Scott, Kansas, in the summer and fall of 1863. Colonel Crawford exerted every effort to prepare the 2d Kansas Colored for front-line service. After the regiment relocated to Fort Smith in late October, he purged his ranks of 200 physically unfit enlisted men and subjected the remainder to a strict regimen of training and discipline. He also closely screened soldiers from white commands who applied for commissions in the 2d Kansas Colored.

In March 1864, the 2d Kansas Colored joined the 14,000-man army that Major General Frederick Steele drew from the Union garrisons at Little Rock and Fort Smith to invade southwest Arkansas. While at Camden on 18 April, Crawford learned that Confederate troops had refused to spare any black personnel captured from the 1st Kansas Colored Infantry in a fight at Poison Spring, about eleven miles away. Crawford conferred with his officers, and they resolved "that in future the regiment would take no prisoners so long as the Rebels continued to murder our men." The 2d Kansas Colored kept that pledge at the battle of Jenkins' Ferry, 30 April, when it charged two enemy cannon. The enraged black soldiers bayoneted every gray gunner within reach except for an officer and five men.

In September 1864, delegates from Kansas regiments stationed at Fort Smith attended the Republican State Convention at Topeka and successfully promoted Crawford's nomination for governor. Crawford returned home to campaign, but interrupted politics for eleven days in October to serve as a volunteer aide when Major General Sterling Price and Confederate cavalry raided through Missouri and threatened eastern Kansas. Crawford's exploits at Westport and Mine Creek enhanced his political appeal, and he carried the election on 8 November. Two years later, Kansans elected him to a second term.

Governor Crawford wrestled with daunting problems stemming from the war, Reconstruction, economic development, and frontier expansion. Incensed by bloody Indian raids on Kansas homesteads, he resigned his office on 4 November 1868 to take command of the 19th Kansas Cavalry, a volunteer regiment that cooperated with the regular army in operations against the Southern Plains tribes.

Crawford aspired to a seat in the U.S. Congress, but that prize eluded him. He harmed his political fortunes by joining the Liberal Republicans in 1872, and he fared no better when he ran for the House of Representatives as a Greenbacker in 1876 and 1878.

Crawford tasted success again as a claims agent in Washington, D.C., from 1877 to 1891. He also practiced law in Washington, tested new agricultural methods on a farm in Kansas, and published his memoirs. The independent soldier/politician died in Topeka on 21 October 1913.

—*Gregory J. W. Urwin*

See also Kansas; United States Colored Troops; Westport, Battle of.

For further reading:

Cornish, Dudley Taylor. "Kansas Negro Regiments in the Civil War." *Kansas Historical Quarterly* (May 1953).

Crawford, Samuel J. *Kansas in the Sixties* (1911).

Hoig, Stan. *The Battle of the Washita* (1976).

Plummer, Mark A. *Frontier Governor: Samuel J. Crawford of Kansas* (1971).

Urwin, Gregory J.W. "'We Cannot Treat Negroes…as Prisoners of War': Racial Atrocities and Reprisals in Civil War Arkansas." *Civil War History* (1996).

CREEK INDIANS

Inhabiting the area between the Arkansas and Canadian rivers in eastern Indian Territory, the people of the Creek Nation viewed the onset of the American Civil War with mixed emotions. Factions existed within the Creek Nation, but these divisions had endured since the mid-eighteenth century when English and Scottish fur traders established ties with the Lower Creeks in Georgia and Alabama. Intermarriage led to an increase of mixed-bloods among the Lower Creeks and the appearance of Creek leaders with names such as McGillivray and McIntosh. The Lower Creeks voluntarily complied with the United States' removal policy of the 1830s endorsed by their mixed-blood leaders, while the Upper Creeks had to be forcibly removed from their traditional homelands. These two Creek factions remained separated in Indian Territory, but they were able to put their animosity aside long enough to establish a seat of government, devise a phonetic written language, draft a slave code, and build schools (with the aid of missionaries) in the 1840s and 1850s.

On 10 July 1861, Principal Chief Motey Kinnard and Daniel N. and Chilly McIntosh (sons of William McIntosh—former principal chief of the Lower Creeks) met with Special Commissioner Albert Pike of the Confederate Bureau of Indian Affairs and together signed a treaty of alliance with the Confederacy. The McIntoshes also promised to raise a regiment of Creeks, provided they would only have to fight within the borders of Indian Territory. However, in the fall of 1861 thousands of loyal and neutral Upper Creeks refused to recognize the treaty of alliance with the Confederacy signed by the Lower Creeks, and prepared to march with their leader, Opothleyahola, to Kansas and safety. A force of Lower Creeks under the McIntosh brothers opposed them. In November, sporadic violence between the two factions began and quickly intensified. Pike ordered Colonel Douglas H. Cooper to take charge of the situation and restore tranquility among the Creeks while the special commissioner departed for the Confederate capital. Cooper called on other Indian home guard units to aid in his efforts to end the hostilities and prevent the Upper Creeks from leaving Indian Territory. In doing so, Cooper began what amounted to a civil war within the borders of the territory.

When Cooper arrived near the Canadian River, he discovered almost 4,000 Upper Creek men, women, and children as well as Indians from assorted other nations crowded into encampments along with their livestock, wagons, and worldly possessions. About one-third of these Indians were armed. After failing to dissuade the Upper Creeks from their mission, Cooper chose to use force. Considering these Indians to be a threat to Confederate authority in Indian territory, Cooper assembled a body of 1,400 mounted soldiers composed of six companies of his Choctaw and Chickasaw regiment, Daniel McIntosh's Lower Creek regiment, Chilly McIntosh and John Jumper's battalion of Creeks and Seminoles, and 500 whites of the 9th Texas Cavalry. On 5 November 1861, the ever-growing group of loyal Creeks and refugees left their encampments and moved north toward Kansas. Two weeks later, Cooper attacked the slow-moving caravan at Round Mountain, near the junction of the Cimarron and Arkansas rivers. The loyal Creeks fought back, managing to escape at dusk after setting a prairie fire to impede Cooper's progress.

Slowed but undaunted, Cooper resumed the chase, now reinforced by John Drew's Cherokee regiment, which was ordered by Cooper to aid in the operation. On 9 December, Cooper found Opothleyahola and the loyal Creeks waiting for him at Chusto-Talasah, or Caving Banks, on Bird Creek near present-day Tulsa. Cooper engaged the Upper Creeks for four hours before Opothleyahola finally withdrew his band. All told, Cooper lost fifteen men killed and thirty-seven wounded, and failed once again to cut off the fleeing loyalists.

Although claiming a victory, Cooper nevertheless withdrew to Fort Gibson near Tahlequah and waited for reinforcements from Texas and Arkansas. With the arrival of 1,380 Confederate troopers under Colonel James McIntosh, Cooper had the luxury to plan a combined attack against Opothleyahola's band utilizing the converging columns of his own and McIntosh's troops. The Confederates once again took to the field, but unfortunately were unable to synchronize their convergence on the Creek camp at Chustenahlah. Rather than wait for Cooper's badly delayed troops,

McIntosh chose to engage Opothleyahola's numerically superior forces on 26 December. Weakened by exhaustion, cold weather, and lack of adequate food, the loyal Creeks could not withstand the Confederate onslaught. Warriors mixed with men, women, and children fled the field in panic pursued by white Confederate cavalrymen and the recently arrived mixed-blood Cherokee regiment under Stand Watie. Watie's 300 men killed or captured many of the stragglers who were too weak to flee. Those who did escape finally made their way to Kansas and safety. There they fared little better, owing to a lack of adequate food, clothing, and shelter for the winter. U.S. Indian agents in Kansas were unable to aid the refugees, whose numbers eventually swelled to over 10,000. Eventually hunger and disease took their toll.

In the spring of 1862, Brigadier General James G. Blunt, commander of the Union Department of Kansas, decided to return the loyal Indian refugees to their home in Indian Territory. The resulting operation resulted in frequent skirmishes with Confederate forces as the refugee column and its Federal escort entered Cherokee country north of the Arkansas River. The return of this contingent of loyal Creeks to Indian Territory fanned the flames of factionalism within the Creek Nation. While Creek soldiers participated in conventional military operations such as those that led to the battle of Honey Springs on 17 July 1863, the real fateful combat for the two factions of the Creek Nation came in the form of guerrilla raids upon each other that sowed the seeds for continued strife well after the war's end.

—*Alan C. Downs*

See also Cherokee Indians; Honey Springs, Battle of; Indian Territory; Pike, Albert; Watie, Stand.

For further reading:
Hauptman, Laurence M. *Between Two Fires: American Indians in the Civil War* (1995).
Josephy, Alvin M. *The Civil War in the American West* (1991).

CRIMPING

The American Civil War spilled over U.S. boundaries to affect the British North American provinces in a variety of ways. Historians estimate that perhaps 40,000 provincials fought in Civil War armies and navies as volunteers (more for the Union than the Confederacy because of proximity and colonial sympathies). They were often led to service by so-called crimps, who were free-lance recruiters working on commission. Despite the severe manpower demands of the war, the American government denounced crimping. However, state and local officials needed men to fill their quotas and often ignored Federal policy. Inside the United States, crimps worked immigrant communities and boarding houses, using local gamblers, idlers, and even the police in Boston, Portland (Maine), and New York City to find potential recruits. Methods ranged from press-gang tactics, to bribes and trickery, to honest appeals.

Crimps mostly lured colonials from Canada into Union regiments and the navy. They roamed borderland towns and waterfronts from Nova Scotia to the Detroit River. Using such devices as newspaper advertisements, they cajoled not only the idle and the young, but also mature men with military experience. At Fredericton, New Brunswick, in spring 1861 they led thirty 62d Regiment redcoats south. Many British tars headed for American service rather that suffer Royal Navy pay and discipline. In 1861 crimpers prowled Montreal and Toronto disguised as hiring agents for railroads and cotton mills. They recruited from black refugee communities in Canada West for black regiments such as the 54th Massachusetts.

Crimpers offered free drink, money, clothing, and free transport to a border state, where the official recruiting took place. They got what they could from their victims, although bounties, at first $15 to $25 for each recruit, provided most of their income. State and local governments offered bounties that could reach $300 per head. Massachusetts paid out $13 million in such bounties throughout the war. The Conscription Acts of 1862 and 1863 created another source of income for crimps because draftees could now legally pay for substitutes. Some offered as much as $1,000 to avoid military service.

Britain's 1819 and 1854 Foreign Enlistment Acts and the proclamation of Neutrality in the Civil War on 14 May 1861 made crimping illegal on British soil. Secretary of State William Henry Seward became cautious about infringement on British neutrality and deflected British North Americans who offered to raise troops or asked for military commissions. Official proclamations did nothing, however, to stop crimping in Canada. The reward for turning in a crimp was $50, but "victims" often refused to testify against the accused. In any case, penalties were light. Abuses increased in number and extent, and in 1864 John A. Macdonald issued a circular to all county attorneys in Canada West to search out crimps. He recruited a body of detectives to aid them. These men patrolled border towns under cover and used soldiers from local garrisons in entrapment schemes. The reward for catching a crimp rose to $200 and any American convicted was fined $160 and handed six months of hard labor. But rising profits counterbalanced the low risk of discovery and prosecution, so crimping ended only with the Civil War itself.

—*Reginald C. Stuart*

See also Conscription, U.S.A.

For further reading:

Geary, James W. "Civil War Conscription in the North: A Historiographical Review." *Civil War History* (1986).

Hamer, Marguerite B. "Luring Canadian Soldiers into Union Lines during the War Between the States." *Canadian Historical Review* (1946).

Marquis, Greg. "Mercenaries or Killer Angels? Nova Scotians in the American Civil War." *Collections of the Royal Nova Scotia Historical Society* (1996).

Rany, William F. "Recruiting and Crimping in Canada for the Northern Forces, 1861–1865." *Mississippi Valley Historical Review* (1923).

CRITTENDEN COMPROMISE
(1860–1861)

The lame-duck session of the Thirty-sixth U.S. Congress convened in December 1860 with the Lower South boiling with secessionist zeal in the aftermath of Abraham Lincoln's election as president. Congressional leaders responded by creating two special committees whose sole purpose was to find a formula that would prevent the South from leaving the Union: a "Committee of Thirty-Three" in the House and a "Committee of Thirteen" in the Senate. Public hopes for a peaceful settlement to the looming crisis especially focused on a member of the latter body, John J. Crittenden of Kentucky, a man whose political career had been largely defined by his association with Henry Clay, the man who had forged Union-saving compromises in 1820, 1833, and 1850. The seventy-three-year-old Crittenden rose to the occasion. On 18 December he presented a package of six amendments to the Senate designed to provide both a comprehensive and permanent solution to the slavery issue.

The first of Crittenden's proposed amendments denied the federal government the ability to abolish slavery or its property in slave states; the second stated that Congress had no power to interfere with the transportation of slaves across state or territorial lines; the third mandated that the federal government would compensate slave owners who were unable to recover fugitive slaves as a result of mob action and authorized the attorney general to sue counties where the recovery of fugitives was thwarted; the fourth prohibited the abolition of slavery in the District of Columbia without the consent of the inhabitants or the previous abolition of slavery in Maryland and Virginia; and the fifth resolved the territorial issue by prohibiting slavery north of the Missouri Compromise line of 36°30' while slavery was recognized and guaranteed throughout the territorial stage in all land south of the line "now held, or hereafter acquired." The final amendment Crittenden proposed was designed to ensure the permanence of the compromise. It exempted the first five from the process of amendment and prohibited any future amendment that gave the federal government the ability to interfere with slavery in any state, constrained the slave owner's constitutional right to recover fugitive slaves, or altered the three-fifths clause of the Constitution. Crittenden also called upon Congress to adopt resolutions that asserted the constitutionality of the Fugitive Slave Law and commit the government to its rigid enforcement, declared state laws that conflicted with that law null and void and advocated their repeal, deleted clauses in the law that offended Northern sensibilities, and committed Congress to strengthening and rigorously executing laws prohibiting the foreign slave trade.

This was not a true compromise. Crittenden's plan conceded everything to the South that it could possibly want, while offering little to the North. Nonetheless, Northern Democrats led by Stephen A. Douglas and the New York business community joined border state Unionists in stepping forward to throw their support behind Crittenden and his plan. Even some Republicans, most prominently Thurlow Weed and William H. Seward, flirted with the idea of accepting the compromise, even though it asked them to disavow the commitment to keeping slavery out of the territories that held their party together.

The most important Republican, Abraham Lincoln, was not willing to do this. Although not unalterably opposed to compromise, when the outlines of Crittenden's plan became clear, the president-elect took up his pen and instructed his fellow Republicans to "entertain no proposition for a compromise in regard to the *extension* of slavery....There is no possible compromise upon it....On that point hold firm, as with a chain of steel."

Lincoln's actions effectively killed whatever chance there was for passage of Crittenden's plan by bolstering Republican resistance to surrendering their platform, which steeled the opposition of their Lower South counterparts to compromise. The Committee of Thirteen rejected the omnibus of compromise measures by a vote of seven to six on 22 December, two days after South Carolina adopted its ordinance of secession, with Republican members voting unanimously against it.

Crittenden did not give up, however. On 3 January 1861, he brought the compromise to the Senate floor and called for a national referendum to determine its fate. Again Lincoln responded by urging his fellow Republicans to remain firm. At stake, he told them, was no less than the nation's claim to possess a government of, by, and for the people. "We have just carried an election on principles fairly presented to the people," he wrote on 11 January. "Now we are told...the government will be broken up, unless we surrender to those we have beaten....[I]f we surrender, it is the end of us, and of the government."

On 16 January the Senate dealt the final blow to compromise efforts by voting twenty-five to twenty-three to reject Crittenden's call for a national referendum, even though Horace Greeley would later concede that had such a plebiscite occurred the compromise would probably have commanded a popular majority. Henceforth, hopes that the Union could be restored without war would rest upon the silent majority

of Southern Unionists who Lincoln believed did not need concessions on slavery to rise up and overthrow the secession movement in the South.

—*Ethan S. Rafuse*

See also Crittenden, John J.; Republican Party; Thirteenth Amendment.
For further reading:
Basler, Roy P., ed. *The Collected Works of Abraham Lincoln* (1953–1955).
Kirwan, Albert D. *John J. Crittenden: The Struggle for the Union* (1962).
Potter, David M. *Lincoln and His Party in the Secession Crisis* (1942).
Stampp, Kenneth M. *And the War Came: The North and the Secession Crisis, 1860–1861* (1950).

CRITTENDEN, GEORGE BIBB
(1812–1880)
Confederate general

George Bibb Crittenden was born into a prominent political family in Russellville, Kentucky, on 20 March 1812. His father, John Jordan Crittenden, was a longstanding Kentucky statesman who attempted a final compromise to keep the Union together. As the eldest son in his family, George Bibb later attended West Point to receive a military education. He graduated in 1832, finishing twenty-sixth in his class of forty-five.

After graduation, Crittenden stayed in the army because he enjoyed its excitement. He was a brevet second lieutenant in the Black Hawk War (1832), and after that conflict was stationed at various locations across the South. With no war to feed his sense of adventure, Crittenden resigned his commission to study law at Transylvania University in Lexington, Kentucky. When his studies became cumbersome, he headed southwest in 1842 to fight with the Texans. He participated in the 1843 Meir expedition in pursuit of Mexican raiders, during which he was taken captive in Mexico. Crittenden and his fellow prisoners were forced to draw lots to see who would be executed. He drew a white bean, signifying that he would survive, but gave it to a fellow Kentuckian because the man was married and had children. Crittenden drew again, picked another white bean, and this time kept it. Crittenden's political connections helped to free him from prison, and he returned to Kentucky. He returned to the southwest to fight during the Mexican-American War (1846–1848), and afterward remained in the army.

In June 1861 Crittenden resigned his post in the New Mexico Territory and returned to Kentucky. He found his father trying to stop Southern secession by effecting a compromise that was acceptable to both sides. To the chagrin of his father, George had Southern sympathies. George joined the Confederate army and was made brigadier general. At the same time, George's younger brother, Thomas Leonidas, joined the Union as a brigadier general. The Crittendens thus exemplified the divided nation, fighting a war that pitted brother against brother.

Just two days after he was commissioned major general on 9 November 1861, George Crittenden was assigned command of the Cumberland Mountain region, where he defended an area from southeastern Kentucky to eastern Tennessee. Crittenden's only major Civil War battle experience occurred two months later in southeastern Kentucky.

Crittenden was commanding with General Felix Zollicoffer in January 1862, when the two officers met at Mill Springs on the south bank of the Cumberland River. Zollicoffer decided to take his troops to Beech Grove on the opposite bank, which angered Crittenden because of its poor defensive location. Meanwhile, Union forces were advancing in the rain under General George H. Thomas. Crittenden knew that much of his army would perish if it stayed at Beech Grove, so he decided to take the initiative and planned an attack. Crittenden's surprise attack was aimed at catching the Union armies off guard while they were separated by the rain-swollen Fishing Creek.

The battle—variously known as Mill Springs, Logan's Cross Roads, and Fishing Creek—occurred on 19–20 January 1862. The separated Union forces were able to cross Fishing Creek and join the previously engaged forces, thus giving them a decided advantage. Also, Zollicoffer's death during the battle demoralized the Southern troops. Crittenden led the Confederate retreat to Tennessee, abandoning his horses, wagons, and artillery. Crittenden's miscalculation of the river level and the size of the opposing Union army had crushed his troops.

The defeat caused Confederate officials to look for a scapegoat, and they decided on George Crittenden. He was accused of drunkenness during battle and of having Union sympathies because of his family connections. A court of inquiry found Crittenden innocent of treason, but guilty of intoxication.

Crittenden was given a chance for redemption by commanding a reserve corps that Confederate general Albert Sidney Johnston was building in northern Mississippi. But on 1 April 1862, in Iuka, Mississippi, Major General William J. Hardee found Crittenden drunk and his soldiers in disarray. Crittenden was arrested and court-martialed. His disappointing Civil War career ended on 23 October 1862, when he resigned from the Confederate army.

After the Civil War, Crittenden returned to Frankfort, where his bravery and loyalty were recognized by the state of Kentucky. He later became a state librarian from 1867 to 1871. George Bibb Crittenden died 27 November 1880, in Danville, Kentucky, and was buried with his family in Frankfort.

—Nathan R. Meyer

See also Crittenden, John J.; Crittenden, Thomas L.; Logan's Cross Roads, Battle of; Zollicoffer, Felix K.
For further reading:
Coleman, Ann Mary. *The Life of John J. Crittenden, with Selections from His Correspondence and Speeches.* (1871).

CRITTENDEN, JOHN JORDAN
(1786–1863)
U.S. senator, congressman, attorney general

John Jordan Crittenden, best known for his eleventh-hour attempts to forestall secession by compromise in the winter of 1860–1861, played a key role in U.S. politics from James Monroe's administration through the first two years of the Civil War. Crittenden served in the cabinet of three different presidents, was elected to the U.S. Senate on five occasions, and was offered a position on the Supreme Court by both John Quincy Adams and Abraham Lincoln. After spending much of his career as Henry Clay's top political lieutenant, Crittenden inherited Clay's mantle of compromise during the secession crisis. Despite Crittenden's failure to prevent war, Unionists in central Kentucky sent him in 1861 to Congress, where he became a spokesman for the old Union and against weakening slavery. Crittenden declined renomination in 1863 for health reasons and died that summer.

Crittenden began his political career in the Kentucky House of Representatives in 1811. After serving as a general's aide during the Thames River campaign in the War of 1812, Crittenden returned to Kentucky, spent three terms as speaker of the state House and won election to the U.S. Senate in 1817. He played an important, albeit minor, role in the development of the second party system. After Henry Clay engineered the House of Representatives' selection of John Quincy Adams as president in 1825, Crittenden advised Clay to accept Adams's offer of the State Department. Clay's agreement, partly resulting from Crittenden's guidance, led to charges of a corrupt bargain by partisans of defeated candidate Andrew Jackson, who then worked to organize the Democratic Party. Crittenden joined the opposition to President Jackson and became a key figure in the Whig Party. After the election of the first Whig president, William Henry Harrison, Crittenden entered the cabinet as attorney general. In 1842, after John Tyler's repeated rejection of a national bank, Crittenden resigned his post and replaced Clay in the U.S. Senate.

Crittenden perhaps deserved most of the credit for Zachary Taylor's election to the presidency in 1848. Although he had loyally stood by Clay for decades, Crittenden became an early supporter of General Taylor. Asserting that three-time loser Clay could not win, Crittenden turned to the popular general, who was soon "identified as his candidate." Crittenden's efforts gave political cover to many pro-Taylor Whigs in Kentucky. Once it became clear that Clay could not command the support of his own state, Whigs chose Taylor rather than their venerable champion. However, Crittenden refused his share of the spoils; rather than become Taylor's secretary of state, he opted to remain governor of Kentucky, a position he had accepted only to strengthen Whig prospects in the state. After Taylor's death in 1850, Crittenden agreed to become Millard Fillmore's attorney general, helping the president assist the Compromise of 1850.

Once Henry Clay died in 1852, Crittenden became Kentucky's most famous politician. He returned to the U.S. Senate in 1855, spending his term as a moderate against the extremes of both sections, such as the admission of Kansas under the Lecompton Constitution and the dangerous new Republican Party. In 1860, Crittenden became one of the leading figures in the new Constitutional Union Party, seeking a middle ground between proslavery Democrats and antislavery Republicans. After Lincoln's election, Crittenden became the Senate's chief advocate of compromise to prevent secession and civil war. Crittenden proposed a series of constitutional amendments to guarantee the rights of Southerners and preserve sectional peace. His compromise included dividing all territory along the old Missouri Compromise line into free and slave areas, prohibiting Congress from interfering with the interstate slave trade, compensating owners for fugitive slaves liberated by mobs in the North, and preventing certain clauses of the Constitution from being amended. Although the Crittenden Compromise seemed to have widespread popular support in the winter of 1860–1861, his appeal to sacrifice in the name of Union fell on deaf ears. Republicans refused to yield; Deep South states continued to secede. Only part of Crittenden's proposal received approval. An amendment forbidding federal interference with slavery in the states passed Congress with the necessary majorities and went to the states before war intervened. In March 1861, at the end of his term, Crittenden returned home to Kentucky.

Once war broke out in April 1861, Crittenden used his considerable influence to prevent the secession of Kentucky. Like the state, however, his family was divided by the conflict as his two sons, George B. Crittenden and Thomas L. Crittenden, parted ways to serve in the Confederate and Union armies, respectively. Meanwhile, Crittenden was part of an extralegal committee that originated Kentucky's policy of neutrality in the early months of the conflict. While the state remained aloof from battle, Crittenden and other Unionists worked hard to solidify support for the Federal war effort. To aid the Union cause, Crittenden consented to run for Congress in the May elections.

Although secessionists tried mightily to embarrass Unionists by defeating the legendary Crittenden, he prevailed. In the House, Crittenden quickly worked to confirm the conservative purposes of the war and to reassure Kentucky Unionists. His resolutions on Federal war aims, which passed Congress with little opposition, blamed the war on Southern disunionists and declared that the government sought only the restoration of the Union. Despite this initial success, Crittenden spent most of his term in the minority. He opposed any attempts to confiscate Rebels' land or slaves as grossly unconstitutional, argued against creating the Committee on the Conduct of the War, denounced the Emancipation Proclamation, protested the use of black soldiers, and fought the creation of West Virginia. Crittenden also resisted conscription, asserting that the government's lack of personnel proved that the war had become more radical than the American people would support. Although his views placed him in a minority in Congress, Crittenden echoed the concerns of many Kentuckians who had loyally backed the Union only to feel betrayed when the government changed the purpose of the war. Crittenden could have won another term in Congress, but his distaste for the government's conduct, along with his rapidly failing health, led him to retire. He died on 26 July 1863.

—*Christopher M. Paine*

See also Crittenden Compromise; Crittenden, George B.; Crittenden, Thomas L.; Kentucky.
For further reading:
Coleman, Ann Mary. *The Life of John J. Crittenden, with Selections from His Correspondence and Speeches* (1871).
Kelly, Jack. "John J. Crittenden and the Constitutional Union Party." *Filson Club History Quarterly* (1974).
Kirwan, Albert D. *John J. Crittenden: The Struggle for the Union* (1962).
Zacharias, Donald W. "John J. Crittenden Crusades for the Union and Neutrality in Kentucky." *Filson Club History Quarterly* (1964).

CRITTENDEN, THOMAS LEONIDAS
(1819–1893)
Union general

Thomas Leonidas Crittenden was born in Russellville, Kentucky, on 15 May 1819, the second son of a powerful political family. Crittenden's father was John Jordan Crittenden, the eminent Kentucky statesman who attempted a final compromise in 1861 in an effort to save the Union.

Thomas Crittenden spent much of his youth being educated by his father, who taught his son law. Crittenden passed the bar in 1840 and soon afterward began his legal career in Frankfort, Kentucky. His tenure as a lawyer was short-lived because of the Mexican War (1846–1848). The war began Crittenden's military

Thomas L. Crittenden (*Library of Congress*)

career: he recruited Kentucky soldiers and was made a lieutenant colonel in the United States Army. When the war ended, he returned to his legal career, but soon thereafter became a businessman. Because of their relationship established in the Mexican War, President Zachary Taylor appointed Crittenden consul to Liverpool.

The secession crisis threw the Crittenden household into turmoil. Senator John Crittenden tried to fashion a compromise to preserve the Union, but Thomas's older brother, George Bibb, sympathized with the South and eventually became a general in the Confederacy. For his part, Thomas opposed slavery and secession. When the war began, he volunteered for the Union army and was commissioned a brigadier general of volunteers on 17 July 1861. The Crittenden family exemplified a divided nation and a war that pitted brother against brother.

Crittenden's commission as a general angered many within the Union army. He had little military experience, had never attended military school, and had obviously benefitted from the political influence of his powerful father. Crittenden's unpopularity also could

have been due to his arrogance and his drinking, which usually caused him to use profane language. One observer described Crittenden as having a "thin, staring face, and hair hanging to his coat collar—a very wild appearing major general, but quite a kindly man in conversation."

Despite Crittenden's lack of experience, the war began well for him and his command. Crittenden took command of the 5th Division of the Army of the Ohio under General Don Carlos Buell before the battle of Shiloh in April 1862. At Shiloh, Crittenden rendered gallant and notable service and was promoted to major general of volunteers on 17 July 1862.

On 8 October 1862 Crittenden participated in the battle of Perryville, Kentucky. He made a critical mistake when a small number of Confederate horsemen, about one-tenth the size of his army, bluffed him into withdrawing his troops from the battle, a blunder that may have saved the Confederate forces from a crushing defeat.

On 24 October 1862 Crittenden was transferred to the Army of the Cumberland under General William Rosecrans. His first important experience with the Army of the Cumberland came on 31 December 1863 at the battle of Stones River in Tennessee. Crittenden appeared to have rebounded from Perryville and performed admirably. His behavior at Stones River quickly earned the respect and trust of Rosecrans, and he was breveted for gallantry.

As fall approached in 1863 Crittenden and the Army of the Cumberland continued the fight toward Chattanooga, Tennessee. That September, General Crittenden was commanding the 21st Corps of the Army of the Cumberland during the battle of Chickamauga, when he was driven back after weakening his forces to reinforce General George Thomas. Later, rumors circulated that his troops had deserted him. In any event, Crittenden's corps was routed, and his actions were investigated. He was relieved of command and sent to Indianapolis for an inquiry.

Crittenden's fellow Kentuckians were outraged by what they regarded as an inquisition, so on 14 December 1863 the Kentucky legislature forwarded a demand to President Lincoln for a rehearing. The following February a court in Louisville, Kentucky, honorably acquitted him, but the whole affair damaged Crittenden's military reputation.

Crittenden spent the rest of the war with the Army of the Potomac during the Virginia campaign. His resignation on 13 December 1864 ended his Civil War service.

Thomas Crittenden rejoined the army after the Civil War in July 1866. He served until May 1881, when advancing age forced his retirement. Crittenden died at Staten Island, New York, on 23 October 1893. He is buried with his family in Frankfort, Kentucky.

—*Nathan R. Meyer*

See also Chickamauga, Battle of; Crittenden Compromise; Crittenden, George B.; Crittenden, John J.; Perryville, Battle of.

For further reading:

Bowers, John. *Chickamauga and Chattanooga: The Battles that Doomed the South* (1994).

Cozzens, Peter. *This Terrible Sound: The Battle of Chickamauga* (1992).

Foote, Shelby. *The Civil War: A Narrative* (1958–1974).

McDonough, James L. *Stones River–Bloody Winter in Tennessee* (1980).

U. S. War Department. *The War of the Rebellion: A Compilation of the Official Records of the Union and Confederate Armies* (1880–1901).

CROCKER, MARCELLUS MONROE
(1830–1865)
Union general

Marcellus M. Crocker was born in Indiana but moved with his family to Illinois in 1830, and then, a few years later, to Jefferson County, Iowa. He was able to secure an appointment to the military academy at West Point when he was sixteen. He attended West Point for more than two years, but health problems and family hardship prevented him from graduating.

In 1849, at age nineteen, Crocker began to study law in Fairfield, Iowa, and was admitted to the Iowa bar in 1851. His first law practice was in Keokuk County, Iowa, where he earned a reputation as a successful lawyer. When he was twenty-five he moved to Des Moines, the state capital, where he worked in two law offices and was active in the Democratic Party. In 1858 he ran and was defeated for the position of district judge.

In April 1861, news reached Des Moines that Fort Sumter had been fired on and that war had begun. The result of this news was an explosion of war fever across the state. Des Moines, like most Iowa communities, was the scene of mass rallies and public displays of patriotism. Crocker was a Democrat, but he was also a strong defender of the Union. He attended the largest of the city's war rallies and took the stage to make an impassioned speech in defense of the old flag. In that speech, he called for 100 volunteers, enough men to fill a military company, to follow him into Dixie. Within a few minutes he had more than he requested.

Crocker was elected captain of the new company, and on 4 May 1861 he and his volunteers left for the mustering center at Keokuk to be enlisted in the Union army as Company D, 2d Iowa Volunteer Infantry. Crocker was made major of the regiment, and four months later was commissioned lieutenant colonel. The regiment participated in campaigns in Missouri throughout the summer and fall of 1861, and Crocker earned a reputation as an efficient leader and firm disciplinarian and drillmaster.

Crocker was transferred from the 2d Iowa in October 1861, promoted to full colonel, and placed in command of the newly formed 13th Iowa Volunteer Infantry. Crocker led the 13th Iowa at the battle of Shiloh in April 1862, where he was acknowledged by his commanding officer for his coolness and bravery and his ability to inspire his men to stand by their colors while under severe fire.

After Shiloh the 11th, 13th, 15th, and 16th Iowa infantry regiments were organized as the Iowa Brigade and placed under Crocker's command. He led the new brigade at the battle of Corinth and so impressed his superiors that he was promoted to brigadier general in November 1862. He commanded the Iowa Brigade until April 1863, when he was placed in command of the 7th Division of XVII Corps of the Army of the Tennessee. He led the division in the battles of Jackson and Champion's Hill during the Vicksburg campaign in the summer of 1863 and served, briefly, on General Ulysses S. Grant's staff in May 1863.

Crocker's health was nearly broken by consumption during the Vicksburg campaign, and under General Grant's personal advice he went home on sick leave in June 1863. Republican leaders in Des Moines ignored Crocker's history as a Democrat and actively sought to make him the party's candidate for governor. Crocker declined the honor, saying, "If a soldier is worth anything he cannot be spared from the field; if he is worthless, he will not make a good governor."

Crocker returned to service in less than a month and was given command of the 4th Division of XIII Corps of the Army of the Tennessee, which he commanded for the rest of the summer. From the fall of 1863 to May 1864 he was back with XVII Corps serving under General William T. Sherman in the Meridian and Atlanta campaigns.

Crocker's health worsened throughout the winter, and in May 1864 he submitted his resignation. Rather than accept the offered resignation, General Sherman arranged for him to be transferred to New Mexico in the hopes that the climate there would help him recover his health. He remained in New Mexico throughout the summer and fall, but in December he requested active duty and was sent to the Army of the Cumberland in Tennessee. After less than three months in his new position, his health finally failed him, and he was then transferred to Washington, D.C.

Crocker died in Washington on 26 August 1865. He was thirty-five years old. His wife traveled to Washington and escorted his body back to Des Moines, where he was buried with full military honors.

—*Kenneth L. Lyftogt*

See also Meridian Campaign; Vicksburg Campaign.

For further reading:

Brigham, Johnson. *Iowa: Its History and Its Foremost Citizens* (1916).

Gue, Benjamin F. *A History of Iowa* (1903).

Iowa General Assembly. *Roster and Record of Iowa Soldiers in the War of the Rebellion: Together with Historical Sketches of Volunteer Organizations, 1861–1866* (1908–1911).

Stuart, A.A. *17th Iowa Infantry. Iowa Colonels and Regiments: Being a History of Iowa Regiments in the War of the Rebellion* (1891).

Throne, Mildred. "Iowans and the Civil War." *Palimpsest* (1969).

CROOK, GEORGE
(1828–1890)
Union general

George Crook was born on 8 September 1828 near Taylorsville, Ohio, the ninth of ten children in a relatively prosperous farming family. His father's status as a locally prominent Whig drew Crook an appointment to the U.S. Military Academy, and after first preparing at nearby Dayton Academy, he entered West Point with the class of 1852.

After a mediocre cadet career, Crook was posted to the 4th Infantry and spent his antebellum years on the Pacific Coast. There he saw action in the Rogue River War, gaining experience in guerrilla-style warfare and carefully observing frontier administration and diplomacy. Returning east upon the outbreak of the Civil War, he received command of the 36th Ohio Volunteer Infantry and took the field in western Virginia. On 23 May 1862, Crook defeated a larger Confederate force at Lewisburg, an action for which he was brevetted a major in the regular army. After promotion to brigadier general of volunteers, he led a brigade of the Kanawha Division at South Mountain and Antietam, where he helped force the hotly contested crossing at "Burnside's bridge" on the Confederate right.

Crook then briefly returned to western Virginia before joining General William S. Rosecrans's Army of the Cumberland for the Tullahoma campaign in the summer of 1863. Later that fall, he led the 2d Cavalry Division into battle at Chickamauga and helped cover the routed Union army's retreat to Chattanooga. Reassignment back to West Virginia gave the young general an opportunity to exercise independent command at Cloyd's Mountain, where he won a complete victory and earned his men's lasting respect. Crook took part in David Hunter's Valley campaign and was also prominent at Cedar Creek—a victory for which Crook bitterly believed Philip Sheridan ungraciously accepted largely undeserved credit.

While in command of the Department of West Virginia, Crook gained the peculiar and unfortunate wartime distinction of being captured in his own bed. In February 1865, Captain Jesse McNeill's Confederate guerrillas snatched the sleeping general from a hotel bed in Cumberland, Maryland, and held him captive until exchanged a short time later. Humiliated, Crook returned to West Virginia to find his department assigned to Winfield Scott Hancock. General Ulysses S. Grant restored Crook's honor by giving him command of the Army of the Potomac's cavalry, which Crook led during the war's last days around Petersburg, at Dinwiddie Court House, Sayler's Creek, and Appomattox.

After the war, on 22 August 1865, Crook married Mary Dailey, daughter of the hotel owner where he had been captured. The marriage never assumed a prominent role in Crook's life, and Mary usually remained in Maryland during the general's frontier service, venturing west only for short visits. In November 1866, after several months of Reconstruction duty in North Carolina, Crook returned west in command of the 23d Infantry to the Idaho Territory.

Crook's frontier operations were innovative and often departed from conventional military wisdom. He employed "friendly" Indians against their hostile tribe members, a practice that he stubbornly defended against popular and professional criticism. In 1871, he was given command of the troubled Department of Arizona after achieving striking success in the Northwest. In Arizona, he again fielded Indian auxiliaries and employed pack mules instead of supply wagons to gain mobility in pursuit of hostile Apaches. Crook's techniques proved effective, and by the spring of 1873 the Arizona Territory enjoyed temporary peace.

The same tactics were applied less successfully on the plains, where, as commander of the Department of the Platte, Crook participated in the Sioux War of 1876. His reputation suffered from controversial actions taken at Rosebud Creek in June 1876. His failure to continue northward after the battle led to speculation that his decision contributed to Custer's massacre at the Little Big Horn. It was also during this period that his humanitarian views on federal Indian policy became more public. Paternalistic attempts to acculturate Indians made him a sort of hero among eastern reformers and provided a basis for his "tough but fair" administrative doctrine. Upon returning to Arizona in 1882, he attempted to permanently settle the Apaches into an agricultural lifestyle. This solution was dealt a severe blow when Geronimo and several others broke from the reservation and raided along the border.

After the subsequent campaign ended in broken promises by both Geronimo and the government, Crook felt discredited and requested reassignment, believing that external interference would never allow his methods to achieve enduring success. He ended his career as commander of the Division of the Missouri and remained an active campaigner for Indian rights. On 21 March 1890, Crook died of a heart attack in Chicago, Illinois, and was buried in Oakland, Maryland.

—*Ronald G. Machoian*

See also Cedar Creek, Battle of; Cloyd's Mountain, Battle of; McNeill, John and Jesse.
For further reading:
Bourke, John G. *On the Border with Crook* (1891; reprint, 1971).
Greene, Jerome A. "George Crook." In *Soldiers West: Biographies from the Military Frontier* (1987).
King, James T. "George Crook: Indian Fighter and Humanitarian." *Arizona and the West* (1967).
Schmitt, Martin F., ed. *General George Crook: His Autobiography* (1960).
Utley, Robert M. *Frontier Regulars: The United States Army and the Indian, 1866–1891* (1973).

CROSS KEYS, BATTLE OF
(8 June 1862)

The battle of Cross Keys was the fifth battle of Lieutenant General Thomas J. "Stonewall" Jackson's Shenandoah Valley campaign and was fought the day before the larger battle of Port Republic. The battle occurred near the small village of Cross Keys, six miles southeast of Harrisonburg and seven miles northwest of Port Republic.

At Cross Keys on 7 June, three brigades of Confederate troops, about 5,000 men commanded by Major General Richard S. Ewell, prepared to meet a Union attack by 10,500 men under Major General John C. Frémont, who had moved down the Valley Pike through Harrisonburg. Frémont, moving in from the northwest, and Brigadier General James Shields, closing from the northeast, hoped to trap Jackson's force between them.

Ewell had charge of defending Jackson's western flank. He established excellent defensive positions along a ridge facing northwest and fronted by several hundred acres of open fields with maple woods protecting both flanks. He positioned his artillery batteries in the center of the line to block the road to Port Republic. Brigadier General George Steuart's brigade held the Confederate left; Brigadier General Isaac Trimble's brigade, the right. Brigadier General Arnold Elzey's infantry brigade was in reserve.

Jackson was at Port Republic. He positioned his men there just north of that town to be able to deal with Shields's division approaching from the northeast. Jackson was thus in supporting distance of Ewell, although Ewell fought his own battle at Cross Keys against Frémont.

The battle of Cross Keys opened at about 10:00 A.M. on 8 June with a half-hearted advance by Frémont's infantry. Brigadier General Louis Blenker's division of German immigrants slowly pushed back the Confederate advance elements. The 15th Alabama Infantry of Trimble's brigade held the Union troops for about a half hour. A long-range artillery duel followed. The 44th Virginia Regiment and 1st Maryland then beat back several Union attacks.

Frémont mounted his major attack with a brigade of Blenker's Germans against Trimble's brigade on the Confederate right. Displaying excellent discipline, Trimble's men held their fire until the Union troops were close, then fired a series of volleys that repulsed the assault. Confederates located in the woods on the right flank exacted a heavy toll on the Union troops.

Trimble's men then advanced about a mile. Trimble was confident he could flank the entire Union line and asked Ewell for reinforcements. Even though the Confederates had sustained few casualties, Ewell declined. Two of his brigade commanders, Elzey and Steuart, had been slightly wounded by shell fragments, and Ewell had received reports of a Union turning movement against the Confederate left.

Meanwhile, Jackson had sent Colonel John M. Patton's brigade and Brigadier General Richard Taylor's brigade to Ewell. They arrived in the afternoon and Ewell placed them in the center of his line. Later when Frémont failed to mount an attack on the Confederate left, Ewell ordered his men forward, and by nightfall they had occupied the Union positions of that morning.

Trimble wanted a night attack, but Ewell refused, reluctant to put too much distance between himself and Jackson. Ewell gave Trimble permission to approach Jackson who told him, "Consult General Ewell and be guided by him." To give his subordinate Ewell such latitude was high praise from Jackson. Trimble then tried a second time to convince Ewell, who again refused.

The fight at Cross Keys was more a skirmish than a real battle. Ewell had lost 288 men, of whom 41 were dead. Frémont, on the other hand had lost 684, nearly half of them dead or mortally wounded. (In his report to Jackson, containing the entire Union order of battle captured during the fight, Ewell claimed 2,000 Union casualties.)

Jackson then sent orders to Ewell to leave only a holding force (Trimble's brigade) in position facing Frémont while the rest of his men marched to join him at Port Republic. Jackson hoped that once Shields had been defeated they could then both return and complete the work of destroying Frémont. Ewell's march to reinforce Jackson at Port Republic began at dawn on 9 June; the remaining Confederate troops withdrew from Cross Keys on Jackson's subsequent order later on 9 June.

—*Spencer C. Tucker*

See also Elzey, Arnold; Ewell, Richard S.; Frémont, John C.; Jackson, Thomas J.; Port Republic, Battle of; Shenandoah Valley campaign (May–June 1862); Steuart, George H.; Taylor, Richard; Trimble, Isaac.
For further reading:
Collins, Darrell L. *Jackson's Valley Campaign. The Battles of Cross Keys and Port Republic, June 8–9, 1862* (1993).
Tanner, Robert G. *Stonewall in the Valley. Thomas J. "Stonewall" Jackson's Shenandoah Valley Campaign, Spring 1862* (1976; reprint 1996).

CULLUM, GEORGE WASHINGTON
(1809–1892)
Union general

Born to Arthur Cullum and Harriet Sturges Cullum in New York City, George Cullum moved with his parents to Pennsylvania while he was still a child. He was educated locally before receiving an appointment to the U.S. Military Academy. He graduated third of forty-three from the class of 1833. Commissioned into the Corps of Engineers, Cullum worked on a variety of projects including coastal fortifications, the expansion of the buildings at West Point, and harbor improvements during the pre–Civil War years.

As the Civil War approached, Cullum had reached the rank of major and was serving in Newport, Rhode Island. With the secession crisis becoming more serious in early 1861, he tried to bring the town to some defensive readiness but could not persuade the civilian authorities in the town that a crisis was at hand. Beginning in April 1861 he served as aide-de-camp to General Winfield Scott. Cullum held this position until August 1861, at which point he was promoted to colonel. In the fall of that year he transferred west. On 1 November 1861, Cullum became brigadier general of volunteers and chief of staff to General Henry Halleck. During his first months with Halleck, he also served as the general's chief engineer.

Halleck gave Cullum a great deal of leeway in carrying out the general's orders. Cullum traveled throughout the theater reporting back to Halleck the condition of troops and the quality of officer performance. He also did not hesitate to urge commanders to be more aggressive if necessary. Halleck also relied on Cullum, given his extensive engineering background, to inspect fortifications throughout the theater, and when short-handed would send Cullum to command those fortifications until a suitable officer could be found.

In July 1862, Halleck was summoned to Washington to serve as commanding general of Union armies. Cullum accompanied his commander to act as chief of staff in Washington. Cullum was to find his duties in Washington far more bureaucratic than serving a general in the field. He handled much of Halleck's communication with generals scattered throughout the country, but did not travel to the scene of action as he had done in the West. Cullum also served on several boards during his time in Washington. In December 1862, Secretary of War Edwin Stanton appointed Cullum to a commission to study the defenses of Washington, D.C. The following year Cullum served on a board to look at the defense of the Potomac Aqueduct and another looking again at Washington's defenses.

In March 1864, Halleck's position was considerably reduced when Ulysses S. Grant became commanding general. In fact, Halleck became Grant's chief of staff, thus reducing Cullum's role substantially. Cullum remained for several months on Halleck's staff, but in September 1864 accepted appointment as superintendent of the U.S. Military Academy. He remained in that position for two years.

Upon leaving West Point in 1866, Cullum was promoted to colonel in the regular army and served as an engineer until his retirement in 1874. He married for the first time the following year Elizabeth Hamilton Halleck, General Halleck's widow. For the remainder of his life, Cullum indulged a variety of interests including active membership in the National Geographical Society and efforts as a founder of the Association of Graduates of the U.S. Military Academy. He also wrote history and compiled and wrote much of the *Biographical Register of the Officers and Graduates of the United States Military Academy*, one of the most useful reference works on the officer corps of the nineteenth century. Cullum died in New York City on 28 February 1892, leaving a large fortune to his various causes.

—*David S. Heidler and Jeanne T. Heidler*

See also Halleck, Henry Wager.
For further reading:
Livermore, William Roscoe. "Biographical Notice of George Washington Cullum." *Proceedings of the Academy of Arts and Sciences.*

CUMMING, KATE
(ca. 1828–1909)
Confederate nurse

Kate Cumming is credited with writing the most detailed and poignant narrative of Confederate hospital life. A matron in the Confederate Army of Tennessee, Cumming traveled to Okolona and Corinth, Mississippi, after the battle of Shiloh in April 1862 and worked continuously until the spring of 1865. Having assessed the tremendous need for helping hands early in the war, she advocated hospital work and criticized those who discouraged elite women from volunteering. She kept a journal throughout her tour of duty, which records early Confederate jubilation, strong religious faith, anti-Union sentiments, frustrations with hospital staff, and increasing despondency at the prospect of food shortages and Confederate loss.

Cumming was born in Leith, Scotland, around 1828. Her father, David, who worked in commerce, moved his large family to Montreal while Kate was still a child (there were eventually ten children). There Kate received her only formal education, but her letters indicate a highly engaged intellect and an eloquent style. An intermediate move to New York and a final one to Mobile, Alabama, probably in the 1840s, resulted in Kate's strong association with the South. By the time of the Civil War, her views on slavery and states' rights made Cumming seem more Southern than many born in Dixie.

Cumming first became involved in hospital work when a neighboring clergyman conducted a band of churchwomen to Confederate hospitals established in Okolona and Corinth after Shiloh. The conditions at Tishomingo Hotel, where Confederate wounded were laid out all over the floors, were so foul that only Cumming and one other woman remained beyond the first week. With inadequate space, supplies, and staff, Cumming was so busy that she could not change her bloodstained dress for ten days and was compelled to sleep, when she could steal a few hours, on boxes. She was halfway through washing a soldier's face before she realized that he had died with no one near him. "These are terrible things," she wrote, "and what is more heart-rending, no one seems to mind them."

She returned home in June, but by early fall was bound for Chattanooga, where she served at Newsom Hospital (named for Ella King Newsom) until Braxton Bragg's forces withdrew from the city in the summer of 1863. Letters to her father from Chattanooga suggest that she was responsible for locating and managing laundresses, a job she disliked intensely. She also delivered food and medicine, kept clothing and bedding fresh, wrote letters, and even cooked when slaves were not available. From 1863 to the end of the war, Cumming was constantly on the move with Surgeon Samuel Stout's medical corps in the Army of Tennessee. Known for developing a system of "flying hospitals," the precursor to twentieth-century mobile surgical units, Stout's corps was plagued by frequent and sudden mobilizations as Sherman's army invaded Georgia and the Carolinas. Cumming complained that it was bad luck whenever a new hospital kitchen was completed because the army would inevitably be called to retreat the next day.

Before the war was over, she would travel to the Georgia cities of Dalton, Ringgold, Kingston, Cherokee Springs, Newnan, Americus, and Griffin, sometimes working in field hospitals. On duty during the siege of Vicksburg and the battles of Chickamauga and Lookout Mountain, Cumming despaired at the "moral leprosy eating at the very vitals of the Confederacy," or the graft that resulted from severe food shortages by 1864. By the autumn of 1864, she went for six weeks without writing in her journal because she had no paper.

Cumming left Newnan to travel the 385 miles to Mobile in May 1865. The trip took several weeks because of broken rail lines and lack of funds. Taking command of her father's household, Kate immersed herself in readying her journal for publication. In 1866, she paid a Louisville publisher to print the book with borrowed funds, but could not repay the loan for several years—a fact that caused her considerable anguish. Working as a governess and Sunday-school teacher, she

scraped together income to help with family expenses. The Cummings moved to Birmingham in 1874, where Kate settled into a round of teaching and participated in Confederate memorial activities. Always single, she adopted a nephew in the 1870s and produced a series of novels, none of which was ever published. In 1890 she republished a sanitized version of her journal called *Gleanings from Southland*, which was more successful in a market hungry for "the romance of reunion," a term coined by historian Nina Silber to denote North-South reconciliation. When Cumming died in 1909, she was better off financially than were nurses who had donated their substantial fortunes to the Lost Cause.

—*Jane E. Schultz*

See also Nurses.
For further reading:
Cumming, Kate. *A Journal of Hospital Life in the Confederate Army of Tennessee* (1866).
Faust, Drew Gilpin. *Mothers of Invention: Women of the Slaveholding South in the American Civil War* (1996).
Harwell, Richard B., ed. *Kate: The Journal of a Confederate Nurse* (1959).
Schultz, Jane E. *Women at the Front: Female Hospital Workers in Civil War America* (2000).

CURRENCY, C.S.A.

The Confederate government could not enact more than a shade of taxation for fear of causing immediate economic and political dislocations. The Davis administration was especially concerned that taxation would arouse suspicion of central authority at a time when the war effort required the unqualified support of the people. The Confederacy consequently tried to rely on disappointing loans from domestic bond issues and foreign creditors as well as nominal tariffs and taxes. The result was an insoluble financial dilemma wherein the inadequacy of Confederate finance became apparent in the opening days of the new government's existence. Within weeks of taking the post, Secretary of the Treasury Christopher Memminger tried to pay for the exploding costs of the Civil War with treasury notes.

These treasury notes were the legendary currency whose inflationary proliferation still stuns the imagination. To his credit, Memminger never succumbed to the easy delusion that currency is money. Too many Southerners, however, at least for a time slipped into the error because currency can act just as money does in the right circumstances. Yet currency and money fundamentally differ in that money has an intrinsic value apart from any form it takes. Gold has value even if it is not minted into coin. Yet currency, in the form of treasury notes for instance, has no value other than that artificially imparted to it. Currency can act as money only when markets are confident that its value derives from a stable source, such as a proportionate amount of specie or a healthy and responsible government. In fact, in the absence of any other support, such as specie, a robust government and calm political environment become paramount. The Confederacy had neither. As the government's effectiveness diminished under the fracturing burdens of war and internal discord, it was inevitable that the viability of Confederate currency would collapse as well and destroy the Southern economy.

Shortages of almost everything, including specie, plagued the Confederacy in 1861. Even the special paper used to print currency and the engraving expertise necessary to design it were hard for the government to procure. When the government resorted to issuing treasury notes that would have been redeemable in specie two years after the war, it inaugurated a long slide of depreciation that by 1863 had attained a staggering rate of acceleration. Paper currency in all denominations, even as low as fifty cents, spewed from printing presses as costs mounted. At the end of 1861, the Confederate dollar was worth approximately eighty cents in gold. In the first two months of 1862, it lost twenty cents of that value, and a year later the dollar reached a low of 20 cents. Value plummeted like a stone after that as military misfortunes occurred, placing the dollar's value at eight cents in the summer of 1863. When Lee surrendered at Appomattox, the Confederate dollar had a value of approximately 1.5 cents in gold.

The main cause for this rapid decline was rampant inflation. Using the standard axiom that high value is a result of scarcity and low value of overabundance, the astronomical numbers of treasury notes in circulation simply gutted their value. Yet other factors also contributed to the fiscal disaster. Localities ranging from the state to the county level added to the problem by circulating their own paper currency, and the variety and crudity of notes encouraged counterfeiting. The decision not to designate the treasury notes as legal tender was designed to inspire faith in their value, but it also did not require anybody to accept them as payment for goods and services. When their declining value became their most obvious feature, the currency in some instances simply became worthless. Prices rose about 300 percent in 1862, and by 1865 an ordinary suit of clothes in Richmond could cost as much $2,500. By then, the ocean of paper had become just another aspect of Confederate disintegration and collapse.

—David S. Heidler and Jeanne T. Heidler

See also Financing, C.S.A.

For further reading:

Lerner, Eugene M. "The Monetary and Fiscal Programs of the Confederate Government, 1861–1865." *Journal of Political Economy* (1954).

Schwab, John C. *The Confederate States of America, 1861–1865; A Financial and Industrial History of the South during the Civil War* (1901; reprint, 1968).

Todd, Richard Cecil. *Confederate Finance* (1954).

CURTIN, ANDREW GREGG
(1817–1894)
Northern politician and statesman

Born 22 April 1817, in Bellefonte, Pennsylvania, a son of Roland and Jane Curtin, Andrew G. Curtin was educated at the Harrisburg and Milton academies and at Dickinson School of Law. Curtin was a prosperous attorney before the war and served as secretary of the commonwealth and head of public education under Governor James Pollock from 1855 to 1857. Elected in 1860 by a 32,000-vote majority over Democrat Henry Foster, Curtin served as governor of Pennsylvania from 1861 to 1865 and was the first Republican to hold that office. While often overshadowed by such luminaries as John Andrew of Massachusetts and Horatio Seymour of New York, Andrew Curtin was an astute politician and a tireless defender of the Union and of the Lincoln administration.

Curtin was seemingly the only Northern politician (Lincoln included) who comprehended the gravity of the situation in 1861. It had been one of his first acts as governor to send agents into the Confederacy to ascertain the true state of affairs there. Hence, while most Northerners dismissed Southern threats as being mere bombast, Curtin never doubted that Southerners were in earnest. He quietly began to prepare his state for war. Pennsylvania under Curtin was one of the first states to answer the president's call for volunteers after Fort Sumter. The state provided more troops than the government could handle and many had to be turned away. Rather than send them home, as the War Department recommended, Curtin instead formed them into a semi-independent state command known as the Pennsylvania Reserves. Curtin's foresight in retaining these troops was soon born out after the Union disaster at First Bull Run in July 1861, when a frantic War Department, panicked by the prospect of an attack on the capital, urgently wired Curtin to send the reserves at once.

Among his contributions to the Union war effort were his tireless efforts to improve the lot of ordinary soldiers. Governor Curtin was the driving force behind the establishment of the National Cemetery at Gettysburg, organized a state commission to minister to sick and wounded soldiers, and worked especially hard to ensure that Pennsylvania's war dead be brought home for burial. Curtin was also responsible for the establishment of a state school for war orphans. It was because of these and countless other humanitarian endeavors that Curtin became known affectionately as "the Soldiers' Friend."

Perhaps Curtin's most significant contribution to Union victory was the 1862 Altoona Governors' Conference, which Curtin not only hosted but, together with Governor Andrew of Massachusetts, also drafted its concluding resolutions calling upon Lincoln to make another request for 300,000 men for the war. This statement, coming as it did in the wake of the Union defeats at the Seven Days' and Bull Run battles and the bloodletting at Antietam, not only relieved Lincoln of the politically onerous task of issuing another such call for troops, but was instrumental in rallying support from the Northern governors at what must have seemed the darkest hours for the Union cause.

So instrumental was Curtin in rallying support for the Union cause within Pennsylvania that many deemed it essential that he seek a second term in 1863 despite poor health and Lincoln's offer of a foreign ambassadorship. His decision to accept the Republican nomination would subject Curtin to one of the bitterest campaigns in the state's history. Despite the bitter and personal nature of the opposition's attacks, Curtin easily won reelection over his Democratic opponent George Woodward, an avowed Copperhead and ally of Ohio congressional representative Clement Vallandigham. Curtain's victory not only served to discourage antiwar Democrats, but would also prove to be a bellwether for Democratic fortunes in 1864, when Lincoln would handily defeat former Commander of the Army of the Potomac general George B. McClellan.

After the war, Curtin continued as governor until 1866 and later was appointed by President Grant as minister to Russia. There was a great deal of talk within the Republican Party of Curtin being nominated for vice president or even president. The manipulations of his chief political rival, former Secretary of War Simon Cameron, denied Curtin these opportunities, however. The feud with Cameron would not only deny Curtin a chance at higher office, but would eventually cause him to switch to the Democrats in 1878. It was as a member of that party that Curtin won election to Congress in 1880, 1882, and 1884. He served as chairman of the House Foreign Affairs Committee. After leaving Congress in 1885, Curtin retired to his home in Bellefonte, where he died on 7 October 1894. To the end of his days, he remained a staunch promoter of harmony and reconciliation between North and South.

—*Ken A. Dietreich*

See also Cameron, Simon; Pennsylvania; Woodward, George W.

For further reading:

Armor, William C. *Lives of the Governors of Pennsylvania with the Incidental History of the State, from 1609 to 1872* (1877).

Curtin, Andrew G. *Annual Message of the Governor of Pennsylvania, Andrew G. Curtin, to the Legislature of Pennsylvania, at Harrisburg, 7 January 1864* (1864).

Egle, William H., ed. *Life and Times of Andrew Gregg Curtin* (1895).

Goas, Thomas Stewart. *The Contribution of Andrew Gregg Curtin to the Union: Honors to Andrew Gregg Curtin* (1869).

CURTIS, BENJAMIN ROBBINS
(1809–1874)
U.S. Supreme Court justice

The son of Benjamin Curtis III, a merchant marine officer who lost his life at sea, and Lois Robbins, Curtis grew up in Watertown, Massachusetts. He received an A.B. from Harvard in 1829 and then entered Harvard's law school. After a brief career as a country lawyer in the rural Massachusetts town of Northfield, Curtis accepted a position in a Boston law firm owned by his relative Charles Pelham Curtis. Benjamin Robbins Curtis thrived in the new firm, and he soon represented some of the more affluent merchants in the city. He likewise became prominent in Boston's Whig Party, and he served two terms as a state representative.

There was little in Curtis's professional or political background that would suggest anything other than a moderate political philosophy—particularly on the two most divisive issues of his day: slavery and states' rights. In one case, for instance, Curtis argued that Southerners had rights to bind their slaves as property even while visiting Northern states in which slavery was outlawed. Curtis was likewise one of Daniel Webster's leading advisors in drafting a defense of the Fugitive Slave Law of 1850 that created such furor among Northern abolitionists. Thus, as he had been true to moderate Whig principles, and having distinguished himself as an exceptionally gifted attorney, Curtis was appointed by President Millard Fillmore—on the advice of Daniel Webster—to the high court in 1851 to fill the vacancy created by the death of Justice Levi Woodbury.

During his short tenure on the bench, Curtis's legal positions tended to side more often than not with the majority, dominated by Southern Democrats, and he strove to maintain the dual federalism that characterized most of the Taney court's legal opinions. The two most famous cases in which Curtis is most often noted involved his majority opinion in *Cooley v. Board of Wardens* (1852) and his dissenting opinion in *Scott v. Sandford* (1857), the former establishing the doctrine that the commerce clause did not give the federal government exclusive power of regulation, while the latter rendered the Missouri Compromise unconstitutional.

Often viewed as the classic example of dual federalism jurisprudence, Curtis's opinion in *Cooley* established what some legal scholars refer to as the doctrine of selective exclusiveness. Curtis wrote that when a uniform national rule with respect to objects of commerce is necessary, the federal government has exclusive right to regulate such commercial activity. However, his opinion likewise asserted that when no such rule is necessary, states are free to regulate at their discretion. Clearly then a moderate on states' rights and the respective powers of the federal and state governments, Curtis was well respected by his co-justices, who regarded his legal opinions highly.

Yet, in 1857, when the famous *Dred Scott* case was argued before the Supreme Court, Curtis broke with the court and rendered one of the most memorable dissents in American legal history. The majority opinion, prepared by Chief Justice Taney, asserted that a slave was not automatically freed by spending time in free territory. The opinion likewise stated that slaves could not be citizens of the United States; that they had no rights to sue in federal courts; and, as the most controversial aspect of the ruling, that Congress had had no constitutional authority to establish the Missouri Compromise line in 1820.

Curtis's dissent thoroughly repudiated the majority opinion from several angles. First, Curtis showed that African-Americans had been citizens of at least five states at the time of the ratification of the Constitution, and, he argued, as that had been true, federal citizenship automatically conferred to them in 1789. Therefore, he asserted, a person of African descent could indeed be a citizen of the United States, an assertion in direct contrast to Taney's racially based argument. Second, with respect to Congressional authority to regulate slavery in the territories—an action Taney asserted was unconstitutional—Curtis described fourteen precedents when Congress had in fact lawfully regulated slavery. Therefore, he argued, the Missouri Compromise line was constitutional and Congress had had full authority to disallow the expansion of slavery north of 36° 30'.

It has been argued that Curtis's dissent, in which he so forcefully argued the constitutionality of the Missouri Compromise, literally forced the majority to expand their decision beyond what was necessary to settle the case. In other words, had Curtis not broached the subject, the majority would not have felt compelled to render such a controversial opinion. Such an indictment of Curtis lacks credibility, and in all likelihood Curtis wrote his dissent in response to the majority opinion once he realized the full implications of its pro-Southern position. Curtis had never been a firebrand on the slavery issue, yet he clearly could not follow a decision that would destroy the Missouri Compromise line and Congress's power to regulate slavery in the territories.

Due to the furor over the *Dred Scott* decision and the deep resentment among the justices raised by that ruling, Curtis lost all confidence in the Court and its ability to rule impartially. Thus, in September 1857, after only six terms as an associate justice, Curtis resigned from the bench and returned to Boston and to private practice. The breach among the justices and Curtis's resignation over the *Dred Scott* decision were but the first in a long series of schismatic events that culminated in the secession winter of 1860–1861.

—*Robert Saunders, Jr.*

See also Dred Scott Case; Supreme Court U.S.

For further reading:
Curtis, Benjamin R., ed. *The Life and Writings of Benjamin Robbins Curtis* (1879).
Fehrenbacher, Don E. *The Dred Scott Case: Its Significance in American Law and Politics* (1978).
Leach, Richard H. "Benjamin R. Curtis: Case Study of a Supreme Court Justice" (Ph.D.dissertation, 1951).

CURTIS, NEWTON MARTIN
(1835–1910)
Union general

Born in De Peyster, New York, to Jonathan Curtis and Phebe Rising Curtis, Newton Martin Curtis received his education locally and at Gouverneur Wesleyan Seminary. Before the outbreak of the Civil War, he taught school, served as the De Peyster postmaster, studied law, and farmed.

Abraham Lincoln's call for volunteers caused Curtis to raise a local company that became a part of the 16th New York. Curtis was commissioned a captain in the regiment and went with the unit to Washington. He fought at First Bull Run. In the Peninsula campaign the following year, Curtis was wounded on 7 May at West Point, Virginia. He was unable to return to duty for some months, and when he did in the fall he was promoted to lieutenant colonel in the 142d New York. He became the regiment's colonel in January 1863. Still not fully recovered from his wounds, Curtis did not see significant action until the following year, though he served briefly at the end of 1863 in the Department of the South, headquartered at Hilton Head, South Carolina.

Curtis returned to the Army of the Potomac in the spring of 1864 and fought at Cold Harbor. In June 1864 he was given command of a brigade. In October 1864 Curtis was recommended for promotion to brigadier general for his actions at New Market Heights at the end of September.

At the end of the year, Curtis became part of the Army of the James under Benjamin F. Butler and was assigned to the Fort Fisher, North Carolina, expedition. He was a part of the aborted December assault and the successful one on 15 January 1865. In the latter engagement, Curtis commanded the attack on the northwest corner of the fort and was credited with being the first man into the fort. He was hit in the head by Confederate canister and lost his left eye. On 28 May 1891, Curtis was awarded the Medal of Honor for his actions at Fort Fisher. He was promoted shortly after the battle to brigadier general dating from 15 January.

Because of the seriousness of his injury, Curtis was unable to return to duty until 15 April. On 24 April he became the chief of staff for the Army of Virginia. The

Newton Martin Curtis (*Library of Congress*)

Story of the Sixteenth New York Infantry Together with Personal Reminiscences (1906).

CURTIS, SAMUEL RYAN
(1805–1866)
Union general

Born on 3 February 1805 near Champlain, New York, Samuel R. Curtis grew up in central Ohio. He attended the U.S. Military Academy at West Point and graduated twenty-seventh in a class of thirty-three in 1831.

After only one year of service, Curtis resigned his commission and returned to Ohio to begin a successful engineering career. He worked on the National Road and later designed plans to make the Muskingum River in Ohio and the Des Moines River in Iowa navigable. He spent three distinguished years as the city engineer for St. Louis. During the Mexican-American War, Curtis mustered Ohio troops into service and then commanded the 3d Ohio Infantry. Returning to Iowa in 1853, Curtis surveyed and advocated several routes for a transcontinental railroad. In early 1856 he was elected mayor of Keokuk, and in the fall he surprisingly won a seat in Congress as a Republican. Narrowly reelected in 1858 and 1860, Curtis said his championship of the Pacific railway caused his success.

After Fort Sumter, Curtis equipped and mustered Iowa's first volunteer regiments, and the 2d Iowa Infantry unanimously elected him colonel. He resigned from Congress in August 1861 to accept a promotion to brigadier general. Assigned to John C. Frémont's command in St. Louis, Curtis brought calm and order to the city. When Henry Halleck succeeded Frémont, he ordered Curtis in December 1861 to remove organized Confederate resistance in southwest Missouri. On 7–8 March 1862, General Earl Van Dorn's 16,000 Confederates attacked Curtis's army of 10,500 entrenched near Pea Ridge, Arkansas. Although surprised by two aggressive flanking attacks, Curtis quickly reversed his front while maintaining his composure and interior lines of communication. After several desperate assaults at Elkhorn Tavern, the exhausted Confederate army disintegrated. The victory saved Missouri for the Union and earned Curtis a promotion to major general. His subsequent two-month campaign to capture Little Rock failed, but the Confederacy also lost northern Arkansas.

After Halleck's promotion to general-in-chief, Curtis became commander of the Department of the Missouri in September 1862. Military and political difficulties immediately plagued him. The acceleration of Grant's campaign to capture Vicksburg drained troops from Curtis's department. Southern Missouri experienced

following month, he served on a board to examine the qualifications for advancement for colonels. In June 1865 he was recommended for promotion to major general of volunteers. At the end of the year, he commanded the District of Southwest Virginia. Curtis left the army in early 1866 with the mustering out of the volunteers and returned home to New York.

After the war, Curtis held the position of customs collector and U.S. Treasury special agent in his home county. In the 1880s he became involved in politics, serving in the New York state legislature before being elected to the U.S. House of Representatives in 1890. He served three terms in that body. Curtis's other interests included agricultural experimentation as well as several reform movements. He worked diligently to achieve more humane treatment for the mentally ill and to abolish capital punishment. In his retirement he wrote extensively, including a memoir of the Civil War. Curtis died on 8 January 1910 in New York City.

—*David S. Heidler and Jeanne T. Heidler*

See also Fort Fisher.
For further reading:
Curtis, Newton Martin. *From Bull Run to Chancellorsville, the*

increased guerrilla activity, and Curtis's relationship with General John M. Schofield, his senior general in the field, was characterized by mutual pettiness. Curtis also clashed with conservative Missouri politicians. Governor Hamilton R. Gamble, in particular, accused Curtis of being a Radical Republican interested in substituting martial law for civil authority. Curtis's zealous crackdown on guerrilla activity and the continuation of assessments, a levy placed upon suspected Southern sympathizers, aggravated matters. Eventually Lincoln intervened, ending the assessment policy and, in May 1863, replacing Curtis with Schofield.

Upon Kansas senator James H. Lane's insistence, Lincoln assigned Curtis to command the newly created Department of Kansas in January 1864. Curtis negotiated this politically charged environment more carefully. He faced few military threats until October 1864, when Confederate general Sterling Price's invasion of central Missouri turned toward Kansas and the supply depot at Fort Leavenworth. With only 4,000 regular troops and 10,000 unreliable militia, Curtis tried unsuccessfully to stop Price's 9,000 veterans at the Big Blue River on 21 October. Forced back to Westport, Curtis's army offered stiff resistance on 23 October until General Alfred Pleasonton's cavalry threatened Price from the rear. Price beat a hasty retreat to the south with Curtis in aggressive pursuit. Curtis decimated the Confederate rear guard before Price crossed the Arkansas River to safety.

Unenthusiastic about an impending Indian war in midwinter, Curtis requested reassignment in January 1865. After the war, he helped negotiate a treaty with the Sioux and became a commissioner for the transcontinental railroad. Curtis died suddenly on 26 December 1866 at Council Bluffs, Iowa. He is buried in Keokuk.

Curtis's methodical nature and an engineer's concern for detail characterize his wartime performance. He could be "slow and unimaginative, but at the same time steady and tenacious." Advancing age and political turmoil perhaps made Curtis a marginal figure after 1863, but his success in the field secured the trans-Mississippi for the Union.

—M. *Philip Lucas*

See also Gamble, Hamilton; Kansas; Missouri; Pea Ridge, Battle of; Price's Missouri Raid; Schofield, John M.

For further reading:
Castel, Albert. "A New View of the Battle of Pea Ridge." *Missouri Historical Review* (1968).
Colton, Kenneth E., ed. "With Fremont in Missouri in 1861: Letters of Samuel Ryan Curtis." *Annals of Iowa* (1942).
Gallaher, Ruth A. "Samuel Ryan Curtis." *Iowa Journal of History and Politics* (1927).
Parrish, William E. *Turbulent Partnership: Missouri and the Union, 1861–1865* (1963).
Shea, William L., and Earl J. Hess. *Pea Ridge: Civil War Campaign in the West* (1992).

CUSHING, ALONZO HERSFORD
(1841–1863)
Union officer

Alonzo Cushing came from a family that distinguished itself during the Civil War. His brother, William B. Cushing, was one of the U.S. Navy's great heroes, specializing in commando-type raids. Another brother, Howard B. Cushing, served as a private in various artillery units in 1862 and 1863. After Gettysburg, Howard Cushing was commissioned into the U.S. 4th Artillery, his late brother's regiment. Howard Cushing remained in the U.S. Army following the war, transferred to the cavalry, and died in action in 1871 fighting the Apaches in Arizona.

Alonzo Cushing was born in Waukesha City, Wisconsin on 19 January 1841. In 1857 he was appointed to West Point from the state of New York. George Armstrong Custer was one of his classmates. Cushing graduated twelfth in his class on 24 June 1861. That day he received both his commission as a second lieutenant and a simultaneous promotion to first lieutenant in the regular army. It was the only substantive promotion he would ever receive. Immediately following graduation, Cushing reported to the 4th Artillery. He would remain in that unit for the rest of his short life.

Cushing fought in many of the major battles of the Civil War, including First Bull Run, Fair Oaks, Second Bull Run, Antietam, and Fredericksburg. He received a brevet promotion to captain for his actions at Fredericksburg on 13 December 1862. In February 1863, Cushing assumed command of Battery A, 4th Artillery and led that unit at Chancellorsville. In the subsequent Union retreat, his battery was the last unit to cross the Rappahannock River. Cushing received a brevet promotion to major for his actions at Chancellorsville on 2 May 1863.

On 1 July 1863, the first day of the battle of Gettysburg, the Union troops were forced back upon Cemetery Ridge about the same time Major General Winfield Scott Hancock arrived on the field to take command. One of his first acts was to press Cushing into temporary duty as his aide. For twelve hours Cushing moved about the battlefield, conveying orders and guiding newly arriving units to their assigned positions. All the while he was exposed to heavy Confederate fire.

Returning to Battery A, Cushing and his cannoneers remained in position on Cemetery Ridge and saw relatively little action on 2 July. Battery A's position in the Union line was just to the north of the Copse of Trees that became the orienting point of the Confederate attack on 3 July. Cushing's six 3-inch ordnance rifles were less than ten yards away from the Angle in the stone fence that fronted the Federal position. Preparatory to the charge of Pickett's and Pettigrew's

Alonzo Cushing (*Library of Congress*)

Divisions, Confederate guns pounded the Union lines for almost three hours. During the cannonade Cushing's battery returned fire, but took heavy casualties in the process. By the time the shelling lifted, Battery A had lost four of its six guns, and Cushing himself was severely wounded in the right shoulder and groin.

Refusing to relinquish his command or submit to medical attention, Cushing continued to fight at his battery. When the Confederate artillery fire ceased, the Union troops knew that the ground attack would follow shortly. Cushing moved his two surviving guns forward to the edge of the stone wall and prepared to resist the Southern onslaught. He ordered all of his battery's remaining canister rounds consolidated at the two pieces. He also ordered his cannoneers to arm themselves with trail spikes and rammer staffs in anticipation of hand-to-hand combat with the Confederate infantry.

When the attack came, Cushing's guns fired spherical case and solid shot until the Confederates came within canister range. As the leading Southern troops closed to within fifty yards of his position, Cushing's men commenced firing double canister. Shortly after that, Cushing was hit in the face by a bullet and died at his Number 4 gun. Although he had been bleeding heavily and in severe pain, Cushing remained at his post and in command for more than one and a half hours after first being wounded. He was only 22 when he died.

Immediately after Cushing fell, his German-born first sergeant, Frederick Fuger, assumed command of what was left of Battery A and fired triple canister until Pickett's troops overran their position. The Union cannoneers then engaged the Confederate infantrymen in hand-to-hand combat until a counterattack by the 72d Pennsylvania Infantry broke the Southern momentum. The attack faltered and then failed. Brigadier General Lewis Armistead died immediately to the left of Battery A's Number 4 gun, only a few yards from where Cushing fell. At the end of the battle, more than 600 dead Confederate soldiers lay directly in front of Battery A's position.

While most of the soldiers killed at Gettysburg were buried close to where they fell, Cushing's body was guarded by his loyal first sergeant until Cushing's brother could arrive to claim it. The Cushing family had the body buried in the West Point cemetery, where Cushing lies today next to Major General John Buford. Curiously enough, Cushing received a posthumous brevet promotion to lieutenant colonel for his actions as Hancock's aide on 1 July, but no formal recognition of his heroism on 3 July.

The gallant First Sergeant Fuger received a battlefield commission for his actions on 3 July, and later in the Civil War he received two more brevet promotions. In 1896 Fuger also received the Medal of Honor for his heroism at Gettysburg. He retired from the U.S. Army in 1900 as a colonel.

—*David T. Zabecki*

See also Cushing, William B.
For further reading:
Brown, Kent Masterson. *Cushing of Gettysburg: The Story of a Union Artillery Commander* (1993).
Downey, Fairfax. *The Guns at Gettysburg* (1958).
Naisawald, L. Van Loan. *Grape and Canister: The Story of the Field Artillery of the Army of the Potomac* (1983).

CUSHING, WILLIAM BARKER
(1842–1874)
U.S. Navy commando

No U.S. Navy officer emerged from the Civil War better known or more respected than William Barker Cushing. By 1865 Cushing was a living legend in the navy and, although he never obtained wartime rank above that of lieutenant commander, was more popular among Northerners than the U.S. Navy's highest ranking officers, with the exception of Admiral David G. Farragut. One of Cushing's many admirers observed that, "As Farragut was its glory and its hero…Cushing [was] the darling of the American navy." A determined and intrepid young seaman, Cushing's daring commando-like raids behind enemy lines outwitted and bedeviled Confederate forces. Rear Admiral David D. Porter described Cushing as a "'free-lance,' who was always ready to perform any act of daring…and whether fortunate or not in his undertakings, he was sure to create a sensation."

Cushing created a sensation from the days of his boyhood. Born on 4 November 1842, he was the fourth son of Milton and Mary Barker Cushing, who made their home at the time near the present-day town of Delafield, Wisconsin. (William's well-known older brother Alonzo would die while commanding a battery of the 4th U.S. Artillery in defense of Cemetery Ridge at Gettysburg on 3 July 1863.) After her husband's untimely death in 1847, Mary Cushing moved her children to Fredonia, New York. There young Will grew up a rambunctious, fearless, and prideful young man fond of pranks who never backed down from a fight.

Cushing's undisciplined nature haunted him at the U.S. Naval Academy in Annapolis, Maryland, where, at the age of fourteen, he was appointed to the class of 1861. Although intelligent and bright, Cushing acquired numerous demerits for skylarking instead of studying. Disappointed by Cushing's bad conduct and poor work habits, the academy's superintendent forced the young midshipman's resignation on 23 March 1861, just ten weeks before graduation. The official reason for Cushing's dismissal was a "deficiency in Spanish."

The outbreak of war in April 1861 heightened the need for sailors to serve in Lincoln's navy. Cushing was given a chance to redeem himself when, with the assistance of his friend Lieutenant Charles W. Flusser, Cushing was appointed a midshipman in the U.S. Navy. Encouraged by the renewed faith shown in him, Cushing vowed to make a name for himself in the war or die trying.

For the first year of the conflict, Cushing served meritoriously on board blockading vessels off the coast of the Carolinas. During June and July 1861, Cushing was with the USS *Wabash* on the blockade at Charleston, South Carolina. In August 1861, he fought with the USS *Minnesota* at the capture of Forts Hatteras and Clark on the Outer Banks of North Carolina. As a crewman on board the USS *Cambridge* from the autumn of 1861 to the spring of 1862, Cushing made a name for himself as a dependable and brave volunteer on "cutting-out" expeditions against Confederate positions in tidewater Virginia.

Impressed by the courageous young seaman, the U.S. Navy appointed Cushing lieutenant on 16 July 1862. Only nineteen years old, Cushing jumped the two commissioned grades of master and ensign with his promotion. The following month Lieutenant Cushing became executive officer of the gunboat *Commodore Perry*, commanded by his old friend Lieutenant Commander Charles Flusser.

Cushing quickly increased his reputation for bravery.

On the Blackwater River in Virginia on 3 October 1862, he helped serve a boat howitzer in the repulse of an enemy assault, thus saving the *Commodore Perry* from capture. Rear Admiral S. Phillips Lee, head of the North Atlantic Blockading Squadron, awarded Cushing with command of the USS *Ellis*, a captured Confederate steamer, on 13 October 1862. Less than a week after assuming his new command, Cushing captured and burned his first enemy vessel, the laden schooner *Adelaide*, at New Topsail Inlet, North Carolina.

In late November 1862, Cushing boldly steamed the *Ellis* up the New River to raze salt works, and to capture boats and the little town of Jacksonville, North Carolina. After some measured success, the *Ellis* ran aground trying to exit the river and was destroyed in a crossfire from Confederate shore batteries. Nevertheless, Cushing managed to escape with his crew in a captured schooner and was subsequently commended by Admiral Lee for his "coolness, courage and conduct."

Between December 1862 and January 1863, Cushing made three attempts to enter the Cape Fear River in the schooner *Home* and kidnap pilots at Wilmington, North Carolina. Calm winds spoiled each endeavor, so Cushing shifted his efforts to Little River, South Carolina, fifty miles south of Wilmington. On 5 January, Cushing staged a bold raid up Little River, overrunning a blockhouse, driving off its Confederate defenders, and capturing provisions.

Most of 1863 found Cushing on assignment again in southeastern Virginia, where he received the thanks of the Navy Department for his good fighting on the Nansemond River and at Chuckatuck in the battle for Suffolk. Cushing returned to the Cape Fear, where he spent the longest stint of his wartime service, when he was placed in command of the gunboat *Shokokon* on 9 August 1863. By then Wilmington was the Confederacy's premier blockade running seaport.

Shortly after reporting for duty with the Wilmington blockading squadron, Cushing commanded the *Shokokon* in battle for possession of the derelict blockade runner *Hebe* near New Inlet, the northern-most entrance into the Cape Fear River, on 18 August 1863. Aroused by the excitement of the *Hebe* skirmish, Cushing steamed the *Shokokon* up to New Topsail Inlet, where he discovered and destroyed the Northern blockade running schooner *Alexander Cooper* on 22 August. In a letter to Secretary of the Navy Gideon Welles, Admiral Lee called Lieutenant Cushing a "zealous and able young officer." The 20-year-old Fredonian and Naval Academy dropout had been with the Wilmington squadron less than three weeks and was already earning high praise from the navy high command.

Consequently, when Cushing's ship, the *Shokokon*, proved unseaworthy, the department quickly provided him with the sturdier *Monticello* on 5 September 1863. Commanding the *Monticello*, Cushing kept a vigilant watch for blockade runners operating in and out of Wilmington.

On the night of 29 February 1864, Cushing initiated a daring raid through Old Inlet, the southern entrance into the Cape Fear River, to kidnap Confederate brigadier general Louis Hébert, commander of the Lower Cape Fear defenses and headquartered at the town of Smithville, two miles inside the bar. Though he missed General Hébert who happened to be in Wilmington upriver that night, Cushing and his men managed to capture Captain Patrick Kelly, Hébert's chief engineer. Cushing may have failed to bag his main quarry, but his "gallantry and success" again earned him the compliments of the U.S. Navy Department.

When the Monticello ran into and sank the USS Peterhoff on blockade duty at the Cape Fear on 6 March 1864, the Navy Department overlooked Cushing's responsibilty in the accident. The Navy could ill afford to lose Cushing, a daring commando who would be harder to replace than the Peterhoff.

On 23 June 1864, Cushing and a small group of sailors from the Monticello again entered the Cape Fear River, this time hoping to find and destroy the ironclad CSS Raleigh, which had recently tried to break the Federal blockade at New Inlet. Unaware that the Raleigh had run aground and sunk in the river, Cushing and his men spent three days reconnoitering the area, kidnapping passers-by and committing acts of sabotage. Again the Navy Department extended its gratitude to Cushing for his boldness. U.S. rear admiral David D. Porter later wrote that "There was not a more daring adventure than this during the course of the war."

During the summer of 1864 Admiral S. Phillips Lee selected Cushing to lead an expedition to destroy the Confederate ironclad ram Albemarle near Plymouth, North Carolina. Cushing set out immediately for New York to select the small boats he would use in the attempt to place a torpedo against the Albemarle's hull.

Cushing selected two thirty-foot steam-powered launches. One, however, was destroyed in a storm coming down to North Carolina. Therefore he set out with thirteen other men aboard the one boat on the night of 27 October 1864 to destroy the Albemarle. He and his men entered the Roanoke River and were quickly spotted as they neared their target. They were fired upon but managed to draw close to the Albemarle only to discover that the ship was surrounded by logs chained together to prevent someone from placing a torpedo against the hull. The men managed to get their boat over the logs but knew they would not have the momentum to recross the barrier once they had placed the torpedo. As Cushing maneuvered the torpedo at the end of a long pole against the hull of the ship, several bullets tore through his clothes. He remained calm while going about his work and once he had succeeded, the

resulting explosion swamped his small craft. He instructed the men to swim for shore, though most were captured before they could make an attempt. The Albemarle began to sink.

Cushing made it into the river and over the next several hours struggled against a strong current finally to make it to the riverbank. The next day he trudged through a swamp and stole a rowboat from a Confederate work party. He rowed for ten hours out to the Federal fleet. Once he arrived, he was treated as a hero and sent to Hampton Roads to make his report. As a result of his efforts the Federals were able to take Plymouth, North Carolina. The mission also earned Cushing a navy promotion to lieutenant commander, the thanks of the U.S. Congress, and everlasting fame as "Albemarle Cushing."

When the Federals attacked Fort Fisher, the Confederacy's largest and strongest seacoast fortification and main guardian of Wilmington, at Christmas 1864, Cushing commanded Admiral David D. Porter's flagship USS Malvern. Cushing also led a boat expedition to take soundings of New Inlet while under heavy cannon fire from Fort Fisher.

At Second Fort Fisher, 13–15 January 1865, Cushing and forty of his men from the Monticello, which he again commanded, volunteered to fight onshore with a column of more than 2,000 seamen in conjunction with the army's ground assault against Fort Fisher. Despite the failure of the navy's shore arm in the attack, Fort Fisher fell to Union forces, thus closing the harbor to blockade running and severing the Confederacy's lifeline.

Three days after the capture of Fort Fisher, Cushing took possession of abandoned Confederate fortifications on Oak Island at Old Inlet and accepted the surrender of Smithville from the town's mayor. He also declared himself governor of the province. Cushing then concocted a scheme to lure unsuspecting blockade runners into the Cape Fear estuary, now in Union hands. This led to Cushing's capture of the blockade runner Charlotte out of Bermuda on the night of 20 January 1865.

While the Federal high command made plans to advance on Wilmington, Cushing led several expeditions upriver to reconnoiter Confederate defenses and waterway obstructions. On the night of 11 February 1865, Cushing stole ashore at Fort Anderson, the strongest interior fortification protecting Wilmington, to witness a Confederate pep rally. He barely escaped with his life.

During the battle of Fort Anderson on 18 February 1865, Cushing employed a Quaker monitor of his own design against the Confederates in an effort to get them to explode their torpedoes in the river. The effort failed but did not dissuade Cushing from boasting to President Abraham Lincoln that his sham monitor, dubbed Old

Bogey and *Albemarle No. 2*, had caused the Confederates to abandon Fort Anderson. Wilmington fell on 22 February 1865, and the Confederacy collapsed soon thereafter.

Five times during the war the Navy Department rendered William B. Cushing thanks for his gallant feats and daring deeds. He also received the thanks of the U.S. Congress and high praise from President Lincoln himself. Cushing "would undertake the most desperate adventures, where it seemed impossible for him to escape death or capture," observed Admiral David D. Porter, "yet he always managed to get off with credit to himself and loss to the enemy."

Cushing's critics, who considered him vain, arrogant and foolish, believed his hazardous undertakings behind enemy lines gained little and risked or cost the lives of good seamen. Yet, as one Cushing admirer later remarked, "there was more method in [Cushing's missions] than appeared on the surface and important information was sometimes obtained, to say nothing of the brilliant example of courage and enterprise...."

Cushing remained in the navy after the war, serving in the Pacific Squadron, cruising for Chinese pirates and performing administrative duties at both the Boston and Washington Navy Yards. In Fredonia, New York, on 22 February 1870, he married Katherie Louisa Forbes. They had two daughters.

For some time after the war, Cushing's friends and family noticed symptoms of a "diseased brain." They believed the disease was brought on by "exposure and high excitement" of his wartime duties. By early December 1874, Cushing had become so violent and uncontrollable that he was confined to the Government Hospital for the Insane in Washington, D.C. He died on 17 December. The official cause of death listed on his pension papers was "acute mania."

Ironically, "Albemarle Cushing" was buried with full military honors in the cemetery on Bluff Point at the U.S. Naval Academy, the school that had ejected him only thirteen years before. Midshipmen at the Naval Academy still study the life and exploits of William B. Cushing. An admirer wrote that the young commando's life was a "fascinating story of glorious achievement and dauntless courage" that placed him "among the veritable heroes of the age."

—*Chris E. Fonvielle, Jr.*

See also *Albemarle*, CSS; Fort Fisher.

For further reading:
Cushing, William B. *The Journal of Lieutenant Comdr. William B. Cushing, 1861–1865* (1976).
Edwards, E.M.H. *Commander William Barker Cushing of the United States Navy* (1896).
Fonvielle, Chris E., Jr. "William B. Cushing: Commando at the Cape Fear." *Blue & Gray Magazine* (1997).
Roske, Ralph J. and Charles Van Doren. *Lincoln's Commando: The Biography of Commander William B. Cushing, U.S. Navy* (1957; reprint ed., 1995).

CUSHMAN, PAULINE
(1833–1893)
Union spy

Described by her 1865 biographer as a woman of "entrancing form," "flashing eye," and "most wondrous beauty," Pauline Cushman was a professional actress at the time the Civil War began. Born in the New Orleans, Louisiana, she was raised on the Michigan frontier where she developed a taste for adventure and equestrian skills that would serve her effectively during the Civil War.

In 1863 Cushman found herself at Wood's Theater in politically divided Louisville, Kentucky, where she had come with her acting troupe to perform a play. On her own initiative, Cushman turned the occasion into an opportunity to embark on a stint as a Union spy, courier, and scout. When some Confederate officers dared her to interrupt one of her performances to offer a toast to Confederate president Jefferson Davis, Cushman consulted with the Union army's local provost marshal, suggesting that she might offer the toast to Davis, but only as a means of misleading her audience about her political loyalties and thereby to establish a cover for herself as an intelligence agent for the Union. The provost marshal agreed to her plan, and subsequently "banished" her to Union-held Nashville, where she sought out Colonel William Truesdail, the Union army's chief of police for the Army of the Cumberland, for further instructions.

The precise nature of the instructions Truesdail gave to Cushman are not on record, but over the next several months Cushman served as a Federal courier, riding through Kentucky, Tennessee, northern Georgia, Alabama, and Mississippi. In the course of her travels, Cushman assumed a variety of disguises, including a soldier's uniform, in order to gather information on Confederate fortifications and troop movements. She strove at the same time to identify for Union officials the names of dangerous Confederate spies and activists across the region.

At some point during her service Cushman received an honorary military commission from either General William S. Rosecrans or General James A. Garfield in recognition of her daring and loyal service. Not long after she set out on her chosen mission for the Union, however, Cushman's activities began to provoke suspicion, and late in the spring of 1863 none other than Confederate general John Hunt Morgan arrested her near Shelbyville, Tennessee. Morgan turned Cushman over to General Nathan Bedford Forrest, who interrogated her at length and, convinced of her duplicity, sentenced her to death by hanging. Whether Forrest actually would have carried out the sentence is unclear. Fortunately for Cushman, Union troops arriving in

Shelbyville drove Forrest and his men away and effected Cushman's release.

Cushman continued to serve the Union to the best of her ability after this, but because of her remarkable beauty and the attention that she received as a result of her capture by Morgan, her spying days were cut short.

When Cushman visited New York City in 1864, her presence was noted in the local papers, which described her as a dedicated scout and spy for the Union. To the end of her life she would be remembered by many in this way, although her postwar years were hardly glorious. After the war Cushman resumed her stage career, often presenting monologues related to her wartime espionage activities and sometimes dressing in the uniform of a soldier. As time passed, however, popular interest in her adventures declined, and Cushman—who took up sewing to earn an income—fell victim to alcohol and possibly drug abuse, perhaps to cope with a physical disability related to her wartime exploits. Cushman married twice (she had also been married before the war to a man who soon left her a widow) and bore two children, who died in infancy. She died in 1893 in San Francisco. When the members of a local veterans group learned of her death, they claimed her body from the morgue and buried it in full military style, with an honor guard and a gun salute.

—Elizabeth D. Leonard

See also Espionage; Women.
For further reading:
Brockett, Linus P. *The Camp, the Battlefield and the Hospital; or, Light and Shadows of the Great Rebellion* (1866).
Kane, Harnett T. *Spies for the Blue and Gray* (1954).
Leonard, Elizabeth D. *All the Daring of the Soldier: Women of the Civil War Armies* (1999).
Sarmiento, F. L. *Life of Pauline Cushman: The Celebrated Union Spy and Scout* (1865).
Young, Agatha. *The Women and the Crisis: Women of the North in the Civil War* (1959).

CUSTER, GEORGE ARMSTRONG
(1839–1876)
Union general

George Armstrong Custer entered the Civil War fresh out of West Point and emerged as the most famous member of a generation of so-called boy generals noted for their dash and aggressiveness. Born in New Rumley, Ohio, on 5 December 1839, Custer entered the U.S. Military Academy in 1857. He scored low in academics and conduct, but displayed leadership ability in the boisterous pranks so dear to his fellow cadets and the young officers who instructed them. Thanks to the indulgence of the latter, Custer managed to graduate last in the class of June 1861.

Early on 21 July 1861, 2d Lieutenant Custer reported to Company G, 2d U.S. Cavalry, and rode into the battle of the First Bull Run a few hours later. During the organization of the Army of the Potomac in the months after Bull Run, Custer served briefly on the staff of Brigadier General Philip Kearny, whose imperious command style deeply impressed the young aide.

The opening of the Peninsula campaign in March 1862 found Custer on loan to the Topographical Engineers. A daring reconnaissance earned him an appointment as a temporary captain and aide-de-camp to Major General George Brinton McClellan, the charismatic commander of the Army of the Potomac. McClellan's dismissal in November 1862 left Custer a first lieutenant in the regular army, but he soon joined the staff of Brigadier General Alfred Pleasonton. Pleasonton's subsequent elevation to major general and command of the Army of the Potomac's Cavalry Corps brought Custer increased responsibilities and opportunities.

On 28 June 1863, Major General George Gordon Meade granted Pleasonton's request and named Custer a brigadier general of U.S. Volunteers. The elated twenty-three year old, then the youngest general in the Union army, took charge of the Michigan Cavalry Brigade in Brigadier General H. Judson Kilpatrick's 3d Cavalry Division.

Custer and his "Wolverines" proved themselves a potent combat team. On 3 July 1863, they bore the brunt of the fight that stopped Major General J. E. B. Stuart and his Confederate cavalry from turning the Union right at Gettysburg. Custer closed the action by leading a single regiment in a headlong charge that helped halt two rebel brigades. Custer continued to grow as a general in the many mounted skirmishes that filled the summer and fall of 1863. Although Custer gloried in thundering saber charges, he developed a talent for employing troopers armed with repeating rifles and carbines as mounted infantry. His most striking trait was his willingness to lead every charge himself, which caused his men to idolize him. As one Wolverine wrote: "For all that this Brigade has accomplished all praise is due to General Custer. So brave a man I never saw and as competent as brave. Under him a man is ashamed to be cowardly. Under *him* our men can achieve wonders."

Major General Philip H. Sheridan replaced Pleasonton as commander of the Cavalry Corps in March 1864, but Custer quickly won the confidence of his new chief. At Yellow Tavern on 11 May 1864, Custer ensured the success of Sheridan's Richmond Raid with a charge that culminated in the fatal wounding of Jeb Stuart. When Sheridan assumed command of the Army of the Shenandoah in August, Custer accompanied him. For turning Lieutenant General Jubal A. Early's left flank at the third battle of Winchester on 19 September,

George A. Custer, ca. 1864 (*Library of Congress*)

Custer received command of the 3d Cavalry Division. He proceeded to mold that unit into the hardest-hitting Union horsemen in the Eastern theater, winning new laurels at Tom's Brook, Cedar Creek, and Waynesboro. By the close of Sheridan's Valley campaign, Custer wore the stars of a major general, and his division was setting records in capturing Confederate cannon.

Custer excelled himself as a soldier during the Appomattox campaign. His division's timely arrival steadied Sheridan's wavering line at the battle of

Dinwiddie Court House, 31 March 1865. The next day at Five Forks, Custer swamped the enemy's right flank as Sheridan destroyed a major portion of General Robert E. Lee's Army of Northern Virginia. Lee reacted to Five Forks by abandoning Richmond and fleeing west, but Custer pursued him with a zeal that outshone the efforts of Sheridan's other cavalry commanders. Custer's troopers delivered telling blows against their prey at Namozine Church and Sayler's Creek, and they blocked Lee's retreat route at Appomattox Station on the evening of 8 April. On the basis of the nine hectic days that doomed Lee's army, some historians rank Custer second only to Sheridan as the best cavalry commander ever produced by the Union army.

With the return of peace, Custer reverted to the rank of lieutenant colonel in the regular army. He reported to the Kansas frontier in late 1866 as the acting commander of the newly formed 7th U.S. Cavalry Regiment. His career as an Indian fighter began badly in 1867. Indian tactics baffled him, and he ended up getting suspended from rank and pay for a year for shooting deserters without trial and abandoning his own command. After Sheridan had him return to duty before the expiration of his sentence, the humbled cavalier redeemed himself by destroying a small Cheyenne village in a surprise attack along the Washita River in Indian Territory on 27 November 1868. Custer followed that controversial triumph with successful operations against the Southern Plains tribes in the winter of 1868–1869, skirmishes with the Sioux along the Yellowstone River in 1873, and a much-publicized reconnaissance of the Black Hills in 1874.

On 25 June 1876, Custer located a large village of Sioux and Cheyenne in the Little Bighorn Valley in Montana Territory. Sure his foes were about to flee, Custer divided the 7th Cavalry into three battalions and attempted to head them off. By the time Custer realized that the Indians intended to stand and fight, it was too late to reunite his regiment, which was defeated in detail. Custer and the 210 troopers under his immediate command were wiped out. This disaster ensured Custer's lasting immortality in history and legend, but it eclipsed his many Civil War victories.

—*Gregory J. W. Urwin*

See also Cavalry, U.S.A.; Kilpatrick, Hugh Judson; Shenandoah Valley Campaign (1864–1865); Sheridan, Philip H.; Yellow Tavern, Battle of.

For further reading:

Hutton, Paul A., ed. *The Custer Reader* (1992).

Longacre, Edward G. *Custer and His Wolverines: The Michigan Cavalry Brigade, 1861–1865* (1997).

Urwin, Gregory J.W. *Custer Victorious: The Civil War Battles of General George Armstrong Custer* (1990).

Utley, Robert M. *Cavalier in Buckskin: George Armstrong Custer and the Western Military Frontier* (1988).

Wert, Jeffry D. *Custer: The Controversial Life of George Armstrong Custer* (1996).

CYCLORAMA

After the Civil War, artists were commissioned to paint large murals commemorating battle scenes. Called cycloramas, derived from the Greek words kyklos (circular) and horama (a view), they were large, 360-degree paintings that surrounded the viewing area and were housed in round buildings. Some credit an Irish prisoner with inventing the concept in 1788.

Cycloramas were created to earn profits as well as educate and entertain. Individuals invested in cyclorama stock and thus served as patrons to artists. Paintings usually depicted a dramatic historic incident such as a battle or Biblical story, with scenes displayed chronologically. Many cycloramas featured elaborately detailed landscapes and used vast areas of canvas to portray characters and items both in life size and in varying scales for uncanny visual effects. These artistic techniques made paintings extraordinarily realistic.

After the Civil War, several hundred cycloramas were painted and shown in Europe and North America. Their viewing became a popular social and cultural activity, encouraging interest in the war and its veterans. Designed to appeal to all spectators, the paintings depicted the heroism of both Union and Confederate forces. Some cycloramas promoted political candidates by portraying their Civil War valor. By the twentieth century, most of these murals had been damaged or lost, and few cycloramas depicting Civil War events have survived.

Perhaps the best-known Civil War cyclorama is *The Battle of Atlanta*. Considered the world's largest painting at 50 feet high and 400 feet in circumference, the Atlanta Cyclorama depicts the events of 22 July 1864. During the war, *Harper's Weekly* had secured General William T. Sherman's permission for artist Theodore Davis to record the battle. Davis observed the fighting at its intensity on the afternoon of 22 July. Twenty-one years later, the American Panorama Company in Milwaukee, Wisconsin, used Davis's sketches to create the Atlanta Cyclorama. The company's manager, William Wehner, examined European cycloramas and recruited German artists who had painted cycloramas featuring the Franco-Prussian War. Each artist specialized in some aspect of cyclorama painting, such as landscapes, people, or animals. This team first completed another cyclorama, entitled *The Battle of Missionary Ridge*, before focusing on the Atlanta mural. Davis served as technical adviser for both projects. According to tradition, the Atlanta Cyclorama was originally planned to promote former Civil War general John A. Logan's 1884 vice presidential bid, but if so, it was not ready in time.

During the summer of 1885, the American Panorama Company artists traveled to Atlanta for several months to study the battlefield site. Davis shared his 22 July 1864 sketches with the artists, who also interviewed veterans and civilian witnesses about their recollections of that day. A forty-foot wooden tower was built at the intersection of Moreland Avenue and the Georgia Railroad so the artists could locate landmarks mentioned in official reports and shown on military maps. They prepared oil sketches to record topographical details such as the red dirt roads, tree lines, and gullies. Returning to Milwaukee, the artists used scaffolding to paint sections of the massive mural. Because of their careful analysis of the site, they achieved high accuracy in placing specific components of the battle.

The completed cyclorama began its tour in Detroit, Michigan, on 26 February 1887, and then traveled to Minneapolis, Minnesota. When the cyclorama arrived in Indianapolis, Indiana, legal problems concerning Wehner's stock company forced him give the painting to property owners where it was displayed. In 1890, the Atlanta Cyclorama's new owners sold it to Paul Atkinson of Madison, Georgia.

Atkinson also owned the Missionary Ridge cyclorama and had exhibited it in Chattanooga until he purchased the Atlanta painting. The Missionary Ridge cyclorama was moved to Atlanta and then to Nashville, where it was damaged by a tornado. The Atlanta Cyclorama was relocated to a "drum-like structure" on Edgewood Avenue in Atlanta and was opened for display on 22 February 1892. Charles W. Hubner, former telegraph corps chief for Confederate generals Joseph E. Johnston and John B. Hood, presented lectures to audiences. The *Atlanta Constitution* described how viewers stood on a platform surrounded by the canvas. The newspaper claimed the cyclorama was so realistic that birds flying above the building tried to land in painted trees and that General Logan's wife fainted when she saw his artistic image.

Veterans enjoyed pointing out people and events, and descendants visited to see where their ancestors had fought. Although some inaccuracies had found their way into the painting (such as the presence of the 8th Wisconsin's mascot, an eagle named Old Abe), the artists also included precise details such as hair colors, clothing, and wounds. The cyclorama included scenes of railroad destruction, hand-to-hand combat, ambulances transporting casualties, and an abandoned drum lying on the field. From one perspective, troops appeared to be marching toward the viewer. The painting consisted of five sections sequentially illuminated during the lecture explaining the battle.

By January 1893, attendance had decreased. Then a snowstorm caved in the building's roof, damaging the painting. To satisfy debts, the Fulton County sheriff sold the cyclorama at public auction on 1 August 1893. George V. Gress and Charles Northen bought the cyclorama to preserve it as a memorial to wartime Atlanta. Gress, who had given the animals to establish the city's zoo in Grant Park, suggested that the city provide adja-

cent park space for the cyclorama and charge a maximum of ten cents for admission, the proceeds to be donated to charity. He gave the cyclorama to Atlanta upon the stipulation that the city repair the painting and build a structure to house it. The Atlanta Cyclorama reopened for the 1898 reunion of Confederate veterans, who reacted emotionally to the artistic rendering of vividly recalled combat. In 1921, a fireproof building became the permanent home of the cyclorama as well as the *Texas*, the locomotive that had pursued Andrews's Raiders. A diorama that skillfully blends three-dimensional figures into scenes on the canvas was added in the 1930s, and an extensive restoration has rescued the painting from the ravages of time and exposure. Other recent improvements to the facility include a rotating platform with amphitheater seating that synchronizes viewing of the battle scenes with dramatic lighting, sound effects, narration, and music. The Atlanta Cyclorama and Civil War Museum commemorated its centennial in 1992 and is visited annually by thousands of Civil War enthusiasts.

The Gettysburg Cyclorama portrays Pickett's Charge. Paul Philippoteaux, a professional cyclorama artist from France, surveyed the battlefield in 1879 and interviewed veterans and witnesses. He sketched the terrain and hired a photographer to shoot a panoramic photograph of the battle site before creating the painting with oil-based pigments on canvas. The resulting cyclorama measured 360 feet long and 26 feet high and weighed almost three tons. First displayed in Chicago in 1882, the Gettysburg Cyclorama was so successful that Philippoteaux agreed to paint an identical cyclorama for display in Boston. The latter painting was featured at the 1913 anniversary of the battle and remained at Gettysburg afterward. The National Park Service eventually bought the painting to display in the National Park Service Cyclorama Center accompanied by a twenty-minute sound and light show. Two additional copies of this cyclorama were produced. What happened to one of these is unknown; the other was cut up to be used as tents on an Indian reservation. The original Gettysburg Cyclorama was sold to a private collector.

Other cycloramas include a painting by Philippoteaux, entitled *Cyclorama of the Second Battle of Manassas*, that was displayed in Washington, D.C., in 1887. A veteran wrote to General James Longstreet to criticize this cyclorama's inaccuracies in representing troop placements and battle conditions. Philippoteaux also prepared a 400-foot-long, 50-foot-wide canvas showing Niagara Falls that toured Europe. In 1888, a special cyclorama building in Buffalo, New York, exhibited Karl Frosch's *Jerusalem on the Day of the Crucifixion*. Circa 1890, the Buffalo cyclorama building displayed Philippoteaux's *Gettysburg*. Yet by the turn of the century, cycloramas no longer enjoyed wide popular appeal, and museums increasingly turned to dioramas to depict battle scenes in smaller spaces.

—*Elizabeth D. Schafer*

See also Art; Photography.

For further reading:

Carroll, John M. *Cyclorama of General Custer's Last Fight: A Reproduction of the Original Document Complete in All Respects, and with an Introduction* (1988).

Cecchini, Bridget Theresa. "The Battle of Atlanta Cyclorama (1885–1886) As Narrative Indicator of a National Perspective on the Civil War" (M.A. thesis, 1998).

Historical Conservation Project, Inc. "Cyclorama: The Restoration of *The Battle of Atlanta*" (videotape, 1982).

Kurtz, Wilbur G. *The Atlanta Cyclorama: The Story of the Famed Battle of Atlanta* (1954).

McGinnis, Karen Hertel. "Moving Right Along: Nineteenth Century Panorama Painting in the United States" (Ph.D. dissertation, 1983).